FEMINIST POSTCOLONIAL THEORY

A READER

Edited by
Reina Lewis and Sara Mills

EDINBURGH UNIVERSITY PRESS

Selection and editorial material © Reina Lewis and Sara Mills, 2003

Edinburgh University Press Ltd
22 George Square, Edinburgh

Typeset in Sabon and Gill Sans
by Servis Filmsetting Ltd, Manchester, and
printed and bound in Great Britain by
Cromwell Press, Trowbridge, Wilts

A CIP Record for this book is available from
the British Library

ISBN 0 7486 1350 1 (hardback)
ISBN 0 7486 1349 8 (paperback)

The right of the contributors to be identified
as authors of this work has been asserted in
accordance with the Copyright, Designs and
Patents Act 1988.

CONTENTS

ACKNOWLEDGEMENTS

We would like to thank the following people for their help in suggesting essays for this reader and for reading through and discussing with us the ideas in the introduction, particularly Suzanne Biggs, Merle Storr, Teresa Hefferman, Caroline Evans, Peggy Gough, Marsha Bryant and Tony Brown. We are very grateful to those people who allowed us to reproduce their essays without a permissions fee. Our thanks go also to those authors who kindly supported this project but whose work we were not able to include. We would also like to thank Jackie Jones for commissioning this anthology and Carol Macdonald for piloting us through the treacherous waters of permissions negotiations.

Grateful acknowledgement is made to the following sources for permission to reproduce material previously published elsewhere. Every effort has been made to trace the copyright holders but, if any have been inadvertently overlooked, the publisher will be pleased to make the necessary arrangements at the first opportunity.

Audre Lorde, 'The Master's Tools Will Never Dismantle The Master's House', in *This Bridge Called My Back* (eds), Cherríe Moraga and Gloria Anzaldúa (New York: Third Woman Press), 1983;

Adrienne Rich, 'Notes Towards a Politics of Location', from *Blood, Bread and Poetry: Selected Prose 1979–1985*, © Little, Brown and W. W. Norton and Company;

Gita Sahgal and Nira Yuval-Davis, 'The Uses of Fundamentalism', from *Women Against Fundamentalisms*, no. 5, 1994, 7–9;

Chandra Mohanty, 'Under Western Eyes: Feminist Scholarship and Colonial Discourses', from *Feminist Review*, 30, 1988, 65–88 (http://www.tandf.co.uk/journals) © Taylor & Francis Ltd.;

Chela Sandoval, 'U.S. Third World Feminism: The Theory and Method of Oppositional Consciousness in the Postmodern World', from *Genders* 10, 1–24 © 1991 by the University of Texas Press. All rights reserved;

Vron Ware, 'To Make the Facts Known: Racial Terror and the Construction of White Femininity' from *Beyond the Pale: White Women, Racism and Industry*, 1992, 169–224 © the author;

Natalie Zemon Davis, 'Iroquois Women, European Women', from *Women,*

'*Race*', *and Writing* edited by Margo Hendricks and Patricia Parker, 1992, 243–58 © Taylor & Francis;

Jane Haggis, 'White Women and Colonialism: Towards a Non-Recuperative History', from *Gender and Imperialism* edited by Clare Midgley, 1998, 45–75 © Manchester University Press;

Ien Ang, 'I'm a feminist but . . . : "Other" women and postnational feminism', from *Transitions: New Australian Feminisms* edited by B. Caine and R. Pringle, 1995, 57–73 © Allen and Unwin;

bell hooks, 'The Oppositional Gaze: Black Female Spectators', from *Black Looks: Race and Representation*, 1992, 115–31 © Turnaround (PSL) Ltd.;

Hazel V. Carby, ' "On the Threshold of Woman's Era": Lynching, Empire, and Sexuality in Black Feminist Theory', from *Critical Inquiry* 12 (Autumn 1985), 262–77 © The University of Chicago Press;

Ania Loomba, 'Dead Women Tell No Tales: Issues of Female Subjectivity, Subaltern Agency and Tradition in Colonial and Post-colonial Writings on Widow Immolation in India', from *History Workshop Journal*, no. 36, 209–27 © Oxford University Press;

Deniz Kandiyoti, 'End of Empire: Islam, Nationalism and Women in Turkey', from *Women, Islam and the State*, 1991, 22–47 © Macmillan Ltd. and Temple University Press;

Kirin Narayan, 'How Native is a "Native" Anthropologist?', from *American Anthropologist*, 95 (3), 671–86. Reproduced by permission of the American Anthropological Association from *American Anthropologist* 95 (3) and Kirin Narayan. Not for sale or further reproduction;

Gayatri Chakravorty Spivak, 'Three Women's Texts and a Critique of Imperialism', from *Critical Inquiry*, 1985, 243–61. Reproduced by permission of Gayatri Chakravorty Spivak;

Rey Chow, 'Where Have All the Natives Gone?', from *Displacements: Cultural Identities in Question* edited by Angelika Bammer, 1994, 125–51 © Indiana University Press;

Angela Davis, 'Racism, Birth Control and Reproductive Rights', from *Women, Race and Class*, 1982. Reproduced by permission of The Women's Press Ltd and Random House, Inc.;

Françoise Lionnet, 'Feminisms and Universalisms: "Universal Rights" and the Legal Debate Around the Practice of Female Excision in France', from *Inscriptions*, vol. 6, 1992;

Aihwa Ong, 'State Versus Islam: Malay Families, Women's Bodies and the Body Politic in Malaysia', from *Bewitching Women, Pious Men: Gender and Body Politics in Southeast Asia*, edited by Aihwa Ong and Michael G. Peletz, 1995, 160–94 © The Regents of the University of California;

Alison Murray, 'Debt-Bondage and Trafficking: Don't Believe the Hype', from *Global Sex Workers: Rights, Resistance and Redefinition* edited by Kamala Kempadoo and Jo Doexema, 1998, 51–64 © Taylor & Francis, Inc.;

Mrinalini Sinha, 'Reconfiguring Hierarchies: The Ilbert Bill Controversy,

1883–84', from *Colonial Masculinity: The 'Manly Englishman' and the 'Effeminate Bengali' in the Late Nineteenth Century*, 1995, 33–68 © Manchester University Press;

Joseph A. Boone, 'Vacation Cruises; or, The Homoerotics of Orientalism', *PMLA*, vol. 110, no. 1, 1995, 89–107. Reprinted by permission of the Modern Language Association of America;

Fatima Mernissi, 'The Meaning of Spatial Boundaries', from *Beyond the Veil: Male-Female Dynamics in Muslim Society*, 1975, 137–47 and 41–5 © Al Saqi Books;

Sarah Graham-Brown, 'The Seen, the Unseen and the Imagined: Private and Public Lives', from *Images of Women: The Portrayal of Women in Photography of the Middle East 1860–1950*, 1988, 70–91 © Columbia University Press;

Reina Lewis, 'On Veiling, Vision and Voyage: Cross-cultural Dressing and Narratives of Identity', from *Interventions*, vol. 1 (4) 1999, 500–20. Reproduced by permission of Taylor and Francis (http://www.tandf.co.uk) and the Author;

Meyda Yeğenoğlu, 'Veiled Fantasies: Cultural and Sexual Difference in the Discourse of Orientalism', from *Colonial Fantasies: Towards a Feminist Reading of Orientalism*, 1998, 39–175. Reproduced by permission of Cambridge University Press and Meyda Yeğenoğlu;

Winifred Woodhull, 'Unveiling Algeria', from *Genders* 10, 112–31. Copyright © 1991 by the University of Texas Press. All rights reserved;

Fadwa El Guindi, 'Veiling Resistance', from *Fashion Theory*, vol. 3, issue 1, 51–80 © Berg Publishers. Printed in Oxford;

Avtar Brah, 'Diaspora, Border and Transnational Identities', from *Cartographies of Diaspora*, 1996, 178–210. Reprinted by permission of Routledge and Avtar Brah;

Anne McClintock, 'Imperial Leather: Race, Cross-Dressing and the Cult of Domesticity', from *Imperial Leather: Race, Gender and Sexuality in the Colonial Contest*, 1995, 132–80 © Routledge;

Jane Jacobs, 'Earth Honoring: Western Desires and Indigenous Knowledges', from *Writing Women and Space: Colonial and Postcolonial Geographies* edited by A. Blunt and G. Rose, 1994, 169–96 © Routledge;

Sara Mills, 'Gender and Colonial Space', from *Gender, Place and Culture*, vol. 3, no. 2, 125–47, 1996 © Taylor & Francis Ltd.;

Alison Blunt, 'Spatial Stories under Siege: British Women Writing from Lucknow in 1857', from *Gender, Place and Culture*, vol. 7, no. 3, 229–46, 2000 © Taylor & Francis Ltd.;

Library of Congress, Washington for 'Porte centrale de la cour de Suleymaniye' – Central Gate of the Courtyard of the Suleymaniye (Mosque) (Chapter 5.2, Plate 1); Cairo street scene: Tancrède, Dumas, probably 1870s (Chapter 5.2, Plate 2); 'Veiled Ladies in a Carriage'. On the shores of the Bosporus, Turkey, late nineteenth century (Chapter 5.2, Plate 4);

Bibliothèque nationale de France for 'Mussulman Ladies at Home' (Chapter 5.2, Plate 3);

Collection Roger-Viollet for 'Members of the Harem of Sultan Abdul Hamid with two Eunuchs Setting off to Exhibit Themselves in Vienna after the Sultan had been Deposed'. Probably Istanbul, 1909 (Chapter 5.2, Plate 5);

Sykes Collection, Middle East Centre, St Antony's College, Oxford, for 'Women and children in a park, Tehran, Iran, 1860s–90s' (Chapter 5.2, Plate 7);

Museum voor Volkenkunde for 'Day for Women to Visit the Commercial, Industrial and Agricultural Exhibition at Cairo', 18 March 1931 (Chapter 5.2, Plate 8).

INTRODUCTION

Reina Lewis and Sara Mills

This book marks an attempt to resituate postcolonial theory in relation to feminism. This is not to suggest that much postcolonial theory does not engage with questions of gender. Indeed many researchers in the field would define themselves as feminist and some of the most important contributions have come from women. But, as postcolonial studies has become established in the Western academy, to the extent that it is now de rigueur to have at least some work on this theme available at graduate and undergraduate level, we note that the dynamism that feminism provided for the early development of critical studies in colonialism, imperialism, race and power has often been overlooked. It is far more common to see allegiances proffered to the line of male greats (for example, Frantz Fanon, Edward Said and Homi Bhabha) than to acknowledge the contributions of women scholars and activists (such as Angela Davis, Adrienne Rich, Audre Lorde or bell hooks, although it must be noted that Gayatri Spivak tends to be very visible as the exceptionally cited female voice). This is not entirely surprising: as new fields develop and solidify into nascent academic disciplines – even in projects like postcolonialism which, for many, was seen to be essentially about challenging existing boundaries – lines of legitimacy become established and are invoked by practitioners as a way to confirm their own authority.[1] But, of course, these emergent orthodoxies develop with the characteristics common to all bodies of knowledge. As Michel Foucault has shown, the establishment of knowledges and disciplines is never innocent: knowledges are also formations of power which not only delineate specific inclusions but enforce overt and covert exclusions (Foucault, 1980).

It is the marginalisation and exclusion of a separate trajectory of feminist thought about race, power, culture and empire that this collection seeks to redress: to locate again this history of feminist thinking and activism in relation to mainstream postcolonial theory. This is an attempt not to create an alternative orthodoxy, but to suggest a different genealogy to contemporary thinking about colonial power and postcolonial relations. This differently complexioned route to theory cannot be totally inclusive (like all editors of such readers, we were haunted by the number of wonderful sources we did not have space to include and beset by a desire for the 'whole picture' which we know to be as fictitious as it is practically impossible), but it can be suggestive. And it is in this spirit that we offer this selection of essays: a chance to, in some cases, revisit some of the early feminist hopes, dreams, angers and conflicts that inspired scholars, activists and artists in their attempts to make sense of and ultimately to change the oppressive power relations encoded in the name of race, nation and empire, as well as those of gender, class and sexuality, and, in other cases, to trace a path of feminist postcolonial concerns. In making more accessible some of the writings on this subject which have been marginalised, this reader is also, therefore, a project of recuperative publishing.

It is clear that current feminist postcolonial theory still exerts a pressure on mainstream postcolonial theory in its constant iteration of the necessity to consider gender issues. In the past, feminist postcolonial theorists have criticised male theorists for assuming that the behaviour of British men could be taken to stand for the behaviour of imperial subjects in general or to symbolise the empire as a whole. In contrast to Ronald Hyam's exclusive focus on British men in *Empire and Sexuality: the British Experience* (1990), for example, feminist scholars such as Jenny Sharpe and Vron Ware have shown that for the Victorian public British female sexuality within the empire was a subject of much discussion and indeed legislation (Sharpe, 1993, Ware, 1992, and this volume). Edward Said's seminal study *Orientalism* itself included little attention to female agency and discussed very few female writers (Said, 1978; but see also Said, 1993; and, on Said, see Lowe, 1991; Miller, 1990). Whilst one feminist response has been to insert a study of women's experiences and cultures (as colonisers, colonised and those 'at home' in the metropolitan centres of empire, Chaudhuri and Strobel, 1992; Jayawardena, 1995), another has been to engage with studies in masculinity to decentre the presumed privilege of a normative male subject. It has taken the sustained effort of feminist theorists such as Mrinalini Sinha (1995 and this volume), in her work on colonial masculinity, to position male British imperialists as gendered rather than as universalised and hence neutral subjects. Sinha shows how the stereotyping of the 'manly Englishman' and the 'effeminate Bengali' led to controversy over such issues as whether Indian judges could preside in cases which involved white defendants or Indian doctors examine English women. The current concern with colonial masculinity and indeed postcolonial masculinities, for example, has been a direct result of feminist interventions in mainstream postcolonial theory (Bristow, 1991; Phillips, 1997). Specifying those elements of colonial subjectivities which are masculine rather than general has enabled theorists to disentangle the complex process of construction of national subjectivity and the elision of the masculine with the national. This has also led to an examination of the process whereby femininity and female stereotyping is entangled with the process of constructing a nationalist anti-colonial symbolism, the female signifying the pre-colonial, the traditional and the untouched domestic space (Innes, 1994; Sharpe, 1993; and see Ong, this volume).

We have divided this collection of essays into six thematic parts (Gendering Colonialism and Postcolonialism/Racialising Feminism; Rethinking Whiteness; Redefining the 'Third World' Subject; Sexuality and Sexual Rights; Harem and the Veil; and Gender and Post/Colonial Spatial Relations). These six parts focus on some of the key issues and debates which have taken place in feminist postcolonial theory and articulate an overlapping set of concerns with gender, economics, sexuality, representation and the development of effective political activism. These divisions should not be seen as absolute: indeed many of the authors could have featured in more than one part. Rather, we would prefer readers to see the parts in dialogue with each other – just as the authors featured within them often make direct reference to each other's work. Sometimes this dialogue is one of agreement, at other times of dispute, indicating the continued vibrancy of the feminist postcolonial field. The authors represented here stand as emblematic of debates also engaged in by many other feminist postcolonial writers (we have given indicative references to further reading throughout this introduction). The historical and geographical scope of this book is not exhaustive. We have concentrated on sources dealing with nineteenth- and twentieth-century material and thus we have not included much material which deals with early modern colonial experiences (see Zemon Davis, this volume; see also Hendricks and Parker, 1994). Our geographical range is necessarily partial. Although the papers in this reader feature a number of different colonial and postcolonial situations, we have not attempted to provide 'world coverage'. Indeed, we would want to emphasise the necessity of attending to the specificity of each historical situation; of rooting the theories we use in the analysis of the historical; of recognising that it is only in certain moments that particular practices currently beloved of postcolonial theory, such as colonial mimicry (Bhabha, 1984), have the potential to be counter-insurgent;[2] and that the very category 'postcolonial' cannot adequately be applied to every situation of the modern world (Frankenberg and Mani, 1993). However, despite these restrictions of scope – a necessity in producing anthologies of any kind – these essays give an indication of the debates and issues which have shaped postcolonial feminism and politics.

GENDERING COLONIALISM AND POSTCOLONIALISM/RACIALISING FEMINISM

Feminist postcolonial theory has engaged in a two-fold project: to racialise mainstream feminist theory and to insert feminist concerns into conceptualisations of colonialism and postcolonialism. Feminist activism and struggle, including most pertinently struggles with other feminists, is where we situate ourselves: these are our intellectual antecedents, the ideas that formed us. It seems perverse that it has become more difficult to talk about race just as European ethno-centrism is challenged in the academy and non-Western writers, histories and case studies are increasingly included in the syllabus (Shohat and Stam, 1994; Goldberg, 1993). In the 1990s it seemed as if a prob-lematisation of race could be taken as read in some quarters, as was an atten-tion to gender. It was almost déclassé to harp on too much about such politics. But, in the new century, the glass ceiling continues to stymie women in work and racial prejudice continues to mar public life, while race hate still kills (Lakoff, 2001; Butler, 1997).[3] So, in this context, public testimony to such anti-racist and feminist allegiances becomes again ever more crucial.

Feminist anti-racist politics was born out of recognition of the differences between women and out of the anti-imperialist campaigns of 'first-' and 'third-world' women. We have given feminist anti-racist political writing a prominent place in this anthology because, for many women (white and not), these debates within the women's movement were an important foundational moment. Tensions and struggles within the women's movement faced white women with the necessity of recognising that gender is always racialised. Second wave Anglo-American feminist theory had generalised from Western middle-class women's experiences and developed a form of theorising – 'sisterhood is global' – which assumed that those white concerns were the concerns of women every-where. This type of essentialising led to a silencing of Black and third-world women's interventions within early Anglo-American feminist theory. What seemed self-evidently universal to second wave Western feminists – for example, the right to sexual self-determination and the so-called sexual libera-tion of the 1960s – seemed to Muslim feminists to be a degradation of women's sexuality and a misguided defining of women's freedom in terms of men's inter-ests (a view with which many Western feminists today might concur). Resulting from the critique by Black and third-world feminist theorists of this over-generalising of white concerns has been a thoroughgoing rethinking of the cat-egory gender itself. Developed initially as a term to describe the social constructedness of 'women' and 'men' in opposition to the apparently simple biological differences of 'sex', gender seemed to be a more nuanced and his-toricised concept. The social construction model of gender gained widespread acceptance and proved useful as a way of talking about masculinity and femi-ninity without recourse to biological determinism. But, although using the term 'gender' prevented lapsing into biologism, it made it difficult to talk about 'women' as a generic group once the variety of concerns and values of women in other cultures were taken into account, something which is essential for many feminists in creating allegiances and solidarity in struggles within the international sphere (Butler, 1990).

Black feminist theorists, such as hooks (1984; 1989), Carby (1982), Bhavnani and Coulson (1986) and Amos and Parmar (1984), have argued that white Western feminist theory needs to confront its implicit racism and racial stereotyping (see Mirza, 1997 for an overview; see also Bhavnani, 2001). Some critics, such as Sandoval (this volume), have drawn attention to the erasure from consideration of the very different intellectual and political contexts of feminist theory. She stresses the need to acknowledge the intellectual and political debt that the white feminist consciousness-raising movement of the 1960s and 1970s owed to the Black Civil Rights Movement. Furthermore, a white Western feminist separatist strategy of aligning with other women and rejecting men did not accord with the concerns of many Black British and African-American feminist theorists who wished to take part in campaigns about racial discrimination with their Black male colleagues. Arguments about the interlocking nature of race and gender were forcefully made by the Combahee River Collective, whose manifesto from 1978 was reprinted in Barbara Smith's influential anthology of Black feminist writing, *Home Girls: A Black Feminist Anthology* (1983). The collective spoke against feminist separatism on the grounds that concentrating on gender oppression alone would never make sense for Black women who always experienced sexual and racial oppression as linked and compounded by each other: 'sexual politics under patriarchy is as pervasive in Black women's lives as are the politics of class and race. . . . [W]e know that there is a such a thing as racial-sexual oppression which is neither solely racial nor solely sexual' (Smith, 1983: p. 275). This explanation of why all gender relations – not just Black women's experiences – needed always to be seen as racialised provided tools for analysis and served as a rallying point for feminist and anti-racist action.

Some of the most forceful critiques of the unthinking racism of second wave feminism in the West were proffered by the African-American poet and writer Audre Lorde (this volume). She insisted that white women must learn to recognise that their relative privilege within a patriarchal status quo was achieved at the cost of Black and third-world women's lives. Rather than be fearful of facing these differences, feminists who learned to understand them as forms of interdependency could channel this awareness into a feminist political process for change. Written in the fulcrum of late 1970s and early 1980s internationalist feminism, Lorde's clarion call to undertake fearlessly radical change (rather than colluding in reform) pre-empts Anglo-American debates in the late 1980s and 1990s about the limitations of the tolerance model propounded by multiculturalism.

In a similar vein, Adrienne Rich provided an injunction to women to see themselves, their experiences and their knowledges as situated – always already marked by race and ethnicity (Rich, this volume). Reconceptualising subjectivity as not just gendered but also firmly embodied, she positioned the female gendered body as an antidote to the Marxist universalising of male experience as the (disembodied) abstract norm. This resulted in a 'politics of location' that recognised the relationality of identity formation without tipping into the apolitical despair that came to be associated for some with the loss of modernity's certainties and grand narratives. Rather, it recognised that women's involvement in complex patterns of power and oppression could be seen as the conditions of possibility for the emergence of new forms of international feminist agency – forms that sought alliances with other women rather than allowing educated Western white women to speak on behalf of 'all women'. But Rich was not positing identity as the pre-eminent arbiter of analysis (something which was often critiqued in so-called identity politics – in which a presumed hierarchy of oppression effectively silenced women who could not claim an experiential knowledge of the subject under review).[4] Instead, Rich used the embodiment of politics to argue for the possibility of dialogue between women.

The publication of work by Black feminists in Britain and America worked as a corrective to the lack of non-white voices in previous feminist publications and campaigns, and writing (both creative, critical and polemical) was valued as a political contribution. Books, such as *The Bridge Called my Back: Writings by Radical Women of Color* edited by Cherríe Moraga and Gloria Anzaldúa (1983), *All the Women are White, All the Blacks are Men, But Some of Us are Brave: Black Women's Studies*, edited by Gloria T. Hull (1982) and *The Heart of the Race: Black Women's Lives in Britain* edited by Beverly Bryan, Stella Dadzie and Suzanne Scafe (1985), worked in dialogue with Smith's *Home Girls* to establish a framework for considering the intersections of gender and race, and sexuality and class. It is hard to overestimate the significance of books such as these for the development of feminist postcolonial theory. Yet these polemics, often but not always produced outside of the academy, are frequently overlooked in contemporary thinking about the postcolonial.

Continuing the activism of second wave interventionist politics, the London-based group Women Against Fundamentalisms (WAF) was formed in 1989 to 'challenge the use of fundamentalisms in all religions'.[5] WAF has importantly shifted the definition of fundamentalism away from one of religious observance to a political critique of how all religious fundamentalisms (whatever their differences) aim to control women through the reinforcement of the patriarchal family unit (Sahgal and Yuval-Davis, this volume).

RETHINKING WHITENESS

Feminist theorists such as Jayawardena and Ware have analysed the complexities of white women's involvement in empire, not only at the level of symbolism, as many postcolonial theorists have, but as a material presence in terms of the running, sustaining and even financing of imperial and colonial projects (Chaudhuri, 1992; Jayawardena, 1995; Ware, 1992). Zemon Davis (this volume) has focused on the striking similarities of position of Iroquois and white women in the colonial encounter, rather than the conventional assumption of difference. As well as maintaining the importance of gender in the analysis of colonial and imperial subjectivity, feminist postcolonial theorists have tried to examine the various forms which exploitation took in the imperial period. Not just restricting themselves to the analysis of imperial rule in terms of the relations between governments, feminist theorists have focused on the relations which were played out 'on the ground'. For example, Jane Haggis has examined the relations between British women missionaries and their indigenous assistants (this volume). This detailed work has enabled an examination of the texture of imperial rule, rather than the abstract rhetoric of imperial ideology alone.

White feminists have begun to focus on their own racial identities, rather than assuming that race is a term which can only be used in discussions about Black people. Just as theorists, such as Celia Kitzinger and Sue Wilkinson, have begun to open up the discussion of heterosexuality, forcing straight feminists to see their own sexuality as a set of choices and privileges rather than as 'natural', many theorists are now turning to the choices and privileges involved in whiteness (Kitzinger and Wilkinson, 1993). Alongside Richard Dyer's groundbreaking (1997) work on whiteness, white feminists have started to interrogate the constructions of white identities and the intersection of class and racial identities (Frankenberg, 1993; Brown, Gilkes and Kaloski-Naylor, 1999; (charles), 1992). The resurgence of scholarship on the construction and significance of whiteness marks the re-animation of concerns that were central to feminist practice in the 1970s and 1980s. One important element of feminist activity in the Western academy was the establishment of courses and programmes in women's studies and the inclusion of material by and on women in diverse programmes in the arts and humanities and, to a lesser extent, in the sciences. But, in the rush to secure an institutional place for feminist scholarship, some of the radical race politics that were most challenging within the women's movement were sidelined. Conversely, the move to recognise non-British literatures in English, which enriched the syllabus and spawned many programmes in postcolonialism in British and North American universities, tended to align itself with European 'high' literary theory and to sideline gender. This can leave elements of material analysis (particularly those of class, gender and sexuality) subsumed under a postcolonial rationale.

Black feminist analysis of white racism led to some extremely productive theoretical and political work by white feminists. However, 'white guilt' has developed as a term to describe white inertia in the face of the problematic of race. Many white feminists assumed that it was so easy to 'get it wrong' in relation to the discussion of race, that it was more prudent simply to work on other issues or ignore race altogether. This white guilt developed from the awareness that Western powers within the nineteenth century had subjugated a large portion of the world and exploited these territories and their populations for material gain, and that white people had benefited directly and indirectly from that exploitation. Materially, Western economies and industrial infrastructures prospered as a result of the appropriation of land, the extraction of raw materials, the use of slave and indentured labour, and the opening up of new markets in countries such as Africa and India. This prosperity and the political dominance of Britain and other Western powers in the nineteenth century and America in the twentieth century has been a consistent focus of attention of

Black and third-world postcolonial and anti-imperialist theorists, and indeed forms the bedrock of anti-capitalist thinking. The link between past exploitation and present affluence, and indeed the deeds of past colonialists and oneself, is one which white people have found difficult to deal with in constructive ways. White guilt is one of the least productive responses to this history.

REDEFINING THE THIRD-WORLD SUBJECT

As some of the essays in the previous section showed, feminist postcolonial theory is concerned, among other things, to analyse the relations between Western women and, broadly speaking, indigenous women. In the nineteenth century particularly, at the height of European colonialism in Africa and India, some Western women used their campaigning skills to argue for the rights of oppressed indigenous women in colonies. In drawing attention to the seemingly self-evident nature of indigenous women's oppression through campaigns around the issues of 'sati' and female seclusion, which presupposed Western women's relative freedom, British women were forced to confront the ways in which they themselves and other women within Britain were 'secluded' within the private sphere of the home. However, in the process of campaigning on behalf of Indian and African women, they also constructed for themselves a political voice which led ultimately to suffrage for British women and women in the 'white' settled colonies (Burton, 1992; Jayawardena, 1995). It is debatable whether their campaigns led to significant improvement in the lives of indigenous women. Often, the very process of having Western women aligned with their cause repositioned issues such as the veil and sati – newly inflecting them as traditional and religious practices symbolising the nationalist and anti-colonialist movement. Sati and veiling thus began to function as symbols of resistance to colonial rule, rather than as symbols of the oppression of women. Sati in particular has been the subject of much feminist debate by both Indian and Western feminists; Ania Loomba's essay in this section draws on Lata Mani and Rajeswari Rajan's important works in order to trace the three main bodies of writing on sati (colonial, Western and Indian feminist and current writings). She traces the difficulty of figuring the burning widow without portraying her as an archetypal victim as Western feminists have, nor as a free agent as is often done in nationalist writings (Mani, 1992; Sunder Rajan, 1993). In the case of Turkish nationalism as discussed by Deniz Kandiyoti (this volume), women's liberation may be undertaken by the state as part of a nationalist modernising programme in advance of the mass articulation of women's own demands (unlike the progress of Western feminism where legislation usually lagged behind changes in public attitudes to female emancipation). Kandiyoti contributes to the recent re-examination of Turkish historiography an analysis of how the figure of woman was struggled over by all sides in the crises of the late Ottoman empire and continued as a definitional trope in the formation of Turkish nationalism (see Ong, this volume).

Partly because of the problematic history of intervention by Western women on behalf of indigenous women, feminist postcolonial theory now faces a delicate and difficult task in intervening in the political situations of the developing world at present. This is particularly in relation to debates about female circumcision/female genital mutilation and about the use of the burqa, the veil and seclusion, as we discuss later in this introduction. Rather than assuming that third-world women can be spoken for and that these practices are simply oppressive, as they seem to many Western feminists, women in other cultures need to be consulted and worked alongside so that they set the agenda for political action. Thus, for many Western feminist postcolonial theorists, it is a question of positioning oneself differently in relation to other women, according them the same degree of agency one would expect for oneself.

Feminist postcolonial theory is now aware that Western feminist theory has often made generalisations about 'third-world' women, assuming a homogeneity amongst very diverse groups of women and has relied on a tokenist inclusion of a single or few Black women to represent all Black and third-world women. Mohanty (this volume) argues that this move on the part of Western feminists is akin to colonialism. Trinh T. Minh-ha is particularly sceptical about the devotion of special issues of Western feminist journals to 'Third-World Women' or to the inclusion of one woman from a minority group on conference panels (Min-ha, 1989). Thus the diversity of women in developing countries has had to be confronted by Western feminists. Ang (this volume) argues that white women, wishing to 'include' non-white women within a broader feminism, need to remake feminism so that difference is not absorbed, nor ambivalence and ambiguity erased. Kirin Narayan's article (1997) on the complex position of the indigenous informant in anthropological work highlights the diversity of indigenous women and the impossibility of one group of women having any necessary unmediated access to others' experiences. She draws attention to the distance that there often is between educated Indian women informants and the Indian peasant women that they survey and suggests, therefore, that we need to confront the diversity within the terms 'Indian women' or 'third-world women'.

Western feminist focus on the writings of white women in the colonial period was critiqued by many Black and third-world feminists since it often led to the perspective of those white colonial women being accepted as the 'correct' interpretation of the colonial experience. Some early accounts which retrieved colonial women's history were read uncritically in a celebratory way, hailing white colonial women as proto-feminists or remarkable individuals, whilst often ignoring the wider impact of their actions within the colonial context. However, much of the later feminist writing focused on white women's complicity with colonialism as well as their resistance (Chaudhuri and Strobel, 1992). The focus on the white female heroine in literary texts written within the colonial period often led to a lack of attention to Black female characters on whom the process of liberation for the protagonist rested. Gayatri Spivak's seminal 1985 article (reprinted here) radically resituated *Jane Eyre*, previously celebrated as a proto-feminist account of one woman's (Jane's) progress to emancipated adulthood, as a colonial novel by focusing on seemingly marginalised characters such as Bertha Mason. Reading *Jane Eyre* alongside Jean Rhys's *Wide Sargasso Sea*, Spivak showed that the foregrounded production of the white heroine's subjectivity forces the figures of Bertha and the Black maid Christophine to the background. Yet it could be contended that these characters are crucial to the questions and identifications which produce and undermine that notion of a 'white' subjectivity for the heroine. Spivak calls for a refocusing in colonial texts on central yet marginalised figures such as this and takes the argument beyond the literary text to demonstrate that this process of marginalisation has a wider emblematic status for the production of white subjectivity in general (on *Jane Eyre*, see also Meyer, 1989; Sharpe, 1993; on feminist Orientalism in the literary field, see Zonana, 1993; and, on the visual arts, see Cherry, 2000).

The focus on white women's colonial texts has also led to a particular view of indigenous women being adopted, sometimes leading to a generalisation that all the women described in white women's texts (generally either aristocrats or servants) represented the women in that nation. This marginalising or stereotyping of indigenous women led some feminists to try to access other women's voices, particularly those from the nineteenth century, to counter some of these representations. Essay collections, such as Kumkum Sangari and Sudesh Vaid's (1990) *Recasting Women: Essays in Colonial History*, examine Indian women's role in Indian history, characterising Indian women as agents in political struggle rather than as passive victims of patriarchal oppression. Hazel Carby's work is part of this wider project of rediscovering the agency of Black women in struggles against slavery and oppression (this volume). The very difficulty of finding such sources has led to a focus on the subaltern, the member of a subjugated group whose position has been hidden from history, which often tended to an unquestioning heroicisation of the oppressed and to a mis-labelling of all third-world women as generically subaltern. Spivak has to some extent questioned this trend, analysing the possibility, or perhaps the impossibility, of the subordinated subaltern female being able to articulate anything other than the dominant discourses (Spivak, 1993).[6] Further, she argued against the assumption that all indigenous subjects were automatically in radical opposition to the imperial powers. This would entail ignoring instances of collaboration by colonial elites and those in positions of relative power within colonised regimes, and would fail to analyse how and why dominant discourses of Western rationality and modernity were often adopted by many of the colonised to serve their own ends.

White Western women's relative ignorance of the situation of women in other countries has often been highlighted. Spivak in particular has been most vocal in her calls for white feminists to find out more about the rest of the world, so that they could challenge their own ignorance about the situations of women in other countries, rather than assuming that 'third-world' women are universally oppressed, held in purdah, uneducated and abused by their husbands and male relatives (Spivak, 1990; 1993b). Whilst it is essential to describe the abuses that women in other countries suffer and to document the resistance movements that they have formed, such as the Chipko movement and other environmental movements, it is also essential not to romanticise those movements or to simply focus on single-issue struggles out of context.

Responding to the romanticisation of native experience and to Spivak's work on subalternity, Rey Chow (this volume) problematises the quest to find the authentic 'native' voice. Such recoveries, she contends, can end up perpetuating the construction of the native as a differentiating category that will always position the native outside of the unmarked normative subject of Western modernity. Retaining this logic by trying to replace bad/inauthentic images with good/true images of the native will not do. Instead she proposes the radical benefits of conceptualising the impossibility of discovering the true native whilst holding onto the epistemic violence that transforms the pre-native into this symptom of colonialism.

SEXUALITY AND SEXUAL RIGHTS

This part is concerned with sexuality and with sexual and reproductive rights – in relation to contemporary struggles against the abuse of women's control of their bodies; in relation to the pivotal role such campaigns have had historically in revealing the fault-lines of race relations within feminism; and in relation to how work on the racialisation of sexuality has also led to the rethinking of masculinity in the colonial and postcolonial context.[7] The control of reproduction and the protection of sexual rights have been central to the agenda of European and North American feminism since the earliest days of campaigns for female emancipation in the eighteenth century. For white feminists, the right to control one's own body, for it not to be regarded as a man's property, was essential to the conceptualisation of female sovereign subjectivity and citizenship. Feminists were outraged at the exploitation and abuse of women's sexual rights (such as the notorious Contagious Diseases Acts of the 1850s).[8] Campaigns against the Contagious Diseases Acts in Britain and in India did eventually serve to end despicable infringements on the bodily rights of women working as, or presumed to be working as, prostitutes. But, constructed as part of 'women's mission to women', they can also be seen to have relied on and endorsed a hierarchical sense of the classed and racialised differences between the largely bourgeois white women running the campaigns and the working-class and colonised women who were positioned as the grateful recipients of their imperial philanthropy.

By the 1970s, a woman's right to choose an abortion on demand had become one of the defining rallying points of Western feminism and operated almost as an article of faith. But, as Angela Davis demonstrates, any campaign which claims to speak on behalf of all women is highly likely to be premised on a disregard for or inability to see the structural differences between women – of race, ethnicity and class – which will impact on women's experience of the sexual and reproductive oppressions fought against (Davis, this volume). Writing in

1981, she analyses what white feminists saw as an apparent lack of enthusiasm among Afro-American women for improved abortion legislation. For Black women – affected by the historic refusal of colonialism and slavery to let them have children and keep them – the desire for legal and safe abortion could never be seen outside of the wider sexual rights discriminations of institutionalised rape, racist eugenics and enforced sterilisation. Thus, rather than freedom to have an abortion, the issue for many Black women, then and now, is freedom not to have contraception forced upon them.[9] This emphatic refusal to permit the deracination of reproductive rights politics serves as a reminder of how the particular imperial, colonial and class dynamics, which structure the abuse of women's sexual and reproductive rights, are simultaneously also implicated in the formation of resistance to such abuses.

As such, the case of female circumcision/female genital mutilation (FC/FCM)[10] covered in this section is not only important as a difficult-to-discuss but widespread infringement of women's sexual rights, it is also illustrative of how the inequities of postcolonialism create particular and gendered dilemmas for those who resist it. Practised in some African and Arab countries and their diasporic communities (Sudan, Somalia, Yemen, Egypt, Mali, Kenya, Ethiopa, for example), FC/FGM is regarded by many as an abuse against women (El Saadawi, 1980; Rifaat, 1990; Dorkeno, 1994; Hosken, 1994). But those, including women, who defend FC/FGM present it as a traditional and often religious practice (Lightfoot-Klein, 1989; Rahman and Toubia, 2000). Indeed, like the more visible veil, the status of FC/FGM has been heightened in a postcolonial context since it is now defended as a long-held tradition under attack by neo-imperialist reformers who lack respect for indigenous custom. We have included material on FC/FGM because, as well as being a subject of grave concern to feminists, this issue operates as a limit case for the cultural relativist approach that has held sway in the conceptualisation of postcolonial cultural politics. As Toubia (1997) demonstrates in her study of FC/FGM in Sudan, configuring the practice as religious (generally, though not exclusively, Muslim) rather than as social discourages an understanding of how FC/FGM operates as a form of social control over women, the continuation of which has come to rest significantly on its recently developed status as a cultural institution to be protected from Western inroads. The difficulties for health care professionals in dealing with women who have been circumcised are addressed by international organisations such as RAINBO (Research, Action, and Information Network for Bodily Integrity of Women).[11] They aim not only to empower communities to reject the practice but also to educate health providers in Africa and the first world to deal sensitively and effectively with circumcised female bodies. To do this, without further objectifying the African female body or disempowering the women concerned as primitive, unenlightened or ignorant, is one of the great struggles faced by those who tackle such an issue in a postcolonial context. The difficulty of speaking out against FC/FGM in the face of support from women in the circumcising communities positions feminist against feminist within and across the lines of racial and ethnic divide

(Walker and Palmer, 1993; on their collaboration, *Warrior Marks*, see also Murungi, 1994). In an argument about who has the right to represent the interests of women at risk of FC/FGM, the difficulties of location (Rich, this volume), of the place from which one enunciates become critically pronounced (see also Spivak, 1993a).

Françoise Lionnet examines how immigrant subjectivities are (re)created and acted upon by the state legal system when practices coded as traditional (in this case in Mali) are relocated to postcolonial France, taking on new meanings for their proponents in a diaspora context. Within a gendered racialising discourse, members of an immigrant community, normally denied recognition as citizens, find themselves interpolated as subjects of the French state in order to be prosecuted for transgressing the rights of their daughters (now constructed as *citoyennes* in need of protection from alien barbarity). This ignores the call to create through consultation a situation in which legal reform can be welcomed by women faced with circumcision so that they might be confident that the law can defend their sexual rights without attacking their communities. Thus, a reformist intent from outside the circumcising community can end up once again acting on Black/African/third-world women's bodies in a continuation of a colonial discourse whose interest in reforming 'native' savageries and protecting 'brown women from brown men [or brown women]' (Spivak, 1993a) obscures the other violences of colonial and postcolonial power. Similarly, the potentially obsessive focus by Western feminist and non-governmental organisations (NGOs) on FC/FGM to the exclusion of other sexual rights infringements runs the risk of perpetuating a longstanding prurient interest in a sexualised 'African' female body (see, for example, Gilman, 1985) and of distracting attention away from other pressing women's health issues in the developing world (El Saadawi, 1997).

FC/FGM is not the only issue of concern in this area. Indeed, as sexual subjects positioned by global capital, the bodies of third-world women (and men) are mapped by a series of economic, religious and cultural powers. Aihwa Ong (this volume) analyses the way that Malaysian women are positioned by conflicting discourses of sexuality, nationalism, modernity and religion. However, Ong focuses on the way in which these discourses are negotiated with differently by women from different class positions. She challenges the notion that women's responses to Islamic revivalism and modernisation can be framed in terms of collusion or resistance, since university women in Malaysia often wear a full body covering, whilst working-class women in factories do not. Neither of these forms of dress can be seen simply to align these women to the poles of Islam or the West.

Alison Murray (this volume) tackles prostitution and prostitutes' rights within the postcolonial context, another perennial feminist preoccupation. Arguing that the prominent emphasis on sex trafficking is often fuelled by an implicit or explicit agenda to end prostitution, Murray suggests that sex work should be seen as a viable choice of income generation. She redefines trafficking as a form of economic migration, contending that the difference between forced and unforced prostitution is irrelevant. Her contentious argument takes issue with those feminists who regard all prostitution as a form of patriarchal oppression that needs to be eradicated. Murray insists that it is the criminalisation of sex work that creates the conditions in which sex workers can be exploited, rather than the nature of the work itself. This allows her to point up the continuity of salacious and sensationalist characterisations of a sexual slave trade circulated by anti-trafficking campaigns with previous missions of 'rescue work', many of which, such as nineteenth-century missions to save 'fallen women', aimed to reform women of their immoral earning capacities rather than to protect them as workers in a chosen field. The economic inequalities, which make sex work a viable and attractive occupation for Asian or any other women, mean that such a choice must be regarded as constrained by the same variables of privilege or dispossession within global capital that prompt all economic migrants (such as domestic workers). Indeed, Murray ponders, might not the critical interest in American sex tourism to Asia serve to mask the other elements of American neo-imperial capitalism and government policy which similarly exploit Asian labour (both male and female) abroad and at home?

Another approach to the discourses of sexualised difference that facilitates sex tourism is taken by Joseph A. Boone (this volume). In an antidote to the usual attention to the heterosexual male exoticisation and eroticisation of the female Oriental body, Boone examines the related sexualisation of the male Oriental body and its significance for the construction of Western masculinities. His focus on the racialisation of sexual desire and the sexualisation of race links contemporary gay sex tourism to heterosexual 'adventures' in the nineteenth century. In this he relates visual and literary cultural consumption to the bodily consumption of sex acts, exploring how the sexual exchange is differently experienced by subjects produced through different psycho-sexual formations (see also Nanda, 1993).

THE HAREM AND THE VEIL

The image of the secluded and veiled Oriental/Muslim woman, the hidden secret presumed to lie at the heart of the Orient, has fascinated the West for centuries. The harem walls or their sartorial extension by means of the veil have not just stood for a thwarted Western male desire to gaze upon forbidden female beauty but have also figured as the obstacle that maintains the mystery of the impenetrable realm of the Orient itself. The trope of the veiled woman is so powerful a motif that, as Meyda Yeğenoğlu (this volume) argues, 'whether he likes it or not, for the European subject there is always more to the veil than the veil'. This simple garment is invested with the potency to hide or reveal the 'truth' about the Orient which the West ultimately seeks. It is clear from the earliest Western accounts of travellers that the response to the veil is always overdetermined, reliant on a series of gendered, imperial and classed dynamics which respond to the seclusion of women in a variety of ways but which always privilege the veil as a symbol of the hidden order of Oriental society and as proof of its inimical difference from the West.

Although the veil is inevitably identified as an exclusively Muslim practice and claimed as such by many advocates of female veiling, this method of ensuring the public modesty of women was, for centuries, observed by diverse populations in the Middle East, including Druze, Christian and Jewish communities (Keddie, 1991). A preserve often of the wealthy and the urban, veiling was traditionally found less often in the country where women were required to labour out of doors and where markers of social status were differently observed. Indeed, it is the issue of status preservation that lies at the heart of veiling and of spatial methods of seclusion such as the harem and the high-caste Hindu institution of zenana. As Leslie Pierce (1993) explains, the division of the harem space derives from the requirement to seclude and protect that which is holy or forbidden (*haram*). Applying initially to religious sites and the body of the sultan, who, as caliph, embodied the religious leadership of the *umma*, the notion of harem operated to sequester the sacred from contact with the unholy. As Peirce makes clear, to map on to the harem a European notion of public and private, with public as the domain of politics and power and private as outside the workings of power, is to misrecognise that, within the spatial relations of seclusion, it was proximity to the interior of the imperial household that bespoke power and status, not distance from it in some outside public domain.[12]

Beyond the imperial harem, Fatima Mernissi argues that there is an experiential and ideological divide in Muslim society between the public world of the *umma*, coded as male, and the secluded world of the home and harem, coded as female and familial. This separation is preserved by the veil which allows women to pass through the spaces of the public without losing the security of seclusion. This protects the *umma* from the chaos of *fitna*, or illicit sexual behaviours, that would be unleashed if women's sexuality were permitted to run untrammelled. As Mernissi points out (1975, and this volume), Islam differs from the West in seeing female sexuality as dangerously active (rather than as intrinsically passive) and thus as something in need of control (see Ong, this volume).

But, as Sarah Graham-Brown demonstrates in her analysis of the web of female relationships within and without the harem space, the supposedly imprisoning harem was in fact the site of female society, structured by its own internal hierarchies and permeated by visitors and workers as well as by journeys out by its inhabitants.[13] This vision of the harem as the social space of the household inhabited by women and children is at odds with the Western fixation on it as a brothel-like sexual prison that animated so much cultural production in the last two centuries (see Nochlin, 1983; Lewis, 1996; Benjamin, 1997). Whilst Mernissi conceives the *umma* as a public realm contrasted to the private of the home and harem, others extend this to argue that the network of relations inside and between harems constitutes another public in which women could play important roles as cultural producers and consumers for a female public that was, of course, invisible to most Western and all male observers (Micklewright, 1999).

Western women travellers found their accounts were in great demand since they could show the 'real' harem about which men were so curious. But they might undercut the long-treasured illusions that helped create a market for their insider accounts in the first place. As Billie Melman (1992) has demonstrated, women's representation of the harem tended to be determined by their own concerns about European gender relations. Thus, the harem appeared as oppressive (evidencing the potential for sexual enslavement) or liberating (the ability of Muslim women to own property) in relation to local anxieties about female agency (see also Suleri, 1992b).

The extent to which Western stereotypes impinged on the self-representation of women produced as Orientalised subjects is seen in Reina Lewis's analysis of the photographs of cross-cultural dressing by the English writer Grace Ellison and the Ottoman Zeyneb Hanum in the early twentieth century (Lewis, this volume). Part of a growing interest in the self-conscious manipulation of Orientalist cultural codes by those produced as its objects (see also Codell and Macleod, 1998; Beaulieu and Roberts, 2002), Lewis examines the photographs which illustrate Ellison and Zeyneb Hanum's accounts of harem life. Analysing the inherent problem in their performance of racialised and gendered identities she argues that, within the unequal power relations of Orientalist discourse, the iterative elements that make a performance recognisable do not translate equally across cultures. Nor are they equally available to differently racialised writing subjects. It is here that the overdetermined nature of the veil comes into play for, although it functions for the Occident as guarantor of Zeyneb Hanum's authentic Turkish female identity, her self-presentation in 'Turkish' dress in a book about her time in Europe is not simply anachronistic. It also reconstructs her Turkish past in the terms of European fantasy – since in Istanbul she, like most elite women, would have worn Paris fashions at home. When worn in Europe the veil's marking of racialised bodies and gendered spaces produces a haremisation effect (Apter, 1992) that newly reveals the gender segregations of Europe's own structures of public and private.

The Western obsession with the harem reveals the harem's efficacy within European discourse as a stereotypical or generic space (see Mills, this volume). As such, it operates as an eminently flexible counterweight to the other domestic of the European home to which it was posed in such absolute alterity. And this relational dynamic structured the experience and forms of activism taken by Orientalised women too. Inderpal Grewal's study of women in India in the nineteenth and early twentieth centuries demonstrates the links between the colonial stereotype of the harem and the construction of 'home' in Indian nationalist discourse (Grewal, 1996). In this, purdah and the zenana were recast as a morally superior space presided over and signified by the new and, significantly, relational category of 'Indian woman' that came to characterise emergent nationalist discourse. This process of reframing female identity and spaces re-inscribed local patriarchal structures as signs of moral superiority in contrast to the immorality attributed to the unsegregated memsahib scandalously mingling in public with men. On the other side of the equation, European women's tendency to desexualise the zenana is seen to be driven by a desire to avoid having all women, themselves included, suffused with the immorality attributed to the harem stereotype, whilst also seeking to maintain a racialised superiority (see also Nair, 1990). Grewal explores the different dynamics of rescue work when undertaken by a colonised rather than colonial subject, such as in the case of the Indian reformer Pandita Ramabai and her establishment of missionary-style 'homes' for prostituted women and Hindu widows.

Meyda Yeğenoğlu takes a psychoanalytic approach to the veil (see also Copjec, 1994), arguing that the veil – symbolising the truth of the ultimately different Orient – is essential to the constitution of the European colonial subject. This process of subject formation, she contends, relies on cultural differences which are relentlessly sexualised. This is testified to by the central recurrent fantasy of penetrating the veil (fantasies that are sexual, territorial and epistemological). But she also explores how the experience of the veil and its various usages as a barrier and a mode of (apparent) revelation can testify to the agency of resisting colonised subjects. She analyses the way that Algerian nationalist women changed tactics once the French realised they were carrying arms under their veils. Selectively unveiling, they were able to move past French soldiers who, reading their uncovered Algerian female bodies as signs that they had been won over by the West, were unable to recognise them as a security threat. Disrupting rather than simply reversing the logic of Orientalist binaries (veiled/unveiled, traditional backwardness/progressive Europeanised modernity), the colonised Algerian women veiled, unveiled and re-veiled to bewildering effect. Their displacement also produced new and previously unimaginable significations for the veil within local structures of meaning – though these opportunities for the veil to sign female insurgency are historically contingent and fleeting, as the subsequent events discussed by Winifred Woodhull demonstrate.

Woodhull, in her reading (this volume) of the political significance of the representation of the veil, shows that the nationalists as well as the colonialists saw the Algerian woman as the embodiment of the whole country, whether she be a symbol of Europeanised modernity or of tradition coded as anti-imperialist.[14] This tendency, she argues, has operated to the detriment of Algerian women whose exclusion from political and economic power has been a feature of postcolonial government in which female liberation becomes demonised as a Western, read imperialist, intrusion. Whether worn through choice or compunction, the veil continues to be a changing form of bodily presentation whose efficacy must be understood as relational. As such, the increased prevalence of veiling through choice by a younger generation of women in the West and the East can be seen as a response to local and international changes. Fadwa El Guindi (this volume) draws attention to the 'new veiling' in Egypt in the 1970s – when young college-educated women took up the veil as part of an Islamic revivalism that revitalised Islamic dress for a new generation. She does so in order to reinsert the tradition of religious feminism into the historiography of Middle-Eastern feminism of the late nineteenth and early twentieth century where local interest in Western discourses of modernity and progress have often been privileged (see also Badran, 1996; Baron, 1994; Nelson, 1996). Arguing that the new veiling originates in female agency (rather than being mandated by male clerics), she highlights how in some circumstances Islamic religiosity is seen to offer women true emancipation – in contrast to the false emancipation of Western women, exploited and sexualised in Western consumer society (see also Nader, 1989). But, again, this female agency needs to be situated historically in relation to the international rise of fundamentalisms in many religions (on contestations of the new veiling by feminists and by state apparatuses in Turkey, see Göçek, 1999; on veiling in postcolonial France, see Blank, 1999).

The meanings of dress acts and spatial behaviours are never singular (Kondo, 1997). Observance can act as an alibi for women's behaviour, legitimating work and travel outside the home and permitting activities impossible without a visible proof of respectability (Abu Odeh, 1993). The veil's meaning for its wearers will vary in each period and locale and is differently legible to different observers. These meanings are not, it must be noted, just determined by whether the observer is a Muslim or not, a Westerner or not, but will be nuanced by differences of class, region, religiosity, generation and politics and need to be located in relation to other sartorial expressions of postcolonial racialised identity (Donnell, 1999). To look for a singular meaning to the veil would be an error of Orientalist proportions.

GENDER AND POST/COLONIAL SPATIAL RELATIONS

Space has become a central issue in feminist discussions of the relations between the colonial and the colonised, and the 'third world', broadly speaking, and the first world (Massey, 1994; Rose, 1993). Brah re-animates Adrienne Rich's concept of the politics of location to discuss the new theoretical models of diaspora, displacement, home and the border that are needed to formulate a response to the (gendered) effects of late capitalism's global relations (Brah, this volume). Several theorists have focused on the domestic economy within the colonial context. McClintock focuses on the erotics of the metropolitan domestic sphere in relation to Arthur Munby and his servant Hannah Cullwick, while Rose focuses on the way that the domestic is figured in the context of the Siege of Lucknow, that crucial moment for conceptualising both Indian nationalism and British imperial decline (McClintock and Blunt, both this volume).

Western women, travelling to other countries within the colonial period, seem to point up some of the tensions in colonial relations and the way that these conflicts were worked out in the relation between British and indigenous women and men (McEwan, 2000; Mills, 1991). Some of them travelled alone or with indigenous male companions because, protected as they were by the colonial authority, an attack on them would be treated as an attack on the colonial authorities. However, Blake (1990) questions the assumption that women's colonial travel writing is necessarily different, more empathetic, than male writing, arguing that there is a difference of context, audience and status rather than one of gender. Mills also describes the complexities of colonial space, arguing that masculine space must be set alongside and in the context of the other (and often overlapping) spaces of British and indigenous women (this volume).

Critics, such as Schaffer, have examined women's relation to the wilderness or, in the Australian context, the bush, which has always been one of complex negotiation (Schaffer, 1988). The Australian outback was, and is still, seen as a space of national self-defining, conceptualised as feminine, an all-absorbing mother earth, which yet was seen as restricted to males alone. Many of the most important narratives in Australian exploration history have been the preserve of white male writers who have pitted themselves in heroic struggles of endurance to survive in the Australian desert regions and to cross from North to South or to discover a mythical inland sea (Ryan, 1996). This symbolisation of the bush, as the testing site for a certain type of Australian white male subjectivity, affects the way that spatial relations are conceptualised for Aboriginal people who largely inhabit these areas of wilderness (when they are not restricted to reservations nearer to the white inhabited coastal regions) and have claims to ownership of large areas of these supposed off-limits and dangerous places (Gelder and Jacobs, 1998).

The sense of possible alliances between Aboriginal and Western women is the focus of Jane Jacobs's article (this volume). Jacobs remains sceptical about some of the motives of the ecofeminist involvement in Aboriginal land right campaigns, examining, in particular, the role of ecofeminist campaigners in the action by the Arrernte people of central Australia in trying to stop the flooding of women's sacred sites in the proposed building of a dam. Whilst it would seem that Australian and British ecofeminists, within this context, would be sensitive to issues of difference, Jacobs traces the way that there may still remain a sediment of unthought through colonial assumptions within their actions and also essentialist, but European, notions of women's and Aboriginal relation to the land. The actions of the ecofeminist campaigners around this sacred site bear striking resemblances to the actions of Western women in the nineteenth century in trying to 'open up' the harem and campaign on behalf of oppressed women; in this instance, the campaigners' actions, trying to protect the site, led to the 'opening up' of the site which, by its very nature as a sacred site, needed to remain secret.

CONCLUSION

Compiling this book has been both a delight and a nightmare for us. Re-reading voices from the past has reminded us how important it is to historicise and theorise the position of the present. It has reaffirmed for us how much a knowledge of feminist theory and praxis can help to make sense of varied postcolonial experiences. These sources also remind us that, whilst gender will always be imbricated in the matrix of power, exploitation and resistance that characterises colonialism and the postcolonial, it is not always the predominant factor in people's consciousness nor is it always the most effective rallying point. We have included feminist theorising from a range of disciplines in order to examine not just the textual and discursive nature of colonial and postcolonial discourse in relation to gender but also the material effects of the postcolonial condition on the practices developed in relation to it. The dialogue between feminists that this book represents also demonstrates how political and scholarly opinion is formed in specific historical, personal and geographical circumstances, endlessly reframed in response to changes in the global picture.

There are many areas of concern that we have not been able to include here (our original proposal had over sixty pieces that have now been whittled down to the current thirty-three) and we want to end this introduction by sketching some of those areas for further work. AIDS and HIV have become an urgent concern and excellent work has been done in this area, analysing the cruel productivity of interconnecting discourses of racialised sexuality with international capital and regional gender relations (see for example, Bhatt, 1997; Patton, 1992). We would also like to highlight the interest in globalisation and transnational identities (heralded in this book by Brah and Ong) and to signal the hugely expanded field of feminist political theory and development studies which has tackled many of the same concerns articulated by sources in this volume (Visvanathan et al, 1997). Similarly a great deal of productive work has been done on representation in the fields of literary and media and cultural studies (in addition to works already cited, see also Levy,1991; Ferguson, 1992; Paxton, 1992; Jordan and Weedon, 1995; and the anthologies by Williams and Chrisman, 1993; and Ashcroft, Griffiths and Tiffin, 1995). This research work and the selection of essays which we have included in this anthology help to foreground feminist theorisings of race and racism and feminist analyses of gender issues within the colonial and postcolonial sphere. Whilst many have suggested that postcolonial theory, in its present institutionalised form, is perhaps overburdened with the abstract, unable to focus on the specific and the concrete, perhaps paradoxically even on the political, and thus has come to the end of its 'moment' in mainstream theory, the vibrancy and situatedness of feminist theory in this area, as demonstrated by the essays included here, speak of a consistent concern with the particularities of the way identities and political positions are worked out within the postcolonial context. This may indicate a way in which, rather than discarding postcolonial theory for a 'new' concern, postcolonial theory itself can be re-examined and seen as one important trajectory among others for the discussion of the postcolonial.

NOTES

1. A similar movement can be seen to have occurred in the development of postmodernist theory, where an initial reliance on feminist theorising for insights into theoretical problems was soon transmuted into a masculinist orthodoxy which erased all trace of that intellectual legacy (see Morris, 1988).
2. Indira Ghose in conversation.
3. Like many people working in this area, we have found that the crisis in Afghanistan has brought a renewed contemporaneity to this material, but the imperialist activities of the Bush/Blair-led alliance against terrorism have of course yet again paid little attention to women's real needs. Rather, the alliance has used the figure of the veiled Afghan woman as the symbol par excellence of Islamic oppression, leading to a frantic rush to get the first photograph of the first de-burqaed Afghan woman as proof of the West's magnanimous 'liberation' of third-world women. See also 'Women Reflect on the New World Dis-Order: Special Issue', *Trouble and Strife*, no. 43, Summer 2002.
4. On identity politics and critiques thereof see *Feminist Review*, 31, 1989.
5. For a statement of WAF's aims see their website: www.gn.apc.org/waf
6. For a recent overview of the subaltern debate see 'Revisiting the Subaltern in the New Empire: special issue', *Cultural Studies*, vol. 17, no. 1, Fall 2003.
7. See also 'Queer Transexions of Race, Nation and Gender; special issue', *Social Text*, pp. 52–3, 1997; and also Parker et al., 1992.
8. These acts aimed to restrict male sexual activity and hence the spread of sexually transmitted disease by the detention and enforced examination of any woman assumed to be a prostitute.
9. On the enforced use of Depo-Provera for Black women in South Africa, see Wicomb, 1994.
10. Female circumcision is also referred to as female genital mutilation (FGM) in an effort to challenge the apparently more neutral medicalised term 'circumcision'. The use of the term 'mutilation' also aims to emphasise that procedures such as cliteridectomy and infibulation have far more profound and damaging effects on women's reproductive health and psychology than is usually the case with male circumcision. But neither appellation is straightforward since some women who have been circumcised may prefer not to be labelled as mutilated nor seen as the mutilators of their daughters. As Nahid Toubia (in conversation) argues, 'any terminology which brands people as mutilated or as mutilators is just as offensive as the practice itself'. However, as she also notes, the term FGM, in wide use since the 1980s, 'has been a very effective policy and advocacy tool' (Rahman and Toubia 2000: p. x).
11. Information about RAINBO can be found at www.rainbo.org
12. Thus from the sixteenth century as the sultan became increasingly located in one place and brought his female dependants into the spatial relations of the imperial harem, women, generally older women, were able to exercise considerable power within and from the imperial household (Peirce, 1993).
13. In North Africa and other societies where there is seclusion, it should be noted that the term 'women's quarters' rather than the term 'harem' is often used. This practice excludes certain groups of men from what are seen as women's spaces, allowing male relatives into the household on women's terms. Women in North Africa, in Gadames in Southern Libya for example, have a different way of getting around cities; rather than using the streets they go from house to house over the rooftops, thus enabling them to travel within the city without contact with males.
14. On comparable struggles over the appearance of women in Iran, see De Groot, 1988; Paidar, 1996.

PART I
GENDERING COLONIALISM AND POSTCOLONIALISM/RACIALISING FEMINISM

1.1

'THE MASTER'S TOOLS WILL NEVER DISMANTLE THE MASTER'S HOUSE'

Audre Lorde

I agreed to take part in a New York University Institute for the Humanities conference a year ago, with the understanding that I would be commenting upon papers dealing with the role of difference within the lives of american women; difference of race, sexuality, class and age. For the absence of these considerations weakens any feminist discussion of the personal and the political.

It is a particular academic arrogance to assume any discussion of feminist theory in this time and in this place without examining our many differences, and without a significant input from poor women, black and third-world women and lesbians. And yet, I stand here as a black lesbian feminist, having been invited to comment within the only panel at this conference where the input of black feminists and lesbians is represented. What this says about the vision of this conference is sad, in a country where racism, sexism and homophobia are inseparable. To read this program is to assume that lesbian and black women have nothing to say of existentialism, the erotic, women's culture and silence, developing feminist theory or heterosexuality and power. And what does it mean in personal and political terms when even the two black women who did present here were literally found at the last hour? What does it mean when the tools of a racist patriarchy are used to examine the fruits of that same patriarchy? It means that only the most narrow perimeters of change are possible and allowable.

From: Audre Lorde (1983), 'The Master's Tools Will Never Dismantle the Master's House', pp. 94–101, in Cherríe Moraga and Gloria Anzaldúa (eds), *This Bridge Called My Back: Writings by Radical Women of Color* (New York: Kitchen Table Press).

The absence of any consideration of lesbian consciousness or the conscious-ness of third world women leaves a serious gap within this conference and within the papers presented here. For example, in a paper on material relation-ships between women, I was conscious of an either/or model of nurturing which totally dismissed my knowledge as a black lesbian. In this paper there was no examination of mutuality between women, no systems of shared support, no interdependence as exists between lesbians and women-identified women. Yet it is only in the patriarchal model of nurturance that women 'who attempt to emancipate themselves pay perhaps too high a price for the results', as this paper states.

For women, the need and desire to nurture each other is not pathological but redemptive, and it is within that knowledge that our real power is rediscovered. It is this real connection, which is so feared by a patriarchal world. For it is only under a patriarchal structure that maternity is the only social power open to women.

Interdependency between women is the only way to the freedom which allows the 'I' and 'be', not in order to be used, but in order to be creative. This is a difference between the passive 'be' and the active 'being'.

Advocating the mere tolerance of difference between women is the grossest reformism. It is a total denial of the creative function of difference in our lives. For difference must be not merely tolerated, but seen as a fund of necessary polarities between which our creativity can spark like a dialectic. Only then does the necessity for interdependency become unthreatening. Only within that interdependency of different strengths, acknowledged and equal, can the power to seek new ways to actively 'be' in the world generate, as well as the courage and sustenance to act where there are no charters.

Within the interdependence of mutual (non-dominant) differences lies that security which enables us to descend into the chaos of knowledge and return with true visions of our future, along with the concomitant power to effect those changes which can bring that future into being. Difference is that raw and powerful connection from which our personal power is forged.

As women, we have been taught either to ignore our differences or to view them as causes for separation and suspicion rather than as forces for change. Without community, there is no liberation, only the most vulnerable and tem-porary armistice between an individual and her oppression. But community must not mean a shedding of our differences, nor the pathetic pretense that these differences do not exist.

Those of us who stand outside the circle of this society's definition of accept-able women; those of us who have been forged in the crucibles of difference; those of us who are poor, who are lesbians, who are black, who are older, know that *survival is not an academic skill*. It is learning how to stand alone, unpop-ular and sometimes reviled, and how to make common cause with those other identified as outside the structures, in order to define and seek a world in which we can all flourish. It is learning how to take our differences and make them strengths. *For the master's tools will never dismantle the master's house.* They may allow us temporarily to beat him at his own game, but they will never enable us to bring about genuine change. And this fact is only threatening to those women who still define the master's house as their only source of support.

Poor and third world women know there is a difference between the daily manifestations and dehumanizations of marital slavery and prostitution, because it is our daughters who line 42nd Street. The Black panelists' observation about the effects of relative powerlessness and the differences of relationship between black women and men from white women and men illustrate some of our unique problems as black feminists. If white american feminist theory need not deal with the differences between us and the resulting difference in aspects of our oppressions, then what do you do with the fact that the women who clean your houses and tend your children while you attend conferences on feminist theory are, for the most part, poor and third world women? What is the theory behind racist feminism?

In a world of possibility for us all, our personal visions help lay the groundwork for political action. The failure of the academic feminists to recognize difference as a crucial strength is a failure to reach beyond the first patriarchal lesson. Divide and conquer, in our world, must become define and empower.

Why weren't other black women and third world women found to participate in this conference? Why were two phone calls to me considered a consultation? Am I the only possible source of names of black feminists? And although the black panelist's paper ends on an important and powerful connection of love between women, what about interracial co-operation between feminists who don't love each other?

In academic feminist circles, the answer to these questions is often 'We did not know who to ask.' But that is the same evasion of responsibility, the same cop-out, that keeps black women's art out of women's exhibitions, black women's work out of most feminist publications except for the occasional 'Special Third World Women's Issue'[1] and black women's texts off of your reading lists. But, as Adrienne Rich pointed out in a recent talk, white feminists have educated themselves about such an enormous amount over the past ten years, how come you haven't also educated yourselves about black women and the differences between us – white and black – when it is key to our survival as a movement?

Women of today are still being called upon to stretch across the gap of male ignorance and to educate men as to our existence and our needs. This is an old and primary tool of all oppressors to keep the oppressed occupied with the master's concerns. Now we hear that it is the task of black and third world women to educate white women, in the face of tremendous resistance, as to our existence, our differences, our relative roles in our joint survival. This is a diversion of energies and a tragic repetition of racist patriarchal thought.

Simone de Beauvoir once said: 'It is in the knowledge of the genuine conditions of our lives that we must draw our strength to live and our reasons for acting.' Racism and homophobia are real conditions of all our lives in this place and this time. *I urge each one of us here to reach down into that deep place of knowledge inside herself and touch that terror and loathing of any difference that lives there. See whose face it wears.* Then the personal as the political can begin to illuminate all our choices.

NOTE

1. *Conditions* of Brooklyn, NY is a major exception. It has fairly consistently published the work of women of color before it was 'fashionable' to do so. [editor's footnote]

1.2

'NOTES TOWARD A POLITICS OF LOCATION'

Adrienne Rich

I am to speak these words in Europe,[1] but I have been searching for them in the United States of America. A few years ago I would have spoken of the common oppression of women, the gathering movement of women around the globe, the hidden history of women's resistance and bonding, the failure of all previous politics to recognize the universal shadow of patriarchy, the belief that women now, in a time of rising consciousness and global emergency, may join across all national and cultural boundaries to create a society free of domination, in which 'sexuality, politics . . . work, . . . intimacy . . . thinking itself will be transformed'.[2]

I would have spoke these words as a feminist who 'happened' to be a white United States citizen, conscious of my government's proven capacity for violence and arrogance of power, but as self-separated from that government, quoting without second thought Virginia Woolf's statement in *Three Guineas* that 'as a woman I have no country. As a woman I want no country. As a woman my country is the whole world'.

This is not what I come here to say in 1984. I come here with notes but without absolute conclusions. This is not a sign of loss of faith or hope. These notes are the marks of a struggle to keep moving, a struggle for accountability.

Beginning to write, then getting up. Stopped by the movements of a huge early bumblebee which has somehow gotten inside this house and is reeling,

From: Adrienne Rich (1984), 'Notes Towards a Politics of Location', pp. 210–31, in Adrienne Rich, *Blood, Bread and Poetry: Selected Prose 1979–1985* (London: Little Brown & Co.).

bumping, stunning itself against windowpanes and sills. I open the front door and speak to it, trying to attract it outside. It is looking for what it needs, just as I am, and, like me, it has gotten trapped in a place where it cannot fulfill its own life. I could open the jar of honey on the kitchen counter and perhaps it would take honey from that jar; but its life process, its work, its mode of being cannot be fulfilled inside this house.

And I, too, have been bumping my way against glassy panes, falling half-stunned, gathering myself up and crawling, then again taking off, searching.

I don't hear the bumblebee any more and I leave the front door. I sit down and pick up a secondhand, faintly annotated student copy of Marx's *The German Ideology*, which 'happens' to be lying on the table.

I will speak these words in Europe, but I am having to search for them in the United States of North America. When I was ten or eleven, early in World War II, a girlfriend and I used to write each other letters which we addressed like this:

Adrienne Rich
14 Edgevale Road
Baltimore, Maryland
The United States of America
The Continent of North America
The Western Hemisphere
The Earth
The Solar System
The Universe

You could see your own house as a tiny fleck on an every-widening land-scape, or as the center of it all from which the circles expanded into the infinite unknown.

It is that question of feeling at the center that gnaws at me now. At the center of what?

As a woman I have a country; as a woman I cannot divest myself of that country merely by condemning its government or by saying three times 'As a woman my country is the whole world'. Tribal loyalties aside, and even if nation-states are now just pretexts used by multinational conglomerates to serve their interests, I need to understand how a place on the map is also a place in history within which a woman, a Jew, a lesbian, a feminist I am created and trying to create.

Begin, though, not with a continent or a country or a house, but with the geography closest in – the body. Here at least I know I exist, that living human individual whom the young Marx called 'the first premise of all human history'.[3] But it was not as a Marxist that I turned to this place, back from philosophy and literature and science and theology in which I had looked for myself in vain. It was as a radical feminist.

The politics of pregnability and motherhood. The politics of orgasm. The politics of rape and incest, of abortion, birth control, forcible sterilization. Of prostitution and marital sex. Of what had been named sexual liberation. Of prescriptive heterosexuality. Of lesbian existence.

And Marxist feminists were often pioneers in this work. But, for many women I knew, the need to begin with the female body – our own – was understood not as applying a Marxist principle *to* women, but as locating the grounds from which to speak with authority *as* women. Not to transcend this body, but to reclaim it. To reconnect our thinking and speaking with the body of this particular living human individual, a woman. Begin, we said, with the material, with matter, mma, madre, mutter, moeder, modder, etc., etc.

Begin with the material. Pick up again the long struggle against lofty and privileged abstraction. Perhaps this is the core of revolutionary process, whether it calls itself Marxist or Third World or feminist or all three. Long before the nineteenth century, the empirical witch of the European Middle Ages, trusting her senses, practicing her tried remedies against the anti-material, anti-sensuous, anti-empirical dogmas of the Church. Dying for that, by the millions. 'A female-led peasant rebellion'? – in any event, a rebellion against the idolatry of pure ideas, the belief that ideas have a life of their own and float along above the heads of ordinary people – women, the poor, the uninitiated.[4]

Abstractions severed from the doings of living people, fed back to people as slogans.

Theory – the seeing of patterns, showing the forest as well as the trees – theory can be a dew that rises from the earth and collects in the rain cloud and returns to earth over and over. But if it doesn't smell of the earth, it isn't good for the earth.

I wrote a sentence just now and x'd it out. In it I said that women have always understood the struggle against free-floating abstraction even when they were intimidated by abstract ideas. I don't want to write that kind of sentence now, the sentence that begins 'Women have always . . .' We started by rejecting the sentences that began 'Woman have always had an instinct for mothering' or 'Women have always and everywhere been in subjugation to men'. If we have learned anything in these years of late twentieth-century feminism, it's that that 'always' blots out what we really need to know: when, where and under what conditions has the statement been true?

The absolute necessity to raise these questions in the world: where, when and under what conditions have women acted and been acted on as women? Wherever people are struggling against subjection, the specific subjection of women, through our location in a female body, from now on has to be addressed. The necessity to go on speaking of it, refusing to let the discussion go on as before, speaking where silence has been advised and enforced, not just about our subjection, but about our active presence and practice as women. We believed (I go on believing) that the liberation of women is a wedge driven into all other radical thought, can open out the structures of resistance, unbind the imagination, connect what's been dangerously disconnected. Let us pay attention now, we said, to women: let men and women make a conscious act of attention when women speak; let us insist on kinds of process which allow more women to speak; let us get back to earth – not as paradigm for 'women', but as place of location.

Perhaps we need a moratorium on saying 'the body'. For it's also possible to abstract 'the' body. When I write 'the body', I see nothing in particular. To write 'my body' plunges me into lived experience, particularity: I see scars, disfigurements, discolorations, damages, losses, as well as what pleases me. Bones well nourished from the placenta; the teeth of a middle-class person seen by the dentist twice a year from childhood. White skin, marked and scarred by three pregnancies, an elected sterilization, progressive arthritis, four joint operations, calcium deposits, no rapes, no abortions, long hours at a typewriter – my own, not in a typing pool – and so forth. To say 'the body' lifts me away from what has given me a primary perspective. To say 'my body' reduces the temptation to grandiose assertions.

This body. White, female; or female, white. The first obvious, lifelong facts. But I was born in the white section of a hospital which separated Black and white women in labor and Black and white babies in the nursery, just as it separated Black and white bodies in its morgue. I was defined as white before I was defined as female.

The politics of location. Even to begin with my body I have to say that from the outset that body had more than one identity. When I was carried out of the hospital into the world, I was viewed and treated as female, but also viewed and treated as white – by both Black and white people. I was located by color and sex as surely as a Black child was located by color and sex – though the implications of white identity were mystified by the presumption that white people are the center of the universe.

To locate myself in my body means more than understanding what it has meant to me to have a vulva and clitoris and uterus and breasts. It means recognizing this white skin, the places it has taken me, the places it has not let me go.

The body I was born into was not only female and white, but Jewish – enough to geographic location to have played, in those years, a determining part. I was a *Mischling*, four years old when the Third Reich began. Had it been not Baltimore, but Prague or Lódz or Amsterdam, the ten-year-old letter writer might have had no address. Had I survived Prague, Amsterdam or Lódz and the railway stations for which they were deportation points, I would be some body else. My center, perhaps, the Middle East or Latin America, my language itself another language. Or I might be in no body at all.

But I am a North American Jew, born and raised three thousand miles from the war in Europe.

Trying as women to see the center. 'A politics', I wrote once, 'of asking women's questions'.[5] We are not 'the woman question' asked by somebody else; we are the women who ask the questions.

Trying to see so much, aware of so much to be seen, brought into the light, changed. Breaking down again and again the false male universe. Piling piece by piece of concrete experience side by side, comparing, beginning to discern patterns. Anger, frustration with Marxist or Leftist dismissals of these questions, this struggle. Easy now to call this disillusionment facile, but the anger was deep, the frustration real, both in personal relationships and political organizations. I wrote in 1975:

> Much of what is narrowly termed 'politics' seems to rest on a longing for certainty even at the cost of honesty, for an analysis which, once given, need not be reexamined. Such is the deadendedness – for women – of Marxism in our time.[6]

And it has felt like a dead end wherever politics has been externalized, cut off from the ongoing lives of women or of men, rarefied into an elite jargon, an enclave, defined by little sects who feed off each others' errors.

But, even as we shrugged away Marx along with the academic Marxists and the sectarian Left, some of us, calling ourselves radical feminists, never meant anything less by women's liberation than the creation of a society without domination; we never meant less than the making new of all relationships. The problem was that we did not know whom we meant when we said 'we'.

'The power men everywhere wield over women, power which has become a model for every other form of exploitation and illegitimate control.'[7] I wrote these words in 1978 at the end of an essay called 'Compulsory Heterosexuality and Lesbian Existence'. Patriarchy as the 'model' for other forms of domination – this idea was not original with me. It has been put forward insistently by white Western feminists, and in 1972 I had quoted from Lévi-Strauss: 'I would go so far as to say that even before slavery or class domination existed, men built an approach to women that would serve one day to introduce differences among us all.'[8]

Living for fifty-some years, having watched even minor bits of history unfold, I am less quick than I once was to search for single 'causes' or origins in dealings among human beings. But suppose we could trace back and establish that patriarchy has been everywhere the model. To what choices of action does that lead us in the present? Patriarchy exists nowhere in a pure state; we are the latest to set foot in a tangle of oppressions grown up and around each other for centuries. This isn't the old children's game where you choose one strand of color in the web and follow it back to find your prize, ignoring the others as mere distractions. The prize is life itself, and most women in the world must fight for their lives on many fronts at once.

> We . . . often find it difficult to separate race from class from sex oppression because in our lives they are most often experienced simultaneously. We know that there is such a thing as racial-sexual oppression which is neither solely racial nor solely sexual . . . We need to articulate the real class situation of persons who are not merely raceless, sexless workers but for whom racial and sexual oppression are significant determinants in their working/economic lives.

This is from the 1977 Combahee River Collective statement, a major document of the US women's movement, which gives a clear and uncompromising Black-feminist naming to the experience of simultaneity of oppressions.[9]

Even in the struggle against free-floating abstraction, we have abstracted. Marxists and radical feminists have both done this. Why not admit it, get it said, so we can get on to the work to be done, back down to earth again? The faceless, sexless, raceless proletariat. The faceless, raceless, classless category of 'all women'. Both creations of white Western self-centeredness.

'To come to terms with the circumscribing nature of (our) whiteness.'[10] Marginalized though we have been as women, as white and Western makers of theory, we also marginalize others because our lived experience is thoughtlessly white, because even our 'women's cultures' are rooted in some Western tradition. Recognizing our location, having to name the ground we're coming from, the conditions we have taken for granted – there is a confusion between our claims to the white and Western eye and the woman-seeing eye,[11] fear of losing the centrality of the one even as we claim the other.

How does the white Western feminist define theory? Is it something made only by white women and only by women acknowledged as writers? How does the white Western feminist define 'an idea'? How do we actively work to build a white Western feminist consciousness that is not simply centered on itself, that resists white circumscribing?

It was in the writings but also in the actions and speeches and sermons of Black United States citizens that I began to experience the meaning of my whiteness as a point of location for which I needed to take responsibility. It was in reading poems by contemporary Cuban women that I began to experience the meaning of North America as a location which had also shaped my ways of seeing and my ideas of who and what was important, a location for which I was also responsible. I traveled then to Nicaragua, where, in a tiny impoverished country, in a four-year-old society dedicated to eradicating poverty, under the hills of the Nicaragua-Honduras border, I could physically feel the weight of the United States of North America, its military forces, its vast appropriations of money, its mass media, at my back; I could feel what it means, dissident or not, to be part of that raised boot of power, the cold shadow we cast everywhere to the south.

I come from a country stuck fast for forty years in the deep freeze of history. Any United States citizen alive today has been saturated with Cold War rhetoric, the horrors of communism, the betrayals of socialism, the warning that any collective restructuring of society spells the end of personal freedom. And, yes, there have been horrors and betrayals deserving open opposition. But we are not invited to consider the butcheries of Stalinism, the terrors of the Russian counter-revolution alongside the butcheries of white supremacism and Manifest Destiny. We are not urged to help create a more human society here in response to the ones we are taught to hate and dread. Discourse itself is frozen at this level. Tonight as I turned a switch searching for 'the news', that shinily animated silicone mask was on television again, telling the citizens of my country we are menaced by communism from El Salvador, that communism – Soviet variety, obviously – is on the move in Central America, that freedom is imperiled, that the suffering peasants of Latin America must be stopped, just as Hitler had to be stopped.

The discourse has never really changed; it is wearingly abstract. (Lillian Smith, white anti-racist writer and activist, spoke of the 'deadly sameness' of abstraction.)[12] It allows no differences among places, times, cultures, conditions, movements. Words that should possess a depth and breadth of allusions – words like *socialism*, *communism*, *democracy*, *collectivism* – are stripped of their historical roots, the many faces of the struggles for social justice and independence reduced to an ambition to dominate the world.

Is there a connection between this state of mind – the Cold War mentality, the attribution of all our problems to an external enemy – and a form of feminism so focused on male evil and female victimization that it, too, allows for no differences among women, men, places, times, cultures, conditions, classes, movements? Living in the climate of an enormous either/or, we absorb some of it unless we actively take heed.

In the United States large numbers of people have been cut off from their own process and movement. We have been hearing for forty years that we are the guardians of freedom, while 'behind the Iron Curtain' all is duplicity and manipulation, if not sheer terror. Yet the legacy of fear lingering after the witch hunts of the fifties hang on like the aftersmell of a burning. The sense of obliquity, mystery, paranoia surrounding the American Communist party after the Khrushchev Report of 1956: the party lost 30,000 members within weeks, and few who remained were talking about it. To be a Jew, a homosexual, any kind of marginal person was to be liable for suspicion of being 'Communist'. A blanketing snow had begun to drift over the radical history of the United States.

And, though parts of the North American feminist movement actually sprang from the Black movements of the sixties and the student left, feminists have suffered not only from the burying and distortion of women's experience, but from the overall burying and distortion of the great movements for social change.[13]

The first American woman astronaut is interviewed by the liberal-feminist editor of a mass-circulation women's magazine. She is a splendid creature, healthy, young, thick dark head of hair, scientific degrees from an elite university, an athletic self-confidence. She is also white. She speaks of the future of space, the potential uses of space colonies by private industry, especially for producing materials which can be advantageously processed under conditions of weightlessness. Pharmaceuticals, for example. By extension one thinks of chemicals. Neither of these two spirited women speaks of the alliances between the military and the 'private' sector of the North American economy. Nor do they speak of Depo-Provera, Valium, Librium, napalm, dioxin. *When big companies decide that it's now to their advantage to put a lot of their money into production of materials in space . . . we'll really get the funding that we need,* say, the astronaut. No mention of who 'we' are and what 'we' need funding for; no questions about the poisoning and impoverishment of women here on earth or of the earth itself. Women, too, may leave the earth behind.[14]

The astronaut is young, feels her own power, works hard for her exhilaration. She has swung out over the earth and come back, one more time passed all the tests. It's not that I expect her to come back to earth as Cassandra. But this experience of hers has nothing as yet to do with the liberation of women. A female proletariat – uneducated, ill nourished, unorganized, and largely from the Third World – will create the profits which will stimulate the 'big companies' to invest in space.

On a split screen in my brain I see two versions of her story: the backward gaze through streaming weightlessness to the familiar globe, pale blue and green and white, the strict and sober presence of it, the true intuition of relativity battering the heart;

   and the swiftly calculated move to a farther suburb, the male technocrats and the women they have picked and tested, leaving the familiar globe behind: the toxic rivers, the cancerous wells, the strangled valleys, the closed-down urban hospitals, the shattered schools, the atomic desert blooming, the lilac suckers run wild, the blue grape hyacinths spreading, the ailanthus and kudzu doing their final desperate part – the beauty that won't travel, that can't be stolen away.

A movement for change lives in feelings, actions and words. Whatever circumscribes or mutilates our feelings makes it more difficult to act, keeps our actions reactive, repetitive: abstract thinking, narrow tribal loyalties, every kind of self-righteousness, the arrogance of believing ourselves at the center. It's hard to look back on the limits of my understanding a year, five years ago – how did I look without seeing, hear without listening? It can be difficult to be generous to earlier selves, and keeping faith with the continuity of our journeys is especially hard in the United States, where identities and loyalties have been shed and replaced without a tremor, all in the name of becoming 'American'. Yet how, except through ourselves, do we discover what moves other people to change? Our old fears and denials – what helps us let go of them? What makes us decide we have to re-educate ourselves, even those of us with 'good' educations? A politicized life ought to sharpen both the senses and the memory.

The difficulty of saying I – a phrase from the East German novelist Christa Wolf.[15] But once having said it, as we realize the necessity to go further, isn't there a difficulty of saying 'we'? *You cannot speak for me. I cannot speak for us.* Two thoughts: there is no liberation that only knows how to say 'I'; there is no collective movement that speaks for each of us all the way through.

And so even ordinary pronouns become a political problem.[16]

- 64 cruise missiles in Greenham Common and Molesworth.
- 112 at Comiso.
- 96 Pershing II missiles in West Germany.
- 96 for Belgium and the Netherlands.

That is the projection for the next few years.[17]

- Thousands of women, in Europe and the United States, saying *no* to this and to the militarization of the world.

An approach which traces militarism back to patriarchy and patriarchy back to the fundamental quality of maleness can be demoralizing and even paralyzing . . . Perhaps it is possible to be less fixed on the discovery of 'original causes'. It might be more useful to ask, How do these values and behaviors get repeated generation after generation?[18]

The valorization of manliness and masculinity. The armed forces as the extreme embodiment of the patriarchal family. The archaic idea of women as a 'home front' even as the missiles are deployed in the backyards of Wyoming and Mutlangen. The growing urgency that an anti-nuclear, anti-militarist movement must be a feminist movement, must be a socialist movement, must be an anti-racist, anti-imperialist movement. That it's not enough to fear for the people we know, our own kind, ourselves. Nor is it empowering to give ourselves up to abstract terrors of pure annihilation. The anti-nuclear, anti-military movement cannot sweep away the missiles as a movement to save white civilization in the West.

The movement for change is a changing movement, changing itself, demasculinizing itself, de-Westernizing itself, becoming a critical mass that is saying in so many different voices, languages, gestures, actions: *It must change; we ourselves can change it.*

We who are not the same. We who are many and do not want to be the same.

Trying to watch myself in the process of writing this, I keep coming back to something Sheila Rowbotham, the British socialist feminist, wrote in *Beyond the Fragments*:

> *A movement helps you to overcome some of the oppressive distancing of theory and this has been a . . . continuing creative endeavour of women's liberation. But some paths are not mapped and our footholds vanish . . . I see what I'm writing as part of a wider claiming which is beginning. I am part of the difficulty myself. The difficulty is not out there.*[19]

My difficulties, too, are not out there – except in the social conditions that make all this necessary. I do not any longer *believe* – my feelings do not allow me to believe – that the white eye sees from the center. Yet I often find myself thinking as if I still believed that were true. Or, rather, my thinking stands still. I feel in a state of arrest, as if my brain and heart were refusing to speak to each other. My brain, a woman's brain, has exulted in breaking the taboo against women thinking, has taken off on the wind, saying, *I am the woman who asks the questions.* My heart has been learning in a much more humble and laborious way, learning that feelings are useless without facts, that all privilege is ignorant at the core.

The United States has never been a white country, though it has long served what white men defined as their interests. The Mediterranean was never white. England, northern Europe, if ever absolutely white, are so no longer. In a Leftist bookstore in Manchester, England, a Third World poster: *WE ARE HERE BECAUSE YOU WERE THERE.* In Europe there have always been the Jews, the original ghetto dwellers, identified as a racial type, suffering under pass laws and special entry taxes, enforced relocations, massacres: the scapegoats, the aliens, never seen as truly European but as part of that darker world that must be controlled, eventually exterminated. Today the cities of Europe have new scapegoats as well: the diaspora from the old colonial empires. Is anti-Semitism the model for racism, or racism for anti-Semitism? Once more, where does the question lead us? Don't we have to start here, where we are, forty years after the Holocaust, in the churn of Middle Eastern violence, in the midst of decisive ferment in South Africa – not in some debate over origins and precedents, but in the recognition of simultaneous oppressions?

I've been thinking a lot about the obsession with origins. It seems a way of stopping time in its tracks. The sacred Neolithic triangles, the Minoan vases with staring eyes and breasts, the female figurines of Anatolia – weren't they concrete evidence of a kind, like Sappho's fragments, for earlier woman-affirming cultures, cultures that enjoyed centuries of peace? But haven't they also served as arresting images, which kept us attached and immobilized? Human activity didn't stop in Crete or Çatal Hüyük. We can't build a society free from domination by fixing our sights backward on some long-ago tribe or city.

The continuing spiritual power of an image lives in the interplay between what it reminds us of – what it *brings to mind* – and our own continuing actions in the present. When the labrys becomes a badge for a cult of Minoan goddesses, when the wearer of the labrys has ceased to ask herself what she is doing on this earth, where her love of women is taking her, the labrys, too, becomes abstraction – lifted away from the heat and friction of human activity. The Jewish star on my neck must serve me both for reminder and as a goad to continuing and changing responsibility.

When I learn that, in 1913, mass women's marches were held in South Africa which caused the rescinding of entry permit laws; that, in 1956, 20,000 women assembled in Pretoria to protest pass laws for women, that resistance to these laws was carried out in remote country villages and punished by shootings, beatings and burnings; that, in 1959, 2,000 women demonstrated in Durban against laws which provided beerhalls for African men and criminalized women's traditional home brewing; that, at one and the same time, African women have played a major role alongside men in resisting apartheid, I have to ask myself why it took me so long to learn these chapters of women's history, why the leadership and strategies of African women have been so unrecognized as theory in action by white Western feminist thought. (And in a book by two men, entitled *South African Politics* and published in 1982, there is one entry under 'Women' [franchise] and no reference anywhere to women's political leadership and mass actions.)[20]

When I read that a major strand in the conflicts of the past decade in Lebanon has been political organizing by women of women, across class and tribal and religious lines, women working and teaching together within refugee camps and armed communities, and of the violent undermining of their efforts through the civil war and the Israeli invasion, I am forced to think.[21] Iman Khalife, the young teacher who tried to organize a silent peace march on the Christian–Moslem border of Beirut – a protest which was quelled by the threat of a massacre of the participants – Iman Khalife and women like her do not come out of nowhere. But we Western feminists, living under other kinds of conditions, are not encouraged to know this background.

And I turn to Etel Adnan's brief, extraordinary novel *Sitt Marie Rose*, about a middle-class Christian Lebanese woman tortured for joining the Palestinian Resistance, and read:

> She was also subject to another great delusion believing that women are protected from repression, and that the leaders considered political fights to be strictly between males. In fact, with women's greater access to

certain powers, they began to watch them more closely, and perhaps with even greater hostility. Every feminine act, even charitable and seemingly unpolitical ones, were regarded as a rebellion in this world where women had always played servile roles. Marie Rose inspired scorn and hate long before the fateful day of her arrest.[22]

Across the curve of the earth, there are women getting up before dawn, in the blackness before the point of light, in the twilight before sunrise; there are women rising earlier than men and children to break the ice, to start the stove, to put up the pap, the coffee, the rice, to iron the pants, to braid the hair, to pull the day's water from the well, to boil water for tea, to wash the children for school, to pull the vegetables and start the walk to market, to run to catch the bus for the work that is paid. I don't know when most women sleep. In big cities at dawn women are traveling home after cleaning offices all night, or waxing the halls of hospitals, or sitting up with the old and sick and frightened at the hour when death is supposed to do its work.

In Peru:

> Women invest hours in cleaning tiny stones and chaff out of beans, wheat and rice; they shell peas and clean fish and grind spices in small mortars. They buy bones or tripe at the market and cook cheap, nutritious soups. They repair clothes until they will not sustain another patch. They . . . search . . . out the cheapest school uniforms, payable in the greatest number of installments. They trade old magazines for plastic washbasins and buy second-hand toys and shoes. They walk long distances to find a spool of threat a slightly lower price.[23]

This is the working day that has never changed, the unpaid female labor which means the survival of the poor.

In minimal light I see her, over and over, her inner clock pushing her out of bed with her heavy and maybe painful limbs, her breath breathing life into her stove, her house, her family, taking the last cold swatch of night on her body, meeting the sudden leap of the rising sun.

In my white North American world they have tried to tell me that this woman – politicized by intersecting forces – doesn't think and reflect on her life. That her ideas are not real ideas like those of Karl Marx and Simone de Beauvoir. That her calculations, her spiritual philosophy, her gifts for law and ethics, her daily emergency political decisions are merely instinctual or conditioned reactions. That only certain kinds of people can make theory; that the white-educated mind is capable of formulating everything; that white middle-class feminism can know for 'all women'; that only when a white mind formulates is the formulation to be taken seriously.

In the United States, white-centered theory has not yet adequately engaged with the texts – written, printed and widely available – which have been for a decade or more formulating the political theory of Black American feminism:

the Combahee River Collective statement, the essays and speeches of Gloria I. Joseph, Audre Lorde, Bernice Reagon, Michele Russell, Barbara Smith, June Jordan, to name a few of the most obvious. White feminists have read and taught from the anthology *This Bridge Called My Back: Writings by Radical Women of Color*, yet often have stopped at perceiving it simply as an angry attack on the white women's movement. So white feelings remain at the center. And, yes, I need to move outward from the base and center of my feelings, but with a corrective sense that my feelings are not *the* center of feminism.[24]

And if we read Audre Lorde or Gloria Joseph or Barbara Smith, do we understand that the intellectual roots of this feminist theory are not white liberalism or white Euro-American feminism, but the analyses of Afro-American experience articulated by Sojourner Truth, W. E. B. Du Bois, Ida B. Wells-Barnett, C. L. R. James, Malcolm X, Lorraine Hansberry, Fannie Lou Hamer, among others? That Black feminism cannot be marginalized and circumscribed as simply a response to white feminist racism or an augmentation of white feminism; that it is an organic development of the Black movements and philosophies of the past, their practice and their printed writings? (And that, increasingly, Black American feminism is actively in dialogue with other movements of women of color within and beyond the United States?)

To shrink from or dismiss that challenge can only isolate white feminism from the other great movements for self-determination and justice within and against which women define ourselves.

Once again: Who is *we*?

This is the end of these notes, but it is not an ending.

NOTES

1. Talk given at the First Summer School of Critical Semiotics, Conference on Women, Feminist Identity and Society in the 1980s, Utrecht, Holland, June 1, 1984. Different versions of this talk were given at Cornell University for the Women's Studies Research Seminar, and as the Burgess Lecture, Pacific Oaks College, Pasadena, California.
2. Adrienne Rich, *Of Woman Born: Motherhood as Experience and Institution* (New York: W. W. Norton, 1976), p. 286.
3. Karl Marx and Frederick Engels, *The German Ideology*, ed. C. J. Arthur (New York: International Publishers, 1970), p. 42.
4. Barbara Ehrenreich and Deirdre English, *Witches, Midwives and Nurses: A History of Women Healers* (Old Westbury, NY: Feminist Press, 1973).
5. Adrienne Rich, *On Lies, Secrets, and Silence: Selected Prose 1966–1978* (New York: W. W. Norton, 1979), p. 17.
6. *Ibid.*, p. 193. [A.R., 1986: For a vigorous indictment of dead-ended Marxism and a call to 'revolution in permanence' see Raya Dunayevskaya, *Women's Liberation and the Dialectics of Revolution* (Atlantic Highlands, NJ: Humanities Press, 1985).]
7. Adrienne Rich, 'Compulsory Heterosexuality and Lesbian Existence', in *Blood, Bread and Poetry* (London: Virago, 1987), p. 68.
8. Rich, *On Lies, Secrets, and Silence*, p. 84.
9. Barbara Smith, ed., *Home Girls: A Black Feminist Anthology* (New York: Kitchen Table/Women of Color Press, 1983), pp. 272–283. See also Audre Lorde, *Sister Outsider: Essays and Speeches* (Trumansburg, NY: Crossing Press, 1984). See Hilda

Bernstein, *For Their Triumphs and for Their Tears: Women in Apartheid South Africa* (London: International Defence and Aid Fund, 1978), for a description of simultaneity of African women's oppressions under apartheid. For a biographical and personal account, see Ellen Kuzwayo, *Call Me Woman* (San Francisco: Spinsters/Aunt Lute, 1985).

10. Gloria I. Joseph, 'The Incompatible Ménage à Trois: Marxism, Feminism and Racism', in *Women and Revolution*, ed. Lydia Sargent (Boston: South End Press, 1981).

11. See Marilyn Frye, *The Politics of Reality* (Trumansburg, NY: Crossing Press, 1983), p. 171.

12. Lillian Smith, 'Autobiography as a Dialogue between King and Corpse', in *The Winner Names the Age*, ed. Michelle Cliff (New York: W. W. Norton, 1978), p. 189.

13. See Elly Bulkin, 'Hard Ground: Jewish Identity, Racism, and Anti-Semitism', in E. Bulkin, M. B. Pratt, and B. Smith, *Yours in Struggle: Three Feminist Perspectives on Anti-Semitism and Racism* (Brooklyn, NY: Long Haul, 1984; distributed by Firebrand Books, 141 The Commons, Ithaca, NY 14850).

14. *Ms.* (January 1948): p. 86.

15. Christa Wolf, *The Quest for Christa T*, trans. Christopher Middleton (New York: Farrar, Straus & Giroux, 1970), p. 174.

16. See Bernice Reagon, 'Turning the Century', in Smith, *Home Girls*, pp. 356–368; Bulkin, pp. 103, 190–193.

17. Information as of May 1984, thanks to the War Resisters League.

18. Cynthia Enloe, D*oes Khaki Become You? The Militarisation of Women's Lives* (London: Pluto Press, 1983), ch. 8.

19. Sheila Rowbotham, Lynne Segal and Hilary Wainwright, *Beyond the Fragments: Feminism and the Making of Socialism* (Boston: Alyson, 1981), pp. 55–56.

20. *Women under Apartheid* (London: International Defence and Aid Fund for Southern Africa in cooperation with the United Nations Centre Against Apartheid, 1981), pp. 87–99; Leonard Thompson and Andrew Prior, *South African Politics* (New Haven: Yale University Press, 1982). An article in *Sechaba* (published by the African National Congress) refers to 'the rich tradition of organization and mobilization by women' in the Black South African struggle ([October 1984]: p. 9).

21. Helen Wheatley, 'Palestinian Women in Lebanon: Targets of Repression', *TWANAS, Third World Student Newspaper*, University of California, Santa Cruz (March, 1984).

22. Etel Adnan, *Sitt Marie Rose*, trans. Georgina Kleege (Sausalito, CA: Post Apollo Press, 1982), p. 101.

23. Blanca Figueroa and Jeanine Anderson, 'Women in Peru', *International Reports: Women and Society* (1981). See also Ximena Bunster and Elsa M. Chaney, *Sellers and Servants: Working Women in Lima, Peru* (New York: Praeger, 1985) and Madhu Kishwar and Ruth Vanita, *In Search of Answers: Indian Women's Voices from 'Manushi'* (London: Zed, 1984), pp. 56–57.

24. Gloria Anzaldúa and Cherríe Moraga, eds. *This Bridge Called My Back: Writings by Radical Women of Color* (Watertown, MA: Persephone, 1981; distributed by Kitchen Table/Women of Color Press, Albany, NY).

1.3

'THE USES OF FUNDAMENTALISM'

Gita Sahgal and Nira Yuval-Davis*

The key question Jan Pieterse asks in his survey of the use of the term 'fundamentalism' is whether it is either a good analytical or political tool. As members of Women Against Fundamentalism, our answer is perhaps obvious. Yet while we disagree strongly with his overall conclusions we find much to agree with in his article. However, Pieterse bases his view of the different uses of the term on a set of binary oppositions. In describing these he unfortunately falls into the error that he describes – setting up a straw figure in order to combat it.

While objecting to the English term 'fundamentalism' Pieterse approves of the French term 'integrisme'. However, our definition of 'fundamentalism' is very similar to his definition of 'integrisme'. Having moved away from the narrow theological definition within Christian Protestantism, WAF (and we are by no means alone in this) have adopted a wider definition of fundamentalism. In our founding statement we say,

> By fundamentalism we are not referring to religious observance, which we see as a matter of individual choice, but rather to modern political movements which use religion as a basis for their attempt to win or consolidate power and extend social control.

---

*A response to Jan Nederveen Pieterse, 'Fundamentalism Discourse: Enemy Images' (1994), pp. 2–6, in *Women Against Fundamentalisms Journal*, no 5, also available at www.gn.apc.org/waf

From: Gita Sahal and Nira Yuval-Davis (1994), 'The Uses of Fundamentalism', pp. 7–9, in *Women Against Fundamentalisms*, no. 5

This rather compressed definition also takes into account use of the media and in other ways the sense of newness of the movements. Fundamentalism is not merely a defence of tradition in our definition. Pieterse has ignored this widely held definition. When we translated an article on France for the WAF journal the term 'integrisme' was translated as fundamentalism. It referred to the crusade of the Catholic right 'to re-establish the reign of our Lord' armed with the slogan 'God, Family, Fatherland'. Ann Rossiter's writings on Ireland have examined the historic roots of Catholic fundamentalism in Ireland and its relation to the state.

Pieterse also mentions the Indian term 'communalism'. The history and use of this term is instructive. The historian Bipin Chandra has defined this term as the 'belief that, because a group of people follow a particular religion, they have, as a result, common social, political and economic interests'.[1] It applies not only to rivalry and competition between religious groups but also between caste groups. The term is in very common use in India today and has pejorative overtones, inherited from its nationalist origins. As a term of abuse, it is used by the most 'politically correct' in Indian politics – the left and the liberals, who define it in opposition to the modernising project of nation building. Used in this sense, the term (and the phenomenon) have a very modern usage, gradually developed by Indian nationalists in the 1920s and 30s, who saw communalism as a political threat and found it necessary to name and discuss the problem in order to expose it.

But, this use of the word had originated in colonial discourse about Indian society.

> Communalism captured for the colonialist what they had conceptualised as a basic feature of Indian society – its religious bigotry and its fundamentally irrational character – long before the term came to be used in its Indian sense. Like tribalism and factionalism, communalism is given, endemic, inborn. Like them, it denies consciousness and agency to the subjected peoples of the colonised world. 'History' happens to these people; it can hardly be a process in which they play a significant part. (Pandey, 1990)[2]

While communalism was an ahistorical phenomenon in most colonialist discourses, nationalists tended to hisoricise it and situate it in modern times.

While it is important to be aware of different words used in different historical, cultural and linguistic contexts, the appropriation of fundamentalism, from its strictly Protestant origins to a term used across religious movements, is inevitable in anglophone discourse. In any culture, references to religious movements are clothed in the language of the dominant religious influence. No other word was so readily available for appropriation in transatlantic discourse but its use has spread far beyond that.[3] Rather than abandoning it, it would be more useful to import it back into English usage in relation to the self rather than the other. In other words instead of using it only to describe an outside threat, an 'alien other', it could be held up as a mirror to the dominant culture – to the huge influence that the various groupings that Pieterse discusses have on American politics and the ideology of the right. Even in England, relatively small sects such as the Plymouth Brethren have had a disproportionately large influence. With some well-placed lobbying they managed to get teaching on HIV and Aids removed from the National Curriculum, as a compulsory subject. Compare that with the persistent and relatively unsuccessful demand for voluntary aided status for private religious schols which are not Christian (mostly Muslim, but also of other minorities including black Christian sects). In a Christian country such as Britain, even one that is by no means fundamentalist, the space for white Christian fundamentalists to push their demands is considerable.

The spectre of fundamentalism has been used selectively in areas like the Middle East by both Israel and the US. All those who object to Pax Americana can be tarred with the fundamentalist brush. However, just because the word is used by discredited proponents does not mean that it is not valid. Jan Pieterse himself points out that fundamentalism is used very selectively as a bogey when it is in conflict with Western security interests. Many would not abandon the ideas of solidarity and mutuality embodied by the term socialism even though it was co-opted by authoritarian states, nor the concept of empowerment, now used by the World Bank and the IMF. The struggle to rescue the language of human rights, not only from a liberal capitalist ethic in which it originated but the specific aims of the American security establishment, was most poignantly demonstrated by the hundreds of groups lobbying the UN Human Rights conference in Vienna with their tales of torture and dispossession. Many of them came from countries allied with the USA – indigenous peoples from Latin America, dissidents from South Korea. Language is an area of contested meanings. Usages shift and change according to context – and historical developments.

Fundamentalist movements arise in all major religions and are a reaction to the crisis in/of modernity. As we have written in the introduction to *Refusing Holy Orders*:

> The recent rise of fundamentalism is linked to the crisis of modernity of social orders based on the belief in the principles of enlightenment, rationalism and progress. Both capitalism and communism have proved unable to fulfil people's material, emotional and spiritual needs. A general sense of despair and disorientation has opened people to religion as a source of solace. Religion provides a compass and an anchor; it gives people a sense of stability and meaning as well as a coherent identity.[4]

It is in relation to fundamentalism and modernity that Pieterse's constructions of discourses around fundamentalism as a series of binary oppositions breaks down. As he acknowledges, 'The dichotomic view of modernity/tradition is misleading.' For those of us for whom fundamentalism was not merely a polemical concept, this is of no great importance. In fact, it is impossibly reductive to squeeze all discussions of such a diverse and shifting phenomenon into 'binarism'.

Since Pieterse does not recognise 'fundamentalism' as a valid description, he has not discussed the common ground in discourses within fundamentalist movements: the sense of danger from outside, irrespective of whether the religious collectivity is a minority or majority; the claim of purity and authenticity; the right to interpret the religious text and to insist that this is the only true version of it; the imposition of social control on members of the collectivity and the drawing of boundaries of legitimacy of the collectivity; and above all the use of state media and other resources to capture power or maintain control.

In many respects, though, fundamentalist movements do not present themselves as homogeneous phenomena. Fundamentalism can align itself with different political trends in different countries. It can appear as a form of orthodoxy – a maintenance of traditional values – or as a revivalist radical phenomenon dismissing impure and corrupt forms of religion 'to return to original sources'. It can grow among persecuted minorities or among the powerful with backing of international resources. The fundamentalist gospel can rely heavily on sacred religious texts, but it can also be more experiential and linked to specific charismatic leadership.

Examining the concept of nationalism might help us to understand better the multiple, contemporary meanings of the term fundamentalism. Both cover such a variety of movements in very different historical circumstances. Though many have examined nationalist discourses such as Gellner[5] and Anderson,[6] they have not waved a wand to reduce the phenomenon to a series of discourses about it. Yet to say that Nelson Mandela and Radovan Karadic are both rationalists is to state the near impossibility of defining it. Here is one definition, describing some of the characteristics of nationalism:

> The discourse of nationalism is part of the post enlightenment discourse of modernity, of progress of human capability: but as a discourse of modernity it bears the distinct marks of an earlier age. Consequently, nationalism has everywhere a deeply divided relation to 'community' . . . On the one hand, nationalism must speak the language of rationality, of the equality of all individuals and of 'construction', the possibility of making the world as we want it; on the other it needs the language of blood and sacrifice, of historical necessity, of ancient (God-given) status and attributes – which is part of the discourse of community, as it were, and not of individual rationality.[7]

The most astonishing omission is Pieterse's discussion of the feminist use of the term, particularly his silence on the work of his colleague Amrita Chhachhi (mentioned in the bibliography but not in the article). Far from being an attack on a transhistorical structure called patriarchy, feminist theorists and activists have produced complex works detailing particular social and historical configurations which have led to the growth of fundamentalist movements and demands. Their work on the state is particularly important. Amrita Chhachhi's article on 'Forced Identities: the State, Communalism, Fundamentalism, and Women in India' is a part of a major contribution to the debate on the relationship between the state, capitalism, fundamentalism and women's rights/position in very specific case studies.

Because we differentiate between religion and fundamentalism, collapsing the two together can be especially dangerous in discourses about religion. It is precisely women from within various religious traditions who are in the strongest position to analyse the effects of fundamentalist control over them. They can see that the fundamentalist project is definitely a new development. The reference to scripture may allow space for women, for instance, to fight female genital mutilation as an un-Islamic practice,[8] or it may circumscribe what is permitted by tradition, like banning dancing and singing at weddings.[9] Either way, it is clearly a break with tradition not a continuation of it. Greater scriptural authority will not necessarily convert the devotee who uses her knowledge of her religion to follow the dictates of her heart. 'I am willing to be judged by God,' said one, 'but not by the mullahs of this world.'

Many members of WAF are in constant contact with women who remain within their religious traditions, many of whom have reinvented their religions to fulfil/satisfy very private needs. There may well be a difference between these women who have often led transgressive lives and those who are members of what Pieterse has termed 'new religious movements'. But it is the business of academics not WAF to make painstaking classifications about who is or is not an enemy 'other' and who a potential ally. We must focus our energies on finding ways to resist oppressive practices and increase areas of autonomy for women. Rayah Feldman says:

> Female genital mutilation has been shown not to be fundamentally an issue of religion. Yet many people believe that it is a religious requirement. Paradoxically, as seems to be happening in Sudan, religion may provide a forum from which to resist the practice. On the other hand, some fundamentalists may use it as a further means of repressing women. Clearly this issue, as others, shows that we need to draw distinctions between different genres of institutionalised religion, and engage in dialogues with religious opponents of AGM: Our role in WAF is obviously solidarity with those campaigning against FGM. What 'Female Genital Mutilation. Proposals for Change' teaches is that such solidarity cannot be given cheaply as a kneejerk reaction to the strong arm of fundamentalist men, but requires a close political analysis of the issues it raises.[10]

Politically, it is very important for WAF to use a term which is not specific to one movement such as Islam, because this would support a more narrow and confined reading – a racist usage of the term. (Although, this does not prevent us from using specific terms when referring to specific movements.) It would also prevent us from looking at the the the commonalities across religions and cultures. Far from wiping out divergence it is precisely our view of religious movements as social and political movements which alerts us to the dangers inherent in the politics of identity.[11] We can also see the problems in the left viewing of all anti-imperialism as a sort of sacred cow and their disastrous failure to recognise the character of the Khomeini regime in Iran.

Retaining the general term 'fundamentalism' has proven to be very important for WAF speakers who have found that that women from diverse backgrounds can relate to the phenomena we are describing. This sense of common experience is fundamental for political mobilising and creates links across religious and cultural specifics. As it does not deny difference in context and circumstances it is a very different response to earlier homogenising and ethnocentrist 'sisterhood is powerful' feminism.

Yes, divergency is important; so is coalition politics.[12] As Gayatri Chakravorty Spivak remarked:

> Deconstruction does not say anything against the usefulness of mobilising unities. All it says is that because it is useful it ought not to be monumentalised as the way things really are.[13]

NOTES

1. Bipin Chandra, *Communism in Modern India*, Delhi: 1984.
2. Gyanendra Pandey, *The Construction of Communalism in Colonial North India*, Delhi: OUP, 1990.
3. Fundamentalism as a present and increasing threat to women's human rights, *WAF* no. 4, ibid., A resolution adopted by women from over 20 countries.
4. Gita Sahgal and Nira Yuval-Davis (eds), *Refusing Holy Orders*, London, Virago, 1992.
5. Ernest Gellner, *Nations and Nationalism*, Oxford: Basil Blackwell, 1983.
6. Benedict Anderson, *Imagined Communities*, London: Verso, 1983.
7. Pandey, *The Construction of Communalism in Colonial North India*.
8. Rayah Feldman, 'Book review of *Female Genital Multilation: Proposals for Change*', *WAF* no. 4, Winter 92/93.
9. Gita Sahgal, 'Secular Space: the Experience of Asian Women Organising' in Sahgal and Yuval-Davis, *Refusing Holy Orders*, ibid.
10. Rayah Feldman, book review of *Female Genital Multilation*.
11. Julia Bard, 'Women Against Fundamentalism and the Jewish Community', *WAF* no. 4, Winter 92/93.
12. Nira Yuval-Davis, 'Women, Ethnicity, Empowerment', Institute of Social Studies Working Paper, Series no 151, 1993 (a revised version forthcoming in *Feminism and Psychology*, Spring 1994).
13. Gayatri Chakravorty Spivak, 'Reflections on Cultural Studies in the Post Colonial Conjecture', *Critical Studies*, vol. 3, no. 1, 1991.

'UNDER WESTERN EYES: FEMINIST SCHOLARSHIP AND COLONIAL DISCOURSES'

Chandra Talpade Mohanty

It ought to be of some political significance at least that the term 'colonization' has come to denote a variety of phenomena in recent feminist and left writings in general. From its analytic value as a category of exploitative economic exchange in both traditional and contemporary Marxisms (cf. particularly such contemporary scholars as Baran, Amin and Gunder-Frank) to its use by feminist women of colour in the US, to describe the appropriation of their experiences and struggles by hegemonic white women's movements,[1] the term 'colonization' has been used to characterize everything from the most evident economic and political hierarchies to the production of a particular cultural discourse about what is called the 'third world.'[2] However sophisticated or problematical its use as an explanatory construct, colonization almost invariably implies a relation of structural domination and a discursive or political suppression of the heterogeneity of the subject(s) in question. What I wish to analyse here specifically is the production of the 'Third World Woman' as a singular monolithic subject in some recent (western) feminist texts. The definition of colonization I invoke is a predominantly *discursive* one, focusing on a certain mode of appropriation and codification of 'scholarship' and 'knowledge' about women in the third world by particular analytic categories employed in writings on the subject which take as their primary point of reference feminist interests as they have been articulated in the US and western Europe.

My concern about such writings derives from my own implication and

From: Chandra Talpade Mohanty (1988), 'Under Western Eyes: Feminist Scholarship and Colonial Discourses', pp. 65–88, in *Feminist Review*, no. 30.

investment in contemporary debates in feminist theory and the urgent political necessity of forming strategic coalitions across class, race and national boundaries. Clearly, western feminist discourse and political practice are neither singular nor homogeneous in their goals, interests or analyses. However, it is possible to trace a coherence of *effects* resulting from the implicit assumption of 'the west' (in all its complexities and contradictions) as the primary referent in theory and praxis. Thus, rather than claim simplistically that 'western feminism' is a monolith, I would like to draw attention to the remarkably similar effects of various analytical categories and even strategies which codify their relationship to the Other in implicitly hierarchical terms. It is in this sense that I use the term 'western feminist'. Similar arguments pertaining to questions of methods of analysis can be made in terms of middle-class, urban African and Asian scholars producing scholarship on or about their rural or working-class sisters which assumes their own middle-class culture as the norm and codifies peasant and working-class histories and cultures as Other. Thus, while this article focuses specifically on western feminist discourse on women in the third world, the critiques I offer also pertain to identical analytical principles employed by third-world scholars writing about their own cultures.

Moreover, the analytical principles discussed below serve to distort western feminist political practices and limit the possibility of coalitions among (usually white) western feminists and working-class and feminist women of colour around the world. These limitations are evident in the construction of the (implicitly consensual) priority of issues around which apparently *all* women are expected to organize. The necessary and integral connection between feminist scholarship and feminist political practice and organizing determines the significance and status of western feminist writings on women in the third world for feminist scholarship, like most other kinds of scholarship, does not comprise merely 'objective' knowledge about a certain subject. It is also a directly political and discursive *practice* insofar as it is purposeful and ideological. It is best seen as a mode of intervention into particular hegemonic discourses (for example, traditional anthropology, sociology, literary criticism, etc.) and as a political praxis which counters and resists the totalizing imperative of age-old 'legitimate' and 'scientific' bodies of knowledge. Thus, feminist scholarly practices exist within relations of power – relations which they counter, redefine or even implicitly support. There can, of course, be no apolitical scholarship.

The relationship between Woman – a cultural and ideological composite Other constructed through diverse representational discourse (scientific, literary, juridical, linguistic, cinematic, etc.) – and women – real, material subjects of their collective histories – is one of the central questions the practice of feminist scholarship seeks to address. This connection between women as historical subjects and the representation of Woman produced by hegemonic discourses is not a relation of direct identity or a relation of correspondence or simple implication.[3] It is an arbitrary relation set up in particular cultural and historical contexts. I would like to suggest that the feminist writing I analyse here discursively colonizes the material and historical heterogeneities of the lives of women in the third world, thereby producing/representing a composite, singular 'third-world woman' – an image which appears arbitrarily constructed but nevertheless carries with it the authorizing signature of western humanist discourse.[4] I argue that assumptions of privilege and ethnocentric universality, on the one hand, and inadequate self-consciousness about the effect of western scholarship on the 'third world' in the context of a world system dominated by the west, on the other, characterize a sizable extent of western feminist work on women in the third world. An analysis of 'sexual difference' in the form of a cross-culturally singular, monolithic notion of patriarchy or male dominance leads to the construction of a similarly reductive and homogeneous notion of what I shall call the 'third-world difference' – that stable, ahistorical something that apparently oppresses most if not all the women in these countries. It is in the production of this 'third-world difference' that western feminisms appropriate and colonize the constitutive complexities which characterize the lives of women in these countries. It is in this process of discursive homogenization and systematization of the oppression of women in the third world that power is exercised in much of recent western feminist writing and this power needs to be defined and named.

In the context of the west's hegemonic position today, of what Anouar Abdel-Malek calls a struggle for 'control over the orientation, regulation and decision of the process of world development on the basis of the advanced sector's monopoly of scientific knowledge and ideal creativity',[5] western feminist scholarship on the third world must be seen and examined precisely in terms of its inscription in these particular relations of power and struggle. There is, it should be evident, no universal patriarchal framework which this scholarship attempts to counter and resist – unless one posits an international male conspiracy or a monolithic, transhistorical power structure. There is, however, a particular world balance of power within which any analysis of culture, ideology and socio-economic conditions has to be necessarily situated. Abdel-Malek is useful here, again, in reminding us about the inherence of politics in the discourses of 'culture':

> Contemporary imperialism is, in a real sense, a hegemonic imperialism, exercising to a maximum degree a rationalized violence taken to a higher level than ever before – through fire and sword, but also through the attempt to control hearts and minds. For its content is defined by the combined action of the military – industrial complex and the hegemonic cultural centers of the West, all of them founded on the advanced levels of development attained by monopoly and finance capital, and supported by the benefits of both the scientific and technological revolution and the second industrial revolution itself.[6]

Western feminist scholarship cannot avoid the challenge of situating itself and examining its role in such a global economic and political framework. To do any less would be to ignore the complex interconnections between first- and third-world economies and the profound effect of this on the lives of women in *all* countries. I do not question the descriptive and informative value of most western feminist writings on women in the third world. I also do not question the existence of excellent work which does not fall into the analytic traps I am concerned with. In fact I deal with an example of such work later on. In the context of an overwhelming silence about the experiences of women in these countries, as well as the need to forge international links between women's political struggles, such work is both path-breaking and absolutely essential. However, it is both to the *explanatory potential* of particular analytic strategies employed by such writing and to their *political effect* in the context of the hegemony of western scholarship that I want to draw attention here. While feminist writing in the US is still marginalized (except perhaps from the point of view of women of colour addressing privileged white women), western feminist writing on women in the third world must be considered in the context of the global hegemony of western scholarship – i.e., the production, publication, distribution and consumption of information and ideas. Marginal or not, this writing has political effects and implications beyond the immediate feminist or disciplinary audience. One such significant effect of the dominant 'representations' of western feminism is its conflation with imperialism in the eyes of particular third-world women.[7] Hence the urgent need to examine the *political* implications of our *analytic* strategies and principles.

My critique is directed at three basic analytical presuppositions which are present in (western) feminist discourse on women in the third world. Since I focus primarily on the Zed Press 'Women in the Third World' series, my comments on western feminist discourse are circumscribed by my analysis of the texts in this series.[8] This is a way of focusing my critique. However, even though I am dealing with feminists who identify themselves as culturally or geographically from the 'west', as mentioned earlier, what I say about these presuppositions or implicit principles holds for anyone who uses these analytical strategies, whether third-world women in the west or third-world women in the third world writing on these issues and publishing in the west. Thus, I am not making a culturalist argument about ethnocentrism; rather, I am trying to uncover how ethnocentric universalism is produced in certain analyses. As a matter of fact, my argument holds for any discourse that sets up its own authorial subjects as the implicit referent, i.e., the yardstick by which to encode and represent cultural Others. It is in this move that power is exercised in discourse.

The first analytical presupposition I focus on is involved in the strategic location or situation of the category 'women' vis-à-vis, the context of analysis. The assumption of women as an already constituted and coherent group with identical interests and desires, regardless of class, ethnic or racial location, implies a notion of gender or sexual difference or even patriarchy which can be applied universally and cross-culturally. (The context of analysis can be anything from kinship structures and the organization of labour to media representations.)

The second analytical presupposition is evident on the methodological level, in the uncritical way 'proof' of universality and cross-cultural validity are provided. The third is a more specifically political presupposition, underlying the methodologies and the analytic strategies, i.e., the model of power and struggle they imply and suggest. I argue that as a result of the two modes – or, rather, frames – of analysis described above, a homogeneous notion of the oppression of women as a group is assumed, which, in turn, produces the image of an 'average third-world woman'. This average third-world woman leads an essentially truncated life based on her feminine gender (read: sexually constrained) and being 'third world' (read: ignorant, poor, uneducated tradition-bound, religious, domesticated, family-oriented, victimized, etc.). This, I suggest, is in contrast to the (implicit) self-representation of western women as educated, modern, as having control over their own bodies and sexualities and the 'freedom' to make their own decisions. The distinction between western feminist re-presentation of women in the third world and western feminist self-presentation is a distinction of the same order as that made by some Marxists between the 'maintenance' function of the housewife and the real 'productive' role of wage-labour, or the characterization by developmentalists of the third world as being engaged in the lesser production of 'raw materials' in contrast to the real 'productive' activity of the first world. These distinctions are made on the basis of the privileging of a particular group as the norm or referent. Men involved in wage-labour, first-world producers and, I suggest, western feminists who sometimes cast third-world women in terms of 'ourselves undressed'[9] all construct themselves as the normative referent in such a binary analytic.

'WOMEN' AS CATEGORY OF ANALYSIS OR: WE ARE ALL SISTERS IN STRUGGLE

By women as a category of analysis, I am referring to the crucial presupposition that all of us of the same gender, across classes and cultures, are somehow socially constituted as a homogeneous group identifiable prior to the process of analysis. The homogeneity of women as a group is produced not on the basis of biological essentials, but rather on the basis of secondary sociological and anthropological universals. Thus, for instance, in any given piece of feminist analysis, women are characterized as a singular group on the basis of a shared oppression. What binds women together is a sociological notion of the 'sameness' of their oppression. It is at this point that an elision takes place between 'women' as a discursively constructed group and 'women' as material subjects of their own history.[10] Thus, the discursively consensual homogeneity of 'women' as a group is mistaken for the historically specific material reality of groups of women. This results in an assumption of women as an always-already constituted group, one which has been labelled 'powerless', 'exploited', 'sexually harassed', etc., by feminist scientific, economic, legal and sociological discourses. (Notice that this is quite similar to sexist discourse labelling women as weak, emotional, having math anxiety, etc.) The focus is not on uncovering the material and ideological specificities that constitute a group of women as 'powerless' in a particular context. It is rather on finding a variety of cases of 'powerless' groups of women to prove the general point that women as a group are powerless.[11]

In this section I focus on five specific ways in which 'women' as a category of analysis is used in western feminist discourse on women in the third world to construct 'third-world women' as a homogeneous 'powerless' group often located as implicit *victims* of particular cultural and socio-economic systems. I have chosen to deal with a variety of writers – from Fran Hosken, who writes primarily about female genital mutilation, to writers from the Women in International Development school who write about the effect of development policies on third-world women for both western and third-world audiences. I do not intend to equate all the texts that I analyse, nor will I ignore their respective strengths and weaknesses. The authors I deal with write with varying degrees of care and complexity; however, the *effect* of the representation of third-world women in these texts is a coherent one. In these texts women are variously defined as victims of male violence (Fran Hosken); victims of the colonial process (M. Cutrufelli); victims of the Arab familial system (Juliette Minces); victims of the economic development process (B. Lindsay and the – liberal – WID school); and finally, victims of the economic basis of *the* Islamic code (P. Jeffery). This mode of defining women primarily in terms of their *object status* (the way in which they are affected or not affected by certain institutions and systems) is what characterizes this particular form of the use of 'women' as a category of analysis. In the context of western women writing about and studying women in the third world, such objectification (however benevolently motivated) needs to be both named and challenged. As Valerie Amos and Pratibha Parmar argue quite eloquently, 'Feminist theories which examine our cultural practices as "feudal residues" or label us "traditional", also portray us as politically immature women who need to be versed and schooled in the ethos of western feminism. They need to be continually challenged.'[12]

Women as Victims of Male Violence

Fran Hosken, in writing about the relationship between human rights and female genital mutilation in Africa and the Middle East, bases her whole discussion and condemnation of genital mutilation on one privileged premise: the goal of genital mutilation is 'to mutilate the sexual pleasure and satisfaction of woman'.[13] This, in turn, leads her to claim that woman's sexuality is controlled as is her reproductive potential. According to Hosken, 'male sexual politics' in Africa and around the world 'share the same political goal: to assure female dependence and subservience by any and all means'. Physical violence against women (rape, sexual assault, excision, infibulation, etc.) is, thus, carried out 'with an astonishing consensus among men in the world'.[14] Here, women are defined systematically as the *victims* of male control – the 'sexually oppressed'. Although it is true that the potential of male violence against women circumscribes and elucidates their social position to a certain extent, defining women as archetypal victims freezes them into 'objects-who-defend-themselves', men into 'subjects-who-perpetrate-violence' and (every) society into a simple opposition between the powerless (read: women) and the powerful (read: men) groups of people. Male violence (if that indeed is the appropriate label) must be theorized and interpreted *within* specific societies, both in order to understand it better, as well as in order to effectively organize to change it.[15] Sisterhood cannot be assumed on the basis of gender; it must be forged in concrete historical and political praxis.

Women as Universal Dependants

Beverley Lindsay's conclusion to the book, *Comparative Perspectives on Third World Women: The impact of race, sex and class*, states: 'Dependency relationships, based upon race, sex and class, are being perpetuated through social, educational, and economic institutions. These are the linkages among Third World Women.'[16] Here, as in other places, Lindsay implies that third-world women constitute an identifiable group purely on the basis of shared dependencies. If shared dependencies were all that was needed to bind us together as a group, third-world women would always be seen as an apolitical group with no subject status! Instead, if anything, it is the *common context* of political struggle against class, race, gender and imperialist hierarchies that may constitute third-world women as a strategic group at this historical juncture. Lindsay also states that linguistic and cultural differences exist between Vietnamese and Black American women, but 'both groups are victims of race, sex and class'. Again, Black and Vietnamese women are characterized and defined simply in terms of their victim status.

Similarly, examine statements like: 'My analysis will start by stating that all African women are politically and economically dependent.'[17] Or: 'Nevertheless, either overtly or covertly, prostitution is still the main if not the only source of work for African women.'[18] *All* African women are dependent. Prostitution is the only work option for African women as a *group*. Both statements are illustrative of generalisations sprinkled liberally through a Zed Press publication, *Women of Africa: Roots of oppression*, by Maria Rosa Cutrufelli, who is described on the cover as an 'Italian Writer, Sociologist, Marxist and Feminist'. In the 1980s is it possible to imagine writing a book entitled 'Women of Europe: Roots of oppression'? I am not objecting to the use of universal groupings for descriptive purposes. Women from the continent of Africa can be descriptively characterized as 'Women of Africa'. It is when 'women of Africa' becomes a homogeneous sociological grouping characterized by common dependencies or powerlessness (or even strengths) that problems arise – we say too little and too much at the same time.

This is because descriptive gender differences are transformed into the division between men and women. Women are constituted as a group via dependency relationships vis-à-vis men, who are implicitly held responsible for these relationships. When 'women of Africa' (versus 'men of Africa' as a group?) are seen as a group precisely because they are generally dependent and oppressed, the analysis of specific historical differences becomes impossible, because reality is always apparently structured by divisions between two mutually exclusive and jointly exhaustive groups, the victims and the oppressors. Here the sociological is substituted for the biological in order, however, to create the same – a unity of women. Thus, it is not the descriptive potential of gender difference but the privileged positioning and explanatory potential of gender difference as the *origin* of oppression that I question. In using 'women of Africa' (as an already constituted group of oppressed peoples) as a category of analysis, Cutrufelli denies any historical specificity to the location of women as subordinate, powerful, marginal, central or otherwise, vis-à-vis particular social and power networks. Women are taken as a unified 'powerless' group prior to the historical and political analysis in question. Thus, it is then merely a matter of specifying the context *after the fact*. 'Women' are now placed in the context of the family or in the workplace or within religious networks, almost as if these systems existed outside the relations of women with other women and women with men.

The problem with this analytical strategy is, let me repeat, that it assumes men and women are already constituted as sexual–political subjects prior to their entry into the arena for social relations. Only if we subscribe to this assumption is it possible to undertake analysis which looks at the 'effects' of kinship structures, colonialism, organization of labour, etc. on women who are defined in advance as a group. The crucial point that is forgotten is that women are produced through these very relations as well as being implicated in forming these relations. As Michelle Rosaldo argues, 'woman's place in human social life is not in any direct sense a product of the things she does (or even less, a function of what, biologically, she is) but the meaning her activities acquire through concrete social interactions.'[19] That women mother in a variety of societies is not as significant as the value attached to mothering in these societies. The distinction between the act of mothering and the status attached to it is a very important one – one that needs to be stated and analysed contextually.

Married Women as Victims of the Colonial Process
In Lévi-Strauss's theory of kinship structures as a system of the exchange of women, what is significant is that exchange itself is not constitutive of the subordination of women; women are not subordinate because of the *fact* of exchange, but because of the *modes* of exchange instituted and the values attached to these modes. However, in discussing the marriage ritual of the Bemba, a Zambian matrilocal, matrilineal people, Cutrufelli in *Women of Africa* focuses on the fact of the marital exchange of women before and after western colonization, rather than the value attached to this exchange in this particular context. This leads to her definition of Bemba women as a coherent group affected in a particular way by colonization. Here again, Bemba women are constituted rather unilaterally as the victims of western colonization.

Cutrufelli cites the marriage ritual of the Bemba as a multi-stage event 'whereby a young man becomes incorporated into his wife's family group as he takes up residence with them and gives his services in return for food and maintenance'.[20] This ritual extends over many years and the sexual relationship varies according to the degree of the girl's physical maturity. It is only after the girl undergoes an initiation ceremony at puberty that intercourse is sanctioned and the man acquires legal rights over the woman. This initiation ceremony is the most important act of the consecration of women's reproductive power, so that the abduction of an uninitiated girl is of no consequence, while heavy penalty is levied for the seduction of an initiated girl. Cutrufelli asserts that the effect of European colonization has changed the whole marriage system. Now the young man is entitled to take his wife away from her people in return for money. The implication is that Bemba women have now lost the protection of tribal laws. However, while it is possible to see how the structure of the traditional marriage contract (as opposed to the post-colonial marriage contract) offered women a certain amount of control over their marital relations, only an analysis of the political significance of the actual practice which privileges an initiated girl over an uninitiated one, indicating a shift in female power relations as a result of this ceremony, can provide an accurate account of whether Bemba women were indeed protected by tribal laws *at all times*.

However, it is not possible to talk about Bemba women as a homogeneous group within the traditional marriage structure. Bemba women *before* the initiation are constituted within a different set of social relations compared to Bemba women *after* the initiation. To treat them as a unified group, characterized by the fact of their 'exchange' between male kin, is to deny the specificities of their daily existence and the differential *value* attached to their exchange before and after their initiation. It is to treat the initiation ceremony as a ritual with no political implications or effects. It is also to assume that in merely describing the *structure* of the marriage contract, the situation of women is exposed. Women as a group are positioned within a given structure, but there is no attempt made to trace the effect of the marriage practice in constituting women within an obviously changing network of power relations. Thus, women are assumed to be sexual–political subjects prior to entry into kinship structures.

Women and Familial Systems

Elizabeth Cowie, in another context,[21] points out the implications of this sort of analysis when she emphasizes the specifically political nature of kinship structures which must be analysed as ideological practices which designate men and women as father, husband, wife, mother, sister, etc. Thus, Cowie suggests, women as women are not simply *located* within the family. Rather, it is in the family, as an effect of kinship structures, that women as women are *constructed*, defined within and by the group. Thus, for instance, when Juliette Minces cites *the* patriarchal family as the basis for 'an almost identical vision of women' that Arab and Muslim societies have, she falls into this very trap.[22] Not only is it problematical to speak of a vision of women shared by Arab and Muslim societies, without addressing the particular historical and ideological power structures that construct such images, but to speak of the patriarchal family or the tribal kinship structure as the origin of the socio-economic status of women is again to assume that women are sexual–political subjects prior to their entry into the family. So, while on the one hand women attain value or status within the family, the assumption of a singular patriarchical kinship system (common to all Arab and Muslim societies, i.e., over twenty different countries) is what apparently structures women as an oppressed group in these societies! This singular, coherent kinship system presumably influences another separate and given entity, 'women'. Thus all women, regardless of class and cultural differences, are seen as being similarly affected by this system. Not only are *all* Arab and Muslim women seen to constitute a homogeneous oppressed group, but there is no discussion of the specific *practices* within the family which constitute women as mothers, wives, sisters, etc. Arabs and Muslims, it appears, don't change at all. Their patriarchical family is carried over from the times of the Prophet Muhammad. They exist, as it were, outside history.

Women and Religious Ideologies

A further example of the use of 'women' as a category of analysis is found in cross-cultural analyses which subscribe to a certain economic reductionism in describing the relationship between the economy and factors such as politics and ideology. Here, in reducing the level of comparison to the economic relations between 'developed' and 'developing' countries, the question of women is denied any specificity. Mina Modares, in a careful analysis of women and Shi'ism in Iran, focuses on this very problem when she criticizes feminist writings which treat Islam as an ideology separate from and outside social relations and practices, rather than a discourse which includes rules for economic, social and power relations within society.[23] Patricia Jeffery's otherwise informative work on Pirzada women in purdah considers Islamic ideology as a partial explanation for the status of women in that it provides a justification for the purdah.[24] Here, Islamic ideology is reduced to a set of ideas whose internalization by Pirzada women contributes to the stability of the system. The primary explanation for purdah is located in the control that Pirzada men have over economic resources and the personal security purdah gives to Pirzada women. By taking a specific version of Islam as *the* Islam, Jeffery attributes a singularity and coherence to it. Modares notes: ' "Islamic Theology" then becomes imposed on a separate and given entity called "women".' A further unification is reached: 'Women (meaning *all women*), regardless of their differing positions within societies, come to be affected or not affected by Islam. These conceptions provide the right ingredients for an unproblematic possibility of a cross-cultural study of women.'[25] Marnia Lazreg makes a similar argument when she addresses the reductionism inherent in scholarship on women in the Middle East and North Africa:

> A ritual is established whereby the writer appeals to religion as *the* cause of gender inequality just as it is made the source of underdevelopment in much of modernization theory. In an uncanny way, feminist discourse on women from the Middle East and North Africa mirrors that of theologians' own interpretation of women in Islam. . . .
>
> The overall effect of this paradigm is to deprive women of self-presence, of being. Because women are subsumed under religion presented in fundamental terms, they are inevitably seen as evolving in nonhistorical time. They have virtually no history. Any analysis of change is therefore foreclosed.[26]

While Jeffery's analysis does not quite succumb to this kind of unitary notion of religion (Islam), it does collapse all ideological specificities into economic relations and universalizes on the basis of this comparison.

Women and the Development Process

The best examples of universalization on the basis of economic reductionism can be found in the liberal 'Women in Development' literature. Proponents of this school seek to examine the effect of development on third-world women, sometimes from self-designated feminist perspectives. At the very least, there is an evident interest in and commitment to improving the lives of women in 'developing' countries. Scholars like Irene Tinker, Ester Boserup and Perdita Huston[27] have all written about the effect of development policies on women in the third world. All three women assume that 'development' is synonymous with 'economic development' or 'economic progress'. As in the case of Minces' patriarchal family, Hosken's male sexual control and Cutrufelli's western colonization, 'development' here becomes the all-time equalizer. Women are seen as being affected positively or negatively by economic development policies, and this is the basis for cross-cultural comparison.

For instance, Perdita Huston states that the purpose of her study is to describe the effect of the development process on the 'family unit and its individual members' in Egypt, Kenya, Sudan, Tunisia, Sri Lanka and Mexico. She states that the 'problems' and 'needs' expressed by rural and urban women in these countries all centre on education and training, work and wages, access to health and other services, political participation and legal rights. Huston relates all these 'needs' to the lack of sensitive development policies which exclude women as a group. For her, the solution is simple: improved development policies which emphasize training for women field-workers, use women trainees and women rural development officers, encourage women's cooperatives, etc. Here, again women are assumed to be a coherent group or category prior to their entry into 'the development process'. Huston assumes that all third-world women have similar problems and needs. Thus, they must have similar interests and goals. However, the interests of urban, middle-class, educated Egyptian housewives, to take only one instance, could surely not be seen as being the same as those of their uneducated, poor maids. Development policies do not affect both groups of women in the same way. Practices which characterize women's status and roles vary according to class. Women are constituted as women through the complex interaction between class, culture, religion and other ideological institutions and frameworks. They are not 'women' – a coherent group – solely on the basis of a particular economic system or policy. Such reductive cross-cultural comparisons result in the colonization of the specifics of daily existence and the complexities of political interests which women of different social classes and cultures represent and mobilize.

Thus it is revealing that for Perdita Huston women in the third-world countries she writes about have 'needs' and 'problems', but few if any have 'choices' or the freedom to act. This is an interesting representation of women in the third world, one which is significant in suggesting a latent self-presentation of western women which bears looking at. She writes, 'What surprised and moved me most as I listened to women in such very different cultural settings was the striking commonality – whether they were educated or illiterate, urban or rural – of their most basic values: the importance they assign to family, dignity, and service to others.'[28] Would Huston consider such values unusual for women in the west?

What is problematical, then, about this kind of use of 'women' as a group, as a stable category of analysis, is that it assumes an ahistorical, universal unity among women based on a generalized notion of their subordination. Instead of analytically *demonstrating* the production of women as socio-economic political groups within particular local contexts, this analytical move – and the presuppositions it is based on – limits the definition of the female subject to gender identity, completely bypassing social class and ethnic identities. What characterizes women as a group is their gender (sociologically not necessarily biologically defined) over and above everything else, indicating a monolithic notion of sexual difference. Because women are, thus, constituted as a coherent group, sexual difference becomes coterminous with female subordination and power is automatically defined in binary terms: people who have it (read: men) and people who do not (read: women). Men exploit, women are exploited. Such simplistic formulations are both historically reductive; they are also ineffectual in designing strategies to combat oppressions. All they do is reinforce binary divisions between men and women.

What would an analysis which did not do this look like? Maria Mies's work is one such example. It is an example which illustrates the strength of western feminist work on women in the third world and which does not fall into the traps discussed above. Maria Mies's study of the lace-makers of Narsapur, India, attempts to analyse carefully a substantial household industry in which 'housewives' produce lace doilies for consumption in the world market.[29] Through a detailed analysis of the structure of the lace industry, production and reproduction relations, the sexual division of labour, profits and exploitation, and the overall consequences of defining women as 'non-working housewives' and their work as 'leisure-time activity', Mies demonstrates the levels of exploitation in this industry and the impact of this production system on the work and living conditions of the women involved in it. In addition, she is able to analyse the 'ideology of the housewife', the notion of a woman sitting in the house, as providing the necessary subjective and socio-cultural element for the creation and maintenance of a production system that contributes to the increasing pauperization of women and keeps them totally atomized and disorganized as workers. Mies's analyses show the effect of a certain historically and culturally specific mode of patriarchal organization, an organization constructed on the basis of the definition of the lace-makers as 'non-working housewives' at familial, local, regional, statewide and international levels. The intricacies and the effects of particular power networks are not only emphasized, they also form the basis of Mies's analysis of how this particular group of women is situated at the centre of a hegemonic, exploitative world market.

This is a good example of what careful, politically focused, local analyses can accomplish. It illustrates how the category of woman is constructed in a variety of political contexts that often exist simultaneously and overlaid on top of one another. There is no easy generalization in the direction of 'women' in India, or 'women in the third world', nor is there a reduction of the political construction of the exploitation of the lace-makers to cultural explanations about the passivity or obedience that might characterize these women and their situation. Finally, this mode of local, political analysis, which generates theoretical categories from within the situation and context being analysed, also suggests corresponding effective strategies for organizing against the exploitations faced by the lace-makers. Here Narsapur women are not mere victims of the production process, because they resist challenge and subvert the process at various junctures. This is one instance of how Mies delineates the connections between the housewife ideology, the self-consciousness of the lace-makers and their interrelationships as contributing to the latent resistances she perceives among the women:

> The persistence of the housewife ideology, the self-perception of the lace-makers as petty commodity producers rather than as workers, is not only upheld by the structure of the industry as such but also by the deliberate propagation and reinforcement of reactionary patriarchal norms and institutions. Thus, most of the lace-makers voiced the same opinion about the rules of *purdah* and seclusion in their communities which were also propagated by the lace exporters. In particular, the *Kapu* women said that they had never gone out of their houses, that women of their community could not do any other work than housework and lace work, etc. but in spite of the fact that most of them still subscribed fully to the patriarchal norms of the *gosha* women, there were also contradictory elements in

their consciousness. Thus, although they looked down with contempt upon women who were able to work outside the house – like the untouchable *Mala* and *Madiga* women or women of other lower castes, they could not ignore the fact that these women were earning more money precisely because they were *not* respectable housewives but workers. At one discussion, they even admitted that it would be better if they could also go out and do coolie work. And when they were asked whether they would be ready to come out of their houses and work in one place in some sort of a factory, they said they would do that. This shows that the *purdah* and housewife ideology, although still fully internalized, already had some cracks, because it has been confronted with several contradictory realities.[30]

It is only by understanding the *contradictions* inherent in women's location within various structures that effective political action and challenges can be devised. Mies's study goes a long way towards offering such an analysis. While there is now an increasing number of western feminist writings in this tradition,[31] there is also unfortunately a large block of writing which succumbs to the cultural reductionism discussed earlier.

METHODOLOGICAL UNIVERSALISMS, OR: WOMEN'S OPPRESSION IS A GLOBAL PHENOMENON

Western feminist writings on women in the third world subscribe to a variety of methodologies to demonstrate the universal cross-cultural operation of male dominance and female exploitation. I summarize and critique three such methods below, moving from the most simple to the most complex methodologies.

First, proof of universalism is provided through the use of an arithmetic method. The argument goes like this: the higher the number of women who wear the veil, the more universal is the sexual segregation and control of women.[32] Similarly, a large number of different, fragmented examples from a variety of countries also apparently add up to a universal fact. For instance, Muslim women in Saudi Arabia, Iran, Pakistan, India and Egypt all wear some sort of a veil. Hence, this indicates that the sexual control of women is a universal fact in those countries in which the women are veiled.[33] Fran Hosken writes: 'Rape, forced prostitution, polygamy, genital mutilation, pornography, the beating of girls and women, purdah (segregation of women) are all violations of basic human rights.'[34] By equating purdah with rape, domestic violence and forced prostitution, Hosken asserts its 'sexual control' function as the primary explanation for purdah, whatever the context. Institutions of purdah are, thus, denied any cultural and historical specificity and contradictions and potentially subversive aspects are totally ruled out. In both these examples, the problem is not in asserting that the practice of wearing a veil is widespread. This assertion can be made on the basis of numbers. It is a descriptive generalization. However, it is the analytic leap from the practice of veiling to an assertion of its general significance in controlling women that must be questioned. While there may be a physical similarity in the veils worn by women in Saudi Arabia and Iran, the specific meaning attached to this practice varies according to the cultural and ideological context. In addition, the symbolic space occupied by the practice of purdah may be similar in certain contexts, but this does not automatically indicate that the practices themselves have identical significance in the social realm. For example, as is well known, Iranian middle-class women veiled themselves during the 1979 revolution to indicate solidarity with their veiled working-class sisters, while in contemporary Iran mandatory Islamic laws dictate that all Iranian women wear veils. While in both these instances similar reasons might be offered for the veil (opposition to the Shah and western cultural colonization in the first case, and the true Islamicization of Iran in the second), the concrete *meanings* attached to Iranian women wearing the veil are clearly different in the two historical contexts. In the first case, wearing the veil is both an oppositional and revolutionary gesture on the part of Iranian middle-class women, in the second case, it is a coercive, institutional mandate.[35] It is on the basis of such context-specific differentiated analysis that effective political strategies can be generated. To assume that the mere practice of veiling women in a number of Muslim countries indicates the universal oppression of women through sexual segregation is not only analytically reductive, but also proves to be quite useless when it comes to the elaboration of oppositional political strategy.

Second, concepts, like reproduction, the sexual division of labour, the family, marriage, household, patriarchy, etc., are often used without their specification in local cultural and historical contexts. These concepts are used by feminists in providing explanations for women's subordination, apparently assuming their universal applicability. For instance, how is it possible to refer to 'the' sexual division of labour when the *content* of this division changes radically from one environment to the next and from one historical juncture to another? At its most abstract level, it is the fact of the differential assignation of tasks according to sex that is significant; however, this is quite different from the *meaning* or *value* that the content of this sexual division of labour assumes in different contexts. In most cases the assigning of tasks on the basis of sex has an ideological origin. There is no question that a claim such as 'women are concentrated in service-oriented occupations in a large number of countries around the world' is descriptively valid. Descriptively, then, perhaps the existence of a similar sexual division of labour (where women work in service occupations, like nursing, social work, etc., and men in other kinds of occupations) in a number of different countries can be asserted. However, the concept of the 'sexual division of labour' is more than just a descriptive category. It indicates the differential *value* placed on 'men's work' versus 'women's work'.

Often the mere existence of a sexual division of labour is taken to be proof of the oppression of women in various societies. This results from a confusion

between and collapsing together of the descriptive and explanatory potential of the concept of the sexual division of labour. Superficially similar situations may have radically different, historically specific explanations and cannot be treated as identical. For instance, the rise of female-headed households in middle-class America might be construed as indicating women's independence and progress, whereby women are considered to have *chosen* to be single parents, there are increasing numbers of lesbian mothers, etc. However, the recent increase in female-headed households in Latin America,[36] where women might be seen to have more decision-making power, is concentrated among the poorest strata, where life choices are the most constrained economically. A similar argument can be made for the rise of female-headed families among Black and Chicana women in the US. The positive correlation between this and the level of poverty among women of colour and white working-class women in the US has now even acquired a name: the feminization of poverty. Thus, while it is possible to state that there is a rise in female-headed households in the US and in Latin America, this rise cannot be discussed as a universal indicator of women's independence, nor can it be discussed as a universal indicator of women's impoverishment. The *meaning* and *explanation* for the rise must obviously be specified according to the socio-historical context.

Similarly, the existence of a sexual division of labour in most contexts cannot be sufficient explanation for the universal subjugation of women in the workforce. That the sexual division of labour does indicate a devaluation of women's work must be shown through analysis of particular local contexts. In addition, devaluation of *women* must also be shown through careful analysis. In other words, the 'sexual division of labour' and 'women' are not commensurate analytical categories. Concepts like the sexual division of labour can be useful only if they are generated through local, contextual analyses.[37] If such concepts are assumed to be universally applicable, the resultant homogenization of class, race, religious and daily material practices of women in the third world can create a false sense of the commonality of oppressions, interests and struggles between and amongst women globally. Beyond sisterhood there is still racism, colonialism and imperialism!

Finally, some writers confuse the use of gender as a superordinate category of organizing analysis with the universalistic proof and instantiation of this category. In other words, empirical studies of gender differences are confused with the analytical organization of cross-cultural work. Beverley Brown's review of the book *Nature, Culture and Gender* (1980) best illustrates this point.[38] Brown suggests that nature:culture and female:male are superordinate categories which organize and locate lesser categories (like wild/domestic and biology/technology) within their logic. These categories are universal in the sense that they organize the universe of a system of representations. This relation is totally independent of the universal substantiation of any particular category. Her critique hinges on the fact that rather than clarify the generalizability of nature:culture::female:male as superordinate organizational categories,

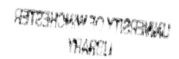

Nature, Culture and Gender, the book construes the universality of this equation to lie at the level of empirical truth, which can be investigated through field-work. Thus, the usefulness of the nature:culture::female:male paradigm as a universal mode of the organization of representation within any particular socio-historical system is lost. Here, methodological universalism is assumed on the basis of the reduction of the nature:culture::female:male analytic categories to a demand for empirical proof of its existence in different cultures. Discourses of representation are confused with material realities, and the distinction between 'Woman' and 'women' is lost. Feminist work on women in the third world which blurs this distinction (a distinction which interestingly enough is often present in certain western feminists' self-representation) eventually ends up constructing monolithic images of 'Third World Women' by ignoring the complex and mobile relationships between their historical materiality on the level of specific oppressions and political choices on the one hand and their general discursive representations on the other.

To summarize: I have discussed three methodological moves identifiable in feminist (and other academic) cross-cultural work which seeks to uncover a universality in women's subordinate position in society. The next and final section pulls together the previous sections, attempting to outline the political effects of the analytical strategies in the context of western feminist writing on women in the third world. These arguments are not against generalization as much as they are for careful, historically specific generalizations responsive to complex realities. Nor do these arguments deny the necessity of forming strategic political identities and affinities. Thus, while Indian women of different backgrounds might forge a political unity on the basis of organizing against police brutality towards women,[39] an *analysis* of police brutality must be contextual. Strategic coalitions which construct oppositional political identities for themselves are based on generalization and provisional unities, but the analysis of these group identities cannot be based on universalistic, ahistorical categories.

THE SUBJECT(S) OF POWER

This last section returns to an earlier point about the inherently political nature of feminist scholarship and attempts to clarify my point about the possibility of detecting a colonialist move in the case of a structurally unequal first/third-world relation in scholarship. The nine texts in the Zed Press 'Women in the Third World' series that I have discussed[40] focused on the following common areas in discussing women's 'status' within various societies: religion, family/kinship structures, the legal system, the sexual division of labour, education and, finally, political resistance. A large number of western feminist writings on women in the third world focus on these themes. Of course, the Zed texts have varying emphases. For instance, two of the studies, *We Shall Return: Women of Palestine* (1982) and *We Shall Smash This Prison: Indian Women in struggle* (1980), focus explicitly on female militancy and political involvement, while

The House of Obedience: Women in Arab society (1980) deals with Arab women's legal, religious and familial status. In addition, each text evidences a variety of methodologies and degrees of care in making generalizations. Interestingly enough, however, almost all the texts assume 'women' as a category of analysis in the manner designated above. Clearly this is an analytical strategy which is neither limited to these Zed Press publications, nor symptomatic of Zed Press publications in general. However, in the particular texts under question, each text assumes 'women' have a coherent group identity within the different cultures discussed, prior to their entry into social relations. Thus, Omvedt can talk about 'Indian Women' while referring to a particular group of women in the State of Maharashtra, Cutrufelli about 'Women of Africa' and Minces about 'Arab Women' as if these groups of women have some sort of obvious cultural coherence, distinct from men in these societies. The 'status' or 'position' of women is assumed to be self-evident because women as an already constituted group are *placed* within religious, economic, familial and legal structures. However, this focus on the position of women whereby women are seen as a coherent group across contexts, regardless of class or ethnicity, structures the world in ultimately binary, dichotomous terms, where women are always seen in opposition to men, patriarchy is always necessarily male dominance, and the religious, legal, economic and familial systems are implicitly assumed to be constructed by men. Thus, both men and women are always seen as preconstituted whole populations, and relations of dominance and exploitation are also posited in terms of whole peoples – wholes coming into exploitative relations. It is only when men and women are seen as different categories or groups possessing different *already constituted* categories of experience, cognition and interests as *groups* that such a simplistic dichotomy is possible.

What does this imply about the structure and functioning of power relations? The setting up of the commonality of third-world women's struggles across classes and cultures against a general notion of oppression (primarily the group in power – i.e., men) necessitates the assumption of something like what Michel Foucault calls the 'juridico-discursive' model of power,[41] the principal features of which are: 'a negative relation' (limit and lack); an 'insistence on the rule' (which forms a binary system); a 'cycle of prohibition'; the 'logic of censorship'; and a 'uniformity' of the apparatus functioning at different levels. Feminist discourse on the third world which assumes a homogeneous category – or group – called 'women' necessarily operates through such a setting up of *ordinary* power divisions. Power relations are structured in terms of a unilateral and undifferentiated source of power and a cumulative reaction to power. Opposition is a generalized phenomenon created as a response to power – which, in turn, is possessed by certain groups of people. The major problem with such a definition of power is that it locks all revolutionary struggles into binary structures – possessing power versus being powerless. Women are powerless, unified groups. If the struggle for a just society is seen in terms of the move from powerless to powerful for women as a *group*, and this is the implication in feminist discourse which structures sexual difference in terms of the division between the sexes, then the new society would be structurally identical to the existing organization of power relations, constituting itself as a simple *inversion* of what exists. If relations of domination and exploitation are defined in terms of binary divisions – groups which dominate and groups which are dominated – surely the implication is that the accession to power of women as a group is sufficient to dismantle the existing organization of relations? But women as a group are not in some sense essentially superior or infallible. The crux of the problem lies in that initial assumption of women as a homogeneous group or category ('the oppressed'), a familiar assumption in western radical and liberal feminisms.[42]

What happens when this assumption of 'women as an oppressed group' is situated in the context of western feminist writing about third-world women? It is here that I locate the colonialist move. By contrasting the representation of women in the third world with what I referred to earlier as western feminism's self-presentation in the same context, we see how western feminists alone become the true 'subjects' of this counter-history. Third-world women, on the other hand, never rise above the debilitating generality of their 'object' status.

While radical and liberal feminist assumptions of women as a sex class might elucidate (however inadequately) the autonomy of particular women's struggles in the west, the application of the notion of women as a homogeneous category to women in the third world colonizes and appropriates the pluralities of the simultaneous location of different groups of women in social class and ethnic frameworks; in doing so it ultimately robs them of their historical and political *agency*. Similarly, many Zed Press authors, who ground themselves in the basic analytic strategies of traditional Marxism, also implicitly create a 'unity' of women by substituting 'women's activity' for 'labour' as the primary theoretical determinant of women's situation. Here again, women are constituted as a coherent group not on the basis of 'natural' qualities or needs, but on the basis of the sociological 'unity' of their role in domestic production and wage labour.[43] In other words, western feminist discourse, by assuming women as a coherent, already constituted group which is placed in kinship, legal and other structures, defines third-world women as subjects *outside* of social relations, instead of looking at the way women are constituted as women *through* these very structures. Legal, economic, religious and familial structures are treated as phenomena to be judged by western standards. It is here that ethnocentric universality comes into play. When these structures are defined as 'underdeveloped' or 'developing' and women are placed within these structures, an implicit image of the 'average third-world woman' is produced. This is the transformation of the (implicitly western) 'oppressed woman' into the 'oppressed third-world woman'. While the category of 'oppressed woman' is generated through an exclusive focus on gender difference 'the oppressed third-world woman' category has an additional attribute

– the 'third-world difference'! The 'third-world difference' includes a paternalistic attitude towards women in the third world.[44] Since discussions of the various themes identified earlier (e.g., kinship, education, religion, etc.) are conducted in the context of the relative 'underdevelopment' of the third world (which is nothing less than unjustifiably confusing development with the separate path taken by the west in its development, as well as ignoring the unidirectionality of the first/third-world power relationship), third-world women as a group or category are automatically and necessarily defined as: religious (read 'not progressive'), family oriented (read 'traditional'), legal minors (read 'they-are-still-not-conscious-of-their-rights'), illiterate (read 'ignorant'), domestic (read 'backward') and sometimes revolutionary (read 'their-country-is-in-a-state-of-war; they-must-fight!'). This is how the 'third-world difference' is produced.

When the category of 'sexually oppressed women' is located within particular systems in the third world which are defined on a scale which is normed through Eurocentric assumptions, not only are third-world women defined in a particular way prior to their entry into social relations, but since no connections are made between first- and third-world power shifts, it reinforces the assumption that people in the third world just have not evolved to the extent that the west has. This mode of feminist analysis, by homogenizing and systematizing the experiences of different groups of women, erases all marginal and resistant modes of experiences.[45] It is significant that none of the texts I reviewed in the Zed Press series focuses on lesbian politics or the politics of ethnic and religious marginal organizations in third-world women's groups. Resistance can thus only be defined as cumulatively reactive, not as something inherent in the operation of power. If power, as Michel Foucault has argued recently, can really be understood only in the context of resistance,[46] this misconceptualization of power is both analytically as well as strategically problematical. It limits theoretical analysis as well as reinforcing western cultural imperialism. For in the context of a first/third-world balance of power, feminist analyses which perpetrate and sustain the hegemony of the idea of the superiority of the west produce a corresponding set of universal images of the 'third-world woman', images like the veiled woman, the powerful mother, the chaste virgin, the obedient wife, etc. These images exist in universal ahistorical splendour, setting in motion a colonialist discourse which exercises a very specific power in defining, coding and maintaining existing first/third-world connections.

To conclude, then, let me suggest some disconcerting similarities between the typically authorizing signature of such western feminist writings on women in the third world, and the authorizing signature of the project of humanism in general – humanism as a western ideological and political project which involves the necessary recuperation of the 'East' and 'Woman' as Others. Many contemporary thinkers like Foucault, Derrida, Kristeva, Deleuze and Said have written at length about the underlying anthropomorphism and ethnocentrism which constitutes a hegemonic humanistic problematic that repeatedly confirms and legitimates (western) Man's centrality.[47] Feminist theorists like Luce Irigaray, Sarah Kofman, Hélène Cixous and others have also written about the recuperation and absence of woman/women within western humanism.[48] The focus of the work of all these thinkers can be stated simply as an uncovering of the political *interests* that underlie the binary logic of humanistic discourse and ideology whereby, as a valuable recent essay puts it:

> the first (majority) term (Identity, Universality, Culture, Disinterestedness, Truth, Sanity, Justice, etc.), which is, in fact, secondary and derivative (a construction), is privileged over and colonizes the second (minority) term (difference, temporality, anarchy, error, interestedness, insanity, deviance, etc.), which is in fact, primary and originative.[49]

In other words, it is only in so far as 'Woman/Women' and 'the East' are defined as *Others* or as peripheral that (western) Man/Humanism can represent him/itself as the centre. It is not the centre that determines the periphery, but the periphery that, in its boundedness, determines the centre. Just as feminists like Kristeva, Cixous, Irigaray and others reconstruct the latent anthropomorphism in western discourse, I have suggested a parallel strategy in this article in uncovering a latent ethnocentrism in particular feminist writings on women in the third world.[50]

As discussed earlier, a comparison between western feminist self-presentation and western feminist representation of women in the third world yields significant results. Universal images of 'the third-world woman' (the veiled woman, chaste virgin, etc.), images constructed from adding the 'third-world difference' to 'sexual difference', are predicated on (and hence obviously bring into sharper focus) assumptions about western women as secular, liberated and having control over their own lives. This is not to suggest that western women *are* secular and liberated and have control over their own lives. I am referring to a *discursive* self-presentation, not necessarily to material reality. If this were a material reality there would be no need for feminist political struggle in the west. Similarly, only from the vantage point of the west is it possible to define the 'third world' as underdeveloped and economically dependent. Without the overdetermined discourse that creates the *third* world, there would be no (singular and privileged) first world. Without the 'third-world woman', the particular self-presentation of western women mentioned above would be problematical. I am suggesting, in effect, that the one enables and sustains the other. This is not to say that the signature of western feminist writings on the third world has the same authority as the project of western humanism. However, in the context of the hegemony of the western scholarly establishment in the production and dissemination of texts, and in the context of the legitimating imperative of humanistic and scientific discourse, the definition of 'the third-world woman' as a monolith might well tie into the larger economic and ideological praxis of 'disinterested' scientific inquiry and pluralism which are the surface manifestations of a latent economic and cultural colonization of the 'non-western' world. It is time to move beyond the ideological framework in which even Marx found it possible to say: They cannot represent themselves; they must be represented.

NOTES

1. See especially the essays in Cherrie Moraga and Gloria Anzaldúa (eds), *This Bridge is Called My Back: Writings by radical women of color*, New York: Kitchen Table Press, 1983; Barbara Smith (ed.), *Home Girls: A black feminist anthology*, Kitchen Table Press: New York, 1983; Gloria Joseph and Jill Lewis, *Common Differences: Conflicts in black and white feminist perspectives*, Beacon Press: Boston, MA, 1981; and Cherrie Moraga, *Loving in the War Years*, South End Press: Boston, MA, 1984.

2. Terms like 'third' and 'first' world are very problematical both in suggesting over-simplified similarities between and amongst countries labelled 'third' or 'first' world, as well as implicitly reinforcing existing economic, cultural and ideological hierarchies. I use the term 'third world', with full awareness of its problems, only because this is the terminology available to us at the moment. The use of quotation marks is meant to suggest a continuous questioning of the designation 'third world'. Even when I do not use quotation marks, I mean to use the term critically.

3. I am indebted to Teresa de Lauretis for this particular formulation of the project of feminist theorizing. See especially the introduction to her *Alice Doesn't: Feminism, semiotics, cinema*, Indiana University Press: Bloomington, 1984; see also Sylvia Winter, 'The politics of domination', unpublished manuscript.

4. This argument is similar to Homi Bhabha's definition of colonial discourse as strategically creating a space for a subject peoples through the production of knowledge and the exercise of power (Homi Bhabha, 'The other question – the stereotype and colonial discourse', *Screen*, 24, 6, 1983, p. 23). The full quote reads: '[colonial discourse is] an apparatus of power . . . an apparatus that turns on the recognition and disavowal of racial/cultural/historical differences. Its predominant strategic function is the creation of a space for a "subject peoples" through the production of knowledges in terms of which surveillance is exercised and a complex form of pleasure/unpleasure is incited. It [i.e., colonial discourse] seeks authorization for its strategies by the production of knowledges by colonizer and colonized which are stereotypical but antithetically evaluated.'

5. Anouar Abdel-Malek, *Social Dialectics. Nation and revolution*, State University of New York Press: Albany, 1981, esp. p. 145.

6. Ibid., pp. 145–6.

7. A number of documents and reports on the UN International Conferences on Women, Mexico City 1975 and Copenhagen 1980, as well as the 1976 Wellesley Conference on Women and Development attest to this. Nawal el Saadawi, Fatima Mernissi and Mallica Vajarathon in 'A critical look at the Wellesley Conference' (*Quest*, IV, 2, Winter 1978, pp. 101–7) characterize this conference as 'American-planned and organized', situating third-world participants as passive audiences. They focus especially on the lack of self-consciousness of western women's implication in the effects of imperialism and racism in their assumption of 'international sisterhood'. Amos and Parmar characterize Euro-American feminism which seeks to establish itself as the only legitimate feminism as 'imperial' (Valerie Amos and Pratibha Parmar, 'Challenging imperial feminism', *Feminist Review*, 17, 1984).

8. The Zed Press 'Women in the Third World' series is unique in its conception. I choose to focus on it because it is the only contemporary series of books I have found which assumes that 'Women in the Third World' is a legitimate and separate study of research. Since 1985, when this essay was first written, numerous new titles have appeared in the Zed 'Women in the Third World' series. Thus, I suspect that

Zed has come to occupy a rather privileged position in the dissemination and construction of discourses by and about third-world women. A number of books in this series are excellent, especially those which deal directly with women's resistance struggles. In addition, Zed Press consistently publishes progressive, feminist, antiracist and anti-imperialist texts. However, a number of texts written by feminist sociologists, anthropologists and journalists are symptomatic of the kind of western feminist work on women in the third world that concerns me. Thus, an analysis of a few of these particular texts in this series can serve as a representative point of entry into the discourse I am attempting to locate and define. My focus on these texts is, therefore, an attempt at an internal critique: I simply expect and demand more from this series. Needless to say, progressive publishing houses also carry their own authorizing signatures.

9. Michelle Rosaldo's term: 'The use and abuse of anthropology: reflections on feminism and cross-cultural understanding', Signs, 5, 3, 1980, pp. 389–412, esp. p. 392.

10. Elsewhere I have discussed this particular point in detail in a critique of Robin Morgan's construction of 'women's herstory' in her introduction to Morgan (ed.), Sisterhood is Global: The international women's movement anthology, Anchor Press/Doubleday: New York; Penguin: Harmondsworth, 1984. (See Chandra Mohanty, 'Feminist encounters: locating the politics of experience', Copyright 1, 'Fin de siècle 2000', 1987, pp. 30–44, esp. pp. 35–7.)

11. My analysis in this section of the paper has been influenced by Felicity Eldhom, Olivia Harris and Kate Young's excellent discussions ('Conceptualising women', Critique of Anthropology, 'Women's issue', 3, 1977). They examine the use of the concepts of 'reproduction' and the 'sexual division of labour' in anthropological work on women, suggesting the inevitable pull towards universals inherent in the use of these categories to determine 'women's position'.

12. Valerie Amos and Pratibha Parmar, 'Challenging imperial feminism', Feminist Review, 17, 1984, p. 7.

13. Fran Hosken, 'Female genital mutilation and human rights', Feminist Issues, 1, 3, 1981, pp. 3–24, esp. p. 11. Another example of this kind of analysis is Mary Daly's Gyn/Ecology. Daly's assumption in this text, that women as a group are sexually victimized, leads to her very problematic comparison between the attitudes towards women witches and healers in the west, Chinese foot binding and the genital mutilation of women in Africa. According to Daly, women in Europe, China and Africa constitute a homogeneous group as victims of male power. Not only does this label (sexual victims) eradicate the specific historical realities which lead to and perpetuate practices like witch-hunting and genital mutilation, but it also obliterates the differences, complexities and heterogeneities of the lives of, for example, women of different classes, religions and nations in Africa. As Audre Lorde has pointed out, women in Africa share a long tradition of healers and goddesses that perhaps binds them together more appropriately than their victim status. However, both Daly and Lorde fall prey to universalistic assumptions about 'African women' (both negative and positive). What matters is the complex, historical range of power differences, commonalities and resistances that exist among women in Africa which construct African women as 'subjects' of their own politics. See Mary Daly, Gyn/Ecology: The metaethics of radical feminism, Beacon Press: Boston, MA, 1978, pp. 107–312, and Audre Lorde, 'An open letter to Mary Daly', in Cherríe Moraga and Gloria Anzaldúa (eds), This Bridge Called My Back: Writings by radical women of color, New York: Kitchen Table Press, 1983.

14. Hosken, 'Female genital mutilation and human rights', p. 14.

15. See Eldhom et al., 'Conceptualizing Women', for a good discussion of the necessity to theorize male violence within specific societal frameworks, rather than to assume it as a universal fact.

16. Beverley Lindsay (ed.), Comparative Perspectives of Third World Women: The impact of race, sex and class, Praeger: New York, 1983, esp. pp. 298, 306.

17. Maria Ross Cutrufelli, *Women of Africa: Roots of oppression*, Zed Press: London, 1983, esp. p. 13.
18. Ibid., p. 33.
19. Michelle Rosaldo, 'The use and abuse of anthropology: reflections on feminism and cross-cultural understanding', *Signs*, 5, 3, 1980, p. 400.
20. Cutrufelli, *Women of Africa*, p. 43.
21. Elizabeth Cowie, 'Woman as sign', *m/f*, 1, 1978, pp. 49–63.
22. Juliette Minces, *The House of Obedience: Women in Arab society*, Zed Press: London, 1980, esp. p. 23.
23. Mina Modares, 'Women and Shi'ism in Iran', *m/f*, 5–6, 1981, pp. 62–82.
24. Patricia Jeffery, *Frogs in a Well: Indian women in purdah*, Zed Press: London, 1979.
25. Modares, op. cit., p. 63.
26. Marnia Lazreg, 'Feminism and difference: the perils of writing as a woman on women in Algeria', *Feminist Issues*, 14, 1, 1988, p. 87.
27. These views can also be found in differing degrees in collections like: Wellesley Editorial Committee (ed.), *Women and National Development: The complexities of change*, University of Chicago Press: Chicago, 1977, and *Signs*, Special Issue, 'Development and the sexual division of labor', 7, 2, Winter 1981. For an excellent introduction to WID issues see ISIS, *Women in Development: A resource guide for organization and action*, New Society Publishers: Philadelphia, PA, 1984. For a politically focused discussion of feminism and development and the stakes for poor third-world women, see Sita Sen and Caren Grown, *Development Crises and Alternative Visions: Third world women's perspectives*, Monthly Review Press: New York, 1987.
28. Perdita Huston, *Third World Women Speak Out*, Praeger: New York, 1979, p. 115.
29. Maria Mies, *The Lace-makers of Narsapur: Indian wives produce for the world market*, Zed Press: London, 1982.
30. Ibid, p. 157.
31. See essays by Vanessa Maher, Diane Elson and Ruth Pearson, and Maila Stevens in Kate Young, Carol Walkowitz and Roslyn McCullagh (eds), *Of Marriage and the Market: Women's subordination in international perspective*, CSE Books: London, 1981; and essays by Vivian Mota and Michelle Mattelart in June Nash and Helen I. Safa (eds), *Sex and Class in Latin America: Women's perspectives on politics, economics and the family in the third world*, Bergin & Garvey: South Hadley, MA, 1980. For examples of excellent self-conscious work by feminists writing about women in their own historical and geographical locations, see Lazreg, 'Feminism and the difference', on Algerian women; Gayatri Chakravorty Spivak's 'A literary representation of the subaltern: a woman's text from the third world', in her *In Other Worlds: Essays in cultural politics*, Methuen: London and New York, 1987, and Lata Mani's essay 'Contentious traditions: the debate *on sati* in colonial India', *Cultural Critique*, 7, Fall 1987, pp. 119–56.
32. Ann Deardon (ed.), *Arab Women*, Minority Rights Group Report No. 27: London, 1975, pp. 4–5.
33. Ibid., pp. 7, 10.
34. Hosken, 'Female genital mutilation', p. 15.
35. For a detailed discussion of these instances see Azar Tabari, 'The enigma of the veiled Iranian women', *Feminist Review*, 5, 1980.
36. Olivia Harris, 'Latin American women – an overview', in Harris (ed.), *Latin American Women*, Minority Rights Group Report No. 57: London, 1983, pp. 4–7. Other MRG reports include Deardon, *Arab Women*, and Rounaq Jahan (ed.), *Women in Asia*, Minority Rights Group Report No. 45: London, 1980.
37. See Eldhom 'Conceptualizing Women', for an excellent discussion of this.
38. Beverly Brown, 'Displacing the difference – review *Nature, Culture and Gender*', *m/f*, 8, 1983. Marilyn Strathern and Carol McCormack (eds), *Nature, Culture and Gender*, Cambridge University Press: Cambridge, 1980.

39. For a discussion of this aspect of Indian women's struggles, see Madhu Kishwar and Ruth Vanita, *In Search of Answers: Indian women's voices from Manushi*, Zed Press: London, 1984.

40. List of Zed Press publications: Patricia Jeffery, *Frogs in a Well: Indian women in purdah*, 1979; Latin American and Caribbean Women's Collective, *Slaves of Slaves: The challenge of Latin American women*, 1980; Gale Omvedt, *We Shall Smash This Prison: Indian women in struggle*, 1980; Juliette Minces, *The House of Obedience: Women in Arab society*, 1980; Bobby Siu, *Women of China: Imperialism and women's resistance in 1900–1949*, 1981; Ingela Bendt and James Downing, *We Shall Return: Women of Palestine*, 1982; Maria Rosa Cutrufelli, *Women of Africa: Roots of oppression*, 1983; Maria Mies, *The Lace-makers of Narsapur: Indian housewives produce for the world market*, 1983; Miranda Davis (ed.), *Third World/Second Sex; Women's struggles and national liberation*, 1983.

41. Michel Foucault, *Power/Knowledge*, Pantheon: New York, 1980, pp. 134–45.

42. For succinct discussion of western radical and liberal feminisms, see Hester Eisenstein, *Contemporary Feminist Thought*, G. K. Hall & Co.: Boston, MA, 1983, and Zillah Eisenstein, *The Radical Future of Liberal Feminism*, Longman: New York, 1981.

43. See Donna Haraway, 'A manifesto for cyborgs: science, technology and socialist feminism in the 1980s', *Socialist Review*, 80, 1985, pp. 65–108, esp. p. 76.

44. Amos and Parmar, 'Challenging imperial feminism', p. 9, describe the cultural stereotypes present in Euro-American feminist thought: 'The image is of the passive Asian woman subject to oppressive practices within the Asian family, with an emphasis on wanting to "help" Asian women liberate themselves from their role. Or there is the strong, dominant Afro-Caribbean woman, who despite her "strength" is exploited by the "sexism" which is seen as being a strong feature in relationships between Afro-Caribbean men and women.' These images illustrate the extent to which *paternalism* is an essential element of feminist thinking which incorporates the above stereotypes, a paternalism which can lead to the definition of priorities for women of colour by Euro-American feminists.

45. I discuss the question of theorizing experience in my 'Feminist encounters', and in Chandra Mohanty and Biddy Martin, 'Feminist politics: what's home got to do with it?', in Teresa de Lauretis (ed.), *Feminist Studies/Critical Studies*, Indiana University Press: Bloomington, IN, 1986.

46. This is one of Foucault's central points in his reconceptualization of the strategies and workings of power networks. See *History of Sexuality Volume One*, Random House: New York, 1978, and *Power/Knowledge*.

47. Michel Foucault, *History of Sexuality* and *Power/Knowledge*; Jacques Derrida, *Of Grammatology*, John Hopkins University Press: Baltimore, MD, 1974; Julia Kristeva, *Desire in Language*, Columbia University Press: New York, 1980; Edward Said, *Orientalism*, Random House: New York, 1978; and Giles Deleuze and Felix Guattari, *Anti-Oedipus: Capitalism and schizophrenia*, Viking: New York, 1977.

48. Luce Irigaray, 'This sex which is not one' and 'When the goods get together', in Elaine Marks and Isabel de Courtivron (eds), *New French Feminisms*, Schocken Books: New York, 1981; Hélène Cixous, 'The laugh of the Medusa', in ibid. For a good discussion of Sarah Kofman's work, see Elizabeth Berg, 'The third woman', *Diacritics*, Summer 1982, pp. 11–20.

49. William V. Spanos, 'Boundary 2 and the polity of interest: humanism, the "center elsewhere", and power', *Boundary 2*, XII, 3/XIII, 1, Spring/Fall 1984.

50. For an argument which demands a *new* conception of humanism in work on third-world women, see Lazreg, 'Feminism and difference'. While Lazreg's position might appear to be diametrically opposed to mine, I see it as a provocative and potentially positive extension of some of the implications that follow from my arguments. In criticizing the feminist rejection of humanism in the name of 'essential Man', Lazreg points to what she calls an 'essentialism of difference' within these very feminist

projects. She asks: 'To what extent can western feminism dispense with an ethics of responsibility when writing about "different" women? The point is neither to subsume other women under one's own experience nor to uphold a separate truth for them. Rather, it is to allow them to *be* while recognizing that what they are is just as meaningful, valid, and comprehensible as what "we" are. . . . Indeed, when feminists essentially deny other women the humanity they claim for themselves, they dispense with any ethical constraint. They engage in the act of splitting the social universe into "us" and "them", "subjects" and "objects"' (pp. 99–100).

This essay by Lazreg and an essay by S. P. Mohanty entitled 'Us and them: on the philosophical bases of political criticism', *The Yale Journal of Criticism*, 2, 2, March 1989, suggest positive directions for self-conscious cross-cultural analyses, analyses which move beyond the deconstructive to a fundamentally productive mode in designating overlapping areas for cross-cultural comparison. The latter essay calls not for a 'humanism' but for a reconsideration of the question of the 'human' in a post-humanist context. It argues that (1) there is no necessary 'incompatibility between the deconstruction of western humanism' and such 'a positive elaboration' of the human; and moreover that (2) such an elaboration is essential if contemporary political–critical discourse is to avoid the incoherencies and weaknesses of a relativist position.

'US THIRD-WORLD FEMINISM: THE THEORY AND METHOD OF OPPOSITIONAL CONSCIOUSNESS IN THE POSTMODERN WORLD'[1]

Chela Sandoval

The enigma that is US third-world feminism has yet to be fully confronted by theorists of social change. To these late twentieth-century analysts it has remained inconceivable that US third-world feminism might represent a form of historical consciousness whose very structure lies outside the conditions of possibility which regulate the oppositional expressions of dominant feminism. In enacting this new form of historical consciousness, US third-world feminism provides access to a different way of conceptualizing not only US feminist consciousness but oppositional activity in general; it comprises a formulation capable of aligning such movements for social justice with what have been identified as world-wide movements of decolonization.

Both in spite of and yet because they represent varying internally colonized communities, US third-world feminists have generated a common speech, a theoretical structure which, however, remained just outside the purview of the dominant feminist theory emerging in the 1970s, functioning within it – but only as the unimaginable. Even though this unimaginable presence arose to reinvigorate and refocus the politics and priorities of dominant feminist theory during the 1980s, what remains is an uneasy alliance between what appears on the surface to be two different understandings of domination, subordination and the nature of effective resistance – a shot-gun arrangement at best between what literary critic Gayatri Spivak characterizes as 'hegemonic feminist theory'[2] on the one side and what I have been naming 'US third-world feminism' on the

From: Chela Sandoval (1991), 'US Third World Feminism: the Theory and Method of Oppositional Consciousness in the Postmodern World', pp. 1–24, in *Genders*, no. 10.

other.[3] I do not mean to suggest here, however, that the perplexing situation that exists between US third-world and hegemonic feminisms should be understood merely in binary terms. On the contrary, what this investigation reveals is the way in which the new theory of oppositional consciousness considered here and enacted by US third-world feminism is at least partially contained, though made deeply invisible by the manner of its appropriation, in the terms of what has become a hegemonic feminist theory.

US third-world feminism arose out of the matrix of the very discourses denying, permitting and producing differences. Out of the imperatives born of necessity arose a mobility of identity that generated the activities of a new citizen-subject, and which reveals yet another model for the self-conscious production of political opposition. In this essay I will lay out US third-world feminism as the design for oppositional political activity and consciousness in the United States. In mapping this new design, a model is revealed by which social actors can chart the points through which differing oppositional ideologies can meet, in spite of their varying trajectories. This knowledge becomes important when one begins to wonder, along with late twentieth-century cultural critics such as Fredric Jameson, how organized oppositional activity and consciousness can be made possible under the co-opting nature of the so-called 'postmodern' cultural condition.[4]

The ideas put forth in this essay are my rearticulation of the theories embedded in the great oppositional practices of the latter half of this century especially in the United States – the Civil Rights movement, the women's movement and ethnic, race and gender liberation movements. During this period of great social activity, it became clear to many of us that oppositional social movements which were weakening from internal divisions over strategies, tactics and aims would benefit by examining philosopher Louis Althusser's theory of 'ideology and the ideological state apparatuses'.[5] In this now fundamental essay, Althusser lays out the principles by which humans are called into being as citizen/subjects who act – even when in resistance – in order to sustain and reinforce the dominant social order. In this sense, for Althusser, all citizens endure ideological subjection.[6] Althusser's postulations begin to suggest, however, that 'means and occasions'[7] do become generated whereby individuals and groups in opposition are able to effectively challenge and transform the current hierarchical nature of the social order, but he does not specify how or on what terms such challenges are mounted.

In supplementing Althusser's propositions. I want to apply his general theory of ideology to the particular cultural concerns raised within North American liberation movements and develop a new theory of ideology which considers consciousness not only in its subordinated and resistant yet appropriated versions – the subject of Althusser's theory of ideology – but in its more effective and persistent oppositional manifestations. In practical terms, this theory focuses on identifying forms of consciousness in opposition, which can be generated and coordinated by those classes self-consciously seeking affective oppositional stances in relation to the dominant social order. The idea here, that the subject-citizen can learn to identify, develop, and control the means of ideology, that is, marshal the knowledge necessary to 'break with ideology' while also speaking in and from within ideology, is an idea which lays the philosophical foundations enabling us to make the vital connections between the seemingly disparate social and political aims which drive yet ultimately divide liberation movements from within. From Althusser's point of view, then, the theory I am proposing would be considered 'science of oppositional ideology'.

This study identifies five principal categories by which 'oppositional consciousness' is organized and which are politically effective means for changing the dominant order of power. I characterize them as 'equal rights', 'revolutionary', 'supremacist', 'separatist', and 'differential' ideological forms. All these forms of consciousness are kaleidoscoped into view when the fifth form is utilized as a theoretical model which retroactively clarifies and gives new meaning to the others. Differential consciousness represents the strategy of another form of oppositional ideology that functions on an altogether different register. Its power can be thought of as mobile – not nomadic but rather cinematographic: a kinetic motion that maneuvers, poetically transfigures, and orchestrates while demanding alienation, perversion, and reformation in both spectators and practitioners. Differential consciousness is the expression of the new subject position called for by Althusser – it permits functioning within yet beyond the demands of dominant ideology. This differential form of oppositional consciousness has been enacted in the practice of US third-world feminism since the 1960s.

This essay also investigates the forms of oppositional consciousness that were generated within one of the great oppositional movements of the late twentieth century, the second wave of the women's movement. What emerges in this discussion is an outline of the oppositional ideological forms which worked against one another to divide the movement from within. I trace these ideological forms as they are manifested in the critical writings of some of the prominent hegemonic feminist theorists of the 1980s. In their attempts to identify a feminist history of consciousness, many of these thinkers believe they detect four fundamentally distinct phases through which feminists have passed in their quest to end the subordination of women. But viewed in terms of another paradigm, 'differential consciousness', here made available for study through the activity of US third-world feminism, these four historical phases are revealed as sublimated versions of the very forms of consciousness in opposition which were also conceived within post-1950s US liberation movements.

These earlier movements were involved in seeking effective forms of resistance outside of those determined by the social order itself. My contention is that hegemonic feminist forms of resistance represent only other versions of the forms of oppositional consciousness expressed within all liberation movements active in the United States during the later half of the twentieth century. What I want to do here is systematize in theoretical form a theory of oppositional consciousness as it comes embedded but hidden within US hegemonic feminist theoretical tracts. At the end of this essay, I present the outline of a corresponding theory which engages with these hegemonic feminist theoretical forms while at the same time going beyond them to produce a more general theory and method of oppositional consciousness.

The often discussed race and class conflict between white and third world feminists in the United States allows us a clear view of these forms of consciousness in action. The history of the relationship between first and third world feminists has been tense and rife with antagonisms. My thesis is that at the root of these conflicts is the refusal of US third-world feminism to buckle under, to submit to sublimation or assimilation within hegemonic feminist praxis. This refusal is based, in large part, upon loyalty to the differential mode of consciousness and activity outlined in this essay but which has remained largely unaccounted for within the structure of the hegemonic feminist theories of the 1980s.

Differential consciousness is not yet fully theorized by most contemporary analysts of culture, but its understanding is crucial for the shaping of effective and ongoing oppositional struggle in the United States. Moreover, the recognition of differential consciousness is vital to the generation of a next 'third-wave' women's movement and provides grounds for alliance with other decolonizing movements for emancipation. My answer to the perennial question asked by hegemonic feminist theorists throughout the 1980s is that yes, there *is* a specific US third-world feminism: it is that which provides the theoretical and methodological approach, the 'standpoint' if you will, from which this evocation of a theory of oppositional consciousness is summoned.

A BRIEF HISTORY

From the beginning of what has been known as the second wave of the women's movement, US third-world feminists have claimed a feminism at odds with that being developed by US white women. Already in 1970 with the publication of *Sisterhood Is Powerful*, black feminist Francis Beal was naming the second wave of US feminism as a 'white women's movement' because it insisted on organizing along the binary gender division male/female alone.[8] US third world feminists, however, have long understood that one's race, culture, or class often denies comfortable or easy access to either category, that the interactions between social categories produce other genders within the social hierarchy. As far back as the middle of the last century, Sojourner Truth found it necessary to remind a convention of white suffragettes of her female gender with the rhetorical question 'Ain't I a woman?'[9] American Indian Paula Gunn Allen has written of Native women that 'the place we live now is an idea, because whiteman took all the rest'.[10] In 1971, Toni Morrison went so far as to write of US third world women that 'there is something inside us that makes us different from other people. It is not like men and it is not like white women'.[11] That same year Chicana Velia Hancock continued: 'Unfortunately, many white

women focus on the maleness of our present social system as though, by implication, a female dominated white America would have taken a more reasonable course' for people of color of either sex.[12]

These signs of a lived experience of difference from white female experience
in the United States repeatedly appear throughout US third world feminist
writings. Such expressions imply the existence of at least one other category of
gender which is reflected in the very titles of books written by US feminists
of color such as *All the Women are White, All the Blacks are Men, But Some
of Us Are Brave*[13] or *This Bridge Called My Back*,[14] titles which imply that
women of color somehow exist in the interstices between the legitimated categories of the social order. Moreover, in the title of bell hooks' 1981 book, the
question 'Ain't I a Woman' is transformed into a defiant statement,[15] while Amy
Ling's feminist analysis of Asian American writings, *Between Worlds*,[16] or the
title of the journal for US third-world feminist writings, *The Third Woman*,[17]
also calls for the recognition of a new category for social identity. This in-
between space, this third gender category, is also explored in the writings of
such well-known authors as Maxine Hong Kingston, Gloria Anzaldúa, Audre
Lorde, Alice Walker, and Cherríe Moraga, all of whom argue that US third-
world feminists represent a different kind of human – new 'mestizas'.[18] 'Woman
Warriors' who live and are gendered 'between and among' the lines.[19] 'Sister
Outsiders'[20] who inhabit a new psychic terrain which Anzaldúa calls 'the
Borderlands', 'a neuva Frontera'. In 1980, Audre Lorde summarized the US
white women's movement by saying that 'today, there is a pretense to a homogeneity of experience covered by the word SISTERHOOD in the white
woman's movement. When white feminists call for "unity", they are mis-
naming a deeper and real need for homogeneity'. We began the 1980s, she says,
with 'white women' agreeing 'to focus upon their oppression as women' while
continuing 'to ignore difference'. Chicana sociologist Maxine Baca Zinn rearticulated this position in a 1986 essay in *Signs*, saying that 'there now exists in
women's studies an increased awareness of the variability of womanhood' yet
for US feminists of color 'such work is often tacked on, its significance for feminist knowledge still unrecognized and unregarded'.[21]

How has the hegemonic feminism of the 1980s responded to this other kind
of feminist theoretical activity? The publication of *This Bridge Called My Back*
in 1981 made the presence of US third-world feminism impossible to ignore on
the same terms as it had been throughout the 1970s. But soon the writings and
theoretical challenges of US third-world feminists were marginalized into the
category of what Alison Jaggar characterized in 1983 as mere 'description',[22]
and their essays deferred to what Hester Eisenstein in 1985 called 'the special
force of poetry',[23] while the shift in paradigm I earlier referred to as 'differential consciousness', and which is represented in the praxis of US third world
feminism, has been bypassed and ignored. If, during the eighties, US third world
feminism had become a theoretical problem, an inescapable mystery to be
solved for hegemonic feminism, then perhaps a theory of difference – but

imported from Europe – could subsume if not solve it. I would like to provide an example of how this systematic repression of the theoretical implications of US third-world feminism occurs.

THE GREAT HEGEMONIC MODEL

During the 1980s, hegemonic feminist scholars produced the histories of feminist consciousness which they believed to typify the modes of exchange operating within the oppositional spaces of the women's movement. These feminist histories of consciousness are often presented as typologies, systematic classifications of all possible forms of feminist praxis. These constructed typologies have fast become the official stories by which the white women's movement understands itself and its interventions in history. In what follows I decode these stories and their relations to one another from the perspective of US third-world feminism, where they are revealed as sets of imaginary spaces, socially constructed to severely delimit what is possible within the boundaries of their separate narratives. Together, they legitimize certain modes of culture and consciousness only to systematically curtail the forms of experiential and theoretical articulations permitted US third-world feminism. I want to demonstrate how the constructed relationships adhering between the various types of hegemonic feminist theory and consciousness are unified at a deeper level into a great metastructure which sets up and reveals the logic of an exclusionary US hegemonic feminism.

The logic of hegemonic feminism is dependent upon a common code that shapes the work of such a diverse group of thinkers as Julia Kristeva, Toril Moi, Gerda Lerna, Cora Kaplan, Lydia Sargent, Alice Jardine or Judith Kegan Gardiner. Here I follow its traces through the 1985 writings of the well-known literary critic Elaine Showalter;[24] the now classic set of essays published in 1985 and edited by Hester Eisenstein and Alice Jardine on *The Future of Difference* in the 'women's movement'; Gale Greene and Coppelia Kahn's 1985 introductory essay in the collection *Making a Difference: Feminist Literary Criticism*;[25] and the great self-conscious prototype of hegemonic feminist thought encoded in Alison Jaggar's massive dictionary of feminist consciousness, *Feminist Politics and Human Nature*, published in 1983.

Showalter's well-known essay, 'Towards a Feminist Poetics', develops what she believes to be a three-phase 'taxonomy, if not a poetics, of feminist criticism'.[26] For Showalter, these three stages represent succeedingly higher levels of women's historical, moral, political, and aesthetic development.

For example, according to Showalter, critics can identify a first-phase 'feminine' consciousness when they detect, she says, women writing 'in an effort to equal the cultural achievement of the male culture'. In another place, feminist theorist Hester Eisenstein concurs when she writes that the movement's early stages were characterized by feminist activists organizing to prove 'that differences between women and men were exaggerated, and that they could be reduced' to a common denominator of sameness.[27] So, too, do historians Gayle

Greene and Coppelia Kahn also claim the discovery of a similar first-phase feminism in their essay on 'Feminist Scholarship and the Social Construction of Woman'.[28] In its first stage, they write, feminist theory organized itself 'according to the standards of the male public world and, appending women to history' as it has already been defined, left 'unchallenged the existing paradigm'. Matters are similar in political scientist Alison Jaggar's book *Feminist Politics and Human Nature*. Within her construction of four 'genera' of feminist consciousness which are 'fundamentally incompatible with each other' though related by a metatheoretical schema, the first phase of 'liberal feminism' is fundamentally concerned with 'demonstrating that women are as fully human as men'.[29]

In the second phase of this typology, shared across the text of hegemonic feminist theory, Showalter claims that female writers turn away from the logics of the 'feminine' first phase. Under the influence of a second 'feminist' phase, she states, writers work to 'reject' the accommodation of 'male culture', and instead use literature to 'dramatize wronged womanhood'.[30] Elsewhere, Eisenstein also insists that first-phase feminism reached a conclusion. No longer were women the same as men, but, rather, 'women's lives WERE different from men and . . . it was precisely this difference that required illumination'.[31] In Greene and Kahn's view, feminist scholars turned away from the 'traditional paradigm' of first-phase feminism and 'soon extended their enquiries to the majority of women unaccounted for by traditional historiography, "in search of the actual *experiences* of women in the past"', asking questions about 'the quality of their daily lives, the conditions in which they lived and worked, the ages at which they married and bore children; about their work, their role in the family, their class and relations to other women; their perception of their place in the world; their relation to wars and revolutions'.[32] If women were not like men, but fundamentally different, then the values of a patriarchal society had to be transformed in order to accommodate those differences. Jaggar argued that it was during this second phase that feminists undermined 'first-phase liberal feminism' by turning toward Marxism as a way of restructuring a new society incapable of subordinating women.[33]

In Showalter's third and, for her, final 'female' phase of what I see as a feminist history of consciousness, Showalter argues that 'the movement rejected both earlier stages as forms of dependency' on men, or on their culture and instead turned 'toward female experience as a source of a new, autonomous art'.[34] It is in this third phase, Eisenstein asserts, that 'female differences originally seen as a source of oppression appear as a source of enrichment'.[35] Under the influence of this third-phase feminism, women seek to uncover the unique expression of the essence of 'woman' which lies underneath the multiplicity of her experiences. Eisenstein reminds us that this feminism is 'woman-centered', a transformation within which 'maleness' – not femaleness – becomes 'the difference' that matters: now, she says, 'men were the Other'.[36] Greene and Kahn also perceive this same third-phase feminism within which 'some historians of women posit the existence of a separate woman's culture, even going so far as to suggest that women and men within the same society may have different experiences of the universe'.[37] Jaggar's typology characterizes her third-phase feminism as an 'unmistakably twentieth-century phenomenon which is the first approach to conceptualizing human nature, social reality, and politics 'to take the subordination of women as its central concern'. Her third-phase feminism contends that 'women naturally know much of which men are ignorant', and takes as 'one of its main tasks . . . to explain why this is so'. Jaggar understands this third phase as generating either 'Radical' or 'Cultural' feminism.[38]

Now, throughout what can clearly be viewed as a three-phase feminist history of consciousness, as white feminist Lydia Sargent comments in her 1981 collection of essays on *Women and Revolution*, 'racism, while part of the discussion, was never successfully integrated into feminist theory and practice'. This resulted, she writes, in powerful protests by women of color at each of these three phases of hegemonic feminist praxis 'against the racism (and classism) implicit in a white feminist movement, theory and practice'.[39] The recognition that hegemonic feminist theory was not incorporating the content of US third world feminist 'protests' throughout the 1970s suggests a structural deficiency within hegemonic feminism which prompted certain hegemonic theorists to construct a fourth and for them a final and 'antiracist' phase of feminism.

The fourth category of this taxonomy always represents the unachieved category of possibility where the differences represented by race and class can be (simply) accounted for, and it is most often characterized as 'socialist feminism'. Eisenstein approaches her version of fourth-phase feminism this way: 'as the women's movement grew more diverse, it became *forced* [presumably by US feminists of color] to confront and to debate issues of difference – most notably those of race and class'.[40] Jaggar laments that first-phase liberal feminism 'has tended to ignore or minimize all these differences' while second-phase Marxist feminism 'has tended to recognize only differences of class', and the third-phase 'political theory of radical feminism has tended to recognize only differences of age and sex, to understand these in universal terms, and often to view them as determined biologically'. By contrast, she asserts, a fourth-phase 'socialist feminism' should recognize differences among women 'as constituent parts of contemporary human nature'. This means that the 'central project of socialist feminism' will be 'the development of a political theory and practice that will synthesize the best insights' of the second- and third-phase feminisms, those of the 'radical and Marxist traditions', while hopefully escaping 'the problems associated with each'. Within Jaggar's metatheoretical schema socialist feminism represents the fourth, ultimate and 'most appropriate interpretation of what it is for a theory to be impartial, objective, comprehensive, verifiable and useful'.[41]

Socialist feminist theorist Cora Kaplan agrees with Jaggar and indicts the previous three forms of hegemonic feminism – liberal, Marxist and radical – for failing to incorporate an analysis of power relations, beyond gender relations, in their rationality. Most dominant feminist comprehensions of gender, she believes, insofar as they seek a unified female subject, construct a 'fictional landscape'. Whether this landscape is then examined from liberal, psychoanalytic or semiotic feminist perspectives, she argues, 'the other structuring relations of society fade and disappear, leaving us with the naked drama of sexual difference as the only scenario that matters'. For Kaplan, differences among women will only be accounted for by a new socialist feminist criticism which understands the necessity of transforming society by coming 'to grips with the relationship between female subjectivity and class identity'.[42] Unfortunately, however, socialist feminism has yet to develop and utilize a theory and method capable of achieving this goal, or of coming to terms with race or culture, and of thus coming 'to grips' with the differences existing between female subjects. Though continuing to claim socialist feminism as 'the most comprehensive' of feminist theories, Jaggar allows that socialist feminism has made only 'limited progress' toward such goals. Rather, she regretfully confesses, socialist feminism remains a 'commitment to the development' of 'an analysis and political practice' that will account for differences among and between women rather than a commitment to a theory and practice 'which already exists'.[43] Finally, Jaggar grudgingly admits that, insofar as socialist feminism stubbornly 'fails to theorize the experiences of women of color, it cannot be accepted as complete'.[44]

We have just charted our way through what I hope to have demonstrated is a commonly cited four-phase feminist history of consciousness consisting of 'liberal', 'Marxist', 'radical/cultural' and 'socialist' feminisms, and which I schematize as 'women are the same as men', 'women are different from men', 'women are superior', and the fourth catch-all category, 'women are a racially divided class'. I contend that this comprehension of feminist consciousness is hegemonically unified, framed and buttressed with the result that the expression of a unique form of US third-world feminism, active over the last thirty years, has become invisible outside of its all-knowing logic. Jaggar states this position quite clearly in her dictionary of hegemonic feminist consciousness when she writes that the contributions of feminists of color (such as Paula Gunn Allen, Audre Lorde, Nellie Wong, Gloria Anzaldúa, Cherríe Moraga, Toni Morrison, Mitsuye Yamada, bell hooks, the third world contributors to *Sisterhood Is Powerful*, or the contributors to *This Bridge*, for example) operate 'mainly at the level of description', while those that *are* theoretical have yet to contribute to any 'unique or distinctive and comprehensive theory of women's liberation'.[45] For these reasons, she writes, US third-world feminism has not been 'omitted from this book' bur rather assimilated into one of the 'four genera' of hegemonic feminism I have outlined earlier.

US third-world feminism, however, functions just outside the rationality of the four-phase hegemonic structure we have just identified. Its recognition will require of hegemonic feminism a paradigm shift which is capable of rescuing its theoretical and practical expressions from their exclusionary and racist forms. I am going to introduce this shift in paradigm by proposing a new kind of taxonomy which I believe prepares the ground for a new theory and method of oppositional consciousness. The recognition of this new taxonomy should also bring into view a new set of alterities and another way of understanding 'otherness' in general, for its demands that oppositional actors claim new grounds for generating identity, ethics and political activity.

Meanwhile, US third-world feminism has been sublimated, both denied yet spoken about incessantly, or, as black literary critic Sheila Radford-Hill put it in 'rhetorical platform' which allows white feminist scholars to 'launch arguments for or against' the same four basic configurations of hegemonic feminism.[46] It is not surprising, therefore, that the writings of feminist third world theorists are laced through with bitterness. For, according to bell hooks in 1982, the sublimation of US third-world feminist writing is linked to racist 'exclusionary practices' which have made it 'practically impossible' for any new feminist paradigms to emerge. Two years before Jaggar's *Feminist Politics and Human Nature*, hooks wrote that although 'feminist theory is the guiding set of beliefs and principles that become the basis for action', the development of feminist theory is a task permitted only within the 'hegemonic dominance' and approval 'of white academic women'.[47] Four years later Gayatri Spivak stated that 'the emergent perspective' of hegemonic 'feminist criticism' tenaciously reproduces 'the axioms of imperialism'. Clearly, the theoretical structure of hegemonic feminism has produced enlightening and new feminist intellectual spaces, but these coalesce in what Spivak characterizes as a 'high feminist norm' which culminates in reinforcing the 'basically isolationist' and narcissistic 'admiration' of hegemonic feminist thinkers 'for the literature of the female subject in Europe and Anglo America'.[48]

We have just charted our way through a four-phase hegemonic typology which I have argued is commonly utilized and cited – self-consciously or not – by feminist theorists as the way to understand oppositional feminist praxis. I believe that this four-phase typology comprises the mental map of the given time, place and cultural condition we call the US white women's movement. From the perspective of US third-world feminism this four-category structure of consciousness as presently enacted interlocks into a symbolic container which sets limits on how the history of feminist activity can be conceptualized, while obstructing what can be perceived or even imagined by agents thinking within its constraints. Each category of this typology along with the overriding rationality that relates the categories one to the other is socially constructed, the structure and the network of possibilities it generates are seen by feminists of color as, above all, *imaginary* spaces which, when understood and enacted as if self-contained, rigidly circumscribe what is possible for feminists and their relations across their differences. Hegemonic feminist theoreticians and activists are trapped within the rationality of this structure, which sublimates or disperses the theoretical specificity of US third-world feminism.

Despite the fundamental shift in political objectives and critical methods which is represented by hegemonic feminism, there remains in its articulations a limited and traditional reliance on what are previous, *modernist* modes of understanding oppositional forms of activity and consciousness. The recognition of a specific US third-world feminism demands that feminist scholars extend their critical and political objectives even further. During the 1970s, US feminists of color identified common grounds upon which they made coalitions across profound cultural, racial, class and gender differences. The insights perceived during this period reinforced the common culture across difference comprised of the skills, values and ethics generated by subordinated citizenry compelled to live within similar realms of marginality. During the 1970s, this common culture was reidentified and claimed by US feminists of color, who then came to recognize one another as countrywomen – and men – of the same psychic terrain. It is the methodology and theory of US third-world feminism that permit the following rearticulation of hegemonic feminism, on its own terms, and beyond them.

Toward a theory of oppositional consciousness

Let me suggest, then, another kind of typology, this one generated from the insights born of oppositional activity beyond the inclusive scope of the hegemonic women's movement. It is important to remember that the form of US third-world feminism it represents and enacts has been influenced not only by struggles against gender domination, but by the struggles against race, class and cultural hierarchies which mark the twentieth century in the United States. It is a mapping of consciousness in opposition to the dominant social order which charts the white and hegemonic feminist histories of consciousness we have just surveyed, while also making visible the different ground from which a specific US third-world feminism rises. It is important to understand that this typology is not necessarily 'feminist' in nature, but is rather a history of oppositional consciousness. Let me explain what I mean by this.

I propose that the hegemonic feminist structure of oppositional consciousness be recognized for what it is, reconceptualized and replaced by the structure which follows. This new structure is best thought of not as a typology, but as a *'topography'* of consciousness in opposition, from the Greek word 'topos' or place, insofar as it represents the charting of realities that occupy a specific kind of cultural region. The following topography delineates the set of critical points around which individuals and groups seeking to transform oppressive powers constitute themselves as resistant and oppositional subjects. These points are orientations deployed by those subordinated classes which have sought subjective forms of resistance other than those forms determined by the social order itself. They provide repositories within which subjugated citizens can either occupy or throw off subjectivities in a process that at once both enacts and yet decolonizes their various relations to their real conditions of existence. This kind of kinetic and self-conscious mobility of consciousness is utilized by US third-world feminists as they identify oppositional subject positions and enact them *differentially*.

What hegemonic feminist theory has identified are only other versions of what I contend are the various modes of consciousness which have been most effective in opposition under modes of capitalist production before the postmodern period, but in their 'feminist' incarnations. Hegemonic feminism appears incapable of making the connections between its own expressions of resistance and opposition and the expressions of consciousness in opposition enacted amongst other racial, ethnic, cultural or gender liberation movements. Thus, I argue that the following topography of consciousness is not necessarily 'feminist' in nature, but represents a history of oppositional consciousness.

Any social order which is hierarchically organized into relations of domination and subordination creates particular subject positions within which the subordinated can legitimately function.[49] These subject positions, once self-consciously recognized by their inhabitants, can become transformed into more effective sites of resistance to the current ordering of power relations. From the perspective of a differential US third-world feminism, the histories of consciousness produced by US white feminists are, above all, only other examples of subordinated consciousness in opposition. In order to make US third-world feminism visible within US feminist theory, I suggest a topography of consciousness which identifies nothing more and nothing less than the modes the subordinated of the United States (of any gender, race or class) claim as politicized and oppositional stances in resistance to domination. The topography that follows, unlike its hegemonic feminist version, is not historically organized, no enactment is privileged over any other, and the recognition that each site is as potentially effective in opposition as any other makes possible another mode of consciousness which is particularly effective under late capitalist and postmodern cultural conditions in the United States. I call this mode of consciousness 'differential' – it is the ideological mode enacted by US third-world feminists over the last thirty years.

The first four enactments of consciousness that I describe next reveal hegemonic feminist political strategies as the forms of oppositional consciousness most often utilized in resistance under earlier (modern, if you will) modes of capitalist production. The following topography, however, does not simply replace previous lists of feminist consciousness with a new set of categories, because the fifth and differential method of oppositional consciousness has a mobile, retroactive and transformative effect on the previous four forms (the 'equal rights', 'revolutionary', 'supremacist', and 'separatist' forms) setting them into new processual relationships. Moreover, this topography compasses the perimeters for a new theory of consciousness in opposition as its gathers up the modes of ideology-praxis represented within previous liberation movements into the fifth, differential and postmodern paradigm.[50] This paradigm can, among other things, make clear the vital connections that exist between feminist theory in general and other theoretical modes concerned with issues of social hierarchy, race marginality and resistance. US third-world feminism, considered as an enabling theory and method of differential consciousness, brings the following oppositional ideological forms into view:

1. Under an 'equal rights' mode of consciousness in opposition, the subordinated group argue that their differences – for which they have been assigned inferior status – are only in appearance, not reality. Behind their exterior physical difference, they argue, is an essence the same as the essence of the human already in power. On the basis that all individuals are created equal, subscribers to this particular ideological tactic will demand that their own humanity be legitimated, recognized as the same under the law, and assimilated into the most favored form of the human in power. The expression of this mode of political behavior and identity politics can be traced throughout the writings generated from within US liberation movements of the post-World War II era. Hegemonic feminist theorists have claimed this oppositional expression of resistance to social inequality as 'liberal feminism'.

2. Under the second ideological tactic generated in response to social hierarchy, which I call 'revolutionary', the subordinated group claim their *differences* from those in power and call for a social transformation that will accommodate and legitimate those differences, by force if necessary. Unlike the previous tactic, which insists on the similarity between social, racial and gender classes across the differences, there is no desire for assimilation within the present traditions and values of the social order. Rather, this tactic of revolutionary ideology seeks to affirm subordinated differences through a radical societal reformation. The hope is to produce a new culture beyond the domination/subordination power axis. This second revolutionary mode of consciousness was enacted within the white women's movement under the rubric of either 'socialist' or 'Marxist' feminisms.

3. In 'supremacism', the third ideological tactic, not only do the oppressed claim their differences, but they also assert that those very differences have provided them access to a superior evolutionary level than those currently in power. Whether their differences are of biological or social origin is of little practical concern, of more importance is the result. The belief is that this group has evolved to a higher stage of social and psychological existence than those currently holding power, moreover, their differences now comprise the essence of what is good in human existence. Their mission is to provide the social order with a higher ethical and moral vision and consequently a more effective leadership. Within the hegemonic feminist schema 'radical' and 'cultural' feminisms are organized under these precepts.

4. 'Separatism' is the final of the most commonly utilized tactics of opposition organized under previous modes of capitalist development. As

in the previous three forms, practitioners of this form of resistance also recognize that their differences have been branded as inferior with respect to the category of the most human. Under this mode of thought and activity, however, the subordinated do not desire an 'equal rights' type of integration with the dominant order, nor do they seek its leadership or revolutionary transformation. Instead, this form of political resistance is organized to protect and nurture the differences that define it through complete separation from the dominant social order. A utopian landscape beckons these practitioners . . . their hope has inspired the multiple visions of the other forms of consciousness as well.

In the post-WWII period in the United States, we have witnessed how the maturation of a resistance movement means not only that four such ideological positions emerge in response to dominating powers, but that these positions become more and more clearly articulated. Unfortunately, however, as we were able to witness in the late 1970s white women's movement, such ideological positions eventually divide the movement of resistance from within, for each of these sites tend to generate sets of tactics, strategies, and identities which historically have appeared to be mutually exclusive under modernist oppositional practices. What remains all the more profound, however, is that the differential practice of US third-world feminism undermines the appearance of the mutual exclusivity of oppositional strategies of consciousness; moreover, it is US third-world feminism which allows their reconceptualization on the new terms just proposed. US feminists of color, insofar as they involved themselves with the 1970s white women's liberation movement, were also enacting one or more of the ideological positionings just outlined, but rarely for long and rarely adopting the kind of fervid belief systems and identity politics that tend to accompany their construction under hegemonic understanding. This unusual affiliation with the movement was variously interpreted as disloyalty, betrayal, absence, or lack: 'When they *were* there, they were rarely there for long' went the usual complaint or 'they seemed to shift from one type of women's group to another'. They were the mobile (yet ever present in their 'absence') members of this particular liberation movement. It is precisely the significance of this mobility which most inventories of oppositional ideology cannot register.

It is in the activity of weaving 'between and among' oppositional ideologies as conceived in this new topological space where another and fifth mode of oppositional consciousness and activity can be found.[51] I have named this activity of consciousness 'differential' insofar as it enables movement 'between and among' the other equal rights, revolutionary, supremacist and separatist modes of oppositional consciousness considered as variables, in order to disclose the distinctions among them. In this sense the differential mode of consciousness operates like the clutch of an automobile: the mechanism that permits the driver to select, engage and disengage gears in a system for the transmission of power.[52] Differential consciousness represents the variant, emerging out of correlations, intensities, junctures, crises. What is differential functions through hierarchy, location and value – enacting the recovery, revenge or reparation; its processes produce justice. For analytic purposes I place this mode of differential consciousness in the fifth position, even though it functions as the medium through which the 'equal rights', 'revolutionary', 'supremacist' and 'separatist' modes of oppositional consciousness became effectively transformed out of their hegemonic versions. Each is now ideological and *tactical* weaponry for confronting the shifting currents of power.

The differences between this five-location and processual topography of consciousness in opposition, and the previous typology of hegemonic feminism, have been made available for analysis through the praxis of US third-world feminism understood as a differential method for understanding oppositional political consciousness and activity. US third-world feminism represents a central locus of possibility, an insurgent movement which shatters the construction of any one of the collective ideologies as the single most correct site where truth can be represented. Without making this move beyond each of the four modes of oppositional ideology outlined above, any liberation movement is destined to repeat the oppressive authoritarianism from which it is attempting to free itself and become trapped inside a drive for truth which can only end in producing its own brand of dominations. What US third-world feminism demands is a new subjectivity, a political revision that denies any one ideology as the final answer, while instead positing a *tactical subjectivity* with the capacity to recenter depending upon the kinds of oppression to be confronted. This is what the shift from hegemonic oppositional theory and practice to a US third-world theory and method of oppositional consciousness requires.

Chicana theorist Aida Hurtado explains the importance of differential consciousness to effective oppositional praxis this way: 'by the time women of color reach adulthood, we have developed informal political skills to deal with State intervention. The political skills required by women of color are neither the political skills of the White power structure that White liberal feminists have adopted nor the free spirited experimentation followed by the radical feminists.' Rather, 'women of color are more like urban guerrillas trained through everyday battle with the state apparatus'. As such, 'women of color's fighting capabilities are often neither understood by white middle-class feminists' nor leftist activists in general, and up until now, these fighting capabilities have 'not been codified anywhere for them to learn.'[53] Cherríe Moraga defines US third-world feminist 'guerrilla warfare' as a way of life: 'Our strategy is how we cope' on an everyday basis, she says, 'how we measure and weigh what is to be said and when, what is to be done and how, and to whom . . . daily deciding/risking who it is we can call an ally, call a friend (whatever that person's skin, sex, or sexuality).' Feminists of color are 'women without a line. We are women who contradict each other'.[54]

In 1981, *Anzaldúa* identified the growing coalition between US feminists of color as one of women who do not have the same culture, language, race or 'ideology, nor do we derive similar solutions' to the problems of oppression. For US third-world feminism enacted as a differential mode of oppositional consciousness, however, these differences do not become 'opposed to each other'.[55] Instead, writes Lorde in 1979, ideological differences must be seen as 'a fund of necessary polarities between which our creativities spark like a dialectic. Only within that interdependency', each ideological position 'acknowledged and equal, can the power to seek new ways of being in the world generate, as well as the courage and sustenance to act where there are no charters'.[56] This movement between ideologies along with the concurrent desire for ideological commitment are necessary for enacting differential consciousness. Differential consciousness makes the second topography of consciousness in opposition visible as a new theory and method for comprehending oppositional subjectivities and social movements in the United States.

The differential mode of oppositional consciousness depends upon the ability to read the current situation of power and of self-consciously choosing and adopting the ideological form best suited to push against its configurations, a survival skill well known to oppressed peoples.[57] Differential consciousness requires grace, flexibility, and strength: enough strength to confidently commit to a well-defined structure of identity for one hour, day, week, month, year; enough flexibility to self-consciously transform that identity according to the requisites of another oppositional ideological tactic if readings of power's formation require it; enough grace to recognize alliance with others committed to egalitarian social relations and race, gender and class justice, when their readings of power call for alternative oppositional stands. Within the realm of differential consciousness, oppositional ideological positions, unlike their incarnations under hegemonic feminist comprehension, are tactics – not strategies. Self-conscious agents of differential consciousness recognize one another as allies, countrywomen and men of the same psychic terrain. As the clutch of a car provides the driver the ability to shift gears, differential consciousness permits the practitioner to choose tactical positions, that is, to self-consciously break and reform ties to ideology, activities which are imperative for the psychological and political practices that permit the achievement of coalition across differences. Differential consciousness occurs within the only possible space where, in the words of third world feminist philosopher Maria Lugones, 'cross-cultural and cross-racial loving' can take place, through the ability of the self to shift its identities in an activity she calls 'world traveling'.[58]

Perhaps we can now better understand the overarching utopian content contained in definitions of US third-world feminism, as in this statement made by black literary critic Barbara Christian in 1985 who, writing to other US feminists of color, said: 'The struggle is not won. Our vision is still seen, even by many progressives, as secondary, our words trivialized as minority issues', our oppositional stances 'characterized by others as devisive. But there is a deep philosophical reordering that is occurring' among us 'that is already having its effects on so many of us whose lives and expressions are an increasing revelation of the INTIMATE face of universal struggle'.[59] This 'philosophical reordering', referred to by Christian, the 'different strategy, a different foundation' called for by hooks are, in the words of Audre Lorde, part of 'a whole other structure of opposition that touches every aspect of our existence at the same time that we are resisting'. I contend that this structure is the recognition of a five-mode theory and method of oppositional consciousness, made visible through one mode in particular, differential consciousness, or US third-world feminism, what Gloria Anzaldúa has recently named 'la conciencia de la mestiza' and what Alice Walker calls 'womanism'.[60] For Barbara Smith, the recognition of this fundamentally different paradigm can 'alter life as we know it' for oppositional actors.[61] In 1981, Merle Woo insisted that US third-world feminism represents a 'new framework which will not support repression, hatred, exploitation and isolation, but will be a human and beautiful framework, created in a community, bonded not by color, sex or class, but by love and the common goal for the liberation of mind, heart, and spirit'.[62] It has been the praxis of a differential form of oppositional consciousness which has stubbornly called up utopian visions such as these.

In this essay I have identified the hegemonic structure within which US feminist theory and practice are trapped. This structure of consciousness stands out in relief against the praxis of US third-world feminism, which has evolved to center the differences of US third-world feminists across their varying languages, cultures, ethnicities, races, classes and genders. I have suggested that the 'philosophical reordering' referred to by Christian is imaginable only through a new theory and method of oppositional consciousness, a theory only visible when US third-world feminist praxis is recognised. US third-world feminism represents a new condition of possibility, another kind of gender, race and class consciousness which has allowed us to recognize and define differential consciousness. Differential consciousness was utilized by feminists of color within the white women's movement; yet it is also a form of consciousness in resistance well utilized among subordinated subjects under various conditions of domination and subordination. The acknowledgement of this consciousness and praxis, this thought and action, carves out the space wherein hegemonic feminism may become aligned with different spheres of theoretical and practical activity which are also concerned with issues of marginality. Moreover, differential consciousness makes more clearly visible the equal rights, revolutionary, supremacist and separatist, forms of oppositional consciousness, which when kaleidescoped together comprise a new paradigm for understanding oppositional activity in general.

The praxis of US third-world feminism represented by the differential form of oppositional consciousness is threaded throughout the experience of social marginality. As such it is also being woven into the fabric of experiences belonging to more and more citizens who are caught in the crisis of late capitalist conditions and expressed in the cultural angst most often referred to as the postmodern dilemma. The juncture I am proposing, therefore, is extreme. It is a location wherein the praxis of US third-world feminism links with the aims of white feminism, studies of race, ethnicity and marginality, and with post-modern theories of culture as they crosscut and join together in new relationships through a shared comprehension of an emerging theory and method of oppositional consciousness.

NOTES

1. This is an early version of a chapter from my book in progress on 'Oppositional Consciousness in the Postmodern World'. A debt of gratitude is owed the friends, teachers and politically committed scholars who made the publication of this essay possible, especially Hayden White, Donna Haraway, James Clifford, Ronaldo Balderrama, Ruth Frankenberg, Lata Mani (who coerced me into publishing this now), Rosa Maria Villafañe-Sisolak, A. Pearl Sandoval, Mary John, Vivian Sobchak, Helene Moglan, T. de Lauretis, Audre Lorde, Traci Chapman and the Student of Color Coalition. Haraway's own commitments to social, gender, race and class justice are embodied in the fact that she discusses and cites an earlier version of this essay in her own work. See especially her 1985 essay where she defines an oppositional post-modern consciousness grounded in multiple identities in her 'A Manifesto for Cyborgs: Science, Technology, and Socialist Feminism in the 1980s', *Socialist Review*, no. 80 (March 1985). At a time when theoretical work by women of color is so frequently dismissed, Haraway's recognition and discussion of my work on oppositional consciousness has allowed it to receive wide critical visibility, as reflected in references to the manuscript that appear in the works of authors such as Sandra Harding, Hancy Hartsock, Biddy Martin and Katherine Hayles. I am happy that my work has also received attention from Caren Kaplan, Katie King, Gloria Anzaldúa, Teresa de Lauretis, Chandra Mohanty and Yvonne Yarboro-Bejarano. Thanks also are due to Frederic Jameson, who in 1979 recognized a theory of 'oppositional consciousness' in my work. It was he who encouraged its further development.

    This manuscript was first presented publically at the 1981 National Women's Studies Association conference. In the ten years following, five other versions have been circulated. I could not resist the temptation to collapse sections from these earlier manuscripts here in the footnotes; any resulting awkwardness is not due to the vigilance of my editors. This essay is published now to honor the political, intellectual, and personal aspirations, of Rosa Maria Villafañe-Sisolak, 'West Indian Princess', who died April 20, 1990. Ro's compassion, her sharp intellectual prowess and honesty, and her unwavering commitment to social justice continue to inspire, guide and support many of us. To her, to those named here and to all new generations of US third-world feminists, this work is dedicated.

2. Gayatri Spivak, 'The Rani of Sirmur' in *Europe and Its Others*, ed. F. Barker vol. 1 (Essex: University of Essex, 1985), p. 147.

3. Here, US third-world feminism represents the political alliance made during the 1960s and 1970s between a generation of US feminists of color who were separated by culture, race, class or gender identifications but united through similar responses to the experience of race oppression.

    The theory and method of oppositional consciousness outlined in this essay is visible in the activities of the recent political unity variously named 'US third-world feminist', 'feminist women of color', and 'womanist'. This unity has coalesced across differences in race, class, language, ideology, culture and color. These differences are painfully manifest: materially marked physiologically or in language, socially value laden, and shot through with power. They confront each feminists of color in any gathering where they serve as constant reminders of their undeniability. These constantly speaking differences stand at the crux of another, mutant unity, for this unity does not occur in the name of all 'women', nor in the name of race, class, culture, or 'humanity' in general. Instead, as many US third-world feminists have pointed out, it is unity mobilized in a location heretofore unrecognized. As Cherríe Moraga argues, this unity mobilizes 'between the seemingly irreconcilable lines – class lines, politically correct lines, the daily lines we run to each other to keep difference and desire at a distance', it is *between* these lines 'that the truth of our connection lies'. This connection is a mobile unity, constantly weaving and reweaving an interaction of differences into coalition. In what follows I demonstrate how it is that inside this coalition, differences are viewed as varying survival tactics constructed in response to recognizable power dynamics. See Cherríe Moraga, 'Between the Lines: On Culture, Class and Homophobia', in *This Bridge Called My Back: Writings by radical women of color*, eds Cherríe Moraga and Gloria Anzaldúa (Watertown, MA: Persephone Press, 1981), p. 106.

During the national conference of the Women's Studies Association in 1981, three hundred feminists of color met to agree that 'it is white men who have access to the greatest amount of freedom from necessity in this culture, with women as their "helpmates" and chattels, and people of color as their women's servants. People of color form a striated social formation which allow men of color to call upon the circuits of power which charge the category of "male" with its privileges, leaving women of color as the final chattel, the ultimate servant in a racist and sexist class hierarchy. US third-world feminists seek to undo this hierarchy by reconceptualizing the notion of "freedom" and who may inhabit its realm'. See Sandoval, 'The Struggle Within: A Report on the 1981 NWSA Conference', published by the Center for Third World Organizing, 1982, reprinted by Gloria Anzaldúa in *Making Faces Making Soul, Haciendo Caras* (San Francisco: Spinsters/Aunt Lute, 1990), 55–71. See also 'Comment on Krieger's *The Mirror Dance*', a US third-world feminist perspective in *Signs* 9, no. 4 (Summer 1984): p. 725.

4. See Fredric Jameson's 'Postmodernism, or the Cultural Logic of Late Capitalism', *New Left Review* 146 (July–August 1984). Also, footnote no. 50, this essay.

5. Louis Althusser, 'Ideology and Ideological State Apparatuses (Notes Towards an Investigation)', in *Lenin and Philosophy and Other Essays* (London: New Left Books, 1970), pp. 123–73.

6. In another essay I have identified the forms of consciousness encouraged within subordinated classes which are resistant – but not self-consciously in political *opposition* to the dominant order. In Althusser's terms, the repressive state apparatus and the ideological state apparatus all conspire to create subordinated forms of *resistant* consciousness that I characterize as 'human', 'pet', 'game', and 'wild'. The value of each of these subject positions is measured by its proximity to the category of the most-human; each position delimits its own kinds of freedoms, privileges and resistances. Whatever freedoms or resistances, however, their ultimate outcome can only be to support the social order as it already functions. This four-category schema stems from the work of the anthropologist Edmund Leach, who demonstrates through his examples of English and Tibeto-Burman language categories that human societies tend to organize individual identity according to perceived distance from a male self and then into relationships of exchange Leach characterizes as those of the 'sister', 'cousin', or 'stranger'. He suggests that these relationships of value of distance are replicated over and over again throughout many cultures and serve to support and further the beliefs, aims and traditions of whatever social order is dominant. Edmund Leach, 'Anthropological Aspects of Language: Animal Categories and Verbal Abuse', in *New Directions in the Study of Language*, ed. Eric Lenneberg (Cambridge: MIT, 1964), p. 62.

7. Althusser, 'Ideology', p. 147.

8. Francis Beal, 'Double Jeopardy: To Be Black and Female', in *Sisterhood Is Powerful: An Anthology of Writings from the Women's Liberation Movement*, ed. Robin Morgan (New York: Random House, 1970), p. 136.

9. Soujourner Truth, 'Ain't I a Woman?' in *The Norton Anthology of Literature by Women* (New York: Norton, 1985), p. 252.
10. Paula Gunn Allen, 'Some Like Indians Endure', in *Living the Spirit* (New York: St. Martin's Press, 1987), p. 9.
11. Toni Morrison, in Bettye J. Parker, 'Complexity: Toni Morrison's Women – an Interview Essay', in *Sturdy Black Bridges: Visions of Black Women in Literature*, eds Roseanne Bell, Bettye J. Parker and Beverly Guy-Sheftall (New York: Anchor/Doubleday, 1979).
12. Velia Hancock, 'La Chicana, Chicano Movement and Women's Liberation', *Chicano Studies Newsletter* (February–March 1971).

    The sense that people of color occupy an 'in-between/outsider' status is a frequent theme among third world liberationists who write both in and outside of the United States. Rev. Desmond Mpilo Tutu, on receiving the Nobel prize, said he faces a 'rough passage' as intermediary between ideological factions, for he has long considered himself 'detribalized'. Rosa Maria Villafañe-Sisolak, a West Indian from the island of St. Croix, has written: 'I am from an island whose history is steeped in the abuses of Western imperialism, whose people still suffer the deformities caused by Euro-American colonialism, old and new. Unlike many third world liberationists, however, I cannot claim to be descendent of any particular strain, noble or ignoble. I am, however, 'purely bred' – descendent of all the parties involved in that cataclysmic epoch. I . . . despair, for the various parts of me cry out for retribution at having been brutally uprooted and transplanted to fulfill the profit-cy of "white" righteousness and dominance. My soul moans that part of me that was destroyed by that callous righteousness. My heart weeps for that part of me that was the instrument . . . the gun, the whip, the book. My mind echoes with the screams of disruption, desecration, destruction.' Alice Walker, in a controversial letter to an African-American friend, told him she believes that 'we are the African and the trader. We are the Indian and the Settler. We are oppressor and oppressed . . . we are the mestizos of North America. We are black, yes, but we are "white", too, and we are red. To attempt to function as only one, when you are really two or three, leads, I believe, to psychic illness: "white" people have shown us the madness of that.' And Gloria Anzaldúa, 'You say my name is Ambivalence: Not so. Only your labels split me.' Desmond Tutu, as reported by Richard N. Osting, 'Searching for New Worlds', *Time Magazine*, Oct. 29, 1984, Rosa Maria Villafañe-Sisolak, from a 1983 journal entry cited in *Haciendo Caras, Making Face Making Soul*, ed. Gloria Anzaldúa; Alice Walker, 'In the Closet of the Soul: A Letter to an African-American Friend', *Ms. Magazine* 15 (November 1986): pp. 32–35; Gloria Anzaldúa, 'La Prieta', *This Bridge Called My Back: Writings by Radical Women of Color* (Watertown, MA: Persephone Press, 1981), pp. 198–209.
13. Gloria T. Hull, Patricia Bell Scott and Barbara Smith, *All the Women Are White, All the Blacks Are Men, But Some of Us Are Brave: Black Women's Studies* (New York: Feminist Press, 1982).
14. Cherríe Moraga and Gloria Anzaldúa, *This Bridge Called My Back: Writings by radical women of color* (Watertown, MA: Persephone Press, 1981).
15. bell hooks, *Ain't I a Woman: Black Women and Feminism* (Boston: South End Press, 1981).
16. Amy Ling, *Between Worlds* (New York: Pergamon Press, 1990).
17. Norma Alarcon, ed., *The Third Woman* (Bloomington, IN: Third Woman Press, 1981).
18. See Alice Walker, 'Letter to an Afro-American Friend', *Ms. Magazine*, 1986. Also Gloria Anzaldúa, *Borderlands, La Frontera: The New Mestiza* (San Francisco: Spinsters/Aunt Lute, 1987).
19. Maxine Hong Kingston, *The Woman Warrior* (New York: Vintage Books, 1977); Cherríe Moraga and Gloria Anzaldúa, *This Bridge Called My Back: Writings by radical women of color*.

20. Audre Lorde, *Sister Outsider* (New York: The Crossing Press, 1984).
21. Maxine Baca Zinn, Lynn Weber Cannon, Elizabeth Higginbotham and Bonnie Thornton Dill, 'The Costs of Exclusionary Practices in Women's Studies', in *Signs: Journal of Women in Culture and Society* 11, no. 2 (Winter 1986), p. 296.
22. Alison Jaggar, *Feminist Politics and Human Nature*: (Totawa: Rowman and Allanheld, 1983), p. 11.
23. Hester Eisenstein, *The Future of Difference* (New Brunswick, NJ: Rutgers University Press, 1985), p. xxi.
24. Elaine Showalter, ed., *The New Feminist Criticism: Essays on Women, Literature and Theory* (New York: Pantheon Books, 1985). See especially the following essays: 'Introduction: The Feminist Critical Revolution', 'Towards a Feminist Poetics', and 'Feminist Criticism in the Wilderness', pp. 3–18, 125–43 and 243–70.
25. Gayle Greene and Copelia Kahn, eds., *Making a Difference: Feminist Literary Criticism* (New York: Methuen, 1985). See their chapter 'Feminist Scholarship and the Social Construction of Woman'. pp. 1–36.
26. Showalter, *New Feminist Criticism*, p. 128.
27. Eisenstein, *The Future of Difference*, p. xvi.
28. Greene and Kahn, *Making a Difference*, p. 13.
29. Jaggar, *Feminist Politics*, p. 37.
30. Showalter, 'New Feminist Criticism', p. 138.
31. Eisenstein, *The Future of Difference*, p. xviii.
32. Greene and Kahn, *Making a Difference*, p. 13.
33. Jaggar, *Feminist Politics*, p. 52.
34. Showalter, 'New Feminist Criticism', p. 139.
35. Eisenstein, *The Future of Difference*, p. xviii.
36. Ibid., p. xix.
37. Greene and Kahn, *Making a Difference*, p. 14.
38. Jaggar, *Feminist Politics*, p. 88.
     Like US hegemonic feminism, European feminism replicates this same basic structure of feminist consciousness. For example, Toril Moi and Julia Kristeve argue that feminism has produced 'three main strategies' for constructing identity and oppositional politics. They represent feminist consciousness as a hierarchically organized historical and political struggle which they schematically summarize like this:

     1. Women demand equal access to the symbolic order. Liberal feminism. Equality.
     2. Women reject the male symbolic order in the name of difference. Radical feminism. Femininity extolled.
     3. (This is Kristeva's own position.) Women reject the dichotomy between masculine and feminine as metaphysical.

     Toril Moi, *Sexual/Textual Politics: Feminist Literary Theory* (New York: Methuen, 1985), 12. Note that the second category here combines the second and third categories of US feminism, and the third category dissolves 'the dichotomy between masculine and feminine' altogether. Luce Irigaray is considered a 'radical feminist' according to this schema.
39. Lydia Sargent, *Women and Revolution: A Discussion of the Unhappy Marriage of Marxism and Feminism* (Boston: South End Press, 1981), p. xx.
     Indeed we can see how those 'protests' pressed hegemonic feminist theory into recentering from its one 'phase' to the next. This hegemonic typology of feminist consciousness, that women are the same as men, that women are different from men, and that women are superior, was challenged at its every level by US third-world feminists. If women were seen as the same as men – differing only in form, not in content – then feminists of color challenged white women for striving to represent themselves as versions of the male, and especially of the dominant version of the 'successful' white male. When the class of women *recognized* and *claimed* their differences from men, then, as feminists of color pointed out, these differences were

understood, valued and ranked according to the codes and values of the dominant class, race, culture and female gender. The response to this challenge is the third phase, which sees any feminist expression as valid as any other as long as it is an expression of a higher moral and spiritual position, that of 'woman'. But US feminists of color did not feel at ease with the essence of 'woman' that was being formulated. If ethical and political leadership should arise only from that particular location, then for feminists of color, who did not see themselves easily identifying with any legitimized form of female subject, Sojourner Truth's lingering question 'Ain't I a woman?' rang all the more loudly. This schema of forms does not provide the opportunity to recognize the existence of another kind of woman – to imagine another, aberrant form of feminism. We could go so far as to say that each hegemonic feminist expression generates equivalent forms of racist ideology.

40. Eisenstein, *The Future of Difference*, p. xix [emphasis mine].
41. Jaggar, *Feminist Politics*, p. 9.
42. Cora Kaplan 'Pandora's Box: Subjectivity, Class and Sexuality in Socialist Feminist Criticism', in Greene and Kahn, *Making a Difference*, pp. 148–51.
43. Jaggar, *Feminist Politics*, p. 123.
44. Ibid. p. 11.
45. Ibid.
46. Sheila Radford-Hill, 'Considering Feminism as a Model for Social Change', in *Feminist Studies/Critical Studies*, ed. Teresa de Lauretis (Bloomington: Indiana University Press, 1986), p. 160.
47. bell hooks, *Feminist Theory from Margin to Center* (Boston: South End Press, 1984), p. 9.
48. Gayatri Chakravorty Spivah, 'Three Women's Texts and a Critique of Imperialism', *Critical Inquiry* 12 (Autumn 1985): pp. 243–61.
49. In another essay I characterize such legitimized idioms of subordination as 'human', 'pet', 'game', and 'wild'.
50. The connection between feminist theory and decolonial discourse studies occurs within a contested space claimed but only superficially colonized by first world theorists of the term 'postmodernism'. Within this zone, it is generally agreed that Western culture has undergone a cultural mutation unique to what Frederic Jameson calls 'the cultural logic of late capital'. There is, however, profound *disagreement* over whether the new cultural dominant should be opposed or welcomed. Jameson's essay on postmodernism, for example, is a warning which points out how the new cultural dominant creates a citizen who is incapable of any real oppositional activity, for all novelty, including opposition, is welcomed by its order. Forms of oppositional consciousness, he argues, the 'critical distance' available to the unitary subjectivities of a Van Gogh or a Picasso under previous modernist conditions, are no longer available to a postmodern subject. The critical distance by which a unitary subjectivity could separate itself from the culture it lived within, and which made parodic aesthetic expression possible, has become erased, replaced by an 'exhilatory' superficial affect, 'schizophrenic' in function, which turns all aesthetic representations into only other examples of the plethora of difference available under advanced capital social formations. Given these conditions, Jameson can only see the first world citizen as a tragic subject whose only hope is to develop a new form of opposition capable of confronting the new cultural conditions of postmodernism. For Jameson, however, the catch is this: 'There may be historical situations in which it is not possible at all to break through the net of ideological constructs' that make us subjects in culture and this is 'our situation in the current crises'. Jameson's own attempt to propose a new form of 'cognitive mapping' capable of negotiating postmodern cultural dynamics dissipates under the weight of his hopelessness, and in my view, his essay coalesces into a eulogy to passing modes of Western consciousness.

What Jameson's essay does not take into account, however, is the legacy of decolonial discourse which is also permeating the cultural moment first world subjects now inherit. In the intersections between the critical study of decolonial discourse and feminist theory is a form of consciousness in opposition once only necessary to the socially marginalized citizen, but which postmodern cultural dynamics now make available to all first world citizens. The content of this form of oppositional consciousness is rather naively celebrated and welcomed by other (primarily white, male) first world theorists of postmodernism. But whether welcoming or rejecting the variously construed meanings of the new cultural dominant, both camps share the longing for a regenerated hope and new identity capable of negotiating the crumbling traditions, values, and cultural institutions of the West; in the first example by celebrating a passing modernist form of unitary subjectivity, in the second by celebrating an identity form whose contours are comparable to the fragmenting status of present Western cultural forms.

Interesting to certain third world scholars is the coalescing relationship between these theories of postmodernism (especially between those which celebrate the fragmentations of consciousness postmodernism demands) and the form of differential oppositional consciousness which has been most clearly articulated by the marginalized and which I am outlining here. The juncture I am analyzing in this essay is that which connects the disorientated first world subject, who longs for the postmodern cultural aesthetic as a key to a new sense of identity and redemption, and the form of differential oppositional consciousness developed by subordinated and marginalized Western or colonized subjects, who have been forced to experience the aesthetics of a 'postmodernism' as a requisite for survival. It is this constituency who are most familiar with what citizenship in this realm requires and makes possible.

The juncture between all of these interests is comprised of the differential form of oppositional consciousness which postmodern cultural conditions are making available to all of its citizenry in an historically unique democratization of oppression which crosses class, race and gender identifications. Its practice contains the possibility for the emergence of a new historical movement – a new citizen – and a new arena for unity between peoples. See Jameson, 'Postmodernism', pp. 53–92.

51. Gloria Anzaldúa writes that she lives 'between and among' cultures in 'La Prieta', *This Bridge Called My Back*, p. 209.
52. Differential consciousness functioning like a 'car clutch' is a metaphor suggested by Yves Labissiere in a personal conversation.
53 Aida Hurtado, 'Reflections on White Feminism: A Perspective from a Woman of Color' (1985), 25, from an unpublished manuscript. Another version of this quotation appears in Hurtado's essay, 'Relating to Privilege: Seduction and Rejection in the Subordination of White Women and Women of Color', in *Signs* (Summer 1989): pp. 833–55.
54. Moraga and Anzaldúa, p. xix. Also see the beautiful passage from Margaret Walker's *Jubilee* which enacts this mobile mode of consciousness from the viewpoint of the female protagonist. See the Bantam Books edition (New York, 1985), pp. 404–407.
55. Gloria Anzaldúa, 'La Prieta', *This Bridge Called My Back*, p. 209.
56. Audre Lorde, comments at 'The Personal and the Political Panel', Second Sex Conference, New York, September 1979. Published in *This Bridge Called My Back*, 98. Also see 'The Uses of the Erotic' in *Sister Outsider*, pp. 58–63, which calls for challenging and undoing authority in order to enter a utopian realm only accessible through a processual form of consciousness which she names the 'erotic'.
57. Anzaldúa refers to this survival skill as 'la facultad, the capacity to see in surface phenomena the meaning of the deeper realities' in *Borderlands, La Frontera*, p. 38.

The consciousness which typifies la facultad is not naive to the moves of power: it is constantly surveying and negotiating its moves. Often dismissed as 'intuition', this kind of 'perceptiveness', 'sensitivity', consciousness if you will, is not determined by race, sex or any other genetic status, neither does its activity belong solely to the 'proletariat', the 'feminist', nor to the oppressed, if the oppressed is considered a unitary category, but it is a learned emotional and intellectual skill which is developed amidst hegemonic powers. It is the recognization of 'la facultad' which moves Lorde to say that it is marginality, 'whatever its nature . . . which is also the source of our greatest strength', for the cultivation of la facultad creates the opportunity for a particularly effective form of opposition to the dominant culture within which it is formed. The skills required by la facultad are capable of disrupting the dominations and subordinations that scar US culture. But is is not enough to utilize them on an individual and situational basis. Through an ethical and political commitment, US third-world feminism requires the development of la facultad to a methodological level capable of generating a political strategy and identity politics from which a new citizenry arises.

Movements of resistance have always relied upon the ability to read below the surfaces – a way of mobilizing – to resee reality and call it by different names. This form of la facultad inspires new visions and strategies for action. But there is always the danger that even the most revolutionary of readings can become bankrupt as a form of resistance when it becomes reified, unchanging. The tendency of la facultad to end in frozen, privileged 'readings' is the most divisive dynamic inside of any liberation movement. In order for this survival skill to provide the basis for a differential and unifying methodology, it must be remembered that la facultad is a process. Answers located may be only temporarily effective, so that wedded to the process of la facultad is a flexibility that continually woos change.

58. Maria Lugones, 'Playfulness, World-Travelling, and Loving Perception', from *Hypatia: A Journal of Feminist Philosophy* 2, no. 2 (1987).

Differential consciousness is comprised of seeming contradictions and difference, which then serve as tactical interventions in the other mobility that is power. Entrance into the realm 'between and amongst' the others demands a mode of consciousness once relegated to the province of intuition and psychic phenomena, but which now must be recognized as a specific practice. I define differential consciousness as a kind of anarchic activity (but with method), a form of ideological guerrilla warfare and a new kind of ethical activity which is being privileged here as the way in which opposition to oppressive authorities is achieved in a highly technologized and disciplinized society. Inside this realm resides the only possible grounds of unity across differences. Entrance into this new order requires an emotional commitment within which one experiences the violent shattering of the unitary sense of self, as the skill which allows a mobile identity to form takes hold. As Bernice Reagon has written, 'most of the time you feel threatened to the core and if you don't, you're not really doing no coalescing'. Citizenship in this political realm is comprised of strategy and risk. Within the realm of differential consciousness there are no ultimate answers, no terminal utopia (through the imagination of utopias can motivate its tactics), no predictable final outcomes. Its practice is not biologically determined, restricted to any class or group, nor must it become static. The fact that it is a process capable of freezing into a repressive order – or of disintegrating into relativism – should not shadow its radical activity.

To name the theory and method made possible by the recognition of differential consciousness 'oppositional' refers only to the ideological effects its activity can have under present cultural conditions. It is a naming which signifies a realm with constantly shifting boundaries which serve to delimit, for differential consciousness participates in its own dissolution even as it is in action. Differential consciousness under postmodern conditions is not possible without the creation of another ethics, a new morality, which will bring about a new subject of history. Movement into this realm is heralded by the claims of US third-world feminists, a movement which makes manifest the possibility of ideological warfare in the form of a theory and method, a praxis of oppositional consciousness. But to think of the activities of US

third-world feminism thus is only a metaphorical avenue which allows one conceptual access to the threshold of this other realm, a realm accessible to all people.

59. Barbara Christian, 'Creating a Universal Literature: Afro-American Women
Writers', *KPFA Folio*, Special African History Month Edition, February 1983, front
page. Reissued in *Black Feminist Criticism: Perspectives on Black Women Writers*
(New York: Pergamon Press, 1985), p. 163.

60. Alice Walker coined the neologism 'womanist' as one of many attempts by femi-
nists of color to find a name which could signal their commitment to egalitarian
social relations, a commitment which the name 'feminism' had seemingly betrayed.
See Walker, *In Search of Our Mother's Gardens: Womanist Prose* (New York:
Harcourt Brace Jovanovich, 1983), pp. xix–xiii. Anzaldúa, *Borderlands, La Nueva
Frontera*.

61. bell hooks, 'Feminist Theory: From Margin to Center', 9; Audre Lorde. 'An
Interview: Audre Lorde and Adrienne Rich' held in August 1979, *Signs* 6, no. 4
(Summer 1981); and Barbara Smith, *Home Girls: A Black Feminist Anthology*, p.
xxv.

62. Merle Woo, *This Bridge Called My Back*, p. 147.

PART 2
RETHINKING WHITENESS

2.1

'TO MAKE THE FACTS KNOWN: RACIAL TERROR AND THE CONSTRUCTION OF WHITE FEMININITY'

Vron Ware

You see, the white man has never allowed his women to hold the sentiment 'black but comely', on which he has so freely acted himself. Libertinism apart, white men constantly express an open preference for the society of black women. But it is a sacred convention that white women can never feel passion of any sort, high or low, for a black man. Unfortunately facts don't always square with convention; and then, if the guilty pair are found out, the thing is christened an outrage at once and the woman is practically forced to join in hounding down the partner of her shame.[1]

A vital project awaits any historian interested in exploring the social and political dynamics of race, class and gender in nineteenth-century Britain: quite simply, to identify and describe the anti-colonial movement that was formed in opposition to the rapacious growth of Empire. While there are separate studies of anti-imperialist campaigns, organizations and individuals, I do not believe there has been a single work that attempts either to document or to analyse the early formation of anti-imperialism as a movement. It would be an enormous task as it would require a study of the nascent nationalist groupings in the different colonies, their supporters in England, Scotland, Ireland and Wales, and the network of various philanthropic organizations that campaigned at the heart of Empire. Yet a single account would never be enough; the history of

From: Vron Ware (1992), 'To Make the Facts Known: Racial Terror and the Construction of White Femininity', pp. 169–224, in Vron Ware, *Beyond the Pale: White Women, Racism and Industry* (London: Verso).

anti-imperialism would benefit from endless debate and reframing, from being scrutinized from different points of view, and from being constantly referred back to other social and political movements of that period. Just as the history of abolitionism has both added to and been influenced by an understanding of the early women's rights movement, so a compendium of anti-imperialist thought and practice would enrich current perceptions of nineteenth-century feminism.

Feminist history has credited individual women with expressing criticism of Empire: women like Annie Besant, for example, who immersed herself in the Indian nationalist movement, or Olive Schreiner, who wrote about colonial relations in her native South Africa. It would be possible to list many other extraordinary women whose names have arisen in the context of particular struggles – women like Lady Florence Dixie and Harriet Colenso, who each played a decisive role in negotiations between the Zulu people and the British government, or Daisy Bates, who left her husband and son in Australia to live with aborigines. Their individual stories are always highly intriguing, and in most cases require far greater study than has so far been given to them. However, when they are added together, the existing accounts immediately suggest the need for an analysis of the role that women played in the anti-imperialist movement in late Victorian Britain – an analysis which considers, at the same time, their relationship to feminism.

There has been an enormous amount of useful feminist research on the different strands of feminism that competed with each other during the late nineteenth century. In *Faces of Feminism*, Olive Banks has described the development of different political agendas among feminists in Britain and America, showing how, by the end of the nineteenth century they were involved in 'contradictions between different definitions of feminism and different and indeed opposing concepts of femininity'.[2] In this essay I want to bring this interpretation to bear on a study of a particular episode in the history of anti-imperialism. It centres on the formation of a political grouping which came together in England to campaign against lynching in America and its relevance for this project of connecting race, class and gender stems from three main sources. First, the campaign was initiated and largely sustained by women; second, it was a product of collaboration between white English women and a black American woman who galvanized the campaign with a coherent political analysis based on her own research and experience; and finally, through addressing issues of sexuality and femininity, the short-lived anti-lynching movement not only forced a division between different kinds of feminism, but actually made possible a radical politics that acknowledged the connection between the domination of black people and the subordination of women.

Lynch law

'Lynching is a peculiarly American tradition', wrote Manning Marable in his book *How Capitalism Underdeveloped Black America*.[3] The word is now used so carelessly that its meaning has lost much of its association with racial terror. It was first used to describe the system devised during the American Revolution by a Quaker political leader called Charles Lynch to curb criminal behaviour in a community which was two hundred miles away from the nearest court of law. The accused man was given the opportunity to defend himself, but if convicted, was sentenced to a punishment deemed appropriate to the crime. This practice, started in a town in Virginia, known today as Lynchburg and famous for Jack Daniels whisky, was fairly common in the Southern states until the end of the eighteenth century, when it came to mean the actual execution of the allegedly guilty person.

It was not until twenty years after the end of the Civil War that the murder of untried suspects became a means of political administration in the South, one which particularly affected black people. By the late 1880s a new generation of blacks and whites had grown up without any direct experience of slavery. Southern society had seen enormous social and economic disintegration, and where ideas about black behaviour and pathology were once governed by the institution of slavery, they were now informed by theories of race and biological difference. As the decade moved from prosperity to recession, racist diatribes on black criminality and bestiality came to be accepted by whites as the observable truth, and in 1889 there began an orgy of lynching. From then on the practice became a specific form of racial terror: the great majority of those who were lynched in the years from 1882 to 1930 were black: of the 4,761 recorded deaths by lynching, 1,375 were of whites.[4] In the period 1889–93, which saw an unprecedented number, 579 blacks and 260 whites were lynched – and 134 of the total 839 took place outside the South. By the turn of the century, from 1899 to 1903, only 27 of the total 543 recorded lynchings were of whites.

The statistics themselves reveal nothing of what lynching actually involved. With the tolerance, and usually the participation of the local establishment, suspects were sometimes taken from gaols after their arrest; at other times the mere rumour of a crime was enough to send out a lynch mob in search of a victim and in such cases people were seized without any evidence whatsoever. Far from being a spontaneous act of revenge, a lynching was frequently publicized a day or two in advance, sometimes even beyond the area in which it was to take place. Public transport might be organized for those wishing to watch and tickets were sold in advance. The event itself often became a mass spectacle involving ritual torture – usually castration – and execution, watched by thousands of people, including children. Photographs and eyewitness accounts describe how families flocked to witness lynchings and then fought to get a souvenir from the victim's charred and dismembered remains. On one occasion a gramophone record was said to have been made of the victim's screams.[5] The event was usually written up in detail by the local press.[6]

The fact that the local law-enforcement officers were often directly involved in these practices meant that when they began to spread in the late 1880s there was almost no opposition from white institutions in the South. In the North, which had by then withdrawn its occupying army, lynchings came to be seen as a natural outcome of abolition; it was thought inevitable that former slaves would wish to take revenge on whites, who would feel threatened by their liberty. It was also assumed that the crimes which precipitated lynchings were invariably of a sexual nature – in other words, that black men were assaulting white women. It was this assumption that made millions of people throughout the United States condone the behaviour of the lynch mobs, either through silence or by voicing approval. Lynching was certainly 'the ultimate of historical white justice and black death'[7] – and it was carried out in the name of defending the honour of white women. Few thought to question this apparent justification, and to relate the pattern of lynching to the political and economic fate of black Southerners after Reconstruction.

By 1892, when the number of lynchings reached a peak, the laws that guaranteed black citizens legal and constitutional equality with whites had been dismantled or overridden by state legislation in most of the Southern states. Segregation was enforced on public transport, in places of entertainment, hotels and schools, and voting rights were in the process of being removed either by law or by intimidation of black voters at the polling booths. The old anti-slavery movement had fallen apart after emancipation, and although there was a great deal of protest and opposition, this made little impact on the federal government which had already sanctioned these developments.

The British anti-slavery movement had also disintegrated, although many former activists retained an interest in conditions in both the Caribbean and America. However, it was in Britain that the first concerted public campaign against lynching took place. 1893 saw a resurgence of activity in support of African-Americans, inspired and largely maintained by the efforts of a few British women who were determined to organize a protest movement. Against a background of Empire mania in their own country, these women, who came from different political and social backgrounds, were briefly united in an alliance with black people across the Atlantic. Their motivation came partly from the horror they felt when reading about lynching; but it was their understanding of the role of white women in justifying the practice that made their involvement so important. This essay will begin by looking at the background to the campaign, before moving on to discuss the arguments and conflicts that came up during its course.

SUPPORT FROM BRITAIN

In 1894 the Anti-Lynching Committee was set up in London sponsored by an impressive list of editors, politicians and public figures.[8] Its aim was

> to obtain reliable information on the subject of lynching and mob outrages in America, to make the facts known, and to give expression to public opinion in condemnation of such outrages in whatever way might best seem calculated to assist the cause of humanity and civilization.[9]

The catalyst for this group of people was the young African-American journalist, Ida B. Wells, who had spent several months in 1893 and again in the following year touring Britain in an attempt to draw attention to the way blacks in the United States were being systematically denied the legal justice and equality guaranteed them in the constitution.

Ida. B. Wells's lecture tours were not particularly unusual, as an increasing number of African-Americans had visited Britain from the 1830s onwards to campaign against slavery and to raise money for black projects. The networks, both personal and organizational, which had invited and received American abolitionists were still very much in existence following the Civil War and many of the friendships that had resulted were carried on by the younger generations on both sides. When Frederick Douglass made his last visit to Britain in 1886–87 it was primarily to see his friends rather than to make new political contacts; however, he was often called upon at social gatherings to make speeches about the situation in post-war America.[10] In the course of one of these meetings in London he met Catherine Impey, who was ultimately to be responsible for the anti-lynching campaign on the British side of the Atlantic. They met again a few weeks later at the home of Helen Bright Clark, daughter of the radical MP John Bright, who had met Douglass as a child when he was befriended by her father. Catherine Impey described her second meeting with Frederick Douglass in her diary:

> During the evening . . . Mr Douglass gave us a luminous half hour's address on the present condition of the coloured population in America, speaking of the caste barriers that everywhere blocked their way, of the iniquitous truck system, their oppression, and their total inability to protect themselves without the ballot of which they had been deprived by cruel persecution and the fraudulent manipulation of the ballot box.[11]

Shortly after this encounter, in 1888, Catherine Impey launched a magazine called *Anti-Caste* which was 'devoted to the interests of the coloured race'. She wrote a substantial part of it herself, but relied on correspondents in America and different parts of the British Empire to supply her with first-hand information and newspaper cuttings about the maltreatment of black people by white. When Frederick Douglass invited her to visit his home in Washington, Catherine was overjoyed and three years later, while in America on family business, spent several days with him learning about the realities of life for black people after emancipation.[12] It was during the same trip that she arranged to meet Ida B. Wells, whose outspoken condemnation of lynching had brought her to the attention of Frederick Douglass.

Shortly after her return, Catherine Impey was sent a report of a lynching in Alabama that had appeared in a local newspaper, complete with graphic photograph. She published the picture on the front page of *Anti-Caste* with a caption that drew attention to the children posing by the body of the hanged man.[13] In doing so she was risking her own reputation, not so much because of the explicit nature of the photograph, but because she was raising the forbidden subject of rape, and even worse, defending the perpetrators of a particularly terrible crime. It would have required very strong convictions for a woman to have brought it to public attention anyway, let alone as a white woman defending black men against charges of assaulting her fellow white women. At that time the circulation of the journal was small, but those who saw it were horrified. A newspaper editor in Liverpool criticized her strongly in his own paper, assuming that the picture was a drawing and had been embellished by the artist. When, however, he was told that it was a photograph sent out by the lynchers themselves, his disapproval of Catherine turned to outrage at what the photograph depicted, and he became one of Catherine's most influential supporters.

Only days after this edition of *Anti-Caste* was published, Catherine Impey read an account of a lynching so sadistic that it had reached even the pages of the British press. A black man in Paris, Texas, was arrested and charged with raping and murdering a five-year-old girl. While he was in prison but before any semblance of a trial, preparations were made to burn him alive with the full consent of the authorities. Schoolchildren were given a day's holiday and trains carried people from the surrounding countryside to watch the event which was carried out in broad daylight. The local papers described in detail how the prisoner was tortured with red-hot irons for hours before the flames were eventually lit; after it was over the mob fought over the ashes for souvenirs in the form of bones, buttons and teeth.

Catherine Impey wrote the same day to Frederick Douglass asking him to arrange for someone, preferably Ida. B. Wells, to come to Britain to help influence public opinion and campaign against lynching from outside the United States. She was encouraged to do so by an acquaintance, Isabella Fyvie Mayo, a Scottish widow whose own philanthropic tendencies had led her to take in lodgers from different parts of the world.[14] Isabella Mayo's reaction to the lynching question was at first cautious as, like most people, she assumed that there must have been evidence of some dreadful crime, presumably of a sexual nature, to justify the revenge of the lynch mob. Catherine's account of her meeting with Ida B. Wells the previous year intrigued Mayo enough to want to meet the outspoken American woman, and plans were immediately made for a speaking tour. Two months later, in April 1893, Ida B. Wells disembarked at Liverpool and after a brief trip to Somerset to recover from the journey, the three women set to work in Mayo's house in Aberdeen planning the tour.

Through Catherine Impey's contacts in the newspaper world and her membership of the Society of Friends, and through Mayo's Scottish connections, meetings and publicity were quickly arranged and Ida B. Wells was accompanied on a rigorous circuit of engagements. A new organization was set up, called the Society for the Recognition of the Universal Brotherhood of Man (SRUBM), which declared itself fundamentally opposed to the system of race separation by which the despised members of a community are cut off from the social, civil and religious life of their fellow man. It regards lynchings and other forms of brutal justice inflicted on the weaker communities of the world as having their root in race prejudice, which is directly fostered by the estrangement, and lack of sympathy consequent on race separation.

Years later, Ida B. Wells wrote down the details of her trips to Britain in her autobiography, *Crusade for Justice*. She quoted numerous press reports and the interviews she gave, in addition to comments on the places she visited and the reactions of the people who met her. She also wrote regular dispatches for the Chicago paper *Inter-Ocean*, becoming the first black overseas columnist for any paper in America. In an interview with *The Sun*, a sympathetic American paper, Ida B. Wells described the reaction to her lectures while she was in England:

> Well, you know that the English people are very undemonstrative. At first everything I said was received in absolute silence, but I saw that their interest was intense. . . . What I told them about the negro lynchings in the South was received with incredulity. It was new to them, and they could not believe that human beings were hanged, shot, and burned in broad daylight, the legal authorities sometimes looking on. . . . They could not believe that these acts were done, not by savages, not by cannibals who at least would have had the excuse of providing themselves with something to eat, but by people calling themselves Christian, civilized American citizens.[15]

Ida B. Wells had anticipated a sceptical reaction and came well armed with evidence to support her argument that black people in the South were being systematically denied access to the same processes of law that were available to whites. All her examples came from Southern newspaper reports, so that no one could accuse her of exaggerating the details, and she had carefully recorded the circumstances of each incident to demonstrate that the lynch mobs were prepared to murder without a shred of evidence of any 'crime' committed.

Her audiences consisted 'of all classes, from the highest to the lowest' as she travelled round churches, social clubs, political and social reform gatherings, and even drawing-room meetings requested by 'fashionable ladies'. Like many of the African-American lecturers who had preceded her in the years before the Civil War, she was surprised to find that many white people in Britain, whatever their class background, were prepared to be receptive and sympathetic to her cause, in contrast to her experience at home. In the same interview in *The Sun*, Ida B. Wells was asked whether she encountered any race prejudice in Britain. According to the report she replied 'enthusiastically':

> No, it was like being born again in a new condition. Everywhere I was received on a perfect equality with the ladies who did so much for me and

my cause. In fact, my color gave me some agreeable prominence which I might not otherwise have had. Fancy my feeling when in London I saw the Lady Mayoress taking a negro African Prince about at a garden party and evidently displaying him as the lion of the occasion.

In her autobiography Ida B. Wells expanded on the subject, describing her acquaintance with Ogontula Sapara, a young African medical student who volunteered to help with the campaign in 1894. He once visited her at her hotel in London, accompanied by six fellow-students, also from Africa: 'Such excitement you never saw, and several of the residents of the hotel said that they had never seen that many black people in their lives before.'[16] Sapara entertained Ida with stories of how some of his patients, who had never seen a black man, refused to let him touch them. But she was convinced that this was nothing compared to the hatred and prejudice she was accustomed to in America. Her enthusiasm, however, must be read as an index of the racism in the South rather than of the lack of it in Britain, where resident black people were all too aware of what Catherine Impey called 'the dark spirit of Caste, which so often lurks hidden behind the scenes'.[17]

IDA B. WELLS'S ANALYSIS

The press reports of Ida B. Wells's lectures and interviews during both her visits are witness to her remarkable ability to move her audiences to condemn racism. She evidently spoke quietly, which many found impressive, and was ready to draw on personal experience as well as presenting a carefully argued analysis of the failure of the American legal system to protect black people. Born into slavery in Mississippi in 1862, Ida grew up in the early days of the post-emancipation South, receiving an unusually comprehensive education in a college set up by the Freedmen's Aid. However, by the time she was twenty-two years old she had already been disillusioned of any ideals of equality for blacks under the law when she became the first person to contest newly introduced legislation permitting segregation on the railways. When she went to sit in the women's compartment of a first-class carriage she was ordered by the guard to remove herself to the smoking carriage. After a physical struggle in which she was virtually dragged out of the compartment, much to the delight of the white passengers, she left the train with her ticket intact and returned to Memphis to bring a suit against the railway company.

Her argument was that under the law, black people were permitted separate but equal accommodation on the trains, and that as there had been only one first-class carriage, she was entitled to sit in it. She won the first round and was awarded $500 damages, but the railway company appealed and the case was decided against Ida on the grounds that she had intended all along to harass the company and 'her persistence was not in good faith to obtain a comfortable seat for a short ride'.[18]

Ida B. Wells wrote in her diary:

I felt so disappointed because I had hoped such great things for my people generally. I have firmly believed that the law was on our side and would, when we appealed to it, give us justice. I feel shorn of that belief and utterly discouraged, and just now, if it were possible, would gather my race in my arms and fly away with them.[19]

However disappointed Ida felt with the power of the law to protect black people in the South, she never lost her commitment to fighting for legal justice. Her politics became more sharply focused when she abandoned her career as a teacher and took over as editor of *Free Speech*, a black newspaper in Memphis. It was at this point in her life that she first turned her attention to lynching and its function in Southern society. In her autobiography she wrote that once she too had 'accepted the idea . . . that although lynching was irregular and contrary to law and order, unreasoning anger over the terrible crime of rape led to the lynching; that perhaps the brute deserved death anyhow and the mob was justified in taking his life'.[20] When, however, one of her best friends was murdered in cold blood with the sanction of the white establishment, she realized that the lynch law was becoming a primary means of controlling black social and economic life.

In her autobiography, Ida gives a detailed account of this incident, which was to change her life dramatically. Three black businessmen, Thomas Moss, Calvin MacDowell and Henry Stewart, were arrested after some white men were wounded in a street fight. Fearing more violence, the black community organized a guard outside the gaol where they were held for two nights. On the third night, a crowd of armed white men entered the police prison, took the three prisoners out and shot them a mile outside the town. One of the daily newspapers delayed its appearance in order to give full details of the lynching.

The men who died had opened a grocery shop in a crowded black suburb, threatening the custom of a white grocer who had until then had a monopoly in the neighbourhood. They were well known and liked in the community and news of their murder came as a terrible shock. A crowd gathered outside their shop, the People's Grocery Company, to talk about the incident, but there was no violence. However, when word came back to the courts that 'Negroes were massing', orders were given to the sheriff to take a hundred men and 'shoot down on sight any Negro who appears to be making trouble'. The white mob swarmed into the grocery, destroying what they could not eat or drink, while the black onlookers were forced to submit to all kinds of insults. A few days later the shop was closed by the creditors and the white grocer was able to continue his business without competition.

It was reported in the newspaper that the last words of Thomas Moss, a close friend of Ida B. Wells, who had pleaded with the murderers to spare him for the sake of his wife and unborn child, were, 'Tell my people to go West – there is no justice for them here.' Ida B. Wells's paper, *Free Speech*, urged people to take this advice, arguing that there was no protection for black people in Memphis if they dared to compete in business with whites. Within a few weeks there was a great exodus of black families from the city. White business was practically at a standstill as it relied heavily on black custom. Even the transport system was affected as people preferred to walk in order to save their money for the journey west. When anxious executives from the City Railway Company came to the offices of *Free Speech* to ask them to use their influence, Ida B. Wells wrote up the interview with them and urged readers to continue to keep their money for themselves. She then travelled out west herself, spending three weeks in Oklahoma reporting on the successes of the new settlers in order to counteract the fabrications of white newspapers in Memphis, which were now urging blacks to stay in the city. Immediately after this she accepted an invitation to speak at a conference in Philadelphia, and from there she intended to make a short trip to New York before returning to Memphis. On her arrival in New York she was greeted by the news that the white establishment in Memphis was out for her blood. Her paper had been closed down and orders had been given to punish with death anyone who tried to start it again. Her friends wrote to her warning her not even to consider returning as there were white men watching every train ready to kill her on sight. Ida knew that it was her support of the economic boycott that had driven the white authorities to try and suppress her paper, but it was the final editorial, published while she was in Philadelphia, that had provoked the mob to destroy her offices and to attempt to lynch her as well.

In the three months following the death of her friend, Ida B. Wells had thought a great deal about the way in which the white establishment was able to prevent black businesses from competing successfully. The law was totally inadequate in protecting blacks from intimidation and murder and, more than this, the highest figures of authority were frequently implicated in organizing this violence. Meanwhile the rest of the country condoned lynching because of a readiness to believe that it was a spontaneous outburst of revenge against black rapists and child molesters. Ida began to investigate reports of lynchings and discovered that in every incident in which white women were said to have been assaulted, the facts had actually been distorted out of recognition. There was almost no evidence to support the rape theory, except that in each case there was a white woman who had been found to have been associating with a black man of her own free will. In one example, the sheriff's seventeen-year-old daughter was traced to the cabin of one of her father's farm-hands, who was then lynched by the mob in order to salvage the young woman's reputation. The press reported that 'The big burly brute was lynched because he had raped the seventeen-year-old daughter of the sheriff.'

The final editorial of *Free Speech* was direct in its denunciation of this example of the notorious Southern chivalry:

> Eight Negroes lynched since last issue of *Free Speech*. Three were charged with killing white men and five with raping white women. Nobody in this

section believes the old thread-bare lie that Negroes assault white women. If Southern white men are not careful they will over-reach themselves and a conclusion will be reached which will be very damaging to the moral reputation of their women.[21]

Following her exile to the North, Ida B. Wells expanded her theoretical observations, comparing the widespread rape and abuse of black women and girls by white men under slavery with the savagery they showed towards any white woman suspected of intimacy with a black man. She had become convinced that the Southerner had not recovered from the shock of losing his slaves and of seeing free black men and women working for themselves and enjoying their constitutional rights to education, voting and holding public office. The racism of the whites, constantly refined and developed as the economy of the South went into a severe depression following Reconstruction, invoked a hysterical fear of black male sexuality which made any contact between black men and white women a danger. If a black man so much as looked a white woman in the eye he risked being accused of lechery or insolence, and in some cases this was as good as committing an actual assault. As long as white women were seen to be the property of white men, without power or a voice of their own, their 'protectors' could claim to be justified in taking revenge for any alleged insult or attack on them. Whenever the reputation of white women was 'tainted' by the suggestion of immoral behaviour, it could always be saved by the charge that they had been victims of black lust.

Lynching was a way of reinforcing white supremacy by rule of terror. Black people had learned that any action that might cause annoyance to whites, however trivial, could provoke a violent reaction for which there was no redress in law; and the most plausible justification for this kind of violence was the prospect of the sexual assault of a white female by a black male. The young black woman's instigation of an economic boycott had been damaging enough to the white authorities in Memphis; her slur against the white womanhood of the South, implied in her last editorial, made her own lynching an inevitability if she dared to return home.

Ida B. Wells's analysis of the economic and political treatment of blacks in the post-Reconstruction South was received cautiously in the North, which prided itself on its comparative liberalism. The complacency which followed from abolishing slavery had led to a general apathy on matters of race while attitudes and behaviour towards black people had scarcely changed. However, she had just begun to make a name for herself when she was invited, through Frederick Douglass, to go to Britain in the hope of gaining a more sympathetic hearing.

BRITISH RESPONSES

In many ways, Ida B. Wells's audiences outside America were more shocked than those at home by her portrayal of Southern justice. The main hostility that she encountered came from those who thought that the British had no right to criticize Americans, especially over what appeared to be a complicated internal issue of law and order. *The Times* expressed this view in a scathing denunciation of the Anti-Lynching Committee, which had written to the governor of Alabama asking him to verify certain reports of lynching in that state. *The Times* had obtained a copy of the governor's reply which it used to illustrate its point. In a familiar tone, the paper's editorial professed to have no sympathy with lynching, and none with 'anti-lynching' either, portraying the committee as a 'large number of well-known Dissenters' who were meddling in affairs that had nothing to do with them:

> Nor do we suppose that those who are responsible for the unfortunate letter have the least suspicion that it was likely to be represented as a piece of officious impertinence. Burning with sympathy for the much trampled on negro, they betray no consciousness of the magnitude and delicacy of the problem in which they are intervening. We should not be surprised if the Anti-Lynching Committee's well-meant letter multiplied the number of negroes who are hanged, shot, and burnt by paraffin, not only in Alabama, but throughout the Southern states. This would be a bitter stroke of irony. But it is the fate which frequently attends a fanatical anxiety to impose our own canons of civilisation upon people differently circumstanced.[22]

In an attempt to be humorous the editorial paid almost as much attention to the grammar of both letters as to the content, even to the extent of suggesting that the committee's secretary, Florence Balgarnie, was in danger of being 'lynched by a mob of enraged grammarians'. It gave far greater space and weight to the governor's reply, and after proposing that this was not the occasion to discuss lynching itself, went on to display the very attitudes that condoned it. While condemning it as a form of race hatred, since it was only blacks who were being lynched, the writer then felt compelled to point out:

> [A]lthough the negro, it must be acknowledged, does something to justify such differential treatment by the frequency and atrocity of his outrages on white women. That is a circumstance which ought to weigh with Miss Balgarnie and the numerous ladies upon the Anti-Lynching Committee.

The Anti-Lynching Committee would not have been at all surprised by this reaction from *The Times* as it represented the most conservative sections of the ruling class. However, the facetious tone and arrogant racism that lay behind it could not obscure the point that it was hypocritical to criticize other countries for their standards of behaviour when comparable atrocities were being carried out nearer home. Just as pro-slavery agitators had claimed that the terrible conditions in Britain's growing industrial centres were far worse than those on most slave plantations, so the protagonists of American racism could point to the treatment of many of Britain's colonial subjects. The savage repression of the

1857 uprising in India, for example, was a case in point. British criticism of the handling of the 'race problem' in the South must have seemed continuous with their condemnation of slavery in the decade before the Civil War, and many resented both the interference and the tone of moral superiority that often accompanied it. In Britain it was indeed relatively easy to express horror at the way white Americans turned illegal executions into mass spectacles, but this outrage did not necessarily have the effect of challenging forms of racism that existed within the country and throughout the colonies.

On the other hand, as far as commentators like *The Times* were concerned, those who defended black people in America might as well be defending all blacks, whether in the Caribbean, India or Africa. By the late nineteenth century, theories of so-called scientific racism had sought to prove that all people with darker skin were biologically different from and inferior to whites. Serious uprisings in the Caribbean and in India had made these theories more attractive to those who supported the idea of the British Empire, which by now had been extended throughout Africa, Australia and the Indian subcontinent. Those who actively supported organizations like the Anti-Lynching Committee or the Society for the Recognition of the Universal Brotherhood of Man earned themselves the epithet 'nigger philanthropists' among those who believed in white supremacy. It was not surprising then that the anti-lynching campaign launched by Ida B. Wells brought together individuals from different backgrounds who were prepared to make connections between racism at home and abroad, and who realized their own responsibility to challenge it.

At the centre of this group of people, including the 'numerous ladies' referred to in *The Times* editorial, was the journal *Anti-Caste* and its editor, Catherine Impey. The name 'Anti-Caste' itself meant virtually the same as 'anti-racism', which might seem strangely modern for a period more commonly associated with jingoism. The paper was produced from Catherine Impey's house in Street, Somerset, on a monthly basis, with the help of her mother and sister, and sold for a nominal sum of a halfpenny to cover the cost of postage. It relied on subscriptions and donations for immediate support, though the main costs were borne personally by the editor. Catherine Impey's family and many of her subscribers belonged to the Society of Friends: Street was one of the largest Quaker communities in southern England. At its centre was the Clark shoe factory which was run by William Clark, also from a Quaker family. He was married to Helen Bright, who had retained many of her father's radical connections after he died, and who was part of a network of English feminists and philanthropists. Yet although Catherine Impey received a great deal of support from local Friends, little evidence of her work has survived and all her papers have disappeared without trace. The loss of her diaries is tragic as they would have contained so much information about the networks of antiracist sympathizers, as well as more insights into Catherine herself. Apart from a few surviving letters and essays and invaluable personal recollections from friends and more distant relatives in Street who remember her towards the end of her life, the main sources of information about her are to be found in Ida B. Wells's autobiography and in *Anti-Caste*.

Catherine was an unusual woman, not just because of her commitment to what we would now call anti-racism, but because she made a conscious decision to remain independent and devote her life to various social and political causes. Her father, who ran a small business selling agricultural equipment, died when she was thirty-eight and Catherine was given the opportunity to carry on the family business. In a letter to a friend, however, she wrote that her sister had taken over the business, which allowed her to continue with her 'social reform' work, as she called it: 'I am very glad not to be obliged to work for my living, but it is a more serious matter than it seems to some – to deliberately choose a life of independence.'[23]

It is hard to do more than speculate on Catherine's early political influences. Judging from the support her mother gave her, and the number of local names and addresses on her early subscription lists, she seems to have been part of a network of politically sympathetic families, many of whom were Quakers who had been active in the anti-slavery movement. In the first issue of *Anti-Caste* she wrote that she believed all arbitrary distinctions between people to be 'contrary to the mind of Christ', and that 'of all such distinctions the meanest and most cruelly irritating to the victims are those which are based purely upon *physical* characteristics – sex, race, complexion, nationality – in fact, form or deformity of any kind'. In the tradition of most Victorian philanthropists she relied on the power of religious language to express her own views on what she felt to be right and wrong, and biblical references and quotations permeated her writing. But although she referred to all kinds of discrimination and oppression as 'evil', she was also quite specific about what she meant. At the beginning of her fourth year as editor she wrote:

> While Religion teaches men that God is the Father of *all*, that we are all 'brethren', that of 'one blood hath He made all nations of men for to *dwell together*', the 'Father of Lies' goes up and down in the world, teaching that the God of Heaven created separate races of men, to dwell apart – separated from each other, that a fair skin is always superior to a dark one, that fellowship between differing races is contrary to man's nature, that the strong should *compel* the submission of the weak, crushing and if necessary, exterminating those who resist. From such a doctrine spring the horrors, whose echoes reach us from all quarters of the Globe, from Central Africa, to ice-bound Siberia, from the United States with her slaughtered Indian babes and women and her down-trodden millions of dark-hued workers, to thoughtful cultured India under the heel of British militarism, from the Australian forests, to the islands of the Southern Seas.[24]

Apart from equality between the races, Catherine Impey's ideal of human brotherhood included the abolition of the alcohol traffic, an end to militarism, a respect for the environment and the humane treatment of animals – she was also a strict vegetarian. She often wrote about these issues in the 'Village Album', a monthly collection of essays and correspondence kept by the Quaker community in Street. In the last twenty years of her life she became a Poor Law Guardian, though sadly very little is known about this period of her life. Her obituary in the Quaker journal, *The Friend*, remembered how her 'warm and generous sympathies had ever been at the service of the many interests to which she was wholeheartedly devoted'. 'Nevertheless,' it continued, it was 'the colour question, which enlisted her closest sympathy, and on which she held deep convictions in her consistent advocacy of equal rights for the white and coloured people.'[25]

By the time she founded *Anti-Caste*, Catherine Impey had already visited the USA three times, and had made important contacts with black writers, clergy and teachers. Among those she listed as her personal acquaintances in the first issue of her journal were Frederick Douglass, Amanda Smith (a preacher who passed through England on her way to Africa), Judge Albion Tourgee, author of the first novel to deal with Reconstruction, Thomas Fortune, editor of the *New York Freeman* and an influential figure in black politics, Fanny Jackson Coppin, President of the Institute of Coloured Youth In Philadelphia, and Frances E. Harper, head of the black women's section of the Women's Christian Temperance Union, and with Coppin and four other black women, a speaker at the World's Congress of Representative Women, which was held as part of the Colombian Exposition in Chicago in 1893.[26] Many of these friends kept up a correspondence with Catherine which must have given her great encouragement: 'My friend and sister,' wrote Frances E. Harper, 'permit me to say go on with your work in the name of Him who honoured our common humanity by respecting it.'[27]

Catherine Impey also relied upon friends and contacts throughout the Empire to supply her with information. She was particularly concerned about the situation in India – both the exploitation of workers on tea plantations and of the state of the nationalist movement. In one issue she wrote: 'We are sure the comfortable tea-drinking public little knows at what a cost of human lives their cheap tea is procured.'[28] She went on to describe the conditions under which the coolies of the Assam tea gardens were forced to work, comparing the abuse of the system to slavery in America and the West Indies. Quoting an article in the *Indian Messenger* which claimed that many of the British did not regard Indians 'as in any way superior to lower animals', Catherine agreed: 'This is strongly put, but it is undoubtedly the feeling of many of our Indian fellow-subjects. And what wonder! when race prejudice is manifested towards their converts even by the men to whom has been entrusted the solemn responsibility of introducing the Christian religion in the East.' She then cited a new book that exposed the corrupt behaviour of missionaries in India, given to her by a 'Christian working man'. His own verdict of the book had been that 'if this is the state of affairs . . . I feel I should be doing God's service more by circulating this work, than by contributing to the Missionary Society.'[29]

Reports from Australia, the Caribbean, South America, Africa, China – wherever the British or white Americans were responsible for injustices – appeared regularly, although Catherine Impey was careful to keep her journal short 'so that it may be read even by busy people'. She was also quick to condemn racism in England itself, most notably when Lord Salisbury, the prime minister, referred to Indians as 'black men'. Although his remarks were given wide publicity in the press, and he was forced to apologize by Queen Victoria, Salisbury had evidently felt he was expressing a view held privately by many others. Catherine pointed out that it was this underlying racism which was as much a problem as its open manifestation: 'On the whole we feel somewhat glad that the dark spirit of Caste, which so often lurks hidden behind the scenes – the prompter of so many a cowardly and bloody act on the part of our rulers – for once allowed his face to be openly seen.' This was followed by a long extract from another paper, the *Pall Mall Gazette*, which attributed Salisbury's use of the phrase to a 'certain mental defect . . . which is probably the direct result of his aristocratic training'. His sneer at darker-skinned people would not have been felt as much if whites had not dominated them: 'The white man is the aristocrat of the world, and he sums up his superiority in his own estimation when he sneers at the blackamoor, and the taunt goes all the more surely home because the darker-skinned man is more or less in subjection.'[30]

Apart from providing her readers with information, Catherine Impey was also adamant that *Anti-Caste* should be a space for black writers to 'present their case'.[31] She advertised and often supplied pamphlets written by black men and women, and reprinted extracts from black newspapers or even letters sent to her personally. Educational achievements were of particular interest and when visitors like Hallie Quinn Brown came to Britain to raise funds for schools and universities for black children in America, she gave them her full support.

From reading *Anti-Caste* over the eight years it was published, it is clear that Catherine Impey's own political vision was continually developing, particularly as a result of her contact with black activists such as Ida B. Wells and Frederick Douglass. This is illustrated most forcefully by the alterations she made to the subtitle of her paper. *Anti-Caste* began life as a journal 'devoted to the interests of coloured races'. Some eighteen months later this masthead was amended to: 'Advocates the brotherhood of mankind irrespective of colour or descent'. The editorial explained the reasons for the change:

> True, it has been, as it said from the first: 'devoted to the interests of coloured races' but that declaration of its object imperfectly indicated the standpoint from which those interests were treated. Among the aristocracy of Europe, thousands are 'devoted to the interests of' the working classes. Alas! few are there who 'advocate the *brotherhood*' of rich and poor as the basis of their 'devotion'. 'Anti-Caste' advocates the brotherhood of Mankind irrespective of colour or descent. Its purpose, however feebly fulfilled, is to awaken in the breasts of others some of that aching

sense of wounded love that should stir a brother's or sister's heart, in view of the shameless cruelty under which the most defenseless of God's family on earth are being helplessly crushed. Our money they do not need, though they are poor; nor our patronage, nor cheap condescension . . .[32]

Six years later, in the final year of its publication, the subtitle changed again. As a result of a personal rift between Isabella Mayo and herself, Catherine Impey may have felt obliged to clarify her aims still further. She wrote that *Anti-Caste* now 'Assumes the brotherhood of the entire human family, and claims for the dark races of Mankind their equal right to protection, personal liberty, equality of opportunity and human fellowship'.[33]

Shortly after this the journal ceased publication altogether, and we can only speculate on the reasons for this. One, almost certainly, was that Hannah Impey, Catherine's mother, became ill in 1895 and died within a few months. She had always been supportive of her daughter's activities and it is likely that Catherine would have missed her intensely, especially because her sister Nellie suffered from ill-health as well. But there was another reason for *Anti-Caste's* demise – one which accounted also for a gap in publication the previous year. Catherine's passionate belief in the equality of black and white led to a situation that jeopardized the whole anti-lynching campaign in Britain, and exposed a range of different attitudes towards questions of race, gender and sexuality.

FEMININITY AND THE 'FEMALE ACCUSATION'

Scarcely one month after she had arrived in Britain, Ida B. Wells witnessed what she later described as one of the most painful scenes of her life.[34] During the two weeks which she had spent in Aberdeen with Isabella Mayo and Catherine Impey preparing for the campaign, she wrote that she had very much enjoyed the 'atmosphere of equality, culture, refinement, and devotion to the cause of the oppressed darker races'. The three women were helped by Isabella's lodgers, one of whom was George Ferdinands, a dental student from Ceylon, as it was known then, who had trained and qualified while in Aberdeen under his host's patronage. The tour began when Ida accompanied Isabella Mayo on a visit of Scottish towns and cities while Catherine went ahead to prepare the way in northern England. Soon after she had left Scotland, Catherine wrote to George Ferdinands proposing marriage, and he professed to be so shocked by her letter that he forwarded it immediately to his benefactor. Ida was shown the letter by a scandalized Isabella Mayo, who more or less ordered her to denounce Catherine at once. Catherine was summoned and asked to explain herself.

In the offending letter, Catherine had declared that she 'returned the affection' that she was sure Ferdinands felt for her and that she was taking the initiative because she knew he hesitated to do so, being 'of a darker race'. She had already written to her family announcing her intention of marrying him and saying that she 'rejoiced to give this proof to the world of the theories she had approved – the equality of the brotherhood of man'. Catherine was at this time forty-five years old, an age at which hopes of marriage for a single Victorian woman would have receded. According to a cousin she was once engaged to a member of the Clark family in her home town, but the marriage was called off, possibly for financial reasons.[35] However, there is no evidence that she ever expressed regret at not having a husband and, as we have seen, was positive about the independent life she felt she had chosen. George Ferdinands, about whom we know next to nothing, apparently 'revered' Catherine for her work on India, but never dreamed of her in any romantic connection. It is hard to believe that Catherine would have made the proposal without any encouragement, and the whole episode remains a mystery. However, what is very clear is that for Isabella Mayo, her colleague's behaviour was completely unacceptable. She insisted that Catherine was a disgrace to the movement and that she was 'the type of maiden lady who used such work as an opportunity to meet and make advances to men'. Ida recalled that Mayo even called Catherine a nymphomaniac, and demanded the destruction of the edition of *Anti-Caste* which had their name as joint editors. Catherine, who was devastated, was evidently no match for the older woman's 'scorn and withering sarcasm'.

Having been forced by Isabella to choose between them, Ida spent a sleepless night 'praying for guidance'. Although she felt that Catherine had been mistaken in acting so impulsively, she had not committed any crime by falling in love and was certainly not likely to do it again. Moreover, she had already proved by her work that she was genuinely concerned about equality and justice for black people and Ida was not prepared to desert her just to appease Isabella Mayo. She also knew it would be impossible to explain to people at home, who had immense respect for Catherine Impey and her work, why she had abandoned her. She begged Mayo to change her mind, but, 'stern upright Calvinistic Scotchwoman that she was', she cast the two women 'into outer darkness' and Ida never saw her again.

In spite of being humiliated by Isabella Mayo, Catherine refused to withdraw from the work. She accompanied Ida on a tour of Newcastle, Birmingham and Manchester, arranging interviews with newspapers to obtain maximum publicity. They then returned to Street to plan the next stage of the itinerary. Isabella Mayo, who had tried to prevent Ida from continuing with her engagements, insisted that if she went to London she must at least be escorted by a more 'suitable' companion. The alternative was presumably that Mayo would publish scurrilous reports of Catherine's behaviour which would cast a bad light on Ida. Mayo had already sent details to her friends in America, criticizing Ida's behaviour and denouncing Catherine. Ida attended a few meetings in London in May of that year and then returned home, leaving her friend full of bitterness and self-reproach that the tour had ended without more success.

In her autobiography, Ida B. Wells explained that she had only written about the episode to remove any misunderstandings that might have arisen. She remained friends with Catherine for several years, inviting her to her wedding in 1895 and having her pamphlets distributed from Catherine's home address.

In subsequent meetings she often referred to Catherine's work, expressing 'the gratitude of the colored races' to her for her efforts.[36] It seems that the quarrel, which, as I shall explain shortly, continued to disrupt the unity of the campaign, also affected Ida's relationship with Frederick Douglass, to whom Mayo wrote complaining about Ida's ingratitude towards her English hosts. But however difficult it is to piece together the narrative, the subject matter of the dispute raises intriguing questions about the politics of race, gender and sexuality. What exactly was the nature of the crime that Catherine Impey had committed in Isabella Mayo's eyes? Was it that she dared to proposition a man, or that she was attracted to a black man? In other words, did she transgress the accepted bounds of her gender or was it her racial identity that she betrayed? The evidence suggests that it was probably both. And what was the significance of Ida, a black woman, supporting Catherine, and what does this imply about her sexual politics? Possible answers to these questions emerged more clearly as the anti-lynching campaign gathered pace.

Shortly after Ida B. Wells returned to America, the anti-lynching campaign was relaunched, a feat which Mayo credited to her own efforts. She enlisted the help of a Caribbean writer and editor called Celestine Edwards who agreed to take over the leadership of the newly formed Society for the Recognition of the Universal Brotherhood of Man. In July 1893, Edwards launched a new paper called *Fraternity*, which was to be its mouthpiece. The aim of the society, which Edwards explained in his first editorial, was 'to direct its attention to the work of removing inequality and wrongs from races, whom we feel sure will, with greater opportunity and freedom, do as much credit to themselves as any nation in Europe'. *Fraternity*'s format was very similar to that of *Anti-Caste*, with editorials, letters, information about events in India, Africa or America, prayers, poems – anything thought to be relevant to the cause of abolishing racism.

If Mayo hoped that Catherine would be snubbed by the revitalized society, she was mistaken, for Edwards had clearly been an admirer of *Anti-Caste* for some time and knew its editor personally. His attitude towards Catherine Impey bears out her reputation in Britain and America as a serious political crusader. The first sentence of his new paper read:

> For years one has been longing for the opportunity to plead the cause of the oppressed and helpless, and when we first came into contact with *Anti-Caste* years ago, we thought that there was at least a prospect of helping those who were actually doing a work which our own experience (in all the countries in which the work of this Society will extend) convinced us was very much indeed. For more than six years *Anti-Caste* has been doing a quiet work in England, slowly but surely permeating society, and winning the hearts of good men and true women to the cause of the struggling helpless races in America, India, Africa, and Australia, and wherever tribes, races, and nations have been oppressed by the accursed enemy of mankind – Caste.[37]

Edwards was born in Dominica, the youngest of nine children, but had settled in England in the 1870s when he was in his late teens. By that time he had become a convinced Christian and a champion of the temperance movement. He quickly made a name for himself, campaigning first in Scotland and then all over England. He was a popular speaker, and used to draw crowds of over a thousand at his public meetings. At the time when he was approached by Mayo to front the SRUBM he was editing another magazine, *Lux*, which was a 'weekly Christian Evidence Newspaper' that frequently expressed the same anti-imperialist views as *Fraternity*. In one editorial Edwards wrote that 'the British Empire will come to grief unless it changes its methods of dealing with the aboriginal races'. He went on to warn that 'the day is coming when Africans will speak for themselves. . . . The day is breaking and . . . the despised African, whose only crime is his colour, will yet give an account of himself'.[38]

Whether or not Edwards knew what had caused the rift between Catherine Impey and Isabella Mayo, we shall never know, but he obviously attempted to steer a middle course between them. He relied heavily on Catherine's help with contributions for *Fraternity*; for a few months both editors continued to publish their own journals, until *Anti-Caste* temporarily suspended publication in 1894 and Catherine donated all her material to Edwards. Another example of Catherine's continuing involvement, and of her undamaged reputation, was given during the weeks that followed Ida B. Wells's visit. The second edition of *Fraternity*, published in August 1893, carried a report of a meeting in Newcastle where 'thousands' gathered to hear Edwards lecture on 'Black and White in America'. The chairman, who had been a missionary in Jamaica, opened the proceedings by giving a 'high testimony to the earnest zeal of Miss C. Impey . . . the originator of the society, who, almost unaided, has carried on the work up to the present time'.

Isabella Mayo was continually frustrated in her attempts to dissociate the campaign from Catherine Impey. When Edwards died of illness and exhaustion in 1894, she took the opportunity in writing his obituary of giving a revised version of his leadership. She explained how he had been

> hampered by a small clique, who had gained some footing in the society, even in the brief interval which necessarily elapsed between the first startling appearance of difficulty and Mr Celestine Edwards' obtaining power to grapple with it. The object of this clique has been to force upon the society's councils a person of admitted mental instability – the victim of 'hallucination' – one, too, who on being expostulated with on the matter, had given promises of absolute withdrawal from active and official relations with the society, which promises were immediately afterwards broken.[39]

This 'clique' to which Mayo referred consisted of Catherine and her friends and supporters who had apparently taken control of the society by unconstitutional means soon after Edwards left the country in a desperate attempt to recover his health. They had been helped by the fact that Edwards had not managed to find time to record the preliminary sessions, according to Mayo, who resolved to keep control of the journal until the society was again in the hands of a properly elected council.

Edwards's greatest achievement as leader of the SRUBM was to organize a second tour for Ida B. Wells, who returned in March 1894 and stayed for several months. Mayo still refused to have anything to do with her, so it is quite likely that Catherine Impey instigated the tour, even if she was to keep a lower profile this time. During Ida's visit, which was followed closely in the pages of *Fraternity*, Mayo took the opportunity to publish her most damning indictment of Catherine's behaviour in order to humiliate her into silence. It was deliberately published next to Ida's final report, shortly after Edwards had been forced to give up work as editor. Headed 'The Female Accusation', it is worth quoting at length, partly because it reveals more about its writer than its intended victim, but mainly because it throws more light on the nature of the quarrel between the two women:

> Seeing the frequency of 'female accusation' in the case of the lynched negroes, too little attention seems to have been given to certain morbid peculiarities well known to medical men and matrons of experience. There are women who will 'fancy' anything which will give them a sensation and a little passing notoriety. In wild countries, where terrible crimes will occasionally occur, such diseased imaginations will fasten upon these, and imagine a criminal and an attempted crime in any innocent stranger. Under happier social circumstances the morbid egotists may only imagine that 'men fall in love with them'. Be it remembered that even this 'imagination', if indulged in by a 'white woman', regarding a 'nigger' in some of the States, would mean *the death of the man*, perhaps the more ignominious death, if he ventured to say in self-defence that the 'imagination' was wholly baseless, or must have been derived from some of the natural and proper civilities paid by youth and strength to age and manifest infirmity. For it must be noted that female sufferers from this diseased egotism are not necessarily young and flighty. They are often elderly, dowdy, and disappointed. Nor are they invariably recognised by their nearest connections as fit objects for pity and care. Their friends often leave them to wander among unsuspecting strangers, heedless of the annoyance and hindrance they give. Such kinsfolk are ready enough to crave for mercy and to plead hereditary mental affliction and general weakness, and instability, if even from this unfortunate woman's own statements they think she is likely to get *herself* into serious trouble; but they are prepared to recall all their words *when only the interests of others, or even of great public causes, are concerned*!
>
> We have just risen from perusal of the documents in a strikingly typical case of this kind, in which all the points of diseased vanity, prurient

insinuation, and the self-contradictory selfishness of 'kinsfolk' are strongly brought out.[40]

Isabella Mayo's continued assertion that Catherine had behaved in a way that would have caused a lynching in the Southern states must have been extraordinarily wounding – it was intended to be so. After a plea to all sensible men and women to avoid 'these poor creatures', Mayo suggested that the sufferer should retire for the sake of her mental health: 'And can anything be more wholesome for this complaint (which in its earliest stages is, as the best lunacy authorities assert, simply vanity and the basest egotism), that the knowledge that the active outbreak of these symptoms will leave the sufferer to "go softly" all her days.'

Mayo's parting shot gives an interesting slant on her understanding of the lynching question:

> If the women in the South were all 'pure in heart and sound in head', we should hear of fewer lynchings; and if British philanthropy, whenever forewarned gently set aside the dubious help of these diseased imaginations . . . many good works which now flag and falter, would go on apace.

This suggests a conservative approach both to women's sexuality and to the question of race. Her use of the phrase 'pure in heart' implies that it was not acceptable for women to take an active role in relations with men. This was a conventional attitude towards female sexuality which was shared by many women – feminists and non-feminists alike. The idea that madness contributed to white women's attraction to black men is harder to interpret. Possibly Mayo meant that in a climate hostile to interracial relationships a woman would have to be 'unsound in head' to risk the consequences both to herself and to her lover. I find it strange that her argument is at odds with Ida B. Wells's analysis of the situation in the South, and this suggests to me that her motives for backing the anti-lynching campaign had been different from Catherine's from the start.[41]

Isabella Mayo wrote as though it was the immoral and irresponsible behaviour of white women which contributed to the increase of lynching, taking a moralistic view of the activities of actual women. It was true, as Ida frequently pointed out, that friendships between black men and white women were often initiated by the woman, and that it was invariably the man who was punished as a result. Instead of blaming white women for immorality, her demand was that such voluntary relationships should be allowed to exist in the open, just as they were between white men and white women, and that if there was any element of coercion, the guilty party should be brought to trial according to the law of the land. In other words, Ida B. Wells was not interested in criticizing the behaviour of the white women who were implicated in lynchings; her argument was based on a perception of white womanhood as an ideological component of American racism. The 'sacred convention that white women can never feel passion of any sort, high or low, for a black man' was, in her eyes, incompatible with the evidence she had collected during her research. This conviction helps to explain her decision to support Catherine who, she thought, had made a mistake but not committed a crime. The ultimate significance of this episode is that it dramatized important aspects of Ida B.Wells's analysis of lynching. By exposing Isabella Mayo's conservative views on female sexuality which were expressed in response to Catherine Impey's unorthodox feminine behaviour, it forced a division between the two women who had made the campaign possible in the first place.

THE SIGNIFICANCE OF ANTI-LYNCHING POLITICS FOR WHITE WOMEN'S FEMINISM

[Ida Wells and Frances Willard, an American women's rights campaigner, had engaged in a bitter dispute during Wells's second visit to Britain in 1894.] The detail of this controversy is important, I think because it illustrates the range of positions that different women took in their attempts to formulate a political outlook that acknowledged both gender and race. It is also significant that the public quarrel between Frances Willard and Ida B. Wells first surfaced in England and was carried back to the United States where it had originated. This was partly due to circumstance, in that Frances Willard happened to be in Britain when the Society for the Recognition of the Universal Brotherhood of Man was being set up. But as a young, unknown black woman in her own country, Ida B. Wells would never have been able to attract public support for her criticism of a figure of Frances Willard's calibre. Yet in London her relative obscurity seemed to add weight to her argument; she believed that the British public felt more sympathy for her after the two temperance leaders threatened to use their influence to silence her. It would be wrong, however, to attribute Ida's moral victory solely to what she perceived as the British sense of fair play. The support that she was shown indicates that there was a substantial current of anti-imperialist thought in Britain at that time, which was able to make sense of and accept her political analysis of racial terror in America with all its implications for the social and political relations of race and gender elsewhere. But this makes me wonder whether this analysis was acceptable because it was made in an American context, or whether it was also seen to hold good in British colonial societies, where segregation and racial subordination were also part of everyday life. Why did Ida B. Wells not face more opposition in Britain than she did, since her description of social relations in the South were often uncomfortably close to those in parts of the Empire? As she herself frequently pointed out, the hardest part of her work in Britain was to convince people that black men were not 'wild beasts after white women'.[42] When *The Times* drew the attention of Florence Balgarnie and 'the numerous ladies upon the Anti-Lynching Committee' to the 'frequency and atrocity of his outrages on white women', it was not just referring to the black man in America, but to everywhere where a man with a darker skin could come into contact with whites.

This belief, which lurked in the recesses of the imperial imagination, had been more widely expressed, not in the context of the British experience of slavery and abolition, but in reaction to uprisings of black colonial subjects in India and the Caribbean – in particular the Indian 'Mutiny' of 1857 and the Morant Bay uprising of 1865, both discussed in Part I.[43] Although responses to the uprisings were part of a much more complex debate about the nature of democracy at home and the legitimation of imperial rule abroad, these rebellions and the manner in which they were suppressed occupied an indelible place in the memory of racial dominance. Yet it does not appear that the British anti-lynching campaigners saw useful analogies between the situation in the Empire and conditions in the Southern states of America. Their opponents in the South, however, were quick to cite the cruel suppression of the Sepoy rebellion as an example of barbarity committed by the hypocritical British. While the 'ladies' involved in the Anti-Lynching Committee would have been too young to remember the actual events surrounding the insurrections, they would have been familiar with the mythologies that developed as a result. Not being American, they might have been less sensitive to the outrage caused by Ida B. Wells's remarks about Southern white women enjoying intimate friendships with former slaves, but they would certainly have been aware of the impact of such arguments had they been made in the context of British colonial society. The way that Isabella Mayo reacted to Catherine Impey's proposal to her lodger was evidence that even when friendship between black men and white women was possible, marriage was an entirely different matter.

I shall now consider what motivated the women who rallied behind Frances Willard and Lady Henry Somerset to defend the name of white women in America. The details of the controversy belie the simple conclusion that it was a conflict between middle-class white women who saw themselves as representing what they understood to be women's interests and middle-class white women who were more concerned with the idea of helping oppressed people than fighting for their own rights as women. By focusing on the writings of Frances Willard, Catherine Impey and Florence Balgarnie, it is possible to explore the political beliefs that these white women shared as well as where they disagreed with each other.

Frances Willard belonged to a body of women who believed that society needed moral reform and that woman's equality was justified by her ability to provide moral and spiritual guidance rather than as an end in itself. Ultimately, the Women's Christian Temperance Union (WCTU) was a conservative organization, although many of its actual policies suggested some degree of radicalism, intersecting with both socialism and feminism. There was a constant tension within the network around its identification with feminist aims – the demand for 'rights for women' was considered 'too strident', for example.[44] However, by the beginning of the twentieth century, the movement for social purity was in decline, as Victorian ideas on morality became outdated. Frances Willard died in 1896, and her life and her philosophy – summed up by the call for 'a white life' – were very soon identified with an era that had passed.

It is no coincidence that Willard's views on race were also more appropriate to an earlier historical period. She was, as she claimed so proudly on many occasions, a child of the abolitionist movement, and it is significant that in the 1890s she still felt this was sufficient proof of her freedom from racial prejudice. 'I was born an abolitionist, taught to read out of the "Slave's Friend",' she announced at the beginning of her interview in the New York *Voice*. The propaganda of abolitionism was often directed at women in their capacity as guardians of a superior morality, and it appealed to many because of its support for basic domestic values, the most important one being the defence of the family. For thousands of women, campaigning against slavery was entirely compatible with demanding equal rights for women outside the home, as long as they still accepted that women were basically responsible for the moral and spiritual welfare of the family. As we have already seen, Willard's views on the liberation of black people *beyond* emancipation appear to have been confined to a general sympathy for educated blacks and support for the policy of repatriation.

Catherine Impey, whose views on racism were expressed through her columns in *Anti-Caste*, was also born into an anti-slavery tradition. However, the changes she made to the masthead of *Anti-Caste* from 1888 to 1895 revealed that she was more in touch with the aspirations and achievements of black people than Frances Willard was. As we have already seen, the aim of her journal moved from being 'devoted to the interests of coloured races' to claiming black peoples' equal right 'to protection, personal liberty, equality of opportunity and human fellowship'. This change reflected a shift from a conventional philanthropic stance, in keeping with her Quaker background, to a more active recognition of the autonomy of black struggles for racial justice.

Like Frances Willard, Catherine Impey, who lived in a household of women, was in no way dependent on a man for her upkeep. Although this does not necessarily mean that she believed women should be active in a wider sphere, her writings and involvement in the anti-imperialist network all take for granted an assumption that women should be as free as men in expressing their political opinions. She recognized that women had a particular role to play in the anti-lynching campaign, though whether this was due to a sense of women's philanthropic mission is not clear. Her first issue of *Anti-Caste* stated her belief that purely physical differences between people, such as those arising from 'sex, race, complexion, nationality', were arbitrary. However, as far as we know she did not campaign specifically for women's rights, nor was she a member of any campaign for women's suffrage during this period. Superficially – and there is so little evidence to take it further – her views on suffrage and women's role in the public sphere were entirely compatible with Willard's.

In the only surviving writing by Catherine on this subject – an article written for the Street 'Village Album' – she tried to address the arguments that were frequently raised against women's demand for the vote.[45] Her reasoning was not without its own contradictions. She first pointed out the dangers of women achieving political power at the expense of losing their influence at home. This was not the conventional line that it was women's job to raise the children while the men took care of life outside, but an attempt to understand the basic objection to women's suffrage expressed by its opponents – that it was 'unnatural'. Her theory was that 'very few political or social arrangements of permanence have originated solely in evil' and therefore it was vital to the success of the reform movement to understand why those arrangements evolved. People, she suggested, were generally very slow to realize that as society changed so these old systems became inappropriate and 'obnoxious'. But it was a mistake to think that everything about the outdated system was automatically wrong and override it by 'the iron wheels of modern theory-in-action'.

Catherine's argument was that the time was right for women to vote and take part in political life because the family – 'historically the unit of all our political systems' – had changed radically. She explained how the 'Division of Labour principle' accounted for the greater involvement of men in certain activities, but this was for immutable physical reasons rather than ideological ones. It is significant that she turned to examples of 'primitive "village communities" in parts of the East' to demonstrate the influence that women had in the absence of their men. It was more often the case that proponents of women's rights throughout the nineteenth century tried to distance themselves from 'primitive' society by arguing that women's subordination was an index of lack of civilization.

Apart from the fact that the family unit had changed so that women were now often heads of households just as men were, the importance of that 'external life', which men traditionally saw as their domain, had altered as well. She wrote: 'We must realise a state of things where national life and organisation (in which men ruled) was, compared with today, feeble and of small account and where local, even family life and organisation, where women ruled, was full of life, importance and variety.' The loss, in modern 'artificial' society, was that women's influence and responsibility were diminished at the expense of society as a whole. Now that the public political sphere was so much more pervasive and accessible to both men and women, it made sense for women to be equally involved. At the same time Catherine made it clear that she still believed that it was women who were primarily responsible for maintaining family life. It was wrong to place too much hope on endowing women with political power:

> Even at present there are too many instances that women when suffered to enter the professions, the political positions which have been formerly men's alone, have adopted some of the very modes of thought and feeling which it was hoped women's influence in these spheres would correct. Especially we have to guard in the present days of this movement against anything that tends to the undervaluing of family life which is the basis, humanly speaking, of the religion and true civilisation of the world.

Clearly there are important overlaps between the politics of Frances Willard and Catherine Impey, illustrated by this last sentence. Catherine was also an active member of her local temperance organization and was very likely to have been an admirer of the WCTU leader before the campaign against lynching began.

By the time that Catherine Impey wrote her article, the suffrage issue was just beginning to attract greater popular support from women in Britain. The trade union movement was rapidly expanding, and many middle-class women involved themselves in employment issues with or on behalf of working-class women. In 1885, Florence Balgarnie was appointed secretary of the Central Committee of the National Society for Women's Suffrage. She had already made a name for herself by her skills in both organizing and public speaking, and she was widely respected for her commitment to women's rights. In 1889 she was one of a group of women who founded the Women's Trade Union Association, and she was also, through her work as a journalist, closely involved in the British Women's Temperance Association. An interview with Balgarnie in the *Women's Penny Paper* revealed that she felt most at home when addressing meetings of working people, particularly men.[46] Born and brought up in Scarborough, Yorkshire, daughter of a Scottish Congregational Minister, her favourite book as a child had been *Uncle Tom's Cabin*. Education was another cause that interested her and she helped set up the Scarborough branch of the University Extension Scheme; for two years she sat on the school board there, having been elected alongside men. In the same interview she named Ruskin, John Stuart Mill and Mazzini as writers who had influenced her greatly, although she also lectured on the life and works of her other favourite author, Charlotte Brontë.

Florence Balgarnie was, like Catherine Impey, an independent woman engaged in reform work. More of a 'conventional' feminist by virtue of the fact that she belonged to suffrage and women's rights organizations, she encountered the anti-lynching campaign through her work as a journalist and was not able to pass it by without becoming deeply involved. After being elected secretary of the Anti-Lynching Committee in 1894, she wrote an article about Ida B. Wells in a popular magazine called *Great Thoughts*. It began:

> The age of chivalry is not dead nor dying. It is gloriously real and present with us. This so-called prosaic nineteenth century thrills with romance, the very air palpitates with deeds of daring and heroism. We have brave knight-errants in many a field, and, better still, women, the Jeanne d'Arcs of today, are not wanting.[47]

Despite the purple prose, Florence Balgarnie's account of her young life and her analysis of lynching accords completely with Ida's own version. For instance, she contrasted the treatment of white women by black men with that of black women by white men, and drew attention, using Ida's own words, to the fact that black men were being lynched for rape when the relationship between the victim lynched and the alleged victim of the assault was 'voluntary, clandestine, and illicit'. The article went on to describe Ida's success in Britain and its effect on her work back in America, where at last an anti-lynching campaign seemed to be gathering momentum. Balgarnie was aware that Great Britain 'should be the last to condemn another nation' when it came to race prejudice, but that it was in the spirit of '*goodwill, brotherly kindness, and large human affection*' that they were pressing for equality between black and white in America.

The key to the connection between Florence Balgarnie and Catherine Impey can be found in their use of language. It was this concept of 'human brotherhood' that inspired many of those who actively supported anti-racist causes. Throughout the nineteenth century the word 'brotherhood' had been an ideal most often expressed in religious language, but as the socialist movement gathered pace, it acquired more secular and literal connotations. The development of *Fraternity* into an overtly socialist publication illustrates this process perfectly. In 1895 the SRUBM became the International Society for the Recognition of the Brotherhood of Man (ISRBM), and the motto 'Fellow-Workers' was adopted. A statement in the magazine declared: 'We are endeavouring to widen the scope of our work in order the better to serve the interests of the weak and oppressed in all lands'. The revised aims of the new society were:

> To declare the Unity of the Human Race and to further the Brotherhood of Mankind.
>
> To influence public opinion in the promotion of Justice and Sympathy between all Races, Classes, Creeds, and Communities.
>
> To discourage and denounce Race Separation, Race Animosity, and Race Arrogance wheresoever displayed.
>
> To assert the Inter-dependence of Nations and the Responsibilities and Reciprocities, and especially to insist upon the duty of the strong (Nation) to protect the weak (Nation).[48]

These aims have a significantly different tone to the opening editorial in *Anti-Caste*, which had renounced all forms of inequality, including those between men and women. Women continued to be involved in *Fraternity*, however. Isabella Mayo claimed to be the founder of the new society, and her own politics were radically influenced by the new socialist spirit. Introducing Caroline Martin as the new editor, she wrote that 'brighter days are now dawning for our work! For we have at last gained a firm standpoint in that very section of society which we dared to enlist with us, *the workers of the world*, all of whom we long to see banded together as *fellow-workers*, since only they can stand against the world's forces of wrong and robbery.'[49] Caroline Martin, who died only weeks after taking up her post, was about to become trade union organizer for the north of Scotland, having written and lectured extensively on 'Labour matters'. She too was a Christian, as Mayo was at pains to point out, and 'was led on to her most advanced standpoints, not by "revolutionary" pamphlets, nor even by "economic" considerations . . . but by the earnest study of the New Testament itself'.[50]

Fraternity was evolving during a period of popular imperialism, which demanded new arguments and new tactics. In the 1896 annual meeting of the ISRBM, a resolution was put forward which lamented 'the present outbreak of "Jingoism"' and condemned the policy which had led to attempts by different European countries to divide up Africa. The man who proposed the motion argued that the society should try to educate the working man in the true principles of fraternity and persuade him that the notion that trade follows the flag was all 'nonsense'.[51] This emphasis on the working man dominated the magazine in the last few months of its life under the editorship of Frank Smith, who succeeded Caroline Martin in 1896. In one of its last editions he published an article in favour of women's suffrage in an attempt to redress the imbalance of language. The writer began by saying that he – or she – had never considered the fact that 'fraternity' was a masculine word until asked to write for the paper. The argument was the familiar one that 'the world wants mothering, and it can't get it until women are free and have their full share in the management of it'.[52] Readers were exhorted to think of the 'national home, of the great human home of the race, denied even the participation of women in the management of its affairs, and say if you can wonder that it falls so far short of being ideal'.

The changing language of *Fraternity* expressed perfectly the transition of the anti-lynching campaign from a generally middle-class philanthropic concern to a more concerted attempt to involve the working class in a protest against imperialism in general. As the movement became more infused with socialist ideas and dedicated to the task of converting workers to its cause, so the concept of 'fraternity' became more literal. Despite the attempts of women workers to form and join trade unions, the ethic of labour politics was predominantly masculine and the word 'fraternity' inevitably came to be associated with men, losing its previous humanitarian meaning. The vision of 'human brotherhood' shared by Catherine Impey and Florence Balgarnie had included justice and equality for all, regardless of sex, race, nationality or class. At that time there was no language to express the particular connections between women and black people, beyond the vocabulary of slavery and emancipation, yet it was through the anti-lynching campaign that those connections were made explicit.

This was ultimately the significance of the short-lived movement. It showed the possibility of an alliance between black and white women in which white women went beyond sisterly support for black women; by confronting the racist ideology that justified lynching, these white women also began to develop a radical analysis of gender relations that intersected with class and race. Whether or not they were 'feminist' can be judged perhaps by the way they lived their lives and identified themselves with social and political issues – the implications of their own independence were that they believed women should be free to choose how and with whom they lived or associated themselves. By refusing to accept the portrait of innocent and vulnerable white women painted by those who supported or ignored lynchings in the United States, they were not only defending the rights of the black population but also claiming a different and more active version of femininity. As a result, they threw into relief a range of conservative beliefs about both women and black people, not just those held by their opponents but also the beliefs of those who considered themselves progressive.

There was not a clear cut division between the politics of the women who supported Ida B. Wells and those who tried to silence her, but there were two main differences. Where Frances Willard and others in the temperance movement saw themselves as largely representing women's interests, both Catherine Impey and Florence Balgarnie declared themselves to be advocates of human brotherhood, which expressed, as we have just seen, a desire for universal equality across race, class and gender. The second difference was that those who were offended by Ida B. Wells failed to see the centrality of racism which worked both to oppress black people and, in the case of lynching, to undermine more radical ideas about women as well.

NOTES

1. Interview with Ida B. Wells in the *Westminster Gazette*, 10 May 1894; also quoted in David M. Tucker, 'A Memphis Lynching', *Phylon: Atlanta University Review of Race and Culture*, vol. XXXII, no 2, Summer 1971, p. 120.
2. Olive Banks, *Faces of Feminism: A Study of Feminism as a Social Movement*, Martin Robertson, Oxford, 1981, p. 102.
3. Manning Marable, *How Capitalism Underdeveloped Black America: Problems in Race Political Economy and Society*, South End Press, Boston, 1983, p. 15.
4. Jacqueline Dowd Hall, *Revolt Against Chivalry: Jesse Daniel Ames and the Women's Campaign Against Lynching*, Columbia University Press, New York, 1979, pp. 134–5.
5. R. M. Brown, *Strain of Violence: Historical Studies of American Violence and Vigilantism*, Oxford University Press, New York, 1975; H. A. Bulhan, *Frantz Fanon and the Psychology of Oppression*, Plenum Press, New York, 1985, ch. 8.
6. See, for example, Ralph Ginzburg, *100 Years of Lynchings*, Black Classic Press, Baltimore, 1962/1988, a book compiled entirely from press reports during the period 1880–1961.
7. Bulhan, *Franz Fanon and the Psychology of Oppression*, p. 157.
8. The source of information for much of this part of the book is Alfreda M. Duster ed., *Crusade for Justice: The Autobiography of Ida B. Wells*, University of Chicago Press, Chicago, 1970. For further reading about the life and political influence of Ida B. Wells, who is now being acknowledged as one of the most important black figures of her generation, see Joanne M. Braxton, *Black Women Writing Autobiography: A Tradition Within a Tradition*, Temple University Press, Philadelphia, 1989, pp. 102–38; Hazel V. Carby, *Reconstructing Womanhood: The Emergence of the Afro-American Woman Novelist*, Oxford University Press, New York/Oxford, 1987, pp. 108–16; Angela Y. Davis, *Women, Race, and Class*, Random House, New York, 1981; Paula Giddings, *When and Where I Enter: The Impact of Black Women on Race and Sex in America*, William Morrow, New York, 1984; Dorothy Sterling, *Black Foremothers*, The Feminist Press, New York, 1988, pp. 61–118.
9. *The Times*, 1 August 1894.
10. Douglass made the trip to Europe with his second wife; he also achieved a long-held ambition to visit Egypt before he grew too old.
11. *Anti-Caste*, vol. VII, April 1895.
12. Ibid.

13. *Anti-Caste*, vol. VI, January 1893.
14. Isabella Mayo was also a novelist who wrote under the pseudonym of Edward Garrett. She later wrote an autobiography called *Recollections of What I Saw, What I Lived Through and What I Learned during More than Fifty Years of Social and Literary Experience* (John Murray, London, 1910) which unfortunately contains almost no reference to her political activities.
15. *The Sun*, 26 August 1894.
16. Duster, *Crusade for Justice*, p. 214.
17. *Anti-Caste*, vol. VII, January 1889. For more information on racism in Britain at this time see Douglas A. Lorimer, *Colour, Class and the Victorian: English Attitudes to the Negro in the Mid-Nineteenth Century*, Leicester University Press, 1978; James Walvin, *Black and White: The Negro and English Society*, 1855–1945, Allen Lane, London, 1973; Peter Fryer, *Staying Power: The History of Black People in Britain*, Pluto, London, 1984.
18. Duster, *Crusade for Justice*, p. 20.
19. Duster, *Crusade for Justice*, p. xvii.
20. Duster, *Crusade for Justice*, p. 64. See chapters 6 to 8 for Ida B. Wells's own account of her realization that lynching was a form of political and economic terror.
21. Duster, *Crusade for Justice*, p. 65.
22. *The Times*, 6 November 1894.
23. Letter to Frederick Chesson, 1886, Rhodes House Library, Oxford (Ref: C138/163–74).
24. *Anti-Caste*, vol. IV, January 1891 (supplement).
25. *The Friend*, 4 January 1924.
26. For a discussion of this occasion see Carby, pp. 3–19.
27. *Anti-Caste*, vol. IV (supplement) January 1891.
28. *Anti-Caste*, vol. III, January 1890.
29. *Anti-Caste*, vol. III, June 1890.
30. *Anti-Caste*, vol. II, January 1889.
31. Her actual words were: 'We hope little by little to give some insight into the evils of Caste as it prevails in countries where our white race habitually ostracises those who are even partially descended from darker races; and by circulating in our pages the current writings of prominent and thoughtful persons of coloured races hope to give them fresh opportunities of presenting their case before white races.' *Anti-Caste*, vol. I, March 1888.
32. *Anti-Caste*, vol. II, August 1989.
33. *Anti-Caste*, vol. VII, March 1895.
34. For Ida B. Wells's account of this, see Duster, *Crusade for Justice*, ch. 14, 'An Indiscreet Letter'. The only account that remains of this incident is Ida B. Well's autobiography, compiled years later after Ida had lost touch with Catherine. However, assuming that she kept a diary and that her memory was good, there is no reason to suspect Ida of embroidering on the affair, especially as she was implicated in it as well.
35. I am indebted to Stephen Morland for his help and interest in remembering Catherine Impey, or Katie, as she was known, as an elderly relative – one of the pleasanter ones – who visited his family when he was young, and for suggesting further contacts.
36. *The Friend*, 1 June 1894.
37. *Fraternity*, vol. I, July 1893. See Fryer, *Staying Power* (p. 278) who puts forward the interesting theory that *Fraternity* was a large step towards the production in Britain of a politically-committed Pan-African press. In fact Edwards was editor for only a short period due to his bad health, and subsequent editors were white socialists, which affected the orientation of the journal considerably.
38. Fryer, *Staying Power*, pp. 278–9.
39. *Fraternity*, vol. II, September 1894.

40. *Fraternity*, vol. II, August 1894.
41. This suggestion is supported by Ida B. Wells's account of Catherine Impey's first conversation with Isabella Mayo about lynching: in response to Mayo's question about why 'the United States of America was burning human beings alive in the nineteenth century . . . Miss Impey's reply was evidently not satisfactory' (Duster, *Crusade for Justice*, p. 85).
42. Duster, *Crusade for Justice*, p. 220.
43. Lurid accounts of slave violence in the Caribbean dating back to the eighteenth century were also used to stoke up opposition to the abolition of slavery in America. See Forrest G. Wood, *Black Scare: The Racist Response to Emancipation and Reconstruction*, University of California Press, Berkeley, C.A, 1970, p. 28.
44. Barbara Leslie Epstein, *The Politics of Domesticity: Women, Evangelism, and Temperance in Nineteenth-Century America*, Wesleyan University Press, Middleton, CT, 1981, p. 147.
45. Catherine Impey, 'Some Thoughts on the Women's Suffrage Question', Street 'Village Album', c. 1887.
46. *Women's Penny Paper*, vol. 1, no 21, 16 March 1889.
47. *Great Thoughts*, 1894, p. 384.
48. *Fraternity*, vol. IV, January 1897.
49. *Fraternity*, vol. III, July 1896.
50. Ibid.
51. *Fraternity*, vol. III, June 1896.
52. *Fraternity*, vol. IV, January 1897.

2.2

'IROQUOIS WOMEN, EUROPEAN WOMEN'

Natalie Zemon Davis

In the opening years of the seventeenth century in the Montagnais country, Pierre Pastedechouan's grandmother loved to tell him how astonished she had been at the first sight of a French ship. With its large sails and many people gathered on the deck, she had thought the wooden boat a floating island. She and the other women in her band immediately set up cabins to welcome the guests.[1] The people on a floating island appeared also to a young Micmac woman of the Saint Lawrence Gulf in a dream which she recounted to the shaman and elders of her community and which came true a few days later when a European ship arrived.[2]

Across the Atlantic, Mother Marie Guyart de l'Incarnation also first saw the Amerindian lands in a dream-vision, a vast space of mountains, valleys and fog to which the Virgin Mary and Jesus beckoned her and which her spiritual director then identified as Canada. By the time she had boarded the boat in 1639, she hoped to 'taste the delights of Paradise in the beautiful and large crosses of New France'. Once at Québec, she and her sister Ursulines kissed the soil, Marie finding the landscape just like her dream except not so foggy. The Christianized Algonquin, Montagnais and Huron girls, 'freshly washed in the blood of the lamb, seem[ed] to carry Paradise with them'.[3]

The similarities and differences in the situation and views of these women in the sixteenth and first half of the seventeenth centuries is my subject in this essay. I want to look at the Amerindian women of the eastern woodlands in

From: Natalie Zemon Davis (1994), 'Iroquois Women, European Women', pp. 243–58, in Margo Hendricks and Patricia Parker (eds), *Women, Race, and Writing* (London: Taylor & Francis Ltd).

terms of historical change – and not just change generated by contact with Europeans, but by processes central to their own societies. I want to insist on the absolute simultaneity of the Amerindian and European worlds, rather than viewing the former as an earlier version of the latter, and make comparisons less polarized than the differences between 'simple' and 'complex' societies. I want to suggest interactions to look for in the colonial encounter other than the necessary but overpolarized twosome of 'domination' and 'resistance', and attribute the capacity for choice to Indians as to Europeans. The Amerindian case may also be a source of alternative examples and metaphors to illumine the European case. Indeed, an ideal sequel to this essay would be an inquiry about the history of European women that made use of Iroquois tropes and frames.

The term 'Iroquois women' in my title is a shorthand for both the Hurons and the Iroquois among the nations speaking the Iroquoian languages, from whom many of my examples will be drawn, and in some instances for women of the groups speaking Algonquian languages, peoples from primarily hunting, fishing and gathering communities such as the Montagnais, Algonquins, Abenakis and Micmacs. On the whole, I will stay within the region penetrated by the French, though the woodlands Indians themselves ranged well beyond its reach. My sources are the classic travel accounts and the Jesuit and other religious relations from the eastern woodlands (including the writings of Marie de l'Incarnation and the women Hospitalers of Québec); ethnographic studies, including those based on archeological research and material culture; and collections of Amerindian tales and legends and customs made over the last 150 years and more.[4]

The Hurons and Iroquois alike lived from a digging-stick agriculture gathering, fishing and hunting.[5] The men opened the fields for cultivation, but the women were the farmers, growing maize, beans, squash and, in some places, tobacco. The women also were the gatherers, picking fruits and other edible food and bringing in all the firewood. When villages changed their base, as they did every several years, it was sometimes in fear of their enemies, but ordinarily because the women declared the fields infertile and the suitable wood exhausted for miles around. The men were in charge of hunting, fishing, and intertribal trading, but the active women might well accompany their husbands or fathers on these expeditions when not held back by farming or cabin tasks. Along the way the women were expected to do much of the carrying, although, if there were male prisoners with the band, their masters would have them help the women.[6] Warfare was in the hands of the men.

Responsibility for the crafts and arts was similarly divided. Men made weapons and tools of stone, wood and sometimes bits of copper, carved the pipes, built the cabins and constructed frames for canoes and snowshoes. Women were in charge of anything that had to do with sewing, stringing and weaving, preparing thread and laces by hand-spinning and winding, stringing snowshoes and making baskets, birchbark kettles, nets, and rush mats. Once the men had made a kill at the hunt, the animal was the women's domain, from skinning and preparing the hide, softening and greasing the furs, to making garments and moccasins. The women were the potters and also made all the decorative objects of porcupine quills, shells (including wampum necklaces and belts), beads and birchbark. They painted the faces and bodies of their husbands and sons so that they would look impressive when they went visiting and decorated each other for dances and feasts. As for the meals, the women took care of them all, pounding the corn into flour and cooking much of the food in a single kettle. (Similar work patterns were found among the Algonquian-speaking peoples, where horticulture was only occasionally practiced and where the women were thus on the move much of the time with the men.)

This division of labor looked very lopsided to the French men who first reported it, presumably contrasting it with European agriculture, where men did the ploughing, where women did the weeding and gardening and where both did woodcutting and carrying, and with European crafts like leather and pottery, where men had a predominant role. 'The women work without comparison more than the men,' said Jacques Cartier of the Iroquois whom he had met along the Saint Lawrence in 1536; 'the women do all the servile tasks, work[ing] ordinarily harder than the men, though they are neither forced or constrained to do it,' said the Recollet Gabriel Sagard of the Huron women in 1623. 'Real pack-mules,' a Jesuit echoed a few years later.[7] Marie de l'Incarnation, in contrast, took the women's heavy work for granted, perhaps because she heard about it from the Huron and Algonquin women in a matter-of-fact way in the convent yard rather than seeing it, perhaps because she herself had spent her young womanhood in a wagoner's household, doing everything from grooming horses and cleaning slops to keeping the accounts.[8] In any case, Sagard noted that the Huron women still had time for gaming, dancing and feasts, and 'to chat and pass the time together'.[9]

The differences that even Marie de l'Incarnation could not fail to recognize between her life in France and that of Huron and Iroquois women concerned property, kinship structures, marriage and sexual practice. Whereas in France private or at least family property was increasingly freeing itself from the competing claims of distant kin and feudal lords, among both the Iroquois and the Hurons collective property arrangements – village, clan, band or tribal – prevailed in regard to hunting and gathering areas and to farming plots. Matrilineality and matrilocality seem to have been more consistently practiced among the Iroquois than among the Hurons,[10] but for both societies the living unit was a long-house of several related families, in which the senior women had a major say about what went on. (The Algonquian-speaking peoples counted descent patrilineally and dwelt in smaller wigwams and summer lodges.)

Parents often suggested potential marriage partners to their children (among the Iroquois, it was the mothers who took the initiative), but then the younger generation had to act. A Huron youth would ask the permission of the parents of a young woman and give her a substantial present of a wampum collar or beaver robe; if, after a sexual encounter for a few nights, she gave her consent, the wedding feast took place.[11] As there was no dowry and dower but only a bride gift, so there was no property in the way of inheritance: the deceased took some of his or her mats and furs and other goods away to the other world, while the bereaved kin were given extensive gifts 'to dry their tears' by the other members of their village and clan.[12]

Without property inheritance and without firm notions about the father's qualities being carried through sexual intercourse or the blood,[13] sexual relations between men and women were conducted without concern about 'illegitimate' offspring. There could be several trial encounters and temporary unions before a marriage was decided on, and openly acknowledged intercourse with other partners was possible for both husband and wife. When a Huron father was questioned one day by a Jesuit about how, with such practices, a man could know who his son was, the man answered, 'You French love only your own children; we love all the children of our people.' When Hurons and Algonquins first saw the Québec Hospital nuns in 1639 – three women all in their twenties – they were astonished (so one of the sisters reported) 'when they were told that we had no men at all and that we were virgins'.[14]

Clearly there was room in the Iroquoian long-house and Algonquian wigwam for many quarrels: among wives at their different long-house fires, among daughters and parents about consent to a suitor,[15] among husbands and wives about competing lovers.[16] One Jesuit even claimed in 1657 that some married women revenged themselves on their husbands for 'bad treatment' by eating a poisonous root and leaving the men with 'the reproach of their death'.[17] Much more often, an unsatisfactory marriage simply ended in divorce, with both man and woman free to remarry and the woman usually having custody of the children.[18]

In such a situation the debate about authority had a different content from that in Renaissance and early seventeenth-century Europe, where a hierarchical model of the father-dominated family was at best moderated by the image of companionate marriage or reversed by the husband-beating virago. Among the Amerindians, physical coercion was not supposed to be used against anyone within the family, and decisions about crops, food consumption and many of the crafts were rightfully the women's. If a man wanted a courteous excuse not to do something he could say without fear of embarrassment 'that his wife did not wish it'.[19]

When we leave the long-house fire and kettle for the religious feast or dance and council meeting, we have a different picture again. Religious belief among both the Algonquian- and Iroquoian-speaking peoples was diverse and wide-ranging, their high divinities, sacred manitous and omnipresent lesser spirits remembered, pondered over and argued about through decentralized storytelling. Recollets and Jesuits, hearing such accounts, would challenge the speakers: 'How can the creator Yoscaha have a grandmother Aataentsic if Yoscaha is the first god?' they would ask a Huron. 'And how could Aataentsic's daughter get pregnant with Yoscaha and his evil twin Tawiscaron if men had not yet been created?' 'Was Atahocan definitely the first creator?' they would ask a Montagnais. Huron or Montagnais would then reply that he did not know for sure: 'Perhaps it was Atahocan; one speaks of Atahocan as one speaks of a thing so far distant that nothing sure can be known about it.' Or that he had the account from someone who had visited Yoscaha and Aataentsic or had seen it in a dream. Or, politely, that the French beliefs about 'God' were fine for Europe but not for the woodlands. Or, defiantly, that he would believe in the Jesuits' God when he saw him with his own eyes.[20]

The Recollets and Jesuits reported such exchanges only with men, Father Lejeune even adding, 'there are among them mysteries so hidden that only the old men, who can speak with credit and authority about them, are believed'.[21] Marie de l'Incarnation, always attentive to women's roles and pleased that Abenaki belief included the virgin birth of the world-saver Messou, said only that traditional accounts of the 'Sauvages' were passed on 'from fathers to children, from the old to the young'.[22] Women were certainly among the listeners to Amerindian creation accounts, for the 'ancient tales' were told, for instance, at gatherings after funerals,[23] but were they among the tellers of sacred narratives? Speculation from the existing evidence suggests the following picture: during the sixteenth and early seventeenth centuries, men, especially older men, were the tellers of creation stories at male assemblies (as for the election of a chief)[24] and at mixed gatherings, but women recounted Aataentsic's doings along with many other kinds of narrative to each other and to their children.[25] If this be the case, then the situation of women in the eastern woodlands was rather like that of their Catholic contemporaries in Europe. There, for the most part, Catholic belief systems were formally taught by doctors of theology and male preachers and catechizers, and women reflected on such doctrine among themselves in convents and told Christian stories to their children.

To the all-important realm of dreams, however, Amerindian women and men had equal access. Huron and Iroquois notions of 'the soul' and 'the self' were more inflected, articulated or pluralistic than Christian notions of the living person, where a single soul animated the body and where reason, will and appetite were functions warring or collaborating within. Huron and Iroquois saw 'the soul' as 'divisible' (to use Father Brébeuf's term about the Huron), giving different names and some independence to different soul-actions: animation, reason, deliberation, and desire. The desiring soul especially spoke to one in dreams – 'this is what my heart tells me, this is what my appetite desires' (*ondayee ikaton onennoncwat*); sometimes the desiring soul was counseled by a familiar *oki* or spirit who appeared in a dream in some form and told it what it needed or wanted, its *ondinoc*, its secret desire.[26] In France, dreams and the time between sleeping and waking were the occasion for extraordinary visits from Christ, the saints, the devil, or the ghosts of one's dead kin. In the American woodlands, dreams were a visit from part of oneself and one's *oki*, and their prescriptions had wider effect, forestalling or curing illness and pre-dicting, sanctioning or warning against future events of all kinds.

Amerindian women and men thus took their dreams very seriously, describ-ing, evaluating and interpreting them to each other and then acting on them with intensity and determination. For a person of some standing, the village council might decide to mobilize every cabin to help fulfill a dream. So a woman of Angoutenc in the Huron country went outside one night with her little daughter and was greeted by the Moon deity, swooping down from the sky as a beautiful tall woman with a little daughter of her own. The Moon ordered that the woman be given many presents of garments and tobacco from sur-rounding peoples and that henceforth she dress herself in red, like the fiery moon. Back in her long-house, the woman immediately fell ill with dizziness and weak muscles and learned from her dreams that only a curing feast and certain presents would restore her. The council of her birth-village of Ossassané agreed to provide all she needed. Three days of ritual action followed, with the many prescribed gifts assembled, the woman in her red garments walking through fires that did not burn her limbs and everyone discussing their dream desires through riddles.[27] She was cured in an episode that illustrates to us how an individual woman could set in motion a whole sequence of collective relig-ious action.[28]

Women also had important roles in dances intended to placate the *oki* spirits or to drive out evil spirits from the sick. Among the Hurons, a few women who had received a dream sign might be initiated along with men into a society whose curative dance was considered 'very powerful against the demons'; among the Iroquois, women were received in several healing and propitiary societies.[29] To be sure, women were accused of witchcraft – that is, of causing someone's death by poisoning or charms – but no more than Huron and Iroquois men, and *okis* or *manitous* in mischievous action were not gendered female more than male.[30]

The major asymmetry in religious life in the sixteenth and seventeenth cen-turies concerned the shamans. The Arendiwane, as the Hurons called them ('sorcerers' or 'jugglers' in the language of the Jesuits), comprised the master shamans, who diagnosed and cured illness by dealing with the spirit world, and the lesser religious leaders, who commanded winds and rains, predicted the future or found lost objects. The Jesuits scarcely ever described women in these roles among either the Algonquian-speaking or Iroquoian-speaking peoples, and Marie de l'Incarnation mentioned none at all. An Algonquin woman was known 'to be involved in sorcery, succeeding at it better than the men'; a woman 'famous' among the Hurons for her 'sorcery' sought messages from the *Manitou* about what kinds of feasts or gifts would cure an illness; a Montagnais woman entered the cabin where the male shamans consulted the spirits of the air and through shaking the tent-posts and loud singing was able to diagnose an illness and foresee an Iroquois attack.[31] Indeed, soothsaying seems to have been the one shamanic function in which women were welcome, as with the old woman of Teanaostaiaë village in the Huron country, who saw events in distant battles with the Iroquois by looking into fires, and the Abenaki 'Pythonesses' who could see absent things and foretell the future.[32]

Most of the time, however, a woman was simply an aide, marking on a 'triangular stick' the songs for the dead being sung by a Montagnais medicine man so their order would be remembered; walking around the shaman and his male performers at a prescribed moment in a ritual to kill a far-away witch.[33] Surely the herbal remedies known to be used by later Amerindian women must have had their antecedents in the female lore of the sixteenth and early seventeenth centuries,[34] and it is hard to imagine that there were no religious specialists associated with the menstrual cabins of the Iroquian communities and the Montagnais. It may have been precisely the beliefs about defilement that barred women from handling the sacred shamanic objects and rattle used in spirit cures. Across the Atlantic, the powers and dangers of menstruation kept European *religieuses* from touching altars and chalices too directly and kept Catholic laywomen away from the mass during their periods. Among the Hurons, the presence of a pregnant woman made a sick person worse, but was required for the extraction of an arrow; among the French Catholics, the glance of a post-partum woman brought trouble to people in streets and roadways. Among the Amerindians, medicine men were to abstain from sexual intercourse before their ceremonies; among the Europeans, Catholic priests were to abstain from sexual intercourse all the time.[35]

The most important asymmetry among Indian men and women was political. In the female world of crops, cooking and crafts, women made the decisions; in lodge and long-house, their voice often carried the day. Village and tribal governance, however, was in the hands of male chiefs and councils, and, apart from the Iroquois, women's influence on it was informal. (Only among the Algonquian peoples of southern New England and the mid-Atlantic coast do we hear of women sometimes holding authority as sunksquaws along with the more numerous male sachems.)[36] Huron villages and Algonquin and Montagnais settlements often had two or more chiefs, their access to this honor partly hereditary but even more based on assessments of their eloquence, wisdom, generosity or past prowess. The chiefs presided over frequent local council meetings, where women and young warriors were rarely present and where pipe-smoking men gave their views, the eldest among them being accorded particular respect. At larger assemblies of several clans and villages, the young men were invited as well, and sometimes the women.[37] When council or assembly decisions required embassies to other villages or nations – to seek support in war or to resolve disputes – the envoys were chiefs and other men.

In Iroquois communities, women had more formal roles in political decisions than elsewhere. Here, to women's advantage, succession to chieftancies was more strictly hereditary, passing matrilineally to a sister's son or another male relative named by the woman. Here among the Onondagas – so we learn from the pen of Marie de l'Incarnation – there were 'women of quality' or

'Capitainesses' who could affect decisions at local council meetings and select ambassadors for peace initiatives.[38] At least by the eighteenth century important women could attend treaty councils of the Iroquois nations, and perhaps they did so earlier.[39]

Now it is precisely in regard to this political life that major historical changes had occurred in the American/Canadian woodlands and villages from the fourteenth through sixteenth centuries. The evidence for these changes comes in part from archeologists: tobacco-pipes become more elaborate, pottery and sea shells are found further from their place of origin and human bones in ossuaries show signs of being 'cut, cooked and split open to extract the marrow'.[40] The evidence comes also from the collective memory of Hurons and Iroquois after European contact and from Indian stories and legends.

A double picture emerges. First, warfare became more prevalent and intense, with the seizure of women as wives[41] and the adoption of some male captives and the torture and cannibalization of others. European contact then added to the complicated history of enmity and exchange between Iroquois and Hurons. As a Huron chief recalled to some Onondagas in 1652:

> Have you forgotten the mutual promises our Ancestors made when they first took up arms against each other, that if a simple woman should take it on herself to uncover the Sweat-house and pull up the stakes that support it, that the victors would put down their arms and show mercy to the vanquished?[42]

The two roles assigned to women by intensified warfare – the woman-adoptor of an enemy and the woman-enemy incorporated as wife – must have had important consequences for consciousness. Let us consider here only the enemy wife, a position in which women living in Europe rarely found themselves (even though the foreign queens of Spain and France might have felt divided loyalties when their husbands went to war in 1635, the marriages had been made as peaceful alliance).[43] In the eastern American woodlands, Algonquin and Huron captives became Iroquois wives; Iroquois captives became Huron wives. Nor was their origin forgotten: Pierre Esprit Radisson among the Mohawks in 1652 discovered that his adoptive mother had been taken from the Huron country in her youth; Father Le Moyne among the Onondagas the next year was approached by a Huron wife who 'wanted to pour out her heart to him'.[44] This suggests that to the Amerindian habit of self-discovery through dream analysis was added for the enemy wife another source for self-definition: the experience of being forcibly transplanted, alone or with only a few of her kin, to a people who had a different language and burial ground from her ancestors. When the enemy wife was also a Christian in a non-Christian village, the impulse toward self-definition might be all the stronger, but the process predated conversion.

This setting for self-consciousness is rather different from those in which Renaissance historians usually locate the discovery of 'the individual' or of a renewed sense of self among European Christians. There we stress how persons set themselves off against those whom they resembled, against their own kind and kin: some of Montaigne's best self-discovery occurred when he played himself off against his friend La Boétie and against his own father. The Amerindian enemy wife (and the adopted male enemy as well) represent a contrasting historical trajectory. Still, they should make us more attentive to European situations where the experience of 'foreignness' and 'strangeness' could prompt consciousness of self as well as of group. The emergence of Jewish autobiography by the early seventeenth century is a case in point.[45]

Along with intensified warfare, a second associated change took place in the eastern American woodlands in the fifteenth, sixteenth and early seventeenth centuries: intertribal political federations appeared along with a new peacemaking diplomacy. The Huron League, or League of the Ouendats as they called themselves, was made up of four nations or tribes, two of them establishing themselves as 'brother' and 'sister' with a grand council in the fifteenth century, the other two being adopted, one in the last decades of the sixteenth century and the other in the early seventeenth century.[46] The Iroquois League of the Five Nations, the Houdénosaunee – three Elder Brothers and two Younger Brothers – was probably founded around 1500.[47] Its origin was memorialized in the Deganawidah Epic about a divine Iroquois seer, Deganawidah, who preached peace, converted a Mohawk chief Hiawatha away from cannibalism, and then together with him transformed the wicked and obstructive Onondaga chief Thadodaho into a willing collaborator. (Women enter the epic through Deganawidah's grandmother, who foresaw his peace-bringing role in a dream; his mother, who received divine guidance in hidden seclusion and then gave birth to Deganawidah as a virgin; and the daughter of Hiawatha, who died sacrificially in the encounter with Thadodaho.)[48]

Among the many fruits of the League formation was the development of a language of politics and diplomacy: a set of rules and styles of communication that operated around the local council fire, on embassies to rouse for war or make amends for a murder, at large assemblies and at general councils of the federation. At council meetings, where many opinions were given, matters opened with the leader's appreciative words about the men's safe arrival, no one lost in the woods or fallen in the stream or slain by an enemy. A special tone of voice was used for all the comments and opinions – the Hurons called it *acouentonch* – 'a raising and lowering of the voice like the tone of a Predicant à l'antique, an old style Preacher', said a Jesuit in 1636.[49] Always the men spoke slowly, calmly and distinctly, each person reviewing the issues before giving his opinion. No one ever interrupted anyone else, the rhythm of taking turns aided by the smoking of pipes. No matter how bitter the disagreement – as when some Huron villages wanted to rebury their ancestors' bones in a separate grave – courteous and gentle language was sought. The Hurons said of a good council, *Endionraondaoné*, 'even and easy, like level and reaped fields'.[50]

In more elaborate public speeches, for example, as an envoy or at a large assembly or to make a treaty, still another tone of voice was used – 'a Captain's tone', said a Jesuit, who tried to imitate it among the Iroquois in 1654. Mnemonic devices were used 'to prop up the mind', such as marked sticks and, for a major event, the ordered shells on a wampum necklace or belt. Arm gestures and dramatic movements accompanied the argument, and the speaker walked back and forth, seeming 'marvelous' to Jacques Cartier in 1535 and, to the later Jesuits, 'like an actor on a stage'.[51] At the 1645 treaty between the Iroquois, the French, the Algonquins, and the Montagnais, the tall Mohawk chief Kiotseaeton arose, looked at the sun and then at all the company and said (as taken from a rough French translation):

> 'Onotonio [the French governor], lend me ear. I am the whole of my country; thou listenest to all the Iroquois in hearing my words. There is no evil in my heart; I have only good songs in my mouth. We have a multitude of war songs in our country; we have cast them all on the ground; we have no longer anything but songs of rejoicing'. Thereupon he began to sing; his countrymen responded; he walked about that great space as if on the stage of a theatre; he made a thousand gestures; he looked up to Heaven; he gazed at the Sun; he rubbed his arms as if he wished to draw from them the strength that moved them in war.[52]

Throughout, in all political speech, many metaphors and circumlocutions were used, which made it difficult to follow for anyone who had not learned the system. 'Kettle' could denote hospitality ('to hang the kettle') hostility or killing ('to break the kettle', 'to put into the kettle') and ritual reburial of ancestors ('Master of the Kettle', the officer for the Feast of the Dead).[53]

Meanwhile, the persons who were literally in charge of the kettle and who literally reaped the cornfields so that they were easy and even were not deliverers of this oratory. Women strung the shells for the wampum necklaces and belts used in all diplomacy, but they did not provide the public interpretations of their meaning. (Even the Algonquian sunksquaws of the central Atlantic coast are not known for their speeches, and it is significant that Mary Rowlandson, captive of the sunksquaw Weetamoo in 1676, said of her mistress only that 'when she had dressed herself, her work was to make Girdles of Wampom and Beads'.)[54] To be sure, councils had to accede to the request of any woman to adopt a prisoner who would replace her slain or dead male relative, but this desire could be discovered by a word or gesture. Only one occasion has come down to us where a Huron woman gave a speech at an assembly: during the smallpox epidemic of 1640 at a large and tumultuous gathering of Ataronchronons, an older woman denounced the Jesuit Black Robes as devils spreading disease.[55] Even in the most favored case of the Iroquois, where the chiefs had been enjoined by Hiawatha to seek the advice of their wisest women about resolving disputes and where captains' wives might accompany an embassy, women never orated as ambassadors – the Five Nations never 'spoke through their mouths' – and their opinion at treaty councils was given by a male Speaker for the Women.[56]

Indian men trained their sons in oratory: 'I know enough to instruct my son,' said an Algonquin captain in refusing to give his son to the Jesuits. 'I'll teach him to give speeches.' Huron men teased each other if they made a slip of the tongue or mistake, and accorded the eloquent speaker praise and honor. When the Mohawk chief Kiotseaeton wanted to persuade the Hurons to take part in a peace treaty with the Iroquois, he presented a wampum necklace 'to urge the Hurons to hasten forth to speak. Let them not be bashful [*honteux*] like women.' The Hurons 'call us Frenchmen women,' said the Recollet Sagard, 'because too impulsive and carried away [*trop précipités et bouillants*] in our actions, [we] talk all at the same time and interrupt each other.'[57]

It seems to me that connections between political change, eloquence and gender can be similarly constructed in the North American villages and woodlands and in Western Europe in the fifteenth, sixteenth and early seventeenth centuries. Renaissance political oratory, emerging in both republics and monarchies, and the art of formal diplomacy were part of a masculine political culture. As Leonardo Bruni said, 'Rhetoric in all its forms – public discussion, forensic argument, logical fencing and the like – lies absolutely outside the province of women.' The privileged few with a right to public pronouncement – the queens or queen regents and a rare learned woman – required exceptional strategies if their voice were to have an authoritative ring.[58]

Some European women sought the chance to speak publicly (or semi-publicly) in religion instead: members of radical and prophetic sects from the first Anabaptists to the Quakers; Protestants in the early days of the new religion, before Paul's dictum that women should not speak in church, was strictly enforced; Catholics in the new religious orders, like Marie de l'Incarnation's Ursulines and the Visitation of Jeanne de Chantal, where women preached to and taught each other.[59]

Can we find evidence for a similar process in the eastern American woodlands, that is, did Amerindian women try to expand their voice in religious culture while Amerindian men were expanding political oratory? Conceivably, the role of women in dream analysis (which, as we have seen, involved describing one's dreams publicly and playing riddle games about them at festive fires) may have increased in the course of the sixteenth century. In 1656 an Onondaga woman used her dream-swoon to unmask the Christian Paradise to her fellow Iroquois: she had visited 'Heaven', she announced to them, and had seen the French burning Iroquois.[60] Conceivably, the women soothsayers whom the Jesuits met were not simply filling a timeless function open to women, but were recent shamanic innovators. Conceivably, the Iroquois Ogiweoano society of Chanters for the Dead, described in nineteenth-century sources as composed of all or predominantly women, was not a timeless institution, but a development of the sixteenth and seventeenth centuries.[61]

The evidence we do have concerns Amerindian women who converted to

Christianity. Some of them used the new religion to find a voice beyond that of a shaman's silent assistant, even while Jesuits were teaching them that wives were supposed to obey their husbands. Khionrea the Huron was one such woman, her portrait drawn for seventeenth-century readers by Marie de l'Incarnation. Brought to the Ursuline convent by her parents in 1640, when she was about twelve, Khionrea had been given the name Thérèse, Marie de l'Incarnation's *favorite* saint, and had learned to speak both French and Algonquin and to read and write. Two Huron men from her village came to the convent two years later and she preached to them through the grill:

> They listened to this young woman with unrivalled attention, and one day, when they were on the point of being baptized, one of them pretended no longer to believe in God and so she need no longer speak to him of faith or baptism. Our fervent Thérèse . . . became disturbed and said, 'What are you talking about? I see the Devil has overturned all your thoughts so that you will be lost. Know you well that if you died today, you would go to Hell where you would burn with Devils, who would make you suffer terrible torments!' The good man laughed at everything she said, which made her think that he spoke with a spirit of contempt. She redoubled her exhortations to combat him, but failing, she came to us in tears. 'Ah,' she said, 'he is lost; he's left the faith; he will not be baptized. It hurt me so to see him speak against God that if there had not been a grill between us, I would have thrown myself on him to beat him.' We went to find out the truth . . . and the man affirmed that he had done this only to test her faith and zeal.[62]

Several months afterward Khionrea's parents came to take her back to her village to marry, expecting her to be 'the example of their Nation and the Teacher (Maîtresse) of the Huron girls and women'. Instead her party was captured by Iroquois, a number were slain and Thérèse was married to a Mohawk. A decade later, in 1653, she was the mistress of the several families of her Iroquois long-house, still praying to her Christian God and leading others publicly in prayer.[63] Khionrea may have been placating *oki* spirits as well – though Marie de l'Incarnation would have hated to think so – and inspired non-Christian women in her village to experimental religious action. One thinks especially of how Christian forms and phrases could have been appropriated to elaborate and lengthen Indian propitiary prayer.

Cécile Gannendaris is another example of a Huron woman who found an authoritative voice through a new religious mix. Her biography was left by the Sisters of the Québec Hospital where she died at an advanced age in 1669, her Christian 'virtue' being demonstrated not only by her fighting off 'seducers' in her youth with smoldering logs and spanking her children 'when they deserved it', but by giving spiritual guidance to her first and second husbands. Especially she taught and preached, 'converting numerous Savages and encouraging them to live more perfectly'.

> She was so solidly instructed in our mysteries and so eloquent in explaining them that she was sent new arrivals among the Savages who were asking to embrace the faith. In a few days she had them ready for baptism, and had reduced the opinionated ones beyond defense by her good reasoning.

The French were impressed with her as well, the Jesuits learning the Huron language from her lips, the newly established Bishop of Québec coming to visit her in her cabin, and the Frenchwomen sending her gifts of food. The Hospital Sisters thought that Gannendaris's clarity of expression and discernment were a break with her Huron past, or, as they put it, 'had nothing of the savage [*rien de sauvage*] about them'. We would interpret these talents differently, as drawing on a Huron tradition of lucid male discussion around the council fire and on a long-house practice of women's teaching, here transformed by Christian learning and opportunity into a new realm of speech.[64]

When Iroquois women became interested in Christianity, the oratorical force of young converts struck them right away. In the fall of 1655, an Onondaga embassy came to Québec to confirm peace with the Hurons and their French allies and to invite the Black Robes to their villages. A chief's wife ('*une Capitainesse*', in the words of Marie de l'Incarnation) visited the Ursulines with other Onondagas several times and listened to the Huron, Marie Aouentohons, not yet fifteen and able to read and write in French, Latin and Huron. Aouentohons catechized her sister seminarians before the company and made a speech (*une harangue*) both to the chief and his wife:

> Send me as many of my Iroquois sisters as you can. I will be their older sister. I will teach them. I will show them how to pray and to worship the Supreme Parent of All. I will pass on to them what my teachers have taught me.

She then sang hymns in Huron, French and Latin. The Capitainesse asked the Ursulines how long it would take their daughters to acquire such accomplishments.[65]

Religious eloquence was not, of course, the only kind of expressiveness that attracted some Indian women to Christianity.[66] The spirituality of the 'Servant of God' Katherine Tekakwitha, daughter of a Mohawk chief and an enemy-wife Algonquin, was marked by heroic asceticism, intense female companionship and absorption in mental prayer. Her holy death in 1680 at age twenty-four was followed by shining apparitions of her and by miracles at her tomb near Caughnawaga. But even Tekakwitha's life involved teaching, as she spoke to the women while they did their cabin tasks of the lives of the saints and other sacred themes and as, toward the end of her life, she instructed those drawn by her reputation on the virtues of virginity and chastity. As her confessor reported it, 'At these times her tongue spoke from the depths of her heart.'[67]

In one striking way, then, Iroquois and Huron women faced what European historians could call a 'Renaissance' challenge in regard to voice and some of them made use of religious tools and the 'Catholic Reformation' to meet it. But neither rebirth nor a return to a privileged past would be an image of change that came readily to them. In the thought of the Algonquian- and Iroquoian-speaking peoples of Marie de l'Incarnation's day, sacred time turned around on itself, but there was no historical golden age from which humankind had declined and to which it might hope to return. When people died, their souls divided into two, one part gradually moving toward the setting sun to the Village of the Dead, the other part remaining with the body 'unless someone bears it again as a child'.[68] There was no fully developed theory of reincarnation among the Hurons, however. Gaps were filled not so much by rebirth as by adoption: the adoption of the dead person's name, which otherwise could not be mentioned; the adoption of a captured enemy to replace a slain son. Things could be created anew, like wampum, which came from the feathers of a fierce and huge wampum bird, slain to win the hand of an Iroquois chief's daughter and then put to the new uses of peacemaking.[69] Institutions could be created anew by joint divine and human enterprise, as with Deganawidah and Hiawatha and the confederating of the Five Iroquois Nations.

Models for abrupt change were also available. One was metamorphosis, the sudden and repeatable change from bear to man to bear, from trickster to benefactor to trickster – changes emerging from the double possibilities in life, the ever-present destabilizing potentiality for twinning[70] (a potentiality that makes interesting comparison with the sixteenth-century fascination with Ovidian metamorphosis). A second model was the sudden fall to a totally different world. The first fall was at creation, when the pregnant woman Aataentsic plunged from the sky through the hole under the roots of a great tree (according to one version recounted to the Jesuit Brébeuf), landed on the back of a great turtle in the waters of this world and, after dry land had been created, gave birth to the deity Yoscaha and his twin brother. Falls through holes, especially holes under trees, are the birth canals to experiences in alternative worlds in many an Indian narrative.[71] A seventeenth-century Huron woman, describing Marie de l'Incarnation's life, might say that she tried to fulfill the promptings of a dream, as a person must always do, but what she thought would only be a boat trip turned out to be a fall down a hole. What that alternative world would become remained to be seen.

I hope that one of the Amerindian women in Marie's convent yard told her a seventeenth-century version of the Seneca tale of the origin of stories. We know it from the version told by the Seneca Henry Jacob to Jeremiah Curtin in 1883, where a hunting boy is its protagonist;[72] perhaps a woman's version 230 years before would have used a wooding girl instead. Set in the forest, the tale called to my mind Marguerite de Navarre's rather different storytelling field in the Pyrenees – a conjoining of alternative worlds. An Orphan Boy was sent each day into the woods by his adoptive mother to hunt for birds. One day he came upon a flat round stone in the midst of a clearing. When he sat upon it he heard a voice asking, 'Shall I tell you stories?' 'What does it mean – to tell stories?' the boy asked. 'It is telling what happened a long time ago. If you will give me your birds, I'll tell you stories.'

So each day the Orphan sat on the stone, heard stories and left birds, bringing home to his mother only what he could catch on the way back. His mother sent other boys from the long-house and even men to follow him to find out why his catch had diminished, but they too were captivated by the stories and would say 'haa, haa' with approval now and again. Finally, the stone told the Orphan Boy that he should clear a larger space and bring everyone in the village to it, each of them with something to eat. The boy told the chief and, for two days at sunrise, all the men and women of the village came, put food on the stone and listened to stories till the sun was almost down. At the end of the second day the stone said:

> I have finished! You must keep these stories as long as the world lasts. Tell them to your children and your grandchildren. One person will remember them better than another. When you go to a man or a woman to ask for one of these stories, bring a gift of game or fish or whatever you have. I know all that happened in the world before this; I have told it to you. When you visit one another, you must tell these things. You must remember them always. I have finished.

NOTES

An initial version of this essay was given on May 2, 1992, at the University of Chicago Centennial Colloquium 'Do We Need "The Renaissance"?' A somewhat different version appears in the papers of the conference, edited by Philippe Desan, Richard Strier and Elissa Weaver.

1. Paul Le Jeune, *Relation de ce qui s'est passé en la Nouvelle France en l'année 1633* (Paris, 1634), in Reuben Gold Thwaites, *The Jesuit Relations and Allied Documents* (henceforth *JR*), 73 vols (Cleveland, Ohio: Burrows Brothers, 1896–1901), 5 pp. 118–21, 283 n. 33. Pierre Pastedechouan was born about 1605 and taken to France around 1618 by the Recollet brothers, then returned to Canada in 1625, living sometimes with the Jesuits and much of the time with the Montagnais. See also Gabriel Sagard, *Le Grand Voyage du pays des Hurons* (1632), ed. Réal Ouellet (Quebec: Bibliothèque québécoise, 1990), p. 58.
2. 'The Dream of the White Robe and the floating island/Micmac', in Ella Elizabeth Clark, *Indian Legends of Canada* (Toronto: McClelland and Stewart, 1991, pp. 151–2; also Silas Rand, *Legends of the Micmac* (New York: Longmans Green, 1894). For another Amerindian telling of the floating island and the coming of Europeans, see the excerpt from William Wood (1634) in William S. Simmons, *Spirit of the New England Tribes: Indian History and Folklore* (Hanover, NH: University Press of New England, 1986), p. 66. For a use of the floating island to describe origins of the Amerindians from a race of white giants, see 'The Beginning and the End of the World (Okanogan of the Salishan Languages)', in Paula Gunn Allen (ed.), *Spider Woman's Granddaughters: Traditional Tales and Contemporary Writing by Native American Women* (Boston: Beacon Press, 1989), pp. 106–7. For references to the motif-type 'Island canoe', see Stith Thompson (ed.), *Tales of North American Indians* (Cambridge, Mass.: Harvard University Press, 1929), p. 275 n. 14.
3. Marie de l'Incarnation and Claude Martin, *La Vie de la vénérable Mère Marie de*

l'Incarnation première supérieure des Ursulines de la Nouvelle France (Paris: Louis Billaine, 1677; facsimile ed. Solesmes: Abbaye Saint-Pierre, 1981), pp. 228–30, 400, 408. Marie de l'Incarnation, *Correspondance*, ed. Dom Guy Oury (Solesmes: Abbaye Saint-Pierre, 1971), no. 28, pp. 64–5, no. 41, p. 91.

4. General bibliographical orientation can be found in Dean R. Snow, *Native American Prehistory: A Critical Bibliography* (Bloomington: Indiana University Press for the Newberry Library, 1979); Neal Salisbury, *The Indians of New England: A Critical Bibliography* (Bloomington: Indiana University Press for the Newberry Library, 1982); James P. Ronda and James Axtell, *Indian Missions: A Critical Bibliography* (Bloomington, Indiana University Press for the Newberry Library, 1978). The writings of James Axtell have been pioneering in the study of the American Indians in their encounter with Europeans: *The European and the Indian: Essays in the Ethnohistory of Colonial North America* (Oxford and New York: Oxford University Press, 1981); *The Invasion Within: The Contest of Cultures in Colonial North America* (New York and Oxford: Oxford University Press, 1985); *After Columbus: Essays in the Ethnohistory of Colonial North America* (New York and Oxford: Oxford University Press, 1988); *Beyond 1492: Encounters in Colonial North America* (New York and Oxford: Oxford University Press, 1992). A general historical and ethnographical orientation to the Amerindian peoples of Canada is R. Bruce Morrison and C. Roderick Wilson (eds), *Native Peoples: The Canadian Experience* (Toronto: McClelland and Stewart, 1986). Bruce G. Trigger's *Natives and Newcomers: Canada's 'Heroic Age' Reconsidered* (Kingston and Montréal: McGill-Queen's University Press, 1985) is an excellent presentation of both archeological and historical evidence. Important studies of Iroquoian-speaking peoples include Elisabeth Tooker, *An Ethnography of the Huron Indians, 1615–1649* (Washington, DC: Smithsonian Institution for the Huronia Historical Development Council, 1964); Conrad Heidenreich, *Huronia: A History and Geography of the Huron Indians* (Toronto: McClelland and Stewart, 1971); Bruce G. Trigger, *The Children of Aataentsic, A History of the Huron People to 1660*, new edn (Kingston and Montréal: McGill-Queen's University Press, 1987) [with much archaelogical material from before the seventeenth century]; Lucien Campeau, *La mission des Jésuites chez les Hurons, 1634–1650* (Montreal: Editions Bellarmin, 1987), especially pp. 1–113 on the pre-contact Hurons); Francis Jennings, *The Ambiguous Iroquois Empire: The Covenant Chain Confederation of Indian Tribes with English Colonies from Its Beginnings to the Lancaster Treaty of 1744* (New York: W. W. Norton, 1984); Francis Jennings, William Fenton, Mary Druke and David R. Miller (eds), *The History and Culture of Iroquois Diplomacy. An Interdisciplinary Guide to the Treaties of the Six Nations and Their League* (Syracuse: Syracuse University Press, 1985); and Daniel K. Richter, *The Ordeal of the Longhouse: The Peoples of the Iroquois League in the Era of European Colonization* (Chapel Hill: University of North Carolina Press for the Institute of Early American History and Culture, 1992). Important studies of Algonquian-speaking peoples include Alfred Goldsworthy Bailey, *The Conflict of European and Eastern Algonkian Cultures, 1504–1700*, 2nd edn (Toronto: University of Toronto Press, 1969); Simmons, *Spirit of the New England Tribes*; Colin G. Calloway (ed.), *Dawnland Encounters: Indian and Europeans in Northern New England* (Hanover, NH and London: University Press of New England, 1991); W. Vernon Kinietz, *The Indians of the Western Great Lakes, 1615–1760* (Ann Arbor: University of Michigan Press, 1965); Richard White, *Indian, Empires, and Republics in the Great Lakes Region, 1650–1815* (Cambridge: Cambridge University Press, 1991). Penny Petrone provides an introduction to Amerindian literary genres in *Native Literature In Canada. From the Oral Tradition to the Present* (Toronto: Oxford University Press, 1990). A major study of the art and material culture of Amerindian peoples, with much early historical evidence, is *The Spirit Sings: Artistic Traditions of Canada's First Peoples* (Toronto: McClelland & Stewart for the Glenbow-Alberta

Institute, 1988). Special studies of Iroquois women have a long history behind them: a collection of essays from 1884 to 1989 is W. G. Spittal (ed.), *Iroquois Women: An Anthology* (Ohsweken: Iroqrafts, 1990). Marxist and feminist approaches opened a new chapter in the study of Indian women of northeastern America in the work of Judith K. Brown, 'Economic Organization and the Position of Women among the Iroquois', initially published in *Ethnohistory*, 17 (1970) and reprinted in *Iroquois Women*, pp. 182–98, and Eleanor Leacock, 'Montagnais Women and the Jesuit Program for Colonization', in Mona Etienne and Eleanor Leacock (eds), *Women and Colonization. Anthropological Perspectives* (New York: Praeger, 1980), pp. 25–42. Karen Anderson's *Chain Her by One Foot: The Subjugation of Women in Seventeenth-Century France* (London and New York: Routledge, 1991) does not carry the conceptual argument beyond Leacock's pioneering essay. A new historical and ethnographical study of Iroquois women is under way by Carol Karlsen. An introduction to the history of Amerindian women of many regions is Carolyn Niethammer, *Daughters of the Earth: The Lives and Legends of American Indian Women* (New York: Macmillan, 1977). Paula Gunn Allen has published several works that draw on a mix of historical examples, legends and women's values and lore in her own Lakota family in order (as she says in the subtitle to *The Sacred Hoop*) 'to recover the feminine in American Indian traditions': *The Sacred Hoop: Recovering the Feminine in American Indian Traditions*, 2nd edn (Boston: Beacon Press, 1992); *Spider Woman's Granddaughters*; and *Grandmothers of the Light. A Medicine Woman's Sourcebook* (Boston: Beacon Press, 1991).

5. Among many primary sources for this information on the division of labor are Sagard, *Grand Voyage*, Part 1, ch. 7 and passim, and *JR*, vol. 5, pp. 132–3.
6. On women being assisted in carrying tasks by male prisoner, see Marc Lescarbot, *The History of New France*, trans. W. L. Grant, 3 vols (Toronto: Champlain Society, 1907–1914), Book 6, ch. 17, 3: pp. 200, 412.
7. Jacques Cartier, 'Deuxième voyage de Jacques Cartier (1535–1536)', ed. Théodore Beauchesne, in Charles A. Julien (ed.), *Les Français en Amérique pendant la première moitié du 16e siècle* (Paris: Press Universitaires de France, 1946), p. 159. Sagard, *Grand Voyage*, p. 172. Sagard applied to the Huron women what Lescarbot had said in his *Histoire de la Nouvelle France* (1609), about women of the Micmacs and other Algonquian-speaking groups:

   > J'ay dit au chapitre de la Tabagie [on banquets] qu'entre les Sauvages les femmes ne sont point en si bonne condition qu'anciennement entre les Gaullois et Allemans. Car (au rapport même de Iacques Quartier) 'elles travaillent plus que les hommes,' dit-il, 'soit en la pecherie, soit au labour, ou autre chose.' Et neantmoins elles ne sont point forcées, ne tourmentées, mais elles ne sont ni en leurs Tabagies [at their banquets], ni en leurs conseils, et font les oeuvres serviles, à faute de serviteurs.

   Lescarbot, *New France* 3, p. 411. *JR*, vol. 4 pp. 204–5 ('ces pauvres femmes sont de vrais mulets de charge').
8. Marie de l'Incarnation, *Correspondance*, no. 97, p. 286; no. 244, pp. 828–9. Marie de l'Incarnation and Claude Martin, *Vie*, pp. 41–3, 54–5.
9. Sagard, Grand Voyage, Part 1, ch. 7, 172.
10. Heidenreich (*Huronia*, p. 77) gives two sources for Huron matrilineality. First, a single sentence from Samuel Champlain where, after noticing that Hurons are not always sure of the father of a child because of permitted sexual promiscuity in marriage, he goes on,

   > in view of this danger, they have a custom which is this, namely that the children never succeed to the property and honors of their fathers, being in doubt, as I said, of their begetter, but indeed they make their successors and heirs the children of their sisters, from whom these are certain to be sprung and issued.

(*The Works of Samuel Champlain*, trans. H. P. Biggar, 6 vols [Toronto: Champlain Society, 1922–1936], 3: 140). Second, an unclear description of cross-cousin marriage by Sagard (*Grand Voyage*, Part 1, ch. 11, p. 199) that could apply to either a patrilineal or matrilineal situation. Elsewhere Sagard said that after divorce Huron children usually stayed with their father (p. 201). Heidenreich concluded that matrilocality was sometimes practiced, sometimes not (p. 77). In *Children of Aataentsic*, Trigger talks of a 'matrilineal' preference among the Iroquoians more generally, but adds that their 'kinship terminology and incest prohibitions seem to reflect a bilateral ideal of social organization'. He suggests that Huron boys in the lineages of chiefs lived with their mother's brother, and that when they married their wives came to live with them rather than following the matrilocal principle (pp. 55, 100–2). See also Trigger's *Natives and Newcomers*, pp. 117, 208 and Richter, *Ordeal of the Longhouse*, p. 20. Lucien Campeau shows from evidence about specific Huron families described in the *Jesuit Relations* that the Hurons were not consistent in matrilocal living arrangements nor in the matrilineal passing of chiefly honors (*Mission des Jésuites*, pp. 54–8). Karen Anderson takes Huron matrilineality and matrilocality for granted, but does not review the Jesuit evidence or mention Campeau's book (*Chain Her by One Foot*, pp. 107, 193). A mixed practice in regard to lineage and dwellings creates an interesting and variegated situation for Huron women.

11. Sagard, *Grand Voyage*, Part 1, ch. 11, pp. 198–9; *JR*, vol. 14: pp. 18–19, vol. 27: pp. 30–1; vol. 30 pp. 36–7; Claude Chauchetière, *The Life of the Good Katharine Tegakoüita, Now Known as the Holy Savage* (1695) in Catholic Church, Sacred Congregation of Rites, *Positio . . . on the Introduction of the Cause for Beatification and Canonization and on the Virtues of the Servant of God Katharine Tekakwitha, the Lily of the Mohawks* (New York: Fordham University Press, 1940), pp. 123–5; Pierre Cholenec, *The Life of Katharine Tegakoüita, First Iroquois Virgin* (1696) in Catholic Church Sacred Congregation of Rites, *Cause for Beatification*, pp. 273–5. Tooker, *Ethnography*, pp. 126–7; Trigger, *Children of Aataentsic*, p. 49.

12. Sagard, *Grand Voyage*, Part 1, ch. 1, pp. 291–2. *JR*, vol. 10: pp. 264–71. The remaining goods of the deceased were not given to his or her family, but after burial were given to 'recognize the liberality of those who had made the most gifts of consolation' at the funeral (*JR*, vol. 43: pp. 270–1).

13. Intercourse itself as the sole source of conception was problematized in folktales in which females get pregnant from passing near male urination or scratching themselves with an object used by a male (Claude Lévi-Strauss, *Histoire de lynx* [Paris: Plon, 1991], pp. 21–2). Among some Amerindian peoples today, pregnancy is believed to occur only through many occasions of intercourse (Niethammer, *Daughters of the Earth*, p. 2). Among the Hurons in the seventeenth century, it was believed that the body-soul of a deceased person might sometimes enter the womb of a woman and be born again as her child (*JR*, vol. 10: pp. 285–7). When an adult male died, and especially an important male, such as a chief, his name was given to another person, not necessarily kin to the bereaved, and he then took up the deceased person's role and attributes (*JR*: vol. 10: pp. 274–7, vol. 23: pp. 164–9; Alexander von Gernet, 'Saving the Souls: Reincarnation Beliefs of the Seventeenth-Century Huron', in Antonia Mills and Richard Slobodin, *Amerindian Rebirth: Reincarnation Belief among North American Indians and Inuit* [Toronto: University of Toronto Press, 1993]). These adoptive practices carry with them a very different sense of the succession of qualities from that current in sixteenth- and seventeenth-century Europe, where lineage and stock were so important.

14. *JR*, vol. 6: pp. 254–5. Jeanne-Françoise Juchereau de St Ignace and Marie Andrée Duplessis de Ste Hélène, *Les Annales de l'Hôtel-Dieu de Québec, 1636–1716*, ed. Albert Jamet (Québec: Hôtel-Dieu, 1939), p. 20.

15. Sagard reported a 'grand querelle' between a daughter and a father who refused to give his consent to the suitor she desired, so the latter seized her (*Grand Voyage*,

Part 1, ch. 11, pp. 199–201; this story was already recounted by Lescarbot, ibid., p. 203 n. 4). Marie de l'Incarnation, *Correspondance*, no. 65, p. 163.

16. In addition to occasional reports in the *Jesuit Relations* of jealousy among spouses are the legends about a wife who goes off with a bear lover and the husband's efforts at retrieval or revenge. Lévi-Strauss, *Histoire de lynx*, p. 146; 'The Bear Walker (Mohawk)', in Herbert T. Schwarz (ed.), *Tales from the Smokehouse* (Edmonton, AL.: Hurtig Publishers, 1974), pp. 31–5, 101. A similar theme with a buffalo lover in 'Apache Chief Punishes His Wife (Tiwa)', in Richard Erdoes and Alfonso Ortiz (eds), *American Indian Myths and Legends* (New York: Pantheon Books, 1984), pp. 291–4.

17. *JR*, vol. 43: pp. 270–1.

18. *JR*, vol. 8: pp. 151–2; vol. 23: pp. 186–7; vol. 28: pp. 50–3 ('en leurs mariages les plus fermes, et qu'ils estiment les plus conformes à la raison, la foy qu'ils se donnent n'a rien de plus qu'une promesse conditionelle de demeurer ensemble, tandis qu'un chacun continuera à rendre les services qu'ils attendent mutuellement les uns des autres, et n'offensera point l'amitié qu'ils se doivent; cela manquant on iuge le divorce estre raisonnable du costé de celuy qui se voit offensé, quoy qu'on blasme l'autre party qui y a donné occasion'). On women ordinarily having custody of the children, *JR*, vol. 5: pp. 136–9; Marie de l'Incarnation, *Correspondance*, no. 52, p. 123 ('c'est la coûtume du païs que quand les personnes mariées se séparent, la femme emmène les enfans').

19. *JR*, vol. 5: pp. 172–3, 180–1. For an example of a wife using the need for her husband's assent to allow her infant to be baptized (possibly an excuse to cover her own reluctance), see *JR*, vol. 5; pp. 226–9.

20. Sagard, *Grand Voyage*, Part 1, ch. 18, pp. 253–7; *JR*, vol. 5: pp. 152–7; vol. 6: pp. 156–63; vol. 7: pp. 100–3; vol. 8: pp. 118–21; vol. 10: pp. 128–39, 144–8. Marie de l'Incarnation, *Correspondance*, no. 270, pp. 916–17. Tooker, *Ethnography*, pp. 145–8 and Appendix 2; Elisabeth Tooker (ed.), *Native North American Spirituality of the Eastern Woodlands. Sacred Myths, Dreams, Visions, Speeches, Healing Formulas, Rituals and Ceremonials* (New York: Paulist Press, 1979); Campeau, *Mission des Jésuites*, ch. 7; Axtell, *Invasion Within*, pp. 13–19.

21. *JR*, vol. 8: pp. 117–19. *JR*, vol. 30: pp. 60–1, for an evidently all-male gathering to elect a new captain among the Hurons:

> Ils ont coustume en semblables rencontres de raconter les histoires qu'ils ont appris de leurs ancestres et les plus éloignées, afin que les ieunes gens qui sont presens et les entendent, en puissent conserver la memoire et les raconter à leur tour, lors qu'ils seront devenus vieux.

Creation accounts were among the tales told at the gathering.

22. Marie de l'Incarnation, *Correspondance*, no. 270, pp. 917–18. Also, Jean de Brébouf on the Hurons: 'Or cette fausse creance qu'ils ont des ames s'entretient parmy-eux, par le moyen de certaines histoires que les peres racontent à leurs enfans' (*JR*, vol. 10: pp. 148–9).

23. *JR*, vol. 43: pp. 286–7.

24. *JR*, vol. 30: pp. 58–61: Paul Ragueneau describes the telling of creation stories by men at meeting for the election of a chief, where 'les anciens du païs' were assembled.

25 Women storytellers are documented among the Amerindians in the early nineteenth century (Clark, *Indian Legends of Canada*, pp. x–xi; Jeremiah Curtin (ed.), *Seneca Indian Myths* [New York: E. P. Dutton, 1922], pp. 243, 351; Marius Barbeau (ed.), *Huron-Wyandot Traditional Narratives in Translations and Native Texts* [Ottawa: National Museum of Canada, 1960], pp. 2–3), and individual women can be traced back to the eighteenth century (e.g., the Seneca grandmother of Johnny John, who told her grandson 'A Man Pursued by his Uncle and by His Wife' and whom John described in 1883 as having lived 'to be one hundred and thirty years old' [Curtin,

Seneca Indian Myths, p. 307]; the Huron-Wyandot Nendusha, who lived to a hundred and told the traditional tales to her grandson, an elderly man in 1911 [Barbeau, *Huron-Wyandot Narratives*, p. 2]). According to Penny Petrone, herself an honorary chief of the Gulf Lake Ojibway and specialist on Amerindian tales, some oral narratives were the 'private property' of certain tribes, societies within tribes, or of particular persons and families. These could be told and heard only by certain persons (*Native Literature in Canada*, p. 11). Petrone does not mention gender as a factor in these exclusions and has herself collected sacred tales from Tlingit women; but the cultural habit of restricting the pool of tellers for certain narratives might account for the fact that formal recitals of creation accounts were attributed by the Jesuits and even by Marie de l'Incarnation to men. On the other hand, these sacred stories could not have been successfully passed on if the women with good memories and narrative skills had not also told them on many occasions. (For a woman with evident storytelling skills, see *JR*, vol. 22: pp. 292–5: the blind woman's story about how her grandfather got a new eye.) Petrone thinks my speculation about different settings in which men and women told the sacred stories in the early period is plausible (phone conversation of January 18, 1993). Paula Gunn Allen maintains that Amerindian stories about 'women's matters' were for the most part told by women to other women (Allen (ed.), *Spider Woman's Granddaughters*, pp. 16–17).

26. *JR*, vol. 8: pp. 22–3; vol. 10: pp. 140–1, 168–73; vol. 17: pp. 152–5; vol. 33: pp. 188–91. Tooker, *Ethnography*, pp. 86–91 and Iroquois evidence, pp. 86, n. 62, 87, n. 63. Dreams could also involve the departure of the rational soul from the body to observe distant events or places.

27. *JR*, vol. 17: pp. 164–87.

28. *JR*, vol. 43: pp. 272–3 for an Iroquois woman who came to Québec to get a French dog of which her nephew had dreamed and, discovering the dog had been taken elsewhere, took a voyage of over four hundred miles through snow, ice and difficult roads to find the animal.

29. *JR*, vol. 30: pp. 22–3. On the Huron 'confraternities', Campeau, *Mission des Jésuites*, p. 105. Brébeuf's description of a special dance group for curing a man of madness had eighty persons in it, six of whom were women (*JR*, vol. 10: pp. 206–7). Games of lacrosse were also ordered for healing purposes (Ibid.: pp. 184–7), but this would be only for men. Shafer, 'The Status of Iroquois Women', (1941) in Spittal, (ed.), *Iroquois Women*, pp. 88–9. For an early eighteenth-century picture of Iroquois women and men doing a curing dance together, see the illustration to *Aventures du Sr. C. Le Beau*, reproduced by Ruth Phillips, 'Art in Woodlands Life: the Early Pioneer Period', in *The Spirit Sings*, p. 66.

30. *JR*, vol. 10: pp. 222–3, for the Amerindian definition of *sorciers*: 'ceux qui se meslent d'empoisonner et faire mourir par sort', who, once declared as such, can have their skulls smashed by anyone who comes upon them without the usual amends for a murder (compensatory gifts to the bereaved kin). For old men accused and punished as sorcerers: *JR*, vol. 13: pp. 154–7, vol. 15: pp. 52–3. Tooker, *Ethnography*, pp. 117–20. The Jesuits also use the word 'sorcerer' as one of several pejorative terms for all the various medicine men and shamans among the Amerindians, though there was some uncertainty among the fathers about whether they were actually assisted by Satan (*JR*, vol. 6: pp. 198–201; vol. 10: pp. 194–5, Brébeuf: 'Il y a donc quelque apparence que le Diable leur tient la main par fois').

31. *JR*, vol. 14: pp. 182–3; vol. 8: pp. 26–61; vol. 9: pp. 112–15. A Montagnais *sorcière* received messages from a Manitou (*JR*, vol. 31: pp. 242–3). Huron women were prepared to blow on a sick person when no medicine man was around to do it (*JR*, vol. 24: pp. 30–1).

32. *JR*, vol. 8: pp. 124–7; vol. 38: pp. 36–7. The Huron soothsayer is the only reference given to women shamans in Tooker, *Huron Indians*, pp. 91–101. Leacocks's statement that 'Seventeenth-century accounts . . . referred to female shamans who

might become powerful' ('Montagnais Women', p. 41) gives as supporting evidence *JR*, vol. 6: p. 61, which includes no reference whatsoever to this topic, and vol. 14: p. 183, the woman 'involved in sorcery,' mentioned in my text. Robert Steven Grumet gives seventeenth-century evidence for women 'powwows' or 'pawwaws' among the central coast Algonquians of southern New England ('Sunsquaws, Shamans, and Tradeswomen: Middle Atlantic Coastal Agonkian Women during the 17th and 18th Centuries', in Etienne and Leacock (eds), *Women and Colonization*, p. 53).

33. *JR*, vol. 6, pp. 204–7. On sticks as mnemonic devices, see William N. Fenton, 'Structure, Continuity, and Change in the Process of Iroquois Treaty Making', in Jennings (ed.), *Iroquois Diplomacy*, vol. 17. *JR*, vol. 6: pp. 194–9: at this ceremony, intended to make a distant enemy die, all the women were sent from the cabin but one, who sat next to the shaman and moved around the backs of all the men once during a specified point in the ceremonies. A similar ceremonial role in the sacrifice of the corpse of a person dead by drowning or freezing (*JR*, vol. 10: 162–5). To appease the sky's anger, the body is cut up by young men and thrown into the fire. Women walk around the men several times and encourage them by putting wampum beads in their mouths. Among the Hurons, if a pregnant woman entered the cabin of a sick person, he or she would grow sicker (*JR*, vol. 15: pp. 180–1). By the presence of a pregnant woman and the application of a certain root, an arrow could be extracted from a man's body. In all of these examples, it is the female body, pregnant or not-pregnant, which is the source of power or danger.

34. Niethammer, *Daughters of the Earth*, pp. 146–63 on herbal medicine and medicine women. Her examples of women shamans come from a later period and, except for Menominee story about Hunting Medicine (collected 1913), are all from regions other than those of the Algonquian- and Iroquoian-speaking peoples. In *Grandmothers of the Light* and *The Sacred Hoop*, Paula Gunn Allen develops a modern medicine woman's culture based on Amerindian values and tales of goddesses. Her examples of women shamans are all from the late nineteenth and twentieth centuries (*Sacred Hoop*, pp. 203–8). On the earlier period: 'Pre-contact American Indian women valued their role as vitalizers because they understood that bearing, like bleeding, was a transformative ritual act' (ibid., p. 28).

35. Champlain, *Works*, vol. 3: pp. 97–8; Sagard, *Grand Voyage*, part 1, ch. 4, pp. 132–3. The critical issue may be the menstrual taboos, which would allow women to deal with certain matters, but, as Niethammer points out, would prevent women from handling 'the sacred bundle' of the shaman (*Daughters of the Earth*, p. xii). Pregnant women: *JR*, vol. 15: pp. 180–1; vol. 17: pp. 212–13. Sexual restraint for men before shamanic ceremonial: *JR*, vol. 15: pp. 180–1. Menstrual separation and the power of the glance of the menstruating woman: *JR*, vol. 29: pp. 108–9; vol. 9: pp. 122–3. Separation of post-partum women among Algonquian peoples: Nicholas Perrot, *Memoir on the Manners, Customs, and Religion of the Savages of North America* (c. 1680), in Emma Helen Blair (ed. and trans.), *The Indian Tribes or the Upper Missippi Valley and Region of the Great Lakes*, 2 vols (Cleveland, Ohio: Arthur Clark, 1911; New York: Klaus Reprint, 1969), vol. 1: p. 48.

36. The best study is Grumet, 'Sunsquaws, Shamans, and Tradeswomen', pp. 46–53. See also Niethammer, *Daughters of the Earth*, pp. 139–41; Carolyn Thomas Foreman, *Indian Women Chiefs* (Muscogee: Hoffman Printing Co., 1966); Samuel G. Drake, *The Aboriginal Races of North America*, 15th edn (Philadelphia: Charles Desilver, 1860), Book IIII, chs 1, p. 4 on the Wampanoag sunksquaws Weetamoo and Awashonks.

37. Descriptions of government and councils from Champlain, *Works*, vol. 3: pp. 157–9; Sagard, *Grand Voyage*, Part 1, ch. 17, pp. 229–32; Brébeuf in *JR*, vol. 10: pp. 229–63; Bailey, *Algonkian Cultures*, pp. 91–2; Heidenreich, *Huronia*, pp. 79–81; Campeau, *Mission des Jésuites*, ch. 5; Fenton, 'Iroquois Treaty Making', pp. 12–14. Evidence in regard to women: Champlain on men's conduct on council

meetings: 'ils usent bien souvent de ceste façon de faire parmy leurs harangues au conseil, où il n'y que les plus principaux, qui sont les antiens: Les femmes et enfans n'y assistent point' (vol. 1: p. 110); Sagard, pp. 230–1, talking about local council meetings: 'Les femmes, filles et jeunes hommes n'y assistent point, si ce n'est en un conseil général, où les jeunes hommes de vingt-cinq à trente ans peuvent assister, ce qu'il connaissent par un cri particulier qui en est fait' pp. 230–1; Brébeuf, on the council chamber:

> la Chambre de Conseil est quelque fois la Cabane du Capitaine, parée de nattes, ou ionchées de branches de Spain, avec divers feux, suivant la saison de l'année. Autrefois chacun y apportoit sa busche pour mettre au feu; maintenant cela ne se pratique plus, les femmes de la Cabane supportent cette dépense, elles font les feux, et ne s'y chauffent pas, sortant dehors pour ceder la place à Messieurs le Conseillers. Quelquefois l'assemblée se fait au milieu du Village, si c'est en Esté [this may have been the time when women could most easily attend and listen, NZD], et quelquefois aussi en l'obscurité des forests à l'ecart, quand les affaires demandent le secret.
>
> *(JR, vol. 10: p. 250);*

Paul Le Jeune on the Huron community of both 'pagans' and Christians at Saint Joseph (Silléry): The Christian elders decided:

> d'assembler les femmes pour les presser de se faire instruire et de recevoir le sainct Baptesme. On les fit donc venir, et les ieunes gens aussi. Le bon fut qu'on les prescha si bien que le iour suivant une partie de ces pauvres femmes, rencontrant le Pere de Quen, lay dirent, 'Où est un tel Pere, nous le venons prier de nous baptiser, *hier les hommes nous appellerent en Conseil, c'est la premiere fois que iamais les femmes y sont entrées*'
>
> (italics mine; *JR*, vol. 18: p. 104).

Drawing from a general description of Huron civility, in which Brébeuf talks of marriages, feasting, and other kinds of sociability and comments

> Ce qui les forme encor dans le discours sont les conseils qui se tiennent quasi tous les iours dans les Villages en toutes occurrences: et quoy que les anciens y tiennent le haut bout, et que ce soit de leur iugement qui dépende la decision des affaires; neantmoins s'y trouve qui veut et chacun a droit d'y dire son advis
>
> *(JR, vol. 10: p. 212),*

Karen Anderson assumes that women could be present at any Huron council meeting and speak whenever they wanted (*Chain Her by One Foot*, p. 124). But this is in contradiction to other evidence, including more specific evidence given some pages later by Brébeuf himself. Brébeuf was following the usual practice in men's writing in the sixteenth and seventeenth centuries and using 'chacun' (and other general nouns and pronouns) to refer to men; the paragraph in question is describing male civility.

38 Marie de l'Incarnation, *Correspondance*, no. 161, p. 546, September 24, 1654 ('Ces capitainesses sont des femmes de qualité parmi les Sauvages qui ont voix delibérative dans les Conseils, et qui en tirent des conclusions comme les hommes, et même ce furent elles qui déléguèrent les premiers Ambassadeurs pour traiter de la paix'); no. 191, p. 671. In 1671, Father Claude Dablon said of Iroquois women of high rank that they:

> are much respected; they hold councils, and the Elders decide no important affair without their advice. It was one of these women of quality who, some time ago, took the lead in persuading the Iroquois of Onnontagué, and afterward the other nations, to make peace with the French.
>
> *(JR, vol. 54: pp. 280–1).*

This is surely the same Onodaga 'capitainesse' who visited the Ursuline convent during the embassy of 1654. In contrast, in the early eighteenth century, Pierre-François-Xavier de Charlevoix claimed of the Iroquois that 'the men never tell the women anything they would have to be kept secret, and rarely any affair of consequence is communicated to them, though all is done in their name' (quoted in W. M. Beauchamp, 'Iroquois Women', *Journal of American Folklore*, 13 [1900], reprinted in Spittal (ed.), *Iroquois Women*, pp. 42–3). Carol Karlsen, currently engaged in a study of Iroquois women, says she has found considerable variation from period to period and nation to nation: in some instances, women attend council, in some they have meetings of their own and their views are communicated to the council (Lecture at Princeton University, March 25, 1993). Daniel Richter, in his important recent study *The Ordeal of the Longhouse*, describes women's roles in naming which man in a hereditary chiefly family would assume the role of leadership and concludes that there 'appears to have been a form of gender division of political labor corresponding to the economic and social categories that made women dominant within the village and its surrounding fields while men dealt with the outside world' (p. 43).

39. Jennings (ed.), *Iroquois Diplomacy*, p. 124.
40. Trigger, *Natives and Newcomers*, pp. 94–108. An example of the archeological work that allows one to historicize the Amerindian past is James F. Pendergast and Bruce G. Trigger, *Cartier's Hochelaga and the Dawson Site* (Montréal and London: McGill University Press, 1972), see especially pp. 155–6, 158–61.
41. Sagard mentions women and girls kept by Hurons from war as wives or to be used as gifts, *Grand Voyage*, Part 1, ch. 17, p. 239. *JR*, vol. 9: pp. 254–5: Le Jeune, talking of some Iroquois prisoners seized by Algonquins, comments more generally: 'Il est vray que les Barbares ne font point ordinairement de mal aux femmes, non plus qu'aux enfans, sinon dans leurs surprises, voire mesme quelque ieune homme ne fera point de difficulté d'épouser une prisonniere, si elle travaille bien, et par apres elle passe pour une femme du pays.'
42. *JR*, vol. 40: pp. 180–1.
43. Elizabeth of France, sister of Louis XIII, was the wife of Philip IV of Spain; Anne of Austria, sister of Philip IV, was the wife of Louis XIII. John Elliott, *Richelieu and Olivares* (Cambridge: Cambridge University Press, 1984), pp. 12, 113.
44. Pierre Esprit Radisson, *The Explorations of Pierre Esprit Radisson*, ed. Arthur T. Adams (Minneapolis: Ross & Haines, 1961), vol. 26. *JR*, vol. 41: pp. 102–3.
45. I treat and give further bibliography on the issues in this paragraph in 'Boundaries and the Sense of Self in Sixteenth-Century France', in Thomas Heller, Morton Sosna and David Wellbery (eds), *Reconstructing Individualism. Autonomy, Individuality, and the Self in Western Thought* (Stanford: Stanford University Press, 1986), pp. 53–63, 332–5 and 'Fame and Secrecy: Leon Modena's Life as an Early Modern Autobiography', in Mark Cohen, trans., *The Autobiography of a Seventeenth-Century Venetian Rabbi: Leon Modena's 'Life of Judah'* (Princeton: Princeton University Press, 1988), pp. 50–70.
46. *JR*, vol. 16: pp. 226–9; Trigger, *Children of Aataentsic*, pp. 58–9, *Natives and Newcomers*, p. 104; Campeau, *Mission Jésuites*, pp. 22–6.
47. Fenton, 'Structure, Continuity, and Change', in Jennings (ed.), *Iroquois Diplomacy*, p. 16; Jennings, *Iroquois Empire*, pp. 34–40; Trigger, *Children of Aataentsic*, pp. 162–3, and Richter, *Ordeal of the Longhouse*, ch. 2. Grumet talks of 'Coastal Algonkian confederacies' in the 'early historic contact period' ('Sunksquaw', p. 47), but he may be referring to alliances rather than federations. White, *The Middle Ground* does not give evidence for Algonquin confederations in the Great Lakes region until the late eighteenth century. Of course, these alliances must also have stimulated diplomatic and oratorical skills.
48. Horatio Hale (ed.), *The Iroquois Book of Rites* (Philadelphia: D. G. Brinton, 1883), ch. 2: 'a historical telling of the founding work of Deganiwidah and Hiawatha,

collected during Hale's visits to the Reserve of the Iroquois nations in the 1870s; pp. 180–3: the stories he collected about the death of Hiawatha's daughter. J. N. B. Hewitt, 'Legend of the Founding of the Iroquois League', *American Anthropologist*, 5 (April 1892): pp. 131–48 (the legend of Deganiwidah, Hiawatha and Thadodaho, collected by Hewitt in 1888). Clark, *Indian Legends*, pp. 138–45; Erdoes and Ortiz, *American Indian Myths and Legends*, pp. 193–9. Fenton, 'Structure, Continuity, and Change', pp. 14–15; J. N. B. Hewitt, 'The Status of Woman in Iroquois Polity before 1784', in *Iroquois Women*, pp. 61–3.

49. Brébeuf in *JR*, vol. 10: pp. 256–7. 'Ils haussent et flechissent la voix comme d'un ton de Predicateur à l'antique'. 'Raise and lower the voice' would seem a better translation than 'raise and quiver the voice', the translation given on p. 257.

50. Champlain, *Works*, vol. 1: p. 110; Sagard, *Grand Voyage*, Part 1, ch. 15, p. 220; and especially Brébeuf in *JR*, vol. 10: pp. 254–63. Le Jeune on the Montagnais, *JR*, vol. 5: pp. 24–5: 'They do not all talk at once, but one after the other, listening patiently'.

51. On mnemonic devices and wampum belts strung by women, see Fenton, 'Structure, Continuity, and Change', pp. 17–18, and Michael K. Foster, 'Another Look at the Function of Wampum in Iroquois-White Councils', in Jennings (ed.), *Iroquois Diplomacy*, pp. 99–114. Captain's tone and walking back and forth: *JR*, vol. 41: pp. 112–13. Cartier, 'Deuxième voyage', p. 132: 'Et commença ledict agoahanna . . . à faire une prédication et preschement à leur modde, en démenant son corps et membres d'une merveilleuse sorte, qui est une sérymonye de joye et asseurance'.

52. Barthélemy Vimont in *JR*, vol. 27: pp. 252–3. Vimont himself was depending on an interpreter for the words, and admitted that he was getting only 'some disconnected fragments' (pp. 264–5).

53. Brébeuf in *JR*, vol. 10: pp. 256–9, 278–9. Fenton, 'Structure, Continuity, and Change', p. 16 and 'Glossary of Figures of Speech in Iroquois Political Rhetoric', in Jennings (ed.), *Iroquois Diplomacy*, pp. 115–24; Petrone, *Native Literature*, pp. 27–8.

54. 'Narrative of the Captivity of Mrs. Mary Rowlandson, 1682', in Charles H. Lincoln (ed.), *Narratives of the Indian Wars, 1675–1699* (New York: Charles Scribner's Sons, 1913), p. 150. It would be interesting to know what speech strategies Weetamoo used when she negotiated her support for King Philip in his war against the English in the 1670s. When a Wyattanon woman spoke to President Washington together with other delegates from Prairie Indian communities in 1793, she did so only because her uncle, Great Joseph, had died and she was representing him. In the transcription made by Thomas Jefferson, she said:

> He who was to have spoken to you is dead, Great Joseph. If he had lived you would have heard a good man, and good words flowing from his mouth. He was my uncle, and it has fallen to me to speak for him. But I am ignorant. Excuse, then, these words, it is but a woman who speaks.

Thomas Jefferson, *The Writings of Thomas Jefferson*, ed. Andrew A. Lipscomb, 20 vols (Washington, DC: Thomas Jefferson Memorial Association, 1903), vol. 16: pp. 386–7.

55. Marie de l'Incarnation to Mother Ursule de Ste Catherine, September 13, 1640, *Correspondance*, no. 50, pp. 117–18. This is the only account we have of the woman's speech; Marie must have heard about it from one of the Jesuits on the Huron mission and, with her characteristic sensitivity to women's words and actions, included it in her letter to the Mother Superior at her former convent at Tours. In the *Relation* of 1640, the Jesuit Superior Jerome Lallemant talks about the conflict about the Jesuits at this same 'conseil general', but does not mention a woman speaker (*JR*, vol. 19: pp. 176–9).

56. 'Hiawatha the Unifier', in Erdoes and Ortiz, *American Indian Myths*, p. 198; Marie de l'Incarnation, *Correspondance*, no. 168, p. 565. Jennings (ed.), *Iroquois*

Diplomacy, pp. 13, 124, 249. 'Speaking through my mouth' is the phrase used by envoys and ambassadors: 'Escoute, Ondessonk, Cinq Nations entieres te parlent par ma bouche' (*JR*, vol. 41: p. 116).

57. *JR*, vol. 5: pp. 180–1; vol. 10: pp. 258–9; vol. 27: pp. 262–3; Sagard, *Grand Voyage*, Part 1, ch. 15, p. 220. Le Jeune also comments on Montagnais reaction to the French talking all at the same time: 'A Sagamore, or Captain, dining in our room one day, wished to say something; and not finding an opportunity, because [we] were all talking at the same time, at last prayed the company to give him a little time to talk in his turn, and all alone, as he did' (*JR*, vol. 5: pp. 24–5).

58 Leonardo Bruni, 'Concerning the Study of Literature, A Letter to . . . Baptista Malatesta', in W. H. Woodward, *Vittorino da Feltre and other Humanist Educators* (Cambridge: Cambridge University Press, 1897; reprinted New York: Teachers College of Columbia University, 1963), p. 126. Margaret L. King, Women of the Renaissance (Chicago: University of Chicago Press, 1991), p. 194. For a few well-born Italian women with training in good letters who managed to give orations, see Margaret L. King and Albert Rabil, Jr, *Her Immaculate Hand. Selected words by and about the Women Humanists of Quattrocento Italy* (Binghamton: Medieval & Renaissance Texts & Studies, 1983), nos. 2, 4, 6, 7. For an overview of queenly strategies, see N. Z. Davis, 'Women in Politics', in Natalie Zemon Davis and Arlette Farge (eds), *A History of Women in the West*, p. 3: *Renaissance and Enlightenment Paradoxes*, (Cambridge, MA.: Harvard University Press, 1993), ch. 6.

59. Phyllis Mack, *Visionary Women: Ecstatic Prophecy in Seventeenth-Century England* (Berkeley: University of California Press, 1992). [Margaret Fell Fox], *Women's Speaking Justified, Proved and Allowed of by the Scriptures* (London, 1666 and 1667). Natalie Zemon Davis, 'City Women and Religious Change', *Society and Culture in Early Modern France* (Stanford: Stanford University Press, 1975), ch. 3. Elizabeth Rapley, *The Dévotes: Women and Church in Seventeenth-Century France* (Montréal and Kingston: McGill-Queen's University Press, 1990). Linda Lierheimer, 'Female Eloquence and Maternal Ministry: The Apostolate of Ursuline Nuns in Seventeenth-Century France' (Ph.D. diss., Princeton University, 1994).

60. *JR*, vol. 43: pp. 288–91.

61. Ann Eastlack Shafer, 'The Status of Iroquois Women' in Spittal (ed.), *Iroquois Women*, p. 108; Tooker, *Ethnography*, p. 91, n. 75. It has been suggested that the False Face society was created among the Iroquois during the 1630s (Trigger, *Natives and Newcomers*, p. 117) and that the Midewiwin society of shamans developed in the central Great Lakes region in the course of the eighteenth century (Phillips, 'Art in Woodlands Life', pp. 64–5). Could one find archeological, visual, or other evidence that would allow one to historicize the relation of Amerindian women to religious action in the healing and other shamanic societies?

62. Marie de l'Incarnation, *Correspondance*, no. 65, pp. 165–6.

63. Marie de l'Incarnation, *Correspondance*, no. 65, pp. 165–9; no. 73, p. 201; no. 97, p. 281; Appendix, no. 9, p. 975; no. 11, p. 977 (letter from Thérèse); no. 18, p. 988, (letter from an Ursuline, almost certainly Marie, to Paul Le Jeune, 1653:

> Nous avons appris que nostre Séminariste Huronne, qui fut prise il y a environ dix ans par les Iroquois, estoit mariée en leur pays; qu'elle estoit la maistresse dans sa cabane, composée de plusieurs familles; qu'elle priot Dieu tous les jours et qu'elle le faisoit prier par d'autres.

Campeau provides the name Khionrea (*La Mission des Jésuites*, p. 86).

64. Juchereau and Duplessis, *Hôtel-Dieu de Québec*, pp. 161–3.

65. Marie de l'Incarnation to Claude Martin, 12 October 1655 in *Correspondance*, no. 168, pp. 565–6. François du Creux, *The History of Canada or New France*, trans. Percy J. Robinson, 2 vols (Toronto: The Champlain Society, 1951–2), vol. 2: pp. 698–700. Du Creux's report was based on the letters sent to him by Marie de

l'Incarnation (referred to in her *Correspondance*, pp. 642, 719), which he simply incorporated into his *Historia canadensis* (Paris: Sébastien Cramoisy, 1664).

66. See the fine discussion of Jacqueline Peterson in her essay 'Women Dreaming: The Religiopsychology of Indian White Marriages and the Rise of Metis Culture', in Lillian Schlissel, Vicki Ruiz and Janice Monk (eds), *Western Women: Their Land, Their Lives* (Albuquerque: University of New Mexico Press, 1988), pp. 49–68. I am treating the relation of Amerindian women to Christianity from other points of view in my chapter on Marie de l'Incarnation in *Women on the Margins* (Cambridge, MA: Harvard University Press, 1995).

67. Cholenec, *Life of Katharine Tegakoüita* in *The Cause for Beatification and Canonization . . . of the Servant of God Katharine Tekakwitha*, pp. 257, 299.

68. *JR*, vol. 10: pp. 286–7. Alexander von Gernet analyzes the evidence for Huron beliefs regarding souls after death and the various ways in which the qualities of the dead could be saved for the living in a remarkable essay, 'Saving the Souls', in Mills and Slobodin (eds), *Amerindian Rebirth*.

69. 'The first wampum (Iroquois and Huron-Wyandot)', in Clark, *Indian Legends*, pp. 55–6 from a story collected by Erminnie A. Smith, in 1883 (pp. 170, 176). Another Iroquois version of the origin of wampum, which also connects it indirectly with feathers and directly with treaty use, in 'Hiawatha and the Wizard (Onondaga)', ibid., pp. 138–41, from a story collected by J. N. B. Hewitt in 1892 (pp. 172, 174). See Hewitt, 'Legend of the Iroquois', pp. 134–5.

70. The twin motif is widely discussed in regard to Indian stories (for example, Erdoes and Ortiz (eds), *American Indian Myths and Legends*, p. 73 ff.) and is the central theme of Lévi-Strauss, *Histoire de lynx*.

71. Brébeuf, *JR*, vol. 19: pp. 126–9. Erdoes and Ortiz discuss the 'fall through a hole' as a motif in *American Indian Myths and Legends*, p. 75, and there are several examples analyzed in Lévi-Strauss, *Histoire de lynx*.

72. Curtin (ed.), *Seneca Indian Myths*, pp. 70–5. Curtin collected myths in the Seneca reservation in Versailles, NY in 1883 as an agent of the Bureau of Ethnology of the Smithsonian Institute (v). Curtin's version given in Clark (ed.), *Indian Legends*, pp. 37–40, and in Susan Feldmann (ed.), *The Story-Telling Stone: Traditional Native American Myths and Tales* (New York: Dell, 1991), pp. 161–6.

2.3

'WHITE WOMEN AND COLONIALISM: TOWARDS A NON-RECUPERATIVE HISTORY'

Jane Haggis

Only in the last few years has the white woman found a voice in colonial histories. Her voice questions the myth of the ignorant, jealous memsahib who turned the happy Arcadia of early race relations into a bitter segregation. However, almost as soon as she spoke up, the white woman has been told to shut up again. She is told that she speaks from a selective memory; she paints her role in colony-making in the most favourable light; and she refuses to understand the deep-seated class and race oppression which characterises all colonies.[1]

In this quotation from a recent article, Chilla Bulbeck encapsulates the tensions currently felt by many feminist historians working in the specialism of gender and imperialism, particularly those who focus on uncovering and understanding the presences and participations of white women in imperial contexts and colonial locations. A number of studies have convincingly challenged the caricature of the white woman as responsible for the segregations and petty bigotries of colonial societies. These have revealed the gender biases of colonial writers such as Kipling, who helped concoct and popularise the stereotype, and the male historians who have built on and continued the memsahib image, charging the white woman with the ruin and loss of empire.[2] However, as Bulbeck's somewhat bitter words indicate, some of these studies have received a sharply critical response from other feminist writers and historians, myself

From: Jane Haggis (1998), 'White Women and Colonialism: Towards a Non-Recuperative History' pp. 45–75, in Clare Midgley (ed.), *Gender and Imperialism* (Manchester: Manchester University Press).

included, who have criticised the new histories for not being new enough, and for continuing the colonising and Eurocentric discourses of mainstream colonial and imperial histories in their narration of white women's stories.[3] In her response, Bulbeck draws on her account of the experiences of expatriate women in Papua New Guinea to charge that such criticisms result from adopting questions 'produced by male colonisers and male colonial historians', in effect importing a 'non-feminist' discourse into feminist history by relegating 'gender' to a subsidiary analytical role.[4]

This sharp exchange of views is informed by a broader debate over the nature of the feminist historical project.[5] Is the task primarily to restore women's presences to the past and the historical account, or is it a broader endeavour to draw on the conceptual absence of women and gender to fundamentally challenge and reinscribe history writing and our accounts of the past? Joan Scott has summarised this wider debate as that between historians of women and historians of gender.[6]

Historians of women take the category of 'women' as their primary conceptual focus and seek to uncover women's 'voices' and 'experiences', placing them within a past presumed knowable and transparently reconstructed in the historian's narrative. Scott identifies several variants within this approach, not all of which see themselves or would be identified as feminist. The feminist variant sees a specific women's history as distinct from and parallel to the men's history of mainstream history, constructing a separate sphere of historical endeavour, distinct in its subject, themes and causal frameworks.

Gender history, in Scott's typology, is influenced by post-structuralist literary theory, and focuses on meaning and discourse rather than experience and voice. The categories 'woman' and 'man' are not viewed as fixed identities or natural entities, but as constructions of gender with variable meanings across culture and time. Gender itself is analytically conceived as an aspect of social organisation constructed through discourses of power and knowledge which ascribe historically and culturally contingent meanings to sexual difference. Within this schema, the gender historian's praxis is a reflexive art of constructing narratives which are relative, partial and fundamentally contemporary in their resonance. Thus, bringing gender (and women) into historical narrative involves challenging the taken-for-granted assumptions of positivist history, going beyond a recuperative exercise to embrace a new theoretical and methodological agenda for the writing of history, an agenda overtly political in its feminist intent to make explicit, and to challenge, the 'ways in which hierarchies of differences – inclusions and exclusions – have been constituted'.[7]

For many women's history practitioners, Scott's agenda is threatening to, rather than enabling of, a specific feminist history. A focus on a relativist conception of gender, fractured by multiple aspects of difference, seems to erode the visibility of women as specific historical agents just as their presence is being written into our accounts of the past. A core tenet of feminism – the historic and continuing subjugation of women by a dominant patriarchy – appears undermined, even dismissed, when attention is focused on other relations of power, such as class and race, which undercut the commonality of women's subordination. As Stanley and Birkett and Wheelwright comment, the awareness of women's absence from the historical stage has often fuelled a desire to find 'the perfect feminist heroines for us to admire, feel close to, inspired by and even imitate'[8] and encouraged a tendency to 'romanticise'[9] or explain away 'unpalatable facts'.[10] Birkett and Wheelwright suggest that the way to guard against such dangers is to allow 'these historical figures to live within their context' rather than '[t]o rewrite history to conform more exactly with current received notions'.[11] From this perspective, then, concerns of the present should not impinge on the recovery of the past. Issues of difference which might fracture or question the restoration of women to the historical account can thus be seen as contemporary distractions, their place in history writing limited to a contextual preamble for today's readership rather than as thematic aspects of the past, integral to the historical narrative. Such a view of the feminist historical project, however, has some problematic implications when applied to the history of empire.

The recuperative drive to place women in the history of colonialism and imperialism takes the texts and reminiscences of white women as literal accounts of their experiences, authentic and significant in their meaning – a meaning directly available to the historian and providing a readily comprehensible and valid, if partial, account of the past. Retrieving the voice and experience of white women in colonial settings, these histories place it alongside the existing 'male' narrative as an autonomous account of the past, while the histories of the colonised – male and female – are presumed to be another, different project, by implication awaiting the attentions of 'native' historians themselves.

A kind of pluralism is implicit in this approach. 'History' consists of a series of distinct strands, each largely independent of each other. The respective accounts are given their priority by the historians, from their defined historical goals. Thus, to paraphrase Bulbeck, for a feminist historian of white women (as against a male or 'third world' one) the task is to privilege gender, understood as the voice of the white female subject, as the primary analytical perspective. The singular perspective of the white woman and her prior exclusion from the existing male account becomes the connection between the different strands: the white woman's authenticity is confirmed by her taken-for-granted status as subordinate to, indeed outside of, the male-defined world of colonialism.

This exteriority, buttressed by an unexamined assumption of a shared woman-ness with her colonised counterparts, permits a double recuperation of the white woman. She is restored to the account of the past in her own authenticity, refuting a male-constructed invisibility and presumed irrelevance, while giving the lie to the fitful male inclusion of the negative memsahib. The white woman, by her own account, is rendered irresponsible, a victim of the white male colonising adventure, who, through this exclusion, is uniquely positioned, nevertheless, to forge a different, more benevolent, colonial relation with her 'native' sisters in the interstices of the masculine project, by virtue of her shared experience of being a woman in a male world. Where such benevolence and positive interaction is not borne out in the words and actions of the white woman, it is, again, not her responsibility, but a logical outcome of the constraints of the roles accorded her in a patriarchal world – a world where the clash between being a good mother and a dutiful wife in the midst of the masculine adventure of the colonial frontier led many women to negative appraisals of their colonial surroundings and an understandable desire to isolate themselves and their children from the dangers of an alien and 'uncivilised' environment.[12]

I have pointed out elsewhere how such recuperative histories of white women risk colonising gender for white men and women rather than gendering colonialism as a historical process.[13] Centring a singular female subjectivity fosters an inability to deal with the power relations of colonialism, privileging the White Woman as benevolent victim of the imperialist White Man. The colonised are relegated to an ungendered background against which the white genders act out their historical roles. Race, class and the asymmetry of colonial domination cannot be addressed without risking the fragmentation of the subject 'woman'. Bulbeck's assertion that these other dimensions of power are 'non-feminist' discourses, external to a cohesive category of gender, ignores the subtleties of colonial social relations, reducing the ambivalences of the peculiar location of white women in the colonial hierarchy, where, 'although race and class might intersect to accumulate her power, her sex did not'.[14] Focusing on gender to the exclusion of race or class does little to capture the nature of relations between women across the colonial divide, while white women's own historical agency is limited by her all-encompassing status as patriarchal victim.

Segregating gender and race as either/or categories ignores the ways in which the two aspects of social organisation are imbricated with each other. Framed as a dichotomy, an implicit ranking exercise is imposed on the analysis such that one or other of the two categories must be prioritised in any given context. A reductionism results, whereby gender is captured only in the veracity accorded white women's voice and experience. Race is reduced to behaviour and the accusatory issue of whether the historical subjects were guilty of racism or not. Hence Bulbeck's response to the critics of the new histories of white women is to charge them with silencing her historical subjects. The dualism informing her recuperative model provides only two positions for the white woman to assume in the feminist historical record: a vocality likely to leave her vulnerable to a new version of the negative stereotypes of mainstream, male, history, or a guilty silence, repentant in its compliance with the norms of a contemporary feminist political correctness.

Presenting the voices of white women in a singular authenticity reduces the historical narrative to a series of parallel tracks essentially unrelated to each other. In an attempt to retheorise the politics of difference in women's history away from such a recuperative framework, Elsa Barkley Brown uses a musical analogy particularly apt in capturing the dilemmas of writing a history of white women and colonisation. She contrasts the 'classical score' of much Western knowledge, which demands 'surrounding silence – of the audience, of all the instruments not singled out as the performers in this section',[15] with the 'gumbo ya-ya' of African-Americans' ways of conversing and recounting their stories to each other: 'They do this simultaneously because, in fact, their histories are joined – occurring simultaneously, in connection, in dialogue with each other. To relate their tales separately would be to obliterate that connection.'[16] Instead of a classical singularity the 'gumbo ya-ya' echoes the democratic individualism of Afro-American jazz music – 'the various voices in a piece of music may go their own ways but still be held together by their relationship to each other'.[17] Thus, history becomes, by analogy, expressive of difference and interrelatedness, 'everybody talking at once, multiple rhythms being played simultaneously',[18] but held together, in a particular narrative, by the explicit awareness of inter-relatedness.

This awareness of inter-relatedness is crucial in going beyond paying lip service to difference within feminist discourses, where, as Barkley Brown observes, the tendency is either to acknowledge differences between women and then proceed to ignore them, or to see differences as pertaining to 'otherness' such that – to take white women and colonialism – race is something pertaining to colonised people and not an inherent part of the identity of the white woman (despite the racial marker of colour identifying her specificity).[19] Difference thus remains a mark of deviance from the norm, rather than a concept disrupting the complacent authority of the dominant discursive presence.

Writing a feminist history of white women and colonialism sensitive to issues of difference involves more than capturing the complex qualities of hierarchy embedded in past narratives. As Spivak and Said have demonstrated, even where texts of the past are not overtly about empire, the power dynamics of imperialism form an underlying structure of reference, forming an essential, taken-for-granted part of the fabric of metropolitan life and its imaginative representations.[20] Any non-recuperative history of white women and colonialism must also engage with the hierarchies of the present or risk producing a discourse which, as post-colonial critics of contemporary Western academic discourses have revealed, continues colonising the non-Western 'other' even where the express intention is to challenge such oppressions and exploitations.[21]

Such arguments indicate the dual nature of the problems raised in writing feminist histories of colonialism and imperialism. On the one hand there are the issues associated with how to deal with the remnants and records of the past, in their incompleteness and partialities, and on the other are the related issues of writing history in a late-twentieth-century context of post-coloniality. How does one try to write a non-recuperative history that confronts the contemporary challenges of acknowledging difference and attempts to construct a 'gumbo ya-ya' of gender and imperialism while nevertheless trying to avoid the problem identified by Birkett and Wheelwright, of rewriting history to conform to the present rather than the past? In the remainder of this chapter I want to draw on my own experiences of researching and writing about British women missionaries in South India during the nineteenth century to suggest the kinds of issues and strategies which might form part of such an endeavour.

As yet no comprehensive history of women's involvements in the British foreign missionary movement that emerged out of the evangelical revival of the late eighteenth century has been written. Drawing on the work done by feminist and other historians on American missionary women,[22] I was interested in exploring the British context to see how missionary women were located as actors within both the metropolitan gender order and the arena of empire and colonialism and what the connections were between the two. Based on a study of the publications and archival records of the major British Protestant missionary societies active in India during the nineteenth century, I undertook a detailed investigation of one such society, the London Missionary Society (LMS). Drawing on the official archive of the LMS, I traced the involvement of women in the Society from the national organisation in Britain through to the workings of a particular mission district, South Travancore, in South India.[23] Writing this history in a way which addresses both the integrity of the past as it emerges from a partial and incomplete historical record, and my contemporary awareness of the feminist and post-colonial politics of difference has involved questions of power, authority and voice. At least three histories are imbricated in this particular process of history writing: my story of gender and imperialism; the missionaries' account of their endeavours; and the story of Indian women. In the remainder of this chapter I make explicit the discursive procedure by which I brought these three histories into an uneasy and unequal relationship in an attempt to write a feminist, post-colonial history of British women missionaries.

LABOURS OF LOVE

Though missionary work was originally conceived of as purely a male endeavour, by 1899 it was estimated that women missionaries outnumbered men in the 'foreign field' by over a thousand.[24] This numerical ascendancy reflected the recruitment of single women as missionaries by the major missionary societies during the last three decades of the century. One writer calculated that in 1879 there were no more than 400 single women serving in the entire foreign mission field (covering the Protestant missions from Britain, the USA and Europe),[25] yet in the seven years 1887–1894, the Church Missionary Society alone sent 214 women overseas as 'lady missionaries'.[26]

This chronology of the feminisation of the missionary endeavour parallels that trajectory revealed by historians looking at middle-class women's entry into formal education and paid employment in the second half of the nineteenth century – a trajection intimately caught in the emergence of Victorian feminism as an initiator of and vocal participant in a rapidly changing social context. The single lady missionary, as she was known, assumes a position analogous to that of her sisters entering the sphere of paid employment as office workers, teachers, nurses and even medical doctors,[27] forming part of that shift feminist historians have charted 'out of the garden, out of idleness, out of ignorance, and into wisdom, service and adventure',[28] leaving behind 'the confining domestic world of married women'.[29]

However, a closer inspection of the missionary archive reveals a more nuanced, more subtle and lengthier process of female involvement in the missionary movement. This was an agency that turned less on the activism of single women in breaching the walls of a patriarchal domesticity, than on the efforts of missionary wives to carve out a separate sphere of 'women's work', as it was called, within the boundaries of conventional ideologies of gender. It was this women's work, initiated, developed and promoted by the wives of missionaries, which instigated the recruitment of single women, eventually in numbers sufficient to displace the male missionary's numerical ascendancy. As Davidoff and Hall have noted, there was a degree of ambiguity in evangelical notions of appropriate male and female roles: '[b]etween the recognition of influence and the marking out of a female sphere there was contested ground'.[30] It was precisely this 'contested ground' upon which women argued for their inclusion within the missionary movement. As one anonymous woman wrote in 1797, 'Why are females alone excluded from . . . these labours of love? . . . Nor let it be argued that their own familiar and domestic concerns afford the only sphere of their exertions. Here, indeed they ought undoubtedly to begin, but they are not called upon to stop there.'[31]

Her plea was a response to the exclusion of women from membership of the new societies. Women's role was to be limited to being 'the Mothers of the Missionaries', as one sermon put it.[32] However, by the 1820s missionary wives, most notably in India, were pushing the boundaries of female involvement well beyond the role of mother, carving out a separate sphere of women's work in female education. Wherever there was a missionary wife a school for girls was established.[33] To a degree the activism of missionary wives was appropriate to their role within the missionary marriage – a role the husband, wife and missionary society assumed would extend beyond that of simply intimate companion and domestic keeper to their spouse.[34] However, the endorsement by the missionary societies stopped short of according a separate status to wives' efforts at missionary work. Their labours were assumed to be part of their husbands' work and, as such had no claim on the funds and resources raised for missionary work, understood as the work of the ordained in converting men.

In a way, a division of labour emerged in the field which the ideology of the missionary marriage as a single labour did not acknowledge. It was against this background that the need for female education began to be articulated by wives and their supporters as a distinct aspect of the mission – as an appeal for funds, supporters and workers over and above those being devoted to the labours of the (male) missionaries, and outside the official concerns of the missionary societies. With no direct claims on society funds, wives established their own links to sources of material support amongst their friends and sympathisers in Britain and India.

This separate sphere of female endeavour assumed distinctive organisational form in 1834 with the founding of the Society for the Propagation of Female Education in the East (SPFEE) in London, which had the aim of supporting the efforts of wives both financially and by recruiting single women as teachers to go to India and other fields to further female education. It was the first systematic British initiative to send single women abroad as part of the general missionary endeavour. The justification for such an innovation was argued on the grounds of the 'Asiatic' practice of secluding women, which meant only 'ladies' had any chance of 'being welcomed to their seclusion, and can win upon their confiding affection'.[35] Without this specific female effort, moreover, 'the great work' of 'our revered fathers and brethren' to evangelise the world would be at risk: 'What help would a young Christian receive from an ignorant, idolatrous wife?'[36] The aim of female education was thus to produce the good wives and mothers deemed essential if the converts of the male missionaries were to establish solid Christian families and communities as the critical bulwark against 'heathenism'.

The idea of sending single women out as teachers to the 'East' does not seem to have come as a shock or generated much opposition,[37] in part because the groundwork had already been laid. The work of wives in the mission field had developed and fleshed out the need of a separate sphere of women's work, while married and single women were continuing to expand and organise their religious philanthropy in Britain.[38] Evangelical doctrine and the Woman Question were coming together in new formulations of the most appropriate roles for women and men, which, even at their most prescriptive, condoned an active Christian engagement for women that could extend well beyond the home.

Another reason for the acceptance of the initiative to send single women abroad also seems to lie in the ideology of separate spheres which informed the establishment of the SPFEE and the way it went about its purpose. The historian of the SPFEE explained the reasons behind the Society's formation thus: 'as a Committee of gentlemen would be manifestly incompetent to select [female teachers] and superintend their preparatory training, it followed of course that a Ladies Society could alone meet the emergency. Their discernment and discrimination are thus most usefully brought to bear upon a matter of serious responsibility.' Even if the existing missionary societies were prepared to finance and manage the endeavour 'it would still be advisable to adopt the principle . . . of a division of labour with a specific female society'.[39]

The missionary societies were not prepared to take the responsibility anyway. Missionary wives had petitioned the societies to sponsor single women teachers but, while the need was acknowledged, propriety prevented any action.[40]

The SPFEE dealt with such issues in several ways. Candidates for 'lady teachers' were carefully vetted in an exhaustive selection process which placed considerable emphasis on character as well as education and training.[41] The Society was also careful to act, and be seen to act, as a facilitator rather than an initiator of women's work, limiting itself to responding to requests from wives in the field rather than instituting new arenas of work. Its teachers were represented as helpers to missionary wives rather than as autonomous workers. To the SPFEE and its supporters, if single women could be attached in some way, their presence in the foreign field was less contentious or open to the husband-hunting charge.[42] The link with the missionary couple served as a respectable alternative to fatherly or brotherly protection. At the same time, however the missionary wives, the Society and their supporters made a virtue of the unmarried state. Only single women were able to bring to bear the 'distinct agency' capable of carrying the work forward. In the words of the Society's historian: '[T]he great design of the Society is to maintain a distinct agency for a specific purpose, which shall be undistracted by relative interests, and at full liberty to devote its whole time and its undivided energy to the work assigned it.'[43] Thus by 1847 the SPFEE had sent out fifty single women as teachers to India, Africa and Southeast Asia, and associated organisations had been established in Scotland, Basle, Geneva and Berlin, while in England Committee members 'wrote letters, and encouraged candidates, . . . took some journeys . . . held drawing-room meetings, and formed associations in aid of the Society'.[44] Women in the mission field had established a separate organisation for the conduct of a female mission – the women's work of educating the female 'heathen'. The ambiguities between wife and lady worker were resolved by portraying the missionary wife as the critical grass-roots actor, defining, initiating and overseeing the work, thus conforming to the proprieties of gender. This portrayal was predicated on the existence of women's work as a separate sphere of organisation and endeavour which allowed the female agency, married or single, to operate outside the immediate structures of a masculine world.

By the 1870s, however, the role of the SPFEE in providing an organisational form for 'women's work' in the foreign field was largely redundant as the major missionary societies moved to recruit single women as foreign missionaries. The directors of the LMS announced their decision in 1875, giving a range of reasons, including a huge expansion of openings for work with women in 'the East' beyond the scope of missionary wives to fill; the increasing availability of suitable lady candidates; and the willingness of the public at home to finance such an effort.[45] The directors' resolutions reflect profound social changes occurring during this period both at home and in India, particularly the circumstances of British middle-class women, often lacking the support, fiscal and otherwise, of husband, father or brother presumed in the Victorian gender ideology of domesticity and the 'angel in the house'. In India, the assumption of direct imperial authority by the Crown in 1857 provided the missionary movement with a more secure and legitimate base for their endeavours, endeavours which elicited a somewhat unexpected and often disconcerting response, as whole communities of low caste people converted *en masse* to Christianity, particularly in South India. To the chagrin of many in the missionary movement, access to, influence over and conversion of the upper caste elites of India remained frustratingly limited. It was these poor and lowly converts who made up the bulk of the pupils in the schools run by missionary wives and the lady teachers recruited by the SPFEE. During the 1860s, however, a new agency was developed by missionary women – *zenana* visitation – intended to side-step the strictures of seclusion and caste which often prevented easy contact with high caste women, by taking Christian teaching and influence into any high caste homes they could gain access to. Thus by the 1870s new demands were being placed on women's work in terms of finance, organisation and personnel, while the relative success of *zenana* visitation in gaining access to, if not converts from, upper caste homes, and the need to 'civilise' the masses of low caste converts, brought women's work more centrally into the concerns of the mainstream missionary societies. It was now no longer seen as a useful adjunct to the main mission of converting men, but rather as a potentially powerful way to achieve precisely that end.

The recruitment of single women as lady missionaries by the major missionary societies marked the beginning of a process of incorporation and professionalisation of women's work. It signals a shift in gender protocols as single women no longer risked breaking the 'proprieties' by being cast, and casting themselves, as active agents and initiators in missionary work. There is more than a tinge of irony in this shift, however, as missionary wives, in a reversal of the earlier imagery and role, are increasingly portrayed as helpers to the lady missionaries. However, the separate sphere of women's work was not immediately dismantled with the shift into the mainstream, but was initially reconstituted within the boundaries of the male society.

In the LMS the 1875 decision to recruit women as missionaries involved the setting up of a Ladies Committee of well-known women drawn from the Congregational circles from which the LMS drew its closest supporters and affiliations. The Committee was to oversee all aspects of women's work, including fund-raising, recruitment and training of suitable candidates, and all matters pertaining to the employment of lady missionaries in the field.[46] This organisational form for women's work continued until 1890, when the Ladies Committee threatened to break with the Society and form an independent *zenana* society if it was not accorded representation on the board.[47] The board responded to this demand without much ado, reconstituting the Committee as the Ladies Examination Committee, which, unlike its predecessor, was formally integrated into the structure of the Society as one of seven Standing Committees, another of which was the Male Examination Committee, with its nine female members given seats on the Board of Directors.

While this reorganisation satisfied the demand for representation, the new committee was only a shadow of its former self, responsible only for the examination and selection of lady candidates, while its proceedings were now conducted by the Home Secretary of the LMS. All other issues to do with lady missionaries and women's work were now dealt with in the same organisational manner and structure as the work and employment of male missionaries.[48] The separate sphere of women's work appears to have been dissolved into the general mission, except in terms of a narrow division of labour and mark of difference between male and female candidates. In 1907 the male and ladies committees were amalgamated into a single Examination Committee, completing the image of incorporation.

The period during which the Ladies Committee was responsible for the application and selection process of lady missionaries, from 1875 to 1890, negotiates the transition and transformation of women's work from a labour of love carried out by missionary wives on the basis of their influence as 'good Christian women' to a professional and paid employment of single women, predicated as much on education and training as it was on Christian and feminine influence. The minute books and other records of the Ladies Committee depict a kind of balancing act in the application and selection process established for the post of lady missionary. On the one hand, the Committee maintained determined and exhaustive expectations of education and training, formal and vocational, for the work, a work now extending beyond teaching to embrace nursing, medicine and industrial work (the term used for the embroidery, lace and other money-making ventures which were set up to train and employ poor low caste women in 'respectable' occupations while at the same time generating useful funds for the work). On the other hand, the Committee was rigorous in ascertaining that the quality of being a 'lady' pertained to all candidates deemed suitable, regardless of an individual's otherwise exemplary training, experience, religiosity and sense of mission.

Being a lady meant demonstrating the qualities of respectable femininity – culture, civility and manners – in the milieu of the home (usually by invitation to tea at a Committee member's house), qualities deemed intrinsic to the exercise of that specifically female influence women's work was predicated upon.[49] The image of the true lady not only negotiated the complexities of class; it also ensured that the lady missionary, despite all the emphasis on training, experience and work, remained cast within a rubric of femininity rooted in the ideology of the private sphere of domesticity where home was the heart of culture and the powerful underpinning of female influence. Thus the proprieties of gender were still at work, interlaced with class, in constituting the lady missionary, although in a somewhat different configuration from those the SPFEE negotiated in the 1840s and 1850s. In the missionary archive and literature this transformation is articulated and accorded a legitimacy through the discursive construction of a 'mission of sisterhood', a process I explore below. For now, I want to briefly turn to the conduct of women's work in the field, where gender and class are reworked in a colonial patterning of this process of professionalisation.

I have argued in this section that over the course of the nineteenth century women's work shifted from being a labour of love carried out by missionary wives to a professional employment for single female missionaries. However, the impact of this shift on the ways in which women's work was actually conducted in the mission field was minimal. In effect, the lady missionary largely continued the pattern of work already established by wives in the preceding decades. The primary role undertaken by both wives and lady missionaries in the field was that of superintendence of the work, their responsibilities and activism portrayed as organisational and inspirational, as they managed and supervised a work largely carried out by a labour force of Indian Christian women, overwhelmingly drawn from the ranks of the lowest communities in the Indian caste hierarchy. It was these women who, by the last quarter of the century, actually did most of the teaching, nursing and training being carried out under the rubric of women's work.[50]

Ironically, whereas the single lady missionary was displacing the missionary wife as the principal actor, these Indian Christian women were overwhelmingly married or widowed, many apparently with dependent children still requiring care.[51] Another irony lay in the fact that it was primarily their credentials as 'good Christian women' which first accorded evangelical women, as wives of missionaries, the sense of mission and influence which instigated a specific female sphere of women's work in the mission field. It was this same essence of good woman that the single woman had to retain as lady in order to be considered effective as a missionary, her influence of superior Christian womanhood thus assured. This essence of goodness was closely connected, as I stated earlier, to the idealised versions of femininity dominant in Victorian gender ideologies, which connected the good woman so closely with home and hearth. The inversions threatened in the missionary wives' activisms and the lady missionaries' flight from home are contained by the religious rubric: a call from, and service to, God. Yet in their efforts at women's work, to produce 'good Christian wives and mothers', it is the Bible women who are actually produced, as working women earning a wage, not evangelical philanthropists – more in the image of the lady missionary than the domestic ideal of the angel in the house. At the same time, the very appellation 'Bible women' denotes the ways in which discourses of class and race as well as gender intersect the relational configurations of women's work in the field. However much the Bible women of South India come to resemble the lady missionary in qualification, effort and dedication, they are never accorded the title 'lady' while their attributes as teachers, trainers, evangelists or nurses are always prefaced by the qualifying 'native'.[52] 'Lady', as a designation of Indian femininity, is reserved for the upper caste women of the *zenanas*, although even their assumed superior class qualities remain confined by the racial signifier – as 'native ladies'.

The history I have recounted here documents how women's work in the mission field shifted in meaning and identity from being a service and duty carried out largely by the wives of male missionaries, to an occupation and relation of employment conducted by single missionary women by the turn of the century. In effect, I document another aspect of the emancipation of Victorian single middle-class women from the bounds of domesticity and economic dependency on men – one that demonstrates a broader and more ambiguous chronology of female agency and escape 'out of the garden' than that charted in the available feminist historiography of middle-class women's entry into the world of education, employment and profession. Moreover, the lady missionary negotiates her way out of the garden along a path of convention rather than a path of rebellion, as a religious rubric couches the aspirations of the missionary women in an idiom compatible with the conventionalities of Victorian ideals of gender. It is moreover, a path firmly caught within the intricate web of race, class and gender that underpinned the age of empire. This is a very different story from that depicted in the missionary texts themselves. In the following section I will briefly outline their portrayal of women's work, before returning to the methodological issues of power and authority raised in the initial part of the chapter.

THE MISSION OF SISTERHOOD

The missionary movement in Britain was prolific in its production of texts to advertise, promote and celebrate its efforts. A vast publishing effort, of books, tracts and periodicals ranging from serious treatises on the theological basis of the mission impulse through to Sunday school texts for children, has, along with the extensive archival collections, left a rich source for the historian trying to track the movement and its understandings of itself. A significant subsection of this textual record was devoted specifically to proselytising and recording the needs, activities and achievements of women's work. Taken together, the missionary literature evinces a remarkable degree of consistency in its portrayal of the work over the course of the century.

In the missionary text a mission of sisterhood was constructed, in which British women were cast as the saviours of Indian women, liberating them from the degradation of a vindictive Hindu culture and religion. As one missionary wife put it: 'The daughters of India are unwelcomed at their birth, untaught in childhood, enslaved when married, accursed as widows, and unlamented at their death.'[53] Indian women were portrayed as innocent and passive victims of a merciless system which used and abused them as daughters and as wives. In contrast, British women are portrayed as having the virtues and responsibilities of their free-born and independent situation. Not for them the walls of a domestic prison; rather they are portrayed as intelligent, respected agents in their own right, as well as help-meets in male endeavours, secure in their own sphere of usefulness and purpose: women's work. It is in the setting up of this opposition of stereotypes that the 'mission' of English women to their Indian counterparts is constructed, and in emotional, graphic language they are urged to respond: 'Hear the wail of India's women! Millions, millions, to us cry, They to us for aid appealing . . . "Come to us!" with hands uplifted and with streaming eyes they plead.'[54]

These two contrasting stereotypes – the passive, pitiable Indian woman and the active, independent British lady missionary – were nevertheless brought together in a very close relation indeed. For it is as sisters that British ladies are urged to respond to India's call. The argument as to why British women should assume responsibility for this mission of enlightenment and rescue to Indian women started from a common basis. Both Indian and British women, by virtue of being women, are seen alike as innately religious, spiritual and moral, in ways that men (by implication and regardless of race) are not. However, at the same time as sisterhood is constructed on a shared womanly identity, a set of differences around axes of class, religion and race-nation were drawn, which break down this assumed identity into constituent parts, in keeping with the dichotomised stereotypes described above. British ladies were also accorded a superior gendered authority, as better women. The endeavour women mission-aries are involved in becomes not one simply to convert, educate or enlighten, but to impose/introduce a very specific set of gender roles and models belong-ing to Victorian middle-class culture. In the specific milieu of South India this meant transforming Indian women into good wives and mothers as well as active Christian workers, much in the image of their missionary teachers.

This ambition was reinforced by the explicit linkage made between the relig-ious aims of the missionary movement and British imperial rule: 'This great empire has . . . been delivered into our hands . . . not, surely to gratify us, but to use our influence in elevating and enlightening the vast myriads of her people.'[55] In particular, 'It is to alleviate that misery as God may enable us and bless our efforts, and to deliver our sisters out of it, that we English women are called and selected in the providence of God – a wondrous honour [and] responsibility of the deepest solemnity.'[56]

PROBLEMS OF REPRESENTATION

The portrayal of this mission of sisterhood in the missionary texts confronted me with a number of dilemmas over issues of representation and discursive practice. Put simply, I did not believe the missionary account of women's work in the mission field. From the perspective of feminist history, Victorian women are not seen as liberated and free, but constrained by the boundaries of a patri-archal gender order. Also, to the contemporary eye of someone in the 1990s, the colonising and imperialist nature of the missionary discourse and construc-tion of the mission of sisterhood is obvious, particularly in the stereotype of the *zenana* victim. Both contemporary stances thus question the emancipation offered to Indian women by the claim of sisterhood and the energies of women's work in the mission field.

One way of dealing with my disbelief would be to dismiss the missionary view, deconstructing the mission of sisterhood as a colonising artifice. This would reveal the missionary women as racist agents of an imperial state. At the same time, they would appear as gullible victims of a patriarchal fiction, with a false consciousness of themselves as free women, flying in the face of the historical 'fact' of their subordinate and unfree status in the Victorian social order. But where would this leave their representations of Indian women as pitiful victims of a domesticity cruel and relentless in its captivity? Not to say of Indian culture at large. By dismissing the mission of sisterhood did I leave their depiction of India intact?

The problem was exaggerated by the limits of the historical sources I had to rely upon. As yet no substantive history of Indian women or gender transformation in South India exists and documentary resources are few. The chronicle of the missionary texts was the primary available story of the missionary endeavours in the indigenous locale. In these texts Indian voices, male or female, were few and embedded within the missionary narrative. There was no easily available Indian story to replace or set against the mission of sisterhood.

Moreover, I had a growing respect for the integrity of my historical subjects – the missionary women – and the sense they clearly made of their world. This was a sense which often challenged the stereotypes I held of them as subordinate to Victorian patriarchy. Yet I was unwilling to accept or simply re-present their views of themselves and their Indian sisters. My dilemma was threefold. While I sought to present the authenticity of the past, I also felt compelled to respect my own scepticism, a scepticism which rested on my secular location in the post-colonial world of the late twentieth century. I sought to address, with some degree of equivalence, three distinct interests: my subjects – the missionaries; their Indian subjects; and my own purpose: a feminist post-colonial history.

Facts and fictions

In seeking a way to address these three interests I have drawn on the work of Hayden White, Talal Asad and Edward Said. Influenced by post-structuralist and post-colonial critical theory, these three writers treat with issues of authority, power and voice in ways which usefully extend the feminist critiques of recuperative history discussed at the outset of this chapter. By developing the notion of translation variously addressed by White, Asad and Said, I am able to construct a discursive framework for writing my history.

In *Tropics of Discourse* White has argued that, put simply, there is no 'real' history of events beyond the historian's text – no 'true story' that historians discern – to uncover 'what must have been'. Rather, White argues, the historian translates facts into 'fictions' – culturally familiar story forms, thus rendering the strange and exotic past comprehensible to the contemporary reader. Even these 'facts', the grounding of the historian's translation, are not to be treated as given, but as *constructed* 'by the kinds of questions which the investigator asks of the phenomena'.[57] In White's analysis, therefore, the 'single correct view' is replaced by 'many correct views'. The basis of judgement is no longer that of correspondence to 'fact' but effective choice of metaphor and mode of representation.

There is a seductive quality about White's analysis, offering, as it seems to do, the individual writer of history a free choice (within the bounds of culture) to 'translate' and 'encode' her/his 'fiction'. But doubts persist. If history as knowing the past becomes a series of culturally specific but varied stories from the present, all equally true as representations and translations of historical remnants, what are the implications for feminist and post-colonial histories? To be one among a plurality of true stories might take more than it seems to give. Are all interpretations, regardless of form, accorded equivalent authority as true stories? The effects of White's dismantling of a positivist singularity risks flattening out 'history'. If there is no one 'true story' neither is there, it seems, any disparity between them in effect or authority; all are portrayed as equally recognised and available as a construction of the past.

Social anthropologists, from whom White borrows his methodological model, have, however, begun to cast a critical eye over the notion of 'translation' in ways which challenge White's straightforward co-option of the term for historical method. Talal Asad has argued that 'the process of cultural "translation" is inevitably enmeshed in conditions of power – professional, national, international'.[58] Within anthropology, Asad argues, the method of translation is based on the privilege accorded the anthropologist to ascertain the real meaning of what his informants say. The ethnographer becomes author, not translator, a displacement of authority which takes particular effect in the institutional context of the anthropological exercise. The 'real' meaning discerned by the anthropologist is not simply an alternative or parallel text to that produced by its ethnographic subjects. Rather the anthropologist's translation is accorded a privileged authority which threatens to undermine the self-knowledge of her/his informants, given the global circumstances of its production. At no stage of the translation process does a dialogical relationship exist between the two sets of meanings: '[I]n the long run . . . it is not the personal authority of the ethnographer, but the social authority of his ethnography that matters. And that authority is inscribed in the institutionalised forces of industrial capitalist society which are constantly *tending* to push the meanings of various Third World countries in a single direction.'[59]

Asad's critique of anthropological translations raises a number of points relevant to White's historical method. Clearly, the historian can never hope to construct a dialogue between her/his 'translation' and an authentic original – they (usually) being dead and we dealing with textual remnants. This does not, however, exonerate historians from dealing with the issues of power and authority Asad raises.

White's identification of the multiple meanings and fictional nature of historical narrative and method fails to acknowledge precisely the wider contexts within which the historian's story takes effect. His critique appears to be addressed primarily to fellow practitioners of history in contemporary North America and Europe. Revealing the fictional qualities of their discourse does not dislodge the authoritative status accorded their texts by the broader society – as history it is *their* stories which inscribe meaning in the past as part of the metropolitan canon of knowing its others. Even within the academy, the struggles for recognition fought by those writing histories from the perspective of a subordinate gender, class or race demonstrate the different authority lent some stories over others. No less than the anthropologist's ethnography, the historian's history is a powerful invention beyond any aspirations of the author her/himself.

It is not only the worldliness of the historian's discursive products that White fails to address, but also that of the historical texts which form the basis of his/her translations. White rightly challenges the positivist claim to discern a real history beyond the limits of the textual evidence, a claim similar to the anthropologist's search for an implicit meaning in its assumption of objective perspicacity. In the process, however, he conceives of the historical text as a disembodied entity whose potential meanings are entirely constructed by the reader/historian. White's historical methodology therefore obtains a doubly fictive character, the historian as translator effectively mediating between two free-floating texts anchored only by the disciplinary location of their author.

Edward Said, however, cogently argues that this fails to acknowledge that: '[T]exts are worldly, to some degree they are events, . . . a part of the social world, human life, and of course the historical moments in which they are located and interpreted.'[60] Taking as his example Macaulay's Minute of 1835 on Indian education and the English language, Said argues that the text cannot be viewed as an opinion of Macaulay's nor as simply an instance of ethnocentrism: 'For it is that and more. Macaulay's was an ethnocentric opinion with ascertainable results. He was speaking from a position of power where he could translate his opinions into the decision to make an entire subcontinent of natives submit to studying in a language not their own.'[61] Macaulay's Minute does not simply form part of a powerful administrative nexus however. It is representative of nineteenth-century thought more generally. As Said points out, no European writer, however critical of the status quo, could avoid, at that time, expressing a hierarchy which positioned themselves 'above' and 'interior' to those others 'below' and 'exterior'.[62] It was the discourse providing the culturally available means of ordering and representing their thought. More than this, in a context of European imperialism and colonial domination, the nineteenth-century corpus contributed to a powerful cultural hegemony which effectively imposed this discourse on colonised societies to the extent that even oppositional anti-colonial thought could be caught within the parameters of this Eurocentric discourse.[63]

Said's intervention complicates rather than denies White's claim that there is no historical reality beyond the text for the historian to discern. Acknowledging the worldly nature of a historical document does not overcome the distance of the past, or facilitate some kind of authentic reconstruction of what it must have been. What it does, surely, is to provide a potential limitation on the historian's choice of enplotment for her/his translated narrative. To continue Said's nineteenth-century example, failure to take into account the imperialist discourse within which such texts were constructed risks re-presenting material whose complicity in past relations of domination assumes a contemporary relevance in the global context of Western economic and political domination, precisely the warning Asad directs to social anthropologists.

Such an awareness is, of course, thoroughly contemporary to the 1990s. In this sense, White's depiction of historical writing as fictional remains an accurate and important qualifier to the issues of power and meaning raised by Asad and Said. The ability to problematise the hierarchies of race and culture present in Macaulay's text is a consequence of late-twentieth-century sensibilities and politics reinforced by a particular knowledge of the consequences his Minute helped engender. To explicate Macaulay's words from such a position is to create a 'fiction' in terms of any relationship to the original meanings the Minute might have held for its author or those implicated in its application, while establishing a truism for the contemporary readership.

So where does this leave me and my writing of the mission of sisterhood? The comparative frame I bring White, Asad and Said within provides me with a discursive methodology which holds out the potential to address the twin tasks of contextualising the subject while avoiding the pitfalls of a singular, exclusive focus. By utilising White's depiction of history as fiction and narrative I am able to juxtapose the missionary chronicle of the mission of sisterhood and my own *translation* of that representation in ways which facilitate precisely the acknowledgement of power and context both Asad and Said, in different ways, insist upon. In doing so I am thus able to avoid the dichotomies of good and bad women which structure a woman-centred historiography, whilst making difference a central axis of my history.

Different stories

The missionary texts recount a story about Indian women and the efforts of British 'ladies' to emancipate them from the bounds of both culture and religion. Women's work in the mission field is the *mechanism* through which this liberation is attempted.

The mission of sisterhood turns on a comparison between the unfree Indian woman and her free British counterpart, portrayed most starkly in the contrast between the confining Indian household or *zenana* and the freedoms of the British home, drawn as a harmony of companionate marriage. Such a picture assumes an artificial gloss in the light of the contemporary feminist understanding of the nineteenth-century middle-class home and family to be a place of confinement and site of rebellion for many Victorian women, an image more nearly like that of the *zenana* of missionary imagination than the suburban ideal of the British home portrayed in the missionary literature.

Across the distance of time, the image of the Indian woman seems more an artifice with which the narrative of women's work in the mission field is able to negotiate the boundaries of a Victorian gender order rather than a rendition of Indian circumstances – a point of view reinforced by the knowledge that strict female seclusion and *zenanas* were a phenomenon specific to time, place, caste and class in India. By constructing the gap of culture and religion represented by the image of the *zenana* victim, the need and legitimation for women's work in the foreign field is established within a conventional frame of feminine action and agency. Yet despite the rhetoric of making good wives and mothers of the *zenana* inmates, the interventions of women's work do not produce images of domesticity or of freedom from the *zenana*. Rather, the images are of intellectual development and occupational industry by the Bible women – the low caste and low class women who, in the circumstances of South India, never were inhabitants of the *zenana*. The missionary women write of themselves engaged in educating their pupils for posts as – good Christian – teachers and nurses, and even, by the end of the century, for university entrance. It is a picture that most nearly captures the agency of the missionary women themselves, hardly the good wives and mothers of the stereotypical 'home', embroiled as they were in the demands of the work, demands which, as the century progressed, often precluded marriage.

The story I tell reverses the configuration of character and agency which in the missionary texts situates women's work as the means of emancipating Indian women. In my narrative, women's work takes centre stage as the means of emancipating not Indian women, but the missionary women themselves, albeit in ultimately ambiguous ways. The key aspect in my documentation of the professionalisation of missionary women's work is how the colonial context played a vital role in articulating these changes in the configuration of gender and work. My analysis turns on the ways in which the representation of Indian women, the ostensible subjects of women's work, mediates the participation of British women in the mission of sisterhood.

The missionary discourse of women's work is revealed, I argue, as a process of 'othering' which constructs Indian women as the converse of their free and active British sisters through the image of the *zenana* victim. The point of reference is precisely the measure of difference between the 'lady' and the 'Indian sister', forming the space in which women's work takes shape. The effect, however, is contrary. It is not the other of the *zenana* who is 'made' in this process, but her British sister, as the professional, and single, lady missionary. The *zenana* inmate remains a stereotype, the representation around which the agency of the missionary woman obtains its feasibility. In my translation Indian women are no longer the subjects of the narrative, but the textual device around which the missionary story turns. The difference between my narrative and that of the mission of sisterhood thus raises those issues of fact, fiction and translation dealt with by White, Asad and Said. The basis of my 'translation' turns on my stance in the late twentieth century and the 'knowledge' this distance of time gives me about the missionary past, in a sense, constructing a prism through which I represent the missionaries.

The key to the missionary texts' representation of the missionary women as free, emancipated, devoted workers, while nevertheless archetypes of conventional Christian womanhood, lay in the religious rubric in which it was couched. It was the higher call of God which legitimated the efforts and ambitions of the missionary women and the conduct of women's work. This call was not simply an injunction to carry out scriptural commands to spread the word, but a call to assume fully the particular role allocated to Christian women, a role perceived of as equivalent to, though not the same as, that of their male counterparts, and fully documented from the annals of biblical history. It was a role which could overcome bounds of familial obligation, sending daughters thousands of miles from parental care, and casting the role of missionary wife as 'an independent sphere of labour and responsibility', both nevertheless expressed in terms of selflessness, duty and obedience – to God.[64] It is, however, precisely this religious rubric which sets off the missionary narrative from my own.

From the more secular viewpoint of the 1990s, nineteenth-century Britain is not caught in a trajectory of Christian mission and selflessness, as the missionary literature assumes. Rather, it is the chronicle of the development of capitalism and a secular individualism conceived of as a cultural and psychological as well as an economic and social configuration. It is this secular history which provides the prism within which I am able to make sense, for myself, of the missionary literature and through which I discern an alternative story based not on duty, selflessness and service to God but independence, individual aspiration and material transformations.

It is through this play-off between the religious perspective of the missionaries and my own secular reading of these texts that I am able to document the transformation in the meanings of women's work around which my analysis turns. Precisely because of the place allocated the nineteenth century in the development of contemporary capitalist society, the missionary narrative of women's work provides both evidence and point of departure for my argument. I document the transition from their meaning of women's work, of work as duty and service, to one closer to the contemporary meanings of my own culture and time, as individual ambition and waged employment. Thus, despite the limitations of my prism, I do accord the missionary view of work a validity as fact as well as fiction in the shift from a labour of love for God to a professional employment relation.

Further, it is not just the racial hierarchies explicit in the idioms and images of the missionary narrative which make these texts 'worldly' in the context of empire and colonialism, but also the circumstances of their production. As I mentioned earlier, Indian contributions to these texts are caught firmly within the purview of the missionary narrative, forming part of a literature which stood alone in its powerful authority to represent both itself and its subjects to a British audience increasingly engaged with the ideals of empire. The missionary account of India and its women was, if not the main, then undoubtedly a primary contributor to the public perceptions of India as an appropriate subject of British imperial rule.[65]

A failure to 'translate' the mission of sisterhood into our contemporary discourses of post-colonialism would risk, therefore, contributing to precisely those global relations of power Talal Asad is concerned to take account of in anthropological ethnography, rather than to an ethical integrity towards the past. My dilemma thus becomes the reverse of Asad's, however, for it is only by imposing my translation on the historical chronicle that I can attempt to avoid contributing to our contemporary inequalities.

The last word

Acknowledging the fictional quality of my narrative and the ways in which I am constrained in my treatment of the missionary sources does not overcome the problems of translation identified by Asad. The historical, rather than contemporary ethnographic, relationship reverses but does not avoid the dilemmas of imposition and allocation of meaning. I am unable to believe or simply reproduce the missionary narrative of the mission of sisterhood but, rather than dismissing that account entirely, I have tried to present both narratives – the missionaries' and my own – rather than simply my translation; marking the missionary language as distinct from my own and making explicit the points at which the translation occurs, in an attempt to represent both as contingently available versions of the historical events.

But of course, this does not solve the problem. My 'distant primitives' – the missionaries – are given a relevance and integrity within their own time and culture, but there is no dialogical relationship established between the two narratives. I tell a story about the ways in which a group of Victorian middle-class women experienced the transformation to a professional employment relationship and the ways, from my point of view, a colonial subject facilitated this process. It is not a story of the mission of sisterhood and labours of love designed to emancipate Indian women.

The duality of my text is artificial, reserving for my narrative the authority of determining meaning – the last word. At best, by making explicit the ways in which the two narratives meet, I am able to indicate the ways in which the missionary view of women's work had a sense which not only differs from, but in some ways is both inaccessible and unacceptable to, my own.

There is one other narrative implicit in this historical chronicle, that of Indian women. By showing how the image of the *zenana* victim acted as a literary device and artifice of the missionary women's *self-representation* to their home audience, as professional workers who, by virtue of the contrast with a colonial other, maintain a conventional quality of good women despite their independence and unmarried state, I am able to suggest the fictional quality of the missionary portrayal of Indian women. By revealing how their subject status operated as device for the story of women's work, however, I risk duplicating the emancipatory efforts of the mission of sisterhood. I have tried to avoid this possibility by purposely refusing to tell a story of Indian women. Instead, I have attempted to place them as outside either the liberation effort of women's work or my agenda of professional 'ladies'. I have sought to suggest that, buried in the as yet inaccessible past, lies yet another account of emancipation but one which turned on very different axes to those of the missionaries or myself.

The principal Indian voices to come through in the missionary texts are the Bible women, Christian converts who, in South India, assisted the missionary women by actually doing the work of reaching the 'heathen women'. They are present in fragments of their work diaries, submitted to the missionary women who supervised their work. These reports were translated into English and edited by the missionaries for inclusion in missionary reports and articles. Hence, they are very far from any 'authentic voice'. However, what at first glance seems a complicit reflection of the mission of sisterhood's emancipatory aims, takes on another sheen when read against the backdrop of the emerging history of colonial South India – a history conceived of from within an indigenous milieu, rather than from a stance which assumes a universalising presence for the forces of colonialism.[66] While the story is far from complete yet, even within the constraints of the Bible women's fragments, one can discern a struggle in which the missionary women's efforts at education and emancipation assume a secondary role as a resource mobilised by Indian women to wage their own struggles about issues of class and caste.[67]

CONCLUSION

My approach to the missionary discourse on women's work was dictated by my scepticism of their representation of the mission of sisterhood as an effort to emancipate Indian women. A contemporary post-colonial sensibility ensured I was unwilling to simply reproduce the missionary account. This was reinforced by a secular understanding of the nineteenth century as a chronicle of developing capitalism rather than of true religion. Thus, I translate the mission of sisterhood into a narrative of the emancipation of British 'ladies'[68] – an emancipation achieved, in the missionary texts, through the discursive mechanism of the colonial other: Indian women.

However, I have tried to avoid simply dismissing the missionary account as indicative of either false consciousness or of propaganda, by presenting it as a contingently available version of the historical events. Thus, while I have resolutely located the mission of sisterhood within an imperialist context of colonial domination based on distinctions of both class and race, I have refrained from labelling these professional ladies and working wives either 'good' or 'bad' women, to parody the various approaches to white women and colonialism in the literature. Issues of imperialism and race, as a politics of postcolonialism, are explicitly located within my contemporary 'fiction' of the past, their salience one of the 1990s rather than the 1890s.

My ability to construct a dual (though not a dialogical) text rests in large part on the distance I assume between the 'exotic' past and the mundane present, the former conceived of as beyond the semantic knowing of the latter. In particular, it is the religious idioms and images of the missionary discourse which allow me to articulate this difference and make my translations explicit. I am able, therefore, to portray the coherence of the self-representations of the missionary women.

Despite the distance I assume between my present and the Victorian past, it is an assumption based on the knowledge that this distance nevertheless forms part of a continuum, one I have labelled the development of a capitalist social formation. However, I cannot assume a similar continuum between my present and the past of the Indian women who, in the fragmented voices of the Bible women, occasionally impinge on the missionary record. While India, over the same time-span, has also experienced the development of capitalism, it has done so as part of a very different context, one which cannot be assumed to fit the framework of secular individualism which underpins my counterpoint to the missionary chronicle of true religion.

Yet this same distance and sense of difference which reveals the internal integrity of women's work uncovers another, profoundly disturbing, continuity. I have also laid bare the origins of another contemporary relationship. The mission of sisterhood and its trope of emancipation bear an uncanny resemblance to the contemporary relationship drawn between 'Western' feminism and 'third world' women. Replacing the images of veiled Islamic women or the brides of arranged marriages in some contemporary Western feminist texts with that of the *zenana* inmate is an unnerving experience. The legacy is surely made explicit in that claim to universal sisterhood which galvanised second-wave feminism as much as it appears to have done the Victorian women of my study. While the slogan is currently much the worse for wear, its sentiment continues to resonate.

To return to the debates over women's and gender history with which I began this chapter, have I succeeded in my aim of constructing a 'gumbo-ya-ya' rather than a 'symphonic' history? Not entirely. The limitations of historical sources, particularly the lack of an Indian narrative, mean I am only able to suggest the space such a story would fill. As well, the over-riding authority given my 'translation' precludes the kind of democracy Barkley Brown seems to claim for 'gumbo-ya-ya'.[69] However, by adopting a post-structuralist discursive method, I am able to overcome the dualisms of a recuperative history in a way which does not tell white women – either of the past or the present – to 'shut up'. By making explicit the ways in which I 'translate' the missionary narrative I am able to avoid either dismissing or apologising for the missionary women's accounts of their presences and actions. Instead, it is revealed as a historically contingent and coherent version of events. My lady missionaries may not emerge as feminist heroines, but neither are they caught in a historical behavioural vacuum, charged with racism. The actions and agencies of the missionary women are accorded meaning by treating the missionary archive as textual representations located within the logics of metropolitan trajectories of social change and gender relations. Thus the depiction of Indian women as other assumes an effect within the history of the professionalisation of middle-class women's occupations and employments in Britain. The consequences of this, and of the activities of the missionary women, for Indian histories, are neither assumed nor denied, but given a potentiality in terms of their local context. In the process, it seems to me that the concept of 'women' as a putative category of identity and relation is not deconstructed to the point of incoherence. Rather, it is given a complexity across time and place which surely facilitates a sound, if shifting, base for writing feminist histories able to contribute fully to contemporary feminisms.[70]

NOTES

This chapter is a revised version of a paper first published as *The Past in the Present: Writing the History of the Mission of Sisterhood*, Discussion Papers in Women's Studies, Centre for Women's Studies, University of Waikato, Hamilton, NZ, ed. Professor Anna Yeatman, 1992.

1. Chilla Bulbeck, 'New histories of the memsahib and missus: the case of Papua New Guinea', *Journal of Women's History*, 3:2 (1991), p. 82.
2. See especially Claudia Knapman, *White Women in Fiji 1835–1930: The Ruin of Empire?* (Sydney, Allen and Unwin, 1986), Helen Callaway, *Gender, Culture and Empire: European Women in Colonial Nigeria* (London, Macmillan, 1987); Margaret Macmillan, *Women of the Raj* (London, Thames and Hudson, 1988); C. Bulbeck, *Australian Women in Papua New Guinea: Colonial Passages 1920–1960* (Cambridge, Cambridge University Press, 1992), for studies which explicitly engage with the stereotype of the racist memsahib. Other works which look at the way male historians have portrayed white women as the inaugurators of racist relations in the colonies are: Margaret Strobel, *European Women and the Second British Empire* (Bloomington and Indianapolis, Indiana University Press, 1991); Nupur Chaudhuri and Margaret Strobel (eds), *Western Women and Imperialism: Complicity and Resistance* (Bloomington and Indianapolis, Indiana University Press, 1992); and Kumari Jayawardena, *The White Woman's Other Burden: Western Women and South Asia During British Rule* (New York and London, Routledge, 1995).
3. Janaki Nair, 'Reconstructing and reinterpreting the history of women in India', *Journal of Women's History*, 3 (1991), pp. 8–34, and Jane Haggis, 'Gendering colonialism or colonising gender? Recent women's studies approaches to white women and the history of British colonialism', *Women's Studies International Forum*, 12 (1990), pp. 105–12.
4. Bulbeck, 'New histories', p. 99.
5. This debate has been wide-ranging and prolific. Some key texts are: L. Newman, 'Critical theory and the history of women: what's at stake in deconstructing women's history'; J. Williams, 'Domesticity as the dangerous supplement of liberalism'; L Vogel, 'Telling tales: historians of our own lives'; J. Newton, 'A feminist scholarship you can bring home to dad?'; all in *Journal of Women's History*, 2:3 (1911), pp. 58–105, E. Fox-Genovese, 'Placing women's history in history', *New Left Review*, 133 (1982), pp. 5–29; G. Bock, 'Women's history and gender history: aspects of an international debate', *Gender and History*, 1:1 (1989), pp. 7–30; D. Riley, *'Am I That Name?' Feminism and the Category of 'Women' in History* (Minneapolis, University of Minnesota, 1988); J. Scott, *Gender and the Politics of History* (New York, Columbia University Press, 1988); J. A. Bennett, 'Feminism and history', *Gender and History*, 1:3 (1989), pp. 251–72; J. L. Newton, 'History as usual? 'Feminism and the "new historicism"', in H. Aram Veeser (ed.), *The New Historicism* (London and New York, Routledge, 1989), D. Clark Hine, 'Black women's history, white women's history: the juncture of race and class', and R. Roach Pierson, 'Colonization and Canadian women's history', both in *Journal of*

Women's History, 4:2 (1992), pp. 125–56; E. Barkley Brown, '"What has happened here": the politics of difference in women's history and feminist politics', and I. Berger, 'Categories and contexts: reflections on the politics of identity in South Africa', Symposium: Intersections and collision courses: women, blacks, and workers confront gender, race, and class, *Feminist Studies*, 18:2 (1992), pp. 284–312; R. Roach Pierson, 'Experience, difference and voice in the writing of Canadian women's history', in K. Offen, R. Roach Pierson and J. Rendall (eds), *Writing Women's History: International Perspectives* (Bloomington and Indianapolis, Indiana University Press, 1991), pp. 79–106.

6. Scott, 'Gender and the politics of history', esp. ch. 1.
7. Ibid., p.10
8. D. Birkett and J. Wheelwright, 'How could she? Unpalatable facts and feminists' heroines', *Gender and History*, 2:1 (1990), p. 49.
9. L. Stanley, 'Moments of writing: is there a feminist auto/biography?', *Gender and History*, 2:1 (1990), p. 58.
10. Birkett and Wheelwright, 'How could she?', p. 49.
11. Ibid., p. 46.
12. The tension between the roles of mother and wife in the lives of expatriate women in the colonies, and how this impacted on their view of the colonial environment, has been explored in several studies. Knapman, *White Women in Fiji*, and Callaway, *Gender, Culture and Empire*, draw on a conceptual framework similar to Bulbeck's, suggesting white women were essentially outside the masculine sphere of colonial authority. P. Grimshaw, *Paths of Duty: American Missionary Wives in Nineteenth Century Hawaii* (Honolulu, Hawaii University Press, 1989), and M. Jolly, '"To save the girls for brighter and better lives": Presbyterian missions and women in the south of Vanuatu – 1848–1870', *Journal of Pacific History*, 26:1 (1991), pp. 27–48, situate white women in a more relational context in which norms of gender ideologies dictate the specific aspects of white women's involvements in domestic and non-domestic life.
13. See Haggis, 'Gendering colonialism'.
14. M. Jolly, 'Colonising women: the maternal body and empire', undated mimeo, p. 21.
15. Barkley Brown, '"What has happened here"', p. 298.
16. Ibid., p. 297
17. Ibid.
18. Ibid.
19. Ibid., p. 299.
20. See particularly G. Chakravorty Spivak, 'Three women's texts and a critique of imperialism', *Critical Inquiry*, 12:1 (1985), pp. 243–61, and E. W. Said, *Culture and Imperialism* (London, Chatto and Windus, 1993).
21. See particularly C. Talpade Mohanty, 'Under Western eyes: feminist scholarship and colonial discourses', in C. Talpade Mohanty, A. Russo and L Torres (eds), *Third World Women and the Politics of Feminism* (Bloomington and Indianapolis, Indiana University Press, 1991) pp. 51–80, and G. Chakravorty Spivak, 'French feminism in an international frame', in *In Other Worlds: Essays in Cultural Politics* (New York and London, Methuen, 1987), pp. 134–53.
22. R. Pierce Beaver, *American Protestant Women in World Mission: History of the First Feminist Movement in North America* (Grand Rapids, Eardmans, 1980); S. S. Garrett, 'Sisters all: feminism and the American Women's Missionary Movement', in T. Christensen and W. R. Hutchinson, (eds), *Missionary Ideologies in the Imperialist Era 1880–1920* (Denmark, Aros, 1982), pp. 221–30; P. R. Hill, *The World Their Household: The American Women's Foreign Mission Movement and Cultural Transformation 1870–1920* (Ann Arbor, University of Michigan Press, 1985); J. Hunter, *The Gospel of Gentility: American Women Missionaries in Turn-of-the-Century China* (New Haven and London, Yale University Press, 1984);

Grimshaw, *Paths of Duty*; S. M. Jacobs, 'Give a thought to Africa: black women missionaries in Southern Africa', in Chaudhuri and Strobel, *Western Women and Imperialism*, pp. 207–28; M. King, 'American women's open door to Chinese women: which way does it open?', *Women's Studies International Forum*, 13:4 (1990), pp. 369–79; G. B. Paul, 'Presbyterian missionaries and the women of India during the nineteenth century', *Journal of Presbyterian History*, 62 (1982), pp. 230–36.

23. The London Missionary Society was established in 1795. Although putatively non-denominational, the Society was closely associated with the Congregational community in England. Its first missionary undertaking was to the 'South Seas' in 1796. The Society launched its mission to India by smuggling two men in via the Danish territory of Tranquebar in South India, as a consequence of the East India Company's opposition to missionary activities in territories under its jurisdiction. One of these, a Prussian named Ringeltaube, found his way to Travancore, a Hindu kingdom on the far south-west coast of India, in 1807. The South Travancore District was, by 1851, the most successful of the Society's Indian establishments with one of the largest convert communities of any missionary station in India, a position it retained for much of the nineteenth century. The South Travancore District extended to Quilon in the north and the border between Travancore and Madras Presidency in the east, at which points the Church Missionary Society, affiliated with the Church of England, assumed territorial rights to convert loyalties.

24. J. S. Dennis, *Christian Missions and Social Progress: A Sociological Study of Foreign Missions* (Edinburgh and London, Oliphant, Anderson & Ferrier, 1899), vol. 2, p. 46.

25. E. R. Pitman, *Heroines of the Mission Field: Biographical Sketches of Female Missionaries Who Have Laboured in Various Lands Among the Heathen* (London, Cassell, Petter, Galpin & Co., c. 1881), p. 7.

26. E. Stock, *The History of the Church Missionary Society* (London, Church Missionary Society, 1899), vol. 3, p. 369.

27. The movement of middle-class women into the labour force during the years 1870 to 1914 has been called a 'white blouse revolution': see G. Anderson (ed.), *The White Blouse Revolution: Female Office Workers Since 1870* (Manchester, Manchester University Press, 1988). There was a massive increase in the percentage of women employed in teaching, nursing, shop and clerical occupations and the civil service. One estimate puts the overall increase at 161 per cent between 1881 and 1911: see L. Holcombe, *Ladies At Work Middle Class Working Women in England and Wales, 1850–1914* (Hamden, Connecticut, Archon Press, 1973).

28. M. Vicinus, *Independent Women: Work and Community for Single Women, 1850–1920* (London, Virago, 1985), p. 1.

29. Vicinus, *Independent Women*, p. 33.

30. L. Davidoff and C. Hall, *Family Fortunes: Men and Women of the English Middle Class 1780–1850* (London, Hutchinson, 1987), p. 117.

31. G. K. Hewat, *Vision and Achievement 1796–1956: A History of the Foreign Missions of the Churches United in the Church of Scotland* (Edinburgh, Thomas Nelson, 1960), p. 11.

32. Stock, *History of the Church Missionary Society*, vol. 1, p. 108.

33. Mrs Marshman, of the Baptist Missionary Society, is credited with having established the first girls' school at some point soon after her arrival in Bengal in 1799: M. Weitbrecht, *Women of India and Christian Work in the Zenana* (London, J. Nisbett, 1875), p. 145.

34. Commenting on the departure of the first missionary couples despatched to Ceylon in 1804, the Directors of the LMS wrote: 'Mrs Vos and Mrs Palm have also an important service to occupy their zeal, in the instruction of the female natives, and in assisting in the education of children': R. Lovett, *The History of the London Missionary Society 1795–1895*, vol. 2 (London, H. Frowde, 1899), p. 18. Fiancees

and wives were vetted by the missionary societies as part of the application process for missionary candidates. In 1837, Mr Abbs applied as a missionary to the LMS. Confidential references were called regarding his fiancee's suitability to accompany him as his wife, her pastor describing her as a valuable teacher in the Sunday school, with a 'zeal and heartiness in the cause of the Redeemer'. *Council for World Mission*, Home and General, Candidates Papers, Box 1, Envelope 1, Letter Dryden, 1 August 1837.

35. *History of the Society for Promoting Female Education in the East* (London, E. Suter, 1847), p. 5.

36. *History of SPFPE*, p. 6.

37. Although Jemima Luke, an early member of the SPFEE, wrote in her memoirs that 'opposition and sarcasm have given place to respect and sympathy', I have as yet found no evidence of any concerted or organised opposition to the establishment of the SPFEE and its operations. J. Luke, *Early Years of My Life* (London, Hodder and Stoughton, 1900), p. 155.

38. See F. Prochaska, *Women and Philanthropy in Nineteenth Century England* (Oxford, Oxford University Press, 1980), for a general history.

39. *History of SPFEE*, p. 5.

40. Ibid., p. 45.

41. Mrs Corrie was the first to approach the Church Missionary Society in this regard in 1815. The Committee responded that it would be against 'Christian decorum and propriety' to send single women out to India unless they were 'sisters accompanying or joining their brothers': Stock, *History of the Church Missionary Society*, vol. 1, p. 125; see also J. S. Isherwood, 'An analysis of the role of single women in the work of the Church Missionary Society 1804–1904', University of Manchester, Theology MA (1979).

42. The SPFEE had a clause in its bylaws binding all appointed agents, should they voluntarily relinquish their post or leave to marry within five years, to repay the Committee 'the sum expended by them on her less one fifth deducted for each year she did her job', *History of SPFEE*, p. 280. In 1842, one of the ladies sent out by the Edinburgh Society married one of the male missionaries who had been amongst those most eager for 'a lady from Scotland' to be sent to his mission to start women's work there. The Society felt so strongly about this that they tried, unsuccessfully, to demand compensation from the male missionary's society: A. S. Swan, *Seed Time and Harvest: The Story of the Hundred Years Work of the Women's Foreign Mission of the Church of Scotland* (London, Thomas Nelson and Sons, 1937), pp. 47–9.

43. *History of SPFEE*, p. 31.

44. Luke, *Early Years*, p. 73.

45. CWM, Home and General, Committee Minutes, Ladies Committee, Box 1, Printed Notice, 13 July 1875.

46. CWM, Home and General, Committee Minutes, Ladies Committee, Box 1, Printed Letter, 13 July 1975.

47. LMS, Annual Report, 1891.

48. CWM, Home and General, Committee Minutes Ladies Committee Box 1, 9 June 1891.

49. The vetting process is particularly visible in the case of candidates who were ambiguously located in class terms. Susannah Hodge had earned her own living as a milliner, maintaining herself out of a sense of 'duty' to her widowed mother, she wrote in a letter to the Committee (CWM, Candidates Papers, Box 7, Envelope 46, Letter, 5 July 1890). Her minister wrote that 'she had received a better education than is usual with persons in her position; and I should think she has come from a home of some refinement' (CWM, Candidates Papers, Box 7, Envelope 46, Letter, 17 June 1890). However, despite attending an interview and completing the Printed Questionnaire required of all candidates, the Committee still felt they required a

'more intimate knowledge'. Only after Committee members had seen Susannah in their homes and had reported 'the favourable impression produced on them . . . by her manner and personal appearance' was her application accepted, six months after her initial enquiry (CWM, Committee Minutes, Ladies Committee, Box 1, 15 July 1890 and 4 November 1890).

50. The importance of Indian Christian women in actually carrying out missionary 'work' is also noted by Geraldine Forbes in her brief study of single women missionaries who served with the Society for the Propagation of the Gospel in Bombay between 1858 and 1914. Forbes emphasises the important role of Indian Christian women in the development of female education, a point borne out in my own research. G. H. Forbes, 'In search of the "Pure Heathen": missionary women in nineteenth century India', *Economic and Political Weekly*, 21 (1986), Review of Women's Studies, WS2–WS8.

51. One missionary, serving in South Travancore in the 1880s, related in his Annual Report how a star graduate from his wife's boarding school had been sent, under mission auspices, to undertake midwifery training at a medical school for women in North Travancore, a considerable distance from her home: 'As she had a family of four young children it was not an easy matter for her to leave her home and go for two years with only occasional holidays to a place over sixty miles off. . . . Her husband who is a schoolmaster . . . felt it very difficult of course to spare his wife for two years and take charge himself for so long a time of three or four young children but he finally decided to do so' (CWM/Home and General/India/South India/Travancore/Reports/Box 3/1888).

52. For a more detailed consideration of the class, race and gender dimensions of the representation of the Bible women see J. Haggis, 'Good wives and mothers or dedicated workers: contradictions of domesticity in the Mission of Sisterhood, Travancore, South India', in K. Ram and M. Jolly (eds), *Maternities and Modernities: Colonial and Postcolonial Experiences in Asia and the Pacific* (Cambridge, Cambridge University Press, 1998).

53. *India's Women*, vol. 1 (1880), preliminary issue, p. 3.

54. *India's Women*, 1:9 (1882), p. 134.

55. *India's Women*, 4:22 (1884), p. 180.

56. *India's Women*, vol. 1 (1880), preliminary issue, p. 3.

57. H. White, *Tropics of Discourse: Essays in Cultural Criticism* (Baltimore, Johns Hopkins University Press, 1978), p. 43.

58. T. Asad, 'The concept of cultural translation in British social anthropology', in J. Clifford and G. E. Marcus (eds), *Writing Culture: The Poetics and Politics of Ethnography* (Berkeley, University of California Press, 1986), p. 163.

59. Asad, 'The concept of cultural translation', p. 163, emphasis in original.

60. E. W Said, *The World, the Text and the Critic* (Cambridge, Mass., Harvard University Press, 1983), p. 4.

61. Ibid., p. 12.

62. Ibid., p. 13.

63. E. W. Said, *Orientalism* (Harmondsworth, Penguin, 1985); see also R Chatterjee, *Nationalist Thought and the Colonial World: A Derivative Discourse* (London, Zed Books Ltd., 1986).

64. Weitbrecht, *Women of India*, p. 194.

65. J. M. MacKenzie, *Propaganda and Empire: The Manipulation of British Public Opinion 1880–1960* (Manchester, Manchester University Press, 1984).

66. See D. Ludden, *Peasant History in South India* (Delhi, Oxford University Press, 1989), and S. Bayly, *Saints, Goddesses and Kings: Muslims and Christians in South Indian Society 1700–1900* (Cambridge, Cambridge University Press, 1990), for histories of South India which attempt to set colonialism within the context of an existing indigenous historical dynamic.

67. See Haggis, 'Good wives and mothers'.

68. See A. Burton, *Burdens of History: British Feminists, Indian Women and Imperial Culture 1865–1915* (Chapel Hill, University of North Carolina Press, 1994).

69. Barkley Brown draws a direct analogy between the description of jazz music as a 'true democracy, and history as 'everybody talking at once' (p. 297). However, she does not really address in her article the problems of power and authority as an issue for the writing of history I've tried to raise here.

70. On the issue of feminist history and its contribution to feminist theory see Antoinette Burton, ' "History" is now: feminist theory and the production of historical feminism', *Women's History Review*, 1:1 (1992), pp. 25–38.

2.4

'I'M A FEMINIST BUT ... "OTHER" WOMEN AND POSTNATIONAL FEMINISM'

Ien Ang

For some time now, the problematic of race and ethnicity has thrown feminism into crisis. I am implicated in this crisis. As a woman of Chinese descent, I suddenly find myself in a position in which I can turn my 'difference' into intellectual and political capital, where 'white' feminists invite me to raise my 'voice', *qua* a non-white woman, and make myself heard. Anna Yeatman suggests that voices such as mine are needed to contest and correct the old exclusions of the established feminist order, and that they will win non-white women authorship and authority within a renewed, less exclusionary feminism.[1] In this sense, feminism acts like a nation; just like Australia, it no longer subscribes to a policy of assimilation but wants to be multicultural.

I want to complicate this scenario by looking at the *problems* of such a desire. Rather than positively representing a 'Chinese' or 'Asian' contribution to Australian feminism – which would only risk reinforcing the objectification and fetishisation of 'Asianness' – I want to argue that the very attempt to construct a voice for self-presentation in a context already firmly established and inhabited by a powerful formation (what is now commonly called, rather unreflexively, 'white/Western feminism') is necessarily fraught with difficulty. To me, non-white, non-Western women in 'white/Western' societies can only begin to speak with a hesitating 'I'm a feminist, but ...', in which the meaning and substance of feminism itself become problematised. Where does this leave femi-

From: Ien Ang (1995), 'I'm a Feminist but ... "Other" Women and Postnational Feminism', pp. 57–73, in B. Caine and R. Pringle (eds), *Transitions: New Australian Feminisms* (London: Allen & Unwin).

nism? Feminism must stop conceiving itself as a nation, a 'natural' political designation for all women, no matter how multicultural. Rather than adopting a politics of inclusion (which is always ultimately based on a notion of commonality and community), it will have to develop a self-conscious politics of partiality, and imagine itself as a *limited* political home, which does not absorb difference within a pre-given and predefined space but leaves room for ambivalence and ambiguity. In the uneven, conjunctural terrain so created, white/ Western feminists too will have to detotalise their feminist identities and be compelled to say: 'I'm a feminist, but . . .'

THE POLITICS OF DIFFERENCE AND ITS LIMITS

In the early days of the second wave, feminist theory and practice were predicated on the assumption of women's common identity *as* women, and of a united global sisterhood. It was the universalisation of white, middle-class women's lives as representative of *the* female experience which made it possible for modern Western feminism to gather momentum and become such an important social movement. In this sense feminism, like any other political philosophy, is an 'interested universalism' (Yeatman, 1993), based on the postulate that women have common experiences and share common interests *qua* women.

Today, it is precisely this homogenising idea of sisterhood which has come under increasing attack within feminism itself. After all, not all women share the same experience of 'being a woman', nor is shared gender enough to guarantee a commonality in social positioning. As Elizabeth Spelman (1988: p. 14) rightly states, 'even if we say all women are oppressed by sexism we cannot automatically conclude that the sexism all women experience is the same'. This is an important realisation which undermines any reductionist, essentialising definition of 'women's oppression' as a universal female experience. It also means the end of the authority of the category of 'women' as the 'natural' binding factor for feminist politics. Instead, as Judith Butler (1990: p. 3) notes, '*women* has become a troublesome term, a site of contest, a cause for anxiety'.

It is now widely acknowledged that differences between women undermine the homogeneity and continuity of 'women' as a social category: differences produced by the intersections of class, race, ethnicity, nationality, and so on. So 'difference' has become an obligatory tenet in feminist discourse in the 1990s, and feminism's ability to 'deal with it' is often mentioned as a condition for its survival as a movement for social change. The so-called politics of difference recognises the need to go beyond the notion of an encompassing sisterhood and acknowledges that feminism needs to take account of the fact that not all women are white, Western and middle class and take into consideration the experiences of 'other' women as well. In Australian feminism, this trend is evidenced in important recent publications such as *Intersexions: Gender/ Class/Culture/Ethnicity* (Bottomley et al. 1991), *Living in the Margins: Racism, Sexism and Feminism* (Pettman 1992) and *Feminism and the Politics of Difference* (Gunew and Yeatman, 1993).

What does it mean, however, to 'deal with difference'? Pettman (1992: p. 158) suggests among other things that it means 'recognising unequal power and conflicting interests while not giving up on community or solidarity or sisterhood'. But this sounds all too deceptively easy, a formula of containment that wants to have it both ways, as if differences among women could unproblematically be turned into a 'unity in diversity' once they are 'recognised' properly. Yeatman (1993: p. 241) suggests that the politics of difference should encourage 'the complexity of dialogue' between differently situated feminists (e.g., Aboriginal and Anglo-Australian women) who are not positioned as mutually exclusive selves versus others, but 'who understood themselves to be complexly like and different from each other'. However, isn't 'women' being surreptitiously smuggled back in here as the essential way in which the interlocutors are assumed to resemble each other?

The way difference should be 'dealt with', then, is typically imagined by the feminist establishment through such benevolent terms as 'recognition', 'understanding' and 'dialogue'. The problem with such terms is first of all that they reveal an overconfident faith in the power and possibility of open and honest communication to 'overcome' or 'settle' differences, of a power-free speech situation without interference by entrenched presumptions, sensitivities and preconceived ideas. It is a faith in our (limitless?) capacity not only to speak, but, more importantly, to listen and hear. Spelman, speaking to fellow white feminists, relentlessly questions the (white) feminist ability to listen in this regard.

> Is the reason we haven't heard from them before that they haven't spoken, or that we haven't listened (. . .) Are we really willing to hear anything and everything that they might have to say, or only what we don't find too disturbing? Are we prepared to hear what they say, even if it requires learning concepts or whole languages that we don't yet understand? (Spelman 1988: p. 163).

Spelman's very phrasing brings to bear a deep and disturbing gulf between 'us' and 'them' (i.e., 'other' women). This suggests that 'difference' cannot be 'dealt with' easily, and can certainly not just be 'overcome'.

Therefore, I want to stress here the *difficulties* of 'dealing with difference'. These difficulties cannot be resolved through communication, no matter how complex the dialogue. Indeed, the very desire to resolve them in the first place could result in a premature glossing-over of the social irreducibility and inescapability of certain markers of difference and the way they affect women's lives. To focus on *resolving* differences between women as the ultimate aim of 'dealing with difference' would mean their containment in an inclusive, encompassing structure which itself remains uninterrogated; it would mean that 'these differences must comply with feminism's (. . .) essentialising frame' (Kirby 1993: p. 29). In such a case, difference is 'dealt with' by absorbing it into an already existing feminist community without challenging the naturalised legitimacy and status of that community *as* a community. By dealing with difference in this way, feminism resembles the multicultural nation – the nation that, faced with cultural differences within its borders, simultaneously recognises and controls those differences amongst its population by containing them in a grid of pluralist diversity (Bhabha 1991). However, reducing difference to diversity in this manner is tantamount to a more sophisticated and complex form of assimilation. As Chandra Talpade Mohanty puts it:

> The central issue (. . .) is not one of merely *acknowledging* difference; rather, the more difficult question concerns the kind of difference that is acknowledged and engaged. Difference seen as benign variation (diversity), for instance, rather than as conflict, struggle, or the threat of disruption, bypasses power as well as history to suggest a harmonious, empty pluralism. On the other hand, difference defined as asymmetrical and incommensurate cultural spheres situated within hierarchies of domination and resistance cannot be accommodated within a discourse of 'harmony in diversity'. (Mohanty 1989: p. 181)

To take difference seriously, then, we need to examine the sources and effects of the threat of disruption Mohanty talks about. Concretely, it would mean a focus on how the gulf between mainstream feminism and 'other' women is constructed and reproduced, and paying attention to, rather turning our gaze away from, those painful moments at which communication seems unavoidably to *fail*.[2] Rather than assuming that ultimately a common ground can be found for women to form a community – on the *a priori* assumption that successful communication is guaranteed – we might do better to start from point zero and realise that there are moments at which no common ground exists whatsoever, and when any communicative event would be nothing more than a speaking past one another. I want to suggest, then, that these moments of ultimate failure of communication should not be encountered with regret, but rather should be accepted as the starting point for a more modest feminism, one which is predicated on the fundamental *limits* to the very idea of sisterhood (and thus the category 'women') and on the necessary *partiality* of the project of feminism as such.

In other words, I suggest that we would gain more from acknowledging and confronting the stubborn solidity of 'communication barriers' than from rushing to break them down in the name of an idealised unity. Such an idealised unity is a central motif behind a politics of difference which confines itself to repairing the friction between white women and 'other' women. The trouble is that such reparation strategies often end up appropriating the other rather than fully confronting the incommensurability of the difference involved. This is the case, for example, in well-intentioned but eventually only therapeutic attempts on the part of white women to overcome 'our own racism' through conscious-raising, a tendency particularly strong in some strands of American liberal feminism. White feminists worried about their own race privilege typically set out to overcome their feelings of guilt by identifying with the oppressed other. Thus, Ann Russo (1991: p. 308) claims that her ability to 'connect with women of color' is greater when she faces the ways in which she herself has been oppressed in her own life as a white, middle-class woman. She would be less able to empathise, she says, if she would see herself 'as only privileged' and 'as only an oppressor', because then she would see herself as 'too different' from 'women of color'. In other words, the white woman can become a 'politically correct' anti-racist by disavowing the specificity of the experience of being a racialised 'other', reducing it to an instance of an oppression essentially the same as her own, gender-based oppression. This form of appropriation only reinforces the security of the white point of view as the point of reference from which the other is made same, a symbolic annihilation of otherness which is all the more pernicious precisely because it occurs in the context of a claimed solidarity with the other. The very presumption that race-based oppression can be understood by paralleling it with gender-based oppression results in a move to reinstate white hegemony. Such a move represses consideration of the cultural repercussions of the structural ineluctability of white hegemony in Western societies. (I have used the terms 'white' and 'Western' in an overgeneralising way here, but will specify them later.)

Of course, the most powerful agents of white/Western hegemony are white middle-class males,[3] but white middle-class females too are the bearers of whiteness which, because of its taken for grantedness, is 'a privilege enjoyed but not acknowledged, a reality lived in but unknown' (Cathy Thomas, quoted in Frankenberg 1993). To her credit, Russo (1991: p. 308) is aware of the possible ramifications of this shared whiteness: 'While white feminists have directed our anger at white men for their sexual (and other) atrocities, there remains a common historical and cultural heritage which carries with it a certain familiarity and even subconscious loyalty to our skin and class privilege.' These comments elucidate the fact that white privilege does not have to do necessarily with overt or explicit forms of racism, but with a much more normalised and insidious set of assumptions which disremember the structural advantage of being white, and which generalise specifically white cultural practices and ways of seeing and being in the world as normal (Frankenberg 1993).

The extent to which this white self-exnomination permeates mainstream feminism should not be underestimated. It is a core, if unconscious, aspect of (white/Western) feminism, which appears unaware that even some of its apparently most straightforward ideas and beliefs reveal its embeddedness in particular orientations and tendencies derived from 'white/Western' culture. For example, the well-known maxim 'When a woman says no, she means no!' to articulate the feminist stance on rape and sexual harassment invokes an image of the ideal feminist woman as assertive, determined, plain-speaking and confrontational. The slogan does not just speak to men (who are commanded to take no for an answer), but also implicitly summons women to take up these feministically approved qualities and mean no when they say it. However, these qualities are far from culturally neutral: they belong to a repertoire of rules for social interaction which prizes individualism, conversational explicitness, directness and efficiency – all Western cultural values which may not be available or appeal to 'other' women. Asian women, for example, may well deal with male dominance in culturally very different, more circuitous (and not necessarily less effective) ways. In other words, far from being culturally universal, 'When a woman says no, she means no!' implies a feminist subject position and style of personal politics that are meaningful chiefly for those women who have the 'right' cultural resources. I am not saying that the maxim itself is ethnocentric: what is ethnocentric is the assumption that it represents all women's experiences and interests in sexual relations (arguably it doesn't even represent those of all 'white/Western' women). Even more perniciously, this universalist feminist assumption implicitly finds wanting all women who do *not* have these cultural resources. As a result, these different women are, as Mohanty says about Third World women, 'stripped of their existence as concrete historical subjects living, working, acting and fighting in particular societal circumstances, and are objectified as a generalised, always-already oppressed "other woman" (e.g., the veiled woman, the chaste virgin)' (Mohanty 1984: p. 353), against whom Western women become elevated as the self-professed avant-garde of liberated womanhood (see also, e.g., Chow 1991; Jolly 1991; Kirby 1993; Ong 1988).

In acknowledgment of the need to deconstruct such universalising assumptions of white/Western feminism, feminist theories have begun to concern themselves with the issue of representation, of 'who is permitted to speak on behalf of whom'. If speaking in the name of the other is no longer politically acceptable, how then should the other be represented? Or should white feminists refrain from representing 'other' women at all? Would the problem be gradually solved if more 'other' women would start raising their voices and presenting 'their' points of view? Here again, the implicit assumption is that a diversification of discourse would eventually lead to a broader, more inclusive representation of 'all' women. However, what implications the resulting contestatory discourses can and should have for feminist politics remain glaringly unresolved. In other words, where does the emanating 'complexity of dialogue' lead us?

Let me address this question through an example, again derived (mainly) from American feminist criticism. As is well known, there has been much controversy in the academy about the cultural and sexual politics of the pop singer Madonna. Her many white feminist defenders see her as a postmodern proto-feminist heroine, a woman who manages to create a cultural space where she can invent and play with daring representations of feminine sexuality while remaining in control and in charge (see Schwichtenberg 1993). While white critics have generally appreciated Madonna in terms of her clever subversion of male dominance.[4] However, the black feminist critic bell hooks argues that Madonna's gender politics can only be interpreted as liberating from a 'white' perspective:

> In part, many black women who are disgusted by Madonna's flaunting of sexual experience are enraged because the very image of sexual agency that she is able to project and affirm with material gain has been the stick this society has used to justify its continued beating and assault on the black female body. (hooks 1992: pp. 159–60)

According to hooks, what Madonna's white feminist fans applaud her for – namely her power to act in sexually rebellious ways without being punished – cannot be experienced as liberating by the vast majority of black women in the US, as dominant myths of black females as sexually 'fallen' force them to be 'more concerned with projecting images of respectability than with the idea of female sexual agency and transgression' (hooks 1992: p. 160). In other words, hooks contends, Madonna's status as a feminist heroine makes sense only from a white woman's perspective, and any deletion of this specification only slights the black woman's perspective.

The point I want to make is not that the white feminist interpretation is wrong or even racist, or that hook's view represents a better feminism, but that we see juxtaposed here two different points of view, constructed from two distinct speaking positions, each articulating concerns and preoccupations which make sense and are pertinent within its own reality. The meaning of Madonna, in other words, depends on the cultural, racially marked context in which her image circulates, at least in the US. Nor can either view be considered the definitive white or black take on Madonna; after all, any interpretation can only be provisional and is indefinitely contestable, forcing us to acknowledge its inexorable situatedness (Haraway 1988). Nevertheless, a reconciliation between these points of view is difficult to imagine. And this is not a matter of 'communication barriers' that need to be overcome, of differences that need to be 'recognised'. What we see exemplified here is a fundamental *incommensurability* between two competing feminist knowledges, dramatically exposing an irreparable chasm between a white and a black feminist truth. No harmonious compromise or negotiated consensus is possible here.

This example illuminates the limits of a politics of difference focused on representation. The voice of the 'other', once raised and taken seriously in its distinctiveness and specificity, cannot be assimilated into a new, more totalised feminist truth. The otherness of 'other' women, once they come into self-representation, works to disrupt the unity of 'women' as the foundation for feminism. This is the logic of Butler's (1990: p. 15) claim that '[i]t would be wrong to assume in advance that there is a category of "women" that simply needs to be filled in with various components of race, class, age, ethnicity, and sexuality in order to become complete'. That is, there are situations in which 'women' as signifier for commonality would serve more to impede the self-presentation of particular groups of female persons – in this case African-American women struggling against racist myths of black female sexuality – than to enhance them. White women and black women have little in common in this respect. Teresa de

Lauretis (1988: p. 135) has put it this way: 'the experience of racism changes the experience of gender, so that a white woman would be no closer than a Black man to comprehending a Black woman's experience'. So we can talk with each other, we can enter into dialogue – there is nothing wrong with learning about the other's point of view – provided only that we do not impose a premature sense of unity as the desired outcome of such an exchange.

CONSIDERING WHITE/WESTERN HEGEMONY

But there is more. It is clear that, while white critical discourse could afford to be silent about the racial dimension of the cultural meaning(s) of Madonna and could assume a stance of seeming racial neutrality,[5] hooks (1992) is only too aware of the marginal situatedness of her own point of view. She does not share the sense of entitlement which empowers white women to imagine a world in which they are 'on top', as it were, successfully turning the tables on men (white and black). Yet this is the quintessence of the all-powerful fantasy Madonna offers white women. Black women like hooks operate in the certainty that they will *never* acquire the power to rule the world; they know that this world – white-dominated, Western, capitalist modernity – is quite simply *not theirs*, and can never be. This fundamental sense of permanent dislocation, this feeling of always being a foreigner in a world that doesn't belong to you,[6] is what all those who are 'othered' – racialised or ethnicised – in relation to white/Western hegemony share.

It is important to emphasise, at this point, that white/Western hegemony is not a random psychological aberration but the systemic consequence of a global historical development over the last 500 years – the expansion of European capitalist modernity throughout the world, resulting in the subsumption of all 'other' peoples to its economic, political and ideological logic and mode of operation. Whiteness and Westernness are closely interconnected; they are two sides of the same coin. Westernness is the sign of white hegemony at the international level, where non-white, non-Western nations are by definition subordinated to white, Western ones. It is the globalisation of capitalist modernity which ensures the structural insurmountability of the white/non-white and Western/non-Western divide, as it is cast in the very infrastructure – institutional, political, economic – of the modern world (Wallerstein 1974). In other words, whether we like it or not, the contemporary world system is a *product* of white/Western hegemony, and we are all, in our differential subjectivities and positionings, implicated in it.

We are not speaking here, then, of an *ontological* binary opposition between white/Western women and 'other' women. Nor is it the case that white feminists are always-already 'guilty' (another psychologising gesture which can only paralyse). But the fracturing of the category of 'women' is historically and structurally entrenched, and cannot be magically obliterated by (white) feminism through sheer political will or strategy. As a consequence, in the words of de Lauretis (1988: p. 136):

the feminist subject, which was initially defined purely by its status as colonised subject or victim of oppression, becomes redefined as much less pure [and] as indeed ideologically complicitous with 'the oppressor' whose position it may occupy in certain sociosexual relations (though not others), on one or another axis.

Complicity, in other words, is a structural inevitability which we can only come to terms with by recognising it as determining the *limits* of political possibilities, not as something that we can work to undo (by consciousness-raising, for example). In other words, it is important to realise that the white/'other' divide is a historically and systematically imposed structure which cannot yet, if ever, be superseded.

Until now I have deliberately used the term 'other' to encompass all the disparate categories conjured up to classify these 'others': for example, 'black women', 'women of color', 'Third World women', 'migrant women' or, a specifically Australian term circulating in official multicultural discourse, 'NESB (non-English-speaking-background) women'. Of course these different categories, themselves labels with unstable and shifting content and pasting over a multitude of differences, cannot be lumped together in any concrete, historically and culturally specific sense. In structural terms, however, they occupy the same space insofar as they are all, from a white perspective, relegated to the realm of racialised or ethnicised 'otherness', a normalising mechanism which is precisely constitutive of white/Western hegemony. As we have seen, feminism in Australia and elsewhere is not exempt from such hegemonising processes: in most feminist theory, too, whiteness is the umarked norm against which all 'others' have to be specified in order to be represented. Spelman (1988: p. 169) points this out astutely: 'Black women's being Black somehow calls into question their counting as straightforward examples of "women", but white women's being white does not.'

What difference can a politics of difference make in the face of this fundamental, binary asymmetry? Sneja Gunew (1993: p. 1) claims that '[t]he dismantling of hegemonic categories is facilitated by the proliferation of difference rather than the setting up of binary oppositions that can merely be reversed, leaving structures of power intact'. This postmodern celebration of a 'proliferation of difference' as a utopian weapon in the destruction of hegemonic structures of power is also proposed by Jane Flax, as in this oft-quoted statement:

> Feminist theories, like other forms of postmodernism, should encourage us to tolerate and interpret ambivalence, ambiguity, and multiplicity as well as expose the roots of our needs for imposing order and structure no matter how arbitrary and oppressive these needs may be. If we do our work well, reality will appear even more unstable, complex and disorderly than it does not. (Flax 1990: pp. 56–7)

For reasons which will become clear, I am generally sympathetic to Flax's emphasis on ambivalence, ambiguity and multiplicity as theoretical principles in our approach to 'reality'. But she surreptitiously displays another form of psychological reductionism when she ascribes the imposition of order and structure to the obscurity of 'our needs', and suggests that we should learn to 'tolerate' ambivalence, ambiguity and multiplicity. To be sure, the consequence of Flax's postmodern equation of 'doing our work well' with making reality 'appear even more unstable, complex and disorderly' is an underestimating of the historical tenacity and material longevity of oppressive orders and structures, such as those entailing sedimented consequences of white/Western hegemony. This postmodern optimism, I suspect, can only be expressed from a position which does not have to cope with being on the receiving end of those orders and structures. Flax's 'we', therefore, can be read as a white 'we': it is white needs for order and structure which she implicitly refers to and whose roots she wants to expose (and, by implication, do away with), and it is only from a white perspective that 'tolerating' ambivalence and disorder would be a 'progressive', deuniversalising step. The problem is, of course, that the order and structure of white/Western hegemony cannot be eliminated by giving up the 'need' for it, simply because its persistence is not a matter of 'needs'.

From the perspective of 'other' women (and men), then, there is no illusion that white, Western hegemony will wither away in any substantial sense, at least not in the foreseeable future. The nature of global capitalist modernity is such that these 'other' peoples are left with two options: either enter the game or be excluded. At the national level, either integrate/assimilate or remain an outsider; at the international level, either 'Westernise' or be ostracised from the 'world community', the 'family of nations'. This ensures that the position of the non-white in a white-dominated world and the non-Western in a Western-dominated world is always necessarily and inescapably an 'impure' position, always dependent on and defined *in relation to* the white/Western dominant.[7] Any resistance to this overwhelming hegemony can therefore only ever take place from a position always-already 'contaminated' by white/Western practices, and can therefore only hope to carve out spaces of *relative* autonomy and freedom *within* the interstices of white/Western hegemony.

It is in this historical sense that the hierarchical binary divide between white/non-white and Western/non-Western should be taken account of as a master-grid framing the potentialities of, and setting limits to, all subjectivities and all struggles. Feminists and others need to be aware of this systemic inescapability when 'dealing with difference'. This is where I find Flax's insistence on ambivalence, ambiguity and multiplicity useful, not to celebrate 'difference' as a sign of positive postmodern chaos, but to describe the *necessary condition of existence* of those who are positioned, in varying ways, as peripheral others to the white, Western core. There is no pure, uncontaminated identity outside of the system generated by this hegemonic force. Despite hooks's largely autonomist stance on the African-American political struggle and counter-hegemonic

practice (see for example, her essays in hooks 1990), it is clear that the very construction of Black identity in the US is intimately bound up with the history of
slavery and segregation, just as contemporary Aboriginal 'identity' in Australia
cannot erase the effects of 200 years of contact and conflict with European
colonisers (see Attwood 1989), and the 'identity' of Third World nations,
mostly postcolonial, cannot be defined outside the parameters of the international order put in place by the unravelling of European colonial and imperial
history. The irony is that while all these 'identities' are affected by the objectification of 'others' by white/Western subjects, they have become the necessary
and inescapable points of identification from which these 'others' can take
charge of their own destinies in a world not of their own making. Ambivalence,
ambiguity and multiplicity thus signal the unfinished and ongoing, contradictory, and eternally unresolved nature of this double-edged process of simultaneous objectification/subjectification. Seen this way, the politics of difference,
while bitterly necessary now that 'other' voices are becoming increasingly insistent, has not resulted in a new feminist consensus and never will. There will
always be a tension between difference as benign diversity and difference as
conflict, disruption, dissension.

AUSTRALIAN WHITENESS, THE POSTCOLONIAL AND THE MULTICULTURAL

I have used the terms 'white' and 'Western' rather indiscriminately so far.
This is problematic, especially given the rapidity with which these terms
have become 'boo-words', signifying irredeemable political incorrectness. To
counter such sloganeering and to clarify my argument, I should stress that I
have used these concepts first of all as generalising categories which describe *a
position in a structural, hierarchical interrelationship* rather than a precise set
of cultural identities. Thus, being white in Australia is not the same as being
white in Britain, France or the United States, as whiteness does not acquire
meanings outside of a distinctive and overdetermined network of concrete
social relations. Even who counts as white is not stable and unchanging – we
should not forget, for example, that in the postwar period Southern European
immigrants to Australia (Italians, Greeks) were perceived as non-white, thus
'black'! Whiteness, then, is not a biological category but a political one.
Therefore, we need to go beyond the generalisations of generic whiteness and
undifferentiated Westernness if we are to understand the specific cultural
dynamics in which these interrelationships are played out in any particular
context. In other words, analysing and interrogating the culturally specific ways
in which whiteness, including white femininity, has been historically constructed and inflected in Australia is a necessary condition if Australian feminism is to effectively deuniversalise the experience of white women in feminist
theory and practice.[8]

Australia is implicated in the global configuration of white/Western hegemony in ways which are particular to its history – of European settlement and
Aboriginal genocide, of the White Australia policy, official multiculturalism,

and the current 'push toward Asia'. Despite this, Australia remains predominantly populated by Anglo-Celtic people, who inhabit exnominated whiteness in this country. Its main social institutions and basic cultural orientations are identifiably Western, and as a nation it is categorised in the international order as a part of 'the West'. Yet it is important to note that Australian whiteness is itself relatively marginal in relation to world-hegemonic whiteness. The fact that Australia itself is on the periphery of the Euro-American core of 'the West' (and as such is often forgotten or ignored by that core), produces a sense of non-metropolitan, postcolonial whiteness whose structures of feeling remain to be explored. Meaghan Morris (1992) has begun to capture the distinctive ambiguities of Australian whiteness with the term 'white settler subjectivity', a subject position which, Morris notes, oscillates uneasily between identities as coloniser and colonised. In this respect, Australian whiteness is itself steeped in a deep sense of the ambivalence, ambiguity and multiplicity so valued by Flax. Here again, however, it doesn't get us very far to celebrate these conditions as inherently positive principles. Rather, they signal a historically specific cultural predicament which has led Morris (1992: p. 471) to describe the Australian social formation as both 'dubiously postcolonial' and 'prematurely postmodern'. I want to suggest that the precariousness and fragility of this antipodean whiteness, so different from (post)imperial British whiteness or messianic, superpower American whiteness, inscribes and affects the way in which white Australia relates to its non-white 'others'. I will finish this essay then, by sketching briefly how Australian feminism is implicated in this.

Being Asian in Australia necessarily implies a problematic subject positioning. It is well known that the White Australia policy effectively excluded Asian peoples from settling in the country, because Australia wanted to be white, an outpost of Europe. Since the abandonment of this policy, however, 'we' are allowed in. And the politics of multiculturalism even encourages us to contribute to the cultural diversity of Australia. Still, the presence of Asians is not naturalised. A while ago I bumped into a middle-aged white woman in the supermarket. Such small accidents happen all the time; they are part of the everyday experience of sharing a space, including national space. But she was annoyed and started calling me names. 'Why don't you go back to your own country!' she shouted. I am familiar with this exhortation: it is a declaration of exclusion racialised and ethnicised people have to put up with all the time. But what does such as comment mean in Australia? I want to suggest that, placed in the larger context of Australian cultural history, the racism expressed here is not just ordinary prejudice. There is a measure of spite in the insistence with which this white woman proclaims Australia as her 'home' while emphatically denying me the right to do the same thing. It shocked me, because I thought this kind of thing was possible in Europe, not in a settler society such as Australia. In declaring herself to be a native threatened by alien immigrants, she displays an historical amnesia of (British) colonialism which actively erases the history of Aboriginal dispossession of the land. In other words, in her claim that Asians don't belong in this country, she simultaneously reproduces, in a single appropriative gesture, the exclusion of Aboriginal people. A disturbing bunker mentality is expressed in this peculiar double-edgedness of white Australian ethnocentrism, a mentality of tenaciously holding on to what one has which, I suggest, is sourced precisely in the precariousness and fragility, the moot legitimacy and lack of historical density of white settler subjectivity.[9]

Australian feminism has to take into account this two-sided antagonism, in which white Australia constitutes and asserts itself by demarcating itself from the immigrant on the one hand and the indigene on the other by racialising and/or ethnicising both, naturalising its own claim to nativeness in the process. It is clear that an Australian feminist politics of difference needs to dismantle and deconstruct the hierarchical relations involved in this complex and contradictory, three-pronged structure of mutual exclusivism, in which 'white' is the constitutive centre. This quotation from anthropologist Margaret Jolly typifies the problematic as it is currently seen through 'white' feminist eyes:

> There is the general problem of white feminists dealing with Australian women of colour, the rainbow spectrum of ethnic identities resulting from a long process of migration. *But the problem is more acute* with indigenous women because they identify us not so much as Anglo-inhabitants of Australia, but as the white invaders of their land. There is a strong and persistent sense of racial difference and conflict born out of the history of colonialism in our region. (Jolly 1991: p. 56; emphasis added)

My quarrel with this comment is that it reinstates the white feminist subject as the main actor, for whom the Aboriginal other and the migrant other are two competing interlocutors, kept utterly separate from each other. One result of this is that the differing relations between indigenous peoples and various groups of settlers remains unaddressed,[10] and that the Anglo centre – *its* problems and concerns pertaining to identity and difference – remains the main focus of attention. In intellectual terms, this amounts to a non-dialogue between the postcolonial and the multicultural problematic, the serial juxtapositioning of the two conditional entirely upon the distributive power of the hegemonic Anglo centre. From a white (Anglo) perspective, it may be understandable that priority be given to Anglo-Aboriginal relations (as Jolly suggests), as it is this relation which marks the original sin foundational to Australian white settler subjectivity, which can now no longer be repressed. However, this intense investment in the postcolonial problematic – which is the locus of the distinctively Australian quandary of 'white guilt' – may be one important reason why there is so little feminist engagement with the challenge of constructing a 'multicultural Australia'. 'Migrant women', lumped together in homogenising and objectifying categories such as NESB, are still mostly talked about, not spoken with and heard (Martin 1991); they remain within the particularist ghetto of ethnicity and are not allowed an active, constructive role in the ongoing construction of 'Australia' (see for example Curthoys 1993).

Multiculturalism remains, as Gunew (1993b: p. 54) complains, 'the daggy cousin of radical chic postcolonialism'.

It is this context which makes it problematic to construct an 'Asian' voice in Australian feminism. Despite the regular presence of Asians in contemporary Australia and despite the recurrent official rhetoric that Australia is 'part of Asia', Asianness remains solidly defined as external to the symbolic space of Australianness, in contrast with Aboriginality which – certainly since Mabo – has now been accepted by white Australia, albeit reluctantly, as occupying an undeniable place, however fraught by the injustices of history, in the heart of Australian national identity. To define myself as Asian, however, necessarily means writing myself out of the boundaries of that identity and into the margins of a pregiven, firmly established Australian imagined community. The only escape from this ghetto, from this perspective, would be the creation of a symbolic space no longer bounded by the idea(l) of national identity; a space, that is, where 'Australia' no longer has to precede and contain, in the last instance, the unequal differences occurring within it. Of course, such a space is utopian, given the fact that 'Australia' no longer has to precede and contain, in the last instance, the unequal differences occurring within it. Of course, such a space is utopian, given the fact that 'Australia' is not a floating signifier but the name for an historically sedimented national state. Yet the imagination of such a space is necessary to appreciate the permanent sense of displacement experienced by racialised and ethnicised people, including, I want to stress, Aboriginal people.[11]

What does this tell us, finally, about the feminist politics of difference? As I have already said, too often the need to deal with difference is seen in the light of the greater need to save, expand, improve or enrich feminism as a political home which would ideally represent all women. In this way, the ultimate rationale of the politics of difference is cast in terms of an overall politics of *inclusion*: the desire for an overarching feminism to construct a pluralist sisterhood which can accommodate all differences and inequalities between women. It should come as no surprise that such a desire is being expressed largely by white, Western, middle-class women, whom Yeatman (1993) calls the 'custodians of the established order' of contemporary feminism. Theirs is a defensive position, characterized by a reluctance to question the status of feminism *itself* as a political home for all women, just as Australia will not – and cannot, in its existence as a legislative state – question its status as a nation despite its embrace of multiculturalism. Yeatman herself, for example, considers the politics of difference as an 'internal politics of emancipation *within* feminism' (1993: p. 230, emphasis added). In this conception, difference can only be taken into consideration insofar as it does not challenge the rightfulness of feminism as such. Feminism functions as a nation which 'other' women are invited to join without disrupting the ultimate integrity of the nation. But this politics of inclusion is born of a liberal pluralism which can only be entertained by those who have the *power* to include, as pointed out poignantly by Spelman (1988: p. 163): 'Welcoming someone into one's own home doesn't represent an attempt to undermine privilege; it expresses it.'

Taking difference seriously necessitates the adoption of a politics of *partiality* rather than a politics of inclusion. A politics of partiality implies that feminism must emphasise and consciously construct the *limits* of its own field of political intervention. While a politics of inclusion is driven by an ambition for universal representation (of all women's interests), a politics of partiality does away with that ambition and accepts the principle that feminism can never ever be an encompassing political home for all women, not just because different groups of women have different and sometimes conflicting interests, but, more radically, because for many groups of 'other' women other interests, other identifications are sometimes more important and politically pressing than, or even incompatible with, those related to their being women.

Yeatman (1993: p. 228) acknowledges the necessary partiality of the feminist project when she points to the incommensurability of its insistence on the primacy of gender oppression with the political foci of movements against other forms of social subordination. It is this structural incommensurability that feminists need to come to terms with and accept as drawing the unavoidable limits of feminism as a political project. In short, because all female persons 'do not inhabit the same sociohistorical spaces' (Chow 1991: p. 93), (white/Western) feminism's assumption of a ' "master discourse" position' (ibid.: p. 98) can only be interpreted as an act of symbolic violence which disguises the fundamental structural divisions created by historical processes such as colonialism, imperialism and nationalism. As Butler (1990: p. 4) puts it, 'the premature insistence on a stable subject of feminism, understood as a seamless category of women, inevitably generates multiple refusals to accept the category'. It compels us to say, 'I'm a feminist, but . . .'

NOTES

1. See Anna Yeatman, Chapter 4, in B. Caine and R. Pringle (eds), *Transitions: New Australian Feminisms* (London: Allen and Unwin, 1995).
2. On the theoretical importance of emphasising failure rather than success, see Ien Ang 1994.
3. For a historical analysis of the construction of this hegemonic masculine identity in imperial Britain, see Hall 1992.
4. While most white feminist critics have come out as Madonna enthusiasts, there are exceptions. See, for example, Bordo 1993.
5. See, however, Patton 1993.
6 See Kristeva 1991.
7. It should be added that 'whiteness', too, is a structurally impure position, deriving its very meaning from suppressing and othering that which is not white. But, while the centre, by virtue of its being the centre, can subsequently repress the marginalized other in its sense of identity, the marginal(ised) always has to live under the shadow of the centre and be constantly reminded of its own marginality.
8. For this kind of interrogation by white feminists in Britain and the US, see Ware 1992 and Frankenberg 1993.
9. I would suggest that it is for this reason that the scare campaign against Mabo relied so much on a popular hysteria focused around 'people's backyards'.

10. For example, I have not come across any discussion about the relations between Asian and Aborigine women.
11. In this sense, the theme of reconciliation is more important to the peace of mind of white Australians than to Aboriginal people, for whom reconciliation will never compensate for their permanent displacement from their land.

REFERENCES

Ang, I., 'In the Realm of Uncertainty: The global village in the age of capitalist postmodernity', in D. Crowley and D. Mitchell (eds), *Communication Theory Today* (Oxford: Polity Press, 1994).

Attwood, B., *The Making of the Aborigines* (Sydney: Allen and Unwin, 1989).

Bhabha, H., 'The Third Space', in J. Rutherford (ed.), *Identity: Community, Culture, Difference* (London: Lawrence and Wishart, 1991).

Bordo, S., ' "Material Girl": The effacements of postmodern culture', in C. Schwichtenberg (ed.), Madonna Connection: *Representational Politics, Subcultural Identities and Cultural Theory* (Boulder, CO: Westview Press, 1993).

Bottomley, G. et al. (eds), *Intersexions: Gender/Class/Culture/Ethnicity* (Sydney: Allen and Unwin, 1991).

Butler, J., *Gender Trouble: Feminism and the Subversion of Identity* (New York: Routledge, 1990).

Chow, R., 'Violence in the Other Country: China as crisis, spectacle and woman', in C. T. Mohanty et al. (eds), *Third World Women and the Politics of Feminism* (Bloomington, IN: Indiana University Press, 1991).

Curthoys, A., 'Feminism, Citizenship and National Identity', in *Feminist Review*, no. 44, pp. 19–38.

de Lauretis, T., 'Displacing Hegemonic Discourses: Reflections on feminist theory in the 1980s', in *Inscriptions*, nos 3–4, pp. 127–44.

Flax, J., 'Postmodernism and Gender Relations in Feminist Theory', in L. Nicholson (ed.), *Feminism/Postmodernism* (New York: Routledge, 1990).

Frankenberg, R., *White Women, Race Matters* (Minneapolis, MN: University of Minnesota Press, 1993).

Gunew, S., 'Feminism and the Politics of Irreducible Differences: Multiculturism/ethnicity/race', in S. Gunew and Anna Yeatman (eds), *Feminism and the Politics of Difference* (Sydney: Allen and Unwin, 1993).

Gunew, S., 'Multicultural Multiplicities: US, Canada, Australia', in D. Bennet (ed.), *Cultural Studies: Pluralism and Theory* (Melbourne: Melbourne University Press, 1993b).

Gunew, S. and A. Yeatman (eds), *Feminism and the Politics of Difference* (Sydney: Allen and Unwin, 1993).

Hall, C., *White, Male and Middle Class* (Oxford: Polity Press, 1992).

Haraway, D., 'Situated Knowledges: The science question in feminism and the privilege of partial perspective', in *Feminist Studies*, vol. 14, no. 3, pp. 575–99.

hooks, b., *Yearning: Race, Gender and Cultural Politics* (Boston, MA: South End Press).

hooks, b., *Black Looks: Race and Representation* (Boston, MA: South End Press).

Jolly, M., 'The Politics of Difference: Feminism, colonialism and decolonisation of Vanuatu', in Bottomley, G. et al. (eds), *Intersexions: Gender/Class/Culture/Ethnicity* (Sydney: Allen and Unwin, 1991).

Kirby, V, ' "Feminism, Reading, Postmodernisms": Rethinking complicity', in S. Gunew and A Yeatman (eds), *Feminism and the Politics of Difference* (Sydney: Allen and Unwin, 1993).

Kristeva, J., *Strangers to Ourselves* (New York: Columbia University Press, 1991).

Martin, E., *The woman in the Body: A cultural analysis of reproduction* (Milton Keynes: Open University Press, 1987).

Mohanty, C. T., 'Under Western Eyes: Feminist scholarship and colonial discourses', in Boundary 2, vol. 13, no. 1, pp. 333–58.

Mohanty, C. T, 'On Race and Voice: Challenges for liberal education in the 1990s', in *Cultural Critique*, no. 14, pp. 179-208.

Morris, M., 'Afterthoughts on "Australianism"', in *Cultural Studies*, vol. 6, no. 3, pp. 468–75.

Ong, A, 'Colonialism and Modernity: Feminist re-presentations of women non-Western societies', in *Inscriptions*, nos 3–4, pp. 79–93.

Patton, C., 'Embodying Subaltern Memory: Kinesthesia and the problematics of gender and race', in C. Schwichtenberg (ed.), *Madonna Connection* (Boulder, CO: Westview Press, 1993).

Pettman, J, *Living in the Margins* (Sydney: Allen and Unwin, 1992).

Russo, A., ' "We Cannot Live Without Our Lives": White women, antiracism and feminism', in C. T. Mohanty et al. (eds), *Third World Women and the Politics of Feminism* (Bloomington, IA: Indiana University Press, 1991).

Schwichtenberg, C. (ed.), *Madonna Connection: Representational Politics, Subcultural Identities and Cultural Theory* (Boulder, CO: Westview Press, 1993).

Spelman, E, *Inessential Women: Problems of exclusion in feminist thought* (Boston, MA: Beacon Press, 1988).

Wallerstein, I., *The Modern World System* (London: Academic Press, 1974).

Ware, V, *Beyond the Pale: White women, racism and history* (London: Verso, 1992).

Yeatman, A., 'Voice and Representation in the Politics of Difference', in Gunew, S. and A. Yeatman (eds), *Feminism and the Politics of Difference* (Sydney: Allen and Unwin, 1993).

2.5

'THE OPPOSITIONAL GAZE: BLACK FEMALE SPECTATORS'

bell hooks

When thinking about black female spectators, I remember being punished as a child for staring, for those hard intense direct looks children would give grown-ups, looks that were seen as confrontational, as gestures of resistance, challenges to authority. The 'gaze' has always been political in my life. Imagine the terror felt by the child who has come to understand through repeated punishments that one's gaze can be dangerous. The child who has learned so well to look the other way when necessary. Yet, when punished, the child is told by parents, 'Look at me when I talk to you.' Only, the child is afraid to look. Afraid to look, but fascinated by the gaze. There is power in looking.

Amazed the first time I read in history classes that white slave-owners (men, women, and children) punished enslaved black people for looking, I wondered how this traumatic relationship to the gaze had informed black parenting and black spectatorship. The politics of slavery, of racialized power relations, were such that the slaves were denied their right to gaze. Connecting this strategy of domination to that used by grown folks in southern black rural communities where I grew up, I was pained to think that there was no absolute difference between whites who had oppressed black people and ourselves. Years later, reading Michel Foucault, I thought again about these connections, about the ways power as domination reproduces itself in different locations employing similar apparatuses, strategies, and mechanisms of control. Since I knew as a child that the dominating power adults exercised over me and over my gaze was

From: bell hooks (1992), 'The Oppositional Gaze: Black Female Spectators', pp. 115–31, in bell hooks, *Black Looks: Race and Representation* (London: Turnaround (PSL) Ltd).

never so absolute that I did not dare to look, to sneak a peep, to stare danger-ously, I knew that the slaves had looked. That all attempts to repress our/black people's right to gaze had produced in us an overwhelming longing to look, a rebellious desire, an oppositional gaze. By courageously looking, we defiantly declared: 'Not only will I stare. I want my look to change reality.' Even in the worse circumstances of domination, the ability to manipulate one's gaze in the face of structures of domination that would contain it, opens up the possibility of agency. In much of his work, Michel Foucault insists on describing domina-tion in terms of 'relations of power' as part of an effort to challenge the assump-tion that 'power is a system of domination which controls everything and which leaves no room for freedom'. Emphatically stating that in all relations of power 'there is necessarily the possibility of resistance', he invites the critical thinker to search those margins, gaps and locations on and through the body where agency can be found.

Stuart Hall calls for recognition of our agency as black spectators in his essay 'Cultural Identity and Cinematic Representation'. Speaking against the con-struction of white representations of blackness as totalizing, Hall says of white presence: 'The error is not to conceptualize this "presence" in terms of power, but to locate that power as wholly external to us – as extrinsic force, whose influence can be thrown off like the serpent sheds its skin.' What Franz Fanon reminds us, in *Black Skin, White Masks*, is how power is inside as well as outside:

> . . . the movements, the attitudes, the glances of the Other fixed me there, in the sense in which a chemical solution is fixed by a dye. I was indig-nant; I demanded an explanation. Nothing happened. I burst apart. Now the fragments have been put together again by another self. This 'look' from – so to speak – the place of the Other, fixes us, not only in its vio-lence, hostility and aggression, but in the ambivalence of its desire.[1]

Spaces of agency exist for black people, wherein we can both interrogate the gaze of the Other but also look back, and at one another, naming what we see. The 'gaze' has been and is a site of resistance for colonized black people glo-bally. Subordinates in relations of power learn experientially that there is a crit-ical gaze, one that 'looks' to document, one that is oppositional. In resistance struggle, the power of the dominated to assert agency by claiming and cultivat-ing 'awareness' politicizes 'looking' relations – one learns to look a certain way in order to resist.

When most black people in the United States first had the opportunity to look at film and television, they did so fully aware that mass media was a system of knowledge and power reproducing and maintaining white supremacy. To stare at the television, or mainstream movies, to engage its images, was to engage its negation of black representation. It was the oppositional black gaze that responded to these looking relations by developing independent black cinema. Black viewers of mainstream cinema and television could chart the progress of political movements for racial equality *via* the construction of images, and did so. Within my family's southern black working-class home, located in a racially segregated neighborhood, watching television was one way to develop critical spectatorship. Unless you went to work in the white world, across the tracks, you learned to look at white people by staring at them on the screen. Black looks, as they were constituted in the context of social movements for racial uplift, were interrogating gazes. We laughed at television shows like *Our Gang* and *Amos 'n' Andy*, at these white representations of blackness, but we also looked at them critically. Before racial integration, black viewers of movies and television experienced visual pleasure in a context where looking was also about contestation and confrontation.

Writing about black looking relations in 'Black British Cinema: Spectatorship and Identity Formation in Territories', Manthia Diawara identifies the power of the spectator: 'Every narration places the spectator in a position of agency; and race, class and sexual relations influence the way in which this subjecthood is filled by the spectator.' Of particular concern for him are moments of 'rupture' when the spectator resists 'complete identification with the film's discourse'. These ruptures define the relation between black spectators and dominant cinema prior to racial integration. Then, one's enjoyment of a film wherein representations of blackness were stereotypically degrading and dehumanizing co-existed with a critical practice that restored presence where it was negated. Critical discussion of the film while it was in progress or at its conclusion maintained the distance between spectator and the image. Black films were also subject to critical interrogation. Since they came into being in part as a response to the failure of white-dominated cinema to represent blackness in a manner that did not reinforce white supremacy, they too were critiqued to see if images were seen as complicit with dominant cinematic practices.

Critical, interrogating black looks were mainly concerned with issues of race and racism, the way racial domination of blacks by whites overdetermined representation. They were rarely concerned with gender. As spectators, black men could repudiate the reproduction of racism in cinema and television, the negation of black presence, even as they could feel as though they were rebelling against white supremacy by daring to look, by engaging phallocentric politics of spectatorship. Given the real life public circumstances wherein black men were murdered/lynched for looking at white womanhood, where the black male gaze was always subject to control and/or punishment by the powerful white Other, the private realm of television screens or dark theaters could unleash the repressed gaze. There they could 'look' at white womanhood without a structure of domination overseeing the gaze, interpreting, and punishing. That white supremacist structure that had murdered Emmet Till after interpreting his look as violation, as 'rape' of white womanhood, could not control black male responses to screen images. In their role as spectators, black men could enter an imaginative space of phallocentric power that mediated racial negation. This gendered relation to looking made the experience of the black male spectator radically different from that of the black female spectator. Major early black male independent filmmakers represented black women in their films as objects of male gaze. Whether looking through the camera or as spectators watching films, whether mainstream cinema or "race" movies such as those made by Oscar Micheaux, the black male gaze had a different scope from that of the black female.

Black women have written little about black female spectatorship, about our moviegoing practices. A growing body of film theory and criticism by black women has only begun to emerge. The prolonged silence of black women as spectators and critics was a response to absence, to cinematic negation. In 'The Technology of Gender', Teresa de Lauretis, drawing on the work of Monique Wittig, calls attention to 'the power of discourses to "do violence" to people, a violence which is material and physical, although produced by abstract and scientific discourses as well as the discourses of the mass media'.[2] With the possible exception of early race movies, black female spectators have had to develop looking relations within a cinematic context that constructs our presence as absence, that denies the 'body' of the black female so as to perpetuate white supremacy and with it a phallocentric spectatorship where the woman to be looked at and desired is 'white'. (Recent movies do not conform to this paradigm but I am turning to the past with the intent to chart the development of black female spectatorship.)

Talking with black women of all ages and classes, in different areas of the United States, about their filmic looking relations, I hear again and again ambivalent responses to cinema. Only a few of the black women I talked with remembered the pleasure of race movies, and even those who did, felt that pleasure interrupted and usurped by Hollywood. Most of the black women I talked with were adamant that they never went to movies expecting to see compelling representations of black femaleness. They were all acutely aware of cinematic racism – its violent erasure of black womanhood. In Anne Friedberg's essay 'A Denial of Difference: Theories of Cinematic Identification' she stresses that 'identification can only be made through recognition, and all recognition is itself an implicit confirmation of the ideology of the status quo'. Even when representations of black women were present in film, our bodies and being were there to serve – to enhance and maintain white womanhood as object of the phallocentric gaze.

Commenting on Hollywood's characterization of black women in *Girls on Film*, Julie Burchill describes this absent presence:

> Black women have been mothers without children (Mammies – who can ever forget the sickening spectacle of Hattie MacDaniels waiting on the simpering Vivien Leigh hand and foot and enquiring like a ninny, 'What's ma lamb gonna wear?') . . . Lena Horne, the first black performer signed to a long term contract with a major (MGM), looked gutless but was actually quite spirited. She seethed when Tallulah Bankhead complimented her on the paleness of her skin and the non-Negroidness of her features.[3]

When black women actresses like Lena Horne appeared in mainstream cinema most white viewers were not aware that they were looking at black females unless the film was specifically coded as being about blacks. Burchill is one of the few white women film critics who has dared to examine the intersection of race and gender in relation to the construction of the category 'woman' in film as object of the phallocentric gaze. With characteristic wit she asserts: 'What does it say about racial purity that the best blondes have all been brunettes (Harrow, Monroe, Bardot)? I think it says that we are not as white as we think.' Burchill could easily have said 'we are not as white as we want to be', for clearly the obsession to have white women film stars be ultra-white was a cinematic practice that sought to maintain a distance, a separation between that image and the black female Other; it was a way to perpetuate white supremacy. Politics of race and gender were inscribed into mainstream cinematic narrative from *Birth of A Nation* on. As a seminal work, this film identified what the place and function of white womanhood would be in cinema. There was clearly no place for black women.

Remembering my past in relation to screen images of black womanhood, I wrote a short essay, 'Do you remember Sapphire?' which explored both the negation of black female representation in cinema and television and our rejection of these images. Identifying the character of 'Sapphire' from *Amos 'n' Andy* as that screen representation of black femaleness I first saw in childhood, I wrote:

> She was even then backdrop, foil. She was bitch – nag. She was there to soften images of black men, to make them seem vulnerable, easygoing, funny, and unthreatening to a white audience. She was there as man in drag, as castrating bitch, as someone to be lied to, someone to be tricked, someone the white and black audience could hate. Scapegoated on all sides. *She was not us.* We laughed with the black men, with the white people. We laughed at this black woman who was not us. And we did not even long to be there on the screen. How could we long to be there when our image, visually constructed, was so ugly. We did not long to be there. We did not long for her. We did not want our construction to be this hated black female thing – foil, backdrop. Her black female image was not the body of desire. There was nothing to see. She was not us.[4]

Grown black women had a different response to Sapphire; they identified with her frustrations and her woes. They resented the way she was mocked. They resented the way these screen images could assault black womanhood, could name us bitches, nags. And in opposition they claimed Sapphire as their own, as the symbol of that angry part of themselves white folks and black men could not even begin to understand.

Conventional representations of black women have done violence to the image. Responding to this assault, many black women spectators shut out the image, looked the other way, accorded cinema no importance in their lives.

Then there were those spectators whose gaze was that of desire and complicity. Assuming a posture of subordination, they submitted to cinema's capacity to seduce and betray. They were cinematically 'gaslighted'. Every black woman I spoke with who was/is an ardent moviegoer, 'a lover of the Hollywood film, testified that to experience fully the pleasure of that cinema they had to close down critique, analysis; they had to forget racism. And mostly they did not think about sexism. What was the nature then of this adoring black female gaze – this look that could bring pleasure in the midst of negation? In her first novel, *The Bluest Eye*, Toni Morrison constructs a portrait of the black female spectator; her gaze is the masochistic look of victimization. Describing her looking relations, Miss Pauline Breedlove, a poor working woman, maid in the house of a prosperous white family, asserts:

> The onliest time I be happy seem like was when I was in the picture show. Every time I got, I went, I'd go early, before the show started. They's cut off the lights, and everything be black. Then the screen would light up, and I's move right on in them picture. White men taking such good care of they women, and they all dressed up in big clean houses with the bath tubs right in the same room with the toilet. Them pictures gave me a lot of pleasure.[5]

To experience pleasure, Miss Pauline sitting in the dark must imagine herself transformed, turned into the white woman portrayed on the screen. After watching movies, feeling the pleasure, she says, 'But it made coming home hard.'

We come home to ourselves. Not all black women spectators submitted to that spectacle of regression through identification. Most of the women I talked with felt that they consciously resisted identification with films – that this tension made moviegoing less than pleasurable; at times it caused pain. As one black woman put, 'I could always get pleasure from movies as long as I did not look too deep.' For black female spectators who have 'looked too deep' the encounter with the screen hurt. That some of us chose to stop looking was a gesture of resistance, turning away was one way to protest, to reject negation. My pleasure in the screen ended abruptly when I and my sisters first watched *Imitation of Life*. Writing about this experience in the 'Sapphire' piece, I addressed the movie directly, confessing:

> I had until now forgotten you, that screen image seen in adolescence, those images that made me stop looking. It was there in *Imitation of Life*, that comfortable mammy image. There was something familiar about this hard-working black woman who loved her daughter so much, loved her in a way that hurt. Indeed, as young southern black girls watching this film, Peola's mother reminded us of the hardworking, churchgoing, Big Mamas we knew and loved. Consequently, it was not this image that captured our gaze; we were fascinated by Peola.[6]

Addressing her, I wrote:

> You were different. There was something scary in this image of young
> sexual sensual black beauty betrayed – that daughter who did not want
> to be confined by blackness, that 'tragic mulatto' who did not want to be
> negated. 'Just let me escape this image forever,' she could have said. I will
> always remember that image. I remembered how we cried for her, for our
> unrealized desiring selves. She was tragic because there was no place in
> the cinema for her, no loving pictures. She too was absent image. It was
> better then, that we were absent, for when we were there it was humiliat-
> ing, strange, sad. We cried all night for you, for the cinema that had no
> place for you. And like you, we stopped thinking it would one day be dif-
> ferent.[7]

When I returned to films as a young woman, after a long period of silence, I
had developed an oppositional gaze. Not only would I not be hurt by the
absence of black female presence, or the insertion of violating representation, I
interrogated the work, cultivated a way to look past race and gender for aspects
of content, form, language. Foreign films and US independent cinema were the
primary locations of my filmic looking relations, even though I also watched
Hollywood films.

From 'jump', black female spectators have gone to films with awareness of
the way in which race and racism determined the visual construction of gender.
Whether it was *Birth of A Nation* or Shirley Temple shows, we knew that white
womanhood was the racialized sexual difference occupying the place of
stardom in mainstream narrative film. We assumed white women knew it too.
Reading Laura Mulvey's provocative essay, 'Visual Pleasure and Narrative
Cinema', from a standpoint that acknowledges race, one sees clearly why black
women spectators not duped by mainstream cinema would develop an oppositional gaze. Placing ourselves outside that pleasure in looking, Mulvey argues,
was determined by a 'split between active/male and passive/female'. Black
female spectators actively chose not to identify with the film's imaginary subject
because such identification was disenabling.

Looking at films with an oppositional gaze, black women were able to critically assess the cinema's construction of white womanhood as object of phallocentric gaze and choose not to identify with either the victim or the
perpetrator. Black female spectators, who refused to identify with white womanhood, who would not take on the phallocentric gaze of desire and possession, created a critical space where the binary opposition Mulvey posits of
'woman as image, man as bearer of the look' was continually deconstructed.
As critical spectators, black women looked from a location that disrupted, one
akin to that described by Annette Kuhn in *The Power of The Image*:

> . . . the acts of analysis, of deconstruction and of reading 'against the
> grain' offer an additional pleasure – the pleasure of resistance, of saying

'no' not to 'unsophisticated' enjoyment, by ourselves and others, of culturally dominant images, but to the structures of power which ask us to
consume them uncritically and in highly circumscribed ways.[8]

Mainstream feminist film criticism in no way acknowledges black female
spectatorship. It does not even consider the possibility that women can construct an oppositional gaze via an understanding and awareness of the politics
of race and racism. Feminist film theory rooted in an ahistorical psychoanalytic
framework that privileges sexual difference actively suppresses recognition of
race, reenacting and mirroring the erasure of black womanhood that occurs in
films, silencing any discussion of racial difference – of racialized sexual difference. Despite feminist critical interventions aimed at deconstructing the category 'woman' which highlight the significance of race, many feminist film critics
continue to structure their discourse as though it speaks about 'women' when
in actuality it speaks only about white women. It seems ironic that the cover of
the recent anthology *Feminism and Film Theory* edited by Constance Penley
has a graphic that is a reproduction of the photo of white actresses Rosalind
Russell and Dorothy Arzner on the 1936 set of the film *Craig's Wife* yet there
is no acknowledgment in any essay in this collection that the woman 'subject'
under discussion is always white. Even though there are photos of black women
from films reproduced in the text, there is no acknowledgment of racial difference.

It would be too simplistic to interpret this failure of insight solely as a gesture
of racism. Importantly, it also speaks to the problem of structuring feminist film
theory around a totalizing narrative of woman as object whose image functions
solely to reaffirm and reinscribe patriarchy. Mary Ann Doane addresses this
issue in the essay 'Remembering Women: Psychical and Historical Construction
in Film Theory':

> This attachment to the figure of a degeneralizible Woman as the product
> of the apparatus indicates why, for many, feminist film theory seems to
> have reached an impasse, a certain blockage in its theorization . . . In
> focusing upon the task of delineating in great detail the attributes of
> woman as effect of the apparatus, feminist film theory participates in the
> abstraction of women.[9]

The concept 'Woman' effaces the difference between women in specific socio-
historical contexts, between women defined precisely as historical subjects
rather than as *a* psychic subject (or non-subject). Though Doane does not focus
on race, her comments speak directly to the problem of its erasure. For it is only
as one imagines 'woman' in the abstract, when woman becomes fiction or
fantasy, can race not be seen as significant. Are we really to imagine that feminist theorists writing only about images of white women, who subsume this
specific historical subject under the totalizing category 'woman' do not 'see' the
whiteness of the image? It may very well be that they engage in a process of

denial that eliminates the necessity of revisioning conventional ways of thinking about psychoanalysis as a paradigm of analysis and the need to rethink a body of feminist film theory that is firmly rooted in a denial of the reality that sex/sexuality may not be the primary and/or exclusive signifier of difference. Doane's essay appears in the anthology, *Psychoanalysis and Cinema* edited by E. Ann Kaplan, where, once again, none of the theory presented acknowledges or discusses racial difference, with the exception of one essay, 'Not Speaking with Language, Speaking with No Language', which problematizes notions of orientalism in its examination of Leslie Thornton's film *Adynata*. Yet in most of the essays, the theories espoused are rendered problematic if one includes race as a category of analysis.

Constructing feminist film theory along these lines enables the production of a discursive practice that need never theorize any aspect of black female representation or spectatorship. Yet the existence of black women within white supremacist culture problematizes, and makes complex, the overall issue of female identity, representation, and spectatorship. If, as Friedberg suggests, 'identification is a process which commands the subject to be displaced by an other; it is a procedure which breeches the separation between self and other, and, in this way, replicates the very structure of patriarchy'. If identification 'demands sameness, necessitates similarity, disallows difference – must we then surmise that many feminist film critics who are 'over-identified' with the mainstream cinematic apparatus produce theories that replicate its totalizing agenda? Why is it that feminist film criticism, which has most claimed the terrain of woman's identity, representation, and subjectivity as its field of analysis, remains aggressively silent on the subject of blackness and specifically representations of black womanhood? Just as mainstream cinema has historically forced aware black female spectators not to look, much feminist film criticism disallows the possibility of a theoretical dialogue that might include black women's voices. It is difficult to talk when you feel no one is listening, when you feel as though a special jargon or narrative has been created that only the chosen can understand. No wonder then that black women have for the most part confined our critical commentary on film to conversations. And it must be reiterated that this gesture is a strategy that protects us from the violence perpetuated and advocated by discourses of mass media. A new focus on issues of race and representation in the field of film theory could critically intervene on the historical repression reproduced in some arenas of contemporary critical practice, making a discursive space for discussion of black female spectatorship possible.

When I asked a black woman in her twenties, an obsessive moviegoer, why she thought we had not written about black female spectatorship, she commented: 'We are afraid to talk about ourselves as spectators because we have been so abused by 'the gaze'. An aspect of that abuse was the imposition of the assumption that black female looking relations were not important enough to theorize. Film theory as a critical 'turf' in the United States has been and continues to be influenced by and reflective of white racial domination. Since feminist film criticism was initially rooted in a women's liberation movement informed by racist practices, it did not open up the discursive terrain and make it more inclusive. Recently, even those white film theorists who include an analysis of race show no interest in black female spectatorship. In her introduction to the collection of essays *Visual and Other Pleasures*, Laura Mulvey describes her initial romantic absorption in Hollywood cinema, stating:

> Although this great, previously unquestioned and unanalyzed love was put in crisis by the impact of feminism on my thought in the early 1970s, it also had an enormous influence on the development of my critical work and ideas and the debate within film culture with which I became preoccupied over the next fifteen years or so. Watched through eyes that were affected by the changing climate of consciousness, the movies lost their magic.[10]

Watching movies from a feminist perspective, Mulvey arrived at that location of disaffection that is the starting point for many black women approaching cinema within the lived harsh reality of racism. Yet her account of being a part of a film culture whose roots rest on a founding relationship of adoration and love indicates how difficult it would have been to enter that world from 'jump' as a critical spectator whose gaze had been formed in opposition.

Given the context of class exploitation, and racist and sexist domination, it has only been through resistance, struggle, reading, and looking 'against the grain', that black women have been able to value our process of looking enough to publicly name it. Centrally, those black female spectators who attest to the oppositionality of their gaze deconstruct theories of female spectatorship that have relied heavily on the assumption that, as Doane suggests in her essay, 'Woman's Stake: Filming the Female Body', 'woman can only mimic man's relation to language, that is assume a position defined by the penis-phallus as the supreme arbiter of lack'.[11] Identifying with neither the phallocentric gaze nor the construction of white womanhood as lack, critical black female spectators construct a theory of looking relations where cinematic visual delight is the pleasure of interrogation. Every black woman spectator I talked to, with rare exception, spoke of being 'on guard' at the movies. Talking about the way being a critical spectator of Hollywood films influenced her, black woman film-maker Julie Dash exclaims, 'I make films because I was such a spectator!' Looking at Hollywood cinema from a distance, from that critical politicized standpoint that did not want to be seduced by narratives reproducing her negation, Dash watched mainstream movies over and over again for the pleasure of deconstructing them. And of course there is that added delight if one happens, in the process of interrogation, to come across a narrative that invites the black female spectator to engage the text with no threat of violation.

Significantly, I began to write film criticism in response to the first Spike Lee movie, *She's Gotta Have It*, contesting Lee's replication of mainstream patriarchal cinematic practices that explicitly represents woman (in this instance black woman) as the object of a phallocentric gaze. Lee's investment in patriarchal filmic practices that mirror dominant patterns makes him the perfect black candidate for entrance to the Hollywood canon. His work mimics the cinematic construction of white womanhood as object, replacing her body as text on which to write male desire with the black female body. It is transference without transformation. Entering the discourse of film criticism from the politicized location of resistance, of not wanting, as a working-class black woman I interviewed stated, 'to see black women in the position white women have occupied in film forever', I began to think critically about black female spectatorship.

For years I went to independent and/or foreign films where I was the only black female present in the theater. I often imagined that in every theater in the United States there was another black woman watching the same film wondering why she was the only visible black female spectator. I remember trying to share with one of my five sisters the cinema I liked so much. She was 'enraged' that I brought her to a theater where she would have to read subtitles. To her it was a violation of Hollywood notions of spectatorship, of coming to the movies to be entertained. When I interviewed her to ask what had changed her mind over the years, led her to embrace this cinema, she connected it to coming to critical consciousness, saying, 'I learned that there was more to looking than I had been exposed to in ordinary (Hollywood) movies'. I shared that though most of the films I loved were all white, I could engage them because they did not have in their deep structure a subtext reproducing the narrative of white supremacy. Her response was to say that these films demystified 'whiteness', since the lives they depicted seemed less rooted in fantasies of escape. They were, she suggested, more like 'what we knew life to be, the deeper side of life as well'. Always more seduced and enchanted with Hollywood cinema than me, she stressed that unaware black female spectators must 'break out', no longer be imprisoned by images that enact a drama of our negation. Though she still sees Hollywood films, because 'they are a major influence in the culture' – she no longer feels duped or victimized.

Talking with black female spectators, looking at written discussions either in fiction or academic essays about black women, I noted the connection made between the realm of representation in mass media and the capacity of black women to construct ourselves as subjects in daily life. The extent to which black women feel devalued, objectified, dehumanized in this society determines the scope and texture of their looking relations. Those black women whose identities were constructed in resistance, by practices that oppose the dominant order, were most inclined to develop an oppositional gaze. Now that there is a growing interest in films produced by black women and those films have become more accessible to viewers, it is possible to talk about black female spectatorship in relation to that work. So far, most discussions of black spectatorship that I have come across focus on men. In 'Black Spectatorship: Problems of Identification and Resistance' Manthia Diawara suggests that 'the components of "difference" ' among elements of sex, gender, and sexuality give rise to different readings of the same material, adding that these conditions produce a 'resisting' spectator. He focuses his critical discussion on black masculinity.[12]

The recent publication of the anthology *The Female Gaze: Women as Viewers of Popular Culture* excited me, especially as it included an essay, 'Black Looks', by Jacqui Roach and Petal Felix that attempts to address black female spectatorship. The essay posed provocative questions that were not answered: Is there a black female gaze?[13] How do black women relate to the gender politics of representation? Concluding, the authors assert that black females have 'our own reality, our own history, our own gaze – one which the sees the world rather differently from "anyone else"'. Yet, they do not name/describe this experience of seeing 'rather differently'. The absence of definition and explanation suggests they are assuming an essentialist stance wherein it is presumed that black women, as victims of race and gender oppression, have an inherently different field of vision. Many black women do not 'see differently' precisely because their perceptions of reality are so profoundly colonized, shaped by dominant ways of knowing. As Trinh T. Minh-ha points out in 'Outside In, Inside Out': 'Subjectivity does not merely consist of talking about oneself . . . be this talking indulgent or critical.'[14]

Critical black female spectatorship emerges as a site of resistance only when individual black women actively resist the imposition of dominant ways of knowing and looking. While every black woman I talked to was aware of racism, that awareness did not automatically correspond with politicization, the development of an oppositional gaze. When it did, individual black women consciously named the process. Manthia Diawara's 'resisting spectatorship' is a term that does not adequately describe the terrain of black female spectatorship. We do more than resist. We create alternative texts that are not solely reactions. As critical spectators, black women participate in a broad range of looking relations, contest, resist, revision, interrogate, and invent on multiple levels. Certainly when I watch the work of the black women film-makers, Camille Billops, Kathleen Collins, Julie Dash, Ayoka Chenzira, Zeinabu Davis, I do not need to 'resist' the images even as I still choose to watch their work with a critical eye.

Black female critical thinkers concerned with creating space for the construction of radical black female subjectivity, and the way cultural production informs this possibility, fully acknowledge the importance of mass media, film in particular, as a powerful site for critical intervention. Certainly Julie Dash's film *Illusions* identifies the terrain of Hollywood cinema as a space of knowledge production that has enormous power. Yet, she also creates a filmic narrative wherein the black female protagonist subversively claims that space. Inverting the 'real-life' power structure, she offers the black female spectator representations that challenge stereotypical notions that place us outside the realm of filmic discursive practices. Within the film she uses the strategy of

Hollywood suspense films to undermine those cinematic practices that deny black women a place in this structure. Problematizing the question of 'racial' identity by depicting passing, suddenly it is the white male's capacity to gaze, define and know that is called into question.

When Mary Ann Doane describes in 'Woman's Stake: Filming the Female Body' the way in which feminist film-making practice can elaborate 'a special syntax for a different articulation of the female body', she names a critical process that 'undoes the structure of the classical narrative through an insistence upon its repressions'.[15] An eloquent description, this precisely names Dash's strategy in *Illusions*, even though the film is not unproblematic and works within certain conventions that are not successfully challenged. For example, the film does not indicate whether the character Mignon will make Hollywood films that subvert and transform the genre or whether she will simply assimilate and perpetuate the norm. Still, subversively, *Illusions* problematizes the issue of race and spectatorship. White people in the film are unable to 'see' that race informs their looking relations. Though she is passing to gain access to the machinery of cultural production represented by film, Mignon continually asserts her ties to black community. The bond between her and the young black woman singer Esther Jeeter is affirmed by caring gestures of affirmation, often expressed by eye-to-eye contact, the direct unmediated gaze of recognition. Ironically, it is the desiring objectifying sexualized white male gaze that threatens to penetrate her 'secrets' and disrupt her process. Metaphorically, Dash suggests the power of black women to make films will be threatened and undermined by that white male gaze that seeks to reinscribe the black female body in a narrative of voyeuristic pleasure where the only relevant opposition is male/female, and the only location for the female is as a victim. These tensions are not resolved by the narrative. It is not at all evident that Mignon will triumph over the white supremacist capitalist imperialist dominating 'gaze'.

Throughout *Illusions*, Mignon's power is affirmed by her contact with the younger black woman whom she nurtures and protects. It is this process of mirrored recognition that enables both black women to define their reality, apart from the reality imposed upon them by structures of domination. The shared gaze of the two women reinforces their solidarity. As the younger subject, Esther represents a potential audience for films that Mignon might produce, films wherein black females will be the narrative focus. Julie Dash's recent feature-length film *Daughters of the Dust* dares to place black females at the center of its narrative. This focus caused critics (especially white males) to critique the film negatively or to express many reservations. Clearly, the impact of racism and sexism so over-determine spectatorship – not only what we look at but who we identify with – that viewers who are not black females find it hard to empathize with the central characters in the movie. They are adrift without a white presence in the film.

Another representation of black females nurturing one another via recognition of their common struggle for subjectivity is depicted in Sankofa's collective work *Passion of Remembrance*. In the film, two black women friends, Louise and Maggie, are from the onset of the narrative struggling with the issue of subjectivity, of their place in progressive black liberation movements that have been sexist. They challenge old norms and want to replace them with new understandings of the complexity of black identity, and the need for liberation struggles that address that complexity. Dressing to go to a party, Louise and Maggie claim the 'gaze'. Looking at one another, staring in mirrors, they appear completely focused on their encounter with black femaleness. How they see themselves is most important, not how they will be stared at by others. Dancing to the tune 'Let's get Loose', they display their bodies not for a voyeuristic colonizing gaze but for that look of recognition that affirms their subjectivity – that constitutes them as spectators. Mutually empowered they eagerly leave the privatized domain to confront the public. Disrupting conventional racist and sexist stereotypical representations of black female bodies, these scenes invite the audience to look differently. They act to critically intervene and transform conventional filmic practices, changing notions of spectatorship. *Illusions*, *Daughters of the Dust*, and *A Passion of Remembrance* employ a deconstructive filmic practice to undermine existing grand cinematic narratives even as they retheorize subjectivity in the realm of the visual. Without providing 'realistic' positive representations that emerge only as a response to the totalizing nature of existing narratives, they offer points of radical departure. Opening up a space for the assertion of a critical black female spectatorship, they do not simply offer diverse representations, they imagine new transgressive possibilities for the formulation of identity.

In this sense they make explicit a critical practice that provides us with different ways to think about black female subjectivity and black female spectatorship. Cinematically, they provide new points of recognition, embodying Stuart Hall's vision of a critical practice that acknowledges that identity is constituted 'not outside but within representation', and invites us to see film 'not as a second-order mirror held up to reflect what already exists, but as that form of representation which is able to constitute us as new kinds of subjects, and thereby enable us to discover who we are'.[16] It is this critical practice that enables production of feminist film theory that theorizes black female spectatorship. Looking and looking back, black women involve ourselves in a process whereby we see our history as counter-memory, using it as a way to know the present and invent the future.

NOTES

1. Franz Fanon, *Black Skin, White Masks* (London: Pluto, 1986 [1952]).
2. Teresa de Lauretis, *The Technology of Gender: Essays on theory, film and fiction* (Bloomington, IN: Indiana University Press, 1987).
3. Julie Burchill, *Girls on Film* (New York: Pantheon, 1986).
4. bell hooks, unspecified publication.
5. Toni Morrison, *The Bluest Eye* (New York: Holt, Rinehart and Winston, 1970).
6. bell hooks, unspecified publication.

7. bell hooks, unspecified publication.
8. Annette Kuhn, *The Power of the Image: Essays on representation and sexuality* (New York: Routledge, 1985).
9. Mary Ann Doane, 'Remembering Women: Psychical and historical constructions in film theory', in E. Ann Kaplan (ed.), *Psychoanalysis and Cinema* (London: Routledge, 1990).
10. Laura Mulvey, *Visual and Other Pleasures* (Bloomington, IN: Indiana University Press, 1989).
11. Mary Ann Doane, 'Woman's Stake: Filming the female body', in Constance Penley (ed.), *Feminism and Film Theory* (New York: Routledge, 1988)
12. Manthia Diawara, 'Black Spectatorship: Problems of identification and resistance', in *Screen*, Fall 1988, vol. 29, no. 4.
13. Jacqui Roach and Petal Felix, 'Black Looks', in Lorraine Gammon and Margaret Marshment (eds), *The Female Gaze: Women as Viewers of Popular Culture* (London: Women's Press, 1988).
14. Trinh T. Minh-ha, 'Outside In, Inside Out', in Jim Pines (ed.), *Questions of Third World Cinema* (London: British Film Institute, 1989).
15. Doane, 'Woman's Stake'.
16. Stuart Hall, unspecified publication.

FILMOGRAPHY

Arzner, D., *Craig's Wife* (US, 1936).
Blackwood, Maureen and Isaac Julien, *The Passion of Remembrance* (US, 1986).
Dash, J. *Daughters of the Dust* (US, 1991).
Dash, J., *Illusions* (US, 1983).
Griffith, D. W., *Birth of a Nation* (US, 1915).
Lee, S, *She's Gotta Have It* (US, 1986).
Stahl, J. M., *Imitation of Life* (US, 1934).
Thornton, L., *Adynata* (US, 1983).

2.6

'"ON THE THRESHOLD OF WOMAN'S ERA": LYNCHING, EMPIRE AND SEXUALITY IN BLACK FEMINIST THEORY'

Hazel V. Carby

If the fifteenth century discovered America to the Old World, the nineteenth is discovering woman to herself. . . .

Not the opportunity of discovering new worlds, but that of filling this old world with fairer and higher aims than the greed of gold and the lust of power, is hers. Through weary, wasting years men have destroyed, dashed in pieces, and overthrown, but to-day we stand on the threshold of woman's era, and woman's work is grandly constructive. In her hand are possibilities whose use or abuse must tell upon the political life of the nation, and send their influence for good or evil across the track of unborn ages.

[Frances E. W. Harper, 'Woman's Political Future']

The world of thought under the predominant man-influence, unmollified and unrestrained by its complementary force, would become like Daniel's fourth beast: 'dreadful and terrible, and *strong* exceedingly;' 'it had great iron teeth; it devoured and brake in pieces, and stamped the residue with the feet of it;' and the most independent of us find ourselves ready at times to fall down and worship this incarnation of power.

[Anna Julia Cooper, *A Voice from the South*]

My purpose in this essay is to describe and define the ways in which Afro-American women intellectuals, in the last decade of the nineteenth century, the-

From: Hazel V. Carby (1985), '"On the Threshold of Woman's Era": Lynching, Empire and Sexuality in Black Feminist Theory', pp. 262–77, in *Critical Inquiry*, no. 12.

orized about the possibilities and limits of patriarchal power through its manipulation of racialized and gendered social categories and practices. The essay is especially directed toward two academic constituencies: the practitioners of Afro-American cultural analysis and of feminist historiography and theory. The dialogue with each has its own peculiar form, characterized by its own specific history; yet both groups are addressed in an assertion of difference, of alterity, and in a voice characterized by an anger dangerously self-restrained. For it is not in the nature of Caliban to curse; rather, like Caliban, the black woman has learned from the behaviour of her master and mistress that if accommodation results in a patronizing loosening of her bonds, liberation will be more painful.

On the one hand, Afro-American cultural analysis and criticism have traditionally characterized the turn of the century as the age of Booker T. Washington and W. E. B. Du Bois. Afro-American studies frame our response to that period within a conceptual apparatus limiting historical interpretation to theories of exceptional male intellectual genius as exemplified in the texts *Up from Slavery* and *The Souls of Black Folk*. I wish to reconsider the decade of the 1890s as the 'woman's era' not merely in order to insert women into the gaps in our cultural history (to compete for intellectual dominance with men) but to shift the object of interpretation from examples of individual intellectual genius to the collective production and interrelation of forms of knowledge among black women intellectuals. The intellectual discourse of black women during the 1890s includes a wide variety of cultural practices. This essay, however, will concentrate on the theoretical analyses of race, gender, and patriarchal power found in the essays of Anna Julia Cooper, the journalism of Ida B. Wells, and the first novel of Pauline Hopkins.

On the other hand, feminist theory and its academic practice, 'women's studies', appear if not content with, then at least consistent in, their limited concern with a small minority of the women of the planet: those white, middle-class inhabitants of the metropoles. Although feminist scholarship has made the histories of these women visible, it has done so by reconstituting patriarchal power on another terrain rather than by promising a strategy for its abolition. This leaves us with the same complaint as our nineteenth-century black foremothers: feminist theory supports and reproduces a racist hierarchy. Feminist investigations of nineteenth-century women writers actively ignore nonwhite women; some of the most recent, exciting, and innovative thinking on sexuality relegates black women to a paragraph and secondary sources. Ellen Carol DuBois and Linda Gordon, in their essay 'Seeking Ecstasy on the Battlefield: Danger and Pleasure in Nineteenth-Century Feminist Sexual Thought', argue that 'the black women's movement conducted a particularly militant campaign for respectability, often making black feminists spokespeople for prudery in their communities', without direct reference to one of these black feminists or their work. Their subject is 'how feminists conceptualized different sexual dangers, as a means of organizing *resistance* to sexual oppression'; their motivation is to be able to examine how these strategies changed and to learn what historical understanding can be brought to contemporary feminist campaigns.[1] I hope that a discussion of Cooper, Wells and Hopkins in the context of the black women's movement will direct readers to consider more seriously how black feminists conceptualized the possibilities for resisting sexual oppression than the dismissal implied in 'prudery' allows.

The decade of the 1890s was a time of intense activity and productivity for Afro-American women intellectuals. It opened with the publication of Frances Harper's *Iola Leroy*, Cooper's *Voice from the South*, and Wells' *Southern Horrors: Lynch Law in All Its Phases*.[2] In 1893, as part of the World's Columbian Exposition, the World's Congress of Representative Women met in Chicago. Among others, Hallie Q. Brown, Anna Julia Cooper, Fannie Jackson Coppin, Sarah J. Early, Frances Harper, Fannie Barrier Williams, and Frederick Douglass – six black women and one black man – addressed the gathering. Harper told her audience that she felt they were standing 'on the threshold of women's era'; in 1894, *Woman's Era* was the name chosen for the journal run by the Woman's Era Club in Boston.[3] The club movement grew rapidly among Afro-American women and culminated in the first Congress of Colored Women of the United States, which convened in Boston in 1895. In 1896, the National Federation of Colored Women and the National League of Colored Women united in Washington, DC, to form the National Association of Colored Women (NACW). For the first time, black women were nationally organized to confront the various modes of their oppression.[4]

The decade opened and closed with the publication of novels by black women: Harper's *Iola* and the first of Hopkins' four novels, *Contending Forces* (1900). Both authors intended that their texts contribute to the struggle for social change in a period of crisis for the Afro-American community. Their novels were meant to be read as actively attempting to change the structure of the Afro-American culture of which they were a part. As an integral part of a wider movement among black women intellectuals, these books both shaped and were shaped by strategies for resisting and defeating oppression. Organizing to fight included writing to organize. The novels do not merely reflect constituencies but attempt to structure Afro-American struggles in particular directions; both are loci of political and social interests that try to form, not just reveal, their constituencies. Afro-American women were attempting to define the political parameters of gender, race and patriarchal authority and were constantly engaged with these issues in both fiction and nonfiction. The formation of the NACW provided a forum for the exchange of ideas among Afro-American women intellectuals, within a structure that disseminated information nationally. Black women's clubs provided a support for, but were also influenced by, the work of their individual members. Hopkins, for example, read from the manuscript of *Contending Forces* to the members of the Woman's Era Club in Boston; in turn, those members were part of the constituency that Hopkins tried to mobilize to agitate against Jim Crow segregation and the terrorizing practices of lynching and rape.

As intellectuals, these women organized around issues that addressed all aspects of the social organization of oppression. Arrival at the threshold of woman's era did not lead to concentration on what could be narrowly construed as women's issues – whether domestic concerns or female suffrage. Cooper characterized the opportunity this way: 'To be a woman of the Negro race in America, and to be able to grasp the deep significance of the possibilities of the crisis, is to have a heritage . . . unique in the ages' (V, p. 144). Cooper saw the responsibility of the black woman to be the reshaping of society: 'Such is the colored woman's office. She must stamp weal or woe on the coming history of this people' (V, p. 145). To illustrate the process of exchange of ideas within the discourse of the woman's era, I will concentrate on one object of analysis: a theory of internal and external colonization developed in the works of Cooper and Wells and finally figured in the fiction of Hopkins.

As indicated in the epigraphs to this essay, both Harper and Cooper associated imperialism with unrestrained patriarchal power. Prefiguring Hopkins, Harper and Cooper reassessed the mythology of the founding fathers in terms of rampant lust, greed and destruction: they portray white male rule as bestial in its actual and potential power to devour lands and peoples. Cooper developed a complex analysis of social, political and economic forces as being either distinctly masculine or feminine in their orientation and consequences. She saw an intimate link between internal and external colonization, between domestic racial oppression and imperialism. While her critique of imperialism and institutionalized domestic racism is a particularly good example of her larger theories of masculine and feminine practices and spheres of influence, it is important to stress that her categories were not dependent on biological distinction. Cooper made it clear in her application of such analyses that women could conform to masculinist attitudes and practices and men could display womanly virtues.

Cooper saw the imperialist or expansionist impulse, with its ideology of racial categorization, as a supreme manifestation of patriarchal power. She argued that the source of such flagrant abuse had to be questioned, challenged, and opposed:

> Whence came this apotheosis of greed and cruelty? Whence this sneaking admiration we all have for bullies and prize-fighters? Whence the self-congratulation of 'dominant' races, as if 'dominant' meant 'righteous' and carried with it a title to inherit the earth? Whence the scorn of so-called weak or unwarlike races and individuals, and the very comfortable assurance that it is their manifest destiny to be wiped out as vermin before this advancing civilization? (V, p. 51)

Cooper refers to Lowell's *Soul of the Far East*, an imperialist treatise which predicted the death of all Asian peoples and cultures, '"before the advancing nations of the West"'. She indicts the author as a 'scion of an upstart race' who felt confident that, with the stroke of a pen, he could consign 'to annihilation one-third the inhabitants of the globe – a people whose civilization was hoary headed before the parent elements that begot his race had advanced beyond nebulosity' (V, p. 52). The world under a dominant male influence is compared to the beast from the Book of Daniel, devouring all before it and demanding that it be worshiped as an incarnation of power. The complementary force, the female influence, is unable to restrain 'the beast'; the rampant will to dominate and despise the weak is also present in the racist attitudes of white women. Cooper saw patriarchal power revealed in the imperialist impulse, but she also saw that that power was nurtured and sustained at home by an elite of white women preoccupied with maintaining their caste status (see V, pp. 86–7).

Cooper felt strongly that the only effective counter to patriarchal abuse of power – the feminine – had to be developed through the education of women. Education held possibilities for the empowerment of women, who could then shape the course of a future society which would exercise sensitivity and sympathy toward all who were poor and oppressed. White women, however, rarely exercised their power in sympathy with their black sisters. Cooper was well aware of this, and some of her most vituperative work attacks the exclusionary practices and discourse of white women's organizations which presumed to exist for and address the experiences of 'women'. Cooper challenged white women, as would-be leaders of reform, to revolutionize their thinking and practices. She challenged them to transform their provincial determination to secure gender and class interests at the expense of the rights of the oppressed (see V, pp. 123–4).

These gender and class interests were disguised when the issue of justice began to be displaced by debates about the dangers of social equality – debates that concerned the possible status of subject peoples abroad as well as the position of blacks in the United States. Cooper recognized – and condemned as fallacious – the concept of social equality with its implications of forced association between the races. This was not the social justice which blacks demanded. On the contrary, Cooper asserted, forced association was the manacled black male and the raped black woman, both internally colonized. Social equality masked the real issue: autonomy and the right to self-determination.

Cooper understood that the smoke screen of social equality obscured questions of heritage and inheritance which appeared in the figure of 'blood' and gained consensual dominance both North and South (see V, pp. 103–4). She became convinced that the key to understanding the unwritten history of the United States was the dominance of southern 'influence, ideals, and ideas' over the whole nation. Cooper saw that the manipulative power of the South was embodied in the southern patriarch, but she describes its concern with 'blood', inheritance, and heritage in entirely female terms and as a preoccupation that was transmitted from the South to the North and perpetuated by white women. The South represented not red blood but blue:

If your own father was a pirate, a robber, a murderer, his hands are dyed in red blood, and you don't say very much about it. But if your great great great grandfather's grandfather stole and pillaged and slew, and you can prove it, your blood has become blue and you are at great pains to establish the relationship. . . . [The South] had blood; and she paraded it with so much gusto that the substantial little Puritan maidens of the North, who had been making bread and canning currants and not thinking of blood the least bit, began to hunt up the records of the Mayflower to see if some of the passengers thereon could not claim the honor of having been one of William the Conqueror's brigands, when he killed the last of the Saxon Kings and, red-handed, stole his crown and his lands. (V, pp. 103–4)

Ridicule effectively belittles and undermines the search for an aristocratic heritage and proof of biological racial superiority; it also masks a very serious critique of these ideologies that Hopkins was to develop in her fiction. The juxtaposition of 'red' with 'blue' blood reveals the hidden history of national and nationalist heritage to be based on the principles of murder and theft – piracy. Hopkins drew from this analysis of the methods of expansionism, as it applied to the colonization of the Americas and to the imperialist ventures of the United States, as she demystified the mythological pretensions of the American story of origins in her fiction.

By linking imperialism to internal colonization, Cooper thus provided black women intellectuals with the basis for an analysis of how patriarchal power establishes and sustains gendered and racialized social formations. White women were implicated in the maintenance of this wider system of oppression because they challenged only the parameters of their domestic confinement; by failing to reconstitute their class and caste interests, they reinforced the provincialism of their movement. Ultimately, however, Cooper placed her hopes for change on the possibility of a transformed woman's movement. She wanted to expand the rubric defining the concerns of women to encompass an ideal and practice that could inspire a movement for the liberation of all oppressed peoples, not just a movement for the defence of parochial and sectional interests in the name of 'woman' (see V, p. 125).

The pen of Ida B. Wells was aimed at a different target – lynching, as a practice of political and economic repression. Wells' analysis of the relation between political terrorism, economic oppression, and conventional codes of sexuality and morality has still to be surpassed in its incisive condemnation of the patriarchal manipulation of race and gender.[5] Her achievement drew upon the support of club women but also provided the impetus for the formation of antilynching societies. *Southern Horrors*, on the one hand, was dedicated to the Afro-American women of New York and Brooklyn, whose contributions had made publication of the pamphlet possible. On the other hand, Wells claimed in her autobiography that the meetings to organize her first antilynching lecture and the forum itself were 'the real beginning of the club movement among the colored women' in the United States.[6] The gathering of black women from Philadelphia, New York, Boston, and other cities indicated that organization was already embryonic. The meeting on one particular issue, lynching, was a catalyst for the establishment of numerous clubs and a general movement that would extend beyond any one single issue.

Wells established in *Southern Horrors* that the association between lynching and rape was strictly a contemporary phenomenon; she argued that there was no historical foundation for that association, since 'the crime of rape was unknown during four years of civil war, when the white women of the South were at the mercy of the race which is all at once charged with being a bestial one' (*SH*, p. 5). She indicted the miscegenation laws, which, in practice, were directed at preventing sexual relations between white women and black men. The miscegenation laws thus pretended to offer 'protection' to white women but left black women the victims of rape by white men and simultaneously granted to these same men the power to terrorize black men as a potential threat to the virtue of white womanhood. Wells asserted that 'there are many white women in the South who would marry colored men if such an act would not place them at once beyond the pale of society and within the clutches of the law'. The miscegenation laws, in her opinion, only operated against 'the legitimate union of the races' (*SH*, p. 6). In her publications and speeches, Wells increasingly used evidence from the white press – statistics on lynchings and reports that substantiated her claims that black male/white female sexual relationships were encouraged by white women. Wells used the white press in this way not only to avoid accusations of falsification or exaggeration but also because she wanted to reveal the contradictions implicit in the association of lynching with the rape of white women. She wanted to condemn the murderers out of their own mouths (see *RR*, p. 15).

Wells recognized that the Southerners' appeal to Northerners for sympathy on the 'necessity' of lynching was very successful. It worked, she thought, through the claim that any condemnation of lynching constituted a public display of indifference to the 'plight' of white womanhood. Wells demonstrated that, while accusations of rape were made in only one-third of all lynchings, the cry of rape was an extremely effective way to create panic and fear. Lynching, she argued, was an institutionalized practice supported and encouraged by the established leaders of a community and the press they influenced. The North conceded to the South's argument that rape was the cause of lynching; the concession to lynching for a specific crime in turn conceded the right to lynch any black male for any crime: the charge of rape became the excuse for murder. The press acted as accomplices in the ideological work that disguised the lesson of political and economic subordination which the black community was being taught. Black disenfranchisement and Jim Crow segregation had been achieved; now, the annihilation of a black political presence was shielded behind a 'screen of defending the honor of [white] women' (*SH*, p. 14). Those that remained silent while disapproving of lynching were condemned by Wells for being as guilty as the actual perpetrators of lynching.

The lesson the black community should learn, Wells argued, was to recognize its economic power. The South owed its rehabilitation to Northern capital, on the one hand, and to Afro-American labor, on the other: 'By the right exercise of his power as the industrial factor of the South, the Afro-American can demand and secure his rights.' But economic power was only one force among the possible forms of resistance, she concluded: 'a Winchester rifle should have a place of *honor* in every black home' (*SH*, p. 23). Wells knew that emancipation meant that white men lost their vested interests in the body of the Negro and that lynching and the rape of black women were attempts to regain control. The terrorizing of black communities was a political weapon that manipulated ideologies of sexuality. Wells analysed how ideologies of manhood – as well as of citizenship – were embodied in the right to vote. The murder of blacks was so easily accomplished because they had been granted the right to vote but not the means to protect or maintain that right. Thus, Wells was able to assert that the loss of the vote was both a political silencing and an emasculation which placed black men outside the boundaries of contemporary patriarchal power. The cry of rape, which pleaded the necessity of revenge for assaulted white womanhood, attempted to place black males 'beyond the pale of human sympathy' (*RR*, p. 12). Black women were relegated to a place outside the ideological construction of 'womanhood'. That term included only white women; therefore the rape of black women was of no consequence outside the black community.

Wells' analysis of lynching and her demystification of the political motivations behind the manipulation of both black male and female and white female sexuality led her into direct confrontation with women like Frances Willard, president of the Woman's Christian Temperance Union, who considered themselves progressive but refused to see lynching as an institutionalized practice. Willard's attitude and *Wells'* conclusion that Willard was 'no better or worse than the great bulk of white Americans on the Negro questions' are indicative of the racism that Cooper condemned in white women's organizations (*RR*, p. 85). As Harper also pointed out, there was not a single black woman admitted to the southern WCTU. What Cooper called the white woman's concern with caste was evident in the assumption of many 'progressive' white women that rape actually *was* the crime to which lynching was the response.[7]

For Cooper, imperialism linked all those oppressed under the domination of the United States. Patriarchy, for her, was embodied in these acts of violence; therefore she ultimately placed her focus and hopes for the future on a transformed woman's movement. Wells, in her analysis of lynching, provided for a more detailed dissection of patriarchal power, showing how it could manipulate sexual ideologies to justify political and economic subordination. Cooper had failed to address what proved central to the thesis of Wells – that white men used their ownership of the body of the white female as a terrain on which to lynch the black male. White women felt that their caste was their protection and that their interests lay with the power that ultimately confined them. Although Cooper identified the relation between patriarchal power and white women's practice of racial exclusion, she did not examine and analyse what forged that relation. She preferred to believe that what men taught women could be unlearned if women's education was expanded. Wells was able to demonstrate how a patriarchal system, which had lost its total ownership over black male bodies, used its control over women to attempt to completely circumscribe the actions of black males. As black women positioned outside the 'protection' of the ideology of womanhood, both Cooper and Wells felt that they could see clearly the compromised role of white women in the maintenance of a system of oppression.

Black women listened, organized, and acted on the theses of both Wells and Cooper, but very few white women responded to their social critiques. Cooper was right to argue that a transformed woman's movement, purged of racism, would have provided a liberating experience for white women themselves. But racism led to concession, to segregated organizations, and, outside the anti-lynching movement, to a resounding silence about – and therefore complicity in – the attempt to eliminate black people politically, economically and, indeed, physically.

Pauline Hopkins shared this very real fear that black people were threatened with annihilation. She addressed her plea to 'all Negroes, whether Frenchmen, Spaniards, Americans or Africans to rediscover their history as one weapon in the struggle against oppression'.[8] Hopkins challenged the readers of her work to bear witness to her testimony concerning the international dimensions of the crisis.

> The dawn of the Twentieth century finds the Black race fighting for existence in every quarter of the globe. From over the sea Africa stretches her hands to the American Negro and cries aloud for sympathy in her hour of trial. . . . In America, caste prejudice has received fresh impetus as the 'Southern brother' of the Anglo-Saxon family has arisen from the ashes of secession, and like the prodigal of old, has been gorged with fatted calf and 'fixin's'.[9]

As a black intellectual, Hopkins conceived of her writing as an inspiration to political action, a pattern for encouraging forms of resistance and agitation, and an integral part of the politics of oppression.

Hopkins regarded fiction in particular as a cultural form of great historical and political significance. In the preface to her first novel, *Contending Forces* (1900), she asserted its 'religious, political and social' value and urged other black writers to *'faithfully portray the inmost thoughts and feelings of the Negro with all the fire and romance which lie dormant in our history'*.[10] History is the crucial element in Hopkins' fiction: current oppressive forces, she argued, must be understood in the context of past oppression. 'Mob-law is nothing new. . . . The atrocity of the acts committed one hundred years ago are dupli-cated today, when slavery is supposed no longer to exist' (*CF*, pp. 14, 15). This thesis is a cornerstone of *Contending Forces*. Drawing upon the theoretical per-spectives of women like Cooper and Wells as well as the central concerns of the black woman's movement as a whole, Hopkins figures lynching and rape as the two political weapons of terror wielded by the powers behind internal coloni-zation.

Contending Forces opens with a brief recounting of family history. Charles Montfort, a West Indian planter, decides to move his family and estate of slaves from Bermuda to North Carolina in response to the increasing agitation in the British Parliament for the abolition of slavery. Montfort acts to protect his com-mercial interests and profits. Hopkins is careful to remove any motivation or intention on his part that could be attributed to cruelty or personal avaricious-ness. Thus she establishes the economic basis of slavery as the primary factor in this decision which precipitates all the events and conditions in the rest of the text. Once the Montfort estate has been established in North Carolina, the focus of the novel gravitates toward Grace Montfort and the suspicion, which becomes rumor, that her blood is 'polluted' by an African strain. Hopkins uti-lizes what Cooper had identified as the American obsession with 'pure blood' and reveals its mythological proportions. It is actually irrelevant whether Grace Montfort is a black or a white woman. Her behaviour is classically that of 'true womanhood' – but her skin is a little too 'creamy'. The reader is not apprised of her actual heritage; what is important is the mere suspicion of black blood. This results in the social ostracism of her whole family, while Grace herself, denied her station on the pedestal of virtue, becomes the object of the illicit sexual desire of a local landowner, Anson Pollock. The possibility that Grace might be black leads directly to the murder of Charles Montfort, the rapes of Grace and her black foster sister Lucy, and the enslavement of the two Montfort sons, Jesse and Charles.

Grace Montfort rejects the advances of Pollock, who then plots to avenge his wounded pride and satisfy his sexual obsession. Under the pretence of quelling an imminent rebellion by Montfort's slaves, Pollock uses the 'committee on public safety' – in fact, a vigilante group – to raid the Montfort plantation. Montfort himself is quickly dispatched by a bullet in the brain, leaving Grace prey to Pollock. In a graphic and tortured two-page scene, Hopkins represents a brutal rape in a displaced form: Grace is whipped by two members of the 'committee'. Her clothes are ripped from her and she is 'whipped' alternately 'by the two strong, savage men'. Hopkins' replacement of the phallus by the 'snaky leather thong' is crude but effective, and the reader is left in no doubt about the kind of outrage that has occurred when 'the blood stood in a pool about her feet' (*CF*, p. 69).

Grace commits suicide, in the tradition of outraged virtue, and Pollock takes Lucy, Grace's black maid and slave, as his mistress instead. But the actual and figurative ravishing of 'grace' at the hand of Southern brutality establishes the link that Hopkins is drawing between rape and its political motivation as a device of terrorism. Both Charles and Grace Montfort are punished because they threatened to break the acceptable codes that bound the slave system. The possibility of miscegenation represented the ultimate violation of the white woman's social position and required the degradation of the transgressor and the relegation of her offspring to the status of chattel. The two sons represent two possible histories. Charles junior is bought and eventually grows up 'white' in Britain. Jesse escapes into the black communities of Boston and, later, New Hampshire; he is the ancestor of the black family which is the main subject of the novel.

This preliminary tale acts as an overture to the main body of *Contending Forces*, containing the clues and themes that will eventually provide the resolutions to the crises of relations between the main characters. Living in Boston at the turn of the century, the Smith family inherits this tale of its ancestors: the tale appears remote from their everyday lives but is retained in the naming of the children. Ma Smith, her husband dead, runs a lodging house with her son, William Jesse Montfort, and her daughter, Dora Grace Montfort. The two other main characters are both lodgers, John P. Langley, engaged to Dora, and Sappho Clark, a woman who is mysteriously hiding her personal history. All these characters cannot move forward into the future until their relation to the past is revealed. Hopkins displaces a direct attack on the increasing separation of the races onto issues of inheritance, heritage, and culture – issues where bloodlines between the races are so entangled that race as a biological category is subordinated to race as a political category. The historical importance of rape is crucial to the construction of *Hopkins'* fictionalized history: it is through the rapes of Grace and Lucy that the two races share an intertwined destiny.

Shifting contemporary debates about race from the biological to the political level was a crucial move for Hopkins to make in her fiction. At the height of debate about the consequences of colonizing overseas territories, Hopkins attempted to disrupt imperialist discourse concerning empires composed primarily of nonwhite peoples. The grounds of imperialist argument derived their problematic from the experience of the internal colonization of native American Indians and Africans. At the moment when black Americans were again being systematically excluded from participation in social institutions, the status of people who lived in what the United States now deemed its 'possessions' was an integral component of the contemporary discourse on race. 'Mixing blood' was seen as a threat to the foundations of North American civilization.[11]

Hopkins intended to disrupt this imperialist discourse through the figuration of an alternative set of historical consequences. The degradation of a race is not represented as being the result of amalgamation but of an abuse of power – the use of brutality against an oppressed group equates with savagery, in *Hopkins'* terms. She quotes Ralph Waldo Emerson on her title page and again in the body of the text: '*The civility of no race can be perfect whilst another race is degraded.*' The link that Hopkins establishes between Britain and the West Indies makes visible a colonial relationship that enables her to direct a critique of imperial relations to an American readership. Hopkins carefully demonstrates that blacks are a colonized people for whom it is a necessity that history be rewritten. The histories of the externally colonized and the internally colonized are interwoven in many ways but primarily through questions of rightful inheritance. In Hopkins' fictional world, one consequence of external colonization is that a debt must be paid from the profits of the slave trade and Charles Montfort's plantation. For the purposes of this essay, however, I want to concentrate on Hopkins' presentation of the two main weapons of terror of internal colonization: lynching and rape.

At the heart of the text are two tales told at a public gathering by Luke Sawyer, who is black. In the first, a lynching is the central focus of concern; in the second, a rape. Both tales confirm the privileging of these two acts in Hopkins' thesis of 'contending forces'. The first history that Luke tells is of his father, whose success in trade resulted in competition with white traders, threats on his life, and, ultimately, a mob attack on his home and family. His act of self-defence – firing into the mob – is punished by lynching; the women are whipped and raped to death, the two babies slaughtered.

The second tale follows from the first. Luke escapes into the woods and is found by a black planter, Beaubean, who rescues him and takes him into his home to raise as a son. Beaubean has a wealthy and politically influential white half brother, who assumes a stance of friendship toward the whole family but particularly toward Beaubean's daughter, Mabelle. At the age of fourteen, Mabelle is kidnapped by this uncle, raped, and left a prisoner in a brothel. After weeks of searching, Beaubean finds Mabelle and confronts his brother with the crime – only to be asked 'What does a woman of mixed blood, or any Negress, for that matter, know of virtue?' (*CF*, p. 261). Beaubean is offered a thousand dollars by his brother which he rejects with a threat to seek justice in a federal court. Beaubean's threat is promptly met with mob action: his house is set on fire and its occupants shot. Luke escapes with Mabelle and places her in a convent.

Hopkins concentrates on the practices of oppression – the consequences of white supremacy – in reconstructing the history of her characters. The predominance of mulattoes and octoroons in the novel is not intended to glorify the possibilities of the black race if only it would integrate with (and eventually lose itself within) the white.[12] On the contrary, Hopkins states categorically in this novel and throughout her work that 'miscegenation, either *lawful* or *unlawful*, we *do not want*' (*CF*, p. 264). The presence of racially mixed characters throughout the text emphasizes particular social relations and practices and must be understood historically. Such characters are often the physical consequences of a social system that exercised white supremacy through rape. Use of the mulatto figure, as a literary device, has two primary functions: it enables an exploration of the relation between the races while, at the same time, it expresses the relation between the races. It is a narrative mechanism of mediation frequently used in a period when social convention dictated an increased and more absolute distance between black and white. The figure of the mulatto allows for a fictional representation and reconstruction of the socially proscribed. Hopkins' particular use of such figuration is intended, in part, to demythologize concepts of 'pure blood' and 'pure race'. More important, however, it is an attempt to demonstrate the crucial role of social, political, and economic interests in determining human behaviour by negating any proposition of degeneracy through amalgamation. Hopkins transposes contemporary accusations that miscegenation is the inmost desire of the nonwhite peoples of the earth by reconstructing miscegenation as the result of white rape.

Hopkins saw clearly that the threat to white supremacy was not black sexuality but the potential of the black vote. Rape, she argued, should be totally separated from the issue of violated white womanhood and then recast as part of the social, political, and economic oppression of blacks:

> 'Lynching was instituted to crush the manhood of the enfranchised black. Rape is the crime which appeals most strongly to the heart of the home life. . . . *The men who created the mulatto race, who recruit its ranks year after year by the very means which they invoked lynch law to suppress*, bewailing the sorrows of violated womanhood!
>
> 'No; it is not rape. If the Negro votes, he is shot; if he marries a white woman, he is shot . . . or lynched – he is a pariah whom the National Government cannot defend. But if he defends himself and his home, then is heard the tread of marching feet as the Federal troops move southward to quell a "race riot".' (*CF*, pp. 270–1)

The analysis of rape and its links to lynching as a weapon of political terror is, obviously, shaped by the arguments and indictments of Wells. In *Hopkins'* fictional reconstruction of the social relations between white and black, the two parts of the text move across generations and thus, through historical knowledge, invalidate the understanding of cause and effect then being reasserted through white patriarchal supremacy. Hopkins offers her readers an alternative story of origins where the characters are not holistic creations but the terrain on which the consequences of the authorial assertion of history are worked through. This can be clearly seen in the creation of Sappho Clark, the dominant female figure in the text, who has two identities.

The disguise – that which hides true history – is Sappho, the poet of Lesbos, who was admired and loved by both men and women, though her erotic poetry was addressed to women. The Sappho of *Contending Forces* embodies the potential for utopian relationships between women and between women and men; she represents a challenge to a patriarchal order. To Dora, whose duties running the boarding house confine her to a domestic existence, Sappho is the independent woman who, in their intimate moments together, talks of the need for suffrage and the political activity of women (see *CF*, p. 125). Sappho disrupts Dora's complacency – Dora will 'generally accept whatever the men tell me as right' and leads her to reassess the importance of friendships with women. But Sappho as an ideal of womanhood does not exist except as a set of fictional possibilities. In order to function, to work and survive, Sappho's younger self, Mabelle Beaubean, a product of miscegenation and the subject of rape, has had to bury her violated womanhood and deny her progeny. Like Sappho of Lesbos, Sappho Clark has a child, 'whose form is like gold flowers'.[13] But unlike Sappho of Lesbos, Mabelle exists in a patriarchal order, her body is colonized, her child the fruit of rape. Sappho Clark journeys toward the retrieval of a whole identity, one which will encompass a combination of the elements of Sappho and Mabelle. Such an identity leads to an acceptance of a motherhood which, like that of Sappho of Lesbos, does not require that a male occupy the space of father.

The most significant absence in the network of social forces is the black father. In narrative, the father is a figure that mediates patriarchal control over women; in most texts by nineteenth-century black women, this control is exercised by white men who politically, socially, and economically attempt to deny patriarchal power to black men. The absent space in fiction by black women confirms this denial of patriarchal power to black men, but Hopkins uses that space to explore the possibilities of alternative black male figures. Black men are depicted in peer relations, as brothers, or as potential partners/lovers. Women are not seen as the subject of exchange between father and husband; neither are their journeys limited to the distance between daughter and wife. As partners, sexual or nonsexual, the narrative impulse is toward utopian relations between black men and black women.

Nineteenth-century black feminists cannot be dismissed simply as 'spokespeople for prudery in their communities'. Their legacy to us is theories that expose the colonization of the black female body by white male power and the destruction of black males who attempted to exercise any oppositional patriarchal control. When accused of threatening the white female body, the repository of heirs to property and power, the black male, and his economic, political, and social advancement, is lynched out of existence. Cooper, Wells, and Hopkins assert the necessity of seeing the relation between histories: the rape of black women in the nineties is directly linked to the rape of the female slave. Their analyses are dynamic and not limited to a parochial understanding of 'women's issues'; they have firmly established the dialectical relation between economic/political power and economic/sexual power in the battle for control of women's bodies.

A desire for the possibilities of the uncolonized black female body occupies a utopian space; it is the false hope of Sappho Clark's pretend history. Black feminists understood that the struggle would have to take place on the terrain of the previously colonized: the struggle was to be characterized by redemption, retrieval, and reclamation – not, ultimately, by an unrestrained utopian vision. Sappho could not deny the existence of the raped Mabelle but, instead, had to reunite with the colonized self. Thus, these black feminists expanded the limits of conventional ideologies of womanhood to consider subversive relationships between women, motherhood without wifehood, wifehood as a partnership outside of an economic exchange between men, and men as partners and not patriarchal fathers. As DuBois and Gordon have argued so cogently, we have '150 years of feminist theory and praxis in the area of sexuality. This is a resource too precious to squander by not learning it, in all its complexity'.[14]

But let us learn *all* of it, not only in its complexity but also in its difference, and so stand again on the 'threshold of woman's era' – an era that can encompass all women.

NOTES

1. Ellen Carol Dubois and Linda Gordon, 'Seeking Ecstasy on the Battlefield: Danger and Pleasure in Nineteenth-Century Feminist Sexual Thought', in Carole S. Vance (ed.) *Pleasure and Danger: Exploring Female Sexuality* (Boston, 1984), pp. 34, 33.
2. See Frances E. W. Harper, *Iola Leroy: or, Shadows Uplifted* (Philadelphia, 1892), and Anna Julia Cooper, *A Voice from the South: By a Black Woman of the South* (Xenia, Ohio, 1892); all further references to this work, abbreviated *V*, will be included in the text. See also Ida B. Wells-Barnett, *On Lynchings; Southern Horrors; A Red Record; Mob Rule in New Orleans* (New York, 1969); all further references to *Southern Horrors* and *A Red Record*, respectively abbreviated *SH* and *RR*, are to this collection and will be included in the text. These were preceded by a novel by Emma Dunham Kelley ('Forget-me-not' [Emma Dunham Kelley], *Megda* [Boston, 1891]) and followed by the publication of a short story by Victoria Earle (Victoria Earle Matthews, *Aunt Lindy: A Story Founded on Real Life* [New York, 1893]) and a survey by Gertrude Mossel (Mrs. N. F. [Gertrude] Mossell, *The Work of the Afro-American Woman* [Philadelphia, 1894]).
3. Harper, 'Woman's Political Future', in May Wright Sewell (ed.), *World's Congress of Representative Women*, 2 vols. (Chicago, 1894), 1: 433–4.
4. This paragraph draws upon material from my forthcoming book, *Uplifting as They Write: The Emergence of the Afro-American Woman Novelist*.
5. Wells' pamphlet *Southern Horrors: Lynch Law in All Its Phases* was published in 1892; *A Red Record: Tabulated Statistics and Alleged Causes of Lynchings in the United States, 1892–1893–1894* was published in 1895; and *Mob Rule in New Orleans* was published in 1900. All three have been reprinted; see Wells, *On Lynchings* (New York, 1969). My account of some of her arguments is oversimplified and extremely adumbrated.
6. Wells, quoted in Alfreda M. Duster (ed.), *Crusade for Justice: The Autobiography of Ida B. Wells* (Chicago, 1970), p. 81.
7. See Bettina Aptheker (ed.), *Lynching and Rape: An Exchange of Views*, American Institute for Marxist Studies Occasional Paper 25 (San Jose, CA, 1977), p. 29.
8. Pauline Hopkins, 'Toussaint L'Overture', *Colored American Magazine* 2 (Nov. 1900): 10, 24.
9. Hopkins, 'Heroes and Heroines in Black', *Colored American Magazine* 3 (Jan. 1903): 211.
10. Hopkins, *Contending Forces: A Romance Illustrative of Negro Life North and South* (1900: Carbondale, IL, 1978), pp. 13, 14; all further references to this work, abbreviated *CF*, will be included in the text.
11. See Robert L. Allen, *Reluctant Reformers: Racism and Social Reform Movements in the United States* (Garden City, NY, 1975) and Christopher Lasch, *The World of Nations: Reflections on American History, Politics, and Culture* (New York, 1973), pp. 70–9.

12. Gwendolyn Brooks misunderstands Hopkins to be arguing for integration; see Brooks, afterword to Hopkins, *Contending Forces*, pp. 403–9.
13. Sappho, fragment 132, quoted in Sarah B. Pomeroy, *Goddesses, Whores, Wives, and Slaves: Women in Classical Antiquity* (New York, 1975), p. 54.
14. DuBois and Gordon, 'Seeking Ecstasy on the Battlefield', p. 43.

PART 3
REDEFINING THE 'THIRD-WORLD' SUBJECT

3.1

'DEAD WOMEN TELL NO TALES: ISSUES OF FEMALE SUBJECTIVITY, SUBALTERN AGENCY AND TRADITION IN COLONIAL AND POSTCOLONIAL WRITINGS ON WIDOW IMMOLATION IN INDIA'

Ania Loomba

Sati has been a focal point not only for the colonial gaze on India, but also for recent work on post-coloniality and the female subject, for nineteenth- and twentieth-century Indian discourses about tradition, Indian culture and femininity, and, most crucially, for the women's movement in India.[1] Reading these various discourses against each other and in the context of the specific cultural moments and inter-cultural tensions in which they are produced is often a frustrating task because of the astounding circularity of language, arguments and even images that marks discussions on sati from the late eighteenth century till today. This circularity has sometimes been used to indicate the enormous shaping power of a colonial past on contemporary India society, or 'to question', as Lata Mani puts it, 'the "post" in "post-colonial"'.[2] While such an emphasis has been useful in indicating the continued economic, cultural and epistemological hegemony of the West, and salutary in questioning Eurocentric intellectual paradigms, it has also contributed to a lack of focus on the crucial shifts from colonial to post-colonial governance and culture. To isolate the study of colonialism from that of its later evolution is to deflect attention from the narratives of nationalism, communalism and religious fundamentalism which are the crucibles within which gender, class, caste or even neo-colonialism function today.[3]

Widow immolation is one of the most spectacular forms of patriarchal violence; each burning was and is highly variable, and is both produced by and

From: Ania Loomba (1993), 'Dead Women Tell No Tales: Issues of Female Subjectivity, Subaltern Agency and Tradition in Colonial and Postcolonial Writings on Widow Immolation in India', pp. 209–27, in *History Workshop Journal*, no. 36.

helps to validate and circulate other ideologies that strengthen the oppression of women. But for the most part, representations of sati have tended to homogenize the burnings and to isolate them from the specific social, economic and ideological fabric in which they are embedded. Thus the spectacularity of widow immolation lends itself to a double violence: we are invited to view sati as a unique, transhistorical, transgeographic category and to see the burnt widow as a woman with special powers to curse or bless, as one who feels no pain, and one who will be rewarded with everlasting extra-terrestrial marital bliss. She is marked off from all other women by her will; thus her desire, her 'decisions' are to be revered by the community even as theirs are consistently erased. Paradoxically but necessarily, this process also casts the burning widow as a sign of normative femininity: in a diverse body of work, she becomes the privileged signifier of either the devoted and chaste, or the oppressed and victimized Indian (or sometimes even 'third world') woman.

In this essay, I will attempt to locate, within the apparent repetitions of arguments, the differences in what is at stake in the three most substantial bodies of writings on sati: the first being the colonial debate on widow immolation, the second the work of feminists working in the Western academy (both diasporic Indians and non-Indians), and the third is the spate of writings produced in India following the burning of a young woman, Roop Kanwar, in the village of Deorala, Rajasthan, in October 1987. These historical and conceptual differences, I shall suggest, are crucial to our reconceptualising the burning widow as neither an archetypal victim nor a free agent, and to analysing the interconnections between colonialism and its aftermath. In order to trace the roots and trajectories of the different ideologies and representations of widow immolation, I shall move freely between these three sets of writings.

Despite widespread references to sati, there were surprisingly few extended studies of it between Edward Thompson's well-known colonial commentary on the subject published in 1928 and the Deorala episode in 1987.[4] Even now, apart from Lata Mani's work, the most thought-provoking accounts have been shorter essays, although several book-length studies are now available.[5] Curiously too, the most prestigious historians of colonial India (either British or Indian) have not written at any length on the subject, and nor does the influential revisionist series Subaltern Studies deal with it.[6] There is no conclusive evidence for dating the origins of sati, although Romilla Thapar points out that there are growing textual references to it in the second half of the first millennium AD.[7] It began as a ritual confined to the Kshatriya caste (composed of rulers and warriors) and was discouraged among the highest caste of Brahmins. She suggests that it provided a heroic female counterpart to the warrior's death in battle: the argument was that the warrior's widow would then join him in heaven. The comparison between the widow who burns herself and heroic male deaths has been a recurrent feature of the discourse on sati from the earliest comments till the present day and has been used to distinguish sati from mere suicide: the argument is that the sati, like the warrior, dies positively for something, instead of negatively to escape a miserable life.[8] Such a comparison obviously deflects attention from the miserable fate that awaited and still threatens most Indian widows; it also led to the contention that the heroic sati feels no pain in death. Thapar suggests a correlation between the rise of sati and the decline of niyoga or the practice of a widow being married to her dead husband's brother; widow immolation reduced the possibilities of women marrying others within the family, or outsiders, and thus creating complications regarding inheritance. In a useful commentary on sati, Dorothy Stein points out that it was not unique to India: 'there are accounts of widow sacrifice among the Scandinavians, Slavs, Greeks, Egyptians, Chinese, Finns, Maories and some American Indians.'[9] This was Edward Thompson's view too: 'the rite' he says, 'belongs to a barbaric substratum which once overlay the world, including India.'[10] Like several others of his time (notably, for example, Rider Haggard), Thompson subscribes to the idea of a globally shared and primitive past from which Europe had emerged and from which England could liberate India too. This notion of sati being a sort of global practice is also an idea that recent writers like Ashis Nandy return to, in their attempt to read widow immolation as the result of [a universal] male anxiety about female sexuality.[11]

The earliest historical record of widow burning is a Greek commentary on the death of a Hindu general in a battle with the Greeks in 316 BC. The elder of his two wives was not allowed to burn because of 'her condition' (which could mean she was either pregnant or menstruating). The death of the younger one is described in some detail, especially her clothing and her ornaments, and the commentator concludes that she 'ended her life in heroic fashion. . . . The spectators were moved, some to pity and some to exhuberant praise. But some of the Greeks present found fault with such customs as savage and inhumane.'[12] That this first recorded comment includes all the dominant ingredients of responses to sati till today – the fascination, the horror mingled with admiration, the voyeurism, the oscillation between regarding the widow as victim or as sovereign agent – is a measure of the representational stasis or circularity to which I earlier alluded.

The growth of colonial enterprises in India shaped the tone as well as frequency of comments by Europeans on the idea as well as the spectacle of sati.[13] With increasing English involvement, the accounts proliferate; simultaneously, the commentator becomes enmeshed in the scenario he describes, and the burning widow herself is progressively pictured as reaching out to the white man watching her: 'I stood close to her, she observed me attentively,' writes William Hodges;[14] Mandelso claims that she gives him a bracelet; Thomas Bowery receives some flowers from another's hair. By the late eighteenth/early nineteenth century, the recurrent theme of what Spivak calls 'white men saving brown women from brown men' has crystallized.[15] Legend has it that Job Charnock, the founder of Calcutta, rescued from the flames a Brahmin widow and lived with her for fourteen years till her death; European fiction from Jules

Verne's *Around the World in Eighty Days* to M. M. Kaye's *The Far Pavilions* is obsessed with such rescues. Sati became, as is well known, simultaneously the moral justification for empire and an ideal of female devotion. Katherine Mayo's *Mother India* had blamed all of India's ills on the Indian male's 'manner of getting into the world and his sex-life thenceforward'. London's *New Statesman and Nation* said that the book demonstrated 'the filthy personal habits of even the most highly educated classes in India – which, like the denigration of Hindu women, are unequalled even among the most primitive African or Australian savages'.[16] Sati was emblematic of this denigration; at the same time, even the harshest colonial criticism included a sneaking admiration for the sati as the ideal wife who represented 'the wholly admirable sentiment and theory, that the union of man and woman is lifelong and the one permanent thing in the world'.[17] The idealisation of the burning widow, of course, goes back much earlier: Montaigne, for example, in his essay, 'Of Virtue', writes at length about the resolute widow, 'with a gay countenance, as if going, as she says, to sleep with her husband'.[18] John Master's novel about the thuggee cult, *The Deceivers*, is particularly interesting in this regard – its British hero, who is an administrator in a small district of central India, disguises himself as an Indian man to prevent his wife from committing sati. During the course of the story, this impersonation is transformed into a psychic drama whereby his British and Christian identities conflict with his passionate fascination with and seduction by the cult of thuggee and its patron goddess, Kali, so that at the end of the novel he helps the same widow to immolate herself.

These contradictory responses to sati – as a powerful male fantasy of female devotion and an instance of Hindu barbarism – both fuelled the voyeuristic fascination of the colonial gaze and impelled the narrative division, in the first half of the colonial debate on widow immolation in nineteenth-century India, of satis into good and bad ones. In the initial years of imperial rule, following their declared policy of non-interference with native religions and customs, the British made no efforts to stop the practice (although Albuquerque had prohibited it within the Portuguese territory of Goa in 1510), ostensibly because of their declared policy of non-interference in native customs and religion. The Mughal emperor Akbar disliked it and is supposed to have ridden nearly 100 miles to save the Raja of Jodhpur's daughter-in-law from burning against her will. Edward Thompson sympathised with Akbar's position – as a 'foreign' ruler, he could 'only insist that it be always voluntary'. This was precisely the nature of the first British intervention: hence the sanctioned voluntary sati was separated from the illegal coerced one, and both the idea of [Indian] woman as victim [of Hindu barbarism] and that of women as supreme devotee of man, could be maintained.

In 1813 a legislation was enacted which defined sati as legal if it met certain criteria, chief among which was that it be a voluntary act. From then on, the government's strategy was simply to make it increasingly difficult to achieve the state of legality, hence the age, caste, and the physical state of the 'ideal' sati were increasingly regulated. One obvious implication here is that once these criteria were met, sati could be sanctioned: an implication that re-surfaced in the post-Deorala debate when pro-sati commentators insisted on the voluntary status of the true sati. It is relevant to note here that, between 1813 and 1816, it is estimated that only ten illegal satis were prevented out of a total of 400 that occurred in the Presidency of Bengal.[19]

Lata Mani's is the most extensive commentary on the entire colonial debate; she shows how, prior to the 1813 legislation, the colonial administration 'generated' a particular kind of information about the practice by extensively questioning pundits resident at the courts. The pundits were instructed to respond with 'a reply in conformity with the scriptures'.[20] In the process, a scriptural sanction and a religion tradition were constructed for a practice which had been diverse, variable and uneven. Veena Das reaches a similar conclusion: by annexing the category of 'vyavahara', or usage to the category of law, she says, 'what may have been contextual and open to interpretation, or limited to certain castes only, became frozen as "law"'.[21] Hence the British virtually orchestrated the articulation of a textual tradition and scriptural sanction for widow immolation, made pundits the spokesmen for a vast and heterogeneous Hindu population, and thereby calcified in new and dangerous ways the existing hierarchies of Hindu society. Because they had strategically divided sati into illegal and legal, involuntary and voluntary ones, British officials were directed to be present at each burning and tabulate its details, to see that no coercion was used. But conversely officials were sometimes reprimanded for disallowing a legal immolation![22]

Following the 1813 legislation, most commentators agree, there was a sharp increase in the number of satis. From 378 in 1815, it went up to 839 in 1818. This increase spurred the movement for straightforward abolition; Raja Ram Mohan Roy published his first pamphlet on the subject, and in England there was a spate of protests. The final abolition in 1829 is regarded as a sort of landmark in the history of Indian women; commentators allot the credit for it to different people according to their own ideological positions: hence Thompson attributes it entirely to the efforts of William Bentinck, the then Governor General, as does V. N. Datta; Ashis Nandy predictably gives Roy pride of place,[23] and only Lata Mani traces the complex interpenetration of interests in a way that takes into account the entire spectrum of positions on this subject. Comments on the increase of satis in 1818 are also significant; many British officials simply attributed it to a cholera epidemic. Edward Thompson, like some others, read it as a sign of excessive native obedience to British law: 'I think there can be no doubt that the sanction of the Government was sometimes misrepresented as an order that widows should burn.[24] Ashis Nandy interprets the increase as precisely the opposite of this, as a form of subaltern disobedience: 'the rite', he suggests, 'became popular in groups made psychologically marginal by their exposure to Western impact . . . the opposition to sati constituted . . . a threat to them. In their desperate defence of the rite they were also trying to defend their traditional self-esteem'.[25] Certain statistics seem to support such a conclusion; for example, a modification of the legislation in 1817 forbade widows of the Brahmin caste to commit sati as it was contrary to the shastras. In 1823, out of a total of 576 satis, 235 were Brahmin widows. Nandy's analysis has also been contested on the grounds that there is no easy correlation between this increase in widow burning and the 'marginalised groups' he identifies,[26] but it remains important for at least two reasons.

First, by arguing that the colonial conflict calcified indigenous patriarchal practices, Nandy's was one of the pioneering attempts to trace the multiple connections between colonial power and gender relations. Later feminist work on British India has considered in greater depth and with most sophistication how the colonial disenfranchisement of Indian men led to a situation whereby women became the grounds and signs for the colonial struggle. Indian nationalisms of different shades produced their own versions of the good Hindu wife, each of which became emblematic of Indian-ness and tradition, a sign of rebellion against colonial authority and a symbol of the vision of the future.[27] In the process, women's own questioning of patriarchal authority – both indigenous and colonial – were specifically marginalised. While writings on sati have been a fruitful ground for drawing attention to the ways in which women become signifiers of the colonial conflict (and here Lata Mani provided the most detailed account), they have not sufficiently proved *why* the signs acquired the meanings they did for both Indians and the British, or considered the process whereby the divisions between masculine and feminine, public and private, active and passive, colonial and native came to acquire overlapping meanings. Such questions are necessary if one is not to assume that these terms carry universal and always already constituted meanings. Here other work on women in colonial India has been more nuanced. Rosalind O'Hanlon's essay on widows in Western India, for example, suggests that the colonial state severed 'the sphere of Hindu social relations and ritual practice from their pre-colonial incorporation within the realm of politics and state structure, and . . . designate[d] them as matters of purely "social" concern'; this 'process was couched in terms of a version of contemporary Western distinctions between domains of public and private' and carried

a colonial invitation to the exercise of new kinds of power. It offered public participation in the moral and judicial discourses, many of the most intensely contested of which concerned women, through which a generalized Hindu tradition was defined, represented and made the basis not only of colonial legislation, but, in different forms, of contemporary nationalists' own efforts to construct a cultural equivalent for India as a political entity . . . The employment of woman as a sign thus instituted a strong naturalizing parallelism in this particular form of detached authority: authority over a tradition whose essential qualities were characterized in terms of a feminine, and authority to pronounce upon and sometimes to determine in very real ways what should be the proper status and forms of freedom allowed to Hindu women.[28]

Such studies can be read as fleshing out and critiquing the skeletal connections made by Nandy. The *second* outcome of his work has not been as felicitous; it is worth tracing its somewhat involved trajectory here because it warns against the dangers of easy explanations of indigenous patriarchies as merely responses to colonial power and also because it encodes the problems – of separating colonial and post-colonial histories, and of recovering and theorizing female agency – with which I began this essay.

In 1987, following the burning of 25-year-old Roop Kanwar in Deorala, Nandy began to write in terms of a division between 'the idea of sati in mythical times and sati in historical time, between sati as event or ghatana and sati as system or pratha, between an authentic sati and an inauthentic one, between those who only respect it and those who organise it in our time', valorizing the first in each of these oppositions.[29] As he acknowledged, these distinctions are not his contribution to the debate; they are, we can see, a curious mixture of those made by the British and the ones offered by Indian men of different political persuasions, reformers as well as advocates of sati. Nandy evoked them, in the charged post-Deorala atmosphere, to defend what he called the ability of 'the traditional Indian' to discriminate between the ideal of the authentic sati and its corrupt contemporary manifestations.[30]

Nandy had, as I have pointed out, been one of the pioneers of historicising sati, of analysing sati as a form of specifiable political economic social and psychic cultures. This, ironically, was the thrust of feminist writings following the Deorala episode of 1987. Feminists insisted that the death of Roop Kanwar should be viewed not as a remnant of a feudal past but as an expression of distinctly modern economies and the contemporary denigration of women. They pointed out that huge amounts of money had been made following the murder of Roop Kanwar by those who turned the sati into a commercial spectacle involving hundreds of thousands of people; that Roop Kanwar was an educated girl, not a simple embodiment of rural femininity (a fact that pro-sati lobbyists used to argue that it was a case of 'free choice'); and that the leaders of the pro-sati movement 'constitute a powerful regional elite' who had much to gain from constructing sati anew as emblematic of their 'tradition'.[31]

> Thus, what was essentially a women's rights issue had been distorted into an issue of 'tradition' versus 'modernity', a struggle of the religious majority against an irreligious minority.[32]

Now, these are almost exactly the terms in which Lata Mani, in essays written before the Deorala incident, had described the colonial discourse on the subject. Brilliantly unravelling the rhetorical and ideological overlaps between seemingly opposed views in the debates between the colonial government, the nationalist reformers and the indigenous pro-sati lobby, Mani points out that 'the entire issue was debated within the framework of the scriptures'.[33] Even Indian reformers, epitomised by Raja Ram Mohan Roy, argued against sati by contending that it had no scriptual sanction and that it was custom and not the Hindu religion that had fostered the practice.

At first glance, then, it seems that little has changed between the colonial situation and 1987. But Nandy's own analytical moves – towards subscribing to a division that he had earlier analysed, and invoking an ideal of mythical sati that represents an Indian tradition, a tradition that he had earlier seen as constructed out of the tensions of colonialism – help us identify the definitive contextual shifts. His conflation of 'respect' for an ideal sati with rural India, native authenticity and the canny cultural instincts of the average Indian clearly positions him as a sophisticated example of the nativism which Gayatri Spivak has repeatedly targeted as a major pitfall for the post-colonial intellectual. It is significant that such nativism, like its earlier counterparts, bases itself on a posited notion of an ideal woman or femininity.

Significantly too, the target of Nandy's anger today is not the colonial state but Indian feminists who are seen as deculturalised, inauthentic, westernised and alienated from an appreciation of their own culture, which their village sisters embody in the act of immolating themselves. Here Nandy has a wide range of allies: Mark Tully, BBC's veteran correspondent in New Delhi, endorsed such a view. In his essay on the Deorala sati, he pitted the 'Committee for the Protection of Religion', under whose banner 100,000 Rajputs assembled in Jaipur to hear speeches calling on them to defend Hinduism against the Westernized elite, 'independent women', urban 'journalists – as fundamentalist in their blind faith in modernity as the young Rajputs were in their beliefs', against 'academics' and most significantly, against 'those feminists who jumped at the opportunity the tragedy of Deorala gave to promote their views on women's rights'.[34] American sociologist Patrick Harrigan too launched his defence of sati on the shoulders of an attack on westernised feminists who were out of touch, he claimed, with the sentiments of their rural sisters, who in turn were emblematic of 'Bharat Mata' or Mother India.[35] The conservative Hindi press spoke in similar terms, as did various pundits and sadhus.[36] All of them zeroed in on 'azad kism ki auratein' [types of free woman] and pitted them against archetypes of the good Hindu woman and of the present-day average/authentic rural woman. The Rajput lobby was vociferous in condemning women in trousers and with short hair who were now going to tell 'their' women what not to do. As we can see, the division between the west and India, crass materialism and spirituality, is angrily and sanctimoniously re-worked to guard against the spectre of organized women's movements.

Thus, while the post-Deorala debates seems cast entirely in the mould of the tradition/modernity dichotomy Mani speaks of, the distinctively new factor is the women's movement, a movement which has 'been the single most important factor in changing the terms of the public debate on issues like rape, domestic violence, women's employment [etc] . . . if it were not for this, the incident at Deorala would not have been a national issue'.[37] We can unravel, via these overlaps between intellectual, religious, journalistic and other patriarchs, what it means for a writer like Nandy to celebrate the idea of sati at a time when, not only had a widow been immolated, but the ideologies behind female immolation were being re-invoked and aggressively re-circulated. The ire against feminist makes strange bedfellows.

While discussions of the textual tradition figured after Deorala, the question of the widow's choice was at the core of all debates. The idea of the voluntary sati as an expression of a peculiarly Indian mode of femininity was repeated ad nauseam by the pro-sati lobby – contradictorily invoked both via Roop Kanwar's modern education as well as via her supposed distance from other educated Indian women. The struggle now was clearly over female volition – with feminists claiming that the entire notion of a voluntary sati is retrogressive and the pro-sati lobby insisting on the freedom of choice. This brings us to the frustrating core of past and present representations of, and debates over, sati.

For the Indian woman to be cast as Mother India and to serve a wide spectrum of political interests in colonial times, she had to be rewritten as more-than-victim. As an agent of Hindu tradition, or nationalist interests, a certain amount of volition, and even desire had to be attributed to her. This rewriting is evident in the drama of sati abolition.

Two petitions were put forward by the Indian pro-sati lobby protesting the abolition in 1828, one to the King and the second to William Bentinck, the then Governor-General. In both a death-wish on the part of the loving, faithful widow becomes the emblem of Hindu resistance to colonial law:

> And on what grounds can strangers to our Faith, even though Rulers, assume the right to determine that the option which an Holy Religion thus expressly gives, shall exist no longer, and what right can they have to choose for us? . . . [The widow is] the Devotee who, superior to this world, and fitted for heaven, voluntarily dies, after every means which filial affection and human consideration have vainly employed in persuasion. . . . the Devotee never can be persuaded from her purpose, and if prevented by force or authority she only survives a few days. [Thus abolition is] an unjust and intolerant dictation in matters of conscience.[38]

Here, the *desire* of the Hindu wife for her husband is accorded a recognition that is otherwise entirely absent in patriarchal discourses. Ironically but hardly surprisingly, this recognition of desire and of subjectivity, and of agency, leads to the annihilation of the woman; hence female desire is allowed but a spectacular moment, a swan's song that announces her ceasing to be.[39]

After the Deorala incident, it was not only the pro-sati lobby that invoked the widow's desire. The new legislations on sati introduced by the Indian Government and the Rajasthan State Government, both of which were avowedly concerned with effectively eradicating widow immolation as well as its 'glorification', implicitly cast the woman herself as agent of the crime. The Commission of Sati (Prevention) Act, 1987, states:

> whoever attempts to commit sati and does any act towards the commission shall be punishable with imprisonment for a term which shall be not less than one year but which may extend to five years and shall also be liable to a fine which shall not be less than five thousand rupees but which may also extend to twenty thousand rupees.

The widow who survives is to be punished by a prison sentence of one to five years. As Vasudha Dhagamwar, a feminist legal expert pointed out, the relevant clauses 'do not distinguish between voluntary and involuntary sati. But in effect they treat all sati as voluntary. That is why the woman is punished and that is why those who kill her are punished for abetment and not for murder.'[40] The invocation of female will here can be seen to work against the woman herself.

Lata Mani's central argument has been that the entire colonial debate on sati was concerned with re-defining tradition and modernity, that 'what was at stake was not women but tradition' (p. 118) and that women 'become sites on which various versions of scripture/tradition/law are elaborated and contested' (p. 115). Hence, she argues, nowhere is the sati herself a subject of the debate, and nowhere is her subjectivity represented. Thus, we learn little or nothing about the widows themselves, or their interiority, or in fact of their pain, even from reformers such as Ram Mohan Roy.

Mani's conclusions have set the terms for subsequent work on sati, especially that which is concerned with the relationship between gender and colonialism. The critical recovery of the sati's consciousness and subjectivity has become a recurrent but fraught project, consonant with the recent preoccupation in writings on colonial discourse in general and South Asian historiography in particular with the agency of the oppressed subject.[41] Anand Yang laments the lack of focus on the satis themselves in existing writings, but largely repeats statistical data about the women's age, caste and region.[42] Gayatri Spivak, in at least three influential essays, reads the absence of women's voices in the colonial debate as representative of the difficulty of recovering subject positions in general and as indicative of the violence of colonialism and of indigenous patriarchy in particular: the discourses on sati are read as proof that 'there is no space from where the subaltern [sexed] subject can speak'.[43]

The silence of Spivak's subaltern is both a critique and, more disturbingly, an echo of a notoriously recurrent theme in the writings of British colonialists, Indian nationalists, Hindu orthodoxy, and indeed British feminists of the nineteenth century. The silence of Indian women enabled British feminists to claim a speaking part for themselves.[44] In an editorial comment in *The Storm-bell* of June 1898, Josephine Butler commented that Indian women were

> indeed between the upper and nether millstone, helpless, voiceless, hopeless. Their helplessness appeals to the heart, in somewhat the same way

in which the helplessness and suffering of a dumb animal does, under the knife of a vivisector. Somewhere, halfway between the Martyr Saints and the tortured 'friend of man', the noble dog, stand, it seems to me, these pitiful Indian women, girls, children, as many of them are. They have not even the small power of resistance which the western woman may have . . .[45]

Butler and others could thus claim the necessity of representing their mute sisters, and hence legitimize themselves as 'the imperial authorities on "Indian womanhood"'.[46] Although she contests precisely the legacy of such politics, it is not surprising that the silence of Spivak's subaltern is a pre-condition for her own project of representation. She writes:

> As Sarah Kofman has shown, the deep ambiguity of Freud's use of women as a scapegoat is a reaction-formation to an initial and continuing desire to give the hysteric a voice, to transform her into the subject of hysteria. The masculist-imperialist ideological formation that shaped that desire into 'the daughter's seduction' is part of the same formation that constructs the monolithic 'third world woman'. . . . Thus, when confronted with the questions, Can the subaltern speak? and Can the subaltern (as woman) speak?, our efforts to give the subaltern a voice in history will be doubly open to the dangers run by Freud's discourse.[47]

Spivak contends that both Foucault and the Subaltern school of South Asian historians succumbs to these dangers in trying to recover the voice of the marginalised subject. In both cases the idea of a sovereign subject creeps back and undercuts their own concerns – in the case of Foucault, s/he is imperialist, in the case of the subaltern historians, a nativist. Spivak thus signals the necessity of adapting the Gramscian maxim – 'pessimism of the intellect, optimism of the will' – by combining a philosophical scepticism about recovering any subaltern agency with a political commitment to making visible the positioning of the marginalised. Thus she makes her case for the validity of the representation of the subaltern by the post-colonial feminist intellectual:

> The subaltern cannot speak. There is no virtue in global laundry lists with 'woman' as a pious item. Representation has not withered away. The female intellectual as intellectual has a circumscribed task which she must not disown with a flourish.[48]

The intellectual whom Spivak here calls to arms is almost by definition the Indian woman academic working in the metropolitan academy, a woman who must struggle against the neo-colonial impulses of that space without succumbing to the nostalgic gestures of her counterpart in the third world.

It is no accident that such a project focuses on the immolated widow, who, in Spivak's work, becomes the ground for formulating a critique of colonialism, of indigenous patriarchy, of contemporary critical and cultural theories and of revisionist historiographies. She provides the most suitable language for talking about silence: she is, after all, a conceptual and social category that comes into being only when the subject dies. The to-be-sati is merely a widow, the sati is by definition a silenced subject. Caught between the notion of representation that comes too easily, as in the case of the nineteenth-century British feminists, and another that recognises its contingencies and difficulties, like Spivak's, the Indian woman remains silent: she still 'cannot speak'. An insistence on subaltern silence is disquieting for those who are engaged in precisely the task of recovering such voices; it can be linked to Spivak's curious detachment, in these essays, from the specificities of post-colonial politics. But her argument for the validity, indeed necessity, of representation ironically takes on, as I hope to show below, a specially urgent resonance in the very arena she does not address: the struggles of third world feminists in their own countries, and in this case, India.

From the earliest commentaries onwards, only two options are offered for the dead widow: she either wanted to die or was forced to. Each option marks a dead end for feminist investigations. In the first case, we are dangerously close to the 'radiant heroism' of the willing widow which is suggested by both British and Indian male commentators. In the second case, fears have been voiced that if we refuse to 'grant sati the dubious status of existential suicide' we will find ourselves 'in another bind, that of viewing the sati as inexorably a victim and thereby emptying her subjectivity of any function or agency'.[49] Edward Thompson, in a section called 'The Psychology of the "Satis"' easily combined both ideas:

> I had intended to try and examine this; but the truth is, it has ceased to be a puzzle to me. Obviously the mental state of the women who were sacrificed varied infinitely, as that of martyrs for religion or patriotism. The Rajput lady who died when a foe girdled her city and her whole sex was swept away, or who ascended the pyre with her lord newly slain in battle, was in a mood that had no contact or resemblance with the mood of the cowed and unwilling slave-girl.[50]

In those essays where Lata Mani uncovers the common ground on which dichotomies between willing and unwilling satis were constructed, she declares that she herself is 'not concerned here with what the practice of sati meant to those who undertook it', suggesting in a footnote that we turn to Ashis Nandy's essay, which, however, does not concern itself at all with the points of view of satis or would-be satis.[51] It seems to me that, until very recently, Mani was unable to proceed significantly beyond Edward Thompson's dichotomies.[52] Thompson, to give credit where it is due, speaks at length about how societies construct desire – whether this be manifested as the devotion of the sati or in the patriotism of soldiers. In fact, in the aftermath of Deorala, Thompson's rhetoric sounded less offensive than that of the pro-sati lobby which, as I earlier mentioned, harped in different ways about the free-will of the authentic sati. In the context where feminist-bashing poised itself precisely on the question of free-will, formulations such as Lata Mani's that 'the volition of some widows can justifiably be seen as equal to the resistance of others' had a rather disturbing resonance.[53] Feminists in India, I should note here, have repeatedly stressed that 'there is no such things as a voluntary sati'.[54]

Rajeswari Sunder Rajan attempts to break this impasse by drawing on Elaine Scarry's work on the 'radical subjectivity' of pain.[55] Arguing that neither colonial commentators, nor Indian reformers, nor even the feminist work on sati have sufficiently focused on the pain of the dying woman, and showing also how the pro-sati lobby has always insisted that the sati feels none, Sunder Rajan claims that 'an inherent resistance to pain is what impels the individual or collective suffering subject towards freedom. It is therefore as one who acts/reacts, rather than as one who invites assistance, that one must regard the subject in pain' (p. 9). A recent essay by Lata Mani can be read as in dialogue with Sunder Rajan and other feminists working in India.[56] Mani now mines colonial eyewitness accounts of widow burning for signs of the struggles and vacillations of potential satis and shows how pain may impel a woman to try to escape the pyre, contrary to her own earlier resolution to die. She thereby moves beyond her earlier notion of 'complex subjectivity' for satis, which had seemed to merely oscillate between various static states of being. Significantly, she now clearly states that there is no such things as a voluntary sati and is anxious, too, that we avoid 'globalizing the local . . . granting colonialism more power than it achieved'. She wants also to 'make sure that the things in my work that speak to the context of the U.S. are not . . . counter-productive in the struggle of progressives in India'.[57] Such a note is rare in work on colonial discourse within the Western academy and it leads Lata Mani to a crucial reformulation:

> The question 'can the subaltern speak?' then, is better posed as a series of questions: Which groups constitute the subalterns in any text? What is their relationship to each other? How can they be heard to be speaking or not speaking in a given set of materials? With what effects? Rephrasing the question in this way enables us to retain Spivak's insight regarding the positioning of women in colonial discourse *without conceding to colonial discourse what it, in fact, did not achieve – the erasure of women.*[58]

Let me attempt to answer these questions by returning to the question of the subaltern's experience and her pain as they figure in Sunder Rajan's essay, which searches the postcolonial discourse on sati for representations of the widow's pain. Analysing the law, the media, feminist analyses, and the Indian women's movement, she finds that the pain of the sati is represented only in 'forms of agit-prop representations in theatre, film and posters' which bring 'us closer to the "reality" of sati than does either the liberal discourse denouncing it or the popular and religious discourse glorifying it' (p. 16). It is significant, I think, that an essay which begins with an inquiry into subjectivity and the individual subject ends up with what in fact is one of the most succinct accounts of the political situation after the Deorala sati. Sunder Rajan discusses how the Indian media and others writing on the Deorala incident persistently attempted to reconstruct the subjectivity of Roop Kanwar, and shows how the assumption that the 'answer to such a complex mystery is to be sought in knowing the sati herself, leads all too often to a closure of analysis, her death creating a condition of definitional unknowability'.[59] She herself is forced to conclude 'that an exclusive focus on choice and motivation in constructing the subjectivity of the sati in some representations leads either to mystification or to cognitive closure'. I say she is 'forced to conclude' because Sunder Rajan does not draw out the implications of her own work. Why is it that a project which seeks to unravel subjectivity ends up by describing, and by valorising (albeit somewhat uneasily) the representation of sati in agitprop posters and by social movements?

Even though I find her use of the subject-in-pain model somewhat problematic, I think Sunder Rajan's essay is crucial in implicitly moving towards a collective subjectivity of agents – in this case this would not be a collectivity of satis or even of widows but rather of huge, if not all, sections of Indian women who suffer from the consequences of the ideology of sati. I would like to suggest that 'the subaltern' 'in the text of sati', if we must locate one, cannot be understood simply as the immolated widow. The sati is produced by and functions to recirculate ideologies which target and seek to position a larger body of women, whose experiences, articulations and silences are crucial to understanding the relations of power and insubordination which are central to any analysis of 'the subaltern'.

It is entirely true that to focus on the pain of the burning widow is at once to draw attention to the shared indifference to women on the part of both defenders and abolitionists of sati, then and now, and to remind ourselves that sati is not just a symbol and a figuration, but a tortuous experience. However, recovering that experience, or locating agency within the temporal and experiential boundaries of the act of widow immolation is fraught with the dangers of succumbing to its grotesque power and its ideal authenticity at the expense of understanding how and why it is produced in the first place. Joan Scott's critique of 'experience' as a foundational historical category is useful in drawing attention to the dangers of Scarry's epistemology of pain even when it is used as cautiously as it is by Sunder Rajan. Scott points out that

> experience works as a foundation providing both a starting point and a conclusive kind of explanation, beyond which few questions need to or can be asked. And yet it is precisely the questions precluded – questions about discourse, difference and subjectivity, as well as about what counts as experience and who gets to make that determination – that would enable us to historicize experience, to reflect critically on the history we write about it, rather than to premise our history upon it.[60]

If we are not to take either identity or experience for granted, we should look at how they are 'ascribed, resisted or embraced', she writes.

Such an exercise points to several directions in which work on sati still needs to be done. Colonial accounts voyeuristically focus on the spectacle of burning and obsessively describe the beautiful young widow as she strips herself of clothes and ornaments to ascend the fire.[61] An alternative view that exposes the pain and ugliness of the event must also guard against sealing it off from what precedes or follows it. The sati's experience is not limited to the pain of a death: a whole life is brought to the violence of that event, which, if unpacked, can be seen as constructed – not just crudely by her fears of a miserable life as a widow, not just by familial economic designs on her property, not even by male anxieties about her sexuality, but by social and ideological interactions, pressures and configurations that connect her immediate situation to the politics of her community, and indeed of the nation, and to the crucial articulations of gender within each of them. Some feminist work produced in India has been moving towards making these connections visible. Kumkum Sangari and Sudesh Vaid have meticulously documented specific cases of sati and delineated their 'contexts'.[62] Their writings certainly speculate on the ideologies that connect one burning to another, but they also focus on what was at stake in staging each immolation.

To use the word 'staging' is problematic in as much as it might be seen to deny the part played by the individual psyche and drives in enabling the violence of a sati. Such a denial is, unfortunately, emblematic of much feminist work produced in India, and elsewhere I touch upon how it is sometimes produced by a suspicion of 'western feminist theory' which is thereby flattened out and cast entirely as 'liberal-humanist' or as focussing on the psychic, the sexual and the individual at the expense of the political and the social.[63] This is not the space to discuss the debilitating effects of recasting a divide between the East and the West on the grounds of feminist studies, although it should be obvious that such a dichotomy works to the detriment of nuanced understandings of gender politics anywhere. There is no necessary contradiction between focusing on the social and the psychic: Jacqueline Rose has pointed out that 'ideology is effective . . . because it works at the most rudimentary levels of psychic identity and its drives'.[64] In such an understanding, the individual psyche and the social exist in a constitutive, *traumatic*, reciprocity; the violence and pathologies of the one being symptomatic of the other. In the case of sati, this violent reciprocity is the reason why 'choice' has no meaning apart from its multiple determinations. Sangari and Vaid do not address this traumatic relation, but they do point out the ways in which the widow's desire is understood only when it is expressed as a willingness to die. Hence the sati's 'power' lies in her will to die and comes into being only when she expresses that will.[65] Therefore it is visible only when it is compliant with dominant ideologies.

The 1987 episode of sati was particularly frightening for feminists in India precisely because it was embedded within a context in which various types of murders are constructed as questions of female choice. When wives are burnt for dowry it is alleged that they committed suicide. The systematic abortion of female foetuses in contemporary India, it has been argued, is only a question of 'choice' on the part of the mothers-to-be. The debate over these amniocentesis-determined abortions also highlights the dubious status of women's experience and of a feminist politics that valorises it.[66] Then there was the case of Shahbano, where the elderly Muslim divorcee petitioned the courts for alimony, a right granted by the civil code of the country but not by the Muslim personal Law. When she won the case, Muslim fundamentalists forced her to withdraw her petition in the name of her religion. It was then argued that women's groups had no right to petition further since the individual woman had made her choice. These groups, however, continued to 'represent', not Shahbano the individual, but the politics of gender and of community identity which the case had thrown up.[67] All of these issues were articulated, by communal, nationalist or patriarchal voices, as issues of female and individual choice. In each of them, such a formulation pushed for a cognitive and discursive closure that would protect existing inequalities for women, or create new ones. And in each case, feminists had to insist on their right to represent other women, although they did not speak merely *for* the subaltern as much as insist that much was at stake for women's groups, for larger bodies of women, and for the Indian polity at large.[68]

The debate on sati, then, signals the need to take into account two sorts of collective subjects in order to reposition the individual subject within them – the first is the collectivity of women at large, and the second a politically organised collectivity of women. The first would highlight that, despite its spectacular nature, the sati is not an isolated event; the second would indicate the ways in which female agency is wrought out of precariously achieved political intervention. Taken together, the two collectives do not seek to bypass, devalue or erase the suffering, the pain or the determinations of the individual subject. They do, however, extend Spivak's notion of representation: the 'truth' about Roop Kanwar is not exclusively or best represented by the post-colonial feminist intellectual, but by an intersection of the two collectivities mentioned above. In the post-Deorala debates, statements by rural women showed that they often believed in sati as a possibility even as they questioned that Roop Kanwar was a 'true' sati. But at the same time, they questioned various aspects of women's oppression in India, and showed an awareness of women's movements even when these had not touched their own lives.[69]

Such an exercise, of listening to other women's voices to position the individual sati, and of detailing the individual circumstances and nuances of each immolation, is obviously easier to attempt in the present context. But I want to suggest here that if we look back, from the vantage point of a contemporary widespread backlash against the women's movement, at the bedfellows of the colonial controversy, and find that women are somehow erased there, we should not simply suppose that they were merely the grounds on which other concerns were articulated. We may modify Lata Mani's conclusions to suggest that women were, *then as now*, the targets as well as the grounds of the debates over transition.

This, however, calls for us to *suppose a presence which at first cannot be found*, an exercise that Spivak critically endorses in the case of the subaltern school of Indian historians. If women are and have always been at stake, we must look for them, both within discourses which seek to erase their self-representation and elsewhere. The writings of women who worked alongside, within or in opposition to the nationalist movements are increasingly becoming available for feminist scholars and invaluable in understanding what was at stake in nineteenth-century widow immolations.[70] These writings help us understand that the debate over traditional and modernity did not merely use *woman* as a 'site', but specifically targeted those who challenged or critiqued the patriarchal underpinnings of nationalist discourses. The more feminist research uncovers these hitherto hidden and erased voices, the clearer it becomes that the precursors of today's feminists, as individuals and as a potential collectivity, constituted a threat and were thus at least partially the target of earlier rewritings of 'tradition'. The bitter lessons of the present resurgence of communalism in India should make this easier to understand. Today, Hindu communalism does not simply resort to the image of a traditional, passive woman but offers its own versions of militant womanhood to counter those produced by feminist struggles.[71] Indeed, the latest ironic manifestation of this is the fact that the most aggressive and masculist face of recent Hindu communalism is embodied by two women leaders, Sadhvi Rithambara and Uma Bharati.[72] Communalism articulates itself as both traditional and modern, and so does nationalism; both tradition and modernity are thus fluid terms, invoked freely to serve specific class and gender interests.

I have been arguing that we can re-position the sati by looking not just at the widow who died but at those who survived to tell the tale. This tale, however, will only underline that subaltern agency, either at the individual level or at the collective, cannot be idealised as pure opposition to the order it opposes; it works both within that order and displays its own contradictions. Finally, identity is not just a matter of self-perception. In an article called 'The Plight of Hindu Widows as Described by a Widow Herself', which first appeared in *The Gospel of All Lands* in April 1889, the writer describes the misery of a wife following the death of her husband:

> None of her relatives will touch her to take her ornaments off her body. That task is assigned to three women from the barber caste . . . those female fiends literally jump all over her and violently tear all the ornaments from her nose, ears etc. In that rush, the delicate bones of the nose and ear are sometimes broken. Sometimes . . . tufts of hair are also plucked off . . . At some times grief crashes down on the poor woman from all sides . . . there is nothing in our fate but suffering from birth to death. When our husbands are alive, we are their slaves; when they die, our fate is even worse . . . Thousands of widows die after a husband's death. But far more have to suffer worse fates throughout their lives if

they stay alive. Once, a widow who was a relative of mine died in front of me. She had fallen ill before her husband died. When he died, she was so weak that she could not even be dragged to her husband's cremation. She had a burning fever. Then her mother-in-law dragged her down from the cot onto the ground and ordered the servant to pour bucketfuls of cold water over her. After some eight hours, she died. But nobody came to see how she was when she was dying of the cold. After she died, however, they started praising her, saying she had died for the love of her husband . . . If all [such] tales are put together they would make a large book. The British government put a ban on the custom of sati, but as a result of that several women who could have died a cruel but quick death when their husbands died now have to face an agonizingly slow death.[73]

The widows in this narrative come close to those constructed by colonial records and accounts. The speaker herself offers a functionalist explanation of the sati's desire to die. And yet, she herself, a potential sati, did not die. In speaking, she reveals not just a tremulous or vacillating subjectivity but an awareness of the traumatic constructedness of one's own 'experience'. Identity is both self-constructed, and constructed for us.

To conclude, feminist theory is still working out the connections between social determinations and individual subjectivity. The work on sati demonstrates how the contexts of utterance and intervention still determine which of these two will be stressed, but it also marks a space where a fruitful dialogue has begun to emerge. Widow immolation is thus neither the burning of the exceptional woman nor the sign of the special devotion/victimisation of the average Indian or 'third world' woman; in becoming a vanishing point for a theory of female subjectivity, it signals both worthwhile directions in which revisionist histories of Indian women and theories of subaltern agency might move, and the problems they will encounter.

NOTES

1. I would like to thank Rajeswari Sunder Rajan and Rukun Advani for their generous help with materials; Nivedita Menon, Priyamvada Gopal and Andrew Parker for their responses and, above all, Suvir Kaul for his extensive comments and his illuminating editorial pencil. I use the term 'sati', which has itself been the subject of much debate, for the act as well as the practice of widow immolation, as well as for the woman who dies. Colonial writings spelt it as 'suttee'; and, recently, Sudesh Vaid and Kumkum Sangari 'use the words "widow immolation" to designate the primary violence and the word "sati" to indicate those structures of belief and ideology which gain consent for widow immolation', 'Institutions, Beliefs, Ideologies: Widow Immolation in Contemporary Rajasthan', *Economic and Political Weekly*, Vol. XXVI, no. 17, April 27 1991, p. WS-3. 'Dead women tell no tales' in my title refers both to Pamela Philipose and Teesta Setalvad's casual use of the phrase ('Demystifying Sati', *The Illustrated Weekly of India*, March 13 1988, p. 41) and to the obsession of the dead widow's desire in discourses on sati.
2. Lata Mani, 'Contentious Traditions: The Debate on Sati in Colonial India', in *Recasting Women* Kumkum Sangari and Sudesh Vaid (eds), New Delhi, 1989, p. 126 n. 97.

3. For an elaboration of this argument, see my 'Overworlding the "third world"', *Oxford Literary Review*, 3: 1–2, 1991, pp. 164–92.
4. Edward Thompson, *Suttee: A Historical and Philosophical Enquiry into the Hindu Rite of Widow-Burning*, 1928.
5. See, for example, Arvind Shama, *Sati, Historical and Phenomenological Essays*, Delhi, 1988; VN Datta, *Sati: a Historical, Social and Philosophical Enquiry into the Hindu Rite of Widow Burning*, New Delhi, 1988. I have been unable to review *Sati, the Blessing and the Curse; The Burning of Wives in India*, John Stratton Hawley (ed.), New York, 1993.
6. *Subaltern Studies*, Vols 1–8, Ranajit Guha (ed.), Delhi, 1982–92.
7. Romila Thapar, 'Traditions Versus Misconceptions', in *Manushi*, no. 42–3, 1987, p. 8. See also her essay, 'In History', in *Seminar*, no. 342 ('Sati: a symposium on widow immolation and its social contexts'), February 1988, pp. 14–19.
8. Dorothy K. Stein, 'Women to Burn: Suttee as a Normative Institution', *Signs*, 4: 2, 1978, argues that the difference between satis and warriors is the narrowness of the cause for which the women die. Feminists in India have, instead, repeatedly stressed that the difference lies in the fact that the group from which satis are drawn is marginalised and oppressed, unlike the group from which soldiers are produced.
9. Ibid., p. 253.
10. Edward Thompson, *Suttee*, p. 26.
11. Ashis Nandy, 'Sati: A Nineteenth Century Tale of Women, Violence and Protest', in *At the Edge of Psychology: Essays in Politics and Culture*, Delhi, 1980, pp. 1–31.
12. Quoted by Arvind Sharma, pp. 2–3. This episode is referred to by many commentators, including Thompson and Stein.
13. A translation of 'M. Caesar Fredericke [Federici], Marchant of Venice' in 1558 describes with puzzlement the Indian women who 'so wilfully burne themselves against nature and law' (quoted by Thomas Hahn, 'Indians East and West: primitivism and savagery in English discovery narratives of the sixteenth century', *The Journal of Medieval and Renaissance Studies*, 8: 1, 1978, p. 103). The (16th-century) Jesuit missionary de Nobili was impressed 'by the ecstatic devotion with which many of these young widows went to their deaths'.
14. Quoted in Lata Mani, 'Cultural Theory, Colonial Texts: Reading Eyewitness Accounts of Widow Burning', in Lawrence Grossberg, Cary Nelson and Paula Treichler (eds), *Cultural Studies*, New York and London, 1992, p. 400.
15. Gayatri Chakravorty Spivak, 'Can the Subaltern Speak?' in Cary Nelson and Lawrence Grossberg, *Marxism and the Interpretation of Culture*, Urbana and Chicago, 1988, p. 297.
16. Katherine Mayo, *Mother India*, New York, 1927, p. 22; the review is quoted by Rama Joshi and Joanne Liddle, *Daughters of Interdependence: Gender, Caste and Class in India*, 1986, p. 31.
17. George Macmun, *The Religious and Hidden Cults of India*, 1931, p. 174.
18. 'Of Virtue', in *The Complete Essays of Montaigne*, translated by Donald M. Frame, Stanford, 1958, p. 535.
19. Vasudha Dhagamwar, 'Saint, Victim or Criminal', *Seminar*, no. 342, Feb. 1988, p. 35.
20. Mani, 'Contentious Traditions' p. 98. One example is worth quoting in detail:

> The question posed to the pundit was whether sati was enjoined by scriptural texts. The pundit responded that the texts did not enjoin but merely permitted sati in certain instances . . . Nevertheless based on this response the Nizamat Adalat concluded that 'The practice, generally speaking, being thus recognized and *encouraged* by the doctrines of the Hindoo religion, it appears evident that the course which the British government should follow, according to the principle of religious tolerance . . . is to allow the practice in those cases in which it is counternanced by their religion; and to prevent it in others in which it is by the same authority prohibited (p. 99).

21. Veena Das, 'Strange Response', *The Illustrated Weekly of India*, February 28 1988, p. 31. See also her 'Gender Studies, Cross-cultural Comparisons and the Colonial Organization of Knowledge', *Berkshire Review*, 21 (1986), pp. 58–76.

22. The *Calcutta Review* commented that 'the Government and the Sudder Court were, in fact, getting into a dilemma by attempting to introduce justice and law into what was, in itself, the highest kind of illegality, the most palpable injustice and the most revolting cruelty (Thompson, *Suttee*, p. 65).

23. Ashis Nandy, 'Sati', pp. 1–31.

24. Thompson, *Suttee*, p. 65. The presence of British officers at the immolations are supposed to have 'thrown the ideas of the Hindoos upon the subject into a complete state of confusion', according to one Mr. C. Smith, a second judge of the Sudder Court, '. . . they conceive our power and our will to be commensurable' (pp. 64–5). The ironies attendant upon policing sati do not stop there: in 1987, the Indian government passed The Commission of Sati (Prevention) Act which sought to intensify the existing ban on sati by outlawing its spectacle: hence witnessing a sati became a potential abetment of the crime. Ironically, where the British half-measure necessitated that each sati event be policed, watched, observed and documented, the latest act has led to a paradoxical situation where surveillance is criminal; now, as Rajeswari Sunder Rajan has acutely observed, to report sati is to render oneself vulnerable to law so that today, when a woman dies, a 'collective amnesia' suggests that 'her death never occurred', 'The Subject of Sati: Pain and Death in the Contemporary Discourse on Sati', *Yale Journal of Criticism*, 3: 2, 1990, p. 13.

25. Nandy, 'Sati', p. 7.

26. Anand Yang, 'Whose Sati? Widow Burning in Early 19th Century India', *Journal of Women's History*, pp. 19–21; Sanjukta Gupta and Richard Gombrich, 'Another View of Widow-Burning and Womanliness in Indian Public Culture', *Journal of Commonwealth and Comparative Politics* 22, 1984, p. 256. But the later article also endorses the tired (and potentially communal) claim that the Hindu emphasis on chastity was a consequence of the Muslim threat to the purity of Hindu women (pp. 255–6).

27. See for example, Partha Chatterjee, 'The Nationalist Resolution of the Women's Question' in *Recasting Women*, pp. 233–53.

28. Rosalind O'Hanlon, 'Issues of Widowhood in Colonial Western India', in *Contesting Power, Resistance and Everyday Social Relations in South Asia*, edited by Douglas Haynes and Gyan Prakash, Delhi, 1991, p. 77–9.

29. Ashis Nandy 'The Human Factor', *The Illustrated Weekly of India*, January 17 1988, p. 22.

30. Here Nandy claimed Rabindranath Tagore as an illustrious predecessor in severing the 'idea' of sati from the practice, and also extensively referred to Anand Coomaraswamy's notorious defense of sati in his influential book *The Dance of Shiva*.

31. It is significant that now the tradition or culture being defended by the pro-sati lobby was that of the Rajputs, whereas once the pan-Indian-ness of sati was stressed. Of course, in this instance, the 'Rajput' become encoded as the essence of Indian-ness.

32. Madhu Kishwar and Ruth Vanita, 'The Burning of Roop Kanwar', *Manushi*, no. 42–3, 1987, p. 16. See also Sudesh Vaid, 'The Politics of Widow Immolation', *Seminar*, no. 342, February 1988, pp. 20–3.

33. Mani, 'Contentious Traditions', p. 110.

34. Mark Tully, 'The Deorala Sati', in *No Full Stops in India*, pp. 210–36.

35. 'Tyranny of the Elect? Bringing Bharat Mata Up to Date', *Statesman*, Delhi edition, Nov. 5 1987.

36. For an analysis of some of these positions, see Kumkum Sangari, 'Perpetuating the Myth', *Seminar*, no. 342, Feb. 1988, pp. 24–30.

37. Pamela Philipose and Teesta Setalvad, 'Demystifying Sati', p. 41.
38. Quoted by Stein in 'Women to Burn', pp. 260–1.
39. In contemporary pro-sati discourses, the sati is repeatedly spoken of in terms of her love for her husband, a love whose everyday expression is subjection and service to him and which is marked by a consistent erasure of the self. All other forms of female desire are, within such discourses, repellant and abnormal.
40. Dhagamwar, 'Saint, Criminal or Victim', p. 38.
41. Rosalind O'Hanlon's essay, 'Recovering the Subject: *Subaltern Studies* and Histories of Resistance in Colonial South Asia', *Modern Asian Studies*, 22: 1, 1988, pp. 189–224, perceptively reviews these materials.
42. Anand Yang, 'Whose Sati?' pp. 8–33 and 'The Many Faces of Sati in The Early Nineteenth Century', *Manushi*, no. 42–3, 1987, pp. 26–9.
43. Gayatri Chakravorty Spivak, 'Can the Subaltern Speak? Speculations on Widow-Sacrifice', *Wedge*, Winter/Spring 1985, pp. 120–30, p. 120, and p. 129. The other two essays are, 'Can the Subaltern Speak?' in *Marxism and the Interpretation of Culture*, pp. 271–313 and 'The Rani of Sirmur', *History and Theory*, 24: 3, 1987, pp. 247–72.
44. Antoinette M. Burton, 'The White Woman's Burden, British Feminists and "The Indian Woman", 1865–1915', in *Western Women and Imperialism* edited by Nupur Chaudhuri and Margaret Strobel, Bloomington, 1992, pp. 137–57, suggests that feminists in Britain constructed 'the Indian woman' as a foil against which to gauge their own progress; for them empire was an integral and enabling part of 'the woman question' (p. 139). See also Barbara N. Ramusack, 'Cultural Missionaries, Maternal Imperialists, Feminists Allies, British Women Activists in India, 1865–1945' in the same volume, pp. 119–36.
45. Burton, 'The White Woman's Burden, p. 144.
46. Ibid., p. 148.
47. Spivak, 'Can the Subaltern Speak?', *Marxism and the Interpretation of Culture*, p. 296.
48. Ibid., p. 308. See also her 'Subaltern Studies: Deconstructing Histoiography' in *Subaltern Studies IV: Writings on South Asian History and Society* edited by Ranajit Guha, Delhi, 1985.
49. Sunder Rajan, 'The Subject of Sati', p. 5.
50. Thompson, *Suttee*, 137–8.
51. Mani, 'Contentious Traditions', p. 92.
52. Mani writes: 'It is difficult to know how to interpret these accounts, for we have no independent access to the mental or subjective states of widows outside of these overdetermined colonial representations of them. In any case, the meaning of consent in a patriarchal context is hard to assess. Still, it is fair to assume that the mental states of widows were complex and inconsistent. Some widows were undoubtedly coerced: the decisions of others would be difficult to reduce to "force".' ('Contentious Traditions').
53. Mani, 'Contentious Traditions', *Cultural Critique*, no. 7, fall 1987, p. 97. This sentence was, significantly, dropped in later versions; Loomba, 'Overworlding', p. 187.
54. See, for example, Kumkum Sangari, 'There is no such thing as voluntary sati', *The Times of India*, Sunday Review, Oct. 25 1987.
55. Elaine Scarry, *The Body in Pain: The Making and Unmaking of the World*. New York and Oxford, 1985.
56. Lata Mani, 'Cultural Theory, Colonial Texts: Reading Eyewitness Accounts of Widow Burning, in Lawrence Grossberg, Cary Nelson and Paula A. Treichler, (eds) *Cultural Studies*, New York and London, 1992, pp. 392–408.
57. Ibid., p. 408. See also Mani's discussion of the different resonances of her work in the US, in India and in Britain in 'Multiple Mediations: Feminist Scholarship in the Age of Multinational Reception', *Feminist Review*, no. 36, 1989, pp. 21–41.
58. Mani, 'Cultural Theory, Colonial Texts', p. 403.

59. Sunder Rajan, 'The Subject of Sati', p. 14.
60. Joan Scott, 'Experience', in Judith Butler and Joan W. Scott (eds), *Feminists Theorize the Political*, New York and London, 1992, p. 33.
61. Satis were of course not always or even mostly the nubile young things they are portrayed as in such accounts, as Anand Yang and Lata Mani both indicate.
62. See Sudesh Vaid and Kumkum Sangari, 'Sati in Modern India: A 'Report', *Economic and Political Weekly*, 16: 31, August 1 1981, pp. 1284–88, and 'Institutions, Beliefs, Ideologies, Widow Immolation in Contemporary Rajasthan', *Economic and Political Weekly*, 26: 17, April 27 1991, pp. WS-2–WS-18.
63. 'The feminine mystique unveiled', *The Indian Express*, Sunday Magazine, August 25 1991.
64. Rose, *Sexuality in the Field of Vision*, 1986, p. 5.
65. The relationship between 'will' and 'willingness' is worth considering in this context.
66. See Nivedita Menon, 'Abortion and the Law: Problems for Feminism', *Canadian Journal of Women and the Law*, 6: 1, 1993, pp. 103–18.
67. The silence of Shahbano did not stifle the voices of Indian women on the subject of religion, the state and the female subject. See Zakia Pathak and Rajeswari Sunder Rajan, 'Shahbano' in *Feminists Theorize the Political*, pp. 257–79.
68. 'Their pain from the sati incident', concluded Veena Das 'stems from the manner in which they see their own lives as intrinsically bound with the lives of women such as Roop Kanwar', 'Strange Response', p. 31.
69. See Kavita, Shobha, Shobita, Kanchan and Sharad, 'Rural Women Speak', *Seminar*, no. 342, February 1988, pp. 40–4.
70. Susie Tharu and K. Lalita, *Women Writing in India*, Volume 1, New Delhi, 1991 and Volume 2, New York, 1993 are valuable recent resources for feminists working in this area.
71. See Tanika Sarkar, 'The Woman as Communal Subject', *Economic and Political Weekly*, 26: 35, August 1991, pp. 2057–67.
72. See Tapan Basu, Pradip Datta, Sumit Sarkar, Tanika Sarkar and Sambuddha Sen, *Khaki Shorts and Saffron Flags: A Critique of the Hindu Right*, New Delhi, 1993. But this issue needs deeper analysis, as do the images of femininity and female militancy among the Indian left.
73. Basu, et al., *Women Writing in India*, pp. 359–63.

3.2

'END OF EMPIRE: ISLAM, NATIONALISM AND WOMEN IN TURKEY'

Deniz Kandiyoti

It is commonly conceded that among Muslim nations Turkey distinguishes herself by comprehensive, and as yet unparalleled, reforms with respect to the emancipation of women. These reforms, initiated by Mustafa Kemal Ataturk, the founder of the Turkish Republic, were part of a spate of legislation which amounted to a radical break with Ottoman Islam and its institutions. World War I had resulted in the dismemberment of the defeated empire and the occupation of the Anatolian provinces by the Allied powers. The active hostility of the last Ottoman Sultan-Caliph to Kemal's nationalist struggle in Anatolia, and his collaboration with the Allies, culminated in the abolition of the Sultanate by the Ankara government in 1922. The Turkish Republic was proclaimed on 29 October 1923. A few days earlier, on 24 October, the Istanbul head of police had taken an administrative decision desegregating public transport, so that men and women would no longer be separated by curtains or special compartments. Thereafter, a systematic onslaught on Ottoman institutions took place.

In a single day, on 3 March 1924, the Caliphate was abolished, education was made a monopoly of the state, and the *medrese* (religious education) system was terminated. Religious affairs and the administration of the *vakif* (pious foundations) were henceforth allocated to directorates attached to the office of the prime minister. This was followed by the elimination of religious courts in April of the same year. The *tarikats* (mystic religious orders) were

From: Deniz Kandiyoti (1991), 'End of Empire: Islam, Nationalism and Women in Turkey', pp. 22–47, in Deniz Kandiyoti (ed.), *Women, Islam and the State* (Basingstoke: Macmillan Ltd; Philadelphia: Temple University Press)

banned in 1925. The constitutional provision accepting Islam as the religion of the state was finally abrogated in 1928.

It is against this background that the Turkish Civil Code, inspired by and almost identical to the Swiss Civil Code, was adopted in 1926. Unlike previous attempts at legislative reform which remained mindful of the provisions of the *Shar'iah*, this Code severed all links with it. Polygyny was outlawed and marriage partners were given equal rights to divorce and child custody. Although veiling was not legally banned, a vigorous propaganda campaign led by Ataturk himself exhorted women to adopt modern styles of dress, and dissenters were dealt with severely.[1] The enfranchisement of women followed in two steps: women were granted the vote at local elections in 1930 and at the national level in 1934. This meant that Turkey could present herself as a democratic nation electing women to parliament at a time when dictatorships held sway over some European states (namely Nazi Germany and Fascist Italy).[2]

Analyses of women's emancipation in Turkey have either tended to focus on the strategic aims of the first Turkish Republic, often stressing their radical break with the past, or to present the republican reforms as the logical culmination of earlier attempts at modernisation and westernisation, starting with the era of Ottoman reforms during the *Tanzimat* period (1839–76). These tendencies both reveal and obscure important aspects of a more complex picture. It is indeed after the *Tanzimat*, a period of intense encroachment by Western powers, that the 'woman question' appeared on the Ottoman political agenda, never to leave it again. The predominantly male polemicists on questions relating to women and the family used the condition of women to express deeper anxieties concerning the cultural integrity of the Ottoman/Muslim polity in the face of Western influence.[3] There have been some critical shifts in discourses on women between the *Tanzimat* and the Republic, however, prefiguring though not fully predictive of the eventual Kemalist position on this issue.

The transformation of the 'woman question' in Turkey between the latter half of the 19th century and the beginning of this century has involved a progressive distancing from Islam as the only form of legitimate discourse on women's emancipation, in favour of a cultural nationalism appropriating such emancipation as an indigenous pattern. The argument I will develop in this chapter is that the current parameters of the 'woman question' were shaped by the historically specific conditions of the rise of Turkish nationalism, starting with the Second Constitutional period (1908–19) and leading to the Kemalist republican regime. Although the tensions between Westernism, nationalism and Islam are by no means resolved and continue to occupy a prominent place in current political debate, I am suggesting that the specificity of the Turkish case with respect to the emancipation of women can be fully appreciated only through an examination of the process of her emergence from an empire based on the multi-ethnic *millet* (national and religious communities) system to the Anatolia-based secular nation-state.

THE REFORM ERA: *TANZIMAT* 'WESTERNISM' AND ITS CONSEQUENCES

The drive for Ottoman modernisation is commonly associated with the *Tanzimat* period (1839–76) despite earlier attempts at technical and administrative reform in the military sphere. The decline of the empire, signalled by two centuries of military defeat and territorial retreat, called for more radical and comprehensive measures. It is significant that the *Tanzimat* was officially announced on 3 November 1839, at a point when the Ottoman government was threatened by its Egyptian vassal, Mehmed Ali Pasha, whose own reforms made it possible to support a powerful modem army. Resit Pasha, then Minister of Foreign Affairs, saw the introduction of reforms as the only way of both matching Mehmed Ali's efficiency and winning British support against his claims. Capitalising upon Ottoman military misadventures to wrest trade concessions from them was in any case a well-established trend, as in the case of the Commercial Treaty of 1838 which opened up the vast Ottoman market to British manufactures by lifting trade restrictions and tariff walls. The *Tanzimat* edict, penned by Resit Pasha but supported and approved by the British, set the scene for extensive reforms with far-reaching consequences in the fields of administration, legislation and education.

The centralisation of power, which had already started under Mahmud II's reign (1808-39) with the abolition of the Janissary Corps, went further with the elimination of tax farming and the introduction of direct taxation in the context of a reformed provincial administration which limited the power of provincial landowners. The independent position of the *ulema* (the clergy) was undermined both by the introduction of state control of the *vakif*, the religious foundations which procured their most important income, and the inception of secular education in parallel to the *medrese* system. Power was increasingly concentrated in the hands of a new class of Ottoman imperial bureaucrats, who were relatively secure in their position within a secularised bureaucratic hierarchy. In the process of its modernisation the apparatus of the Ottoman state appeared to be more monolithic and authoritarian and more enmeshed in ties of dependence to the West than it had ever been.

The *Tanzimat* reforms have given rise to conflicting evaluations, denounced by some as total capitulation to the West and assumed by others to provide the foundation of all later developments in the creation of a secular state.[4] It seems beyond doubt that the Ottoman empire had suffered serious peripheralisation vis-à-vis European powers since the 16th century. It is thus not unreasonable to argue that the reforms had, among other things, the effect of creating a central bureaucracy which could become an instrument for the smooth integration of the Ottoman state into the world economy.[5] Indeed, the official document that ushered in the *Tanzimat*, the *Gulhane Hatt-i Humayunu* (Imperial Rescript of Gulhane) guaranteeing the life, honour and property of all Ottoman subjects regardless of their creed and religion, had as its net effect the extension of legal assurances to non-Muslim and non-Turkish mercantile groups affiliated to European commercial interests.

The new role that the *Tanzimat* bureaucracy had to assume meant that it had to adapt itself to the requirements of modernisation and to the expectations of Western powers in a manner that alienated the groups and classes which were excluded from the new 'modernised' structures (such as craftsmen, artisans, the urban lower middle class, petty civil servants and the lower ranks of the *ulema*). These classes were to become the focus of a resistance which often took Islamic forms. Thus the *Tanzimat* reforms were to create deep cleavages in Ottoman society, reflected both at the institutional level and at that of culture more generally.

The movement of the Young Ottomans, among whom were Şinasi, Ziya Pasha, Namik Kemal and Ali Suavi, emerged as a reaction to the authoritarianism, extreme Westernism and superficiality of *Tanzimat* policies. Their ideology involved a complex blend of Ottoman nationalism, Islamism and constitutionalism.[6] Influenced by European ideas of nationalism and liberalism, they were none the less conservatives attempting to achieve a synthesis between Western notions of 'progress' and a harmonious Islamic state. It is not uncommon, if slightly misleading, to find prominent Young Ottomans cited as the earliest advocates of women's emancipation, preparing the ground for later reforms. Şinasi's satirical play *Şair Evlenmesi* (The Poet's Wedding) written in 1859 is considered one of the earliest criticisms of the arranged marriage system. Namik Kemal was also vocal in his criticisms of the more oppressive and unjust aspects of marriage and family life, as well as women's overall position in society. He used the newspaper he edited, *Ibret*, to call for reforms in women's education and denounce the state of ignorance in which Ottoman women were kept. His novels *Intibah* (The Awakening) and *Zavalli Çocuk* (Poor Child) also offer critical commentaries on women's condition. It is worth noting that the most ardent reformists of women's condition were at the same time the most outspoken critics of *Tanzimat* 'Westernism'. Mardin suggests that the cultural tensions between a Western-oriented bureaucratic elite and popular classes committed to and protected by Ottoman communitarian conservatism were worked through in the post-*Tanzimat* novel, via biting satires of Western-struck upper-class males.[7] Those same authors, such as Ahmed Mithat Efendi, strongly advocated changes in women's position and denounced the practices of forced marriage, concubinage and polygamy as 'social ills'. Ahmet Mithat's works, *Diplomali Kiz* (The Girl with a Diploma), *Felsefe-i Zenan* (Women's Philosophy), *Teehhül* (Marriage) and *Eyvah* (Alas) touch upon a wide range of such concerns.

I have argued elsewhere[8] that the male reformers of the time found the plight of women a powerful vehicle for the expression of their own restiveness with social conventions they found particularly stultifying and archaic. 'Modern' men often felt alienated from Ottoman patriarchal structures which curtailed their own freedom considerably, even though women were the more obvious victims of the system.[9] They thus made a case for the emancipation of women in moralistic, sentimental and 'civisational' terms, whilst at the same time condemning and bemoaning the moral decay occasioned by Western influences in Ottoman society. However, as Mardin points out, the unity established with the masses of people against Western-struck male behaviour was undermined when women's independence was at stake. Conservatism in this area had long been a hallmark of popular resistance and figured prominently in all protests against innovation.[10] As will become clearer in the discussion of ideological currents during the Second Constitutional period (1908–19), later debates on women would both reveal and create bitter cleavages among the Ottoman elite itself, when the condition of women became more self-consciously identified as the touchstone of Ottoman cultural 'integrity' or 'backwardness', as the case might be.

The early reformers inscribed themselves on the one hand in a modernist Islamic perspective, arguing that their demands were compatible with the dictates of Islam, and on the other in an instrumentalist framework suggesting that changes in women's condition would benefit the 'health' of society as a whole. In contrast to the feminist-nationalist stance of later periods, Islam was the only legitimate terrain in which issues relating to women could be debated.

Fatma Aliye Hanim, the first Ottoman woman to engage in such debates, was the daughter of Cevdet Pasha, an enlightened member of the *ulema* and main author of the *Mecelle*, the Ottoman Civic Code. As a member of the upper class, she had benefited from private education and even taught herself French.[11] She distinguished herself through a polemic with the conservative Mahmud Esad Efendi who had published a series of articles in favour of polygyny, defending it both as a law of nature and as an article of the *Shar'iah*. She exposed her own views in a book entitled *Nisvan-i Islam* (Muslim Women) in 1891, which pre-dates Qasim Amin's influential *Tahrir-i al Mara* (Liberation of Women) and foreshadows many of his arguments. It is also significant that the longest lived woman's weekly of the time, *Hanimlara Mahsus Gazete* (The Ladies' Own Gazette), to which Fatma Aliye Hanim was an important contributor, proclaimed on its title page that it served three principles: being a good mother, a good wife and a good Muslim.

However, the very fact that conservatives of Mahmud Esad's persuasion had to adopt a defensive tone and rally around polygyny attested to the inroads made by new ideas in Ottoman society and to the growing strength of the constituency upholding them. In that sense, the *Tanzimat* may be said to have ushered in a painful and often bitter process of negotiation and compromise between the pressures of foreign powers, the requirements of modernity as perceived by different sections of the Ottoman elite, and the resistance of those most threatened by changes in the Ottoman order.

Ottoman legislative reforms are indicative of these tensions. The vizier Ali Pasha was in favour of the wholesale adoption of the 1804 French Civic Code. This initiative was blocked by the *ulema* and Cevdet Pasha used his scholarly authority to propose a modern Ottoman code based on the principles of the Hanefi school of Islamic law (*fiq'h*). A commission headed by Cevdet Pasha produced the *Mecelle-i Ahkami Adliyye*, a home-grown Ottoman Civic Code. However, a religious opposition headed by the *Sheyh-ul Islam* (chief canonical functionary of the empire) persuaded Abdulhamid II to disband the commission in 1888 once it had completed its work on commercial transactions, thereby blocking any further legislation in the fields of the family and inheritance. The religious authorities were claiming the sphere of personal status as their own, and were doing so in an environment where their overall influence had been shrinking. This led to a dual juridical system whereby secular courts (*mahkeme-i nizamiye*) operated under the aegis of the Ministry of Justice while religious courts (*mahkeme-i şer'iyye*) remained under the jurisdiction of the *Sheyh-ul Islam*. It was not until 1917 that a new Family Law would be put on the agenda and that the total monopoly of religious authorities in this area would be challenged. This coincided, as we shall later see, with a period when the Ottoman state was for the first time formulating a family policy in line with the nationalist, regenerative ideals of the Committee for Union and Progress.

For all the polemics around issues concerning women and the family, actual legislative advances had been relatively modest. The 1858 Land Law (*Arazi Kanunu*) extended and consolidated women's rights of inheritance. The imperial decrees banning female slavery (issued in 1854 for white slaves and 1857 for blacks) became effective with the ratification of international treaties in 1880 and 1890. Reforms in the educational field were more significant. The Medical School started training local midwives under the direction of European instructresses from 1842, secondary schooling for girls (*Kiz Rüştiyeleri*) started in 1858, a girls' vocational school (*Kiz Sanayi Mektebi*) was opened in 1869 and a women's teacher-training college (*Dar-ul Muallimat*) started operating in 1870. Taşkiran in her evaluation of these initiatives comments on the pressures resulting from the strict segregation of the sexes and the scarcity of trained female teachers.[12] These constituted an important advance if one considers that apart from private tutoring for upper-class women, frequently involving foreign governesses, there were no provisions at all for women's education beyond the barest rudiments of religious instruction at the primary level.[13]

It is a matter of some debate whether the thirty-year absolutist rule of Abdulhamit II and its Islamist backlash, following an abortive attempt at constitutional monarchy (1876–8), actually held in check or reversed the progress achieved. There was certainly a higher level of police interference and surveillance over women's movements as well as attire (such as the banning of the diaphanous *feradje* in favour of the black *charshaf*).[14] Women's publications continued despite severe censorship (as in the case of Fatma Aliye Hanim's book, *Nisvan-i Islam*, mentioned earlier) and so did their education. However, some foreign observers commenting on the sorry state of women's education under the Hamidian regime describe the *Dar-ul Muallimat* (teachers' training college) in the following terms: 'It was under the direction of a sleepy old Effendi who spent his time lying on a divan in his office smoking a narghilé, and drinking coffee; and classes were conducted when it was thought best, always with the attempt not to place too great a strain on the nervous system and delicate organisms of youth and beauty'.[15] This remark was a prelude to their eulogy of state sponsored 'feminism' during the Second Constitutional Period (1908–19).

WOMEN UNDER THE YOUNG TURKS: THE ERA OF PATRIOTIC FEMINISM

The overthrow of Abdulhamit's autocratic regime in 1908 by the Young Turks, members of the Committee of Union and Progress (hereafter referred to as CUP) who had been fighting for a return to Constitutional rule, was followed by a period of intense social upheaval and ideological ferment. Women's rights issues were no exception. Impressed by the changes she witnessed and by the policies of the CUP, a visiting Englishwoman, Grace Ellison was to exclaim: 'A Turkish Feminist Government! To Western Europe this sounds strange.'[16] Tunaya lists no less than a dozen women's associations founded between 1908 and 1916, ranging from primarily philanthropic organisations to those more explicitly committed to struggle for women's rights.[17] Among these, *Teali-i Nisvan Cemiyeti* (The Society for the Elevation of Women) founded in 1908 by Halide Edib had links with the British suffragette movement (and required a knowledge of English from its members). The *Müdafaa-i Hukuk-i Nisvan Cemiyeti* (The Society for the Defence of Women's Rights) was the best known and the most militant, fighting to secure women's access to paid professions.[18] New journals such as *Mahasin, Kadin* (Woman) and *Kadinlar Dünyasi* (Woman's World) played an active role in shaping public opinion.

It seems pertinent to reflect on the prominence of women's rights issues at this particular juncture. At least three sets of new influences appear to have been at work: the rise of Turkism as a dominant ideology among the intellectual currents of the Second Constitutional Period, the requirements of a war economy spanning the period from the Balkan War (1912) to the end of World War I, and their joint effects on the social and economic policies of the CUP.

The *Tanzimat* reforms which aimed at a consolidation of the empire signally failed to stem the tide of nationalism in the Christian Balkan provinces, whilst strengthening the hand of local Christian merchants who were the preferred trading partners of European powers in Ottoman lands. In Berkes' terms, the more Westernisation proceeded the more Turks felt excluded from it.[19] The Committee for Union and Progress who were the architects of the 1908 revolution did not delay in seeing that the Ottoman nationalism which united Muslim and non-Muslim subjects in a bid for 'freedom' during the overthrow of Abdulhamit's despotic rule would not arrest the progress of the secessionist movements in the ethnically heterogenous provinces. Toprak suggests that Turkish nationalism which was born from the liberal currents of 1908 also represented a reaction against such liberalism, especially against the economic liberalism which had cost the Muslim artisan so dear.[20]

The search for alternatives to liberalism produced a major shift in thinking about the economy and society. The dominant ideology in the CUP represented a blend of solidarism emanating from French corporatist thought and Ottoman guild traditions.[21] Throughout the war years the CUP consistently struggled to create a middle class consisting of Turkish-Muslim entrepreneurs, persistently stressing the ethnic dimension of the problem and favouring Muslim over non-Muslim. The same effort was apparent in the creation of trained local cadres. For instance, in 1916 a law was passed imposing Turkish as the language of correspondence on all foreign firms operating in the Ottoman empire. These firms, which had previously employed foreigners, now had the choice of either folding up or recruiting local employees. Meanwhile vocational evening classes, especially on commerce and banking, were started by CUP Clubs in an attempt to create skilled cadres that were competent in these fields. The University opened its doors to women in 1914 and the demand was such that the Ministry of Education instituted a women's section (*Inas Dar-ul-fununu*) which soon afterwards merged with the men's classes (producing irate reactions from traditionalist circles, in particular the *Sheyh-ul Islam* Mustafa Sabri). In this context, special business classes for women were also started when the Advanced School for Commerce opened a section for women, which was so popular that a second one soon had to be added.[22] The necessities of general mobilisation carved out a new space for women. Later, in the Republican period, women would be called upon to replenish the ranks of trained professional cadres.[23] In the Second Constitutional Period, it was primarily the war effort that drew them out into the workforce in unprecedented numbers.[24]

WOMEN AND WAR

Already during the Balkan War middle-class women were involved in social welfare activities, bringing relief to war orphans and attending to the wounded. The women's branch of the Red Crescent Society had started training Turkish nurses. Halide Edib's memoirs convey a powerful impression of the mood of shock and despondency that shook the nation as invalids and war refugees started flocking into Istanbul.[25] One also senses that women's 'patriotic' activities legitimised both their greater mobility and their visibility.

It was during World War I that the massive loss of male labour to the front created a demand for women's labour. The growth of female employment did not remain confined to white-collar jobs in post offices, banks, municipal services and hospitals but involved attempts at wider mobilisation throughout the Anatolian provinces. A law passed in 1915 by the Ministry of Trade instituted a form of mandatory employment which rapidly swelled the ranks of women workers.[26] Women volunteers were organised into workers' platoons to help the army with support services. In the agrarian sector, the Fourth Army (Syria and Palestine) formed Women Workers' Brigades. The Islamic Association for the Employment of Ottoman Women was founded in 1916 and aimed at promoting the employment of women under conditions that ensured them an 'honest' living. The first pro-natalist policies of the empire had the employees of the Association as their target. Marriage was made mandatory for women by the age of 21 and for men by 25, weddings were generously sponsored and financial incentives offered for the birth of each child.[27]

Whilst objective conditions may have stimulated an increased female presence in the labour force, it is clear that this was viewed with considerable ambivalence. Some accommodations had to be made, as evidenced by the imperial decree issued in 1915 allowing women to discard the veil during office hours. However, they were apparently often forced by the police to return home if their skirts were shorter than the officially prescribed length.[28] Indeed, the right to go out into the streets and to places of entertainment, and a limited right to work with freedom from police harassment were among the demands voiced by the women's press of the time, demands which were clearly very modest by later standards. There is little doubt that this period must have been fraught with confusion and contradictions. An announcement posted on Istanbul walls by the police in September 1917 gives us some indication of this:

> In the last few months shameful fashions are being seen in the streets of the Capital. All Muslim women are called upon to lengthen their skirts, refrain from wearing corsets and wear a thick *charshaf*. A maximum of two days is allowed to abide by the orders of this proclamation.

This announcement was the subject of such indignation and furore that higher level administrators were forced to rebuke their over-zealous subordinates and retract the order. The new announcement read as follows:

> The General Directorate regrets that old and retrograde women were able to induce a subaltern employee to publicise an announcement ordering Muslim women to go back to old fashions. We announce that the previous orders are null and void.[29]

One has to consider that the CUP itself was divided and that 1917 was the year when, in the midst of war, a committee was set up to discuss the suitable length for women's skirts. Enver Pasha, who held particularly conservative views, actually removed one of his commanders in the Dardanelles on the grounds that his daughters were seen sunning themselves on the Bosphorus.[30] The earlier progressive leanings of the CUP were to prove short-lived, as they instituted their own autocracy. Significantly, a woman's periodical would proclaim on the fifth anniversary of the Constitution that it was 'Men's National Celebration Day', giving voice to women's dashed hopes.[31]

WOMEN AND THE IDEOLOGICAL CURRENTS OF THE SECOND CONSTITUTIONAL PERIOD

During the Second Constitutional Period, debates on women and the family became more tightly and self-consciously integrated into ideological positions representing different recipes for salvaging the floundering empire. These can be identified as the Islamist, Westernist and Turkist positions.

The Islamists, despite their internal differences, thought that the reasons for imperial decline had to be sought in the subversion and abandonment of Islamic institutions and laws.[32] They advocated a return to the unadultered application of the *Shari'ah* and their political solution revolved around the idea of a pan-Islamic empire consolidated around the institution of the Caliphate. Although the adoption of Western technology and material progress were deemed to be inevitable, Western culture must on no account be allowed to contaminate the values of Islam. The position of women represented the touchstone of such contamination, and discussions on veiling, polygyny and divorce became bitterly political. The main proponents of conservative views on women among the *ulema* were Mustafa Sabri and Musa Kazim (both of whom held the office of *Sheyh-ul Islam*) who used the periodical *Beyan-ul Haq* as a platform. Musa Kazim exhorted the government to take punitive measures against the violators of the Islamic rules of veiling (*tesettur*). Mustafa Sabri emphatically rejected the views of apologists who maintained that women did not hold an inferior status in Islam: 'Muslim religion does not need such lying and ignorant defenders . . . To distort the truth and attempt to reconcile the views of the adversary, and thereby approve such views, is not a service to Islam but treason'.[33] The initially more reformist Islamist periodical *Sirat-i Mustakim* hardened its position and reappeared under the name *Sebilürreşat*. The poet Mehmet Akif and Sait Halim Pasha were among the most prominent figures of this tendency. Mehmet Akif joined the polemic on women by translating Farid Wajdi's refutation of Qasim Amin's influential *Tahrir-al Mara*. This translation was first serialised in *Sirat-i Mustakim* and then published in book form under the title *Müslüman Kadını* (The Muslim Woman).[34] Akif's short preface makes his sympathy to Farid Wajdi quite clear. Sait Halim's views were equally uncompromising.

The Westernists were also heterogenous in their views, but united around certain major themes. Foremost among these was the conviction that the superiority of the West did not reside simply in its advanced technology but also in its rationalistic and positivistic outlook, which was free of the shackles of religious obscurantism and stifling superstitions. To varying degrees, they held Islam responsible for both obscurantism and what they saw as the debased condition of women, which they considered as one of the major symptoms of Ottoman backwardness. Of these, Celal Nuri Ileri, the author of *Kadinlarimiz* (Our Women) and Halil Hamit, author of *Islamiyette Feminizm* (Femisnism in Islam) held moderate views, arguing that Islam was in no way inimical to the equality of women. Salahattin Asim's *Türk Kadınlğinin Tereddisi* (The Degeneration of Turkish Womanhood) takes a much more radical and uncompromising stance. Asim held religion directly responsible for what he considered as the progressive degeneration of Turkish womanhood into an abject state of subjection. He went as far as advocating a complete change in family laws. The poet Tevfik Fikret was equally radical in his denunciation of Islam and preached humanistic ideals. The combination of Western positivism, humanitarian ideals and respect for Islam finds one of its most contradictory expressions in the person of Abdullah Cevdet. His defence of women's rights was more indebted to biological materialism and the ideas of Ribot, a French disciple of Darwinism, than to humanitarian considerations. He took a frankly eugenistic position by claiming that, whatever the social extraction of their father, children born of enslaved women would in time lead to the degeneration of the race.[35] The rehabilitation of the mothers of the nation could thus be defended on 'scientific' grounds.

It is when the Turkists entered the fray, under their leading ideologue Ziya Gökalp, that the debates on women and the family really came to a head. Berkes comments that the Turkist theses raised such a tempest among the Islamists that 'their opposition to the Westernists assumed the appearance of a summer breeze'.[36] The Turkism of the Second Constitutional Period represented an attempt at recuperating a sense of national identity which did not rest solely on Islam. This was in many ways a fraught enterprise. As Berkes points out, the Turks were the last to achieve a sense of nationality in the whole Ottoman formation.[37] In the Ottoman context, Turkish nationalism could be perceived as divisive in a situation where other ethnic minorities were restive, and certainly found no favour among the Islamists, for whom the notion of a Turkish nation constituted a threat to the Islamic *umma*.[38]

The nationalism of the Turkish-Tatar intelligentsia in tsarist Russia provided the Turkist movement not only with ideas but also with its cadres when its leading ideologues emigrated to the Ottoman empire.[39] The earlier national awakening of Turks in Russia was both a reaction to the rising oppression of nationalities due to pan-Slavic ideology, and a reflection of the fact that the Turkish-Tatar bourgeoisie had matured to the point of evolving its own nationalist ideals. Soon after the 1908 revolution, Yusuf Akçura, Ahmet Ağaoğlu, Hüseyinzade Ali and others migrated to the Ottoman capital. Taking advantage of the freedoms afforded by the Constitution they set up their own organizations, the most important being *Türk Ocaği* (the Turkish Hearth) officially established in 1912, with its associated journal *Türk Yurdu* (Turkish Homeland). Among its prominent members were Ziya Gökalp, Mehmet Emin Yurdakul and Halide Edib Adivar. The nationalism of Ottoman Turkists in the nineteenth century had remained confined to the cultural arena and had not yet challenged the state ideologies of Ottomanism and pan-Islamism. By the turn of the century these ideologies were no longer tenable. The Young Turks, who initially were quite heterogenous politically, increasingly turned to Turkism as successive military defeats threatened the empire further. After 1913, they began to pursue the intensive policy of economic and cultural Turkification referred to earlier. In time, cleavages were to develop between pan-turkist nationalism and the non-irredentist Turkish nationalism which gave birth to Kemalist ideology.[40]

The leading ideologue of this transition period was undoubtedly Ziya Gökalp (1876–1924), the author of *The Principles of Turkism*. In his extensive analysis of Gökalp's work and ideas, Parla suggests that Gökalp's framework fixed the parameters within which mainstream political action has been conducted in Turkey.[41] This has certainly been the case for the politics of women's emancipation throughout the period of republican reforms. Gökalp, who was deeply influenced by Durkheim's sociology, replaced his notion of society with that of 'nation', emphasising the national-cultural rather than Islamic sources of morality. His search for national-cultural roots led him to an ecclectic examination of myths, legends, archaeological and anthropological evidence of pre-Islamic Turkic patterns, which he claimed were still alive in popular culture despite the superimposition of alien civilisational influences, the latter including those of Islam as well. In his *Principles of Turkism* he spells out the programmatic implications of Turkism in the fields of language, aesthetics, morality, law, religion, economy and philosophy.

Gökalp's views on 'moral Turkism', especially on the family and sexual morality, represent a significant departure from earlier approaches to the woman question. He suggested that family morality based on ancient Turkish cultural values included norms such as communal ownership of land, democracy in the 'parental' family as opposed to the autocracy of the patriarchal family, the equality of men and women, and monogamous marriage. He traces some of the origins of what he labels as 'Turkish feminism' (using these exact words) to the fact that Shamanistic religion and rituals were based on the sacred power vested in women. This made the sexes ritualistically equal, an equality which he thought permeated every aspect of life including the political sphere. The patrilineal and matrilineal principles were equally important, children belonged to both parents, women could control their own independent property, and interestingly, were excellent warriors (amazons, to use Gökalp's own words). This amounted to a pre-Islamic 'golden age' for women which was made much of by subsequent republican feminists. Gökalp was concerned that the Turks had lost their old morality under the impact of alien influences, most notably that of the Persians and Byzantines. The degradation of women's status was one of the symptoms of this loss. A return to cultural authenticity would automatically restore women their lost status and dignity:

> When the ideal of Turkish culture was born was it not essential to remember and revitalise the beautiful rules of old Turkish lore? It is for this reason that as soon as the current of Turkism was born in our country the ideal of feminism was born with it. The reason why the Turkists are both populist and feminist is not simply because these ideals are valued in this century; the fact that democracy and feminism were the two main principles of ancient Turkish life is a major factor in this respect.[42]

This position was greeted with a certain amount of scepticism in some quarters. Mehmet Izzet, for instance, suggested that Gökalp's ideas might have been greatly influenced by pragmatic considerations:

> At a time when Islamic law was being abolished, improvements in women's position sought and changes in family life along the Western model were being introduced, interpreting this movement as a return to

ancient Turkish law and national identity would ensure greater goodwill and sympathy.[43]

Halide Edib is even more candid in her introduction to her book *Turkey Faces West*:

> In the recent changes in Turkey, a great many intellectuals believe that there is a tendency to return to our origins. What is more important is that this belief is consciously propagated by a considerable number of intellectuals, partly for the sake of making these changes acceptable to the masses.[44]

On the subject of Gökalp, whom she praises for his feminist leanings, she adds: 'He probably stretched the point, to produce the necessary psychological effect in the minds of the people.'[45] Indeed, with respect to the position of women what might have been rather unpalatable in the form of Western influence gained a new legitimacy when it was recuperated by nationalist discourse.

Although Turkism may have provided a new ideological framework to debate these questions, Unionist family policies must ultimately be understood as an attempt to extend state control and intervention into the private realm of the family. Toprak suggests that this intervention was motivated by the necessity to follow up the political revolution of 1908 by a social revolution that would remould Ottoman society along more egalitarian and nationalistic lines. The Unionists attempted to hasten this transformation by adopting a new family model.[46] Their 'National Family' (*Milli Aile*) was nuclear and monogamous in contrast to the traditional Ottoman patriarchal family. It was not simply emulative of European ways, but rather grounded in the indigenous patterns referred to in our previous discussion of Gökalp. However, the encroachment of the state in this delicate realm was to prove extremely problematic. The compromises apparent in the 1917 Family Code are indicative of some of the difficulties. This law, which is the first written family code in the Muslim world, aimed at completing the task left unfinished by the *Mecelle* (the Ottoman Civic Code) by legislating aspects of personal status which had been totally abandoned to the rulings of religious authorities.[47] Apart from common clauses it had separate sub-sections applying to Muslim, Christian and Jewish subjects, who were still bound by their own religious laws. The intention to provide women with greater security in the conjugal contract was displayed by stipulating the presence of a specially empowered state employee alongside the two witnesses required by the *Shar'iah*, a clear step in the direction of secularisation. Marriages without consent were decreed illegal and divorce was made more difficult by the introduction of a conciliation procedure. However, not only was polygyny not abolished but it was actually legalised, although its practice was made more difficult by stipulating the consent of the first wife. Needless to say this law failed to satisfy either those who wanted to see fundamental changes in a family system considered to be in crisis, or those who saw these changes as clear-cut infractions of Koranic law. Minorities were also discontented with what they considered a curtailment of the power of their own religious authorities. In 1919, at the end of the war, they complained to the Allied forces then occupying Istanbul and obtained a repeal of the clauses pertaining to non-Muslim marriages. This law none the less remained in force until 1926 in Turkey, and until much later in the Ottoman periphery. It represented a timid move towards secularisation under precarious conditions in which a beleaguered central state was ultimately unable to wrest control from religious and communal interests. The secular project of the state, already incipient at this period, was to be realised under the Kemalist republic.

WOMEN AND KEMALISM: THE ADVENT OF CITIZENSHIP

At the end of World War I the Ottoman empire was defeated and the Anatolian provinces were occupied by the Allied powers. The landing of Greek forces in Izmir in May 1919 and the occupation of Istanbul by the British, French and Italian forces unleashed a wave of popular protest in which women took part, not merely as anonymous participants but as public speakers in open-air meetings where they made impassioned calls for the defence of the motherland.[48] One of the few first-hand chronicles of the different phases of the struggle for national liberation is to be found in the second volume of Halide Edib's memoirs, *The Turkish Ordeal*.[49] She was part of the small group who had joined the resistance movement in Anatolia, one of those facing a death sentence issued by the Istanbul government, and awarded the rank of corporal for her services by the Ankara government. Associations for Patriotic Defence started being formed in the Anatolian provinces. Women did not join those directly but set up their own parallel organisations. The Anatolian Women's Association for Patriotic Defence was founded in Sivas in November 1919. Studies of some branches of the Association suggest that the active members were the wives, daughters and sisters of local provincial notables and higher level state employees, who were the main supporters of the nationalist struggle, as well as some teachers and educational administrators. In other words, these were the women of the nascent local middle class which the Second Constitutional Period did so much to nurture.

During the global mobilisation occasioned by the War of National Liberation, peasant women in Anatolia also played critical roles which were celebrated and glorified in public monuments and patriotic rhetoric alike. Yet the coalition of nationalist forces which united behind Mustafa Kemal included men of religion who were going to remain totally inflexible on the question of women's emancipation. The First National Assembly which led the struggle for national independence was dominated by a conservative majority who systematically blocked any attempt to give women equal citizenship rights. More progressive deputies such as Tunali Hilmi Bey were repeatedly attacked and insulted for being 'feminist'. It is indicative that among the indictments directed at the then Minister of Education, Hamdullah Suphi, in 1921, and which led to his resignation, was the fact that he had conducted a mixed-sex teachers' congress.[50] The political opponents of Mustafa Kemal, the so-called Second Group of the First Assembly, were marginalised in the 1923 elections so that the Second Assembly consisted mainly of Kemalist loyalists. Nevertheless, there remained an important nucleus of resistance and procrastination on the question of women's rights. For instance, during the debate on the 1924 Constitution the clause concerning every Turk's right to vote was understood and interpreted by some deputies quite literally to denote every Turk of voting age, regardless of sex. However, the opposition was such that the clause had to be amended to specify 'every male Turk', and even some progressive deputies argued that the time was not ripe for such a drastic change.

An even clearer indication of the prevailing social conservatism can be found in the draft Family Law which was presented to the National Assembly on 27 November 1923 and went through several rounds of debates in 1923 and 1924. The commission in charge of formulating the new law actually cancelled some of the advances gained through the 1917 Code by endorsing polygyny, eliminating the need for consent by the first wife and lowering the legal marriage-age for girls to nine years. This proposal, which was subsequently rejected, was clearly part of the playing out of the opposition between religious and Kemalist forces, an opposition which was finally crushed by the abolition of the Caliphate and the abrogation of the *Shari'ah* in favour of secular codes and laws.[51] Berkes points out that this was also the first instance of a clear divergence between Gökalpist and Kemalist views manifesting itself in the field of legislation.[52] Indeed, while Gökalp had taken an accommodationist stance arguing for the mutual compatibility of Islam, Turkish culture and contemporary civilisation, Kemal had opted for a model that required the total privatisation of religion and the full secularisation of social life. There is little doubt that the woman question became one of the pawns in the Kemalist struggle to liquidate the theocratic remnants of the Ottoman state, a struggle in which male protagonists engaged each other while women by and large remained surprisingly passive onlookers.[53] Not only did women hardly participate in the debates on Family Law but the 'protest' reunion they were practically forced to stage was unable to generate any coherent suggestions. In fact, some progressive men went as far as using newspaper columns to take women to task over their acquiescent posture.[54] Despite other evidence of women's activism, especially later on the question of suffrage, this suggests that the process of mobilisation and co-optation of women into the ideological struggles of the Republic followed a path that was quite distinct from early feminist movements in the West. In the latter, the women's struggle took place against a background where legislation was lagging considerably behind the socio-economic realities of advancing industrialism and a growing labour movement. In Turkey, it was an ideological lever operating on a substantially unchanged economic base, at least as far as women's economic and familial options were concerned.

The decisive actions of Kemalism with respect to women's emancipation were the evacuation of Islam from the legislative and broader institutional sphere, and the inclusion of women into a new notion of 'citizenship' dictated by the transition from a monarchy to a populist republic. While it is by and large correct to suggest that the dominant legitimising discourse for women's emancipation in republican Turkey is a nationalism which has its roots in the Turkism of the Second Constitutional Period, it is also important to acknowledge the ideological break represented by Kemalism. Indeed, Mustafa Kemal was to distance himself from Islam to a much greater extent than Gökalp and other Turkists could ever have envisaged. This was possibly due partly to the specific historical circumstances of the struggle for national independence. Although initially most of the Associations for Patriotic Defence had a clearly Islamic outlook and couched the defence of the motherland in religious terms (as a *jihad* or holy war against the infidel), the Istanbul government headed by the Sultan-Caliph had reached an agreement with the occupying powers to stamp out Kemalist resistance. In April 1920 the *Sheyh-ul Islam* issued a *fetva* (canonical proclamation) declaring a holy war against the 'Ankara rebels'. A military court condemned Ataturk and a group of his supporters to death in absentia. Civil war and the defection of his forces to the Army of the Caliphate were only averted after the outrage created by the humiliating treaty of Sèvres. Henceforth religious reaction (*irtica*) was to be identified as one of the main enemies of Kemalist nationalism. Moreover, it was not merely the official Islam of the centre, which was seen to have acted treasonably by abetting imperialist designs on Turkey, that Mustafa Kemal condemned. He also took an uncompromising stand on popular Islam. This was the Islam practised by the diverse religious sects, the *tarikats*, which he considered to be centres of obscurantism, superstition, passivity and laziness; in short, representatives of a world-view totally incompatible with his Enlightenment vision of progress, with its twin components of rationalism and positivism. The fact that they were also the focuses of local allegiances and particularisms which the central bureaucracy sought to eliminate in favour of more universalistic principles of association was clearly relevant. Thus, whatever the politically strategic motives informing the timing and content of Kemal's emancipatory reforms, it must be recognised that they fitted in well with his conception of 'civilisation' and with republican notions of citizenship.

It would be a serious misrepresentation, however, to suggest that these were merely the culmination of earlier attempts at Westernisation. In fact, Kemal's attitude to nineteenth century Ottoman statesmen was dismissive if not outright hostile, since he considered them as 'the gendarmes of foreign capital',[55] and their brand of Westernism as a shameful capitulation. He sought to break away from the fetters of an Ottoman past he considered as decadent and to forge a radically new sense of nationhood.

This attempt is nowhere more apparent than in the 'Turkish History Thesis' which was launched in the 1930s. It was Afet Inan, Mustafa Kemal's adoptive daughter, who was entrusted with the task of setting the historical record right on the question of the origins of Anatolian civilisations and of the role of Turks within them. This thesis stated that the Turks' contribution to civilisation had started long before their incorporation into the Ottoman empire and their conversion to Islam. They originated from an urban civilisation in Central Asia from which many subsequent civilisations of Asia Minor and Mesopotamia had sprung. As such, they were the true heirs of their Anatolian homeland and could claim their rightful place in the development of world civilisations. Berktay suggests that the history thesis had an orientation to the Ottoman past which is reminiscent of that of the French revolution to its *ancien régime*.[56] It constituted a break from the 'sacred' histories of Ottoman chroniclers, who presented the empire as a glorious chapter in the history of Islam, and resulted in a 'laicisation' of Turkish history through its integration into the mainstream of world civilisations. It seems quite clear that the early 'romantic phase' of Turkish nationalism was inspired at least in part by a reaction to the extremely negative and ethnocentric views of European historians. Assumptions about the elevated position of women in Central Asiatic societies can be seen to emanate from this 'romantic phase', and have continued to influence republican rhetoric on Turkish women. A case in point is Afet Inan's classic book, *The Emancipation of the Turkish Women*, in which she devotes an important section to the status of women before the advent of Islam.[57] She suggested that the transition to Islam brought about a decline in the status of Turkish women, although she puts this down to the social customs of Arabs and Persians rather than to Islam per se. Thus, the 'new woman' of the republic had ancient and respectable antecedents to invoke.

The 'new woman' of the Kemalist era became an explicit symbol of the break with the past, a symbolism which Mustafa Kemal himself did much to promote. He did so personally through the inclusion of Latife Hanim, his wife, in his public tours, through his relations with his adoptive daughters, one of whom, Afet Inan, became a public figure in her own right, and through his broader endorsement of women's visibility, attested to by photographs of the period ranging from ballroom dancing to official ceremonies. This has had a decisive influence on the socialisation of a whole generation of women who internalised the Kemalist message and forged new identities as professionals as well as patriots.[58]

The extent to which the paternalistic benevolence of the Kemalist era actually fostered or hindered women's political initiatives has never really been explicitly addressed. On the one hand, it is during the first republic that women achieved their highest level of representation in parliament. In the 1937 general election, following the enfranchisement of women in 1934, eighteen women deputies were elected, making up 4.5% of the National Assembly. This was an all-time high, never to be equalled again. This level of representation slipped steadily back, especially from 1946 onwards after the transition to a multiparty democracy when the quasi-automatic election of women by an 'enlightened' party vanguard could no longer operate.

On the other hand, there is evidence that women's autonomous political initiatives were actively discouraged. The first such instance was the refusal to authorise the Women's People's Party founded in June 1923. This coincided with the preparations for the foundation of the Republican People's Party and was therefore considered untimely and divisive. Despite women's subsequent appointment of a male figurehead as their party leader, Ankara withheld its consent and advised women to found an association.[59] This led to the creation of the Turkish Women's Federation in 1924, which was disbanded in 1935, a fortnight after it had hosted the 12th Congress of the International Federation of Women. The choice of Istanbul as a venue for the Congress was clearly inspired by the advent of women's suffrage in Turkey and was meant to be an international display and celebration of this momentous event. Indeed, all the foreign delegates, including Huda Sharawi of Egypt, were expressing their gratitude to Atatürk on behalf of world womanhood. How is it possible to explain the self-elimination of the Federation, under directives from Ankara, so soon after this obvious success? Toprak points out that one of the prominent themes of the Congress was peace and that the Turkish delegates were swayed by the pacifist appeals of the British, American and French delegates who dominated the Congress. (Germany and Italy did not participate.) Turkey had unwittingly been made a tool of allied propaganda through the feminist platform of the Congress. On the eve of a major conflagration in Europe and at a time when defence spending was increasing its share of the national budget. Turkish feminists' stand on disarmament was inopportune, to say the least.[60] The public rationale offered by its president, Latife Bekir, for the closure of the Federation and the dispersal of its assets is none the less quite telling. She claimed that Turkish women had achieved complete equality with full constitutional guarantees, and that the goals of the Federation having thus been totally fulfilled there was no further justification for its continued existence. This ended the brief career of women's sole attempt at political organisation during the single-party era.

Thus, the republican regime opened up an arena for state-sponsored 'feminism', but at one and the same time circumscribed and defined its parameters. It would be quite erroneous to single out the women's movement as a privileged target of state control, since workers' associations and cultural clubs (such as the influential Turkish Hearths referred to earlier) were similarly abolished. This accorded well with the corporatist populism of the single-party era, which negated the existence of class and other sectional interests in the body politic, and saw the party as the representative of the whole nation. This is in no way specific to Turkey, but quite typical of many post-independence and post-revolutionary Third World states. What singles out the Turkish case, especially in the broader context of the Muslim Middle East, is a particular positioning of Islam vis-à-vis nationalism, and the important implications deriving from it. This positioning cannot be understood without considering the nature of the Ottoman state and the 'secular' tendencies of Ottoman Islam itself,[61] not without taking account of the specific characteristics of Turkish republican ideology. Despite the dramatic changes and realignments currently taking place in state and society, the imprint of this formative moment has to be reckoned with.

CONCLUSION

This chapter traces some of the critical transformations that Turkey underwent in the transition from a multi-ethnic empire to a secular nation state. I have attempted to show how the appearance of women, first as objects of political discourse and later as political actors and citizens, was intimately bound up with the changing nature of the Ottoman/Turkish polity.

It is no accident that issues relating to women first became 'ideologised' during the *Tanzimat* period, when pressures to Westernise created a climate of enhanced self-awareness and soul-searching among the Ottoman elite. It is noteworthy that at this stage both progressives and traditionalists invoked Islam as the sole pradigm within which issues pertaining to the position of women could be debated, against a more distant background of Western notions of 'progress'. Few women actually participated in these debates. The first outspoken would-be reformers of women's condition were not the *Tanzimat* Westernists, but the Young Ottomans, whose position could best be defined as a modernist Islamism, indicating an early link between nationalist discourse and concerns over the condition of Turkish womanhood.

It is after the 1908 revolution, which brought the Young Turks to power, that women emerged as activists, forming their own associations and expanding the volume of their publications. Among the complex set of influences at work, I singled out rising Turkish nationalism in the threatened empire, and more specifically the effects of Turkist ideology and CUP's drive to create a national bourgeoisie. Women first demanded their rights under the banner of patriotism, as participants in the war effort and the broader goals of national mobilisation. Turkism as a legitimising ideology of women's emancipation created a discursive space in which nationhood could be invoked alongside Islam. However, the position of women was so closely identified with Ottoman cultural integrity that it continued to elicit conservative reflexes which united men, sometimes across political persuasions, well into the republican period. Indeed, the vagaries of successive legislative exercises with respect to personal status and the family attest to the difficulties of reformative action in this domain until Atatürk severed the gordian knot of the *Sha'riah*.

Women's emancipation under Kemalism was part of a broader political project of nation-building and secularisation. It was a central component of both the liquidation of the 'theocratic remnants' of the Ottoman state and of the establishment of a republican notion of citizenship. It was also the product of a Western cultural orientation, which despite its anti-imperialist rhetoric, inscribed Kemalism within an Enlightenment perspective on progress and civilisation. However, the authoritarian nature of the single-party state and its attempt to harness the 'new woman' to the creation and reproduction of a uniform citizenry aborted the possibility for autonomous women's movements.

A separate history of Turkish women's movements still remains to be written. Establishing the extent to which women of different social extraction colluded with patriarchal definitions of their place in society, or were able to carve out a relatively autonomous political project would require further meticulous investigation. The more limited objective of this chapter has been to capture, at a time when the Kemalist legacy is being actively contested and reappropriated by different political tendencies, some of the basic ingredients of Turkey's specificity and to promote a better understanding of the baseline from which future women's movements have to operate.

NOTES

1. Caporal mentions trials and short prison sentences for those spreading counter-propaganda. B. Caporal, *Kemalizm ve Kemalizm Sonrasinda Türk Kadını* (Ankara: Türkiye Iş Bankasi Kültür Yaylınları, 1982), p. 649.
2. Tekeli argues that this was one of the strategic goals sought by the Kemalist regime in enfranchising women. S. Tekeli, 'Women in Turkish Politics', in N. Abadan-Unat (ed.), *Women in Turkish Society* (Leiden: E. J. Brill, 1981), pp. 293–310.
3. D. Kandiyoti, 'Women and the Turkish State: Political Actors or Symbolic Pawns?', in N. Yuval-Davis and F. Anthias (eds), *Woman – Nation – State* (London: Macmillan, 1989).
4. N. Berkes, *The Development of Secularism in Turkey* (Toronto: McGill University Press, 1964); S. J. Shaw and E. K. Shaw, *History of the Ottoman Empire and Modern Turkey* (Cambridge: Cambridge University Press, 1977), Vol. 2; B. Lewis, *The Emergence of Modern Turkey* (London: Oxford University Press, 1961); T. Timur, *Türk Devrimi: Anlamı ve Felsefi Temeli* (Ankara: Sevinç Matbaası, 1968); I. Ortaylı, *Imparatorluğun En Uzun Yüzyılı* (Istanbul: Hil Yayīn, 1983).
5. H. Inan, 'Osmanli Tarihi ve Dünya Sistemi: Bir Değerlendirme,' *Toplum ve Bilim*, 23 (1983) pp. 9–39. For a broader discussion of the different phases of the articulation between state, bureaucracy and society see Ç. Keyder, 'Class and State in the Transformatiion of Modern Turkey' in F. Halliday and H. Allavi (eds), *State and Ideology in the Middle East and Pakistan* (London: Macmillan, 1988).
6. Ş. Mardin, *The Genesis of Young Ottoman Thought* (Princeton: Princeton University Press, 1962).
7. Ş. Mardin, 'Superwesternization in Urban Life in the Ottoman Empire in the last quarter of the 19th century' in P. Benedict and E. Tumer'ekin (eds), *Turkey: Geographical and Social Perspectives* (Leiden: E. J. Brill, 1974).
8. D. Kandiyoti, 'Slave Girls, Temptresses and Comrades: Images of Women in the Turkish Novel', *Feminist Issues*, 8 (1988) no. 1, pp. 33–50.
9. This alienation appears as a persistent theme in literary works. It is expressed eloquently by Ömer Seyfettin who ridicules the right controls imposed on the younger generation and bemoans the absence of female companionship and romantic love in Turkish men's lives: 'Here in our surroundings, the surroundings of the Turks, love is strictly forbidden. It is as forbidden as an infernal machine, a bomb, a box of dynamite . . .' *Aşk Dalgası* (Istanbul: Bilgi Yayımevi, 1964), p. 52.
10. Ş. Mardin, ;Superwesternisation in Urban Life . . .', p. 442.
11. E. Işin, 'Tanzimat, Kadin ve Gündelik Hayat', *Tarih ve Toplum*, 51 (1988), pp. 150–5.
12. T. Taşkıran, *Cumhuriyetin 50. Yılında Türk Kadın Haklari* (Ankara: Başbakanlık Basimevı, 1973).
13. For further details on women's education see F. Davis, *The Ottoman Lady: A Social*

History 1718–1918 (London: Greenwood Press, 1986).

14. On state control over Ottoman women's attire, see N. Seni, 'Ville Ottomane et Représentation du Corps Feminin', *Les Temps Modernes*, no. 456–7 (1984) pp. 66–95.

15. E. D. Ellis and F. Palmer, 'The Feminist Movement in Turkey', *Contemporary Review*, 105 (January–June 1914) p. 859.

16. G. Ellison, *An Englishwoman in a Turkish Harem* (London: Methuen, 1915), p. 81.

17. T. Z. Tunaya, *Türkiyede Siyasi Partiler* (Istanbul: Hürriyet Vakfı Yayınları, 1984), Vol. 1.

18. As in the case of Bedriye Osman, who applied to become an employee of the Telephone Company but was not hired. This was made a matter of public debate by the Society and led to the backing down of the Company, which from then on had to employ women. T. Z. Tunaya, *Türkiyede Siyasi Pariler*, p. 482.

19. N. Berkes, *Batıcılık, Ulusçuluk ve Toplumsal Devrimler* (Istanbul: Yön Yayınları, 1965).

20. Z. Toprak, *Türkiyede Milli Iktisat (1908–1918)* (Ankara: Yurt Yayınları, 1982).

21. Z. Toprak, 'Türkiyede Korporatizmin Doğusu', *Toplum ve Bilim*, 12 (1980) pp. 41–9.

22. Z. Toprak, *Türkiyede Milli Iktisat*, p. 83.

23. A. Önctü, 'Turkish Women in the Professions: Why so Many?' in Abadan-Unat (ed.), *Women in Turkish Society*, pp. 81–193.

24. S. Tekeli, *Kadınlar ve Siyasal Toplumsal Hayat* (Istanbul: Birikim Yayınları, 1982), p. 198; N. Abadan-Unat, 'Social Change and Turkish Women', in *Women in Turkish Society*, p. 8.

25. H. Edib, *The Memoirs of Halide Edib* (London: John Murray, 1926).

26. A new stocking factory set up in Urfa employed 1,000 women. In the Izmir, Ankara, Sivas and Konya provinces, 4,780 women were employed in carpet production. In Aydin 11,000 and in Kütahya, Eskisehir and Karahisar 1,550 were employed in textile manufacture. In Diyarbakir they replaced me at 1,000 looms.

27. Z. Toprak, *Türkiyede Milli Iktisat*, 317–18; Z. Toprak, 'Osmanlı Kadmınları Çaliştirma Cemiyeti, Kadın Askerler ve Milli Aile', *Tarih ve Toplum*, 51 (March 1988) pp. 162–6.

28. E. Yener, 'Eski Anakara Kıyafetleri ve Eski Giyiniş Tarzları', *Dil, Tarih ve Coğrafya Fakültesi Dergist*, 3 (1955) no. 13, pp. 123–9.

29. J. Melia, *Mustafa Kemal ou la Rénovation de la Turquie* (Paris), 1929, quoted in B. Caporal, *Kemalizmde ve Kemalizm Sonrasinda Türk Kadini*, pp. 147–8.

30. F. Rifki Atay, *Barişılık Yılları*, quoted in Ş. Mardin, 'Superwesternization in Urban Life', pp. 433–4.

31. T. Taşkıran, *Cumhuriyetin 50. Yılında*, p. 38.

32. T. Z. Tunaya, *Islamcılık Cereyanı* (Istanbul: Baha Matbaası, 1962).

33. Mustafa Sabri, *Mes' eleler* (Istanbul: Sebil Yayınevi, 1984; 2nd edition), p. 95.

34. It has gone into several printings in modern Turkish. See M. F. Vecdi (translator Mehmet Akif Ersoy), *Müslüman Kadını* (Istanbul: Sinan Yayınevı, 1982; 3rd edition, first published in 1909).

35. M. S. Hanioğlu, *Doktor Abdullah Cevdet ve Dönemi* (Istanbul: Üçdal Neşriyat, 1981).

36. N. Berkes, *The Development of Secularim*, p. 390.

37. N. Berkes, *Batıcılık, Ulusçuluk ve Toplumsal Devrimler*, pp. 52–3. Also on this question see W. H. Hadded 'Nationalism in the Ottoman Empire' in W. H. Haddad and W. L. Oshsenwald (eds), *Nationalism in a non-National State: The Dissolution of the Ottoman Empire* (Columbus: Ohio State University Press, 1977).

38. For a discussion of the tensions between Islamism and nationalism see T. Z. Tunaya, *Islamcılık Cereyani*, pp. 77–86.

39. For details see F. Georgeon, *Aux Origines du Nationalisme Turc: Yusuf Akçura (1876–1935)* (Paris: Editions ADPF, 1980); D. Kushner, *The Rise of Turkish*

Nationalism (1876–1908) (London: Frank Cass & Co. Ltd., 1977); T. Timur, 'The Ottoman Heritage' in I. C. Schick and E. A. Tonak (eds), *Turkey in Transition: New Perspectives* (New York, Oxford: Oxford University Press, 1987).

40. J. Landau, *Pan-Turkism in Turkey: A Study in Irredentism* (London: Hurst & Co Ltd., 1981).
41. T. Parla, *The Social and Political Thought of Ziya Gökalp 1876–1924* (Leiden: E. J. Brill, 1985).
42. Z. Gökalp, *Türkçülüğün Esasları* (Istanbul: Inkilap ve Aka Kitabevleri, 1978), p. 148.
43. Mehmet Izzet, quoted in M. Eröz, *Türk Ailesi* (Istanbul: Milli Eğitim Basımevi, 1977), p. 13.
44. Halide Edib, *Turkey Faces West* (New Haven: Yale University Prerss, 1930).
45. Ibid., p. 213/
46. Z. Toprak, 'The Family Reminism and the State during the Young Turk period, 1908–1918', paper presented at the 'Workshop on Turkish Family and Domestic Organisation', New York, 23–35 April 1986.
47. Z. F. Findıkoğlu, *Essai sur la Transformation du Code Familial en Turquie* (Paris: Editions Berger-Levrault, 1936).
48. T. Taşkıran, *Cumhuriyetin 50. Yılında*, pp. 68–73.
49. Halide Edib, *The Turkish Ordeal* (London: John Murray, 1928) was first published in English while she was in political exile. It was not translated into Turkish until much later, since it was at variance on many points with the 'official' account of this period which is mainly based on Mustafa Kemal's own memoirs and speeches. It was first serialised in a periodical in 1959–60, and published in book form in 1962.
50. T. Taşkıran, *Cumhuriyetin 50. Yılında*, pp. 91–100.
51. P. Benedict, 'Başılik Parası ve Mehr', in A. Güriz and P. Benedict (eds), *Türk Hukuku ve Toplumu Üzerinde Incelemeler* (Ankara: Sevinç Matbaası, 1974), p. 19.
52. N. Berkes, *Türkiyede Cağdaşlaşma* (Istanbul: Doğu-Bati Yayinlari, 1978), p. 519.
53. T. Taşkıran, *Cumhuriyetin 50. Yılında*, pp. 106–9.
54. Such as Necmettin Sadak, 'Hanıimlarimiz ve Aile Hukuku Karanamesi', *Akşam*, 21 January 1924, quoted in Taşkıran, *Cumhuriyetin 50. Yılında*, p. 109. Sadak wrote an inflammatory article suggesting that the republic was insulting women with its laws while they were being incomprehensibly passive.
55. G. Ökçün, *Türkiye Iktisat Kongresi – 1923 Izmiri: Haberler, Belgeler, Yorumlar* (Ankara: Ankara Universitesi Siyasal Bilgiler Fakültesi Yayınlari, 1968).
56. H. Berktay, *Cumhiriyet Ideolojisi ve Fuat Köprülü* (Istanbul: Kaynak Yayınlari, 1983).
57. Afet Inan, *The Emancipation of the Turkish Women* (Paris: UNESCO, 1962).
58. A. Durakbaşa, *The Formation of 'Kemalist Female Identity': A Historical-Cultural Perspective*, unpublished M. A. thesis, Istanbul: Bogazici University, 1987.
59. Z. Toprak, 'Halk Firkasindan Önce Kurulan Parti: Kadınlar Halk Firkası', *Tarih ve Toplum* 51 (March 1988) pp. 30–1.
60. Z. Toprak, '1935 Istanbul Uluslarasi "Feminizm Kongresi" ve Bariş', *Düşün* (March 1986), pp. 24–9.
61. Ş. Mardin, 'Turkey: Islam and Westernization', in C. Caldarola (ed.), *Religion and Societies* (Berlin: Mouton, 1982).

3.3

'HOW NATIVE IS A "NATIVE" ANTHROPOLOGIST?'

Kirin Narayan

How 'native' is a native anthropologist? How 'foreign' is an anthropologist from abroad? The paradigm polarizing 'regular' and 'native' anthropologists is, after all, part of received disciplinary wisdom. Those who are anthropologists in the usual sense of the word are thought to study Others whose alien cultural worlds they must painstakingly come to know. Those who diverge as 'native', 'indigenous', or 'insider' anthropologists are believed to write about their own cultures from a position of intimate affinity. Certainly, there have been scattered voices critiquing this dichotomy. Arguing that, because a culture is not homogeneous, a society is differentiated, and a professional identity that involves problematizing lived reality inevitably creates a distance, scholars such as Aguilar (1981) and Messerschmidt (1981a: p. 9) conclude that the extent to which anyone is an authentic insider is questionable. Yet such critiques have not yet been adequately integrated into the way 'native' anthropologists are popularly viewed in the profession.

In this essay, I argue against the fixity of a distinction between 'native' and 'non-native' anthropologists. Instead of the paradigm emphasizing a dichotomy between outsider/insider or observer/observed, I propose that at this historical moment we might more profitably view each anthropologist in terms of shifting identifications amid a field of interpenetrating communities and power relations. The loci along which we are aligned with or set apart from those whom we study are multiple and in flux. Factors such as education,

From: Kirin Narayan (1997), 'How Native Is a "Native" Anthropologist?', pp. 671–86, in *American Anthropologist*, vol. 95, no. 3.

gender, sexual orientation, class, race or sheer duration of contacts may at different times outweigh the cultural identity we associate with insider or outsider status. Instead, what we must focus our attention on is the quality of relations with the people we seek to represent in our texts: are they viewed as mere fodder for professionally self-serving statements about a generalized Other, or are they accepted as subjects with voices, views, and dilemmas – people to whom we are bonded through ties of reciprocity and who may even be critical of our professional enterprise?

I write as someone who bears the label of 'native' anthropologist and yet squirms uncomfortably under this essentializing tag. To highlight the personal and intellectual dilemmas invoked by the assumption that a 'native' anthropologist can represent an unproblematic and authentic insider's perspective, I incorporate personal narrative into a wider discussion of anthropological scholarship. Tacking between situated narrative and more sweeping analysis, I argue for the *enactment of hybridity* in our texts; that is, writing that depicts authors as minimally bicultural in terms of belonging simultaneously to the world of engaged scholarship and the world of everyday life.

THE PROBLEM IN HISTORICAL PERSPECTIVE

The paradigm that polarizes 'native' anthropologists and 'real' anthropologists stems from the colonial setting in which the discipline of anthropology was forged: the days in which natives were genuine natives (whether they liked it or not) and the observer's objectivity in the scientific study of Other societies posed no problem. To achieve access to *the native's* point of view (note the singular form), an anthropologist used the method of participant-observation among a variety of representative natives, often singling out one as a 'chief informant' (Casagrande 1960). A chief informant might also be trained in anthropological modes of data collection so that the society could be revealed 'from within'. As Franz Boas argued, materials reported and inscribed by a trained native would have 'the immeasurable advantage of trustworthiness, authentically revealing precisely the elusive thoughts and sentiments of the native' (Lowie 1937: p. 133, cited in Jones 1970: p. 252). Or better yet, a smart and adequately Westernized native might go so far as to receive the education of a bona fide anthropologist and reveal a particular society to the profession with an insider's eye. Ordinary people commenting on their society, chief informants friendly with a foreign anthropologist, or insiders trained to collect indigenous texts were all in some sense natives contributing to the enterprise of anthropology. Yet, it was only those who received the full professional initiation into a disciplinary fellowship of discourse who became the bearers of the title 'native' anthropologist.

Even if such a 'native' anthropologist went on to make pathbreaking professional contributions, his or her origins remained a perpetual qualifier. For example, writing the foreword to M. N. Srinivas's classic monograph on the Coorgs, Radcliffe-Brown emphasized that the writer was 'a trained anthropologist, himself an Indian' and went on to add that he had 'therefore an understanding of Indian ways of thought which it is difficult for a European to attain over many years' (Srinivas 1952: p. v). As Delmos Jones has charged, it is likely that 'natives' who could get 'the inside scoop' were first admitted into the charmed circle of professional discourse because they were potential tools of data collection for white anthropologists (Jones 1970: p. 252). Admittedly, in an era prior to extensive decolonization and civil rights movements, that 'natives' were allowed to participate at all in professional discourse was remarkable. In this context, calling attention to, rather than smoothing over, 'native' identity perhaps helped to revise the ingrained power imbalances in who was authorized to represent whom.

Viewed from the vantage point of the 1990s, however, it is not clear that the term *native anthropologist* serves us well. Amid the contemporary global flows of trade, politics, migrations, ecology, and the mass media, the accepted nexus of authentic culture/demarcated field/exotic locale has unraveled (Appadurai 1990, 1991; Clifford 1992; Gupta and Ferguson 1992). Although many of the terms of anthropological discourse remain largely set by the West, anthropology is currently practiced by members (or partial members) of previously colonized societies that now constitute the so-called Third World (Altorki and El-Solh 1988; Fahim 1982; Kumar 1992; Nakhleh 1979; Srinivas, Shah and Ramaswamy 1979). These scholars often have institutional bases in the Third World, but some have also migrated to Europe and the United States. Furthermore, in the First World, minority anthropologists also hold university positions and their contributions to ongoing discourse have helped to realign, if not overthrow, some of the discipline's ethnocentric assumptions (Gwaltney 1981; Jones 1970; Limón 1991). Feminist scholarship questioning the formulation of 'woman as Other' has underscored the differences between women and the multiple planes along which identity is constructed, thus destabilizing the category of 'Other' as well as 'Self' (Abu-Lughod 1990; Alarcon 1990; Lauretis 1986; Mani 1990; Mohanty and Russo 1991; Strathern 1987). It has also become acceptable to turn the anthropological gaze inward, toward communities in Western nations (Ginsburg 1989; Ginsburg and Tsing 1990; Martin 1987; Messerschmidt 1981b; Ortner 1991). The 'field' is increasingly a flexible concept: it can move with the travels of Hindu pilgrims (Gold 1988), span Greek villagers and New Age American healers (Danforth 1989) or even be found in automobile garages of South Philadelphia (Rose 1987). In this changed setting, a rethinking of 'insider' and 'outsider' anthropologists as stable categories seems long overdue.

MULTIPLEX IDENTITY

'If Margaret Mead can live in Samoa,' my mother is reputed to have said when she moved to India, 'I can live in a joint family.' The daughter of a German father and American mother, she had just married my Indian father. Yet these terms – *German, American, Indian* – are broad labels deriving from modern nation-states. Should I instead say that my mother, the daughter of a Bavarian father and a WASP mother who lived in Taos, New Mexico, became involved with her fellow student at the University of Colorado: my Indian-from-India father? Yet, for anyone familiar with India shouldn't I add that my father's father was from the Kutch desert region, his mother from the dense Kathiawari forests, and that while he might loosely be called 'Gujarati' his background was further complicated by growing up in the state of Maharashtra? Should I mention that Mayflower blood supposedly mingles with that of Irish potato famine immigrants on my maternal grandmother's side (I'm told I could qualify as a 'DAR'), or that as temple builders, members of my paternal grandfather's caste vehemently claimed a contested status as Brahman rather than lower-ranking carpenter? Should I add that my father was the only Hindu boy in a Parsi school that would give him a strictly British education, inscribing the caste profession-based title 'Mistri' (carpenter) onto the books as the surname 'Contractor'? Or would it better locate my father to say that he remembers the days when signs outside colonial clubs read 'No Dogs or Indians'? Also, is it useful to point out that my mother – American by passport – has now lived in India for over 40 years (more than two-thirds of her life) and is instructed by her bossy children on how to comport herself when she visits the United States?

I invoke these threads of a culturally tangled identity to demonstrate that a person may have many strands of identification available, strands that may be tugged into the open or stuffed out of sight. A mixed background such as mine perhaps marks one as unauthentic for the label 'native' or 'indigenous' anthropologist; perhaps those who are not clearly 'native' or 'non-native' should be termed 'halfies' instead (cf. Abu-Lughod 1991). Yet, two halves cannot adequately account for the complexity of an identity in which multiple countries, regions, religions, and classes may come together. While my siblings and I have spent much of our lives quipping that we are 'haylf' (pronounced with an American twang) and 'hahlf' (with a British-educated accent), I increasingly wonder whether any person of mixed ancestry can be so neatly split down the middle, excluding all the other vectors that have shaped them. Then too, mixed ancestry is itself a cultural fact: the gender of the particular parents, the power dynamic between the groups that have mixed, and the prejudices of the time all contribute to the mark that mixed blood leaves on a person's identity (cf. Spickard 1989).

Growing up in Bombay with a strongly stressed patrilineage, a Hindu Indian identity has weighed more than half in my self-definition, pushing into the background the Pilgrim fathers and Bavarian burghers who are also available in my genealogical repertoire. This would seem to mark me as Indian and, therefore, when I study India, a 'native' anthropologist. After all, researching aspects of India, I often share an unspoken emotional understanding with the people with whom I work (cf. Ohnuki-Tierney 1984). Performing fieldwork in Nasik on storytelling by a Hindu holy man whom I called 'Swamiji', I had the benefit of years of association with not just Swamiji himself but also the language and wider culture. Since Nasik was the town where my father grew up, a preexisting identity defined by kinship subsumed my presence as ethnographer (cf. Nakhleh 1979). Similarly, researching women's songs and lives in the Himalayan foothills, I bore the advantage of having visited the place practically every year since I was fifteen, and of my mother having settled there. All too well aware of traditional expectations for proper behavior by an unmarried daughter, in both places I repressed aspects of my cosmopolitan Bombay persona and my American self to behave with appropriate decorum and deference (cf. Abu-Lughod 1988).

In both Nasik and in Kangra, different aspects of identity became high-lighted at different times. In Nasik, when elderly gentlemen wearing white Congress caps arrived and Swamiji pointed me out as 'Ramji Mistri's grand-daughter', my local roots were highlighted, and I felt a diffuse pride for my association with the Nasik landmark of the Victorian bungalow that my grandfather had built in the 1920s. Visiting Nathu Maharaj, the barber with buckteeth and stained clothes, to discuss interpretations of Swamiji's stories, I felt uncomfortable, even ashamed, of the ways in which my class had allowed me opportunities that were out of reach for this bright and reflective man. My gender was important in the observance of menstrual taboos not to touch Swamiji or the altar – injunctions that left me so mortified that I would simply leave town for several days. Borrowing the latest Stevie Wonder tapes from one of 'the foreigners' – a disciple from New Jersey – I savored a rowdy release, becoming again a woman who had lived independently in a California university town. When Swamiji advised that in written texts I keep his iden-tity obscure ('What need do I have for publicity?' – yet his doctor took me aside to advise that I disregard such modesty and identify him by name, 'so people abroad will know his greatness'), I felt my role as culture broker with the dubious power to extend First World prestige to Third World realities. Yet, when Swamiji challenged my motives for taking his words on tape 'to do a business', I was set apart from all planes of locally available identification, thrown outside a circle of fellowship forged by spiritual concerns, and lumped instead with academics who made it their business to document and theorize about other people's lives (Narayan 1989: pp. 59–62).

For my second extended research project in the Himalayan foothills region of Kangra, I had no deep local roots. I was unmoored from a certain base for identification, and the extent to which *others* can manipulate an anthropolo-gist's identity came into dizzying focus (Dumont 1978; Stoller 1989). Explaining my presence, some of the village women I worked with asserted that I was from such-and-such village (where my mother lives), hence local. At other times I was presented as being 'from Bombay', that is, a city dweller from a distant part of the country although still recognizably Indian. A wrin-kled old woman I once fell into step with on an outing between villages asked if I was a member of the pastoral Gaddi tribe (to her, the epitome of a close-by Other). At yet other times, and particularly at weddings where a splash of foreign prestige added to the festivities, I was incontrovertibly stated to be 'from America . . . she came *all* the way from there for this function, yes, with her camera and her tape recorder!' In the same household at different times, I was forced to answer questions about whether all Americans were savages (*jangli log*) because television revealed that they didn't wear many clothes, and to listen as a member of a spellbound local audience when a dignified Rajput matron from another village came by to tell tales about how she had visited her emigrant son in New Jersey. In the local language, she held forth on how, in America, people just ate 'round breads' of three sizes with vegetables and *masalas* smeared on top (pizza); how shops were enormous, with everything you could imagine in them, and plastic bags you could rip off like leaves from a tree; how you put food in a 'trolley' and then a woman would press buttons, giving you a bill for hundreds and hundreds of rupees! Bonded with other entranced listeners, my own claims to authoritative experience in this faraway land of wonders seemed to have temporarily dropped out of sight.

Now it might be assumed that I had experienced these shifting identifications simply because of my peculiar background, and that someone who was 'fully' Indian by birth and upbringing might have a more stable identity in the field. For a comparison, I could turn to Nita Kumar's lively and insightful *Friends, Brothers, and Informants: A Memoir of Fieldwork in Banaras* (1992), which makes many of the same points. Instead, I look further back (to pre-postmodern times) and draw out some of the implications about identity from M. N. Srinivas's compelling ethnography, *The Remembered Village* (1976). Srinivas is one of India's most respected anthropologists, although given the division of labor between anthropologists as those who focus on the Other (tribal groups) and sociologists who research the Self (village and urban dwellers), in India he is known as a sociologist. Srinivas was educated in Oxford in the 1940s. On Radcliffe-Brown's advice, he planned to do fieldwork in a multicaste village called Rampura in Mysore (Karnataka State). Srinivas's ancestors had moved several generations before from neighboring Tamil Nadu to rural Mysore; his father had left his village for the city so that his children could be educated. In returning from Oxford to live in a village, Srinivas stated his hope that 'my study . . . would enable me better to understand my personal cultural and social roots' (1976: p. 5).

But did the presence of these roots mean that he was regarded as a 'native' returning home to blend smoothly with other 'natives'? No, he was an educated urbanite and Brahman male, and the power of this narrative ethnography lies very much in Srinivas's sensitivity to the various ways in which he interacted with members of the community: sometimes aligned with particular groups, sometimes set apart. As he confesses, 'It was only in the village that I realized how far I (and my family) had travelled away from tradition' (1976: p. 18). From his account, one gets the impression that the villagers found him a very entertaining oddity. He struggled regularly with villagers' expectations that he behave as a Brahman should (1976: p. 33–40). Growing up in the city, he had not internalized rules of purity and pollution to the extent that they bound local Brahmans, and he found himself reprimanded by the headman for shaving himself *after* rather than before a ritual bath. On the other hand, a political activist criticized him for his involvement with the headman, rather than with all sections and factions of the village (1976: p. 22). When he did move throughout the village, he found himself received with affection: 'word must have gone round that I did not consider myself too high to mix with poor villagers' (1976: p. 24). Yet, as he was a respected guest and outsider, villagers as a group also colluded in keeping details of unpleasant 'incidents' regarding sex, money and vendettas from him (1976: pp. 40–7). In a lighter vein, many villagers knew him by the exotic object he sported, a camera that fulfilled not just their ends (such as the use of photographs in arranging marriages) but also his anthropological responsibilities of record-ing for a foreign audience. He became 'the camera man – only they trans-formed "camera" into "chamara" which in Kannada means the fly-whisk made from the long hair of yak tails' (1976: p. 20). Villagers plied him with questions about the English, and the headman even planned a tour of England in which Srinivas was to be adopted as guide (1976: p. 29). In short, his rela-tionships were complex and shifting: in different settings, his caste, urban background, unintended affiliations with a local faction, class privilege, attempts to bridge all sectors of the community, or alliance with a faraway land could be highlighted.

Even as insiders or partial insiders, in some contexts we are drawn closer; in others we are thrust apart. Multiple planes of identification may be most painfully highlighted among anthropologists who have identities spanning racial or cultural groups (Abu-Lughod 1988, 1991; Kondo 1986, 1990; Lavie 1990). Yet, in that we all belong to several communities simultaneously (not least of all the community we were born into and the community of profes-sional academics), I would argue that *every* anthropologist exhibits what Rosaldo has termed a 'multiplex subjectivity' with many crosscutting identifi-cations (Rosaldo 1989: pp. 168–95). Which facet of our subjectivity we choose or are forced to accept as a defining identity can change, depending on the context and the prevailing vectors of power. What Stuart Hall has written about cultural identity holds also for personal identity:

> Cultural identities come from somewhere, have histories. But like every-thing which is historical, they [identities] undergo constant transforma-tion. Far from being eternally fixed in some essentialised past, they are subject to the continuous 'play' of history, culture, and power. Far from being grounded in a mere 'recovery' of the past, which is waiting to be found, and which, when found, will secure our sense of ourselves into eternity, identities are the names we give to the different ways we are

positioned by, and position ourselves within, the narratives of the past. (Hall 1989: p. 70)

RETHINKING CONNECTIONS THROUGH FIELDWORK

We are instructed as anthropologists to 'grasp the native's point of view, his relation to life, to realize *his* vision of *his* world' (Malinowski 1961 [1922]: p. 25). Yet who is this generic subject, 'the native'? To use a clump term is to assume that all natives are the same native, mutually substitutable in presenting the same (male) point of view. Yet even received anthropological wisdom tells us that in the simplest societies, gender and age provide factors for social differentiation. To extend conceptual tools forged for the study of heuristically bounded, simple societies to a world in which many societies and subgroups interact amid shifting fields of power, these very tools must be reexamined. We would most certainly be better off looking for the natives' points of view to realize *their* visions of *their* worlds while at the same time acknowledging that 'we' do not speak from a position outside 'their' worlds, but are implicated in them too (cf. Mani 1990; Mohanty 1989; Said 1989): through fieldwork, political relations and a variety of global flows.

Arjun Appadurai (1988) has persuasively teased out some of the underlying assumptions in anthropological use of the term *native* for groups who belong to parts of the world distant and distinct from the metropolitan West. As he argues, the concept is associated with an ideology of *authenticity*: 'Proper natives are somehow assumed to represent their selves and their history, without distortion or residue' (1988: p. 37). Those in the position to observe 'natives', however, exempt themselves from being authentic and instead represent themselves in terms of complexity, diversity, and ambiguity. Furthermore, the term is linked to *place*. 'Natives' are incarcerated in bounded geographical spaces, immobile and untouched yet paradoxically available to the mobile outsider. Appadurai goes on to show how in anthropological discourse, 'natives' tied to particular places are also associated with particular *ideas*: one goes to India to study hierarchy, the circumMediterranean region for honor and shame, China for ancestor worship, and so on, forgetting that anthropological preoccupations represent 'the temporary *localization* of ideas from *many* places' (1988:46, emphasis in original).

The critique that Appadurai levels at the term *native* can also be extended to *native anthropologist*. A 'native' anthropologist is assumed to be an insider who will forward an authentic point of view to the anthropological community. The fact that the profession remains intrigued by the notion of the 'native' anthropologist as carrying a stamp of authenticity is particularly obvious in the ways in which identities are doled out to non-Western, minority or mixed anthropologists so that exotic difference overshadows commonalities or complexities. That my mother is German-American seems as irrelevant to others' portrayal of me as 'Indian' as the American mothers of the 'Tewa' Alfonso Ortiz, the 'Chicano' Renato Rosaldo or the 'Arab' Lila Abu-Lughod. For those of us who are mixed, the darker element in our ancestry serves to define us with or without our own complicity. The fact that we are often distanced – by factors as varied as education, class, or emigration – from the societies we are supposed to represent tends to be underplayed. Furthermore, it is only appropriate (and this may be the result of our own identity quests) that sooner or later we will study the exotic societies with which we are associated. Finally, while it is hoped that we will contribute to the existing anthropological pool of knowledge, we are not really expected to diverge from prevailing forms of, discourse to frame what Delmos Jones has called a genuinely 'native' anthropology as 'a set of theories based on non-Western precepts and assumptions' (1970:251).

'Native' anthropologists, then, are perceived as insiders regardless of their complex backgrounds. The differences between kinds of 'native' anthropologists are also obliviously passed over. Can a person from an impoverished American minority background who, despite all prejudices, manages to get an education and study her own community be equated with a member of a Third World elite group who, backed by excellent schooling and parental funds, studies anthropology abroad yet returns home for fieldwork among the less privileged? Is it not insensitive to suppress the issue of location, acknowledging that a scholar who chooses an institutional base in the Third World might have a different engagement with Western-based theories, books, political stances, and technologies of written production? Is a middle-class white professional researching aspects of her own society also a 'native' anthropologist?

And what about non-'native' anthropologists who have dedicated themselves to long-term fieldwork, returning year after year to sustain ties to a particular community? Should we not grant them some recognition for the different texture this brings to their work? It is generally considered more savvy in terms of professional advancement to do fieldwork in several different cultures rather than returning to deepen understandings in one. Yet to use people one has lived with for articles and monographs, and not maintain ties through time, generates a sort of 'hit-and-run' anthropology in which engagement with vibrant individuals is flattened by the demands of a scholarly career. Having a safe footing to return to outside the field situation promotes 'a contemplative stance . . . [that] pervades anthropology, disguising the confrontation between Self and Other and rendering the discipline powerless to address the vulnerability of the Self' (Dwyer 1982: p. 269). Regular returns to a field site, on the other hand, can nourish the growth of responsible human ties and the subsuming of cultural difference within the fellowship of a 'We-relation' (Schutz 1973: p. 16–17). As George Foster and the other editors of the book *Long-Term Field Research in Social Anthropology* point out in their concluding comments, an ongoing personal involvement with people in the communities studied often makes for an interest in 'action' or 'advocacy' work

(Foster et al. 1979: p. 344). Looking beyond the human rewards to the professional ones, long-term fieldwork leads to the stripping away of formal self-presentations and the granting of access to cultural domains generally reserved for insiders, thus making better scholarship. Returns to the field allow for a better understanding of how individuals creatively shape themselves and their societies through time. Finally, repeated returns to the field force an anthropologist to reconsider herself and her work not just from the perspective of the academy but also from that of the people she purports to represent. As Paul Stoller has written about his long-term fieldwork among the Songhay in Niger:

> Besides giving me the perspective to assess social change, long-term study of Songhay has plunged me into the Songhay worlds of sorcery and possession, worlds the wisdom of which are closed to outsiders – even Songhay outsiders. My insistence on long-term study forced me to confront the interpretive errors of earlier visits. Restudying Songhay also enabled me to get a bit closer to 'getting it right'. But I have just begun to walk my path. As Adamu Jenitongo once told me, 'Today you are learning about us, but to understand us, you will have to grow old with us.' (Stoller 1989: p. 6)

While Stoller was not born Songhay, his ongoing engagement has given him a niche in the society, a place from which he is invited to 'grow old' *with* his teacher. Like all long-term relationships, his encounters in the field have had exhilarating ups and cataclysmic downs, yet persevering has brought the reward of greater insight. Do not anthropologists who engage sensitively in long-term fieldwork also deserve respect from their professional colleagues as partial insiders who have through time become bicultural (cf. Tedlock 1991)? Need a 'native' anthropologist be so very different?

It might be argued that the condescending colonial connotations of a generic identity that cling to the term *native* could be lessened by using alternative words: *indigenous* or *insider*, for example. Yet the same conceptual underpinnings apply to these terms too: they all imply that an authentic insider's perspective is possible, and that this can unproblematically represent the associated group. This leads us to underplay the ways in which people born within a society can be simultaneously both insiders and outsiders, just as those born elsewhere can be outsiders and, if they are lucky, insiders too. Also, as Elizabeth Colson has bluntly stated, ' "Indigenous" is a misnomer, for all of us are indigenous somewhere and the majority of anthropologists at some time deal with their own communities' (Fahim et al. 1980: p. 650). We are *all* 'native' or 'indigenous' anthropologists in this scheme, even if we do not appear so in every fieldwork context. Rather than try to sort out who is authentically a 'native' anthropologist and who is not, surely it is more rewarding to examine the ways in which each one of us is situated in relation to the people we study.

SITUATED KNOWLEDGES

Visiting Nasik as a child, I knew better than to touch Maharaj, the chubby Brahman cook, as he bent over to fill our shining steel *thalis* on the floor; yet, if asked, I would never have been able to explain this in terms of 'purity and pollution'. I knew that servants were frequently shouted at and that they wore ill-fitting, cast-off clothes, but I did not call this 'social inequalities'. I observed that my girl cousins were fed after the boys and that although they excelled in school they were not expected to have careers, but I did not call it 'gender hierarchy'. I listened raptly when the Harveys, a British couple who had stayed on after 1947, told us stories about viceroys and collectors, but I did not know the words 'colonization' or 'decolonization'. When, amid the volley of British authors who shaped our minds in school, we finally came across poems by Rabindranath Tagore, I noticed that these were different but could not call them 'nationalist'. Reflecting on India with the vocabulary of a social analyst, I find that new light is shed on many of the experiences that have shaped me into the person – and professional – I am today.

In some ways, the study of one's own society involves an inverse process from the study of an alien one. Instead of learning conceptual categories and then, through fieldwork, finding the contexts in which to apply them, those of us who study societies in which we have preexisting experience absorb analytic categories that rename and reframe what is already known. The reframing essentially involves locating vivid particulars within larger cultural patterns, sociological relations, and historical shifts. At one further remove, anthropological categories also rephrase these particulars as evidence of theoretical issues that cross cultures and are the special province of trained academics.

Yet, given the diversity within cultural domains and across groups, even the most experienced of 'native' anthropologists cannot know everything about his or her own society (Aguilar 1981). In fact, by opening up access to hidden stores of research materials, the study of anthropology can also lead to the discovery of many strange and unfamiliar aspects of one's own society (cf. Stewart 1989: p. 14). I have learned, for example, a good deal more about village life, regional differences and tribal groups than what my urban upbringing supplied. Institutions and belief systems that I took for granted as immutable reality – such as caste or Hinduism – have been dismantled as historical and discursive constructions. Even for a purported insider, it is clearly impossible to be omniscient: one knows about a society from particular locations within it (cf. Srinivas 1966: p. 154).

As anthropologists, we do fieldwork whether or not we were raised close to the people whom we study. Whatever the methodologies used, the process of doing fieldwork involves getting to know a range of people and listening closely to what they say. Even if one should already be acquainted with some of these people before one starts fieldwork, the intense and sustained engagements of fieldwork will inevitably transmute these relationships. Fieldwork is a common plane binding professional anthropologists, but the process and outcome vary so widely that it is difficult to make a clear-cut distinction between the experiences of those with prior exposure and those who arrive as novices. As Nita Kumar writes in her memoir of fieldwork in Banaras (which she had only visited before as the sheltered, Anglicized daughter of a highly placed Indian government official): 'Fieldwork consists of experiences shared by all anthropologists; the personal and the peculiar are significant as qualities that *always* but *differently* characterize each individual experience' (1992: p. 6, emphasis in original).

To acknowledge particular and personal locations is to admit the limits of one's purview from these positions. It is also to undermine the notion of objectivity, because from particular locations all understanding becomes subjectively based and forged through interactions within fields of power relations. Positioned knowledges and partial perspectives are part of the lingo that has risen to common usage in the 1980s (Clifford 1986, 1988; Haraway 1988; Kondo 1986; Rosaldo 1989). Yet, let us not forget the prescient words of Jacques Maquet from an article in which he argued that decolonization laid bare the 'perspectivist' character of anthropology in Africa, showing anthropology's claim to objectivity as entwined with power relations in which one group could claim to represent another. Arguing against objectivity in a polemic at least twenty years ahead of its time, he writes:

> A perspectivist knowledge is not as such non-objective: it is partial. It reflects an external reality but only an aspect of it, the one visible from the particular spot, social and individual, where the anthropologist was placed. Non-objectivity creeps in when the partial aspect is considered as the global one. (Maquet 1964: p. 54)

ENACTING HYBRIDITY

'Suppose you and I are walking on the road,' said Swamiji, the holyman whose storytelling I was researching in 1985. 'You've gone to University. I haven't studied anything. We're walking. Some child has shit on the road. We both step in it. "That's shit!" I say. I scrape my foot; it's gone. But educated people have doubts about everything. You say, "What's this?" and you rub your foot against the other.' Swamiji shot up from his prone position in the deck chair and, placing his feet on the linoleum, stared at them with intensity. He rubbed the right sole against the left ankle. 'Then you reach down to feel what it could be,' his fingers now explored the ankle. A grin was breaking over his face. 'Something sticky! You lift some up and sniff it. Then you say, "Oh! This is *shit*."' The hand that had vigorously rubbed his nose was flung out in a gesture of disgust.

Swamiji turned back toward me, cheeks lifted under their white stubble in a toothless and delighted grin. Everyone present in the room was laughing uncontrollably. I managed an uncomfortable smile.

'See how many places it touched in the meantime,' Swamiji continued. 'Educated people always doubt everything. They lie awake at night thinking, "What was that? Why did it happen? What is the meaning and the cause of it?" Uneducated people pass judgment and walk on. They get a good night's sleep.'

I looked up at Swamiji from my position on the floor and tried to avoid the eyes of the others, who watched me with broad smiles on their faces. 'What was that? Why did it happen? What is the meaning and the cause of it?' rang in my ears as a parody of my own relentless questioning as an anthropologist interviewing both Swamiji and his listeners. I had to agree that among the academics I represented analysis could often become obsessive. But I also felt awkward, even a little hurt. This parable seemed to dismiss all the years that education had dominated my life. It ridiculed my very presence in this room. In his peculiar mixture of sternness and empathy, Swamiji must have read the discomfort on my face. When he settled back into his deck chair, he turned to me again. 'It's not that you shouldn't study,' he said, voice low and kind. 'You should gain wisdom. But you should realize that in the end this means nothing.'

Once again, Swamiji was needling any possible self-importance that might be ballooning inside me as self-appointed documenter and analyst of what to others was everyday life. While others enjoyed his stories and learned from them, I brought the weightiness of perpetual enquiry to the enterprise. Every action was evaluated (at least partially) in terms of my project on folk narrative as a form of religious teaching. Now Swamiji had turned his technique of instruction through stories on me. Through a parable, he dramatized how we both coexisted in shared time and space, 'walking the same road', yet each with a different awareness. The power relations of "structured inequality" (Dwyer 1982; Rabinow 1977) that allow anthropologists to subsume their subjects in representation had been turned upside down with such a critique.

This uncomfortable scene dramatizes how the issue of who is an insider and who is an outsider is secondary to the need for dismantling objective distance to acknowledge our shared presence in the cultural worlds that we describe. Pioneering works on 'native' anthropology emphasized the need for such anthropologists to achieve distance. Yet, distance, as Dorinne Kondo (1986) has observed, is both a stance and a cognitive-emotional orientation that makes for cold, generalized, purportedly objective and yet inevitably prejudiced forms of representation. As Kondo argues, it can be replaced with the acceptance of 'more experiential and affective modes of knowing' (1986: p. 75) in which the ethnographer's identity and location are made explicit and informants are given a greater role in texts. This is what Michael Jackson (1989) more recently called 'radical empiricism': a methodology and discursive style that emphasizes the subject's experience and involvement with others in the construction of knowledge (cf. Stoller 1992).

To question the discipline's canonical modes of objective distance is not, however, to forfeit subjective distance and pretend that all fieldwork is a celebration of communitas. Given the multiplex nature of identity, there will inevitably be certain facets of self that join us up with the people we study, other facets that emphasize our difference. In even the closest of relationships, disjunctures can swell into distance; ruptures in communication can occur that must be bridged. To acknowledge such shifts in relationships rather than present them as purely distant or purely close is to enrich the textures of our texts so they more closely approximate the complexities of lived interaction. At the same time, frankness about actual interactions means that an anthropologist cannot hide superficial understandings behind sweeping statements and is forced to present the grounds of understanding. Further, as Lila Abu-Lughod has argued in regard to what she calls 'ethnographics of the particular', by writing in terms of 'particular individuals and their changing relationships, one would necessarily subvert the most problematic connotations of culture: homogeneity, coherence, and timelessness' (1991: p. 154).

These insights hold radical implications for anthropological modes of representation. As I see it, there are currently two poles to anthropological writing: at one end stand accessible ethnographies laden with stories, and at the other end stand refereed journal articles, dense with theoretical analyses. We routinely assign narrative ethnographies in 'Intro to Anthro' classes (even if these are written not by professional anthropologists, but by their wives [Fernea 1965; Shostak 1981]) because it is through narratives lively with people, places and events that we know recalcitrant undergraduates are likely to be seduced by the discipline. Reading these ethnographies, we ourselves may forget we are judgmental professionals, so swept along are we in the evocative flow of other people's experiences. Narrative ethnography is one arena in which the literary critic Mary Louise Pratt's blunt diagnosis that ethnographic writing is boring (1986:33) simply does not apply. Journal articles, on the other hand, tend to be exclusively of interest to academics initiated into the fellowship of professional discourse, and subscribing members of a particular, academically formed society. Journal articles are written according to formulas that include a thesis introduced in the beginning and returned to at the end, and the convention that theoretical frameworks and generalized statements should be emphasized, suppressing vivid particulars. We read these articles with our minds more than our hearts, extorting ideas and references from their pages.

Need the two categories, compelling narrative and rigorous analysis, be impermeable? Increasingly, they seep into each other, and here I want to argue for an emerging style in anthropological writing that I call the *enactment of hybridity* (cf. Abu-Lughod 1992; Behar 1993; Jackson 1989; Kondo 1990; Lavie 1990; Rosaldo 1989; Rose 1987; Stoller 1989; Tedlock 1992). In using the word 'enactment', I am drawing on Dorinne Kondo's view that 'the specificity of . . . experience . . . is not opposed to theory; it *enacts* and *embodies* theory' (1990, emphasis in original): any writing, then, represents an enactment of some sort of theory. By 'hybridity', I do not mean only a condition of people who are mixed from birth, but also a state that all anthropologists partake of but may not consciously include in our texts. As Edward Bruner (1993) has elegantly phrased it, every anthropologist carries both a personal and an ethnographic self. In this scheme, we are all incipiently bi- (or multi-) cultural in that we belong to worlds both personal and professional, whether in the field or at home. While people with Third World allegiances, minorities or women may experience the tensions of this dual identity the most strongly, it is a condition of everyone, even of that conglomerate category termed 'white men'. Whether we are disempowered or empowered by prevailing power relations, we must all take responsibility for how our personal locations feed not just into our fieldwork interactions but also into our scholarly texts. When professional personas altogether efface situated and experiencing selves, this makes for misleading scholarship even as it does violence to the range of hybrid personal and professional identities that we negotiate in our daily lives.

Adopting a narrative voice involves an ethical stance that neither effaces ourselves as hybrid nor defaces the vivid humanity of the people with whom we work. Narrative transforms 'informants' whose chief role is to spew cultural data for the anthropologist into subjects with complex lives and a range of opinions (that may even subsume the anthropological enterprise). At a moment in which scholarship has a 'multinational reception' (cf. Mani 1990), it seems more urgent than ever that anthropologists acknowledge that it is *people* and not theoretical puppets who populate our texts, and that we allow these people to speak out from our writings. Also, narratives are not transparent representations of what actually happened, but are told for particular purposes, from particular points of view: they are thus incipiently analytical, enacting theory. Analysis itself is most effective when it builds directly from cases evoked through narrative, providing a chance to step away, reflect on, and reframe the riveting particulars of the story at hand. In including the perspective of the social analyst along with narratives from or about people studied, a stereoscopic 'double vision' can be achieved (Rosaldo 1989: pp. 127–43). Some skillfully constructed analyses are as gripping as good mystery stories, starting from a conundrum, then assembling clues that finally piece together. Narrative and analysis are categories we tend to set up as opposites, yet a second look reveals that they are contiguous, with a border open even to the most full-scale of crossovers.

Calling for a greater integration of narrative into written texts does not mean that analysis is to be abandoned, but rather that it moves over, giving vivid experience an honored place beside it. By translating professional jargon into 'the language of everyday life' (cf. Abu-Lughod 1991: p. 151), analysis can also be made intriguing to audiences who would otherwise be compelled only by narrative. Admittedly, writing cannot single-handedly change the inequalities in today's world; yet, in bearing the potential to change the attitudes of readers, ethical and accessible writing unquestionably takes a step in the right direction. As companions clothed in nontechnical language, narrative and analysis join to push open the doors of anthropological understanding and welcome in outsiders.

CONCLUSIONS

I have argued for a reorientation in the ways that we perceive anthropologists as 'outside' or 'inside' a society. The traditional view has been to polarize 'real' anthropologists from 'native' anthropologists, with the underlying assumption that a 'native' anthropologist would forward an authentic insider's view to the profession. This view sprang from a colonial era in which inegalitarian power relations were relatively well defined: there was little question about the 'civilized' outsider's ability to represent "primitive" peoples, and so it was worthy of note when a person excluded from dominant white culture was allowed to describe his or her own society. With changing times, however, the scope of anthropology has shifted to include industrialized societies, even as it is also practiced in 'Third World' countries and by minority and 'Third World' scholars. Identity, always multiplex, has become even more culturally complex at this historical moment in which global flows in trade, politics, and the media stimulate greater interpenetration between cultures.

In this changed setting, it is more profitable to focus on shifting identities in relationship with the people and issues an anthropologist seeks to represent. Even if one can blend into a particular social group without the quest of fieldwork, the very nature of researching what to others is taken-for-granted reality creates an uneasy distance. However, even if one starts out as a stranger, sympathies and ties developed through engaged coexistence may subsume difference within relationships of reciprocity. 'Objectivity' must be replaced by an involvement that is unabashedly subjective as it interacts with and invites other subjectivities to take a place in anthropological productions. Knowledge, in this scheme, is not transcendental, but situated, negotiated and part of an ongoing process. This process spans personal, professional and cultural domains.

As we rethink 'insiders' and 'outsiders' in anthropology, I have argued that we should also work to melt down other, related divides. One wall stands between ourselves as interested readers of stories and as theory-driven professionals; another wall stands between narrative (associated with subjective knowledge) and analysis (associated with objective truths). By situating ourselves as subjects simultaneously touched by life-experience and swayed by professional concerns, we can acknowledge the hybrid and positioned nature of our identities. Writing texts that mix lively narrative and rigorous analysis involves enacting hybridity, regardless of our origins.

ACKNOWLEDGMENTS

This essay emerged from fieldwork in Nasik between June and September 1983 and July and October 1985, as well as an association with the place since birth. Formal fieldwork in Kangra took place between September 1991 and August 1992, although I have visited there since 1975. I am extremely grateful for an array of grants and fellowships through the years. In building on insights garnered collectively from research enabled by these different funding sources, I lump them together here: a National Science Foundation Graduate Fellowship, a University of California at Berkeley Graduate Humanities Research Grant, a Robert H. Lowie Fellowship, a Charlotte W. Newcombe Dissertation Writing Fellowship, support from the University of Wisconsin Graduate School, an American Institute of Indian Studies Senior Fellowship, and a National Endowment for the Humanities Fellowship. My deep thanks to Ruth Behar, Eytan Bercovitch, Ed Bruner, Janet Dixon-Keller, Ann Gold, Smadar Lavie, Maria Lepowsky, Renato Rosaldo, Janis Shough, Paul Stoller, Barbara Tedlock, Anna Tsing and Kamala Visweswaran for conversations about and comments on issues raised in this essay.

Works Cited

Abu-Lughod, Lila
  1988. 'Fieldwork of a Dutiful Daughter', in *Arab Women in the Field*, S. Altorki and C. Fawzi El-Solh, eds. pp. 139–61. Syracuse: Syracuse University Press.
  1990. 'Can There Be a Feminist Ethnography?', *Women and Performance: A Journal of Feminist Theory*, 5 vol. 7–27.
  1991. 'Writing Against Culture' in *Recapturing Anthropology*, Richard Fox, ed. pp. 137–62. Santa Fe, NM: School of American Research Press.
  1992. *Writing Women's Worlds; Bedouin Stories*. Berkeley: University of California Press.

Aguilar, John
  1981. 'Insider Research: An Ethnography of a Debate', in *Anthropologists at Home in North America*. Donald Messerschmidt, ed. pp. 15–26. Cambridge: Cambridge University Press.

Alarcon, Norma
  1990. 'The Theoretical Subject(s) of This Bridge Called My Back in Anglo-American Feminism', in *Making Face/Making Soul: Creative and Criticial Perspectives on Women of Color*. G. Anzaldua, ed. pp. 356–69. San Francisco: Aunt Lute Foundation.

Altorki, Soraya, and Camillia Fawzi El-Solh, eds.
  1988. *Arab Women in the Field: Studying Your Own Society*. Syracuse: Syracuse University Press.

Appadurai, Arjun
  1988. 'Putting Hierarchy in Its Place' *Cultural Anthropology*, vol. 3, pp. 36–49.
  1990. 'Disjuncture and Difference in the Global Cultural Economy', *Public Culture* vol. 2, pp. 21–24.
  1991. 'Global Ethnoscapes: Notes and Queries for a Transnational Anthropology', in *Recapturing Anthropology*, Richard Fox, ed. pp. 191–210. Santa Fe, NM: School of American Research Press.

Behar, Ruth
  1993. *Translated Woman: Crossing the Border with Esperanza's Story*. Boston: Beacon Press.

Bruner, Edward M.
  1993. 'Introduction: The Ethnographic Self and the Personal Self', in *Anthropology and Literature*, Paul Benson, ed. pp. 1–26. Urbana: University of Illinois Press.

Casagrande, Joseph, ed.
    1960. *In the Company of Men: Twenty Portraits by Anthropologists*. New York: Harper and Row.
Clifford, James
    1986. 'Introduction: Partial Truths', in *Writing Culture: The Poetics and Politics of Ethnography*, James Clifford and George Marcus, eds. pp. 1–26. Berkeley: University of California Press.
    1988. *The Predicament of Culture*. Cambridge, MA: Harvard University Press.
    1992. 'Travelling Cultures', in *Cultural Studies*, L. Grossberg, C. Nelson, and Paula Treichler, eds. pp. 96–116. New York: Routledge.
Danforth, Loring
    1989. *Firewalking and Religious Healing: The Anasteria of Greece and the American Firewalking Movement*. Princeton: Princeton University Press.
Dumont, Jean Paul
    1978. *The Headman and I*. Austin: University of Texas Press.
Dwyer, Kevin
    1982. *Moroccan Dialogues: Anthropology in Question*. Prospect Heights, IL: Waveland Press.
Fahim, Hussein
    1982. *Indigenous Anthropology in Non-Western Countries*. Durham, NC: Carolina Academic Press.
Fahim, Hussein, Katherine Helmer, Elizabeth Colson, T. N. Madan, Herbert C. Kelman and Talal Asad
    1980. 'Indigenous Anthropology in Non-Western Countries: A Further Elaboration', *Current Anthropology*, vol. 21, 644–63.
Fernea, Elizabeth
    1965. *Guests of The Sheik: An Ethnography of an Iraqi Village*. New York: Doubleday.
Foster, George M., T. Scudder, E. Colson and R. V. Kemper, eds
    1979. *Long-Term Field Research in Social Anthropology*. New York: Academic Press.
Ginsburg, Faye
    1989. *Contested Lives: The Abortion Debate in an American Community*. Berkeley: University of California Press.
Ginsburg, Faye and Anna Lowenhaupt Tsing
    1990. *Uncertain Terms: Negotiating Gender in American Culture*. Boston: Beacon Press.
Gold, Ann
    1988. *Fruitful Journeys: The Ways of Rajasthani Pilgrims*. Berkeley: University of California Press.
Gupta, Akhil, and Ferguson, James
    1992. 'Beyond "Culture": Space, Identity, and the Politics of Difference', *Cultural Anthropology* vol. 6, pp. 6–23.
Gwaltney, John L.
    1981. 'Common Sense and Science: Urban Core Black Observations', in *Anthropologists at Home in North America: Methods and Issues in the Study of One's Own Society*, D. Messerschmidt, ed. pp. 46–61. Cambridge: Cambridge University Press.
Hall, Stuart
    1989. 'Cultural Identity and Cinematic Representation', *Framework* vol. 36, pp. 68–81.

Haraway, Donna
  1988. 'Situated Knowledges: The Science Question in Feminism and the Privilege of Partial Perspective', *Feminist Studies* vol. 14, pp. 575–99.
Jackson, Michael
  1989. *Paths Towards a Clearing: Radical Empiricism and Ethnographic Enquiry.* Bloomington: Indiana University Press.
Jones, Delmos J.
  1970. 'Toward a Native Anthropology', *Human Organization* vol. 29, pp. 251–9.
Kondo, Dorinne
  1986. 'Dissolution and Reconstitution of Self: Implications for Anthropological Epistemology', *Cultural Anthropology* vol. 1, pp. 74–96.
  1990. *Crafting Selves: Power, Gender and Discourses of Identity in a Japanese Workplace.* Chicago: University of Chicago Press.
Kumar, Nita
  1992. *Friends, Brothers, and Informants: Fieldwork Memoirs of Banaras.* Berkeley: University of California Press.
Lauretis, Teresa de
  1986. 'Feminist Studies/Critical Studies: Issues, Terms, and Contexts', in *Feminist Studies/Critical Studies*, T. de Lauretis, ed. pp. 1–19. Bloomington: Indiana University Press.
Lavie, Smadar
  1990. *The Poetics of Military Occupation.* Berkeley: University of California Press.
Limón, José
  1991. 'Representation, Ethnicity, and the Precusory Ethnography: Notes of a Native Anthropologist', in *Recapturing Anthropology*, Richard Fox, ed. pp. 115–36. Santa Fe, NM: School of American Research Press.
Lowie, Robert
  1937. *A History of Ethnological Theory.* New York: Holt, Reinhart and Winston.
Malinowski, Bronislaw
  1961 [1922]. *Argonauts of the Western Pacific.* New York: E. P. Dutton.
Mani, Lata
  1990. 'Multiple Mediations: Feminist Scholarship in the Age of Multinational Reception', *Feminist Review* vol. 35, pp. 24–41.
Maquet, Jacques
  1964. 'Objectivity in Anthropology', *Current Anthropology* vol. 5, pp. 47–5.
Martin, Emily.
  1987. *The Woman in the Body: A Cultural Analysis of Reproduction.* Boston: Beacon Press.
Messerschmidt, Donald
  1981a. 'On Anthropology "at Home"', in *Anthropologists at Home in North America: Methods and Issues in the Study of One's Own Society*, D. Messerschmidt, ed. pp. 1–14. Cambridge: Cambridge University Press.
  1981b. [ed.] *Anthropologists at Home in North America: Methods and Issues in the Study of One's Own Society.* Cambridge: Cambridge University Press.
Mohanty, Chandra and Ann Russo, eds.
  1991. *Third World Women and the Politics of Feminism.* Bloomington: Indiana University Press.
Mohanty, Satya
  1989. 'Us and Them', *New Formations* vol. 8, pp. 55–80.
Nakhleh, Khalil
  1979. 'On Being a Native Anthropologist', in *The Politics of Anthropology: From*

Colonialism and Sexism to the View from Below, G. Huizer and B. Mannheim, eds. pp. 343–52. The Hague: Mouton.

Narayan, Kirin
1989. *Storytellers, Saints, and Scoundrels: Folk Narrative in Hindu Religious Teaching.* Philadelphia: University of Pennsylvania Press.

Ohnuki-Tierney, Emiko
1984. ' "Native" Anthropologists', *American Ethnologist* vol. 11, p. 584–6.

Ortner, Sherry
1991. 'Reading America: Preliminary Notes on Class and Culture', in *Recapturing Anthropology*, Richard Fox, ed. pp. 163–89. Santa Fe, NM: School of American Research Press.

Pratt, Mary Louise
1986. 'Fieldwork in Common Places', in *Writing Culture*, James Clifford and George Marcus, eds. pp. 27–50. Berkeley: University of California Press.

Rabinow, Paul
1977. *Reflections on Fieldwork in Morocco.* Berkeley: University of California Press.

Rosaldo, Renato
1989. *Culture and Truth: The Remaking of Social Analysis.* Boston: Beacon Press.

Rose, Dan
1987. *Black American Street Life: South Philadelphia, 1969–71.* Philadelphia: University of Pennsylvania Press.

Said, Esard
1989. 'Representing the Colonized: Anthropology's Interlocutors', *Critical Inquiry* vol. 15, pp. 205–25.

Schutz, Alfred
1973. *Collected Papers, Volume 1: The Problem of Social Reality.* The Hague: Mouton.

Shostak, Marjorie
1981. *Nisa: The Life and Words of a !Kung Woman.* Cambridge, MA: Harvard University Press.

Spickard, Paul R.
1989. *Mixed Blood: Intermarriage and Ethnic Identity in Twentieth Century America.* Madison: University of Wisconsin Press.

Srinivas, M. N.
1952. *Religion and Society among the Coorgs of Southern India.* New Delhi: Oxford University Press.
1966. 'Some Thoughts on the Study of One's Own Society', in *Social Change in Modern India*, M. N. Srinivas, ed. pp. 147–63. Berkeley: University of California Press.
1976. *The Remembered Village.* Berkeley: University of California Press.

Srinivas, M. N., A. M. Shah and E. A. Ramaswamy
1979. *The Fieldworker and the Field: Problems and Challenges in Sociological Investigation.* Delhi: Oxford University Press.

Stewart, John D.
1989. *Drinkers, Drummers, and Decent Folk: Ethnographic Narratives in Village Trinidad.* Albany: State University of New York Press.

Stoller, Paul
1989. *The Taste of Ethnographic Things.* Philadelphia: University of Pennsylvania Press.
1992. *The Cinematic Griot: The Ethnography of Jean Rouch.* Chicago: University of Chicago Press.

Strathern, Marilyn
    1987. 'An Awkward Relationship: The Case of Feminism and Anthropology', *Signs* vol. 12, pp. 276–94.
Tedlock, Barbara
    1991. 'From Participant Observation to the Observation of Participation: The Emergence of Narrative Ethnography', *Journal of Anthropological Research* vol. 47, pp. 69–94.
    1992. *The Beautiful and the Dangerous: Encounters with the Zuni Indians*. New York: Viking.

3.4

'THREE WOMEN'S TEXTS AND A CRITIQUE OF IMPERIALISM'

Gayatri Chakravorty Spivak

It should not be possible to read nineteenth-century British literature without remembering that imperialism, understood as England's social mission, was a crucial part of the cultural representation of England to the English. The role of literature in the production of cultural representation should not be ignored. These two obvious 'facts' continue to be disregarded in the reading of nineteenth-century British literature. This itself attests to the continuing success of the imperialist project, displaced and dispersed into more modern forms.

If these 'facts' were remembered, not only in the study of British literature but in the study of the literatures of the European colonizing cultures of the great age of imperialism, we would produce a narrative, in literary history, of the 'worlding' of what is now called 'the Third World'. To consider the Third World as distant cultures, exploited but with rich intact literary heritages waiting to be recovered, interpreted, and curricularized in English translation fosters the emergence of 'the Third World' as a signifier that allows us to forget that 'worlding', even as it expands the empire of the literary discipline.[1]

It seems particularly unfortunate when the emergent perspective of feminist criticism reproduces the axioms of imperialism. A basically isolationist admiration for the literature of the female subject in Europe and Anglo-America establishes the high feminist norm. It is supported and operated by an information-retrieval approach to 'Third World' literature which often employs a deliberately 'nontheoretical' methodology with self-conscious rectitude.

From: Gayatri Chakravorty Spivak (1985), 'Three Women's Texts and a Critique of Imperialism', pp. 243–61, in *Critical Inquiry* no. 12.

In this essay, I will attempt to examine the operation of the 'worlding' of what is today 'the Third World' by what has become a cult text of feminism: *Jane Eyre*.[2] I plot the novel's reach and grasp, and locate its structural motors. I read *Wide Sargasso Sea* as *Jane Eyre*'s reinscription and *Frankenstein* as an analysis – even a deconstruction – of a 'worlding' such as *Jane Eyre*'s.[3]

I need hardly mention that the object of my investigation is the printed book, not its 'author'. To make such a distinction is, of course, to ignore the lessons of deconstruction. A deconstructive critical approach would loosen the binding of the book, undo the opposition between verbal text and the biography of the named subject 'Charlotte Brontë', and see the two as each other's 'scene of writing'. In such a reading, the life that writes itself as 'my life' is as much a pro-duction in psychosocial space (other names can be found) as the book that is written by the holder of that named life – a book that is then consigned to what *is* most often recognized as genuinely 'social': the world of publication and dis-tribution.[4] To touch Brontë's 'life' in such a way, however, would be too risky here. We must rather strategically take shelter in an essentialism which, not wishing to lose the important advantages won by US mainstream feminism, will continue to honor the suspect binary oppositions – book and author, individual and history – and start with an assurance of the following sort: my readings here do not seek to undermine the excellence of the individual artist. If even minimally successful, the readings will incite a degree of rage against the imperialist narra-tivization of history, that it should produce so abject a script for her. I provide these assurances to allow myself some room to situate feminist individualism in its historical determination rather than simply to canonize it as feminism as such.

Sympathetic US feminists have remarked that I do not do justice to Jane Eyre's subjectivity. A word of explanation is perhaps in order. The broad strokes of my presuppositions are that what is at stake, for feminist individualism in the age of imperialism, is precisely the making of human beings, the constitution and 'interpellation' of the subject not only as individual but 'individualist'.[5] This stake is represented on two registers: childbearing and soul making. The first is domestic-society-through-sexual-reproduction cathected as 'companionate love'; the second is the imperialist project cathected as civil-society-through-social-mission. As the female individualist, not-quite/not-male, articulates herself in shifting relationship to what is at stake, the 'native female' as such (*within* dis-course, *as* a signifier) is excluded from any share in this emerging norm.[6] If we read this account from an isolationist perspective in a 'metropolitan' context, we see nothing there but the psychobiography of the militant female subject. In a reading such as mine, in contrast, the effort is to wrench oneself away from the mesmerizing focus of the 'subject-constitution' of the female individualist.

To develop further the notion that my stance need not be an accusing one, I will refer to a passage from Roberto Fernández Retamar's 'Caliban'.[7] José Enrique Rodó had argued in 1900 that the model for the Latin American intel-lectual in relationship to Europe could be Shakespeare's Ariel.[8] In 1971 Retamar, denying the possibility of an identifiable 'Latin American Culture', recast the model as Caliban. Not surprisingly, this powerful exchange still excludes any specific consideration of the civilizations of the Maya, the Aztecs, the Incas or the smaller nations of what is now called Latin America. Let us note carefully that, at this stage of my argument, this 'conversation' between Europe and Latin America (without a specific consideration of the political economy of the 'worlding' of the 'native') provides a sufficient thematic description of our attempt to confront the ethnocentric and reverse-ethnocentric benevolent double bind (that is, considering the 'native' as object for enthusiastic information-retrieval and thus denying its own 'worlding') that I sketched in my opening paragraphs.

In a moving passage in 'Caliban', Retamar locates both Caliban and Ariel in the postcolonial intellectual:

> There is no real Ariel-Caliban polarity: both are slaves in the hands of Prospero, the foreign magician. But Caliban is the rude and unconquerable master of the island, while Ariel, a creature of the air, although also a child of the isle, is the intellectual.
>
> The deformed Caliban – enslaved, robbed of his island, and taught the language by Prospero – rebukes him thus: 'You taught me language, and my profit on't / Is, I know how to curse.' ('C', pp. 28, 11)

As we attempt to unlearn our so-called privilege as Ariel and 'seek from [a certain] Caliban the honor of a place in his rebellious and glorious ranks', we do not ask that our students and colleagues should emulate us but that they should attend us ('C', p. 72). If, however, we are driven by a nostalgia for lost origins, we too run the risk of effacing the 'native' and stepping forth as 'the real Caliban', of forgetting that he is a name in a play, an inaccessible blankness circumscribed by an interpretable text.[9] The stagings of Caliban work alongside the narrativization of history: claiming to *be* Caliban legitimizes the very individualism that we must persistently attempt to undermine from within.

Elizabeth Fox-Genovese, in an article on history and women's history, shows us how to define the historical moment of feminism in the West in terms of female access to individualism.[10] The battle for female individualism plays itself out within the larger theatre of the establishment of meritocratic individualism, indexed in the aesthetic field by the ideology of 'the creative imagination'. Fox-Genovese's presupposition will guide us into the beautifully orchestrated opening of *Jane Eyre*.

It is a scene of the marginalization and privatization of the protagonist: 'There was no possibility of taking a walk that day. . . . Out-door exercise was now out of the question. I was glad of it', Brontë writes (*JE*, p. 9). The movement continues as Jane breaks the rules of the appropriate topography of withdrawal. The family at the center withdraws into the sanctioned architectural space of the withdrawing room or drawing room; Jane inserts herself – 'I slipped in' – into the margin – 'A small breakfast-room *adjoined* the drawing room' (*JE*, p. 9; my emphasis).

The manipulation of the domestic inscription of space within the upwardly mobilizing currents of the eighteenth- and nineteenth-century bourgeoisie in England and France is well known. It seems fitting that the place to which Jane withdraws is not only not the withdrawing room but also not the dining room, the sanctioned place of family meals. Nor is it the library, the appropriate place for reading. The breakfast-room 'contained a bookcase' (*JE*, p. 9). As Rudolph Ackerman wrote in his *Repository* (1823), one of the many manuals of taste in circulation in nineteenth-century England, these low bookcases and stands were designed to 'contain all the books that may be desired for a sitting-room without reference to the library'.[11] Even in this already triply off-center place, 'having drawn the red moreen curtain nearly close, I [Jane] was shrined in double retirement' (*JE*, pp. 9–10).

Here in Jane's self-marginalized uniqueness, the reader becomes her accomplice: the reader and Jane are united – both are reading. Yet Jane still preserves her odd privilege, for she continues never quite doing the proper thing in its proper place. She cares little for reading what is *meant* to be read: the 'letter-press'. *She* reads the pictures. The power of this singular hermeneutics is precisely that it can make the outside inside. 'At intervals, while turning over the leaves of my book, I studied the aspect of that winter afternoon'. Under 'the clear panes of glass', the rain no longer penetrates, 'the drear November day' is rather a one-dimensional 'aspect' to be 'studied', not decoded like the 'letter-press' but, like pictures, deciphered by the unique creative imagination of the marginal individualist (*JE*, p. 10).

Before following the track of this unique imagination, let us consider the suggestion that the progress of *Jane Eyre* can be charted through a sequential arrangement of the family/counter-family dyad. In the novel, we encounter, first, the Reeds as the legal family and Jane, the late Mr Reed's sister's daughter, as the representative of a near incestuous counter-family; second, the Brocklehursts, who run the school Jane is sent to, as the legal family and Jane, Miss Temple, and Helen Burns as a counter-family that falls short because it is only a community of women; third, Rochester and the mad Mrs. Rochester as the legal family and Jane and Rochester as the illicit counter-family. Other items may be added to the thematic chain in this sequence: Rochester and Céline Varens as structurally functional counter-family; Rochester and Blanche Ingram as dissimulation of legality – and so on. It is during this sequence that Jane is moved from the counter-family to the family-in-law. In the next sequence, it is Jane who restores full family status to the as-yet-incomplete community of siblings, the Riverses. The final sequence of the book is a *community of families*, with Jane, Rochester, and their children at the center.

In terms of the narrative energy of the novel, how is Jane moved from the place of the counter-family to the family-in-law? It is the active ideology of imperialism that provides the discursive field.

(My working definition of 'discursive field' must assume the existence of discrete 'systems of signs' at hand in the socius, each based on a specific axiomatics.

I am identifying these systems as discursive fields. 'Imperialism as social mission' generates the possibility of one such axiomatics. How the individual artist taps the discursive field at hand with a sure touch, if not with transhistorical clairvoyance, in order to make the narrative structure move I hope to demonstrate through the following example. It is crucial that we extend our analysis of this example beyond the minimal diagnosis of 'racism'.)

Let us consider the figure of Bertha Mason, a figure produced by the axiomatics of imperialism. Through Bertha Mason, the white Jamaican Creole, Brontë renders the human/animal frontier as acceptably indeterminate, so that a good greater than the letter of the Law can be broached. Here is the celebrated passage, given in the voice of Jane:

> In the deep shade, at the further end of the room, a figure ran backwards and forwards. What it was, whether beast or human being, one could not . . . tell: it grovelled, seemingly, on all fours; it snatched and growled like some strange wild animal: but it was covered with clothing, and a quantity of dark, grizzled hair, wild as a mane, hid its head and face. (*JE*, p. 295)

In a matching passage, given in the voice of Rochester speaking *to* Jane, Brontë presents the imperative for a shift beyond the Law as divine injunction rather than human motive. In the terms of my essay, we might say that this is the register not of mere marriage or sexual reproduction but of Europe and its not-yet-human Other, of soul making. The field of imperial conquest is here inscribed as Hell:

> 'One night I had been awakened by her yells . . . it was a fiery West Indian night. . . .
>
> ' "This life," said I at last, "is hell! – this is the air – those are the sounds of the bottomless pit! *I have a right* to deliver myself from it if I can. . . . Let me break away, and go home to God!" . . .
>
> 'A wind fresh from Europe blew over the ocean and rushed through the open casement: the storm broke, streamed, thundered, blazed, and the air grew pure. . . . It was true Wisdom that consoled me in that hour, and showed me the right path. . . .
>
> 'The sweet wind from Europe was still whispering in the refreshed leaves, and the Atlantic was thundering in glorious liberty. . . .
>
> ' "Go," said Hope, "and live again in Europe. . . . You have done all that God and Humanity require of you." ' (*JE*, pp. 310–11; my emphasis)

It is the unquestioned ideology of imperialist axiomatics, then, that conditions Jane's move from the counter-family set to the set of the family-in-law. Marxist critics such as Terry Eagleton have seen this only in terms of the ambiguous *class* position of the governess.[12] Sandra Gilbert and Susan Gubar, on the other hand, have seen Bertha Mason only in psychological terms, as Jane's dark double.[13]

I will not enter the critical debates that offer themselves here. Instead, I will develop the suggestion that nineteenth-century feminist individualism could conceive of a 'greater' project than access to the closed circle of the nuclear family. This is the project of soul making beyond 'mere' sexual reproduction. Here the native 'subject' is not almost an animal but rather the object of what might be termed the terrorism of the categorical imperative.

I am using 'Kant' in this essay as a metonym for the most flexible ethical moment in the European eighteenth century. Kant words the categorical imperative, conceived as the universal moral law given by pure reason, in this way: 'In all creation every thing one chooses and over which one has any power, may be used *merely as means*; man alone, and with him every rational creature, is an *end in himself*.' It is thus a moving displacement of Christian ethics from religion to philosophy. As Kant writes: 'With this agrees very well the possibility of such a command as: *Love God above everything, and thy neighbor as thyself*. For as a command it requires respect for a law which *commands love* and does not leave it to our own arbitrary choice to make this our principle.'[14]

The 'categorical' in Kant cannot be adequately represented in determinately grounded action. The dangerous transformative power of philosophy, however, is that its formal subtlety can be travestied in the service of the state. Such a travesty in the case of the categorical imperative can justify the imperialist project by producing the following formula: *make* the heathen into a human so that he can be treated as an end in himself.[15] This project is presented as a sort of tangent in *Jane Eyre*, a tangent that escapes the closed circle of the *narrative* conclusion. The tangent narrative is the story of St. John Rivers, who is granted the important task of concluding the *text*.

At the novel's end, the *allegorical* language of Christian psychobiography – rather than the textually constituted and seemingly *private* grammar of the creative imagination which we noted in the novel's opening – marks the inaccessibility of the imperialist project as such to the nascent 'feminist' scenario. The concluding passage of *Jane Eyre* places St. John Rivers within the fold of *Pilgrim's Progress*. Eagleton pays no attention to this but accepts the novel's ideological lexicon, which establishes St. John Rivers' heroism by identifying a life in Calcutta with an unquestioning choice of death. Gilbert and Gubar, by calling *Jane Eyre* 'Plain Jane's progress', see the novel as simply replacing the male protagonist with the female. They do not notice the distance between sexual reproduction and soul making, both actualized by the unquestioned idiom of imperialist presuppositions evident in the last part of *Jane Eyre*:

> Firm, faithful, and devoted, full of energy, and zeal, and truth, [St. John Rivers] labours for his race. . . . His is the sternness of the warrior Greatheart, who guards his pilgrim convoy from the onslaught of Apollyon. . . . His is the ambition of the high master-spirit[s] . . . who stands without fault before the throne of God; who share the last mighty victories of the Lamb; who are called, and chosen, and faithful. (*JE*, p. 455)

Earlier in the novel, St. John Rivers himself justifies the project: 'My vocation? My great work? . . . My hopes of being numbered in the band who have merged all ambitions in the glorious one of bettering their race – of carrying knowledge into the realms of ignorance – of substituting peace for war – freedom for bondage – religion for superstitution – the hope of heaven for the fear of hell?' (*JE*, p. 376). Imperialism and its territorial and subject-constituting project are a violent deconstruction of these oppositions.

When Jean Rhys, born on the Caribbean island of Dominica, read *Jane Eyre* as a child, she was moved by Bertha Mason: 'I thought I'd try to write her a life.'[16] *Wide Sargasso Sea*, the slim novel published in 1965, at the end of Rhys' long career, is that 'life'.

I have suggested that Bertha's function in *Jane Eyre* is to render indeterminate the boundary between human and animal and thereby to weaken her entitlement under the spirit if not the letter of the Law. When Rhys rewrites the scene in *Jane Eyre* where Jane hears 'a snarling, snatching sound, almost like a dog quarrelling' and then encounters a bleeding Richard Mason (*JE*, p. 210), she keeps Bertha's humanity, indeed her sanity as critic of imperialism, intact. Grace Poole, another character originally in *Jane Eyre*, describes the incident to Bertha in *Wide Sargasso Sea*: 'So you don't remember that you attacked this gentleman with a knife? . . . I didn't hear all he said except "I cannot interfere legally between yourself and your husband". It was when he said "legally" that you flew at him"' (*WSS*, p. 150). In Rhys' retelling, it is the dissimulation that Bertha discerns in the word 'legally' – not an innate bestiality – that prompts her violent *re*action.

In the figure of Antoinette, whom in *Wide Sargasso Sea* Rochester violently renames Bertha, Rhys suggests that so intimate a thing as personal and human identity might be determined by the politics of imperialism. Antoinette, as a white Creole child growing up at the time of emancipation in Jamaica, is caught between the English imperialist and the black native. In recounting Antoinette's development, Rhys reinscribes some thematics of Narcissus.

There are, notably, many images of mirroring in the text. I will quote one from the first section. In this passage, Tia is the little black servant girl who is Antoinette's close companion: 'We had eaten the same food, slept side by side, bathed in the same river. As I ran, I thought, I will live with Tia and I will be like her. . . . When I was close I saw the jagged stone in her hand but I did not see her throw it. . . . We stared at each other, blood on my face, tears on hers. It was as if I saw myself. Like in a looking glass' (*WSS*, p. 38).

A progressive sequence of dreams reinforces this mirror imagery. In its second occurrence, the dream is partially set in a *hortus conclusus*, or 'enclosed garden' – Rhys uses the phrase (*WSS*, p. 50) – a Romance rewriting of the Narcissus topos as the place of encounter with Love.[17] In the enclosed garden, Antoinette encounters not Love but a strange threatening voice that says merely 'in here', inviting her into a prison which masquerades as the legalization of love (*WSS*, p. 50).

In Ovid's *Metamorphoses*, Narcissus' madness is disclosed when he recognizes his Other as his self: 'Iste ego sum.'[18] Rhys makes Antoinette see her *self* as her Other, Brontë's Bertha. In the last secton of *Wide Sargasso Sea*. Antoinette acts out *Jane Eyre*'s conclusion and recognizes herself as the so-called ghost in Thornfield Hall: 'I went into the hall again with the tall candle in my hand. It was then that I saw her – the ghost. The woman with streaming hair. She was surrounded by a gilt frame but I knew her' (*WSS*, p. 154). The gilt frame encloses a mirror: as Narcissus' pool reflects the selfed Other, so this 'pool' reflects the Othered self. Here the dream sequence ends, with an invocation of none other than Tia, the Other that could not be selfed, because the fracture of imperialism rather than the Ovidian pool intervened. (I will return to this difficult point.) 'That was the third time I had my dream, and it ended. . . . I called "Tia" and jumped and woke' (*WSS*, p. 155). It is now, at the very end of the book, that Antoinette/Bertha can say: 'Now at last I know why I was brought here and what I have to do' (*WSS*, pp. 155–6). We can read this as her having been brought into the England of Brontë's novel: 'The cardboard house' – a book between cardboard covers – 'where I walk at night is not England' (*WSS*, p. 148). In this fictive England, she must play out her role, act out the transformation of her 'self' into that fictive Other, set fire to the house and kill herself, so that Jane Eyre can become the feminist individualist heroine of British fiction. I must read this as an allegory of the general epistemic violence of imperialism, the construction of a self-immolating colonial subject for the glorification of the social mission of the colonizer. At least Rhys sees to it that the woman from the colonies is not sacrificed as an insane animal for her sister's consolation.

Critics have remarked that *Wide Sargasso Sea* treats the Rochester character with understanding and sympathy.[19] Indeed, he narrates the entire middle section of the book. Rhys makes it clear that he is a victim of the patriarchal inheritance law of entailment rather than of a father's natural preference for the firstborn: in *Wide Sargasso Sea*, Rochester's situation is clearly that of a younger son dispatched to the colonies to buy an heiress. If in the case of Antoinette and her identity, Rhys utilizes the thematics of Narcissus, in the case of Rochester and his patrimony, she touches on the thematics of Oedipus. (In this she has her finger on our 'historical moment'. If, in the nineteenth century, subject-constitution is represented as childbearing and soul making, in the twentieth century, psychoanalysis allows the West to plot the itinerary of the subject from Narcissus [the 'imaginary'] to Oedipus [the 'symbolic']. This subject, however, is the normative male subject. In Rhys' reinscription of these themes, divided between the female and the male protagonist, feminism and a critique of imperialism become complicit.)

In place of the 'wind from Europe' scene, Rhys substitutes the scenario of a suppressed letter to a father, a letter which would be the 'correct' explanation of the tragedy of the book.[20] 'I thought about the letter which should have been written to England a week ago. Dear Father . . .' (*WSS*, p. 57). This is the first instance: the letter not written. Shortly afterward:

Dear Father. The thirty thousand pounds have been paid to me without question or condition. No provision made for her (that must be seen to). . . . I will never be a disgrace to you or to my dear brother the son you love. No begging letters, no mean requests. None of the furtive shabby manoeuvres of a younger son. I have sold my soul or you have sold it, and after all is it such a bad bargain? The girl is thought to be beautiful, she is beautiful. And yet . . . (*WSS*, p. 59)

This is the second instance: the letter not sent. The formal letter is uninteresting; I will quote only a part of it:

Dear Father, we have arrived from Jamaica after an uncomfortable few days. This little estate in the Windward Islands is part of the family property and Antoinette is much attached to it. . . . All is well and has gone according to your plans and wishes. I dealt of course with Richard Mason. . . . He seemed to become attached to me and trusted me completely. This place is very beautiful but my illness has left me too exhausted to appreciate it fully. I will write again in a few days' time. (*WSS*, p. 64)

And so on.

Rhys' version of the Oedipal exchange is ironic, not a closed circle. We cannot know if the letter actually reaches its destination. 'I wondered how they got their letters posted', the Rochester figure muses. 'I folded mine and put it into a drawer of the desk. . . . There are blanks in my mind that cannot be filled up' (*WSS*, p. 64). It is as if the text presses us to note the analogy between letter and mind.

Rhys denies to Brontë's Rochester the one thing that is supposed to be secured in the Oedipal relay: the Name of the Father, or the patronymic. In *Wide Sargasso Sea*, the character corresponding to Rochester has no name. His writing of the final version of the letter to his father is supervised, in fact, by an image of the *loss* of the patronymic: 'There was a crude bookshelf made of three shingles strung together over the desk and I looked at the books, Byron's poems, novels by Sir Walter Scott, *Confessions of an Opium Eater* . . . and on the last shelf, *Life and Letters of* . . . The rest was eaten away' (*WSS*, p. 63)

Wide Sargasso Sea marks with uncanny clarity the limits of its own discourse in Christophine, Antoinette's black nurse. We may perhaps surmise the distance between *Jane Eyre* and *Wide Sargasso Sea* by remarking that Christophine's unfinished story is the tangent to the latter narrative, as St. John Rivers' story is to the former. Christophine is not a native of Jamaica; she is from Martinique. Taxonomically, she belongs to the category of the good servant rather than that of the pure native. But within these borders, Rhys creates a powerfully suggestive figure.

Christophine is the first interpreter and named speaking subject in the text. 'The Jamaican ladies had never approved of my mother, "because she pretty like pretty self" Christophine said', we read in the book's opening paragraph (*WSS*, p. 15). I have taught this book five times, once in France, once to students who had worked on the book with the well-known Caribbean novelist Wilson Harris, and once at a prestigious institute where the majority of the students were faculty from other universities. It is part of the political argument I am making that all these students blithely stepped over this paragraph without asking or knowing what Christophine's patois, so-called incorrect English, might mean.

Christophine is, of course, a commodified person. ' "She was your father's wedding present to me" ' explains Antoinette's mother, ' ' "one of his presents" ' ' (*WSS*, p. 18). Yet Rhys assigns her some crucial functions in the text. It is Christophine who judges that black ritual practices are culture-specific and cannot be used by whites as cheap remedies for social evils, such as Rochester's lack of love for Antoinette. Most important, it is Christophine alone whom Rhys allows to offer a hard analysis of Rochester's actions, to challenge him in a face-to-face encounter. The entire extended passage is worthy of comment. I quote a brief extract:

> 'She is Creole girl, and she have the sun in her. Tell the truth now. She don't come to your house in this place England they tell me about, she don't come to your beautiful house to beg you to marry with her. No, it's you come all the long way to her house – it's you beg her to marry. And she love you and she give you all she have. Now you say you don't love her and you break her up. What you do with her money, eh?' [And then Rochester, the white man, comments silently to himself] Her voice was still quiet but with a hiss in it when she said 'money'. (*WSS*, p. 130)

Her analysis is powerful enough for the white man to be afraid: 'I no longer felt dazed, tired, half hypnotized, but alert and wary, ready to defend myself' (*WSS*, p. 130).

Rhys does not, however, romanticize individual heroics on the part of the oppressed. When the Man refers to the forces of Law and Order, Christophine recognizes their power. This exposure of civil inequality is emphasized by the fact that, just before the Man's successful threat, Christophine had invoked the emancipation of slaves in Jamaica by proclaiming: 'No chain gang, no tread machine, no dark jail either. This is free country and I am free woman' (*WSS*, p. 131).

As I mentioned above, Christophine is tangential to this narrative. She cannot be contained by a novel which rewrites a canonical English text within the European novelistic tradition in the interest of the white Creole rather than the native. No perspective *critical* of imperialism can turn the Other into a self, because the project of imperialism has always already historically refracted what might have been the absolutely Other into a domesticated Other that consolidates the imperialist self.[21] The Caliban of Retamar, caught between Europe and Latin America, reflects this predicament. We can read Rhys' reinscription of Narcissus as a thematization of the same problematic.

Of course, we cannot know Jean Rhys' feelings in the matter. We can, however, look at the scene of Christophine's inscription in the text. Immediately after the exchange between her and the Man, well before the conclusion, she is simply driven out of the story, with neither narrative nor characterological explanation or justice. ' "Read and write I don't know. Other things I know." She walked away without looking back' (*WSS*, p. 133).

Indeed, if Rhys rewrites the madwomen's attack on the Man by underlining of the misuse of 'legality', she cannot deal with the passage that corresponds to St. John Rivers' own justification of his martyrdom, for it has been displaced into the current idiom of modernization and development. Attempts to construct the 'Third World Woman' as a signifier remind us that the hegemonic definition of literature is itself caught within the history of imperialism. A full literary reinscription cannot easily flourish in the imperialist fracture or discontinuity, covered over by an alien legal system masquerading as Law as such, an alien ideology established as only Truth, and a set of human sciences busy establishing the 'native' as self-consolidating Other.

In the Indian case at least, it would be difficult to find an ideological clue to the planned epistemic violence of imperialism merely by rearranging curricula or syllabi within existing norms of literary pedagogy. For a later period of imperialism – when the constituted colonial subject has firmly taken hold – straightforward experiments of comparison can be undertaken, say, between the functionally witless India of *Mrs. Dalloway*, on the one hand, and literary texts produced in India in the 1920s, on the other. But the first half of the nineteenth century resists questioning through literature or literary criticism in the narrow sense, because both are implicated in the project of producing Ariel. To reopen the fracture without succumbing to a nostalgia for lost origins, the literary critic must turn to the archives of imperial governance.

In conclusion, I shall look briefly at Mary Shelley's *Frankenstein*, a text of nascent feminism that remains cryptic, I think, simply because it does not speak the language of feminist individualism which we have come to hail as the language of high feminism within English literature. It is interesting that Barbara Johnson's brief study tries to rescue this recalcitrant text for the service of feminist autobiography.[22] Alternatively, George Levine reads *Frankenstein* in the context of the creative imagination and the nature of the hero. He sees the novel as a book about its own writing and about writing itself, a Romantic allegory of reading within which Jane Eyre as unself-conscious critic would fit quite nicely.[23]

I propose to take *Frankenstein* out of this arena and focus on it in terms of that sense of English cultural identity which I invoked at the opening of this essay. Within that focus we are obliged to admit that, although *Frankenstein* is ostensibly about the origin and evolution of man in society, it does not deploy the axiomatics of imperialism.

Let me say at once that there is plenty of incidental imperialist sentiment in *Frankenstein*. My point, within the argument of this essay, is that the discursive field of imperialism does not produce unquestioned ideological correlatives for the narrative structuring of the book. The discourse of imperialism surfaces in a curiously powerful way in Shelley's novel, and I will later discuss the moment at which it emerges.

Frankenstein is not a battleground of male and female individualism articulated in terms of sexual reproduction (family and female) and social subject-production (race and male). That binary opposition is undone in Victor Frankenstein's laboratory – an artificial womb where both projects are undertaken simultaneously, though the terms are never openly spelled out. Frankenstein's apparent antagonist is God himself as Maker of Man, but his real competitor is also woman as the maker of children. It is not just that his dream of the death of his mother and bride and the actual death of his bride are associated with the visit of his monstrous homoerotic 'son' to his bed. On a much more overt level, the monster is a bodied 'corpse', unnatural because bereft of a determinable childhood: 'No father had watched my infant days, no mother had blessed me with smiles and caresses; or if they had, all my past was now a blot, a blind vacancy in which I distinguished nothing' (*F*, pp. 57, 115). It is Frankenstein's own ambiguous and miscued understanding of the real motive for the monster's vengefulness that reveals his own competition with woman as maker:

> I created a rational creature and was bound towards him to assure, as far as was in my power, his happiness and well-being. This was my duty, but there was another still paramount to that. My duties towards the beings of my own species had greater claims to my attention because they included a greater proportion of happiness or misery. Urged by this view, I refused, and I did right in refusing, to create a companion for the first creature. (*F*, p. 206)

It is impossible not to notice the accents of transgression inflecting Frankenstein's demolition of his experiment to create the future Eve. Even in the laboratory, the woman-in-the-making is not a bodied corpse but 'a human being'. The (il)logic of the metaphor bestows on her a prior existence which Frankenstein aborts, rather than an anterior death which he reembodies: 'The remains of the half-finished creature, whom I had destroyed, lay scattered on the floor, and I almost felt as if I had mangled the living flesh of a human being' (*F*, p. 163).

In Shelley's view, man's hubris as soul maker both usurps the place of God and attempts – vainly – to sublate woman's physiological prerogative.[24] Indeed, indulging a Freudian fantasy here, I could urge that, if to give and withhold to/from the mother a phallus is *the* male fetish, then to give and withhold to/from the man a womb might be the female fetish.[25] The icon of the sublimated womb in man is surely his productive brain, the box in the head.

In the judgment of classical psychoanalysis, the phallic mother exists only by virtue of the castration-anxious son; in *Frankenstein*'s judgment, the hysteric father (Victor Frankenstein gifted with his laboratory – the womb of theoretical reason) cannot produce a daughter. Here the language of racism – the dark side of imperialism understood as social mission – combines with the hysteria of masculism into the idiom of (the withdrawal of) sexual reproduction rather than subject-constitution. The roles of masculine and feminine individualists are hence reversed and displaced. Frankenstein cannot produce a 'daughter' because 'she might become ten thousand times more malignant than her mate . . . [and because] one of the first results of those sympathies for which the demon thirsted would be children, and a race of devils would be propagated upon the earth who might make the very existence of the species of man a condition precarious and full of terror' (F, p. 158). This particular narrative strand also launches a thoroughgoing critique of the eighteenth-century European discourses on the origin of society through (Western Christian) man. Should I mention that, much like Jean-Jacques Rousseau's remark in his Confessions, Frankenstein declares himself to be 'by birth a Genevese' (F, p. 31)?

In this overly didactic text, Shelley's point is that social engineering should not be based on pure, theoretical, or natural-scientific reason alone, which is her implicit critique of the utilitarian vision of an engineered society. To this end, she presents in the first part of her deliberately schematic story three characters, childhood friends, who seem to represent Kant's three-part conception of the human subject: Victor Frankenstein, the forces of theoretical reason or 'natural philosophy'; Henry Clerval, the forces of practical reason or 'the moral relations of things', and Elizabeth Lavenza, that aesthetic judgment – 'the aerial creation of the poets' – which, according to Kant, is 'a suitable mediating link connecting the realm of the concept of nature and that of the concept of freedom . . . (which) promotes . . . *moral* feeling' (F, pp. 37, 36).[26]

This three-part subject does not operate harmoniously in *Frankenstein*. That Henry Clerval, associated as he is with practical reason, should have as his 'design . . . to visit India, in the belief that he had in his knowledge of its various languages, and in the views he had taken of its society, the means of materially assisting the progress of European colonization and trade' is proof of this, as well as part of the incidental imperialist sentiment that I speak of above (F, pp. 151–2). I should perhaps point out that the language here is entrepreneurial rather than missionary:

> He came to the university with the design of making himself complete master of the Oriental languages, as thus he should open a field for the plan of life he had marked out for himself. Resolved to pursue no inglorious career, he turned his eyes towards the East as affording scope for his spirit of enterprise. The Persian, Arabic, and Sanskrit languages engaged his attention. (F, pp. 66–7)

But it is of course Victor Frankenstein, with his strange itinerary of obsession with natural philosophy, who offers the strongest demonstration that the multiple perspectives of the three-part Kantian subject cannot co-operate harmoniously. Frankenstein creates a putative human subject out of natural philosophy alone. According to his own miscued summation: 'In a fit of enthusiastic madness I created a rational creature' (*F*, p. 206). It is not at all farfetched to say that Kant's categorial imperative can most easily be mistaken for the hypothetical imperative – a command to ground in cognitive comprehension what can be apprehended only by moral will – by putting natural philosophy in the place of practical reason.

I should hasten to add here that just as readings such as this one do not necessarily accuse Charlotte Brontë the named individuals of harboring imperialist sentiments, so also they do not necessarily commend Mary Shelley the named individual for writing a successful Kantian allegory. The most I can say is that it is possible to read these texts, within the frame of imperialism and the Kantian ethical moment, in a politically useful way. Such an approach presupposes that a 'distinterested' reading attempts to render transparent the interests of the hegemonic readership. (Other 'political' readings – for instance, that the monster is the nascent working class – can be advanced.)

Frankenstein is built in the established epistolary tradition of multiple frames. At the heart of the multiple frames, the narrative of the monster (as reported by Frankenstein to Robert Walton, who then recounts it in a letter to his sister) is of his almost learning, clandestinely, to be human. It is invariably noticed that the monster reads *Paradise Lost* as true history. What is not so often noticed is that he also reads Plutarch's *Lives*, 'the histories of the first founders of the ancient republics', which he compares to 'the patriarchal lives of my protectors' (*F*, pp. 123, 124). And his *education* comes through 'Volney's *Ruins of Empires*', which purported to be a prefiguration of the French Revolution, published after the event and after the author had rounded off his theory with practice (*F*, p. 113). It is an attempt at an enlightened universal secular, rather than a Eurocentric Christian, history, written from the perspective of a narrator 'from below', somewhat like the attempts of Eric Wolf or Peters Worsley in our own time.[27]

This Caliban's education in (universal secular) humanity takes place through the monster's eavesdropping on the instruction of an Ariel – Safie, The Christianized 'Arabian' to whom 'a residence in Turkey was abhorrent' (*F*, p. 121). In depicting Safie, Shelley uses some commonplaces of eighteenth-century liberalism that are shared by many today: Safie's Muslim father was a victim of (bad) Christian religious prejudice and yet was himself a wily and ungrateful man not as morally refined as her (good) Christian mother. Having tasted the emancipation of woman, Safie could not go home. The confusion between 'Turk' and 'Arab' has its counterpart in present-day confusion about Turkey and Iran as 'Middle Eastern' but not 'Arab'.

Although we are a far cry here from the unexamined and covert axiomatics of imperialism in *Jane Eyre*, we will gain nothing by celebrating the time-bound pieties that Shelley, as the daughter of two antievangelicals, produces. It is more interesting for us that Shelley differentiates the Other, works at the Caliban/Ariel distinction, and *cannot* make the monster identical with the proper recipient of these lessons. Although he had 'heard of the discovery of the American hemisphere and *wept with Safie* over the helpless fate of its original inhabitants', Safie cannot reciprocate his attachment. When she first catches sight of him, 'Safie, unable to attend to her friend [Agatha], rushed out of the cottage' (*F*, pp. 114 [my emphasis], 129).

In the taxonomy of characters, the Muslim-Christian Safie belongs with Rhys' Antoinette/Bertha. And indeed, like Christophine the good servant, the subject created by the fiat of natural philosophy is the tangential unresolved moment in *Frankenstein*. The simple suggestion that the monster is human inside but monstrous outside and only provoked into vengefulness is clearly not enough to bear the burden of so great a historical dilemma.

At one moment, in fact, Shelley's Frankenstein does try to tame the monster, to humanize him by bringing him within the circuit of the Law. He 'repair[s] to a criminal judge in the town and . . . relate[s his] history briefly but with firmness' – the first and disinterested version of the narrative of Frankenstein – 'marking the dates with accuracy and never deviating into invective or exclamation. . . . When I had concluded my narration I said, 'This is the being whom I accuse and for whose seizure and punishment I call upon you to exert your whole power. It is your duty as a magistrate' (*F*, pp. 189, 190). The sheer social reasonableness of the mundane voice of Shelley's 'Genevan magistrate' reminds us that the absolutely Other cannot be selfed, that the monster has 'properties' which will not be contained by 'proper' measures:

> "I will exert myself [he says], and if it is in my power to seize the monster, be assured that he shall suffer punishment proportionate to his crimes. But I fear, from what you have yourself described to be his properties, that this will prove impracticable; and thus, while every proper measure is pursued, you should make up your mind to disappointment." (*F*, p. 190]

In the end, as is obvious to most readers, distinctions of human individuality themselves seem to fall away from the novel. Monster, Frankenstein, and Walton seem to become each others' relays. Frankenstein's story comes to an end in death; Walton concludes his own story within the frame of his function as letter writer. In the *narrative* conclusion, he is the natural philosopher who learns from Frankenstein's example. At the end of the *text*, the monster, having confessed his guilt toward his maker and ostensibly intending to immolate himself, is borne away on an ice raft. We do not see the conflagration of his funeral pile – the self-immolation is not consummated in the text: he too cannot be contained by the text. In terms of narrative logic, he is 'lost in darkness and distance' (*F*, p. 211) – these are the last words of the novel – into an existential temporality that is coherent with neither the territorializing individual imagination (as in the opening of *Jane Eyre*) nor the authoritative scenario of Christian psychobiography (as at the end of Brontë's work). The very relationship between sexual reproduction and social subject-production – the dynamic nineteenth-century topos of feminism-in-imperialism – remains problematic within the limits of Shelley's text and, paradoxically, constitutes its strength.

Earlier, I offered a reading of woman as womb holder in *Frankenstein*. I would now suggest that there is a framing woman in the book who is neither tangential, nor encircled, nor yet encircling. 'Mrs. Saville', 'excellent Margaret', 'beloved Sister' are her address and kinship inscriptions (F, pp. 15, 17, 22). She is the occasion, though not the protagonist, of the novel. She is the feminine *subject* rather than the female individualist: she is the irreducible *recipient-*function of the letters that constitute *Frankenstein*. I have commented on the singular appropriative hermeneutics of the reader reading with Jane in the opening pages of *Jane Eyre*. Here the reader must read with Margaret Saville in the crucial sense that she must *intercept* the recipient-function, read the letters *as* recipient, in order for the novel to exist.[28] Margaret Saville does not respond to close the text as frame. The frame is thus simultaneously not a frame, and the monster can step 'beyond the text' and be 'lost in darkness'. Within the allegory of our reading, the place of both the English lady and the unnamable monster are left open by this great flawed text. It is satisfying for a postcolonial reader to consider this a noble resolution for a nineteenth-century English novel. This is all the more striking because, on the anecdotal level, Shelley herself abundantly 'identifies' with Victor Frankenstein.[29]

I must myself close with an idea that I cannot establish within the limits of this essay. Earlier I contended that *Wide Sargasso Sea* is necessarily bound by the reach of the European novel. I suggested that, in contradistinction, to reopen the epistemic fracture of imperialism without succumbing to a nostalgia for lost origins, the critic must turn to the archives of imperialist governance. I have not turned to those archives in these pages. In my current work, by way of a modest and inexpert 'reading' or 'archives', I try to extend, outside of the reach of the European novelistic tradition, the most powerful suggestion in *Wide Sargasso Sea*: that *Jane Eyre* can be read as the orchestration and staging of the self-immolation of Bertha Mason as 'good wife'. The power of that suggestion remains unclear if we remain insufficiently knowledgeable about the history of the legal manipulation of widow-sacrifice in the entitlement of the British government in India. I would hope that an informed critique of imperialism, granted some attention from readers in the First World, will at least expand the frontiers of the politics of reading.

NOTES

1. My notion of 'worlding of the world' upon what must be assumed to be uninscribed earth is a vulgarization of Martin Heidegger's idea; see 'The Origin of the Work of Art', *Poetry, Language, Thought*, trans. Albert Hofstadter (New York, 1977), pp. 17–87.
2. See Charlotte Brontë, *Jane Eyre* (New York, 1960); all further references to this work, abbreviated *JE*, will be included in the text.
3. See Jean Rhys, *Wide Sargasso Sea* (Harmondsworth, 1966); all further references

to this work, abbreviated *WSS*, will be included in the text. And see Mary Shelley, *Frankenstein; or, The Modern Prometheus* (New York, 1965); all further references to this work, abbreviated *F*, will be included in the text.

4. I have tried to do this in my essay 'Unmaking and Making in *To the Lighthouse*', in *Women and Language in Literature and Society*, Sally McConnell-Ginet, Ruth Borker and Nelly Furman (eds) (New York, 1980), pp. 310–27.

5. As always, I take my formula from Louis Althusser, 'Ideology an Ideological State Apparatuses (Notes towards an Investigation)', *'Lenin and Philosophy' and Other Essays*, trans. Ben Brewster (New York, 1971), pp. 127–86. For an acute differentiation between the individual individualism, see V. N. Vološinov, *Marxism and the Philosophy of Language*, trans. Ladislav Matejka and I. R. Titunik, Studies in Language, vol. 1 (New York, 1973), pp. 93–3 and 152–3. For a 'straight' analysis of the roots and ramifications of English 'individualism', see C. B. MacPherson, *The Political Theory of Possessive Individualism: Hobbes to Locke* (Oxford, 1962). I am grateful to Jonathan Rée for bringing this book to my attention and for giving a careful reading of all but the very end of the present essay.

6. I am constructing an analogy with Homi Bhabha's powerful notion of 'not-quite/not-white' in his 'Of Mimicry and Man: The Ambiguity of Colonial Discourse', *October* 28 (Spring 1984): 132. I should also add that I use the word 'native' here in reaction to the term 'Third World Woman'. I cannot, of course, apply with equal historical justice to both the West Indian and the Indian contexts nor to contexts of imperialism by transportation.

7. See Roberto Fernández Retamar, 'Caliban: Notes towards a Discussion of Culture in Our America', trans. Lynn Garafola, David Arthur McMurray and Robert Márquez, *Massachusetts Review* 15 (Winter–Spring 1974): 7–72; all further references to this work, abbreviated 'C', will be included in the text.

8. See José Enrique Rodó, *Ariel*, ed. Gordon Brotherston (Cambridge, 1967).

9. For an elaboration of 'an inaccessible blankness circumscribed by an interpretable text', see my 'Can the Subaltern Speak?' in *Marxist Interpretations of Culture*, Cary Nelson (ed.) (Urbana, Ill., forthcoming).

10. See Elizabeth Fox-Genovese, 'Placing Women's History in History', *New Left Review* 133 (May–June 1982): 5–29.

11. Rudolph Ackerman, *The Repository of Arts, Literature, Commerce, Manufactures, Fashions, and Politics* (London, 1823), p. 310.

12. See Terry Eagleton, *Myths of Power: A Marxist Study of the Brontës* (London, 1975); this is one of the general presuppositions of his book.

13. See Sandra M. Gilbert and Susan Gubar. *The Madwoman in the Attic: The Woman Writer and the Nineteenth-Century Literary Imagination* (New Haven, Conn., 1979), pp. 360–2.

14. Immanuel Kant, *Critique of Practical Reason, The "Critique of Pure Reason," the "Critique of Practical Reason" and Other Ethical Treatises, the "Critique of Judgement,"* trans. J. M. D. Meiklejohn et al. (Chicago, 1952), pp. 328, 326.

15. I have tried to justify the reduction of sociohistorical problems to formulas or propositions in my essay 'Can the Subaltern Speak?' The 'travesty' I speak of does not befall the Kantian ethic in its purity as an accident but rather exists within its lineaments as a possible supplement. On the register of the human being as child rather than heathen, my formula can be found, for example, in what is Enlightenment? Kant, *"Foundations of the Metaphysics of Morals," 'What Is Englightenment?" and a Passage from "The Metaphysics of Morals,"* trans. and ed. Lewis White Beck (Chicago, 1950). I have profited from discussing Kant with Jonathan Rée.

16. Jean Rhys, in an interview with Elizabeth Vreeland, quoted in Nancy Harrison, *Jean Rhys and the Novel as Woman's Text* (Chapel Hill, NC; London: University of North Carolina Press, 1988). This is an excellent, detailed study of Rhys.

17. See Louise Vinge, *The Narcissus Theme in Western European Literature Up to the Early Nineteenth Century*, trans. Robert Dewsnap et al. (Lund, 1967), chap. 5.

18. For a detailed study of this text, see John Brenkman, 'Narcissus in the Text', *Georgia Review* 30 (Summer 1976): 293–327.

19. See, e.g., Thomas F. Staley, *Jean Rhys: A Critical Study* (Austin, Tex. 1979), pp. 108–16; it is interesting to note Staley's masculist discomfort with this and his consequent dissatisfaction with Rhys' novel.

20. I have tried to relate castration and suppressed letters in my 'The Letter As Cutting Edge', in *Literature and Psychoanalysis; The Question of Reading: Otherwise*, Shoshana Felman (ed.) (New Haven, C, 1981), pp. 208–26.

21. This is the main argument of my 'Can the Subaltern Speak?'

22. See Barbara Johnson, 'My Monster/My Self', *Diacritics* 12 (Summer 1982): 2–10.

23. See George Levine, *The Realistic Imagination: English Fiction from Frankenstein to Lady Chatterley* (Chicago, 1981), pp. 23–35.

24. Consult the publications of the Feminist International Network for the best overview of the current debate on reproductive technology.

25. For the male fetish, see Sigmund Freud, 'Fetishism', *The Standard Edition of the Complete Psychological Works of Sigmund Freud*, ed. and trans. James Strachey et al., 24 vols. (London, 1953–74), 21:152–7. For a more 'serious' Freudian study of *Frankenstein*, see Mary Jacobus, 'Is There a Woman in This Text?', *New Literary History* 14 (Autumn 1982): 117–41. My 'fantasy' would of course be disproved by the 'fact' that it is more difficult for a woman to assume the position of fetishist than for a man; see Mary Ann Doane, 'Film and the Masquerade: Theorising the Female Spectator', *Screen* 23 (Sept.–Oct. 1982): 74–87.

26. Kant, *Critique of Judgement*, trans. J. H. Bernard (New York, 1951), p. 39.

27. See [Constantin François Chasseboeuf de Volney], *The Ruins; or, Meditations on the Revolutions of Empires*, trans. pub. (London, 1811). Johannes Fabian has shown us the manipulations of time in 'new' secular histories of a similar kind; see *Time and the Other: How Anthropology Makes Its Object* (New York, 1983). See also Eric R. Wolf, *Europe and the People Without History* (Berkeley and Los Angeles, 1982), and Peter Worsley, *The Third World*, 2d ed. (Chicago, 1973); I am grateful to Dennis Dworkin for bringing the latter book to my attention. The most striking ignoring of the monster's education through Volney is in Gilbert's otherwise brilliant 'Horror's Twin: Mary Shelley's Monstrous Eve', *Feminist Studies* 4 (June 1980): 48–73. Gilbert's essay reflects the absence of race-determinations in a certain sort of feminism. Her present work has most convincingly filled in this gap; see, e.g., her recent piece on H. Rider Haggard's *She* ('Rider Haggard's Heart of Darkness', *Partisan Review* 50, no. 3 [1983]: 444–53).

28. 'A letter is always and *a priori* intercepted, . . . the "subjects" are neither the senders nor the receivers of messages. . . . The letter is constituted . . . by its interception' (Jacques Derrida, 'Discussion', after Claude Rabant, 'Il n'a aucune chance de l'entendre', in *Affranchissement: Due transfert et de la lettre*, René Major (ed.) [Paris, 1981], p. 106; my translation). Margaret Saville is not made to appropriate the reader's 'subject' into the signature of her own 'individuality'.

29. The most stiking 'internal evidence' is the admission in the 'Author's Introduction' that, after dreaming of the yet-unnamed Victor Frankenstein figure and being terrified (thought, yet not quite through, him) by the monster in a scene she later reproduced in Frankenstein's story, Shelley began her tale 'on the morrow . . . with the words 'It was on a dreary night of November"' (*F*, p. xi). Those are the opening words of chapter 5 of the finished book, where Frankenstein begins to recount the actual making of his monster (see *F*, p. 56).

3.5

'WHERE HAVE ALL THE NATIVES GONE?'

Rey Chow

THE INAUTHENTIC NATIVE

A couple of years ago, I was serving on a faculty search committee at the University of Minnesota. The search was for a specialist in Chinese language and literature. A candidate from the People's Republic of China gave a talk that discussed why we still enjoy reading the eighteenth-century classic, *The Dream of the Red Chamber*. The talk was a theoretical demonstration of how no particular interpretation of this book could exhaust the possibilities of reading. During the search committee's discussion of the various candidates afterwards, one faculty member, an American Marxist, voiced his disparaging view of this particular candidate in the following way: 'The talk was not about why we still enjoy reading *The Dream of the Red Chamber*. It was about why she enjoys reading it. She does because she likes capitalism!'

This colleague of mine stunned me with a kind of discrimination that has yet to be given its proper name. The closest designation we currently have for his attitude is racism, that is, a reduction of someone from a particular group to the stereotypes, negative *or* positive, we have of that group. But what is at stake here is not really 'race' as much as it is the assumption that a 'native' of communist China ought to be faithful to her nation's official political ideology. Instead of 'racial' characteristics, communist beliefs became the stereotype with which my colleague was reading this candidate. The fact that she did not speak from such beliefs but instead from an understanding of the text's irreducible plurality (an understanding he equated with 'capitalism') greatly disturbed him;

From: Rey Chow (1994), 'Where Have all the Natives Gone?', pp. 125–51, in Angelika Bammer (ed.), *Displacements: Cultural Identities in Question* (Bloomington: Indiana University Press).

his lament was that this candidate had betrayed our expectation of what communist 'ethnic specimens' ought to be.

My colleague's disturbance takes us to the familiarly ironic scenarios of anthropology, in which Western anthropologists are uneasy at seeing 'natives' who have gone 'civilized' or who, like the anthropologists themselves, have taken up the active task of shaping their own culture. Margaret Mead, for instance, found the interest of certain Arapesh Indians (in Highland New Guinea) in cultural influences other than their own 'annoying' since, as James Clifford puts it, '*Their* culture collecting complicated hers' (p. 232). Similarly, Claude Lévi-Strauss, doing his 'fieldwork' in New York on American ethnology, was troubled by the sight, in the New York Public Library reading room where he was doing research for his *Elementary Structures of Kinship*, of a feathered Indian with a Parker pen. As Clifford comments:

> For Lévi-Strauss the Indian is primarily associated with the past, the 'extinct' societies recorded in the precious Bureau of American Ethnology *Annual Reports*. The anthropologist feels himself 'going back in time'. . . . In modern New York an Indian can appear only as a survival or a kind of incongruous parody. (p. 245)

My colleague shares the predicament of Mead and Lévi-Strauss insofar as the stereotypical 'native' is receding from view. What confronts the Western scholar is the discomforting fact that the natives are no longer staying in their frames. In the case of the faculty search at Minnesota, what I heard was not the usual desire to *archaize* the modern Chinese person,[1] but rather a valorizing, on the part of the Western critic, of the official political and cultural difference of the People's Republic of China as the designator of the candidate's supposed 'authenticity'. If a native from the People's Republic of China espouses capitalism, then she has already been corrupted. An ethnic specimen that was not pure was not of use to him.

THE NATIVE AS IMAGE

In the politics of identifying 'authentic' natives, several strands of the word 'identification' are at stake: How do we identify the native? How do we identify with her? How do we construct the native's 'identity'? What processes of identification are involved? We cannot approach this politics without being critical of a particular relation to *images* that is in question.

In his volume of essays exploring film culture, Fredric Jameson writes that 'The visual is *essentially* pornographic. . . . Pornographic films are . . . only the potentiation of films in general, which ask us to stare at the world as though it were a naked body' (p. 1).[2] This straightforward definition of the visual image sums up many of the problems we encounter in cultural criticism today, whether or not the topic in question is film. The activity of watching is linked by projection to physical nakedness. Watching is theoretically defined as the primary agency of violence, an act that pierces the other, who inhabits the place of the passive victim on display. The image, then, is an aggressive sight that reveals itself in the other; it is the site of the aggressed. Moreover, the image is what has been devastated, left bare, and left behind by aggression – hence Jameson's view that it is naked and pornographic.

For many, the image is also the site of possible change. In many critical discourses, the image is implicitly the place where battles are fought and strategies of resistance negotiated. Such discourses try to inhabit this image-site by providing alternative sights, alternative ways of watching *that would change the image*. Thus one of the most important enterprises nowadays is that of investigating the 'subjectivity' of the other-as-oppressed-victim. 'Subjectivity' becomes a way to change the defiled image, the stripped image, the image-reduced-to-nakedness, by showing the truth behind/beneath/around it. The problem with the reinvention of subjectivity as such is that it tries to combat the politics of the image, a politics that is conducted on surfaces, by a politics of depths, hidden truths, and inner voices. The most important aspect of the image – its power precisely as image and nothing else – is thus bypassed and left untouched.[3] It is in this problematic of *the image as the bad thing to be replaced* that I lodge the following arguments about the 'native'.

The question in which I am primarily interested is: Is there a way of 'finding' the native without simply ignoring the image, or substituting a 'correct' image of the ethnic specimen for an 'incorrect' one, or giving the native a 'true' voice 'behind' her 'false' image? How could we deal with the native in an age when there is no possibility of avoiding the reduction/abstraction of the native as image? How can we write about the native by not ignoring the defiled, degraded image that is an inerasable part of her status – that is, by not resorting to the idealist belief that everything would be all right if the inner truth of the native were restored because the inner truth would lead to the 'correct' image? I want to highlight the native – nowadays often a synonym for the oppressed, the marginalized, the wronged – because I think that the space occupied by the native in postcolonial discourses is also the space of error, illusion, deception and filth. How would we write this space in such a way as to refuse the facile turn of sanctifying the defiled image with pieties and thus enriching ourselves precisely with what can be called the surplus value of the oppressed, a surplus value that results from *exchanging* the defiled image for something more noble?

The Native As Silent Object

The production of the native is in part the production of our postcolonial modernity. Before elaborating on the relation between 'native' and 'modernity', however, I want to examine how current theoretical discussions of the native problematize the space of the native in the form of a symptom of the white man. Following Lacan, I use 'symptom' not in the derogatory sense of a dispensable shadow but in the sense of something that gives the subject its ontological consistency and its fundamental structure. Slavoj Žižek explains the non-pejorative sense of 'symptom' this way:

> If, however, we conceive the symptom as Lacan did in his last writings and seminars, namely as a particular signifying formation which confers on the subject its very ontological consistency, enabling it to structure its basic, constitutive relationship towards enjoyment (*jouissance*), then the entire relationship [between subject and symptom] is reversed, for if the symptom is dissolved, the subject itself disintegrates. In this sense, 'Woman is a symptom of man' means that man himself exists only through woman qua his symptom: his very ontological consistency depends on, is 'externalized' in, his symptom. ('Rossellini' p. 21)

As the white man's symptom, as that which is externalized in relation to the white-man-as-subject, the space occupied by the native is essentially objective, the space of the object.

Because of the symptomatic way non-white peoples are constructed in post-coloniality and because 'symptom' is conventionally regarded in a secondary, derivative sense, many critics of colonialism attempt to write about these peoples in such a way as to wrest them away from their status as symptom or object. The result is a certain inevitable subjectivizing, and here the anti-imperialist project runs a parallel course with the type of feminist project that seeks to restore the truth to women's distorted and violated identities by theorizing female subjectivity. We see this in Frantz Fanon's formulation of the native. Like Freud's construction of woman (which, though criticized, is repeated by many feminists), Fanon's construction of the native is Oedipal. Freud's question was 'What does woman want?' Fanon, elaborating on the necessity of violence in the native's formation, asks, 'What does the black man want?'[4] The native (the black man) is thus imagined to be an angry son who wants to displace the white man, the father. While Freud would go on to represent woman as lack, Fanon's argument is that the native is someone from whom something has been stolen. The native, then, is also lack.

This Oedipal structure of thinking – a structure of thinking that theorizes subjectivity as compensation for a presumed lack – characterizes discourses on the non-West in a pervasive manner, including, occasionally, the discourse of those who are otherwise critical of its patriarchal overtones. In her reading of Julia Kristeva's *About Chinese Women*, for instance, Gayatri Spivak criticizes Kristeva's ethnocentric sense of 'alienation' at the sight of some Chinese women in Huxian Square. Kristeva's passage goes as follows:

> An enormous crowd is sitting in the sun: they wait for us wordlessly, perfectly still. Calm eyes, not even curious, but slightly amused or anxious: in any case, piercing, and certain of belonging to a community with which we will never have anything to do. (p. 11)

Citing this passage, which is followed a few pages later by the question, 'Who is speaking, then, before the stare of the peasants at Huxian?' (p. 15), Spivak charges Kristeva for being primarily interested in her own identity rather than in these other women's. While I agree with this observation, I find Spivak's formulation of these other women's identity in terms of 'envy' troubling:

> Who is speaking here? An effort to answer that question might have revealed more about the mute women of Huxian Square, *looking with qualified envy* at the 'incursion of the West'. ('French Feminism', p. 141; my emphasis)

Doesn't the word 'envy' here remind us of that condition ascribed to women by Freud, against which feminists revolt – namely, 'penis envy'? 'Envy' is the other side of the 'violence' of which Fanon speaks as the fundamental part of the native's formation. But both affects – the one of wanting to *have* what the other has; the other, of destroying the other so that one can *be* in his place – are affects produced by a patriarchal ideology that assumes that the other at the low side of the hierarchy of self/other is 'lacking' (in the pejorative, undesirable sense). Such an ideology, while acknowledging that a lack cannot be filled, also concentrates on how it might be filled (by the same thing), even if imperfectly. The fate of the native is then like that of Freud's woman: Even though she will never have a penis, she will for the rest of her life be trapped within the longing for it and its substitutes.

What we see in the accounts by Kristeva and Spivak is a battle for demonstrating the *unspeaking* truth of the native. While Spivak shows how the articulation of the Western critic is itself already a sign of her privileged identity, for Kristeva it is the limits of Western articulation and articulation itself that have to be recognized in the presence of the silent Chinese women. Throughout Kristeva's encounter with these women, therefore, we find descriptions of the others' looking – their 'calm eyes', their 'indefinable stare' (p. 13), and so on – that try to capture their undisturbed presence. If these others have been turned into objects, it is because these objects' gaze makes the Western 'subject' feel alienated from her own familiar (familial) humanity:

> They don't distinguish among us man or woman, blonde or brunette, this or that feature of face or body. As though they were discovering some weird and peculiar animals, harmless but insane. (p. 11)

> I don't feel like a foreigner, the way I do in Baghdad or New York. I feel like an ape, a martian, an *other*. (p. 12)

Between a critical desire to subjectivize them with envy and a 'humble' gesture to revere them as silent objects, is there any alternative for these 'natives'?

Kristeva's way of 'giving in' to the strangeness of the other is a philosophical and semiotic gesture that characterizes many European intellectuals, whose discourse becomes self-accusatory and, *pace* Rousseau, confessional when confronted by the other.[5] When that other is Asia and the 'Far East', it always seems as if the European intellectual must speak in absolute terms, making this other an utterly incomprehensible, terrifying and fascinating spectacle. For example, after visiting Japan, Alexandre Kojève, who had asserted that history had come to an end (he was convinced of this in the United States, where he thought he found the 'classless society' predicted by Marx as the goal of human history), wrote a long footnote to the effect that his experience with the Japanese had radically changed his opinion about history. For Kojève in 1959, like Roland Barthes about a decade later, the formalized rituals of Japanese society suggested that the Japanese had arrived at the end of history three centuries earlier. As Barthes would say, semiologically, that Japanese culture is made up of empty signs, Kojève writes:

> all Japanese without exception are currently in a position to live according to totally *formalized* values – that is, values completely empty of all 'human' content in the 'historical' sense. Thus, in the extreme, every Japanese is in principle capable of committing, from pure snobbery, a perfectly 'gratuitous' *suicide*. . . . (p. 162)[6]

Michel Serres, on the other hand, also finds 'the end of history' when he goes east, but it is in agricultural China that he finds the absolute totality of the other. Confronted with the Chinese who have to make use of every bit of land for cultivation, Serres comments with statements like the following in an essay called 'China Loam':

> Farming has covered over everything like a tidal wave.
> It is the totality.
> This positiveness is so complete, so compact, that it can only be expressed negatively. There is no margin, no gap, no passes, no omission, no waste, no vestiges. The fringe, the fuzzy area, the refuse, the wasteland, the open-space have all disappeared: no surplus, no vacuum, no history, no time. (p. 5)
>
> Here the utmost limit of what we call history had already been reached a thousand years ago. (p. 6)

To the extent that it is our own limit that we encounter when we encounter another, all these intellectuals can do is to render the other as the negative of what they are and what they do. As Serres puts it, the spectacle of China's total rationality is so 'positive, so rational, so well-adapted that one can only speak of it in negative terms' (p. 5). As such, the 'native' is turned into an absolute entity in the form of an image (the 'empty' Japanese ritual or 'China loam'), whose silence becomes the occasion for *our* speech.[7] The gaze of the Western scholar is 'pornographic' and the native becomes a mere 'naked body' in the sense described by Jameson. Whether positive or negative, the construction of the native remains at the level of image-identification, a process in which 'our' own identity is measured in terms of the degrees to which we resemble her and to which she resembles us. Is there a way of conceiving of the native beyond imagistic resemblance?

This question is what prompts Spivak's bold and provocative statement, 'The subaltern cannot speak'.[8] Because it seems to cast the native permanently in the form of a silent object, Spivak's statement foreseeably gives rise to pious defences of the native as a voiced subject and leads many to jump on the bandwagon of declaring solidarity with 'subalterns' of different kinds. Speaking sincerely of the multiple voices of the native woman thus, Benita Parry criticizes Spivak for assigning an absolute power to the imperialist discourse:

> Since the native woman is constructed within multiple social relationships and positioned as the product of different class, caste and cultural specificities, it should be possible to locate traces and testimony of women's voice on those sites where women inscribed themselves as healers, ascetics, singers of sacred songs, artisans and artists, and by this to modify Spivak's model of the silent subaltern. (p. 35)

In contrast to Spivak, Parry supports Homi Bhabha's argument that since a discursive system is inevitably split in enunciation, the colonist's text itself already contains a native voice – ambivalently. The colonial text's 'hybridity', to use Bhabha's word, means that the subaltern has spoken (pp. 39–43).[9] But what kind of an argument is it to say that the subaltern's 'voice' can be found in the *ambivalence* of the imperialist's speech? It is an argument which ultimately makes it unnecessary to come to terms with the subaltern since she has already 'spoken', as it were, in the system's gaps. All we would need to do would be to continue to study – to deconstruct – the rich and ambivalent language of the imperialist! What Bhabha's word 'hybridity' revives, in the masquerade of deconstruction, anti-imperialism and 'difficult' theory, is an old functionalist notion of what a dominant culture permits in the interest of maintaining its own equilibrium. Such functionalism informs the investigatory methods of classical anthropology and sociology as much as it does the colonial policies of the British Empire. The kind of subject constitution it allows, a subject constitution firmly inscribed in Anglo-American liberal humanism, is the other side of the process of image-identification, in which we try to make the native more like us by giving her a 'voice'.

The charge of Spivak's essay, on the other hand, is a protest against the *two* sides of image-identification, the *two* types of freedom the subaltern has been allowed – object formation and subject constitution – which would result either in the subaltern's protection (as object) from her own kind or her achievement as a voice assimilable to the project of imperialism. That is why Spivak concludes by challenging precisely the optimistic view that the subaltern has already spoken: 'The subaltern cannot speak. There is no virtue in global laundry lists with "woman" as a pious item" ('Subaltern', p. 308).

Instead, a radical alternative can be conceived only when we recognize the essential *untranslatability* from the subaltern discourse to imperialist discourse. Using Jean-François Lyotard's notion of the *différend*, which Spivak explains as 'the inaccessibility of, or untranslatability from, one mode of discourse in a dispute to another' ('Subaltern' p. 300), she argues the impossibility of the sub-altern's constitution *in life*.[10] The subaltern cannot speak, not because there are not activities in which we can locate a subaltern mode of life/culture/subjectiv-ity, but because, as is indicated by the critique of thought and articulation given to us by Western intellectuals such as Lacan, Foucault, Barthes, Kristeva and Derrida (Spivak's most important reference), 'speaking' itself belongs to an already well-defined structure and history of domination. As Spivak says in an interview: 'If the subaltern can speak then, thank God, the subaltern is not a subaltern any more' ('New Historicism' p. 158).

It is only when we acknowledge the fact that the subaltern cannot speak that we can begin to plot a different kind of process of identification for the native. It follows that, within Spivak's argument, it is a *silent* gesture on the part of a young Hindu woman, Bhuvaneswari Bhaduri, who committed suicide during her menstruation so that the suicide could not be interpreted as a case of illicit pregnancy, that becomes a telling instance of subaltern writing, a writing whose message is only understood retrospectively ('Subaltern' pp. 307–8). As such, the 'identity' of the native is inimitable, beyond the resemblance of the image. The type of identification offered by her silent space is what may be called symbolic identification. In the words of Slavoj Žižek:

> in imaginary identification we imitate the other at the level of resemblance – we identify ourselves with the image of the other inasmuch as we are 'like him', while in symbolic identification we identify ourselves with the other precisely at a point at which he is inimitable, at the point which eludes resemblance. (*Sublime Object*, p. 109)

LOCAL RESURRECTIONS, NEW HISTORIES

As an issue of postcoloniality, the problem of the native is also the problem of modernity and modernity's relation to 'endangered authenticities' (Clifford, p. 5). The question to ask is not whether we can return the native to her authen-tic origin, but what our fascination with the native means in terms of the irre-versibility of modernity.

There are many commendable accounts of how the native in the non-Western world has been used by the West as a means to promote and develop its own intellectual contours.[11] According to these accounts, modernism, especially the modernism that we associate with the art of Modigliani, Picasso, Gauguin, the novels of Gustave Flaubert, Marcel Proust, D. H. Lawrence, James Joyce, Henry Miller and so forth, was possible only because these 'first world' artists with famous names incorporated into their 'creativity' the culture and art work of the peoples of the non-West. But while Western artists continue to receive attention specifically categorized in time, place and name, the treatment of the works of non-Western peoples continues to partake of systemic patterns of exploitation and distortion.

Apart from the general attribution of 'anonymity' to native artists, 'native works' have been bifurcated either as timeless (in which case they would go into art museums) or as historical (in which case they would go into ethnographic museums). While most cultural critics today are alert to the pitfalls of the 'timeless art' argument, many are still mired in efforts to invoke 'history', 'contexts', and 'specificities' as ways to resurrect the native. In doing so, are they restoring to the native what has been stolen from her? Or are they in fact avoiding the genuine problem of the native's status as object by providing *something* that is more manageable and comforting – namely, a phantom history in which natives appear as our equals and our images, in our shapes and our forms? Nancy Armstrong summarizes our predicament this way:

> The new wave of culture criticism still assumes that we must either be a subject who partakes in the power of gazing or else be an object that is by implication the object of a pornographic gaze. The strategy of identifying people according to 'subject positions' in a vast and intricate differential system of interests and needs is perhaps the most effective way we now have of avoiding the problem incurred whenever we classify political interests by means of bodies inscribed with signs of race, class, and gender. But even the 'subject' of the critical term 'subject position' tends to dissolve too readily back into a popular and sentimental version of the bourgeois self. By definition, this self grants priority to an embodied subject over the body as an object. To insist on being 'subjects' as opposed to 'objects' is to assume that we must have certain powers of observation, classification, and definition in order to exist; these powers make 'us' human. According to the logic governing such thinking as it was formulated in the nineteenth century, only certain kinds of subjects are really subjects; to be human, anyone must be one of 'us'. (p. 33)

As we challenge a dominant discourse by 'resurrecting' the victimized voice/self of the native with our readings – and such is the impulse behind many 'new historical' accounts – we step, far too quickly, into the otherwise silent and invisible place of the native and turn ourselves into living agents/witnesses for her. This process, in which *we* become visible, also neutralizes the untranslatability of the native's experience and the history of that untranslatability. The hasty supply of original 'contexts' and 'specificities' easily becomes complicitous with the dominant discourse, which achieves hegemony precisely by its capacity to convert, recode, make transparent and thus represent even those experiences that resist it with a stubborn opacity. The danger of historical contextualization turning into cultural corporations is what leads Clifford to say:

> I do not argue, as some critics have, that non-Western objects are properly understood only with reference to their original milieux. Ethnographic contextualizations are as problematic as aesthetic ones, as susceptible to purified, ahistorical treatment. (p. 12)

The problem of modernity, then, is not simply an 'amalgamating' of 'disparate experience'[12] but rather the confrontation between what are now called the 'first' and 'third' worlds in the form of the *différend*, that is, the untranslatability of 'third world' experiences into the 'first world'. This is because, in order for her experience to become translatable, the 'native' cannot simply 'speak' but must also provide the justice/justification for her speech, a justice/justification that has been destroyed in the encounter with the imperialist.[13] The native's victimization consists in the fact that the active evidence – the original witness – of her victimization may no longer exist in any intelligible, coherent shape. Rather than saying that the native has already spoken because the dominant hegemonic discourse is split/hybrid/different from itself, and rather than restoring her to her 'authentic' context, we should argue that it is the native's silence which is the most important clue to her displacement. That silence is at once the *evidence* of imperialist oppression (the naked body, the defiled image) and what, in the absence of the original witness to that oppression, must act in its place by *performing* or *feigning* as the preimperialist gaze.

A Brown Man's Eye for a White Man's Eye

As part of my argument, I read an anti-imperialist text whose intentions are both antipornographic (anti-the-bad-'image'-thing) and restorative. Despite such intentions, this text is, I believe, an example of how cultural criticism can further engender exploitation of the native, who is crossed out not once (by the imperialist forces of domination), nor twice (by the cultural processes of subjection), but three times – the third time by the anti-imperialist critic himself.

In his book, *The Colonial Harem*, Malek Alloula focuses on picture post cards of Algerian women produced and sent home by the French during the early decades of the twentieth century. Alloula's point is a simple one, namely, that these native women have been used as a means to represent a European phantasm of the Oriental female. The mundane postcard therefore supports, through its pornographic gaze at the female native, the larger French colonial project in Algeria. Alloula describes his own undertaking as an attempt 'to return this immense postcard to its sender' (p. 5).

There is no return to any origin which is not already a construction and therefore a kind of writing. Here Alloula writes by explicitly identifying with the naked or half-naked women: 'What I read on these cards does not leave me indifferent. It demonstrates to me, were that still necessary, the desolate poverty of *a gaze that I myself*, as an Algerian, *must have been the object of* at some moment in my personal history; (p. 5; my emphasis). This claim of identification with the women as image and as object notwithstanding, the male critic remains invisible himself. If the picture postcards are the kind of *evidence-and-witness* of the oppression of the native that I have been talking about, then what happens in Alloula's text is an attempt to fill in the space left open by the silent women by a self-appointed gesture of witnessing, which turns into a second gaze at the 'images' of French colonialism. The Algerian women are exhibited as objects not only by the French but also by Alloula's discourse. Even though the male critic sympathizes with the natives, his status as invisible writing subject is essentially *different from*, not identical with, the status of the pictures in front of us.

The anti-imperialist charge of Alloula's discourse would have us believe that the French gaze at these women is pornographic while his is not. This is so because he distinguishes between erotism and pornography, calling the picture postcards a 'suberotism' (which is the book title in French and the title of the last chapter). In her introduction to the book, Barbara Harlow supports the point of Alloula's project by citing Spivak's statement, 'brown women saved by white men from brown men' (p. xviii).[14] In effect, however, because Alloula is intent on captivating the essence of the colonizer's discourse as a way to retaliate against his enemy, his own discourse coincides much more closely with the enemy's than with the women's. What emerges finally is not an identification between the critic and the images of the women as he wishes, but an identification between the critic and the gaze of the colonialist-photographer *over the images of the women*, which become bearers of multiple exploitations. Because Alloula's identification is with the gaze of the colonialist-photographer, the women remain frozen in their poses.[15] The real question raised by Alloula's text is therefore not, 'Can brown women be saved from brown men by white men?', but 'Can brown women be saved from white men by brown men?'

Alloula writes: 'A reading of the sort that I propose to undertake would be entirely superfluous if there existed photographic traces of the gaze of the colonized upon the colonizer' (p. 5). The problem of a statement like this lies in the way it hierarchizes the possibilities of native discourse: had there been photographs that reciprocate in a symmetrical fashion the exploitative gaze of the colonizer, he says, he would not have to write his book. His book is second best. The desire for revenge – to do to the enemy *exactly* what the enemy did to him, so that colonizer and colonized would meet eye to eye – is the fantasy of envy and violence that has been running throughout masculinist anti-imperialist discourse since Fanon. This fantasy, as I have already suggested, is Oedipal in structure.

To make his project what he intended it to be – a *symbolic* identification, as defined by Žižek, with the native women not only as images but also as oppressed victims with their own stories – Alloula would need to follow either one of two alternatives. The first of these would require, in a manner characteristic of the poststructuralist distrust of anything that seems 'spontaneous' or 'self-evident', a careful reading of the materiality of the images.[16] Such a reading would show that what is assumed to be pornographic is not necessarily so, but is more often a projection, on to the images, of the photographer's (or viewer's) own repression.[17] As it stands, however, Alloula's 'reading' only understands the images in terms of *content* rather than as a signifying process which bears alternative clues of reading that may well undo its supposed messages. Alloula bases his reading on very traditional assumptions of the visual as the naked, by equating photography with a 'scopic desire' to unveil what is 'inside' the women's clothes, etc. Thus he not only confirms Jameson's notion that 'the visual is essentially pornographic' but unwittingly provides a demonstration of how this is so in his own anti-pornographic writing.

On the other hand, if the problem with poststructuralist analysis is that it too happily dissolves the pornographic obviousness of the images and thus misses their abusive structuration, then a second alternative would have been for Alloula to exclude images from his book. Alloula's entire message could have been delivered verbally. Instead, the images of the Algerian women are exposed a second time and made to stand as a transparent medium, a homoerotic link connecting the brown man to the white man, connecting 'third world' nationalism to 'first world' imperialism. What results is neither a dissembling of the pornographic apparatus of imperialist domination nor a restoration of the native to her 'authentic' history, but a perfect symmetry between the imperialist and anti-imperialist gazes, which cross over the images of native women as silent objects.

THE NATIVE IN THE AGE OF DISCURSIVE REPRODUCTION

Modernity is ambivalent in its very origin. In trying to become 'new' and 'novel' – a kind of primary moment – it must incessantly deal with its connection with what *precedes* it – what was primary to it – in the form of a destruction. As Paul de Man writes, 'modernity exists in the form of a desire to wipe out whatever came earlier, in the hope of reaching at last a point that could be called a true present, a point of origin that marks a new departure' (p. 148). If the impetus of modernity is a criticism of the past, then much of our cultural criticism is still modernist.

Many accounts of modernity view the world retrospectively, in sadness. The world is thought of as a vast collection, a museum of lives which has been more or less stabilized for/by our gaze. To an anthropologist like Lévi-Strauss in the 1940s a city like New York 'anticipates humanity's entropic future and gathers up its diverse pasts in decontextualized, collectible forms' (Clifford p. 244). The cosmopolitanizing of humanity also signals the vanishing of human diversity, an event the modern anthropologist laments. Isn't there much similarity between the nostalgic culture-collecting of a Lévi-Strauss and what is being undertaken in the name of 'new historicism', which always argues for preserving the 'specifics' of particular cultures? Despite the liberalist political outlook of many of its practitioners, the new historical enterprise often strikes one as being in agreement with Francis Fukuyama's pronouncement about 'the end of history':

> In the post-historical period there will be neither art nor philosophy, just the perpetual caretaking of the museum of human history. I can feel in myself, and see in others around me, a powerful nostalgia for the time when history existed. (p. 18)

Why are we so fascinated with 'history' and with the 'native' in 'modern' times? What do we gain from our labor on these 'endangered authenticities' which are presumed to be from a different time and a different place? What can be said about the juxtaposition of 'us' (our discourse) and 'them'? What kind of *surplus value* is derived from this juxtaposition?

These questions are also questions about the irreversibility of modernity. In the absence of that original witness of the native's destruction, and in the untranslatability of the native's discourse into imperialist discourse, natives, like commodities, become knowable only through routes that diverge from their original 'homes'. Judging from the interest invested by contemporary cultural studies in the 'displaced native', we may say that the native is precisely caught up in the twin process of what Arjun Appadurai calls 'commoditization by diversion' and 'the aesthetics of decontextualization', a process in which

> value . . . is accelerated or enhanced by placing objects and things in unlikely contexts . . . Such diversion is . . . an instrument . . . of the (potential) intensification of commoditization by the enhancement of value attendant upon its diversion. This enhancement of value through the diversion of commodities from their customary circuits underlies the plunder of enemy valuables in warfare, the purchase and display of 'primitive' utilitarian objects, the framing of 'found' objects, the making of collections of any sort. In all these examples, diversions of things combine the aesthetic impulse, the entrepreneurial link, and the touch of the morally shocking. (p. 28)

Appadurai, whose intention is to argue that 'commodities, like persons, have social lives' (p. 3), refrains from including human beings in his account of commodities. By centering the politics of commoditization on *things* in exchange, he anthropomorphizes things but avoids blurring the line between things and people, and thus preserves the safe boundaries of an old, respectable humanism. However, the most critical implication of his theory begins precisely where he stops. Where Appadurai would not go on, we must, and say that *persons, like things, have commodified lives*: The commoditization of 'ethnic specimens' is *already* part of the conceptualization of 'the social life of things' indicated in the title of his volume. The forces of commoditization, as part and parcel of the 'process' of modernity, do not distinguish between things and people.

To elaborate this, let us turn for a moment to the texts of that great modernist, Walter Benjamin. I have in mind 'Eduard Fuchs: Collector and Historian', 'The Work of Art in the Age of Mechanical Reproduction', and 'Theses on the Philosophy of History'. Together these texts offer a writing of the native that has yet to be fully recognized.

Benjamin was himself a passionate collector of books, art and other objects.[18] As an allegorist, Benjamin's writing is often remarkable for the way it juxtaposes dissimilar things, allowing them to illuminate one another suddenly and unexpectedly. Such is the way he reads the 'modernity' of the collector and the making of literature by a poet like Baudelaire. Like the process of 'commoditization by diversion' described by Appadurai, Baudelaire's poetry specializes in wresting things from their original contexts. Following Benjamin's allegorical method, I juxtapose his description of Baudelaire with anthropologist Sally Price's description of modernist art collecting:

> Tearing things out of the context of their usual interrelations – which is quite normal where commodities are being exhibited – is a procedure very characteristic of Baudelaire. (Benjamin, 'Central Park' p. 41)

> Once rescued from their homes among the termites and the elements, the objects come into the protective custody of Western owners, something like orphans from a Third-World war, where they are kept cool, dry, and dusted, and where they are loved and appreciated. (Price p. 76)

Such a juxtaposition makes way for a reading of Benjamin's theses of *history* against the background of primitive art in civilized places (to allude to the title of Price's book). What emerges in this reading is not so much the violence of Benjamin's messianism as the affinity and comparableness between that violence and the violence of modernist collecting. Think, for instance, of the notion of 'a fight for the history of the oppressed'. If we refuse, for the time being, the common moralistic reading of this notion (a reading which emphasizes the salvational aspect of Benjamin's writings and which dominates Benjamin scholarship) and instead insert 'the oppressed' into the collection of things that fascinate Benjamin, we see that 'the oppressed' shares a similar status with a host of other cultural objects – books, antiques, art, toys and prostitutes. The language of fighting, plundering, stealing and abducting is uniformly the language of 'wresting objects from native settings' (Price p. 74). The violent concept that is often quoted by Benjamin lovers as a way to read against 'progress' – the concept of blasting open the continuum of history[19] – is as much a precise description of imperialism's relentless destruction of local cultures as it is a 'politically correct' metaphor for redeeming the history of 'the oppressed'.

By underlining the mutual implication of Benjamin's discourse and the discourse of imperialism, my aim is not that of attacking the 'ambiguous' or 'problematic' moral stance of Benjamin the writer. Rather, it is to point out the ever-changing but ever-present complicity between our critical articulation and the political environment at which that articulation is directed. Because of this, whenever the oppressed, the native, the subaltern, and so forth are used to represent the point of 'authenticity' for our critical discourse, they become at the same time the place of myth-making and an escape from the impure nature of political realities. In the same way that 'native imprints' suggest 'primitivism' in modernist art, we turn, increasingly with fascination, to the oppressed to locate a 'genuine' critical origin.

Consider now Benjamin's argument in the essay with which we are all familiar, 'The Work of Art in the Age of Mechanical Reproduction'. The usual understanding of this essay is that Benjamin is describing a process in which the technology of mechanical reproduction has accelerated to such a degree that it is no longer relevant to think of the 'original' of any art work. The age of mechanical reproduction is an age in which the aura of art – its ties to a particular place, culture, or ritual – is in decline. Benjamin is at once nostalgic about the aura and enchanted by its loss. While the aura represents art's close relation with the community that generates it, the loss of the aura is the sign of art's emancipation into mass culture, a new collective culture of 'collectibles'.

For our present purposes, we can rethink the aura of an art object as that 'historical specificity' which makes it unique to a particular place at a particular time. The vast machines of modernist production and reproduction now make this 'historical specificity' a thing of the past and a concept in demise. Instead of the authentic, mysterious work with its irreproducible aura, we have technologically reproduced 'copies' which need not have the original as a referent in the market of mass culture. The original, marked by some unique difference that sets it apart from the mass-produced copies, becomes now a special prize of collectors with exquisite but old-fashioned 'taste'.

Benjamin's notion of the aura and its decline partakes of the contradictions inherent to modernist processes of displacement and identification. The displaced object is both a sign of violence and of 'progress'. Purloined aggressively from its original place, this displaced object becomes infinitely reproducible in the cosmopolitan space. Displacement constitutes identity, but as such it is the identity of the ever-shifting. Benjamin shows how the new reproductive technology such as film brings the object within close proximity to the viewer and at the same time allows the viewer to experiment with different viewing positions. From the perspective of the 1990s, the irony of Benjamin's 1936 essay is that while he associated the new perceptive possibilities brought by mechanical reproduction with communist cultural production, he was actually describing the modes of receptivity that have become standard fare for audiences in the capitalist world.[20]

Such contradictions help in some way to explain the double-edged process in which we find ourselves whenever we try to resuscitate the 'ethnic specimen' or 'native cultures'. Once again, we need to extend Benjamin's conceptualization, a conceptualization that is ostensibly only about objects – works of art and their mechanical reproduction – to human beings. Once we do that, we see that in our fascination with the 'authentic native', we are actually engaged in a search for the equivalent of the aura even while our search processes themselves take us farther and farther away from that 'original' point of identification. Although we act like good communists who dream of finding and serving the 'real people', we actually live and work like dirty capitalists accustomed to switching channels constantly. As we keep switching channels and browsing through different 'local' cultures, we produce an infinite number of 'natives', all with predictably automaton-like features that do not so much de-universalize Western hegemony as they confirm its protean capacity for infinite displacement. The 'authentic' native, like the aura in a kind of *mise en abîme*, keeps receding from our grasp. Meanwhile our machinery churns out inauthentic and imperfect natives who are always already copies. The most radical message offered to us by Benjamin's texts is that the commodified aspects of mass reproduction, often described with existentialist angst as alienated labor, are actually a displacement *structural* to the modernist handling of history, in which the problematic of the authentic native now returns with a vengeance. We could rewrite the title of Benjamin's essay as 'The Native in the Age of Discursive Reproduction'.

In his lecture at the Annual Conference of the Semiotic Society of America in the fall of 1990, J. Hillis Miller returns to Benjamin's remarkable essay as part of a discussion about cultural studies in the age of digital reproduction.[21] One of the scandalous points Miller makes is that Benjamin's formulation of communism and fascism in terms of the 'politicization of art' and the 'aestheticization of politics' is actually a reversible one.[22] Therein lies its danger. What Miller means is that what begins as a mobilization for political change based on an interest in/respect for the cultural difference of our others (the politicization of art) can easily grow into its ugly opposite. That is to say, the promotion of a type of politics that is based on the need to distinguish between 'differences' may consequently lead, as in the case of the Nazis, to an oppression that springs from the transformation of 'difference' into 'superiority'. Any pride that 'we' are stronger, healthier and more beautiful can become, in effect, the aestheticization of politics.

Accordingly, it is ironic that in much of the work we do in cultural studies today, we resort to cultural/ethnic/local 'difference' not as an open-ended process but as a preordained fact. The irony is that such a valorization of cultural difference occurs at a time when difference-as-aura-of-the-original has long been problematized by the very availability – and increasing indispensability – of our reproductive apparatuses. Following the drift of Benjamin's argument, Miller writes:

> this celebration of cultural specificity has occurred at a time when that specificity is being drastically altered by technological and other changes that are leading to internationalization of art and of culture generally. The work of cultural studies inevitably participates in that uprooting. . . . [A]rchival work . . . is another form of the digital reproduction that puts everything on the same plane of instant availability. . . . By a paradox familiar to anthropologists, the effort of understanding, preservation, and celebration participates in the drastic alteration of the cultures it would preserve. The more cultural studies try to save and empower local cultures the more they may endanger them. (p. 18)

For Miller, to hang on to the 'local' as the absolutely different – that is, absolutely identical with itself – means to attempt to hang onto a rigid stratification of the world in the age of digital reproduction:

if the politicizing of art is only the specular image of the aestheticizing of politics, can the former as exemplified in cultural studies be exempt from the terrible possibilities of the aestheticizing of politics? . . . [T]he more cultural studies works for the celebration, preservation, and empowerment of subordinated cultures the more it may aid in the replication of just those political orders it would contest. . . . Are not cultural studies caught in a form of the penchant of all national aestheticisms and aesthetic nationalisms toward war? (pp. 19–20)

The Native as other and Other

So far my argument has demonstrated a few things. I present the place of the native as that of the image and the silent object, which is often equated with a kind of 'lack' in a pejorative sense. After Fanon, we tend to fill this lack with a type of discourse that posits envy and violence as the necessary structure of the native's subjectivity. Corresponding to this is the wave of 'new history' which wants to resurrect the native by restoring her to her original context. But new historicism, as a modernist collecting of culture specimens, inevitably comes up against its own aporia, namely, that the possibility of *gathering* 'endangered authenticities' is also the possibility of dispensing with the authentic altogether. This is indicated by the collage of Benjamin's critical items – history, collecting, and the mechanical reproduction of art – in which the aura is experienced only in ruin. We are left with the question of how cultural difference can be imagined without being collapsed into the neutrality of a globalist technocracy (as the possibilities of mechanical reproduction imply) and without being frozen into the lifeless 'image' of the other that we encounter in Alloula's book.

Alloula's book is disturbing because its use of the image, albeit a problematic one, nonetheless confronts us with the reality of a *relation* which is neither innocuous nor avoidable. This is the relation between technological reproduction and cultural displacement. If technological reproduction is inevitable, is not cultural displacement also? If cultural displacement is conceived derogatorily, must technological reproduction be condemned moralistically then? Does the necessity of the first make the second a necessary virtue, or does the problematic nature of the second render the first equally problematic? This nexus of questions becomes most poignant when the representation of the 'native' is not only in the form of a visual other, but explicitly in the form of a pornographic image produced by the technology of photography. Should the criticism of this kind of image lead to 1) the criticism of the visual image itself (if, as Jameson says, the visual is essentially pornographic); 2) an alternative form of conceiving of 'otherness' that is completely free of the image; and 3) a subsequent construction of the 'native' as 'truth' rather than 'falsehood'?

While we have no simple answer to these questions, we know that 'false' images are going to remain with us whether or not we like it. That is not simply because they are willfully planted there by individuals desiring to corrupt the world; rather it is because the image itself is traditionally always regarded with suspicion, as a site of duplicity if not of direct degeneration. Is there a way in which we can re-imagine our relation to the 'pornographic' image of the native?

Ever since Jean-Jacques Rousseau, the native has been imagined as a kind of total other – a utopian image whose imaginary self-sufficiency is used as a stage for the incomplete (or 'antagonistic')[23] nature of human society. Rousseau's savage is 'self-sufficient' because he possesses *nothing* and is in that sense indifferent and independent. The true difference between the savage and civil man is that man is completable only through others; that is, his identity is always obtained through otherness:

> the savage lives within himself; social man lives always outside himself; he knows how to live only in the opinion of others, it is, so to speak, from their judgment alone that he derives the sense of his own experience. (p. 136)

Rousseau's formulation of the native is interesting not simply because of its idealism. To be sure, this idealism continues to be picked up by other intellectuals such as Kristeva, Barthes, Serres, and others, who (mis)apply it to *specific other cultures*. In doing so, they limit and thus demolish the most important aspect of Rousseau's text, which is that the idealized native is, literally, topographically *nowhere*. No cruise ship ever takes us to see a self-sufficient 'native', nor are the remains of any such person to be found at any archeological site.

Rousseau's savage is, then, not simply a cultural 'other', but, in Lacanian language, the Other (big Other) that exists before 'separation', before the emergence of the *object petit a*, the name for those subjectivized, privatized; and missing parts of the whole.[24] Why is this important? Because it enables us to imagine the native in a way that has been foreclosed by the Manichaean aesthetics[25] in which she is always already cast – as the white man's other, as the degraded and falsified image, as the subject constituted solely by her envy and violence, *and* as the 'identity' that can never free itself of any of this 'pornography'. My invocation of the big Other is hence not an attempt to depoliticize the realities of displaced identities in the postimperialist world; rather, it is an attempt to broaden that politics to include more *general* questions of exploitation, resistance and survival by using the historical experience of the 'native' as its shifting ground.

A moment in Homi Bhabha's reading of Fanon suggests a similar attempt at a more extended politics when he points out how Fanon, writing in times of political urgency, has limited it to the colonial situation:

> At times Fanon attempts too close a correspondence between the *mise-en-scène* of unconscious fantasy and the phantoms of racist fear and hate that stalk the colonial scene; he turns too hastily from the ambivalences of identification to the antagonistic identities of political alienation and cultural discrimination; he is too quick to name the Other, to personalize its presence in the language of colonial racism – 'the real Other for the white

man is and will continue to be the black man. And conversely'. These attempts, in Fanon's words, to restore the dream to its proper political time and cultural space can, at times, blunt the edge of Fanon's brilliant illustrations of the complexity of psychic projections in the pathological colonial relation. ("'What Does the Black Man Want?"' p. 121)

While not giving up the politically urgent sense in which Fanon wrote, Bhabha indicates that the criticism of the history of colonialism via the problematic of the native's (the black man's) identification can in fact lead to an understanding of the larger problems of otherness that do not necessarily emerge exclusively in anticolonial discourse. This openness, which is not as expediently committed to a particular 'position' as most self-declared political discourses are, is to be differentiated from the kind of idealization of another *culture* in the form of a totality that is absolutely different (and indifferent) to our own. This openness is not an attempt to recuperate an originary, primordial space before the sign. Rather, it is a total sign, the Other, the *entire* function of which is to contest the limits of the conventional (arbitrary) sign itself.[26] We may call this big Other the big Difference.

How does the big Other work? It works by combatting the construction of the native as the straightforward or direct 'other' of the colonizer. Instead, it adds to this 'image' of the native the ability to look, so that the native is 'gaze' as well. But this is not the gaze of the native-as-subject, nor the gaze of the anti-imperialist critic like Alloula; rather it is a simulation of the gaze that witnessed the native's oppression prior to her becoming image. (For instance, it is the video camera that records policemen beating their black victim, Rodney King, with clubs in Los Angeles, as he 'resists arrest' by pleading for his life.) The big Other thus functions to supplement the identification of the native-as-image in the form of *evidence-cum-witness* that I have been talking about.[27]

In other words, the agency of the native cannot simply be imagined in terms of a resistance against the image – that is, *after* the image has been formed – nor in terms of a subjectivity that existed *before*, beneath, inside, or outside the image. It needs to be rethought as that which bears witness to its own demolition – in a form that is at once image and gaze, but a gaze that exceeds the moment of colonization.

What I am suggesting is a mode of understanding the native in which the native's existence – that is, an existence before becoming 'native' – precedes the arrival of the colonizer. Contrary to the model of Western hegemony in which the colonizer is seen as a primary, active 'gaze' subjugating the native as passive 'object', I want to argue that it is actually the colonizer who feels looked at by the native's gaze. This gaze, which is neither a threat nor a retaliation, makes the colonizer 'conscious' of himself, leading to his need to turn this gaze around and look at himself, henceforth 'reflected' in the native-object. It is the self-reflection of the colonizer that produces the colonizer as subject (potent gaze, source of meaning and action) and the native as his image, with all the pejorative meanings of 'black' attached to the word 'image'. Hegel's story of human 'self-consciousness' is then not what he supposed it to be – a story about Western Man's highest achievement – but a story about the disturbing effect of Western Man's encounter with those others that Hegel considered primitive. Western Man henceforth became 'self-conscious', that is, uneasy and uncomfortable, in his 'own' environment.

Because this 'originary' *witnessing* is, temporally speaking, lost forever, the native's defiled image must act both as 'image' (history of her degradation) *and* as that witnessing gaze. In the silence of the native-as-object – a silence not immediately distinguishable from her ascribed silence/passivity – the indifference of the 'originary' witness appears again – in simulation. Like the silent picture postcards reproduced by Alloula, this simulated gaze is *between* the image and the gaze of the colonizer. Where the colonizer undresses her, the native's nakedness stares back at him both as the defiled image of his creation *and* as the indifferent gaze that says, there was nothing – no secret – to be unveiled underneath my clothes. That secret is your fantasm.

THE NATIVE IS NOT THE NON-DUPED

I conclude by returning to the issue with which I began, the issue of authenticity. As anthropologist Brian Spooner writes:

> In seeking authenticity people are able to use commodities to express themselves and fix points of security and order in an amorphous modern society. But the evolving relationship between the search for personal authenticity inside and the search for authenticity in carefully selected things outside has received relatively little attention. (p. 226)

My argument *for* the native's status as an indifferent defiled image is really an attempt to get at the root of the problem of the image, in which our cultural studies is deeply involved whenever it deals with 'the other'. Because the image, in which the other is often cast, is always distrusted as illusion, deception and falsehood, attempts to salvage the other often turn into attempts to uphold the other as the non-duped – the site of authenticity and true knowledge. Critics who do this can also imply that, having absorbed the primal wisdoms, they are the non-duped themselves.

In his 1990 essay, 'How the Non-Duped Err', Žižek describes the paradox of deception. Žižek, as Jonathan Elmer writes, 'concurs with Lacan that *"les non-dupes errent"*, that those who think they are undeceived are the fools' (p. 122). In his work, Žižek often refers to the classic topos in Lacan, the topos that only human beings can 'deceive by feigning to deceive', or deceive by telling the truth (p. 3).[28] That this can happen depends on the fact that we all assume that there is always something else under the mask. One deep-rooted example is that under the mask of civilization we are 'savages' the savage/primitive/native is then the 'truth', that is outside/under the symbolic order. The cultural critic who holds on to such a notion of the native is, by analogy, a psychotic subject:

the psychotic subject's distrust of the big Other, his *idée fixe* that the big Other (embodied in his intersubjective community) is trying to deceive him, is always and necessarily supported by an unshakable belief in a consistent, Other, an Other without gaps, an 'Other of the Other' . . . a non-deceived agent holding the reins. His mistake does not consist in his radical disbelief, in his conviction that there is a universal deception – here he is quite right, the symbolic order is ultimately the order of a fundamental deception – his mistake lies on the contrary in his being too easy of belief and supposing the existence of a hidden agency manipulating this deception, trying to dupe him. . . . (Žižek p. 12)

For us working in anti-imperialist discourse, this 'hidden agency manipulating . . . deception' would be precisely 'imperialism', 'colonialism', 'capitalism', and so forth. According to Žižek, our identification with the native in the form of a radical *disbelief* in the defiled images produced by these symbolic orders would not be wrong. What is problematic is our attempt to point to them as if they were one consistent manipulator that is trying to fool us consistently. Our fascination with the native, the oppressed, the savage and all such figures is therefore a desire to hold onto an unchanging certainty somewhere outside our own 'fake' experience. It is a desire for being 'non-duped', which is a not-too-innocent desire to seize control.

To insist on the native as an indifferent, defiled image is then to return to the native a capacity for distrusting and resisting the symbolic orders that 'fool' her, while not letting go of the 'illusion' that has structured her survival. To imagine the coexistence of defilement and indifference *in* the native: object is not to neutralize the massive destructions committed under such orders as imperialism and capitalism. Rather, it is to invent a dimension beyond the deadlock between native and colonizer in which the native can only be the colonizer's defiled image and the anti-imperialist critic can only be psychotic. My argument is: Yes, 'natives' are represented as defiled images – that is the fact of our history. But must we represent them a second time by turning history 'upside down', this time giving them the sanctified status of the 'non-duped'? Defilement and sanctification belong to the same symbolic order.

So where have all the 'natives' gone? They have gone . . . between the defiled image and the indifferent gaze. The native is not the defiled image and not not the defiled image. And she stares indifferently, mocking our imprisonment within imagistic resemblance and our self-deception as the non-duped.

NOTES

1. I discuss this in the first chapter of *Woman and Chinese Modernity*. One criticism that Sinologists deeply invested in the culture of ancient China often make about contemporary Chinese people is that they are too 'Westernized'.
2. Jameson's notion of pornography owes its origins in part at least, to fictional explorations of the relations between sexual images and technology such as J. G. Ballard's *Crash* (first published by Farrar, Straus & Girous, Inc. in 1973), described by its author as 'the first pornographic novel based on technology'. See Ballard,

'Introduction to the French Edition' (first published in French in 1974 and in English in 1975), p. 6. I am grateful to Chris Andre of Duke University for pointing this out to me.

3. Jean Baudrillard's theory of 'seduction' offers a strong critique of modern theory's tendency to go toward depths, thus ignoring the subversive potential of the superficial. See his *Seduction*.

4. See Homi Bhabha, 'What Does the Black Man Want?' Bhabha's argument is that 'the black man wants the objectifying confrontation with otherness' (p. 120). This essay is based on Bhabha's introduction to Frantz Fanon's *Black Skin, White Masks*.

5. As Jacques Derrida writes of Lévi-Strauss: 'the critique of ethnocentrism, a theme so dear to the author of *Tristes Tropiques*, has most often the sole function of constituting the other as a model of original and natural goodness, of accusing and humiliating oneself, of exhibiting its being-unacceptable in an anti-ethnocentric mirror?' (p. 114).

6. Barthes's reading of Japan is found in his *Empire of Signs*. For a discussion of Kojève's conception of Japan's 'post-historic' condition, see Miyoshi and Harootunian, Introduction, 'Postmodernism and Japan'. In his *Suicidal Narrative in Modern Japan*, Alan Wolfe offers an astute reading of Kojève's problematic pronouncement and its Orientalist assumptions against the complex background of modern Japanese literature and culture. See especially pp. 216–17 and pp. 220–2 of Wolfe's book.

7. 'However impeccably the content of an 'other' culture may be known, however anti-ethnocentrically it is represented, it is its location as the 'closure' of grand theories, the demand that, in analytic terms, it be always the 'good' object of knowledge, the docile body of difference, that reproduces a relation of domination and is the most serious indictment of the institutional powers of critical theory' (Bhabha, 'The Commitment to Theory', p. 124).

8. See 'Can the Subaltern Speak?' p. 308. The Spivak of this essay is very different from the one who speaks of 'envy' on behalf of the silent Chinese women in 'French Feminism in an International Frame', precisely because she does not read the subaltern in Oedipalized terms.

9. Bhabha's view is expressed in many of his essays. See, for instance, 'The Other Question'; 'Of Mimicry and Man'; 'Signs Taken for Wonders'. See also 'DissemiNation'.

10. Jean-François Lyotard:

> I would like to call a differend *differend* [*différend*] the case where the plaintiff is divested of the means to argue and becomes for that reason a victim. . . . A case of differend between two parties takes place when the 'regulation' of the conflict that opposes them is done in the idiom of one of the parties while the wrong suffered by the other is not signified in that idiom (p. 9).

11. See, for instance, Sally Price; Marianna Torgovnick; the many essays in Clifford and Marcus; and Marcus and Fischer.

12. This is T. S. Eliot's view of the poet's mind when it is 'perfectly equipped for its work' (p. 64). This well-known discussion of the metaphysical poets' relevance to modernity was in part a criticism of Samuel Johnson's remark of them that 'the most heterogeneous ideas are yoked by violence together' (Eliot, p. 60).

13. See Lyotard's definition of the *différend*, cited in note 10.

14. Spivak's statement, 'White men are saving brown women from brown men', is found in 'Subaltern' (pp. 296–7). She is describing the British intervention in *sati* (widow sacrifice) in British India, whereby the colonizer attempted to coopt native women under the pretext of freeing them from oppression by their own men.

15. See a similar criticism made by Winifred Woodhull. Because Alloula never really addresses the question of women's interests, Woodhull argues, he ultimately 'repeats the gesture of the colonizer by making of the veiled woman the screen on

which he projects his fantasy . . . of an Algerian nation untroubled by questions of women's oppression (p. 126). See also Mieke Bal for an argument about the complicity between the critic of colonial visual practice and colonial exploitation itself. Alloula's book is one of several Bal shows as lacking in a careful critique of the critic's own sexist and colonizing position.

16. Deconstructionist anti-colonial critics such as Bhabha have, for instance, elaborated on the 'ambivalence' of the image in the following terms:

> the image – as point of identification – marks the site of an ambivalence. Its representation is always spatially split – it makes *present* something that is *absent* – and temporally deferred – it is the representation of a time that is always elsewhere, a repetition. The image is only ever *appurtenance* to authority and identity; it must never be read mimetically as the 'appearance' of a 'reality'. The access to the image of identity is only ever possible in the *negation* of any sense of originality or plenitude through the principle of displacement and differentiation (absence/presence, representation/repetition) that always renders it a liminal ('What Does the Black Man Want?, p. 120).

17. For an example of a poststructuralist analysis of how pornography is in the eye of the beholder, see Judith Butler.

18. In the brief introduction to 'Eduard Fuchs', 'the editors of *The Essential Frankfurt School Reader* write: 'the presentation of Fuchs, the collector and often crude materialist, must also be read as one of Benjamin's self-presentations, and even as an *apologia pro vita sua* in the face of criticism' (Arato and Gebhardt, p. 225).

19. History is the subject of a structure whose site is not homogeneous, empty time, but time filled by the presence of the now [*Jetztzeit*]. Thus, to Robespierre ancient Rome was a past charged with the time of the now which he blasted out of the continuum of history'. 'The awareness that they are about to make the continuum of history explode is characteristic of the revolutionary classes at the moment of their action' (Benjamin, 'Theses', p. 261).

20. See also Benjamin's similar argument in 'The Author as Producer'.

21. Miller s reading of 'aura' is poststructuralist.

> The fact that the modern work of art is reproducible casts its shadow back not just to remove the aura from traditional works but to reveal that aura was always an ideological formation. That is what Benjamin means by saying film in itself, as a means of mechanical reproduction, is revolutionary criticism of traditional concepts of art. As the technological changes Benjamin describes have proceeded apace, the opposition between traditional man or woman and the masses disappears and with it the pertinence of the idea of a people with a specific culture. We are all to some degree members of what Benjamin invidiously calls the 'masses'. We are members of a transnational, multilinguistic, worldwide technological culture that makes the pieties of nationalism seem more and more outdated, nostalgic, perhaps even dangerously reactionary. (p. 10)

A substantially modified version of Miller's essay is found in his book *Illustrations*, many of the views of which I do not share. My present discussion, however, is based entirely on the earlier lecture.

22. 'The problem with all Benjamin's symmetrical oppositions is that they tend to dissolve through the effort of thinking they facilitate' (Miller, p. 10).

23. The notion of a radical 'antagonism' that structures sociality by making it incapable of self-identification or closure is argued by Laclau and Mouffe. See especially chapter three, 'Beyond the Positivity of the Social: Antagonisms and Hegemony'.

24. Gilles Deleuze and Félix Guattari make a comparable point when they, criticizing Freudian psychoanalysis as an anthropomorphic representation of sex, equate Lacan's 'big Other' with what they call 'nonhuman sex' (see p. 295; pp. 308–10). Deleuze and Guattari's notion of 'part objects' or 'partial objects' is, of course,

very different. They are not 'part' of any 'whole', but molecular machinic flows and breaks.

25. I take this phrase from Abdul R. JanMohamed.

26. In Saussure, the linguistic sign (made up of a relationship between signifier and signified) is arbitrary because it is conventional – in the sense that it works only within a coherent system of differences.

27. This essay was completed in mid-1991. The subsequent verdict on the King beating in 1992 demonstrated once again the dominant culture's ability to manipulate images to its own advantage by sabotaging the witnessing function crucial to any evidence of abuse. Once it succeeds in divorcing the act of witnessing from the image, the dominant culture can appoint itself as the 'true' witness whose observation and interpretation of the image is held as the most accurate one. The Rodney King video and the racial riots that followed the verdict thus became 'evidence' not for the historical white discrimination against blacks, but for how necessary that discrimination is!

28. Žižek quotes the Freudian joke about Polish Jews often mentioned by Lacan: 'one of them asks the other in an offended tone: "Why are you telling me that you are going to Lemberg, when you are really going to Lemberg?"' ('How the Non-Duped Err', p. 3; see also *Sublime Object*, p. 197).

WORKS CITED

Alloula, Malek, *The Colonial Harem*. Trans. Myrna Godzich and Wlad Godzich. Minneapolis: U of Minnesota P, 1986.

Appadurai, Arjun. 'Introduction: Commodities and the Politics of Value'. *The Social Life of Things: Commodities in Cultural Perspective*. Ed. Arjun Appadurai. Cambridge: Cambridge UP, 1986, pp. 3–63.

Arato, Andrew and Eike Gebhardt, eds. *The Essential Frankfurt School Reader*. New York: Urizen, 1978.

Armstrong, Nancy. 'The Occidental Alice'. *differences* 2.2 (1990): pp. 3–40.

Bal, Mieke, 'The Politics of Citation'. Diacritics 21.1 (1991): pp. 25–45.

Ballard, J. G. *Crash*. First Vintage Books Edition, 1985.

Barthes, Roland. *Empire of Signs*. Trans. Richard Howard. New York: Hill, 1982.

Baudrillard, Jean. *Seduction*. Trans. Brian Singer. New York: St. Martin's, 1990.

Benjamin, Walter. 'The Author as Producer'. Trans. Edmund Jephcott. Arato and Gebhardt pp. 254–69.

——. 'Central Park'. Trans. Lloyd Spencer (with the help of Mark Harrington). *New German Critique* 34 (1985: pp. 32–58.

——. 'Edward Fuchs: Collector and Historian'. Trans. Knut Tarnowski. Arato and Gebhardt. pp. 225–53.

——. *Illuminations*. Ed. Hannah Arendt. Trans. Harry Zohn. New York: Schocken, 1969.

——. 'Theses on the Philosophy of History'. *Illuminations*. pp. 253–64.

——. 'The Work of Art in the Age of Mechanical Production'. *Illuminations*. pp. 217–51.

Bhabha, Homi K. 'The Commitment to Theory'. *Questions of Third Cinema*. Ed. Jim Pines and Paul Willemen. London: British Film Inst., 1989.

——. 'DisseminNation: Time, Narrative, and the Margins of the Modern Nation'. *Nation and Narration*. Ed. Homi K. Bhabha. London: Routledge, 1990. pp. 291–322.

——. 'Of Mimicry and Man: The Ambivalence of Colonial Discourse'. *October* 28 (1984): pp. 125–33.

——. 'The Other Question – the Stereotype and Colonial Discourse'. *Screen* 24.6 (1983): pp. 18–36.

——. 'Signs Taken for Wonders: Questions of Ambivalence and Authority under a Tree

Outside Delhi, May 1817'. *Critical Inquiry* 12.1 (1985): pp. 144–65. Rept. in
'*Race', Writing and Difference*. Ed. Henry Louis Gates, Jr. Chicago: U of Chicago
P, 1985. pp. 163–24.

——. '"What Does the Black Man Want?"' *New Formations* 1 (1987): pp. 118–24.

Butler, Judith. 'The Force of Fantasy: Feminism, Mapplethorpe, and Discursive Excess'.
differences 2.2 (1990): pp. 105–25.

Chow, Rey. *Woman and Chinese Modernity: The Politics of Reading between West and
East*. Minneapolis: U of Minnesota P, 1991.

Clifford, James. *The Predicament of Culture: Twentieth-Century Ethnography,
Literature, and Art*. Cambridge: Harvard UP, 1988.

Clifford James and George E. Marcus, ed. *Writing Culture: The Poetics and Politics of
Ethnography*. Berkeley: U of California P, 1986.

Deleuze, Gilles and Félix Guattari. Anti-Oedipus: *Capitalism and Schizophrenia*.
Preface Michel Foucault. Trans. Robert Hurley, Mark Seem and Helen R. Lane.
Minneapolis: U of Minnesota P, 1983.

de Man, Paul. *Blindness and Insight: Essays in the Rhetoric of Contemporary Criticism*.
Minneapolis: U of Minnesota P, 1983.

Derrida, Jacques. *Of Grammatology*. Trans. Gayatri Chakravorty Spivak. Baltimore:
Johns Hopkins UP, 1976.

Eliot, T. S. 'The Metaphysical Poets'. *Selected Prose of T. S. Eliot*. Ed. Frank Kermode.
New York: Harcourt; Farrar, 1975.

Elmer, Jonathan. Review of Slavoj Žižek's *The Sublime Object of Ideology*. *Qui Parle*
4.1 (1990): pp. 117–23.

Fanon, Frantz. *Black Skin, White Masks*. London: Pluto, 1986.

Fukuyama, Francis. 'The End of History?' *The National Interest* 16 (1989): pp. 3–18.

Harlow, Barbara. Introduction. Alloula. pp. ix–xxii.

Jameson, Fredric. *Signatures of the Visible*. New York: Routledge, 1990.

JanMohamed, Abdul R. *Manichean Aesthetics: The Politics of Literature in Colonial
Africa*. Amherst: U of Massachusetts P, 1983.

Kojève, Alexandre. *Introduction to the Reading of Hegel: Lectures on the
Phenomenology of Spirit*. Assembled by Raymond Queneau. Ed. Allan Bloom.
Trans. James H. Nichol, Jr. Ithaca: Cornell UP, 1989.

Kristeva, Julia. *About Chinese Women*. Trans. Anita Barrows. New York: Marion
Boyars, 1977, 1986.

Laclau, Ernesto and Chantal Mouffe. *Hegemony and Socialist Strategy: Towards a
Radical Democratic Politics*. Trans. Winston Moore and Paul Cammack. London:
Verso, 1985.

Lyotard, Jean-François. *The Differend: Phrases in Dispute*. Trans. Georges Van Den
Abbeele. Minneapolis: U of Minnesota P, 1988.

Marcus, George E. and Michael M. J. Fischer, eds. *Anthropology as Cultural Critique:
An Experimental Moment in the Human Sciences*. Chicago: U of Chicago P, 1986.

Miller, J. Hillis. *Illustration*. Cambridge: Harvard UP, 1992.

——. 'The Work of Cultural Criticism in the Age of Digital Reproduction'. Annual
Conference of the Semiotic Society of America. Manuscript. 1990.

Miyoshi, Masao, and H. D. Harootunian. Introduction. 'Postmodernism and Japan'.
The South Atlantic Quarterly 87.3 (1988): pp. 392–94. Rpt. as *Postmodernism and
Japan*. Ed. Masao Miyoshi and H. D. Harootunian. Durham: Duke UP, 1989.

Parry, Benita. 'Problems in Current Theories of Colonial Discourse'. *Oxford Literary
Review* 9.1–2 (1987): pp. 27–58.

Price, Sally. *Primitive Art in Civilized Places*. Chicago: U of Chicago P, 1989.

Rousseau, Jean-Jacques. *A Discourse on Inequality*. Trans. Maurice Cranston. London:
Penguin, 1984.

Saussure, Ferdinand de. *Course in General Linguistics*. Trans. Wade Baskin. Ed. Charles Bally et al. Glasgow: Fontana/Collins, 1974.

Serres, Michel. *Detachment*. Trans. Genevieve James and Raymond Federman. Athens: Ohio UP, 1989.

Spivak, Gayatri Chakravorty. 'Can the Subaltern Speak?'. *Marxism and the Interpretation of Culture*. Ed. Cary Nelson and Lawrence Grossberg. Urbana: U of Illinois, 1988. pp. 271–313.

——. 'French Feminism in an International Frame'. *In Other Worlds: Essays in Cultural Politics*. London: Methuen, 1987. pp. 134–53.

——. 'The New Historicism: Political Commitment and the Postmodern Critic'. *Post-Colonial Critic: Interviews, Strategies, Dialogues*. Ed. Sarah Harasym. London: Routledge, 1990. pp. 152–68.

Spooner, Brian. 'Weavers and Dealers: The Authenticity of an Oriental Carpet'. *The Social Life of Things: Commodities in Cultural Perspective*. Ed. Arjun Appaduran. Cambridge: Cambridge UP, 1986: pp. 195–235.

Torgovnick, Marianna. *Gone Primitive: Savage Intellects, Modern Lives*. Chicago: U of Chicago P, 1990.

Wolfe, Alan. *Suicidal Narrative in Modern Japan: The Case of Dazai Osamu*. Princeton: Princeton UP, 1990.

Woodhull, Winifred. 'Unveiling Algeria'. *Genders* 10 (1991): pp. 121–26.

Žižek, Slavoj. 'How the Non-Duped Err'. *Qui Parle* 4.1 (1990): pp. 1–20.

——. 'Rossellini: Woman as Symptom of Man'. *October* 54 (1990): pp. 18–44.

——. *The Sublime Object of Ideology*. New York: Verso, 1989.

PART 4
SEXUALITY AND SEXUAL RIGHTS

4.1

'RACISM, BIRTH CONTROL AND REPRODUCTIVE RIGHTS'

Angela Davis

When nineteenth-century feminists raised the demand for 'voluntary motherhood', the campaign for birth control was born. Its proponents were called radicals and they were subjected to the same mockery as had befallen the initial advocates of woman suffrage. 'Voluntary motherhood' was considered audacious, outrageous and outlandish by those who insisted that wives had no right to refuse to satisfy their husbands' sexual urges. Eventually, of course, the right to birth control, like women's right to vote, would be more or less taken for granted by US public opinion. Yet in 1970, a full century later, the call for legal and easily accessible abortions was no less controversial than the issue of 'voluntary motherhood' which had originally launched the birth control movement in the United States.

Birth control – individual choice, safe contraceptive methods, as well as abortions when necessary – is a fundamental prerequisite for the emancipation of women. Since the right of birth control is obviously advantageous to women of all classes and races, it would appear that even vastly dissimilar women's groups would have attempted to unite around this issue. In reality, however, the birth control movement has seldom succeeded in uniting women of different social backgrounds, and rarely have the movement's leaders popularized the genuine concerns of working-class women. Moreover, arguments advanced by birth control advocates have sometimes been based on blatantly racist

From: Angela Davis (1982), 'Racism, Birth Control and Reproductive Rights', pp. 202–71, in Angela Davis, *Women, Race and Class* (London: The Women's Press; New York: Random House, Inc.).

premises. The progressive potential of birth control remains indisputable. But in actuality, the historical record of this movement leaves much to be desired in the realm of challenges to racism and class exploitation.

The most important victory of the contemporary birth control movement was won during the early 1970s when abortions were at last declared legal. Having emerged during the infancy of the new Women's Liberation movement, the struggle to legalize abortions incorporated all the enthusiasm and the militancy of the young movement. By January, 1973, the abortion rights campaign had reached a triumphant culmination. In *Roe v. Wade* (410 US) and *Doe v. Bolton* (410 US), the US Supreme Court ruled that a woman's right to personal privacy implied her right to decide whether or not to have an abortion.

The ranks of the abortion rights campaign did not include substantial numbers of women of color. Given the racial composition of the larger Women's Liberation movement, this was not at all surprising. When questions were raised about the absence of racially oppressed women in both the larger movement and in the abortion rights campaign, two explanations were commonly proposed in the discussions and literature of the period: women of color were overburdened by their people's fight against racism; and/or they had not yet become conscious of the centrality of sexism. But the real meaning of the almost lily-white complexion of the abortion rights campaign was not to be found in an ostensibly myopic or underdeveloped consciousness among women of color. The truth lay buried in the ideological underpinnings of the birth control movement itself.

The failure of the abortion rights campaign to conduct a historical self-evaluation led to a dangerously superficial appraisal of Black people's suspicious attitudes toward birth control in general. Granted, when some Black people unhesitatingly equated birth control with genocide, it did appear to be an exaggerated – even paranoiac – reaction. Yet white abortion rights activists missed a profound message, for underlying these cries of genocide were important clues about the history of the birth control movement. This movement, for example, had been known to advocate involuntary sterilization – a racist form of mass 'birth control'. If ever women would enjoy the right to plan their pregnancies, legal and easily accessible birth control measures and abortions would have to be complemented by an end to sterilization abuse.

As for the abortion rights campaign itself, how could women of color fail to grasp its urgency? They were far more familiar than their white sisters with the murderously clumsy scalpels of inept abortionists seeking profit in illegality. In New York, for instance, during the several years preceding the decriminalization of abortions in that state, some 80 percent of the deaths caused by illegal abortions involved Black and Puerto Rican women.[1] Immediately afterward, women of color received close to half of all the legal abortions. If the abortion rights campaign of the early 1970s needed to be reminded that women of color wanted desperately to escape the back-room quack abortionists, they should have also realized that these same women were not about to express pro-abortion sentiments. They were in favor of *abortion rights*, which did not mean that they were proponents of abortion. When Black and Latina women resort to abortions in such large numbers, the stories they tell are not so much about their desire to be free of their pregnancy, but rather about the miserable social conditions which dissuade them from bringing new lives into the world.

Black women have been aborting themselves since the earliest days of slavery. Many slave women refused to bring children into a world of interminable forced labor, where chains and floggings and sexual abuse for women were the everyday conditions of life. A doctor practicing in Georgia around the middle of the last century noticed that abortions and miscarriages were far more common among his slave patients than among the white women he treated. According to the physician, either Black women worked too hard or,

> as the planters believe, the blacks are possessed of a secret by which they destroy the fetus at an early stage of gestation . . . All country practitioners are aware of the frequent complaints of planters (about the) . . . unnatural tendency in the African female to destroy her offspring.[2]

Expressing shock that 'whole families of women fail to have any children',[3] this doctor never considered how 'unnatural' it was to raise children under the slave system. The previously mentioned episode of Margaret Garner, a fugitive slave who killed her own daughter and attempted suicide herself when she was captured by slave-catchers, is a case in point.

> She rejoiced that the girl was dead – 'now she would never know what a woman suffers as a slave' – and pleaded to be tried for murder. 'I will go singing to the gallows rather than be returned to slavery!'[4]

Why were self-imposed abortions and reluctant acts of infanticide such common occurrences during slavery? Not because Black women had discovered solutions to their predicament, but rather because they were desperate. Abortions and infanticides were acts of desperation, motivated not by the biological birth process but by the oppressive conditions of slavery. Most of these women, no doubt, would have expressed their deepest resentment had someone hailed their abortions as a stepping stone toward freedom.

During the early abortion rights campaign it was too frequently assumed that legal abortions provided a viable alternative to the myriad problems posed by poverty. As if having fewer children could create more jobs, higher wages, better schools, etc., etc. This assumption reflected the tendency to blur the distinction between *abortion rights* and the general advocacy of *abortions*. The campaign often failed to provide a voice for women who wanted the *right* to legal abortions while deploring the social conditions that prohibited them from bearing more children.

The renewed offensive against abortion rights that erupted during the latter half of the 1970s has made it absolutely necessary to focus more sharply on the needs of poor and racially oppressed women. By 1977 the passage of the Hyde

Amendment in Congress had mandated the withdrawal of federal funding for abortions, causing many state legislatures to follow suit. Black, Puerto Rican, Chicana and Native American women, together with their impoverished white sisters, were thus effectively divested of the right to legal abortions. Since surgical sterilizations, funded by the Department of Health, Education and Welfare, remained free on demand, more and more poor women have been forced to opt for permanent infertility. What is urgently required is a broad campaign to defend the reproductive rights of all women – and especially those women whose economic circumstances often compel them to relinquish the right to reproduction itself.

Women's desire to control their reproductive system is probably as old as human history itself. As early as 1844 the *United States Practical Receipt Book* contained, among its many recipes for food, household chemicals and medicines, 'receipts' for 'birth preventive lotions'. To make 'Hannay's Preventive Lotion', for example

> Take pearlash, 1 part; water, 6 parts. Mix and filter. Keep it in closed bottles, and use it, with or without soap, immediately after connexion.[5]

For 'Abernethy's Preventive Lotion'

> Take bichloride of mercury, 25 parts; milk of almonds, 400 parts; alcohol, 100 parts; rosewater, 1000 parts. Immerse the glands in a little of the mixture . . . Infallible, if used in proper time.[6]

While women have probably always dreamed of infallible methods of birth control, it was not until the issue of women's rights in general became the focus of an organized movement that reproductive rights could emerge as a legitimate demand. In an essay entitled 'Marriage', written during the 1850s, Sarah Grimke argued for a 'right on the part of woman to decide *when* she shall become a mother, how often and under what circumstances'.[7] Alluding to one physician's humorous observation, Grimke agreed that, if wives and husbands alternatively gave birth to their children, 'no family would ever have more than three, the husband bearing one and the wife two'.[8] But, as she insists, 'the *right* to decide this matter has been almost wholly denied to woman'.[9]

Sarah Grimke advocated women's right to sexual abstinence. Around the same time the well-known 'emancipated marriage' of Lucy Stone and Henry Blackwell took place. These abolitionists and women's rights activists were married in a ceremony that protested women's traditional relinquishment of their rights to their persons, names and property. In agreeing that, as husband, he had no right to the 'custody of the wife's person',[10] Henry Blackwell promised that he would not attempt to impose the dictates of his sexual desires upon his wife.

The notion that women could refuse to submit to their husbands' sexual demands eventually became the central idea of the call for 'voluntary motherhood'. By the 1870s, when the woman suffrage movement had reached its peak, feminists were publicly advocating voluntary motherhood. In a speech delivered in 1873, Victoria Woodhull claimed that:

> The wife who submits to sexual intercourse against her wishes or desires, virtually commits suicide; while the husband who compels it, commits murder, and ought just as much to be punished for it, as though he strangled her to death for refusing him.[11]

Woodhull, of course, was quite notorious as a proponent of 'free love'. Her defense of a woman's right to abstain from sexual intercourse within marriage as a means of controlling her pregnancies was associated with Woodhull's overall attack on the institution of marriage.

It was not a coincidence that women's consciousness of their reproductive rights was born within the organized movement for women's political equality. Indeed, if women remained forever burdened by incessant childbirths and frequent miscarriages, they would hardly be able to exercise the political rights they might win. Moreover, women's new dreams of pursuing careers and other paths of self-development outside marriage and motherhood could only be realized if they could limit and plan their pregnancies. In this sense, the slogan 'voluntary motherhood' contained a new and genuinely progressive vision of womanhood. At the same time, however, this vision was rigidly bound to the lifestyle enjoyed by the middle classes and the bourgeoisie. The aspirations underlying the demand for 'voluntary motherhood' did not reflect the conditions of working-class women, engaged as they were in a far more fundamental fight for economic survival. Since this first call for birth control was associated with goals which could only be achieved by women possessing material wealth, vast numbers of poor and working-class women would find it rather difficult to identify with the embryonic birth control movement.

Toward the end of the nineteenth century the white birth rate in the United States suffered a significant decline. Since no contraceptive innovations had been publicly introduced, the drop in the birth rate implied that women were substantially curtailing their sexual activity. By 1890 the typical native-born white woman was bearing no more than four children.[12] Since US society was becoming increasingly urban, this new birth pattern should not have been a surprise. While farm life demanded large families, they became dysfunctional within the context of city life. Yet this phenomenon was publicly interpreted in a racist and anti-working class fashion by the ideologues of rising monopoly capitalism. Since native-born white women were bearing fewer children, the specter of 'race suicide' was raised in official circles.

In 1905 President Theodore Roosevelt concluded his Lincoln Day Dinner speech with the proclamation that 'race purity must be maintained'.[13] By 1906 he blatantly equated the falling birth rate among native-born whites with the impending threat of 'race suicide'. In his State of the Union message that year Roosevelt admonished the well-born white women who engaged in 'willful sterility – the one sin for which the penalty is national death, race suicide'.[14]

These comments were made during a period of accelerating racist ideology and of great waves of race riots and lynchings on the domestic scene. Moreover, President Roosevelt himself was attempting to muster support for the US seizure of the Philippines, the country's most recent imperialist venture.

How did the birth control movement respond to Roosevelt's accusation that their cause was promoting race suicide? The President's propagandistic ploy was a failure, according to a leading historian of the birth control movement, for, ironically, it led to greater support for its advocates. Yet, as Linda Gordon maintains, this controversy 'also brought to the forefront those issues that most separated feminists from the working class and the poor'.[15]

> This happened in two ways. First, the feminists were increasingly empha-sizing birth control as a route to careers and higher education – goals out of reach of the poor with or without birth control. In the context of the whole feminist movement, the race-suicide episode was an additional factor identifying feminism almost exclusively with the aspirations of the more privileged women of the society. Second, the pro-birth control fem-inists began to popularize the idea that poor people had a moral obliga-tion to restrict the size of their families, because large families create a drain on the taxes and charity expenditures of the wealthy and because poor children were less likely to be 'superior'.[16]

The acceptance of the race-suicide thesis, to a greater or lesser extent, by women such as Julia Ward Howe and Ida Husted Harper reflected the suffrage movement's capitulation to the racist posture of Southern women. If the suffra-gists acquiesced to arguments invoking the extension of the ballot to women as the saving grace of white supremacy, then birth control advocates either acqui-esced to or supported the new arguments invoking birth control as a means of preventing the proliferation of the 'lower classes' and as an antidote to race suicide. Race suicide could be prevented by the introduction of birth control among Black people, immigrants and the poor in general. In this way, the pros-perous whites of solid Yankee stock could maintain their superior numbers within the population. Thus class-bias and racism crept into the birth control movement when it was still in its infancy. More and more, it was assumed within birth control circles that poor women, Black and immigrant alike, had a 'moral' obligation to restrict the size of their families'.[17] What was demanded as a 'right' for the privileged came to be interpreted as a 'duty' for the poor.

When Margaret Sanger embarked upon her lifelong crusade for birth control – a term she coined and popularized – it appeared as though the racist and anti-working-class overtones of the previous period might possibly be overcome. For Margaret Higgens Sanger came from a working-class background herself and was well acquainted with the devastating pressures of poverty. When her mother died, at the age of forty-eight, she had borne no less than eleven chil-dren. Sanger's later memories of her own family's troubles would confirm her belief that working-class women had a special need for the right to plan and space their pregnancies autonomously. Her affiliation, as an adult, with the Socialist movement was a further cause for hope that the birth control campaign would move in a more progressive direction.

When Margaret Sanger joined the Socialist party in 1912, she assumed the responsibility of recruiting women from New York's working women's clubs into the party.[18] *The Call* – the party's paper – carried her articles on the women's page. She wrote a series entitled 'What Every Mother Should Know', another called 'What Every Girl Should Know', and she did on-the-spot coverage of strikes involving women. Sanger's familiarity with New York's working-class districts was a result of her numerous visits as a trained nurse to the poor sections of the city. During these visits, she points out in her autobiography, she met countless numbers of women who desperately desired knowledge about birth control.

According to Sanger's autobiographical reflections, one of the many visits she made as a nurse to New York's Lower East Side convinced her to undertake a personal crusade for birth control. Answering one of her routine calls, she discovered that twenty-eight-year-old Sadie Sachs had attempted to abort herself. Once the crisis had passed, the young woman asked the attending physician to give her advice on birth prevention. As Sanger relates the story, the doctor recommended that she 'tell [her husband] Jake to sleep on the roof'.[19]

> I glanced quickly to Mrs. Sachs. Even through my sudden tears I could see stamped on her face an expression of absolute despair. We simply looked at each other, saying no word until the door had closed behind the doctor. Then she lifted her thin, blue-veined hands and clasped them beseechingly. 'He can't understand. He's only a man. But you do, don't you? Please tell me the secret, and I'll never breathe it to a soul. Please!'[20]

Three months later Sadie Sachs died from another self-induced abortion. That night, Margaret Sanger says, she vowed to devote all her energy towards the acquisition and dissemination of contraceptive measures.

> I went to bed, knowing that no matter what it might cost, I was finished with palliatives and superficial cures; I resolved to seek out the root of evil, to do something to change the destiny of mothers whose miseries were as vast as the sky.[21]

During the first phase of Sanger's birth control crusade, she maintained her affiliation with the Socialist party – and the campaign itself was closely associated with the rising militancy of the working class. Her staunch supporters included Eugene Debs, Elizabeth Gurley Flynn and Emma Goldman, who respectively represented the Socialist party, the International Workers of the World and the anarchist movement. Margaret Sanger, in turn, expressed the anti-capitalist commitment of her own movement within the pages of its journal, *Woman Rebel*, which was 'dedicated to the interests of working women'.[22] Personally, she continued to march on picket lines with striking workers and publicly condemned the outrageous assaults on striking workers. In 1914, for example, when the National Guard massacred scores of Chicano miners in Ludlow, Colorado, Sanger joined the labor movement in exposing John D. Rockefeller's role in this attack.[23]

Unfortunately, the alliance between the birth control campaign and the radical labor movement did not enjoy a long life. While Socialists and other working-class activists continued to support the demand for birth control, it did not occupy a central place in their overall strategy. And Sanger herself began to underestimate the centrality of capitalist exploitation in her analysis of poverty, arguing that too many children caused workers to fall into their miserable predicament. Moreover, 'women were inadvertently perpetuating the exploitation of the working class', she believed, 'by continually flooding the labor market with new workers'.[24] Ironically, Sanger may have been encouraged to adopt this position by the neo-Malthusian ideas embraced in some socialist circles. Such outstanding figures of the European socialist movement as Anatole France and Rosa Luxemburg had proposed a 'birth strike' to prevent the continued flow of labor into the capitalist market.[25]

When Margaret Sanger severed her ties with the Socialist party for the purpose of building an independent birth control campaign, she and her followers became more susceptible than ever before to the anti-Black and anti-immigrant propaganda of the times. Like their predecessors, who had been deceived by the 'race suicide' propaganda, the advocates of birth control began to embrace the prevailing racist ideology. The fatal influence of the eugenics movement would soon destroy the progressive potential of the birth control campaign.

During the first decades of the twentieth century the rising popularity of the eugenics movement was hardly a fortuitous development. Eugenic ideas were perfectly suited to the ideological needs of the young monopoly capitalists. Imperialist incursions in Latin America and in the Pacific needed to be justified, as did the intensified exploitation of Black workers in the South and immigrant workers in the North and West. The pseudoscientific racial theories associated with the eugenics campaign furnished dramatic apologies for the conduct of the young monopolies. As a result, this movement won the unhesitating support of such leading capitalists as the Carnegies, the Harrimans and the Kelloggs.[26]

By 1919 the eugenic influence on the birth control movement was unmistakably clear. In an article published by Margaret Sanger in the American Birth Control League's journal, she defined 'the chief issue of birth control' as 'more children from the fit, less from the unfit'.[27] Around this time the ABCL heartily welcomed the author of *The Rising Tide of Color Against White World Supremacy* into its inner sanctum.[28] Lothrop Stoddard, Harvard professor and theoretician of the eugenics movement, was offered a seat on the board of directors. In the pages the ABCL's journal, articles by Guy Irving Birch, director of the American Eugenics Society, began to appear. Birch advocated birth control as a weapon to 'prevent the American people from being replaced by alien or

Negro stock, whether it be by immigration or by overly high birth rates among others in this country'.[29] By 1932 the Eugenics Society could boast that at least twenty-six states had passed compulsory sterilization laws and that thousands of 'unfit' persons had already been surgically prevented from reproducing.[30] Margaret Sanger offered her public approval of this development. 'Morons, mental defectives, epileptics, illiterates, paupers, unemployables, criminals, prostitutes and dope fiends' ought to be surgically sterilized, she argued in a radio talk.[31] She did not wish to be so intransigent as to leave them with no choice in the matter; if they wished, she said, they should be able to choose a lifelong segregated existence in labor camps.

Within the American Birth Control League, the call for birth control among Black people acquired the same racist edge as the call for compulsory sterilization. In 1939 its successor, the Birth Control Federation of America, planned a 'Negro Project'. In the Federation's words:

> The mass of Negroes, particularly in the South, still breed carelessly and disastrously, with the result that the increase among Negroes, even more than among whites, is from that portion of the population least fit, and least able to rear children properly.[32]

Calling for the recruitment of Black ministers to lead local birth control committees, the Federation's proposal suggested that Black people should be rendered as vulnerable as possible to their birth control propaganda. 'We do not want word to get out', wrote Margaret Sanger in a letter to a colleague, 'that we want to exterminate the Negro population and the minister is the man who can straighten out that idea if it ever occurs to any of their more rebellious members'.[33] This episode in the birth control movement confirmed the ideological victory of the racism associated with eugenic ideas. It had been robbed of its progressive potential, advocating for people of color not the individual right to *birth control*, but rather the racist strategy of *population control*. The birth control campaign would be called upon to serve in an essential capacity in the execution of the US government's imperialist and racist population policy.

The abortion rights activists of the early 1970s should have examined the history of their movement. Had they done so, they might have understood why so many of their Black sisters adopted a posture of suspicion toward their cause. They might have understood how important it was to undo the racist deeds of their predecessors, who had advocated birth control as well as compulsory sterilization as a means of eliminating the 'unfit' sectors of the population. Consequently, the young white feminists might have been more receptive to the suggestion that their campaign abortion rights include a vigorous condemnation of sterilization abuse, which had become more widespread than ever.

It was not until the media decided that the casual sterilization of two Black girls in Montgomery, Alabama, was a scandal worth reporting that the Pandora's box of sterilization abuse was finally flung open. But, by the time the case of the Relf sisters broke, it was practically too late to influence the politics of the abortion rights movement. It was the summer of 1973 and the Supreme Court decision legalizing abortions had already been announced in January. Nevertheless the urgent need for mass opposition to sterilization abuse became tragically clear. The facts surrounding the Relf sisters' story were horrifyingly simple. Minnie Lee, who was twelve years old, and Mary Alice, who was fourteen, had been unsuspectingly carted into an operating room, where surgeons irrevocably robbed them of their capacity to bear children.[34] The surgery had been ordered by the HEW-funded Montgomery Community Action Committee after it was discovered that Depo-Provera, a drug previously administered to the girls as a birth prevention measure, caused cancer in test animals.[35]

After the Southern Poverty Law Center filed suit on behalf of the Relf sisters, the girls' mother revealed that she had unknowingly 'consented' to the operation, having been deceived by the social workers who handled her daughters' case. They had asked Mrs. Relf, who was unable to read, to put her 'X' on a document, the contents of which were not described to her. She assumed, she said, that it authorized the continued Depo-Provera injections. As she subsequently learned, she had authorized the surgical sterilization of her daughters.[36]

In the aftermath of the publicity exposing the Relf sisters' case, similar episodes were brought to light. In Montgomery alone, eleven girls, also in their teens, had been similarly sterilized. HEW-funded birth control clinics in other states, as it turned out, had also subjected young girls to sterilization abuse. Moreover, individual women came forth with equally outrageous stories. Nial Ruth Cox, for example, filed suit against the state of North Carolina. At the age of eighteen – eight years before the suit – officials had threatened to discontinue her family's welfare payments if she refused to submit to surgical sterilization.[37] Before she assented to the operation, she was assured that her infertility would be temporary.[38]

Nial Ruth Cox's lawsuit was aimed at a state which had diligently practiced the theory of eugenics. Under the auspices of the Eugenics Commission of North Carolina, so it was learned, 7,686 sterilizations had been carried out since 1933. Although the operations were justified as measures to prevent the reproduction of 'mentally deficient persons', about 5,000 of the sterilized persons had been Black.[39] According to Brenda Feigen Fasteau, the ACLU attorney representing Nial Ruth Cox, North Carolina's recent record was not much better. 'As far as I can determine, the statistics reveal that since 1964, approximately 65% of the women sterilized in North Carolina were Black and approximately 35% were white.'[40]

As the flurry of publicity exposing sterilization abuse revealed, the neighboring state of South Carolina had been the site of further atrocities. Eighteen women from Aiken, South Carolina, charged that they had been sterilized by a Dr. Clovis Pierce during the early 1970s. The sole obstetrician in that small town, Pierce had consistently sterilized Medicaid recipients with two or more children. According to a nurse in his office, Dr. Pierce insisted that pregnant welfare women 'will have to submit (sic!) to voluntary sterilization' if they wanted him to deliver their babies.[41] While he was 'tired of people running around and having babies and paying for them with my taxes'.[42] Dr. Pierce received some $60,000 in taxpayers' money for the sterilizations he performed. During his trial he was supported by the South Carolina Medical Association, whose members declared that doctors 'have a moral and legal right to insist on sterilization permission before accepting a patient, if it is done on the initial visit'.[43]

Revelations of sterilization abuse during that time exposed the complicity of the federal government. At first the Department of Health, Education and Welfare claimed that approximately 16,000 women and 8,000 men had been sterilized in 1972 under the auspices of federal programs.[44] Later, however, these figures underwent a drastic revision. Carl Shultz, director of HEW's Population Affairs Office, estimated that between 100,000 and 200,000 sterilizations had actually been funded that year by the federal government.[45] During Hitler's Germany, incidentally, 250,000 sterilizations were carried out under the Nazis' Hereditary Health Law.[46] Is it possible that the record of the Nazis, throughout the years of their reign, may have been almost equalled by US government-funded sterilizations in the space of a single year?

Given the historical genocide inflicted on the native population of the United States, one would assume that Native Americans would be exempted from the government's sterilization campaign. But, according to Dr. Connie Uri's testimony in a Senate committee hearing, by 1976, twenty-four per cent of all Native American women of childbearing age had been sterilized.[47] 'Our blood lines are being stopped,' the Choctaw physician told the Senate committee, 'Our unborn will not be born . . . This is genocidal to our people'.[48] According to Dr. Uri, the Indian Health Services Hospital in Claremore, Oklahoma, had been sterilizing one out of every four women giving birth in that federal facility.[49]

Native Americans are special targets of government propaganda on sterilization. In one of the HEW pamphlets aimed at Native American people, there is a sketch of a family with *ten children* and *one horse* and another sketch of a family with *one child* and *ten horses*. The drawings are supposed to imply that more children mean more poverty and fewer children mean wealth. As if the ten horses owned by the one-child family had been magically conjured up by birth control and sterilization surgery.

The domestic population policy of the US government has an undeniably racist edge. Native American, Chicana, Puerto Rican and Black women continue to be sterilized in disproportionate numbers. According to a National Fertility Study conducted in 1970 by Princeton University's Office of Population Control, twenty per cent of all married Black women had been permanently sterilized.[50] Approximately the same percentage of Chicana women had been rendered surgically infertile.[51] Moreover, forty-three per cent of the women sterilized through federally subsidized programs were Black.[52]

The astonishing number of Puerto Rican women who have been sterilized reflects a special government policy that can be traced back to 1939. In that year President Roosevelt's Interdepartmental Committee on Puerto Rico issued a statement attributing the island's economic problems to the phenomenon of overpopulation.[53] This committee proposed that efforts be undertaken to reduce the birth rate to no more than the level of the death rate.[54] Soon afterward an experimental sterilization campaign was undertaken in Puerto Rico. Although the Catholic Church initially opposed this experiment and forced the cessation of the program in 1946, it was converted during the early 1950s to the teachings and practice of population control.[55] In this period over 150 birth control clinics were opened, resulting in a twenty per cent decline in population growth by the mid-1960s.[56] By the 1970s over thirty-five per cent of all Puerto Rican women of childbearing age had been surgically sterilized. [57] According to Bonnie Mass, a serious critic of the US government's population policy:

> if purely mathematical projections are to be taken seriously, if the present rate of sterilization of 19,000 monthly were to continue, then the island's population of workers and peasants could be extinguished within the next 10 or 20 years . . . [establishing] for the first time in world history a systematic use of population control capable of eliminating an entire generation of people.[58]

During the 1970s the devastating implications of the Puerto Rican experiment began to emerge with unmistakable clarity. In Puerto Rico the presence of corporations in the highly automated metallurgical and pharmaceutical industries had exacerbated the problem of unemployment. The prospect of an ever-larger army of unemployed workers was one of the main incentives for the mass sterilization program. Inside the United States today, enormous numbers of people of color – and especially racially oppressed youth – have become part of a pool of permanently unemployed workers. It is hardly coincidental, considering the Puerto Rican example, that the increasing incidence of sterilization has kept pace with the high rates of unemployment. As growing numbers of white people suffer the brutal consequences of unemployment, they can also expect to become targets of the official sterilization propaganda.

The prevalence of sterilization abuse during the latter 1970s may be greater than ever before. Although the Department of Health, Education and Welfare issued guidelines in 1974, which were ostensibly designed to prevent involuntary sterilizations, the situation has nonetheless deteriorated. When the American Civil Liberties Union's Reproductive Freedom Project conducted a survey of teaching hospitals in 1975, they discovered that forty per cent of those institutions were not even aware of the regulations issued by HEW.[59] Only thirty per cent of the hospitals examined by the ACLU were even attempting to comply with the guidelines.[60]

The 1977 Hyde Amendment has added yet another dimension to coercive sterilization practices. As a result of this law passed by Congress, federal funds for abortions were eliminated in all cases but those involving rape and the risk of death or severe illness. According to Sandra Salazar of the California Department of Public Health, the first victim of the Hyde Amendment was a twenty-seven-year-old Chicana woman from Texas. She died as a result of an illegal abortion in Mexico shortly after Texas discontinued government-funded abortions. There have been many more victims – women for whom sterilization has become the only alternative to the abortions, which are currently beyond their reach. Sterilizations continue to be federally funded and free, to poor women, on demand.

Over the last decade the struggle against sterilization abuse has been waged primarily by Puerto Rican, Black, Chicana and Native American women. Their cause has not yet been embraced by the women's movement as a whole. Within organizations representing the interests of middle-class white women, there has been a certain reluctance to support the demands of the campaign against sterilization abuse, for these women are often denied their individual rights to be sterilized when they desire to take this step. While women of color are urged, at every turn, to become permanently infertile, white women enjoying prosperous economic conditions are urged, by the same forces, to reproduce themselves. They therefore sometimes consider the 'waiting period' and other details of the demand for 'informed consent' to sterilization as further inconveniences for women like themselves. Yet whatever the inconveniences for white middle-class women, a fundamental reproductive right of racially oppressed and poor women is at stake. Sterilization abuse must be ended.

NOTES

1. Edwin M. Gold, et al., 'Therapeutic Abortions in New York City: A twenty-year review', in *American Journal of Public Health*, vol. LV, July 1965, pp. 964–72. Quoted in Lucinda Cisla, 'Unfinished Business: Birth control and women's liberation', in Robin Morgan (ed.), *Sisterhood Is Powerful: An anthology of writings from the women's liberation movement* (New York: Vintage Books, 1970), p. 261. Also quoted in Robert Staples, *The Black Woman in America* (Chicago: Nelson Hall, 1974), p. 146.
2. Herbert Gutman, *The Black Family in Slavery and Freedom, 1750–1925* (New York: Pantheon Books, 1976), pp. 80–1, note.
3. Ibid., pp. 80–1, note.
4. Herbert Aptheker, 'The Negro Woman', in Herbert Aptheker (ed.), *Masses and Mainstream*, vol. 11, no. 2, p. 12.
5. Quoted in Rosalyn Baxandall, Linda Gordon and Susan Reverby (eds), *America's Working Women: A documentary history – 1600 to the present* (New York: Random House, 1976), p. 17.
6. Ibid., p. 17.
7. Lerner, Gerda (ed.), *The Female Experience: An American documentary* (Indianapolis, IN: Bobbs-Merrill Educational Publisher, 1977), p. 91.
8. Ibid., p. 91
9. Ibid., p. 91.
10. 'Marriage of Lucy Stone Under Protest', in *History of Women Suffrage*, vol. 1. Quoted in Miriam Schneir, *Feminism: The essential historical writings* (New York: Vintage Books, 1972), p. 104.
11. Speech by Virginia Woodhull, 'The Elixir of Life'. Quoted in Schneir, *Feminism*, p.153.

12. Mary P. Ryan, *Womanhood in America from Colonial Times to the Present* (New York: Franklin Watts Inc., 1975), p. 162.
13. Melvin Steinfeld, *Our Racist Presidents* (San Ramon, CA: Consensus Publishers, 1972), p. 212.
14. Bonnie Mass, *Population Target: The political economy of population control in Latin America* (Toronto: Women's Education Press, 1977), p. 20.
15. Linda Gordon, *Woman's Body, Woman's Right: Birth control in America* (New York: Penguin Books, 1976), p. 157.
16. Ibid., p. 158.
17. Ibid., p. 158.
18. 18, Margaret Sanger, *An Autobiography* (New York: Dover Press, 1971) p. 75.
19. Ibid., p. 90.
20. Ibid., p. 91.
21. Ibid., p. 92.
22. Ibid., p. 106.
23. Mass, *Population Target*, p. 27.
24. Bruce Dancis, 'Socialism and Women in the United States, 1900–1912', *Socialist Revolution*, 27, vol. VI, no. 1, January–March 1976, p.85.
25. David M. Kennedy, *Birth Control in America: The career of Margaret Sanger* (New Haven, CT, and London: Yale University Press, 1976), pp. 21–2.
26. Mass, *Population Target*, p. 20.
27. Gordon, *Woman's Body, Woman's Right*, p. 281.
28. Mass, *Population Target*, p. 20.
29. Gordon, *Woman's Body, Woman's Right*, p. 283.
30. Herbert Aptheker, 'Sterilization Experimentation and Imperialism', *Political Affairs*, vol. LIII, no. 1, January 1974, p. 44.
31. Gena Corea, *The Hidden Malpractice* (New York: A Jove/HBJ Book, 1977), p. 149.
32. Gordon, *Woman's Body, Woman's Right*, p. 332.
33. Ibid., pp. 332–3.
34. Aptheker, 'Sterilization', p. 38. See, also, Anne Braden, 'Forced Sterilization: Now women can fight back', *Southern Patriot*, September 1973.
35. Ibid.
36. Jack Slater, 'Sterilization, Newest Threat to the Poor', *Ebony*, vol. XXVIII, no. 12, October 1973, p. 150.
37. Braden, 'Forced Sterilization'.
38. Les Payne, 'Forced Sterilization for the Poor?', San Francisco Chronicle, 26 February 1974.
39. Harold X., 'Forced Sterilization Pervades South', *Muhammed Speaks*, 10 October 1975.
40. Slater, 'Sterilization, Newest Threat to the Poor'.
41. Payne, 'Forced Sterilization'.
42. Ibid.
43. Ibid.
44. Aptheker, 'Sterilization', p. 40.
45. Payne, 'Forced Sterilization'.
46. Aptheker, 'Sterilization', p. 48.
47. Arlene Eisen, 'They're Trying to Take Our Future – Native American Women and Sterilization', *The Guardian*, 23 March 1972.
48. Ibid.
49. Ibid.
50. Quoted in a pamphlet issued by the Committee to End Sterilization Abuse, Box A244, Cooper Station, New York 10003.
51. Ibid.
52. Ibid.
53. Gordon, *Woman 's Body, Woman's Right*, p. 338.

54. Ibid., p. 338.
55. Mass, *Population Target*, p. 92.
56. Ibid., p. 91.
57. Gordon, *Woman's Body, Woman's Right*, p. 401. See, also, pamphlet issued by the Committee to End Sterilization Abuse.
58. Mass, *Population Target*, p. 108.
59. Rahemah Aman, 'Forced Sterilization', *Union Wage*, 4 March 1978.
60. Ibid.

4.2

'FEMINISMS AND UNIVERSALISMS: "UNIVERSAL RIGHTS" AND THE LEGAL DEBATE AROUND THE PRACTICE OF FEMALE EXCISION IN FRANCE'

Françoise Lionnet

In the American academy, the experience of the last two decades of literary and cultural criticism seems to have created almost insurmountable differences between 'Western' modes of analysis of the concrete status of women in various non-Western cultures, on the one hand, and non-Western women's subjective experience of their own position, on the other hand.[1] Is it possible, in such a climate, for a critic based in the academy to 'illuminate', as Fatima Mernissi has put it, non-Western social contexts within which the 'structural dissymmetry' of gender is embedded?[2] To attempt to do so, I would like to take as case in point the issue of female genital excision which has again come to the attention of public opinion in France and other Western European countries where African immigrants are having it performed on their daughters.

To address such an issue, interdisciplinary work of the kind with which the past two decades of academic feminisms have made us familiar remains important. Feminisms (in the plural) have been a major intellectual tool for interrogating the production (and the reproduction) of knowledge across the academy. Feminist scholars in history, sociology, anthropology, psychology, psychoanalysis, philosophy, legal theory and literary criticism have provided us with paradigms that have broadened our understanding of the politics of representation across time and place and, more specifically, the representation of women as the object of patriarchal knowledge – across disciplinary and cultural boundaries.

From: Françoise Lionnet (1992), 'Feminisms and Universalisms: "Universal Rights" and the Legal Debate Around the Practice of Female Excision in France', pp. 97–113, in *Inscriptions*, vol. 6.

Because of the cross-fertilization among different disciplines that has occurred thanks in large part to this kind of inquiry, I believe that feminism has, in many ways, lived up to its early promise of interrogating the nineteenth-century model of the university organized around disciplines and periods. As Naomi Schor and Elizabeth Weed have recently put it in an issue of *differences* devoted to 'Feminism and the Institution', to question *that* traditional model of the university is 'not only to critique and resist disciplinarization within the university, but to struggle against the split between inside and outside . . . The challenge of academic feminism has always been to displace the very categories constituting the academy and its other [i.e. what is also called the 'real world' and it is that challenge that US feminists of color and Italian feminisms are, in different ways, reasserting today.'[3] It is of course true, as Elaine Marks affirms in the pages of the same journal, that one of the most surprising developments about women's studies and feminist theory in general has been 'the reproduction of familiar discourses and paradigms that existed – whether in the United States, or France, or England, or Italy – within other political, intellectual and pedagogical fields, as if the "feminist" inquiry were imprisoned in national, sometimes chauvanist modes of thinking and writing.' And Marks goes on to add: 'Feminist studies' worst enemies have been those who have treated "feminism" like a new religion with dogmas that can allow for only one possible interpretation.'[4] I think that the only way out of that fundamentalist feminist impasse is, and will continue to be, through the awareness of the multicultural dimensions of women's real lives in and out of the academy – and that's where working between disciplines becomes imperative.

For my purposes in this paper, I'd like to focus on the legal debates that now exists in France on the issue of rights, bodily integrity and female excision. The fact that this practice exists in Europe began to surface at a time when the rights of all children were also being widely debated, fostering new legislation to protect them from various forms of physical and sexual abuse.

On February 2, 1981, a new law was introduced in the French penal code with the express purpose of repressing violence against minors. Article 312–2 of the code states the various types of legal sanctions that can be used to punish those found guilty of assault and battery or 'coups et blessures volontaires á enfants de moins de 15 ans'. During the following decade, several interesting judicial cases that raised complex cultural questions would be tried on the basis of this law. They all involve African families whose daughters were subjected to this custom. Viewed as intolerable by Western critics since colonial times, excision consists primarily of clitoridectomy, but can also be accompanied by the excision of all or part of the labia and by infibulation (or the stitching together) of the two sides of the vulva. It can be fatal and is increasingly considered – in the West – as a violation of basic human rights.[5]

Transferred by immigrants from their own countries to their new homeland, this rite of passage is meant to mark entrance into adulthood and is normally accompanied by extensive psychological preparation in the form of religious teachings and ritualized observances. When performed in France, however, much of the ritual apparatus is absent. This was the case when Mantessa Baradji, a five-week-old baby girl died of a slow but fatal haemorrhage on April 3, 1983, the day after she had been excised. This case, as well as two other non-fatal ones, involving Batou Doukara and Assa Traore, excised respectively at the ages of three months in 1980, and one week in 1984, were tried in criminal court, and suspended jail terms of one to three years were given to the parents. Several other cases are pending, and the justice system is becoming ever more severe in its attempt to suppress the practice. But at the same time, a serious legal controversy has emerged around these decisions.

The debate opposes two apparently conflicting versions of human rights, one based on the Enlightenment notion of the sovereign individual subject, and the other on a notion of collective identity grounded in cultural solidarity. Critics of the Enlightenment version of human rights have opposed to it the more culturally-specific concept of human dignity, stating that 'concepts of human dignity do indeed vary. They are embedded in cultural views of the nature of human beings, which interm reflect the social organization of particular societies', and adding that 'in Africa, idealized versions of human dignity reflect idealized interpretations of pre-colonial structure'.[6] When emphasis is on the group, protection of the individual *qua* sovereign individual subject can be at odds with her development as a fully-functioning member of her own society. By criminalizing the practice and sending to jail the parents of the excised girls, the French courts have judged individuals guilty of an act of violence which they had, in fact, no intention of committing, since their behavior was in accordance with deeply-held socio-cultural and religious beliefs about the nature of femininity and the function of sexuality in their respective collectivities. Anthropologists and social critics have argued that such sanctions will have little if any positive impact, since families may continue to have the excision performed either clandestinely in France (and with greater risk to the girls' life and health) or back in Africa during school vacations.

Geneviève Guidicelli-Delage has pointed out that France is the only European country confronted with this issue that actually prosecutes 'les auteurs et complices d'excision'.[7] This, she says, presents serious judicial risks since 'le prétoire pénal est le lieu où l'on juge exclusivement des comportements individuels et non un lieu où l'on débat de pratiques collectives'.[8] Despite these warnings, the most recent jury trial at the Paris *Courd'assises* on March 6, 7 and 8, 1991, concluded with the harshest punishment ever: a five-year jail term for Aramata Keita, a resident of France and a member of the caste of women ironworkers who traditionally perform excision in Mali, and a five years' suspended sentence with two years' probation for the parents, Sory and Sémite Coulibaly, who had their six daughters excised by Keita in 1982 and 1983.

As *Le Monde* reported, in its coverage of the trial, the presence of the three accused in the dock seemed but 'a pretext, were it not for the fact that they were risking imprisonment'.[9] Although three individuals were sent to jail, it seems as though the courts tried the practice rather than the persons involved: 'The three accused listened to proceedings without understanding them. Their two interpreters did not translate the debate being conducted in court – which occasionally took the air of a symposium.'[10] The woman public prosecutor dismissed experts' arguments regarding the pressures of ethnic customs and the ways in which such a practice forms part of a whole social system. She stressed the fact that Keita received a financial reward for her services (ostensibly the symbolic and documented offering of a *pagne* and some soap, but presumably other unacknowledged monies totalling approximately one hundred francs) and because of this, the prosecutor demanded – and got – an exemplary decision from the jury, stating: 'From today on, it must be made quite clear to every African family that excision has become a money-making activity which risks incurring a very heavy sentence.'[11] Under the guise of protecting young girls from a 'barbaric mutilation', the French legal system has victimized three individuals who were not themselves treated as persons in their own right during the trial, since it was clear that intentions, motivations and responsibility – which are the foundations of individual guilt before the law – could not be interpreted as criminal.[12] As the respected ethnopsychiatrist Michel Erlich has explained, the reasons for the continued performance of this practice are compelling psychosexual ones for those involved, since it is embedded in a cultural context that encodes it as a beautifying and enriching phenomenon without which girls do not become women and will therefore never be able to marry, have some degree of economic security and lead 'full' female lives.

However objectionable the practice, and many women and men in Africa and the Middle East have denounced it, putting complex 'strategies for eradication'[13] in place in countries like Senegal, Sierra Leone or Egypt, experts in the field agree that education remains the essential tool, whereas legal action cannot even be justified on judicial or juridical grounds, since there exists no law in France that specifically forbids excision, only the above-mentioned art. 312–3 which must be *interpreted* as relevant to these particular cases in order for it to apply. The social, economic and psychological consequences of jail for the families of the condemned parties are ignored by the courts, which thus manifest a blatant disregard for collective, familial and community values, and under the pretext of protecting the abstract rights of an individual child, penalize the child by arbitrarily sentencing her parents for the purposes of making an example of them.

It is to reflect upon the contradictions and difficulties that arise from these complex human rights issues that a working group or 'Atelier Droits des Peuples et Droits de l'Homme' was created at the *Centre Droit et Cultures* of the University of Paris–Nanterre. The first series of essays pertaining to excision was recently published in the journal of the centre, *Droit et Cultures*, and I would like to briefly survey the preliminary results of this workshop because of the importance that they will have in defining the discourse about identity and sexuality within immigrant communities in France, and because it re-opens the question of universal rights in an unprecedented way.

The increasing diversity and plurality of French society has given rise to cultural conflicts that continue to erupt around topics such as citizenship, habitation, schooling, dress and the rhetoric of difference and equality, or integration and xenophobia, that has characterized political discourse in the 1980s. These are forcing a reexamination of the principles of universal democracy and natural rights that had theoretically been taken for granted since the Revolution of 1789. As Raymond Verdier explains, it has become necessary to rethink the familiar Western dialectic based on the oppositional paradigm of the individual versus society and to conceptualize in its place 'des droits dits de la solidarité'.

> Cessant de prendre pour point de départ le sujet individuel mais envisageant l'homme comme membre d'une communauté humaine diversifiée, l'approche proposée entend échapper tant à un pur relativisme culturel qui mettrait en pièce l'unité du genre humain qu'à un pseudo-universalisme totalitaire et impérialiste qui méconnaitrait tout droit à la différence et conduirait à la négation de toute identité culturelle et religieuse, selon 'la configuration moderne indivualiste des valeurs'.
>
> Difficile conciliation à promouvoir qui nécessite d'un cotée la connaissance profonde des traditions culturelles, de leur évolution et de leur transformation, de l'autre un regard critique sur la nation d'identité qui nous évite de tomber dans les pièges de l'ethnocentrisme. (p. 149)[14]
>
> [The approach we propose would not take the individual subject as its point of departure, but would look at the human being as a member of a diversified community. This would avoid the recourse to either the pure cultural relativism that undermines the unity of the human race of the totalitarian pseudo-universalism that would refuse the right to difference and lead to the negation of all cultural and religious identity, in keeping with 'the modern individualist configuration of values'.
>
> This is a difficult conciliation, and it requires a deep understanding of cultural traditions, of their evolution and transformation on the one hand, and on the other, a critical look at the notion of identity as as to avoid falling into the traps of ethnocentrism.]

The practice of female excision is a kind of ideal test-case, since it apparently illustrates absolute and total cultural conflict between the rights of the individual to bodily integrity on the one hand, and her need to be satisfactorily integrated into a community on the other. But, as Michel Erlich reminds us, this right to bodily integrity is by no means an absolute value in Western society, since male circumcision, tonsillectomy and appendectomy – which can be viewed as ritual forms of surgery comparable to ethnic 'mutilations', and which have been the object of controversy among medical professionals – are culturally acceptable, and thus to not fall under art 312–3 of the penal code (pp. 159

ff.) Furthermore, what Erlich calls a form of 'misogynie medicalisée' [medicalized mysogyny] was the reason why excision was frequently performed, (as were ovariectomy and hysterectomy) from the seventeenth to the early twentieth century: to treat nymphomania, hypertrophy of the female genitalia, masturbation and lesbianism. A famous seventeenth-century French surgeon named Dionis credited with being the first one to recommend excision 'comme remède à la lascivité féminine' [as a remedy against feminine lasciviousness].[15] To defend the practice on strictly cultural relativist grounds is thus as misguided as to condemn it on univarsalist and humanitarian ones, since complex psychological phenomena both in Europe and elsewhere have motivated its existence, and only education and information combined with an open and tolerant approach to different definitions of identity and sexuality will eventually help eradicate excision.

Can one oppose the practice on a feminist epistemological ground that might allow us to argue that in all of the above cases, the common denominator is a – conscious or unconscious, individual or collective – example of misogyny and homophobia which aims at curbing all manifestations of female sexuality, and thus represents a universal fear and hatred of women which must be countered by the appeal to a universal approach to human rights, the only means of protection for female children in misogynist cultures? Ideally, perhaps one can. But to condemn excision as a violation of human rights is to arbitrarily presume that such a practice is the only culturally sanctioned form of violence that deserves to be denounced, whereas we know that many other forms of violence are not repressed by law in the Western context, and that some of our own practices are objectionable and shocking to Africans.

Erlich expresses doubts about some of the radical Western feminist arguments, and states that it is 'un étrange paradoxe' that women's right to pleasure and to the integrity of their bodies

> passe par une législation qui légitime l'avortement, mutilation majeure dont la légalisation a effectivement contribué à libération féminine dans notre société, mais qui est encore considérée par bon nombre de nos concitoyens comme un crime et jugée en tant que tel dans ces cultures aux moeurs mutilantes, que notre activisme humanitaire a décidé de traiter par des moyens eux-memes mutilants.[16]

> [is linked to a legislation that legitimates abortion, a major mutilation the legalization of which did indeed contribute to female liberation in our society, but which is still considered a crime by many, and judged as such in those cultures that practice mutilations, and that our humanitarian activism has decided to treat by mutilating means.]

To accept the legality of abortion, but to criminally repress the performance of excision is one of those paradoxes of contemporary legal practice that seem to arbitrarily condemn 'exotic' or 'foreign' barbaric practices regardless of precedents in our own culture that are legal and acceptable to a majority because they are situated within a particular framework of rights and gender that no longer shock our sense of fairness or interfere with our freedom to live according to our own values. Although Erlich does not elaborate on the parallel he draws with abortion, the suggestion is provocative and compelling because it does seem to put the abortion issue within a context of reproductive rights that forces a re-examination of both feminist individualism and modern notions of freedom of choice.

Given the social stigmas that still attach to unwed motherhood among the middle classes, and the financial and emotional difficulties that will continue to be involved in raising a child as a single parent so long as the responsibility for doing so is primarily the mother's, one might argue that there is no real 'freedom of choice' for many women to decide to have an abortion. Indeed, aren't some of them – like the African women influenced by their communities' views on excision – deciding to have an abortion because it is the only possible solution in an economic and cultural context that might force them to choose between a career and motherhood, or to gain acceptance within their own social or professional communities as women who are truly in charge of their own lives and reproductive capacities? The rhetoric in favor of abortion has stressed the rights of women to choose, and that is why the law should protect that right and sustain the legality of the procedure. Note also that the parallel Erlich draws between abortion and excision is *not* based on a religious view of the fetus as different 'person' whose rights are in conflict with those of the mother (as the fundamentalist Christian right would have it), but more on a view of pregnancy as a 'natural' consequence of female sexuality, just as we might see the clitoris as a 'natural' part of the female body. In this view, abortion, like excision, simply imposes cultural constraints on physical reality, and both procedures can arguably be defended by their proponents as cultural steps taken to avoid biological determinism.

The question of choice thus remains problematic when one focuses not just on individual rights, but on the way such rights may be in conflict with the broader social, religious or communitarian values to which an individual woman has to subscribe if she is to remain a respected member of her community, as opposed to being a 'free' agent in our increasingly atomized capitalist culture. Here again, the modern individualist view of freedom leaves much to be desired, since identity remains so closely linked to particularist views of reproductive rights and sexual choices, and in the case of women choosing motherhood, to their – by no means universal – right to health care, day care and social programs that will help in the task of raising children.

What this suggests is that radical individualism is an empty word for women, whether they live in 'traditional' societies that uphold practices that are shocking to us, citizens of modern states that theoretically protect human rights, or are such citizens living under a comforting illusion of choice that does not sustain critical scrutiny whenever we examine the supposedly 'voluntary' acts that involve sexuality and reproduction. Similarly, ritual practices are not adhered to 'voluntarily': the mother, like Sémité Coulibaly, who solicits the services of a woman to excise her daughters, believes that she is conforming to the traditions of her community, and that failing to do so would jeopardize her daughters' chances of being accepted by their community of origin. Furthermore, refusal to allow excision of the daughters runs the risk of endangering the mother's opportunity to engage in the slow process of liberation that now allows African women living in France to oppose polygamy, to work, and to enroll in literacy programs *so long as* they are not perceived by the immigrant community as imposing these 'new' values on their own daughters: 'Si en plus on s'approprie les filles on sera rejetée par tout le monde, renvoyées au village . . .' [If on top of all this we seem to be appropriating the girls, we'll be rejected by everyone, sent back to the village . . .] as one woman exclaimed. Her fear is echoed by most of the Soninké of Mali who participated in the study conducted in Paris by Catherine Quiminal.[17]

At stake is the definition of tradition itself, the way it forms part of a network of power within which conflicting notions of freedom, community, and authority hold ground. Quiminal is well aware of this.

> Comme toutes les traditions, les mutilations sexualles des femmes ne sont traditions que dans la mesure où les intéressés n'one d'autres possibiltés que de les subir sous peine d'être exclues de leur communauté. Dés lors qu'elles sont contestées, les traditions apparaissent pour ce qu'elles sont: expression d'un rapport de force, arguments d'authorité.[18]
>
> [Like all traditions, the sexual mutilation of women is a 'tradition' only to the extent that the women concerned have no choice but to submit to it or else be excluded from their community. As soon as they are contested, traditions are revealed to be but the expression of power relations, arguments of authority.]

Excision makes clear how power relations are inscribed on the female body by virtue of its subjection to particular sexual traditions. Indeed, the reasons for this practice have to do with complex definitions of masculinity and femininity that construct the clitoris and the male prepuce as vestiges of the opposite sex that must be eliminated for a 'proper' sexual identity to exist. Thus, the female body is considered 'too masculine' and socially unacceptable when not marked by excision. Malian women are culturally dependent on this view of sexuality that forms the basis of their feminine identity. This situation illustrates well Michel Foucault's insight that 'the political technology of the body' amounts to a 'system of subjection'[19] of individual persons within a specific cultural code.

It is interesting to note that in the African context, the discourse on female sexuality defines femininity in terms of binary *cultural* inscriptions (male circumcision/female excision) rather than purely biological categories of male/female.[20] One becomes a female person after having submitted to a cultural process, one is not simply born a 'woman'. Similarly, a 'person' is not a person until he/she has been marked by society in a way that gives him/her dignity and social status within a specific ethnic group. Isaac Nguema has stressed that throughout 'traditional' Africa 'la personne humaine n'a de valeur qu'à l'intérieur de son groupe ethnique . . . la personalité juridique . . . s'acquiert au fur et à mesure que la personne franchit les étpes de la vie: à l'occasion de la circoncision . . . du mariage . . . de la naissance des enfants' [the person has value only as a member of her own ethnic group . . . the legal personality . . . develops as one goes through different stages of life: on the occasion of circumcision . . . marriage . . . and the birth of children].[21] Thus, he argues, the African notion of 'person' is a more interactive and dynamic one compared to the Western one which he sees as 'abstraite, mécanique, statique, matérialiste' [abstract, mechanistic, static, materialistic] and intolerant of genuine solidarity since an absolute view of individual rights will necessarily enter in conflict with a genuine form of familial of cultural solidarity.

Problems then arise because the power of Malian culture to invest meaning in the individual body is at odds with the French State's power to construct that body's biological integrity according to modern notions of individual rights. When Malians fall under the authority of the French courts on French territory, their bodies are invested with full responsibility for their actions and intentions, and they become liable to imprisonment, not so much because the performance and/or abetting of excision is a violation of the rights of children, as the application of art. 312–3 would suggest, but because the state locates meaning and identity in the individual, autonomous body of its *citizens*. Because the Coulibalys reside in France, it is the authority and sovereignty of the French courts that are exercised. It is the Coulibaly's identity as immigrants that supercedes their 'Africanness'. Sylvie Fainzang is well aware of the specifically legal aspect of a dilemma which is increasingly familiar in a pluralistic society, and which faces all those who live in two cultures, with a foot in each world:

> L'excision est donc pratiquée pour se conformer à une loi; elle est le résultat d'une conformité à une pratique collective et de la soumission à une contrainte sociale. Les individus se retrouvent pris comme dans un étau entre deux Lois contraires: la conformité à l'une entrainant *ipso facto* le non-respect de l'autre.[22]
>
> [Excision is thus performed in order to obey a law; it results from the need to conform to a collective practice, and from the fact of being subjected to a social constraint. Individuals are thus caught as in a vise between two opposing Laws: to obey the one *ipso facto* leads to breaking the other.]

Both laws represent two systems of power which hold sway over individual responsibility, undermining the very possibility of assigning individual blame. These cases demystify the fiction of the sovereign subject since the subjectivity of the defendants can easily be shown to be the site of conflicting and contradictory constraints. The 'power-knowledge relations'[23] created by the courts' intransigence is a reflection of the absolute non-commensurability of the two cultural systems that interface in these cases.

Indeed, since excision can very well be defined as a 'custom' in the technical sense allowed by French law (according to art. 327 of the penal code), this should exempt it from criminalization, just as corporeal punishment of children is exempt because it is considered an acceptable form of parental behavior sanctioned by 'custom' as understood by this law (Merle & Vitu).[24] The crux of the matter here is clearly a question of which jurisdiction has authority on the persons accused, and what constitutes 'custom' or tradition or precedent under that jurisdiction. Guidicelli-Delage puts it clearly:

> Dans le conflit de cultures que constitue l'excision, toute position qui pourrait laisser croire à une tolérance de cette pratique sur le territoire français est condamnée au nom de l'ordre public interne et des principes fondamentaux de l'homme . La culture qui est la notre ne peut qu'affirmer haut et fort son rejet de l'excision. Mais par quelle voie l'affirmer? La voie judiciaire actuellement pratiquée, la voie législative, ou encore une 'troisième voie' . . .?[25]
>
> [Within the conflict of cultures that excision foregrounds, any position that might suggest a tolerant attitude toward this practice on French territory is condemned in the name of our own internal public order, and of fundamental human principles. Our culture can only proclaim its vigorous opposition to excision. But by which means can it do so? The judicial way, as is currently done, the legislative way, or yet a 'third way' . . . ?]

For Guidicelli-Delage, there is no doubt that the only worthwhile and effective approach is the 'third' one, that is, cooperation with those African countries that are slowly struggling to put in place new cultural forms by educational, and not repressive, means: 'Il faut pour chasser une ancienne coutume qu'une nouvelle prenne sa place, qu'une nouvelle culture se forge at non se volt imposer' [The way to phase out an ancient custom is to allow a new one to replace it, to let a new culture to forge itself, not to impose one from above].[26] To apply abstract Enlightenment values in a rigidly intolerant legal way is to undermine the system's own claim to universality since it thereby condemns practices that form part of a network of social values which are the scaffolding upon which rests the global equilibrium of a *different* culture. These practices are not just irrational and aberrant abuses as many uninformed Western critics would like to believe. It is in fact possible to see them as part of a coherent, rational and workable system, albeit one as flawed and unfair to women as our own can be.

The March 8, 1991 ruling marks the Coulibalys as subjects of/to the French State. Ironically, their identity is thus reconstructed by the same court that might ultimately decide whether or not to grant them citizenship, in accordance with recent decisions about the right of immigrants to full French citizenship. Interestingly, then, it is the same sort of power relations that impose a different 'national' identity (and the customs that go with it) on immigrant families whose right to citizenship is not even clear that is also central to the construction of sexual identity in the cultures that allow excision. Sylvie Fainzang explains:

> L'analyse des discours relatifs à cette pratique révèle qu'il s'agit en fair, avec les mutilations sexuelles, de faconner les individus de manière à les rendre aptes à assumer le role social qui leur est réservé en raison de leur sexe. Cette différenciation sexualle est motivée par une volonté de différenciatioin des statuts sociaux . . . Le marquage sexuel que réalise l'excision est la condition de l'accés à un statut social spécifique, celui de *femme, soumise à l'autorité de l'homme*. La pratique de l'excision repose donc sur la volonté de créer les conditions (physique) de la domination (sociale) de l'homme sur la femme.[27]

> [The analysis of discourses relating to this practice reveals that sexual mutilations are a means of disciplining individuals, of rendering them fit for the social role which is reserved for them because of their gender. This sexual differentiation is motivated by the will to distinguish among different social statuses . . . The sexual marking provided by excision is the necessary condition of access to a specific social status, that is of *woman subjected to the authority of man*. The practice of excision thus depends on the will to create the (physical) conditions of the (social) domination of woman by man.]

On the one hand, we have immigrants who are subordinated to French law, on the other, females brought under the authority of males. In either case, it would seem that we are very far indeed from any individualist conceptions of rights. It is a conception of identity as subordinate to either the state (France) or the ruling patriarchy (in Mali) that governs the (il)legitimacy of parental behaviour. It is therefore pointless to claim that the issue opposes communitarian values to universal ones, since the actual conflict hinges on the opposing claims of two different communities, one of which would like to believe that its culture is a 'universal' one.

What does appear to be 'universal' when we carefully examine the whole cultural contexts within which the debate is situated is the way in which *different* cultures, for better or for worse, impose *similar* constraints on the bodies of their members, especially when those bodies are already marked by the sign of the feminine. Both cultures – the French and the African – have ways of disciplining and socializing the body that denote highly complex socio-cultural organizations, and the work done by the *Centre Droit et Cultures* attests to the long-term educational process that still needs to take place in order for African immigrants to liberate themselves from age-old customs, and for the French legal system to accommodate the increasing diversity that is now French society. This diversity has the incontestable merit of underscoring the injustices and inequalities of our own culture, and of reminding us that 'le barbare, c'est d'abord l'home qui croit à la barbarie' [The barbarian is first and foremost the one who believes in barbarism] as Lévi-Strauss once put it.[28]

NOTES

1. I wish to thank the Rockefeller Foundation and the Center for Advanced Feminist Studies at the University of Minnesota, and the University of California Humanities Research Institute, for supporting my research and writing during the 1991–92 academic year.
2. Fatima Mernissi, *Beyond the Veil: Male-Female Dynamics in Modern Muslim Society* (Indianapolis: Indiana University Press, 1987), p. ix.
3. Naomi Schor and Elizabeth Weed, Editors' 'Preface', 'Notes from the Beehive: Feminism and the Institution', special issue of *differences* 2:3 (Fall 1990), p. vi.
4. Elaine Marks, et al., 'Conference Call', *differences* 2:3 (Fall 1990), pp. 72–3.
5. Allison Slack T., 'Female Circumcision: A Critical Appraisal', *Human Rights Quarterly* 10 (1988).
6. Rhoda E. Howard, *Human Rights in Commonwealth Africa* (New Jersey: Rowman and Littlefield, 1986), p. 17.
7. Geneviève Guidicalli-Delage, 'Excision et droit Pénal', *Droit et Cultures* 20 (1990), p. 207.
8. Ibid., p. 208.
9. Maurice Peyrot, 'Tribal Practices Pose Dilemma for Western Society', *The Guardian Weekly*, March 24th, (1991), p. 16 (Translation of Le Monde Articles).
10. Ibid., pp. 15–16.
11. Ibid., p. 16.
12. Geneviève Guidicalli-Delage, 'Excision et droit Pénal', p. 205.
13. Olayinka Koso-Thomas, *The Circumcision of Women: A Strategy for Eradication* (London: Zed Books, 1987).
14. Raymond Verdier, 'Chercher remède à l'excision: une nécessaire concertation', *Droit et Cultures* 20 (1990), p. 149.
15. Michel Erlich, 'Notions de mutilation et criminalisation de l'excision en France', *Droit et Cultures* 20 (1990), p. 156. This medical 'solution' to the 'problems' of female sexuality reaches its apex during the Victorian era in Britain, and continues to be performed until the 1950s in the United States: 'Reprise par LEVRET, cette solution radical inaugure une stratégie répressive de la sexualité féminine don't le sadisme va s'accentuer tout au long du XIXe siècle. Appliquée pour la première fois en 1822 par GRAFFE au traitement de la 'folie masturbatoire', la clitoridectomie est érigée en panacée quarante ans plus tard par BAKER-BROWN, chirurgien britannique de renom qui passe à la postérité comme le champion de l'excision 'thérapeutique'. A la meme époque, l'américain BATTEY, autre grand mutilateur propose l'ovariectomie q'il qualifie de 'normale', c'est-à-dire la castration féminine, enguise de traitement de divers troubles nerveux. Culminant à lépoque victorienne en Angleterre et aux Etas-Unis, cette mysoginie médicalisée va se prolonger dans ce dernier pays jusqu'au courant du XXe siècle, où elle trouvera encore e'ultimes adeptes jusque dans les années cinquante. Ainsi les indications médicales des mutilations sexualles évoluent du domaine de la pathologie morphologique à celui de la pathologie psychologique' [Adapted by Levret, this medical solution innaugurates a strategy of repression of female sexuality the sadism of which will increase all through the 19th century. Clitoridectomy was first used in 1822 by Graefe to treat 'masturbatory madness', and forty years later, it was chosen as a panacea by Barker-Brown, the famed British surgeon who will be remembered by posterity as the champion of 'therapeutic' excision. At about the same time, Battey, an American, and also a great mutilator, proposes ovariectomy, that is female castration, which he defines as 'normal', as a means of treatment for a number of nervous ailments. This medicalized form of misogyny culminates in England during the Victorian era,

but in the United States, it will continue to be performed during the 20th century, with some doctors still prescribing it in the 1950s. This is how the medical uses of sexual mutiliation evolve from the domain of physical pathology to that of psychological pathology], p. 156).

16. Ibid., p. 161.
17. Catherine Quiminla, Les Soninké en France et au Mali: le débat sur les mutilations sexuelles', *Droit et Cultures* 20 (1990), p. 190.
18. Ibid., p. 183.
19. Michel Foucault, *Discipline and Punish: The Birth of the Prison*, trans. Alan Sheridan (New York: Vintage Books, 1979), p. 26.
20. See Michel Erlich, *La Femme blessée* (Paris: L'Hartman, 1986) and Françoise Lionnet, 'Feminism, Universalism and the Practice of Female Excision', *Passages* 1 (1990).
21. Isaac Nguema, 'Universalité et spécificité des droits de l'homme en Africque: la conception traditionelle de la personne humaine' *Droit et Cultures* 19 (1990), p. 215.
22. Sylvie Fainzang, 'Excision et ordre social', *Droit et Cultures* 20 (1990), p. 180.
23. Michael Foucault *Discipline and Punish*, p. 27.
24. Merle and Vitu. *Traite de droit criminel* (Paris: Cujas 1980).
25. Ibid., pp. 206–7.
26. Ibid., p. 210.
27. Sylie Fainzang, 'Excision et ordre social', *Droit et Cultures* 20 (1990), pp. 177–8.
28. Claude Levi-Strauss, *Race et histoire* (Paris: Gonthier, 1961), p. 22.

4.3

'STATE VERSUS ISLAM: MALAY FAMILIES, WOMEN'S BODIES AND THE BODY POLITIC IN MALAYSIA'

Aihwa Ong

In the summer of 1990, on my annual visit to Malaysia, I noticed that many young Malay women had traded in their black Islamic robes (*hijab*) for pastel colored ones, and that their headcloths (*mini-telekung*) were now embroidered with flowers. The effect was rather like seeing a black and white film in color. In the late 1970s and early 1980s, when Malaysian campuses were the hotbeds of Islamic resurgence, female students shrouded in black robes and veils sometimes appeared like phalanxes of Allah's soldiers. Now university women were dressed in *hijab* outfits that had been transformed by color and more subtle touches in cut, style and decoration. As they walked around campus, many attracted the eyes of young men, who were sometimes rewarded with subdued giggles and responsive glances. The Islamic resurgence of the 1970s, emerging in its black female garb and fiery criticism of Western consumerism, official corruption and the spiritual hollowness of modern life, had settled down as a normalized cultural practice in which people carried on the daily affairs of life of an affluent, developing country.

Competing images of the Malay woman and family are key elements in the social construction of modern Malaysian society. This chapter discusses the social effects of state policies and Islamic resurgence from the 1980s to the early 1990s, as they both negotiated different models of Malay womanhood and

From: Aihwa Ong (1995), 'State Versus Islam: Malay Families, Women's Bodies and the Body Politic in Malaysia', pp. 160–94, in Aihwa Ong and Michael G. Peletz (eds), *Bewitching Women, Pious Men: Gender and Body Politics in Southeast Asia* (California: The University of California Press).

kinship. By seeking out the contrasting logic and tropes of official and resurgent discourses, my interpretation differs from other studies of the secular Malaysian state and the Islamic resurgence. Scholars have examined the impact of state intervention on Malay class differentiation (Jomo 1988; Scott 1985; Shamsul 1986; Wong 1988) while viewing the Islamic resurgence as an anti-government strategy among the politically marginalized (Kessler 1978, 1980; Nagata 1984; Chandra 1986; Hassan 1987). These works on state-peasant relations have focused on the structural reorganization of Malaysian society but have quite misplaced the class emphasis of the Islamic resurgence, and the critical role of gender renegotiation in modern Malay life.

Challenging these views, I argue that the state project and the Islamic resurgence must be seen as competing forms of postcolonial nationalism that fix upon the Malay family and woman as icons of particular forms of modernity. Writing about 'imagined communities', Benedict Anderson (1992) focused on the rise of 'official nationalisms' led by traditional elites in their struggles against colonial rulers, but he quite neglected the importance of what Partha Chatterjee calls the 'narrative of community' that is not domesticated to the requirements of the postcolonial state (1993: pp. 238–39). In Malaysia, state-sponsored development expressed a particular vision of modernity that incited an Islam-inspired backlash among the emergent Malay middle classes attempting to secure their interests against state encroachments that challenge male authority. These tensions in the state-Islamic struggle are frequently ignored by scholars accustomed to interpreting Malaysian political culture in terms of peasant politics and electoral struggles (a major exception is Kessler 1978). For instance, *Fragmented Vision* (Kahn and Loh 1993), a volume that claims to explore different visions of postcolonial Malaysian society, remains heavily focused on intra- and interethnic rivalries while giving short shrift to gender relations in the re-envisioning of modern Malaysia. Such a male bias reproduces an orientalist view whereby Asian women, fetishized as sexual objects (mothers, wives, prostitutes) and cheap docile workers, are disregarded as political subjects and icons in the struggle to redefine communal identity (Ong 1993).

Indeed, the political culture of postcolonial societies is often forged in ideological struggles over the concepts of family, gender and race. For instance, in implementing secular, technocratic development projects, modern states routinely zero in on the domestic unit as the object of social policy. In countries as different as early-twentieth-century France (Donzelot 1979), contemporary Singapore (Salaff 1988), and socialist China (Anagnost 1989), the family has been variously defined, manipulated and generally subjected to the regulation of health, educational, and welfare programs. Such disciplinary interventions are an aspect of what Michel Foucault calls 'bio-power', or the state management of the population to secure its control, welfare and productivity (1978: pp. 141–7). Modern state power is not imposed so much as absorbed into society through the 'capillary' actions of the human sciences and social techniques that penetrate the nooks and crannies of everyday life. In Malaysia, the New Economic Policy (introduced in 1972) represented not only the economic modernization of Malay society, but also a social intervention into its very constitution and understanding of itself. Official policies were introduced to reshape domestic relations, to mark off the domestic from the public and to sponsor the large-scale entry of young women into mass education and industry.

What have been the cultural effects of this state reconstitution of the Malay peasantry? James Scott (1985), insisting upon an indefensible demarcation between state hegemony and Malay peasant culture, maintains that 'everyday forms of resistance' are an index of peasants' agency protesting economic change in the countryside. While Scott's general observations about peasant resentment may have captured the contrary impulses of village Malaysia, his model of individualistic expressions of free will unmediated by larger solidarities as Muslims and as Malays in Malaysia is highly problematic.[1] As Foucault has pointed out, subjects are materially constituted by power relations and are always part of them. Malay peasants' increasingly dense ties to government programs, party politics and patronage networks cannot be discounted in our understanding of their agency. Thus the question of agency, as reformulated by Marilyn Strathern, goes beyond the independent action of individuals and must focus on the interests 'in terms of which they act'; their aims are 'not necessarily . . . independently conceived' (1987: p. 22). Her perspective refines and moves beyond the 'active/passive' model often used in discussions of women's agency. Although I will sometimes talk about the independent actions of individual women and men, in this essay I generally conceive of social agency in terms of 'how social effects are registered' (Strathern 1987: p. 23) in shifting fields of power. For instance, regardless of the motivations and experiences of individuals, tensions between state policies and the Islamic resurgence have incited and intensified concerns about female sex, spaces and actions, and these tensions have gone into shaping the changing social order. Knowledge-power schemes imposed by the state, and the counterdisciplinary actions proposed by Islamic revivalists, have affected women in different classes in different ways. In Malaysia, there are different Islamic resurgent groups (Nagata 1984), and an Islamic party PAS (Patai Islam Se-Malaysia) enjoys broad peasant support in the rural state of Kelantan (Kessler 1978, 1980). However, the widespread popularity of ABIM (Islamic Youth Movement of Malaysia) among the emergent Malay middle class raises the question as to why university-educated men and women in the 1980s came to identify, in their words and bodily presentation, with the ethos of a resurgent, patriarchal form of Islam.

I will begin by briefly discussing the official racial construction of Malayness and the ways in which Islam and local customs concerning community, kinship and gender have shaped an understanding of Malayness in village society. Next, I discuss the state's interventions in Malay peasant society, especially through its family planning policies, its promotion of female out-migration and industrial employment, and its ideology of rural women's duties in 'poverty eradication' campaigns. These changes in Malay society, both in villages and among migrants in the cities, contributed to the rise of a strict form of Islamic culture among young men and women who had benefited directly from government efforts to create a Malay petty bourgeoisie overnight. The next section discusses the ways in which competing state and Islamic resurgent discourses use women as symbols of motherhood, Malay vulnerability, and as boundary markers in their visions of Malaysian modernity. I end by considering the apparently paradoxical problem of educated middle-class women who express their agency by aligning themselves with the patriarchal forces of an alternative Islamic imaginary.

KINSHIP, GENDER AND COMMUNITY IN MALAY PEASANT SOCIETY

Before British intervention in the late nineteenth century, Malays were defined not by race but by their allegiance to sultans in the Malay Peninsula (Milner 1982). Colonial administrators were the first to legally differentiate the sultans' subjects from non-Malay immigrants in racial terms: a Malay was 'a person belonging to any Malay race who habitually speaks the Malay language . . . and professes the Muslim religion.'[2] This racial and behavioral definition was broad enough to embrace immigrants from the Malay archipelago, who could settle in the Peninsula and receive land grants denied to non-Malays. Thus, 'Malays' in contemporary Malaysia, the majority of whom live in the *kampung* (villages), include groups like the Javanese, Bugis, Acehnese and Minangkabau. Collectively racialized by the colonial state as 'Malays', they were categorically opposed to Chinese, Indians and other immigrants to colonial Malaya.

After independence (1957), the UMNO (United Malay National Organization) inherited the practice of defining citizens in racial terms (*bangsa*), distinguishing between Malays, who are all Muslim,[3] and the predominantly non-Muslim Chinese and Indians.[4] Statistics measuring the relative size of the three 'races' and providing evidence of their relative poverty and wealth have been a critical part of modern Malaysian politics and racial consciousness. In 1969, racial riots protesting the poverty of Malays, the majority of whom were peasants, forced a rapid adjustment between the state and the races. The UMNO government introduced a New Economic Policy (NEP) designed to 'eradicate poverty' and to bring an end to the ethnic identification with economic roles. This policy was to have profound social implications for village Malay culture and domestic politics.

Local conditions and the historical interactions of custom (*adat*) with Islam have shaped Malay beliefs and practices concerning kinship, residence and property. Although men traditionally enjoyed prerogatives in religion and property, women were neither confined to the household nor totally dependent on men for economic survival. Malay society is often cited as an example of a Muslim society that permitted relatively egalitarian relations between the sexes (Djamour 1959; Firth 1966; Swift 1963; Karim 1992), compared, say, with the rigid gender segregation found in Bangladesh (Kabeer 1988). However, throughout the twentieth century, and more recently under the NEP, forces linked to economic development and the Islamic resurgence have undermined the *adat* emphasis on bilaterality while strengthening Islamic tenets that increase male control in the emerging Malay middle class.

In 1979 and 1980, I conducted fieldwork in Sungai Jawa (a pseudonym), a village in Kuala Langat, in the state of Selangor. Among the villagers, the sexual division of labor and emphasis on bilateral kinship somewhat attenuated the patrilateral bias of Islamic law. Both men and women tapped rubber and tended coffee trees in their holdings. Until the early 1970s, only *kampung* men sought migrant work; a few women, usually divorcées or widows, were compelled to earn wages outside the village as rubber tappers or domestic servants. In recent years, however, population growth and land scarcity have affected gender relations and peasant householding. The *adat* practice of awarding equal land shares to sons and daughters has been superseded by the Islamic Shafi'i law dictating that sons be entitled to claim shares twice those of their sisters. Female-owned plots too small to be farmed separately are now often bought up by brothers. This emphasis on male inheritance has led to a situation in which most farms are the husband's property. In the sections that follow, I will discuss domestic relations in Sungai Jawa in order to show how concepts of kinship, gender and reproduction have been transformed by state policies and Islamic revivalism.

Malays throughout the Peninsula (excluding the matrilineally-oriented Minangkabau), it has been shown, prefer nuclear households to more complex domestic arrangements (Firth 1966; Laderman 1983). In Sungai Jawa, 80 percent of the 242 households I surveyed were nuclear units. Despite important day-to-day relations between kin and neighbor, the founding of a *rumah tangga* – a 'house served by a single staircase' – was considered essential to male adulthood. A married man compelled to reside with his parents would consider his status diminished. An informant noted that Malays would find intolerable the extended households of rural Chinese, in which different generations pool resources and even set up father-son businesses. It was a question of autonomy (he used the English word 'independence') and control by the adult male. *Adat* required the father to give his son the property in order to establish a new household upon marriage. Once the head of his own household, a man was free from parental claims on his labor and earnings. A married man working on his father's land would expect to be paid like any other hired help.

Second, independent householding by a man made clear his sexual rights in his wife and authority over his daughters and sons. This fact was brought home to me when I first sought residence in Sungai Jawa. Since I am a Chinese woman, villagers advised me against setting up a separate household. Elsewhere, single female nurses and teachers who wished to live in villages stayed in government quarters, their status and reputation protected. As a researcher, however, I did not have such a clearly specified role or this sort of official supervision. If I were to rent a house on my own, I would be perceived as a woman eminently seduceable by village men. I was kindly invited to lodge with a household, on the condition that I take the role of an adopted daughter, thus dispelling suspicions that I might be a mistress to men in the family. In fact, the Malay expression for living together (*bersama*) implies having a sexual relationship, much as the American expression does.

Strathern points out that gender ideas often operate as an indigenous conceptualization of social cause and effect (1987: p. 24). In the Malay village, gender differentiation was commonly expressed not in terms of biological makeup but in terms of morality. A basic aspect of a man's role was guardianship – of his sisters', wife's and daughters' virtue. By extension, all village men were responsible for the moral status of all village women. This code of morality was often explained in terms of men's greater rationality and self-control (*akal*) and women's greater susceptibility to animalistic lust (*nafsu*). This notion of moral capacity was also reflected in the concept of procreation, in which the male seed was considered 'the active principle' nourished by the womb (Banks 1983: pp. 67–8). In accordance with Islamic tradition, Malays considered the children of one man mothered by different women (all bear his name) to be more closely related than the children of one woman fathered by different men. The former relationship was one of clearly defined paternity (*keturunan*), whereas the latter was considered the product of *saudara anjing* or 'dog relations' (Banks 1983: p. 68). (Malays find dogs especially loathsome [*menghina*], and the phrase connotes indiscriminate and impure sexuality on the part of the woman.) However, in practice, *adat* often prevailed over the Islamic law on paternity, by stressing a woman's rights in her children. Thus, children by different fathers were also called 'milk siblings' (*adik beradik susu*). In divorce cases, judges often gave women custody of the children, favoring the *adat* emphasis on maternity ('shared breast'). This custom reflected the belief that children, if they so chose, should remain with their mothers. Nevertheless, a man could contest such a settlement by appealing to the Islamic court, and he could even claim as his own all children conceived during the period in which he had provided his wife support. In return for his provision of food, shelter and clothing, a woman provided for her husband's everyday needs. A man could divorce his wife by simply repudiating (*talak*) her three times, whereas she needed judicial intervention to divorce her husband, on the grounds of his failure to provide support or to consummate the marriage.

Masculinity thus depended to an important degree, though not entirely, on a man's economic power and moral authority over women in his household. The Islamic emphasis on female chastity imposed more rigorous restrictions on unmarried women (called *anak dara* or virgins) than on unmarried youths, although promiscuity in either sex was criticized. Young girls were required to be bashful and modest, but the Islamic emphasis on *aurat* ('nakedness' that should be covered) did not, until recently, extend to covering girls' hair (an erotic feature), which they wore loose or plaited. Everyday dress consisted of loose-fitting long tunics over sarongs (*baju kurong*). Before the recent wave of out-migration for wage work and higher education, adolescent daughters were expected to stay close to home and to keep a circumspect distance from male kinsmen. An important role of young men was to prevent their sisters from interacting with men, a practice that compromised their virtue.

Adat defined adult womanhood in other ways, but always within the Islamic construction of womens' relation to men. In everyday life, married women could move freely in tending to their cash-crop gardens or engaging in petty trade. They were not, however, supposed to sit in coffee shops or to seek male company. Women were the ones who maintained kin and neighborly relations by sharing resources, information, childcare and the work of preparing feasts. *Keluarga*, the word often rendered as 'family' in English, were open-ended kindred circles maintained by female kin between village households. In their own homes, married women customarily held the purse strings, despite the Islamic emphasis on men's keeping and handling money. Most important, women's special knowledge and skills were used in cooking, childbirth, health care (Laderman 1983) and the intensification of sexual pleasure (Karim 1992).[5] Women's *adat* knowledge included the art of preserving their sexual attractiveness to retain their husbands' interest. Married women wore their hair in buns, but on special occasions they dressed up in close-fitting, semitransparent jackets (*kebaya*) and batik sarongs. A lacy shawl (*selendang*) draped loosely over the head and shoulders could be used as a sunscreen and, occasionally, as a means of flirtation. Emphasizing their sexual charms, married women's clothing was in sharp contrast to the modest attire required of unmarried girls. Because sexually experienced and not legally subordinated to any man, previously married women, whether widows or divorcées (called by the same term, *janda*), were considered both vulnerable and dangerous. *Janda* were frequently suspected of trying to steal husbands. The virginity code and sanctions against adultery permitted sex only between spouses.[6] This did not prevent premarital or extramarital sex, but the Islamic ban on *khalwat* (illicit proximity) made having affairs a risky business.

Just as self-control and control of his wife's sexuality defined a man's adult status, regulating the activities of unmarried women – virgins and *janda* – defined the collective identity of *kampung* men. In Sungai Jawa, young men, with the implicit backing of Islamic elders, kept a watch on couples carrying on illicit affairs. If 'caught wet' (*tangkap basah*) and found to be unmarried, a couple would be compelled to marry as soon as possible. If either party were already married, the man would be beaten as a warning to other would-be adulterers. Sometimes the Islamic court would impose fines or even imprisonment, but villagers preferred to police and punish sexual misconduct themselves, as part of their role in safeguarding morality and protecting the boundaries between Malays and non-Malays (Ong 1990). Thus, youths would be more ferocious in their attacks if the paramour were an outsider or a non-Malay man. For instance, a Chinese man who dated a Malay factory girl was attacked and, according to one of my informants, 'left half-dead; he was in a coma for three days'. Male protection of female sexuality delineated the boundaries between male and female spaces (cf. Mernissi 1987: pp. xv–xvii), as well as between Muslims and the wider, multiethnic society.

In *kampung* society, then, Islamic law defined a man's identity in terms of his ability to prepare his sons for independent householding, to control the sexuality of his wife and daughters, and to provide all economic support for his household. However, *adat* practices and kindred relations provided women a measure of autonomy and influence in everyday life that prevented a rigid observation of male authority. In recent years, state policies and capitalist relations have created conditions that make the regulation of female sexuality a major issue. The possibilities for interracial liaisons created by the interweaving of Malay and non-Malay worlds have been perceived as a threat to Malay male rights and as a dangerous blurring of boundaries between Muslim and non-Muslim groups. As we shall see, control over female sexuality has been made a focus of the resulting efforts to strengthen male authority, reinforce group boundaries and ensure the cultural survival of the Malay community undergoing 'modernization'.

State Intervention: Making the Modern Malay Family

Under British rule, numerous laws like land tenure enactments presaged the dramatic postcolonial 'social engineering' of Malay society brought about by the NEP. Under this program, Malays were now legally defined as *bumiputera* or 'sons of the soil'.[7] The most important goal of this indigenization program was to correct interethnic economic imbalances by bringing thirty percent of the nation's wealth under *bumiputera* control by 1990.[8] The new state ideology, *Rukunegara*, produced a view of Malaysian modernity in which Malays were to become capitalists, professionals and workers, a dominant part of the citizenry who, because of their certified status as original natives, had special claims to national wealth. An expansion of state policies to remake the peasantry along these lines gradually increased class differentiation in Malay village society and stimulated the urban migration of young women and men. Such changes in the political economy class and ethnic formations, including state policies affecting the Malay family, contributed to the growing crisis of the Malay peasantry, which became inseparable from a crisis in Malay cultural identity. *Kampung* notions of kinship, conjugal rights, and gender were increasingly subjected to the operation of state policies.

Capitalist Development and Out-migration

Among the complex effects of the NEP was an improvement in living conditions in the *kampung* coupled with a reduction in the ability of most peasants to support their children by farming. For instance, double-cropping introduced into the Muda region, Malaysia's rice-bowl area, increased class differentiation: as a minority of commercial farmers emerged from a growing class of smallholders, the landless were cut adrift from the tenure system and cast upon the urban economy (Scott 1985: pp. 70–7). In Kuala Langat, an expanded state bureaucracy and population pressure on the land also increased class differentiation: well-to-do peasants and civil servants, who had contacts with state and UMNO party officials, benefited more than others did from farm subsidies and loan speculation. In my survey of 242 households, a quarter were landless or owned only their house lot. Sixty-one percent had access to farms under two and a half acres, a size just adequate for supporting a family of four. About sixty-five percent of the household heads (mainly men) were working as day laborers or migrant workers, reflecting a movement out of cash cropping into the wage economy. With land fragmentation, rising land costs and an increasing reliance on wage employment, many village men found themselves unable to pass property on to their children so as to make a *kampung* livelihood. This increasing 'crisis of transmission' was first noted by Banks (1983) among Kedah rice peasants. In Sungai Jawa, only a few years later, many fathers did not have enough land left for their sons. In fact, they were beginning to depend on children's wages to augment the household budget.

Meanwhile, welfare policies seemed to prepare *kampung* children for different places in the wider economy. From independence to 1975, development expenditures in rural areas increased about sixfold (Scott 1985: p. 44). In Kuala Langat, a coeducational high school and a free trade zone were set up. The best students were creamed off through nationally certified examinations and sent to urban schools and colleges or to overseas universities on state scholarships. Like *kampung* youth throughout the country, those high school graduates left in Sungai Jawa rejected farming as a way of life. Many youths preferred to remain unemployed, waiting for a plum job as office boy in some government agency. With the NEP, the outmigration of young *kampung* men and, increasingly, women for higher education and wage work became an irreversible process, dramatically changing parent-child and gender relations.

Family Planning

As in many developing countries, family planning in Malaysia was informed by the postwar World Bank prescription of increasing agricultural development while reducing family size. For instance, in land development schemes Malay settlers were given maternity benefits for only the first three children. Concerned that family policy could be construed as interference in Malay husbands' rights, officials packaged family planning as a 'health programme', emphasizing nutrition and well-being while strategically pushing fertility control. Family planning ideology promoted a model based on the Western conjugal family, using the term *keluarga* (kindred) to designate a 'nuclear family' made up of a working father, housewife, and dependent children. A pamphlet promoting contraceptives depicted family problems caused by a tired and irritable wife burdened with housework and childcare. She was portrayed as inadequate to her husband's needs. Village women were urged to take the Pill in order to spare their husbands 'inconvenience'. But in suggesting that the Pill could improve husband-wife relations, the program was an unwelcome intrusion into an area governed by Islamic law and personal desires.

Not surprisingly, village men actively resisted family planning, using the health services of the 'maternity and children's' clinic in Sungai Jawa to attain the highest birthrate in the district. There is little doubt that throughout the country, in fact, 'family planning' programs contributed to rising birthrates among Malay villagers: during the 1970s and 1980s, fertility rates rose among Malays but fell among the Chinese and Indians (Hirschman 1986). In Sungai Jawa, a survey of 238 ever-married women (from 242 households) showed that they had given birth to an average of five to six children, a higher rate than in previous decades.

Nevertheless, the ideology of family planning increased tensions between husbands and wives. In Sungai Jawa and, I suspect, most villages, the Pill was the main contraceptive provided by government clinics. Villagers noted that women taking the Pill complained of headaches, a 'bloated' appearance and a lethargy that made them 'too lazy to work'. Some husbands even threatened that if their wives got sick from the Pill, they would be refused help. Male hostility to family planning was so strong that men rejected contraceptives even when they were poor and could barely support large families. A twenty-seven-year-old mother of six children under fifteen was seven months' pregnant when I met her; she had wanted to go on the Pill after the fourth child but her husband, a laborer, had refused her permission. She said that most women had children because their husbands wished it, even though women themselves did not desire many children (although they did feel some concern about having children for old-age security). In another case, after a woman had had her sixteenth child – delivered by Caesarean – the nurse had suggested family planning. The woman had refused, saying 'Allah giveth'. Her father and her husband were both devout Muslims.

Family planning challenged *kampung* men's exclusive rights to their wives' sexuality. In addition, the men feared that contraceptives might embolden women to dissent from their husbands' wishes.[9] Villagers and religious leaders often used Islam, citing the hadith (an authorized compilation of the Prophet's words, deeds and exemplary practices) to criticize family planning as 'killing the fetus'. In the villagers' daily conversations the distinctions between miscarriage, abortion and contraception were often blurred. An *imam* told me that the Qur'an allowed abortion when the mother's health was endangered or the family could not possibly support another child, but, as the above examples illustrate, husbands rejected contraception even in such cases.

Since family planning was considered anti-Islam, those who used contraceptives had reason to conceal their decision. The Sungai Jawa clinic kept records on ninety-seven family planning couples, showing that seventy percent of the husbands were wage workers. Most of the wives were between fourteen and twenty-eight years old. I was told that perhaps twenty or more young couples bought their own contraceptives rather than get them free at the clinic. The factory women I interviewed said they did not intend to have more than four children. Young couples who depended mainly or exclusively on wage income had begun to talk about children in terms of 'costs'. Besides creating more expenses, children required help with their schoolwork so that they could later compete for white-collar jobs. Wage employment and family planning together, thus, produced an adjustment in family relations challenging two key elements of masculinity – a man's control of his wife's sexuality, and his ability to raise children.

Whatever the local effects of the family planning program, most Malays viewed the family planning ideology as ultimately a threat to their national survival. Although teachers and other state servants might have been practising contraception in private, in public they loudly proclaimed the practice contrary to Islam. A teacher said that he rejected family planning for Malays because it implied that they were incapable of raising as many children as they desired. He hinted that, as *bumiputera*, Malays were promised government preference in scholarships, jobs, business licenses and credit. Moreover, family planning conflicted in practice with state policies encouraging Malays to have many children as one way of increasing wealth and ensuring the success of the race. Civil servants warned that if contraception were widely adopted, Malays would lose their voting power vis-à-vis the other races. Modern concepts and practices concerning health and sex thus challenged male conjugal rights, their moral authority over women, and Islam. And not only did family planning challenge Islamic culture, but it threatened Malay racial power as well. The recruitment of young women into the labor force offered a further challenge to local norms for regulating female sexuality and social reproduction.

The Deployment of Female Labour in Free Trade Zones

As welfare policy tried to mange the bodily care and reproduction of peasant Malays, social engineering redistributed the younger generations in new locations scattered throughout the wider society. The *Third Malaysia Plan* notes that the general aim of the NEP was to promote the 'progressive transformation of the country's racially-compartmentalized economic system into one in which the composition of Malaysian society is visibly reflected in its countryside and towns, farms and factories, shops and offices.'[10]

Throughout the 1970s, state intervention in the peasant sector generated a steady influx of Malays into cities, a rising number of them young women. Tens of thousands of female migrants collected in urban free trade zones, working in labor-intensive subsidiaries of transnational corporations (Jamilah 1980). These corporations had established electronics firms, garment factories, and other light manufacturing plants in the special zones, where they were legally required to have a thirty percent *bumiputera* representation in their work force. By the late 1970s, some 80,000 *kampung* girls between the ages of sixteen and the mid-twenties had been transformed into industrial laborers (Jamilah 1980).

The industrialization strategy, originally focused on creating a male Malay working class, found itself producing an increasingly female industrial force, largely because of the manufacturing demand for cheaper (female) labor.

This army of working daughters introduced another line of division into the Malay household. In Sungai Jawa, the local free trade zone turned village girls into factory operators. Many peasants eagerly sent their daughters off to earn an income to be put towards household expenses. Most working daughters were induced to hand over part of their paychecks, especially when brothers proved reluctant to share their own earnings, were unemployed or were attending school. Daughters' wages paid for consumer durables and house renovations that broadcast the new wealth of *kampung* families (Ackerman 1984: p. 53). Not unexpectedly, working daughters strengthened the influence of mothers in the household: since it would be shameful for fathers to ask help from daughters, mothers extracted the earnings. Village men found themselves unable to fulfill their duties as fathers and husbands. Some felt humiliated that they depended on daughters' wages and could not keep them at home, their virtue protected (Ackerman 1984: p. 56; Ong 1987: p. 99).

Nationwide, as thousands of peasant girls descended on cities and free trade zones, they came into competition with their male peers. For young men, sisters became an easily tapped source of cash, but as would-be wives working women transgressed the wider arena of male power. So long as unmarried girls were confined to the *kampung* milieu, men's superiority in experience and knowledge could remain unchallenged. Now, young women too were acquiring experience in market situations, situations where they could mingle freely with men. Furthermore, the new class of female workers and college students induced in their male peers a widespread fear of female competition in the changing society.

For the first time in Malay history, a large number of nubile women had the money and social freedom to experiment with a newly awakened sense of self. Many came to define themselves, through work experiences and market choices, as not materially or even morally dependent on parents and kinsmen. Factory women could now save for their weddings, instead of receiving money from their parents, and could therefore choose their own husbands. The increasing number of brides who were wage earners produced a trend toward larger wedding outlays by grooms for feasting and for outfitting the bride and the new household. In Sungai Jawa, many men did not hesitate to emphasize their prestige by spending lavishly. Civil servants had access to government loans for just such expenses. Between 1976 and 1980, wedding payments exceeding M$1,000 (approximately US$500) increased from fifteen to fifty-three percent.[11] These sums were presented in fresh bank notes expertly folded into money trees, a ritual symbolizing masculine power, now subsidized not by fathers but by the government. In the changing *kampung* society, young men and women found themselves dependent on the labor market and the state, rather than on their parents, as they negotiated the path toward adulthood.

Young women, however, came to bear special moral burdens for realizing the image of a modern Malay society.

Work Ethics, Women's Duties, and the Modern Family

In the early 1980s, the state introduced a 'Look East' policy to enforce discipline in modern institutions. Some observers saw bureaucrats as the focus of this campaign (Mauzy and Milne 1983), but in my view, the object of this discourse has been workers, especially Malay female workers in transnational firms, many Japanese-owned (see also Kua 1983). The prime minister lauded Japanese companies for their 'family system', which displayed concern 'for the welfare of their employees', and he remarked on the similarity between Japanese and Malaysian 'morals and ethics' (Das 1982: pp. 38–9). The aim of the policy, an educator explained, was 'to urge Muslims to follow the attitude and work ethics of a successful race [the Japanese] as long as it does not contravene Islamic ideals and principles'.[12] The presumed 'communal spirit' of Japanese enterprises was presented as in keeping with Islamic kinship values.

Whereas health policy pushed a nuclear family ideal, industrial ideology promoted a patrilineal 'family welfare' model said to reflect the *keluarga* emphasis on mutual obligations and loyalty. In the Kuala Langat free trade zone, a company motto proclaimed its goal to be:

> to create one big family,
> to train workers,
> to increase loyalty to company, country and fellow workers.

Despite this corporate 'philosophy', many factory women felt manipulated and harassed by male supervisors whom they were urged to consider as family elders. To some workers, management was implacably the other ('aliens'): it did not speak their language, was not Muslim, profited from their labor, and sometimes treated them as though they were not 'human beings'. Among operators, only fellow workers were considered 'siblings' (*saudara saudari*). Despite factory-induced competition among operators, workers in the same section would help each other and look out for new recruits, as one would for one's *keluarga*. Such mutual dependence, of course, unintentionally reinforced self-regulation, commitment, and discipline among workers – the goals of the 'one big family' ideology.

The 'poverty eradication' program also promoted new concepts of female duty, based on the Western notion of family as a privatized unit of obligations and exclusion (cf. Asad 1987). In the Fifth Malaysia Plan, women were seen as key to improving the lot of 'low-income households'. Rural women were blamed for not being hardworking and for their presumed lack of response to 'modern practices' and 'new opportunities' for improving the well-being of their families. Officials dictated a series of tasks women could undertake to improve the health and wealth of their families. Peasant mothers were instructed to ignore 'customary' practices in preparing their children for 'a progressive society'; they were called upon to raise children with values such as 'efficiency' and 'self-reliance'.[13] A government program called KEMAS ('tidy up') instructed village women in home economics and handicrafts. The new housewife requirements echoed the slogan 'Clean, Efficient and Trustworthy', displayed in factories with largely female work forces. The official discourse on the modern family thus defined women's modern roles: as working daughters who could pull their families out of 'backwardness' and as housewives (*seri-rumah*) who could inculcate 'progressive' values in their children. This privileging of the mother-child relationship reflected the Western family model while ignoring the central role of the Muslim father.

Through various NEP programs, then, the ideology of a modern Malay society unintentionally undermined the source of customary male power. Welfare policies progressively defined a privatized domestic sphere and women's responsibilities in it. This family model seemed to undermine male conjugal and paternity rights while supporting a more assertive role for women at home. Second, the emphasis on *bumiputera* rights greatly raised the expectations of young people without eliminating their sense of uncertainty in the multiethnic society to which they were channeled as students, wage workers, professionals, and unemployed youths. Their cultural dislocation was compounded by the changing sexual division of labor and the new freedoms of daughters, wives, female students and female workers. Moral confusion over the proper roles of men and women and the boundaries between the public and domestic, Muslim and non-Muslim worlds contributed to a crisis of national identity.

ISLAMIC REVIVALISM: ENGENDERING THE *UMMA*

In Malaysia, Islamic resurgent movements are not historically unprecedented: during the struggle for national independence, Islamic reformists challenged traditional Malay systems (Roff 1967), and in post-independence Malaysia, the major opposition party, PAS (*Partai Islam Se Malaysia*), used Islam to articulate the discontent of poor peasants in the east coast states (Kessler 1978). In the 1970s, diverse Islamic revivalist groups, collectively referred to as the *dakwa* (proselytizing) movement, began to develop among the *kampung*-born and educated Malays who had emerged as a new social force under the NEP.[14]

Here, I will focus on the major group, ABIM (*Angkatan Belia Islam Malaysia* or Islamic Youth Movement of Malaysia), which rose to national prominence through the 1970s, at its height numbering some 30,000 members and innumerable sympathizers. Besides its size, it drew on the largest cohort of young Malays to have benefited from mass literacy. They differed from earlier generations of revivalists in that they emphasized a direct engagement with holy texts (the sunnah, hadith and Qur'an), bypassing the received wisdom of traditional religious leaders (*ulama*). ABIM members and supporters were mainly young men and women who, hailing from villages like Sungai Jawa, had migrated into cities for wage employment and higher education. Despite the *bumiputera* rhetoric, they had been made aware of the gulf between them and the older Malay elites who had come to power under British tutelage. Students sent on scholarships to universities in London, Cairo and Islamabad were exposed to the various strands of Islamic resurgence abroad. Upon returning home, many became *dakwa* leaders who railed against the decadent lifestyle of nouveaux-riches Malays, with their pursuit of glittering acquisitions and sensual pleasures and their blithe disregard of Islam (Chandra 1986: pp. 70–1). ABIM's leader, Anwar Ibrahim, proclaimed that Islam opposed 'development which propagates inequality and which is void of moral and spiritual values' (Anwar 1986: p. 5). Embedded in this critique was a class analysis linking upper-class corruption to the impoverishment of the Malay majority (Kessler 1980). Moreover, the *dakwa* perception that non-Malay communities were more successful in the secular milieu produced fears for Malay survival. Looking back, an ABIM leader said: 'After "May 13" [1969; that is, the racial riots] . . . [i]t was all a question of the survival of the *umma*, of the Malay race. Previously, we [thought] about all these problems outside Islam, when actually we could have solved them through Islam' (Zainah 1987: p. 11).

ABIM's search for an Islamic revivalist identity was an assault on a hegemonic construction of *bumiputera*-hood that did not address the cultural problems of Malays living in a secular, multiethnic world. As the above quotation suggests, the recovery of the *umma* (social and religious community) became a central goal in dealing with the breakdown in social boundaries that had traditionally defined Malay group identity. Through *dakwa* activities, ABIM members aimed to awaken a 'broader religious consciousness' among Muslims (Nagata 1984: pp. 81–2). *Dakwa* attacks on capitalism focused on its spawning choices and practices 'based not on divine morality but on sensuality and as such not according to truth and justice' (Mohammad 1981: p. 1046). The 'truth' that Islamic revivalists sought was to be found in an *umma* that would infuse the community as well as the government with revitalized Islamic values (Hassan 1987).[15] By insisting on a stricter adherence to the *umma*, the *dakwa* was urging a social system more gender-stratified than existed in Malay society.

Writing about Islamic revivalism in Morocco, Mernissi noted that the *umma*, which recognized Allah as its only leader, resisted the secular power of the modern state when it spread to previously uncontested areas of domestic relations (1987: pp. 20–2). The *umma* was 'ultimately a society of male citizens who possessed . . . the female half of the population' (Mernissi 1987: p. 169). For Malay revivalists, the *umma* had been unmade by the influx of women into modern schools and offices; a new 'sacred architecture' of sexuality (Mernissi 1987: p. xvi) had to be created, through everyday practices inventing 'Islamic' traditions (Hobsbawm 1983) that would redraw boundaries between Malay men and women, Muslims and non-Muslims. Almost overnight, large numbers of university students, young workers and even professionals began to enact – in prayer, diet, clothing and social life – religious practices borrowed from Islamic history, Middle Eastern societies and South Asian cults. Here, I will present two cases which show that attacks on changing gender and domestic relations were central to the *dakwa* construction of the *umma*.

In Sungai Jawa, villagers felt a general anxiety about the ways in which state policies and secularization had weakened male authority over young women. Parents were torn between wanting their daughters to work and being concerned about keeping their status honorable. With independent earnings, women's agency, formerly channeled through legal superiors (parents, husbands), came to express individual interests in consumption and in dating. Factory women took to wearing revealing Western outfits (such as jeans and miniskirts) and bright makeup. This 'sarong-to-jeans movement' was seen as a license for permissiveness that overturned *kampung* norms of maidenly decorum. In the factories, nubile women were daily supervised by men, many non-Malays, an arrangement that seemed to mock at Malay male authority. Worse, some working women began to date non-Malay men, breaking village norms of sexual and religious segregation. 'It is not a matter of romance, but of social relationships,' one worker commented. Women who were unrestrained (*bebas*) by family guidance in relations with men were derided as being no longer Malay (*bukan Melayu*). Villagers viewed this development of an autonomous female agency as a weakening of male control and of the boundaries between Malays and non-Malaya (see also Peletz 1993).

The religious response to women's assertiveness was exemplified in a speech given at a village celebration of the Prophet Muhammad's birthday in 1979. A young scholar complained that the modern ills afflicting Malays included drug taking, excessive watching of television and communism (he mentioned the Soviet invasion of Afghanistan). Islamic societies were weak not because Islam was weak, but because Muslims were weak human beings who succumbed to their baser nature (*nafsu*). He elaborated this theme by saying that women's roles as mothers and wives had to be strengthened according to Islamic tenets. When a student at Al-Azhar, Cairo, he had had the opportunity to observe the great respect children showed their mothers in societies where Islam was an overwhelming force in everyday life. He urged villagers to raise their children with great respect for authority. And, while all Muslims should obey Islamic laws and respect their elders, women should first and foremost serve their husbands. He then raised the vision of factory women 'letting themselves' be cheated by men, thus 'damaging themselves'. Wage work was presented as dishonorable, inducing women to indulge their indiscriminate passions. He continued by saying that a woman's sensual nature was acceptable only if (his hands sculpting the air to suggest a curvaceous body) her sexual allure were reserved for her husband's pleasure. He ended by calling on village women to emulate the Prophet's wife, Katijah.[16] This call for a strengthening of the Malay race required women to adhere to a stricter Islamic version of male authority and of women's roles as mothers and wives.

The use of foreign Islamic practices to validate increased male authority over women was also evident in the middle-class milieu. In the mid-1980s, a Malay socialist named Kassim Ahmad stirred up a hornet's nest by publishing a modest critique of the hadith, the text used in the everyday teachings of *dakwa* members. Exposing various 'contradictions' between the hadith and the Qur'an, Kassim Ahmad argued that the latter was the only source of truth for Muslims. For instance, contrary to the Qur'an, the hadith was 'anti-women'. It prescribed 'stoning to death' for adulterers (Kassim 1986: pp. 95–6, 101–2) and even claimed that fasting women should submit themselves to their husbands' carnal desires (Kassim 1986: pp. 104–5). This challenge galvanized orthodox *ulama* and Islamic revivals alike into calling for a ban on Kassim Ahmad's book and censuring him in other ways. Although the controversy was mainly phrased in terms of Kassim Ahmad's religious expertise, its very silence over the 'contradictions' specified by Kassim Ahmad revealed the depth of popular sentiment about husbands' control of their wives.[17] Public discussions of the case failed to refer to local Malay traditions that do not condone the punitive measures mentioned in the hadith. This controversy in fact provided an opportunity for Islamic revivalists to insist anew that Muslim men should have total authority over women.

In thus defining a new *umma*, ABIM and other *dakwa* groups were inventing practices harking back to a mythic, homogeneous past, while rejecting their Malay-Muslim cultural heritage. This Arabization of Malay society depended in large part on implementing a rigid separation between male public roles and female domestic ones, a concrete realization of the architecture of male rationality (*akal*) and female eroticism (*nafsu*) that went way beyond any arrangement found in indigenous village arrangements where *akal* and *nafsu* are found in both women and men (see Peletz, this volume). A new radical division between Malay men and women, Muslims and non-Muslims, was thus being constructed in public life, primarily by inscribing a religious spatialization of power on women's bodies.

WOMEN'S AGENCY AND THE BODY POLITIC

Draped in dark veils and robes, women are the most potent symbols of Islamic revivalism. Their presence calls into question feminist assumptions that women in Muslim societies would invariably 'resist' lslamic resurgent movements (see, for example, Kabeer 1988). In Malaysia, women displayed a range of responses, both to modernization and to Islamic revivalism, that cannot be reduced to 'resistance', a term implying only oppositional tactics. Here, I suggest that, among Malay women, agency in terms of autonomy or adherence to interests not independently conceived differed according to class. Whereas working-class women were less morally compromised by working, middle-class women were significantly swayed by the spirit of Islamic resurgence in their understanding of femininity.

It would be erroneous to assume that state policies unambiguously provided Malay women with conditions for employment and individual security. Land scarcity, widespread female wage labor and secularization in many cases reduced men's customary obligation to be the sole supporters of their families where possible. Furthermore, the trend toward female wage employment made all Malay women vulnerable to a reduction or even withdrawal of their husbands' support. At an UMNO Women's meeting, wives of the rural elite complained that government promotion of the 'housewife' did not guarantee women economic support. Leaders reminded village women of their responsibilities for the educational success of their children and the preservation of the UMNO heritage for their grandchildren. However, some women noted that men viewed their wives as having rights only in housework and childcare, with no claim on their husbands' salaries. Invoking the Islamic marriage contract, members proposed that mutual respect and intimacy within marriage would be improved if the state could guarantee that 'housewives' would be paid an 'allowance' drawn from their husbands' salaries. This proposal indicated that even women not caught up in Islamic revivalism felt that social and economic changes made them vulnerable to loss of the male protection provided by Islamic law. Although their demands for payment for housework may seem an echo of Western feminist demands, they were really calling on the government to enforce men's customary role as sole supporters of their families. It is such protests by middle-class women that have resulted in new Islamic family laws for the 'protection of women's rights' regarding divorce. For the first time, Islamic judges nationwide have been ordered to regulate their implementation of family laws.[18] For Malays who consider divorce and polygamy male rights, this law must seem to be yet another instance of state inroads on the power vested in men by Islam.

For unmarried women, the impact of modernizing forces has been greater and more disorienting, especially among the first large generation of Malay university women. Many have found refuge in the *dakwa* movement. On the University of Malaya campus, at least sixty percent of the students showed some commitment to *dakwa* in the early 1980s (Zainah, 1987: p. 33). Whereas ABIM men wore Western shirts and pants, dakwa women put on the *mini-telekung*, a cloth that tightly frames the face and covers the head, hair and chest, considered parts of the *aurat* ('nakedness') that Islam requires women to conceal. This headcloth was usually worn with the customary *baju kurung*. Some women also donned long black robes (*hijab*), socks, gloves and face-veils, denoting a full purdah (*parda*) historically alien to Malay culture.[19] This representation of the female body may be seen as 'subversive *bricolages*' (Comaroff 1985: pp. 197–8) combining elements of different traditions to register protest over cultural dislocations linked to colonial and postcolonial domination.

Students walking around in full purdah were a source of irritation to government officials worried that 'Arabic' robes would scare off foreign investors. In fact, *dakwa* groups were critical of the kind of cultural colonializing promoted by the market, media, and foreign corporations. A female *dakwa* lecturer assailed working women for adopting the consumerist 'feminine false consciousness' promoted by factory culture (Amriah 1989). As a male revivalist remarked, 'I feel that secularism is the biggest threat to the Muslim *umma*' (Zainah 1987: p. 76). *Dakwa* groups sought to provide networks and daily support for Malay women disoriented by the consumerism of modern life.

ABIM recruitment of women was not only a resistance to capitalist culture, but also a reorienting of women's agency to rebuild a Malay-Muslim identity. State policies had 'liberated' women for campuses and the marketplace, but could not offer protection against new self-doubts and social anxieties among women and men. Released from the guidance and protection of their kin, many young women were compelled to act as 'individuals' representing their own interests in the wider society. Furthermore, Malay society for the first time confronted the problem of a large group of unmarried young women, whose unregulated sexuality was seen as symbolic of social disorder (cf. Mernissi 1987: p. xxiv). Fatna Sabbah argues that Muslim women's entry into the modern economy is often seen as a challenge to men's economic role, the basis of their virility; men thus perceive women's participation in modern public life as a form of 'erotic aggression' (Sabbah 1984: p. 17). This reading is highly suggestive for the Malaysian case. The *dakwa* obsession with women's 'modesty' in 'male' and multiethnic spaces was reflected in their insistence that women cover themselves. Women's bodily containment was key to the envisaged order that would contain those social forces unleashed by state policies and the capitalist economy. The *mini-telekung* and long robes marked off the female body as an enclosed, 'pregnant' space, symbolic of the boundaries drawn around Malay society and the male authority within it.

Such dramatic reversals from their brief exposure to personal liberation were more evident among female university students than among blue-collar women. Campuses were the seats of the most intensive *dakwa* campaigns to cover the female body and maintain sexual and ethnic segregation. Women were discouraged from participating in sports that exposed their naked limbs (Nagata 1984: p. 100). A University of Malaya ban on the *mini-telekung* in lecture halls failed to deter many female students from covering their heads. Even female lecturers who rejected the *dakwa* prescription felt sufficiently intimidated to wear headscarves and avoid Western style clothing.

The following two examples illustrate the centrality of sexuality to female students' struggles between autonomy and group identity. One student, who favored leotards and disco dancing, was repeatedly chastised by *dakwa* members over a period of two years. One day her boyfriend urged her to don the *mini-telekung* because, he said, it would help him resist her sexual appeal. When she finally complied, *dakwa* women immediately embraced and salaamed to her (Zainah 1987: pp. 64–7). In another case, a student confided that when she first came to the university she had worn 'miniskirts and low-cut clothes'. She had mixed with Chinese students and attended campus 'cultural' events, but not religious ones. One day she received a letter, signed 'servant of Allah', accusing her of having sinned by befriending Chinese infidels, who would lead her astray. Just for not covering her head, she would burn in hell

(Zainah 1987: p. 60). As these cases indicate, ABIM recruits were often women who had tasted individual 'freedom' but, subjected to pressure and even outright threats, later found security and acceptance in Islamic revivalism. By donning *dakwa* outfits, they could negotiate the urban milieu without being insulted by men. The *dakwa* robes registered the multiple effects of cultural disorientation, protest, and intimidation, enfolding them in a moral community.

Furthermore, through their *dakwa* outfits, women proclaimed the impossibility of interethnic liaisons or marriages, thereby stemming any potential loss in progeny to the Malay race, who form a small majority in Malaysia.[20] *Dakwa* women have thus asserted Malay singularity against Malaysian multiculturalism, at the same time partaking of the aura cast by the global Islamic efflorescence.

Depeasantization, Middle-Class Women, and Religious Nationalism

The Islamic resurgence and all its trappings quickly became associated with upwardly mobile *kampung* and urban middle-class women, rather than peasant or working-class women. In Sungai Jawa, where most young women were employed in factories, only a handful who managed to enter teachers' colleges and the university wore *dakwa* outfits. Village elders noted that the religious clothing, while admirable, was inappropriate for life in the village. An elder woman explained that her granddaughter, clothed in *mini-telekung* and *hijab*, was dressed in the way of 'an educated woman'. In contrast, because she herself was a peasant (*tani*), she could sit comfortably in her carelessly tied blouse and sarong.[21] Hardly any factory woman adopted the *dakwa* robes, although many believed that the intensified religious environment provided them protection against sexual and social abuse in the wider society (Ong 1987: pp. 181–93). Thus, *dakwa* clothing became a symbol of depeasantization,[22] a process of class mobility whereby successful Malay women explored their gender identity in modern Islamic terms.

For many Malay women, depeasantization and higher education were not to be associated with exploring their sexual selves; rather, a higher social and moral status required rigid constraints on sexual expression. Thus many university-educated women were caught between the demands of individualistic competition in higher education and the job market, on the one hand, and their hopes of being married on the other. Indeed, the *dakwa* granddaughter mentioned above, who was in her early twenties, spent her holidays in the village reading British romances, ostensibly to improve her English. Her mother complained anxiously about her lack of suitors, blaming it on her ignorance of the finer aspects of cooking, cleaning and childcare, the important skills of village wives.

Such tensions are reflected in a university survey of a hundred and fifty female seniors who revealed ambivalence about their new status, stating that they did not believe in competing with men in the labor market. They would only seek jobs which involved serving others – for example, as clerks, teachers, nurses or doctors (attending to women and children only). The respondents considered occupations that would put them in authority positions over men forbidden by Islam, because to work in such positions would change the status of women vis-à-vis men (Narli 1981: pp. 131–3; see also Nagata 1984: pp. 74–5). A deep concern among educated women was their postponement of marriage and their fear of being progressively priced out of the marriage market by their academic credentials. By seeking to maintain, rather than challenge, male authority, they would be better assured of finding husbands. They are the ones most likely to don *dakwa* robes that soon became the Malay woman's working uniform, replacing the body-fitting *batik sarung-kebaya* of the days before the Islamic resurgence.

The discourse on Muslim womanhood thus became a countermodel to the government's promotion of working women, the modern family, and the secular 'housewife' ideal. These were all seen as threats to male authority at home and in the public sphere. ABIM members insisted that women's first duties were to their husbands and that wives should obey their husbands just as all Muslims should obey Allah. The moral of wives' obedience seemed to be an appropriate ideology for the urban middle class, among whom divorce has lately declined, possibly because of women's fear of the economic and social losses it would entail, but also because of middle-class men's ability to fulfill the economic and moral implications of the husband/father role (Peletz, this volume). Among working-class women, divorce rates remained high (Azizah 1987: pp. 109–10; Ong 1990: pp. 453–4). The nurturing and self-sacrificing role of women as homebound mothers emphasized in resurgent teachings was more easily realized by middle-class women who did not need to make a living. ABIM members frequently invoked the Qur'anic phrase 'paradise lies beneath [our] mothers' feet' (Nagata 1984: p. 100), to celebrate women's primary responsibility for instilling Islamic values in their children. Women were also urged to spread Islamic values among their female friends. In *dakwa* discourse, the redirection of women's agency from labor force to moral force tapped into the deepseated spiritual unease of women aspiring to be upwardly mobile, yet filled with ambivalence about careers and the solitude of modern life.

Thus, although a substantial number of its members were engaged in a genuine spiritual quest, the *dakwa* movement also reflected a discontent with changing gender roles and the declining force of male authority in the new middle-class family. This analysis helps to explain the apparently paradoxical fact that many young women who had benefited from state policies (which opened up educational and employment opportunities to them in the first place) found the *dakwa* call so appealing. In *dakwa* visions, women are all married and fulfilled. As wives and mothers, they play central roles in rebuilding and preserving Malay society as part of the larger Islamic family (Anwar 1986: p. 5). The Islamic resurgence reminds them of their moral duty to construct and nurture a modern Muslim-Malay community imagined by *dakwa* leaders. In the university survey, most of the women interviewed considered themselves to be 'first and foremost Muslims', arguing that 'nowadays, there is only one tradition – that is, Islamic tradition'. They saw Islam as a 'more comprehensive value system' than Malay customs, one more fit to guide them in this era of rapid change. Some insisted on being reidentified, saying 'I am Muslim rather than Malay' (Narli 1981: pp. 132–3). The *dakwa* movement thus constructs a kind of religious nationalism, divested of many attractive features of indigenous Malay culture, that is based on an invented tradition, and the creation of a strict Muslim patriarchal domination in both public and domestic spheres.

OFFICIAL ISLAM'S NEW WOMEN

The powerful Islamic claim on a Malay moral identity and criticisms of modernization caused the state to launch an Islamization campaign of its own in the early 1980s. Its most important move was to co-opt the charismatic ABIM leader Anwar Ibrahim into the government, putting him in charge of youth and sports. In addition, the state set up official Islamic institutions for banking, university education and missionary programs. More rigorous efforts were made to punish Muslims who broke religious laws forbidding gambling, drinking and sex out of wedlock (Mauzy and Milne 1983). On television, Islamic programs proliferated, some promoting the image of 'ideal mothers' who would put their husbands and children before anything else.

The new religious tone of state programs prepared the stage for a new 'family development' policy. A new language linking development, population and the family articulated the new moral role of Malay women. The government proclaimed a goal of population growth from fourteen to seventy million over the next hundred years in order to meet the anticipated labor needs for sustained capitalist development.[23] Although there was widespread skepticism about the possibility of attaining this goal, the new population policy found support even among Malays disaffected with the UMNO regime. The uncharacteristic silence over racial composition led many to believe that population growth would be encouraged only among Malays. The program seemed to allow natural population growth among Malays to be augmented by the largescale immigration of Indonesians who could easily be absorbed into the *bumiputera* category (Clad 1984: pp. 109–10). Second, in producing a discourse on 'family development' (thus overturning family planning), the state appropriated the *dakwa* themes of defining and empowering Malays in opposition to non-Malays. Despite its technocratic language, the policy explicitly links the success of the Malay family to the strengthening of the body politic. Third, the 'pronatalist' (Stivens 1987) thrust of the message diffused Malay fears of female domination in the labor force while accommodating the *dakwa* insistence on women's primary role as mothers. The prime minister was quoted as saying that women whose husbands could afford it should stay home to raise families of at least five children (Chee 1988: p. 166). Undoubtedly, through such official approval and flattery of middle-class men (who can afford to support non-working wives), the state regained control over the definition of the domestic domain, earning moral and even Islamic legitimacy in the process. The family development campaign suggested that middle-class women should rethink their options since the pregnant body at home can be even more patriotic than the female body at work. Furthermore, male-dominated Malay families are not incompatible with a growing population and capitalist economy.

Thus, despite differences over the issue of economic development, both resurgent Islam and the secular state have made the image of an Islamic modernity, with its powerful claims on women and their bodies, the key element in their competing visions of Malaysian society. The consequence of such ideological competition between official and religious nationalisms has been the intensification of Malay gender difference, segregation and inequality. The intersection of hegemonic and counterhegemonic visions was occasioned in large part by an obsession with racial, political and demographic domination on the one hand, and by an emergent, conservative middle class's need to maintain patriarchal control of the family, on the other.

Soft Nationalism and Sisters in Islam

By the end of the 1980s, the Islamic resurgence had settled in as a low-key but pervasive part of urban Malay culture. Malay women continued to be conservatively dressed in long robes and *mini-telekung*, but their clothes were now cut in colorful, more glamorous styles. Few chose to drape themselves entirely in black. Growing economic affluence among Malays and increasing economic interdependence with other Asian countries had somewhat routinized the fervor of resurgent Islam and instilled a detachment from Middle East events like the Rushdie affair and the Gulf War. While the Islamic resurgence took more militaristic forms in the Middle East, in Malaysia both official and religious nationalisms became low-key integrated into the fabric of a rapidly modernizing society in which the domination of the Malays is now well-assured. As inconsistencies between the *dakwa* political body and the physical body of desire and affluence grew, women's outfits reflected an interesting nexus of religious and fashion consciousness.[24] It is not so much that eroticism is breaking through the *dakwa* body, but rather that the body is being remanaged with a lighter hand.

Talking about another invented tradition in Malaysia, Clive S. Kessler (1992) notes the new expressions of loyalty through popular songs and media images celebrating the subject-leader relationship in Malay culture. On television, women again play important iconic roles, but this time decked out in colorful, stereotypical costumes representing the different ethnic groups, they take turns singing a new patriotic song (*Lagu Setia*). Kessler observes that the song projects patriotism and loyalty as 'a kind of falling in love, a voluptuous yearning, a chaste seduction'. Loyalty, Kessler argues, is 'reimagined and reinvented . . . as something modern, subtle, low-key' (1992: p. 155). In sharp contrast to the forbidding *dakwa* image, this new multiracial female body is seductive, even yielding, tentatively open to outside influences. Such a repackaged 'soft' nationalism, whereby politics, religion, culture and entertainment are inter-woven and inseparable, allows the racial body and, by extension, the wider imagined community of Malaysia to engender a limited kind of multicultural-ism.[25]

As the Muslim-non-Muslim boundaries became less rigid, the state redirected its ideological energy toward the larger Asian arena. Increasingly the state faced off challenges not so much from an Islamic resurgence as from elements in the middle class agitating for the rights of women, political detainees and restive workers. The prime minister became internationally known for his outspoken criticism of the West and defended his occasional curtailment of civil rights by proclaiming a culturally relative notion of 'human rights' in Asian modernity. Anwar Ibrahim, former ABIM leader and the new deputy prime minister, had long set aside his ascetic, firebrand image for expensive batik silks. Perhaps anticipating being the ruler of a rich multiracial country, he speaks cordially of multicultural tolerance among the different races. This muting of racial and religious differences in public discourse also owes something to the fact that Taiwanese Chinese have become the most numerous foreign investors in the country, while the Malaysian government is competing for investments in China. Similarly, the low-key Islamic resurgence has been adjusted to local real-ities. The *hijab* has even become something of a patriotic fashion that is some-times adopted by non-Muslim women to proclaim a generalized loyalty and vision of a multicultural Malaysia.

The merging and muting of state and religious nationalisms have created openings for a renegotiation of gender relations. The moral economy of resur-gent Islam gave women little choice but to inscribe themselves into a 'traditional' subordination, even when that position was itself an invented tradition.[26] Because Malay community, kinship and gender matters are informed by Islamic law, women who may resist their second-class status cannot draw upon civil laws to articulate women's rights. However, the *umma* has nurtured a group of Malay female professionals to invent other Islamic traditions heretofore ignored by male leaders. Calling themselves 'Sisters in Islam', they seek to articulate women's rights within Islam by emphasizing the need to interpret the Qur'an and hadith in their proper historical and cultural contexts. They point out that narrowly literal interpretations of Islamic texts like the right to strike one's wife and polygamy may work against the rights of Muslim women in modern times. Through a careful citing of Islam's holy books, the Sisters identify the universal principle that the sexes are equal, 'members, one of another'.[27] They argue that the Qur'an suggested 'a single strike' against the wife to restore marital peace (verse 4:34) but that this was at a time when violence against women was rampant. Furthermore, they contest the view that polygamy is Islam's answer to 'men's allegedly unbridled lust'. Instead, they call upon men who abuse polyg-amy to seek Islamic guidance to change their promiscuous attitude to 'one of self-discipline and respect for the opposite sex'. Thus, contrary to hegemonic Islamic discourses that oppose male reason to female passion, the Sisters chide men for their lustfulness and lack of discipline: 'It is not Islam that oppresses women, but human beings with all their weaknesses who have failed to understand Allah's intentions.'[28]

Furthermore, by acting as reasoning Sisters in Islam, they present themselves as siblings arguing on equal terms with men and appealing to their much-vaunted male reason in reinterpreting Allah's will regarding women's status. They also criticize other forms of patriarchal practices said to be required by Islam, like the imposed female dress codes and even speech restrictions, as 'mechanisms of control' masquerading as norms promoting feminine modesty. However, the Sisters' strategy unintentionally strengthens the reason-as-to-male versus passion-as-to-female ideology since only by being reasoning sisters can they get respectful male attention concerning the subordination of daughters, wives and mothers (i.e., kinship statuses in which women's passions are experienced as more threatening). Thus women's rights in Islam are being fought for by a group exuding the chaste aura of learned sisters; the division between reason and passion remains, but now men have to be more mindful of their unruly passions and women who work with their minds must be cast as sexually unthreatening.[29]

In contrast to the growing negotiations over middle-class Muslim women's rights, the resurgent Islamic party PAS, working among the rural poor, is agitating for greater controls over Muslims, especially over women. Recently, PAS introduced strict Islamic laws (*hudud*) in Kelantan state to punish offences like theft, robbery, apostasy and unlawful sexual intercourse by stoning, whipping and amputation. The laws are especially discriminatory against women since a rape victim must produce four male eyewitnesses in her defense. Thus just as the nation's Islamic elites have begun the tentative articulation of women's rights, peasant-based revivalists are seeking to impose a stricter kind of Islam, springing in part from an intensified sense of political marginalization and exclusion from the material benefits of capitalism. In Kuala Lumpur, where Malay middle-class religious fervor is tempered by affluence and cosmopolitanism, there is something surreal in the prime minister declaring that 'I don't think we are going to allow them to chop off heads, hands, and feet'.[30] The chaste voluptuous body of affluent Malay nationalism faces off the specter of a truncated one representing patriarchal Islam. Thus, the struggle between state nationalism and Islamic radicalism continues in another guise on other sites rooted in other class, political and regional dynamics, but still focused on regulating women, who symbolize the varied ways Islam may be deployed to loosen or control the body politic in an unevenly modernized country. Indeed, it appears that the newly 'reasonable' resurgent Islam and the newly affluent state are both seeking to regulate not just women's bodies but ultimately *all* bodies.[31]

CONCLUSIONS

In the postcolonial era, many Third World states have had to contend with communally based narratives expressing particular interests that have been overlooked in nationalist struggles against colonialism. In Southeast Asia, as postcolonial states sponsored changes that uprooted peasants, intervened in the conduct of family relations, and created new urban classes, they also produced nationalist ideologies that rationalize these transformations in technocratic (World Bank) terms. Among groups dislocated by these changes, crises in cultural identity created counter ideologies that are obsessively concerned with controlling resources, group boundaries and articulating belonging in transcendental terms. Women, as symbols and agents of change, have to be brought into line with the new orthodoxies. Other scholars have shown that historically, the emerging middle classes have turned to a religious resurgence to construct patriarchal family orders, and to patrol the boundaries between the domestic and public, insiders and outsiders. It bears remembering that all Great Religions – Islam, Christianity, Hinduism and Buddhism – are heavily patriarchal, investing substantial weight in women's roles as wives and mothers. Whether the emerging middle classes turn to Christian fundamentalism (e.g., Ryan 1981) or Islamic resurgence in order to conserve their economic, political and cultural resources, they find in religion an important source of competing nationalist ideologies in modernizing societies.

The twists and turns in gender contestations show vividly that gender politics are seldom merely about gender; they represent and crystallize nationwide struggles over a crisis of cultural identity, development, class formation, and the changing kinds of imagined community that are envisioned. The management and self-managing that women's bodies come to represent is in tandem with the larger forces at work in the construction of the body politic. Religious conservatism, almost always symbolized by confining women's agency and space, may eventually give way to looser mechanisms for controlling women's bodily and social movements, and the boundaries of the imagined community. As the middle class gains more security and confidence, women play a greater role in reworking gender inequality and group boundaries within the religious orthodoxy. In places like late-twentieth-century Malaysia, local conditions and complex racial and cultural features have produced a particular form of rivalry between the ideological state and Islamic revivalists, and conditioned the responses of women who both symbolize and negotiate these contestations over women and imagined communities. Rather than seeing the agency of middle-class Malay women in terms of mere resistance or passivity, I have argued that it has been shaped by the intersection of their own self-interests with their group identity, contingent upon the historical changes in Malay society and in Malaysia over the past two decades. By yielding to religious and class forces, and by working to protect the integrity of their bodies, families and the body politic, women have found new ways of belonging in a changing Malaysia.

NOTES

An earlier and shorter version of this chapter appeared as 'State versus Islam: Malay Families, Women's Bodies, and the Body Politic in Malaysia', *American Ethnologist*

17(2): pp. 258–76, May 1990. I am particularly grateful to Michael Peletz for his thoughtful and helpful suggestions in this new version.

1. Furthermore, Scott's argument that Malaysian state hegemony stops at the village gates and that peasants' everyday resistances are informed by a Malay village subculture unadulterated by wider politics is problematic for two major reasons. It reveals his misreading of the Gramscian notion of hegemony as an ideological formation which dominates through the creation of false consciousness, and which does not allow for oppositional views (Scott 1985: pp. 316–18). Actually, Gramsci was very critical of the 'false consciousness' model, and developed hegemony as an alternative theory of rule by consent (not oppression or mystification), which is an always open-ended process (1971; see also Williams 1977). However, in Scott's view, when Malay peasants challenge hegemonic views of development, they can only do so from a position he artificially defines as outside the realm of state hegemony (Scott 1985: pp. 335–40). He seems to have missed the Gramscian notion of counterhegemony, and its dialectical relationship to hegemonic forms. Thus Scott came to misrepresent social realities in rural Malaysia as a simple dichotomy between a national hegemony and a resistant village subculture. In contrast, other scholars provide a more complex and entangled picture of Malay peasants in their daily lives deeply implicated in the religious, ethnic, and political economic hegemonies prevailing in the country (see Kessler 1978; Shamsul 1986; Ong 1987; Peletz 1995)
2. Federated Malay States Enactment no. 15, 1913.
3. 'Malay' in the Malaysian context denotes persons of a Malay-Muslim identity. They are Sunni Muslims at birth. The term 'Malay' will be used interchangeably with *bumiputera* (sons of the soil). Since the Malay language does not use suffixes to denote the plural condition, words like *kampung* and *bumiputera* will not be suffixed with an 's.'
4. This article deals only with the situation in West (Peninsular) Malaysia. In 1985, there were about 13 million citizens, with Malays making up some 56 per cent, Chinese 33 per cent and Indians 10 per cent of the population (Government of Malaysia 1986: pp. 128–9).
5. It is important to stress that the Malay *kampung* women I interviewed saw Islamic beliefs about sexuality in a positive light. For instance, *kampung* women claimed that female circumcision (partial removal of the clitoral hood) increased a woman's sexual pleasure during intercourse (cf. Reid 1988: p. 149). *Kampung* women use different techniques and tonics (*jamu*) to condition their bodies for enhancing erotic pleasure. Sex was considered essential to good health and a normal life and only viewed negatively when indulged in excessively or with an unsuitable partner.
6. Similar attitudes towards female sexuality outside marriage are found in many Asian, Middle East and Mediterranean societies. See Goddard (1987) who argues that Neapolitan male control of female sexuality is linked to women's role as the bearers of group identity.
7. See Government of Malaysia (1976: pp. 2, 9), and Siddique (1981). In 1970, the Malay share of equity capital was 2.4 percent. The NEP sought to expand that figure by entitling *bumiputera* to equity held in trust by special government agencies. By 1990, *bumiputera* equity still fell short of 30 percent, but the new affluence has made it possible for the government to promote economic growth among the poor in all ethnic communities without holding back wealth accumulation by the bumiputera as a whole.
8. Government of Malaysia (1976: 86–9).
9. Formerly, Malay women could turn to midwives for covert treatment to prevent childbirth, but traditional midwifery is now officially frowned upon (Laderman 1983: pp. 104–105). The modern health system reduces women's role in birth

prevention because men have become more directly involved in decision making affecting women's health.

10. Government of Malaysia (1976: p. 9).

11. In the 1960s, wedding payments were in the range of M$100 to M$500. The increase in payments between 1976 and 1980 also reflected a rise in mean age at first marriage – from late adolescence to twenty-two years for women and twenty-eight years for men.

12. *The New Straits Times*, November 8, 1983, p. 2.

13. Government of Malaysia (1986: pp. 83–4).

14. The term 'Islamic resurgence' is widely used to describe the activities and ideologies of both rural peasant and urban middle-class groups. I focus on the latter here because they were more numerous and had a wider effect on the upper echelons of Malay society. For different interpretations of the causes of the Islamic resurgence, see Lyon (1979), Nagata (1984), Chandra (1986), Kessler (1978, 1980), Mohammad (1981), Muhammad Kamal (1987) and Zainah (1987).

15. The *dakwa* leaders were challenging the legal dualism between religion and government inherited from British colonial rule (see Roff 1967). They wished to expand the scope of Islamic law (*hukum*) to cover areas currently governed by civil and criminal law.

16. He did not mention that Katijah (Ar., Khadija) was many years older than Muhammad and an enterprising business woman in her own right.

17. This rhetorical insistence on the husband's sexual needs ignores the *adat* expectation that husbands and wives will satisfy each other sexually. Good marriages seem to require lively sexual encounters, commonly referred to as 'sparring' (*melawan*). A man's inability to please his wife sexually may become the subject of gossip (Karim 1992).

18. *The New Straits Times*, July 14, 1988, p. 2.

19. See Reid (1988: pp. 85–90) for a brief historical account of Malay clothing from the fifteenth century onward. The coming of Islam induced otherwise bare-chested Malay women and men to wear loose tunics (*baju*) above their sarongs. However, heavily veiled women 'covered from head to foot' were observed only in Makassar (in present-day Indonesia) in the mid-seventeenth century.

20. A. C. Hepburn observes that, in societies dominated by a numerically small majority, the containment of intermarriage is crucial to the maintenance of the existing population structure (1978: p. 4).

21. This grandmother, lounging on her verandah in full view of passersby sometimes opened her blouse and allowed her three-year-old grandson to play with her breasts. She gave the impression that she pitied her granddaughter who was 'having such hard life' as a student and unmarried woman.

22. Soheir Morsy used the word 'depeasantization' to describe the Islamic resurgence in Egypt, where out-migration and education have created a new ideology of the discontented upwardly mobile (personal communication).

23. Government of Malaysia (1984: pp. 21–2). Demographic projections of the various ways the population can grow to 70 million in a hundred years have been worked out by Jones and Lim (1985) and by Chee (1988: p. 167), who argues that the population policy could legitimize using women as a population reserve.

24. Conflicts between the status body and the physical body are a key theme in Takie Lebra's (1994) highly suggestive essay on the imperial family and body politic in Japan.

25. Prasenjit Duara makes a distinction between an incipient nationality with soft boundaries that allow cultural practices to be shared and adopted between groups, and nationalism with hard boundaries, when selected cultural practices are used to mobilize and define the boundaries of a particular group (1993: p. 20). Here I am using 'soft nationalism' in a slightly different way, as one that allows some intermingling of culture at the borders of groups, and as a national identity that can

coexist with nationalism identified with fixed boundaries. I also use 'soft national-ism' to denote the low-key, media-processed patriotism that has overtaken more strident forms like the Islamic resurgence.

26. It is important to note that this 're-traditionalization' (Williams n.d.) is a mythic invention. One should therefore be cautious of statements about the Malay middle class's reconstruction of Malay identity 'through the symbols of a traditional, village-based, feudalistic and patriarchal Malay culture' (Joel Kahn, cited in Kessler 1992: p. 146) when that 'culture' is described in such static and extreme terms. See Banks (1983), Ong (1987), and Peletz (1995) for more complex, ethno-graphically based descriptions of gender relations in different Malay village com-munities.

27. *Asiaweek*, August 9, 1991, p. 27; see also *Asiaweek*, November 17, 1993, p. 17.

28. Ibid.

29. See Peletz 1995, chapter 5, for an extended and careful discussion of how the reason:passion gender ideology is unevenly embraced by Malay women and men as practical knowledge. See also Peletz 1988 for a discussion of the striking impor-tance of the sibling relationship in Malay society as a channel for familial aid, exchange and mediation, but also as a source of ambivalence and hostility.

30. *South Chinese Morning Post*, November 22, 1993, p. 14.

31. This includes the bodies of male transvestites called *pondan/Mak Nyah* (Peletz 1995, chap. 3). I thank Michael Peletz for pointing this out to me.

REFERENCES

Ackerman, Susan. 1984. 'The Impact of Industrialization on the Social Role of Rural Malay Women', in Hing Ai Yun, Nik Safiah Karim and Rokiah Talib, eds., *Women in Malaysia*, pp. 40–70. Petaling Jaya, Malaysia: Pelanduk Publications.

Amriah Buang. 1989. 'Development and Factory Women – Negative Perceptions from a Malaysian Source Area', paper presented at the Commonwealth Geographical Bureau Workshop on Gender and Development. University of Newcastle, April 16–21.

Anagnost, Ann. 1989. 'Prosperity and Counterprosperity: The Moral Discourse on Wealth in Post-Mao China', in Arif Dirlik and Maurice Miesner, eds., *Marxism and the Chinese Experience: Issues in Contemporary Chinese Socialism*, pp. 210–34. Armon, M. E. Sharpe.

Anderson, Benedict R. O'G. 1992. *Imagined Communities: Reflections on the Origins of Nationalism*. 2d ed. London: Verso.

Anwar Ibrahim. 1986. 'Development, Values and Changing Political Ideas', *Sojourn* 1(1): pp. 1–7.

Asad, Talal 1987. 'Conscripts of Western Civilization', unpublished MS.

Azizah Kassim. 1987. 'Women and Divorce among the Urban Malays', in Hing Ai Yun, Nik Safiah Karim and Rokiah Talib, eds., *Women in Malaysia*, pp. 94–112. Petaling Jaya, Malaysia: Pelanduk Publications.

Banks, David. 1983. *Malay Kinship*. Philadelphia: ISHI Publications.

Chandra Muzaffar. 1986. 'Malaysia: Islamic Resurgence and the Question of Development', Sojourn 1(1): pp. 57–75.

Chatterjee, Partha. 1993. *The Nation and Its Fragments: Colonial and Postcolonial Histories*. Princeton: Princeton University Press.

Chee Heng Leng. 1988. 'Babies to Order: Recent Population Policies in Malaysia and Singapore', in Bina Agarwal, ed., *Structures of Patriarchy: The State, the Community, and the Household*, pp. 164–74. London: Zed Books Ltd.

Clad, James. 1984. 'The Patchwork Society', *Far Eastern Economic Review* (April 20): 109–10.

Comaroff, Jean. 1985. *Body of Power, Spirit of Resistance: The Culture and History of a South African People*. Chicago: University of Chicago Press.

Das, K. 1982. 'Mahathir's "Restoration"', *Far Eastern Economic Review* (June 11): pp. 38–9.

——. 1983. 'A Shift in the Balance', *Far Eastern Economic Review* (June 2): pp. 42–3.

Djamour, Judith. 1959. *Malay Kinship and Marriage in Singapore*. London: Athlone Press.

Donzelot, Jacques. 1979. *The Policing of Families*. New York: Random House.

Duara, Prasenjit. 1993. 'Deconstructing the Chinese Nation', *Australian Journal of Chinese Affairs* 30: pp. 1–28.

Federated Malay States Enactment, no. 15. 1913. Ms. *Arkib Negara Malaysia* (National Archives of Malaysia). Petaling Jaya, Malaysia.

Firth, Rosemary. 1966. *Housekeeping among Malay Peasants*. New York: Humanities Press.

Foucault, Michel. 1978. *The History of Sexuality*, trans Robert Hurley. Vol. 1, *An Introduction*. New York: Pantheon.

——. 1980. *Power/Knowledge*, trans. Colin Gordon. New York: Pantheon.

Goddard, Victoria. 1987. 'Honor and Shame: The Control of Women's Sexuality and Group Identity in Naples', in Pat Caplan, ed., *The Cultural Construction of Sexuality*, pp. 166–92. New York: Tavistock Publications.

'Government of Malaysia. 1976. *Third Malaysia Plan, 1976–1980*. Kuala Lumpur: Government Printing Press.

——. 1984. *Mid-Term Review of the Fourth Malaysia Plan*, 1981–1985. Kuala Lumpur: Government Printing Press.

——. 1986. *Fifth Malaysia Plan, 1986–1990*. Kuala Lumpur: Government Printing Press.

Gramsci, Antonio. 1971. *Selections from the Prison Notebooks of Antonio Gramsci*, ed. and trans. Quinten Hoare and Geoffrey Nowell Smith. New York: International Publishers.

Hassan, Muhammad Kamal. 1987. 'The Response of Muslim Youth Organizations to Political Change: HMI in Indonesia and ABIM in Malaysia', in William R. Roff, ed., *Islam and the Political Economy of Meaning*, pp. 180–96. Berkeley: University of California Press.

Hepburn, A. C. 1978. 'Minorities in History', in A. C. Hepburn, ed., *Minorities in History: Papers Read before the Thirtieth Irish Conference of Historians at the New University of Ulster, 1977*, pp. 1–10. London: Edward Arnold.

Hirschman, Charles. 1986. 'The Recent Rise in Malay Fertility: A New Trend or a Temporary Lull in a Fertility Transition?', *Demography* 23(2): pp. 161–84.

Hobsbawm, Eric. 1983. 'Introduction: Inventing Traditions,' in Eric Hobsbawm and Terence Ranger, eds., *The Invention of Tradition*, pp. 1–14. New York: Cambridge University Press.

Jamilah Ariffin. 1980. 'Industrial Development in Peninsular Malaysia and Rural-Urban Migration of Women Workers: Impact and Implications', *Jurnal Ekonomi Malaysia* 1: pp. 41–59.

Jomo K. Sundaram. 1988. *A Question of Class: Capital, the State, and Uneven Development in Malaysia*. New York: Monthly Review Press.

Jones, Gavin, and Lim Lin Lee. 1985. 'Scenarios for the Future Population Growth in Malaysia', *Kajian Malaysia* 3(2): pp. l–24.

Kabeer, Naila. 1988. 'Subordination and Struggle: Women in Bangladesh', *New Left Review* 168: pp. 95–121.

Kahn, Joel S., and Francis K W. Loh, eds. 1993. *Fragmented Vision: Culture and Politics in Contemporary Malaysia*. Honolulu: University of Hawaii Press.

Karim Wazir Jahan. 1992. *Women and Culture: Between Malay Adat and Islam*. Boulder: Westview Press.

Kassim Ahmad. 1986. *Hadis: Satu Penilailan Semula (The Hadith: A Reinterpretation)*. Petaling Jaya, Malaysia: Media Intelek Sdn. Bhd.

Kessler, Clive S. 1978. *Islam and Politics in a Malay State. Kehutan 1838–1969*. Ithaca: Cornell University Press.

——. 1980. 'Malaysia: Islamic Revivalism and Political Disaffection in a Divided Society', *Southeast Asia Chronicle* 75: pp. 3–11.

——. 1992. 'Archaism and Modernity: Contemporary Malay Political Culture', in Joel S. Kahn and Francis K. W. Loh, eds., *Fragmented Vision: Culture and Politics in Contemporary Malaysia*, pp. 133–57. Honolulu: University of Hawaii Press.

Kua Kia Soong. 1983. 'Look East, But Watch for Blemishes.' *Far Eastern Economic Review* (March 31): pp. 69–70.

Laderman, Carol. 1983. *Wives and Midwives: Childbirth and Nutrition in Rural Malaysia*. Berkeley: University of California Press.

Lebra, Takie. 1994. 'Status Dilemma and the Body Politic in Japan', paper presented at the Department of Anthropology, University of California, Berkeley, January 28.

Lyon, Margo. 1979. 'The Dakwah Movement in Malaysia'. *Review of Indonesian and Malaysian Affairs* 13(2): pp. 34–45.

Mauzy, Diane K. and R. S. Milne. 1983. 'The Mahathir Administration in Malaysia: Discipline through Islam', *Pacific Affairs* 55: 617–48.

Mernissi, Fatima. 1987. *Beyond the Veil: Male-Female Dynamics in Modern Muslim Society*. Rev. ed. Bloomington: Indiana University Press.

Milner, A. C. 1982. *Kerajaan: Malay Political Culture on the Eve of Colonial Rule*. Tuscon. University of Arizona Press.

Mohammad Abu Bakar. 1981. 'Islamic Revivalism and the Political Process in Malaysia', *Asian Survey* 21: pp. 1040–59.

Nagata, Judith. 1984. *The Reflowering of Malaysian Islam*. Vancouver: University of British Columbia Press.

Narli, Ayse Nilufer. 1981. 'Development, Malay Women, and Islam in Malaysia: Emerging Contradictions', *Kajian Malaysia* 2: pp. 123–41.

Ong, Aihwa. 1987. *Spirits of Resistance and Capitalist Discipline: Factory Women in Malaysia*. Albany: SUNY Press.

——. 1990. 'Japanese Factories, Malay Workers: Class and Sexual Metaphors in West Malaysia' in Jane M. Atkinson and Shelly Errington, eds., *Power and Difference: Gender in Island Southeast Asia*, pp. 385–422, 453–7. Stanford: Stanford University Press.

——. 'Postcolonial Nationalism: Women and Retraditionalization in the Islamic Imaginary, Malaysia', in Connie Sutton, ed., *Feminism, Nationalism, and Militarism*. Arlington: American Anthropological Association.

Peletz, Michael G. 1988. *A Share of the Harvest: Kinship, Property, and Social History among the Malays of Rembau*. Berkeley: University of California Press.

——. 1993. 'Sacred Texts and Dangerous Words: The Politics of Law and Cultural Rationalization in Malaysia'. *Comparative Studies in Society and History* 35(1): pp. 66–109.

——. 1995. *Reason and Passion: Representations of Gender in a Malay Society*. Berkeley: University of California Press.

Reid, Anthony. 1988. *Southeast Asia in the Age of Commerce, 1450–1680*. Vol. I, *The Lands Below the Winds*. New Haven: Yale University Press.

Roff, William R. 1967. *The Origins of Malay Nationalism*. New Haven: Yale University Press.

Ryan, Mary. 1981. *The Cradle of the Middle Class*. Cambridge: Cambridge University Press.

Sabbah, Fatna A. 1984. *Women in the Muslim Unconscious*. New York: Pergamon Press.

Salaff, Janet W. 1988. *State and Family in Singapore: Restructuring a Developing Society*. Ithaca: Cornell University Press.

Scott, James C. 1985. *Weapons of the Weak: Everyday Forms of Peasant Resistance*. New Haven: Yale University Press.

Shamsul Amri Baharuddin. 1986. *From British to Bumiputera Rule: Local Politics and Rural Development in Peninsular Malaysia*. Singapore: Institute of South East Asian Studies.

Siddique, Sharon. 1981. 'Some Aspects of Malay-Muslim Ethnicity in Peninsular Malaysia', Contemporary Southeast Asia 3(1): pp. 76–87.

Stivens, Maila. 1987. 'Family and State in Malaysian Industrialization: The Case of Rembau, Negri Sembilan, Malaysia', in Haleh Afshar, ed., Women, State and Ideology, pp. 89–110. Albany: SUNYPress.

Strathern, Marilyn. 1987. 'Introduction', in Marilyn Strathern, ed., *Dealing with Inequality: Analysing Gender Relations in Melanesia and Beyond*, pp. 1–32. Cambridge: Cambridge University Press.

Swift, Michael. 1963. 'Men and Women in Malay Society', in Barbara Ward, ed., *Women in the New Asia: The Changing Social Roles of Men and Women in South and Southeast Asia*, pp. 268–86. Paris: UNESCO

Williams, Brackette F., ed. n.d. *Mannish Women: Retraditionalized Female Gender and the Nationality of Domesticity*. New York: Routledge. Forthcoming.

Williams, Raymond. 1977. *Marxism and Literature*. Oxford: Oxford University Press

Wong, Diana. 1988. *Peasants in the Making: Malaysia's Green Revolution*. Singapore: Singapore University Press.

Zainah Anwar. 1987. *Islamic Revivalism in Malaysia*. Petaling Jaya, Malaysia: Pelanduk Publications.

4.4

'DEBT-BONDAGE AND TRAFFICKING: DON'T BELIEVE THE HYPE'

Alison Murray

The anti-trafficking lobby built up through the early 1990s to a peak at the UN Conference on Women/NGO Forum held in Beijing during September 1995, yet trafficking is an aspect of the mythology surrounding Asian sex workers which remains poorly defined even in conventions and laws against the trafficking of women (David 1995). One of the goals of the anti-trafficking lobby at the UN conference was a new UN Convention to replace the 1949 Convention on the Suppression of Trafficking in Persons and the Exploitation of the Prostitution of Others, in which Article 1 condemns anyone who 'procures' or 'exploits' a prostitute, 'even with the consent of that person'. There was relatively little attention paid to 'trafficking' after the 1949 convention, until the late 1980s surge of concern about 'sex tourism'. In April 1993 a conference was organized by the Coalition Against Trafficking of Women (CATW) 'to heighten awareness of the sex trade and to stem the sale of humans into bondage' (*Asia Watch*, 1993: p. 149). The latest intense phase of publicity began with two conferences on trafficking held at the end of 1994: The First International Conference on the Trafficking of Women in Chiang Mai, Thailand from 17–21 October (which established the feminist-based Global Alliance Against Traffic in Women, the GAATW) and the International Conference on Traffic in Persons in Utrecht, the Netherlands from 15–19 November, 1994.

Many people have been misled into thinking that trafficking (and child

From: Alison Murray (1998), 'Debt-Bondage and Trafficking: Don't Believe the Hype', pp. 51–64, in Kamala Kempadoo and Jo Doexema (eds), *Global Sex Workers: Rights, Resistance and Redefinition* (New York: Taylor & Francis, Inc.).

prostitution and sex tourism) are enormous problems for Australia and Southeast Asia. Meanwhile Australian and other sex workers, at the UN conference and through its aftermath, set out an alternative view so that, before people dig in their pockets for a donation, sign a petition or join an anti-trafficking group, they would try to consider the sex workers' perspective and the implications of this lobby for the workers in sex trades. A version of this chapter and a position statement supported by most of the Australian sex workers' rights organizations formed part of the vigorous discussions at Beijing, where the anti-trafficking movement lost much of its credibility.

Sex work is diverse and context-specific, related to the combination of local conditions and the forces of economic globalization, the AIDS discourse and legislation which creates the space for exploitation and violence by criminalizing prostitutes and restricting travel. The most extreme lobby, represented by the Coalition Against Trafficking in Women, formed in the United States in 1991, has an underlying agenda of abolishing prostitution. They try to fulfil this agenda by linking all forms of the sex trade together beneath an emphasis on emotive words like 'trafficking', 'slavery' and 'child prostitution'. Meanwhile, in discussion at Beijing, the Global Alliance has distinguished itself from the Coalition by clarifying that it does not take an abolitionist stand on prostitution and is also open to the sex workers' perspective. Support of sex workers' rights is part of a larger postmodern challenge to conventional feminism, which allows for a cacophony of voices and refuses the binary dichotomy in which all women are constituted as 'other'. Feminism which fails to overcome binary oppositions ends up supporting the status quo, impoverishing women and aligning with right-wing fundamentalism and a discourse which has its genesis in homophobia.

DEFINING TRAFFICKING

There are at least three different 'camps' with different ideas about trafficking: the Coalition Against Trafficking in Women, led by Kathleen Barry, the Global Alliance, which also claims to be feminist but only opposes 'forced' prostitution and various sex workers' rights activists who dismiss the free/forced distinction and claim that the 'harms' of prostitution are actually caused by moral attitudes and their legal consequences. The word trafficking can be applied to any kind of commodities being traded or bartered, however it also has sinister and illicit implications, in this case being used with the implicit assumption that it is women and girls who are being transacted as non-consenting prostitutes to fulfil male sexual desires. The position of Barry and the Coalition is that trafficking is part of the general exploitation of women according to the feminist principle that male sexuality under patriarchy is about power, not sex and thus all prostitution is coercive (see also Sullivan 1996).

If all prostitution is violence against women, it seems that any migration of sex workers can become 'trafficking', as in Coalition member Sheila Jeffreys' statement: 'As men use women in sex tourism in different countries they then demand these women to be trafficked into their country' (*West Australian*, 13 December 1995). Jeffreys has also said that 'prostitution is a form of sexual violence affecting women's bodies, their health and self-image, and undermines other gains women have made . . . Once we remove women's subordination in society there will not be prostitution' (*West Australian*, 13 December 1995). In the *LA Times* another Coalition member, Janice Raymond, has published an editorial, 'Prostitution is rape that's paid for' (11 December 1995).

The Utrecht conference produced a definition emphasizing force rather than the nature of work to be performed in its final statement (1994):

> The traffic in persons is not only for purposes of prostitution, but for a range of other activities as well. . . . It is important to emphasize that the element that defines traffic is force and not the nature of the labor to be performed. . . . The trafficker cannot use as a defense the fact that the person is or was at any time, for example, a prostitute or a domestic worker.

Similarly, after the Chiang Mai conference, the Global Alliance defined trafficking as forced labor where people are lured or deceived into forms of contemporary slavery: more specifically, as a feminist alliance they refer to the movement of 'women' in order to 'subject them to power' (*STV News Bulletin* #3, July 1995). A draft document, 'Standard Minimum Rules for the Treatment of Trafficked Persons' published in the *STV News Bulletin*, says 'the trafficked persons shall be treated as migrant laborers and therefore be protected by the International Labor Organization', the emphasis being on opportunities for retraining and the chance to 'start a new life', the meaning of which is unclear, but implies a moral preference for anything else over prostitution. The Global Alliance worked with sex worker groups at Beijing but their conceptual position is confused, since the 'free/forced' distinction is untenable.

The movement of sex trade workers into and out of Thailand has been a major focus for lobbyists and the subject of the Asia Watch report, *A Modern Form of Slavery: Trafficking of Burmese Women and Girls into Brothels in Thailand*. The report was publicized with a tour of Australia by the researchers from 1–13 May 1995, supported by the International Women's Development Agency (TWDA). *A Modern Form of Slavery* was also the main source for the trafficking section of the Joint Standing Committee on Foreign Affairs, Defense and Trade report on Burma (JSC 1995: pp. 48–53). This report refers to appalling conditions, social ills, victims, etc, without any other evidence, and extends the supposed trafficking to Sydney: 'the main center appears to be Sydney where there were at least twenty brothels' (1995: p. 52). Scarlet Alliance's response notes that the committee failed to contact Australian sex worker organizations which are in touch with Burmese and Thai workers (correspondence, 4 January 1996). While the report says 'there might be 200 Asian prostitutes working in Australia', there are actually around two thousand of whom ninety per cent are Australian residents (Brokett and Murray 1994).

In other usages, the IWDA leaflet says that Burmese women and girls are 'trafficked – sold lured or tricked – into slavery in Thai brothels', while in the media, 'the traffic in flesh is a horror of exploitation that shames the world's conscience' (Hornblower 1993: p. 14). It is not only the media which sensationalizes the issues. A UNESCO report on Contemporary Forms of Slavery (1995) uses the terms trafficking, prostitution and sexual exploitation interchangeably and refers to them as sordid, dangerous and inhuman. As David comments, 'exploitation of prostitution' is a vague term which in itself is not an adequate reason to prohibit prostitution (1995: pp. 1–5). The UNESCO document also makes a reactionary, unsupported and culturally vague demand for 'strengthening the family nucleus and respect for moral values', as a solution to the 'problem'. Conversely, sex workers state that it is precisely the moral hypocrisy of global capitalism and sexual repression, including the criminalization of prostitutes, which creates the space for exploitation, discrimination and negative attitudes towards female sexuality (PROS et al. 1995).

The UN Special Rapporteur on Violence Against Women, Radhika Coomarasway, has made a contexualized report on prostitution and trafficking which states:

> 'A discussion of prostitution must accept the premise that prostitution as a phenomenon is the aggregate of social and sexual relations which are historically, culturally and personally specific. The only common denominator shared by the international community of prostitutes is an economic one: prostitution is an income generating activity' (Coomarasway 1995, Article 205; see also Rubin 1975: p. 175).

She goes on to make the point that sex workers are generally well-paid compared to other workers. Coomarasway's section on trafficking appears to be largely based on the Asia Watch report, describing conditions in Thailand as 'appalling' and referring to an incident where five workers were burned to death when they were chained to the beds in a brothel and could not escape. A contrast can be made with the case of more than two hundred Thai women who burned to death in a Thai toy factory because the exit doors were locked, and similar cases in US sweatshops (Priscilla Alexander, personal correspondence 18 August 1995, also reports in the *New York Times*, 4 August 1995, 12 August 1995, 25 February 1996), the point being that exploitative and dangerous conditions can be found across a range of industries internationally.

The shadowy nature of 'trafficking' may be due to the cunning of the 'traffickers' or it may be because they don't exist. At any rate it is difficult to estimate the scale of these issues. The link with child prostitution makes the debate even more emotive and can be manipulated to sideline the position of Western sex workers (Murray, forthcoming). The Norwegian government has very boldly informed the Council of Europe that 'Every year, one million children are either kidnapped, bought or in other ways forced to enter the sex market' (Black 1994: p. 12). Estimates of 'child' sex workers in Thailand range up to

800,000 under-18-year-olds, according to US Secretary of State for Human Rights John Shattuck, which would mean about a quarter of all teenage girls (*Bangkok Post*, 25 December 1994).

The End Child Prostitution in Asian Tourism (ECPAT) brochure says, 'On a global scale millions of children have been forced into prostitution' and 'tourists create a demand for more than one million "fresh" child prostitutes every year'. None of these figures are referenced, nor do they explain what research has been done, if any. Thai NGOs apparently estimate that there are two million sex workers in Thailand (Asia Watch 1993: p. 16), while the IWDA campaign says that over ten thousand women and girls are trafficked into Thailand each year, as in the Asia Watch report, which also says that fifty to seventy per cent of them become infected with HIV.

A MODERN FORM OF SLAVERY

While it is not clear where the figures for 'trafficking' come from originally, it is books like *A Modern Form of Slavery* which help them to become accepted fact through the repetition of the rhetoric. This report from Asia Watch is written in a quasi-academic style, where tabloid journalism is footnoted, referenced, and hence legitimated. The book is referred to in academic papers, and it is the major source behind sections of Australian government and UN documents. The book and speaking tour put the issue back in the news, although the expert researchers conveniently chose to remain anonymous.

The authors did not actually visit brothels, but interviewed thirty workers ('victims') who had been arrested and taken to shelters or detention centers. While ostensibly giving these workers a voice, their statements are selectively reinterpreted by the 'experts', and may be read differently by other sex workers. On the one hand, it is emphasized that the women say that they did not know the type of work they were going to do. Since prostitution is illegal in Thailand and the workers were interviewed in detention, it seems logical that they would say this to avoid prosecution, as do migrant sex workers everywhere in an effort to avoid deportation. On the other hand, it seems to be the norm for the women to find their own way out of Burma with prior knowledge of where to find brothel agents. The report claims that they are tricked, but if this is the case they seem to be so stupid they can be duped twice, as they are 'taken for deportation to the Thai-Burmese border where they are often lured back into prostitution by brothel agents'. Where they have made it home and boasted about the money they made, this is described as lying to 'save face', even when they have gone on to recruit others for the brothels or returned to work themselves. 'Their return to prostitution was voluntary only in the sense that they saw their first experience as having rendered them unfit for anything else' (*Asia Watch* 1993: p. 74).

The women are described as fleeing the repressive regime and poverty in Burma, which contradicts the stated aim of 'rescuing' the women and returning them home. There is a fairly well-substantiated rumor that HIV-positive

Burmese women returned to Burma have been executed by the ruling SLORC authorities: even if this is untrue it seems inhumane to advocate returning these women to a country where there is no care, support or treatment available for HIV-positive people. The women are described as having limited understanding of HIV or AIDS, in fact the demand for them in Thailand is said to be linked to the myth that Burmese women are free of AIDS. The rapid rise in HIV infections may be related to the growth of the heroin trade and injecting drugs in the border area, or to the sharing of needles for antibiotics and contraceptives at health centers and among the workers themselves, however there is little information available about this.

There is evidence to support the claims of serious abuses by Thai police and immigration authorities. This abuse has been made possible by criminalizing the industry while there continues to be a high demand for female sex workers. The large amounts of money at stake encourage the bribery and corruption of the Thai authorities, and unregulated, substandard working conditions (*Asia Watch* 1993: pp. 67–8). At a conference launching the Asia Watch report in a Thai translation, a Thai police officer named Surasek disputed its findings: 'At present, most of these Burmese girls come here to work in brothels of their own free will. Very few of the women we meet in our day-to-day work say they were lured into the business' (*The Nation*, 5 April 1995). He also pointed out that 'police had great difficulty securing convictions against agents who recruit women for the flesh trade since very few prostitutes are willing to identify or testify against these agents in a court of law'.

It is tempting to wonder why the Asia Watch women want to expose the 'horrors' in Thailand as opposed to some cases in the United States such as HIV prevalence among sex workers in the black housing projects in Oakland, or the treatment of immigrants (even legal ones) in sweatshops and in the United States in general. Meanwhile UNICEF reports that the United States has 300,000 prostitutes under 18, more than its own estimates for all Asian countries put together (*Far Eastern Economic Review*, 14 December 1995). Perhaps the 'researchers' know that as guests in Thailand, which is so dependent on tourism income, they enjoy a level of protection which they would not find in US housing projects.

TRAFFICKING AND FEMALE LABOR MIGRATION

The IWDA campaign over Burmese women tried to link the situation with Thai women arriving in Sydney in its media release. By equating Australian conditions with those in Thailand, they conjured up dens of iniquity full of juveniles held against their will, such as the media periodically sensationalizes. Matheson introduces a typical article:

> One of thousands of women from Thailand, the Philippines, Malaysia and China trafficked to Australia and other First World countries by crime syndicates each year, Susie is the face of contemporary poverty. That her job

as a debt bonded sex worker is the best economic option available to her is a metaphor for most of the world's women, whose grinding impoverishment in the Third World is accelerating (Matheson 1994).

The exaggerations of the anti-trafficking groups only make things worse for the workers, such that representatives of three sex worker organizations in Sydney PROS, SWOP, QEWU, the Sydney Sexual Health Center multicultural health promotion project and Asian sex workers met to develop a policy statement on the alleged trafficking of Asian sex workers in Australia (PROS et al 1995). Thai workers in Australia are variously involved with a complex array of big and small operators, such as agents in Bangkok, passport forgers in Kuala Lumpur and travel agents in Singapore, so that they arrive with debts of up to $30,000. However I have shown elsewhere (Brockett and Murray 1994; and see David 1995) that conditions vary greatly. Most of these women enter their contracts willingly, and if they can pay off their debt, they may become recruiters or brothel managers themselves.

Because the sex industry is not fully decriminalized and sex workers cannot obtain work visas freely, some of the terms and conditions of contracts are exploitative and working conditions may be poor. Australia's own racist policies contribute to exploitation, since young women from the United Kingdom and Canada have no problem getting working visas under bilateral agreements, while, according to Australian immigration officials, 'no young attractive woman, and by that I mean a woman under sixty, is going to get a visa in Bangkok unless she is dripping with gold or has a business background' (David 1995: p. 45). Through their Operation Paper Tiger, the Australian authorities have deported eighty Thai workers in two years under the 1958 Migration Act, and the continuing crackdown pushes up the cost of the bonds. Attempts by women in detention to claim refugee status have so far been unsuccessful. Workers who are persecuted, arrested and deported before they pay off their debts are left with nothing for their hard work and, since they have to pay for deportation, they may end up further indebted. Police and immigration activity depresses business and means that workers have to hide their activities. This makes it harder for them to be contacted by support organizations providing information, condoms and HIV/AIDS information.

Asian workers who seek employment in the sex industry in Australia do so for the money, just as Australian workers do. Workers should be free to move to seek better pay and conditions just as many Australian workers go to work in Japan and Hong Kong. My experience is that workers are aware of the kind of work they will do when they enter the contract; in the very rare cases when workers have been trapped by false promises, of course, this is unacceptable. The Prostitutes Collective of Victoria has argued for working visas to be made available, 'thereby publicly diffusing the mythology of the "coerced innocent"' (PCV 1995), and David (1995) has made a strong case for easier short-term working visas and sponsorship by brothels.

The anti-trafficking campaigns actually have a detrimental effect on workers and increase discrimination as they perpetuate the stereotype of Asian workers as passive and diseased. Clients are encouraged to think of Asian workers as helpless victims who are unable to resist, so they may be more likely to violate the rights of these workers. The campaigns also encourage racism towards Asian workers within the industry (where Australian workers accuse them of undercutting and not using condoms) and in the general community where Asian workers form an ostracized new 'underclass' without equal rights (Brockett and Murray 1994).

The movement of sex workers around the region reflects economic differentials and a transnational division of labor: Thai workers head for Australia, Europe and Japan, while Burmese, Chinese and Indo-Chinese enter Thailand. But sex work is not the only job where the prospects vary so much from place to place that people are prepared to take on debts and forged paperwork. There has been a general rapid increase in migration, from Asia to the West, and a dramatic reversal of the gender balance so that there are now many more women involved in the largest mass migration in human history (see, for example, Heyzer et al. 1994). The majority are employed on a contractual basis as foreign domestic workers (the 'maid trade') in situations which often involve debts, exploitation and sexual abuse – conditions exposed in the media following the 1995 case of Filipina worker, Flor Contemplacion, who was hanged in Singapore. Similarly in Indonesia where domestic workers 'bring in significant foreign revenue and make rich men and women of those in the body business' (IRIP 1995: p. 27), there are frequent reports of exploitation and abuse and yet increasing numbers of migrants.

Expectations are raised by the consumer images beamed in by television, and any life is seen as better relative to a poor existence in the village: sex workers are not idealists any more than they are victims, neither have evil procurers and paedophiles created the whole industry. As Tracy Quan puts it:

> Anyone who travels to a country, believing that the 'streets are paved with gold' is operating out of some form of greed, desire or ambition. . . . There is a saying among the jaded: 'You can't con someone who isn't trying to get away with something'. (personal communication, September 28, 1995)

ABOLITIONISTS CREATING AND MANIPULATING STEREOTYPES

There are now a number of anti-trafficking groups. Not all use an emotive discourse to push an abolitionist, fundamentalist agenda, but some are rooted in the ideology of Catherine MacKinnon (1987) and Kathleen Barry (1981) wherein all sex is prostitution and all prostitution is a violation of human rights – whatever the workers might care to say about it. 'Trafficking' is one of the monsters evoked (like sex tourism and child prostitution) since Western sex workers on our own turf have used our own structures of support and advocacy to challenge some of the middle-class feminists who claim to represent us. Abolitionists have created a new 'other' by victimizing Asian workers and children to enforce the moral condemnation of prostitution, with broad implications for all sex trade workers, freedom of sexual expression and HIV/AIDS prevention.

The trafficking argument depends on the presence of third parties coercing women into prostitution: if any money is offered to the women or their parents it should be as pitiful as possible, whereas the profits being made from their sexual labor should be as enormous as possible. Media reports also emphasize the involvement of organized crime such as Hong Kong triads in the sex industry (e.g. *Far Eastern Economic Review*, 14 December 1995), making a conceptual leap to assume the prostitutes are forced into the work and their lives ruined. According to the *Bangkok Post* (30 October 1995) and *ECPAT Bulletin* (25 November 1995), 'Experts [sic] speak of syndicates systematically buying children from families in poor villages all over Asia, of gangs working in cooperation with police and immigration officials to transport their purchases across national borders and of sophisticated networks of paedophiles exchanging information.'

It is the prohibition of prostitution and restrictions on travel which attract organized crime and create the possibilities for large profits, as well as creating the prostitutes' need for protection and assistance; it is the erotic-pathetic stereotype of the Asian prostitute which creates the possibility for middle-class women's trafficking hysteria. Logically there is no difference between 'debt-bonded' Asian workers and Australian workers choosing to work for Hong Kong triads for more money than they could get in Sydney: it is racism which says that the former are victims and the latter agents. Even the East European workers now being chronically exploited all over the world are rarely constructed as victims in the same way. In Southeast Asia, middle-class feminist groups still claim to represent sex workers and women's NGOs are involved in the anti-trafficking lobby (see, for example, Sancho and Layador 1993). While there are also splits among women's NGOs, these women are often happy to direct attention on to trafficking and Western/Japanese sex tourism and away from the local (largest) part of industry. Anti-trafficking groups such as ECPAT and the Global Alliance (GAATW) do not support abolition per se and are concerned with extreme cases of coercion. However the vagueness of definitions and lack of involvement of the workers themselves enabled the Coalition (CATW) to gather support for a radical abolitionist agenda. The Coalition and a number of other NGOs formed a network, supported by UNESCO, called the NGO Coalition Against Exploitation of Women, to take a petition to the Beijing UN Conference on Women in 1995.

BEIJING, THE UN CONVENTION AND SEX WORKERS' VOICES

The Coalition's petition is for a new 'Convention Against Sexual Exploitation' to replace the 1949 UN Convention on the Suppression of Trafficking in

Persons and the Exploitation of the Prostitution of Others. The 1949
Convention originated with the 'exposure' of the White Slave Trade (which was
later shown to be negligible) by Jewish feminists and the social purity movement in Europe (Truong 1990; Goldman 1970). It 'rests mainly at the conceptual level, i.e. that prostitution is a form of promiscuity which offends public
morality, the family and the community' (Truong 1990: p. 86), and it considers the prostitute as a uniform category, as a source of evil separate from the
socioeconomic environment. Needless to say it ignores the client.

The new Convention Against Sexual Exploitation was previously proposed
by Barry at the UN Human Rights Conference in Vienna, 1993. The proposed
change would ban prostitution completely, not just forced prostitution:
'Legalized prostitution . . . is an open door for traffickers' claims Janice
Raymond, an activist with the US-based 'Coalition Against Trafficking in
Women' (Hornblower 1993: p. 24). Their petition states:

> It is a fundamental human right to be free of sexual exploitation in all its
> forms, from prostitution, sex tourism, trafficking in women, mail-order
> bride selling and pornography to incest, wife abuse, sexual harassment
> and rape. . . . Sexual exploitation abrogates a person's human right to
> dignity, equality, autonomy and physical and mental well-being; it preys
> on women and children made vulnerable by poverty and economic devel-
> opment policies and practices, on refugees and displaced persons, and on
> women in the migrating process; and serves as a vehicle for racism and
> Northern domination (NGO Coalition Against Exploitation of Women,
> 1995).

Sexual exploitation has taken on a life of its own, and everything is conveniently muddled by putting prostitution and pornography in the same sentence
as rape and incest so that people's obvious anathema to non-consensual sex is
extended by implication to all forms of commercial transactions involving sex.
'To equate professional prostitution with domestic violence is to diminish the
horror of the helpless; to equate choiceful sex work with the violence of criminal greed is to deny the value and dignity of the work some women choose to
do . . . it is the criminalizing of sex work that is partly responsible for society's
negative attitudes to ALL women's sexuality' (Helen Vicqua, Scarlet Alliance
internal communication, 19 May 1995). Meanwhile, the Network of Sex Work
Projects (NWSP) coordinated a sex worker presence at Beijing to counter the
anti-trafficking lobby, struggling against a Chinese government which initially
did not allow visas for sex workers and prevaricated in every way possible to
put people off attending. Most sex worker groups do not currently have
resources such as E-mail access, whereas the anti-trafficking lobby is very professional, well organized and au fait with the UN system. However, through
perseverance the NWSP did finally receive accreditation for the main UN conference. According to the Network:

> The dominant ideology about prostitution within the United Nations is that prostitution is a form of sexual exploitation which should be abolished. This view has been legitimized and passed into resolutions and laws at conferences such as Beijing with no input at all from sex workers themselves. Many sex workers feel that it is time to demand that we are heard in such a significant international forum. More than being simply heard it is essential to form some resolutions which reflect our demands for human rights, and have those passed rather than the resolutions which lead to repressive measures to abolish prostitution. To do this sex workers and their supporters need to work to prepare resolutions and to lobby delegates for support at the conference (Doezema 1995).

Abolitionists need to hear that most sex workers, including male and transgender sex workers and men who work with female clients, do the job willingly and do very well out of it relative to other occupations. They need to hear that clients of sex workers come from all walks of life (and include women), they are not monsters, and sex workers as a rule do not hate them. It happens quite frequently that workers and clients develop a personal relationship outside of work, and Asian workers in expatriate bars commonly construct their relationships with clients in emotional, as well as commercial, terms (Law 1996: pp. 80–2).

What can we conclude about the Coalition? Is there an element of titillation in their focus on sex workers, when similar problems are faced by migrant domestic workers and others? Is there an element of self-flagellation due to middle-class white guilt when faced with the rape of Asia by white capitalists? 'Where there is an overlay of North-South exploitation – the Western tourist ruining innocent paradise with his credit card and unleashed libido – this version plays easily in certain, well-meaning ears' (Black 1994: p. 12). At the same time the assumptions of passivity, stupidity and silence on the part of the Asian workers underline the inherent racism and class bias in the Coalition's arguments. In the end, the Beijing declaration was largely decided on before the actual conference and achieved very little in terms of sexual liberation or acknowledgement of women's sexuality due to the strength of Islamic, Catholic and other reactionary groups. Sex work (addressed in terms of trafficking and sexual exploitation) was dealt with in the section on violence against women: existing instruments were recommended to be strengthened and the victims of trafficking supported (UN 1995 Section D). Trafficking is viewed as a global conspiracy which can be dismantled through international co-operation and the paternalistic rehabilitation of victims (assumed female and helpless). The small but staunch sex worker presence at Beijing managed to make a significant impact at the NGO Forum and the UN conference. Some anti-trafficking groups, including GAATW, worked with the sex workers to defeat Section 230(O) of the Draft Platform for Action and to avoid the creation of the new abolitionist Convention on the Elimination of all Forms of Sexual Exploitation as proposed by the Coalition Against Trafficking in Women.

SUMMARY

In the aftermath of Beijing the hysteria is fading, and the abolitionists, especially the CATW, are again out on a limb. The general interest in the topic has spurred more research and more evidence, which has shown up the predominance of local clients and the relatively small part played by 'sex tourists'. It is increasingly hard to maintain unsubstantiated rumors, although those who don't believe the hype are placed in a difficult position of proving a negative (JCNCA 1995: p. 53), while police deficiencies and corruption, the cunning of paedophiles, etc. can be conveniently blamed from the other side for the lack of evidence.

Migration of female labor is increasing due to processes of economic globalization and removal of political boundaries, and clearly this process is accompanied by an increasing degree of coercion and exploitation of women due to prevailing systems of sex and gender in sending and receiving countries such as Thailand. The Utrecht conference statement made a valid point that force and not the type of work should be the issue in 'trafficking' and goes on:

> . . . the individual right to self-determination includes the ability and the right of the individual to decide to work as a prostitute. In order to reduce the vulnerability of prostitutes and others to trafficking in this context, prostitution and other activities in the informal sphere should be recognized as a form of work. Consequently, prostitutes and other sex workers have the right to safe working conditions through the use of occupational health and safety and other labor ordinances (1994).

Truong argues that the industrial production of sexual services requires a continuous supply of sexual labor: 'The effect of this process has been an increase in the use of violence to locate and control sexual labor' (1990: p. 201). Therefore, boundaries and workable definitions (preferably in line with ages of consent and employment) regarding 'underage' sexual labor and controls over the use of force will continue to be necessary. Existing laws and Conventions cover the issues of slavery and similar practices, non-consensual sex and the exploitation of children (Metzenrath 1995), and there is already a Special Rapporteur on the Sale of Children, Child Prostitution and Child Pornography. All states need to ratify and apply (if they have not done so) these conventions, and laws should be introduced or enforced to control the sale of children by their parents, preferably before the sale occurs so that sex workers are not expected to finger their own families to the authorities.

All states need to start decriminalizing prostitution (without creating new categories of good and bad prostitutes), applying occupational health and safety standards to workplaces (including provisions for street workers) and working toward eradicating discrimination. Restrictive immigration policies contribute to the exploitation of migrants and should be reviewed: sex workers should have the right to travel freely and obtain working visas regardless of ethnic background. Governments should follow Australia in funding organizations which provide support and information to Asian workers, and these workers should be supported to form their own groups to achieve greater autonomy (and participate in and strengthen the Asia-Pacific network for sex workers' rights). International networks of sex work projects should aim to inform workers about working conditions and choices. Finally, where sex workers *have* been forced to work against their will they should be offered every support and free transport to their place of origin if they so wish (see also PROS et al. 1995).

It is important to distinguish different types of sex trade work using clearly documented participatory research that involves the workers. Blanket statements about prostitution and the exploitation of women are propaganda from a political agenda which seeks to control the way people think and behave. The situations which the anti-traffickers rail against, insofar as they do exist, are a result of economic, political and gender inequalities, and it is those inequalities which should be our central cause for concern. The vast range of sex industries and contexts requires an understanding of diversity and difference and a realization that prohibition and unitary 'moral values' are part of the problem, not the solution.

ABBREVIATIONS

CATW	The Coalition Against Trafficking in Women
ECPAT	End Child Prostitution in Asian Tourism
GAATW	The Global Alliance Against Traffic in Women
HIV/AIDS	Human Immune-Deficiency Virus/Acquired Immune Deficiency Syndrome
IRIP	Indonesia Resources and Information Project
IWDA	International Women's Development Agency
JCNCA	Joint Committee on the National Crime Authority (Canberra)
JSC	Joint Standing Committee on Foreign Affairs, Defense and Trade (Canberra)
NGO	Non-government organization
PCV	Prostitutes' Collective of Victoria (Melbourne)
PROS	Prostitutes' Rights Organization for Sex Workers (Sydney)
QEWU	Queer and Esoteric Workers' Union (Sydney/Canberra)
SLORC	State Law and Order Restoration Council (Burma)
SWOP	Sex Workers Outreach Project (Sydney)
WISE	Workers in Sex Employment in the ACT (Canberra)

REFERENCES

Asia Watch Women's Rights Project, *A Modern form of Slavery: Trafficking of Burmese Women and Girls into Brothels in Thailand* (Human Rights Watch, 1993).

Black Maggie, 'Home Truths', *New Internationalist*, 252, February 1994.

Brockett, L. and A. Murray, 'Thai Sex Workers in Sydney', in R. Perkins, et al. (eds), *Sex Work and Sex Workers in Australia* (Sydney: UNSW Press, 1994), pp. 191–202.

Coomaraswamy, R., 'Report of the Special Rapporteur on Violence Against Women' (Geneva: UN document, 1995).

David, F., 'Overseas Workers in the Australian Sex Industry: Issues and Options for Reform' (Canberra: unpublished paper, 1995).

Doezema, Jo, 'Choice in Prostitution', in *Changing Faces of Prostitution* (Helsinki: Unioni – The League of Finnish Feminists, 1995).

Doezema, Jo, 'Sex Worker Delegation to the Beijing Conference' (Amsterdam: Network of Sex Work Projects, internal communication, March 1995).

Goldman, E., *The Traffic in Women and Other Essays on Feminism* (New York: Times Change Press, 1970 [1917]).

Heyzer, N., et al. (eds), *The Trade in Domestic Workers: Causes, Mechanisms and Consequences of International Migration* (London: Zed Books, 1994).

Hornblower, M., 'Special Report: The Skin Trade', *Time* vol 8, no. 25, 1993, pp. 18–29.

IRIP, 'Over the Hills and Far Away: Indonesian Migrant Labour', *Inside Indonesia*, vol. 42, March 1995, pp. 27–31.

JCNCA, *Organised Criminal Paedophile Activity* (Canberra: Senate Printing Unit, 1996).

JSC, *A Report on Human Rights and the Lack of Progress Towards Democracy in Burma (Myanmar)* (Canberra: Australian Government Publishing Service, 1995).

Law, L., 'Dancing in Cebu: Mapping Bodies, Subjectivities and Spaces in an Era of HIV/AIDS' (Canberra: ANU, dissertation, 1996).

MacKinnon, C., *Feminism Unmodified: Discourses on Life and Law* (Cambridge, MA: Harvard University Press, 1987).

Matheson, Angela, 'Trafficking in Asian Sex Workers', *Green Left Weekly*, vol. 26, October 1994, p. 1.

Metzenrath, S., 'The Federal Government's Responsibilities Towards Prostitution' (Canberra: WISE discussion paper, 1995).

Murray, A., 'On Bondage, Peers and Queers: Sexual Subcultures, Sex Workers and AIDS Discourses in the Asia-Pacific' (draft manuscript).

NGO Coalition Against Exploitation of Women, 'Petition Against Sexual Exploitation' (Amherst, MA: CATW paper for Beijing, February 1995).

PCV, 'PCV Statement on Trafficking' (St Kilda, unpublished paper, 1995).

PROS, et al., 'Alleged Trafficking of Asian Sex Workers to Australia' (Sydney: discussion paper for Beijing, 1995).

Sancho, N. and M. Layador (eds), 'Traffic in Women: Violation of Women's Dignity and Fundamental Human Rights' (Manila: Asian Women Human Rights Council, 1993).

Sullivan, B., 'Global Prostitution: Sex Tourism and Trafficking in Women' (Glasgow: paper presented to the Annual Meeting of the Law Society Association, University of Strathclyde, 11–13 July 1996).

Troung, Than Dam, *Sex, Money and Morality: The Political Economy of Prostitution and Tourism in south East Asia* (London: Zed Books, 1990). UNESCO, 'Contemporary Forms of Slavery: Draft Programme of Action on the Traffic in Persons and the Exploitation of the Prostitution of Others' (Geneva: UNESCO document 13 June 1995).

4.5

RECONFIGURING HIERARCHIES: THE ILBERT BILL CONTROVERSY, 1883–84

Mrinalini Sinha

On 9 February 1883, the Law Member of the Government of India, C. P. Ilbert, introduced a bill in the Legislative Council to amend the Code of Criminal Procedure of the Indian Penal Code. The Bill, popularly called the Ilbert Bill, proposed to give various classes of native officials in the colonial administrative service limited criminal jurisdiction over European British subjects living in the *mofussil* or country towns in India.[1] The Ilbert Bill, which was widely interpreted as a challenge to the control European capitalists exercised over sources of raw material and labour in the interiors of India, provoked a 'white mutiny' from Anglo-Indian officials and non-officials alike.[2] The opposition secured a victory when the Viceroy Lord Ripon was forced into an agreement or 'concordat' to get a modified bill passed on 25 January 1884, which undermined the original principle of the Ilbert Bill. Although the new Act accorded native magistrates criminal jurisdiction over European British subjects in the *mofussils*, the special legal status of European British subjects was preserved. The European British subjects in the *mofussils* won the right to demand trial by a jury of whom at least half were European British subjects or Americans.

As a crucial moment in the consolidation of a unified Anglo-Indian public opinion in India, the Ilbert Bill controversy has received its share of attention from scholars. Yet while scholars have examined the impact of the Ilbert Bill controversy on the racial polarisation between Anglo-Indians and Indians and

From: Mrinalini Sinha (1995), 'Reconfiguring Hierarchies: The Ilbert Bill Controversy, 1883–84', pp. 33–68, in Mrinalini Sinha, *Colonial Masculinity: The 'Manly Englishman' and the 'Effeminate Bengali' in the Late Nineteenth Century* (Manchester: Manchester University Press).

on the development of an all-India nationalist sentiment, they have scarcely begun to explore the impact of its intersecting gender and racial ideologies on imperialist and nationalist politics in the second half of the nineteenth century.[3] The stereotypes of the 'manly Englishman' and the 'effeminate Bengali *babu*' that structured the Ilbert Bill controversy emerged out of, and helped shape, important shifts in racial and gender ideologies that accompanied the political and economic transformations of the imperial social formation in the late nineteenth century. The politics of colonial masculinity in the Ilbert Bill controversy not only reflected the intersection of racial and gender ideologies, but also enabled those hierarchies to be reconfigured in new ways.

Contemporaries readily acknowledged the gender politics in the racial arguments against the Ilbert Bill. According to the Head of Police Intelligence in Bengal, the agitation against the Bill was instigated by the 'capitalists' in Bengal, but in order to 'make the grievance a general one, they raised the cry of danger to European women and so the agitation spread'.[4] Opponents of the Bill, moreover, expressed their disdain of native civil servants by likening them to 'sweet girl graduates from Girton'.[5] The gender politics of the Anglo-Indian agitation was no doubt underpinned by a patriarchal construct of womanhood. At the same time, however, the Ilbert Bill controversy also witnessed an impressive and unprecedented mobilisation of white women in India. The contribution of white women in India, the *memsahibs* as they were popularly called, provoked a mixed admiration from Anglo-Indian men: 'one circumstance hitherto unexampled in Indian history . . . is that Englishwomen have for the first time thought it necessary to descend into the arena of political controversy'.[6] *The Englishwoman's Review*, one of the leading women's journals in Britain, was more unequivocal in its praise of the racist agitation against the Ilbert Bill for providing Englishwomen in India an opportunity to prove their 'interest in politics'.[7]

Such tensions around women's roles were grist to the mill of an intensified politics of colonial masculinity. For it was precisely the unevenness in the intersection of racial and gender ideologies that gave the politics of colonial masculinity its particular significance in the Ilbert Bill controversy. On the one hand, the agitation against the Ilbert Bill recuperated the challenge of racial equality by rearticulating racial difference in the terms of a pre-given gender hierarchy. On the other, it recuperated the feminist challenge of gender equality by harnessing even a 'New' gender ideology to the agenda of racial hierarchy. Indeed, the impact of the Ilbert Bill controversy was not simply to consolidate traditional racial and gender hierarchies. Rather, the true significance of colonial masculinity in the Ilbert Bill controversy was precisely in rearticulating traditional racial and gender hierarchies to preserve imperial interests in a new guise.

At the first, and perhaps most obvious level, the stereotype of 'effeminacy' performed important ideological service in the Ilbert Bill controversy: it presented the racial privileges of the Anglo-Indians in more acceptable and naturalised gendered terms. The attempt to rationalise racial hierarchy on a supposedly more natural gender hierarchy was based not on homology but on difference. Sir Lepel Griffin, a senior Anglo-Indian official, in his essay entitled 'The Place of Bengalis in Politics' published in 1892 emphasised this difference. He had the following to say of the 'feminine' traits shared by Englishwomen and Bengali men:

> The characteristics of women which disqualify them for public life and its responsibilities are inherent in their sex and are worthy of honour, for to be womanly is the highest praise for a woman, as to be masculine is her worst reproach, but when men, as the Bengalis are disqualified for political enfranchisement by the possession of essentially feminine characteristics, they must expect to be held in such contempt by stronger and braver races, who have fought for such liberties as they have won or retained.[8]

According to Griffin, Englishwomen and Bengali men were disqualified from playing an active part in politics because they both possessed 'feminine' traits; but whereas 'feminine' traits were 'natural' for the former and made them the 'ornaments of life', for the latter it was 'unnatural', and made them the objects of ridicule.

The stereotype of the 'effeminate Bengali *babu*' worked precisely by invoking simultaneously the Victorian British gender ideology and the increasingly embattled status of this ideology: on the one hand, therefore, it invoked the logic of a gender system that associated masculinity with maleness and femininity with femaleness and found in them the basis for the 'natural' division of society into male and female spheres; and, on the other, it also invoked the pressures on the classical bourgeois male public sphere from the inclusion of new social actors, like women and the working class.[9] For as Griffin points out, the 'unnaturalness' of the demands of 'effeminate *babus*' was parallel to the 'unnaturalness' of British feminist demands. To quote Griffin once again:

> Although it would be both impertinent and paradoxical to compare Englishwomen – the most courageous, charming and beautiful of the daughters of Eve – with Bengali agitators, yet it is a curious fact that the question of admitting Bengalis to political power, occupies in British India, the same place that in England is taken by the question of the extension of the vote to women, both may be advocated on somewhat similar grounds and both may be refused in compliance with the necessities of the same arguments.[10]

It was this 'unnaturalness' that was being invoked in the displacement of the racial politics of the Ilbert Bill on to a different register: the supposedly natural division of the sexes.

The need for such a displacement of racial politics was touched off by a debate on the central contradiction of British colonial policy in India: a racial equality that was both promised and endlessly deferred. Although the Bill was initiated innocuously enough as a minor administrative measure, it quickly became the touchstone of the racial policy of the colonial authorities in India. The measure was designed to overcome certain anomalies in the exercise of criminal jurisdiction following the Code of Criminal Procedure of 1872. The Code of 1872 had brought European British subjects in the *mofussils* under the jurisdiction of the *mofussil* courts for the first time; in the past European British subjects in the *mofussils* had to be taken to the High Courts in the Presidency towns for trial on criminal offences. Since an act of 1869 had previously given natives the right to be appointed as Justices of Peace in the *mofussils*, the non-official European population in the *mofussils* were willing to be brought under the *mofussil* courts only if they were to be tried by European British subjects alone. In exchange for being brought under the jurisdiction of the *mofussil* courts, the European British subjects were guaranteed that they would be tried only by Justices of Peace who were themselves European British subjects.[11] The anomalies in the 1872 Code, however, became apparent as natives in the elite Indian civil service gained enough seniority to be appointed as District Officers in the *mofussils*. A native District Magistrate or Sessions Judge, for example, could not try a European British subject in the *mofussil*, but would have to call upon his subordinate, a European Joint Magistrate, to exercise jurisdiction over the case. Moreover, native civilians, who as Presidency Magistrates could exercise jurisdiction over European British subjects in the Presidency towns, would be forced to give up this privilege on promotion as District Officers in *mofussil* towns.

The need for a change in the 1872 Code had been apparent for some time, but the Government decided to proceed cautiously. Hence Act Ten of 1882, which was meant to review the 1872 Code, proposed no changes. Instead, the Government of India decided to take up the issue in a separate amendment to the Code. The proposal for an amendment had been initiated by a Bengali member of the Indian civil service, Behari Lal Gupta.[12] Gupta urged the government to remove the racial disqualification against native members of the senior or 'covenanted' branch of the Indian civil service. Gupta's note of 30 January 1882 was approved by the then Lt.-Governor of Bengal, Sir Ashley Eden, as a 'matter of general policy' and 'administrative convenience'.[13] The Government of India followed up on Eden's recommendation by sending Gupta's proposal for the opinion of other local administrations in India, with the exception of Bengal, whose Lt.-Governor had already approved the proposal. Despite a handful of dissenting opinions from diehard Anglo-Indian officials, there was an 'overwhelming consensus of opinion' that it was time to reconsider the special privilege reserved for Anglo-Indians in the *mofussils* by the Code of 1872.[14] The proposal to amend the 1872 Code was sent to Lord Hartington, the Secretary of State in London; Hartington approved the Government of India's proposal, although he failed to inform the Viceroy of the considerable hostility to the change from some members of his Council, such as Sir Henry Maine.[15] The Viceroy subsequently instructed his Legislative Department to draft a bill incorporating Gupta's proposal; the Bill, now known as the Ilbert Bill, was introduced in the Council on 9 February 1883. Ilbert's Bill, however, went beyond Gupta's original proposal in empowering not just natives in the senior or 'covenanted' branch of the civil service, but various other classes of native civil servants as well.

The Ilbert Bill became the occasion for one of the most significant mobilisations of Anglo-Indian opinion ever in India, even though the changes it proposed would have a very limited impact for many years. For despite the more comprehensive scope of Ilbert's bill, there were too few Indians of sufficient seniority in the civil service actually to qualify to try European British subjects in the *mofussils*. The Government of India, moreover, was willing to concede that at least for some time to come the extension of privilege would be limited only to natives in the senior or 'covenanted' branch of the Indian civil service. The vast majority of Indians in the civil service were not in the 'covenanted', but in the 'uncovenanted' or lower rungs of the administrative service. Native entry into the more prestigious 'covenanted' branch of the civil service was limited, either through the expensive and time-consuming procedure of taking the open competitive examination held in London since 1859 or through government nomination in accordance with the Government of India Act of 1870, which provided for the appointment of 'qualified' natives as 'statutory' civilians to covenanted posts.[16] In 1883 in all of India there were only eleven Indians who had entered the covenanted branch of the Indian civil service through open competition in London. One had left the service, one was dead, two were posted in Bombay, one was posted in the North-West Provinces, and six were posted in Bengal. Even with the inclusion of 'statutory' civilians, the number of Indians in the covenanted civil service was small; and the numbers senior enough to be affected by the change even smaller. In Bengal, for example, including both 'competition' and 'statutory' civilians there was a total of only twelve Indians in the covenanted branch of the civil service.[17] In all of India there were only two Bengali 'competition' civilians who would immediately qualify for the privileges under the Ilbert Bill: S. N. Tagore, of the Bombay civil service, and R. C. Dutt, of the Bengal civil service. Both held appointments as District Magistrates and Sessions Judge and hence confronted the issue of jurisdiction over European British subjects in the *mofussil*. The only other 'competition' civilian with sufficient seniority was B. L. Gupta, who was a Presidency Magistrate in Calcutta. On being moved from Calcutta to a district appointment, Gupta would also have to face the issue of exercising jurisdiction over British subjects. In the next five years only two others, K. G. Gupta and Brajendranath De, both 'competition' civilians serving in Bengal, would be eligible for appointments as District Officers and hence for jurisdiction over European British subjects in the *mofussils*. For another ten years, only nine Indian covenanted civilians, competition and statutory, would qualify for the proposed jurisdiction. Even if the Bill extended the jurisdiction to all classes of native officials, including those in the covenanted as well as the uncovenanted branch of the service, there would be for a long time to come only thirty-seven Indians in all of India able to qualify for the privilege.[18]

The howl of protest from the Anglo-Indian community over the Ilbert Bill thus had less to do with the Bill itself as with the general challenge it posed to the principle of Anglo-Indian racial exclusivity in India. Taken together with other recent measures, the Ilbert Bill was seen as the unfolding of the dubious promise of racial equality made to the colonial subjects. As the *Englishman*, a newspaper of the Anglo-Indian business community in Calcutta, claimed: 'the cause for . . . alarm is to be found in the tendency of the times as exemplified in the (Ilbert) Bill, much more than in the four corners of the Bill itself'.[19] The Government of India was committed, in rhetoric at least, to a policy of racial equality as enunciated in the Charter Act of 1833 and the Queen's Proclamation of 1858. As the time came to fulfil some of these liberal promises, however, the colonial Government found its rhetoric increasingly at odds with the special privileges reserved for Anglo-Indians in India. These underlying contradictions came to a head during the Viceroyalty of Lord Ripon. Ripon, who was an appointee of the Liberal Gladstone Government in Britain, had hoped to cement the loyalty of the Western-educated Indian middle class by removing some of the more glaring racial disqualifications against natives enacted by his predecessors.[20] Ripon's policy, however, set him on a collision course with the vested interests of Anglo-Indian officials and non-officials in India. Members of the Calcutta Bar were enraged that Ripon had appointed a native judge, R. C. Mitter, as the Acting Chief Justice in Calcutta. Ripon's other measures, such as the repeal of the Vernacular Press Acts and the passage of the Local Self-Government Act, were perceived by the Anglo-Indian population as a threat to their exclusive privileges in India. The *Englishman* and the *Civil and Military Gazette* of Lahore blamed Ripon's initiatives for converting India into a 'theatre on which actors play to Radical audiences in England'.[21] Ripon himself was acutely aware of the larger issues at stake in the Anglo-Indian opposition to the Ilbert Bill. In his note to the Secretary of State in London, he admitted that the opposition to the Bill goes 'beyond the Bill and brings into discussion some of the fundamental principles of British policy in India'.[22]

It was indeed precisely these 'fundamental principles of British policy in India' that were at stake in the Ilbert Bill controversy. By the second half of the century, both 'liberal' and 'conservative' Anglo-Indian administrators and intellectuals were forced to reconsider the promise of racial equality as the guiding principle of British policy in India. The pressure for the reconsideration of British colonial policy was over-determined by various economic and political changes in the second half of the nineteenth century: the threat to Britain's economic position from other European nations; the massive increase in British financial investments abroad; and the growing challenge of an Indian middle class who were eager to benefit from the promise of racial equality. In this context, it became increasingly difficult for the colonial authorities to escape the fact that continued British political and economic exploitation of India depended on the maintenance of certain exclusive racial privileges for European British subjects in India. Even such benefits to India as supposedly accrued from the presence of British capital in India were seen as dependent upon the preservation of racial privileges for the British. Hence opponents of the Bill argued that the empowerment of native officials would hinder the smooth operation of British capital in India, leading to a flight of British capital from India.[23]

The gendered politics of colonial masculinity provided the vehicle for the crucial rearticulation of the 'fundamental principles of British policy in India' necessitated by the changes of the second half of the century. For only a few prominent Anglo-Indians like Fitzjames Stephen, a former Law Member of the Viceroy's Council and a Judge of Judicature in England, were willing to disavow unambiguously the liberal principle of racial equality and to celebrate colonial conquest for what it was. In his opposition to Ripon's policies, Stephen 'formulated a doctrine which others had not the ability to put in words or the cynicism to avow'.[24] He argued that the liberal spirit of the Queen's proclamation, known as the Indian 'Magna Carta', was a 'mere expression of sentiment and opinion' and had no legal force in India. The Government of India, he argued, must be guided by a more realistic set of principles. His clear-headed assessment of the nature and purpose of the colonial government in India bears quoting at some length:

> [The Government of India] is essentially an absolute Government founded not on consent, but on conquest. It does not represent the native principles of life or government, and it can never do so until it represents heathenism and barbarism. It represents a belligerent civilization, and no anomaly can be so striking and dangerous as its administration by men who, being at the Head of a Government founded on conquest, implying at every point the superiority of the conquering race, of their ideas, their institutions, their opinions and their principles, and having no justification for its existence except that superiority, shrink from the open, uncompromising straight forward assertion of it, seek to apologize for their own position and refuse from whatever cause, to uphold and support it.[25]

While most Anglo-Indians in the Ilbert Bill controversy demurred from Stephen's frank and cynical position against the Bill, the politics of colonial masculinity served precisely to rearticulate the fundamental principles of British policy in line with Stephen's position.

The strategy of deploying the politics of colonial masculinity against the Ilbert Bill was disingenuous at best: its main purpose was to shift the onus of the debate from a straightforward defence of racial privileges to a question of the fitness of native civil servants. In the popular Anglo-Indian imagination, therefore, the effeminate Bengali *babu* was represented as the chief instigator and the chief beneficiary of the Ilbert Bill. The Ilbert Bill, it was argued, had originated at the instigation of a Bengali *babu*, B. L. Gupta; it was further held that the Bill would benefit disproportionately other Bengali *babus*, like S. N. Tagore and R. C. Dutt. Anglo-Indians singled out middle-class Bengali Hindus in their diatribes against the Bill. Opponents of the Bill suggested frequently that had the provisions of the Bill been limited to natives of provinces other than Bengal or to classes other than the Western-educated middle class there would be little ground for Anglo-Indian opposition to the Bill. One Anglo-Indian writer in the *Pioneer*, a semi-official Anglo-Indian newspaper, was convinced that 'were none but Hindustanis and Punjabis of good birth and education' likely to obtain power under the Ilbert Bill, there would be little to fear from natives abusing their power in trying European British subjects.[26] According to another Anglo-Indian who wrote to the *Englishman*, 'if Bengalis had the finesse of Parsi gentlemen it would be difficult to refuse them the privilege'.[27] Similarly, another writer in the *Englishman* gave the following rationale for the Anglo-Indian opposition to the Bill: 'I fancy most of us would not object to being taken before a fine old Sikh *Hakim* for instance. Is it the Sikhs who are clamouring for our loss of liberty? or is it any one of the warlike races of India?'[28] Yet the Anglo-Indian suspicion that 'none but a few Bengali *babus*' would benefit by the Bill had little basis in the actual proportion of Bengali Hindus who would be empowered by the Bill. W. W. Hunter, a supporter of the Ilbert Bill, presented a breakdown by province and religion of the thirty-three natives in the covenanted and uncovenanted branches of the civil service who would be affected immediately by the provisions of the Bill. Of the thirty-three native civilians, six were Rajputs, eight were Muslims, four were Parsis, five were Hindus from southern India and only ten were Hindus from Bengal. Bengali Hindus made up less than one-third of those who would benefit from the Bill, practically the same ratio they bore to the general population of India.[29] Hunter's argument, however, failed to allay the suspicion of his Anglo-Indian colleagues. Hunter had taken the 'effeminate *babu*' to refer quite narrowly to middle-class Hindus of Bengal, whereas for the opponents of the Bill the term covered more loosely the entire Western-educated Indian middle class.

The opprobrium in the charge of native effeminacy, moreover, was not based simply on likening the unfitness of native civilians to the unfitness of women; rather, it was based on emphasising the very, 'unnaturalness' of the disqualifications of the native civilians. Anglo-Indian opponents claimed that because native officers in the civil service were devoid of both 'manly physique' and 'manly character' they ought not to be placed in a position of authority over a more manly people. The 'constitutional timidity of the race', they argued, made the Bengali civilian unfit to exercise authority over the 'manly Englishman' or even over the other manly native races of India. Anglo-Indian officials declared that the inherent physical weakness or cowardice of the Bengali civilian rendered him incapable of performing his duties as a District Officer. Lord H. Ulick Brown, the Commissioner of Rajshaye and Cooch Behar, claimed that the Bengali officer would cower in fear at the prospect of trying 'burly European loafers' in the *mofussils*, and would only too readily make the case over to his subordinate, a European Joint Magistrate.[30] The Corinthean Theatre in Calcutta staged an updated version of Dave Carson's *Bengali Babu*, replete with contemporary allusions to the Ilbert Bill and the physical incompetence of the Bengali civilians. Contemporary Anglo-Indian satires, such as the immensely popular *A Glance in Advance or What's in Store for '84*, claimed that the Ilbert Bill's policy of placing a weakling race over manlier ones would lead to a total collapse of law and order in India. In such anti-Ilbert Bill pamphlets as *The Conflict of Caste*, moreover, dire consequences were predicted if the Ilbert Bill were passed; it warned that manly European British subjects could not be expected to take their subordination to an effeminate class of Indians lightly when even other native peoples chafed under the authority of such poor specimens of maleness.[31]

The alleged physical incompetence of the Bengali civilian was not just a matter of irrational sentiment or prejudice; it was perceived to have a direct bearing on the Bengali magistrate's ability to sympathise with the more 'sporting' public-school-trained Anglo-Indian who might be brought before him in a criminal case. When C. E. Buckland, a former member of the Board of Revenue in India, alleged at a public meeting in London that no further proof of the unfitness of the Bengali officer was needed than his failure as a 'sportsman', he was drawing attention to what was perceived as a crucial difference between the effeminate native officer and his sport-loving Anglo-Indian colleagues. Buckland reserved his greatest ridicule for Gupta, at whose initiative the Ilbert Bill had been proposed, by citing an incident in which the Bengali civilian had requested to be posted out of a station with 'excellent snipe shooting and a great opportunity for pig sticking'.[32] Although Indian newspapers caustically inquired 'how a proficiency in shooting wild animals can produce an efficiency in trying an offender', Buckland's Anglo-Indian contemporaries would have had no difficulty in recognising the connection between sporting proclivities and the ability to exercise jurisdiction in the *mofussils*.[33] H. H. Risley, Officiating Deputy Commissioner of Manbhoom, for example, expressed concern that since Bengali officers 'do not hunt, shoot, (and) play games', they would not show proper leniency in evaluating criminal charges brought against Anglo-Indians in the *mofussils*.[34] Risley probably had in mind the criminal cases frequently brought against Anglo-Indians by natives in the *mofussils*. A great many of these cases involved accusations against Anglo-Indian hunters and sportsmen, who were frequently responsible for 'accidental' shooting deaths of unwary native peasants, or against Anglo-Indian planters, who were accused of using excessive physical force in 'disciplining' their native employees.[35] In most of these cases, it was impossible to get a conviction against the Anglo-Indian offender from an Anglo-Indian-dominated judicial system. Risley, alluding to the shared interest in 'manly' sports among Anglo-Indians, feared that the more effeminate Bengali Magistrate would be incapable of understanding the 'thoughtless schoolboy spirit in which the injury complained of has been done'.

The further point about the 'unnatural' disqualification of native civilians had to do with the fact that, as many Anglo-Indians believed, races that were 'physically cowardly' were 'rarely morally brave'. In assessing the fitness of native officers, therefore, Anglo-Indians alluded frequently to the various moral deficiencies of character among the 'unmanly' natives. Bengali officers were believed to lack moral courage and to be more prone to falsehood, perjury, sedition, sycophancy, and the blind adherence to social and religious prejudices than any other native race.[36] Even native 'competition' civilians, who had undergone a brief sojourn in England for the purpose of taking the competitive examination and had been exposed to an 'Anglicised' education, were found unfit by English standards of probity, independence, and objectivity. The records of individual Indian 'competition' civilians were thoroughly scrutinised during the Ilbert Bill controversy and examples of their alleged moral shortcomings were publicly aired as proofs of the unfitness of even the most elite of Indian civil servants. The new Lt.-Governor of Bengal, Sir Rivers Thompson, was perhaps the most critical in his official evaluation of the performance of native civilians in the Indian civil service. In concluding his survey of opinions on the Bill, he observed that native civilians suffered from a 'want of nerve' which made it difficult for them to perform their job successfully.[37] In an earlier speech on the question of native jurisdiction, Thompson made a pointed reference to a scandal which had led some years previously to the dismissal of Surendranath Banerjea from the Indian civil service. Banerjea, who later went on to become a prominent Bengali political leader, had been discharged from service on a charge of dishonesty that would most likely have been overlooked had he been a British officer.[38] Allegations against other Indian officers currently serving in the Indian civil service were also repeated in the speeches and writings against the Bill, without much foundation. Henry Sullivan Thomas, in his speech to the Viceroy's Legislative Council, cited a report written by an Anglo-Indian officer on Satyendranath Tagore, the first Indian to join the Indian civil service once entry had been opened through an open competitive examination. Sullivan's purpose was to illustrate that even exceptional Indians who had undergone the rigours of an examination in England that catered primarily for British candidates could not be expected to display the high standards of objectivity expected from officers of the elite service. The report by A. S. Borraidale, District Magistrate of Broach, had suggested that Tagore, because of his own religious prejudices, had been unable to convict a Hindu zealot for murder in a trial that had come before him.[39]

The most telling example of the moral failure attributed to the native civilian, however, was the Anglo-Indian charge that native civilians displayed an 'irrational' or 'emotional' support for the Ilbert Bill. There was a circular logic to this argument; the proof of the unmanly character of the native civil servant alternated between the charge of sycophancy and irrational dislike of Europeans. John Beames, the Commissioner of the Burdwan Division in Bengal and a staunch opponent of the Ilbert Bill, detected in his native subordinate Brajendranath De's advocacy of the Bill a 'tone of dislike to Europeans and almost disrespect towards Government'.[40] For Beames and several like-minded

Anglo-Indian colleagues, this was the strongest argument against giving Western-educated Bengalis a larger share in the administration of the country. The various implications of effeminacy on the physique and character of the native officers were calculated to portray them as uniquely disqualified among all the native classes of India for the privileges of the Ilbert Bill. In so far as the logic of colonial masculinity identified the efforts to grant native civil servants equality as 'unnatural', it reinforced not only the racial hierarchies of colonial rule in India but also the gender hierarchies in both Britain and India.

At a second, and perhaps more important level, the politics of colonial masculinity reconstituted Anglo-Indian racial privileges as the benevolent protection of native and white women. The figure of the woman, therefore, was at the very heart of the definition of Anglo-Indian masculinity and Indian effeminacy in the Ilbert Bill controversy. The effeminacy of Indian men was in proportion to the subordination of Indian women; Indian men were to be disqualified from the privileges of the Ilbert Bill because of the manner in which they treated Indian women. British officials and missionaries in India were sanguine about their own role in 'uplifting' the position of Indian women; the colonial state was thus identified with the civilising role of the 'manly' protector of Indian women. Various scholars, however, have demonstrated that the colonial discourse about the subordination of Indian women served a variety of different functions for the justification of colonial rule. On the one hand, out of considerations of political expediency, the colonial state was often more than willing to compromise with, and even reinforce, orthodox indigenous patriarchal practices. On the other hand, the reforming zeal of the colonial state was directed typically against only select indigenous patriarchal practices; colonial officials and missionaries remained singularly uninterested in the impact of the collaboration between different forms of British and indigenous patriarchal practices.[41] The further point, as Lata Mani has argued, is that women were seldom either the subjects or even the objects of the colonial discourse on the 'woman question'; but, rather, women were merely the grounds on which the ideological struggle was waged between the colonial and the indigenous male elites.[42]

Certain specific manifestations of the subordination of women in orthodox elite and upper-caste Indian practices became the ground for the effeminacy of native men. Opponents of the Ilbert Bill, for example, associated native effeminacy only with particular forms of the subordination of women, such as the seclusion of women in *zenanas* (the female quarters in a native home) or the practice of *purdah* (veiling), found mainly among the elite and upper castes of the north and northeast parts of the country. In the words of one Anglo-Indian woman, 'in Bengal the men are notoriously destitute of manliness' because they 'are most harsh and cowardly in their treatment of the weaker sex'.[43] It was the patriarchal practices of the Bengalis, according to Mr I. Munro, Officiating Commissioner of the Presidency Division in Bengal, that 'hinder[ed] the development in Bengalis of those manly and straightforward qualities which under other conditions are found in Englishmen'.[44]

The opponents of the Bill used the protection of Indian women from such oppressive social practices as a litmus test for granting political concessions to Indians. The Anglo-Indian strategy of using women's subordination in India as a handy stick with which to beat back Indian demands for political equality had converted the 'woman question' into a battleground over the political rights of Indians. Expressing what was a common Anglo-Indian disdain for '*zenana*-bred civilians', a British Deputy Commissioner in Assam wrote: 'Is it seriously meant that natives who practice polygamy treat their wives as caged birds, kept in the dark chiefly for the creation of sons . . . who immolate infants of tender age to marriage, who compel infant widows to remain widows till death – are as such competent to try European men and women?'[45] British officials, non-officials, and missionaries argued that until native men learned to respect the rights of women they were not fit to be granted any political rights. This strategy of deferral was exemplified most famously in the argument of Mr J. J. J. Keswick, a senior partner in the British firm of Jardine, Skinner & Co. At the infamous anti-Ilbert Bill meeting held in the Calcutta Town Hall, Keswick defended the Anglo-Indian position on the Bill on the following grounds:

> when natives have so far advanced that the wives and sisters, daughters and mothers of those of the ranks from which our native civilians are drawn can come openly into Court and give evidence, and can mix with us and with our wives in society, then there will be so much of each other's innate nature known, that Government may seriously consider about giving natives the power they now ask.[46]

Keswick's speech, which echoed a dominant theme in the Anglo-Indian opposition, illustrates a further point about the implication of women in the politics of masculinity and effeminacy: knowledge of women became, in effect, synonymous with knowledge of the 'innate nature' of the British and the Indian people.

Supporters of the Ilbert Bill easily parodied such arguments as in the following verse from a poem entitled 'The Miller and his Men':

> And as we don't know his wife or daughter
> He can't know us as well as he ough'ter . . .
> His principles too are sure to be shady
> As his mother's not trained like an English lady.[47]

When opponents of the Bill brought up the subordination of native women as the cause for their opposition to the Ilbert Bill, they held up, by way of contrast, the norms of the 'English lady' as the qualification for trying European British subjects. If the norms of the 'English lady' were to serve as the standard for granting Indian civil servants privileges under the Ilbert Bill, then, as supporters of the Bill pointed out, it was precisely the female relatives of the class of Western-educated Indians, from which native civil servants were drawn, who were most likely to approximate these norms. For as Hunter, in a speech to the

Legislative Council, pointed out, native officials in the elite Indian civil service were perhaps even 'more English in thought and feeling than the Englishmen themselves'.[48] The female relatives of the Westernised Indian middle class, more than any other class of Indians, were more likely to be exposed to the kind of training expected of an 'English lady'. For, in order to become fit companions to Western-educated husbands, the middle-class Bengali woman or *bhadramahila* was encouraged to conform to at least some of the norms of Victorian bourgeois domesticity.[49] Indeed, the wives of many of the 'competition' Indian civilians were admiringly held up as examples of the modern or new Indian woman. Jnanadanandini Debi, the wife of Tagore, had not only given up *purdah*, but had for long charmed Anglo-Indian circles by her 'great self-possession'. Mohini Debi, the wife of R. C. Dutt, and Suadamini, the wife of B. L. Gupta, had both attended the Native Ladies' Adult and Normal School in Calcutta and had received votes of confidence from their husband's Anglo-Indian colleagues.[50]

Indians were thus struck by the peculiar irony in the Anglo-Indian case against the Bill: opponents who held up the norms of the 'English lady', nevertheless, favoured the orthodox over the more 'Westernised' *babus* for the privileges of the Ilbert Bill. C. E. Gladstone, Deputy Commissioner of Muzuffarnagar, for example, claimed that the orthodox Punjabi had a better understanding of the status of the English lady than the more Westernised Bengali.[51] The contradictions in the Anglo-Indian position drew bitter comment from Bengalis: 'What matter if our women pass F. A. and B. A. exams? They do not know how to clasp the waist and arm of any male and dance in European fashion. Therefore, how is it possible to sanction Ilbert's Bill?'[52] In so far, therefore, as the status of Indian women was made the site for competing political agendas, none of the opposing sides were interested in going beyond a narrow and self-serving model of female emancipation.

The construct of white womanhood was similarly deployed as the basis for the elaboration of British or Anglo-Indian masculinity as the benevolent protection of women. The white woman had traditionally occupied a unique, yet contradictory, position in the masculinist colonial mythology. On the one hand, the white woman was a special object of reverence for white men. Any real or imagined threat to white women was perceived as a threat to the prestige of the entire British race. The political appeal of such a construct of white womanhood was perhaps never more evident than in the immediate aftermath of the rebellion of 1857. Perceptions of real and imaginary assaults by native men on white women became the pretext for the terrible vengeance that Anglo-Indians wreaked on the native population after the defeat of the rebellion.[53] On the other hand, however, ever since white women began arriving in considerable numbers in India from the late eighteenth and early nineteenth centuries, Anglo-Indian society had held white women uniquely responsible for the increase in racial tension in India. Lord Stanley, while presiding over a meeting of the East India Association on racial harmony, noted the sinister role that white women had played in India. He blamed the racial tension in India on white women because, as he argued, 'in all countries, national and race prejudices were more accentuated and more strongly felt and shown by the women then by the men'.[54] Yet, as a senior Anglo-Indian civilian from Madras noted with surprising candour, it was white men who had to make white women aware of their special responsibility for upholding the prestige of the white race in India. He wrote, 'we are in India and we belong to . . . the ruling race, ruling, too, principally by prestige and it is up to us and to our women to do nothing to lower that prestige. The women may not understand but their men ought to.'[55] The masculinist colonial mythology, therefore, required special obligations of, and restrictions on, white women in India. White women in India, for example, were held to an even narrower definition of the appropriate spheres of female activity than their counterparts in Britain.[56] For most of the nineteenth century, even such 'female' pastimes in Britain as philanthropic activities were never entirely acceptable for white women living in India: the primary object of the white woman in India was to reproduce the norms of Victorian British domesticity within the safely circumscribed limits of Anglo-Indian society. The following ironic comment on the lives of white women in India was made by Lady Wilson, the wife of a senior Anglo-Indian civilian, in the early twentieth century:

> You must understand that most Europeans of the old school would not allow a [European] lady to accept an Indian gentleman's proferred hospitality. They, would not permit her to drive through an Indian town, be a spectator of tent-pegging, or receive an Indian as a visitor, far less dine with him. They would, in short, prefer her to be as wholly absent from every kind of society as are the inmates of a *zenana*.[57]

It was in connecting white men's control over white women to their control over native men and women that the colonial construct of white womanhood was integral, as Ann Stoler has argued, to the social hierarchies that sustained colonial rule.[58]

It is not surprising, therefore, that the defence of white womanhood became an especially powerful symbol in the Anglo-Indian agitation against the Ilbert Bill. The prospect of a white woman appearing in public before a native judge in a *mofussil* court triggered the perennial Anglo-Indian anxiety that natives did not hold white women in the esteem which they deserved by virtue of their position in colonial society. Since, as many Anglo-Indians suspected, native men were not suitably impressed by 'the European woman's purity' and engaged in 'revolting and suggestive' parodies of European women and their dances to the applause and appreciation of native audiences, the prospect of a white woman appearing before a native court would demean further the status of all white women in native eyes.[59] Native civil servants, it was argued, were surrounded by 'childish and ignorantly superstitious women' from birth to manhood and, therefore, could have no regard for the 'free' and 'unfettered' white woman. If native judges, moreover, were allowed to handle cases involving such 'delicate' subjects as rape, marriage, or divorce among Europeans, the damage to the prestige of the white race would be unimaginable. Many Anglo-Indians claimed that a growing disrespect towards white women was already evident in the arguments of the native supporters of the Ilbert Bill. The *Ananda Bazar Patrika*, a vernacular newspaper in Bengal, had dared to suggest that white women were so vociferous in their opposition to the Bill because they feared that the presence of native magistrates would embolden their native servants to bring up charges of physical abuse that they had suffered at the hands of the *memsahibs*. Even the faint suggestion that white women might have something other than the noblest of motives in their opposition to the Bill caused a great stir in the Anglo-Indian community. Under the threats of libel and prosecution for sedition the vernacular paper was forced to issue an apology for casting aspersions on the sacrosanct image of white women.[60] For the tarnishing of the image of white women in India was perceived as a blow to the prestige of the entire race. As was argued by a group of white women petitioners, moreover, the loss of prestige for white women went beyond merely the interests of the ruling race; it also had a harmful effect on white women's considerable 'influence for good on which the enlightenment and amelioration of the condition of . . . Native sisters so largely depend'.[61]

So powerful was the appeal of white womanhood in the Anglo-Indian rhetoric against the Bill that even a strong defender of the Bill, like Henry Beveridge, proposed a compromise that would safeguard the prestige of white women. Beveridge anonymously presented a proposal in the columns of the Calcutta *Statesman* that would excuse white women from appearing in court before a native judge.[62] He urged that special concessions ought to be provided for white women in the Ilbert Bill, similar to the concessions already provided to record testimony in cases involving *purdanashin* women (native women who could not appear unveiled in public). Beveridge recommended the exclusion of non-Asiatic women in the extension of the jurisdiction of native magistrates over European British subjects so as to meet the objections of a large majority of Anglo-Indian men and women. While the popular Anglo-Indian press was quick to dismiss Beveridge's proposal as 'absurd', the proposal itself was an important indication of the importance of the figure of the white woman in the agitation against the Bill.[63]

The construct of white womanhood deployed by the opponents of the Bill, moreover, nicely brought together the various racial, gender and class hierarchies in the self-image of the ruling race. Only the wives and female relatives of the more wealthy Anglo-Indians could actually afford the seclusion from native society to sustain the ideology of white womanhood. White women who did not belong to the requisite class background, therefore, posed a special problem to the self-image of whiteness upheld by the colonial elite. The 'common' European woman, like the 'poor white' who was either deported to England or incarcerated in workhouses in India, had an ambiguous status in

Anglo-India.[64] Anglo-Indians feared that such women lowered the prestige of all white women in the eyes of native society. H. Holmswood, the Assistant Magistrate of Meherpore, for example, argued that by fraternising with a common European 'shop-girl' a native civil servant had demonstrated his disrespect of white womanhood: 'I have seen a native gentleman of the Service bring a European female of inferior rank – in fact a shop girl – into the English law courts when he came to report cases, and show surprise that his English companions objected to be associated with her on terms of equality'.[65] For Holmswood, therefore, native men who were not repelled by the coarseness of the 'common' European woman showed no understanding of the status of white womanhood.

The liminal status of the relatively small number of single and unchaperoned white women, mainly missionaries and a handful of other social reformers in India, became a cause for particular concern among Anglo-Indians during the racial polarisation of the Ilbert Bill agitation.[66] The Anglo-Indian response to a much-publicised case involving a female European missionary and a native Christian, tried in the Calcutta High Court in the midst of the Ilbert Bill agitation, was symptomatic of the fear and denial with which Anglo-Indians responded to any possibility of intimacy between white women and native men. While some considered the possibility of such an intimacy as preposterous, others saw the case as underscoring the need for stricter patriarchal control over white women. Mary Pigot, who was in charge of the Church of Scotland's Orphanage and *Zenana* Mission in Calcutta and had close ties with Bengali social reformers, had filed a suit for defamation of character against Revd William Hastie who was in charge of the General Assembly's Institution in Calcutta.[67] Hastie, who had already made himself unpopular with native Christians, had accused Pigot of 'impropriety' with a Mr Wilson, a married man, and with Babu Kali Charan Bannerjee, a native Christian teacher in her school. The case was tried in the Calcutta High Court by Judge J. F. Norris, a staunch opponent of the Ilbert Bill. Perhaps fearing a lengthy public discussion of the alleged intimacy between a white woman and a native man in the midst of the Ilbert Bill controversy, Norris decided to conclude the case hastily. He arrived at a peculiar verdict that awarded Pigot only one *anna* in damages without vindicating her of the charge of impropriety. The Judge felt that Pigot's relations with Bannerjee had not been of a 'proper character'.[68] The following year, however, an Appellate Bench overturned Norris's verdict and vindicated Pigot of any impropriety. Hastie's efforts to take the case to the Privy Council in 1885 were also rejected.

Significantly, Anglo-Indian public opinion in 1883 showed considerable sympathy for Pigot even after Norris's verdict. The Anglo-Indian press questioned the verdict by challenging the very assumption that any white woman would have chosen to be familiar with a native man. The native press, despite substantial support for Pigot, was quick to mock the defence of Pigot adopted in the Anglo-Indian press. One native newspaper had the following to say on the Pigot case:

The *Englishman* refuses to believe that the fair Miranda of the Tempest, recently enacted at the High Court, could possibly go wrong with Caliban . . . we wonder that the revelation in the High court of Babu Kali Charan Bannerjee having got a pair of slippers from Miss Pigot, and of his having had his dinners at her house, has not yet been utilized by our vigilant contemporaries . . . as a damaging fact against Mr. Ilbert's Criminal Procedure Bill.[69]

At least one Anglo-Indian 'District Judge' in Bengal, however, did recognise the implications of the Pigot case for the Anglo-Indian case against the Ilbert Bill. In a letter to the Calcutta *Statesman*, he deplored the fact that young unmarried female missionaries visited the homes of native gentlemen to educate their wives without heed to the propriety of such contact. He claimed that Missionary Societies that allowed 'unmarried ladies' to 'visit alone at houses where they cannot but frequently meet with male members of the Hindoo household in outer apartments' encouraged 'scandals', the implications of which were especially harmful in the context of the Ilbert Bill controversy.[70]

Even though only the more irresponsible sections of the Anglo-Indian community believed that empowering native civil servants posed a real threat to the security of white women in India, the rumours about the potential danger to which white women would be exposed by the Bill had a tremendous impact on the popular perception of the Bill in Britain and in India. For the real test of British masculinity was in the 'chivalric' protection of white women from native men. Englishwomen thus ridiculed the faint-hearted 'chivalry' of Ripon, Ilbert, and their like who had abandoned their duty to their countrywomen in favour of placating effeminate *babus* through the Ilbert Bill. The celebrated Anglo-Indian writer Rudyard Kipling, who was in India during the Ilbert Bill controversy, considered the Bill even years later as a measure that had made white women more vulnerable to the dangers posed by native men.[71] Far-fetched notions of the dangers to white women thus assumed extraordinary importance in the propaganda against the Bill. In the more hysterical and sensational arguments advanced against the Ilbert Bill, it was hinted that effeminate *babus* would use this opportunity to 'wage war' against white women. The Calcutta correspondent of *The Times*, for example, suggested that the Ilbert Bill gave those Indians who lacked proper manly courage the opportunity to express their discontent against British rule by attacking the British in the 'tenderest place': through attacks on innocent white women.[72] The *Englishman* seriously entertained a proposal for setting up a Committee of Safety to protect the honour of white women in the event that the Bill was passed.[73]

The suggestion that Bengali Magistrates might deliberately misuse their powers over European women was made early in the fight against the Bill by an Anglo-Indian who signed himself as 'X'. The melodramatic letter from 'X', which appeared in the *Englishman*, warned as follows: 'One's wife may be walked off for an imaginary offence . . . what would more please our fellow subjects than to bully and disgrace a wretched European woman? The higher her husband's station and the greater her respectabilities, the greater the delight of her torturer'.[74] Another letter in the *Englishman* signed by a 'Junior Official' claimed that a native magistrate would first trump up a case against the *burra memsahib* or senior white woman in the station, and then would try to get into the good books of her husband by 'affording material aid in compromising the case'.[75] A senior officer in the army wrote as follows:

> Many English officers have English servant girls attached to their families in the *mofussil*; a native magistrate, puffed up with importance might set eyes upon one of the girls and make overtures to her. If she refused, as she probably would do, what would be easier than for this native, acting under the smart of disappointment to bring a case against the girl to be tried in his court? A few *annas* would bribe all the native servants of the household and we might guess the result.[76]

Wild rumours that native magistrates would abuse their jurisdiction to fill their harems with white women began to surface in letters to the Anglo-Indian press as well as in the speeches at various anti-Ilbert Bill meetings held all over the country.

Although these arguments were frequently dismissed as 'purely fictitious', they served as extremely effective propaganda against the Bill.[77] The threat that white women living in isolated white settlements faced from the Ilbert Bill was commonly invoked to drum up support for the Anglo-Indian case in Britain. Returning Anglo-Indian officials painted terrible scenarios of the plight of helpless white women in India for British audiences at home. A meeting held at the Limehouse Town Hall in the East End of London, for example, was advertised as an effort to save defenceless Englishwomen in India. A placard in front of the hall bore the words 'Appeal to the people of England from Englishwomen in India', and a second placard outside the building stated that the meeting was being held 'in opposition to Lord Ripon's policy of placing Englishwomen under the criminal jurisdiction of polygamists – Native Magistrates'.[78]

The vague apprehensions about the danger to white women were further compounded by the publicity surrounding a few cases of alleged assault by native servants on white women in Calcutta in the summer of 1883. The local government as well as the Anglo-Indian press in Bengal hinted at a connection between these cases and the Ilbert Bill. The Lt.-Governor of Bengal, Rivers Thompson, appeared to encourage the inflammatory reports about such cases filed by some of his subordinates, such as E. V. Westmacott, the Magistrate of Howrah.[79] In his role as Magistrate, Westmacott regularly dealt with cases involving disputes between white women and native *dhobies* (washermen), *mehters* (sweepers), and *khansamahs* (cooks). He was convinced that there was an increase in the 'insubordination' of native servants in recent months, fuelled by the prospect of the Ilbert Bill. To quote from his official report to the Lt.-Governor: 'I do not suppose the *Baboos* who are agitating and leading the anti-

European tendencies of Government are likely to indulge in rape or murder of Europeans, but I see very clearly what is the outcome of the *Baboo* agitation, when translated into language, intelligible to themselves by natives of the lower classes.'[80] Following through on his dubious political interpretation of these cases, Westmacott justified handing down harsh sentences to native servants to teach them a lesson.

The most widely publicised case was one involving the wife of James Hume.[81] A native *mehter* (sweeper), a former employee in the Hume household, was accused of attempted sexual assault on Mrs Hume. The *Englishman*, commenting on the case, hinted that the accused native was not acting alone but had been urged to commit his 'heinous crime' by the 'superior instigation' of native politicians.[82] Hume was the Public Prosecutor in a case against some Bengali students who had been arrested for protesting against Judge Norris's verdict in a contempt of court case involving the popular native politician Surendranath Banerjea. The rumour that native politicians were deliberately instigating native servants to attack white women made the Hume case a *cause célèbre* for the Anglo-Indian opposition. The case against Hurro Mehter, alias Greedhare Mehter, was tried by a mixed jury of Europeans and natives who found him guilty and convicted him to eight years' rigorous imprisonment. The *mehter* remained undefended and refused to admit his guilt to the end. Senior Anglo-Indian officials who feared that 'natives (might) subscribe to provide counsel for the man and make him another victim of English justice' were relieved that native politicians had displayed considerable restraint despite provocation from the irresponsible comments of some of the Anglo-Indian press.[83] Two years later, Mr A. O. Hume, a cousin of James Hume, informed the then Viceroy Lord Dufferin in a private communication that both James Hume and his wife had deliberately perjured themselves in court; Mrs Hume and Greedhare Mehter had been involved in an intimate relationship for some six months prior to the case. Mr Hume's discovery of this liason had led to the charge against the native of attempted sexual assault.[84] The climate during the Ilbert Bill controversy, however, had precluded a fuller investigation of the case.

Following the Hume case, the Anglo-Indian press reported rumours of other copy-cat cases of native assaults on white women. A female guest at Judge Norris's residence alleged that a native intruder had entered her bedroom while she was asleep one night. However, a thorough examination of the complaint by Mr H. G. Wilkins, the Under-Deputy Commissioner of Police, revealed that the 'failed villainy' was only a delusion in the mind of the young girl.[85] In another case, pursued with characteristic zeal by Westmacott, it was discovered that Mary Watkins, the wife of a railway guard, had charged her native sweeper of assault to get back at him for filing a suit against her husband in the Small Claims Court for the payment of his wages.[86] As the *Statesman*, one of the more liberal Anglo-Indian newspapers, wrote: 'The time is out of joint . . . incidents which, in ordinary times, would have no political significance, are now being seized upon on all hands, and a political significance is attributed to them which, whether it rightly belongs to them or not, has the same effect upon the public mind as if it did.'[87] These cases came to have an important bearing on Anglo-Indian perceptions of the Ilbert Bill: it was alleged that the cases of assaults or attempted assaults by native servants on their white female employers were either instigated by native politicians or else by the native interpretation of the Ilbert Bill as the first step in the reversal of the racial hierarchy of colonial society.

The imminence of a threat to white women created the deepest impression against the Ilbert Bill among Anglo-Indians in India and Britain. At a protest meeting in London, a public telegram received from India on the Hume case had the desired impact. Sir Alexander Arbuthnot, a former high-ranking official in India, led a deputation to the then Secretary of State, Lord Kimberley, in which he alluded to the case as an argument against the Bill.[88] Although Kimberley rebuked Arbuthnot for suggesting a connection between the Hume case and the Ilbert Bill, Arbuthnot's speech met with the approval of several diehard opponents of the Bill in England. Lord Lytton, a former Viceroy of India and a staunch opponent of the Ilbert Bill in the House of Lords, wrote to Arbuthnot approving his deputation to Kimberley; Lytton added 'I thought your speech perfect.'[89] Edward Stanhope, a former Conservative Under-Secretary of State for India, also tried in the House of Commons to raise a question about the 'horrible outrages upon English ladies in Calcutta and Howrah'. Stanhope's efforts, however, were defeated when another member interjected by asking him to 'obtain a statement of annual number of outrages on English women by English men'.[90] Nevertheless, rumours about the dangers to which white women were exposed by the Ilbert Bill did much to weaken support for the Bill in England and in India. Even Queen Victoria was reportedly so shaken by accounts of the outrages on Englishwomen in India that she was led to question in private the appointment of a liberal Viceroy like Ripon as her representative in India.[91] The formidable popularity of the Anglo-Indian case against the Ilbert Bill had to do, at least in part, with the picture of British masculinity as the benevolent protector of both white and native women in India.

Finally, and somewhat paradoxically, the politics of colonial masculinity also licensed a new public role for women, albeit only within the confines of a reconfigured imperial patriarchy. In Britain, feminist demands for greater involvement of women in education, professional employment, and in the public domain, as well as broader late nineteenth-century economic and political changes that brought more middle-class women into the market-place had created a new public visibility for middle-class women. Anglo-India was far slower in being affected by these changes. Although the politics of colonial masculinity did open up an opportunity for the mobilisation of female public opinion, the public participation of white women in the agitation against the Ilbert Bill was symptomatic of another process that Rosemary Hennessy identifies as inseparable from the changes occurring at the turn of the century in Britain: the recuperation of the challenges posed by the 'New Woman' in the racial politics of empire.[92]

The reorientation of racial politics in gendered terms in the Ilbert Bill controversy did open up a space, however limited, for the involvement of women. The involvement of white women in the Ilbert Bill controversy took various forms: white women flooded the Anglo-Indian press with letters against the Bill; they conducted a successful social boycott of the supporters of the Bill in Calcutta; and they took active part in the organisations and associations formed to fight the Bill. The activities of white women contributed substantially to the spread of the Anglo-Indian opposition. Beveridge, one of the few Anglo-Indian civilians who supported the Bill, recalled that 'English ladies appeared to him often to be drawing their skirts away from him as he passed'.[93] The boycott of all the Government House entertainments in Calcutta by the wives of the non-official community proved a great success. The female relatives of elite Anglo-Indian non-officials in India boycotted two full seasons of official entertainments during Ripon's Viceroyalty. Between ninety to a hundred women undertook to absent themselves formally from the Government House Levee and Drawing-Room held in December 1883. According to a report in the *Pioneer*, only 136 women attended the Drawing Room by Public Entry, of whom sixty-nine were new presentations; more than fifty women were noted as being unavoidably absent.[94] The social life of the colonial elite suffered until the arrival of a new Viceroy whose parties white women could attend without compromising their position on the Bill.

Yet the public role assumed by white women in the Ilbert Bill controversy provoked some uneasiness from many an Anglo-Indian male. The public participation of white women threatened the colonial construct of white womanhood. The men were caught in a double bind: they feared that the public participation of women would expose them as more intemperate in their hostility towards natives than white men, thus jeopardising the more sanitised public image of white womanhood. The Home Member of the Viceroy's Council, James Gibbs, suspected that white women were 'far more unreasonable and active in opposition than the male'. The Viceroy, in a note to the Secretary of State, also acknowledged, that 'the ladies are, as is often the case, hotter than the men'.[95] Despite the bad faith in white men's assessment of the 'intemperate' role of white women in the agitation, the public role of white women during the controversy exposed the unrealistic aspirations of the construct of white womanhood. The letters of Flora MacDonald, one of the most intrepid letter-writers against the Bill, is worth quoting at some length:

> Englishmen, try to picture to yourselves a mofussil court, hundreds of miles away from Calcutta – in that Court a Native Magistrate is presiding with the supercilious assurance that a native assumes when he has an Englishman in his power. Before that man stands an English girl in all her maidenly dignity; she has been accused by her ayah (female house-servant) for revenge of a loathsome crime, a crime that is common among native women; the Court is crowded with natives of all castes who have

flocked to hear an English girl being tried for an offence; this motley
crowd laugh and jeer, and stare that English girl in the face, and spit on
the ground to show her the contempt they have for the female sex; scores
of witness are present to give evidence; a native Doctor has also been hired
for that occasion; witnesses are cross-examined by a native pleader; the
most relevant questions are asked, questions that only a native dare to
ask. Picture to yourself that girl's agony of shame! By her stands her only
protector, a widowed mother, who has not the means wherewith to secure
the protection and counsel of her countrymen. That innocent girl, so kind,
so affectionate, so loving, the stay of her widowhood, must go from the
Court with shame, and with a blighted name . . . It cannot be that
Englishmen renowned for chivalry are willing to subject even the hum-
blest of their countrywomen to dishonour.[96]

While Flora Macdonald never spells out the 'loathsome crime' that she claims
is common among native women, her letter reveals a prurient imagination that
was not entirely befitting an 'English lady'.

The white male anxiety about the new public role of white women came to
focus on the Ladies' Committee in Calcutta. Although the wives and female relatives of prominent Anglo-Indian opponents of the Bill had been conspicuous at
various public meetings held to protest the measure, the formation of an independent Ladies' Committee to draft a separate women's petition against the Bill was
seen as particularly controversial. The European and Anglo-Indian Defence
Association, formed during the Ilbert Bill controversy for the purpose of safeguarding Anglo-Indian privileges, had gone as far as appointing a few white
women to its organising committee. The Association had also received generous
financial support from white women, including a donation for ten rupees diverted
from *zenana* work in India.[97] Yet the formation of a separate Ladies' Committee,
albeit under the auspices of the Defence Association, was received with a mixture
of patriarchal condescension and open hostility in the Anglo-Indian community.

At the third meeting of the Defence Association on 22 March 1883, Mr
James Furrell, the vitriolic editor of the *Englishman*, proposed drafting a separate women's petition against the Bill to be sent to the Queen. The petition was
to be drafted with the co-operation of the Defence Association, which would
provide women with organisational aid in obtaining signatures for the petition
and in defraying all the expenses incurred. Furrell's proposal was followed by
an inaugural meeting of nine leading Calcutta *memsahibs*. A separate Ladies'
Committee was formed with Mrs L. R. Tottenham, the wife of a Judge of the
Calcutta High Court, as the Honorary Secretary. Two other meetings of the
Ladies' Committee were held on 31 March 1883 and 7 April 1883. There were
at least twenty-seven women listed as members, including wives of High Court
judges, senior civilians and military men, doctors, barristers, and merchants
from Calcutta. All the members were urged to submit draft proposals to serve
as models for the petition to be submitted to the Queen.[98]

While Anglo-Indian detractors of the Ladies' Committee emphasised its challenge to traditional gender roles, more sympathetic Anglo-Indian observers attempted to trivialise its implications with bemusement at the 'ladies' happy occupation to fill monotonous hours'. The *Civil and Military Gazette* commented tongue-in-cheek about the women's political skills; the paper observed:

> [the] lady who writes most powerfully – as a lady, a woman, and most womanly yet strongly withal – has probably the best chance of posing before the public as the petitioner in propria persona; the intrepid defender – on paper – of her countrywomen's rights. . . . who knows or can guess how many mute, inglorious politicians, how many Chathams, Pitts, Beaconsfields, Gladstones in petticoats may have been hidden away, lost to fame and the gratitude of posterity.[99]

Others, however, were more openly sceptical of the 'fashionable contagion' that had infected white women in India who wrote political letters to the press and met at each other's homes to form a separate committee. The *Pioneer*, for one, reminded the Anglo-Indian public that 'there are special reasons in India which emphasize the soundness of the Athenean proverb that she is the best woman who is least observed'.[100] Even the *Englishman*, a staunch defender of the Ladies' Committee, assured its critics that the Committee was not a permanent association, but had met only twice with the sole purpose of drafting a petition to the Queen. The members of the Ladies' Committee also tried to allay the suspicion of their white male critics by pointing out that 'no desire for publicity nor any ambition to enter the arena of political strife, had prompted (their) movement'.[101]

Whatever challenge the Ladies' Committee could have posed to the existing Anglo-Indian social order was safely circumscribed by the racial and gender politics of colonial masculinity. The petition of the Ladies' Committee was prepared with the help of Mr J. G. Apcar, an Armenian barrister in Calcutta and a prominent member of the Defence Association. The list of signatures was headed by the wife of Judge Norris, and included 5,757 other women; many of the signatures were from Eurasian women and, therefore, not, in the strict sense of the word, European British subjects.[102] The form in which the women had signed their names on the petition – using their appropriate titles 'Miss' or 'Mrs' – further emphasised their dependence on their male relatives. The *Englishman* gently reminded the 'ladies' of their folly in signing their names with their titles: 'Mrs Smith or Miss Smith, as we should have thought every educated person knew, is not a signature but a description.'[103] The petitioners complained of the 'cruel wound' to the self-respect of white women if they were brought under the jurisdiction of men who did not allow their women to appear in public. At the same time, the petitioners also stressed the 'helplessness' of white women if they were left without the watchful eye of their own 'natural protectors': white men.[104] The challenge of white women's political participation was thus safely circumscribed within a traditional gender politics.

Even efforts to mobilise women specifically on the basis of a 'price of womanhood', as was tried by Annette Ackroyd-Beveridge, were recuperated by and for the racial politics of Anglo-India. Beveridge, who had started a college for working women in London in 1854, had come to India on the invitation of Indian social reformers to promote native female education. Following her disputes with Indian social reformers, however, she abandoned her work for female education to marry Henry Beveridge of the Indian civil service.[105] Annette Ackroyd-Beveridge saw herself as a liberal critic of traditional British and Indian patriarchy as well as of blatant Anglo-Indian racism. Together the Beveridges earned a reputation for their hospitality to elite and middle-class Indians. Unlike her husband, however, Beveridge had always been a staunch opponent of political reforms that would empower the educated *babus* of India.[106] Her well-publicised opposition to the Ilbert Bill was expressed in a strong letter to the *Englishman* published on 6 March 1883. Beveridge clarified that her position on the Bill was not based on the 'pride of race', but on something deeper: the 'pride of womanhood'. According to Beveridge, the 'ignorant and neglected' women of India testified to the 'justice of the resentment which English women feel at Mr. Ilbert's proposal to subject civilised women to the jurisdiction of men who have done little or nothing to redeem the women of their race, whose social ideas are still on the outer verge of civilisation'. For Beveridge, this 'pride of womanhood' emanated from the 'form of respect' to which white women were accustomed; and which respect they were not willing 'to abrogate in order to give such advantages to others as are offered by Mr. Ilbert's bill to its beneficiaries'.[107]

In pitting the 'pride of [white] womanhood' against the extension of legal equality to native men, Beveridge evoked what had become a popular strategy in the Anglo-Indian agitation: she both invited white men to serve as the benevolent protectors of white women from native men and excluded native women from the logic of her argument about the 'pride of womanhood'. The limits of Beveridge's alternative politics of womanhood are best illustrated in her allusions to the alleged atrocities committed by native men against white women during the rebellion of 1857:

> Six and twenty years have not elapsed since no inconsiderable portion of the most active classes of North India proved they did not understand what is meant by justice and mercy to the innocent and helpless. Six and twenty years do not suffice to change national characteristics or to educe from savages the qualities at once strong and delicate which make good judges.

As Beveridge's Indian critics pointed out, by the same logic Indian women could also 'claim the privilege of not being tried by the race to which belonged the brutal [British] soldiers', who were accused on numerous occasions of sexual assault on native women.[108] Beveridge's alternative politics of womanhood, no less than the politics of colonial masculinity, was imbricated in what Ania Loomba has called the patriarchal racism of colonial rule.[109]

A gender politics that ignored the ways in which gender relations were imbricated in other social arrangements fell prey to the recruitment of the 'New Woman' for the politics of class domination at home and of racial domination abroad.[110] Hence Beveridge's politics of womanhood became much too easily an unabashed celebration of a 'civilised' British patriarchy over an 'uncivilised' Indian patriarchy. The Bihar Ladies' Petition to the Viceroy, for which Beveridge had campaigned tirelessly among wives of Anglo-Indian officials and planters in Bihar, presented the following case against the Bill: 'we see that in the social systems of India women are ignorant and enslaved . . . we see the men of their races insensible to their degradation, if not contented with it. Therefore, we assert that men born or bred on such a system are unfitted to become the judges of women of a totally different type of society.'[111] Even criticism from liberal public opinion in Britain did not make Beveridge waver from her position. In a letter to her husband defending her position on the Ilbert Bill, she wrote as follows:

> I cannot regret having written the letter to the *Englishman* . . . of a people uncivilized who care about stone idols, enjoy child marriage and seclude their women, and where, at every point the fact of sex is present to the mind – I call it uncivilized in any nation when I see two people together and the notion of their being a man and a woman is the fact suggested by their manner, and not the more commonplace one (as in England) of two people.[112]

Although Beveridge and other white women in India often claimed to have only the interests of native women at heart and no 'unwomanly animosity' against their fellow subjects, they contributed to upholding the social hierarchies of the politics of colonial masculinity.

While some white women, especially in Britain, did express solidarity with Indians over the Ilbert Bill, white feminists during the Ilbert Bill controversy by and large ignored the impact of colonial masculinity on the status of white women. The *Englishwoman's Review*, which devoted space regularly to contributions on the Empire, largely ignored the Ilbert Bill except for noting the opportunity it had provided white women for participating in politics.[113] It is only recently that this moment of Victorian feminism is beginning to be studied in the context of the history of imperialism. As various scholars have noted, not only did the relations between British and Indian women often replicate the hierarchies of imperial and colonial relations, but the stereotype of the 'downtrodden Indian woman' provided an opportunity for British women to exert their influence in India through what Barbara Ramusack characterises as 'maternal imperialism'. Indeed, as Antoinette Burton has demonstrated, the 'Indian woman' was the foil against which imperial Victorian feminism defined its own self-image.[114] The further point, however, is that the impact of imperialism on Victorian feminism went beyond this legacy of racism. For, as the history of white women's involvement in the Ilbert Bill agitation illustrates, it was the racial politics of imperialism that made possible the conservative recuperation of feminist challenges to the existing social order at the turn of the century in Britain.

Although Indian women were less directly involved than white women in the public controversy over the Ilbert Bill, it also had important implications for the construct of modern Indian womanhood. The politics of colonial masculinity in the Ilbert Bill agitation had highlighted the symbolic value of Indian women in the reconstitution of colonial racial politics; for the definition of British masculinity in the controversy rested on the formula that Gayatri Chakravorty Spivak has characterised as 'white men saving brown women from brown men'.[115] Thus the first step in reclaiming Indian masculinity was to substitute Indian men for white men as the benevolent protectors of native women. In the Ilbert Bill agitation, Indian men began by defending Indian women from the disparagement of white men who, in their zeal to condemn native men, often also condemned native women. The 'insulting' references to Indian womanhood in the speeches and writings of Anglo-Indian opponents of the Bill prompted many a 'chivalrous' Indian male to champion the honour of the Indian woman against her Anglo-Indian detractors. Lalmohun Ghose, a Bengali political leader, presented a strong defence of the character of Indian women in castigating the speech of Mr H. H. H. Branson, one of the most vitriolic Anglo-Indian speakers at the infamous Calcutta Town Hall meeting.[116]

Indian public opinion betrayed the same ambivalence towards women's public participation that characterised Anglo-Indian responses to the role of white women in the Ilbert Bill agitation. For even though Indian public opinion was most critical of the role of white women in the Ilbert Bill controversy, it, nevertheless, also recognised the value of an effective response from Indian women to white women. By singling out white women – 'white in complexion . . . [but] black at heart' – as the worst offenders in the Anglo-Indian agitation against the Ilbert Bill, Indian men shared with Anglo-Indian men the hostility towards the new public roles of women. The *Reis and Reyyat* satirised white women's contributions and attributed the defeat of the Ilbert Bill to white women's refusal 'to submit to the jurisdiction of the Calibans lusting after the Mirandas of Anglo-India'.[117] The *Dacca Prakash* referred disparagingly to the 7,000-odd European women who had participated in the agitation as 'white *kalis*'; the *Amrita Bazar Patrika* likened them to 'Lady Macbeths' who had a 'hardening effect upon their husband's hearts'.[118]

At the same time, however, many Indians also invoked the achievements of the modern Indian woman to neutralise the Anglo-Indian case against the Bill. The male editors of the *Amrita Bazar Patrika*, for example, had both Indian and Anglo-Indian society fooled for several months by a native female memorial, allegedly signed by members of the Bengali *bhadramahila*, in response to the white women's petition to the Queen.[119] Even though the native female memorial was exposed as a hoax, the attempt of Indian men to ventriloquise the voice of Indian women reflected a new admission of the significance of the public mobilisation of Indian women. The memorial turned the arguments of the white women petitioners on its head: it argued that native men were qualified to try European British subjects because the modern Indian woman was better educated than the white women who were agitating against the Bill. The memorialists asserted that 'we Indian women are not ignorant and enslaved'. They argued that while there were thousands of ignorant women in India, 'as a like number exists in England', it was unfair to generalise from this and to use it as a disqualification against native men for trying European British subjects. The memorial, unlike the white women's petition, was also signed in the proper manner: 'Binodini, Bhafini, Sundari, Sulochona, Manorama, Thakomani, Chapala, Horu, and others'.[120] The memorial reversed the arguments of the white women by claiming superiority for the native women memorialists against the white women petitioners. The memorial presented the argument thus:

> we are not inferior in intelligence or education to the Englishwoman who have come forward to protest against the Bill . . . some of us have obtained University degrees – among the lady agitators against the Bill there is not a single graduate, Mrs. Tottenham and Mrs. Norris are not B. A.'s, but among us there are B. A.'s who have received first class education at Bethune College. . . . Sir Richard Garth [Chief Justice] and Mr. Croft [Director Public Instruction] may be appointed to bring us and the English ladies who have remonstrated, under severe tests, and see if we are not intellectually superior to them. If our superiority is produced the Bill should become law at once.[121]

The reference to the superiority of the educational qualifications of native women alluded to the fact that the University of Calcutta had admitted female graduates to its degree programme in 1878, before any of the English universities.

There was, moreover, further evidence of the Bengali *bhadramahila's* public involvement in support of the Ilbert Bill. The native female teachers at the Bethune School for women in Calcutta rallied their students to support the Bill. Kamini Sen, a teacher at the school and the wife of a 'statutory' native civilian, organised her female students to wear badges and attend meetings in support of the Bill.[122] The *Bengalee* also commented on the 'unique feature' that encouraged some of the native women's organisations to become involved in politics. The Bengali Ladies' Association, which was not in any way a political organisation, convened a special meeting with about seventy women present to express sympathy with the wife of the Bengali political leader Surendranath Banerjea, who was imprisoned for contempt of court in the midst of the Ilbert Bill controversy. There were several reports of Bengali women publicly protesting Banerjea's imprisonment.[123] But native public opinion, like Anglo-Indian opinion, was not entirely sanguine about women's involvement in the controversy; the *New Dispensation*, for example, deplored the fact that the political conflict over the Ilbert Bill had dragged 'harmless and helpless ladies through the dirt of all this Billingsgate'.[124] Others like the editors of the *Amrita Bazar Patrika* had recognised, somewhat cynically perhaps, the symbolic value of native women's contributions. At a meeting of the Indian Association in 1883, Banerjea urged that the services of Indian women be used 'in the political elevation of the country'. The male-sponsored nature of native women's involvement in the Ilbert Bill controversy prefigured later more successful accommodations of the modern Indian women within a new and reconstituted nationalist Indian patriarch.[125]

The politics of colonial masculinity in the Ilbert Bill controversy thus did more than just reproduce a traditional social order. Rather, it was part of a broader process of political, economic, and ideological realignments in the imperial social formation. The politics of colonial masculinity gave a new lease of life to the racial exclusivity of Anglo-Indians in India: the charge of 'effeminacy' to isolate certain native groups checkmated the demand to extend political rights to Indians; and the 'unnaturalness' in the claims for political and legal equality of these groups extended the rationale for continued Anglo-Indian racial domination. In so far, moreover, as the politics of colonial masculinity allowed for an expansion in the public role of women, it also made the new role of women vulnerable to recuperation in the racial politics of empire. Indeed, the politics of colonial masculinity in the Ilbert Bill controversy links the 'New Woman' in Britain no less than the 'effeminate *babu*' in India to the changing imperatives of the late nineteenth-century imperial social formation.

NOTES

1. For the full text of Ilbert's proposal and of Act 3 of 1884 see *Great Britain Parliamentary Papers 1884*, vol. 60, c. 3952 (Hereafter: *Parliamentary Papers*). The definition of European British subjects given in Section 4 of the Criminal Procedure Code was rather arbitrary. It included persons who were neither European nor British, and excluded persons who may in all respects have been European and British but not of legitimate descent. See *Abstract of the Proceedings of the Council of the Governor General of India Assembled for the Purpose of Making Laws and Resolutions 1883*, vol. 22, p. 13 (Hereafter: *Council Proceedings*), National Archives of India (NAI), New Delhi.
2. See Edwin Hirschmann, *White Mutiny: The Ilbert Bill Crisis in India and the Genesis of the Indian National Congress* (Delhi: Heritage Publishers, 1980). I have drawn largely from Hirschmann's account of the details of the controversy.
3. See Hirschmann, *White Mutiny*; S. Gopal, *The Viceroyalty of Lord Ripon 1880–1884* (London: Oxford University Press, 1953); Christine Dobbin, 'The Ilbert Bill: A Study of Anglo Indian Opinion in India, 1883', *Historical Studies Australia and New Zealand*, 13: 45 (Oct. 1965), 149–66. For an earlier attempt to examine the politics of gender and race in the Ilbert Bill controversy, see Mrinalini Sinha, ' "Chathams, Pitts, and Gladstones in Petticoats": The Politics of Gender and Race in the Ilbert Bill Controversy, 1883–84', in Nupur Chaudhuri and Margaret Strobel (eds), *Western Women and Imperialism: Complicity and Resistance* (Bloomington: Indiana University Press, 1992), pp. 98–116.
4. Quoted in Hirschmann, *White Mutiny*, p. 105.
5. See speech of Major-General Hopkinson, former Chief Commmisioner of Assam, in W. S. Seton-Karr, *The Ilbert Bill: A Collection of Letters, Speeches, Memorials,*

Articles etc. *Stating the Objection to the Bill* (London: W. H. Allen & Co., n.d.), p. 120 (Hereafter: *Ilbert Bill*).

6. *Ilbert Bill*, p. 120.

7. Quoted in Janaki Nair, 'Uncovering the Zenana: Visions of Indian Womanhood in Englishwomen's Writings, 1813–1940', *Journal of Women's History*, 2:1 (Spring 1990), p. 22.

8. Lepel Griffin, 'The Place of Bengalis in Politics', *Fortnightly Review*, 57 (Jan.–June 1892), p. 811.

9. For a discussion of the bourgeois ideology of separate spheres as formative of middle-class life in nineteenth-century Britain, see Leonore Davidoff and Catherine Hall, *Family Fortunes: Men and Women of the English Middle Class, 1780–1850* (Chicago: University of Chicago Press, 1987); and Mary Poovey, *Uneven Developments: The Ideological Work of Gender in Mid-Victorian England* (Chicago: University of Chicago Press, 1988). Although Amanda Vickery challenges the usefulness of the notion of separate spheres for understanding nineteenth-century British women's history, her argument nevertheless does not deny the existence of 'separate spheres' ideology in mid-Victorian Britain. See Amanda Vickery, 'Golden Age to Separate Spheres? A Review of the Categories and Chronology of English Women's History', *Historical Journal*, 36:2 (1993), 383–414.

10. Griffin, 'The Place of Bengalis in Politics', p. 811.

11. For the background to the Ilbert Bill, see Hirschmann, *White Mutiny*, pp. 5–23; and *Council Proceedings*, 2 Feb. 1883, p. 37. For a history of the legal privileges enjoyed by the European British subjects in India, see Nemai Sadhan Bose, *Racism, Struggle for Equality and Indian Nationalism* (Calcutta: Firma KLM Pvt. Ltd, 1981).

12. 'Gutpa in consequence of his position and his station in Calcutta, was simply selected by some of his countrymen to represent their wishes to the Head of the Government', *Bengalee* (Calcutta), 17 Feb. 1884, p. 77. The biographer of R. C. Dutt claims that it was Dutt who had initiated the proposal and prompted Gupta to take it up with the Government. See J. N. Gupta, *Life and Work of R. C. Dutt, CIE.* (Delhi: Gian Publishing House, 1986), p. 93.

13. See H. A. Cockerell, Secretary of Government of Bengal to Secretary Government of India, Home Department, *Legislative Department Papers of Act I–3 of 1884*, 30 Mar. 1882, Paper No. 1 (Hereafter: *Leg. Dept Papers*), NAI. See also *India, Home Department, Establishment Proceedings*, Aug. 1880, Pros. Nos. 43–44 A, NAI.

14. See *Government of India, Legislative Department Proceedings*, May 1884, Nos. 1–401, Pros. No. 2 (Hereafter: *Leg. Dept Pros.*), NAI.

15. See Gopal, *The Viceroyalty of Lord Ripon*, pp. 131–3.

16. For a history of the creation of the 'statutory' appointments, see S. K. Bajaj, 'Indianization of ICS – The Formation of the Statutory Civil Service, 1879', *The Punjab Past and Present*, 5:9 (Apr. 1971), 211–26.

17. See Note from Calcutta High Court, *Leg. Dept Papers*, Paper No. 4.

18. See S. Gopal, *The Viceroyalty of Lord Ripon*, p. 135. Also Hirschmann, *White Mutiny*, p. 25; and *Council Proceedings*, p. 153.

19. *Englishman* (Calcutta), 24 Feb. 1883, p. 1.

20. See S. Gopal, *The Viceroyalty of Lord Ripon*.

21. *Civil and Military Gazette* (Lahore), 22 Jan. 1883, p. 5.

22. Government of India to Secretary of State, 10 Aug. 1883, *Leg. Dept Pros.*, Pros. No. 369.

23. For a summary of the various arguments against the Ilbert Bill, see Hirschmann, *White Mutiny*, pp. 116–40.

24. Ilbert to Justice Markby, 12 Sept. 1884, *Ilbert Papers*, vol. 12, 1882–85, India Office Library and Records (IOLR), London.

25. Letter to *The Times* (London), 1 Mar. 1883, in *Ilbert Bill*, p. 13.

26. *Pioneer* (Allahabad), 26 Mar. 1883, p. 1; 12 Mar. 1883, p. 5; and 20 Mar. 1883, p. 6.

27. *Englishman*, 14 Mar. 1883, p. 2; also 17 Mar. 1883, p. 2.

28. *Englishman*, 2 Mar. 1883, p. 2.

29. Letter to *The Times*, 10 Dec. 1883, in *Opinions in Favour of the Ilbert Bill: Being A Collection of the Recorded Opinions of Some of the Most Eminent Men in Support of That Measure* (Calcutta: Doorga Das Chatterjee, 1885), pp. 65–6 (Hereafter: *Opinions*).

30. *Leg. Dept Papers*, Paper No. 55.

31. APW, *The Conflict of Caste* (Allahabad: Pioneer Press, 1883), pp. 5–6, 27. Also see Hirschmann, *White Mutiny*, p. 232; and Raymond K. Renford, *The Non-Official British In India to 1920* (Delhi: Oxford University Press, 1987), p. 262.

32. Quoted in *Bengalee* (Calcutta), 21 July 1883, p. 341. For the importance of *shikar* or hunting for Anglo-Indians, see Scott Bennett, 'Shikar and the Raj', *South Asia*, 7:2 (Dec. 1984), 72–88; and John M. MacKenzie, *The Empire of Nature*, (Manchester: Manchester University Press, 1988).

33. See *Navavibhakar*, 30 July 1883, in *Report on Native Newspapers of Bengal Presidency*, 1883, No. 32, p. 4645, NAI (Hereafter; *RNBP*). Also *Bengalee*, 4 Aug. 1883, p. 351.

34. *Leg. Dept. Papers*, Paper No. 55.

35. Ram Gopal Sanyal (ed.), *Record of Criminal Cases as Between Europeans and Natives for the Last Sixty Years* (Calcutta: Bengali Press, 1893). Also W. Stobie, 'An Incident of Real Life in Bengal – Injustice in an Indigo Planter's Field', *Fortnightly Review*, 42 (July–Dec. 1888), 329–41.

36. See the arguments of Anglo-Indian officials in *Leg. Dept Papers*, especially Papers Nos. 31, 55 and 70.

37. *Leg. Dept Papers*, Paper No. 55. For Rivers Thompson's speech, see *Council Proceedings*, 9 Mar. 1883, pp. 220–1.

38. See *India, Home Department Establishment Proceedings*, Aug. 1880, Pros. Nos. 43–4 A, NAI. For a discussion of Banerjea's dismissal, see Bose, *Racism*, p. 157.

39. *Leg. Dept Pros.*, Pros. No. 374; and Appendix 5, Pros. No. 441.

40. *Leg. Dept Papers*, Paper No. 55. Also see Brajendranath De, 'Reminiscences of an Indian Member of the Indian Civil Service', *Calcutta Review*, 132:2 (Aug. 1954), 85–98. For a discussion of the hostility between Beames and De, see Barun De, 'Brajendranath De and John Beames – A Study in the Reactions of Patriotism and Paternalism in the ICS at the Time of the Ilbert Bill', *Bengal Past and Present*, 81:151 (Jan.–June 1962), 1–31.

41. See Joanna Liddle and Rama Joshi, 'Gender and Imperialism in British India', *South Asia Research*, 5:2 (1985), 147–65.

42. Lata Mani, 'Contentious Traditions: The Debate on Sati in Colonial India', *Cultural Critique*, 7 (1989), 119–56.

43. *Englishman*, 26 Apr. 1883, p. 2.

44. *Leg. Dept Papers*, Paper No. 55.

45. *Leg. Dept Papers*, Paper No. 51.

46. For the full text of speeches made at the Calcutta Town Hall meeting, see *The Friend of India and Statesman* (Calcutta), 1 Mar. 1883, Supplement (Hereafter: *Statesman*). The argument in Keswick's speech was put to verse in the poem 'Our Peers', quoted in *Bengalee*, 3 Mar. 1883, p. 102.

47. Quoted in *Reis and Reyyet* (Calcutta), 7 Apr. 1883, p. 160.

48. *Council Proceedings*, pp. 193–7.

49. See Meredith Borthwick, *The Changing Role of Women in Bengal, 1849–1905* (Princeton: Princeton University Press, 1984) and Ghulam Murshid, *Reluctant Debutante: Response of Bengali Women to Modernization, 1849–1905* (Rajshahi:

Rajshahi University Press, 1983). For changes in the Muslim community, see B. Metcalf, 'Islam and Custom in 19th-century India', *Contributions to Asian Studies*, 17 (1978), 62–78.

50. See Borthwick, *The Changing Role of Women*, pp. 240–60. Also Sushama Sen, *Memoirs of an Octogenarian* (Simla: Anjali, 1971), p. 10. H. M. Kisch, a colleague of Gupta's in the ICS, had words of praise for Mrs Gupta. See Ethel A. Waley Cohen (ed.), *A Young Victorian in India: Letters of H. M. Kisch* (London: Jonathan Cape, 1957), pp. 171–2.

51. *Leg. Dept Papers*, Paper No. 64.

52. *Samaya*, 28 May 1883, RNBP, No. 23, pp. 262–3.

53. Lady Canning, the wife of the then Viceroy of India, had assured Queen Victoria that there was no 'credible evidence' that the mutineers had sexually assaulted white women in 1857, quoted in Margaret MacMillan, *Women of the Raj* (New York: Thames & Hudson, 1988) p. 102. Also see Nancy L. Paxton, 'Mobilizing Chivalry: Rape in British Novels About the Indian Uprising of 1857', *Victorian Studies*, 36:1 (Fall 1992), 5–30.

54. See Lord Stanley, *East India Association Pamphlet*, p. 14, in *India Office Tracts*, vol. 658, IOLR. For an Englishwoman's protest against such charges, see 'English Women in India', *Calcutta Review*, 80:159 (Jan. 1885), 137–52.

55. W. O. Horne, *Work and Sport in the Old Indian Civil Service* (London: William Blackwood & Sons Ltd, 1928), p. 23.

56. See MacMillan, *Women of the Raj*. Also Maud Diver, *The Englishwoman in India* (London: William Blackwood & Sons Ltd, 1909).

57. Lady Wilson (Anne Campbell Macleod), *Letters from India* (London: William Blackwood & Sons Ltd, 1911), p. 33.

58. Ann Stoler, 'Making Empire Respectable: The Politics of Race and Sexuality in Twentieth-Century Colonial Cultures', *American Ethnologist*, 16:4 (Nov. 1989), 634–60.

59. APW, *Conflict of Caste*, p. 48.

60. *Ananda Bazar Patrika*, 27 Aug. 1883, *RNBP*, No. 36, pp. 549–51. Also see *Englishman*, 4 May 1883, p. 2.

61. Petition of Englishwomen in India to the Queen in *Ilbert Bill*, p. 92.

62. *Statesman*, 27 Mar. 1883, p. 2; and 29 Mar. 1883, p. 2.

63. For the rejection of Beveridge's proposal, see *Englishman*, 28 Mar. 1883, p. 2; 30 Mar. 1883, p. 2; 2 April 1883, p. 2; and 7 Apr. 1883, p. 2.

64. See David Arnold, 'European Orphans and Vagrants in India in the Nineteenth Century', *Journal of Imperial and Commonwealth History*, 7:2 (1979), 104–27.

65. *Leg. Dept Papers*, Paper No. 55.

66. For foreign women missionaries in India, see Geraldine Forbes, 'In Search of the "Pure Heathen": Women Missionaries in Nineteenth-Century India', *Economic and Political Weekly*, 21:17 (26 Apr. 1986), WS2-WS8.

67. For a discussion of the Pigot case, see Kenneth Ballhatchet, *Race, Sex and Class Under the Raj: Imperial Attitudes and Policies and their Critics 1793–1905* (New York: St. Martin's Press, 1980), pp. 112–16.

68. For a full text of the verdict, see *Statesman*, 24 Nov. 1883, Supplement.

69. See *Reis and Reyyet*, 29 Sept. 1883, p. 459; and 15 Sept. 1883, p. 434.

70. *Statesman*, 3 Oct. 1883, p. 2.

71. See Rudyard Kipling, *Something Of Myself For My Friends, Known and Unknown* (New York: Doubleday, Doran & Co., Inc., 1937), pp. 55–6.

72. Quoted in *Reis and Reyyet*, 28 Apr. 1883, p. 195.

73. *Englishman*, 26 June 1883, p. 2.

74. *Englishman*, 10 Feb. 1883, p. 4.

75. *Englishman*, 7 May 1883, p. 2.

76. Quoted in *Reis and Reyyet*, 21 Apr. 1883, p. 182.

77. There were, of course, some Anglo-Indians who were critical of such arguments.

See the letters of 'Gamon de Bon Accord' in the *Statesman*, 7 Mar. 1883, p. 2; and W. S. Blunt, *India Under Ripon* (London: T. Fisher Unwin, 1901), p. 272.

78. Cited in *Bengalee*, 1 Sept. 1883, p. 409.

79. Rivers Thompson to Ripon, *Ripon Papers: Letters of Rivers Thompson*, vol. 54, 17 June 1883, British Museum (BM), London.

80. Ibid. Also see Steuart Bayley to Ripon, enclosing Westmacott to Barnes, *Ripon Papers: Letters of Bayley 1881–84*, 26 June 1883, BM.

81. See Calcutta Town Police Report for 1883 in *India, Home Department Police Proceedings*, Aug. 1884, B, No. 1, NAI. For details of the case, see *Englishman*, 31 July 1883, p. 3. For a discussion of 'rape' in post-1857 colonial fiction, see Jenny Sharpe, *Allegories of Empire: The Figure of Woman in the Colonial Text* (Minneapolis: University of Minnesota Press, 1993), esp. ch. 4.

82. *Englishman*, 26 June 1883, p. 2. Rivers Thompson was to repeat this charge in his communication to the Viceroy; Ripon Papers, vol. 54, 17 June 1883; senior officials were concerned that this view was being repeated by several Anglo-Indians at the time, see Bayley to Ripon, *Ripon Papers: Letters of Bayley*, 25 June 1883.

83. See Bayley to Ripon, *Ripon Papers: Letters of Bayley*, 26 June 1883.

84. Hume to Dufferin, *Dufferin Papers: Correspondence in India, vol. 78, July–Sept. 1885*, 4 July 1885, IOLR.

85. Cited in *Bengalee*, 28 July 1883, p. 351.

86. *Bengalee*, 21 July 1883, p. 338.

87. *Statesman*, 25 June 1883, p. 2.

88. The telegram was read by Sir Roper Lethbridge at a meeting held at the St James Hall in London. See *Ilbert Bill*, p. 19; for Arbuthnot's deputation, see p. 126.

89. Quoted in Lady Constance Arbuthnot (ed.), *Sir Alexander Arbuthnot: Memories of Rugby and India* (London: T. Fisher Unwin, 1910), p. 246.

90. Cited in Hirschmann, *White Mutiny*, p. 189.

91. Blunt, *India Under Ripon*, p. 6.

92. See Rosemary Hennessy, 'New Woman, New History', in *Materialist Feminism and the Politics of Discourse* (New York: Routledge, 1993), pp. 100–38.

93. Quoted in Lord William Beveridge, *India Called Them* (London: George Allen & Unwin Ltd, 1947), p. 39.

94. *Pioneer*, 11 Dec. 1883, p. 1; *Englishman*, 12 Oct. 1883, p. 2; *Bengalee*, 8 Dec. 1885, p. 555. At least one Anglo-Indian memsahib, the wife of a pro-Ilbert Bill Anglo-Indian member of the Viceroy's Council, recorded her extreme displeasure at the social boycott conducted by white women. See Mrs Herbert Reynolds, *At Home in India or Taza be Taza* (London: Henry J. Drane, 1903), p. 185.

95. Gibbs to Ripon, *Ripon Papers: India Miscellaneous Public Documents*, BP 7/6, 18 Nov. 1883, BM (Hereafter: *IMBP*). Also Ripon to Kimberley, *IMBP*, BP 7/3, 2 Dec. 1883.

96. *Englishman*, 13 Mar. 1883, p. 2. See also her letter on 26 Apr. 1883, p. 2.

97. *Englishman*, 23 July 1883, p. 2.

98. See reports in the *Englishman*, 23 Mar. 1883, p. 2; 2 Apr. 1883, p. 3; 3 Apr. 1883, p. 2; and 7 Apr. 1883, p. 1.

99. *Civil and Military Gazette*, 13 Apr. 1883, p. 3.

100. *Pioneer*, 13 Apr. 1883, p. 2.

101. See letter from a Lady on the Committee to the *Englishman*, 3 Apr. 1883, p. 2; also see *Englishman*, 16 Apr. 1883, p. 2.

102. See *Statesman*, 16 June 1883, p. 2.

103. *Englishman*, 25 Apr. 1883, p. 2.

104. For the text of the petition, see *Ilbert Bill*, pp. 90–3.

105. See Pat Barr, *The Memsahibs: The Women of Victorian India* (London: Secker & Warburg, 1976), pp. 161–8, 186–9. For Ackroyd-Beveridge's role in the social reform movement, see Borthwick, *The Changing Role of Women*, pp. 88–92; and Barbara Ramusack, 'Cultural Missionaries, Material Imperialists, Feminist Allies:

British Women Activitists in India, 1865–1945', *Women's Studies International Forum*, 13:4 (Winter 1990), 309–21.

106. For Ackroyd-Beveridge's antipathy towards the *babu*, see Beveridge, *India Called Them*, pp. 166–7; also Barr, *Memsahibs*, pp. 163–4.
107. *Englishman*, 6 Mar. 1883, p. 2.
108. *Bengalee*, 31 Mar. 1883, p. 152. For other comments that singled out Ackroyd-Beveridge's letter for criticism, see *Hindoo Patriot* (Calcutta), 12 Mar. 1883, p. 128 and 26 Mar., 1883, p. 146; *Reis and Reyyet*, 17 Mar. 1883, p. 124 and 14 Apr. 1883, p. 171.
109. Ania Loomba, *Gender, Race, Renaissance Drama* (Delhi: Oxford University Press, 1992).
110. Rosemary Hennessy argues for locating the reconfiguration of the feminine subject in Britain in changing imperial and colonial policy in the late nineteenth century. See Hennessy, 'New Woman, New History'.
111. *Leg. Dept Papers*, Paper No. 28.
112. Quoted in Beveridge, *India Called Them*, p. 248.
113. Cited in Janaka Nair, 'Uncovering the Zenana'. Although the *Bengalee*, 26 May 1883, p. 241 referred to support for the Ilbert Bill from liberal-minded women in London, there was little evidence of interest in the Bill among feminist groups in Britain.
114. See Vron Ware, *Beyond the Pale* (London: Verso 1992); Antoinette Burton, 'The White Woman's Burden: British Feminists and the "Indian Woman", 1865–1915', *Women's Studies International Forum*, 13:4 (Winter 1990), 245–308. Due to the timing of its publication, I was unable to consult Burton's more recent work *Burdens of History: British Feminists, Indian Women and Imperial Culture, 1865–1915* (Chapel Hill: University of North Carolina Press, 1994).
115. Gayatri Chakravorty Spivak, 'Can the Subaltern Speak? Speculations on Widow Sacrifice', *Wedge*, 7/8 (Winter/Spring 1985), p. 121.
116. See *Lal Mohun Ghose* (Madras: G. A. Natesan, 1906), pp. 11–18. For Branson's aspersions on the character of Indian women, see his speech quoted in *Hindoo Patriot*, 5 Mar. 1883, p. 112.
117. *Reis and Reyyet*, 28 Apr. 1883, p. 196.
118. *Amrita Bazar Patrika* (Calcutta), 27 May 1886, p. 4; and *Dacca Prakash*, 24 June 1883; *RNBP*, No. 26, p. 353.
119. The hoax was first reported in the *Bengalee*, 30 June 1883, p. 301; in the meantime the memorial had been widely reproduced in Indian and Anglo-Indian newspapers.
120. Cited in *Civil and Military Gazette*, 7 May 1883, p. 2.
121. Ibid.
122. See Usha Chakraborty, *Conditions of Bengali Women Around the Second Half of the Nineteenth Century* (Calcutta: Burdhan Press, 1963), p. 134. Also see the recollections of Sarala Debi, *Jibaner Jharpatra*, cited in Borthwick, *Changing Role of Women*, p. 339.
123. See *Bengalee*, 19 May 1883, p. 230; and *Statesman*, 14 May 1883, p. 3.
124. See *New Dispensation* (Calcutta), 22 July 1883, quoted in Borthwick, *Changing Role of Women*, p. 339.
125. For a discussion of the reconstitution of Indian patriarchy under colonial rule, see Kumkum Sangari and Sudesh Vaid, 'Recasting Women: An Introduction', in Sangari and Vaid (eds), *Recasting Women: Essays in Indian Colonial History* (New Brunswick: Rutgers University Press, 1990), p. 1–26.

4.6

'VACATION CRUISES; OR, THE HOMOEROTICS OF ORIENTALISM'

Joseph A. Boone

Why the Orient seems still to suggest not only fecundity but sexual promise (and threat) . . . is not the province of my analysis here, alas, despite its frequently noted appearance.

Edward Said (p. 88)

So we had sex, or at least I lay and allowed him to fuck me, and thought as his prick shot in and he kissed my neck, back, and shoulders, that it was a most unappetising position for a world-famous artist to be in.

Joe Orton, in Tangier (p. 174)

Perhaps nowhere else are the sexual politics of colonial narrative so explicitly thematized as in those voyages to the Near East recorded or imagined by Western men. 'Since the time of the Prophet', one of these records proclaims, 'fabulous Araby has reeked of aphrodisiac excitement' (Edwardes and Masters, p. 175). With various shades of prurience and sophistication, similar sentiments echo throughout the writings of novelists, poets, journalists, travel writers, sociologists and ethnographers whose pursuit of eros has brought them, in Rana Kabbani's phrase, 'to the Orient on the flying-carpet of Orientalism' (*Passionate Nomad*, p. x). For such men, the geopolitical realities of the Arabic Orient become a psychic screen on which to project fantasies of illicit sexuality and unbridled excess – including, as Malek Alloula has observed, visions of *'generalized perversion'* (p. 95) and, as Edward Said puts it, 'sexual experience

From: Joseph A. Boone (1995), 'Vacation Cruises; or, The Homoerotics of Orientalism', pp. 89–107, in *PMLA*, vol. 110, no. 1.

unobtainable in Europe', that is 'a different type of sexuality' (p. 190). This appropriation of the so-called East in order to project onto it an otherness that mirrors Western psychosexual needs only confirms the phenomenon that Said calls 'Orientalism' in his book of that name.[1]

But exactly what others are being appropriated here? Despite Alloula's italicizing of the word *perversion*, despite Said's carefully ambiguous rendering of the phrase 'a different, type of sexuality', both Alloula's and Said's analyses of colonialist erotics remain ensconced in conspicuously heterosexual interpretative frameworks.[2] In contrast, the epigraph from Joe Orton's diary makes explicit an aspect of the vacation agendas of many male tourists that remains unspoken in most commentaries on colonial narrative: namely, that the 'sexual promise (and threat)' that Said attributes to the Orient is for countless Western travelers inextricably tied to their exposure abroad to what has come to be known within Western sexual discourse as male homosexual practice (p. 88).[3] Whether these homoerotically charged encounters figure as a voyeuristic spectacle – that is, as one more 'exotic' item that the tourist views from a distance – or as a covert goal of the traveler's journey, the fact remains that the possibility of sexual contact with and between men underwrites and at times even explains the historical appeal of orientalism as an occidental mode of male perception, appropriation and control.

The number of gay and bisexual male writers and artists who have traveled through North Africa in pursuit of sexual gratification is legion as well as legend: André Gide lost his virginity on the dunes of Algeria in 1893 (where Oscar Wilde served as his procurer two years later) and E. M. Forster on the beaches of Alexandria in 1916. Morocco has also served as a mecca for the gay and bisexual literati vacationing in North Africa – many clustered around Tangier's famous resident Paul Bowles – to say nothing of the nonliterati, those celebrities of ambiguous sexual persuasion ranging from Mick Jagger to Malcolm Forbes.[4] Many heterosexually identified men have traveled to the Arabic Orient in pursuit of erotic fulfillment as well, but even these adventurers have had to confront the specter of male-male sex that lurks in their fantasies of a decadent and lawless East; such encounters put into crisis assumptions about male sexual desire, masculinity, and heterosexuality that are specific to Western culture. In the following pages I hope to address the way in which the public and personal texts produced by both straight and nonstraight travelers are implicated in a colonizing enterprise that often 'others' the homosexually inscribed Arab male, a condition that obtains, albeit with differing valences and contexts, whether that 'other' is perceived with dread or with desire. Simultaneously, in nearly all these texts, the imagined or actual encounter with exotic otherness engenders profound anxieties about one's authority to narrate: the threat of being 'unmanned' by the attractive yet dangerous lure of a polymorphous Eastern sexuality that exceeds representation is mirrored in many Western writers' fears, in the face of such excess, of never writing again.

To delineate more precisely these discursive manifestations of displaced and discovered homoeroticism, this essay investigates three categories of occidental tourists whose writings eroticize the Near East. First, it looks at heterosexually identified writers whose transformation of Egypt's perceived sexual bounty into a symbol of polymorphous perversity engenders their obsessive fascination with, and often anguished negotiation of, the homoerotic. Second, it examines the homoerotic undertow in representations of life on the desert, where the act of masquerading as the foreign other, sadomasochism, and gender ambiguities uneasily collide. Third, it turns to gay male enclaves established in the African Mahgreb since the beginning of the twentieth century, in order to consider the implications of the colonially sanctioned tradition of male prostitution for various narratives of gay self-affirmation. Driving and binding all these homo-eroticizing strands of orientalist narrative are a series of interrelated sociopolitical, psychosexual and aesthetic issues: the practice and economics of empire, perceptions of race, the collusion of phallacratic and colonial interests, constructions of sexual 'deviance', questions of narrative authority, crises of representation. Because of the number of texts – biographical, autobiographical, fictional – canvassed in the following pages, highlighting one topos over another is at times necessary, partly but not solely because of space limitations. Working by pastiche, letting the heterogenous strands of my analysis contribute to the illumination of a subject that is necessarily multifaceted and hybrid, rather than forcing each strand to illustrate every aspect of an emerging overview, seems an effective strategy with which to forestall the classic colonizing – and indeed scholarly – move of defining each part in the name of an already assumed whole.

In tracing the trajectories outlined above, my own narrative aims to traverse and unsettle, even as it provisionally inscribes, a number of imposed boundaries – not least those separating 'West' from 'East' and 'heterosexual' from 'homosexual'. What follows is written as part of the growing academic discipline of gay and lesbian studies, whose boundaries I hope to push by showing how contingent and Western its conception of 'homosexuality' – as an identity category, a sexual practice and a site of theoretical speculation – often proves to be when brought into contact with the sexual epistemologies of non-Western cultures, particularly when encounters of 'East' and 'West' are crossed by issues of colonialism, race, nation and class. Taking a cue from Homi K. Bhabha's insightful formulation of the continually 'unfixing' propensities of the colonial stereotype, I present a series of collisions between traditionally assumed Western sexual categories (the homosexual, the pederast) and equally stereotypical colonialist tropes (the beautiful brown boy, the hypervirile Arab, the wealthy Nazarene) – collisions that generate ambiguity and contradiction rather than reassert an unproblematic intellectual domination over a mythic East as an object of desire. For many white gay male subjects, that object of desire remains simultaneously same and other, a source of troubling and unresolved identification and differentiation. It is precisely in the space opened by this gap that a critique of orientalist homoerotics may usefully locate itself and begin the work of dismantling those paradigmatic fictions of otherness that have made the binarisms of West and East, of heterosexuality and homosexuality, at once powerful and oppressive.[5]

(RE)ORIENTING SEXUALITY

The three thematic categories I have outlined map out an imagined terrain of male desire that has specific geographic coordinates. Stretching from the North African countries of Morocco, Algeria and Tunisia to Egypt and thence to the Syrian-Arabic peninsula, this vast territory, whose ethnic and cultural diversities have over the centuries been tenuously linked by a common language and shared Islamic faith,[6] also corresponds to what Richard Burton, in the terminal essay of his 1885–86 translation of the *Thousand Nights and a Night*, dubbed the 'Sotadic Zone'. Within this zone, as Burton argues for forty-some pages of exacting if dubious detail, sodomy, or 'what our neighbors call *Le vice contre*

Fig. 1. An example of Western colonialist fantasy disguised as anthropological study, this anonymous photograph, *The Captives* (c. 1930), purports to take the viewer into the forbidden world of the Near Eastern male brothel. But the presence of various studio props connoting 'enslaved exoticism' (the arranged drapery, manacles, rope, conch shells) belies the photograph's claim to authenticity. (L' Amour bleu: *Die homosexuelle Liebe in Kunst und Literatur des Abendlandes*, ed. Cecile Beurdeley [Berlin: Gmünder, 1988] p. 244. Reproduced by permission of Edita Companie, Lausanne.)

nature', 'is popular and endemic, held at worst to be a mere peccadillo, whilst the races to the North and South of the[se] limits . . . as a rule, are physically incapable of performing the operation and look upon it with the liveliest disgust' (vol. 110 p. 177, 179). What Burton labels a 'popular and endemic' Sotadic practice might more properly be called a 'popular and endemic' stereotype of Eastern perversity, one firmly wedged in the dominant Western imaginary.[7]

By documenting this tradition of 'Eastern' sodomitic 'vice', Burton offers a theory important less for its accuracy than for its frankness in articulating a widespread perception that had hitherto been filtered through codes of vague allusion. Readers of John Hindley's English translation of *Persian Lyrics* (1800), for instance, are informed that 'the disgusting object[s]' of these love poems have been feminized 'for reasons too obvious to need any formal apology' (p. 33). In his classic study of modern Egyptian life (1833–35), Edward W. Lane also draws on the trope of disgust to avoid making explicit the sodomitic antics performed on the streets of Cairo by a trickster and his boy assistant: 'several indecent tricks which he perform[ed] with the boy I must refrain from describing; some of them are abominably disgusting' (p. 391). And yet despite this aura of unmentionability, one can find textual evidence of a fascination with the Near East's rumored homoeroticism scattered through commentaries that reach back to the time of the Crusades.[8] By 1780 Jeremy Bentham could dispassionately write, 'Even now, wherever the Mahometan religion prevails, such practices seem to be attended with but little dispute' (vol. 1: p. 175; see also Crompton, p. 111).

In this light, Said's failure to account for homoerotic elements in orientalist pursuits is a telling omission. Said's theorization of orientalism has proved invaluable in drawing scholarly attention to the discursive paths whereby the Arabic Orient has come to represent 'one [of the West's] deepest and most recurring images of the Other' (p. 1). The threatening excess of this otherness, Said argues, has most often been gendered as feminine and hence sexually available so that it can be penetrated, cataloged and thus contained by the 'superior' rationality of the Western mind (pp. 40, 44, 137–8). Such metaphors for the West's appropriation of the East are at least implicitly heterosexual. But as a close analysis of several specific Western experiences and representations of the Near East reveals, that which appears alluringly feminine is not always, or necessarily, female. A telling example of this reversal of expectation, as I have argued elsewhere, can be located in Said's analysis of the notebooks and journals that Gustave Flaubert kept during his voyage to Egypt in 1849–50 (see 'Mappings', pp. 80–1). Said focuses on Flaubert's heady account of his affair with the professional dancer Kuchuk Hanem. For Said, Flaubert's transformation of Kuchuk's material flesh into an occasion for poetic reverie forms a paradigmatic example of the mechanisms of orientalism: the masculinized, penetrating West possesses for its own purposes the East's fecundity, gendered as female in Kuchuk's 'peculiarly Oriental' sensuality (p. 187). Yet Said overlooks the crucial fact that the first exotic dancer to catch Flaubert's eye is not the female Kuchuk but a famous male dancer and catamite. 'But we have seen male dancers. Oh! Oh! Oh!' exclaims Flaubert in a letter to his best friend as, with barely contained excitement, he details Hasan el-Belbeissi's lascivious pantomime, (semi-)female garb and kohl-painted eyes. This description in turn leads to a discussion of the practice of sodomy among Flaubert's Egyptian acquaintances ('Here it is quite accepted. One admits one's sodomy') and thence to a declaration of his own attempt to 'indulge in this form of ejaculation' at the local bath (p. 83).

Some of the most blatantly heterosexual examples of orientalism – ranging from nineteenth-century travelogues to pseudoscientific surveys of 'Eastern' sexual customs – reveal a similar proximity to the homoerotic.[9] Likewise Burton, a serious orientalist, opens the boundaries of his textual body to a certain destabilizing pressure when he addresses the subject of desire between men in the Arabic Orient. For example, in his introduction to the *Nights*, Burton begins with an anatomical metaphor that bestows on his translation a specifically male body. Prior bowdlerized editions, he complains, have 'castrat[ed]' the tales, producing only 'ennui and disappointment' in the reader, whereas his aim is to 'produce a full, complete, unvarnished, copy of the great original' (vol. 1: pp. xvii, ix). The means by which Burton seeks to restore the text to its 'uncastrated' manhood is curious, however (p. xii); he proceeds to adorn it with footnotes, annotations, and appendixes whose copiousness rivals the primary text, creating a proliferation of multiple (one might argue feminine) sites of textual pleasure (see Naddaff) that threaten to explode the complete and contained male body he has assigned to his translation. Primary among these supplements, moreover, is the terminal essay, whose lengthy fourth section is dedicated to *le vice contre nature*. Burton announces his intention to display this subject – again using a phallic metaphor – 'in decent nudity, not in suggestive fig-leaf' in order to establish once and for all the prevalence of sodomy in the Arab Muslim world (vol. 10: p. 178). The 'unvarnished', uncastrated male body assigned to the text in the introduction, here exposed 'in decent nudity' and without 'fig-leaf', becomes a sodomitic subject in both senses of the phrase.

Moreover, like the language used to frame this discussion of Near Eastern sodomy, the contents of the terminal essay work against Burton's anthropological and orientalist predilection to contain and classify his subject. As his inquiry into sexual relations between men broadens, so too the initially circumscribed Mediterranean 'belt' (vol. 10: p. 201) wherein the vice is said to flourish expands eastward – till, by the conclusion of the essay, it encompasses the Far East and the continents of the precolonized Americas. As East spins back into West, Burton is forced to confirm *le vice*'s growing presence even in 'our modern capitals, London, Berlin, and Paris' (vol. 10: p. 213), although he has earlier set the West off-limits, claiming that the northern European races are 'as a rule . . . physically incapable of performing the operation' (vol. 10: p. 179). Burton's definition of sodomy collapses in contradiction and repeats in its global uncontainability the operation that his notes perform on a textual level, exposing the sanctity of the male body's claim to uncastrated completeness as another masculinist myth. Or to put it another way, as long as Burton can maintain an anthropological pose, he does not mind parading the non-European homosexual subject of the *Nights* in 'decent nudity'; but when he must envision himself as a reader, one whose authority over content yields to vicarious participation in the fictions being relayed, he finds himself restoring the 'fig-leaf' beneath which he has previously declared himself willing to glimpse. For many Western men the act of exploring, writing about, and theorizing an eroticized Near East is coterminous with unlocking a Pandora's box of phantasmic homoerotic desire, desire whose propensity to spread without check threatens to contaminate, if not to re-orient, the heterosexual 'essence' of occidental male subjectivity.

FANTASIZING THE 'DELIGHT . . . AND INFAMY OF THE EGYPTIANS'

Of all the regions of the Near East, Western writers most readily associate ancient and modern Egypt with the spreading 'contagion' of homosexuality. Curiously, Egypt's reputation as 'that classical religion of all abominations', in Richard Burton's phrase (vol. 10: p. 194), has proved to be an irresistible draw to the literary ambitions of a score of occidental writers from Gérard de Nerval and Flaubert to Lawrence Durrell and Norman Mailer – writers intent on producing texts as gargantuan as their (hetero)sexual appetites. In these writers' prose the dazzling spectacle of Cairene and Alexandrian street life is transformed into an emblem of the psyche's overflowing polymorphous desires. As such, this spectacle becomes a convenient screen on which to project fantasies of illicit, unbridled eroticism. In *Colonizing Egypt*, Timothy Mitchell has forcefully shown how such psychological projections onto the foreign other derive from a general Western representational tendency to treat all things Egyptian – including Egyptian visitors to Europe – as objects on display, as exhibition pieces whose 'carefully chaotic' arrangement is orchestrated solely to satisfy the 'isolated gaze' of a European viewer (vol. 1, p. 9). Experiencing Egypt's curiosities as panoramas and tableaux depends, of course, on the illusion of some ineffable but inviolate boundary dividing spectator and spectacle, subject and object, self and other. Despite the strategic mystification of foreign otherness at work in this process, however, Egypt's historical positioning as a conduit between East and West, Europe and Africa, the familiar and the foreign has meant that, contrary to expectation, it has never functioned merely or solely as the Occident's other. Rather, as Antonia Lant suggests, Egypt has come to represent in the Western imagination an intermediate zone, 'a foothold, a staging point', that signifies liminality and indeterminacy itself (p. 98). As a realm of nonfixity, moreover, it has become a ready-made symbol for that interior world of the polymorphously perverse that its Western visitors find uncannily familiar and, as an effect of repression, unimaginably estranging.

Colonized as other but never susceptible to total differentiation from or appropriation by the West, Egypt in all its exotic appeal thus presents the occidental tourist with an unsuspected challenge. Hence the note of hysteria infiltrating the late-eighteenth-century *Travels* of C. S. Sonnini, a former engineer in the French navy, who pauses in his narrative to lament

> [t]he passion contrary to nature . . . [that] constitute[s] the delight, or to use a juster term, the infamy of the Egyptians. It is not for women that their amorous ditties are composed. . . . [F]ar different objects inflame them. . . . This horrid depravation, which, to the disgrace of polished nations, is not altogether unknown to them, is generally diffused all over Egypt: the rich, and poor are equally infected with it. (vol. 1: pp. 251–2)

Part of the horror is that this 'inconceivable appetite' (vol. 1: p. 251) 'is not altogether unknown' to civilized Europe: if the Egyptian vice knows no class ('rich and poor are equally infected with it'), can it be expected to respect the boundaries of colonizer and colonized? Thirty years later, a similar image of unchecked infection appears in Lane's *Manners and Customs of the Modern Egyptians* when the Victorian author addresses, with characteristic understatement, this aspect of Egyptian 'immorality'. 'A vice for which the Memlooks . . . were infamous', Lane writes of the Ottoman rulers, 'was so spread by them in [Egypt] as to become not less rare here than in almost any other country of the East'. Here Egypt is the victim of contagion, the Turks are the culprits, and one assumes (since Lane asserts that 'of late years *it is said* [the vice has] much decreased') that the civilizing machinery of British Empire is the solution (p. 304; emphasis added). Once again, aspersions of 'unnatural' sexuality become markers of larger competing global and colonial interests.

This mythicizing of the magnitude of Near Eastern 'vice' is not unrelated to a Western obsession with the genital size of Egyptian men that filters into even the driest orientalist discourse. For while the figure of the effeminate Asiatic – embodied, for instance, in the transvestic dancer – represents one 'face' of orientalist homoerotic fantasy, the reverse image, that of the hypervirile, mythically endowed sheikh holds equal currency in orientalist homoerotic discourse. Thus Burton, in his *Personal Narrative of a Pilgrimage to Al-Madinah and Meccah* (1893) argues that members of 'the Nilotic race, although commonly called "Arabs"', are more closely related to African blacks because of the size of their sexual organs (vol. 2: p. 83); that this information is buried in a footnote – one written in Latin, no less, to ward off the nonspecialist – would seem to indicate that what is at stake here is a certain European male anxiety or sense of inferiority that needs to be kept under wraps. That white, male, implicitly heterosexual subjectivity is the real issue underlying this prurient obsession with indigenous body parts is made even more blatant in the linking of racial stereotyping with sexual perversion in Jacob Sutor's *L'amour aux colonies* (1893), published under the pseudonym Dr. Jacobus X. An army surgeon posted to various French outposts, Sutor claims that his clinical experience proves beyond a doubt that the Arab, 'an active pederast, is provided with a

genital organ which, for size and length, rivals that of the Negro' (p. 298), and
adds that '[w]ith such a weapon does the Arab seek for anal copulation. He is
not particular in his choice, and age or sex makes no difference' (p. 300). If
foreignness, genital endowment and sodomy are of a piece for Sutor, so too do
exoticism and excess come together to form the more clearly homoerotic frisson
of Allen Edwardes's surveys of Eastern eroticism. 'As hitherto noted, the penile
proportions of the Egyptians were as notorious as their promiscuity', he states
as fact, then proceeds, with more than a touch of prurience, to describe bas-
reliefs that purportedly depict 'Nilotic peasants and labourers with their loin-
clothes' hoisted 'to reveal fleshy genitalia' (*Erotica Judaica*, p. 93); elsewhere
he records the 'impressive sight' presented by orgies of 'round-robin sodomy'
in the Egyptian hammam *(Jewel*, p. 207), where 'well-proportioned' nude bath-
boys service willing customers of all classes (p. 246). The guise of orientalist
scholarship allows Edwardes to express a surfeit of subconscious homoerotic
fantasy.

In a like manner, the autobiographical and literary productions of Flaubert
and Durrell – which I discuss in greater depth elsewhere ('Mappings') – transform Egypt into a landscape of unbridled libidinal desires, a landscape in
which same-sex activity is conspicuously highlighted. Figuratively exploring
such 'foreign' terrain may give these writers an excuse to inhabit textually the
other whom their phallocentrically constituted heterosexuality must otherwise
disavow, but these imaginative ventures into alien territory only highlight the
problematic, indeed unstable, construction of Western discourses of masculinity under the sign of the phallus. And for both Flaubert and Durrell the fantasized projection of sexual otherness onto Egypt eventually occasions a crisis of
writing, of narrative authority, when the writing subject is confronted by (imagined) sensual excess.

Bombarded on his arrival in Egypt by 'such a bewildering chaos of colours
[and sound] that [his] poor imagination is dazzled as though by continuous fireworks', Flaubert quickly embraces the exotic otherness of Egypt as a source of
artistic inspiration and sexual gratification (p. 79). Part of these 'fireworks' is
the erotic dance of the 'marvellous Hasan el-Belbeissi', whose talent at putting
'additional spice into a thing that is already quite clear in itself' injects into
Flaubert's correspondence and diaries a stream of homoerotic banter and speculation that becomes a source of titillation and eventually a spur to experimentation without radically disturbing Flaubert's heterosexual self-definition
('Here . . . it is spoken of at table. Sometimes you do a bit of denying, and then
everyone teases you and you end up confessing' [p. 84]). Simultaneously,
however, the possibilities unlocked by this flirtation with Egyptian sodomy
become the source of a subliminal anxiety linked to Flaubert's literary ambitions. Having traveled to Egypt in search of creative inspiration, Flaubert
expresses his writerly potential in metaphors of (hetero)sexual reproduction
('but – the real thing! To ejaculate, beget the child!' [p. 199]) and conversely
expresses his despair at not having realized his literary goals in images of non-

Fig. 2. Egypt's historical positioning as a meeting point between Europe and Africa, the familiar and the foreign, lends itself to racial and homoerotic codings in George Quaintance's *Egyptian Wrestlers* (1952), where the pharoah's court provides the context for a spectacle of gay erotica pitting two virile, loin-clothed slaves – one African, one Aryan – against each other in a taboo embrace. (*The Art of George Quaintance: Catalogue of the Fifty-Fourth Exhibition of the Janssen Gallery*, ed. Volker Janssen [Berlin: Janssen, 1989] p. 33. Reproduced by permission of Janssen-Verlag, Berlin.)

reproductive sexual play (pp. 198–9); he subtly figures the exotic otherness of sexual perversion as the threat of erasure, the negation of artistic vitality or sap, when 'the lines don't come' (p. 87; see Boone, 'Mappings', p. 102). For all Flaubert's openness to his Near Eastern experiences, then, his encounter with foreign homosexuality triggers an uneasiness about what it means to be a writer and a man; in consciously striving to become one of the West's great writers, Flaubert subconsciously regards his narrative authority as equivalent to, and dependent on, a sexual authority associated with Western codes of heterosexual potency.

A similarly disabling equation of sexual aberration and writerly debilitation haunts Durrell while he is stationed in Egypt during World War II. 'Love, hashish, and boys [are] the obvious solution to anyone stuck here for more than a few years,' he writes Henry Miller from Alexandria in 1944, a few months later adding, 'One could not continue to live here without practising a sort of death – hashish or boys or food' (Wickes, pp, 190, 195). A parallel 'sort of death' faces Darley, the narrator-protagonist of the *Alexandria Quartet*. Confronted with Alexandria's dazzling yet benumbing spectacle of sensual excess – 'the sexual provender that lies at hand is staggering in its variety and profusion', Darley notes on arrival with envy and some fear – this would-be writer experiences a breakdown that is both sexual and textual, finding himself unable to write and 'even to make love' (vol. 1: pp. 4, 11). Darley's feelings of impotence and inadequacy, compounded by Justine's betrayal, increasingly lead him to doubt his 'manhood'. In turn these doubts trigger a flood of repressed memories and events that implicate him in an expanding web of homosexual desire and panic. The welling up of these taboo desires is made possible largely by the psychodramatic resonances that Egypt assumes in Darley's psyche and in Durrell's fiction, its 'foreign' landscape transformed into an emblem of the fragmented, anarchic terrain of the component instincts through which the questing writer must pass on his way to artistic manhood. Ironically, only when Darley has purged himself of all expressions of polymorphous play and perversity can he break through the writer's block that plagues him for four volumes and emerge on the last page of the *Quartet* as a productive writer and successful heterosexual lover.

These displacements shed additional light on Durrell's letter equating the enjoyment of 'hashish or boys or food' with 'death' of the self. For Durrell proceeds to describe the 'wonderful novel on Alexandria' he has just conceived, 'a sort of spiritual butcher's shop with girls on the slab' (vol. 2: p. 196). Underlying this inspiration of the written text of the *Quartet* as a heterosexist fantasy of girls as meat to be devoured glimmers the fear of sodomy as an ultimate indulgence in passive pleasures (like drugs, like food) that spell a 'sort of death' to active, or 'masculine' artistic (pro)creativity. The homoerotic fantasies unleashed by Durrell's projection on to Egypt of the 'dark tides of Eros' hidden within every psyche generate a crisis of masculine subjectivity that compels Durrell to Promethean efforts to contain the very desires on which his exploration of foreign otherness depends (vol. 2: p. 185). To a lesser degree, the same paradox overwhelms Flaubert's exploration of Egyptian sensuality. In the process, 'the homoerotics of orientalism' constantly threatens to become another name for occidental homophobia.

DRESSING DOWN THE DESERT ANDROGYNE

While writers like Flaubert and Durrell locate their visions of a sexualized, mythic Near East in the spectacle and stimulation of Egypt's infinite variety, the homoerotic impulse infiltrating occidental visions of the Near East also manifests itself in adventurers who search out the nomadic life of the desert and embrace ascetic solitude rather than profusion. Seeking to blend into their surroundings by taking on the apparel of the Bedouin, such figures attempt not merely to possess but, more important, to become the desired other. Putting on 'Arab drag' provides the desert androgyne with a disguise that allows for the play of sexual and gender ambiguity. Coupled with a persistent misogyny, this ambiguity issues forth in a complicated modality of homoerotic desire that is expressed sometimes in puritanical asceticism and sublimation, sometimes in sadistic outbreaks of violence, and sometimes in swooning surrender to the desert's harsh beauty. These desert androgynes transform their short lives into the subject of scandal and eventually the stuff of myth – a status that may over-shadow but cannot eclipse the specific scenarios of empire and colonialism that make possible their legendary romances with the desert.

This blend of sexual repression, homosexual yearning, and sadomasochistic surrender finds quintessential expression in T. E. Lawrence, the twentieth

Fig. 3. While T. E. Lawrence's famous white robes were part of his self-constructed image of ascetic masculinity, this photograph, appearing in Lowell Thomas's *With Lawrence in Arabia* (London: Hutchinson, 1924), purports to offer evidence of Lawrence's participation in a more ambiguous form of boundary crossing: 'Lawrence occasionally visited enemy territory disguised as a gipsy woman of Syria'. Thomas's caption reads (facing p. 96). (Courtesy of the estate of Lowell Thomas and Hutchinson Co., London.)

century's most famous icon of the thrill and contradictions of assuming Arab drag. For Lawrence dressing in desert gear was foremost a means of '[quitting him] of [his] English self', of attempting to become the other rather than the colonizer. At the same time he admitted that he 'could not sincerely take on the Arab skin: it was an affectation only' (*Seven Pillars*, p. 30). This contradictory doubleness – which Marjorie Garber links to psychic transvestism (pp. 304–9) and Kaja Silverman to the 'double mimesis' of psychic colonialism (pp. 17–19) – characterized all aspects of Lawrence's life, including the powerful if elusive homoerotic strain that he writes into *The Seven Pillars of Wisdom*, the official story of his engagement in the Arab revolt of 1914–18. The homoerotics of this epic tug in two directions: toward an impossibly idealized Bedouin homosexuality and toward its nightmarish opposite, utter degradation – conditions that both pivot on (dis)simulations of dress and disguise. The first strain is proclaimed in chapter 1, as Lawrence frankly addresses the 'strange longings' that blossom in the 'virile heat' of the desert as his youthful Bedouin followers 'slake one another's few needs in their own clean bodies'. The passion of 'friends quivering together in the yielding sand with intimate hot limbs in supreme embrace', Lawrence continues, is but 'a *sensual* co-efficient of the *mental* passion which was wielding our souls in one flaming effort' (p. 28; emphases added). An erotic ideal thus finds its reflection in a political ideal that, under the sign of male-male love, tenuously combines British colonial interests and the movement toward Arab sovereignty. This idealizing strain is continued in the story of the Bedouin lovers Daud and Saad – 'an instance', Lawrence writes approvingly, 'of the eastern boy and boy affection which the segregation of women [makes] inevitable' (p. 244). Finally, this idealization of love between men is set forth as the raison d'être of Lawrence's participation in the Arab conflict in the volume's dedicatory poem, 'To S. A.', which begins 'I loved you, so I drew these tides of men into my hands . . . To earn you Freedom'. Again, the sexual ideal coexists with and expresses the political goal.

Most biographers agree that the dedication refers to Sheikh Ahmed, otherwise known as Dahoum, the fourteen-year-old water boy with whom Lawrence became infatuated during his first extended stay in the Middle East. Onto this constant companion Lawrence projected an idealized vision of the Arabic race as pure, simple, and untainted by Western culture. The determination with which Lawrence set out to construct Dahoum as an ideal foreign other mirrors the determination with which Lawrence willed his own self-image into being, confident that through sheer self-mastery he could 'mak[e] himself', in his biographer's words, 'a perfected and refined instrument' (Mack, pp, 97, 86). One by-product of this discipline was Lawrence's puritanical sublimation of his homosexual inclinations. Yet in renouncing the flesh, Lawrence also set himself up for a vicious return of the repressed, which in *Seven Pillars* takes the form of the nightmarish inverse of the text's representation of idealized male bonds: the brutal rape he claims he endured when taken prisoner by the Turks at Der'a and the psychologically devastating loss of self-mastery that experience signified for him. These two faces of homosexuality assume unmistakably ideological valences in Lawrence's imaginary: the Arab freedom fighters whose cause he has undertaken engage in 'clean' sex, while the Turks – Britain's foes – are 'beastly' rapists (pp. 28, 452).

But for all the detail with which Lawrence represents his humiliation and degradation – exhibitionistically offering his bloodied body to his readers as a fetishized spectacle – what actually happened at Der'a remains lost in what biographers agree to be Lawrence's inability to distinguish between fact and fantasy. After telling how he spurned the Turkish bey's 'fawn[ing]' (p. 452) sexual advances, Lawrence reports being taken into the hall by the bey's soldiers and repeatedly beaten, lashed, and sodomized. Yet it is indicative of the narrative's confusion that Lawrence's descriptions of torture and sexual abuse are indistinguishable: in the nightmarish fear of sexual contact that forms the inverse of Lawrence's idealization of homoerotic relations, submitting sexually and being tortured are the same fantasy.[10] What emerges is Lawrence's guilt for having surrendered his vaunted self-mastery to the mastery of another; the threat of anal penetration signifies loss of will that in turn signifies a loss of self.

The incredible narrative projections of fear and desire that arise from Lawrence's contemplation of one man's penetration by another are usefully explained by Leo Bersani in his influential essay 'Is the Rectum a Grave?' Bersani argues that phallocentric culture promotes a powerfully subliminal equation between passive anal sex, which represents the breakdown of bodily boundaries, and a shattering of the male ego that is tantamount to death. Underlying the cultural prohibition against being penetrated by another man is the irrational fear of dissolution of the psychic boundaries of the self – a notion that, as Bersani shows, reflects a specifically modern and Western conception of the ego as a self-contained and integral fortress. 'That night the citadel of my integrity [was] irrevocably lost', Lawrence concludes the published account of the Der'a rape (*Seven Pillars* p. 456); in a private explanation to Charlotte Shaw, he confesses, '[T]o earn five minutes respite from . . . pain . . . I gave away the only possession we are born into the world with – our bodily integrity' (*Letters* pp. 47–48).

This specifically male fear of the loss of corporeal integrity and ego boundaries cannot be separated from a concurrent desire to experience sexual surrender, as Bersani also makes clear: the desire expressed in Lawrence's evocation of 'the delicious warmth, probably sexual, . . . swelling through [him]' as he is brutally kicked and then whipped in the groin (*Seven Pillars* p. 454). This experience forces on Lawrence the humiliating knowledge that he can allow himself to experience sexual pleasure only if pain and coercion are part of the scenario – his resistance has to be whipped out of him by an external force. And Lawrence becomes conscious of this hitherto repressed knowledge precisely through his psychodramatic projections onto the Near East of his attraction to and terror of sexual surrender as feminizing (see also Silverman on how this experience transforms Lawrence from a 'reflexive' to a 'feminine' masochist [p. 35]).[11]

Lawrence's masochism marks his subsequent relation to writing. He obsessively rewrites the Der'a incident from 1919 to 1925, elaborating and revising its details, just as he obsessively revises the unruly manuscript of *Seven Pillars*, which has become a text that is out of control, that cannot be mastered. This crisis of narrative authority re-enacts the loss of bodily integrity and sexual control that Lawrence has grafted onto the experience of his rape. As a result, Lawrence increasingly expresses disgust toward the act of writing in terms that conflate authorial and biological functions: 'I can't write . . . since creation . . . is only a nasty vice. You have to be very eager-spirited to overcome the disgust of reproduction' (Mack, p. 423). Ironically, this metaphoric association of textual production and sexual reproduction demonstrates Lawrence's subliminal allegiance to the phallocentric model that inhibits him sexually: a model whose link between regained masculine potency and successful literary production recurs in Flaubert and Durrell. Hence, as the fantasized site of male prowess, of spermatic reproduction, the textual body that arouses Lawrence's 'disgust' mirrors the disgust he expresses in *Seven Pillars* toward his 'soiled' – because mastered – sexual body. And he now equates the 'rankling fraudulence' of this body with his 'daily posturing in alien dress – desert drag no longer serves as an adequate vehicle for mediating his homoerotic urges. The desublimation of his homosexuality through masochistic degradation not only curtails the idealized fantasy of 'clean' Bedouin sex but also forces Lawrence to see his role in 'the national uprising of another race' as a 'fraud' perpetuated by English interests (*Seven Pillars*, p. 514). The man who has traveled to the Arabic desert filled with confidence, privately transforming himself into the foreign other he wants to be (and to have) while publicly transforming himself into the heroic liberator of the land of his desires, returns home to England in self-defeat. Having failed to become the colonial object of his desire, Lawrence settles, ironically, for a pale imitation: psychic existence as a mastered subject, in thrall to an 'imperial' notion of masculine will that transforms his homosexual yearnings into a feminine surrender for which he can only punish himself in rites of degradation and self-abnegation.[12]

The Tourist Trade in Boys

Not all imaginative travelers to the Near East remain so resigned as Lawrence or so resistant as Durrell to the homoerotic pulsations fueling many occidental visions of Arabic sexuality. For over a century, numerous gay men have journeyed to North Africa to discover what they already suspected was there: a colonized Third World in which the availability of casual sex is based on an economics of boys. Seized by the French in 1834, Algeria became a popular cruising site for Gide, Wilde, Alfred Douglas, Ronald Firbank and many other homosexual men of means by the century's end.[13] During the first two decades of the twentieth century, Algeria's reputation for gay tourism was superseded by that of the French-Spanish colony of Morocco. Tangier's establishment as an international zone by Western interests from 1923 to 1956 played a role in this shift by encouraging suspect activities ranging from international monetary speculation and a black market in drugs to underage prostitution.[14] This atmosphere inevitably nurtured a reputation for sexual permissiveness; behaviors unthinkable in much of Europe and America became local badges of honor. Writing in the 1950s, William Burroughs sums up the appeal of Tangier as a haven for those gay, bisexual and otherwise sexually marginalized Anglo-American artists and intellectuals whose desires were a source of persecution back home: 'The special attraction of Tangier can be put in one word: exemption. Exemption from interference, legal or otherwise. Your private life is your own, to act exactly as you please. . . . It is a sanctuary of noninterference' (p. 59).

Given the reality of homosexual persecution that drove a number of Europeans and Americans to make Tangier their home,[15] I do not mean to undervalue the degree to which these gay enclaves created self-affirming communities impossible elsewhere or to overlook the degree to which these

Fig. 4. Best known for his photographs of nude Italian boys of North African origin striking various Hellenic poses, Wilhelm von Gloeden capitalizes on the orientalist motif of the beautiful Arab boy in his portrait series Ahmed, 1890–1900, which was reproduced as tourist postcards. (Collection Lebeck. Reproduced by permission of Agfa Foto-Historama, Cologne.)

expatriate communities, however privileged in their trappings, sometimes allowed for the emergence of desires and practices resistant to the dominant Western erotology of romantic coupling. But the 'sanctuary of non-interference' that Burroughs applauds was no gay utopia. The intersection of this 'sanctuary' for gay men with certain historical and economic factors of Western colonialism allowed a level of exploitation potentially as objectionable as the experience of marginalization and harassment that sent these Western voyagers abroad in the first place. Sex for sale provides an obvious but far from simple example. As Alfred Chester notes, '[i]t is traditional in Morocco to pay for sex', and although the Westerner may find the price nominal, 'to the Moslem it can be enough to live on – and when it is, there is no escaping the fact that, however gilded it is by tradition, prostitution is taking place'. Chester then wickedly adds, in reference to the vaunted primacy of ends over means in Moroccan men's sex practices, 'What makes it adorable to people at either end of the banknote is that, though the Moslem is an employee, he really and truly loves his work' (p. 225). There may be more than a grain of truth in Chester's final turn of phrase: local economies of Moroccan sex can latch on to, participate in and even exploit 'exploitative' Western practices in complex and unpredictable ways. 'Love' of work, however, does not erase the dynamics of power that many employers would rather believe their employees consider mere technicalities of the trade. The novelist Robin Maugham, a longtime Tangier resident, anecdotally sums up the political subtext of such tensions in relating an incident that occurred after the granting of Moroccan independence in 1956. Hassled during a walk with visitors by the persistent propositions of a young boy, one of Maugham's companions snaps, 'Oh do go home'; to this rebuke the boy replies in English, '*You* go home, you go home . . . and don't come back to *my* country' ('Peter Burton', p. 145; emphases added). In a colonial context, what and where is 'home', and whose home is it?

Within this tradition of gay occidental tourism, Gide's 1902 novel of sexual discovery, *L'immoraliste* (*The Immoralist*) is paradigmatic, relentlessly disclosing beneath its veneer of reticence a narrative of homosexual – and specifically pederastic – awakening.[16] The text opens with Michel's confessing to a group of friends summoned from France the story of his marriage and near-fatal honeymoon trip to an Arabic world that, as a scholar of orientalism, he has hitherto possessed only through books. After almost dying in Tunis from a tubercular attack, Michel is nursed back to health in Algeria, where he undergoes a voluptuous awakening to the exotic foreign landscape, which envelops him in its 'richer, hotter blood' and penetrates to 'the most . . . secret fibers of [his] being' (p. 52). The Nietzschean dialectic of freedom versus culture, body versus mind, that evolves as Michel embraces a life of sensual abandon barely covers the homoerotic subtext that the text continually teases the reader to decode.

The first clue to this coded subtext is Gide's representation of Michel's gaze, which uncovers in brief flashes the naked limbs of Arab boys and youths beneath loose clothing. A second, related clue to Gide's gay subtext is the procession of pubescent boys who pass through Michel's quarters or whom Michel encounters on walks during his convalescence. A third clue lies in Michel's growing obsession with masks, deceit and concealment – an obsession, in effect, with the homosexual art of passing and getting away with it. A fourth clue involves Gide's manipulation of Michel's language so that the words always seem on the verge of saying something other than what they ultimately reveal.[17] That the reader is being actively solicited to decode the 'open secret' of these passages is spelled out in an aside in which Michel compares himself to a text – specifically, to a palimpsest beneath whose 'more recent' layers the scholar digs to find the 'more precious ancient text', that of the repressed self (p. 51).

But the possibility of leading (and writing) a double life, coupled with Michel's growing recognition of his own latent desires, breeds profound ambivalence, for in a complex process of internalization that amounts to a fetishizing of the closet, Michel's psyche translates secret desires into necessarily criminal ones. The ultimate measure of Michel's 'criminality' is his neglect of Marceline, whose health has declined as his has improved and whose death Michel guarantees by forcing her to return with him to North Africa, the scene of his homoerotic awakening – symbolically her death ensures that Michel can live as a free man. But to be free translates for Michel into utter immersion in sensual self-gratification at the expense of other selves. 'I'm afraid that what I have suppressed will take its revenge,' he tells his auditors and, then, in a revelation withheld till the novel's final lines, the reader learns of Michel's pederastic relationship with the Kabyl child Ali, whose caresses, 'in exchange for a few sous', are 'what keeps [Michel there] more than anything else' (pp. 170–1), sunk into torpid surrender to inner passions projected outward onto the African landscape. 'This climate, I believe, is what's responsible for the change,' he says. 'Nothing discourages thought so much as this perpetual blue sky. Here any exertion is impossible, so closely does pleasure follow desire' (170).

The disturbing conflation that this conclusion effects between homoerotic surrender and the lure of North African otherness points to the unconscious colonialism involved in Gide's projection of a narrative of gay awakening onto the Near East. Michel's awakening depends on the orientalist move of equating the Near East almost exclusively with the body and with surfeit: for Michel, North Africa can be apprehended only sensually, and that mode of apprehension leaves no room for art or intellect. 'Art is leaving me, I feel it,' says Michel, '[but] to make room for . . . what?' (p. 163). Michel's awakening also depends on his refusal to see the actual foreign others who embody his desire as anything other than objects: boys, once Michel realizes he desires them, form an endless chain of anonymous, available bodies, the means to his awakening, never subjects of their own stories or desires.

The economic underpinnings of this exchange in boys as objects of Western consumption, only hinted at in Gide, are made explicit in Orton's diary account of his and Ken Halliwell's sexual escapades in Tangier in 1967. Orton's diary in fact owes its inspiration to his agent's suggestion that Orton start a 'journal *à la Gide*' of his travels (Lahr, p. 12). The Morocco entries emulate Gide with a vengeance, recording the constant stream of youths trooping in and out of Orton's Tangier flat. The flat, however, is not all that is paid for: Orton takes as a given, indeed as a source of stimulation, that you get what you pay for and pay for what you get in terms of Tangier trade, and he records with cynical humor the bargaining that undergirds sexual pleasure in Morocco. Who could want more, he sardonically muses, than 'the [daily] company of beautiful fifteen-year-old boys who find (for a small fee) fucking with me a delightful sensation'? (p. 186).

A corollary of the occidental tourist's fantasy that all boys are available for the right price is the assumption that they represent interchangeable versions of the same commodity: (nearly) underage sex. The number of identically named Mohammeds that Orton meets thus becomes a running joke in his diary ('His name, inevitably, was Mohammed' [p. 193]), and to keep his schedule of assignations from becoming hopelessly muddled, Orton assigns the boys farcical surnames: Mohammed (I), Mohammed Yellow-jersey, Mohammed Gold-tooth. What may be humorous in the abstract is of course dehumanizing in reality, for such typecasting only reinforces the boys' anonymity and dispensability.[18] Tellingly, Orton not only turns against the one Mohammed who attempts to assert his individuality – proudly declaring to Joe and company that he is off to Gibraltar to make a life for himself, with a legitimate job – but also belittles this ambition as bourgeois careerism and then claims, to top it off, that Mohammed is a bad lay. Not coincidentally, it is also this Mohammed who has asserted his subjectivity by complaining to Orton, 'You give me money, yes – but me want *l'amour*. Me like you. Me want *l'amour*' (p. 174). *L'amour*, of course, is the one item missing from the vacation cruise package Orton has signed up for.

As a gay adventurer in Tangier, then, Orton manifests the contradictions of the colonialist abroad; he hates and mocks the general run of tourists for ruining '*our* town' (p. 187), while at the same time he depends on the hierarchical dynamic of (moneyed) white man/(purchased) brown boy to make his own vacation a success. This doubleness repeats itself in the contradiction between Orton's courageous rebellion against sexual orthodoxy (exemplified in his enjoyment of sex for its own sake) and his basic phallocentrism (categorizing each boy he has had as a 'very valuable addition to [his] collection' [p. 186]). Finally, this appropriation of the East manifests itself on the level where sexual and textual pleasures combine for Orton. For his diary entries, as a record of conquests meant to keep the excitement going, become yet another means of possessing the foreign other, but as textual image rather than as physical body. As Orton writes of one particularly steamy encounter: 'At [that] moment with my cock in his arse the *image* was, and *as I write still* is, overpoweringly erotic' (p. 207; emphases added). If Orton does not manifest the anxieties of textual and sexual authority or the loss of the desire to write present in many writers' homoerotic negotiations with the Near East, it is because Orton's confidence in his gay identity allows him to reassert the coupling of writerly authority and male potency that has always characterized phallocentric discourse, but now in the name of homosexual rather than heterosexual pleasure.

The continuities represented by Gide's and Orton's responses to the North African trade in boys are played out in numerous Western narratives written by gay or bisexual men.[19] In contrast, the Moroccan storyteller Mohammed Mrabet's *Love with a Few Hairs* dramatically recasts the plot of *L'immoraliste* from the perspective of the kept Arab boy: here the sexual object – also named Mohammed – becomes the subject of his own story, a story that renders the Westerner, or Nazarene, the anonymous other.[20] The first sentence of Mrabet's tale – 'Mohammed lived with Mr. David, an Englishman who owned a small hotel near the beach' – introduces the kept-boy theme matter-of-factly, indeed as a fact of life. The reader next learns that 'only [one] thing about Mohammed's life . . . [had] made his father sad . . . during the four years he had been living with Mr. David'. Any expectation that the father's unhappiness may involve the propriety of Mohammed's having maintained a sexual relationship since the age of thirteen with a man the father's age is quickly deflated: the vice that disturbs the father is not sex but alcohol abuse: 'One day soon you'll be getting married. Do you want your wife and children to see you drunk?' (p. 1). Here the structural opposition is between drinking and marriage, not between marriage and a pederastic relationship, for in the narrative that unfolds – the story of Mohammed's ill-fated infatuation with a girl named Mina – the relationship with Mr. David hovers uninterrupted in the background, in a stratum of Tangier life proximate to, but held at a distance from, the story of 'love with a few hairs' – a reference to the magic potion Mohammed procures to make Mina love him.

The text's opening also spells out the economics of the occidental trade in boys, but from a Moroccan perspective. The family, it is clear, looks on Mr. David as a benefactor who periodically brings Mohammed's father 'gifts' that the father can sell on the black market (p. 2). This understood exchange, whereby Mohammed is passed from father to paternal lover, is only one of the many monetary exchanges that Mrabet depicts as affecting all facets of Moroccan life. Within this framework, the Western tourist's guiding principle of promiscuous sexual consumerism – you get what you pay for – gives way to the more pervasive local economies of barter. Sex, as a result, becomes Mohammed's most effective bargaining chip, both in manipulating Mr. David for the money to finance marriage to Mina and in maneuvering to stay in Mr. David's good graces despite the marriage. Here Mrabet's artistry is at its most subtle, as carefully placed variations on the sentence 'That night Mohammed slept with Mr. David' signal the economic and emotional pressures of Mohammed's adjacent heterosexual love life: when he needs money or feels unhappy, Mohammed knows where to go and what to do. In this recasting of the Gidean fantasy from the perspective of the indigenous subject, it is the

Western benefactor and not the Moroccan boy who is kept virtually anonymous: the reader never even learns whether *David* is Mr. David's given name or his surname. Whatever the degree of his seemingly real affection for Mr. David, Mohammed ultimately sees his patron as indistinguishable from the other Nazarenes hanging out in Tangier, and this perspective dramatically reverses the dynamics of otherness that rule in Gide and in Orton.

Yet Mrabet's demystification of the colonialist fantasy of the trade in boys coexists with acceptance of the misogyny and sexism that mark many of the Western narratives discussed here. This contiguity between Eastern and Western sexism is most pronounced in the collusion of Moroccan male culture and of Mr. David's occidental cohorts in supporting Mohammed's scheme to get his marriage annulled by treating Mina so badly that she will beg to be let go. The narrative's entire trajectory works toward a demonstration of the correctness of Mr. David's admonition 'Don't trust any woman' (p. 177), which in turn reinforces Mina's expendability in the plot's economy of desire. While Mr. David takes Mohammed's bisexuality as a given, he also encourages Mohammed to maintain a string of girlfriends, rather than a single relationship. It is Mohammed's acceptance of this advice that forms Mrabet's conclusion: a reformed Mohammed moves back in with Mr. David, 'ha[s] other girls but [does] not let himself love any of them' and lives happily ever after (p. 196). The text's erasure of Mina is finalized when, years later, Mohammed encounters her when he is on the way to visit his father (from whom Mohammed has been estranged because of his marriage to Mina). After escaping Mina, Mohammed hurries, in the text's last line, 'quickly [on] to his father's house' (p. 198). The closing words thus reestablish the alignment between Mohammed's father and Mr. David, between Eastern and Western patriarchy, that opens the narrative, proving that *fathers* know best: 'You should be like the Englishman,' Mohammed's father scolds him in the novel's opening scene. 'He doesn't go out into the street drunk' (p. 2). And one of the last things the reader learns about Mohammed is that he now rarely drinks – he has become not only a 'good' Muslim like his religiously observant father but also a mirror of his Western paternal lover.

These pages trace a number of crossings over hypothetical borders or divisions: East/West, female/male, homosexual/heterosexual, colonized/colonizer, among others. As the lines between these terms blur, neither the dichotomies that these pairings purport to describe nor the hierarchical arrangements they are meant to enforce prove to be so apparent. In particular, by gridding the geographical and sexual oppositions – West/East, heterosexual/homosexual – on to and across each other's axes, I have attempted to call attention to the sexual and textual politics that complicate many Western male travelers' encounters with a homoeroticized Near East. In accounts of orientalism that assume the heterosexuality of the erotic adventurer, for example, the confrontation with the specter of homosexuality that lurks in Western fantasies of Eastern decadence destabilizes the assumed authority of the tourist as a distant, uncontaminated spectator. In narratives where the occidental traveler by virtue of his homosexuality is already the other, the presumed *equivalence* of Eastern homosexuality and occidental personal liberation may disguise the specter of colonial privilege and exploitation encoded in the hierarchy white man/brown boy. And reading Mrabet against Gide's and Orton's narratives shows not only how the *other* other's story can unsettle the assumed hierarchy colonizer/colonized but also how, despite this political critique, a complicitous equivalence between East and West can reestablish itself under the aegis of patriarchy precisely when the tension marking the hierarchy male/female becomes palpable. This return to the gender binary on which sexual hierarchy within patriarchy is based serves as a reminder that the story of many Western men's encounters with the Near East, whatever these tourists' putative sexual orientations, has also been the story of a crisis in male subjectivity – the crisis that by definition is occidental masculinity itself. Every rereading of this story may help Western readers reorient their perceptions of the complex undercurrents of those fantasized geographies of male desire that depend on, even as they resist, the homoerotics of an orientalizing discourse whose phallocentric collusions and resistant excitations this essay has just begun to uncover.[21]

NOTES

1. By *Orient* Said means the Near and Middle East; for insightful critiques of the ways in which Said's terminology unintentionally produces a unified Orient all the more easily dominated by a discursively all-powerful West, see Mani and Frankenberg; Bhabha; and Sharpe. Likewise, while I attempt to make my use of the terms *West* and *East* as specific as possible, it is impossible not to generalize at times; I hope that the context of my statements makes clear when I am using these rhetorical markers as shorthand for much more complex geographic and psychological realities.

2. While Alloula's phrase occurs in a chapter titled 'Oriental Sapphism', his interest lies in the heterosexual viewer for whom images of lesbian love in the harem are created. Said's sidestepping of the homoerotic dimensions of this 'promise (and threat)' is not unique; see the way in which Kabbani raises the specter of homoeroticism only to subsume it into the sexuality of the oriental woman (*Europe's Myths* 80–1). Homosexual practice in the British Empire is addressed by Ronald Hyam, who notes that 'the empire was often an ideal arena for the practice of sexual variation' (5–6); however, his exclusive focus on official British guardians of empire, coupled with his dismissal of feminist criticism, limits his usefulness in analyzing the sexual politics of colonialism. The most thoughtful examination to date of the homoerotic subtexts in Western visions of the Arabic Orient is Marjorie Garber's often dazzling chapter 'The Chic of Araby'.

3. Here terminology becomes, if not a problem, a reminder that defining 'the homosexual' as such is very much a Western enterprise; while male-male sexual practice is plentiful in Muslim culture, there is no Arabic word equivalent to *homosexuality*. The closest approximation is the classical Arabic *liwat*, which designates an act of sodomy performed on or by means of (not with) a boy (Schmitt, pp. 5, 9–11).

4. These literary-artistic vacationers and sojourners have included, among others, Orton, Jean Genet, Tennessee Williams, William Burroughs, Allen Ginsberg, Gregory Corso, Ronald Firbank, Robin Maugham, Angus Stewart, Rupert Croft-Cooke, Michael Davidson, Harold Norse, Truman Capote, Alfred Chester, Ned Rorem and Roland Barthes.

5. In conceiving this project, I am mindful of Jenny Sharpe's warning that '[i]t might well be argued that studies [written within an authorizing Western discourse on] the domination of dominant discourses merely add to their totalizing effects' (p. 138); my presentation attempts to avoid this trap as much as is possible by focusing on an aspect of colonialist discourse – sexuality between men – that remains relatively unauthorized and censored in those 'totalizing' Western discourses to which Sharpe refers. If this investigation owes much to the critiques of European colonialism that have followed in the wake of Said, its gendered analysis is indebted not only to queer theory but also to those many feminist analyses that have engaged issues of colonialism; see Sharpe; Abu-Lughod; El Saadawi; Mernissi; Shaarawi; Lowe; and Woodhull, as well as Spivak's and Mohanty's analyses of the intersections of Western feminist and Third World criticism. I do not focus on same-sex activity between women in this essay, but lesbianism within the harem has also been the subject of much orientalizing commentary since Montesquieu's *Persian Letters*; see the critiques offered by Behdad; Alloula; Croutier. For an account of how some European women have appropriated iconography of the harem as a way of encoding lesbian desire, see Apter's 'Female Trouble',

6. The Arab world that I subsume under the rubric of the Arabic Orient follows, loosely, the definitions unfolded by Bernard Lewis, who traces the historical emergence of an 'Arab' identity that resides as much in a common language, a shared religious faith and a loose confederation of multiple, often highly variable, cultures and nation-states as it does in a single ethnicity or nationality.

7. This assertion is not intended to deny the practice or specificity of sexual relations between males in many strata of Muslim Arabic society. A number of historical factors have influenced the prevalence and (to Western perception) relative tolerance of same-sex love within the nonetheless predominantly heterosexual cultures of the Arabic Orient: the Prophet's relative indifference to male homosexuality (Daniel, p. 40), reflected in stipulations in the Koran that make legal prosecution highly unlikely; the general celebration of all male sexual pleasure in Islamic cultures; the tendency to measure sexuality in terms of activity or passivity rather than in terms of gender; the medieval Persian tradition of pederasty; the latitude offered by sociocommunal codes of propriety and discretion (see Bouhdiba, pp. 103–4, 140–2, 200–10; Daniel 40–42; Schmitt, esp. p. 7; Schmitt and Sofers).

8. For reports of thirteenth- and fourteenth-century testimony, see Boswell, pp. 281–2, and Daniel, p. 62, on Jacques de Vitry's propagandistic (*Oriental History*, William of Ada and Friar Guilliaume Adam. For seventeenth- and eighteenth-century texts reporting the frequency of male-male sexuality in the Near East, see the orientalizing travelogues of Rycaut on Turkey, of Covel on the Levant, and of Sonnini and of Denon on Egypt just before and during the Napoleonic invasion.

9. For further examples of this phenomenon, see my analysis of Hector France's turn-of-the-century travelogue *Musk, Hashish, and Blood* in 'Framing the Phallus' and my reading of the adult film *Sahara Heat* in 'Rubbing Aladdin's Lamp'.

10. Lawrence's collapse of the distinctions between sexual contact and rape should be taken not as a general comment on the physical or psychic abuse experienced by rape victims but as an example of the fantasies engendered by a specifically male cultural fear of anal penetration.

11. After Lawrence returned home to England, the masochistic desire awakened by this shattering of will no longer had to masquerade in Arab drag. For the final ten years of his life, which he spent in England, he engaged in an elaborate ritual of birchings to repeat his original surrender while punishing himself for the pleasure that this punishment stimulated. According to an anonymous eyewitness, Lawrence stipulated that 'the beatings be severe enough to produce a seminal emission' [Mack, p. 433; see also D. Stewart, pp. 244, 275; Maugham, *Escape*, p. 104]).

12. Space limitations prevent me from tracing the homoeroticizing possibilities of donning Arabic dress through their many subsequent permutations. But one might

consider Rudolph Valentino's filmic performances as 'the Sheik'. One might also ponder the homoerotic current that persists even when, as with Isabelle Eberhardt, the white 'man' in Arab drag turns out to be a woman or the frisson that Bowles exploits when Kit Moresby's captor disguises her as an Arab boy in *The Sheltering Sky* (see also Garber, pp. 309–11, 325–6, 335). The pathos of these instances is that the Western subject – real or fictionalized – can imagine male homosexuality only as a total surrender to surfeit, passivity or violation (desired rather than, as with Lawrence, both desired and feared), because the command to yield takes the decision, the agency, out of one's hands. By attempting to become part of a culture whose fatalistic creed is summed up in the saying *mektoub* 'it is written', the occidental tourist recasts 'deviance' as part of an immutable decree beyond individual or authorial control.

13. It is no coincidence that the decade that saw the creation of the pathological category of the homosexual intensified the search for non-European outlets, such as Algeria, for sexual energies increasingly persecuted within Western culture.

14. My phrase 'underage prostitution' begs further definition, as does subsequent use of the term *boys*. Many writers who describe voyages to the Near East use the term *boy* to refer to any male youth from adolescence to late teens and even early twenties. Indeed, the myth of 'younger is better' is so potent a part of gay tourist lore that many Westerners pretend to be engaging in underage sex even when they are not. But for men whose desires are definitionally pederastic, pubescent and prepubescent boys, especially those who come down from the Riffian mountains to eke out a living in the city, are by all accounts readily available. Within a Near Eastern perspective, the term *underage sex* carries little or no meaning and little of the sense of taboo or moral condemnation that it bears within Western constructions of sexuality as an adult activity; a child, particularly one of the peasantry or working class, is never a sexual innocent, indeed is a practicing adult from the time he takes to the streets on his own. See A. Stewart's and Davidson's pederastic narratives, as well as Rossman's survey (pp. 100–2, 116–21) of the North African 'pederast underground'.

15. For example, scandals and prison sentences forced both the respected journalist Michael Davidson (pp. 169–81) and the novelist Rupert Croft-Cooke to leave England for Morocco.

16. For a report of Gide's similar sexual initiation in Algeria, see his autobiography *If It Die . . .* (pp. 267–69, 303), and for a perceptive analysis of the book's colonialist underpinnings, see Michael Lucey ('Gide Writing', p. 30; 'Consequence', pp. 182, 185).

17. Apter identifies the rhetorical strategy whereby the gap in Michel's sentences prefigures an 'unstated subtext of homoeroticism' as anacoluthon (*Gide*, pp. 113–15).

18. Since part of the Moroccan vacation fantasy has to do not simply with availability but with youth, Orton's other means of differentiating among his prospects is to assign an age to each (a 'very attractive fifteen-year-old boy', 'a quite nice looking boy of seventeen, 'a very pretty boy of about eleven' [pp. 174, 184, 209]). And yet so strong is the myth that younger is better that Orton scales down his original estimates: thus Mohammed, 'a very beautiful sixteen-year-old boy' at the beginning of the 9 May entry, is 'about fifteen' by 25 May and 'fourteen' by 11 June (pp. 160, 185, 260).

19. Examples include Maugham's *The Wrong People* (1964), Norse's 'Six for Mohammed Riffi' (1962–63), Chester's 'Glory Hole: Nickel Views of the Infidel in Tangiers' (1963–65), Croft-Cooke's *Exiles* (1970), Angus Stewart's *Tangier: A Writer's Notebook* (1977), Scott Symon's *Helmet of Flesh* (1986), and Aldo Busi's *Sodomies in Eleven Point* (1992).

20. Transcribed and translated from the Maghrebi by Bowles, Mrabet's text also illustrates an ironic 'payoff' of the colonial trade in boys: for Bowles has not only worked indefatigably for over three decades to secure publication and recognition

for rising young Moroccan writers but also made handsome protégés like Mrabet into favored male companions. The implicit power dynamic of Western patron/Moroccan youth underpinning these touted 'literary collaborations' thus participates in and complicates the erotic transactions that form this essay's subject. Another narrative told from the point of view of the kept Moroccan boy is Larbi Layachi's *A Life Full of Holes*.

21. This essay has benefited greatly from the responsive audiences it has met at the University of California, Berkeley; the Humanities Center at the University of California, Davis; Georgetown University's 1990 Conference on Literary Theory; the 1991 Unauthorized Sexual Behaviors conference at the University of California, Riverside; and the University of Southern California's Life of the Mind series. Thanks are also due to Earl Jackson, Ed Cohen, Lee Edelman, David Román. Hilary Schor, Jim Kincaid, Jonathan Strong, and Scott Elledge for their insightful comments, as well as to Parama Roy, Sandra Naddaff, Emily Apter, Karen Lawrence, Michael Lucey, Nancy Paxton and Greg Mullins for sharing ideas, work and citations from related projects.

Works Cited

Abu-Lughod, Lila, *Veiled Sentiments: Honour and Poetry in a Bedouin Society*. Princeton: Princeton UP, 1986.

Alloula, Malek. *The Colonial Harem*. Trans. Myrna Godzich and Wlad Godzich. 1981. Minneapolis: U of Minnesota P, 1986.

Apter, Emily. *André Gide and the Codes of Homotextuality*. Stanford French and Italian Studies 48. Stanford: Stanford UP, 1987.

——. 'Female Trouble in the Colonial Harem'. *Differences* 4.1 (1992): pp. 205–24.

Behdad, Ali. 'The Eroticized Orient: Images of the Harem in Montesquieu and His Precursors'. *Stanford French Review* 13 (1989), pp. 109–26.

Bentham, Jeremy. *Works of Jeremy Bentham*. Ed. John Bowring. 1838–43. 11 vols. New York: Russell, 1962.

Bersani, Leo. 'Is the Rectum a Grave?' *AIDS: Cultural Analysis/Cultural Activism*. Ed. Douglas Crimp. Cambridge: MIT P, 1987: pp. 197–222.

Bhabha, Homi K. 'The Other Question . . . Homi K. Bhabha Reconsiders the Stereotype and Colonial Discourse'. *Screen* 24 (1983): pp. 18–36.

Boone, Joseph A. 'Framing the Phallus in the *Arabian Nights*: Pansexuality, Pederasty, Pasolini'. *Translations/Transformations: Gender and Culture in Film and Literature*. Proceedings of the Literary Studies East and West Conference. Ed. Cornelia Moore and Valerie Wayne. Honolulu: U of Hawaii P, 1993: pp. 22–33.

——. 'Mappings of Male Desire in Durrell's *Alexandra Quartet*'. *Displacing Homophobia*. Spec. issue of *South Atlantic Quarterly* 88 (1989): pp. 73–106.

——. 'Rubbing Aladdin's Lamp'. *Negotiating Lesbian and Gay Subjects*. Ed. Monica Dorenkamp and Richard Henke. New York: Routledge, 1995.

Boswell, John. *Christianity, Social Tolerance, and Homosexuality*. Chicago: U of Chicago P, 1980.

Bouhdiba, Abdelwahab. *Sexuality in Islam*. London: Routledge, 1985.

Burroughs, William S. *Interzone*. New York: Viking. 1989.

Burton, Richard, trans. and ed. The Book of the Thousand Nights and a Night: *A Plain and Literal Translation of the Arabian Nights Entertainments*. Ed. Burton Club. 10 vols. London: n.p., 1885–86.

——. *Personal Narrative of a Pilgrimage to Al-Madinah and Meccah*. 1893. 2 vols. New York: Dover, 1964.

Chester, Alfred. 'Glory Hole: Nickel Views of the Infidel in Tangiers'. *Head of a Sad Angel: Stories, 1953–1966*. Santa Rosa: Black Sparrow, 1990: pp. 217–31.

Covel, John. 'Dr John Covel's Diary (1670–79)'. *Early Voyages and Travels in the Levant*. Ed. J. Theodore Bent. London, Clark: 1893: pp. 101–287.

Croft-Cooke, Rupert. *The Verdict of You All*. London: Allen, 1974.

Crompton, Louis. *Byron and Greek Love: Homophobia in Nineteenth-Century England*. Berkeley: U of California P, 1985.

Croutier, Alev Lytle. *Harem: The World behind the Veil*. New York: Abbeville, 1989.

Daniel, Marc. 'Arab Civilization and Male Love'. 1975–76. *Gay Roots: Twenty Years of Gay Sunshine: An Anthology of Gay History, Sex, Politics, and Culture*. Ed. Winston Leyland. San Francisco: Gay Sunshine, 1991: pp. 33–75.

Davidson, Michael. *The World, the Flesh, and Myself*. 1962. London: GMP, 1985.

Denon, Vivant. *Travels in Upper and Lower Egypt*. 2 vols. New York: n.p., 1803.

Durrell, Lawrence. *Alexandria Quartet*. 4 vols. New York: Pocket, 1957–60.

Edwardes, Allen. *Erotica Judaica: A Sexual History of the Jews*. New York: Julian, 1967.

——. *The Jewel in the Lotus: A Historical Survey of the Sexual Culture of the East*. New York: Julian, 1959.

Edwardes, Allen and R. E. L. Masters. *The Cradle of Erotica*. New York: Julian, 1963.

Flaubert, Gustave. *Flaubert in Egypt: A Sensibility on Tour*. Trans. and ed. Francis Steegmuller. Chicago: Academy Chicago, 1979.

France, Hector. *Musk, Hashish and Blood*. London: n.p., 1900.

Garber, Marjorie. *Vested Interests: Cross-Dressing and Cultural Anxiety*. New York: Routledge, 1992.

Gide, André. *If It Die . . . : An Autobiography*. Trans. Dorothy Bussy. New York: Random, 1935. Trans. of *Si le grain ne meurt*.

——. *The Immoralist*. 1902 Trans. Richard Howard. New York: Vintage, 1970. Trans. of *L'immoraliste*.

Hindley, John. *Persian Lyrics: or, Scattered Poems from the Diwan-i-Hafiz*. London: Harding. 1800.

Hyam, Ronald. *Empire and Sexuality: The British Experience*. Manchester. Manchester UP, 1990.

Kabbani, Rana. *Europe's Myths of Orient: Devise and Rule*. London: Macmillan, 1986.

——. ed *The Passionate Nomad: The Diary of Isabelle Eberhardt*. Boston: Beacon. 1987.

Lahr, John. Introduction. *The Orton Diaries*. New York: Perennial-Harper, 1986: pp. 11–31.

Lane, Edward William. *An Account of the Manners and Customs of the Modern Egyptians*. 1833–35. London: Gardner, 1898.

Lant, Antonia. 'The Curse of the Pharoah; or, How Cinema Contracted Egyptomania'. *October 59* (1992): pp. 86–112.

Lawrence, T. E. *Seven Pillars of Wisdom: A Triumph*. 1926. London: Penguin, 1963.

——. *T. E. Lawrence: The Selected Letters*. Ed. Malcolm Brown. New York: Norton, 1988.

Layachi, Larbi. *A Life Full of Holes*. Trans. Paul Bowles. New York: Grove, 1982.

Lewis, Bernard. *The Arabs in History*. Rev. ed. New York: Torchbooks-Harper, 1960.

Lowe, Lisa. *Critical Terrains: French and British Orientalisms*. Ithaca: Cornell UP, 1991.

Lucey, Michael, 'The Consequence of Being Explicit: Watching Sex in Gide's *Si le grain ne meurt*'. *Yale Journal of Criticism* 4.1 (1990): pp. 174–92.

——. 'Gide Writing Home from Africa; or, From Biskra with Love'. *Qui Parle* 4.2 (1991): pp. 23–42.

Mack, John E. *A Prince of Our Disorder: The Life of T. E. Lawrence*. Boston: Little, 1976.

Mailer, Norman. *Ancient Evenings*. Boston: Little, 1983.

Mani, Lata and Ruth Frankenberg. 'The Challenge of *Orientalism*'. *Economy and Society* May 1985: pp. 174–92.

Maugham, Robin. *Escape from the Shadows*. New York: McGraw, 1973.

——. 'Peter Burton Interviews Robin Maugham'. *The Boy from Beirut and Other Stories*. San Francisco: Gay Sunshine, 1982: pp. 109–60.

Mernissi, Fatima. *Beyond the Veil: Male-Female Dynamics in Modern Muslim Society*. Bloomington: Indiana UP, 1987.

Mitchell, Timothy. *Colonizing Egypt*. Cambridge: Cambridge UP, 1988.

Mohanty, Chandra Talpade. 'Under Western Eyes: Feminist Scholarship and Colonial Discourses'. *Third World Women and the Politics of Feminism*. Eds Mohanty, Ann Russo and Lourdes Torres. Bloomington: Indiana UP, 1991: pp. 51–80.

Mrabet, Mohammed. *Love with a Few Hairs*. Trans. Paul Bowles. 1967. San Francisco: City Lights, 1986.

Naddaff, Sandra. *Arabesque: Narrative Structure and the Aesthetics of Repetition* in The Thousand and One Nights. Evanston: Northwestern UP, 1991.

Orton, Joe. *The Orton Diaries*. Ed. John Lahr. New York: Perennial-Harper, 1986.

Rossman, Parker. *Sexual Experience between Men and Boys: Exploring the Pederast Underground*. New York: Association, 1976.

Rycaut, Paul. *The Present State of the Ottomon Empire*. London: Starkey, 1668.

El Saadawi, Nawal. *The Hidden Face of Eve: Women in the Arab World*. London: Zed, 1980.

Said, Edward. *Orientalism*. New York: Vintage, 1979.

Schmitt, Arno. 'Different Approaches to Male-Male Sexuality/Eroticism from Morocco to Usbekistan'. Schmitt and Sofers, pp. 1–24.

Schmitt, Arno and Jehoeda Sofers, eds. *Sexuality and Eroticism among Males in Moslem Societies*. New York: Harrington Park, 1992.

Shaarawi, Huda. *Harem Years: Memoirs of an Egyptian Feminist*. London: Virago, 1986.

Sharpe, Jenny. 'Figures of Colonial Resistance'. *Modern Fiction Studies* 35 (1989): pp. 137–55.

Silverman, Kaja. 'White Skin, Brown Masks: The Double Mimesis; or, With Lawrence in Arabia'. *Differences* 1.3 (1989): pp. 3–54.

Sonnini, C. S. *Travels in Upper and Lower Egypt*. Trans. Henry Hunter. 3 vols. London: Stockdale, 1807.

Spivak, Gayatri Chakravorty. *In Other Worlds: Essays in Cultural Politics*. New York: Routledge, 1988.

Stewart, Angus. *Tangier: A Writer's Notebook*. London: Hutchinson, 1977.

Stewart, Desmond. *T. E. Lawrence*. New York: Harper, 1977.

Sutor, Jacob [Dr. Jacobus X]. *Untrodden Fields of Anthropology: Observations on the Esoteric Manner and Customs of Semi-civilized Peoples*. 2 vols. Paris: Librarie de Medecine, Folklore et Anthropologie, 1898. Trans. of *L'amour aux colonies*.

Wickes, George. *Lawrence Durrell-Henry Miller: A Private Correspondence*. New York: Dutton, 1963.

Woodhull, Winifred. 'Unveiling Algeria'. *Genders* 10 (1991): pp. 112–31.

PART 5
HAREM AND THE VEIL

5.1

'THE MEANING OF SPATIAL BOUNDARIES'

Fatima Mernissi

Muslim sexuality is territorial: its regulatory mechanisms consist primarily in a strict allocation of space to each sex and an elaborate ritual for resolving the contradictions arising from the inevitable intersections of spaces.[1] Apart from the ritualized trespasses of women into public spaces (which are, by definition, male spaces), there are no accepted patterns for interactions between unrelated men and women. Such interactions violate the spatial rules that are the pillars of the Muslim sexual order. Only that which is licit is formally regulated. Since the interaction of unrelated men and women is illicit, there are no rules governing it. Those people now experiencing sexual desegregation are therefore compelled to improvise. And, whereas imitation is possible, creation is far more difficult.

Boundaries are never established gratuitously. Society does not form divisions purely for the pleasure of breaking the social universe into compartments. The institutionalized boundaries dividing the parts of society express the recognition of power in one part at the expense of the other.[2] Any transgression of the boundaries is a danger to the social order because it is an attack on the acknowledged allocation of power. The link between boundaries and power is particularly salient in a society's sexual patterns.

> Patterns of sexual dangers can be seen to express symmetry or hierarchy. It is impossible to interpret them as expressing something about the actual relation of the sexes. I suggest that many ideas about sexual dangers are

From: Fatima Mernissi (1975), 'The Meaning of Spacial Boundaries', pp. 137–47, in Fatima Mernissi, *Beyond the Veil: Male–Female Dynamics in Muslim Society* (London: Al Saqi Books).

better interpreted as symbols of the relation between parts of society, as mirroring designs of hierarchy or symmetry which apply in the larger social system.[3]

The symbolism of sexual patterns certainly seems to reflect society's hierarchy and power allocation in the Muslim order. Strict space boundaries divide Muslim society into two subuniverses: the universe of men (the *umma*, the world religion and power) and the universe of women, the domestic world of sexuality and the family. The spatial division according to sex reflects the division between those who hold authority and those who do not, those who hold spiritual powers and those who do not.[4] The division is based on the physical separation of the *umma* (the public sphere) from the domestic universe. These two universes[5] of social interaction are regulated by antithetical concepts of human relations, one based on community, the other on conflict.

Membership of the Two Universes

The Public Universe of the Umma
The believers. Women's position in the *umma* universe is ambiguous; Allah does not talk to them directly. We can therefore assume that the *umma* is primarily male believers.

The Domestic Universe of Sexuality
Individuals of both sexes as primarily sexual beings. But because men are not supposed to spend their time in the domestic unit, we may assume that the members are in fact women only.

Principles Regulating Relations Between Members

The Umma
Equality
Reciprocity
Aggregation
Unity, Communion
Brotherhood, Love
Trust

The Family
Inequality
Lack of Reciprocity
Segregation
Separation, Division
Subordination, Authority
Mistrust

COMMUNAL RELATIONSHIP

A social relationship will be so-called 'communal' if and so far as the orientation of social action is based on subjective feeling of the parties, whether affectual or traditional, that they belong together.[6]

The universe of the *umma* is communal; its citizens are persons who unite in a democratic collectivity based on a sophisticated concept of belief in a set of ideas, which is geared to produce integration and cohesion of all members who participate in the unifying task.

CONFLICT RELATIONSHIP

A social relationship will be referred to as a 'conflict' in so far as action within it is oriented intentionally to carrying out the actor's own will against the resistance of the other party or parties.[7]

The citizens of the domestic universe are primarily sexual beings; they are defined by their genitals and not by their faith. They are not united, but are divided into two categories: men, who have power, and women, who obey. Women – who are citizens of this domestic universe and whose existence outside that sphere is considered an anomaly, a transgression – are subordinate to men, who (unlike their women) also possess a second nationality, one that grants them membership of the public sphere, the domain of religion and politics, the domain of power, of the management of the affairs of the *umma*. Having been identified as primarily citizens of the domestic universe, women are then deprived of power even within the world in which they are confined, since it is the man who wields authority within the family. The duty of Muslim women is to obey (as is very clear in the *Muduwana* and in Malik's *al-Muwatta*, from which it is inspired and on which it is based). The separation of the two groups, the hierarchy that subordinates the one to the other, is expressed in institutions that discourage, and even prohibit, any communication between the sexes. Men and women are supposed to collaborate in only one of the tasks required for the survival of society: procreation.

In fact, whenever cooperation between men and women is inevitable, as between the members of a couple, an entire array of mechanisms is set in motion to prevent too great an intimacy from arising between the partners. Sexual segregation thus fuels, and is fuelled by, the conflicts that it is supposed to avoid between men and women. Or better, sexual segregation intensifies what it is supposed to eliminate: the sexualization of human relations.

THE SECLUSION OF WOMEN

In order to prevent sexual interaction between members of the *umma* and members of the domestic universe, seclusion and veiling (a symbolic form of seclusion) were developed. But paradoxically, sexual segregation heightens the sexual dimension of any interaction between men and women.

In a country like Morocco, in which heterosexual encounter is the focus of so many restrictions, and consequently of so much attention, seduction becomes a structural component of human relations in general, whether between individuals of the same sex or between men and women.

I have concentrated my discussion here on heterosexual relations, but our understanding of sexual identity cannot be complete without studies clarifying the interaction among individuals of the same sex. A society that opts for sexual segregation, and therefore for impoverishment of heterosexual relations, is a society that fosters 'homosocial' relations[8] on the one hand and seduction as a means of communication on the other. Seduction is a conflict strategy, a way of seeming to give of yourself and of procuring great pleasure without actually giving anything. It is the art of abstaining from everything while playing on the promise of giving. It is a childish art in that the child has a vital need to protect itself, but for an adult it is the expression of an often uncontrollable emotional avarice. It is very rare that an individual who has invested years in learning seduction as a mode of interchange can suddenly open up and lavish all his (or her) 'emotional treasures' on the person he has finally chosen to love.

In a society in which heterosexual relations are combated, emotional fulfilment is inhibited. As we are taught to fear and mistrust the other sex, and therefore to relate to its members through seduction, manipulation and domination, we become mere puppets who extend the games of seduction, acceptable during adolescence, into our relations as mature men and women.

The hedonistic enhancement of the beauty of the human body seems to have been a pronounced Mediterranean characteristic of Morocco which Islam failed to curb. Body adornment with both jewelry and cosmetics is an integral part of socialization. Even men, at least the generation now in their sixties, used to wear cosmetics to darken their eyelids (*khol*) and lips (*swak*) for religious rituals and festivals. Islam took an unequivocally negative attitude towards body ornamentation, especially for women.[9] It required pious women to be modest in their appearance and hide all ornamentation and eye-catching beauty behind veils.

> And tell the believing women to lower their gaze and be modest, and to display of their adornment only that which is apparent and to draw their veils over their bosoms, and not to reveal their adornment save to their own husbands or fathers or husband's fathers, or their sons or their husband's sons, or their women, or their slaves, or male attendants who lack vigour or children who know naught of women's nakedness. And let them not stamp their feet so as to reveal what they hide of their adornment. And turn unto Allah together, O believers, in order that ye may succeed.[10]

According to Ghazali, the eye is undoubtedly an erogenous zone in the Muslim structure of reality, just as able to give pleasure as the penis. A man can do as much damage to a woman's honour with his eyes as if he were to seize hold of her with his hands.

> To look at somebody else's wife is a sinful act. . . . The look is fornication of the eye, but if the sexual apparatus is not set in motion by it [if the man does not attempt to have sexual intercourse], it is a much more easily pardoned act.[11]

When the Prophet was asking God to protect him from the most virulent social dangers, he asked for help in controlling his penis and his eye from the dangers of fornication.[12]

The theory that seclusion in Islam is a device to protect the passive male who cannot control himself sexually in the presence of the lust-inducing female is further substantiated by verse 60 of sura 24, which explains that elderly women (supposed to be unattractive) can go unveiled. Belghiti's survey of rural women, among whom seclusion is the prevailing mode, reveals that the restrictions on women's movements do not apply to elderly women, who consequently have a greater freedom.[13]

The seclusion of women, which to Western eyes is a source of oppression, is seen by many Muslim women as a source of pride.[14] The traditional women interviewed all perceived seclusion as prestigious. In rural Morocco seclusion is considered the privilege of women married to rich men.[15]

Harems, the ultimate form of seclusion, were considered even more prestigious, since they required huge economic assets. One of the women I interviewed, Salama, lived most of her life as a concubine in a harem. This is unusual even by Moroccan standards, and her experience contrasts sharply with that of most women. Because women are not allowed to leave a harem, sexual segregation is more successfully realized there than in the average, monogamous family. Successful seclusion of human beings requires considerable economic investment, because services must be provided at home for the secluded. Other women, who must go out to shop or go to the baths, are under many restrictions outside the home.

The Deseclusion of Women: on the Street

Traditionally, women using public spaces, trespassing on the *umma* universe, are restricted to few occasions and bound by specific rituals,[16] such as the wearing of the veil. The veil is worn by Moroccan women only when they leave the house and walk through the street, which is a male space. The veil means that the woman is present in the men's world, but invisible; she has no right to be in the street.

If chaperoned, women are allowed to trespass into the men's universe on the traditional visits to the *hammam*, the public bath, and to the tomb of the local saint. According to my data, visits to the *hammam* used to be bi-monthly and to the saint's tomb not more than once or twice a year (usually the twenty-seventh day of Ramadan). Both required the husband's permission. The chaperoning was entrusted to an elderly asexual woman, usually the mother-in-law.

Traditionally, only necessity could justify a woman's presence outside the home, and no respect was ever attached to poverty and necessity. Respectable women were not seen on the street. In class-conscious Morocco, the maid, who has to go wherever she can to find a job, occupies the lowest rung of the social scale, and to be called a maid is one of the commonest insults. Only prostitutes and insane women wandered freely in the streets. One expression for a prostitute is *rajlha zahqa*, 'a woman whose foot is slipping'. The Pascon-Bentahar survey revealed that when a rural youth visits a town he assumes that any woman walking down the street is sexually available.[17]

Women in male spaces are considered both provocative and offensive. Since schooling and jobs both require women to be able to move freely through the streets, modernization necessarily exposes many women to public harassment.[18]

In *The Hidden Dimension*, Edward Hall made two perceptive remarks about the use of space in Middle Eastern, Arab-Muslim societies. First, 'there is no such thing as an intrusion in public. Public means public'.[19] It is not possible for an individual to claim a private zone in a public space. This seems quite true for Morocco and has a particular bearing on women's presence in the street, as one might guess.

Second, space has a primarily social rather than physical quality. The notion of trespassing is related not so much to physical boundaries as to the identity of the person performing the act.[20] A friend, for example, never trespasses, while a foe always does.

A woman is always trespassing in a male space because she is, by definition, a foe. A woman has no right to use male spaces. If she enters them, she is upsetting the male's order and his peace of mind. She is actually committing an act of aggression against him merely by being present where she should not be. A woman in a traditionally male space upsets Allah's order by inciting men to commit *zina*. The man has everything to lose in this encounter: peace of mind, self-determination, allegiance to Allah and social prestige.

If the woman is unveiled the situation is aggravated. The Moroccan term for a woman who is not veiled is *aryana* ('nude'), and most women who frequent schools or hold jobs outside the home today are unveiled. The two elements together – trespassing and trespassing in the 'nude' – constitute an open act of exhibitionism.

> Whether the indictable act consists of words spoken, gestures conveyed, or act performed, the communication structure of the event often consists of an individual initiating an engagement with a stranger of the opposite sex by means of the kind of message that would be proper only if they were on close and intimate terms. Apart from psychodynamic issues, exhibitionists often spectacularly subvert social control that keeps individuals interpersonally distant even though they are physically close to each other. The assault here is not so much directly on an individual as on the system of rights and symbols the individual employs in expressing relatedness and unrelatedness to those about him.[21]

The male's response to the woman's presence is, according to the prevailing ideology, a logical response to exhibitionist aggression. It consists in pursuing the woman for hours, pinching her, if the occasion is propitious, and possibly assaulting her verbally, all in the hope of convincing her to carry her exhibitionist propositioning to its implicit end.

During the Algerian revolution, the nationalist movement used women to carry arms and messages. One of the problems the revolutionary movement faced was the harassment of these women by Algerian 'brothers' who mistook them for prostitutes and interfered with the performance of their nationalist task.[22] A similar incident was reported to have taken place near a refugee camp in Lebanon.

A female Palestinian militant was performing her task as a sentinel. She was posted in a deserted spot a few yards away from the camp, her machine-gun on her shoulder, when a Lebanese civilian who noticed her came by to make a proposition. When the woman rejected his advances with indignant words and gestures, the man got angry and said, 'How do you want me to believe that a woman standing alone in the street the whole night has any honour?' The woman is said to have turned her gun towards her suitor and told him, 'I am here in the street soiling my honour to defend yours because you are unable to do it yourself.'[23] In spite of its revolutionary setting, the anecdote reveals that the female militant shares with the male civilian the belief that her being alone in the street is dishonourable. Her reflex was to justify her presence in the male space, not to claim her right to be there.

THE DESECLUSION OF WOMEN: IN THE OFFICE

The absence of modes of relatedness other than genital encounter helps to explain the form of heterosexual encounters in offices as well as on the street.

The 'office' is a recent development in Moroccan history, a legacy of the centralized bureaucracy set up by the French after 1912. After independence, public administration expanded both in terms of offices and posts and in terms of the portion of public resources it swallows. The state is now by far the most important employer in the country. A substantial number of literate working women are in government offices. These women, who often have not finished high school, are typists and secretaries and usually occupy positions subordinate to their male colleagues.[24]

The situation of the working woman in the office is reminiscent of her position in a traditional household and on the street. These conflicting images are likely to stimulate conflicting patterns of behaviour in men. The boss's typist, like his wife and sister, is in a subordinate position, and he has the right to command her. Like them, she is dependent on him (more or less directly) for economic survival. He administers her salary, which is given to her because she provides him with specific services. Her advancement and promotion depend on him. It is therefore not surprising if he comes to confuse her with the woman he dominates because of his economic superiority and institutional authority (in other words, his wife), a step many men seem to take with ease. In any event, the drift that occurs in relations between the bureaucrat and his secretary, generated by his confusion of his privileges as a man and his rights and privileges as a bureaucrat, are not limited to sexual behaviour. Max Weber identified this confusion as one of the problems of the bureaucratic system.

The confusion is inherent in any bureaucratic structure, but it assumes a particularly exaggerated character in Third World societies in which bureaucratization is relatively recent. Morocco, of course, already had its Makhzencentral, but that institution lacked the structures, resources, equipment, and personnel that it now commands. The harassment of the woman state employee occurs because she has transgressed the boundaries of the male space par excellence, the administration of affairs of state. The conflict and tension experienced by women who work in the state administration is proportional to the insolence of their intrusion into the sanctuaries of male power.

Women's increasing encroachment into traditionally male spaces greatly intensifies the sexual aspect of any encounter between men and women, especially in the urban centres. The process of integration of women into the modern circuits of the production system is now quite advanced, however unplanned or even undesired the process may have been. A growing number of women, both educated and illiterate, are invading the labour market and the modern workshops. The aspiration for a *hadma mezyana* (well-paid job) is now shared by poor illiterate women and their more privileged sisters who have gained access to wealth and education.

When women go to work they are not only trespassing in the universe of the *umma* but are also competing with their former masters, men, for the scarce available jobs. The anxiety created by women seeking jobs in the modern sector, and thus demanding a role traditionally reserved for men, inevitably aggravates tension and conflict because of the scarcity of jobs and the high rate of unemployment among men.

* * *

THE FEAR OF FEMALE SEXUALITY

The perception of female aggression is directly influenced by the theory of women's sexuality. For Freud the female's aggression, in accordance with her sexual passivity, is turned inward. She is masochistic.

> The suppression of woman's aggressiveness which is prescribed for them constitutionally and imposed on them socially favours the development of powerful masochistic impulses, which succeed, as we know, in binding erotically the destructive trends which have been diverted inwards. Thus masochism, as people say, is truly feminine. But if, as happens so often, you meet with masochism in men, what is left for you but to say that these men exhibit very plainly feminine traits.[25]

The absence of active sexuality moulds the woman into a masochistic passive being. It is therefore no surprise that in the actively sexual Muslim female aggressiveness is seen as turned outward. The nature of her aggression is precisely sexual. The Muslim woman is endowed with a fatal attraction which erodes the male's will to resist her and reduces him to a passive acquiescent role. He has no choice; he can only give in to her attraction, whence her identification with *fitna*, chaos, and with the anti-divine and anti-social forces of the universe.

The Prophet saw a woman. He hurried to his house and had intercourse with his wife Zaynab, then left the house and said, 'When the woman comes towards you, it is Satan who is approaching you. When one of you sees a woman and he feels attracted to her, he should hurry to his wife. With her, it would be the same as with the other one.'[26]

Commenting on this quotation, Imam Muslim, an established voice of Muslim tradition, reports that the Prophet was referring to the

fascination, to the irresistible attraction to women God instilled in man's soul, and he was referring to the pleasure man experiences when he looks at the woman, and the pleasure he experiences with anything related to her. She resembles Satan in his irresistible power over the individual.[27]

This attraction is a natural link between the sexes. Whenever a man is faced with a woman, *fitna* might occur: 'When a man and a woman are isolated in the presence of each other, Satan is bound to be their third companion.'[28]

The most potentially dangerous woman is one who has experienced sexual intercourse. It is the married woman who will have more difficulties in bearing sexual frustration. The married woman whose husband is absent is a particular threat to men: 'Do not go to the women whose husbands are absent. Because Satan will get in your bodies as blood rushes through your flesh.'[29]

In Moroccan folk culture this threat is epitomized by the belief in Aisha Kandisha, a repugnant female demon. She is repugnant precisely because she is libidinous. She has pendulous breasts and lips and her favourite pastime is to assault men in the streets and in dark places, to induce them to have sexual intercourse with her and ultimately to penetrate their bodies and stay with them for ever.[30] They are then said to be inhabited. The fear of Aisha Kandisha is more than ever present in Morocco's daily life. Fear of the castrating female is a legacy of tradition and is seen in many forms in popular beliefs and practices and in both religious and mundane literature, particularly novels.

Moroccan folk culture is permeated with a negative attitude towards femininity. Loving a woman is popularly described as a form of mental illness, a self-destructive state of mind. A Moroccan proverb says:

Love is a complicated matter
If it does not drive you crazy, it kills you.[31]

The best example of this distrust of women is the sixteenth-century poet Sidi Abderahman al-Majdoub. His rhymes are so popular that they have become proverbs.

Women are fleeting wooden vessels
Whose passengers are doomed to destruction.

Or:

> Don't trust them [women], so you would not be betrayed
> Don't believe in their promises, so you would not be deceived
> To be able to swim, fish need water
> Women are the only creatures who can swim without it.[32]

And finally:

> Women's intrigues are mighty
> To protect myself I run endlessly
> Women are belted with serpents
> And bejewelled with scorpions.[33]

The Muslim order faces two threats: the infidel without and the woman within.

> The Prophet said, 'After my disappearance there will be no greater source of chaos and disorder for my nation than women.'[34]

The irony is that Muslim and European theories come to the same conclusion: women are destructive to the social order – for Imam Ghazali because they are active, for Freud because they are not.

Different social orders have integrated the tensions between religion and sexuality in different ways. In the Western Christian experience sexuality itself was attacked, degraded as animality and condemned as anti-civilization. The individual was split into two antithetical selves: the spirit and the flesh, the ego and the id. The triumph of civilization implied the triumph of soul over flesh, of ego over id, of the controlled over the uncontrolled, of spirit over sex.

Islam took a substantially different path. What is attacked and debased is not sexuality but women, as the embodiment of destruction, the symbol of disorder. The woman is *fitna*, the epitome of the uncontrollable, a living representative of the dangers of sexuality and its rampant disruptive potential. We have seen that Muslim theory considers raw instinct as energy which is likely to be used constructively for the benefit of Allah and His society if people live according to His laws. Sexuality per se is not a danger. On the contrary, it has three positive, vital functions. It allows the believers to perpetuate themselves on earth, an indispensable condition if the social order is to exist at all. It serves as a 'foretaste of the delights secured for men in Paradise',[35] thus encouraging men to strive for paradise and to obey Allah's rule on earth. Finally, sexual satisfaction is necessary to intellectual effort.

The Muslim theory of sublimation is entirely different from the Western Christian tradition as represented by Freudian psychoanalytic theory. Freud viewed civilization as a war against sexuality.[36] Civilization is sexual energy 'turned aside from its sexual goal and diverted towards other ends, no longer sexual and socially more valuable'.[37] The Muslim theory views civilization as the outcome of satisfied sexual energy. Work is the result not of sexual frustration but of a contented and harmoniously lived sexuality.

> The soul is usually reluctant to carry out its duty because duty [work] is against its nature. If one puts pressures on the soul in order to make it do what it loathes, the soul rebels. But if the soul is allowed to relax for some moments by the means of some pleasures, it fortifies itself and becomes after that alert and ready for work again. And in the woman's company, this relaxation drives out sadness and pacifies the heart. It is advisable for pious souls to divert themselves by means which are religiously lawful.[38]

According to Ghazali, the most precious gift God gave humans is reason. Its best use is the search for knowledge. To know the human environment, to know the earth and galaxies, is to know God. Knowledge (science) is the best form of prayer for a Muslim believer. But to be able to devote his energies to knowledge, man has to reduce the tensions within and without his body, avoid being distracted by external elements, and avoid indulging in earthly pleasures. Women are a dangerous distraction that must be used for the specific purpose of providing the Muslim nation with offspring and quenching the tensions of the sexual instinct. But in no way should women be an object of emotional investment or the focus of attention, which should be devoted to Allah alone in the form of knowledge-seeking, meditation, and prayer.

Ghazali's conception of the individual's task on earth is illuminating in that it reveals that the Muslim message, in spite of its beauty, considers humanity to be constituted by males only. Women are considered not only outside of humanity but a threat to it as well. Muslim wariness of heterosexual involvement is embodied in sexual segregation and its corollaries: arranged marriage, the important role of the mother in the son's life, and the fragility of the marital bond (as revealed by the institutions of repudiation and polygamy). The entire Muslim social structure can be seen as an attack on, and a defence against, the disruptive power of female sexuality.

* * *

NOTES

The version of the Koran used throughout this article is Mohammed Marmaduke Pickthall's *The Meaning of the Glorious Koran* (New York, New American Library, thirteenth printing). Abbreviations used in the notes are:
B for *bab* ('chapter');
H for *hadith* ('verbal tradition of Muhammad');
K for *kitab* ('book');
BESM for *Bulletin Economique et Social du Maroc*.

1. The term 'territoriality', however, is really too primitive for the phenomenon, which is a sophisticated, manifold use of space. Hall's concept of 'proxemics' is more suitable:

   > Proxemics is the term I have coined for the interrelated observations and theories of man's use of space and a specialized elaboration of culture.
   > (Edward Hall, *The Hidden Dimension*, New York 1969, p. 1)

According to Hall, the dangers are great, given the sensuous dimension of any physical interaction, of involving the individuals in an atmosphere of ambiguous signs, unconsciously sent and received.

> Man's sense of space is closely related to his sense of self, which is in an intimate transaction with his environment. Man can be viewed as having visual, kinesthetic, tactile, and thermal aspects of his self which may be either inhibited or encouraged to develop by his environment.
>
> (*The Hidden Dimension*, p. 63.)

2. In *Purity and Danger*, Baltimore 1970, Mary Douglas emphasized the links in social structure between the concept of boundaries, the concept of danger and the concept of power.
3. Ibid., p. 14.
4. In Moroccan folklore women are considered to be the repository of devilish forces: Edmund Doutte, *Magic et Religion dans l'Afrique du Nord*, Algiers 1908, p. 33; also, E. Westermark, *The Belief in Spirits in Morocco*, p. 22. The Moroccan psychologist Abelwanad Radi in 'Processus de socialisation de l'enfant marocain', *Etudes Philosophiques et Littéraires*, no. 4, April 1969, attributes to women the responsibility for introducing children to the world of the irrational, of spirits.
5. The term 'universe' is used here in the sense P. L. Berger and T. Luckman use it in *The Social Construction of Reality*, New York 1967.
6. Max Weber, *The Theory of Social and Economic Organization*, New York 1964, p. 136.
7. Ibid., p. 132.
8. To foster 'homosocial' relations does not necessarily mean to drive members of a society to practise what one Palestinian sociologist has called 'homosociality': the inclination to spend most of one's time, most of one's life, with individuals of the same sex. Homosociality entails fear of the other sex and avoidance or limitation of controls with it. Obviously, homosociality is not peculiar to Arab society. Moreover, any institution or practice that tends to degrade the female body may be considered homosocial, and in this sense the advanced capitalist countries, with their pornography industry, would be prime examples.
9. More specifically, it condemned the practice of wearing wigs, which seems to have been quite common among Arab women in the seventh century (al-Bukhari, *al-Jami' al-Sahih*, p. 447 K: 67). Tattooing, also condemned by Islam, is still practised in Morocco, and some of the tattoos have unequivocal erotic meanings. (J. Herber, 'Tatouage du Pubis au Maroc', *Revue d'Ethnie*, vol. 3, 1922.)
10. Koran, sura 24.
11. Al-Ghazali, *Revivification*, p. 35.
12. Ibid., p. 28.
13. Malika Belghiti, 'Les Relations Féminines et le Statut de la Femme dans la Famille Rurale', *Collection du Bulletin Economique et Social du Maroc*, Rabat 1970, p. 57.
14. The French anthropologist Germaine Tillion (*The Republic of Cousins*, Al Saqï Books, London 1983) noted that peasant women newly arrived to towns usually adopt the practice of veiling. She found it strange that women who were not veiled before adopted the veil willingly. I think that this phenomenon could be very easily interpreted if one remembers that, for the rural woman who has recently emigrated to the town, the veil is a sign of upward mobility – the expression of her newly acquired status as urbanite.
15. M. Belghiti, 'Les Relations Féminines', p. 58.
16. Women are especially restricted when in a space they should have a right to: the mosque. In Morocco they may use only a specified area, usually a narrow, marginal, dark corner behind the male space. Although the Prophet allowed women to go to mosques, their right to be there was, during Islam's fourteen centuries of exis-

tence, frequently in doubt and is often still subject to the husband's authorization. (Al-Bukhari, *al-Jami' al-Sahih*, p. 453, K: 67, B: 115.)

17. P. Pascon and M. Bentahar, '269 Jeunes Ruraux', p. 63.
18. My own experience has been that women are more or less harassed depending on the socio-economic features of the place they are walking. Harassment is more systematic in small and medium-sized than in large cities. It is more intense in the poor neighbourhoods and slums of Rabat and Casablanca than in the middle-class areas of these same cities. It also varies according to the legitimacy of the reason you are on the street: harassment is less intense at a post-office queue than it would be if you succumb to the desire to have an ice cream or some chips in a cafe in a poor neighbourhood. Of course, there are some situations that concern only minorities. In those cases the mechanisms are more difficult to grasp, such as, for instance, the harassment of women who drive cars, which seems to be governed by a completely different system of references. Your chances of being harassed seem to be greater if you drive an old small car than if you are in a big gleaming machine.
19. E. Hall, *The Hidden Dimension*, p. 156.
20. Ibid., p. 163.
21. Erving Goffman, *Behaviour in Public Places*, New York 1966, p. 143.
22. Frantz Fanon, *A Dying Colonialism*, New York 1967, p. 53. It is interesting to note that Fanon thought the incidents were 'funny'. For a man with Fanon's sensitivity to segregation and preoccupation with revolutionary assertion of human rights, his remark is puzzling to say the least.
23. Personal communication to the author.
24. Chérifa Alaoui el-Mdaghri, 'Le Travail féminin: cas de la Fonction publique au Maroc en 1980', Ecole Nationale d'Administration Publique, Rabat, cycle supérieur, no. 11, promotion 1980–1.
25. Sigmund Freud, *New Introductory Lectures on Psychoanalysis*, College Edition, New York 1965, p. 116.
26. Abu Issa al-Tarmidi, *Sunam al-Tarmidi*, Medina n.d., vol. II, p. 413, B: 9, H: 1167.
27. Abu-al-Hasan Muslim, *al-Jami' al-Sahih*, Beirut n.d., vol. III, Book of Marriage, p. 130.
28. Al-Tarmidi, *Sunam al-Tarmidi*, p. 149, B: 16, H: 1181. See, also, al-Bukhari, *Kitah al-Jami' al-Sahih*, Leydon, Holland 1868, vol. III, K: 67, B: 11.
29. Al-Tarmidi, *Sunam al-Tarmidi*, p. 149, B: 17, H: 1172.
30. Edward Westermark, *The Belief in Spirits in Morocco*, Abo, Finland 1920.
31. Edward Westermark, *Wit and Wisdom in Morocco: A study of native proverbs*, London 1926, p. 330.
32. Sidi Abderahman al-Majoub, *Les Quatrains du Mejdoub le Sarcastique, Poèt Maghrébin du XVIième Sciècle*, collected and translated by J. Scelles-Millie and B. Khelifa, Paris 1966, p. 161.
33. Ibid., p. 160.
34. Abu Abdallah Muhammad Ibn Ismal al-Bukhari, *Kitab al-Jami' al-Sahih*, Leydon, Holland 1868, p. 419, K: 67, B: 18.
35. Al-Ghazali, *The Revivification of Religious Sciences*, vol. II, p. 28.
36. Sigmund Freud, *Civilization and Its Discontents*, New York 1962.
37. Sigmund Freud, *A general Introduction to Psychoanalysis*, New York 1952.
38. Al-Ghazali, *Revivification*, p. 32.

5.2

'THE SEEN, THE UNSEEN AND THE IMAGINED: PRIVATE AND PUBLIC LIVES'

Sarah Graham-Brown

Grace Ellison, an Englishwoman who visited Istanbul at the turn of the century as the guest of a well-to-do Turkish family, gave some lectures on her experiences when she returned to London.

> When I said I had actually stayed in a harem, I could see the male portion of my audience, as it were, passing round the wink. 'You may not put the word "harem" on the title of your lecture,' said the secretary of a certain society. 'Many who might come to hear you would stay away for fear of hearing improper revelations, and others would come hoping to hear those revelations and go away disappointed.'[1]

Fantasies about harem life pervaded the Orientalist imagination and did much to cloud understanding of the social, domestic and sexual lives of women in the Middle East. The power of the harem image lay in the notion of a forbidden world of women, of sexuality caged and inaccessible, at least to Western men, except by a leap of imagination. It was this leap of imagination which shaped the literature, paintings, engravings and photographs which purported to reveal the life of women behind the walls and barred windows of the harem. Women appeared first and foremost as possessions: as the playthings of men in the harem, or as objects of commerce in the slave markets which figure in numerous Orientalist paintings.

From: Sarah Graham-Brown (1988), 'The Seen, the Unseen and the Imagined: Private and Public Lives', pp. 70–91, in Sarah Graham-Brown, *Images of Women: The Portrayal of Women in Photography of the Middle East 1860–1950* (Columbia: Columbia University Press).

As Grace Ellison's remarks imply, reactions to these images were of two kinds. The first was to indulge in the excitement of an exotic sexual fantasy beyond the reach of the constraints and taboos of European culture. The harem, pictured in this way, was identified with complete male domination over women's lives and the apparently untrammelled sexual pleasures of four wives and unlimited numbers of concubines. The strict control of women's appearance and behaviour in public was assumed to be the corollary of unbridled licence within the harem.

The other reaction to this vision of promiscuity and indulgence was one of disapproval or disgust, and the denigration of a culture which could permit women to live in conditions apparently akin to those of a brothel. The Middle Eastern scholar Nabia Abbott, writing in the 1950s after living for many years in the United States, observed that in the West, 'the term "harem" has come to connote everything vicious and to exclude everything wholesome in the relationships of the sexes'.[2]

SECLUSION AND SEGREGATION

The word *harim* in Arabic means a sacred, inviolable place, and it also means the female members of the family. From the same root comes also the word *haram*, which bears a double meaning: forbidden, or sacred and protected. But *heram* or *hurma* was also used in upper- and middle-class Arab society as a respectful form of address to a married woman. In Turkey and Iran the equivalent term was *hanum* or *khanum*. But the most common use of the word *harim* (*haremlik* in Turkish) was to denote the space in the family home reserved for women (commonly spelt harem). Among the urban elites of the Arab region, Turkey and Iran, this separation of space was accompanied by the seclusion of the women of the family from the sight of all men except husbands and close relatives.[3]

Segregation of space and control over the visibility of women were forms of patriarchal control which emphasized the need to channel and contain women's sexual power. Some commentators argue that this concept of women's sexual power differs from that which developed in European cultures. The Moroccan sociologist Fatima Mernissi, for example, contends that restrictions placed on women in the Islamic cultures of the Middle East are not based on a view of women's biological inferiority: 'On the contrary, the whole system is based on the assumption that women are powerful and dangerous beings. All sexual institutions (polygamy, repudiation, sexual segregation, etc) can be perceived as a strategy for containing their power.'[4]

This view of women as possessing powerful, even uncontrollable sexual passions has taken many forms, including popular sayings, myths and stories. In Morocco, for example, there is a saying that women are *hbel al-shitan* (Satan's leash) implying that they are capable of dragging men away from virtue and also of tying them up (in Arabic this word is also a euphemism for impotence). Thus women who are not kept under strict control appear, in this imagery, as objects of both fear and blame. Their sexuality needs to be channelled into marriage and their visibility controlled to prevent other men from succumbing to their powerful sexual urges. In this view, men's sexuality is less problematic and they are offered numerous socially acceptable ways of indulging their sexual desires.

Although the idea that women's sexuality is dangerous is evident in many aspects of Christian European culture – as is the desire on the part of men to control it – a variety of strategies, practical as well as ideological, were developed to suppress or sublimate this sexuality. The figure of the nun, the celibate woman who dedicates her life to God, is complemented on the ideological level by the image of the Virgin Mary, the mother figure untouched by human sexuality.[5] In Islam, no equivalent roles have been created for women which similarly defuse the notion of sexual danger.

In practical terms, the desire to control women was often expressed in terms of safeguarding family honour and was manifested primarily in the physical segregation of women's space from that of men. Rules controlling the visibility of women in public were not, of course, confined to the Middle East. They could be found in other Mediterranean societies and, until the late nineteenth century, in 'genteel' society in many parts of Europe. But generally speaking, in the Middle East these rules resulted in a much clearer physical demarcation between male and female society than existed in most European cultures. The boundaries of women's worlds were not, however, set in quite the simple ways suggested by popular Western visions of the harem. Although a high degree of sexual segregation was quite common, strict seclusion of women was practised only by the relatively small proportion of well-to-do urban families in which women did not play an active economic role and could therefore be confined to the home and to the role of childbearers.

In the cities, poorer women would generally veil when they went out in the street and did most of their work at home, but they could not be completely secluded, first because they often had to work to support the family and, second, because their homes were too small to allow for strict seclusion. Eugènie le Brun described the ways different social classes in Cairo practised segregation and seclusion as follows:

> In palaces [the woman] is isolated from the rest of the household by high walls and massive doors; in bourgeois families the demarcation line is simply based on an unwritten law – which does not imply that it is any the less respected. As to the common people, their dwellings are too small to allow any such division, so the men invariably receive [their male guests] in the cafe.[6]

Among the non-Muslim communities of the Middle East, practices relating to the regulation of women's space varied too much to allow any generalization, and depended very much on class and social status. Women in minority urban communities, however, were sometimes subject to an additional constraint on movement – that they were expected to remain within the boundaries of their own neighbourhoods. This was especially the case if the community in question feared hostility or aggression on the part of other groups. It was also common to insist that women marry only members of their own community.

But for the majority of people who lived outside the towns and cities, whether as settled peasants or nomads, the need for women to participate in the family labour force made strict seclusion impossible. Patterns of sexual segregation varied greatly from one community and region to another, but seclusion could be practised only among richer families where women did not need to work.

HIDDEN AWAY FROM THE WORLD?

In the popular Western imagery of seclusion, women were locked away from society and, apart from intrigues and jealousies, had no significant relationships except with their male sexual partners and/or oppressors. Paintings, photographs and literature usually stressed passivity and stillness – not the stillness of inner content, but the stillness of women waiting for the man who was the sole reason for their existence. The only form of power available to them was the power of sexual attraction.

The role of photography in creating and reinforcing this mythology was a singular one, and very influential in shaping popular conceptions. Since seclusion and male control of women's visibility for the most part denied Western photographers access to women in their homes, most 'harem scenes' were studio reconstructions composed by the photographer. In this respect, the photograph, like the painting or engraving, was a figment of imagination, which assumed the privileged position of the voyeur entering this closed and private space, and allowing the viewer to do likewise. But while painting is explicitly an act of imagination, photography is more readily assumed to show 'real' scenes.

For those who travelled in the Middle East, the invisibility of women in urban areas did much to reinforce the idea that their existence was rigidly confined to a hidden private realm from which they could not escape and into which no outsider could enter. In their narratives, Western male travellers frequently treated women's seclusion as a challenge: even the sober E.W. Lane engaged in a little of this voyeurism: 'A man may also occasionally enjoy opportunities of seeing the face of an Egyptian lady when she really thinks herself unobserved; sometimes at an open lattice, and sometimes on a housetop.'[7] In a late edition of his *Account of the Manners and Customs of the Modern Egyptians*, published in 1895, a studio photograph was inserted on the page opposite this statement to emphasize the point. It shows a woman wearing a *burqu* (face veil) at an open lattice window. This was a popular photographic theme which appears in large numbers of late-nineteenth-century studio photographs, and many studios had 'sets' which included a latticework or *mashrabiyya* window.

For the photographer, male or female, seeking to capture glimpses of the

Fig. 1. 'Porte centrale de la cour de Suleymaniye' – Central Gate of the Courtyard of the Suleymaniye (Mosque). Sébah & Joaillier, Istanbul, late nineteenth century.
In this photograph, the camera records the presence of this group of women walking in the street outside the mosque, yet it does not 'see' them as the focus of the picture. Although they dominate the foreground, the composition of the photograph relegates them to being a picturesque detail added to the architectural beauties of the Suleymaniye mosque. The caption further focuses the viewer's attention away from the women's presence in the photograph.

domestic life of women in the cities of the Middle East, there were certainly many difficulties. Homes in most long-established cities in the region generally turned blank walls to the street, or had lattice windows (such as the *mashrabiyya* windows to be seen in Egypt and the cities of Arabia) from which the inhabitants could look out on to the street without being seen. For the traveller, these walls and screens appeared as the definitive boundary between the public and private spheres, and reinforced the notion that this boundary marked off, in an absolute way, the domain of women.

The sense of frustration this provoked in some Westerners can be seen in the following account, by Jane Dieulafoy, a Frenchwoman travelling in Iran in the 1880s with her husband, of her efforts to use her camera to break through this boundary. Her description of how she and her husband managed to snatch a picture of some women in the courtyard of a house makes the taking of a photograph seem an act of intrusion:

Fig. 2.   Cairo street scene: Tancrède Dumas, probably 1870s.
Dumas was a French photographer based in Beirut who also worked in Egypt. Since the
technology of photography at this time did not allow for swift snapshots, this photograph
was probably more posed than is immediately apparent. The unveiled woman in the foreground, gazing directly at the camera, is contrasted with the two veiled women in the background. She might have been a peasant or bedouin woman (who would not normally be
veiled), though among the urban poor, too, veiling was less strictly enforced. However, she
draws her head-veil slightly across her face in the presence of the man behind the camera.

In the centre of a courtyard the head of the household was chatting with
two young women, doubtless his relatives. Unaware that they were being
observed, they had left their faces uncovered . . . [I hid] behind part of the
wall, asked my husband to pass me the cameras, and set them up as
quickly as possible, delighted to have captured such a charming interior
and one so jealously guarded in Persian circles.[8]

Somewhat more detailed and less speculative accounts of harem life began to
emerge in the late nineteenth century as it became fashionable for Western
women travelling or resident in the Middle East to visit a harem, though they
hardly ever took photographs. Some of the most enterprising women travellers
had already visited harems: Sophia Lane Poole and Harriet Martineau in the
1840s in Egypt, and later, Isabel Burton in Syria, Isabella Bird and Ella Sykes
in Iran, and Lady Anne Blunt in Arabia.[9]
The picture painted by these women varies considerably according to their

Fig. 3. 'Mussulman Ladies at Home'. Signed by P. Naumann, published in The Ladies' Realm, *July 1898, accompanying an article by Laura B. Starr, 'Ladies of the Harem'.*
Despite the rich decor of the illustration, Laura Starr, claiming more familiarity with harem life 'than the ordinary tourist', disabuses her readers of the idea that harems at that time were all 'Oriental magnificence'. She claims that, despite 'curious old customs still in force', the women she encountered were often strongly imbued with Western ideas. None the less, she stresses the notion that women in harems were preoccupied with 'visitors, flirtations and intrigues', despite the restrictions imposed by seclusion. The photograph, though entirely unconnected with the writer's experiences, to some extent echoes this idea, with the models posed to convey an air of waiting and expectation.

own ideas and the particular society in question, but as such visits became part of the tourist ritual, the voyeuristic element in these encounters frequently came to the fore. With neither common language nor comprehension of each other's cultures, these encounters could be almost comic in their air of mutual incomprehension. Written accounts of harem visits by the less informed tended to dwell on appearances, especially clothing and decor, and usually confirmed the stereotypes of luxury and indolence.

More knowledgeable and careful observers offered much more diverse opinions, but even women such as Sophia Lane Poole were fascinated by physical appearances and dwelt on them in long descriptive passages. The fact that most of Lane Poole's visits were to the homes of the very rich, including relatives of the Egyptian ruler Muhammad Ali, meant that her descriptions often conform to the Western ideas of the harem as a 'gilded cage'.

In other respects, however, her views did not reflect the usual clichés. While she made clear her disapproval of the system of seclusion, she none the less

remarked on the gentleness, good humour, intelligence and invariable gracious-
ness of manner which she found among the women whom she met in the upper-
class harems of Cairo. She also remarked on the sense of discipline which
prevailed:

> The ideas entertained by many in Europe of the immorality of the harem
> are, I believe, erroneous. True it is, that the chief ladies have much power
> which they might abuse; but the slaves of these ladies are subject to the
> strictest surveillance; and the discipline which is exercised over the young
> women in the Eastern harem can only be compared with that which is
> established in the convent.[10]

A very different view was taken by Harriet Martineau, whose brief visit in
the 1840s to two harems, one in Cairo and one in Damascus, filled her with
horror. She describes the women she saw there as 'the most injured human
beings I have ever seen, the most studiously depressed and corrupted women
whose condition I have ever witnessed'.[11] A highly intelligent woman who had
contributed to the political and social debates of her day, Martineau none the
less rushed to this judgement on the basis of very scant experience. In the case
of the harem she visited in Cairo, she was without even an interpreter and
so could not communicate with the women she saw. The home in Damascus
she found less oppressive but though the women of the harem laughed and
appeared to be enjoying themselves, she emphasized the jealousies between
them. It is hardly surprising that the tiny minority of active, independent
European women should find harem life repugnant in its restrictive narrowness,
but it is perhaps indicative of their attitudes to other cultures that they should
be willing to make such sweeping judgements on the condition of women on
the basis of such limited experience.

There was a handful of European women, however, who went so far as to
suggest that the harem system had its virtues. One of this number was Lucy
Garnett, whose two-volume survey of the lives of Turkish women published in
1890–91 is one of the most detailed Western accounts. In a book which provided a briefer overview she remarked: 'From the foregoing description of the
homes of Osmanlis [Muslim Turks] of all classes, it should, I think, be apparent that the harem, far from being, as is so often supposed, a "detestable
prison" is the most cheerful and commodious division of an Osmanli's house.'[12]

Descriptions of harems by those who experienced life in seclusion were few
and far between, and were mostly written by women who were remarkable for
their self-awareness and interest in the question of women's status: for example
Huda Shaarawi, Halide Edip and Eugènie le Brun. They reflected exclusively
the life of the upper-class harem, but their accounts none the less differ from
those of outside observers in several crucial respects.

While they generally stress, like Sophia Lane Poole, the strict hierarchies
which governed harem life – of old over young, mistress over slave and servant,
and the crucial role of the mother of the male head of household – they also

talk of the web of personal relationships within the harem. They include, inevitably, accounts of bitter rivalries and jealousies, but also of great affection and friendship, particularly between children and older women; and the relationships of dependants which grew up between mistresses and slaves. These relationships were not necessarily confined to members of the household, since for many families paying visits to relatives was a major form of entertainment and social contact. Among the well-to-do, it was also quite common to have female relatives coming to stay for long periods of time. Women whose marriages had broken down might return, sometimes with their young children, to the family home, and some families took in indigent relatives, friends and even former slaves.

Thus women were not entirely cut off from society; even those without wide networks of relatives received information and gossip from the women who came to the homes of the rich as tradespeople, dressmakers, marriage brokers and others who provided services required by wealthy women living in seclusion. Neither do the accounts of these 'insiders' give the impression that women were entirely passive or helpless. Rather they suggest that the limits of women's power and influence depended mainly on their age and status in the household.

By the end of the nineteenth century, the most simplistic Western images of the changeless, passive life of the harem, portrayed in the popular literature and photography of the time as bypassed by history, were less relevant than ever. Even the exotic decor was changing. Grace Ellison related that, in the years just before World War I, she sent a photograph of the women's drawing-room in the harem of an affluent Turkish family to a British newspaper. It showed a rather cluttered room with little to distinguish it from a European drawing-room of the same period. Ellison's caption to the photograph as later published in her own book reads:

> This photograph was taken expressly for a London paper. It was returned with this comment: 'The British public would not accept this as a picture of a Turkish harem.' As a matter of fact, in the smartest Turkish houses European furniture is much in evidence.[13]

The newspaper editor could not accept the picture because it did not conform to the stereotypical photograph taken in a studio, and therefore did not appear 'real'. For his audience, the imaginary notion of the harem was the only acceptable one. The alien quality of this imagery did not allow Europeans to entertain the idea that Middle Eastern harems could even physically resemble their own homes.

What is also striking in this otherwise unremarkable photograph is that, decorating the walls and side tables, are a number of portrait photographs. By this time, in cities such as Istanbul and Cairo it was becoming quite common for members of richer families, women as well as men, to have their photographs taken.

At first there were objections to the photographic portrayal of women who still appeared veiled in public. But gradually the objections became less generalized and women themselves found ways round the prohibition. Dorina Neave, an Englishwoman who lived in Istanbul in the latter part of the nineteenth century, described how women she knew used a small subterfuge to get their pictures taken:

> As they were allowed to take a child to the photographer, they would pretend that they were obliged to hold the child during the process of having his [sic] photograph taken, and if by chance the lady appeared in the picture, no exception could be taken, as they had not been to the photographer for that purpose.[14]

It seems that not only did women find ways of having their pictures taken in the studio, but photographers also visited upper-class and royal harems with the express intention of taking photographs of women. In Egypt, according to feminist historian Margot Badran, male photographers were admitted to such harems from the reign of Khedive Ismail in the 1870s. The women who appeared in these photographs wore indoor clothing – in other words, they were unveiled – and mostly wore Western-style clothes. Certainly by the early twentieth century photographs of secluded women in their homes were quite commonly included in family albums. Clearly they were intended for the eyes of the family alone, but as Badran points out, 'it is an irony that women who remained their whole lives veiled and living strictly segregated lives were posthumously unveiled when, many decades later after their deaths their photographs circulated in public'.[15]

The alterations in fashions and behaviour suggested by photographs of this kind, however, only hint at the wider changes which were affecting the lives of upper-class women, particularly those who lived in large cities such as Cairo and Istanbul. Badran also notes that in Egypt by the 1890s rich families were moving to new European-style villas in the suburbs. The same trend was also evident in Istanbul.

Even for women living in seclusion, certain kinds of travel: to visit relatives, or to perform the pilgrimage, had always been permitted, but by the end of the nineteenth century improvements in transport, both within the Middle East and between the Middle East and Europe, greatly extended the possibilities of travel. Women from wealthy families visiting Paris or London experienced a different lifestyle which, though it sometimes evoked doubts and criticisms, certainly widened their horizons. These changes, combined with the trend towards allowing more upper-class women access to education, encouraged the younger generation of women to question the boundaries, both physical and mental, which were imposed on their lives.

The collapse of the regime of Sultan Abdul Hamid in Turkey in 1908 and the social and political turmoil of the World War I period marked the end of the era of total seclusion for upper-class women in Turkish cities. In Egypt, too, by the 1920s the harem system had effectively broken down. In other parts of the region – North Africa, Syria, Palestine, Iraq and Iran – the same pattern of change was occurring but considerably more slowly.[16] Among the middle classes, and in provincial towns, the physical boundaries of women's lives altered less dramatically, but education and the gradual changes in social norms brought adjustments in the way patriarchal control was exercised. Ann-Marie Goichon, writing of changes in the lives of women in the conservative bourgeoisie of the Moroccan town of Fez, described the gradual relaxation of physical control over women's activities in the 1920s:

> The women would undoubtedly be delighted to enjoy greater freedom. Nevertheless, over the last three or four years there has been quite a noticeable change in this respect – and it is the men who have contributed to it. Four years ago the people of Fez maintained that, 'Even if the idea of going out occurred to them [the women] they would never dare to admit it.' Here we are not speaking of those excursions for which some ingenious pretext has always been found, but rather of outings which do not need to be concealed. These are now much more frequent and travel is seen as both desirable and respectable.[17]

Although it is clear that changes in men's attitudes were crucial to the relaxation of women's seclusion, women themselves played a part in pressing men to allow these changes. Long before there were organized women's movements, some women were trying to alter their positions within their own families. Evidence of women's attitudes towards seclusion in the late nineteenth and early twentieth centuries is only fragmentary and tends to come from those who were the most articulate critics of the harem system.[18]

But it has to be borne in mind that whatever the unwelcome aspects of this form of male control, for many women seclusion also represented the achievement, or the maintenance of social status, a sign that husband or father was able to maintain the family in respectability. In Europe at this time, a comparable indicator of social status might have been that no well-to-do family could countenance its women taking paid employment outside the home.

One of the arguments of those who campaigned against the harem system was that the boundaries imposed on women by seclusion were not just physical, but mental and spiritual. Mrs Badr ol-Moluk Bamdad, one of the early campaigners for women's education in Iran, argued that historically, seclusion had made women '. . . unaware of their own capabilities and spiritual worth. They saw themselves as feeble herbs in society's garden, only able to survive when shaded from the sunshine by robust trees, or when dependent like parasites on strong healthy plants from which they drew sustenance.'[19]

Among the generation of well-to-do women who became adults in the 1920s, a more forceful approach to the subject could be discerned. The following speech, delivered in 1928 to a largely male audience by Doraya Shafiq, a young Egyptian woman in her twenties, directly challenged men's efforts, and by implications their right to impose these physical controls over women's space.

Fig. 4. 'Veiled Ladies in a Carriage'. On the shores of the Bosporus, Turkey, late nineteenth century.
For the photographer, this was an attractive and picturesque scene which would undoubtedly appeal to Westerners; for the women, who from their dress belonged to the upper classes, and therefore probably lived in seclusion, excursions of this kind were among the most popular forms of entertainment. Some years later in 1905, when Huda Shaarawi visited Istanbul from Cairo, she remarked on the relative freedom of movement permitted to Turkish women of her class: 'They go to coffee houses, take boats and drive in carriages with a little black veil on their faces and sometimes go unveiled.'[1] By this time, both the style of dress and attitudes to women appearing in public had also undergone some changes since the late nineteenth century.

She concluded that if men persisted in trying to do so, they would be defied. Yet at the same time she suggested that the observance of religious principles is a better guide to behaviour than seclusion behind high walls:

> You build walls around your daughters and surround them with ever more doors and guards. Have you forgotten, then, that walls can never be high enough to counter feminine guile? Your daughters will always have some servant or old woman to help them communicate with the outside world. You show them the world through the framework of their imagination, so that all they see of it is illusion and, at the first opportunity, they fall into the abyss. The more you restrict them, the stronger will be their reaction. Why do you not draw support from religion? Give your daughters a clear conscience and let them out into the world: their sense of duty will stand them in good stead when the sturdiest of walls would crumble.[20]

Fig. 5. 'Members of the Harem of Sultan Abdul Hamid with two Eunuchs Setting off to Exhibit Themselves in Vienna after the Sultan had been Deposed'. Probably Istanbul, 1909. The unnamed photographer added the following commentary which indicates the ambiguities of both the women's and the photographer's attitude to their intention to 'exhibit themselves'. The imperial harem had been composed mainly of Circassians, many of them brought to Turkey originally as slaves. Some of these women were reclaimed by their families after the Sultan's establishment was broken up but some, like these women it seems, were left to fend for themselves.

'They had arrived in Vienna on 29 September to perform their harem dances. Among them was the Sultan's favourite, Princess Sobrah, the last to enter the harem. When they were turned out of the harem, they had to find some means of livelihood. It was dance that attracted them.'

The photographer continues, asserting that, 'This is a unique event in the history of Turkish women,' and claims that they were the first women ever to put themselves on show, since, even in foreign countries, this is forbidden by the Quran. 'Moreover,' he adds, 'they will appear unveiled. After Vienna, they will tour all the countries of Europe. They have promised themselves that outside their performances they will adhere strictly to the rules of the Quran. The photographer found it extremely difficult to persuade them to pose in front of the camera, and without their veils.' Thus women who had seemed exotic to Westerners because of their seclusion, now became exotic in their public exposure, while apparently in their own minds trying to maintain their own norms of culturally acceptable behaviour.

THE CAMERA AND WOMEN'S HORIZONS

Looking at the mass of early Western photographic images of women in the Middle East, it may be tempting to equate their visibility to the public eye, and therefore to the photographer, with the division of their lives into 'public' and 'private' spheres. This formulation, however, would be just as simplistic as to assume that it was possible to distinguish neatly between a 'public' world of men and a 'private' world of women.

Fig. 6. 'Egyptian Women Visiting the Mahmal at Abbassieh'. S. H. Leeder, Egypt, published in his book The Veiled Mysteries of Egypt, *1912.*
For both men and women it was the height of piety for a Muslim to perform the pilgrimage to Mecca, just as it would be for many Christians and Jews to visit Jerusalem. Women of all classes, whether secluded or not, had gone on the pilgrimage from the earliest days of Islam, and like men, on their return, received the respectful title *hajje.* In this picture, Leeder shows a group of women who could not go to Mecca, but did the next best thing by going to Abbassieh to see the *Mahmal,* the holy carpet carried ceremoniously to Mecca on each year's pilgrimage.

As will become apparent, there were many variations in women's social and economic roles, according to their age and class and to the particular circumstances of their own families and communities. The public/private dichotomy often employed in descriptions of these roles may not prove to be the most illuminating way of seeing them. As anthropologist Roxan Dusen suggests, it may be more useful to examine what she calls the 'social horizons' of particular groups of women. These horizons were set by a variety of factors, most importantly by economic circumstances and by social constraints imposed according to male notions of what constituted proper behaviour for women in that community.

Sexual segregation and seclusion did not mean simply the creation of a boundary between public and private space but the control of women's movements

Fig. 7. Women and children in a park. Tehran, Iran, 1860s–90s.
The exact location of this scene is unknown, but from its layout, this would seem to be a typical upper-class Persian garden with avenues of pine trees intersecting at its centre, and probably fruit trees in the background. This would probably have been a private garden and the women would have been there at the invitation of the owner or the garden-keeper. Judging from their dress, they were evidently quite well-to-do. The light foliage on the trees in the background suggests that it was springtime, and the most likely occasion for this kind of social gathering would have been the *sizdah-be-dar*, thirteen days after New Year. This day was considered ill-omened and people would not stay in their homes. Women and men, in separate groups, would go out and spend the day in a pleasant place such as this. They would have lunch and chat and were sometimes entertained by strolling musicians. The children, boys and girls, could run around and play. This was entirely a social and family occasion, not a religious festival.[2]

and visibility whether they were at home, at work in the fields or walking in the street. Control of the physical space in which women moved took many forms: the segregation of the home into men's and women's quarters; the designation of separate spaces for women in public places and on public transport. An extreme case was the rule enforced in parts of Iran that women had to walk on a designated side of the road. Even in villages, where women's visibility was much greater, it was quite common for there to be unwritten rules about where women could go and how they should conduct themselves in public.[21]

These forms of control over women's use of space, public or private, are very difficult to discern in photographic record, which of its nature lays stress on more tangible factors of visibility and physical appearances. Only in the occasional crowd scene is it possible to see whether that particular society or com-

Fig. 8. 'Day for Women to Visit the Commercial, Industrial and Agricultural Exhibition at Cairo'. 18 March, 1931.
This snapshot appears in the album of a Dutch couple returning to Holland from Indonesia by way of Egypt. Although by the 1930s some women of the elite would attend mixed social gatherings, many middle-class women were not free to do so, and some efforts were made to encourage women to attend public events by having separate times at which women could go, rather than spatial segregation. These women's dress also indicates the gradual change in styles which was occurring – only two of the women in the foreground are still wearing small face veils, though all have their heads covered.

munity imposed spatial segregation on women. Furthermore, not all Western photographers were even aware of the ground rules which governed women's behaviour. The fact that photographic studios produced images which took no account of these rules further confuses the issue.

The camera could record changes which took place in the visibility of well-to-do women who had previously lived in seclusion, showing them unveiled in public places and performing new social and economic roles. But these photographs could also be misleading as to the extent and nature of these changes. Photographs disseminated in the Western media often projected an image of the 'modern woman' in Egypt, Turkey or Iran, suggesting a generalized transformation of women's lives to fit the model of European middle-class women. This did little more to explain the experiences of Middle Eastern women than the older stereotypes of the 'Oriental woman' of the harem.

One of the results of sexual segregation in all classes of society was the creation of largely separate women's worlds, not necessarily confined to the four walls of the home, with their own culture – songs, stories, religious practices – overlapping at times with that of men, but seen by both sexes as different and distinct.

Whether secluded or not, women would at times support each other against their menfolk's demands, or negotiate through older women respected in the family or community. Joy, at a birth or a wedding, and grief at death were usually expressed collectively. Even in peasant societies where women worked with men, in agriculture or crafts, their social lives tended to be more or less separate. Many daily chores – fetching water or firewood, going to market, making food, doing embroidery or weaving – were done by groups of women, both family and neighbours. In urban societies, women went in groups to the public baths, to the cemetery on Fridays or feastdays, or to picnic with their children. Both urban and rural women attended religious festivals and went on pilgrimages. The more private aspects of women's culture were rarely evident in the photographic record but photographs of women's activities which took place in public do exist.

NOTES

1. Zeyneb Khanum, *A Turkish Woman's European Impressions*, edited and translated by Grace Ellison (London: Seeley, Service and Co., 1913), p. xvi.
2. Nabia Abbott, 'Women', in Ruth Nanda Anshen (ed.), *Mid-East: World Center: Yesterday, Today and Tomorrow* (New York: Science of Culture Series, vol. 7, 1956), p. 203.
3. For a detailed description of life in Turkish palace harems, see N. Penzer, *The Harem* (London: Spring Books, 1965). For a general overview of Western ideas about the harem and its imagery, see Annabelle d'Huart and Nadia Tazi, *Harems* (Paris: Chene/Hachette, 1980).
4. Fatima Mernissi, *Beyond the Veil* (London: Al Saqi Books, 1985), p. 19. For a further discussion of women and sexuality in the Middle East, see F. Sabbath, *Women in the Muslim Unconscious* (New York: Pergamon Press, 1984); A. Boudhiba, *Islam and Sexuality* (London: Routledge & Kegan Paul, 1985). For details on *hbel al-shitan*, see Lawrence Rosen, 'The Negotiation of Reality: Male–Female Relations in Sefrou, Morocco', in Lois Beck and Nikki Keddie (eds), *Women in the Muslim World* (Cambridge, MA; London: Harvard University Press, 1982), pp. 566–7 and footnote 3, referring to observations by Kenneth Brown.
5. Marina Warner, *Alone of Her Sex: The Myths and Cult of the Virgin Mary* (London: Weidenfeld & Nicolson, 1976).
6. Madame Rushdi Pasha (Eugènie le Brun), *Harems et musulmanes d'Egypte: Lettres* (Paris: Librarie Felix Juven, 1902), p. 2 (translated from the French).
7. E. W. Lane, *An Account of the Manners and Customs of the Modern Egyptians, Written in Egypt During the Years 1833–35* (London: Garner, 1895), p. 188.
8. Jane Dieulafoy, *La Perse, la Chaldée et la Susiane* (Paris: 1887), p. 36 (translated from the French).
9. Harriet Martineau, *Eastern Life, Present and Past*, 3 vols (London: 1848). Elia

Sykes, *Persia and Its People* (London: Methuen & Co., 1910); *Through Persia on A Sidesaddle* (London: A. D. Innes & Co., 1998). Sophia Lane Poole, *The Englishwoman in Egypt: Letters from Cairo During a Residence There in 1842, 3 and 4. Letters During 1845–6*, Second Series, 3 vols (London; 1844–46). Lady Isabel Burton, *The Inner Life of Syria, Palestine and the Holy Lane: from My Private Journal*, 2 vols (London: H. S. King & Co., 1875). Isabella Bird, *Journeys in Persia and Kurdistan*, 2 vols (London: John Murray, 1891). Lady Anne Isabella Noel Blunt, *A Pilgrimage to Nejd*, 2 vols (London: Frank Cass & Co., 1968). For a discussion of Western women's visits to harems, see Margot Badran, 'Huda Shaarawi and the Liberation of Egyptian Women' (unpublished D.Phil. thesis, St Antony's College, Oxford, 1977), pp. 29–31.

10. Lane Pool. *The Englishwoman in Egypt*, vol. II, p. 74.
11. Martineau, *Eastern Life*, vol. II, p. 167.
12. L. M. J. Garnett, *Turkish Life in Town and Country* (London: George Newnes, 1904), p. 51.
13. Khanum, *A Turkish Woman's European Impressions*, p. 192.
14. Dorina L. Neave, *Twenty-Six Years on the Bosphorus* (London: Grayson & Grayson, 1933), p. 67.
15. Badran, 'Huda Shaarawi and the Liberation of Egyptian Women', p. 36.
16. For changes in urban women's lives in Egypt, see ibid., chapter 2. For a description of women's position in a more conservative urban milieu in the early twentieth century, see A. Jaussen, *Coutumes Palestiniennes I: Naplouse et son district* (Paris: Geuthner, 1927).
17. A. M. Goichon, 'La Femme de la moyenne bourgeoise fasiya', *Revue des Etudes Islamiques*, vol. III, 1929, pp. 64–5.
18. For example, Huda Shaarawi, *Harem Years*, edited and translated by Margot Badran, with an introduction by Badran, (London: Virgo, 1986; New York: Feminist Press, 1987) and Halide Edip, *Memoirs* (New York; London: Century Co., 1926).
19. Bamdad ol-Moluk, *From Darkness into Light: Women's Emancipation in Iran*, edited and translated by F. R. C. Bagley (Smithdown, NY: Exposition Press, 1977), pp. 7–8.
20. Public speech at the commemoration of the death of Qasim Amin, 4 May 1928, quoted in *L'Egyptienne*, June 1928, p. 14 (translated from the French).
21. For discussions of control of women's appearance and visibility and the question of public and private space in the Middle East, see: Nora Seni, 'Ville ottomane et representation du corps féminin', *Les Temps Modernes*, nos 456–7, July/August 1984, pp. 66, ff.; Roxan A. Dusen, 'The Study of Women in the Middle East: Some Thoughts', *MESA Bulletin*, vol. X, no. 2, 1976, pp. 1, ff.; Cynthia Nelson, 'Public and Private Politics: Women in the Middle Eastern World', *American Ethnologist*, vol. I, no. 3, August 1984, pp. 551, ff.

CAPTION NOTES

1. Badran, 'Huda Shaarawi', p. 101.
2. Information from Ali Razavi.

5.3

'ON VEILING, VISION AND VOYAGE: CROSS-CULTURAL DRESSING AND NARRATIVES OF IDENTITY'

Reina Lewis

In 1915 the British feminist and Turkophile Grace Ellison wrote about her visit to Turkey on behalf of a British suffrage organization.[1] Her book *An Englishwoman in a Turkish Harem* aimed to reveal the true state of Turkish women's lives and to challenge Orientalist stereotypes. She emphasized the high standards of education among elite women and the level of support among progressive men for female emancipation. Notably, Ellison also wrote in considerable detail about clothes, especially about the familiarity of elite Ottoman women with European clothes and furniture and the codes of conduct which accompanied these. Although changes in dress were often seen as signs of modernization, Ellison, despite her progressive feminist politics, romanticizes the Ottoman harem system (Melman 1992) and aestheticizes the veil, seeing it not as a mechanism of seclusion but as a fetching head-dress. She herself adores capering about in a veil. These contradictory attitudes are seen most acutely in her 1928 work when she returns to review the new Turkish republic. Although she is thrilled with its modernizing reforms and the advances she sees in women's social position, the veil remains a garment so tantalizing to behold and to wear that, when Mustafa Kemal (Ataturk), propounding his project of national and gender liberation, argues resoundingly that 'All that nonsense is going to cease. Harems, veils, lattice windows . . . must go', Ellison is moved to intervene:

From: Reina Lewis (1999), 'On Veiling, Vision and Voyage: Cross-Cultural Dressing and Narratives of Identity', pp. 500–20, in *Interventions*, vol. 1, no. 4.

> I could not resist the feminine protest, –
> 'But veils are picturesque. No more becoming a head-dress has ever been invented for women.'
> 'We cannot remain in the Dark Ages to supply foreign writers with copy,' was the answer. (Ellison 1928: p. 23)

It is no coincidence that Mustafa Kemal prioritizes getting rid of the veil; not only is he opposed ideologically to the Islamic gender division of society but he is also by now determined to limit the power of the conservative *ulema* (clergy) who had supported the sultan in his opposition to the nationalists (Arat 1994; Kandiyoti 1991; Shaw and Shaw 1994). But what is so delightful about the spectatorial pleasure offered by the figure of the veiled Turkish woman that it threatens the British feminist's political commitment to female emancipation?

In order to think about the significance of the veil and the bodies it surrounds in relation to questions of travel, identity and cross-cultural dressing, I shall be looking at a little-known dialogue between Grace Ellison and her Ottoman Muslim friend, Zeyneb Hanum, whose book *A Turkish Woman's European Impressions*, presented in the form of letters to Ellison, was edited by Ellison and published in 1913. Zeyneb Hanum's account of her travels was written after she and her sister, Melek Hanum, had fled to Europe after having corresponded and met with Pierre Loti, for whose novel *Les Désenchantées* they were the inspiration. In reading these two accounts together, I aim to explore the significance of donning or discarding the veil for the narrative construction of racialized gender identities and to analyse their authors' intervention in disputes about authenticity and cultural authority. In relation to this I want to consider whether recent critical work on the pleasures and politics of cross-cultural dressing can be applied equally to Europeans wearing the veil as to Turkish women wearing French fashions.

In Turkish society, in the late pre-republican and early republican period, women's clothes, in particular the veil, were seen as a crucial index of political and social change by politicians of all persuasions, and inevitably discussed as such by local and foreign commentators (Graham-Brown 1988). Both women's and men's apparel were regularly the subject of sumptuary legislation (Şeni 1995). Since the Tanzimat reforms of the mid-nineteenth century, the partial or wholesale adoption or adaptation of European fashions had become increasingly common among elite women, so women observers might often encounter women wearing the veil in conjunction with elements or adaptations of western dress (Micklewright 1999a).[2] Women might dress entirely in Paris gowns to receive each other at home and often wore European clothes under their veils and cloaks (*feredges*) when outside, though European dress in this latter context would not, of course, be detectable to observers. Sometimes, wearing western clothes was part of a clear political statement but at the very least, dress, like the consumption of other western goods, signalled a vague sense of generally westernized modernity though the advantages of western ways and the extent to which they should be embraced were hotly debated (Berkes 1964; Duben and Behar 1991; Göçek 1996). My focus here is on how dress, both Turkish and European, functions as an element of gender and ethnic performance and how this might register differently with those who wear it and read about it in both Orient and Occident.

Like Zeyneb Hanum, Ellison titles her book with reference to the gender and nation specificities of her view. Calling her book *An English Woman in a Turkish Harem* is an act of bravado for Ellison, who is quite aware that although sales will be prompted by the assumed authenticity of her gendered access to the forbidden realm of the Oriental harem, to associate herself with this sexualized realm was also risky: '[t]o the Western ear, to be staying in a Turkish harem sounds alarming, and not a little – yes, let us confess it – improper' (Ellison 1915: p. 2). The very codes of authenticity which guarantee women's reports on the harem and the world behind the veil also locate them as gendered *participants* in the sexualized space of the segregated harem. For European women travellers and writers, this emphatic presence effectively disallows a scientific mode of detached objectivity and risks contaminating them by too great a proximity to their object of study. As Billie Melman has argued in relation to the nineteenth century (Melman 1992), European women tended to work round this problem by demystifying the fantasy harem of Orientalist stereotype, domesticating it into a counterpart of the European drawing-room and particularizing it with details of individual harems.

In the early twentieth century Grace Ellison similarly sets up a distinction between the claustrophobic and antiquated imperial harem, which can be associated with the potentially morally contaminating elements of the harem myth, and the healthier, more 'normal' elite harems of her friends in which she has been living. This allows her to linger on the luxuries and hospitality of the elite Turkish home which, while evidently a source of great pleasure to her personally, will also provide some of the expected pleasures of Orientalism for her readers: 'In no other land have I met with such lavish hospitality. . . . The courtesy, also, is almost overwhelming. . . . Always, too, I sit in the place of honour' (Ellison 1915: p. 22).

Although Ellison finds that the 'curious resigned happiness' which overtakes her in the harem prevents her from getting on with her writing project – ' "To-morrow", I say, like a true Turkish woman' (Ellison 1915: pp. 3–4) – Turkey is experienced as a refuge of calm and quiet after the noise and rush of 'what we in the West call pleasures of society' (Ellison 1915: p. 2). She is ambivalent about her Orientalized loss of motivation: 'if we in the West possess what is known as the "joy of liberty" have not so many of us been denied the blessing of protection?', and had often longed to return to the 'calm and peace of an Eastern harem' (Ellison 1915: p. 196). The 'contaminating' effects of the Oriental female space may, it would seem, be bewildering, but they are not always unwelcome. Emily Apter attributes such experiences to a haremization effect which challenges the normative phallocentric ordering of western colonial desire (Apter 1992). For western writers, both male and female, she argues, the relentless intrusion of a sapphic subtext into harem narratives reveals as only ever partial the presumed power and sexual omnipotence of the sultan, on whose access to the forbidden multitude of harem women the fantasy Orientalist harem is predicated. This 'other' eroticism that transcends the limitations of the harem regime hints at forms of pleasure (*jouissance* in Apter's Lacanian scenario) outside of a western libidinal economy and makes strange to itself European subjectivity and sexuality.

VEILED IDENTITIES: PLEASURE, PROGRESS AND PHOTOGRAPHY

For Ellison, the impact of haremization is embraced most notably in relation to the pleasures it offers in terms of luxury, wealth and cross-cultural dressing. With her hostess Fatima's connivance, she dresses in a veil to visit the mosque and holy tomb at Eyoub where five years earlier she had 'had the humiliating experience of being refused admission to the tomb because I was wearing a hat; now I am wearing a veil who can tell whether I am Muslim or Christian?' (Ellison 1915: p. 162).

> It was Friday afternoon. The Faithful were at prayer when we arrived. I wanted to see the mosque; but how could I, even as a veiled women, take my place amongst the women? Much as I admire the wonderful solemnity of the Eastern prayers – much as I, a Christian, would have loved to worship Allah with my Muslim sisters – I was just a little frightened; my action might be mistaken for irreverence. We went, however, into the gallery reserved for the Sultan, and through the lattice-work windows we had a good view of the mosque below. (Ellison 1915: p. 164)

However, although she has some qualms about her undercover presence being interpreted badly, as religious and cultural disrespect, she is all laughter at having fooled some Europeans – though this too is presented as unintentional; Fatima and Ellison start to leave when:

> Just before we reached our carriage I saw a dear friend with her accustomed unselfishness escorting some English visitors round as much as they, Christians, could see of the holy city of Eyoub. She recognised my voice, and I was introduced as a Turkish lady to my compatriots.
>
> I felt just a little guilty at their delight in meeting a real Turkish woman, but it was too dangerous to undeceive them in those fanatical surroundings. 'And how well you speak English too!' they said. 'English was the first language I spoke,' I answered truthfully. I wonder whether Miss A. ever told them who I really was. (Ellison 1915: p. 169)

But Ellison is not unaware of the veil's negative qualities. She reports her discussion with the prominent Turkish feminist Halide Edib Adivar:

> Is it [the veil] protection or is it not? Halide-Hanum considers that it creates between the sexes a barrier which is impossible when both sexes

should be working for the common cause of humanity. It makes the woman at once the 'forbidden fruit', and surrounds her with an atmosphere of mystery which, although fascinating, is neither desirable nor healthy. The thicker the veil the harder the male stares. The more the woman covers her face the more he longs to see the features which, were he to see but once, would interest him no more.

Personally I find the veil no protection. In my hat I thread my way in and out of the cosmopolitan throng at Pera. No one speaks to me, no one notices me, and yet my mirror shows I am no more ugly than the majority of my sex. But when I have walked in the park [the new park recently arranged by Abdulhamit on European lines], a veiled woman, what a different experience. Even the cold Englishman has summoned up courage and enough Turkish to pay compliments to our 'silhouettes'. (Ellison 1915: p. 69)

Ellison's delight in receiving the attentions directed (in Turkish) at a supposed Turkish woman indicates her investment in the thrill of passing as 'other'. It is not just that she adores the veil as an item of clothing, but that she also mistakes it for a sleight-of-hand way of temporarily inhabiting another identity. This in part explains her inability to realize the different significance of wearing the veil for Turkish and English women; notably she talks mainly of her scrutiny by European men. The reference to Pera, the foreign quarter of Istanbul, and the new European-style park indicate that the role of veiling is being altered by the new hybrid spaces of the modernizing city. It is hardly surprising that the cross-culturally dressed Ellison should achieve a heightened visibility in Pera, because despite their increased public visibility, veiled women would still be a rarity in this cosmopolitan section of the city and so would be of obvious curiosity to the many tourists and foreigners who resided there. To walk in the park, however, attracts attention from a different audience because the park is a new space designed to allow Turks a mixed gender public life whose social etiquettes are not yet mapped out and where Turkish men also engage in new and potentially perplexing behaviours. This is not to say that men and women never met in public – although ostensibly a segregated society, pleasure trips to the banks of the Sweet Waters of the Bosphorus had long been used as a cover for illicit meetings between men and women. But while these forbidden assignations point to the existence of mixed gender public interactions, they are qualitatively different from the respectable social intercourse which the new parks were intended to facilitate.[3] The new space of the park and Turkish women's increasing licit presence in public present behavioural challenges to men and women:

Five years ago we never walked a step; now we not only saunter through the bazaar, but go to a big dressmaker's in Pera. . . . But not only in the bazaar do we walk; we have walked in the magnificent newly laid-out park, where women are allowed for the first time to walk in a park where there are men. The men I must say, have not yet grown accustomed to the new and extraordinary state of things, and vie with the Levantine 'mashers' in their desire to see the features under the veil. It is not a very comfortable experience for the Turkish woman, but it is the darkness before the dawn. (Ellison 1915: p. 31–2)

Ellison presents the male response as an aping of a Christian/Levantine mode of masculinity, but it also makes sense within a traditional Muslim conceptualization of space as sexualized and segregated. Fatima Mernissi reads the seclusion of women as part of a Muslim binarism which divides space into the public, men's space of the *umma* – the community of believers in which women only exceptionally had a justifiable place – and the women's space of the home, in which men were not encouraged to linger (Mernissi 1985). In this schema, restricting contact between the sexes serves to maintain the purity of the *umma* and to prevent *fitna* – the chaos and disorder threatened by illicit sexual thoughts and/or relations – which could be sparked off by the seductive presence or visibility of women. The veil as a portable means of seclusion, Mernissi argues, allows women to pass through public spaces, symbolically unseen. But the new space of the public park does not accord with these spatial relations and so the Turkish woman, even when veiled, finds herself positioned by Turkish as well as Christian men as a sexualized public spectacle on two counts.[4] The indeterminate nature of the park space emphasizes that, even when veiled, Muslim women should not be in public/men's space unless they have good reason (visiting a shrine, etc.) and since frivolous public dalliance in the park does not count as good reason, women's respectability is bound to be called into question. Combine this with a learned mode of western male voyeurism in which women's bodies are a legitimate object of surveillance, and we can see how the public park activates in Turkish men a mode of behaviour which renders women – even veiled – a spectacle in both Islamic and western terms.

It is interesting to note that although Ellison delights in being mistaken for a Turk, she uses this story to remind her readers of her distance from her Oriental objects of study – male scrutiny is less burdensome to her than to her Turkish friends. This separation from Turkish women is further emphasized when she herself tries to capture the 'features under the veil':

> There is a beautiful old woman in the household whom I long to 'Kodak'. Once I thought I 'had' her as she sat cross-legged on the carpet rolling her quarter-hourly cigarette, but she noticed me, alas! then cursed, screamed, and buried her head in her roomy pantaloons. I shall not try to repeat the experiment. (Ellison 1915: p. 183)

The delightful distinctiveness of the Orient becomes infuriating when it frustrates her scopophilic and ethnographic attempts to gather photographic evidence.[5]

The symbiotic relationship between the new technology of photography and the new investigative social sciences of ethnography and anthropology has been much discussed (Edwards 1990; Pinney 1990; Street 1992). Not only did the new technology and new disciplines develop coterminously, but by the late nineteenth century photography had come to be an established part of the field-work process. Photography did not of course simply document, it played a crucial role in the classification, conceptualization and visualization of 'other' peoples in the protocols of the emerging disciplines, though this was not without its problems and anxieties. As Christopher Pinney discusses, early concerns about the ethics of editing and 'touching up' photographs made in the field became more acute by the early twentieth century as the apparent denotative security of photography was increasingly undermined. In a context where anthropology looked to photography to shore up its classifications, the caption took on a heightened significance (Pinney 1992). For these and other reasons, such as the increase in amateur photography, Elizabeth Edwards identifies 1910 to 1920 as a period in which photography was ceasing to be so central to the professional anthropological endeavour (Edwards 1992).

In Ellison's description of her 'Kodaking' experience we see the would-be amateur ethnographer's classic attempt to assume the invisible viewpoint implicit in early codifications of ethnographic objectivity, just at the point when the role of photography is being reformulated in the profession. The Turkish woman is described in her 'natural' habitat, a local curiosity who is the subject of an 'experiment' to document a dying breed rendered antiquated by the contemporary modernization of Ottoman social life.

While this particular old woman may refuse to be photographed, the looked-for pleasures of Oriental dress are more than adequately represented by photographs of cross-cultural dressing. In the frontispiece to her book, entitled 'The author in Turkish costume' (Plate 1), Ellison simultaneously enacts and frustrates the expectations that her book's title would have created in the minds of her Occidental readers. Having on several occasions identified the erroneous ideas of sex and violence that are aroused in the minds of Europeans at the mere mention of the word harem, she defiantly entitles her book *An Englishwoman in a Turkish Harem* and fronts it with a photograph of herself in 'native' dress. Here, the caption identifies the pictured woman as the author, immediately keying into discourses of experiential realism and literary authority. It also differentiates this photo from other images of women in similar clothes by identifying this woman as English and not Oriental. How else are we to distinguish the racial identity of this figure from that of the unnamed female contributor to the women's magazine, *Kadınlar Dünyası*, illustrated in Plate 2?[6] Both are dark-haired, pale-skinned women in similar clothes and pose.[7] In Plate 1 the clothes are identified as archaic, collective 'costume', utilizing the pseudo-scientific language of ethnographic description which renders 'native' clothing timeless and archaic collective costume, a world far away from the increasingly fast-moving and individualizing fashion industry of the modern western world. But, while Ellison's book often discusses the changing fashions in Turkish dress

Plate 1   'The author in Turkish costume', in Ellison 1915. By permission of The British Library (shelfmark 10125 bb32).

Plate 2   'A contributor to the new Turkish woman's paper 'Kadınlar-Dünyassı' ('The feminine world')', in Ellison 1915. By permission of The British Library (shelfmark 10125 bb32).

and the Turkish adoption of western clothes, it may be that this use of terminology in the captions reflects the publisher's editorial choices rather than
Ellison's own. This puts the images, their captions and the rest of the written
text in a dialectical relationship to each other, all part of the multifaceted narrative sold under Ellison's name but not necessarily all the result of her actual
writing.

Grace Ellison herself has a very peculiar and transitory status in the photographs. She appears as 'the author' at the head of the book yet in 'An Englishwoman wearing a yashmak' (Plate 3), the identity of the woman as well as her
face appears to be veiled. But in fact, both identity and face are only partially
veiled, for this is clearly Ellison, and her face is still quite visible, being only
slightly obscured by the yashmak. This form of veiling was temporarily replaced
by the heavy black veil insisted on by Abdulhamit (Plate 4, showing a 'Turkish
lady in Tcharchaff. Outdoor costume', is from Zeyneb Hanum's book) but the
thinner and more revealing yashmak is described by Ellison as particularly
attractive. When Fatima wears one on their court visit Ellison bewails that 'now,
alas!' it is obsolete, worn only at court, 'for to me it is one of the most becoming of head-dresses, showing the eyes to very great advantage' (Ellison 1915: p.
35). Having plastered her face all over the book, and not herself being bound by
any Islamic scruples about photography, why is Ellison so coy about her identity in this image? To answer this we have to consider the pleasures of cross-cultural dressing and the teasing of her readers in which I think she engages.

Gail Low has written about the pleasures of cross-cultural dressing which,
she argues, are often underpinned by a closely held sense of racialized differentiation. This might initially seem at odds with the profound delight taken by
participants in dressing in local clothes and even passing as native. But for the
westerner, she suggests, the pleasure of wearing an exotic and splendid 'native'
costume is enhanced by the knowledge of the white skin underneath the disguise (Low 1989). For Richard Burton or Kipling's Kim, the ability to pass as
a native is an important talent, both pleasurable (giving access to hidden native
customs) and political (Kim after all spies for the Raj). Clothes, she argues, are
important to the fantasy of cross-dressing because they are 'superficial' and can
always be removed when one needs to revert to type, to reassert one's racial or
cultural superiority. In contrast, Apter maintains that cross-dressing undermines previous conventions of absolute difference, and instances Loti's delight
in passing not only as a Turk, but also as a veiled Turkish woman, as an
example of such fluidity of boundaries. I am inclined to agree with Low that it
is the transitory nature of this boundary-breaking that is significant. For Loti,
as for Ellison, the thrill of cross-cultural dressing is predicated on an implicit
reinvestment in the very boundaries they cross. Clothes operate as visible gate-
keepers of those divisions and, even when worn against the grain, serve always
to re-emphasize the existence of the dividing line. So cross-dressing offers both
the pleasures of consumption – the Orient is a space full of enticing goods to
be bought, savoured and worn – and the deeper thrill of passing as native.

Plate 3 'An Englishwoman wearing a yashmak', in Ellison 1915. By permission of the British Library (shelfmark 10125 bb32).

We see both these pleasures in Ellison's interaction with Turkish clothes. When Fatima puts her entire trousseau at Ellison's disposal, her guest admits that 'I take out these precious gifts sometimes and examine them at leisure' (Ellison 1915: p. 23). This reverie in which she privately indulges suggests the sensual satisfactions obtained from her perusal of the fabulously bejewelled items and hints at the double desirability of Oriental artefacts, whose 'ancient' styles and motifs had been made newly contemporary by Paul Poiret in his attempts to liberate western women from the corsets of the *belle epoque*. This embracing of Oriental style, colour and texture was seen most dramatically in the dance and costumes of the Ballet Russes, whose performances caused a sensation in Paris and London in 1910. I do not know if Ellison saw any of their performances but she and many of her readers would probably have heard of Bakst's sensational costumes and indeed may have visited the displays at London's Selfridges which tied in with this Orientalist craze (Nave 1998; Wollen 1987).

As well as enjoying dressing in Turkish clothes with her women friends, Ellison delights in going out and about in Istanbul in Turkish dress. As we have

Plate 4   'Turkish lady in Tcharchaff. Outdoor costume', in Zeyneb Hanoum 1913.

seen, she is thrilled when she hoodwinks people into thinking that she is Turkish. How does this link to the experience of hoodwinking her readers, who open the book expecting one thing (disreputable 'smoking room' tales of polygamy) and get another? If the logic of the veil is that one cannot identify the wearer, why does the caption 'Englishwoman wearing a yashmak' identify the nationality or race of the subject, but not her name? By presenting herself as willingly acculturated to Turkish life (though we cannot deduce this from the photograph alone, but only from the longer narrative) Ellison suggests the positive aspects of haremization.

But the book also links into another set of pleasures that Low associates with cross-cultural dressing, namely fantasies of power and surveillance. The undercover cross-culturally dressed agent embodies a mode of power based on a 'fantasy of invisibility' which imagines for an imperial gaze a state of omnipotence and omnipresence that is secret and voyeuristic rather than visible, as in the panoptican model (Low 1989: p. 95). Like photography, the undercover agent offers a possibility of seeing without being seen looking. Ellison is well aware that her inquisitive gaze will be defeated if it becomes too apparent. Not just with her Kodak but in the activity of her curious gaze as writer, she admits to a desire to bring the female Orient into view and to represent it for her Occidental readers. But she knows that this is an interactive enquiry and worries about alienating her subjects. Evidently, the masculinist position of objective scientific observer was indeed complicated for women. So perhaps the role of undercover agent was a better, more productive device? If the pleasure of cross-cultural dressing is in knowing that one is white underneath the native garb, perhaps this allows a European woman like Ellison a place from which to demonstrate her impressive local knowledge and contacts. She can revel not only in her gender-specific access to segregated domestic spaces but also in her ability to pass as Muslim and gain access to spaces forbidden to non-believers. By crossing both the gender and religious origins of harem (originally a protection and seclusion of holy space; see Peirce 1993), she can enjoy the pleasures of cultural transgression without having to give up the racial privilege that underpins her authority to represent her version of Oriental reality. Yet, though it is clear that the many advantages offered to Ellison by this cross-cultural dressing are predicated on a reinvestment in discourses of racialized difference, one must not assume that they had no positive potential for her Turkish hosts who often assisted in her sartorial adventures. As an intimate interaction within the social relations of hospitality, dressing up at home provides an obvious chance for friendship and bonding. But, when transposed to public spaces, accompanying Ellison on her cross-dressed outings might vicariously offer a different but related set of transgressive thrills to her Turkish accomplices. Collaborating in the joint misleading of Europeans could provide an opportunity to differently undermine or reposition racialized boundaries for subjects who must themselves have regularly been the recipients of a classificatory Orientalist gaze. Similarly, braving the uncharted social relations of the new park with a woman 'masquerading' as veiled might put quite a different spin on the identificatory and sexualized assumptions projected on to her 'authentically' veiled companions by both European and Turkish men. So, the reinvestment in racialized boundaries that underpins Ellison's cross-cultural dressing might have different connotations for her Turkish hosts than for Ellison herself and her British readers.

In this light, it is significant that while the book discusses and pictures elite Ottoman women's familiarity with western fashions, Ellison herself only appears *à la turque*. Her presence in English dress would be too anti-exoticizing, would disrupt too much the transculturating drive of the book. If one of the declared intentions of the book is to show that Turkish homes are not what Europe imagines them to be, but are in fact full of modern European furniture (to the extent that her hostess shops for 'antiquated' Turkish goods in order to furnish a proper 'Turkish room' for Ellison's next visit), Ellison's visual presence serves to reinforce the exotica that her written text so relentlessly undermines. This suggests why, like her readers who she knows will insist on holding on to outdated stereotypes about the harem, the feminist Ellison could not bear to relinquish Turkey's picturesquely exotic costumes. Despite her best intentions to challenge cultural stereotypes, Ellison is simultaneously interpellated within the larger structures of Orientalism. These power relations are often experienced consciously as an affront to her political sensibilities, yet they also provide the source of much of her determined embrace of cultural difference.

DE-VEILING: PERFORMING THE ORIENT

A different experience of cross-cultural dressing is illustrated by Zeyneb Hanum and Melek Hanum. This is the reverse side of the charade. The power accruing to the European sartorial adventurer who can delight in the white skin underneath the native clothes is not available to two Turkish women who flee the constraints of Istanbul harems for a 'free' life in Europe. Nevertheless, they also start out with similarly fantastical expectations of exoticized difference:

> It seems to me that we Orientals are children to whom fairy tales have been told for too long – fairy tales which have every appearance of truth. You hear so much of the mirage of the East, but what is that compared to the mirage of the West, to which all Orientals are attracted? (Zeyneb Hanum 1913: pp. 186–8)

For these two Turkish women travellers, Europe disappoints on several fronts. Unable to recognize the signs of western freedom as truly valuable (they cannot get over the pointlessness of sport as a leisure pursuit and the crazy pace of a Paris Season), they look through eyes which are both haremized and haremizing, finding the harem in Europe. This is evident when Zeyneb Hanum, writing to Ellison in Istanbul, reports her stay in a 'Ladies' Club' in London and is not impressed with the experience:

> What a curious harem! and what a difference from the one in which you are living at present. . . . The silence of the room was restful . . . [but] it is the peace of apathy. Is this, then, what the Turkish women dream of becoming one day? Is this their ideal of independence and liberty? . . . What I do feel, though, is that a Ladies' Club is not a big enough reward for having broken away from an Eastern harem and all the suffering that has been the consequence of that action. A club, as I said before, is after all another kind of harem, but it has none of the mystery and charm of the Harem of the East. (Zeyneb Hanum 1913: pp. 182–6)

Zeyneb Hanum exerts a haremizing gaze on the west that makes strange its familiar division of space and organization of sexuality. When she writes about the eastern harem she domesticates it into a home. Though she makes no bones about how women are devalued in segregated society, Zeyneb Hanum uses her experience of harem life to challenge the sexualized terms in which it is often represented in western discourse. The recurrent and often sexualized trope of Oriental women's passivity in the face of destiny is here reattributed to the London Ladies' Club. She finds more harems at the Houses of Parliament:

But, my dear, why have you never told me that the Ladies' Gallery is a harem? A harem with its latticed windows! The harem of the Government! . . . How inconsistent are you English! You send your women out unprotected all over the world, and here in the workshop where your laws are made, you cover them with a symbol of protection. (Zeyneb Hanum 1913: p. 194)

Her knowing gaze – 'my dear, why have you never told me?' – sees in the west what the west tries to project on to the east. But Zeyneb Hanum does not only find the harem in Europe, she also brings it with her through her staging of Turkish clothes and interiors. Unlike Ellison, who appears solely photographed in Turkish dress, there are only two culturally cross-dressed photographs in Zeyneb Hanum's book, showing the sisters in European clothes ('Melek on the veranda [sic] at Fontainebleau', Plate 5). The other plate, 'The balcony at the back of Zeyneb's house' (not shown) appears to be Zeyneb Hanum's house in Turkey and, though the photograph is small and indistinct, she seems to be wearing European dress. She is not, however, wearing any form of veil, suggesting that the shot is taken from the interior courtyard. In all the other plates they wear Turkish dress, though even in Turkey they would have had access to Paris fashions.

Although Zeyneb Hanum's references to seeing the outside world without a veil make it clear that the sisters were not veiled in Europe, their written account does not specify what they wear. The picture of Melek Hanum at Fontainebleau shows the existence of a European wardrobe and I suspect this is what they wore most of the time in Europe. Why then do the photographs of them in their book about their travels in Europe mainly show them wearing Turkish clothes? Many of the photographs are captioned with details about Oriental female costume, so I think it is quite likely that these are present as an ethnographic or historical supplement on Turkish female life rather than as a record of their time in Europe. Scenes such as 'Turkish ladies paying a visit' (Zeyneb Hanum 1913: p. 172, not shown) are clearly meant to picture their life in Turkey and complement the written part of the book which mixes accounts of life in Turkey with responses to Europe. The photographs work, I think, to maintain the authors' Turkishness in the face of their potentially acculturating sojourn in Europe. It is, after all, the racialized specificity of their gendered gaze on Europe that supports the rationale of the whole book. So when we turn to photographs like 'Zeyneb in her Paris drawing-room' (Plate 6), we see a mixture of the two – a visibly Turkish woman in her Turkified room in the French capital. If the frontispiece to Ellison's book of her in 'Turkish costume' is designed to testify to the actuality of her visit to Turkish harems, this photograph fronting Zeyneb Hanum's book shows her bringing the harem with her. Wearing a yashmak, even in Paris, is important for the image of the book because the veil proves her authenticity as a Turkish woman in the way most easily recognizable in the west. Zeyneb Hanum cannot start her book with any

Plate 5   'Melek on the veranda at Fontainebleau', in Zeyneb Hanoum 1913.

hint of an unreliable narrator, unlike Ellison, who, as I discussed above, can leave it to captions to distinguish her racialized identity from that of a similarly dressed Turkish woman. In contrast to the free play of Ellison's visual transgressions across racialized boundaries of identification, anchored in a signification of Englishness easier to secure, Zeyneb Hanum's Oriental credentials are emphasized by the structure of the visual narrative in her book.

Although this is the story of two women who resisted the restrictions of the harem system, the book does not permit us to 'see' their unveiled faces for sixty pages. The first picture shows Zeyneb Hanum in a yashmak while the second image in the book, 'Turkish lady in Tcharchaff. Outdoor costume' (Plate 4) makes the unidentified woman even more remote from our gaze. Although this retreat is reversed on page 60, what we see is not another photograph but a sketch by Auguste Rodin of 'Les Désenchantées' (Plate 7). This flimsy drawing sends Melek Hanum and Zeyneb Hanum back to their fictional existence as Loti's heroines, by which they were best known in Europe. The celebrity status of the Loti connection definitely helped to market their book: 'we have not had one free evening. The *Grandes Dames* of France wanted to get a closer view of two Turkish women, and they have all been charming to us' (Zeyneb Hanum

Plate 6   'Zeyneb in her Paris drawing-room', in Zeyneb Hanoum 1913.

1913: p. 156). However, it does not bring us much nearer to the photographic codes of realism promised by the frontispiece. Indeed, the drawing keys into another order of representation and heightens the fantasy elements associated with Loti's *roman à clef*. The visual narrative continues with pictures of the two sisters in Turkey and Europe, punctuated much later by an arresting photograph, 'Zeyneb with a black faceveil thrown back' (Zeyneb Hanum 1913, not shown), suggestive of the emancipatory result promised by the whole project.

The second photograph of 'Zeyneb in her Paris drawing-room' (Plate 6) enacts an identification designed variously to signify Oriental (her Turkish dress and Turkish furnishings) and westernized (being socially able and acculturated in western high society). But what can we make of a Turkish woman wearing western clothes: is this cross-cultural dressing? There is a long-established celebratory mode for dealing with western cross-cultural dressing as one of the pleasures of the imperial theatre, but perhaps if the Oriental does it she not only denies the western gaze of the exotica it expects and demands, but also risks becoming Bhabha's mimic man – an uncanny imitation of the real thing, doomed to inauthenticity (Bhabha 1984). Does the practice of Orientals adopting European dress and behaviours threaten the viability of the west's pleasurable

Plate 7 'Les Désenchantées' by M. Rodin', in Zeyneb Hanoum 1913.

play at fashion *à la turque*? The west wants to play-act at being exotic, but when the referent for that exotic reappears in their midst clad in western clothes the differentiating terms which secure the western masquerade begin to crumble. If by the turn of the century, the 'authentic' Turkish past is already being recommodified as quaint historic interest by the Turks (for both domestic and souvenir markets) what is left for the west to dress in and photograph?

I think it might be useful to consider Zeyneb Hanum and Melek Hanum's identifications as performative, in other words as identifications that work through the reiteration of socially and culturally recognizable signs of difference. Hence the completely unnecessary wearing of the yashmak in the frontispiece makes sense if we allow that the veil (in all its versions) is the ultimate sign by which the west distinguishes the Oriental woman from the Occidental. The non-naturalness of this coding is hinted at by the photographs in the room, some of which also show veiled women. The presence of these mementoes of the Orient in the Occidental room, where Zeyneb Hanum does not need to be veiled, highlights the artificiality of her performance. The dissonance between the montage of photographs and the larger scene in which they figure makes Zeyneb Hanum's 'authentic' Oriental clothing look like drag.[8] This is a woman who has specifically changed her life in order to avoid the veil, alongside other elements of Oriental seclusion, but who dons it here in Europe in order to perform the Oriental identification in terms which the western consumer can understand, aware that her authorial integrity and book sales are both predicated on this. The visual evidence of Zeyneb Hanum's Turkishness makes visible in the text the contradictory nature of her activity as a located writing subject in a way that could not be done by the writing alone.[9] So where does this leave us with cross-cultural dressing? Whereas the cross-dressing of English Ellison works to endorse the racialized boundaries she transgresses, the attempt by Zeyneb Hanum in Europe to dress to type undermines the divisions and encoded identifications she seeks to enact. Rather, it reveals the inventedness of tradition. Like Fatima and her search for authentic artefacts of a now antiquated way of life, this dress becomes a form of historical re-enactment. The photograph shows Zeyneb Hanum dressing up as something which the west imagines she once was, but which was only ever part of the picture, as the rest of her book proceeds to demonstrate.

I want to end by considering whether theories of cross-cultural dressing can be equally applied to all cross-dressing subjects. When I discussed the cross-cultural dressing of Ellison I argued that this marked a reinvestment in the classificatory boundaries that her veiled apparel appeared to cross. In other words, she crosses the boundaries but does not dissolve them. Obviously in taking this line, I am disagreeing with many writers who see cross-dressing, generally cross-gender, as an activity which blurs boundaries and creates new indeterminate categories. Thus the cross-dressed man can be interpreted not as a man dressed as a woman but as a transvestite whose behaviour is allowed different freedoms and faces different restrictions, best illustrated perhaps by the drag queen (Garber 1992).[10] But when I come to Zeyneb Hanum, I do think that her cross-cultural dressing undermines differentiating categories. She becomes an indeterminate subject in a way that Ellison does not. However oppositional Ellison's gender identity is as a feminist in England, when she presents herself in a veil we, her readers, know who she 'really' is underneath. She is not passing as Turkish to us (though she may play with readers' prurient expectations) and her identification of herself as an English woman in Turkish dress keeps classificatory boundaries intact. But Melek Hanum in her European dress is not the equivalent of an English woman in Turkish dress, and neither is Zeyneb Hanum in Turkish dress in Europe the equivalent of an English woman in European dress in Turkey. The sartorial absolutes which can be activated by Ellison do not apply to Zeyneb Hanum and Melek Hanum, whose wardrobes already contained European clothes, though this may be hard for the western observer to recognize or accept. The idea that there is a series of imagined absolute differences, boundaries which can be crossed, cannot adequately describe the late Ottoman attitude to western goods and their use. This did not replicate an Orientalist east/west binarism but saw western commodities as part of a continuum of goods whose partial or wholesale adoption was based on a sense of value concerned as much with rarity as with ideas of cultural difference. So, when Zeyneb Hanum presents herself in Turkish clothes in her book, her native dress no longer looks natural. This is not just because she is in Europe but because the identity she enacts in Europe can only signify in relation to previously existing European classificatory terms. These, with their allegiances to stereotypes of the Oriental woman, are unable to fully recognize her performance of self as an educated, cosmopolitan Turk. The photographs of Zeyneb dressed as a Turk need also to be read alongside photographs reprinted by Sarah Graham-Brown showing elite Middle Eastern women dressed up in peasant costume or the traditional garb of another local ethnic community (Graham-Brown 1988). This indicates the existence of other forms of cross-class and cross-cultural dressing, which destabilize the absolute differences imagined in the Orient/Occident divide.

However, we can also see Zeyneb Hanum's self-presentation in Turkish dress as an activity which knowingly exploits the Orientalist paradigm for her own ends. Without downplaying the frustration of being positioned by and trying to intervene in a western discourse which cannot recognize the nuanced specificity of her Ottoman identification, it is possible that the emigre Turk can manipulate cultural codes to her advantage. In this instance the masquerade as oppressed, veiled, Turkish woman helps her sales just as Ellison's cross-cultural dressing, the epitome of the exoticized Turkish stereotype she claims to challenge, helps hers. Clearly, the shifting significations of the veiled female body offer both women points of resistance and compliance, whose impact on their various audiences they attempt to anticipate. Yet to imagine this was ever an easy process would be to underestimate the complexity of their own subjective investments in cross-cultural codes of dress, narrative and identification.

Acknowledgement

I would like to acknowledge the assistance of the London Library during the preparation of this paper.

Notes

1. *A note on naming conventions*: before the advent of the Turkish republic, Ottomans did not use a second or family name but were known by their first name and an honorific such as hanum, or lady. Zeyneb Hanum's book, though it identities her with the honorific in the frontispiece, uses only her personal name in the captions to the photographs. Though I have retained the honorific in my main text, I have not altered the plate titles – captions are reproduced as they appear in the book. Similarly, I have reproduced certain inconsistencies in my transliteration of Ottoman words. During the early years of the republic the convention for rendering Ottoman and Turkish terms into Latin script changed, seen particularly in the shift from b to p (as in Zeyneb to Zeynep) and from d to t (as in Abdulhamid to Abdulhamit). While I have endeavoured to follow current form in the rendering of names in the public domain, such as Sultan Abdulhamit, I have retained the older transliteration of Zeyneb in keeping with the primary source. But although Zeyneb and Melek Hanum appear in the bibliography as Hanoum, the spelling which

appears on the books, I have elsewhere modernized this to accord with current usage.

As well as the identificatory terms Turkish an Ottoman I also use the term Oriental. Although this is no longer a common classification, it is how Ottoman authors in this period identify themselves. I have adopted it as a constructed, relative term, not as one of neutral, geographic description, using it as a classification for one who has been racialized in the specific terms of an Orientalist discourse which is also, of course, gendered.

2. Western observers were not necessarily equipped to recognize the western-influenced changes to Turkish dress. See also Graham-Brown 1988: 118–43.

3. I am indebted to Nancy Micklewright for her discussion of this point.

4. On the representation of Ottoman gendered spaces in these sources see Lewis 2000.

5. On photography in the Ottoman Empire see Çizgen 1987.

6. Unlike much anthropological photography in that the subjects pictured in Ellison's book tend to be named, thus individuating them rather than producing them as unidentified, essentialized types. The book includes named photographs of Halide Adivar, the two male reformers, Djémal Pasha and Talaat Bey, and so on. The portrait of the Kadınlar Dünyası contributor is unnamed but the partially legible inscription, 'Grace Ellison . . . affection' indicates the existence of some sort of personal relationship.

7. On the difficulty of deciphering ethnicity and nationality in photographs of cross-cultural dressing, see Micklewright 1999b.

8. For an assertion of the 'category crisis' produced by cross-dressing, both gender and cultural, see Garber 1992.

9. On the development of intersubjective and positioned writing in ethnography, see Clifford 1986.

10. Though the heterosexual transvestite and the gay drag queen may share many things, they should not of course be conflated.

REFERENCES

Adivar, H. Edib (1926) *Memoirs of Halide Edib*, London: John Murray.

Apter, E. (1992) 'Female trouble in the colonial harem', *Differences: A Journal of Feminist Cultural Studies* 205–24.

Arat, Z. F. (1994) 'Turkish women and the republican reconstruction of tradition', in F. M. Göçek and S. Balaghi (eds) *Reconstructing Gender in the Middle East: Tradition, Identity and Power*, New York: Columbia University Press.

Berkes, N. (1964) *The Development of Secularism in Turkey*, Montreal: McGill University Press.

Bhabha, H. (1984) 'Of mimicry and man: the ambivalence of colonial discourse', *October* 28: pp. 125–33.

Çelik, Z. (1986) *The Remaking of Istanbul: Portrait of an Ottoman City in the Nineteenth Century*, Seattle: University of Washington Press.

Çizgen, E. (1987) *Photography in the Ottoman Empire 1839–1919*, Istanbul: Haset Kitalevi.

Clifford, J. (1986) 'Introduction: Partial truths', in J. Clifford and G. E. Marcus (eds) *Writing Culture: The Poetics and Politics of Ethnography*, Berkeley: University of California Press.

Duben, A. and Behar, C. (1991) *Istanbul Households: Marriage, Family and Fertility, 1880–1940*, Cambridge: Cambridge University Press.

Edwards, E. (1990) 'Photographic "types": the pursuit of method', *Visual Anthropology*, no. 3: pp. 235–58.

—— (1992) 'Introduction', in E. Edwards (ed.) *Anthropology and Photography 1860–1920*, New Haven, CT: Yale University Press.

Ellison, G. (1915) *An Englishwoman in a Turkish Harem*, London: Methuen.
—— (1928) *Turkey To-day*, London: Hutchinson.
Garber, M. (1992) *Vested Interests: Cross-Dressing and Cultural Anxiety*, London: Routledge.
Göçek, F. M. (1996) *Rise of the Bourgeoisie, Demise of Empire: Ottoman Westernization and Social Change*, New York: Oxford University Press.
Graham-Brown, S. (1988) *Images of Women: The Portrayal of Women in Photography of the Middle East 1860–1950*, London: Quartet.
Kandiyoti, D. (ed.) (1991) *Women, Islam and the State*, Basingstoke: Macmillan.
Keddie, N. R. (1991) 'Introduction: Deciphering Middle Eastern women's history', in N. R. Keddie and B. Baron (eds) *Women in Middle Eastern History: Shifting Boundaries in Sex and Gender*, New Haven, CT: Yale University Press.
Lewis, R. (2000) 'Harems and hotels: segregated city spaces and narratives of identity in the work of oriental women writers', in L. Durning and R. Wrigley (eds) *Gender and Architecture: History, Interpretation and Practice*, London: John Wiley.
Low, G. Ching-Liang (1989) 'White skins/black masks: the pleasures and politics of imperialism', *New Formations*, no. 9 (Winter): pp. 83–103.
Malmsheimer, L. M. (1987) 'Photographic analysis as ethnohistory: interpretive strategies', *Visual Anthropology*, vol. 1, no. 1: pp. 21–36.
Melek Hanoum (1926) 'How I escaped from the harem and how I became a dressmaker', *The Strand Magazine*, February: pp. 129–38.
Melman, B. (1992) *Women's Orients: English Women and the Middle East, 1718–1918. Sexuality, Religion and Work*, Basingstoke: Macmillan.
Mernissi, F. (1985) *Beyond the Veil: Male–Female Dynamics in Muslim Society* (2nd edn), London: al Saqi.
Micklewright, N. (1999a) 'Public and private for Ottoman women of the nineteenth century', in Fairchild D. Ruggles (ed.) *Women and Self-Representation in Islamic Societies*, New York: SUNY.
—— (1999b) 'Photography and consumption in the Ottoman Empire', In D. Quataert (ed.) *Consumption in the Ottoman Empire*, New York: SUNY.
Nava, M. (1998) 'The cosmopolitanism of commerce and the allure of difference: Selfridges, the Russian Ballet and the Tango 1911–1914', *International Journal of Cultural Studies*, vol. 1, no. 2: pp. 163–96.
Peirce, L. (1993) *The Imperial Harem: Women and Sovereignty in the Ottoman Empire*, Oxford: Oxford University Press.
Pinney, C. (1990) 'Classification and fantasy in the photographic construction of caste and tribe', *Visual Anthropology*, no. 3: pp. 259–88.
—— (1992) 'The parellel histories of anthropology and photography', in E. Edwards (ed.) *Anthropology and Photography 1860–1920*, New Haven, CT: Yale University Press.
Quataert, D. (1991) 'Ottoman women, households, and textile manufacturing 1800–1914', in N. R. Keddie and B. Baron (eds) *Women in Middle Eastern History: Shifting Boundaries in Sex and Gender*, New Haven, CT: Yale University Press.
Şeni, N. (1995) 'Fashion and women's clothing in the satirical press of Istanbul at the end of the 19th Century', in T. Sirin (ed.) *Women in Modern Turkish Society*, London: Zed.
Shaw, S. J. and Shaw, E. K. (1994) *History of the Ottoman Empire and Modern Turkey, vol. 2. Reform, Revolution and Republic* (2nd edn), Cambridge: Cambridge University Press.
Street, B. (1992) 'British popular anthropology: exhibiting and photographing the other', in E. Edwards (ed.) *Anthropology and Photography 1860–1920*, New Haven, CT: Yale University Press.
Vaka Brown, D. (1909) *Some Pages from the Life of Turkish Women*, London: Constable.

Wollen, P. (1987) 'Fashion/Orientalism/the body', *New Formations*, no. 1 (Spring): pp. 5–33.

Zeyneb Hanoum (1913) *A Turkish Woman's European Impressions*, ed. G. Ellison, London: Seeley, Service Co.

5.4

'VEILED FANTASIES: CULTURAL AND SEXUAL DIFFERENCE IN THE DISCOURSE OF ORIENTALISM'

Meyda Yeğenoğlu

If one wants to understand the racial situation psychoanalytically . . . considerable importance must be given to sexual phenomena.

Frantz Fanon, *Black Skin, White Masks*

The phantasy is the support of desire; it is not the object that is the support of desire. The subject sustains himself as desiring in relation to an ever more complex signifying ensemble.

Jacques Lacan, *The Four Fundamental Concepts of Psycho-Analysis*

UNVEILING AS POLITICAL DOCTRINE

Erecting a barrier between the body of the Oriental woman and the Western gaze, the opaque, all-encompassing veil seems to place her body out of the reach of the Western gaze and desire. Frustrated with the invisibility and inaccessibility of this mysterious, fantasmatic figure, disappointed with the veiled figure's refusal to be gazed at, Western desire subjects this enigmatic, in Copjec's terms, 'sartorial matter', to a relentless investigation. The practice of veiling and the veiled woman thus go beyond their simple reference and become tropes of the European text in Hayden White's sense: 'the data resisting the coherency of the image which we are trying to fashion of them.'[1] It is no surprise that there are countless accounts and representations of the veil and veiled women in Western discourses, all made in an effort to reveal the hidden secrets of the

From: Meyda Yeğenoğlu (1998), 'Veiled Fantasies: Cultural and Sexual Difference in the Discourse of Orientalism, pp. 39–67, in Meyda Yeğenoğlu, *Colonial Fantasies: Towards a Feminist Reading of Orientalism* (Cambridge: Cambridge University Press)

Orient. The very depiction of the Orient and its women, 'like the unveiling of an enigma, makes visible what is hidden'.[2] The veil is one of those tropes through which Western fantasies of penetration into the mysteries of the Orient and access to the interiority of the other are fantasmatically achieved. The most blatant example of the fear of the other and the associated fantasy of penetration is French colonialism's obsession with the woman's veil in Algeria. As we learn from Fanon, 'the Algerian woman, in the eyes of the observer, is unmistakably "she who hides behind a veil".'[3] Fanon continues: 'this enabled the colonial administration to define a precise political doctrine: "If we want to destroy the structure of Algerian society, its capacity for resistance, we must first of all conquer the women: we must go and find them behind the veil where they hide themselves and in the houses where the men keep them out of sight".'[4]

I propose to take this 'precise political doctrine' seriously, because it provides us with several possibilities at once: first, a critique of the critiques of the ethico-political program of European Enlightenment from the point of view of the double articulation of global-cultural and sexual differences, hence a new way of dealing with the entanglement of questions of imperialism and gender; second, a critique of the critiques of colonial discourse from a feminist point of view, hence the development of a new feminist perspective in the analysis of colonial discourse. I must warn my reader that I claim no privilege for the veil as an object of study. The grand narrative of the imperial, sovereign subject is complex and constantly changing, and the veil is privileged only to the extent that it enables us to see some of the complexity of this narrative.

The question of why the veiled woman has such a high profile in the French colonization of Algeria seems obvious at a first glance: in the colonizer's eye Algerian resistance is condensed in the veil which is seen as an obstacle to his visual control. Conquering the Algerian women is thus equal to conquering Algeria, the land and people themselves. This is surely not a simple military question in a narrow sense, but it is rooted in a problematic of power, which not only takes Algeria as a land to be conquered, but which establishes such conquest in terms of an epistemological superiority.[5] One of the axioms of the European Enlightenment is 'the disenchantment of the world' in which 'knowledge, which is power, knows no obstacles'.[6] In his study on modern forms of discipline, Michel Foucault demonstrated that this problematic of knowledge as power is tied to a social program and strategy according to which space is organized in a particular way which makes its individual occupants and their behavior visible and transparent. With modernity comes a new form of institutional power which is based on visibility and transparency and which refuses to tolerate areas of darkness. The epitome of this modern form of power, Bentham's model prison, the panopticon, embodies the concept of an eye which can see without being seen.[7] For Foucault, the social practice of transparency completes the philosophical ideas of the Enlightenment, for instance Rousseau's well-known dream of a perfectly transparent society (we might also say that it reveals the other side of these ideas).[8] Foucault's view is supported by Jean

Starobinski's interesting study on the theme of transparency and obstacle in Rousseau. Starobinski shows that Rousseau attached a negative value to any-thing hidden or mysterious and elaborated a whole theory of unveiling the truth.[9] Indeed, in the political doctrine of French colonialism, the veiled woman is made 'a case which, at one and the same time, constitutes an object for a branch of knowledge and a hold for a branch of power', and Muslim women are classified as a group of people 'who have to be trained or corrected, clas-sified, normalized, excluded, etc'.[10] As Foucault has succinctly argued, these objects of discourse are not a pure creation of discourse, they are rather objects (and subjects) identified by discourse as problems to be dealt with, and objects to be known and controlled (only once they are identified, they enter into a process of construction in and by discourse). Surely, the veiled woman is already other-ed in her own culture, gender-ed in and by a particular form of dressing, but she is other to the Western subject in a way that differs from her position relative to the dominant male subjects of her culture. I would like to argue here that the case or tropology of the 'veil' is not simply a signifier of a cultural habit or identity that can be liked or disliked, be good or bad, but 'in a world bewitched by the invisible powers of the other' for a subject, i.e., for the European subject in our case, it signifies the production of an 'exteriority', a 'target or threat', which makes possible for that subject to 'postulate a place that can be delimited as its own and serve as the base'.[11] This enables him to produce himself, vis-à-vis an other while simultaneously erasing the very process of this production.

The veil can be seen as the resisting data or tropology of this modern power whose program aims to construct the world in terms of a transparency provided by knowledge as power. However, limiting itself to Europe as the sovereign subject of history, Foucault's analysis of such power has remained blind to the role played by these technologies and their epistemological and subjective import in the European colonization of the world. Gayatri Spivak suggests that we write against the 'possibility that the intellectual is complicit in the persis-tent constitution of other as the self's shadow'. I take her words as a warning:

> The clearest available example of such epistemic violence is the remotely orchestrated, far-flung and heterogenous project to constitute the colonial subject as Other. This project is also the symmetrical obliteration of the trace of that Other in its precarious Subject-ivity. It is well known that Foucault locates epistemic violence, a complete overhaul of the episteme, in the redefinition of sanity at the end of the European eighteenth century. But what if that particular definition was only a part of the narrative of history in Europe as well as in the colonies? What if the two projects of epistemic overhaul worked as dislocated and unacknowledged parts of a vast two-handed engine? Perhaps it is no more than to ask that the subtext of the palimpsestic narrative of imperialism be recognized as 'subjugated knowledge' . . .[12]

The subtext of the palimpsestic narrative of imperialism is demonstrated in the fact that, whether he likes it or not, for the European subject, there is always more to the veil than the veil. A very interesting example is Gaëtan Gatian de Clerambault, the nineteenth-century French psychiatrist who was fascinated with the foldings of North African dressing and took hundreds of photographs of veiled people. Clerambault seems to constitute the unique instance of a subjective approach to North African Islamic culture which needs to be explored further. According to Gilles Deleuze, if Clerambault's interest in Islamic folds 'manifests a delirium, it is because he discovers the tiny hallucinatory perceptions of ether addicts in the folds of clothing'.[13] The Islamic veil is considered by Clerambault and Deleuze as providing a unique form of perception of a world of 'figures without objects'.[14] I see this as a legitimate area of research into the Islamic veil/fold, but I am interested here in a dialectics of seeing and gazing. Although Deleuze considers this a more restricted area of the 'optical fold',[15] I argue that its ethico-political implications exceed its epistemological limits. A general study of the fold and of its varieties remains limited in a different way, if we remember that, writing against the always-already existing possibility of the constitution of the other as the self's shadow, Spivak's 'two-handed engine' would ask for a re-inscription of the Islamic fold/veil as *subjugated knowledge* of the Western imperial palimpsest in Clerambault's psychological 'discoveries'. And Malek Alloula's well-known *The Colonial Harem* undeniably demonstrates the place of sexual difference in the signification of the Islamic fold/veil. Alloula's semiological classification and reading of erotic postcard pictures of half-veiled Algerian women opens up the problematic of cultural difference into a problematic of sexual difference. Although his approach is a semiological/Barthesian one which does not employ a thematics of fold, I suggest that we take this work as a warning for the Deleuzian overlooking of sexual (and cultural) difference in the fold/veil.[16]

THE RHETORIC OF THE VEIL: ORIENTALIST TRAVEL WRITING IN THE NINETEENTH CENTURY

In a sentence which predicts Alloula's work, 'in the Arab world' writes Fanon, 'the veil worn by women is at once noticed by the tourist . . . [it] generally suffices to characterize Arab society'.[17] Can this immediate attention be considered as an instance of the celebrated Lacanian 'triumph of the gaze over the eye'?[18] If I am wary of Foucault's complicity with the very form of power he analyzes because he overlooks its working outside Europe, or of Deleuzian analysis of the fold, I am also wary of a kind of psychoanalysis which is blind to the historical inscription of its conceptual apparatus. The question posed by François Wahl to Jacques Lacan in his seminar on the gaze is instructive in this sense. Against Lacan's insistence that all eye is evil eye, Wahl brings up the example of the 'prophylactic eye' (an eye that protects one from disease) in the Mediterranean cultures. Lacan's answer is that the prophylactic eye is allopathic, i.e., it cures the disease by exciting a dissimilar affection, and that the prophylactic objects are clearly symbols of the phallus. In the same place, he refers to the North African–Islamic 'baraka' and, despite a few places where he admits that he hesitated, concludes that the eye is always maleficent rather than beneficent.[19] I take the hesitation rather than the conclusion as my guide, but I am interested in a deconstruction of the sovereign subject rather than an ethnography of Islamic culture. In other words, I am more interested here in demonstrating the *historical determination* of the Lacanian gaze, of 'the form of a strange contingency, symbolic of what we (they) find on the horizon, as the thrust of our (their) experience, namely the lack that constitutes castration anxiety'.[20] Within such an approach, I consider the European's immediate object of attention in the horizon of Muslim culture as *his* construct: the veiled woman is not simply an obstacle in the field of visibility and control, but her veiled presence also seems to provide the Western subject with a condition which is the inverse of Bentham's omnipotent gaze. The loss of control does not imply a mere loss of sight, but a complete reversal of positions: her body completely invisible to the European observer except for her eyes, *the veiled woman can see without being seen*. The apparently calm rationalist discipline of the European subject goes awry in the fantasies of penetration as well as in the tropological excess of the veil. This is why the precise political doctrine is not simply a military matter, but, as I will demonstrate below, the strategic desire which defines it is structured through fantasy. Drawing upon his experience as a psychiatrist, Fanon emphasizes the violent play of this reversal:

> Thus the rape of the Algerian woman in the dream of a European is always preceded by a rending of the veil . . . Whenever, in dreams having an erotic content, a European meets an Algerian woman, the specific features of his relations with the colonized society manifest themselves . . . With an Algerian woman, there is no progressive conquest, no mutual revelation. Straight off, with the maximum of violence there is possession, rape, near-murder . . . This brutality and this sadism are in fact emphasized by the frightened attitude of the Algerian woman. In the dream, the woman-victim screams, struggles like a doe, and as she weakens and faints, is penetrated, martyrized, ripped apart.[21]

The veil is then part of or an element of a highly charged fantasmatic scene. Nevertheless, the fantasy of penetration is only one aspect of a more complex ideological-subjective formation which oscillates between fascination and anger and frustration. In the nineteenth-century European travellers' obsession with the veil, the 'precise political doctrine' dissolves into a textual inscription which is witness to an underlying enunciative (and subjective) formation traversing different fields of writing. These texts clearly display the veil's specific polysemy. As is well known, in Lacan's approach the gaze is not seen, but is imagined by the subject in the field of the other.[22] Orientalist writing is the European imagination at work in the field of the other. The veil attracts the eye, and forces one to think, to speculate about what is behind it. It is often represented as some kind of a mask, hiding the woman. With the help of this opaque veil, the Oriental woman is considered as not yielding herself to the Western gaze and therefore imagined as hiding something behind the veil. It is through the inscription of the veil as a mask that the Oriental woman is turned into an enigma. Such a discursive construction incites the presumption that the real nature of these women is concealed, their truth is disguised and they appear in a false, deceptive manner. They are therefore other than what they appear to be. Edmondo de Amicis' statements reveal this figure of deception: 'it is impossible to say what they contrive to do with those two veils . . . making them serve at once to *display*, to *conceal*, to *promise*, to *propose* a problem, or to betray some little marvel unexpectedly'[23] (emphasis added).

The figure of the masquerade is frequently employed. Théophile Gautier, in his description of the women of Istanbul, expresses both his denunciation of the veil and his identification of the true nature of the city through this same figure: 'an immense female population – anonymous and unknown – circulates through this mysterious city, which is thus transformed into a sort of vast masquerade – with the peculiarity, that the dominoes are never permitted to unmask.'[24] Edmondo de Amicis describes the women on the streets of Istanbul in a similar manner:

> The first impression is most curious. The stranger wonders whether all those white veiled figures in bright colored wrappers are masquerades, or nuns, or mad women; and as not one is ever seen accompanied by a man, they seem to belong to no one, and to be all girls and widows, or members of some great association of the 'ill-married' . . . One is constrained to stop and meditate upon these strange figures and stranger customs.[25]

The veil gives rise to a meditation: if they wear a mask, or masquerade or conceal themselves, then there must be a behind-the-mask, a knowledge that is kept secret from us. The *mystery* that is assumed to be concealed by the veil is *unconcealed* by giving a figural representation to this mask and to the act of masquerading as an enigmatic figure. However, what is thus concealed, i.e., the 'masquerade', the 'veil', is the *act of concealment itself*. The veiled existence is the very truth of Oriental women; they seem to exist always in this deceptive manner.

This metaphysical speculation or mediation, this desire to reveal and unveil is at the same time the *scene of seduction*. The metaphysical will to know gains a sexual overtone. Troubled with this mask, the Western subject is threatened and seduced at the same time:

> These then, you think, these are really those 'conquerors of the heart', those 'founts of pleasure', those 'little rose leaves', those 'early ripening grapes', those 'dews of the morning', 'auroras', 'vivifiers', and 'full moons'. These are the *hanums* and the mysterious odalisques that we dreamed of when we were twenty years old . . . It is a costume at once

austere and sweet, that has something virginal and holy about it; under which none but gentle thoughts and innocent fancies should have birth.[26]

Since he is devoid of any true perspective on the Oriental woman, Amicis can never be sure. The Oriental woman/Orient is so deceptive and theatrical. With her, everything is an enigma. Amicis continues: 'that jealous veil that, according to the Koran, was to be "a sign of her virtue and a guard against the talk of the world" is now only a semblance.'[27]

This fear of being deceived by the masquerading Oriental woman is also what characterizes Loti's representation of the Oriental woman in *Disenchanted*. In this novel, two Turkish women and a French writer, Marc Helys, write a letter to Loti, simply because they want some divergence from their monotonous life and would like to teach him a lesson by making him an object of ridicule. The women approach Loti under their veils, thus remaining completely incognito.[28] Uncomfortable with their invisible presence, Loti asks them to remove their veils, but they refuse to do so. During their conversations, when the women speak a few Turkish words with each other, Loti immediately warns them that he knows the language sufficiently well and would be aware if any 'uncivil remark' was being uttered about him.

This short scene sums up the whole theme of the novel: it is about how Loti is seduced but at the same time mocked by these veiled women. As they themselves express through their attitude, it is precisely with their veils that Oriental women can seduce, mock, and threaten him. The veil places them at a distance Loti cannot reach. In warning them that he knows Turkish, that he can understand them, he in fact expresses his own anxiety. This anxiety is caused by his lack of a true, fixed perspective; he cannot position himself vis-à-vis them. He reminds them of his knowledge of their language precisely because this knowledge does not seem sufficient to him to gain control over their veiled presence, for they masquerade and their dress is deceptive. It is this incapacity to fix and control that is unsettling and terrifying and yet so seducing.

A variety of reasons are offered by the European subject to explain this obsession with the Oriental veil: 'civilizing', 'modernizing', and thereby 'liberating' the 'backward' Orient and its women, making them speaking subjects. These are the manifest terms of the political doctrine. But then what do we make of the above texts obsessed with the veil? Joan Copjec suggests that no rational explanation can account for the West's preoccupation with lifting the veil, for this is a preoccupation sustained by fantasy and hence belongs to the realm of desire. According to Copjec:

> What was capital in this fantasy was the surplus pleasure, the useless *jouissance* which the voluminous cloth was supposed to veil and the colonial subject, thus hidden, was supposed to enjoy. Every effort to strip away the veil was clearly an aggression against the bloated presence of this pleasure that would not release itself into the universal pool.[29]

Simultaneously attracting and repelling the subject, the veil occupies the place of the *objet petit a*, the object causing desire in Lacanian psycho analysis. Lacan writes that 'the object a in the field of the visible is the gaze'.[30] However, such an object does not exist objectively, in itself, but is constructed retroactively by the subject. Although any object might potentially be an object of desire, what transforms an object into *objet petit a* is, in Slavoj Zizek's words, 'an interested look, a look supported, permeated and distorted by desire'.[31] Such a look is possible within fantasy. Fantasy is basically a scenario filling out the fundamental lack in the subject caused by a splitting in the language. In Heath's words, 'no object can satisfy desire – what is wanting is always wanting, division is the condition of subjectivity'.[32] The concept of fantasy is crucial in Lacan's account of sexual relationship: Jacqueline Rose shows that it is at the level of fantasy that man achieves his identity and wholeness: 'the idea of a complete and assured sexual identity belongs in the realm of fantasy', and 'the man places the woman at the basis of his fantasy, or constitutes fantasy through woman by transposing *objet a* onto the image of woman who then acts as its guarantee. 'The absolute Otherness of the woman, therefore, serves to secure for the man his own self-knowledge and truth.'[33] We have seen above how the veiled Oriental woman is given precisely such a status in Orientalist discourse. In Orientalist writing, *discourses of cultural and sexual difference are powerfully mapped onto each other*. What is crucial in this process is that the very act of representing the veil is never represented; the desire that represents the veil can not be represented. The subject can not represent (see) himself representing (seeing) himself.[34] The metaphorical excess of the veil is thus an effacement of the *process of production* of the subject. Placing desire on the side of the being rather than on that of the thing, Jacques Lacan writes: 'This lack is beyond anything which can represent it. It is only ever represented as a reflection on a veil.'[35]

WOMAN AS VEIL: NIETZSCHE AND DERRIDA, OR LIMITS OF THE DECONSTRUCTION OF METAPHYSICS

We have then a very precise relationship established between the veil, masquerading, truth and woman. These themes are familiar in post-structuralist, psychoanalytic and feminist theories. By a detour through these theories, I am going to argue that, since the veil is a figure essential in the construction of femininity in a patriarchal order, the European's strange obsession with the veiled woman also has implications for a more general analysis of patriarchy.

The representation of 'womanliness as masquerade' finds one of its most powerful expressions in Nietzsche's work, where he associates femininity with the tropes of truth and veil.[36] For him, woman, like the truth, is enigmatic and has a deceptive appearance. She adorns herself and by adorning herself she seduces and fascinates man: 'woman, conscious of man's feelings concerning herself, walking beautifully, dancing, expressing delicate thoughts: in the same way, she practices modesty, reserve, distance – realizing instinctively that in this way the idealizing capacity of man will grow.'[37] She has no truth nor she does or can want enlightenment about herself;[38] Her truth is her adornment and her style is appearance and disguise. She is nothing but a pure spectacle.[39] Here is Nietzsche's description of the feminine:

> Unless a woman seeks a new adornment for herself that way – I do think adorning herself is part of the Eternal-Feminine? – surely she wants to inspire fear of herself – perhaps she seeks mastery. But she does not *want* truth: what is truth to woman? From the beginning nothing has been more alien, repugnant and hostile to woman than truth – her great art is the lie, her highest concern is mere appearance and beauty.[40]

Faced with this destabilizing, fearful and enigmatic figure, we find a perplexed man who tries to grasp the essential femininity that lies behind her mask. Nietzsche's 'nothing but pure spectacle' is only apparently opposite to the veil as a dark figure or as an obstacle to vision. The underlying question is the same as de Amicis' or Loti's: how can he attain the knowledge of this enigma, how can he reveal what lies behind her veiled appearance (i.e., the lie as her great art)? These are the questions de Amicis, Gautier and Loti ask in their search for the truth of the Oriental woman as an appearance of femininity. In their rhetorical and epistemological move which I describe as the double articulation of cultural and sexual difference, culture and gender are other-ed through each other. These European men bring their insight and knowledge, their intuition and contemplation to the task of uncovering her hidden truth, yet they are not successful. Their solution is to posit the truth of a particular culture from within a certain patriarchal metaphorics: deception and dissimulation are essential characteristics of Oriental cultures. According to Nietzsche, however, woman's deceptive style does not mean that she conceals an essence behind her appearance and adornment. She is deceptive *because* she has no essence to conceal. It is her masquerading style which makes one think that she hides an essential truth.

Nietzsche's aim in establishing an association between the tropes of woman, truth, and veil is to develop a critique of the philosophy of truth, which is the problematic commanding European Orientalist writing. An analysis of the veil occupies an important role in his attack on metaphysical discourse and the various set of oppositions established within it. The parallelism he establishes between the movement of truth and the deceptive feminine gesture enables Nietzsche to criticize, but at the same time to reinscribe the tropological system of metaphysics. The veil functions to make 'truth profound, to ensure that there is a depth that lurks behind the surface of things'.[41] It is precisely by attacking this figuring of the veil that Nietzsche is able to take a critical distance from the metaphysics of truth and the essentialism immanent in such discourses as Loti's or de Amicis'. He refutes the idea that there is an essence or 'real' behind the veil and increases the value attached to appearance over truth or real: 'we no longer believe that truth remains truth when the veils are withdrawn; we have lived too much to believe this. Today we consider it a matter of decency not to wish to see everything naked, or to be present at everything, or to understand and "know everything".'[42]

Metaphysical discourse is able to secure the various sets of oppositions it constructs between appearance and reality, surface and depth, precisely through the figuring of the veil as that opaque curtain which conceals, covers, hides or disguises an essential nature. Nietzsche, by distancing himself from the idea of a 'real' residing beneath appearance and by valorizing the appearance over this 'real', attempts to undermine the oppositional structure that characterizes metaphysical discourse. However, as Doane rightly points out, while taking up a critical distance from the metaphysics of truth, Nietzsche reinforces the association between woman and dissimulation or deception, for 'the pronoun *she* plays a major role in delineating the operation of this mode of deception'.[43]

Despite his attempt to devalorize the association of truth with what is behind the veil, Nietzsche's work still retains the categories of deception and femininity as deception. Although, in Nietzsche's philosophy, there are no negative connotations attached to deception and appearance (on the contrary he values them), Doane argues that these categories nevertheless 'place the woman as the privileged exemplar of instability'.[44] In other words, despite his attempt to dissociate the value attached to truth, Nietzsche still remains locked within the binary logic which construes truth and appearance as opposites. What Nietzsche fails to address is posed by Irigaray, as her criticism targets the very opposition between real and appearance itself and the *interest* that resides underneath such an opposition: '*what* that we should question has been *forgotten*, not about a truer truth, a realer real, but *about the profit that underlies the truth/fantasy pair*?'[45]

The profit that underlies the truth/fantasy pair is what I have described as the European's fictional unity and command of experience, i.e., the production of their subjectivity, which de Amicis, Gautier and Loti had managed by a textual proliferation of discourses through the tropology of the veil.

Joan Riviere's important work 'Womanliness as Masquarade' also brings out an implicit criticism of the Nietzschean critique of metaphysics by providing us with a powerful discussion of how the figures of woman or femininity and veil/mask are closely associated in a masculine order.[46] Unlike Nietzsche's approach, Riviere's exposes man as the one who formulates the question: for Riviere, the term 'masquerade' refers to the *male's representation* of woman on the one hand and how this representation constitutes her identity on the other. These two aspects are closely related, for the question of representation is at the same time a question of constitution.

The concept of 'womanliness as masquerade' refers to a male's representation, to masculine construction: 'The masquerade is a representation of femininity, but then femininity is representation, the representation of woman.'[47] This trouble with masquerade is man's trouble: 'the conception of womanliness as a mask, behind which man suspects some hidden danger, throws a little light on the enigma.'[48] It is man's assumption of femininity which turns it into an enigma. As Stephen Heath observes: 'Man's suspicion is the old question, *Was will das Weib?, Das ewig Weibliche* (What does woman want? Eternal feminine) all the others, always the same . . . the masquerade is the woman's thing, hers, but it is also exactly *for* the man, a male representation.'[49] The question 'What does she want?' is paradigmatic here: de Amicis articulates this question when he 'wonders whether all those white veiled figures in bright colored wrappers are masquerades, or nuns, or mad women' or when he cries, in fervor, before the cold mute masks: 'come, more like other men for once! tell us who you are.'[50] We learn from Riviere's psychoanalytic-feminist criticism that the question of what woman wants is the man's question. According to her, it is precisely this characterization of femininity that incites contradictory desires; the desire to know and uncover her truth on the one hand, and the desire to distance her and thus avoid the threat her unpredictability and inaccessibility pose, on the other. Consequently, the man is seduced and mocked and threatened all at the same time. Such a contradictory and ambivalent desire, caused by *the continual displacement of his perspective on or lack of knowledge of the woman*, lends itself to an over-representation (the excess of the veil) and to an endless investigation of the feminine in an effort to evade such a lack and constitute his subjectivity. As such, the instability he experiences is dissipated by projecting it onto the feminine and characterizing her as the sex which is unpredictable and deceptive. At this point we also need to remember Freud's endless attempts to evade his inability to know and conquer the 'darkness' that hovers around the feminine sexuality – *at the same time a darkness he himself construes through his own representation.* For example, he is as confident to study and know men's sexuality as he is totally puzzled by the other sex: 'That of women – partly owing to the stunning effect of civilized conditions and partly owing to their conventional secretiveness and insincerity – is still *veiled* in an impenetrable obscurity' (emphasis added).[51] As Doane suggests, 'the horror or threat of that precariousness (of both sexuality and the visible) is attenuated by attributing it to the woman, over and against the purported stability and identity of the male. The veil is the mark of that precariousness.'[52]

Derrida is another critic of Nietzsche and the last figure in our detour through post-structuralist theory. Although affirming Nietzsche's attack on the metaphysics of truth through the metaphor of woman as the name of untruth, Derrida nevertheless gives it another twist in his *Spurs*. His concern is, like Nietzsche, to undo the metaphysical discourse that sets truth and untruth as opposites. While Nietzsche compares woman's deceptive veiled gesture to the movement of untruth, Derrida compares the feminine gesture to *writing* or *style*. The concept *writing* is one of the central instruments in Derrida's deconstruction of metaphysical binaries. Refuting the idea that woman has an essence, Derrida argues that 'there is no such thing as the truth of woman, but it is because of the abyssal divergence of the truth, because that untruth is "truth". Woman is but one name for that untruth of truth.'[53] The metaphors

Nietzsche uses for femininity such as instability and dissimulation are also deployed by Derrida. In his case, she appears as the figure for undecidability (associated with but repressed by metaphysics), but as a figure nevertheless:

> It is impossible to dissociate the questions of art, style and truth from the question of woman. Nevertheless, the question 'what is woman?' is itself suspended by the simple formulation of their common problematic. One can no longer seek her, no more than one could search for woman's femininity or female sexuality. And she is certainly not to be found in any of the familiar modes of concepts or knowledge. Yet it is impossible to resist looking for her.[54]

Derrida represents a step further than Nietzsche in deconstructing the metaphysics of truth. But his deconstruction of metaphysics by way of associating woman with undecidability and unpredictability implies turning woman into a ground or instrument of deconstruction. However radical this aim is, she becomes a vehicle of deconstruction rather than a subject of it. In Spivak's words, 'as the radically other she does not *really exist*, yet her name remains one of the important names for displacement, the special mark of deconstruction'.[55] As Spivak rightly suggests, to avoid this 'double displacement of woman', what is needed is the deconstruction of the 'opposition between displacement and logocentrism itself'. Spivak further argues that the task of deconstructing the sovereign subject cannot be accomplished if we limit our investigation to the question of what woman is, for this is only another way of asking the question 'what does woman want?' With this question, woman is still posed as the *object* of investigation. Rather, the feminist gesture requires asking the question that will allow the woman the *subject* status and the positioning of a questioning subject: what is man? what does he want? It will then be possible to 'bring back the absolutely convincing deconstructive critiques of the sovereign subject'.[56]

I take Spivak's suggestion that a deconstruction of the opposition between displacement and logocentrism is necessary in order to pose the question of the itinerary of man's desire in an attempt to deconstruct the imperial European subjectivity.[57] The question of what man wants, of 'the itinerary of his desire', does not only make women subjects of inquiry but it also opens the inquiry to a *global socio-economic and cultural inscription*, for which nineteenth-century Orientalist writing is but one remarkable instance. We are now in a better position to ask what 'interest' is involved here and what is 'the profit that underlies the truth/fantasy pair'.

THE CONSTITUTION OF THE EUROPEAN SUBJECT AS SOVEREIGN

Two modes of differentiation, the sexual and the cultural, are thus not simply two distinct, singular moments in the representation of *difference*, but rather, as Homi Bhabha phrases it: 'within the apparatus of colonial power, the discourses of sexuality and race relate in a process of *functional over-determination*.'[58] The structural affinity between the two with respect to the display of difference establishes a chain of equivalence in which woman is the Orient, the Orient is woman; woman like the Orient, the Orient like the woman, exists veiled; she is nothing but the name of untruth and deception. If the Oriental is feminine and if the feminine is Oriental, we can claim that the nature of femininity and the nature of the Orient are figured as one and the same thing in these representations. This equivalence positions the Orientalist/Western colonial subject as masculine: the other culture is always like the other sex.[59] This is why the Western subject, *whether male or female*, is always fascinated by the veil or harem, the truth of culture in the space of woman, in the body of woman. But then what does he see when the mask is lifted? Is it ever lifted? How can the subject of knowledge know and be certain about what lies behind the mask? Nietzsche refutes the view there is an essence behind the veil. Riviere reinscribes the question as man's, but then reads it also as constitution of femininity (which is representation of woman).[60] Irigaray also resists differentiating between the veil and what exists underneath it, by writing that 'beneath the veil subsists only veil'.[61] But for her – and especially we might say, if representation is constitution – there is an interest in the question and a profit in the discourse which it produces.

What do we make of these Orientalist and masculine representations which presuppose and pose a place and a cultural/sexual secret behind the Oriental feminine veil? We have seen that European writers first posit the Oriental veil as an object of investigation and presuppose that there is something behind it, but then this very presupposition is both denied and accepted by the conclusion that the very nature or being of the Orient is veiled. On the surface, this is a process in which the veil is incorporated as an object of discursive and textual play. These two processes however, political and cultural, as separate they are, are not simply chronologically ordered. While the political project has been a precise strategy of unveiling, i.e., an implementation of the European principle of government based on an ideal of transparency and visibility, the textual and conceptual dimension, the inscription of the veil in the European text is witness to a constitution of subjectivity, an imaginary unity and command of experience in the encounter with the other. A careful reading of this constitution might enable us to see that the profit that underlies the truth/fantasy pair is not a simple plus on the side of European subjectivity. Since such profit, such surplus of subjectivity is in the *excess* of the tropology of the veil, it is subjected to a mechanism which remains *beyond its control*. What the Orientalist texts manifest in their paradoxical attempt to other the veil is that the reference is always veiled and remains other to what it signifies. This is the point where 'real' politics (the world of conflict) and textual 'sublation' (*belles lettres*) are necessarily conflated with each other. What appears through this conflation might be called an *ethos*. The ethos in question, that of the sovereign subject of Europe, is described by Marx in his critical reading of Hegel. Gayatri Spivak observes that, according to Marx, 'Hegel's picture of the subject appropriating the object' was really charged by 'a deep hostility'. In Marx's own words, 'the appropriation . . . must proceed from indifferent alienness to real hostile engagement'.[62]

If Europe's outside is made an integral part of its identity and power in discourses such as Orientalism, this is, paradoxically, only by the creation of such outside in terms of an absolute and essential difference. If the veiled woman/ culture remains always different or infinitely dissimulating in Orientalist logic, this is *not* because of the complexity of her/their being-in-the-world, in which one might find continuities as well as discontinuities with one's own culture/subjectivity, but because they are always and absolutely different. They *should* remain different, because I should remain the *same*: they are not/should not be a possibility within my own world, which will thus be different. This is the 'deep hostility' which is pointed out by Spivak and Marx, in resonance with essentialism conceived as a philosophy of the 'proper'. That is to say, such hostility does not refer to a mere prejudice or uncultivated aggressive behavior which can be corrected or repaired by simply taking a more peaceful, good-natured, tolerant or sympathetic attitude. Deep hostility is not merely a subjective or personal characteristic, changing from one person or group to another, and thus adaptable or normalizable. While personal or even group characteristics might well be affected by education, to think that such an education will thus erase the *subject position* is rather disingenuous. It is not a question of liking or disliking the Orientals, their women, and their culture. The hostility expressed here is the force of negation which constitutes the subject *as* sovereign, that stern force which drives the machine of his self-production in the dialectical, restricted economy of the production of the self as same. It is therefore a necessary moment in his encounter with the culturally/sexually different.

MIMICRY AND THE QUESTION OF THE VEIL

I have argued above that if the concept-figure of veil provides the Orientalist with an imaginary control of his colonial displacement, its textual inscription nevertheless remains beyond his control. I have thus located an incessant movement of desire at the center of orientalist discourse. This is part of an attempt to transform and reformulate the very means by which we identify the nature of colonial oppression and hence rethink the problematic dichotomies between self and other, structure and agency, domination and resistance.[63] To rethink Orientalism's discursive field through the psychoanalytic concept of desire enables us to conceive colonial domination as being based on an ambivalent and conflictual economy. To give an account of otherness through the concept of desire implies a formulation of the process of colonial identification not as an affirmation of a pregiven identity, but as a *process* in which both the 'Western subject' and the 'Oriental other' are mutually implicated in each other and thus neither exists as a fully constituted entity. As Bhabha suggests, 'the desire for the Other is doubled by the desire in language, which *splits the difference* between Self and Other so that both positions are partial; neither is sufficient unto itself'.[64] My purpose, in pointing to the complexity and contradiction of desire in the representations of cultural and sexual difference, is twofold: to understand the process of exclusion and differentiation through which the Western self is constituted and achieves the appearance of an autonomous identity precisely by veiling its dependency and indebtedness from its excluded and marginalized other; second, to capture the unavoidable trace of the other in the subject and the consequent resistance it exerts upon him.

The notion of ambivalence and the contradictory economy as developed by Bhabha enables us to understand the excesses or slippages within colonial discourse.[65] Such excesses or slippages imply the impossibility of formulating the relationship between the Western subject and its colonial other in dualistic terms which implies setting up oppression and agency as two different poles of a binary opposition. My reiteration of the concept of desire should thus be conceived of as an effort to displace the notion of colonial discourse as an affirmation of a pregiven Western identity. The crux of my argument is that *not only the very identity of the Western subject is constituted in the movement of desire, but also the potential resistance to this constitution is also inscribed in this very process.* Fanon's observation is pertinent for understanding this dynamic: 'when it encounters resistance from the other, self-consciousness undergoes the experience of *desire* . . . As soon as I *desire* I am asking to be considered.'[66]

Before I proceed to the discussion of the ways in which the veil *might* acquire a subversive quality, I would like to recapitulate what I have been suggesting regarding the moment of colonial resistance. To inquire into the 'mechanism' of the Western subject's constitution through the psychoanalytic concept of desire is not to suggest that its identity is fully determined.[67] On the contrary, it should be seen as an attempt to explain the constituted character of the subject and thereby to argue that both the closure of the subject's identity and the resistance of the other is never final, but always partial and relative. As Judith Butler warns us, it is erroneous to assume the subject in advance so as to protect its agency, because to argue the constituted character of the subject is not to suggest that it is determined. In other words, the power that constitutes the subject does not cease to exist 'after' constituting its subject, for the subject 'is never fully constituted, but is subjected and produced time and again'.[68] Therefore, if we are not in search of an a priori guarantee for the agency of the subject, then we cannot afford not to scrutinize the process of the constitution of the subject. The inquiry into the agency of the subject can be made only when it is not presumed and such an inquiry is contingent upon understanding its constituted character.

How does the desiring subject's ceaseless pursuit of its absent object and the disruption of the stability of this desire refigure itself in the context of colonial discourse? If we claim that the subject can never achieve a full closure in constituting his identity, what role does the unique text-ile of the veil, a text-ile which 'conceals' and 'hides' the other from the colonial gaze, play in this process? How can we seek out the residues, the remains or traces of the veiled other which exceed the phallocentric and Orientalist representations? Where can we locate the moments of recalcitrance? What, if any, role do the unique characteristics of the veil play in this?

We have seen above that the colonial subject's desire to control and dominate the foreign land is not independent from his scopic desire, from his desire to penetrate, through his surveillant eye, what is behind the veil. *The invisibility the veil secures for the colonial other is simultaneously the point at which desire is articulated and the ground upon which the scopic drive of the subject is displaced*, for there is always the threat of the return of the look of the other. In Fanon's words, 'it was the colonialist's frenzy to unveil the Algerian woman, it was his gamble on winning the battle of the veil'.[69] In this battle 'the occupier was *bent on unveiling Algeria*',[70] because 'there is in it the will to bring this woman within his reach, to make her a possible object of possession'.[71] But what explains the obsession with lifting the veil is something that is always-already inscribed in this unique sartorial matter. The veil is seen as a border which distinguishes inside from outside, as a screen or cover, and women are associated with the inside, home and territory in the native Algerian culture.[72] Of course at the same time the veil demarcates a boundary and delimits the colonial power. As Malek Alloula's analysis of the French colonial picture post-cards demonstrates, the veil that covers the Algerian woman indicates a refusal to the French soldier. The photographer, whose scopic desire is discouraged, experiences disappointment and rejection.[73] Similarly for Fanon, since the veil allows women to see without being seen, it disallows reciprocity, and implies that the woman is not yielding herself, making herself available for vision.[74]

It is this disappointment and frustration which disturbs the voyeuristic look of the subject. Unlike looking at a photograph or a screen, by looking at a veiled other, the subject cannot have the security of 'I look at it, but it does not look at me looking at it',[75] because there is always the threat of the return of the look of the other. This implies that the pleasure of seeing is not entirely on the side of the subject, but he himself is subject to a look and hence is not inscribed, to borrow from Metz again, as an 'invisible' subject.[76] The structure of voyeuristic pleasure which is based upon the 'invisibility of the subject' and the 'visibility of the object' is being reversed here into its opposite. Instead of being looked at, the object now looks at.[77]

The subject cannot ignore that he is being looked at as he tries to unveil the other in order to satisfy his voyeuristic pleasure and thus fails to fantasize himself as a full subject.[78] The look that filters through the tiny orifice of the veil is the statement of the absent and invisible other and this statement can be translated, to borrow a formulation from Bhabha, into: 'as even now you look/but never see me'.[79] In other words, the invisible other speaks from its absent location. The countergaze of the other should be located in this absent-presence, in this space of the in-between. It is the veil which enables the Oriental other to look without being seen. This not only disturbs the desire of the

Western/colonial subject to fix cultural and sexual difference, but also enables the colonial other to turn itself into a surveillant gaze. It is in this space of absent-presence that there emerges the challenge of the 'invisible', 'hidden' other. To recapitulate, *it is through the veil that the colonial Western desire to see emerges and is erased simultaneously*, and this is what enables the veiled other to destabilize the identificatory process of the subject. It is this moment of seeing or these eyes that filter through the veil which frustrate the voyeuristic desire of the colonialist and displaces his surveillant eye.

If it is through this uncanny look, which her absence/invisibility provides to her, that the other constitutes its 'I' and thereby unsettles the colonial gaze, then one might ask what the difference is between my account of the other's resistance through its enigmatic absence and the representation of the veil in Orientalist discourse? Are these two discursive systems not based on the recognition of the other as absent, invisible, hidden, and do not both register this absence as enigmatic?

In his discussion of the Algerian liberation struggle, Fanon claims that during the anti-colonial resistance movement, the veil 'has been manipulated, transformed into a technique of camouflage, into a means of struggle'.[80] What transformed the veil from being an element of tradition into an element of strategy of subversion? Fanon at times claims that the veil was used by women as a protective mask in order to carry bombs and weapons for the revolutionary movement – 'every veiled woman, every Algerian woman, became suspect'.[81] But this is not a sufficient explanation because many women during the revolutionary process reveiled themselves in order to affirm 'that it was not true that woman liberated herself at the invitation of France and of General de Gaulle'.[82] Apparently what used to be an 'oppressive' item which confined women to the private domain of the home now enabled them to assert their subjectivity and agency.[83] The affirmation of the veil in the anti-colonial struggle was a direct response to the colonial desire to unveil, reveal, and control the colonized country. It is not surprising after all that women's agency emerged out of the *texture* of their own culture. Or, given the immense significance of the veil for both sides, should we not say that the anti-colonial resistance emerged under the banner of a metaphor – veil – that belongs to, that is woman? However, this culture was no longer the same. In taking up the veil as a constituent symbolic element of their subjectivity, the Algerian women did not simply continue their traditional roles, because the veil had now become the *embodiment of their will to act, their agency*. It was thus reinscribed and re-charged in the colonial situation and acquired a symbolic significance that directly *affected* the struggle. I talk about the consequences of this situation for the relationship between nationalism and women in 'decolonized' societies – the question of the manipulation or control of women by 'post-colonial' nation-states – in chapter 5 of *Colonial Fantasies*, the publication in which this article originally appeared. Now I should like to explain how the veil turned out to be a subversive element. In order to do this, I want to use the concept of mimicry as explained by Luce Irigaray.

In her critique of phallocentrism, Irigaray insists that a mere reversal of this system cannot constitute a subversive politics, for it remains locked within the same economy that it aims to shatter. What could displace and hence shake the ground of the phallocentric representations is a purposeful but distorted imitation of the characteristics attributed to the feminine:

> There is, in an initial phase, perhaps only one 'path', the one historically assigned to the feminine: that of *mimicry*. One must assume the feminine role deliberately. Which means already to convert a form of subordination into an affirmation, and thus to begin to thwart it . . . To play with mimesis is thus, for a woman, to try to recover the place of her exploitation by discourse, without allowing herself to be simply reduced to it. It means to resubmit herself – inasmuch as she is on the side of the 'perceptible', of 'matter' – to 'ideas', in particular to ideas about herself, that are elaborated in/by masculine logic, but so as to make 'visible', by an effect of playful repetition, what was supposed to remain invisible: the cover-up of a possible operation of the feminine in language. It also means 'to unveil' the fact that, if women are such good mimics, it is because they are not simply resorbed in this function. *They also remain elsewhere.*[84]

Following Irigaray's formulation, I suggest that by claiming and playfully repeating the very attributes of concealment and dissimulation, the Algerian women managed to stay elsewhere, indeed to create an 'elsewhere', an 'outside' that displaced the French colonial power. But how does one distinguish between a subversive repetition and a loyal one? For Irigaray, parodic repetition differs from mere loyal repetition, for it consists of simultaneous recognition and denial of the dominant codes of femininity. However, repetition of the dominant norms in and of itself may not be enough to displace them, for there is a risk involved in it. The trap here is becoming complicit by receding back into the old definitions that one seeks to combat. Hence mimicry does not automatically produce a subversive outcome; it can achieve such an effect to the extent that it is, as Braidotti notes, 'being sustained by a critical consciousness'.[85] That is, it can be subversive on the condition that the naturalized gender codes are critically reflected upon. The re-articulation, reworking and re-signification of the discursive characteristics of phallocentrism can open the possibility of an in-between ambivalent zone where the agency of the female subject can be construed. In our case, the colonization of land and culture in Algeria was strategically entangled on the body of women – such is the articulation of the historical and fantasy. This created a unique situation for native women and produced a historically specific kind of critical consciousness. Always-already articulated as the most inner core of culture, of the very nativity and territoriality of culture, Algerian women had become able to embody their difference vis-à-vis the hostile foreign power. It is in this very particular kind of historical conjuncture that the veil shifted from a traditional to a subversive role. This is no doubt a historically specific situation or conjuncture of our modern times, that is repeated in so many anti-colonial and national resistance struggles, a strange and unique historical moment or process in which tradition does not simply disappear in loyalty to the forward march of progress but instead ceases to be traditional and loyal and becomes the signifier of an active, resistant and transformative subjectivity, a moment of empowerment and agency. Surely this is not an unproblematical moment, given the nationalist elite's patriarchal framework. But blindness to women's irreducible power and seeing their difference as simply contained within nationalist leadership is indeed to reinscribe the power of female agency into the grand illusion of the forward march of history.

The Algerian women thus turned the Orientalist representation into an affirmation and thereby instilled a new definition of the act of concealment by, in Mary Ann Doane's words, 'enacting a defamiliarized version' of the Orientalist representations of the veil. What the colonial gaze saw in the Algerian women's disturbing mimicry was a displacement of its own representation of the veil. Hence what was once familiar and recognizable as concealment, mask, masquerading, has now become unfamiliar, disturbing and uncanny. Therefore, what was implied in this manipulative use of the veil was *not* a strategy of reversal of the Orientalist discourse, for such a strategy would have implied an effort to demonstrate that they were hiding *nothing* behind colonialism's so-long-held object of suspicion. Mimicry revealed that there was nothing but the veil behind the veil. In resuming and reclaiming the veil, Algerian women parodied the Orientalist discourse which construed the veil as a mask. Their strategic use of the veil thus *doubled* the Orientalist representation of cultural and sexual difference and this doubling brought a new mode of representation of the veil as a positive, self-affirming political force. The calling into question of Orientalism's claim on the naturalness of the veil through a mimetic repetition enabled women to constitute a space where they engendered their own subjectivity. The subversive quality the veil achieved in this decolonizing gesture was enabled by the very conditions that construed it. There is an affinity between Algerian's women's struggle and deconstruction which, in Derrida's words, 'operate(s) necessarily from the inside, borrowing all the strategic and economic resources of subversion from the old structure, borrowing them structurally'.[86]

Naomi Schor, in reading the meaning(s) of the concept of mimicry in Irigaray, suggests that, in mimicry, difference is signified as a positivity; it refers to the reclaiming of the characteristics attributed to the feminine. The difference that is brought about in this joyful reappropriation is not only beyond masquerade and mimicry, but signifies 'an emergence of the feminine and the feminine can only emerge from within or beneath . . . femininity within which it lies buried. The difference within mimesis *is* the difference within difference'.[87] Following Schor, I would suggest that we see the difference within the Algerian women's mimicry as the difference within difference – a difference that came out of their doubling of the Orientalist/masculinist representations of difference. In other words, what is revealed in this doubling is the sub-sistence of the 'quite Other' behind its mere difference. The difference represented in the subversive mimicry of the Algerian women is the *unrecuperable* or *undomesticated* difference that the colonial Subject has ferociously tried to deny. In Irigaray's words:

> Beneath all those/her appearances, beneath all those/her borrowed finery, that female other still sub-sists. Beyond all those/her forms of life and death, still she is living. And as she is dis-tant – and in 'herself' – she threatens the stability of all values. In her there is always the possibility that truth, appearances, will, power, eternal recurrence . . . will collapse. By mimicking them all more or less adequately, that female other never holds firm to any of them univocally . . . Truth and appearances, and reality, power . . . she is – through her inexhaustible aptitude for mimicry – the living foundation for the whole staging of the world. Wearing different veils according to the historic periods.[88]

In exploring the articulation of sexual and cultural difference in the discourse of Orientalism, I have pointed to the inextricable link between the masculinist and colonialist position the Western subject occupies in relation to its Oriental others. A Western reader, more specifically a feminist reader, might feel uneasy about this suggestion, wondering whether the representations of the Orient, veil and woman might be different if the gender identity of the representing agency were woman.

NOTES

1. Hayden White, *Tropics of Discourse: Essays in Cultural Criticism* (Baltimore and London: The Johns Hopkins University Press, 1982), p. 1.
2. Olivier Richon, 'Representation, the Despot and the Harem: Some Questions Around an Academic Orientalist Painting by Lecomte-Du-Nouy (1885)', in *Europe and its Others*, Proceedings of the Essex Conference on the Sociology of Literature, vol. I, ed. F. Barker et al. (Colchester: University of Essex, 1985), p. 8.
3. Frantz Fanon, *A Dying Colonialism*, trans. Haakon Chevalier (New York: Grove Press, 1965), p. 36.
4. Ibid., pp. 37–38.
5. As Said shows, this is evident in a speech by Lord Balfour in which he spends a lot of effort in denying such a superiority, while at the same time proposing it. Edward Said, *Orientalism* (Harmondsworth: Penguin, 1978), p. 32.
6. Theodor Adorno and Max Horkheimer, *The Dialectic of Enlightenment*, trans. John Cumming (London and New York: Verso, 1979), p. 3.
7. Michel Foulcault, *Discipline and Punish: The Birth of the Prison*, trans. A. Sheridan (New York: Vintage Books, 1979), pp. 200–1; See also the interesting article by Jacques-Alain Miller, 'Jeremy Bentham's Panoptic Device', trans. Richard Miller, *October*, 41 (Summer 1987).
8. Michel Foucault, *Power/Knowledge: Selected Interviews and Other Essays 1972–1977*, ed. Colin Gordon (New York: Pantheon Books, 1977), pp. 152–4. Foucault talks about this emergent modern formation as an 'opinion society'. Of course, we are reminded of de Amicis' cry to Turks whose silence must be the result of a secret agreement or of some malady: 'Come, more like other men, for once! tell us who you are, what you are thinking of, and what you see in the air before you, with those glassy eyes!' Turks seem to be a people without opinions, or worse, a people who hide their opinions. See Edmondo de Amicis, *Constantinople*, trans. Caroline Tilton (New York: Putnam's Sons, 1878), p. 305.

9. Jean Starobiski, *Jean-Jacques Rousseau: Transparency and Obstruction*, trans. A. Goldhammer (Chicago: University of Chicago Press, 1988), pp. 65–80.

10. Foucault, *Discipline and Punish*, p. 191.

11. I am employing Michel de Certeau's definition of 'strategy' here. See his *The Practice of Everyday Life*, trans. Steven Rendall (Berkeley: University of California Press, 1988), pp. 35–6. For a similar application of the concept of strategy, and an astute analysis of the employment of the trope of veil in Iraqi war, see Mahmut Mutman, 'Under Western Eyes' in *Prosthetic Territories: Politics and Hypertechnology*, ed. Gabriel Brahm Jr. and Mark Driscoll (Boulder, CO: Westview Press, 1995). In an admirable study of the colonization of Egypt, Timothy Mitchell has shown, for instance, how Foucauldian power/knowledge technologies were employed by the French and British colonizers in the so-called model villages, in the military barracks and in the educational apparatus. Mitchell argues that the aim of these strategies was to suppress, marginalize or transform the native culture in order to establish a new one which constructs 'the world as picture'. Timothy Mitchell, *Colonizing Egypt* (Cambridge: Cambridge University Press, 1988).

12. Gayatri Chakravorty Spivak, 'Can the Subaltern Speak?' in *Marxism and the Interpretation of Culture*, ed., Cary Nelson and Lawrence Grossberg (Urbana: University of Illinois Press, 1988), pp. 280–1.

13. Gilels Deleuze, *The Fold: Leibniz and the Baroque*, trans. Tom Conley (Minneapolis: University of Minnesota Press, 1993), p. 38.

14. Ibid., p. 94.

15. Ibid., p. 33.

16. Malek Alloula, *The Colonial Harem*, trans. Myrna Godzich and Wlad Godzich (Minneapolis: University of Minnesota Press, 1986).

17. Fanon, *A Dying Colonialism*, p. 35.

18. Jacques Lacan, *The Four Fundamental Concepts of Psychoanalysis*, trans. Alan Sheridan (New York and London: Norton & Company, 1981), p. 103.

19. Ibid., p. 118–19.

20. Ibid., p. 72–4.

21. Fanon, *A Dying Colonialism*, pp. 45–46.

22. Lacan, *Four Fundamental Concepts of Psychoanalysis*, p. 84.

23. de Amicis, *Constantinople*, p. 208.

24. Théophile Gautier, *Constantinople*, trans. Robert H. Gould (New York: Henry Holt and Company, 1875), pp. 193–94.

25. de Amicis, *Constantinople*, p. 206.

26. Ibid., pp. 206–8.

27. Ibid, p. 207.

28. Irene Szyliowich, *Pierre Loti and the Oriental Woman* (Hong Kong: Macmillan, 1988), p. 97.

29. Joan Copjec, 'The Sartorial Superego', *October*, 50 (Fall 1989), p. 87.

30. Lacan, *Four Fundamental Concepts of Psychoanalysis*, p. 105.

31. Slavoj Žižek, 'Looking Awry', *October*, 50 (Fall 1989), p. 34.

32. Stephen Heath, 'Joan Riviere and the Masquerade', in *Formations of Fantasy*, ed. V. Burgin, J. Donald and C. Kaplan (London and New York: Methuen, 1986), p. 52.

33. Jacqueline Rose, 'Introduction II', in *Feminine Sexuality, Jacques Lacan and the École Freudienne*, ed. Juliet Mitchell and Jacqueline Rose (London: Macmillan, 1987), pp. 35, 47–8.

34. I adapt Lacan's formulaic statement. See, Lacan, *Four Fundamental Concepts of Psychoanalysis*, pp. 80–2.

35. Jacques Lacan, *The Seminar of Jacques Lacan II: The Ego in Freud's Theory and in the Technique of Psychoanalysis 1954–1955*, ed. Jacques-Alain Miller, trans. Sylvana Tomaselli (New York and London: Norton and Company, 1991), p. 223.

36. Stephen Heath's reading of Nietzsche's representation of femininity as masquerade is very illuminating. See 'Joan Riviere and the Masquerade'.
37. Friedrich Nietzsche, *The Will to Power*, trans. Walter Kaufmann and R. J. Hollongdale (New York: Vintage Books, 1968), p. 425.
38. Friedrich Nietzsche, *Beyond Good and Evil*, trans. Walter Kaufman (New York: Vintage Books, 1974), p. 163.
39. For a discussion of the figuration of woman in Nietzsche's texts see Eric Blondel, 'Nietzsche: Life as Metaphor', in *The New Nietzsche*, ed. D. Allison (Cambridge and London: The MIT Press, 1988).
40. Nietzsche, *Beyond Good and Evil*, p. 163.
41. Mary Ann Doane, 'Veiling Over Desire', in *Feminism and Psychoanalysis*, ed R. Felstein and J. Roof (Ithaca: Cornell University Press, 1989), pp. 118–19.
42. Friedrich Nietzsche, *The Gay Science*, trans. Walter Kaufman (New York: Vintage Books, 1974), p. 38.
43. Doane, 'Veiling Over Desire', p. 121.
44. Ibid., p. 122.
45. Luce Irigaray, *Speculum of the Other Woman*, trans. Gillian Gill (Ithaca: Cornell University Press, 1985), p. 270.
46. Joan Rivere, 'Womanliness as Masquerade', in *Formations of Fantasy*, ed. V. Burgin, J. Donald and C. Kaplan (London and New York: Methuen, 1986), p. 43. I have benefited greatly from Stephen Heath's reading of Riviere's article: 'Joan Riviere and the Masquerade' in the same collection.
47. Heath, 'Joan Riviere and the Masquerade', p. 51.
48. Riviere, 'Womanliness as Masquerade', p. 53.
49. Heath, 'Joane Riviere and the Masquerade', p. 50.
50. de Amicis, *Constantinople*, p. 206.
51. Sigmund Freud, *Three Essays on the Theory of Sexuality*, trans. James Strachey (New York: Basic Books, 1975), p. 17. I would like to thank Stephen Heath for bringing this to my attention.
52. Doane, 'Veiling Over Desire', p. 107.
53. Jacques Derrida, *Spurs: Nietzsche's Style*, trans. Barbara Harlow (Chicago: University of Chicago Press, 1979), p. 51.
54. Ibid., p. 71.
55. Gayatri Chakravorty Spivak, 'Displacement and the Discourse of Woman', in *Displacement: Derrida and After*, ed. Mark Krupnick (Bloomington: Indiana University Press, 1987), p. 184.
56. Ibid., p. 186.
57. See the quotation from Karl Marx in ibid., p. 191.
58. Homi Bhabha, 'The Other Question', *Screen*, 24/6 (December 1983), p. 26.
59. The reader will notice that I use the pronoun 'he' to refer to the Western/colonial subject. This is not a mere slippage, but a conscious effort on my part to highlight the claim, as developed most notably by Irigaray, that the subject is always-already masculine, and constitutes himself and retains his autonomy at the expense of the feminine, but disavows this dependence.
60. Riviere, 'Womanliness as Masquerade', p. 38.
61. Luce Irigaray, *Marine Lover*, trans. Gilliam Gill (New York: Columbia University Press, 1991), p. 110.
62. Karl Marx quoted in Spivak: 'Displacement and the Discourse of Woman,' p. 191. My thanks go to Mahmut Mutman for drawing my attention to this important quote and sharing his ideas with me.
63. There are a number of theoretical approaches one might use to explain the process of the constitution of the subject, such as Foucault's. The reason for my emphasis on the psychoanalytic theory of desire in understanding this constitution is that it enables us to grasp the process of exclusion and differentiation through which the Western Subject constitutes itself.

64. Homi Bhabha, 'Interrogating Identity: The Postcolonial Prerogative,' in *Anatomy of Racism*, ed. D. T. Goldberg (Minneapolis: University of Minnesota, 1990), p. 193.

65. Homi Bhabha, 'Of Mimicry and Man: The Ambivalence of Colonial Discourse', *October*, 28 (Spring 1984), p. 126.

66. Frantz Fanon, *Black Skin, White Masks* (New York: Grove Press, 1967), p. 218.

67. This is a persistent and unfortunately not a very substantiated criticism that has been advanced by the critiques of post-structuralist theory and psychoanalysis. Such charges of determinism have been brought time and again in the name of defending the notion of agency. What is overlooked in such criticisms is the assumption of a rigid alternative between, to borrow a formulation from Ernesto Laclau and Chantal Mouffe, total autonomy and absolute subordination. See, 'Post-Marxism Without Apologies', in *New Reflections on the Revolution of Our Time*, ed. Erneste Laclau (London and New York: Verso, 1990).

68. Judith Butler, 'The Imperialist Subject', *Journal of Urban and Cultural Studies*, 2/1 (1991), p. 77.

69. Fanon, *A Dying Colonialism*, pp. 46–47.

70. Ibid., p. 63.

71. Ibid., p. 44.

72. When French colonial power identified the veil as a problem and constructed it as an exterior target, it was involved in a reading and writing (or re-writing) of the veil which is different from that of the native culture. In his influential *Outline of a Theory of Practice*, Pierre Bourdieu provides an ethnographic study of the native Muslim patriarchal culture. The historical precondition of such a study is of course the French colonization of Algeria. Bourdieu's observation of the binarism which make the native culture is instructive in this sense. Bourdieu does not mention the veil, but he observes that the opposition between male and female is associated with a number of other oppositions between the outside and inside. In the mythical structure of the native society, woman is associated with the inside, the house and the land. The veiled woman represents an 'inside' that needs to be protected. Pierre Bourdieu, *Outline of A Theory of Practice*, trans. Richard Nice (Cambridge: Cambridge University Press, 1989), pp. 44–5, 90–4, 122–6. The only place where Bourdieu mentions the veil is a native proverb reserved for the son-in-law, 'the veil cast over shame' (ibid., p. 44). Since woman is associated with evil acts, the lesser evil can only be produced by the protection of a man, etc. Despite his apparant criticism of 'legalism', and his recognition of different interests of men and women, Bourdieu re-inscribes the same mythical patriarchal structure based on sexual difference. In Spivak's words, 'the figure of the exchanged woman still produces the cohesive unity of a clan . . .'. See Introduction, *Selected Subaltern Studies*, ed. Ranajit Guha and Gayatri Chakravorty Spivak (New York and Oxford: Oxford University Press, 1988), p. 30.

73. Alloula, *The Colonial Harem*, p. 7.

74. Fanon, *A Dying Colonialism*, p. 44.

75. For this formulation see Christian Metz, quoted in Paul Willemen, 'Voyeurism, The Look and Dwoskin', *Afterimage*, 6 (Summer 1976), p. 41.

76. Even Edward Lane, who stands as one of the solemn and least 'masculine' Orientalists, almost confesses this desire to see: 'A man may also occasionally enjoy opportunities of seeing the face of an Egyptian lady when she really thinks herself unobserved; sometimes at an open lattice, and sometimes on a house-top', *An Account of the Manners and Customs of the Modern Egyptians* (New York: Dover Publications, 1973), p. 177.

77. Willemen, 'Voyeurism, The Look and Dwoskin', p. 48.

78. Mary Ann Doane suggests a similar structure of reversal for understanding the difficulty the masculine subject experiences when woman appropriates the gaze and turns herself from being a passive object of look to a subject of active looking, from spectacle to spectator. See 'Film and the Masquerade'.

79. Bhabha, 'Interrogating Identity', p. 190.
80. Fanon, *A Dying Colonialism*, p. 61.
81. Ibid., p. 62.
82. Ibid., p. 62.
83. To identify Muslim women's gaining her agency and subjectivity by 'moving' outside the home and equating her veiling with confinement implies an unquestioned acceptance of the assumptions of the liberal Western feminism which advocates the unveiling of Muslim women as a means of 'liberation'.
84. Luce Irigaray, *This Sex Which is Not One*, trans. Catherine Porter (Ithaca: Cornell University Press, 1985), p. 76.
85. Rosi Braidotti, *Nomadic Subjects: Embodiment and Sexual Difference in Contemporary Feminist Theory* (New York: Columbia University Press, 1994), p. 7.
86. Jacques Derrida, *Of Grammatology*, trans. Gayatri Chakravorty Spivak, (Baltimore: Johns Hopkins University Press, 1976), p. 24.
87. Naomi Schor, 'This Essentialism Which is Not One: Coming to Grips with Irigaray', *differences*, 1/2 (1989), p. 48.
88. Irigaray, *Marine Lover*, p. 118.

BIBLIOGRAPHY

Adorno, Theodor and Horkheimer, Max *The Dialectic of Enlightenment*, trans. John Cumming (London and New York: Verso, 1979).
Alloula, Malek *The Colonial Harem*, trans. Myrna Godzich and Wlad Godzich (Minneapolis: University of Minnesota Press, 1986).
Amicis, Edmondo de *Constantinople*, trans. Caroline Tilton (New York: Putnam's Sons, 1878).
Bhabha, Homi. 'The Other Question . . .' *Screen*, 24/6 (December 1983).
Certeau, Michel de. *The Practice of Everyday Life*, trans. Steven Rendall (Berkeley: University of California Press, 1988).
Copjec, Joan 'The Sartorial Superego', *October*, 50 (Fall 1989).
Deleuze, Gilles *The Fold: Leibniz and the Baroque* (Minneapolis: University of Minnesota Press, 1993).
Derrida, Jacques *Spurs: Nietzsche's Style*, trans. Barbara Harlow (Chicago: University of Chicago Press, 1979).
Doane, Mary Ann. 'Veiling Over Desire,' in *Feminism and Psychoanalysis*, ed. R. Felstein and J. Roof (Ithaca: Cornell University Press, 1989).
Fanon, Frantz *A Dying Colonialism*, trans. Haakon Chevalier (New York: Grove Press, 1965).
Foucault, Michel *Discipline and Punish: The Birth of the Prison*, trans. Alan Sheridan (Harmondsworth: Penguin, 1977).
—— *Power/Knowledge: Selected Interviews and Other Essays 1972–1977*, ed. Colin Gordon (New York: Pantheon Books, 1980).
Gautier, Théophile *Constantinople*, trans. Robert H. Gould (New York: Henry Holt and Company, 1875).
Irigaray, Luce *Speculum of the Other Woman*, trans. Gillian Gill (Ithaca: Cornell University Press, 1985).
Lacan, Jacques *The Four Fundamental Concepts of a Psychoanalysis*, trans. Alan Sheridan (New York and London: Norton & Company, 1981).
—— *The Seminar of Jacques Lacan II: The Ego in Freud's Theory and in the Technique of Psychoanalysis 1954–1955*, ed. Jacques-Alain Miller, trans. Sylvana Tomaselli (New York and London: Norton and Company, 1991).
Miller, Jacques-Alain 'Jeremy Bentham's Panoptic Device', trans. Richard Miller, *October*, 41 (Summer 1987).
Mitchell, Timothy *Colonizing Egypt* (Cambridge: Cambridge University Press, 1988).

Mutman, Mahmut 'Under Western Eyes', in *Prosthetic Territories: Politics and Hypertechnology*, ed. Gabriel Brahm Jr. and Mark Driscoll (Boulder, Colo.: Westview Press, 1995).

Nietzsche, Friedrich *The Will to Power*, trans. Walter Kaufmann and R. J. Hollingdale (New York: Vintage Books, 1968).

—— *Beyond Good and Evil*, trans. Walter Kaufman (New York: Vintage Books, 1974).

—— *The Gay Science*, trans. Walter Kaufman (New York: Vintage Books, 1974).

Richon, Oliver 'Representation, the Despot and the Harem: Some Questions Around an Academic Orientalist Painting by Lecomte-Du-Nouy (1885)', in *Europe and its Others*, Proceedings of the Essex Conference on the Sociology of Literature, vol. I, ed. F. Barker et al. (Colchester: University of Essex, 1985).

Rose, Jacqueline, 'Introduction II', in *Feminine Sexuality: Jacques Lacan and the École Freudienne*, ed. Juelet Mitchell and Jacqueline Rose (London: Macmillan, 1987).

Said, Edward *Orientalism* (Harmondsworth: Penguin, 1978).

Spivak, Gayatri Chakravorty 'Displacement and the Discourse of Woman', in *Displacement: Derrida and After*, ed. Mark Krupnick (Bloomington: Indiana University Press, 1987).

—— 'Can the Subaltern Speak', in *Marxism and the Interpretation of Culture*, ed. Cary Nelson and Lawrence Grossberg (Urbana: University of Illinois Press, 1988).

Starobinski, Jean *Jean-Jacques Rousseau: Transparency and Obstruction*, trans. A. Goldhammer (Chicago: University of Chicago Press, 1988).

Szyliowich, Irene *Pierre Loti and the Oriental Woman* (Hong Kong: Macmillan, 1988).

White, Hayden *Tropics of Discourse: Essays in Cultural Criticism* (Baltimore and London: Johns Hopkins University Press, 1982).

Žižek, Slavoj 'Looking Awry', *October*, 50 (Fall 1989).

5.5

'UNVEILING ALGERIA'

Winifred Woodhull

THE NATIONAL GUISE

In 1964, Germaine Tillion, a French ethnographer known for her extensive work on male-female relations in Algeria, writes that 'on the Muslim side of the Mediterranean, the veil . . . constitutes not just a picturesque detail of costume, but a veritable border. On one side of this border, female societies stagnate; on the other side there lives and progresses a national society which, by virtue of this fact, is but half a society.'[1] To her credit, Tillion painstakingly emphasizes, in the essay in which this sentence appears, the lines of continuity between social practices in the Northern and Southern parts of the Mediterranean in order to counter the view, widespread among her compatriots, that women's oppression in Muslim societies stems uniquely from the supposed barbarity of Islam. As a survivor of the concentration camps, Tillion is keenly aware of Europe's capacity for savagery toward its own people; and as a critical observer of her country's relation to Algeria, she repeatedly calls her readers' attention to the abuses of colonialism, particularly as they have affected women.[2] Yet in the sentence quoted above, Tillion poses the question of women and nationalism in contemporary Muslim societies in terms which, today, obstruct, as much as they enable, feminist analysis of the problem.

In setting the tradition-bound female sphere in opposition to the modern nation and in underscoring women's exclusion from national life in Muslim societies, Tillion's formulation is typical of much Western scholarship on women

From: Winifred Woodhull (1991), 'Unveiling Algeria', pp. 112–31, in *Genders* no. 10.

in Algeria since the nation achieved independence in 1962. For example, David Gordon states in 1968 that 'with the dawn of independence, confused and economically ominous as the atmosphere was, the expectations of and for women were high. But the force of the legacy of centuries was soon to make itself felt. The gap between promise and reality, law and fact, was to widen. . . . While one does, of course, see women unveiled in the streets, working in ministries, serving as deputies, working by the side of men in welfare centers and such, the role of even these "evolved" women is peripheral.'[3] Nearly twenty years later, Catherine Delcroix poses the problem in similarly dichotomous terms: 'It is certain that, in view of the Algerian woman's higher level of education today, her underrepresentation [in political institutions] can only foster frustration and obstruct the evolution of her personal status, and thus, of her emancipation.'[4] Delcroix contends that responsibility for women's exclusion lies with the traditionalist mentality of the electorate, both female and male, and with 'the ideological system itself, which doesn't sufficiently mobilize the female population, for fear of seeing woman transgress her role as guardian of traditional values' (pp. 138–9). Like the veil, then, which Tillion had identified as 'a veritable border' internally dividing the national territory, 'the ideological system' is said to bar women from meaningful participation in public life.

The opposition that structures the arguments of Tillion, Gordon and Delcroix bears testimony to conditions that prevailed during the Algerian Revolution and at the time of independence, when the emerging nation still held the promise of social equality for women, whose role in the war had been recognized by the National Liberation Front: 'Since 1954, there have been many changes. In most households, men are absent – they are in prison, in combat, or dead. Women have learned to get along on their own; they work, they manage their own money, they take care of their children. It is an established fact of the Revolution; there is no turning back. Habits have changed, too . . . I think men understand that it is in their interest to give their wives some responsibilities, and that they will let them take some initiative, even when peace has been restored.'[5] Unfortunately, the promise of social equality for women faded after 1962, and this failure on the part of the nation that had played an exemplary role in anticolonial struggles provoked bitter disappointment, as Fadela M'rabet's work, for example, makes clear.[6] The realignment of women with tradition, and their consequent exclusion from public life, was considered by feminists to be a betrayal both of the women who had fought for the nation's freedom and of the revolution itself. The oppositional relation between women and the nation thus accounted for an important dynamic of the 1960s, one that is undoubtedly still operative in Algeria today and has a place in feminist analyses which must, of course, affirm the possibility of a nation in which women are on an equal footing with men.

Since independence, however, a quite different relation has emerged between Algerian women and the nation, one which must be taken into account, I believe, if women's situation in Algeria is to be changed. An articulation of this other relation is already apparent in Gordon's 1968 study, which maintains that 'as far as many women are concerned, Algeria lives *between* two worlds, the modern and the traditional'; remarking on the tension between the contradictory aims of the Algerian Revolution – the establishment of a modern socialist nation on the one hand, and, on the other, the restoration of a culture that French colonialism had all but destroyed – Gordon goes on to suggest that 'women are the victims of this tension, and their present condition might be seen as its symbol' (p. 83, my emphasis). Here, women are identified less with tradition as such than with Algeria's 'betweenness', its traversal by irreconcilable modern and traditionalist currents. Tillion situates women in a similar fashion when she says that they are 'the principal victims of the irresistible slippage that draws nomadic populations toward the towns and cities [insofar as it results in stricter practices of seclusion and veiling]. This slippage lies at the source of a conflict, persisting into the present, between two types of structures: the society of citizens, and tribal society. There is conflict *between* individuals, and *within* each one of them. . . . In this conflict, the 'noble personality' opposes the promiscuities that the human density of the cities or towns apparently makes inevitable, for the daily contact with nonrelatives will wound and irremediably compromise this "personality" (p. 30).

As the embodiment of conflicting forces that simultaneously compose and disrupt the nation, women are both the guarantors of national identity – no longer simply as guardians of traditional values, but as *symbols that successfully contain the conflicts of the new historical situation* – and the supreme threat to that identity, insofar as its endemic instability can be assigned to *them*. Gordon's and Tillion's analyses imply, further, that women symbolize, and are called upon to stabilize, Algeria's irreducibly contradictory identity *in* and *through their 'present condition' of subordination*. They are victims, to be sure, but not, as it still appeared in 1968, simply by virtue of their exclusion from a national life that could have included them as equals; rather, women's exclusion increasingly *constitutes* the Algerian nation after independence, just as their veiling – at once a social practice and a powerful symbol – plays a central role in producing and maintaining both Algeria's difference from its colonial oppressor and the uneasy coalition of heterogeneous and conflicting interests under a single national banner.

Writing in 1987, in the wake of Algerian feminism's twenty-five-year struggle against the forms of exclusion and appropriation that have prevailed under the socialist state, Peter R. Knauss recasts the problem Gordon had broached regarding women's symbolic function in the revolution and its aftermath: 'Algerian women became both the revered objects of the collective act of national redemption and the role model for the new nationalist patriarchal family'.[7] Granted, Knauss's rhetoric often echoes Gordon's in its use of antithetical formulations that oppose traditional Algerian culture to modern nationalism as if each were a self-contained entity, albeit one capable of dressing up in the other's clothes (Knauss speaks, for instance, of 'the ideology of cultural restoration wrapped in the mantle of radical nationalism', p. xiii). Nonetheless, Knauss's analyses of present-day male-female relations show that the government's legitimation of traditions that disempower women works to 'contain the social consequences of significant changes that have taken place in education and employment', and does so (this is how his position differs from Delcroix's) in the name of a 'patriarchy which has become part of the warp and woof of Algerian political culture' (pp. 137, 141).

From 1964 on, successive versions of the Charter of Algiers affirm women's formal political equality with men in the new socialist state, calling for their integration into every level of the work force as well as national political organizations. However, Islamic law, eventually formalized in the state's Family Code of 1984, officially sanctions traditional social practices that persist in the post-revolutionary years, practices that effectively cancel the principles set forth in the Charter. Women remain legal minors, for example, until they marry, whereas men attain adult status at age eighteen whether they are married or not; women's, but not men's, decision to marry must be authorized by a guardian; the dowry system is maintained; married women must obey their husbands and must have their husbands' permission to gain employment; while men retain the rights of polygamy and repudiation of their wives, it is difficult and costly for women to initiate divorce; and finally, one man is considered equal to two women in matters of inheritance.[8]

The integration of women into public life is hindered by other factors as well. Despite gains in recent years, large numbers of women continue to be excluded from education, for instance, and birth control is still widely discouraged by both Muslim conservatives and Algerian nationalists, who regard it as 'unnatural' interference in the production of children, an important source of national wealth and family honor.[9] Moreover, because Islamic fundamentalism has gathered new force in Algeria since the Iranian Revolution, there is at present little possibility of change that would ensure women's equality with men. In fact, in the municipal elections of last June, 'the Islamic Salvation Front (FIS), swept every major city in the country, capturing all thirty-three municipal councils in the capital city of Algiers, even those councils in well-to-do neighborhoods populated by wealthy businessmen and Cabinet ministers'.[10] The stunning electoral victory of the fundamentalists bears grim testimony to the growing strength of the claim made nearly a decade ago by President Chadli in response to feminist protests of a 1981 draft of the Family Code: 'No place whatever exists for anarchy [that is, feminist opposition to government policy] in a society that is building itself and constructing the foundations for its future.'[11]

Ever since independence, feminists have deplored the cynicism of political regimes that promote oppressive Islamic traditions and dismiss the relevance of basic civil rights to 'the Arab and Muslim Algerian woman'.[12] If North African feminists are right to argue that the current political function of misogynistic customs is to forge solidarity among men who are otherwise deeply divided, while maintaining what is perceived as a crucial distinction between Muslim and Western societies, then it is reasonable to say that the oppression of women has become *the* national necessity in Algeria.[13]

There has been a vast unemployed or underemployed male population in Algeria for twenty-five years now, as well as ongoing strife between the petty bourgeoisie and the wealthy elite. The events of October 1988 in particular – mass riots to which the government responded with shootings and torture of protesters – mark the degree to which economic divisions are threatening to rend the social fabric in Algeria. The outcome of these violent conflicts was sadly predictable where women's rights are concerned: when the government moved to institute economic reforms, eliminate widespread corruption, and give political parties some freedom to assemble and air their demands, political groups – including the Parti de l'Avant-Garde Socialiste (the reincarnation of Algeria's Communist Party) – refused to call for a single change in the Family Code despite pressure from feminists like Fetouma Ouzegane and Khalida Massaoudi.[14] In its effort, then, to mute economic conflict between men, and also to forestall violent struggle between fundamentalist groups such as the Muslim Brothers and 'progressive' nationalist factions, the state has fixed upon 'the Arab and Muslim Algerian woman' as the indispensable unifying force, a symbol whose power is turned against Algerian women (whether Arab or Berber, Muslim or atheist) in the name of national cohesion and stability.

The government's exploitation of this symbol to erase differences among women, neutralize women's differences with men and overcome men's differences with each other finds its mirror image in the fundamentalists' designation of woman as the *cause* of these differences. In their version, woman embodies *fitna*,[15] the dangerous force that disrupts the community of believers: 'To all the social ills from which Algeria is suffering', writes a group of North African intellectuals in January 1990, 'the fundamentalists ascribe a single origin: woman. They intend to find a way out of the real crisis the country is experiencing by depriving Algerian women, as a group, of their civil and moral rights.'[16]

Clearly, something more, and something other, than women's exclusion from the nation's political life is at stake in Algeria today. For though women are indeed underrepresented in political institutions, silenced in public debates and denounced as anarchists whenever they make themselves heard, they are, at the same time, the *embodiment* of Algerian national life, whether in its 'progressive' or regressive guise. In wearing the veil, Algerian women bear responsibility for the nation's conflicts and assume the risks of its uncertain identity: in covering over the social and psychic divisions in the Algerian 'personality', veiled women present a reassuring aspect; in baring them, they become the objects of fear, hatred and vitriolic attacks, both verbal and physical. Because the women of Algeria have been fashioned as living symbols of the independent nation, feminist analysis must come to terms with, and begin to dismantle, this aspect of national identity, rather than simply call for women's integration into an order whose very constitution depends on their exclusion *as agents* who produce social meanings that contest tradition or, more dangerously still, attest the 'betweenness' of Algeria, which has been projected on to their veiled bodies.

This is not to discount the view, recently put forth by Fatima Mernissi, that 'the conservative wave against women in the Muslim world, far from being a regressive trend, is on the contrary a defense mechanism against profound changes in both sex roles and the touchy subject of sexual identity'.[17] Mernissi shows that unveiled, urban, middle-class women's access to education has put them in competition with the fundamentalist men seeking power, men 'mostly from newly urbanized middle- and lower-middle-class backgrounds' who are calling for the reveiling of their new rivals (p. 9). Access to education has in turn 'dissolved traditional arrangements of space segregation' since it either places women in the classroom with men or, at the very least, encourages the mixing of men and women in public: 'simply to go to school, women have to cross the street!' (p. 11). Finally access to education has produced what Mernissi calls a 'demographic revolution' in Muslim societies by dramatically increasing the number of unmarried adolescent women: 'The concept of an adolescent woman, menstruating and unmarried, is so alien to the entire Muslim family system that it is either unimaginable or necessarily linked with *fitna* (social disorder)' (p. 11).

Mernissi's strategy of underscoring the reality of progressive change in Muslim women's lives constitutes an important challenge to the 'self-representation' of conservatives who claim that Muslim societies are inherently traditional and that 'their women miraculously escape social change and the erosion of time' (p. 8). Still, it seems to me that her flat denial of fundamentalism's regressive character obscures another, equally important reality, namely, fundamentalism's regressive effects in the social field, where it is working to reverse feminist gains by restricting women's mobility and visibility. More and more women are wearing the veil again, whether as an expression of religious faith, a sign of national solidarity or a means of escaping harassment. In the case of Algeria in particular, it is essential to acknowledge the mobilization of the veiled woman as a national symbol that not only defends against the progressive changes Mernissi points to, but also helps to produce a new social configuration in which 'betweenness', rather than 'pure' archaism, works to constrain women. Because it is the political effectiveness of a *representation* that is at issue here, the border dividing culture from politics in feminist analysis must be opened.

REFASHIONING NATIONAL IDENTITIES

The cultural record makes clear that women embody Algeria not only for Algerians in the days since independence, but also for the French colonizers who conquer them militarily, control them administratively, study them as sociologists, ethnographers, and historians, and represent them in both high and popular forms of art and literature. Whether one considers the 'colonial perversion' of nineteenth-century army officers who capture Algerian women, sell them at auction or ship them off to other colonies; the strategies of administrators – including liberals like Maurice Viollette – who institute campaigns for medical assistance and education aimed primarily at women as a means of regulating families; the theories of intellectuals who see the power of Islam as inextricably tied to endogamy and, above all, to women's traditionalism; or the imaginings of writers and painters who exoticize the native population through its figurations of women, it is evident that, for France, Algerian women are key symbols of the colony's cultural identity.[18] They are at once the emblem of Algeria's refusal to accept what the Islamicist Octave Depont calls France's 'emancipatory seed' *and* the gateway to penetration: 'As long as . . . the miserable condition of the native woman is not improved, as long as endogamy causes Muslim society to close in on itself, the door to this society will open to outside influences only with difficulty. We can attempt rapprochement and fusion, but these efforts are liable to weaken, if not shatter, at the feet of this woman, unyielding and faithful guardian of the home, its traditions and, in a word, the preservation and conservation of the race.'[19]

Thus, whether the imagined contact between races or peoples involves a perilous siege or easy pleasure, the point of contact, where Algeria is concerned, is woman. Not surprisingly, in the face of French aggression, including its medical, hygienic, philanthropic, pedagogic and social forms (such as the tea party),[20] Algerians respond with various 'attitudes of refusal' which, according to Abdallah Laroui, mark the emergence of nationalism and the delegitimation of French rule in the 1930s. These attitudes of refusal, which include 'withdrawal into private life, non-cooperation, personal and familial independence, disobedience, slovenliness, and finally, destructive individual revolt',[21] are retroactively symbolized in terms of the veil by Frantz Fanon when, in 1959, the fifth year of the Algerian Revolution, radical changes in women's situation make it possible to ascribe to the veil a 'historic dynamism' dating back to the rise of nationalism in the 1930s. Challenging the idea that Algeria is mere 'prey disputed with equal ferocity by Islam and the Western power, France', and that cultural regression – including anachronistic forms of women's oppression – is Algeria's only alternative to assimilation, Fanon rearticulates the symbolic link between the veil and Muslim traditions in his essay 'Algeria Unveiled'.[22]

In the early phases of the independence struggle, he says, wearing the veil signaled women's allegiance to cultural traditions and forms of existence, such as the extended family, that enabled the emerging nation to forge an identity. This identity, then, grew out of resistance to France's strategy of combating nationalism by 'unveiling' Algeria, that is, regulating private life through assistance campaigns aimed at women and children, and promoting the liberation of Algerian women through education – 'encouraging' them, as Maurice Viollette puts it, in their movement toward Europeanization. Subsequently, according to Fanon, the veil became an instrument in armed resistance to the French forces, once women became actively engaged in guerrilla activity and began hiding explosives under their veils. Later, Algerian women began carrying out their militant actions in Western dress, concealing bombs in their purses rather than in the folds of their veils. When these tactics were discovered by the French, however, militants again wore the veil in order to escape detection by the occupiers. Also, the readoption of the veil came in response to a demonstration that followed the army officers' revolt of May 13, 1958, when officers' wives presided over the public unveiling of Algerian women whose slogan was 'Let's be like the French woman'.[23] In this context, says Fanon, donning the *haïk* showed that 'it isn't true that woman liberates herself at the invitation of France and General de Gaulle' (p. 46).

Fanon's outline of this development is fleshed out by his attention to the historic dynamism of Algerian women's bodies in relation to the veil. It is by means of the veil, he writes, that the nubile body is 'revealed' to the Algerian woman; that is, the veil 'covers the body and disciplines it, tempers it at the very moment when it knows its greatest effervescence' but also 'protects, reassures, insulates'. According to Fanon, who was a psychiatrist at the hospital in Blida-Joinville, dream material shows that the woman accustomed to wearing the veil is disoriented when she begins to move about in public space unveiled; for instance, she has trouble judging distances in the street and even finds it difficult to mark out the contours of her own body: 'the unveiled body seems to get away from itself, to go to pieces. There is an impression of being improperly dressed, even nude.' Accordingly, Fanon argued that during the revolution, the Algerian female combatant in Western dress entered the European district of the city 'completely nude' and so must 'relearn her body, reinstall it in a totally revolutionary way' (p. 42).

In 1959, when Fanon's 'Algeria Unveiled' was first published, it was of undeniable strategic importance to assert a 'historic dynamism of the veil' unfolding within a cultural territory free from French influence, given the fact that the colonizers had positioned Algerian women as living symbols of both the colony's resistance and its vulnerability to penetration. The hypocrisy and brutality of France's stance toward Algerian women at this time is indisputable: shortly after the wives of the rebellious army officers invited Algerian women to 'liberate' themselves by making a public spectacle of their unveiling, the army opened women's prisons for the female combatants they captured and tortured.[24] And clearly, the extension of voting rights to Algerian women in 1958 was intended primarily as a divisive tactic to promote women's support for a French, rather than an independent, Algeria. (By contrast, when the Paris government proposed the same move in 1947, the *Français d'Algérie*, who were in a much stronger position at the time and thus saw no need to make this concession, vigorously opposed it. They responded to the bill with irony – because Algerian women were considered too ignorant and backward to vote – and even made outlandish statements in defense of 'the veil that was being trampled'; 'Tomorrow the young girl, the wife, the mother will be summoned to the disputes of the forum,' they lamented, calling on their (male) 'Muslim friends to stop the evildoers who are weakening the age-old foundation on which *our* households rest.' Here, as in so many other instances, the veil emblematized, for the French, both Muslim tradition *and* the means to effective colonial domination.)[25]

In presenting the 'historic dynamism of the veil' as a fundamentally nationalistic, anti-French development, Fanon does not necessarily succumb to the inevitable limitations of a French-educated secular intellectual in underestimating the force of Islam and its effects on women, as critics of the time claim.[26] Nor does he necessarily allow his *engagé* zeal to blind him to the importance of the colonial relation itself – the implantation of an industrial economy and Western ideology – in preparing the ground for the radical transformation of women's lives during the revolution, as André Adam contends.[27] The writing of 'Algeria Unveiled' cannot be accounted for by invoking the opposition between 'scholarship' (with its supposed disinterestedness and historical 'accuracy') and 'polemic' and situating it, however sympathetically, on the side of the latter, as Adam and others have done. Rather, this essay must be understood as a cultural intervention that both articulates and reinforces a political development whose outcome, in 1959, remains uncertain. 'Algeria Unveiled' is a cultural-political move – a failed one, as it turns out – to *enable* the unveiling of Algeria.

In light of developments since independence, however, it is important, from a feminist standpoint, to note that Fanon's strategy of articulating Algerian feminism as a fundamentally indigenous movement – one as independent from Western feminism as it is inextricably bound up with emergent nationalism – works, *in today's context*, to underwrite nationalism's sacrifice of women's liberation to its own cause. In 'Algeria Unveiled', Fanon elides the positive effects, for Algerian women, of the colonial relation: enfranchisement, education, medical assistance and, for example, the reform of marriage laws in 1959, which henceforth forbad child marriage and required that divorce proceedings be brought before a judge. He also omits reference, for example, to Algerian women's successful manipulation of the ambiguities within both the Muslim and French legal codes, and their productive exploitation of conflicts and gaps between those codes, to improve their economic and social conditions.[28] And finally, Fanon suppresses the emancipatory dimension of ties between Western feminists and Algerian women, both in the 1930s and during the revolution. For example, the sociological and ethnographic studies that Fanon denounces as mere ammunition for the *Bureaux Arabes* (p. 18) include work presented at the *Etats Géneraux du Féminisme* held during the International Colonial Exposition of 1931. They include, too, the work of scholars like Mathéa Gaudry, who applauds the resourcefulness and independence of Kabylian women in terms that complicate (even though they don't negate) the colonialist view of Algerian women as the weak link in the nationalist chain.[29] And as Denise Brahimi shows, the work of Gaudry, Henriette Celarié and other French women writing in the first half of the twentieth century discloses that the writers' sympathy with Algerian women emerges alongside expressions of frustration with the social and political circumstances of women in France where, throughout the 1930s, for example, the National Assembly defeats proposals to extend voting rights to women.[30]

Similarly, though Fanon implicitly aligns the Algerian female combatants in Western dress with the European women of Algeria who are arrested for supporting the liberation struggle in the mid-1950s (p. 44), he makes no explicit mention of *feminist* support for the revolution, support which is manifested most clearly two years after 'Algeria Unveiled', in 1961, when Simone de Beauvoir and other French women working in concert with the Tunisian lawyer Gisèle Halimi protest the arrest and sexual torture of the militant, Djamila Boupacha, by the French forces.[31] In writing that the Algerian female combatant in Western dress enters the European district of the city 'completely nude', Fanon unquestionably strips her of the attire that symbolically links her to Western feminism. Thus, the unveiling performed by Fanon's text, while clearly intended to enable the Algerian woman to 'relearn her body, reinstall it in a totally revolutionary way', nonetheless establishes, between European and Algerian feminism, a border which today's feminist analysis must reopen if women's relation to Algerian national identity is to be refashioned.

According to Mai Ghoussoub, it is the case today, not only in Algeria, but throughout the Arab world, that the streets are filled not with women who have relearned and reinstalled their bodies, but with 'women shrouded in black seeking the respectability of a cloak for their corporeal existence. . . . The bitter reality is that Arab feminism, in the modern sense of the term, exists as a force only in the student milieux of Europe and America to which a privileged few can escape, and in a growing but still very modest academic literature. The double knot tied by the fatal connections in Arab culture and politics between definitions of femininity and religion, and religion and nationality, have all but throttled any major women's revolt so far. Every assertion of the second sex can be charged – in a virtually simultaneous register – with impiety to Islam and treason to the nation.'[32]

In light of this development, it is important for feminist critics to acknowledge the ways cultural texts underwrite nationalism's current exploitation of women – not just as victims of the revolution's betrayal, but as living symbols required to mediate and to contain, as well as to assume responsibility for, threatening social divisions within the nation. Where Algeria is concerned, a reading of Malek Alloula's *The Colonial Harem* can be exemplary in this regard.[33] Alloula analyzes the *scènes et types* postcards circulating widely in Algeria and France between 1900 and 1930. As their name suggests, the postcards are underwritten by the ethnographic alibi of surveying Algerian landscapes and customs. Alloula is concerned with the best-selling subgenre picturing Algerian women in various guises: traversing public space in billowing white veils; imprisoned in the dark recesses of the harem; modeling exotic headdresses and jewelry, in various stages of native dress and undress; and finally, nude women surrounded by the props of the coffee ceremony, entwined in the coils of the hookah or reclining in lascivious abandon on a divan in the manner of the odalisque. Evident in these photographs, Alloula argues convincingly, is the desire of the colonial photographer to render Algeria transparent. His fascination with veiled and unveiled Algerian women betrays his wish to strip Algeria of its cultural identity, deny the existence of its male population and possess it through its women.

This dream of transparency and possession places the photographer in solidarity with the colonial administration whose principled denunciation of the veil (the emblem of women's oppression) is belied by its policies. Its seizure of lands, for instance, disrupts the traditional family patterns of vast numbers of Algerians, forcing displaced rural women into prostitution in the cities.[34] One of the services performed by these displaced and impoverished women is to pose for photographers aiming to capitalize on the fantasies of *pieds noirs* and tourists. The complicity between photographer and administrator extends to the intellectual as well. Mathéa Gaudry's *La Société féminine au Djebel Amour et au Ksel*, for instance, provides striking evidence of the permeable boundary between 'serious' sociological study and its vulgarized forms.[35] Gaudry's book includes photographs, in the style of the postcards, that document women's dress in the region under study. Plate 20 shows an anonymous veiled woman, presumably 'typical' of the region; but in plate 50, *in her place and in the same setting*, there appears a woman unveiled, with hands on hips and a cigarette hanging from her lips: 'Khanoussa, a former courtisan, now a duenna.'

Alloula is thus right to argue that the postcard is embedded in a complex and extensive network of colonialist activity. I would disagree, however, with his claim that as a 'ventrilocal art, the postcard – even and especially when it pretends to be the mirror of the exotic – is *nothing other* than one of the forms of aesthetic justification of colonial violence' (p. 76, my emphasis). Far from merely giving voice to a pre-existing colonial ideology or justifying violence serving 'real' economic and political interests, the postcards articulate a dream of ravishment, a colonizing desire that not only invests and orients administrative activity but helps to produce the interests it serves, for example by establishing a libidinally charged solidarity between *colons* divided by class, ethnicity and nationality. And since postcards form part of the growing tourist industry and the everyday correspondence between France and its colony, they also forge ideologically loaded bonds between the French in Algeria and those in the metropolitan center.[36] In short, they work to make 'L'Algérie Française' a creditable proposition.

That a French Algeria is produced in and through culture, as well as by military and administrative means, is evident from the stated aims of, for example, the International Colonial Exposition held in Paris in 1931. 'The public . . . must realize that the "current miracle" of Greater France rests upon a persistent and longstanding colonizing tradition.'[37] The goals of the Exposition are presented in more aggressive terms by its organizer, Marshall Pierre Lyautey, who wants 'to give the French public a punch in the eye so that it will finally pay attention to the number and quality of our overseas possessions'.[38] In

Algeria, the Centenary celebration of the French conquest in 1830 is one of the most important cultural forces at work. Charles-Robert Ageron shows, for example, that 'a committee was specifically assigned the task of "creating a lasting movement of opinion in metropolitan France in favor of African France"'; 'the French press was subsidized and received 2,075,971 francs to "campaign in favor of Algeria"', despite natives' protests at the prospect of such a humiliating spectacle (pp. 403–4).

The main intent of the Centenary is clearly to create an idealized picture of Algeria as a desirable partner for France, rather than to garner support for concrete improvement of conditions in the colony. For instance, while there is a concerted effort to sell the Centenary celebration in the French schools ('It is above all in the schools that our propaganda must strike,' declares the general secretary of the metropolitan committee on the Centenary), Ageron observes that, when the budget committee extends a credit of one hundred million francs for social assistance and education (based on its 'intuition that France should at least make a charitable gesture in favor of the Muslims'), 'the Financial Delegation [whose members were mainly French Algerians] . . . refused this important credit on the pretext that the Chamber of Deputies had overstepped its powers by designating Algeria as the target of a subsidy. The Financial Delegation reminded the Chamber that it alone controlled the granting of credits in Algeria's budget. This explains why only five million francs were allocated, in the end, for the assistance of natives' (p. 410).

In addition to an intensive press and education campaign, a radio station is set up to broadcast propaganda throughout Algeria and the other French colonies; tourism is encouraged; museums are opened, and art exhibits are organized to demonstrate that 'here [in Algeria] there is truly a new France . . . and that [its] people have but one desire, one ambition: to be intimately fused with the Mother Country'.[39] The postcards analyzed by Alloula must be set within the frame of this mass cultural picture. In this context, it is worth considering Roland Barthes's observation, quoted by Alloula, that 'the age of photography corresponds exactly to the irruption of the private in the public, or rather, to the creation of a new social value, which is the publicity of the private: the private is consumed as such, publicly'.[40] The circulation of postcards placing the natives' private life on display (for purposes of appropriation) complements a politics of the family which is seen as central to the colonizing project as outlined, for example, in the Congress on Rural Colonization held in Algiers in May 1930: 'the creation of [centers of colonization] has entailed the assembly – I would even say mobilization – on the designated point, of many dozens of French families that are in general healthy, fully prolific, and whose conditions of existence encourage fecundity more than they limit it. "A seminary of the French race": the center of colonization presents itself thus.'[41]

At issue, then, in the circulation of the postcards, is not simply the fact that the figures of the harem inscribed on them are hypocritically justified, as Alloula points out, by legends identifying them as mere family portraits. As important as the use of European family ideology to veil sexual exploitation; as important as the postcards' function of putting formerly secluded and veiled Algerian women on public display, ensuring their symbolic availability to the conqueror, is the ideological work of implanting in Algeria the economy of the relation between public and private that is developing in Europe at the time. This comes to have decisive importance after independence when conservative and progressive forces alike justify breaking their promises to grant women basic civil liberties by pointing to the degradation of Western women within the economy of mass culture, as if real or symbolic prostitution represented the only alternative to seclusion and veiling.[42]

The postcard photographer's dream of transparency and possession places him in solidarity not only with the colonial administration in the early twentieth century, but also with the French army's fight against Algerian revolutionaries in the period 1954–1962. The army's antinationalist strategy of dispersing village communities and resettling their inhabitants involves forcing female detainees to unveil before military photographers assigned the task of producing photos for the French national ID cards that these unwilling Algerians are to be required to carry. One of the army photographers, Marc Garanger, denounces the army's policy – and the role he is forced to play in carrying it out – by publishing and exhibiting these photographs in various places during and after the Algerian war, notably in the *Illustré Suisse* in 1961 (when Garanger is still doing his military service in Algeria) and then some twenty years later in a collection entitled *Femmes algériennes 1960*.[43] The forced unveiling documented in these photos at once parallels the unveiling staged by the army officers' wives in May 1958 and, through its critical reframing in Garanger's book, signals the coercion at work in the production of the postcards analyzed by Alloula.

More starkly than the postcards, Garanger's photos disclose the photographer's desire and its collusion with other forms of colonial violence. However, they also mirror the postcards as inscriptions of what Alloula terms the photographer's impotence. On the postcards, as Alloula notes, the haunting images of women in veils, relentlessly opaque rather than transparent, floating rather than fixed within the frame, and also the distracted or downright disgusted look of many of the models, mark the photographer's incapacity to ravish his female subjects. Similarly, the dishevelment and disarray of the women photographed thirty years later during the war bespeak contempt and defiance as much as discouragement and defeat. In his introduction to *Femmes algériennes 1960*, Garanger remembers being 'hit by their look at pointblank range' (p. 3). Leïla Sebbar attributes a similar interpretation of the Garanger photos to the Algerian teenage protagonist of *Shérazade*: 'all of these Algerian women had the same look – intense, ferocious, so savage that the image would only be able to record it, without ever controlling or dominating it'.[44]

But here we encounter a problem regarding Alloula's critique of the colonial photographer's gaze, the global political context in which his critique is generated and the relation of both to Arab feminism. On the one hand, Alloula's analysis discerns in the postcard images contradictions that are specific to the photographic medium in the colonial situation, contradictions which he uses effectively to reflect back to the French photographer a critical image of the gaze he casts on Algeria. By returning these postcards to their sender, Alloula dislocates a set of colonialist male fantasies embodied in the haunting figure of the Algerian woman.

On the other hand, however, Alloula's analysis is itself haunted by a kind of spectral presence, that of an undivided Algeria, an emerging nation in which the conflicting interests of men and women are first and foremost the product of the conqueror's sexual fantasies and administrative policies. Despite occasional references to the postcards' effects on women – for instance, his remark in the final pages that the images represent 'the deceitful expression of [their] symbolic dispossession' (p. 76) – Alloula never really addresses the question of women's interests. Instead, he repeatedly invites readers to deplore the French imposter's efforts either to insinuate himself into the closed space of the harem in order to take what he (the imposter) imagines to be the native man's place or to destroy the forms of solidarity that make anticolonial struggle possible. What Alloula deplores is the rape of an Algeria in which women's differences with men remain veiled.

Implicitly, Alloula subscribes to the same view that Fanon articulates in 'Algeria Unveiled', namely that the affirmation of cultural traditions such as seclusion and veiling of women is necessary at a certain point in Algeria's history. But, in suggesting this, without revision, nearly twenty years after independence, Alloula repeats the gesture of the colonizer by making of the veiled woman the screen on which he projects *his* fantasy (an idealization fueled, perhaps, by his exile in France) – that of an Algerian nation untroubled by questions of women's oppression.[45]

The problem posed to feminism by Alloula's book resurfaces in Barbara Harlow's informative and nuanced introduction to it. Her essay is particularly illuminating insofar as it sets Alloula's analysis in relation to the history of the French occupation of Algeria, including the intellectual and aesthetic strands of that history, which extend through the revolutionary period, for instance in the writing of Camus. Equally helpful is the way it situates the book in relation to the critical rewriting of North African history and culture by influential figures such as Kateb Yacine, Abdelkébir Khatibi and feminists Assia Djebar, Fadela M'rabet and Fatima Mernissi. Valuable as it is, though, it seems to me that Harlow's essay tries to cover over, rather than come to terms with, a fundamental contradiction between the demands of North African feminists and the Maghreb's affirmation of its Islamic identity. This leads Harlow to give undue approval, for example, to 'reforms' of women's civil status in Arab countries, reforms unequivocally denounced by the very feminists she cites.[46]

In her otherwise compelling account, in *Resistance Literature*,[47] of the interconnections between writing, political struggle and imprisonment in the life of Egyptian feminist Nawal al-Saadawi, Harlow likewise ignores the basic conflict between feminism and nationalism in Muslim societies, a conflict which often results in what Mai Ghoussoub calls 'accommodation to obscurantism' by feminists engaged in the struggle against Western imperialism. In the same essay I cited earlier, Ghoussoub asks, 'How many times, over successive generations, as the tides of religious fundamentalism (or opportunism) ebbed and flowed, have we seen women who were once courageous in their rejection of mystification and oppression eventually bow before them and on occasion even end by defending them! Fear of being accused of the contagion of "Occidental values" all too easily leads to discovery of the superior virtues of the Harem, compared to Western marriage and adultery, as many examples show. Some of the most outstanding contemporary feminists, daunted by the scale of the tasks before them and the isolation in which they stand, have changed their tone recently.'[48] Of Nawal al-Saadawi, Ghoussoub writes with bitter irony, 'she too is now starting to claim . . . that Arab women really are more politicized than their Western counterparts, because they are more concerned to change the political system under which they live [a system based on the exploitation of one class by another] than its mere consequences, the superficial features of women's oppression' (p. 18). If Ghoussoub is right – that is, if in Arab countries where there exists an oppositional socialist movement, women are again subordinating the women's struggle to the supposedly 'larger' class struggle; and if, throughout the Arab world, women are bowing to Islamic fundamentalism's antifeminism in the name of nationalism or Arab unity – then it is essential to renew the effort to dismantle modes of cultural-political analysis that ignore or rationalize the suppression of Arab feminism by national and anti-imperial struggles. Among other things, this means attending to the politics of the veil as an urgent question indissociable from issues of national and cultural identity in the Muslim World.

Today, the politics of the veil is the subject of impassioned debate not only with respect to Muslim societies such as Egypt and Algeria but also in France where North African *lycéennes* are demanding the right to wear the veil in school despite injunctions from administrators (defending the national commitment to separation of church and state) and criticism from various sectors of the North African immigrant community (whether liberals favoring assimilation to French national norms or left feminists denouncing the equivalence posited between wearing the veil and exercising a 'right'). Gisèle Halimi, in particular, condemns France's implicit encouragement of reactionary state policies in North Africa.[49]

The issue has sparked reflection on racism in France, the function of human rights discourses in antiracist struggles, relations between national and sexual identity and the effects of one nation's public policy on global politics. The question this raises for Western feminists is how we can best engage with the political and cultural work of Arab feminists in 'the student milieux of Europe and America', while at the same time taking account, self-critically, of the 'boundary problems' cited by Mernissi in her enumeration of forces that are 'tearing the Muslim world apart': colonization ('trespassing by a foreign power on Muslim community space and decision making'); contemporary human rights issues ('the political boundaries circumscribing the ruler's space and the freedoms of the government'); integration of technological information 'without deluging our own Muslim heritage'; international economic dependency; and 'the sovereignty of the Muslim state vis-à-vis voracious, aggressive transnational corporations'.[50] It seems to me that, however we go about it, our efforts will be useful only on condition that we elude fascination by our own counter-ideologies, particularly if they work, paradoxically, to screen out the very voices and bodies they ostensibly address. Above all, this implies, at every moment, guarding against what Ghoussoub calls 'the contemptuous anti-Arab racism of American society, and its hypocritical indignation at the fate of Arab women' (p. 18).

NOTES

1. Germaine Tillion, 'Les Femmes et le voile', in Pierre Marthelot and André Raymond, comps., *Etudes Maghrébines: Mélange Charles-André Julien* (Paris: Presses Universitaires de France, 1964), 29. Future references to this text will appear in parentheses. In *Republic of Cousins: Women's Oppression in Mediterranean Society* (Atlantic Highland, NJ: Humanities Press International, 1983), in which another version of this essay appears, Tillion gives a finely nuanced account of the historical shifts in practices such as veiling, and the disinheritance of daughters as an effect of endogamy, in terms of relations between men and women, urban and rural societies, native and *colon* cultures. It is only the problem of women's relation to the emerging nation that is presented in a dualistic manner.

2. It is true that, in her controversial essay *Algeria: The Realities* (New York: Alfred A. Knopf, 1958), Tillion opposes Algerian independence, mainly on grounds that economic disaster would befall the country if France withdrew. Even here, though, she calls for industrialization, and the guarantee of education and employment for Algerians of both sexes.

3. David C. Gordon, *Women of Algeria* (Cambridge, MA: Harvard University Press, 1968), pp. 61, 64. Future references to this text will appear in parentheses. Similar analyses appear in Attilio Gaudio and Renée Pelletier, *Femmes d'Islam, ou le sexe interdit* (Paris: Denoel, 1980), pp. 89–106, and Juliette Minces, 'Women in Algeria', trans. Nikki Keddie, in Lois Beck and Nikki Keddie, eds., *Women in the Muslim World* (Cambridge, MA: Harvard University Press, 1978), pp. 159–71.

4. Catherine Delcroix, *Espoirs et réalités de la femme arabe (Algérie-Egypte)* (Paris: L'Harmattan, 1986). 139. Future references to this text will appear in parentheses.

5. Interview with a combatant in the National Liberation Front's official organ, *El-Moudjahid* 72 (1 November 1960), in André Mandouze, ed., *La Révolution algérienne par les textes* (Paris: Maspero, 1961), p. 106.

6. Fadela M'rabet, *La Femme algérienne, suivi de les Algériennes* (Paris: Maspero, 1969).

7. Peter R. Knauss, *The Persistence of Patriarchy: Class, Gender and Ideology in Twentieth Century Algeria* (New York: Praeger, 1987), p. xiii. Future references to this text will appear in parentheses.

8. See M'rabet, *La Femme Algérienne*; Knauss, *Patriarchy*, pp. 97–140; Minces, 'Women in Algeria'; and Nadia Aïnad-Tabet, 'Participation des Algériennes à la vie du pays', in Christiane Souriau, ed., *Femmes et politique autour de la méditerranée* (Paris: L'Harmattan, 1980), pp. 235–50.

9. See Aïnad-Tabet, 'Participation', and Camille Lacoste-Dujardin, *Des Mères contre les femmes* (Paris: La Découverte, 1985).

10. 'Islam Fundamentalism Sweeps Over Algeria Like Desert Wind', *Los Angeles Times*, 16 June 1990, sec. A.
11. President Chadli, quoted in Knauss, *Patriarchy*, pp. 134–5.
12. Chadli, quoted in ibid., p. 135.
13. See Ratiba Hadj-Moussa, *Les Femmes algériennes entre l'honneur et la révolution* (Québec: Laboratoire de recherches sociologiques, 1984).
14. See 'No Future à Bab-el-Oued', *L'Express*, 6–12 October 1989, pp. 27–9.
15. See Fatna A. Sabbah, *Woman in the Muslim Unconscious*, trans. Mary Jo Lakeland (New York: Pergamon Press, 1984).
16. *Le Nouvel Observateur*, 22–28 February 1990, p. 23.
17. Fatima Mernissi, 'Muslim Women and Fundamentalism', *Middle East Report* 153 (July–August 1988): 11. This essay is adapted from the introduction to the revised edition of Mernissi's *Beyond the Veil: Male-Female Dynamics in Modern Muslim Society* (Bloomington and Indianapolis: Indiana University Press, 1987).
18. On the fantasies expressed in the official and unofficial writings of army officers, see Mostefa Lacheraf, *L'Algérie: Nation et société* (Paris: Maspero, 1969), pp. 255–6; on the infiltration of Algeria through its families, especially its women, see Maurice Viollette, *L'Algérie vivra-t-elle?* (Paris: Alcan 1931) and le Docteur Calmette, 'Les Principes de la politique française coloniale', in Gabriel Hanotaux, comp., *L'Empire colonial français* (Paris: Plon, 1929), pp. 143–58; on Algeria's endogamy as the 'massive obstacle' to penetration, see E.-F. Gautier, *L'Algérie et la métropole* (Paris: Payot, 1920), p. 249.
19. Octave Depont, *L'Algérie du centenaire* (Bordeaux: Cadoret, 1928), p. 46.
20. In *L'Algérie vivra-t-elle?*, Violette provides evidence of the social pressures to which Fanon claims the Algerian 'évolué(e)s' were subject when he refers, for instance, to tea parties given by his wife, where Algerian women were, in his view, to be encouraged in their 'serious movement' toward Europeanization (pp. 415, 417–18).
21. Abdallah Laroui, *L'Histoire du Maghreb* (Paris: Maspero, 1970), p. 355.
22. Frantz Fanon, 'L'Algérie se dévoile', in *Sociologie d'une révolution* (Paris: Maspero, 1968), p. 23; in English, 'Algeria Unveiled', in *A Dying Colonialism*, trans. Haakon Chevalier (New York: Grove Press, 1967), pp. 35–67. Pierre Bourdieu discusses this dynamic in similar terms in 'Guerre et mutation sociale en Algérie', *Etudes Maghrébines* 7 (April 1960): pp. 25–37.
23. See Hal Lehrman, 'Battle of the Veil', *New York Times Magazine*, 13 July 1958, p. 14, 18. Lehrman notes that Algerian women organized a counterdemonstration and demanded the release of political prisoners. In *L'Aliénation colonialiste et la résistance de la famille algérienne* (Lausanne: La Cité, 1961), Saadia and Lakhdar accuse the French organizers of the May 13 event of coercing their maids, as well as Algerian prostitutes, into participating in this 'grotesque effort', p. 143.
24. On the establishment of women's camps, see Patrick Kessel and Giovanni Pirelli, *Le Peuple algérien et la guerre: Lettres et témoignages d'Algériens* (Paris: Maspero 1962), p. 537, n. 4.
25. Algeron, *Histoire*, p. 609, my emphasis.
26. See Mostefa Lacheraf's comments in *Révolution Africaine*, 7 December 1963, pp. 18–19, and 19 December 1963, pp. 22–3.
27. André Adam, 'Chronique sociale et culturelle', *Annuaire de l'Afrique du Nord* 1 (1962), pp. 545–62. See, for example, 'On National Culture', in *The Wretched of the Earth*, trans. Constance Farrington (New York: Grove Press, 1968), where Fanon points out that 'the colonized man who writes for his people ought to use the past with the intention of opening the future, as an invitation to action and a basis for hope' (p. 232), and that 'we find today the Arab states organically linked once more with societies which are Mediterranean in their culture. The fact is that these states are submitted to modern pressure and to new channels of trade' (p. 216).
28. See Yvonne Knibiehler and Régine Gontalier, *La Femme au temps des colonies*

(Paris: Stock, 1985); 'Kif-Kif la Française', *Time*, 23 February 1959, p. 26; and Jean-Paul Charnay, *La Vie Musulmane en Algérie d'après la jurisprudence* (Paris: Presses Universitaires de France, 1965).

29. See Matthéa Gaudry, *La Femme Chaouïa de l'Aurès: Etude de sociologie berbère* (Paris: Geuthner, 1929) and Laure Bousquet-Lefèvre, *La Femme Kabyle* (Paris: Viard, 1939).

30. Denise Brahimi, *Femmes arabes et soeurs musulmanes* (Paris: Editions Tierce, 1984), pp. 175, 238–39; on women's political and social struggles, Knibiehler and Gontalier, *Colonies*, p. 268, and Knauss, *Patriarchy*, p. 52.

31. Simone de Beauvoir and Gisèle Halimi, *Djamila Boupacha*, trans. Peter Green (New York: Macmillan, 1962).

32. Mai Ghoussoub, 'Feminism – or the Eternal Masculine – in the Arab World', *New Left Review* p. 161 (January–February 1987): pp. 3, 17. Future references to this text will appear in parentheses.

33. Malek Alloula, *The Colonial Harem*, trans. Myrna Godzich and Wlad Godzich (Minneapolis: University of Minnesota Press, 1986). Future references to this text will appear in parentheses.

34. On the displacement of Algerians as a result of colonial land policies, see Lacheraf, *L'Algérie*, pp. 16–25, 70–1, and Pierre Nora, *Les Français d'Algérie* (Paris: Julliard, 1961), pp. 90–3. On the prositution that results, see Knibiehler and Gontalier, *Colonies*, pp. 248, and Jacques Berque, *Le Maghreb entre deux guerres* (Paris: Seuil, 1962), pp. 357–9.

35. Mathéa Gaudry, *La Société féminine au Djebel Amour et au Ksel* (Algiers: Société Algérienne d'Impressions Diverses, 1961).

36. On the second-class status of French Algerians (both economic and cultural) and on Frenchness as the force that mediates ethnic and class conflicts among them by differentiating them from the Algerian natives, see Nora, *Les Français d'Algérie*, pp. 133–43, 150–1.

37. Maurice Besson, 'La Première Exposition Coloniale', *Bulletin du Comité de l'Afrique Française* 2 (February 1931): p. 123.

38. Quoted by C. M., 'Autour de l'Exposition Coloniale', *Bulletin du Comité de l'Afrique Française* 11 (November 1931): p. 734.

39. Text of a speech by Gustave Mercier, general commissioner, 'The Results of the Algerian Centenary', *Bulletin du Comité de l'Afrique Française* 6 (1930): pp. 391, 393.

40. Roland Barthes, *Camera Lucida*, trans. Richard Howard (New York: Hill and Wang, 1982), p. 98.

41. Proceedings of the Congress on Rural Colonization, *Bulletin du Comité de l'Afrique Française* 9 (September 1930): pp. 521–2.

42. The implantation (and negative reinterpretation) of this ideology is evidence from the 1930s through the 1960s. On the Muslim reformers' view of the beaches and dance halls as scenes of 'fornication', see Ali Mérad, *Le Rèformisme musulman en Algérie de 1925 à 1940* (Paris: Mouton, 1967), pp. 328, 329, n. 2. On the official pronouncements of the Algerian government after independence regarding Western women's eternal and inevitable subordination in 'consumer society', see Hadj-Moussa, *Femmes algériennes*, 166–9.

43. Marc Garanger, *Femmes algériennes 1960* (Paris: Contrejour, 1982). In *Révolution en Algérie* (Paris: France Empire, 1956), René Schaefer notes that, during the revolution, certain Algerian women were required to unveil for photos that appeared on food cards needed to obtain provisions (p. 147). On the regrouping of Algerian populations during the revolution, see Lacheraf, *Algérie*, pp. 265–6; Bourdieu, 'Mutation sociale', pp. 32–3; and Patrick Eveno and Jean Planchais, *La Guerre d'Algérie* (Paris: La Découverte, 1989), pp. 221, 223–8.

44. Leïla Sebbar, *Shérazade* (Paris: Stock, 1982), p. 220.

45. In 'Algeria, Conquered by Postcard' (*New York Times Book Review*, 11 January,

1987, p. 24), Carol Schloss remarks, in a similar vein, that, despite Alloula's effort to construct a countermemory by restoring the postcards to their original context, 'the cultural dialogue he initiates remains male-centered and concerned with women as property and as symbolic marks of (dis)honor or status for the men in their families'. However, Schloss accepts Alloula's view of the postcards as a 'surrogate' for political and military conquest. Another brief critique of Alloula's male-centered interpretation appears in Cynthia Enloe, *Bananas, Beaches, and Bases: Making Feminist Sense of International Politics* (London: Pandora Press, 1989), pp. 42, 44.

46. See, for instance, Fatima Mernissi, *Beyond the Veil*, and Assia Djebar, 'Forbidden Sight, Interrupted Sound', *Discourse* 8 (Fall–Winter 1986–87): pp. 39–56.

47. Barbara Harlow, *Resistance Literature* (New York: Methuen, 1987), pp. 137–40.

48. Ghoussoub, p. 17. In the discussion that follows (17–18), she illustrates changes in the work of Ijlal Khalifa, author of books on the history of the women's movement in Egypt and Palestine; Aziza al-Hibri, a feminist Marxist philospher; and the noted Egyptian feminists Leila Ahmed and Nawal al-Saadawi, all of whom have recently defended antifeminist Islamic practices (or denied the fundamental antifeminism of Islam) in the name of national integrity of pan-Arab solidarity.

49. See Diana Johnstone, 'In "great kerchief quarrel" French unite against "Anglo-Saxon ghettos"', in *These Times*, 24–30 January 1990, 10–11.

50. Mernissi, 'Muslim Women', p. 9.

5.6

'VEILING RESISTANCE'

Fadwa El Guindi

In the mid-seventies[1] a phenomenon became noticeable in the streets of Cairo, Egypt that seemed incomprehensible to many observers of the Egyptian scene and bewildering even to the local people. This was the strong, visible and growing presence of a new Egyptian woman, with an appearance unfamiliar to contemporary urban Egypt and to her own parents. The new woman was a young urban college student completely 'veiled' from head to toe, including the face. Confused at the thought of a future 'veiled' doctor, engineer or pharmacist, many observers speculated as to the cause of this development. Was this an identity crisis, *our* version of America's hippie movement, a fad, youth protest or ideological vacuum? An individual psychic disturbance, life-crisis, social dislocation or protest against authority?

THE VEIL BECOMES A MOVEMENT IN EGYPT

The contemporary veiling movement passed through several transitional phases after the 1970s, spreading all over the Arab world and among Muslims worldwide (see Wallace 1956 on processual phases in similar movements). Today the Islamic movement continues to grow strong as it enters its third decade. Dress has played a pivotal symbolic, ritual and political role in this dynamic phenomenon. The new vocabulary and dress style embodies a moral/behavioral code. Islam has struggled to position itself vis-à-vis the Islamic veil. The response of secularists and Western feminists shows how threatening this trend is to their ideological position. Egypt (with other Arab

From: Fadwa El Guindi (1999), 'Veiling Resistance', pp. 51–80, in *Fashion Theory*, vol. 3, no. 1.

countries) has accommodated the new movement and put effort into integrating it politically, despite initial attempts by the state to suppress it. Today the veiled and unveiled interact normally in daily life. Some mothers who originally objected to the veil have adopted it. The Islamic *ziyy* (dress) goes almost unnoticed in Cairo by the local population.

Islamic veiling in Egypt is somewhat different from the situation of the *chador* in Iran. The *chador* is a black head-to-toe wrap that was worn by rural and urban traditional women before the Revolution. The Shah, to Westernize the country, banned it, and the Islamic Revolution, to indigenize tradition, enforced wearing it. In Egypt, the Islamic dress worn after the mid-1970s by women replaced modern secular clothes and is part of a grass-roots activist movement. Unlike Egypt, both Iran and Turkey have long traditions of State-legislated dress reform for both sexes. Although state-discouraged in Egypt, veiling initially met with phenomenal success and spread throughout the urban centers.

As some young Egyptian women took up veiling in the mid-1970s, the government increasingly felt the threat of Islamic militancy and looked for solutions. In 1993, the education minister, Husain Kamal Baha' al-Din, sought to combat the spread of Islamic activism by imposing changes in the area of education, such as the transfer or demotion of teachers with activist leanings, a revision of the curriculum and restrictions on the wearing of the veil (Barraclough 1998: p. 246). However, a ban on wearing the veil at universities was thrown out by the courts. By 1994, attempts to limit the wearing of the veil in schools to students who had their parents' permission were receiving heavy criticism. The minister of education started back-pedaling – conceding that schoolgirls could wear the veil even without parental consent. State interference focusing on the veil remains controversial in Egypt.

In the Ottoman world there were deep roots to the tradition of clothing laws, extending back to the beginning of the empire. And as elsewhere Ottoman clothing laws gave a particular emphasis to head coverings, which typically designated honor and rank. Turbans played a key role in mid-eighteenth century rituals surrounding the Ottoman coronation ceremonies in Istanbul. In the procession, two horsemen each carried turbans of the monarch, tilting them to the right and to the left to receive the homage of the accompanying janissaries. The centrality of the headgear was evident even in the early fourteenth century (Quataert 1997: pp. 403–12).

According to Norton (1997), Turks can judge by appearances and are aware that dress denotes difference, devotion and defiance. 'A glance at what a stranger is wearing is often enough to tell them that person's religious and political stance. Clothes can tell them the wearer's defiance of or devotion to the principles of Kemal Ataturk, the reformer who founded the Turkish Republic and banned the fez' (Norton 1997: p. 149). The present situation in Turkey, like that in most groups in the Islamic world, is such that dress marks the front line in the battle between Islamic advocates and extreme secularists. But whereas the fez was the subject of state legislation, the veil was not, though it was generally discouraged and in some places prohibited. Turkey avoided an outright ban on the veil, the measure the Shah took in Iran, since 'forced unveiling of women' in Iran [is comparable to] the shock that Westerners would experience if women of all ages were forced to go topless in public' (Goldschmidt 1983; Norton 1997).

In the 1970s there was a one-party effort to create 'indigenous dress styles for Muslim women and to legitimize traditional Islamic dress' (Norton 1997: p. 165). Turkish women began to wear long coats and headscarves. Deep divisions formed between secularists and Muslim advocates (Olson 1985). The word 'turban' was introduced in the midst of a headscarf issue. It was ruled that a modern turban may be worn instead of a headscarf. Interestingly, by the mid-1980s in Egypt some of the women who were reluctant at first to wear the *khimar* (a headcovering that covers the hair and extends low to the forehead, comes under the chin to conceal the neck, and falls down over the chest and back) began to wear a turban-like headcovering that had Turkish origins. It was seen as more chic.

AL-ZIYY AL-ISLAMI (ISLAMIC DRESS)

The Code

Women's Islamic dress, known as *al-ziyy al-Islami*, is an innovative construction that was first worn in the mid-1970s by activists. It does not represent a return to any traditional dress form and has no tangible precedent. There was no industry behind it – not one store in Egypt carried such an outfit. Based on an idealized Islamic vision gradually constructed for the early Islamic community in the seventh century, it was made in the homes by the activists themselves. Privacy, humility, piety and moderation are cornerstones of the Islamic belief system. Luxury and leisure await Muslims in the next world. Some elements of this vision can be supported by reference to the *Qur'an*;[2] others find support in the secondary source of Islamic information, the *Sunna*,[3] through the *Hadith*.[4] The 'Prophetic vision' had become idealized through the ages, developing into a model to be emulated via recurring revivalist purifying movements within Islam, just as in the Islamic movement of Egypt in the 1970s.

In the Qur'an (considered the primary and divinely revealed source), but mostly according to the Hadith (a worldly source), evidence suggests that the Prophet Muhammad had paid much attention to a dress code for Muslims in the emerging community, with a specific focus on Muslim men's clothing and bodily modesty during prayer. By comparison, reference to women's body cover is negligible. One such reference, al-Ahzab in *sura* (33:59), distinguishes the status of the Prophet's wives from the rest of the believers, and the other (33:53) protects their privacy from growing intrusions by male visitors.

Men and women in the contemporary Islamic movement who argue for the Islamic dress and behavioral code use as support for their argument two specific *suras* in the Qur'an – al-Nur and al-Ahzab.[5] *Al-Nur*, translates as follows:

And say to the believing men that they should lower their gaze and guard their genitals [and] say to the believing women that they should lower their gaze and guard their genitals, draw their *khimar* to cover their cleavage [breasts], and not display their beauty, except that which has to appear, except to their husbands, their fathers, their husbands' fathers, their sons, their husbands' sons, their brothers or their brothers' sons, or their sisters' sons, or their women, or the slaves, or eunuchs or children under age; and they should not strike their feet to draw attention to their hidden beauty. O ye believers turn to God, that ye may attain bliss (Qur'an 24: 30, 31).

Several points can be drawn from this text: (1) the Arabic notions of lowering the gaze and covering the genitals are central to the code; and (2) men are first mentioned as having to abide by these two prescriptions, to control their gaze at women and suppress their passion and forwardness when interacting with 'strange' women. In the Hadith men especially are enjoined to cover their genitals during worship. Unlike other religions, Islam accepts sexuality as a normative aspect of both ordinary and religious life (Mernissi 1975; Marsot 1979; Nelson 1974) and fluidly accommodates both sacred and worldly activity in the same bi-rhythmic space. There is no contradiction between being religious and being sexual. Sex is to be enjoyed in socially approved marriages.

However, outside marriage, behavior between men and women must be desexualized. Both body and interactive space need to be regulated and controlled and both men and women are required to abide by this temporary desexualization to make public interaction between them possible. This presumes that cross-sex interaction would potentially be sexually charged. Islam accepts sexualized, reproductive men and women and guides them to regulate their public behavior.

As the same *sura* (al-Nur) shows, concealing and revealing is very much tied to cultural notions of respectability or the body parts that are considered sexually charged. Islamic mores were being formulated as the *suras* were revealed. The reference to drawing the headveil to cover a woman's cleavage may have been a reaction to the way women in the region prior to birth of the new community seem to have worn clothes that exposed their bodies. Images from what is now modern Yemen, for example, show women from the low-status group of *al-akhdam* (servants) wearing clothing that revealed the breasts. These suggest, not seductive sexuality, but slovenliness.[6] Another prohibition concerns anklets. The phrase 'not to strike the feet' is a reference to the practice in which women wore decorative jingling anklets made of heavy metal (silver or gold). It is not the anklet per se that is erotic, but the jingling that evokes erotic passions.[7]

Early (1993), in her ethnography on *baladi* (local traditional urban) life in Cairo, describes the traditional *baladi* dress, *milaya laff* (a wrapped black oversheet) draped over a house dress to cover the hair and entire body when in public; the ends of the long wrap are tucked under the arm. From underneath, a tightly knotted scarf covers the hair (p. 70). El-Messiri notes the dimension of sensual playfulness: with high-heeled sandals and tinkling anklets, the dress can combine sexual glamor with modesty (1978: pp. 526, 529).

Within Islam, a woman's sexuality does not diminish her respectability. Islam in fact supports this combined image in womanhood. The Hadith mentions an incident in which the Prophet Muhammad told a woman to color her finger-nails with henna so that her hands were not like the hands of men. What Islamic morality forbids is the public flaunting of sexuality. In general, the Islamic code would consider the behavior of the urban *baladi* women in Egypt described in El-Messiri's and Early's ethnographies as exhibitionist. Dressing and moving in a way that draws sexual attention to the body is *tabarruj* (exhibitionist dress and behavior). It is associated in Islamic perception with Arabian women of *al-Jahiliyya* (the Days of Ignorance or pre-Islamic days) and was frowned upon during the formative years of the Islamic community in the seventh century.

The Dress

In the contemporary revival, the dress code was translated this way: men and women wear full-length *gallabiyyas* (*jilbab* in standard Arabic), loose-fitting to conceal body contours, in solid austere colors made out of opaque fabric. They lower their gaze in cross-sex public interaction and refrain from body or dress decoration or colors that draw attention to their bodies. The dress code for men consists of sandals, baggy trousers with loose-top shirts in off-white or, alter-natively (and preferably), a long loose white *gallabiyya*. They grow a *lihya* (a full beard trimmed short), with an optional moustache. Hair is to be kept shoul-der length. This last feature has not been sustained and was eventually dropped. The general behavioral code of austerity and restraint has support in Qur'anic segments that repeatedly stress the undesirability of arrogance and an exhibi-tionist demeanour.[8]

Similarly, women wear the *hijab* which consists of *al-jilbab* (ankle-length, long-sleeved, loose-fitted dress) and *al-khimar*, a headcovering that covers the hair and extends low to the forehead, comes under the chin to conceal the neck and falls down over the chest and back. The common colors used by women during the first decade of the movement were beige, brown, navy, deep wine, white and black. This dress is worn while engaging fully in daily affairs in public social space in which not only their gender is accepted but also their sexual identity. Austere dress form and behavior therefore are not accompanied by withdrawal, seclusion or segregation.

The voluntary informal dress code extends beyond clothing to a general demeanour characterized by serious behavior and an austere manner, an ideal applied to both sexes. Some women more conservatively add *al-niqab*, which covers the entire face except for the eye slits; at the most extreme, a woman would also wear gloves and opaque socks to cover her hands and feet. This trend has been spreading throughout the Arab world, particularly among university students. Chatty describes a similar trend occurring in south-eastern Arabia (Chatty 1997).

During the first decade of the movement in Egypt the dress code for women corresponded to the degree of Islamic knowledgeability and reading, as well as to a step on a scale of leadership among women. The more intensely covered the college woman, the more 'serious' her public behavior, and the more knowledgeable she is in Islamic sources, the higher she was on the scale of activist leadership among women. She would lead discussions, for example, in mosques and in women students' lounges between lectures. This correspondence dissolved as the movement spread outside the university campuses and as the *hijab* became part of normal life and was integrated with secular life in Cairo and the other major cities.

This Islamic dress was introduced by college women in the movement and was not imposed by the al-Azhar authorities, who ordinarily prescribe Islamic behavior by issuing decrees. Instead, this was a bottom-up movement. By dressing this way in public these young women conveyed their vision of Islamic ideals by becoming exemplary contemporary models. Encoded in the dress style is an affirmation of an Islamic identity and morality and a rejection of Western materialism, consumerism, commercialism and values. The vision behind the Islamic dress is rooted in these women's understanding of early Islam and, as earlier presented, in primary and secondary textual sources. But it is a contemporary movement about contemporary issues.

Clearly, the movement is not simply about a dress code. Like early Islam in Madina, this activism espouses egalitarianism, community, identity, privacy and justice. It condemns exhibitionism in dress and behavior, which was characteristic of *al-jahiliyya* (the pre-Islamic era). Hence, al-Jahiliyya is not just a historical moment, but a state and a condition of society that can recur at any time. Reserve and restraint in behavior, voice and body movement are not restrictions – they symbolize a renewal of traditional cultural identity.

VEILING IN TWO FEMINISMS

The Egyptian feminist movement at the turn of the century was described as a secular movement that 'brought together Muslim and Christian women of the upper and middle classes[9] who identified [themselves] as Egyptians' (Badran 1995b: p. 45). Leila Ahmed does not see it in such monolithic terms. In a discussion linking Western colonialism and feminism, Ahmed distinguishes two strands of feminism propounded by Egypt's 'First Feminists' (1992: pp. 169–88). There is the Westward-looking feminism espoused by Huda Sha'rawi (1879–1947)[10] and another, advocated by Malak Hifni Nasif (1886–1918)[11] that did not affiliate itself with Westernization.

Groundedness of feminists in their own culture has been largely overlooked in the discourse on feminism.[12] Fundamental to a genuine Arabo-Islamic society are mastery of the Arabic language (formal not colloquial) and access to Islamic knowledge. These two cornerstones of the culture had gradually become the domains of men – a masculinization process that distanced many women from the core of their culture. This process is connected to the valuation for 'foreign' languages (at the expense of the Arabic language) that has developed among the urbanized ascribed aristocracy and spread among urban achieved-status groups. Speaking 'soft' Arabic with French loan words became feminine and chic. A corollary practice was the informal adoption of a husband's last name in lieu of one's maiden name. It should be noted in this regard that Arab women have financial autonomy. The legal system requires that a woman should keep her maiden name after marriage. Officially, the state in Arab society does not recognize a husband's name even when it is informally adopted by women. Nasif, true to her views and her self-image, continued to use her natal family name after marriage, whereas Huda first simplified her name from Nur al-Huda (her name at birth) to Huda and then, upon marriage, changed her last name from Sultan (her father's name) to Sha'rawi (her husband's name) – a social (not an official or a legal) practice borrowed by urbanized women to validate their modern, feminine and chic image.

A superficial familiarity with Islamic knowledge acquired casually through male relatives also became the norm among women. One can only speculate about the factors that led to this state of affairs. Women identified with French culture at the expense of Arabic, which was considered *déclassé*. Lacking the necessary command of the Arabic language, Huda Sha'rawi, the pioneer feminist of the Arab world, did not write her own memoirs. Instead she dictated a chronicle of events to her male secretary, who had a command of the Arabic language. Despite her prominence as a feminist leader, she was distanced from her native language and therefore not a complete insider in her own culture. Instead, she mastered foreign languages. 'She was educated at home by tutors in both Turkish and French, the languages of a lady of the time' (Fernea and Bezirgan 1977: p. 193). One must note that those 'ladies' (see Marsot 1978) made up an insignificant percentage of the Egyptian population, and their programs were mostly relevant within their own circles. While Huda was tutored in foreign languages her brother was receiving private Arabic lessons.[13]

This had not always been the case in Egypt. Al-Sayyid Marsot mentions that in the eighteenth century the greater masses of both sexes were illiterate, but 'among the elites both men and women were literate in religion and in language [and] the *ulama* (male religious scholars) and *alimat* (female religious scholars) were more educated than any other sector of society' (1979: pp. 14, 15). Colonial and missionary pressures at the turn of the century as well as consumerist and secularizing trends in the twentieth century led women away from rights they already had in Islam – most importantly the right (with precedents in Islam) to full participation in the Islamic process, teaching and worship. By submitting to these distancing trends, women excluded themselves from the two most relevant spheres (the Arabic language and Islamic studies) that most crucially regulate and sanction their lives, engender dignity and respect and legitimize their rights and privileges. These became dominated by men.

As early as the 1870s and 1880s, before Egyptian organized feminism developed, Egyptian women were publishing their writings and were engaged in public speaking. They wrote poetry, prose, biographies, articles and essays and published them in the mainstream press at a time when publishing was new to Egypt. By the 1890s an emergent 'sisterhood' of exchanges of letters and circulation of books expanded and took new forms. Badran describes the environment of the turn of the century in Egypt as 'an urban harem culture, the site of the first emergence of women's feminist awareness and nascent feminist expression' (Badran 1995a: p. 4). Collective debate grew through 'salons' held by the women of the aristocracy and expanded with the founding by non-aristocratic women of a women's press.

Egyptian women, Muslim and Christian, were positioning their liberation vis-à-vis the simultaneously rising nationalism that grew up in response to colonial intervention.[14] Colonial domination was complete and humiliating, particularly in its very denial of Egyptianness. The British colonizers referred to Egyptians as 'natives' or the 'native race'. Their avoidance of the term 'Egyptian' made Egyptians seem nameless and nationless. It was in this climate that both nationalism and feminism took hold. Egyptianness and women's rights rose simultaneously. Paradoxically, the degree of political or personal affiliation with the colonizer became a barometer of commitment to nationalist activism. It is significant in this regard that, according to Badran, Huda Sha'rawi's father, Sultan Pasha, was implicated in assisting British intervention in Egypt (1995a: p. 11).[15]

Women had already begun to debate their position on these issues when men, in search of factors behind the demise of their country, began questioning existing social practices with regard to gender and formulated what many considered to be feminist positions in the process. These men were highly educated, had legal training and had been exposed to European thought. Consequently, a men's discourse on women's issues (questionably characterized as feminist) emerged in the Arab world (Badran 1995a: pp. 13–16). Unlike women's organized feminism, the veil was central to men's 'feminist' discourse. Women were drawn into the debate and popular periodicals became partisan publications. Three periodicals[16] were 'staunch defenders of the veil [and two][17] condemned the veil . . . Muslims, Jews, and Christians all wrestled with the question of veiling' (Baron 1989: pp. 372, 379).

A prominent Egyptian man who provoked heated controversy and debate was Qasim Amin, who came to be regarded by many as the founder of feminism in Arab culture. The response to his book *Tahrir Al-Mar'a* (The Liberation of Woman), published in 1899, was intense, and opposition to its message was vociferous. In the book, he advocated primary school education for women and reform of the laws on polygyny and divorce. Were these considered radical proposals at the time? Ahmed notes that they were not new. These issues had been proposed in the 1870s and 1880s, perhaps even earlier, by Muslim intellectuals who had argued for women's education and called for reforms in matters of polygyny and divorce 'without provoking violent controversy' (1992: p. 145). By the 1890s the issue of educating women beyond the primary level was uncontroversial and girls' schools were established. So why was there such a strong reaction to Amin's work?

A closer look reveals that Amin called, not for feminist reforms, but rather for a fundamental social and cultural change for Egypt and other Muslim countries, a Europeanization of Arab culture as if were, in which women's issues were embedded. Central to this reform, proposed as the key to change and progress in society, was the call for abolishing the veil.

Tal'at Harb, a wealthy Egyptian industrialist entrepreneur who pioneered modern banking in Egypt, responded strongly to Amin. He is described as having 'defended and upheld Islamic practices' (Ahmed 1992: p. 164). But in fact Harb used Islamic language and selected quotations from Christian and Muslim scriptures and Western and Muslim men of learning to defend and uphold a perspective that is not much different from Amin's Western vision of female domesticity: that the wife's duty was to attend to the physical, mental and moral needs of her husband and children (Harb 1905 [1899]: p. 21). First, these are the same duties ascribed to her by Amin. To modernize Muslim society Amin wanted to abandon its 'backward' ways and follow the Western path, which of course required changing women. His call for women's education was based on the idea that women needed education in order to manage the household, a responsibility that entails many skills. 'It is the wife's responsibility to establish the family budget . . . to manage servants . . . to make her home attractive and appealing to her husband, to enjoy food, drink and sleep, and not seek comfort elsewhere, with neighbors or in public places. But her first and most important duty is to raise and socialize the children, physically, mentally, and morally' (Amin 1976, Vol. 2: p. 31, my translation). Borrowing from Western notions of domesticity and womanhood in order to validate what is characteristically an Arab quality of family relations, Amin wrote that the adult man is nothing but what his mother made him to be from childhood. '*The essence of this book and the message I wish to impart to all men . . . is the special relationship between a man and his mother . . . it is impossible to produce successful men without mothers capable or enabling them to be successful.* This is the noble duty that advanced civilization has given to woman in our age and which she fulfills in advanced societies' (1976, Vol. 2: pp. 78–9; translation mine, emphasis in original).[18] Most significantly, Amin reaffirmed the special and unique mother-son relationship already inherent in Arab society by using European notions of female domesticity.

Second, it is questionable whether Tal'at Harb's views would be characterized as Islamic. Qasim Amin, on the other hand, was explicitly positioned outside the Islamic spectrum. He was a French-educated lawyer whose rationale in calling for change in the position of women and for abolishing the veil was not much different from the colonial/missionary agenda. The ideas espoused by the British colonial official Lord Cromer, who embodied the colonizer's posture and agenda, and the missionaries, whose strategy was to undermine Islam and Arab tradition, were reflected in Amin's book. Amin's text also assumed and declared the inherent superiority of Western civilization and the inherent backwardness of Muslim societies: he wrote that anyone familiar with 'the East' had observed 'the backwardness of Muslims . . . wherever they are'. Among Muslims he saw a hierarchy that put the Egyptians at the bottom[19] – Muslim civilization in general is represented as semi-civilized compared to that of the West. As Ahmed put it: 'In the course of making his argument, Amin managed to express . . . a generalized contempt for Muslims . . . often in lavishly abusive detail' (Ahmed 1992: p. 156). Veiling was not a practice confined to Muslims; it was an urban phenomenon associated mostly with the upper classes. The Coptic intellectual Salama Musa noted in his memoirs that his mother and two married sisters wore the long veil until about 1907 or 1908, and that if was through missionary influence that Christian women began to drop the practice. Also Qasim Amin's wife continued to wear the veil. He tried to enforce unveiling on his daughters despite efforts to the contrary from his own uncle.[20]

Both Amin and Harb claimed to be concerned with women's liberation. They differed in their frameworks but reached similar conclusions. One exception is the veil. Harb's women must veil and Amin's must unveil. The argument between Harb and Amin was not, as it is commonly characterized, feminist versus antifeminist,[21] but rather reflected two muddled versions of domesticity, a Western female domesticity versus an indigenous man's vision of female domesticity. Islam was not in any serious way the ideological basis for either position.[22] Contradictions abound in both. In appropriating a women's issue, men polarized discourse surrounding the veil.

Amin's book, then, can be seen as fuelling feminist debate rather than simple pioneering feminist reform in Egypt. It put on center stage the colonial narrative of women, in which the veil and the treatment of women epitomized Islamic inferiority and entered the colonial agenda of appropriation of resources and culture into mainstream Arabic discourse and programs of reform. The opposition it generated similarly marks 'the emergence of an Arabic narrative developed in resistance to the colonial narrative. This narrative of resistance appropriated, in order to negate them, the symbolic terms of the originating narrative' (Ahmed 1992: p. 164).

By 1910 sensitivity toward the nuances of veiling and unveiling was established. The newspaper al-'Afaf began publication in Cairo in 1910 'proclaiming itself the mouthpiece of women' (Baron 1989: p. 370). In the twenty-sixth issue of its first volume it used as a frontispiece a drawing of a woman standing in front of the pyramids and the sphinx, holding her arm aloft with a banner that read 'modesty is my motto'. Across her face she wore a light, translucent veil. The mouth and nose were revealed through the transparent fabric and the eyes were not covered. Baron (1989: p. 28) notes that the paper was criticized (see al-'Afaf 1911: p. 1)[23] and that three issues later the image was revised. The redrawn veil was thick and non-transparent, and the nose, face and chin were not revealed through it. Revealed, however, are the complex subtleties entailed in the reaction to this visual imagery of the veil and womanhood.

Interestingly, removing the veil was not part of the official feminist agenda at the time. According to Badran (1995a), unveiling, which had been of concern only to urban women, 'had never been part of the EFU's (Egyptian Feminist Union) formal agenda' (pp. 94–6). The phrase used in the discourse surrounding the context of lifting the 'veil' was *raf'al-higab* (the lifting of the *hijab*). Ironically, what secular feminists lifted was the traditional face veil (*burqu'*), which is rooted in cultural tradition and history rather than in Islamic sources, not the *hijab*. In her speech at the Feminist conference in Rome, Sha'rawi specified the face veil (*burqu'* or *yashmik*), not *hijab*, as a barrier to women's advancement (pp. 253, 254; see Kahf 1998). When Huda Sha'rawi dramatically cast off the veil in 1923, it was the face veil she removed, not the *hijab*. Further, the act mirrored a change already taking place, as the debate over the issue of veiling and unveiling shows.

It is not trivial that Huda Sha'rawi only removed the face cover (*burqu'* or *yashmik*) but kept the head covering. Technically, therefore, Sha'rawi never 'lifted the *hijab*'. Some attribute her success in feminist nationalist leadership, compared to Doria Shafiq (1914–1976),[24] for example, to the fact that she respected this tradition. In her *Memoirs* there is a segment in which she mentions being congratulated for 'my success in arriving at lifting the *hijab* . . . but wearing the *hijab shar'i*' (lawful *hijab* – used specifically to mean the Islamic *hijab*) (Sha'rawi 1981: p. 291). The distinction made is important, and becomes central to the debate on contemporary veiling. Sha'rawi lifted the traditional customary veil and wore the *hijab* in the manner that finds support in Islamic sources.[25] Significantly, she was decorated with the state's highest honor, *Nishan al-Kamal* (Medal of Perfection). Badran (1995a) describes how in the first two decades of the twentieth century feminist women like Huda Sha'rawi and Malak Hifni Nasif (Bahithat al-Badiya) retained the veil, because 'uncovering the face was premature [and] society was not ready for it' (Badran 1995a: pp. 22, 23).

Of the early feminists, Nabawiyya Musa, the first college graduate and the one who was not from the aristocracy, removed her face covering unceremonially around 1909. 'Bahithat al-Badiya died in 1918 without having unveiled' (Badran 1995a: p. 23). The comment by Nasif that after social change 'I would approve of unveiling *for those who want it*' (Nasif 1962: pp. 275–9, emphasis added) confirms, contrary to falsely publicized claims, the tolerant stance of early twentieth-century Egyptian feminism with regard to veiling. It also brings out an element in Nasif's feminism absent in other programs – choice on the part of women.

Huda Sha'rawi unveiled ceremonially in a public political feminist act in 1923 upon returning from a feminist meeting in Rome – an act of far-reaching symbolic significance.[26] Its impact and ripple effect was felt beyond her narrow circle of the elite.[27] The gesture has entered the lore on women's liberation and, as lore, is alive and is continually embellished. Evidence in photographs and reports reveals how girls had begun to appear unveiled in schools,[28] in the streets,[29] and in protests between 1910 and 1919 (Baron 1989: p. 379). It has been observed that in Cairo before the First World War Egyptian women were far more advanced than their Lebanese counterparts. Egyptian women, it was observed by a Lebanese writer, are 'more emancipated than us . . . they saw the world with unveiled eyes [unlike our women] who did not see the world except from behind black veils' (Khalidi 1978: p. 64). So unveiling was already publicly visible before 1914. While Sha'rawi's dramatic gesture did not mark the beginning of unveiling, her social and political position in society gave the process celebrity and legitimacy.

The *hijab* worn by Muslim and Christian women at the turn of the century is different in meaning from the *hijab* worn by college women in the 1970s. The first was characterized as 'a national Egyptian dress for upper-class women, then called *al-habara*'.[30] It consisted of a full-length skirt, a head cover and *al-burqu'* (a face covering from below, the eyes down to the chest) and was worn by Muslim and Christian women. In her memoirs, Huda Sha'rawi used the term *izari* (my cloak) in referring to what she commonly wore as a wrap when she went out. She did not seem to use the term *hijab* except in the context of the political act of lifting the veil (Sha'rawi 1981: p. 89).[31] Ahmed notes that Amin's book, the debate it generated and the issues of class and tradition with which the debate became inscribed may be regarded as the precursor and prototype of the debate around the veil (Ahmed 1992: p. 164). This is not quite so, however, since by the time Amin published his work in 1899 the debate had already begun in the press.

Reacting to the writings of European-influenced Egyptian men who advocated the lifting of the veil for women, Malak Hifni Nasif saw a nuanced 'male domination enacted through [their] discourse of the veil' (Ahmed 1992: p. 179). She opposed mandatory unveiling. Badran does not distinguish between the feminism of Nasif and that of Sha'rawi. She sees the latter as a continuation of the same struggle. After Nasif's death at a young age 'Sha'rawi publicly pledged to continue her struggle on behalf of women' (Badran 1995c: p. 230). But Ahmed does.

The two leading women espoused two feminist views: one more authentically Egyptian, the other Western-influenced. This differentiation is important because research increasingly shows that feminism is rooted in culture. It challenges Western feminism's claims of universality, which dominate discourse and research in the West. Differences exist among feminisms and multiple feminist strands can exist within the same society. Background, upbringing, education, social class and political ideology all influence the content of feminism and feminist goals. And just as Western feminism is solidly rooted in European and American cultures, the Egyptian feminism of Western-influenced Egyptians can be different from a feminism that is more deeply and authentically rooted in the culture and tradition of Egypt, despite apparent similarities.

The Arabic language and Islamic knowledge mattered to Malak Hifni Nasif, but were not included in the official feminist agenda as it developed under the leadership of Huda Sha'rawi, which stressed women's suffrage, education reform, health services, and employment opportunities. Nasif, in contrast with Huda Sha'rawi,[32] was highly proficient in the Arabic language. She gave lectures in fluent Arabic and was a prolific Arabic writer. She was comfortable with her roots and well grounded in her native (Arabic) language and Arab culture.

In her *Memoirs* Sha'rawi recounts how the Egyptian delegation to the International Women's conference in Rome in 1923 vowed 'that we would follow in the footsteps of the women in Europe in the awakening of our women so that we could take our land to its rightful place among the advanced nations'[33] (1981: p. 252). The same frame of reference is used in the language of the agenda submitted by the Sha'rawi-led Egyptian Feminist Union to the government. The rationale for the feminist program was couched neither in terms of absolute feminism and women's entitlement, nor in terms espousing the preservation of tradition. Rather, the rationale was in order for Egypt 'to reach a level of glory and might like that reached by the civilized nations' (1981: p. 262).

Looking up to Europeanization of behavior and culture was made integral to the inscripted culture of the aristocracy. Internalizing a valorization of European culture while undermining native culture, its members presented a 'gallicized' public social self. That was the way to convey and validate their class. However, the implication of this colonization of selves and minds is an area of research that has not received sufficient attention.

The principal beneficiaries of the British reform measures and the increased involvement in European capitalism were the European residents of Egypt, the Egyptian upper classes and the new middle class of rural notables and men educated in Western-type secular schools who became the civil servants and the new intellectual elite. Whether trained in the West or in the Western-type institutions established in Egypt, these 'modern' men with their new knowledge challenged the traditionally and religiously trained *ulama* (the al-Azhar authoritative scholars of Islam), displacing them as administrators, bureaucrats and educators to become transmitters of the newly valued secular scholarship and secular approach to society. Traditional knowledge itself became devalued as outmoded and backward. The resulting proposals seemed to have adopted the weaknesses in both cultures, the colonizing and the colonized.

Nasif's agenda stressed two significant elements absent in Sha'rawi's feminist agenda. First, she demanded that all fields of higher education be opened to women. Information on the specific fields that were reserved for men is significant here. In the West the fields that were 'open' for women were mostly the 'soft' fields of art and home economics. American women until recently did not tend to go into the professional schools of medicine and engineering or majors such as mathematics or economics. In the Arab world, studies of patterns in higher education (El Guindi 1985, 1986) show that, when higher education became widely accessible in the 1950s, enrollments were balanced between the sexes. The distribution in 'soft' fields and professional majors was similar for both sexes. Yet while women were significantly present in medicine and engineering (valued or modern society), they were absent in two particular majors: Arabic Studies and Islamic Studies. This is where cultural context is important in determining which obstacles facing women are relevant for their liberation. When Nasif demanded that *all* fields be made open to women, was she concerned about Arabic and Islamic Studies? This very issue would become relevant several decades later in the 1970s.

Second, she demanded that space be made in mosques for women to participate in public prayer. By demanding that mosques be made accessible to women, Nasif had established an agenda that recognizes what is core in the culture (see Nasif 1909). Her agenda was Islamic, her goals feminist. These premises presupposed a strong populist movement that is Islamic feminist.

Clearly, whereas Sha'rawi was socialized into a world that attached high value to French culture above local tradition, Nasif was firmly rooted in Arabo-Islamic culture. But one cannot easily characterize Nasif as a traditionalist. In their ultimate goal of advancing women's rights, Nasif and Sha'rawi did not differ. Had Nasif lived longer, however, it is very likely that two parallel (organized) feminisms would have developed – one grounded in Arabo-Islamic culture, the other in European culture and feminism.

The discourse of colonialism incorporated a language of feminism and used the issue of women's position in Islamic societies as the focus of attack on those societies. Men serving the colonial administration, such as Cromer in Egypt,[34] who ironically opposed feminism in his own country, England, espoused in the colonial context a rhetoric of feminism that attacked Egyptian men for upholding practices that degraded their women. This posture of subversion and appropriation of the colonized culture can be interpreted as the colonizing power's attempt to legitimize its own domination and justify its occupation policies. The kind of feminism emerging out of this colonial context becomes an alternative form of dominance that gives its men and women a sense of superiority. By adopting it, Egyptian men accepted and Egyptian women reproduced their own subordination within their culture as well as their country's subordination to European dominance.

Two Notions of Gender

In the course of my analysis of Islamic activism (El Guindi 1998) two conceptions of gender emerge. The first individuates society,[35] secularizes culture and feminizes social, political and moral issues. Its agenda prioritizes women's problems, mostly independent of cultural constructions and often segregated from society as a whole and from political affairs. While if assumes universality, this notion originates in Western thought and is embedded in cultural values constructed out of a Euro-Christian ethos, relations of domination, and the colonial encounter. It is based on constructs of polarities. Filtered through lenses of Christo-European constructions, efforts to understand the Middle East have resulted in distorted perspectives about Islamic constructions of gender, space and sexuality. For example, gender roles are described as domestic (private) versus public – a division that better describes Western European society but distorts understanding of Arab and Islamic society. Also, piety is mistakenly separated from worldliness and sexuality, leading to the ingrained focus on seclusion and virginity and thus missing nuances characteristic of Islamic space and privacy as they pertain to veiling. Looking at Islamic culture through these lenses of distortion reveals violations of ideal separations between the worldly and the religious, between Church and State, between domestic and public.

Instead of the polarity that characterizes Western constructions, Islamic principles insist on the integration of dualities. Hence we encounter a modality of polarity (Western) versus a modality of relational integration (Arabo-Islamic).

It is within the latter model that we locate the second conception of gender, which is embedded within cultural tradition and Islamic activism and is contextualized in local, regional and cultural history. This conception is more relevant to an objective understanding of Muslim women's activism. Approaching Muslim women's rights through liberal feminist agendas cannot be effective because these agendas are based on the Western experience and derive from Western values; hence they are irrelevant to most issues of concern to Muslim women. Matters pertaining to women and the family are based on scripturalist-derived decrees and laws. To be effective, these issues must be dealt with within the same framework that created them. Feminism within the context of Islam can provide the only path to empowerment and liberation that avoids challenging the whole of the culture (Mir-Hosseini 1996).

But there is another point. Reaffirmation of traditional values and identities also feeds from the same Arabo-Islamic source. One can choose either the liberal feminist or the Islamic feminist path, but in neither can reform be effected or goals be achieved without direct access to primary Islamic knowledge in Arabic. This point had not escaped Doria Shafiq, who struggled to find legitimacy for her feminism even among feminists. She recognized the need to master Islamic knowledge and to communicate in the Arabic language. Any Europeanized activities were considered marginal (see the ethno-biography of Doria Shafik by Nelson (1996)).

The Egyptian college women who pioneered the Islamic movement in the 1970s penetrated precisely these culturally relevant realms. They were reading primary sources, although much of their energy was spent in justifying their newly constructed dress and defending their posture vis-à-vis society. Their dress gradually became a uniform and a model for public demeanour and cross-sex relations. Mainstream society and Islam began to accommodate them. Increasingly, Egyptians dressed more conservatively. Islamic dress was mass-produced and made available at a low cost. Commercial stores specialized in its sale, thereby making it chic and appealing, and hairdressers opened special sections for the *muhaggabat*.

Islamic Feminism

Another feminism, which I label Islamic feminism,[36] set itself unambiguously apart from the two feminisms of Nasif and Sha'rawi when the prominent pioneer, Zaynab al-Ghazali, carved an alternative path. Al-Ghazali was born in 1917, the daughter of an al-Azhar-educated independent religious teacher and cotton merchant. She was privately tutored in Islamic studies in the home, and afterwards attended a public secondary school. Her father encouraged her to become an Islamic leader. She obtained certificates in Hadith and Tafsir.

Al-Ghazali had first begun her activist career by participating in the activities of the secular feminist organization founded by Huda Sha'rawi, who was her mentor, as she was to many prominent women. After joining the Egyptian Feminist Union she became dissatisfied and sought another path for women's rights – one from within Islam. Rejecting the Western woman as a model for Muslim women, Zaynab al-Ghazali abandoned the secular Egyptian Feminist Union and founded, at the age of eighteen, Jama'at al-Sayyidat al-Muslimat (the Muslim Women's Association), which was active from 1936 to 1964.[37] She published and gave weekly lectures to thousands of women at the Ibn Tolon Mosque (Hoffman-Ladd 1995: pp. 64–6). 'The Association published a magazine, maintained an orphanage, offered assistance to poor families, and mediated family disputes' (1995: p. 64). Her public activism and mastery of and leadership in Islamic issues set her apart, and qualified her to lead women within the Islamic fold.

An autonomous, strong-minded woman who was dedicated to learning Islam from childhood and gained credentials that qualified her to teach it, she divorced her first husband who allegedly interfered with her Islamic activities. She espoused Islamic ideals that supported family values while she also developed into a prominent activist leader in Islamic teaching and organizing (Hoffman-Ladd 1995; Hoffman 1985). Neither she nor the Islamic leadership of the Muslim Brotherhood saw her combined roles as contradictory.

When al-Ghazali first joined the Association of Huda Sha'rawi she had established her commitment to women's rights and to serving women's interests. When she switched from the secularist feminist path to the path of Islam to reach these goals, she revealed her own conviction of Islam and awareness of its importance in ordinary people's lives. The movement's success and wide appeal legitimized Islam as potentially liberating for women. When Hassan al-Banna, founder of the Muslim Brotherhood,[38] sought her cooperation and suggested that both associations work together to unify the movement, she insisted on keeping her organization autonomous. Her leadership was not questioned by men or women in the general movement. However, she obviously posed a threat to the state – sufficiently so that she was arrested, imprisoned, and reportedly tortured. She describes her experience in her prison memoirs (al-Ghazali 1977).

The seeds of Islamic feminism were sown long before al-Ghazali formed the organization for Muslim women in 1936. In 1908 some Muslim women in Egypt led by Fatima Rashid, wife of Muhammad Farid Wajdi, owner of the nationalist newspaper *al-Dustur* (The Constitution) formed an organization, *Tarqiyat al-Mar'a* (Refinement of the Woman), through which Rashid urged women to adhere to religion and veiling as 'the symbol of our Muslim grand-mothers' (Rashid 1908a: p. 76; 1908b: p. 84). Modesty, morality and Islamic principles (i.e., the view that Islamic law gives advantages to women) were its founding principles. The newspaper *al-'Afaf* endorsed this affirmation of culture and religion against foreign intervention and customs (Baron 1989: p. 380).

The movement led by Zaynab al-Ghazali was modeled after the other con-temporaneous organized feminist groups and, like them, it was characterized by having a charismatic female leader at the helm. There was a large difference in the size of the organizations' memberships. Records show that membership in the Islamic organization was exponentially larger than in Huda Sha'rawi's. Smaller still was that of Doria Shafik, who was seen as an extremist secularist Europeanized feminist. Her core supporters were from Europe or were family and friends.

The movement that emerged in the 1970s is different. Above all, it is popu-list. It is also grounded in culture and in Islam, and never had any formal organ-ization or membership. It erupted everywhere in the main urban centers of Egypt, particularly in the universities, ultimately spreading outward. It was a grass-roots, voluntary youth movement, possibly begun by women, which mixed backgrounds, lifestyles and social boundaries. Its impact was powerful. Out of it emerged a grass-roots Islamic feminism (El Guindi 1982a, 1982b. 1983, 1992, 1996, 1997).

This thread of Islamic feminism is left out of chronicles of Egyptian feminism. Secularist-bound scholars either deny its existence or ideologically dismiss any scholarly discussion of such formulations (even empirical studies) as apology.[39] Nevertheless, it is feminist because it seeks to liberate womanhood; it is Islamic because its premises are embedded in Islamic principles and values. Yet, in some senses, the liberal Western-influenced feminism of the aristocracy and the Islamic one are not far apart. Both are about emancipation of women. The early feminist lifting of the face veil was about emancipation from exclusion; the vol-untary wearing of the *hijab* since the mid seventies is about liberation from imposed, imported identities, consumerist behaviors, and an increasingly mate-rialist culture. Further, a principal aim has been to allow women greater access to Islamic literacy.

In the 1980s the movement shifted from establishing an Islamic identity and morality to asserting Islamic nationalism, engaging in participatory politics, and resisting local authoritarian regimes, colonial occupation and Western dominance. Embedded in today's *hijab* is imagery that combines notions of respectability, morality, identity and resistance. Women (and men) who oppose the *hijab* are opposing the absence of choice, as in Iran, Turkey, Algeria and Palestine. Resistance through *the hijab* or against it, in tangible form as attire or in intangible form as a code of behavior, has generated a dynamic discourse around gender, Islamic ideals, Arab society and women's status and liberation.

NOTES

1. Fieldwork for data on which this article is partially based was conducted in Egypt on many research trips (1976, 1979, 1980, 1981–2) and annual research trips from 1984 until 1997. Support was provided by a faculty grant from UCLA African Studies Center (1976), a Ford Foundation grant No. 770-0651 (1979, 1980) (as part of the UCLA Interdisciplinary Ford Foundation project, *Rich and Poor States in the Middle East*, directed by the late Malcolm Kerr under the auspices of the Center for Near Eastern Studies) and a Fulbright Fellowship (Islamic Civilization Senior Research Scholarship) grant No. 80-006-IC (1981–82). Subsequent trips were funded by El Nil Research, Los Angeles.

   The author acknowledges with gratitude support from El Nil Research in granting permission to use the ethnographic photos from its archives selected for use in this article. This articule is a shortened version of a chapter that appears in *Veil: Modesty, Privacy and Resistance* (New York: Berg Publishers Ltd, 1999).

2. The word *Qur'an*, derives from words that mean both 'recite' and 'read'. It is based on the oral revelations transmitted to God's messenger, Muhammad, which were recorded upon his request on any available material: cloth, leather, bone, stone, etc. These were meticulously compiled and written up. The *Qur'an* is divided into Suras and the Suras into Ayahs.

3. The *Sunna*, which means 'the path', with reference to the path of the Prophet, consists of actions, sayings and deeds of the Prophet Muhammad as transmitted by reliable sources close to him.

4. The compilation of the *Sunna*, which occurred long after the death of the Prophet, was a scholarly process carried out by Imams; its results were published in written form. The writren books containing the *Sunna* are called *Hadith*, a word that translates as 'Prophetic Narratives'. There are nine recognized Hadith Compendia. Each is divided into books by subject and chapters by constituent topics.

5. The text for this note is missing in the original publication.

6. They are most certainly not suggestive of the eroticism of women's breasts (as in American culture), as there is no ethnographic evidence to that effect. Breasts are traditionally more associated with maternity than with sex, as is the case in many cultures outside the Euro-American fold. The sexualization of breasts is a Western influence.

7. Another part of a Middle Eastern woman's body that is considered erotic is her eyes.

8. *Sura* 4: 36; 17: 37; 28: 83; 31: 18; 40: 75; 57: 23.

9. The classist characterization of Egypt using the tripartite classification of lower, middle and upper that is used in most writings on Egypt is too simple and too ethnocentric to be of value in understanding the groupings in modern urban and traditional urban quarters and rural Egypt. Wealth, education, religion, etc. do not lend themselves to neat 'class' membership. There are very wealthy butchers proud of the *baladi* identity and living in traditional urban quarrers, for example. There are educated, Westernized, urbanized individuals with strong rural backgrounds who visit their relatives in the villages. For the purposes of discussion of urban movements and class organization prior to the Revolution of the 1950s, which is the point where one can (though still simplistically) talk about an emergent middle class, it is best to use the dichtomy that has gone out of use: ascribed-status class and achieved-status class. This would be particularly useful in discussions of the Western-influenced feminist movement.

10. Huda Sha'rawi was born Nur al-Huda Sultan in 1897 in Minya in sourhern Egypt, the daughter of Sultan Pasha, a wealthy landowner, and Iqbal Hanim, a woman of Circassian origin. She was tutored at home and was proficient in French, but learned enough Arabic to memorize the Qur'an (Badran 1995b: pp. 44–6).

11. Malak Hifni Nasif was a feminist activist and writer, known by the pen name Bahithat al-Badiya (Researcher of the Desert). The daughter of a scholar, she entered primary school when the state opened a section for girls in 1895 and received a diploma in 1901. She also enrolled in the Teachers, Training Program at Saniyah School and received a certificate in 1905. After marriage she published and lectured. She sent a list of feminist demands to the Egyptian Congress in 1911 (Badran 1995c: pp. 229–30).

12. Through African-American, Asian-American, Arab-American and Native American women's voices and voices from the non-Western world, discussion of different feminisms is gaining momentum in scholarly debates and activist forums. The dominance of the Western model of feminism is being challenged.

13. It is mentioned in Sha'rawi's *Memoirs* that she secretly bought (run-of-the-mill) novels from women peddlers – her only Arabic reading (see Kahf 1998 for an analysis of the *Memoirs* as literature). Kahf notes how the first eleven chapters of the *Memoirs* 'tell the story of the journey to acquisition of voice by the girl who had been left outside the door of Arabic self-articulation' (1998: p. 65). The question is: what was the role of Huda's secretary, Abd al-Hamid Fahmi Mursi? Was he a passive ghostwriter or a subordinate 'editor' of her verbally transmitted chronicle? The latter is the more likely. In 1892 *Al-'Afaf* started as one in a series of Arabic women's journals and *al-Fatat*, edited by Hind Nawfal, was another. By 1919 over thirty of these periodicals had circulated in Egypt.

14. Badran 1995a describes how, in the second half of the nineteenth century, Egypt experienced growing encroachment by the West on its economic life. The country had become a major source of raw cotton for England following the loss of supplies during the American Civil War. In 1882, the British occupied Egypt on the pretext of safeguarding the khedive and foreign economic interests during the "'Urabi Revolution," a peasant revolt led by 'Urabi Pasha and Egyptian military officers seeking access to the higher ranks monopolized by the Turco-Circassian ruling elite and a broader integration of Egyptians into the civil administration (1995a: 11).

15. Huda's mother participated in establishing a clinic sponsored by the first Lady Cromer (Sha'rawi 1981: 119–20).

16. These were: *Tarquiyat al-Mar'a* (1908), *al-'Afaf* (1892) and *Fatat al-Nil* (1913).

17. These were: *al-Jins al-Latif* (108) and *al-Sufur* (1915). The writer and editor Abd al-Hamid Hamdi founded the latter, which endorsed complete unveiling, progress and reform in all domains (1915: 1(1), pp. 1, 2).

18. The selections from Qasim Amin were in Badran's book *Feminists, Islam, and Nation* (1995a). I checked them against the original and retranslated the extracts myself to capture nuances lost in Badran's translation.

19. Egyptians were 'lazy and always fleeing work', left their children 'covered with dirt and roaming the alleys rolling in the dust like the children of animals', and were sunk in apathy, afflicted, as he put it, 'with a paralysis of nerves so that we are unmoved by anything, however beautiful or terrible' (1976, Vol. 2: p. 134). Nevertheless, over and above such differences between Muslim nationals, Amin asserted, the observer would find both Turks and Egyptians 'equal in ignorance, laziness and backwardness' (1976, Vol. 2: p. 72).

20. This observation is made in the article by Beth Baron (1989: p. 379).

21. Ahmed 1992 observes that analysts (e.g., Cole 1981: pp. 394–407) routinely treat the debate as one between 'feminists', that is, Amin and his allies, and 'antifeminists', that is, Amin's critics. They accept at face value the equation made by Amin and the originating Western narrative: the veil signified oppression; therefore those

who called for its abandonment were feminist and those opposing its abandonment were antifeminists (Ahmed 1992: p. 162).

22. Among the dominant political groups finding voice in the press at the time Amin's work was published was a group that strongly supported the British administration and advocated the adoption of a 'European outlook'. Prominent among its members were a number of Syrian Christians, who founded the pro-British daily *Al-Muqattam*. At the other extreme was a group whose views articulated in the newspaper *Al-Mu'ayyad*, published by Sheikh 'Ali Yusuf, fiercely opposed Western encroachment in any form and were emphatic about the importance of preserving Islamic tradition in all areas. The National Party (Al-Hizb al-Watani), a group led by Mustapha Kamil, was equally fierce in its opposition to the British and to Westernization, but it espoused a position of secular rather than Islamic nationalism. This group held that advancement for Egypt must begin with the expulsion of the British.

   Other groups, including the Umma Party (People's Party), which was to emerge as the politically dominant party in the first decades of the twentieth-century, advocated moderation and an attitude of judicious discrimination in identifying political and cultural goals. Muhammad 'Abdu was an important intellectual influence on the Umma Party, though its members were more secular minded; he had advocated the acquisition of Western technology and knowledge and, simultaneously, the revivification and reform of the Islamic heritage, including reform in areas affecting women. The Umma Party advocated the adoption of the European notion of the nation-state in place of religion as the basis of community. Their goals were to adopt Western political institutions and, at the same time, gradually to bring about Egypt's independence from the British. Umma Party members, unlike Mustapha Kamil's ultra nationalists or the Islamic nationalists, consequently had an attitude, not of hostility to the British, but rather of measured collaboration. Among its prominent members were Ahmad Lutfi al-Sayyid and Sa'd Zaghloul (Ahmed 1992: pp. 144–68).

   To sum up the various political ideological trends, there were: (1) that which supported Europeanization and British colonialism; (2) that which opposed Western encroachment and reaffirmed tradition and Islam; (3) that which opposed colonialism and Westernization, choosing a secular path; and (4) that which called for adopting Western technology and knowledge but chose to revitalize Islamic heritage and reform women's position.

23. Sulayman al-Salimi, *Didd al 'Afaf* (Against Virtue), Vol. 1, No. 28 (29 May 1911: p. 14). This is cited in Baron 1989: p. 383.

24. A contemporary, yet opposite, of Zaynab al-Ghazali in that the former had internalized the superiority of Europe and European ways.

25. Kahf's notion of the *hijab*'s two layers of meaning, concealment versus covering, is polemical and analytically unproductive (1998: p. 79).

26. Baron, like many writers, makes a link between women's veiling, seclusion, and the 'harem system'. This linkage hinders analysis. She mistakenly interprets Huda Sha'rawi's dramatic unveiling as 'the signal for the end of the harem system' (1989: p. 371).

27. Here I disagree with Baron, who suggested that the dramatic unveiling act may have been 'a significant gesture only to those of the elite' (1989: p. 371).

28. A 1910 photograph in the collection of *al-Mathaf al-Markazi al-Qawmi li-Buhuth al-Tarbiya* (the Central National Museum for Educational Research), of Wizarat al-Tarbiya (the Ministry of Education) in Cairo shows students from Abbas girls' school with their faces uncovered. This was noted in Baron 1989.

29. Aflaha Tullab al-Sufur, *al-'Afaf*, 1 (20), 24 March 1911. This is noted in Baron 1989.

30. A photograph taken during the 1919 Revolution shows an unveiled schoolgirl addressing the crowd (Shaarawi 1987: p. 115).

31. This was in a taped interview I recorded with feminist Ceza al-Nabarawi, a contemporary of Huda Sha'rawi, in February 1979 during our participation in the Symposium, 'The Changing Role of Sudanese Women', held in Khartoum, Sudan (22–28 February 1979), in celebration of the 75th anniversary of the founding of Al-Ahfad Schools and Girls' Education.

32. *Izar* is a piece of white calico that covers the whole body like the *habara*, which for a married woman is made of glossy black silk. According to *A Dictioinary of Islam* (Hughes 1885) the *izar* is worn by 'females of the middle classes, who cannot afford to purchase a *habara*' (p. 95). This latter comment indeed cannot be applicable in this case, since Huda Sha'rawi was a wealthy woman from a family belonging to the gentry of Egypt. Most probably, *izar* was used to refer to the more casual attire worn in non-ceremonial outings.

33. However, the biculturalism of Sha'rawi does not translate into 'valorization' of everything European. Her *Memoirs* reveal occasional reluctance to participate in some European social activities. Her Europeanization was not total. She was caught between what is culturally proper and the emblematics of her class.

34. The term used in the *Memoirs* is *al-umam al-raqiya*. *Raqiya* is the same term often used to denote the upper class in Egypt at the time, *al-tabaqa al-raqiya*, meaning the 'refined stratum'. Classist connotations to the usage are to be noted.

35. Earl Cromer, *Modern Egypt*, 2 vols. (New York: Macmillan, 1908, Vol. 2: p. 146), cited in Ahmed 1992.

36. For a sophisticated critique of individuated gender and its relation to the Western notion of equality as both relate to feminism see Nelson and Olesen 1977.

37. I have been working on this concept since I began my fieldwork on the Islamic movement in Egypt, which began in the 1970s (El Guindi 1981, 1982a, 1983, 1987, 1992, 1996).

38. This is separate and different from the Society of Muslim Sisters (*al-Akhawat al-Muslimat*), a branch organization of the Muslim Brothers. According to Ahmed 'women who joined the [Society of Muslim Sisters] wore a head covering', but the position of the organization differed little from the general modernist position (1992: p. 194).

39. The Muslim Brothers (*al-Ikhwan al-Muslimin*), founded by Hassan al-Banna (1906–49) in Egypt in 1928. The Muslim Brothers' platform was anti-colonial, anti-Zionist and anti-Westernization; it was led by the son of a mosque imam who had studied at al-Azhar and was posted to teach in the Suez Canal town of Ismailia. Al-Banna saw the large disparity between rich and poor lifestyles and the language of foreign domination and injustice that permeated Egypt. He founded the organization on principles of purifying Islam, liberating Egypt and Palestine, and opposing Western-influenced parties and government. It was a grass-roots organization that granted needed services to the underprivileged sectors of the population. It grew rapidly. Al-Banna early on emphasized the important role of women in Islamic reform (Mitchell 1969).

40. The bias built into secularist scholarship is not addressed. It raised the question for any theoretical formulation of feminism of whether an individual Muslim woman's personal experiences (childhood abuse or rape) or ideological positions (such as atheism) qualify her formulations to enter a culture-free spectrum of feminism. To what extent is one individual's account of abuse only that? To what extent does an atheist position prejudice discussion on religion? The case of the Bangladeshi physician/writer Taslima Nasrin comes to mind.

REFERENCES

Ahmed, Leila. 1992. *Women and Gender in Islam: Historical Roots of A Modern Debate*. New Haven, CT: Yale University Press.

Amin, Qasim. 1976 [1990]. *Al-A'mal al-Kamilah li-Qasim Amin* (Complete Works of

Qasim Amin), Vol. 2, *al-Mar'a al-Gadida* (*The New Woman*), reprinted and compiled in 'Amarah's work, ed. Muhammad 'Amarah, pp. 115–230. Beirut: al-Mu'assasa al-'Arabiyya lil-Dirasat wal-Nashr.

Badran, Margot. 1995a. *Feminists, Islam, and Nation: Gender and the Making of Modern Egypt*. Princeton, NJ: Princeton University Press.

——. 1995b. 'Huda Sha'rawi', in John L. Esposito (ed.), *The Oxford Enclyclopedia of the Modern Islamic World*, Vol. 4. New York and Oxford: Oxford University Press.

——. 1995c. 'Malak Hifni Nasif (1886–1918)', in John L. Esposito (ed.), *The Oxford Encyclopedia of the Modern Islamic World*, Vol. 3. New York and Oxford: Oxford University Press.

Baron, Beth. 1989. 'Unveiling in Early Twentieth-Century Egypt: Practical and Symbolic Considerations', *Middle Eastern Studies* 25(3) (July): pp. 370–86.

Barraclough, Steven. 1998. 'Al-Azhar: Between the Government and the Islamists', *The Middle East Journal* 52(2) (Spring): pp. 236–50.

Chatty, Dawn. 1997. 'The Burqa Face Cover: An Aspect of Dress in Southeastern Arabia', in N. Lindisfarne-Tapper and Bruce Ingham (eds) *Languages of Dress in the Middle East*, pp. 149–77. London: Curzon with The Centre of Near and Middle Eastern Studies, SOAS.

Cole, Juan Ricardo. 1981. 'Feminism, Class, and Islam in Turn-of-the-Century Egypt', *International Journal of Middle East Studies* 13(4): pp. 394–407.

Cromer, Earl. 1908. *Modern Egypt, 2 vols*. New York: Macmillan.

Early, Evelyn A. 1993. *Baladi Women of Cairo: Playing with an Egg and a Stone*. Boulder, CO and London: Lynne Reinner Publs.

El Guindi, Fadwa. 1981. 'Veiling Infitah with Muslim Ethic: Egypt's contemporary Islamic Movement', *Social Problems* 28(4): pp. 465–85.

——. 1982a. 'From Consciousness to Activism: Dynamics of the Islamic Movement', American Research Center Lecture Series. Cairo: ARCE Office.

——. 1982b. 'Die Ruckkehr zum Schleier: Vom unaufhaltsamen Siegeszug eins konservativen Symbols. Nahost in Flammen', *Der Monat* (285): pp. 165–78.

——. 1983. 'Veiled Activism: Egyptian Women in the Contemporary Islamic Movement', *Peuples Mediterranéans* (Femmes de la Mediterranée) 22–3: pp. 78–89.

——. 1985. 'The Status of women in Bahrain: Social and Cultural Considerations', in J. Nugent and T. Thomas (eds) *Bahrain and the Gulf*, pp. 75–95. Sydney: Croom Helm.

——. 1986. 'The Egyptian Woman: Trends Today, Alternatives Tomorrow', in Lynne B. Iglitzin and Ruth Ross (eds) *Women in the World, 1975–1985: The Women's Decade*, pp. 225–42. Santa Barbara, CA: ABC-CLIO.

——. 1987. 'Das islamische Kleid "al-hidschab",' in G. Volger, K. V. Welck and K. Hackstein (eds) *Pracht und Geheimnis: Kleidung und Schmuck aus Palästina und Jordanie*, pp. 164–67. Cologne: Rautenstrauch-Joest-Museum der Stadt Koln.

——. 1992. 'Feminism Comes of Age in Islam', *Los Angeles Times* (Op-Ed).

——. 1996. 'Feminism Comes of Age in Islam', in Suha Sabbagh (ed.), *Arab Women: Between Defiance and Restraint*, pp. 159–61. New York: Olive Branch Press.

——. 1997. 'Islamic Identity and Resistance', Middle East Institute Annual Conference. National Press Club, Washington DC, Friday, 3 October.

——. 1998. 'Gender in Islamic Activism: The Case of Egypt', McLean, Virginia, 21 May.

El-Messiri, Sawsan. 1978. 'Self Images of Traditional Urban Women in Cairo', in L. Beck and N. Keddie (eds) *Women in Muslim Society*, pp. 522–57. Cambridge, MA: Harvard University Press.

Fernea, Elizabeth W. and Basima Q. Bezirgan. 1977. 'Huda Sha'rawi: Founder of the Egyptian Women's Movement', in Elizabeth W. Fernea and Basima Q. Bezirgan (eds), *Middle Eastern Muslim Women Speak*, pp. 193–200. Austin, TX, and London: University of Texas Press.

Ghazali, Zaynab al-. 1977. *Ayam min Hayati* (Days from My Life) (Arabic). Cairo and Beirut: Dar al-Shuruq.

Goldschmidt, A. Jr. 1983. *A Concise History of the Middle East*. Boulder, CO: Westview Press.

Harb, Tal'at. 1905 [1899]. *Tarbiyet al-Mar'a wa al-hajab* (*Socialization of Women and the Veil*). Cairo: Matba'at al-Manar.

Hoffman, Valerie J. 1985. 'An Islamic Activist: Zeinab al-Ghazali', in Elizabeth W. Fernea (ed.) *Women and the Family in the Middle East: New Voices in Change*. Austin, TX: University of Texas Press.

Hoffman-Ladd, Valerie J. 1995. 'Zaynab Al-Ghazali', in John L. Esposito (ed.), *The Oxford Encyclopedia of the Modern Islamic World*, Vol. 2. New York, Oxford: Oxford University Press.

Hughes, T. Patrick (ed.) (1885). 'Dress', in *A Dictionary of Islam*, pp. 92–9. Lahore: Premier Book House Publishers and Booksellers.

Kahf, Mohja. 1998. 'Huda Sha'rawi's Mudhakkirati: The Memoirs of the First Lady of Arab Modernity', *Arab Studies Quarterly* 20(1) (Winter): pp. 53–82.

Khalidi, 'Anbara Salam al-. 1978. *Jawla fil-Thikrayat bayna Lubnan wa-Falstin* (*A Journey of Memories from Lebanon to Palestine*). Beirut.

Marsot, Afaf L. al-Sayyid. 1978. 'The Revolutionary Gentlewomen in Egypt', in L. Beck and N. Keddie (eds) *Women in the Muslim World*, pp. 261–76. Cambridge, MA: Harvard University Press.

Marsot, Afaf L. al-Sayyid, (ed.). 1979. *Society and the Sexes in Medieval Islam*. Malibu, CA: Undena Publications.

Mernissi, Fatima. 1975. *Beyond the Veil: Male-Female Dynamics in a Modern Muslim Society*. Cambridge, MA: Schenkman.

Mir-Hosseini, Ziba. 1996. 'Women and Politics in Post-Khomeini Iran: Divorce, Veiling and Emergent Feminist Voices', in Haleh Afshar (ed.), *Women and Politics in the Third World*, pp. 142–70. London and New York: Routledge.

Mitchell, Richard P. 1969. *The Society of the Muslim Brothers*. London: Oxford University Press.

Nabarawi, Ceza al-. 1979. Khartoum, Sudan, February: tape-recorded interview.

Nasif, Malak Hifni. 1909. *Nisa'iyyat* (*Feminist Texts*). Cairo: Al-Jarida Press.

Nasif, Majd al-Din Hifni. 1962. *Athar Bahithat al-Badiyah Malak Hifni Nasif: 1886–1918* (*The Influence of Bahithat al-Badiya Malak Hifni Nasif: 1886–1918*). Cairo: Wizarat al-Thaqafah wa-al-Irshad al-Qawmi.

Nelson, Cynthia. 1974. 'Public and Private Politics: Women in the Middle Eastern World', *American Ethnologist* 1: pp. 551–63.

——. 1996. *Doria Shafiq the Feminist: A Woman Apart*. Cairo: American University in Cairo Press.

Nelson, Cynthia and Virginia Olesen. 1977. 'Veil of Illusion: A Critique of the Concept of Equality in Western Feminist Thought', *Catalyst* 10–11: pp. 8–36.

Norton, J. 1997. 'Faith and Fashion in Turkey', in N. Lindisfarne-Tapper and Bruce Ingham (eds), *Languages of Dress in the Middle East*, pp. 149–77. London: Curzon with The Centre of Near and Middle Eastern Studies, SOAS.

Olson, E. A. 1985. 'Muslim Identity and Secularism in Contemporary Turkey: "The Headscarf Dispute",' *Anthropological Quarterly* 58(4): 161–71.

Quataert. Donald. 1997. 'Clothing Laws, State, and Society in the Ottoman Empire, 1720–1829', *International Journal of Middle East Studies* 29: pp. 403–25.

Rashid, Fatima. 1908a. 'Kalima 'an al-Hal al-Hadira' ('A Word on the Present Condition'),' *Tarqiyat al-Mar'a*, 1 (5).

——. 1908b. 'al-Hijab', *Tarqiyat al-Mar'a*, 1 (6).

Sayyid-Marsot, Afaf Lutfi al-. 1995. *Women and Men in Late Eighteenth-Century Egypt*, Modern Middle East Series. Austin, TX: University of Texas Press.

Sha'rawi, Huda. 1981. *Huda Sharawi: Muthakkirat Ra'idat al-Mar'a al-Arabiyya al-Hadith* (*Memoirs of Huda Sharawy, Leader of Modern Arab Women*)

(Introduction by Amina al-Said) (Arabic), Kitab al-Hilal, Silsila Shahriyya. Cairo: Dar al-Hilal.

——. 1987. *Harem Years: The Memoirs of an Egyptian Feminist (1879–1924)*, trans. Margot Badran. New York: The Feminist Press.

Wallace, Anthony F. C. 1956. 'Revitalization Movements', *American Anthropologist* 58: pp. 264–81.

PART 6
GENDER AND POST/COLONIAL
SPATIAL RELATIONS

6.1

'DIASPORA, BORDER AND TRANSNATIONAL IDENTITIES'

Avtar Brah

There has been a rapid increase in migrations across the globe since the 1980s. These mass movements are taking place in all directions. The volume of migration has increased to Australia, North America and Western Europe. Similarly, large-scale population movements have taken place within and between countries of the 'South'. Events in Eastern Europe and the former Soviet Union have provided impetus for mass movements of people. Some regions previously thought of as areas of emigration are now considered as areas of immigration. Economic inequalities within and between regions, expanding mobility of capital, people's desire to pursue opportunities that might improve their life chances, political strife, wars, and famine are some of the factors that remain at the heart of the impetus behind these migrations. People on the move may be labour migrants (both 'documented' and 'undocumented'), highly-qualified specialists, entrepreneurs, students, refugees and asylum seekers or the household members of previous migrants. In 1990, the International Organisation for Migration estimated that there were over eighty million such 'migrants'. Of these, approximately thirty million were said to be in 'irregular situations' and another fifteen million were refugees or asylum seekers. By 1992, some estimates put the total number of migrants at 100 million, of whom twenty million were refugees and asylum seekers (Castles and Miller 1993). The notion of 'economic migrant' as referring primarily to labour migrants was always problematic, not least because it served to conceal the economic proclivities of those

From Avtar Brah (1996), 'Diaspora, Border and Transnational Identities', pp. 178–210, in Avtar Brah, *Cartographies of Diaspora* (London: Taylor & Francis).

who were likely to be placed outside such a definition, for example industrialists or commercial entrepreneurs. However, these new migrations call this construct even more seriously into question, as global events increasingly render untenable such distinctions as those held between the so called 'political' and 'economic' refugees.

These population movements are set against major realignments in the world political order. New transnational configurations of power articulated with fundamental transformations in the political economy of late twentieth-century capitalism. Globalising tendencies set in motion centuries ago acquire new meanings in a world characterised by the increasing dominance of multinational capital; the flexible specialisation of labour and products; and the revolutionising impact of new technologies in production, distribution and communication. The emergent new international division of labour depends quite crucially upon women workers. Indeed, whether working in electronics factories, textile sweatshops, performing outwork from their homes or (rather more untypically) holding jobs in the commanding heights of the economy – women have become emblematic figures of contemporary regimes of accumulation. It is not surprising, therefore, that women comprise a growing segment of migrations in all regions and all types of migrations. This feminisation of migration is especially noticeable in particular instances. For example, women form the majority of Cape Verdian workers migrating to Italy, Filipinos to the Middle East or Thais to Japan. Similarly, women predominate in a number of refugee movements (Castles and Miller 1993).

These recent migrations are creating new displacements, new diasporas. In the context of a proliferation of new border crossings the language of 'borders' and of 'diaspora' acquires a new currency. A variety of new scholarly journals have one or the other of these terms in their titles. Yet, surprisingly, there have been relatively few attempts made to theorise these terms. This is partly because, as James Clifford (1994) rightly observes, it is not easy to avoid the slippage between diaspora as a theoretical concept, diasporic 'discourses' and distinct historical 'experiences' of diaspora. They seem to invite a kind of 'theorising', Clifford continues, that is always embedded in particular maps and histories. Yet, perhaps this embeddedness is precisely why it becomes necessary to mark out the conceptual terrain that these words construct and traverse if they are to serve as theoretical tools.

Here I will attempt to explore the analytical purchase of these terms. I delineate specific features which may serve to distinguish diaspora as a theoretical concept from the historical 'experiences' of diaspora. Inter alia I suggest that the concept of diaspora should be understood in terms of historically contingent 'genealogies' in the Foucauldian sense, that is, as an ensemble of investigative technologies that historicise trajectories of different diasporas, and analyse their relationality across fields of social relations, subjectivity and identity. I argue that the concept of diaspora offers a critique of discourses of fixed origins, while taking account of a homing desire which is not the same thing as desire for a 'homeland'. This distinction is important, not least because not all diasporas sustain an ideology of 'return'. In examining the subtext of 'home' which the concept of diaspora embodies, I analyse the problematic of the 'indigene' subject position and its precarious relationship to 'nativist' discourses.

Inscribed within the idea of diaspora is the notion of 'border'. The second part of this piece is organised around the theme of borders. I address border as a political construct, as well as an analytical category, and explore some of the strengths and limitations of the idea of 'border theory', especially as it has been mobilised via Gilles Deleuze and Felix Guattari's concept of 'deterritorialisation' and applied to the analysis of literary texts.

The concepts of border and diaspora together reference the theme of location. This point warrants emphasis because the very strong association of notions of diaspora with displacement and dislocation means that the experience of *location* can easily dissolve out of focus. The third section of the chapter is centred on this topic and explores the contradictions of and between location and dislocation. As a point of departure, I use the long-standing feminist debate around issues of home, location, displacement and dislocation which came up with the concept of a *'politics of location'* as locationality in contradiction. Self-reflexive autobiographical accounts often provide critical insights into the politics of location. I use two such accounts – an essay by Minnie Bruce Pratt and the autobiography of Angela Davis – as narratives enunciating a white and a black woman's feminist subject position. They do so through an intricate unravelling of those manifold operations of power, which have the effect of naturalising identities, and the different costs involved in maintaining or relinquishing lived certainties attendant upon such identities. What is also crucially important for the discussion at hand is the way in which these autobiographical accounts demonstrate how the same geographical and psychic space comes to articulate different 'histories' and how 'home' can simultaneously be a place of safety and of terror.

The concepts of *diaspora, border* and *politics of location* together offer a conceptual grid for historicised analyses of contemporary trans/national movements of people, information, cultures, commodities and capital. The three concepts are immanent. In part four I discuss a new concept that I wish to propose, namely that of *diaspora space*, as the site of this immanence. Diaspora space is the intersectionality of diaspora, border and dis/location as a point of confluence of economic, political, cultural and psychic processes. It addresses the global condition of culture, economics and politics as a site of 'migrancy' and 'travel' which seriously problematises the subject position of the 'native'. My central argument is that diaspora space as a conceptual category is 'inhabited' not only by those who have migrated and their descendants but equally by those who are constructed and represented as indigenous. In other words, the concept of *diaspora space* (as opposed to that of diaspora) includes the entanglement of genealogies of dispersion with those of 'staying put'.

Throughout I emphasise power relations embedded within discourses, institutions and practices. In so doing I have mobilised a multi-axial performative conception of power. I conclude with the idea of 'creolised theory'.

Thinking through the concept of diaspora

First, a note about the term 'diaspora'. The word derives from the Greek – *dia*, 'through', and *speirein*, 'to scatter'. According to Webster's Dictionary in the United States, diaspora refers to a 'dispersion from'. Hence the word embodies a notion of a centre, a locus, a 'home' from where the dispersion occurs. It invokes images of multiple journeys. The dictionary also highlights the word's association with the dispersion of the Jews after the Babylonian exile. Here, then, is an evocation of a diaspora with a particular resonance within European cartographies of displacement; one that occupies a particular space in the European psyche, and is emblematically situated within Western iconography as the diaspora par excellence. Yet, to speak of late twentieth-century diasporas is to take such ancient diasporas as a point of departure rather than necessarily as 'models' or as what Safran (1991) describes as the 'ideal type'. The dictionary juxtaposition of what the concept signifies in general, as against one of its particular referents, highlights the need to subject the concept to scrutiny, to consider the ramifications of what it connotes or denotes and to consider its analytical value.

At the heart of the notion of diaspora is the image of a journey. Yet not every journey can be understood as diaspora. Diasporas are clearly not the same as casual travel. Nor do they normatively refer to temporary sojourns. Paradoxically, diasporic journeys are essentially about settling down, about putting roots 'elsewhere'. These journeys must be historicised if the concept of diaspora is to serve as a useful heuristic device. The question is not simply about *who travels* but *when, how, and under what circumstances*. What socio-economic, political and cultural conditions mark the trajectories of these journeys? What regimes of power inscribe the formation of a specific diaspora? In other words, it is necessary to analyse what makes one diasporic formation similar to or different from another: whether, for instance, the diaspora in question was constituted through conquest and colonisation as has been the case with several European diasporas. Or it might have resulted from the capture or removal of a group through slavery or systems of indentured labour, as, for example, in the formation respectively of African and Asian diasporas in the Caribbean. Alternatively, people may have had to desert their home as a result of expulsion and persecution, as has been the fate of a number of Jewish groups at various points in history. Or they may have been forced to flee in the wake of political strife, as has been the experience of many contemporary groups of refugees such as the Sri Lankans, Somalis and Bosnian Muslims. Perhaps the dispersion occurred as a result of conflict and war, resulting in the creation of a new nation state on the territory previously occupied by another, as has been the experience of Palestinians since the formation of Israel. On the other hand, a population movement could have been induced as part of global flows of labour, the trajectory of many, for example African-Caribbeans, Asians, Cypriots or Irish people in Britain.

If the circumstances of leaving are important, so, too, are those of arrival and settling down. How and in what ways do these journeys conclude and intersect in specific places, specific spaces and specific historical conjunctures? How and in what ways is a group inserted within the social relations of class, gender, racism, sexuality or other axes of differentiation in the country to which it migrates? The manner in which a group comes to be 'situated' in and through a wide variety of discourses, economic processes, state policies and institutional practices is critical to its future. This 'situatedness' is central to how different groups come to be relationally positioned in a given context. I emphasise the question of relational positioning for it enables us to begin to deconstruct the regimes of power which operate to differentiate one group from another; to represent them as similar or different; to include or exclude them from constructions of the 'nation' and the body politic; and which inscribe them as juridical, political and psychic subjects. It is axiomatic that each empirical diaspora must be analysed in its historical specificity. But the issue is not one that is simply about the need for historicising or addressing the specificity of a particular diasporic experience, important though this is.

Rather, the *concept* of diaspora concerns the historically variable forms of *relationality* within and between diasporic formations. The concept of diaspora centres on the *configurations of power which differentiate diasporas internally as well as situate them in relation to one another*.

Diasporas, in the sense of distinctive historical experiences, are often composite formations made up of many journeys to different parts of the globe, each with its own history, its own particularities. Each such diaspora is an interweaving of multiple travelling; a text of many distinctive and, perhaps, even disparate narratives. This is true of, among others, the African, Chinese, Irish, Jewish, Palestinian and South Asian diasporas. For example, South Asians in Britain have a different, albeit related, history to South Asians in Africa, the Caribbean, Fiji, South East Asia or the USA. Given these differences, can we speak of a 'South Asian diaspora' other than as a mode of description of a particular cluster of migrations? The answer depends crucially upon how the relationship between these various components of the cluster is conceptualised.

I would suggest that it is the *economic, political and cultural specificities linking these components that the concept of diaspora signifies*. This means that these multiple journeys may configure into one journey via a *confluence of narratives* as it is lived and re-lived, produced, reproduced and transformed through individual as well as collective memory and re-memory. It is within this confluence of narrativity that 'diasporic community' is differently imagined under different historical circumstances. By this I mean that the identity of the diasporic imagined community is far from fixed or pre-given. It is constituted within the crucible of the materiality of everyday life; in the everyday stories we tell ourselves individually and collectively.

All diasporic journeys are composite in another sense too. They are embarked upon, lived and re-lived through multiple modalities: modalities, for example, of gender, 'race', class, religion, language and generation. As such, all diasporas are differentiated, heterogeneous, contested spaces, even as they are implicated in the construction of a common 'we'. It is important, therefore, to be attentive to the nature and type of processes in and through which the collective 'we' is constituted. Who is empowered and who is disempowered in a specific construction of the 'we'? How are social divisions negotiated in the construction of the 'we'? What is the relationship of this 'we' to its 'others'? Who are these others? This is a critical question. It is generally assumed that there is a single dominant Other whose overarching omnipresence circumscribes constructions of the 'we'. Hence, there tends to be an emphasis on bipolar oppositions: black/white; Jew/Gentile; Arab/Jew; English/Irish; Hindu/Muslim. The centrality of a particular binary opposition as the basis of political cleavage and social division in a given situation may make it necessary, even imperative, to foreground it. The problem remains, however, as to how such binaries should be analysed. Binaries can all too readily be assumed to represent ahistorical, universal constructs. This may help to conceal the workings of historically specific socio-economic, political and cultural circumstances that mark the terrain on which a given binary comes to assume its particular significance. That is, what are actually the effects of institutions, discourses and practices may come to be represented as immutable, trans-historical divisions. As a consequence, a binary that should properly be an object of deconstruction may gain acceptance as an unproblematic given.

It is especially necessary to guard against such tendencies at the present moment when the surfacing of old and new racisms, violent religious conflicts and the horrors of 'ethnic cleansing' make it all too easy to slide into an acceptance of contexually variable phenomena as trans-historical universalisms that are then presumed to be an inevitable part of human nature. On the contrary, the binary is a socially constructed category whose trajectory warrants investigation in terms of how it was constituted, regulated, embodied and contested, rather than taken as always already present. A bipolar construction might be addressed fruitfully and productively as an object of analysis and a tool of deconstruction; that is, as a means of investigating the conditions of its formation, its implication in the inscription of hierarchies, and its power to mobilise collectivities.

The point is that there are multiple others embedded within and across binaries, albeit one or more may be accorded priority within a given discursive formation. For instance, a discourse may be primarily about gender and, as such, it may centre upon gender-based binaries (although, of course, a binarised construction is not always inevitable). But this discourse will not exist in isolation from others, such as those signifying class, 'race', religion or generation. The specificity of each is framed in and through fields of representation of the other. What is at stake, then, is not simply a question of some generalised notion of, say, masculinity and femininity, but whether or not these representations of masculinity and femininity are racialised; how and in what ways they inflect class; whether they reference lesbian, gay, heterosexual or some other sexualities; how they feature age and generation; how and if they invoke religious authority. Binaries, thus, are intrinsically differentiated and unstable. What matters most is how and why, in a given context, a specific binary – e.g., black/white – takes shape, acquires a seeming coherence and stability, and configures with other constructions, such as Jew/Gentile or male/female. In other words, *how these signifiers slide into one another in the articulation of power*.

We may elaborate the above point with reference to racialised discourses and practices. The question then reformulates itself in terms of the relationship at a specific moment between different forms of racism. Attention is shifted to the forms in which class, gender, sexuality or religion, for instance, might figure within these racisms, and to the specific signifier(s) – colour, physiognomy, religion, culture, etc. – around which these differing racisms are constituted. An important aspect of the problematic will be the relational positioning of groups by virtue of these racisms. How, for instance, are African, Caribbean, South Asian and white Muslims differentially constructed within anti-Muslim racism in present-day Britain? Similarly, how are blacks, Chicanos, Chinese, Japanese or South Koreans in the USA differentiated within its racialised formations? What are the economic, political, cultural and psychic effects of these differential racialisations on the lives of these groups? What are the implications of these effects in terms of how members of one racialised group might relate to those of another? Do these effects produce conditions that foster sympathetic identification and solidarity across groups, or do they create divisions? Of central concern in addressing such questions are the power dynamics which usher racialised social relations and inscribe racialised modes of subjectivity and identity. My argument is that these racisms are not simply parallel racisms but are intersecting modalities of *differential racialisations marking positionality across articulating fields of power*. It is important to note that my use of the term 'differential racialisation' differs from Balibar's use of '*differentialist* racism'. Following P. A. Taguieff, Balibar describes 'differentialist racism' as 'a racism whose dominant theme is not biological heredity but the insurmountability of cultural differences, a racism which, at first sight, does not postulate the superiority of certain groups or peoples in relation to others but only the harmfulness of abolishing frontiers, the incompatibility of lifestyles and traditions' (Balibar 1991: p. 21). Balibar's definition is close to what Barker (1982) describes as the 'new racism'. I, on the other hand, wish to use *differential racialisation* as a concept for analysing processes of *relational multi-locationality within and across formations of power marked by the articulation of one form of racism with another, and with other modes of differentiation*. In my schema, 'new racism' would feature as but one instance of a historically specific racism.

If, as Khachig Tölölian (1991) suggests, contemporary diasporas are the 'exemplary communities of the transnational moment', and the term now overlaps and resonates with meanings of words such as migrant, immigrant, expatriate, refugee, guest worker or exile, then the *concept* of diaspora that I am seeking to elaborate is *an interpretive frame referencing the economic, political and cultural dimensions of these contemporary forms of migrancy*. As such, it interrogates other discourses surrounding the social relations of migrancies in the phase of late twentieth-century capitalism. I now briefly consider how the debate over the construct 'minority' pans out in relation to the concept of diaspora.

DIASPORA AND MINORITY

In Britain there has been a tendency to discuss diaspora primarily along a 'majority/minority' axis. This dichotomy surfaced in post-war Britain as an element underpinning the processes of racialisation. The term 'minority' was applied primarily to British citizens of African, Caribbean and Asian descent – a postcolonial code that operated as a polite substitute for 'coloured people'. The elaboration of the discourse of 'minorities' marks the fraught histories, now widely documented, of immigration control, policing, racial violence, inferiorisation and discrimination that has become the hallmark of daily life of these groups. This discourse also resonates with older connotations of the term in classical liberal political theory, where women, subjugated colonial peoples and working classes tend to be associated with the status of being a 'minor in tutelage' (Spelman 1988; Lloyd 1990; Phillips 1991). Even when the majority/minority dichotomy is mobilised in order to signal unequal power relations, as is the case in studies that document discrimination against 'minorities', its usage remains problematic. This is partly because the numerical referent of this dichotomy encourages a literal reading, reducing the problem of power relations to one of numbers, with the result that the repeated circulation of the discourse has the effect of naturalising rather than challenging the power differential. Moreover, conceptualising social relations primarily in terms of dichotomous oppositions, as I have pointed out above, fails to take full account of the multidimensionality of power.

In the USA, there has been a degree of serious and sustained attempt by some scholars to re-valorise the term from a different perspective. Since I am broadly in agreement with their arguments but also hold some reservations, it is, perhaps, necessary to ask where my argument situates itself with respect to the concept of 'minority discourse' which they offer. This concept was first proposed by JanMohammed and Lloyd in 1986, at a conference entitled 'The Nature and Context of Minority Discourse', held at the University of California, Berkeley. The papers presented at this conference were published in an edited collection of the same title (JanMohammed and Lloyd 1990). This is a theoretically and politically engaged volume whose influence in the USA in sanctioning the concept of 'minority discourse' has been far reaching. The editors define 'minority discourse' as follows:

By 'minority discourse' we mean a theoretical articulation of the political and cultural structures that connect different minority cultures in their subjugation and opposition to the dominant culture.

(JanMohammed and Lloyd 1990: p. ix)

One of the stated aims of the conference was 'to define a field of discourse among various minority cultures'. The project was conceived as a means of 'marginalising the center' and displacing the 'core-periphery model'. As Barbara Christian, invoking the works of other black women such as June Jordan and Audre Lorde, argues in the same volume, it is crucial to 'distinguish the desire for power from the need to become empowered' (ibid.: p. 47) and hence to critique any moves to want to be at the centre. JanMohammed is careful to point out that a minority location is

> not a question of essence (as the stereotypes of minorities in dominant ideologies would want us to believe) but a question of position, subject position that in the final analysis can be defined only in 'political' terms – that is, in terms of the effects of economic exploitation, political disenfranchisement, social manipulation, and ideological domination on the cultural formation of minority subjects and discourses (ibid.: p. 9).

Similarly, David Lloyd's contribution to the collection addresses inter alia the interplay of 'race', gender and class in the construction of minorities as political and cultural categories within the liberal theory of political representation. Pointing to an inextricable linkage of aesthetic and political concepts of representation in 'a western discourse of "the human" conceived as universally valid but effectively ethnocentric' (ibid.: p. 379), Lloyd examines the challenge posed to such hegemonic exercises of power when, as in the works of Jean Genet, there is a refusal of these modes of 'subjection'.

My overall sympathy for this project will be evident from what I have argued so far, not least because JanMohammed and Lloyd are far from endorsing a conception of 'minorities' that does not foreground socio-economic and cultural relations of power. Yet I am less than convinced about the use of the concept of '*minority* discourse'. I have already expressed my concern with respect to the more literal readings that the word minority tends to engender, as well as the related issue to which David Lloyd also draws attention, namely the association in classical liberal political theory of certain categories of 'minorities' with the status of being a 'minor in tutelage'. These connotations have yet to disappear. Moreover, there is a tendency to use the term 'minority' primarily to refer to racialised or ethnicised groups, and I believe that this tendency is not confined to Britain. The discourse then becomes an alibi for pathologised representations of these groups. In other words, given the genealogy of signifying practices centred around the idea of 'minority', the continuing use of the term is less likely to undermine than to reiterate this nexus of meanings.

I am aware that it is possible to turn a term on its head and imbue it with new meanings, and that the construction of this new discourse of 'minority discourse' is intended as just such a project. Nevertheless, in the absence of a political movement such as the Black Power Movement which successfully dislodged the negative associations of black in racist representations, I presently remain sceptical that, irrespective of intent, any moves that perpetuate the circulation of the minority/majority dichotomy will not serve to reinforce the hegemonic relations that inscribe this dichotomy. What category of person is 'minoritised' in a specific discourse? Are dominant classes a 'minority' since, numerically, they are almost always in the minority? If the aim is to use the term as a synonym for subordination and thereby to become all-inclusive by bringing all subordinate classes, genders, ethnicities or sexualities within its orbit, then there would seem to be even less to gain by jettisoning the language of subordination which, at the very least, signals inequities of power. As an alternative, I do not wish to offer some all-embracing panacea, but rather to insist that, in so far as it is possible, the conceptual categories we employ should be able to resist hegemonic cooptation.

The concept of diaspora that I wish to propose here is embedded within a multi-axial understanding of power; one that problematises the notion of 'minority/majority'. A multi-axial performative conception of power highlights the ways in which a group constituted as a 'minority' along one dimension of differentiation may be constructed as a 'majority' along another. And since all these markers of 'difference' represent articulating and performative facets of power, the 'fixing' of collectivities along any singular axis is called seriously into question. In other words, 'minorities' are positioned in relation not only to 'majorities' but also with respect to one another, and vice versa. Moreover, individual subjects may occupy 'minority' and 'majority' positions simultaneously, and this has important implications for the formation of subjectivity.

What this means is that where several diasporas intersect – African, Jewish, Irish, South Asian and so on – it becomes necessary to examine how these groups are similarly or differently constructed vis-à-vis one another. Such relational positioning will, in part, be structured with reference to the main dominant group. But, there are aspects of the relationship between these diasporic trajectories that are irreducible to mediation via metropolitan discourse. India and Africa, for instance, have connections that pre-date by many centuries those initiated via British colonialism. In contemporary Britain, too, the act of conversion to Islam by people of African-Caribbean descent, for instance, cannot be understood exclusively as a reaction to British racism, any more than the positionality of an African, Arab or South Asian Jew in Britain can be encapsulated solely within the European discourse of anti-semitism. There are other transnational histories, diasporic connections – where Europe is not at 'the centre' – which retain a critical bearing on understanding contemporary diasporic formations and their inter-relationships.

By this I do not mean to refer only to those social formations which came under direct European colonial rule. The reconfiguration in modern times of the ancient link between China and Japan, for instance, has not been refracted entirely through the 'Western prism', although the global expansion of both capitalist relations and Western imperialism have, of course, played their part. Chinese and Japanese diasporas in America, therefore, are the bearers of these already entangled histories reconstituted in the modalities of labour migrations to the USA, the politics of World War II (when, for instance, American citizens of Japanese descent were rounded up and interned), the Cold War that followed, in which China was demonised as a communist country, and the present conjuncture when both Japan and China assume, albeit in different ways, a central position in the global social order. The heterogeneity, multiplicity and hybridity of this Asian-American experience, insightfully theorised by Lowe (1991b), articulates these many and varied similarities and differences. What I wish to stress is that the study of diasporic formations in the late twentieth century – as in the case of Chinese and Japanese diasporas in the California of the 1990s – calls for a concept of diaspora in which different historical and contemporary elements are understood, not in tandem, but *in their dia-synchronic relationality*. Such analyses entail engagement with complex arrays of contiguities and contradictions; of changing multilocationality across time and space.

THE HOMING OF DIASPORA, THE DIASPORISING OF HOME

As we noted earlier, the concept of diaspora embodies a subtext of 'home'. What are the implications of this subtext? First, it references another – that of the people who are presumed to be indigenous to a territory. The ways in which indigenous peoples are discursively constituted is, of course, highly variable and context-specific. During imperial conquests the term 'native' came to be associated with pejorative connotations. In the British Empire the transformation of the colonised from native peoples into 'the Native' implicated a variety of structural, political and cultural processes of domination, with the effect that the word Native became a code for subordination. The British diasporas in the colonies were internally differentiated by class, gender, ethnicity (English, Irish, Scottish, Welsh) and so on, but discourses of Britishness subsumed these differences as the term 'British' assumed a positionality of superiority with respect to the Native. The Native became the Other. In the colonies, the Natives were excluded from 'Britishness' by being subjected as natives. But how does this particular nativist discourse reconfigure in present-day Britain? Of course, there is no overt evocation of the term 'native' but it remains an underlying thematic of racialised conceptions of Britishness. According to racialised imagination, the former colonial Natives and their descendants settled in Britain are not British precisely because they are not seen as being native to Britain: they can be 'in' Britain but not 'of' Britain. The term 'native' is now turned on its head. Whereas in the colonies the 'colonial Native' was inferiorised, in Britain the 'metropolitan Native' is constructed as superior. That is, nativist discourse is mobilised in both cases, but with opposite evaluation of the group constructed as the 'native'.

The invocation of native or indigenous status, however, is not confined to dis-courses of nationalism. Oppressed peoples such as Native Americans or Native Australians may also mobilise a concept of the positionality of the indigenous, but with quite a different aim. Here, the native positionality becomes the means of struggle against centuries of exploitation, dispossession and marginality. This native subject position articulates a subaltern location. It is important, therefore, to distinguish these claims from those that go into the constitution of structures of dominance. However, it does not always follow that this sub-altern location will provide automatic guarantees against essentialist claims of belonging. It cannot be assumed in advance that the hegemonic processes of subordination will invariably be resisted without recourse to the indigene subject position as *the* privileged space of legitimate claims of belonging. What is at stake here is the way in which the indigene subject position is constructed, represented and mobilised. Oppositional politics from a subaltern location must contend with all manner of contradictions. Can 'first nationhood' be asserted as a 'native' identity while renouncing nativism? How precisely is the 'first nationhood' of subaltern groups to be distinguished from the claims to this status by groups in positions of dominance? How do subaltern indigenous peoples place themselves vis-à-vis other subordinate groups in a locale? For instance, how do the claims for social justice by Native Americans articulate with and become 'situated' in relation to those made by black Americans? Are such claims marked by a politics of solidarity or competitive antagonism and tension? In one sense, the problematic can only be fully addressed by studying particular cases. But the answer will depend, at least in part, upon the way that the question of 'origins' is treated – in naturalised and essentialist terms, or as historically constituted (dis)placements?

When does a location *become* home? What is the difference between 'feeling at home' and staking claim to a place as one's own? It is quite possible to feel at home in a place and, yet, the experience of social exclusions may inhibit public proclamations of the place as home (Brah 1979; Cohen 1992; Bhavnani 1991; Tizzard and Phoenix 1993). A black British young woman of Jamaican parentage may well be far more at home in London than in Kingston, Jamaica, but she may insist upon defining herself as Jamaican and/or Caribbean as a way of affirming an identity which she perceives is being denigrated when racism represents black people as being outside 'Britishness'. Alternatively, another young woman with a similar background might seek to repudiate the same process of exclusion by asserting a black British identity. The subjectiv-ity of the two women is inscribed within differing political practices and they occupy different subject positions. They articulate different political positions on the question of 'home', although both are likely to be steeped in the highly mixed diasporic cultures of Britain. On the other hand, each woman may embody both of these positions at different moments, and the circumstances of the moment at which such 'choices' are made by the same person are equally critical.

Clearly, the relationship of the first generation to the place of migration is different from that of subsequent generations, mediated as it is by memories of what was recently left behind, and by the experiences of disruption and displacement as one tries to reorientate, to form new social networks, and learns to negotiate new economic, political and cultural realities. Within each generation the experiences of men and women will also be differently shaped by gender relations. The reconfigurations of these social relations will not be a matter of direct superimposition of patriarchal forms deriving from the country of emigration over those that obtain in the country to which migration has occurred. Rather, both elements will undergo transformations as they articulate in and through specific policies, institutions and modes of signification.

The *concept* of diaspora signals these processes of *multi-locationality across geographical, cultural and psychic boundaries.*

THINKING THROUGH BORDERS

Embedded within the concept of diaspora is the notion of the border, and, indeed, it is not possible to address the concept of diaspora without considering its relationship to the idea of borders. It is to this construct that I now turn.

Borders: arbitrary dividing lines that are simultaneously social, cultural and psychic; territories to be patrolled against those whom they construct as outsiders, aliens, the Others; forms of demarcation where the very act of prohibition inscribes transgression; zones where fear of the Other is the fear of the self; places where claims to ownership – claims to 'mine', 'yours' and 'theirs' – are staked out, contested, defended, and fought over.

Gloria Anzaldúa's theorisation of border and borderlands provides important insights. Two are especially important for my purposes here. First, she uses these terms as a means to reflect upon social conditions of life at the Texas–US Southwest/Mexican border where, as she says, 'the Third World grates against the first and bleeds' (Anzaldúa 1987: p. 3). She invokes the concept of the border also as a metaphor for psychological, sexual, spiritual, cultural, class and racialised boundaries. The Anzaldúa text speaks of borders simultaneously as social relation, the everyday lived experience, and subjectivity/identity. Borders are arbitrary constructions. Hence, in a sense, they are always metaphors. But, far from being mere abstractions of a concrete reality, metaphors are part of the discursive materiality of power relations. Metaphors can serve as powerful inscriptions of the effects of political borders.

Each border embodies a unique narrative, even while it resonates with common themes with other borders. Such metaphoric materiality of each border calls attention to its specific features: to the geographical and/or psychic territories demarcated; to the experiences of particular groups of people who are sundered apart or affected in other ways by the creation of a certain border zone; or to the old and new states which may be abolished or installed by the drawing of particular boundaries. How is a border regulated or policed? Who is kept out and why? What are the realities for those stigmatised as *undesirable* border-crossers? The realities, for instance, of proclaiming a gay or lesbian identity in a social context saturated with homophobia and heterosexism, as Anzaldúa shows. Or the realities of present-day labour migrants negotiating the immigration apparatus of the state: difficulties of gaining visas, confronting immigration checks, detentions and deportations, and even facing the possibility in some circumstances of losing one's life.

The USA/Mexico border typifies the conditions of contemporary migrancy. It encapsulates certain common thematics which frequently come into play whenever the 'overdeveloped' countries institute measures to control selectively the entry of peoples from economically 'underdeveloped' segments of the globe. This border speaks the fate of formerly colonised people presently caught up in the workings of a global economy dominated by transnational capital and mediated by politics of 'G-Sevenism' or 'G-Eightism'. These new regimes of accumulation are characterised by 'flexibility' (or what perhaps will increasingly be referred to as 'adaptability', the term favoured by the G7 summit of 10 July 1994) in labour processes, labour markets, commodities, and in patterns of consumption. There is an intensification in the segmentation of the labour market into a comparatively small sector of highly skilled core staff at managerial and professional level, and a much larger group of employees who are often called 'peripheral' workers but whose labour is in fact central to the functioning of the global economy. The core staff hold well-paid full-time permanent jobs with good promotion and retraining prospects. They are expected to be flexible and adaptable and, when required, geographically mobile, but any inconvenience that this may generate is offset by the security of entitlement to pensions, insurance and other benefits. The so-called 'peripheral' employees working in the 'secondary labour market' are generally low paid, and they comprise two distinct sub-groups. The first of these consists of full-time employees performing skilled or semi-skilled jobs. High turnover rates are fairly typical of this type of employment. Providing an even greater level of flexibility is the second group that includes a wide variety of part-timers, temporary staff, fixed-term contract holders, job sharers, and homeworkers. Not surprisingly, as we noted in the last chapter, there is a predominance of women, immigrant and migrant workers (both male and female) and their descendants, as well as other low-paid categories of worker in this secondary labour market.

The late twentieth-century forms of transnational movement of capital and people have ushered in new kinds of diasporic formations. The rapid rate of technological, commercial and organisational innovation is accompanied by a proliferation of new methods of production, new markets, new products and services, and new systems of financing. The accelerated mobility of capital to wherever profitability can be maximised within domestic boundaries or overseas has a particular bearing on population movements. A combination of offshore and onshore relocation of jobs, alongside a continuing demand for migrant labour for certain kinds of low-paid work in the economically advanced 'cores', is resulting in an eruption of new borders, while the old borders are subjected to processes of entrenchment or erosion (Sassen 1988; Rouse 1991; Miles 1993).

Roger Rouse, for example, provides a telling example of the shifting nature of such borders in the face of 'late' capitalism. Using as a case in point his study of US-bound migration since the early 1940s from a rural *municipio* of Aguilla in Mexico, he shows how these migrants have increasingly become part of a transnational network of settlements. By the early 1980s, almost every family in the *municipio* had a member who had worked abroad, and the local economy was heavily dependent on migrant remittances. In time these migrants have established several outposts in the United States, working largely in the service sector as cleaners, dishwashers, gardeners, hotel workers, housekeepers and child care workers. There is frequent traffic and communication between these outposts in the USA and Aguilla, with 'homes' dispersed in several places. In a sense they are *simultaneously migrants and settlers*, negotiating their personal agendas in a political context in which the demand for their labour has been set against increasing political pressure for tighter immigration controls.

The growing polarisation of the labour market in the United States has increased demand for Mexican workers to fill the lowest layers of jobs, in agriculture, on the assembly line and in the service sector. At the same time, new legal restrictions designed to regulate the flow of migrants have been imposed in the face of intensification of racism and growing political pressure against a background of job losses in certain sectors of the economy. Racism is fuelled also by the fact that certain elements of capital find it increasingly more lucrative to locate some aspects of the labour process in Mexico. Mexican workers now suffer resentment for 'taking our jobs' in the USA *and* in Mexico. These tropes of resentment construct the worker as an embodiment of capital rather than its contradiction. Thus there emerges the paradox of the *'undocumented worker' – needed to service lower rungs of the economy, but criminalised, forced to go underground, rendered invisible; that is, cast as a phantom, an absent presence that shadows the nooks and crannies wherever low-paid work is performed.*

The idea of 'border theory'

Increasingly, the idea of 'border theory' is invoked to refer to scholarship that addresses 'borders' both in their geographical and analytical sense. The concept of 'deterritorialisation' proposed by Gilles Deleuze and Felix Guattari has been used in a number of analyses of literary texts presumed to constitute 'border writing' (Lloyd 1990; Hicks 1991; Calderon and Salvidar 1991). Deleuze and Guattari have identified 'deterritorialisation' as a distinctive feature of what they call 'minor literature' – that is, literature with its primary characteristics defined in opposition to canonical writing. Minor literature, they contend, is marked by 'the deterritorialisation of language, the connection of the individual to a political immediacy, and the collective assemblage of enunciation' (Deleuze and Guattari 1986 [1975]: p. 13). The concept of deterritorialisation is understood as describing the displacement and dislocation of identities, persons and meanings, with the moment of alienation and exile located in language and literature. It refers to the effects of a rupture between signifier and signified, so that 'all forms come undone, as do all the significations, signifiers and signifieds to the benefit of an unformed matter of deterritorialised flux, of nonsignifying signs' (ibid.).

While the attraction of such a term in analysing literary texts is understandable, its generalised applicability is much more problematic. The literary trope of 'border writing' can be important in elucidating certain aspects of border encounters. As Emily Hicks suggests, border writing articulates a textual strategy of translation as opposed to representation. She argues that it enacts non-synchronous memory and offers the reader the possibility of practising multi-dimensional perception. The reader enters a multi-layered semiotic matrix, and experiences multi-lingual, cross-cultural realities. I agree with Hicks that 'border writing' offers a rich, multifaceted and nuanced depiction of border histories. My cautionary note here is aimed at the tendency to conflate 'border theory' with analysis of 'border writing', especially when the latter is used as a synonym for literary texts. Literary texts constitute but one element of border textualities. The concept of 'territory' as well as its signifieds and significations is a contested site in diaspora and border positionalities where the issue of territorialisation, deterritorialisation or reterritorialisation is a matter of political struggle. The outcomes of these contestations cannot be predicted in advance. *In other words, the move from a literary text to 'world as text' is much more fraught, contradictory, complex and problematic than is often acknowledged.*

BORDER, DIASPORA AND THE POLITICS OF LOCATION

Together, the concepts of border and diaspora reference a politics of location. This point warrants emphasis, especially because the very strong association of notions of diaspora with displacement and dislocation means that the experience of *location* can easily dissolve out of focus. Indeed, it is the contradictions of and between location and dislocation that are a regular feature of diasporic positioning. Feminist politics have constituted an important site where issues of home, location, displacement and dislocation have long been a subject of contention and debate. Out of these debates emerges the notion of a 'politics of location' as *locationality in contradiction* – that is, a positionality of dispersal; of simultaneous situatedness within gendered spaces of class, racism, ethnicity, sexuality, age; of movement across shifting cultural, religious and linguistic boundaries; of journeys across geographical and psychic borders. Following a strand of the discussion in earlier parts of this chapter I would describe the politics of location *as a position of multiaxial locationality*. But politics is the operative word here, for multi-axial locationality does not predetermine what kind of subject positions will be constructed or assumed, and with what effects.

Self-reflexive autobiographical accounts often provide critical insights into political ramifications of border crossings across multiple positioning. One such account, an essay by Minnie Bruce Pratt entitled 'Identity: Skin, Blood, Heart' (Pratt 1984), has attracted attention in feminist analysis for its commitment to unravelling operations of power that naturalise identities inscribed in positions of privilege, and the different costs involved in maintaining or relinquishing lived certainties attendant upon such positions. This text reveals what is to be gained when a narrative about identity continuously interrogates and problematises the very notion of a stable and essential identity by deconstructing the narrator's own position, in this case that of a white, middle-class, lesbian feminist raised as a Christian in the southern United States. Pratt is able to hold her various 'homes' and 'identities' in perpetual suspension even as she tries to recapture them in re-memory. She enacts her locationality from different subject positions, picking apart her position of racialised class privilege simultaneously as she works through her own experiences of coming out as a lesbian and confronting heterosexism in its many and varied manifestations. A critical strategy that enables this narrative to refuse reductive impulses is that it works at a number of different levels, addressing *the linked materiality of the social, the cultural and the subjective*. As Biddy Martin and Chandra Talpade Mohanty point out:

> the narrative politicises the geography, demography, and architecture of these communities – Pratt's homes at various times of her history – by discovering local histories of exploitation and struggle. These histories are quite unlike the ones she is familiar with, the ones she grew up with. Pratt problematises her ideas about herself by juxtaposing the assumed histories of her family and childhood, predicated on the invisibility of the histories of people unlike her, to whom these geographical sites were also home.

(Martin and Mohanty 1986: p. 195)

Pratt examines how her sense of safety in the world was largely related to her unquestioning acceptance of the normative codes of her social milieu, and the structures of legitimation that underpinned these norms. She is particularly attentive to the workings of racism as one of the central dynamics binding this Southern community together. The tenuous nature of her security and sense of belonging is revealed to her when, as a lesbian mother fighting for the custody of her children, she comes face-to-face with the heterosexism embedded not only in state structures but also in the everyday cultural practices taken for granted by her family, friends and the people she had considered as her 'community'. The withdrawal of emotional support by those whom she had previously loved throws into total disarray the concept of home and community which she had hitherto envisioned. Engulfed by a sense of dislocation and loss, Pratt 'moves home', and she chooses this moment of cultural and psychic journeying to learn about the processes which sustain social relations and subjectivities that had been at the centre of the world she had taken for granted.

While Pratt's narrative addresses the social universe of a white woman growing up in Alabama during the civil rights struggles, Angela Davis's autobiography articulates the positionality of a black woman growing up in Alabama at about the same time. A juxtaposition of these two narratives is helpful in offering related accounts of the operations of racism and class in the constitution of gendered forms of white and black subjectivity against the backdrop of a turbulent period in recent American history. Both women invoke the segregated South of their childhood, but their memories construct an experiential landscape charted from opposite sides of the racial divide. Pratt speaks of the terror endemic in the racist cultural formations of the South. Angela Davis recounts how this terror was unleashed on the black people in her hometown. She relates how she felt when, at the age of four, her family moved into an all-white area:

> Almost immediately after we moved there the white people got together and decided on a borderline between them and us. Center street became the line of demarcation. Provided we stayed on 'our' side of the line (the east side) they let it be known we would be left in peace. If we ever crossed over to their side, war would be declared. Guns were hidden in our house and vigilance was constant.
>
> (Davis 1974 [1990]: p. 78)

Racism was experienced by this four-year-old in the form of hostility from the white elderly couple who now became their neighbours:

> the way they stood a hundred feet away and glared at us, their refusal to speak when we said 'Good Afternoon' . . . sat on the porch all the time, their eyes heavy with belligerence. . . . When a black minister and his wife transgressed the racial border and bought the house next door to the white elderly couple, the minister's house was bombed. As more black families continued to move in the bombings were such a constant response that soon our neighborhood became known as Dynamite Hill.
>
> (ibid.: p. 79)

Davis draws attention to class and gender differences both amongst and between black and white people, and to the conditions under which solidarities across these differentiations are made possible. One of the most poignant moments in the text is when, as a student in France, Davis reads a newspaper report about the racist bombing of a church in Birmingham, Alabama, and realises that the four girls named as killed are her friends. Her fellow students show sympathy but fail to grasp the systematic impact of racism as an institutional and cultural phenomenon underlying such violence, and instead treat the incident as one would a sudden 'accident' – 'as if my friends had just been killed in a crash'. Davis's account, quite rightly, does not ascribe this lack of understanding to their being white, but rather to the absence of an awareness on their part of the history of racism in the USA. Yet, awareness alone might still not have produced an understanding of this history. A deeper engagement with this history would inevitably call for a radical shift in subject position, of the kind that Pratt's narrative demonstrates. The point is that the issue is not simply one of acquiring knowledge but of deconstructing 'whiteness' as a social relation, as well as an experiential modality of subjectivity and identity (see Avtar Brah 1996, chapter 5 on 'difference'; also Breines 1992; Ware 1992; Hall 1992; Frankenberg 1993).

What is especially important for the present discussion about these autobiographical accounts is the way in which they reveal how the same geographical space comes to articulate different histories and meanings, such that 'home' can simultaneously be a place of safety and terror. They also underscore what I have suggested before, namely that diasporic or border positionality does not *in itself* assure a vantage point of privileged insight into and understanding of relations of power, although it does create a space in which experiential mediations may intersect in ways that render such understandings more readily accessible. It is essentially a question of politics. Diasporic identities cannot be read off in a one-to-one fashion straightforwardly from a border positionality, in the same way that a feminist subject position cannot be deduced from the category 'woman'. This point deserves emphasis especially because the proliferation of discourses about 'border crossings' and 'diasporic identities' might be taken to imply a common standpoint or a universalised notion of 'border consciousness'. Rather, there are multiple semiotic spaces at diasporic borders, and the probability of certain forms of consciousness emerging are subject to the play of political power and psychic investments in the maintenance or erosion of the status quo.

DIASPORA SPACE AND THE CREOLISATION OF THEORY

The concepts of diaspora, borders and multi-axial locationality together offer a conceptual grid for historicised analyses of contemporary trans/national movements of people, information, cultures, commodities and capital. The concept of diasporas presupposes the idea of borders. Correspondingly, the concept of border encapsulates the idea of diasporising processes. The two are closely intertwined with the notion of the politics of location or dislocation. The three concepts are immanent. I wish to propose the concept of *diaspora space* as the site of this immanence. Diaspora space is the intersectionality of diaspora, border, and dis/location as a point of confluence of economic, political, cultural, and psychic processes. It is where multiple subject positions are juxtaposed, contested, proclaimed or disavowed; where the permitted and the prohibited perpetually interrogate; and where the accepted and the transgressive imperceptibly mingle even while these syncretic forms may be disclaimed in the name of purity and tradition. Here, tradition is itself continually invented even as it may be hailed as originating from the mists of time. What is at stake is the infinite experientiality, the myriad processes of cultural fissure and fusion that under-write contemporary forms of transcultural identities. These emergent identities may only be surreptitiously avowed. Indeed, they may even be disclaimed or suppressed in the face of constructed imperatives of 'purity'. But they are inscribed in the late twentieth-century forms of syncretism at the core of culture and subjectivity (Hall 1990; Coombes 1992).

The concept of diaspora space references the global condition of 'culture as a site of travel' (Clifford 1992) which seriously problematises the subject position of the 'native'. Diaspora space is the point at which boundaries of inclusion and exclusion, of belonging and otherness, of 'us' and 'them', are contested. My argument is that diaspora space as a conceptual category is 'inhabited', not only by those who have migrated and their descendants, but equally by those who are constructed and represented as indigenous. In other words, the concept of *diaspora space* (as opposed to that of diaspora) includes the entanglement, the intertwining of the genealogies of dispersion with those of 'staying put'. The diaspora space is the site where *the native is as much a diasporian as the diasporian is the native*. However, by this I do not mean to suggest an undifferentiated relativism. Rather, I see the conceptual category of diaspora space in articulation with the four modes of theorising of difference that I have proposed in Chapter Five, where 'difference' of social relation, experience, subjectivity and identity are relational categories situated within multi-axial fields of power relations. The similarities and differences across the different axes of differentiation – class, racism, gender, sexuality, and so on – articulate and disarticulate in the diaspora space, marking as well as being marked by the complex web of power.

In the diaspora space called 'England', for example, African-Caribbean, Irish, Asian, Jewish and other diasporas intersect among themselves as well as with the entity constructed as 'Englishness', thoroughly reinscribing it in the process. Englishness has been formed in the crucible of the internal colonial encounter with Ireland, Scotland and Wales; imperial rivalries with other European countries; and imperial conquests abroad. In the post-war period this Englishness is continually reconstituted via a multitude of border crossings in and through other diasporic formations. These border crossings are territorial, political, economic, cultural and psychological. This Englishness is a new ensemble that both appropriates and is in turn appropriated by British-based African-Caribbean-ness, Asian-ness, Irishness and so on. Each of these forma-tions has its own specificity, but it is an ever-changing specificity that adds to as well as imbues elements of the other. What I am proposing here is that border crossings do not occur only across the dominant/dominated dichotomy, but that, equally, there is traffic within cultural formations of the subordinated groups and that these journeys are not always mediated through the dominant culture(s). In my schema such cultural ensembles as British Asian-ness, British Caribbean-ness, or British Cypriot-ness are cross-cutting rather than mutually exclusive configurations. The interesting question, then, is how these British identities take shape; how they are internally differentiated; how they interrelate with one another and with other British identities; and how they mutually reconfigure and decentre received notions of Englishness, Scottishness, Welshness or Britishness. *My argument is that they are not 'minority' identities, nor are they at the periphery of something that sees itself located at the centre, although they may be represented as such.* Rather, through processes of decentring, these new political and cultural formations continually challenge the minoritising and peripheralising impulses of the cultures of dominance. Indeed, it is in this sense that Catherine Hall (1992) makes the important claim that Englishness is just another ethnicity.

I have argued that feminist theorisation of the politics of location is of critical relevance to understanding border positionalities. This, however, is not to minimise the importance of other theoretical and political strands in illuminating diasporising border processes. Insights drawn from analyses of colonialism, imperialism, class and gay and lesbian politics, for instance, are equally indispensable. Earlier, we noted the growing currency of the term 'border theory' to reference analytical perspectives that, inter alia, address some of these aspects. This term jostles with others, such as 'postcolonial theory' and 'diaspora theory'. Here, I am less concerned about the overlaps or differences between and across these conceptual terrains. The point I wish to stress is that these theoretical constructs are best understood as constituting *a point of confluence and intersectionality* where insights emerging from these fields inhere in the production of analytical frames capable of addressing multiple, intersecting, axes of differentiation. In other words, it is a space of/for theoretical crossovers that foreground processes of power inscribing these interrelationalities; a kind of *theoretical creolisation.* Such creolised envisioning is crucial, in my view, if we are to address fully the contradictions of modalities of enunciation, identities, positionalities and standpoints that are simultaneously 'inside' and 'outside'. It is necessary in order to decode the polymorphous compoundedness of social relations and subjectivity. The concept of diaspora space which I have attempted to elaborate here, and my analysis of 'difference' elsewhere, are firmly embedded in a theoretical creolisation of the type described above.

REFERENCES

Anzaldúa, G., *Borderlands/La Frontera: The New Mestiza* (San Francisco: Spinsters/Aunt Lute, 1987).

Balibar, E., 'Is There a "Neo Racism"?', in E. Balibar and I. Wallerstein, *Race, Nation, Class: Ambiguous Identities* (London and New York: Verso, 1991).

Balibar, E., 'Migrants and Racism', *New Left Review* (1991), p. 186.

Barker, M., *The New Racism* (London: Junction Books, 1982).

Bhavnani, K. K., *Talking Politics* (Cambridge: Cambridge University Press, 1991).

Brah, A., 'Inter-generational and Inter-ethnic Perceptions: A comparative study of South Asian and English adolescents and their parents in Southall, West London' (unpublished PhD thesis, University of Bristol).

Breines, W., *Young, White and Miserable: Growing up Female in the Fifties* (Boston:

Beacon Press, 1992).

Calderon, H. and H. Salvidar, *Criticism in the Borderlands: Studies in Chicano Literature, Culture and Ideology* (Durham, NC: Duke University, 1991).

Castles, S. and M. J. Miller, *The Age of Migration: International Population Movements* (London: Macmillan, 1993).

Clifford, J. 'Travelling Cultures', in L. Grossbeg, C. Nelson and P. Treicher (eds), *Cultural Studies* (New York: Routledge, 1992).

Clifford, J., 'Diasporas', *Cultural Anthropology*, vol. 9, no. 3, pp. 302–38.

Cohen, P., 'The Perversions of Inheritance: studies in the making of multi-racist Britain', in P. Cohen and H. Bains (eds), *Multi-Racist Britain* (London: Macmillan, 1992a).

Cohen, P., *Home Rules: Some Reflections on Racism and Nationalism in Everyday Life* (London: The New Ethnicities Unit, University of East London, 1992b).

Coombes, A. E., 'Inventing the Postcolonial: Hybridity and constituency in contemporary curating', *New Formations*, 18.

Davis, A., *Angela Davis: An Autobiography* (London: The Women's Press, 1981 [1974]).

Deuleuze, G. and F. Gùattari, 'What is a Minor Literature?', in *Kafka: Towards a Minor Literature*, trans. Diana Polan (Minneapolis, MN: University of Minnesota Press, 1986 [1975]).

Frankenberg, R., *White Women, Race Matters: The Social Construction of Whiteness* (London: Routledge, 1993).

Hall, C., *White, Male and Middle Class: Explorations in Feminism and History* (London: Verso, 1992).

Hicks, E., *Border Writing: The Multidimensional Text* (Minneapolis, MN: University of Minnesota Press, 1991).

Lloyd, D., 'Genet's Genealogy: European minorities and the ends of the canon', in A. JanMohammed and D. Lloyd (eds), *The Nature and Context of Minority Discourse* (New York: Oxford University Press, 1990).

Lowe, L., 'Heterogeneity, Hybridity, Multiplicity: Marking Asian-American Differences', *Diaspora*, vol. 1, no. 1, pp. 24–44.

Miles, R., *Racism After 'Race Relations'* (London and New York: Routledge, 1993).

Phillips, A., *Engendering Democracy* (Cambridge: Polity Press, 1991).

Pratt, M. B., 'Identity: Skin, blood, heart', in E. Bulkin, M. B. Prat and B. Smith (eds), *Yours in Struggle: Feminist Perspectives on Racism and Anti-Semitism* (New York: Long Haul, 1984).

Rouse, R., 'Mexican Migration and the Social Space of Postmodernism', *Diaspora*, vol. 1, no. 1, pp. 8–23.

Safran, W., 'Diasporas in Modern Societies: Myths of homeland and return', *Diaspora*, vol. 1, no. 1, pp. 83–99.

Sassen, S., *The Mobility of Labour and Capital: A Study in International Investment and Labour Flow* (Cambridge: Cambridge University Press, 1988).

Spelman, E. V., *Inessential Woman: Problems of Exclusion in Feminist Thought* (London: The Women's Press, 1988).

Tizzard, B. and A. Phoenix, *Black, White or Mixed Race?: Race and Racism in the Lives of Young People of Mixed Parentage* (London and New York: Routledge, 1993).

Tölölian, Khachig, 'The Nation State and Its Others: In lieu of a preface', *Diaspora*, vol. 1, no. 1, pp. 3–7.

Ware, V., *Beyond the Pale: White Women, Racism and History* (London: Verso, 1992).

6.2

'IMPERIAL LEATHER: RACE, CROSS-DRESSING AND THE CULT OF DOMESTICITY'

Anne McClintock

> Wife and servant are the same, but only differ in the name.
>
> *Lady Chudleigh*

> The wife became the head servant.
>
> *Friedrich Engels*

In May 1854, at the age of twenty-five, Arthur Munby stopped a maid-of-all-work in the street. The encounter was as casual as any of the hundreds that filled Munby's wanderings, yet the woman was destined to become his lifelong companion and wife. Almost immediately, Hannah Cullwick and Arthur Munby embarked on an intense but clandestine love affair that lasted the rest of their lives. After nineteen years, they married secretly, though they lived in the same house for only four years and then, to all appearances, only as master and housemaid.

Cullwick and Munby both record in their diaries that they instantly felt destined for each other.[1] In a sense, it was no accident that the maid-of-all-work and the barrister met in the street. In the promiscuous crowd – that element permanently on the verge of social confusion – classes mingle, strangers brush each other, women and men rub shoulders and part. As Benjamin writes: 'A street, a conflagration, or a traffic accident assemble people who are not defined along

From: Anne McClintock (1995), 'Imperial Leather: Race, Cross-Dressing and the Cult of Domesticity', pp. 132–80, in Anne McClintock, *Imperial Leather: Race, Gender and Sexuality in the Colonial Contest* (London: Routledge).

class lines.'[2] Cullwick and Munby took sustenance from the crowd, pitching their strange fantasy life on the borders of social limits – gender and race, paid and unpaid work, domesticity and empire. Their sense of destiny, moreover, bore witness to the social force of the Victorian edicts they so scandalously flouted in private and so decorously affirmed in public. At the same time, the chance encounter, the forbidden meeting across social limits, reveals itself as a recurrent theme in the domestic and racial fetishism that structured their lives, indeed, that structured Victorian society at large.

Leonore Davidoff has vividly evoked the games and fetish rituals Cullwick and Munby staged for their mutual pleasure when together and relived in their diaries when apart.[3] Munby later excised from his diaries the details of the 'training' he claims he gave Cullwick, but we know she chose to address him by the imperial title 'Massa' and that she wore a 'slave-band' on her wrist and a locked chain around her neck (to which only Munby had the key) as proof of her 'bondage'. We know that she would kneel, lick his boots and wash his feet to profess her love and servitude.[4] She posed for numerous photographs: as her working self in 'her dirt'; dressed as an upper-class lady, as a rural maiden, a man, an angel, a male slave and 'almost nude' and blackened from head to foot as a male chimneysweep.

When they married secretly after nineteen years, she dressed as an upper-middle class lady and traveled with Munby around Europe. Back in London, she would arrange to theatrically scrub the front doorsteps on her knees as Munby sauntered down the street, languidly swinging his cane. He checked in at a boardinghouse where she worked, to be served by her as if they were strangers, then to meet her on the clifftops nearby, kissing and giggling and savoring in secret the knowledge of their forbidden liaison. When they lived within reach of each other, Cullwick visited Munby frequently 'in her dirt' after a grueling day's work, her clothes dank and filthy, her face deliberately blackened with boot polish, her hands red and raw; only to pose later that same evening freshly dressed as an upper-class lady in clean finery. They spent happy hours mulling over the ordeals of her workload, ritualistically counting and recounting the incredible number of boots she cleaned. On a couple of occasions at her other employer's house, Cullwick stripped naked except for a blindfold and climbed into the chimney, where she curled in the warm soot 'like a dog', savoring the sensation later in her diary for Munby's delectation. Her diary reveals (as his does not) that she also lifted him in her huge, brawny arms, cradled him on her ample lap and 'nursed' him like a child.

Over the years, Cullwick wrote a voluminous diary, first at Munby's behest, later for more complex reasons of her own, in which she recounted the daily regimen of her domestic work and her curious life with Munby. Both of their diaries reveal, though differently, a profound and mutual involvement in a variety of fetish rituals: slave/master (S/M), bondage/discipline (B/D), hand, foot and boot fetishisms, washing rituals, infantilism (or babyism), cross-dressing and a deep and mutual fascination with dirt. Fundamentally, the scripts for their fantasy life involved theatrically transgressing the Victorian iconographies of domesticity and race, and their fetish rituals took shape around the crucial but concealed affinity between women's work and empire. In what follows, I will argue that their fetishism inhabited the borders of a double disavowal by dominant Victorian society: denial of the value of women's domestic work in the industrial metropolis and the devaluing of colonized labor in the cultures coming under violent imperial rule. What is the meaning of Cullwick and Munby's rituals, belonging as they do in the realm of the fetish? What, in particular, is the relation between fetishism, domesticity and empire?

The Freudian definition of the fetish gives privileged normality to male heterosexuality and the scene of castration. Instead, I wish to explore fetishism as a more complex, historically diverse phenomenon that cannot be reduced to a single, male, sexual narrative of origins. I wish to challenge the primacy of the phallus in the realm of fetishism and open the Freudian and Lacanian theories of fetishism to a more varied and complex history in which class and race play as formative a role as gender.

The presiding contradiction animating Cullwick and Munby's fetishism is, I suggest, the historical dichotomy between women's paid work and women's unpaid work in the home – overdetermined by the contradictions of imperial racism and negotiated by the fetishistic iconographies of slave and master, dirt and cleanliness, rituals of recognition and cross-dressing. In contrast to the idea of fetishism as a quintessentially male preserve, Cullwick takes her place among the countless women for whom fetishism was an attempt – ambiguous, contradictory and not always successful – to negotiate the boundaries of power in ways that do not yield simple lessons about dominance and submission.

The fetish, which inhabits the border of the social and the psychological, throws into sharp relief the invalidity of separating the realms of psychoanalysis and social history. Both psychoanalysis and Marxism took shape around the idea of fetishism as a primitive regression and the disavowal of the social value of domestic work, so it is only fitting that the fetishistic proclivities of an obscure maid-of-all-work should oblige us to begin, again, to renegotiate the relation between psychoanalysis and social history, women's agency and male power, domesticity and the market.

What follows is less an attempt to empirically recover the past than it is an attempt to intervene strategically in historical narratives of race and fetishism, domesticity and empire, in such a way as to throw into question not only the historical force of these relations in Victorian Britain but also their continuing implication for our time.

NO PYGMALION

Ambiguous Agent

Munby and his biographer, Derek Hudson, both portray Cullwick as little more than a cloddish, if charming, marionette, a curiosity trained, costumed and controlled by her 'Massa', lumbering through her awkward theatrical paces to indulge his pleasures.[5] In later years, Munby claimed it was he who apprenticed Cullwick to drudgery: 'training and teaching' her in the 'lowest & most servile kind (of work)', initiating her into subservience and the indecorous degradations of their love.[6] When Cullwick refused to 'enter society' as his wife, Munby lamented that she had heeded his 'training' too well and had become permanently wedded to drudgery. Cullwick is likewise seen by Hudson as little more than the 'product of Munby's training of her in the ways of salvation through drudgery'.[7] Hudson finds, in consequence, that Cullwick's diaries and letters need 'be sampled only briefly'.[8] Even Leonore Davidoff, in an otherwise excellent essay, presents a one-sided portrait of their relationship and sees Munby as the master of ceremonies of Cullwick's life, the impresario and choreographer of their rituals, Svengali to her Trilby. Hudson and Davidoff thereby both become complicit with Munby's self-congratulatory vision of himself as Pygmalion, sculpting Cullwick's values as if from stone and instilling in her an 'over-commitment to drudgery'. 'In many ways', Davidoff writes, 'Hannah was, in fact, a creature of his fancy'.[9] As Davidoff sees it, their relationship was conducted 'on his terms and ultimately at a very high price'. 'All this happens,' she writes, 'at the will of the middle class male protagonist who creates the situation and engineers the transformation.'[10] Once more, the maidservant vanishes from the middle-class narrative.[11]

Liz Stanley, however, in an excellent introduction to Cullwick's diaries, protests these patronizing and dismissive portrayals of Cullwick. To accept only Munby's account of matters and to see Cullwick as no more than Munby's creation runs the very real risk of accepting 'Victorian sexist and classist thinking as an accurate reflection of the social world as it actually was'. Rather, she argues, Munby's writings are 'frequently belied by the reality of experience'.[12] Certainly they are belied by Cullwick's frequently contrasting perspectives. There is ample evidence in her diary and in Munby's, if read against the grain, that Cullwick invented as many of the scenarios and scripted as much of the game-playing as Munby did. It is also clear that she received a good deal of pleasure and power from doing so, despite the unremitting disadvantage of her situation. Far from being a passive drudge, she was stubbornly and steadfastly protective of her own interests and fiercely resisted Munby when her needs came into conflict with his. The critical portrayal of Cullwick as hapless jade and abused plaything serves only to annul the self-respect and agency she struggled so long and so stubbornly to achieve, under circumstances of extreme circumscription. Indeed, the erasure of Cullwick's lifelong resistance to limitation presents a sad irony for, one might say, that the project that animated her obscure and arduous life was the project of the social recognition of women's domestic work.

Certainly it was not Munby who initiated Cullwick into the ambiguous value of pride in working-class labor, for her beloved mother and working-class community, the church, the charity school, the village and the nearby manor had already shaped the foundations of her identity and her attitudes to work. To see

Munby as the only and originary shaper of her identity is to capitulate in a dominant Victorian middle-class fantasy: the fantasy of male philanthropic surveillance and control over the lives of working-class women. At the same time, Cullwick's relationship with Munby was inevitably informed by the discrepancy between her considerable power within the relationship and her social disempowerment outside it, a discrepancy that Munby was not at all averse to exploiting when he could.

I do not wish, however, to give the impression that Cullwick's relation to Munby was one of libertarian equality and mutual power; such a notion is insupportable. I am interested, rather, in the more difficult question of what kind of *agency* is possible in situations of extreme social *inequality*. Cullwick's life expressed a sustained determination to negotiate power within circumstances of great limitations, in ways that raise questions not about her cross-gender and cross-class relations with Munby, but also about her cross-class and inter-gender relations with her female employers. Within domestic households, the unequal burden of women's work, the mutual recriminations, class harassments and class rebellions took place within a combination of class estrangements and gender intimacies. In short, a major theoretical concern of this chapter is to explore the strategic tension between social constraint and social agency.

In what follows, I wish to question one feminist tendency to see women as unambiguous victims, a tendency that equates agency with context, body with situation, and thus annuls possibilities for strategic refusal. In this view, Cullwick is reduced to a victimized drudge, exhibited as the embodiment of female degradation and male dominance. If she was not an unambiguous victim, however, she was also not an unambiguous heroine of female revolt. Her circumstances were unremittingly harsh and disadvantageous; yet within their conscription she engaged in a lifelong negotiation of power, throwing continually into question the binary verities of dominance and resistance, victim and oppressor. What, then, of Cullwick's agency and desires in these curious rituals?

Hannah Cullwick's childhood was the commonplace story of a girl destined for a lifetime of service in Britain's ruling households. Daughter of a lady's maid and a saddler, she was born on May 26, 1833, in the Shropshire village of Shifnal. Her mother, Martha Cullwick, worked for the lady of the Hall and her father worked as a stableman. Her parents thus served the vanishing world of the ancient gentry, where power was invested in land, and the landless classes related to the manorial class through ancestral codes of duty, fealty and paternalism. Although Cullwick died in the village of her birth on July 9, 1909, she spent her life as a lower servant moving between the rural manorial estates and the urban houses of the manufacturing elite in London and Margate.[13] In the imperial dockyards, merchant banks, factories and mills, power was invested in capital and the far-flung lootings of empire, and the working class related to the new masters through the unreliable dynamics of the cash nexus. Cullwick's life thus straddled the dwindling world of the gentry and the ascendant world of industrial manufacture and, if her childhood was in almost every respect ordinary, her life would criss-cross some of the deepest faultlines of the Victorian age.

Born in a rustic cottage in Shropshire, Cullwick spent most of her life in the belching cities, working as a pot girl in an inn, as a nurserymaid, a kitchen maid, a scullion and drudge and a rural stranger in the huge, begrimed houses of the Victorian urban elite. In the heyday of the 'idle woman', she grew muscular with manual labor. Destined by class to wed a laboring man, she married instead a member of the upper-middle-class bureaucracy. As a barrister's wife, Cullwick could have 'entered society' but chose instead to live as a maidservant among her own class, spending very little time under the same roof as her beloved husband. In an age when wifely services were void of economic value, she insisted that her husband pay her monthly wages. At a time when most women devoted two-thirds of their lives to raising children, she remained childless. When most women of the age were illiterate, she could read and write and left behind seventeen diaries, which render in intimate detail the Herculean feats of her domestic toil. Her life was nondescript and her death caused no stir, but in retrospect her diaries offer a rare and important testimony to the life of a Victorian servant. Cullwick's diaries bear invaluable witness to 'the last generation of women that did heavy manual labor in large numbers'.[14]

In 1851 Cullwick traveled with her employers to London, the rhythms of her life following the class logic of their seasonal migrations.[15] In London a prescient vision in the fire showed her Munby's face. In 1854, she returned to London, where Munby approached her in the street. When she returned again the following year, she found lodgings in a cold, tiny room: 'There Massa came to see me again, & there was where I first black'd my face with *oil & lead*'.[16] At Cullwick's instigation, the couple began their lifelong career in domestic and racial fetishism and, soon after, Cullwick began to write the first of her seventeen diaries.

NOTHING TO USE BUT YOUR CHAINS

S/M and Domestic Power

Cullwick and Munby filled their lives with the theatrical paraphernalia of S/M: boots, chains, padlocks, leather, blindfolds, straps, costumes, scripts and photographs – some of them semi-pornographic. Their games included a variety of fetish rituals: transvestism, bondage, foot and leather fetishism, hand fetishism, washing rituals, infantilism, animalism and voyeurism. The primary transformations about which their fantasy games revolved were the central transformations of industrial imperialism: class (servant to mistress), race (white woman to black slave), gender (woman to man), economy (land to city) and age (adult to baby), transformations that were drawn simultaneously from the cult of domesticity and the cult of empire.

As Liz Stanley notes:

> Chains, boot-licking and blacking up the better to show the abasement of a slave to a master aren't just images of servitude in a conventional and often religious sense; they are also images replete with sado-masochistic and sexual overtones.[17]

Yet Stanley quickly rejects 'the usefulness or appropriateness of labeling (their relationship) as sado-masochistic'.[18] For, she argues, while people in S/M scenarios may change roles, we see 'at any one time whoever is the "master" has power and whoever is the "slave" has not'. Since Cullwick was neither powerless nor slavish in this 'conventional' sense, but was rather 'strong, stubborn, independent, assured and competent', the term *sadomasochism*, Stanley contends, has no usefulness for understanding Cullwick and Munby's power games.[19]

Stanley also rejects S/M as no more than the retrospective imposition on the past of images and terminology from the present. Yet it is no accident that the historical subculture of S/M emerged in Europe toward the end of the eighteenth century with the emergence of imperialism in its modern industrial form. As Foucault points out, S/M (which is not simply synonymous with cruelty or brutality) is a highly organized, ritual subculture that 'appeared precisely at the end of the eighteenth century' – a few decades before Cullwick and Munby were born.[20]

Late Victorian racial scientists demonized S/M as the psychopathology of the atavistic individual, a blood flaw and stigma of the flesh.[21] The 'sciences' of man – philosophy, Marxism, anthropology, psychoanalysis – sought to contain the irruptive implication of fetishism by projecting it onto the invented zone of 'degeneration', figuring it as a regression in historical time to the prehistory of racial degradation, the degeneration of the race writ in the pathology of the soul. S/M, however, is less a biological flaw, or a pathological expression of natural male aggression and natural female passivity, than it is an organized subculture shaped around the ritual exercise of social risk and social transformation. As a theater of conversion, S/M reverses and transforms the social meanings it borrows.

To argue that in S/M 'whoever is the "master" has power and whoever is the slave has not', is to read theater for reality; it is to play the world forward. The economy of S/M, however, is the economy of conversion: master to slave, adult to baby, power to submission, man to woman, pain to pleasure, human to animal and back again. S/M, as Foucault puts it, 'constitutes one of the greatest conversions of Western imagination: unreason transformed into delirium of the heart'.[22] S/M is a theater of transformation; it 'plays the world backward'.[23]

Consensual S/M (the collective organization of fetishism) insists on exhibiting the 'primitive' (slave, baby, woman) as a *character* in the historical time of modernity. S/M performs the 'primitive irrational' as a dramatic script; a theatrical, communal performance in the heart of Western reason. The paraphernalia of S/M (boots, whips, chains, uniforms) is the paraphernalia of state power, public punishment converted to private pleasure. S/M plays social power backward, visibly and outrageously staging hierarchy, difference and power, the irrational, ecstasy or alienation of the body, placing these ideas at the center of Western reason. S/M thus reveals the imperial logic of individualism and refuses it as fate, even though it does not finally step outside the enchantment of its own magic circle.

Hence the paradox of S/M. On one hand, S/M parades a slavish obedience to conventions of power. In its reverence to formal ritual, it is the most ceremonial and decorous of practices. S/M is high theater: 'beautifully suited to symbolism'.[24] As theater, S/M borrows its decor, props and costumery (bonds, chains, ropes, blindfolds) and its scenes (bedrooms, kitchens, dungeons, convents, prisons, empire) from the everyday cultures of power. At the same time, with its exaggerated emphasis on costumery, script and scene, S/M reveals that social order is unnatural, scripted and invented.

For Victorian science, nature was the overlord and guarantor of power. Thus for Krafft-Ebing, S/M enacts the male's 'natural' sexual aggression and the female's 'natural' sexual passivity: 'This sadistic force is developed by the natural shyness and modesty of women toward the aggressive manner of the male . . . the final victory of man affords her intense and refined gratification.'[25] The outrage of S/M, however, is precisely its hostility to the idea of nature as the custodian of social power. With the utmost artifice and levity, S/M refuses to read power as fate or nature and outrageously reverses the sacramental edicts of power and abandonment. Since S/M is the theatrical exercise of social contradiction, it is self-consciously *antinature*, not in the sense that it violates natural law, but in the sense that it denies the existence of natural law in the first place. S/M presents social power as sanctioned, neither by nature, fate nor God, but by artifice and convention and thus as radically open to historical change. S/M flouts social order with its provocative confession that the edicts of power are reversible. As such, it is a radically *historical* phenomenon.

S/M AND THE CULT OF DOMESTICITY

Cullwick's lifelong power over Munby lay in her theatrical talent for conversion and her power to play the world backward: to switch from maid to mistress, wife to slave, nurse to mother, white woman to black man. She was the dreamed-of combination, the 'Blessed Anomalie' that allowed Munby to stage in his own private theater of transformation the fateful early contrasts of gender and class that both perplexed and enthralled him. Munby records his first sighting of her in his diary:

> A country girl, she was, a scullion. . . . A tall erect creature, with light firm step and noble bearing: her face had the features and expression of a high born lady, though the complexion was rosy and rustic, & the blue eyes innocent and childlike: her bare arms and hands were large and strong

and ruddy from the shoulder to the finger-tips; but they were beautifully formed. . . . A robust hard-working peasant lass, with the marks of labour and servitude upon her everywhere: yet endowed with a grace and beauty, an obvious intelligence, that would have become a lady of the highest. Such a combination I had dreamt of and sought for; but I have never seen it, save in her.[26]

For Munby, Cullwick was a paragon of ambiguity: a country girl who trod the urban streets, a scullion formed like a high-born lady. She bore the marks of labor, but with aristocratic grace. She was both innocent and worldly-wise. She was a child, but as strong as a man. By playing both drudge and lady, woman and man, Cullwick offered Munby the delirious promise of embodying in one person the contrast of mother and nurse, woman and man, that so excited him: 'Let me,' he wrote, 'at least work out some of my theories upon this tender servant: let me be refreshed and comforted by a mother's love and by that of one so different.'[27] Cullwick's abiding attraction for Munby was her talent to play 'either part so well'. He recalls her sitting after a day's drudgery 'dainty in black silk and drawing-room cap . . . for is she not a servant during the day and a lady in the evening? and fulfills either part so well, that for some time she seems incapable of the other?'[28] 'One moment she is the very pattern of a kitchen drudge, awkward and strong, hard at work in sweat and dirt.' In the next instant, she transforms herself 'into the perfect image of the still and stately queen.'[29]

Cullwick offered Munby the illusion of control over the contradictions that shaped his identity. He relished her muscular brawn and her 'manliness', that allowed him to feel, by contrast, deliciously 'female', yet in such a way as not to endanger his precarious, compulsory manhood.[30] And by indulging the fantasy that he was master of their ceremonies, Munby indulged in what John Berger has called the 'Pygmalion Promise' – the (infantile) desire to shape another being's life according to the dictates of one's own desires. But since Munby's 'mastery' over Cullwick was no more than her theatrical gift to him, which she had the power to withdraw at any time (and did) and, since the contradictions that vexed him were social contradictions that could not be resolved at a personal level, the fetish scene was destined to recur again and again.

S/M is a theater of signs. Munby was helplessly fascinated by the visible and written *signs* of Cullwick's domesticity. The representation of domesticity as social and imperial allegory held him in its thrall. Obsessed with writing, Munby demanded that when Cullwick could not appear physically in the 'sign' of her dirt, she send him verbal signs instead in the form of her diary. And Cullwick, in turn, learned quickly to use her diary and her theatrical performances to manipulate Munby's desires and maintain control over him.

Indeed, it was not so much the actuality of female labor that captivated Munby but the *representation* of labor: labor as spectacle, as photograph, as language, as diary, as sketch, as script, as theatrical scene. He and Cullwick played their fetish games around the theatrical paraphernalia of domesticity: brooms, pails, water, soap, dirt – fetishes that cannot, in my opinion, be usefully reduced to a single-minded phallic logic. In their theater of conversion, mundane household objects became invested with profound fetish power, as ambivalent signs of domestic subordination and domestic power. Why the stress on signs?

As a theater of signs, S/M grants temporary control over social risk. By scripting and controlling the *frame* of representation, in other words, the control frame – the diary, the camera, the theatrical scene – the player stages the delirious loss of control within a situation of extreme control. For Munby, loss of control and confusion of social boundary were mediated by an excessive preoccupation with control. He depended deeply on control frames, by which he managed the staging of social risk. Managing the control frame – the photograph, the sketch, the diary, the script, the circus and, in particular, the exchange of money – was indispensable to his sense of mastery over what were otherwise terrifying ambiguities.

S/M is haunted by memory. By reinventing the memory of trauma and staging loss of control in what is really a situation of excessive control, the player gains symbolic power over perilous memory. S/M affords a delirious triumph over memory and, from this triumph, an orgasmic excess of pleasure. But, since the triumph over memory is theatrical and symbolic, however intensely felt in the flesh, resolution is perpetually deferred. For this reason, the memory (the scene) will recur for perpetual reenactment, and compulsive repetition emerges as a fundamental structuring principle of S/M.

One tendency within feminism has been to demonize heterosexual S/M as the sanctioned exercise of male dominance over women. 'Sadomasochism is self-debasement on all levels that renders wimmin unable to execute truly feminist goals.'[31] But, more often than not, S/M culture often reveals the opposite: 'In the world of the sadomasochist, there is nothing "abnormal" about a male being passive and submissive. Indeed, male passivity is by far the most common phenomenon.'[32] It is therefore not surprising that Munby was what is, in current parlance, called a 'babyist', or 'infantilist', relishing, as he did, to be bathed by Cullwick, lifted in her massive arms and rocked and 'nursed' on her ample lap like a baby.[33] Perhaps in these encounters Munby could surrender deliriously to the memory of his helplessness in his first nurse's arms, to voyeuristic pleasure at the spectacle of a working woman tending his passive body and to forbidden recognition of the social power of working-class women.

The contradiction that Munby faced was his dependence on working-class women whom society stigmatized as subservient. By ritually recognizing Cullwick (like his nurse) as socially powerful, he could acknowledge his forbidden childhood identification with powerful femininity, particularly working-class femininity. His foot-washing fetish was an expiation ritual that symbolically absolved him from guilt and 'dirt' while simultaneously letting him indulge in the forbidden, voyeuristic spectacle of women's work and women's power. Nonetheless, the recognition of domestic work as valuable was socially taboo and had to be mediated and controlled through carefully pre-arranged scripts.

On one occasion, for example, Cullwick asked Munby to visit her at her workplace. Once there, he was plunged into agitation and extreme distress. 'But to see her stand in a drawing room in her servant's dress and know that she is a servant and that the piano, the books, the pictures belonged to her mistress . . . this I could not endure.'[34] Seeing Cullwick in her workplace forced Munby into the agonized recognition that he did not really control, or own, her life. On another occasion he was appalled to visit her workplace and see how truly filthy and exhausted she was. What bothered him to distraction on both occasions was the collapse of his control frame and thus the loss of his illusion of mastery over the scene. Seeing Cullwick at work was a forcible reminder that another woman paid her wages, another woman gave her orders. Just as he was thrown into outrage at the sight of another journalist photographing 'his' pit-brow-women, the sight of Cullwick at work robbed Munby of his illusion that he controlled the dangerous scenario, and he was flung violently into crisis.

Role switching is a common feature of S/M and in their secret society of the spectacle Cullwick and Munby often switched roles. Most S/M is less 'the desire to inflict pain', as Freud argued, than it is the theatrical organization of *social risk*.[35] Contrary to popular perceptions, a great deal of S/M involves no pain at all. Its ritual violations are less violations to the flesh than symbolic reenactments of the memory of violations to selfhood, violations that can take myriad forms. As Weinberg and Kamel argue, 'S&M scenarios are *willingly and co-operatively* produced; more often than not it is the masochist's fantasies that are acted out'.[36] Many S/M fetishists claim that in fact it is the 'bottom' who is in control.

Havelock Ellis points out that much S/M is motivated by love. Far from being the tyrannical exercise of one will upon a helpless other, S/M is more typically collaborative, involving careful initiation rituals, a scrupulous definition of limits and a constant confirmation of reciprocity that can bind the players in an ecstasy of interdependence: abandonment at the very moment of dependence. But because S/M involves the negotiation of perilous boundaries, any violation of the script is fraught with risk, whereas mutual fidelity to the pledge of trust creates an intimacy of a very intense kind. If at any point control is lost or the rules of the game transgressed, either of the players can be plunged into panic. Hence the importance and prevalence of scripting in consensual S/M.

THE SLAVE-BAND

Refusing Abjection

For years Cullwick wore a filthy leather 'slave-band' on her wrist and a chain and locked padlock around her neck. Her original reason for wearing a strap, she tells us, was to support her wrist after a bad sprain.[37] Later she wore it as a 'sign' of her love for and servitude to Munby. When she insisted on wearing the strap while serving dinner, letting it show on her wrist before the invited company, her employer ordered her to remove it. Cullwick declined to obey and was furiously dismissed, preferring, as she proudly records in her diary, to lose her employment rather than take off 'the sign that i'm a drudge & belong to Massa'.[38] What are we to make of Cullwick's slave-band, belonging as it does in the zone of the fetish?

The fetish embodies a crisis in social meaning. In Cullwick's slave-band, three of the formative contradictions of the Victorian era converge: between slave labor and wage labor; between the private realm of domesticity and the public realm of the market; and between metropolis and empire. In the fetish of the slave-band, race, class and gender overlap and contradict each other; the slave-band, like most fetishes, is overdetermined.

Cullwick's transgression was to wear at dinner (the theater of middle-class consumption and female leisure) the forbidden sign of women's work. Cullwick brought scandalously into crisis the incommensurable relation between the Victorian doctrine that women should not work for profit and the visible sign of female domestic labor: the faint, illicit odor of the kitchen, the stain of dirty water, the mark of labor in imperial leather. Cullwick outraged convention by exhibiting, of her own stubborn volition, the public evidence of women's domestic dirt, banished by Victorian decree to kitchen and back-corridor, cellar and garret – the architecture of the unseen. In refusing to take off her band, Cullwick was refusing the social abjection of her labor and domestic dirt.

For Cullwick, the fetish of the slave-band was specific to the recognition of social value. The idea of concealed labor is fundamental to the Marxist analysis of the commodity fetish. The idea of traumatic fixation upon an intense experience is fundamental to the psychoanalytic notion of the sexual fetish. Both ideas fuse in the slave-band. In an important observation William Pietz notes that fetishism often arises from a crisis that 'brings together and fixes into a singularly resonant, unified intensity an unrepeatable event (permanent in memory), a particular object and a localized space'. Paradoxically, this crisis moment, because of its 'degradation from any recognizable value code', becomes 'a moment of infinite value'.[39] The death of Cullwick's mother was just such an unrepeatable moment; the localized space was the architectural space of upper-class domesticity; and the particular object was the imperial fetish of the slave-band. Here the crisis does involve the mother's body, but not in the way that Freud envisaged.

As a child of fourteen, working away from home as a nursemaid, Cullwick was called without warning from the family schoolroom and was summarily told that both her parents had died of illness a few weeks before. Abandoned to cry alone on the floor where she had fallen and refused leave to return home to help her orphaned brothers and sisters, Cullwick felt that the death of her beloved mother stripped her life of all value: 'It seemed as if my care for life or work was all gone.' The crisis took on fetish form, for the violence of the chance encounter with death and her employers' refusal to let her mourn marked a radical break with history and community, costing her not only her family but also the symbolic value of her work and her sense of control over her own life. The death of her mother flung her into intense collision with the power of the upper-class family to subjugate her value to their needs: 'I don't think I ever shall [get over it]. I shall never play again or bowl hoops around the garden.'[40] Henceforth, her mother would be represented by the striving of a memory: 'trying to dream of her ghost.'

With the slave-band, Cullwick turned memory into a repeatable object. In photograph after photograph, she posed in such a way as to display her slave-band to maximum effect. Like all fetishes, the slave-band was contradictory, embodying the power of the upper class to enslave her, while at the same time exhibiting her determination to reclaim the value of her work and the memory of her mother. At the 'marked site' of her wrist, damaged by the trauma of labor, she transformed bondage into the secret sign of self-assertion. By deliberately letting the filthy band show at dinner, she reclaimed her independence and her right to contract her labor as she pleased. By flouncing out of her employment, she claimed her right to control her own body and her own work. By contracting herself to Munby as his symbolic 'slave', she took control, in the symbolic realm, of lack of control in the social realm. Her adamant and entirely unsubservient refusal to take off the band revealed, moreover, that she valued it only as a *symbol* of power over which she had ultimate control. Most importantly, by displaying her wrist filthy with labor, she rejected the stigma of shame attached to domestic work.[41] If the Victorian cult of domesticity voided her work of social recognition, she stubbornly displayed her hands in public to exhibit their *economic* value: 'my hands & arms are tho' chief to *me*, to get my living with.'[42]

Cullwick's fetishistic attachment to her slave-band expressed, I suggest, a lifelong attempt to reinvent the memory of her mother's domestic value in the eyes of the upper class. The upper-class *undervaluation* of her work found its antithesis in her *overvaluation* of her work. Her slave-band and her profound commitment to domestic labor embodied a compulsive determination to maintain control, at whatever physical cost, of the realm of labor in which she was subordinated.

The cross-cultural experiences marked by the fetish fuse in the slave-band: in the triangular relations among slavery as the basis of mercantile capitalism; wage labor as the basis of industrial capitalism; and domestic labor as the basis of patriarchy. By flagrantly wearing on her body the fetish leather of bonded labor, Cullwick threw into question the liberal separation of private and public, insisting on exhibiting her work, her dirt, her *value* in the home: that space putatively beyond both slave labor and wage labor. Exhibiting her filth as value, she gave the lie to the disavowal of women's work and the rational, middle-class control of dirt and disorder.

THE DIRT FETISH

Cullwick's employers' principle objection to her band was its dirt. Cullwick and Munby's rituals – the foot and boot cleaning, the washing rituals Munby's voyeuristic desire to see Cullwick 'in her dirt', Cullwick's deliberate 'blacking', the photographs, the slave band – were organized in complex but repetitive ways around the Victorian dirt fetish. Why did dirt exert such a compulsive fascination over their imaginations, as it did over the Victorian era at large?

Nothing is inherently dirty; dirt expresses a relation to social value and social disorder. Dirt, as Mary Douglas suggests, is that which transgresses social boundary.[43] A broom in a kitchen closet is not dirty, whereas lying on a bed it is. Sex with one's spouse is not dirty, whereas conventionally the same act with a prostitute is. In Victorian culture, the iconography of dirt became deeply integrated in the policing and transgression of social boundaries.

Dirt is what is left over after exchange value has been extracted. In Victorian culture, the bodily relation to dirt expressed a social relation to labor. The male middle class – seeking to dismantle the aristocratic body and the aristocratic regime of legitimacy – came to distinguish itself as a class in two ways: it earned its living (unlike the aristocracy) and it owned property (unlike the working class). Unlike the working class, however, its members, especially its female members, could not bear on their bodies the visible evidence of manual labor. Dirt was a Victorian scandal because it was the surplus evidence of manual work, the visible residue that stubbornly remained after the process of industrial rationality had done its work. Dirt is the counterpart of the commodity; something is dirty precisely *because* it is void of commercial value, or because it transgresses the 'normal' commercial market. Dirt is by definition useless, because it is that which belongs outside the commodity market.

If, as Marx noted, commodity fetishism flamboyantly exhibits the *overvaluation* of commercial *exchange* as the fundamental principle of social community, then the Victorian obsession with dirt marks a dialectic: the fetishized *undervaluation* of human *labor*. Smeared on trousers, faces, hands and aprons, dirt was the memory trace of working class and female labor, unseemly evidence that the fundamental production of industrial and imperial wealth lay in the hands and bodies of the working class, women and the colonized. Dirt, like all fetishes, thus expresses a crisis in value, for it contradicts the liberal dictum that social wealth is created by the abstract rational principles of the market and not by labor. For this reason, Victorian dirt entered the symbolic realm of fetishism with great force.

As the nineteenth century drew on, the iconography of dirt became a poetics of surveillance, deployed increasingly to police the boundaries between 'normal' sexuality and 'dirty' sexuality, 'normal' work and 'dirty' work and 'normal' money and 'dirty' money. Dirty sex – masturbation, prostitution, lesbian and gay sexuality, the host of Victorian 'perversions' – transgressed the libidinal economy of male-controlled, heterosexual reproduction within monogamous marital relations (clean sex that has *value*). Likewise, 'dirty' money – associated with prostitutes, Jews, gamblers, thieves – transgressed the fiscal economy of the male-dominated, market exchange (clean money that has *value*). Like prostitutes and female miners, servants stood on the dangerous threshold of normal work, normal money and normal sexuality, and came to be figured increasingly in the iconography of 'pollution', 'disorder', 'plagues', 'moral contagion' and racial 'degeneration.'

Here a crucial aspect of Victorian imperialism emerges. The relation between the 'normal' economy of heterosexual marriage and the 'normal' economy of capital exchange was legitimized and made natural by reference to a third term: the invention of the 'abnormal' zone of the primitive and the irrational. Money, work and sexuality were seen to relate to each other by negative analogy to the realm of racial difference and empire. Thus, historical contradictions internal to imperial liberalism (the distinctions between private and public; paid work and unpaid work; the formation of the male, propertied individual and the denial that slaves, women and the colonized were 'possessive individuals'; between the rational and the irrational) were contained by displacement onto a third term: the term of race. Class and gender distinctions were displaced and represented as natural racial differences across time and space: the difference between the 'enlightened' present and the 'primitive' past.

Cullwick's slave-band embodies the traces of both personal and historical memory: her own subjugated labor and the slave labor on which industrial capital was built. By the second half of the seventeenth century, black people, brought to Britain by slavers, merchants and plantation owners, lived scattered all over England, though they clustered mostly in London. By the turn of the eighteenth century, London and Bristol were thriving slave ports, continuing for another hundred years to garner huge profits from the murderous transport and sale of human beings. In Britain, the possession of a black slave became an emblem of new imperial wealth and advertisements raising a hue and cry after escaped slaves show that they were 'customarily obliged to wear metal collars riveted round their necks. Made of brass, copper, or silver, the collar was generally inscribed with the owner's name, initials, coat of arms, or other symbol.'[44] At the Lord Mayor's pageant, the annual festival of London's merchant capitalists, black people were obliged to perform in opulent costumes and these fetish collars, exhibiting in public displays of sumptuary excess the wealth of the imperial metropolis and the forced labor on which mercantile capitalism was built.

The slave-collar here embodies a contradiction between the extravagant display of black slaves for their exhibition value and the total denial of the value of their lives and work. Cullwick's slave-collar, as a fetish, thus embodied a double disavowal: the historical erasure both of slave labor and of working-class women's labor as the foundation of modern industrial power. The slave-band and chain-collar brought into the bourgeois home the memory of empire – chains, straps and bondage – at the precise moment when the industrial economy was being transformed from a slave market to a wage market. The fetish slave-band thus stages the history of industrial capital as haunted by the traumatic and ineradicable memory of imperial slavery.

THE LABOR OF LEISURE

Women have always worked – they have not always worked for wages.

Sophonsiba Beckenridge

In a century obsessed with women's work, the idea of the idle woman was born. A commonplace story depicts the middle-class Victorian woman's life as a debauch of idleness. At some point during the eighteenth century, the story goes, the spindle and loom were pried from her fingers and all the 'bustling labor' of the previous century – the candle and soap-making, the tailoring, millinery, straw-weaving, lace-making, carding and wool-sorting, flax-beating, dairy and poultry work – were removed piecemeal to the manufactures.[45] By the end of the eighteenth century, Wanda Neff writes 'the triumph of the useless woman was complete'.[46] Robbed of her productive labor, the middle-class woman became fitted, we are told, only for an ornamental place in society.[47] There, drooping prettily in the faded perfume of watercolors and light embroidery, she lived only to adorn the worldly ambition of her husband, the manufacturer, the city banker, the shipowner.[48] Ensconced after marriage in a bower of ease, she simply exchanged temporary for permanent uselessness.[49] Closeted in her 'cold sepulcher of shame', the virgin in the drawing room blushed at tablelegs and shrank from the pleasures of the body. Her dreamy torpor was ruffled only by hysterical ailments, swooning spells and a plague of obstructive servants.[50] Frigid, neurasthenic and ornamental; wilting in the airless hothouse of Victorian domesticity; fretfully preoccupied by trifles; given to irrationality and hysteria; languishing in ennui; incapable of constancy, decision or stature, the middle-class woman was, until recently, consistently disparaged and her life, as Patricia Branca notes, was dismissed as a 'mass of trifles'.[50a]

At this time, what Nancy Armstrong calls 'economic man' and 'domestic woman' were born.[51] Secluded in the ethic of purity, Coventry Patmore's 'angel in the house' was seen to float in a separate sphere.[52] In the tumult of the commercial marketplace, economic man was seen to live out his destiny as the public actor and maker of history: 'eminently the doer, the creator, the discoverer, the defender.' Domestic woman was shaped to her destiny as sweet preserver and comforter, the vessel and safeguard of tradition. Until the 1970s, most critics simply repeated verbatim this fictional portrayal of the crushed flower of middle-class womanhood, taking Victorian writers at face value and accepting fictional portraits quite literally as documentary portrayals.[53]

For decades, therefore, it was widely assumed that the visible sign of the Victorian middle-class housewife was the sign of leisure.[54] It was as widely assumed that the 'typical' middle-class woman was freed for her conspicuous leisure by employing at least three domestic servants in her home.[55] By common assumption, a typical middle class home was not complete without at least three paid domestics.[56] Yet Patricia Branca, totting up the average yearly wages of a cook, parlormaid, housemaid or nurse, calculates that the family income required to employ this 'necessary trinity' was found only in the tiny, elite-upper and upper-middle classes. Most women of the middle class (itself a broad and shifting category, still under formation) would have to have been content harrying, at best, a single callow girl whose life would, most likely, have been a chronicle of interminable labor and pitiful wages.[57] Wives of the small tradesmen, clerks, grocers and plumbers would probably have made do with the services of only one such maid-of-all work. Perhaps wives of professional men could afford two paid servants, while doctors, clergymen, bank managers and successful businessmen might, by the late Victorian period, have employed three.[58] Arguably, then, neither the typical bourgeois lady nor the typical domestic servant really existed. Little regard has been given to the representational discrepancy between Victorian (largely upper middle class) portrayals of women and the myriad, middling domestic situations that took contradictory shape across the span of the century.[59]

While contemporary historians have noted the *symbolic value* of the serving class in the formation of middle-class identity, few have acknowledged the *economic value* of the domestic serving class as labor.[60] What I suggest is that – apart from the tiny, truly leisured elite – idleness was less a regime of inertia imposed on wilting middle-class wives and daughters than a laborious and time-consuming *character role* performed by women who wanted membership in the 'respectable' class. For most women whose husbands or fathers could not afford enough servants for genuine idleness, domestic work had to be accompanied by the historically unprecedented labor of rendering invisible every sign of that work. For most middling women, the cleaning and management of their large, inefficiently constructed houses took immense amounts of labor and energy. Yet a housewife's vocation was precisely the concealment of this work.

Housewifery became a career in vanishing acts. A wife's vocation was not only to create a clean and productive family but also to ensure the skilled erasure of every *sign* of her work. Her life took shape around the contradictory imperative of laboring while rendering her labor invisible. Her success as a wife depended on her skill in the art of both working and appearing not to work. Her parlor game – the ritualized moment of appearing fresh, calm and idle before the scrutiny of husbands, fathers and visitors – was a theatrical performance of leisure, the ceremonial negation of her work. For most women from the still-disorganized middling classes, I suggest, idleness was less the absence of work than a conspicuous labor of leisure.

The architecture of middle-class homes took shape around this paradox. The parlor marked the threshold of private and public, serving as the domestic space for the spectacular (public) metamorphosis of female work into female leisure. The morning call fulfilled the requirement of being *seen* – idle and scrubbed clean of the telltale signs of labor. As a threshold zone, the parlor also became the domestic space for the display of commodity fetishism. The parlor served to conspicuously display the family's 'best' household commodities: use value was converted to exhibition value. In lower-middle-class houses, the anxious exhibition of 'good' silver, 'good' china and 'clean' furniture (commodities with exhibition value rather than use value) barely cloaked the shabbiness, overwork and anxiety that lay concealed behind the commodity spectacle of female leisure and male buying power. A fresh and pretty housewife presiding at table disavowed the anxious and sweaty hours of labor, cooking, cleaning and polishing, even with the help of an overworked maid. The dilemma for these women was that the more convincingly they performed the labor of leisure, the more prestige they won. But the prestige was gained not through idleness itself but through a laborious mimicry of idleness.

Certainly it was not the spectacle of leisure that mattered in itself, but the undervaluing of women's work that the spectacle achieved.[61] Hence the Victorian fetish with hands, for hands could betray the traces of female work more visibly than a washable apron or disposable gloves. Housewives were advised to rub their hands at night with bacon fat and wear gloves in bed to prevent smearing the oil on the sheets, an imperative that revealed so fundamental an embarrassment at female work that it had to continue even in sleep.

THE INVISIBLE SERVANT

Clearly the most damaging burden of the erasure of domestic labor fell on servants. The housewife's labor of *leisure* found its counterpart in the servant's labor of *invisibility*. Servants were ordered to remain unseen, completing the filthiest work before dawn or late at night, dodging their employers, keeping to the labyrinthine back passages, remaining, at all costs, out of sight. If they had to appear before their 'betters' to answer the master's bell or open the front door to receive a visitor, they were obliged to change instantly from dirty work clothes into fresh, clean white ones – a ritual metamorphosis that rehearsed the century's long transformation of domestic work from the realm of the seen to the unseen.[62] The fetish for clean clothes was eloquent of a systematic attempt to erase from view any visible trace of domestic work. The governess's white gloves, the maid's white apron, the nanny's white sleeves were fetish emblems of the contradiction between women's paid work and women's unpaid work. At the same time, the myriad tools and technologies of work – buckets, brooms, brushes, scuttles, irons, cooking utensils, saucepans and so on – were laboriously hidden from view. Though a tailor's workroom or a smithy's workshop could be visibly eloquent of labor, the domestic labor of women suffered one of the most successful vanishing acts of modern history.[63]

The wife's labor of leisure and the servant's labor of invisibility served to disavow and conceal within the middle-class formation the economic value of women's work. Female servants thus became the embodiment of a central contradiction within the modern industrial formation. The separation of the private from the public was achieved only by paying working-class women for domestic work that wives were supposed to perform for free. Servants' labor was indispensable to the process of transforming wives' *labor* power into their husbands' *political* power. But the figure of the paid female servant constantly imperiled the 'natural' separation of private home and public market. Quietly crossing the thresholds of private and public, home and market, working and middle class, servants brought into the middle-class home the whiff of the marketplace, the odor of cash. Domestic workers thus embodied a double crisis in historic value: between men's paid labor and women's unpaid labor and between a feudal homestead economy and an industrial wage economy.

Small wonder that female servants in Victorian households came to be figured by images of disorder, contagion, disease, conflict, rage and guilt. For this reason, I suggest, domestic space became racialized as the rhetoric of degeneration was drawn upon to discipline and contain the unseemly spectacle of paid women's work.

The Rationalizing of Domesticity

Nancy Armstrong has argued powerfully that eighteenth-century conduct books and domestic manuals reveal a contradiction of historic proportions. The books were written as if they addressed a fairly wide readership with consistent social objectives – a middle class that was not yet there. The new genre of the female conduct book, she argues, implied 'the presence of a unified middle class at a time when other representations of the social world suggest that no such class existed'.[64] What this suggests is that women played a far greater role in the formation of middle-class identity than has been acknowledged. The cult of domesticity was crucial in helping to fashion the identity of a large class of people (hitherto disunited) with clear affiliations, distinct boundaries and separate values – organized around the presiding domestic values of monogamy, thrift, order, accumulation, classification, quantification and regulation – the values of liberal rationality through which the disunited middling classes fashioned the appearance of a unified class identity.

What was specific to rationality in its nineteenth-century form was its single-minded dedication to the principles of capital accumulation for commercial expansion.[65] The full expansion of imperial commerce was not possible without elaborate systems of rational accounting – surveying, map-making, measurement and quantification – organized around the abstract medium of money into the global science of the surface. By the mid nineteenth century, the domestic realm, far from being abstracted from the rational market, became an indispensable arena for the creation, nurturance and embodiment of these values. The cult of industrial rationality and the cult of domesticity formed a crucial but concealed alliance.

The middle-class determination to identify happiness with rational order and the clear demarcation of boundaries manifested itself in precise rules not only for assembling the public sphere but also for assembling domestic space.[66] Household arrangements gradually took shape around a geometry of extreme separation and specialization that came to discipline every aspect of daily life.

Domestic space was mapped as a hierarchy of specialized and distinct boundaries that needed constant and scrupulous policing.

Spatial boundaries were reordered as the large, communal medieval hall was replaced by arrangements of smaller, highly specialized rooms. By the mid nineteenth century, what Barthes calls the 'sensual pleasure in classification' ruled domestic space – in the labeling of bottles, the careful marking of sheets and clothes, the scrupulous keeping of visitors' books, the regular accounting of stocks, the meticulous measuring of food, the strict keeping of account books.[67] Specialized utensils, technologies and timetables were developed for different stages of cooking and eating. The fetish for rational measurement led to an increase in the use of weights and measures. Food was served in obedience to rigid timetables, announced by the ringing of bells. Unlike the medley of sweet and savory, hot and cold courses served all at once in earlier times, meals now followed strict sequential rules, one course following the other with the proper decorum of rational, linear progress.

Domestic space was increasingly disciplined by the obsessive tidying and ordering of ornaments and furniture. Time was rationalized: servants' workloads and children's daily schedules followed strict routines and timetables. Cleaning schedules were divided into increasingly rationalized and rigid calendars: washing on Monday, ironing on Tuesday, polishing on Wednesday and so on. The domestic day itself was measured into mechanical units, marked by the chiming of clocks and the meticulous ringing of bells. The clock presided magisterially over the life of the household, perfectly encapsulating the Victorian fetish for measurement, order and boundary.[68] In short, the cult of domesticity became a crucial arena for rationalizing emergent middle-class identity and its presiding values.

Very little is known about the role of women's labor, attitudes, agency and dilemmas in this process. Even less is known about how working-class women negotiated, opposed or appropriated the cult of domesticity and the rationalizing of the household. Cullwick's diaries, I suggest, offer a rare and important insight into these dynamics, all the more valuable for expressing a working-class perspective. If, as I suggest, a central function of liberal rationality and the cult of domesticity was to disavow the social and economic value of women's manual and domestic work, Cullwick's diaries present the remarkable record of a working-class woman's unflagging attempt to negotiate and accommodate to the rationalizing of housework while at the same time doing precisely what liberal rationalism forbade: stubbornly insisting on the visible economic and social value of her labor power. Cullwick's writings and her fetishistic rituals reveal in glimpses and intimations some of the critical contradictions that bring the discourse of rationality and the cult of domesticity to its conceptual limit. Indeed, her diaries reveal that fetishism, far from being the antithesis of rationalism and progress, as was tirelessly claimed, instead came to inform the domestic cult of rationality as its central logic.

CROSS-DRESSING AND FEMALE FETISHISM

A person without clothes is a person without language.

West African Proverb

Cullwick's abiding power over Munby was her theatrical talent for conversion. Over the years, she revealed a remarkable capacity for adopting different social identities and costumes at will. As a servant, it was her profession and her pride to stage as natural the theatrical rites and pageantries of middle- and upper-middle-class status. One minute she was on her knees scrubbing the grimy floors and closets, her huge arms filthy with fat and water; the next minute she appeared in fresh, dry white, to demurely open the door to a stranger or answer the mistress's bell. One minute she was lifting and carrying menservants around the kitchen table, in gales of hilarity, or heaving heavy luggage, buckets of hot water and loaded coal scuttles up three flights of stairs at a time. Next minute she was bobbing and curtsying to her 'betters', mimicking servility and performing the exaggerated rites of humility required of her station.

In her relationship with Munby, she transformed her servant's skills at mimicry into high theater and a source of considerable power. She cross-dressed as an upper-class mistress, a rural farm worker and a male valet. She costumed herself as a male slave, a chimney sweep, an angel and a fieldhand, and took herself to the photographers to be photographed in her costumery. She cut her hair and dressed as a man and traveled round Europe with Munby as his valet. After they were married, she cross-dressed as an upper-class lady and again toured Europe with Munby, this time as his wife. Munby was helplessly enthralled by 'her talent to play each part so well'.

With her exceptional talent for the ambiguities of identity, Cullwick joins the countless concealed and clandestine female cross-dressers who – according to the edicts of psychoanalytic tradition – do not exist. Robert Stoller proclaims firmly that there is no such thing as the 'transvestite woman': 'fetishistic cross-dressing' in women is 'so rare it is almost non existent'. Unlike Freud, Stoller argues that women 'have no clothing fetish', they simply want to *be* men; a perfectly natural desire.[69] Female cross-dressers cannot be admitted into the house of perversion, for they throw radically into question the centrality of the phallus as the fetishized object around which transvestism is supposed to be organized. However, not only was Cullwick a lifelong cross-dresser, but her fetishism was organized not around the traumas of phallic identity and erotic displacement but around the historic contradictions of women's work and the iconography of empire – chains, blacking, dirt, clothes, boots, buckets, water and brushes. While Cullwick may well have received deferred erotic pleasure from her fetishism, understanding her cross-dressing and fetish rituals as an erotics of the castration scene serves only to reduce her life to a masculinist narrative of sexual interest. Instead, I suggest that her fetishism amounted to a sustained attempt to negotiate the perils attending the Victorian erasure of women's work.

Cross-dressing is not only a personal fetish, it is also a historical phenomenon. What one can call sumptuary panic (boundary panic over clothing) erupts most intensely during periods of social turbulence. In the early modern period, sumptuary laws in Europe and Britain took shape around the upheavals in money and social status engendered by imperialism.[70] As spices from the slave plantations and silver and other precious metals from the slave mines engendered new possibilities for mercantile consumption and surplus, new forms of money and consumption – no longer dependent on land and aristocratic power – began to interfere in old forms of political distinction. These changes led to the promulgation of sumptuary laws all over Europe, restricting 'the wearing of certain furs, fabrics and styles to members of particular social and economic classes, ranks or "states".'[71] Clothing became central to the policing of social boundaries, marking out 'visible and above all legible distinctions of wealth and rank within a society undergoing changes that threatened to even obliterate social distinctions'.[72] Dismantling the aristocratic regime involved, in part, dismantling the aristocratic body as a theater of sumptuary and sexual display.

Sumptuary laws sought to regulate social boundaries by regulating the social legibility of dress.[73] Yet sumptuary laws contain an internal paradox, for the fact that class and rank are made legible by the wearing, or not wearing, of 'cloth of gold, silk or purple' reveals the invented nature of social distinction, throwing into visibility the question of both the origins and the legitimacy of rank and power. The bits and pieces of colored cloth that are the legible insignia of degree are also permanently subject to disarrangement and symbolic theft. For this reason, the historical figure of the cross-dresser becomes invested with a potent and subversive power. As Marjorie Garber puts it in her groundbreaking book, the transvestite is 'the figure that disrupts'.[74]

Garber brilliantly chronicles how 'the specter of transvestism, the uncanny intervention of the transvestite, came to mark and indeed to overdetermine this space of anxiety about fixed and changing identities, commutable or absent selves'.[75] Garber refuses to accept the traditional account of transvestism as a medical pathology or biological anomaly – the crisis of the transvestite, she argues, represents the 'crisis of category itself'.[76] In this way, Garber invites us to take transvestites on their own terms, not as one sex or one gender but as the enactment of ambiguity itself; not even so much a 'blurred sex' as the embodiment and performance of social contradiction. The transvestite inhabits the threshold of category distinction, challenging 'easy notions of binarity and throwing into question the categories of "female" and "male"'.[77] Thus Garber sets herself against the progress narrative theory of cross-dressing, that attempts to uncover a 'real' desired identity, either 'male' or 'female' beneath the transvestite mask. For Garber, by contrast, the transvestite is not equivalent to one sex or another but is rather the figure that inhabits that borderland where oppositions are perpetually disarranged, untidied and subverted.

Nonetheless, Garber herself, by universalizing all cross-dressers as the 'figure that disrupts' and by universalizing all fetishes as the phallus ('the phallus is the fetish, the fetish is the phallus'), cannot, in the final analysis, theoretically explain the wealth of diversity that her own anecdotes reveal. Within the single, cramped Lacanian frame into which she consigns all cross-dressers, diversity, ambiguity and difference are paradoxically lost and each cross-dresser becomes, at the theoretical level, a clone of all the others. Her obedient genu-flection to a single genesis narrative of phallic ambiguity reduces the rich diver-sity she marvelously recounts to an abstract economy of one. Garber is therefore unable to account theoretically for distinctions among subversive, conservative or radical transvestite practices and fetishes. Diversity disappears in the perpetual recurrence of the single 'primal scene'.

In the twilight world of transvestite ambiguity, Cullwick situated her power and her pleasure in that threshold zone where boundaries blur. Her talent for costume, disguise and improvisation was no simple theatrical masquerade; rather, it was a profound engagement with the social edicts that brutally circumscribed her life.

Cullwick celebrated the peculiar freedoms of ambiguity rather than the fixity of one identity. Cross-dressers seldom seek the security of a perfect imitation; rather, they desire that delicious impersonation that belies complete disguise: 'something readable, a foot that is too big, a subtle gesture or the peculiar grain of the voice.'[78] Thus when Cullwick cross-dresses and is photographed as a 'lady', her filthy, callused hand with its dirty strap rests visibly and improbably on her fresh, flounced skirt. Cullwick's insistent display of her hands and strap refuses the historical erasure of women's work. Displaying, in public, the taboo sign of women's private work, she throws into question the naturalness of the categories of dirty work or clean work, dirty women or clean women, insisting that she 'could play either part so well' because both were invention.

It is extremely important to emphasize that Cullwick performed transforma-tions of race and class as well as gender. Cross-dressed as a 'male slave' she posed naked from the waist up, visibly displaying her 'masculine' arms and huge shoulders. Yet, if she appears quite male, on closer examination the gentle curve of her breasts, half-hidden in the shadows, suggests other possibilities. Again, in the 'Rosetti' portrait (hand-tinted for Munby by Rosetti himself, who declared he was sure it was of a 'lady') the slave chain lies visibly and incon-gruously on her gentle bosom.

Cross-dressing became so habitual for Cullwick that she declared in her diary: 'I have got into the way of *forgetting* like, whether I am dressed up as a lady or drest in my apron & cotton frock in the street.'[79] Gautier captures beau-tifully the threshold state that transvestism inhabits in a description that could well have been written by Cullwick: 'I hardly remembered, at long intervals that I was a woman; . . . in truth, neither sex is really mine. . . . I belong to a third sex, a sex apart, that has as yet no name.'[80] Similarly, Cullwick writes of her gender in upper-class houses: 'I was the man in the house.'

On their trip to Europe as man and wife, she started out from the Temple, where she lived as Munby's housemaid, in her old black bonnet and working clothes, performing a complete change of costume at Folkstone. There at the port, where the boundaries of national custom permitted the safe transgression of class convention, Cullwick donned her 'felt hat & plume of cocks feathers and a veil'. The ornamental hat and brooch were the necessary, visible signs of class leisure and wealth, while the veil was the insignia both of male property ownership of female sexuality and protection from the elements (and thus the racial and class disgrace of a sun-darkened skin). Returning from Europe, she put her old plaid shawl over her skirt: 'I've doffed all my best clothes & put my own on again – very dirty cotton frock & apron and my cap.' Her transformations were entirely convincing: 'I wasn't noticed coming into the Temple or going out.'[81]

'SO MUFFLED UP'

Marriage and Resistance

There remain no legal slaves except
the mistress of every house.

J. S. Mill

Cross-dressing signaled Cullwick's refusal of the niggardly social roles allotted her. Cross-dressed as a man, she could travel unquestioned around Europe with Munby. Dressed as a working-class woman, she freely entered bars and music halls, enjoying forms of working-class leisure forbidden 'proper' women. She could walk about after dark without fear of ruination or reprisal. On the other hand, cross-dressed as a lady, she could enjoy the luxury and adventure of the hotels, holiday resorts and sightseeing trips barred to working-class women.

For this reason, Cullwick dreaded the prospect of marriage to Munby and, for some time, steadfastly refused his insistence that she appear in public as his wife. If, for most women, as Christine Delphy argues, 'marriage is a contract into unpaid labor', Cullwick's dogged will to independence expressed itself in a powerful, principled resistance to marriage.[82] Because the 'outward bond' of the legal license threatened to turn her into Munby's real slave, Cullwick found the prospect of marriage unbearably galling. If, on one hand, she called Munby 'Massa' and seemed to genuflect symbolically to Rousseau's dictum that the husband should be a 'master for the whole of life'; on the other hand, there is every evidence that she saw Munby's 'mastery' as purely theatrical.[83] For this reason, she showed nothing but repugnance at the thought of marrying Munby and entering 'proper' society as his wife. When Munby decided that it was high time they married, Cullwick made no bones about her distaste for the idea and relented only when circumstances made it well nigh unavoidable.[84] She was deeply reluctant to move in with Munby and, after four unhappy and lonely years under his roof, she moved out again, against his wishes, to continue their relationship more on her terms than his. Marriage, with its apparently permanent settling of heterosexual identity, struck her as unbearably constrictive: 'It is too much like being a *woman*,' she lamented.

Cullwick's slave-band brings into visibility the triangulated, historic convergence of wife, servant and slave. A long and sorry relation holds between wives and slaves. As Engels points out, the term 'family' derives from 'famulus', which means slave.[85] The status of women as individuals entered classical liberal theory as a central dilemma. If women, like slaves and children, were to be denied the rights to liberty and property ownership, ideological work had to be done. The solution lay in the distinction between the private and the public. Classical liberal theorists constructed as a *political* right the right to contract within the public sphere, but defined conjugal relations as belonging within the sphere of *nature* and thus beyond contract. The domestic sovereignty of the husband over the wife and thus the exclusion of women from possessive individualism, was justified as deriving from natural, not political, law.[86]

Thus when Munby exults that Cullwick was brought to him by 'him who brought Eve to Adam', he speaks in the language, as was only fitting, of the classical liberal contract theorists. For Locke, Adam's sovereignty over Eve has 'a Foundation in Nature for it'.[87] In his 'First Treatise', Locke argues that Eve's natural subjugation is such that 'every Husband hath to order the things of private Concernment in his Family as Proprietor of the Goods and Lands there and to have his Will take place before that of his wife in all things of their common concernment'.[88] For Pufendorf, however, conjugal right, while squaring with 'the condition of human nature' has to be secured 'by her consent, or by a just war'. Yet, because, for Pufendorf, it is 'the most natural thing' for marriages to come about through good will, man's conjugal rights originate in the wife's 'voluntary subjection' to the 'unequal league' of marriage.[89]

Carole Pateman points out that in these redefinitions of contract law a paradox emerges: women are by nature rendered incapable of equal contract with men under political law (since women are naturally subordinate), yet women can and must make marriage contracts (since marriage was to be seen as a matter of consent, not coercion). Through these debates, liberal theory formed an ideological distinction between individual freedom and the right to contract of the political sphere, and the refusal of the right to such political status within the domestic, conjugal sphere. Thus, as Pateman puts it, marriage remained a legal anomaly in that it 'retains a natural status even in civil society'.[90]

The invented distinction between the 'natural' sphere of the family and the 'political' sphere of civic society was indispensable to the formation of middle-class male identity because it was employed to restrict the liberal notion of sovereign individuality to European men of propertied descent. With the alibi of imperial nature, women, slaves, servants and the colonized could be excluded from liberal individuality. The emergence of the rational liberal individual thereby took shape around the reinvention of the domestic sphere as the realm of natural subjugation, just as the realm of the 'primitive' was the realm of natural racial subjugation. Domesticity and empire merge as a necessary element in the formation of the liberal imagination.

Cullwick's slave-band was the visible embodiment of these contradictions. The wife's voluntary, verbal submission: ('I do') represents a ceremonial display of hegemony as the woman 'voluntarily' enters a social relation of inequality with her husband, which grants him henceforth the legal right of coercion over her. In short, the wife's contract is a contract *out* of hegemony *into* coercion.[91] Cullwick's slave-band exposes a fundamental contradiction within classical liberal theory: women are *naturally* like slaves and thus *cannot* make contracts, but women *must* enter into contracts in order to become wives and thereby waive their right to contract-making.

Cullwick tartly brushed aside Munby's patronizing suggestion that she should be grateful to him for marrying her: 'Before the visitors came, Munby show'd me a license he had bought – a marriage licence – for him and me, & he said, "Doesn't this show how much I love you, & what do you say to it?" I told him I had nothing to say about it, but I hoped he would never be sorry for it, nor I. Tho' I seem'd so cool & said so little I really meant what I said. I car'd very very little for the licence or being married either.'[92] She would not brook Munby's condescending notion of their marriage 'as a reward to me for I want no reward', and deeply resented the social reality of the marriage license as an 'outward bond': 'I seem to hate the word marriage in that sense.'[93]

Cullwick's marriage to Munby was, in virtually every respect, an accumulation of transgressions. By insisting on wages from Munby for her services, by contracting herself out to work as she pleased, by keeping her own money (though she asked Munby to manage it for her), Cullwick set herself against the fundamental edicts of Victorian marital law. Indeed, she put quietly and stubbornly into practice what feminists fought for for the rest of the century: the right to control her body, her labor, her money and her reproductive freedom, all the more remarkable and empowering for the fact that it took place within the context of enormous social disempowerment.

By living as Munby's 'symbolic slave', while in effect coming and going as she pleased, Cullwick negotiated a degree of power that would otherwise have been well-nigh impossible. By living independently of a marital household, she avoided contracting herself in marriage as a working-class man's legal possession. 'I made my mind up that it was best & safest to be a slave to a gentleman, nor wife & equal to any vulgar man.'[94] Her marriage to Munby remained a purely titular affair, and she never surrendered her birth name. Most importantly, by refusing to live openly as a wife, Cullwick avoided having children; quite clearly, she had no desire to be a mother. On the contrary, she commented commiseratingly on a cousin of hers: 'I was glad I wasn't a mother of a little family like her . . . for after all however natural it's very troublesome & after they grow up generally a great anxiety.'[95]

Cullwick would not countenance the ennui and dependence of being a wife nor the sacrifices attendant upon having children:

> Ah Ellen – the music's nice, & the easy chair is nice, but for being among the grand folks or drest up like 'em & all that I'd fifty times rather be all black among the grate cleaning. And which is the most lasting of the two, & which is the solidest & real pleasure?

She much preferred the freedom of 'downstairs' and frequently relished the freedom of public mobility her low status gave her:

> I can work at ease. I can go out & come in when I please. . . . all the years I've walked about London nobody has ever spoke to me wrongly, & I don't think they will if you're drest plain & walk on about your own business.[96]

In these complex ways, the realm of fetishism was for Cullwick an arena of contestation and negotiation. She claimed the right to manipulate the theatrical *signs* of lowliness in order to refuse the legitimacy of their value as *nature*. Far from seeing marriage as the gift of progress, she refused the 'grand idea of the nineteenth century' by choosing the value of her work over the muffled ennui and bondage of marriage. Refusing to barter her unruly working-class strength for the halter of respectability, she decked herself in her own symbolic chains and dramatically threw into question the Victorian narrative of progress and the heterosexual Family of Man.

NOTES

1. Cullwick writes that, before she met Munby, God showed her his face in a fiery vision. Munby similarly exults: 'For on the 26th May, 1854, she was brought to me . . . by him who brought Eve to Adam'. Liz Stanley, *The Diaries of Hannah Cullwick: Victorian Maidservant* (New Brunswick: Rutgers University Press, 1984), p. 1. Munby, 'Diary', in Derek Hudson, *Munby, Man of Two Worlds: The Life and Diaires of Arthur J. Munby 1812–1910* (Cambridge: Gambit, 1974), p. 76.
2. Walter Benjamin, *Charles Baudelaire: A Lyric Poet in the Era of High Capitalism* (London: Verso, 1973), p. 62.
3. Leonore Davidoff, 'Class and Gender in Victorian England', in Judith L. Newton, Mary P. Ryan and Judith R. Walkowitz (eds), *Sex and Class in Women's History* (London: Routledge & Kegan Paul, 1983), pp. 16–71. See also Davidoff's brilliant work on domestic relations in 'Above and Below Stairs', *New Society* 26 (1973): pp. 181–3; and 'Mastered for Life: Servant and Wife in Victorian and Edwardian England', *Journal of Social History* 7 (1974): pp. 406–28. I am indebted throughout these pages to Davidoff's work as well as to her collaborative, groundbreaking work with Catherine Hall, *Family Fortunes: Men and Women of the English Middle Class, 1780–1850* (London and Chicago: Hutchinson and Chicago University Press, 1987).
4. Munby was a devotee of Ruskin, and Carlyle's notions of elevation through servitude became the basis for what he regarded as his 'training' of Cullwick in the lessons of domestic submission (though he had no intention of applying Carlyle's principles to himself).
5. Hudson acknowledges that the Munby diaries are as much hers as his, but he proceeds well-nigh to ignore hers, and effectively erases Cullwick's perspective.
6. Munby, 'Diary', July 19, 1894. Quoted in Stanley, *Diaries of Hannah Cullwick*, p. 12. Munby excised the descriptions of these 'trainings' from his diary.
7. Hudson, *Munby*, p. 70.

8. Hudson, *Munby*, p. 4.
9. Davidoff, 'Class and Gender', p. 58.
10. Ibid., pp. 38, 40.
11. It is worth noting, moreover, that Munby is accorded, by all these critics, the social status of an adult, referred to as Munby, while Cullwick is infantilized and denied full social status by being referred to only as 'Hannah'.
12. Stanley, *Diaries of Hannah Cullwick*, p. 11.
13. Ibid., p. 2.
14. Ibid. p. 1. For interpretations of women's work, and of the relations between women's work and economic development, see Davidoff and Hall, *Family Fortunes*; Patricia Branca, *Women in Europe Since 1750* (London: Croom Helm, 1978); Joan W. Scott and Louise Tilly, *Women, Work and Family* (New York: Holt, Reinhart and Winston, 1978); Sally Alexander, 'Women's Work in Nineteenth Century London: A Study of the Years 1820–1850', in Juliet Mitchell and Ann Oakley (eds), *The Rights and Wrongs of Women* (Harmondsworth: Penguin, 1976): Sandra Burman (ed.), *Fit Work for Women* (New York: St. Martin's Press, 1979); Barbara Taylor, 'The Men are as Bad as Their Masters . . .: Socialism, Feminism and Sexual Antagonism in the London Tailoring Trade in the 1830s', in Newton, Ryan and Walkowitz (eds), *Sex and Class*, pp. 187–220; Christine Delphy, trans. Diana Leonard, *Close to Home: A Materialist Analysis of Women's Oppression* (Amherst: University of Massachusetts Press, 1984); and Angela John, *By the Sweat of Their Brow: Women Workers at Victorian Coal Mines* (London: Routledge, 1984).
15. Munby graduated from Trinity College, Cambridge, in 1851, the same year Cullwick arrived in London, and entered Lincoln's Inn in June. For the next five years he lived in lodgings, then entered the chambers on the first floor of 6 Fig Tree Court in the Temple in 1857, which he would retain until his death. On January 2, 1859, Munby began employment as a clerk with the Ecclesiastical Commission.
16. Stanley, *Diaries of Hannah Cullwick*, p. 40.
17. Ibid., p. 14.
18. Ibid., p. 15.
19. Ibid., p. 15.
20. Michel Foucault, *Madness and Civilization* (1961; rpt. London: Routledge, 1993). Let me emphasize here that, by S/M, I refer to the subculture of consensual, reciprocal S/M and not to involuntary abuse. I am also aware that these do not mark absolute extremes but rather a continuum, and that some relationships inhabit the twilight threshold in between.
21. For a detailed exploration of S/M, see my essay on S/M and gender power, 'Maid to Order: Commercial S/M and Gender Power', in Pamela Church Gibson and Roma Gibson (eds), *Dirty Looks* (London: British Film Institute, 1993), pp. 207–31.
22. Foucault, *Madness and Civilization*, p. 124.
23. Erving Goffman, *Frame Analysis* (New York: Harper and Row, 1974), p. 36.
24. Paul H. Gebhard, 'Sadomasochism', in Thomas Weinberg and G. W. Levi Kamel, *S and M: Studies in Sadomasochism* (Buffalo: Prometheus Books, 1983), p. 39.
25. Richard von Krafft-Ebing, 'From *Psychopathia Sexualis*', in Weinberg and Kamel, *S and M*, p. 27.
26. Munby, 'Diary', May 26, 1854, in Hudson, *Munby*, p. 15.
27. Ibid., p. 70. Robert L. Stevenson, likewise, called his nanny: 'My second Mother, my first wife/ The Angel of my infant life' in Janet Adam Smith (ed.), *Collected Poems* (London: Rupert Hart-Davis, 1951), p. 361.
28. Hudson, *Munby*, p. 329.
29. Ibid., p. 108.
30. Munby's own attempts to pose as a working-class man were short-lived and were greeted with much hilarity by Cullwick.

31. In Robin Ruth Linden, et al. (eds), *Against Sadomasochism: A Radical Feminist Analysis* (San Francisco: Frog in the Well, 1982), p. 28.

32. Male 'bottoms' will frequently enact scripts framed by the 'degradation' of female domesticity: compulsive sweeping, cleaning, laundering, under a regime of verbal taunts, insults and calumnies. Some dominatrixes keep 'pets' who regularly do their housework. See McClintock, 'Maid to Order', pp. 207–31.

33. Munby's fetish for infantilism is a common one in S/M: 'There's a whole area of deviant behaviour called Babyism where the client likes to dress up in a nappy, suck a giant dummy or one of her breasts and just be rocked.' Allegra Taylor, *Prostitution: What's Love Got to Do with It?* (London: Optima, 1991), p. 39.

34. Hudson, *Munby*, p. 116.

35. Sigmund Freud, *Three Essays on the Theory of Sexuality* (New York: Basic Books, 1962), p. 23.

36. Weinberg and Levi Kamel, *S and M*, p. 20.

37. Stanley, *Diaries of Hannah Cullwick*, p. 307.

38. Hudson, *Munby*, p. 184.

39. William Pietz, 'The Problem of the Fetish, II', *Res* 13 (Spring 1987): p. 34.

40. Stanley, *Diaries of Hannah Cullwick*, p. 37.

41. As Cullwick observes, 'I have hardly ever met wi' a servant yet who wasn't ashamed o' dirty work.' Stanley, *Diaries of Hannah Cullwick*, p. 96.

42. Ibid., p. 76.

43. Mary Douglas, *Purity and Danger* (London: Routledge and Kegan Paul, 1966). See also Davidoff, 'The Rationalization of Housework', in Diana Leonard and Sheila Allen (eds), *Sexual Divisions Revisted* (Basingstoke: Macmillan, 1991), p. 63.

44. Peter Fryer, S*taying Power: The History of Black People in Britain* (London: Pluto Press, 1984), p. 22. The commercial signs of tobacconists and innkeepers often featured black people as the fetish signs of the trade in humans. Black slaves owned by titled families were customarily decked in showy livery, jeweled eardrops, laced cuffs and ornate waistcoats and breeches.

45. Wanda Fraiken Neff, *Victorian Working Women: An Historical and Literary Study of Women in British Industries and Professions, 1832–1850* (New York: Columbia University Press, 1929).

46. Ibid., p. 186.

47. 'Dismissed from the diary, the confectionary, the store-room, the still-room, the poultry-yard, the kitchen-garden, and the orchard,' as Margaretta Grey put it, 'she shut the doors of laboring society behind her and repaired upstairs for the rest of the century to languish on sofas in haughty listlessness.' Quoted in Pearsall, p. 97.

48. Neff, *Victorian Working Women*, p. 187. Her duty, if one recalls Ruskin's disturbing and memorable essay, 'Of Queens Gardens', was simply 'to assist in the ordering, in the comforting, and in the beautiful adornment of the state'. 'Of Queens Gardens', in E. T. Cook and A. D. O. Wedderburn (eds), *The Complete Works of John Ruskin*, (London, 1902–12.), vol. 18, p. 122.

49. Baldwin Brown exhorted women to comfort their 'world-weary men' in a home 'like a bright, serene, restful, joyful nook of heaven in an unheavenly world'. *Young Men and Maidens: A Pastoral for the Times* (London: Hodder and Stoughton, 1871) pp. 38–9.

50. E. P. Hood, *The Age and Its Architects: Ten Chapters on the English People, in Relation to the Times* (London, 1850, 1852), quoted in Walter Houghton, *The Victorian Frame of Mind* (New Haven: Yale University Press, 1957), p. 354.

50a. Patricia Branca, *Silent Sisterhood: Middle-Class Women in the Victorian Home* (London: Croom Helm 1975).

51. Nancy Armstrong, 'The Rise of the Domestic Woman', in Nancy Armstrong and Leonard Tennenhouse (eds), *The Ideology of Conduct: Essays in Literature and the history of Sexuality* (London: Methuen, 1987).

52. Home, as imagined in Ruskin's exemplary and roseate evocation, became 'the place

of Peace; the shelter, not only from all injury, but from all terror, doubt, and division'. The fortified embrace of Ruskin's 'little rose-covered wall' barricaded the hearth from the bloodied bruit and conflict of trade. Secluded within this 'sacred place, a vestal temple', true womanliness offered a 'centre of order, the balm of distress, and the mirror of beauty'. Beyond the wall of domesticity, 'the wild grass of the horizon, is torn up by the agony of men, and beat level by the drift of their life-blood'. 'Of Queens Gardens', pp. 60, 72, 76.

53. Neff, *Victorian Working Women*, p. 187. Neff sums up a prevailing view: 'The practice of female idleness spread through the middle-class until work for women became a misfortune and a disgrace'. Sir Charles Petrie obediently follows suit, though with no apparent compunction to cite his source: 'It became the sign of a man's importance that he kept his women-folk in idleness . . . The example spread through the middle-class, until work for women became a misfortune and a disgrace.' Petrie concludes: 'Few aspects of modern society are as well documented as the middle-class woman of the nineteenth century, with whom contemporary fiction so largely dealt . . . The Victorian heroine was an almost standardized product.' *The Victorians* (New York: Longmans, 1961). J. A. Banks's influential *Prosperity and Parenthood* only further expanded the idea that the very formation of middle-class identity depended on aping the 'paraphernalia of gentility' of the upper class, at the heart of which was the idea of the 'idle woman', and he has been followed in this by critic after critic. J. A. Banks, *Prosperity and Parenthood: A Study of Family Planning Among the Victorian Middle Classes* (London: Routledge, 1954).

54. 'The lifestyle of the bourgeois lady', as Jeffrey Weeks puts it, 'was purchased at the expense of a large class of servants'. Jeffrey Weeks, *Sex, Politics and Society: The Regulation of Sexuality Since 1800* (London: Longman, 1981), p. 40. The keeping of servants was seen by many historians as the principle source of middle-class identity. In 1899 Seebohm Rowntree took 'the keeping or not keeping of domestic servants' as the dividing line between the 'working classes and those of a higher social scale'. Quoted in Pamela Horn, *The Rise and Fall of the Victorian Servant* (Stroud: Alan Sutton, 1986), p. 17. As the wife of an English surgeon insisted: 'I must not do our household work, or carry our baby out: or I shall lose caste. We must keep a servant.' Horn, p. 18. J. F. C. Harrison concurs that employing servants 'went to the very heart of the idea of class itself'.

55. In 1975, Patricia Branca began to question the image of the middle-class woman as 'an odd museum piece', disparaged either as the butt of criticism or the object of a patronizing sympathy. Critically analyzing domestic, cooking, child-care and housekeeping manuals, Branca began to ask questions about the verisimilitude of the fictional idle woman and the referential authority of the critics' sources. Patricia Branca, *Silent Sisterhood*, p. 186.

56. Ibid., p. 186.

57. In Anthony Trollope's *Last Chronicle of Barset* the family struggles to maintain one servant while their carpets are in rags and the furniture broken.

58. Privileged members of the upper middle classes, such as large farmers or well-heeled rectors, might have enjoyed the services of a coachman or gardener, a cook, a nurse-maid and a couple of housemaids, while the traditional servant-keeping classes, the aristocracy and the large landed families, often kept 'armies' of retainers so large that they constituted a settlement as large as a small village'. Branca, *Silent Sisterhood*, p. 20.

59. See Davidoff and Hall, *Family Fortunes*.

60. E. P. Thompson, for example, notes that domestic work was the largest labor category for women apart from agricultural work, yet he pays no attention whatsoever to the history and conditions of this work. *The Making of the English Working Class* (New York: Vintage, 1966). See Joan Scott's excellent critique of Thompson's gender politics in Scott, *Gender and the Politics of History* (New York: Columbia University Press, 1988), ch. 4.

61. Here one can question Irigaray's notion of mimicry as resistance. This may sometimes be the case; at other times it may not.

62. This was an exhausting aggravation for over-burdened workers and a common source of complaint. Davidoff, 'Class and Gender', p. 54.

63. The very definition of a 'lady' came to be her distance from profit. 'A Lady . . . must not work for profit or engage in any occupation that money can command'. 'The occupations of women engaged in any business or profession . . . must be fully stated. No entry should be made in the case of wives, daughters or other female relatives wholly engaged in domestic duties at home.' Quoted in Sandra Burman, *Fit Work for Women*, p. 67.

64. Armstrong, 'The Rise of the Domestic Woman', pp. 96–141.

65. Max Weber, *The Protestant Ethic and the Spirit of Capitalism* (London: Unwin University Books, 1971), p. 235. Quoted in Davidoff, 'The Rationalization of Housework'. The virtues of a rationalized domestic economy hark back to the morality of Roman husbandry and appear again in European monasticism and again in Puritan and Nonconformist tracts. As Weber put it: 'The Reformation took Christian asceticism and its methodical habits out of the monasteries and placed them in the service of active life in the world.'

66. Davidoff and Hall, *Family Fortunes*.

67. Roland Barthes, *Sade, Fourier, Loyola* (New York: Farrar, Straus and Girioux, 1976).

68. A popular maxim gave eloquent expression to the suffusing of domestic time with rational measurement and commodification: 'Lost yesterday, somewhere between sunrise and sunset/ Two golden hours, each set with sixty diamond minutes.'

69. Robert J. Stoller, *Observing the Erotic Imagination* (New Haven: yale University Press, 1985), p. 155.

70. Marjorie Garber, *Vested Interests: Cross-Dressing and Cultural Authority* (New York: Routledge, 1992), p. 21. As Garber notes (though she does not discuss the relation to empire): 'the term sumptuary is related to "consumption" – the flaunting of wealth by those whose class or other social designation made such display seem transgressive,' p. 21.

71. Ibid., p. 25.

72. Ibid., p. 26.

73. William Jerdan (ed.), 'The Rutland Papers', in *Camden Society Publications*, # 22, p. 247. Quoted in Garber, *Vested Interests*, p. 26.

74. Garber, *Vested Interests*, p. 70.

75. Ibid., p. 32.

76. Ibid., p. 17.

77. Garber, *Vested Interests*, p. 10. Garber argues persuasively that critics of cross-dressing such as Elaine Showalter, Stephen Greenblatt, Sandra Gilbert and Susan Gubar have tended, in different ways, to 'look away from the transsexual as transvestite' seeking a core gender identity beneath the transvestite mask.

78. Garber, *Vested Interests*, p. 149.

79. *Diaries of Hannah Cullwick*, p. 274.

80. Quoted in Garber, *Vested Interests*, pp. 329–30.

81. *Diaries of Hannah Cullwick*, p. 266.

82. Christine Delphy, *Close to Home*, p. 92.

83. Jean Jacques Rousseau, *Emile, or on Education*, trans. by A. Bloom (new York: Basic Books, 1979), p. 404.

84. *Diaries of Hannah Cullwick*, p. 188.

85. In Greek and Roman tradition, the family was, by definition, that extended community of people over which the pater familias had sovereign jurisdiction, owning the rights of life, property and labor of wives, slaves and children. The comparison of wives and slaves continued after the late seventeenth century. Mary Astell opined that all 'women were born slaves'.

86. Carole Pateman, *The Sexual Contract* (Cambridge: Polity with Basil Blackwell, 1988), p. 51.
87. Quoted in Pateman, *The Sexual Contract*, p. 52.
88. Ibid., p. 53.
89. Ibid., p. 51.
90. Ibid., p. 55.
91. Under the law, wives were classed with criminals, idiots and minors. Under coverture, a woman's personal property passed into the absolute possession of her husband. Legally, he could dispose of it in any way he chose. He could legally leave neither his wife nor children anything in his will. If a husband died intestate, the wife received only half at best. If the wife died intestate, all her property remained his absolutely. A wife could not enter into contracts except as her husband's agent. Under coverture, then, marriage was tantamount to systematic, legalized theft.
92. *Diaries of Hannah Cullwick*, p. 253.
93. Cullwick's loathing for the 'outward bond' of marriage is bluntly echoed by Daniel Defoe's *Roxana*, whose heroine proclaims: 'The very Nature of the Marriage-Contract was, in short, nothing but giving up Liberty, Estate, Authority, and everything, to the Man, and the Woman was indeed a mere Woman ever after, that is to say, a Slave.' Quoted in Pateman, p. 120.
94. *Diaries of Hannah Cullwick*, p. 273.
95. Ibid., p. 238.
96. Ibid., p. 181.

6.3

'EARTH HONORING: WESTERN DESIRES AND INDIGENOUS KNOWLEDGES'[1]

Jane M. Jacobs

With each sign that gives language its shape lies a stereotype of which I/i am both the manipulator and the manipulated.[2]

Recent developments in environmentalism and feminism have intensified Western desires to affiliate with indigenous people and to call upon their knowledges and experiences. In settler Australia, alliances have developed between feminists, environmentalists, and Aborigines seeking to have their interests in land recognized. Within the Australian setting, environmentalists have presumed accordance between their interests and those of Aboriginal Australians seeking land rights. Similarly, many non-Aboriginal women's groups have presumed that the land struggles of Aboriginal women resonate with their struggles against patriarchy. As the case of settler Australia testifies, such alliances do not escape the politics of colonialism and patriarchy. In particular, there are specific problems arising from the essentialized notions of Aboriginality and woman that underpin radical environmentalisms and feminisms. Yet to read these alliances only in terms of the reiteration of a politics of Western, masculinist supremacy neglects the positive engagement indigenous women may make with such 'sympathizers' in their efforts to verify and amplify their struggles for land rights.

I will begin with a critical examination of the colonial and patriarchal potentials of recent radical environmentalisms and feminisms. The analysis then

From: Jane M. Jacobs (1994), 'Earth Honoring: Western Desires and Indigenous Knowledges', pp. 169–96, in A. Blunt and G Rose (eds), *Writing Women and Space: Colonial and Postcolonial Geographies* (London: Routledge).

turns to the Australian setting, where I establish a historical context by over-viewing the ways settler discourses have gendered both the Australian land-scape and Aboriginal knowledges of that landscape. I next examine the recent history of political alliances between environmentalists and women's groups and Aborigines. Finally I focus on a specific example of one such political alli-ance, which formed around the struggle by the Arrernte people of central Australia to stop the flooding of women's sacred sites for the purpose of creat-ing a recreational lake/flood mitigation dam for the residents of Alice Springs.[3] This case provides a specific example through which the troubled intersection of environmentalism, feminism, and indigenous rights can be explored.

My analysis of this particular political alliance requires some explanation. In moving from the political terrain of environmentalisms and feminisms to an analysis of practical political alliances, I move into an ethically uncertain realm of describing Aboriginal political discourse and action. In part, my reading of this political alliance focuses on environmentalist and feminist affiliations with the Aboriginal cause. As such, my concern is with non-Aboriginal depictions of Aboriginal interests and the logic of non-Aboriginal expressions of sympathy for the Arrernte struggle. That is, Arrernte discourses are presented in terms of the ways in which they appear within and are spoken about in white settler dis-courses and thereby in relation to the power structures of colonialist Australia.[4] This maneuver may appear politically correct because it is social construction-ist in its emphasis. However, such approaches are not released from certain dif-ficulties that continue to sustain colonialist power relations. Even in the presence of an empowered voice of the 'other', the move to social construction-ism has the potential to more complexly and deeply reinscribe colonialist con-structions and thereby rerender the 'other' passive.

Moreover, such perspectives presume that there is a clear distinction between Arrernte and non-Arrernte discourses/Aboriginal and non-Aboriginal dis-courses, and that there is a line beyond which I (and others) as a non-Aboriginal, a non-Arrernte, cannot step. I believe there are such lines. But I also believe that the politics of difference in contemporary settler nations like Australia exist in an interdiscursive political space, which is neither solely Aboriginal nor non-Aboriginal. Nor is this space singularly a domain of hybrid identity, for essentialist positions are present both as strategic and internally held realities. My concern in this chapter is with this political interspace. And in my efforts to examine this space I not only draw upon non-Aboriginal dis-courses but also take the 'risk' of making contextualized readings of Aboriginal statements and political actions.

New Environmentalisms, Feminisms and Indigenous Knowledges

Recent elaborations in Western environmental and feminist thought have heightened interest in 'non-Western' peoples and peoples of color in the West. In environmentalism this is most clearly expressed within certain strands of Deep Ecology. For feminism, reconciling issues of gender difference with racial difference has been a major challenge and is variously expressed. On the one hand, there has been an embellishment of the concept of universal patriarchy by 'adding' the experiences of Third World women and women of color. In a more radical position, similar to Deep Ecology, ecofeminists turn to 'non-Western' women to provide guidance for an alternative society. Radical environmentalism and environmental feminism both provide a relevant insight into the racial and neocolonial implications of this attention to 'non-Western' peoples.

Environmentalism has long depended upon Western rational thought and in particular upon scientific thought to argue its case against the on-going exploitation of the environment. In this sense it may be interpreted as having depended upon masculinist knowledges in order to challenge exploitative, masculinist and colonialist approaches to the environment.[5] In recent years other forms of knowledge have become more central to environmental philosophy and politics. In particular, there has been a conscious insertion of critical 'otherness' into environmentalist thinking by means of ecocentric and ecofeminist perspectives.[6] Deriving from this movement has been a turn to 'women's knowledges' and to 'indigenous knowledges', which are seized upon as providing cultural models for a modernity that might construct itself not around masculinist anthropocentrism, but through a decentered subjectivity – a part of, and at one with nature. The spiritualism and holistic visions of indigenous peoples readily accords with more radical strands of environmentalism.

Let me turn first to ecocentric environmentalism or Deep Ecology. Ecocentric environmentalism recognizes a moral value in the nonhuman world and stresses the interconnectedness of the living and the nonliving, the human and the nonhuman.[7] Ecocentrism argues against centering human interests (anthropocentrism) and instead locates nonhuman interests as central to decision making. This is a radical subjectivity, a 'transpersonality' that advocates the development of a wider sense of self to include all beings and all things.[8]

Knudston and Suzuki's *Wisdom of the Elders* provides a popular advocacy of such radical subjectivity and explicitly turns to 'Native peoples' and their intellectual and experiential insights for guidance into 'proper human relationships with the natural world'.[9] For Suzuki, the turn to indigenous wisdoms is a specific response to the failure of scientific wisdom. The struggle of indigenous peoples to protect their land has automatic accordance with the objectives of his own environmentalism:

> If biodiversity and ecosystem integrity are critical to salvaging some of the skin of life on earth, then every successful fight to protect the land of indigenous peoples is a victory for all of humanity and other living things.[10]

The diverse cultures that carry the indigenous knowledges Knudston and Suzuki honor are drawn together under the generic descriptor 'the First People of the world'; these are people with a lineage to precolonial and premodern times. Under the generic label of 'First People', cultural diversity is transgressed by a 'shared primary ecological perspective', thereby emptying these groups of the specificities of their histories and geographies. The First People are located within a global chronology, which begins with them and ends with an environmentally sound 'us'. At the hands of Knudston and Suzuki, indigenous knowledges are drawn into more contemporaneous global discourses of environmentalism that seek the preservation of the planet.

James Lovelock's christening of the earth as 'Gaia', after the 'wide-bosomed' earth goddess of Greek mythology, explicitly genders this 'total planetary being'.[11] The feminized 'planet Gaia' is shown 'undisguised love, respect and awe'. It is 'embraced' as 'Mother Earth', guardian of the extended human/non-human family. Deep Ecology center's a specific familial organization which, within Western thought and practice, has long been confined to a feminized domain. The ecocentric perspective struggles to free itself from patriarchal assumptions about sexual difference. Indigenous peoples are seen to be specially placed to understand the feminized planet. It is not surprising that Burger has provided Gaia followers with a much needed 'atlas' of 'First People' – a spatial guide to those 'indispensable partners' in the movement towards a 'sustainable future on our precious plane'.[12] The atlas maps indigenous peoples as the surface custodians of the feminized planet. Marked on the map, the 'West' captures the geography of ecological knowledge. Such mappings of ecological knowledge banks may well be part of the serious and urgent quest for planetary survival; but they are just as likely to circulate, as they do in *Body Shop* marketing, as part of the paraphernalia of global green consumerism – take home souvenirs for the environmentally aware shopper.

Ecofeminism shares with transpersonal ecocentrism a relational image of nature, but ecofeminism stresses the historic and symbolic association of women with nature.[13] Ecofeminists embrace the woman/nature association as a source of empowerment and the basis of a critique of patriarchal domination and the exploitation of both women and nature. Eckersley argues that this is a project that explicitly exposes and celebrates that which was once regarded as 'other' by masculinist visions and consistently reclaims the 'undervalued nurturing characteristics of women'.[14] Ecofeminism engages positively with essentialist understandings of the feminine. Some ecofeminists build upon the 'body-based' assumption that woman's reproductive self predisposes her to being a caregiver, which extends to the nurture of nature. Other ecofeminisms build upon the 'culture-based' assumption that women and nature share the experience of patriarchal oppression and exploitation.[15]

Janet Biehl argues that ecofeminism takes male characterizations of women and turns them into an 'ideology that roots women outside of Western culture altogether'.[16] For example, Spretnak suggests that women have a unique biological disposition that provides them with an ecologically sympathetic sense of 'boundarylessness', allowing them to know all others, natural and cultural.[17] Thus formed, ecofeminism can turn to nonhierarchical pre-Christian cultures and earth-based traditional cultures for validation and inspiration.[18] Biehl refers to this as 'the Neolithic mystique'.[19]

The reclaiming of traditions takes a variety of forms in contemporary ecofeminist writings and practices. Celtic and Neolithic cultures are a popular source of guidance for many Western ecofeminist retrievals, particularly if they are documented as matrilineal or matriarchal and were based around a specifically female deity. Increasingly, however, it is not to the past that ecofeminists turn but to contemporary non-Western cultures. This shift is consistent with, but not identical to, wider trends within feminism that attempt to address the experiences of Third World women and women of color. In countries with colonial histories it is often local indigenous cultures that give guidance. Mellor provides a detailed account of the ways in which matrilineal clan societies of North America have provided environmentalists with a regular and locally relevant inspiration.[20] For example, in Carolyn Merchant's ecohistorical account of development in New England, Native Americans are both victims of colonialism and custodians of knowledges which provide clues for future ecosocieties.[21] Similarly, Rogers argues that the 'experiences of women from societies with remaining links to matrilineal traditions may prove instructive to feminists from industrialised countries who wish to explore a better relationship with the land'.[22]

It should not be presumed that the cultures of Third World women and women of color are only passively appropriated into Western ecofeminist positions. Maori writer Ngahuia Te Awekotuku provides direct testimony concerning the need for the environmentalist project to look to other cultures.[23] Similarly, Vandana Shiva's ecofeminist account of colonialist exploitation of women and nature combines an unusual attention to historical processes with a visionary prescription for the universal adoption of the 'transgendered creative force . . . Prakrita', in order to combat Western gendered objectifications of nature.[24]

Ecofeminist perspectives draw much criticism, not least from other feminists. In the first instance, there is consistent criticism of the way in which the identification of women with nature 'speciously biologizes the personality traits that patricentric society assigns to women'.[25] As Shiva's work shows, even when the women/nature/nurture concept is supplemented by an acknowledgement of its socially constructed form and historical specificity, it remains a central theme in ecofeminist political visions. Biehl argues that this raises important ethical questions about a feminist ecological movement that builds upon an essentialist 'falsehood' of 'woman', the refutation of which has been a key theme in feminist writings since Simone de Beauvoir. Others have criticized ecofeminist retrievals of clan and Neolithic societies for being romanticized reconstructions that neglect evidence of patriarchal domination and environmental exploitation.[26]

The attention to other cultures contained within ecofeminism has the appearance of a feminism sensitive to difference. Radical feminism may presume a history of Western patriarchy, but more spiritually derived versions often neglect imperial histories and the impact they have had on racialized and colonized groups. Concepts of interconnectednes can stop short of incorporating the uneven histories of global capitalism.[27] Breaking down the boundaries within ourselves and between ourselves may be a necessary step on the path to global survival but this path travels across a terrain marked by inequality.[28] The recourse to an original femininity does not necessarily transcend such uneven geographies and Judith Butler argues that such nostalgia leads to exclusionary rather than inclusionary practices.[29]

It is from women of color that the most trenchant criticisms of such feminisms of difference and particularly the ecofeminist desire for indigenous knowledge has come. Winona LaDuke argues that some New Age environmentalisms have 'commodified' indigenous cultures.

> What is happening is that our culture is taken out of context and certain parts of it are sold or just extracted. It's like mining . . . Certain things are taken out and certain people are practising those things in their own ways, and to me, that's appropriation of our culture. It's the same thing as expropriating our wild rice or our land. And it is one of the last things we have. It is our culture.[30]

After a colonial history of subjugation and exploitation, these women are rightly suspicious of the West's new fascination with difference. Western feminisms of differences are placing new pressures upon indigenous women and women of color. Audre Lorde criticizes this process:

> Now we hear that it is the task of black and third world women to educate white women, in the face of tremendous resistance, as to our existence, our differences, our relative roles in our joint survival. This is a diversion of energies and a tragic repetition of racist patriarchal thought.[31]

Ecocentric and ecofeminist environmentalisms are coalitional political formations under a guise of celebrated difference. It should not be presumed that such cross-cultural extensions of ecocentric and ecofeminist environmentalisms can divest themselves of colonialist trappings. These eco-driven reclamation processes are unsettlingly similar to earlier forms of colonialist appropriations, such as the museum practices of imperial science, and retain the potential for reinscribing patriarchal and colonialist constructs and practices.[32] Ecofeminist and ecocentric positions depend upon unifying modes of subjectivity, such as women with nature or Western and premodern/non-Western cultures. At one level they seem to celebrate difference, but at another level they obliterate difference through reductionist concepts of 'oneness'.[33] In such environmentalisms and feminisms, 'otherness' becomes an 'imaginary space' for 'uniting subjectivities' in Western universalist objectives.[34]

There is of course a significant gap between these philosophical positions and the everyday practices of environmentalists and feminists in, say, Australia. Not all environmentalists consciously follow an ecocentric or ecofeminist philosophical position. And certainly most active conservationists and feminists would be shocked to consider their well-meaning support of Aboriginal land issues to be colonialist or patriarchal. This question of consciousness does not seem to concern ecocentric and ecofeminist philosophers. Hay argues that 'ecocentrism is an unarticulated impulse common to most environmentalists'.[35] Carolyn Merchant claims the environmental action of minority women worldwide as part of the ecofeminist movement: 'They might not call themselves ecofeminists, but that is what they are doing.'[36] The relationship between political practices and a consciousness of particular philosophical positions is problematic when attempting to trace connections between the politics of such positionings and everyday political practices. Such linkages may be faintly marked. But in the coalitional politics of environmentalists, feminists, and Aboriginal rights in Australia there is the possibility of seeing more clearly the interweaving of these broader positions and their political effects.

She Land/He Sacred: Land, Gender and Indigenous People in Settler Australia

Kay Schaffer argues that in the early history of masculinist settler Australia a woman's presence was registered through metaphors of landscape. Drawing on Irigaray's notion of woman as 'the scene' of rival exchanges between men, Schaffer argues that Australian colonization was of a land 'imagined, through metaphor, as the body of a woman'. Schaffer continues:

> For centuries Australia existed as an empty space on the map of the world, as a body of desire. Man, as the agent of history, confronted raw nature, as a vast and empty Other, and named it his Australia Felix. The land has taken on the attributes of masculine desire. This desire acts as a generative force in the narratives of exploration and settlement.[37]

Schaffer makes explicit the link between masculine (man, empire, civilization) and the subduing of the feminine (woman, earth, nature) in the settlement of Australia. The colonizing of Australia is enacted through patriarchal constructions of masculinity and femininity in which the land and women were collapsed into a single category.

If the land 'Australia' was feminized in the name of colonization and exploitation, then the indigenous inhabitants of the land were in many renditions conveniently consigned to that feminized nature. The declaration of Australia as *terra nullius* discursively emptied the nation. This emptying was an act of desire challenged by the realities of active Aboriginal resistance or merely a persistent Aboriginal presence. Early depictions of Aboriginal Australians often placed them as part of a feminized nature: sometimes passive, sometimes capricious or wild, but always to be invaded and possessed. Lattas argues, in relation to Australian art, that the land and the Aborigines are simultaneously aestheticized and spiritualized, with Aborigines always depicted as being 'in harmony' with the land. The feminized land, the pacified native, were to be dominated, exploited, possessed.[38] As historians Butcher and Turnbull suggest, the settler's perspectives did not provide the basis for 'an ecologically-sound understanding of the land'.[39] Aboriginal knowledges, they argue, were undervalued and the Aborigines themselves considered simply a nuisance to be Europeanized or eliminated.

Aborigines were not eliminated nor were they ever to become 'European'. Those in the more remote parts of settler Australia, who maintained tradition-oriented ways of life, came under the anthropological gaze. Early anthropological accounts of 'traditional' Aboriginal society were translated through the lens of Western patriarchy. There was a lack of acknowledgment of, or a denigration of, women's 'business', that is, the spiritual and ritual knowledges and practices managed by women. Male anthropologists either ignored the business of women or were denied access to it in accordance with the gender-specific restrictions of Aboriginal society. The spiritual knowledge and ritual practices of men were often assumed to provide for the entire community. Women were viewed as 'profane', participating in 'small-time' rituals and magic unconnected to the more important issues of land and social harmony.[40]

It was only when female anthropologists began entering the profession in Australia that an ethnography of Aboriginal women's business began to emerge.[41] Diane Bell's landmark ethnography of the Kaytej and Warlpiri women of central Australia provided the first detailed study of an empowered and autonomous women's spiritual and ritual life. *Daughters of the Dreaming* shook the foundations of masculinist readings of Aboriginal society. Bell challenged the view of Aboriginal women as 'feeders and breeders' servicing the loftier and more spiritual men. Bell's ethnography was crucial in asserting that Aboriginal women had important land-based traditions and were equally important as the men in maintaining the land. Bell writes:

> Aboriginal women ensure that harmonious relations between people and land will be maintained and that the land will continue to 'come up green'. They perform exclusively female rituals, yawulyu, for the country. . . . There are other ceremonies which men and women perform together. . . . A central responsibility of women is to nurture both people and land.[42]

Bell's ethnography helped redefine the parameters of legitimate claims to land. Women's sites were as important as those of men, they were as 'sacred' as those of men. The Dreaming may have contained songlines depicting male violence against women, but in practice women had much autonomy and power over the management of social relations. Bell's reinterpretation of gender roles and relations in traditional central Australian communities was to prove crucial in land claim controversies throughout the 1980s. It is a reinterpretation that also changed the nature of alliances between Aboriginal women and non-Aboriginal women. The shared experience of the violence of patriarchy was optimistically underwritten by a relic separatist environmentalist possibility contained in Kayetj social organization.

Almost a decade later, the centrality of women's business to Aboriginal culture was reaffirmed in Deborah Bird Rose's land-based history of the Yarralin people of Victoria River, in Western Australia. She explains that in Yarralin culture geographical areas are 'defined in relation to gender' and are 'imbued with the essence and secrets of femaleness or maleness'.[43] In Rose's account women and the feminized earth play a pivotal role:

> Men throughout the Victoria River District recognise that much of their secret ritual and Law ultimately derives from women Dreamings, just as all life originates in mother earth, and as they themselves are born of women.[44]

In Rose's view, 'When Yarralin people speak of mother Earth they speak to a similar understanding' to that of Lovelock's Gaia.[45] For the Yarralin, 'Dreaming and ecology intersect constantly'. But Rose's collapsing of Yarralin women's Dreaming into Western concepts of the 'Earth Mother' has not gone without comment. Swaine, for example, goes so far as to suggest that the notion of Mother Earth uncovered in Rose's ethnography is a 'reinvention', or more precisely, an elaboration, of indigenous concepts through Christian and ecological thought.[46] Swaine's critique rests uncomfortably on a notion of cultural hybridization and is ghosted by the problematic idea of a pristine authentic, that which really is (or was) Aboriginal, and which has been subsequently 'contaminated'.

According to Rose, Yarralin accord with contemporary environimentalism not only through the concept of Mother Earth. They also share the radical decentering of self and the 'boundarylessness' associated with ecocentric/ecofeminist positions:

> Boundaries between species are immutable; they are not, however, impenetrable. Clever people and clever animals can change their shape, disguising themselves as other species and learning to communicate with them. This is what it means to be clever – to be able to cross boundaries.[47]

In Rose's account, the Dreaming is embellished to become the 'Dreaming ecology . . . a political economy of intersubjectivity embedded in a system that has no centre'. Concomitant with this heightened intersubjectivity comes a fundamental wholeness in which 'there is no Other . . . there is only Us'. In her final chapter Rose explicitly links her account of Yarralin life to holistic ecovisions. It is here that the prescriptive role Yarralin life holds for global survival is articulated. Citing Carolyn Merchant, Rose reiterates the ecofeminist view that modernity is secular and that the lack of spiritual understanding has 'killed Nature'. The stories of the Yarralin are offered by Rose as 'possibilities' for finding answers to the 'difficult questions', raised by the damage being wrought upon the 'holistic Earth'.[48]

Diane Bell and Deborah Bird Rose confirm a significant shift in anthropological and academic understandings of Aboriginal knowledges of the land, a shift in which women's business and environmentalist and feminist projects are at one. In their attention to difference, these ethnographies displace ideas of universal patriarchy, but retain and embellish essentialized notions of women as nurturers of nature. While these ethnographies are attempting to reinstate the status of women in non-Aboriginal understandings of Aboriginal society (and in so doing, to write new maps of geography), they are also part of a Western feminist/environmentalist project in which Aboriginal gender and land relations serve a non-Aboriginal revisionary political agenda.

COALITIONAL POLITICS IN AUSTRALIA

Australian environmentalists have long seen Aboriginal Australians as the original conservationists. Sackett has noted the predominance of Aboriginal motifs and music as backdrop to populist 'wilderness' presentations in the media, as well as the abundance of literature on Aboriginal Australia in conservation shops.[49] The philosophical alliance between environmentalism and Aboriginal views of the land have begun to gain expression in political action and social formations. In the early 1980s a group of people of both non-Aboriginal and Aboriginal backgrounds gathered in eastern Australia to celebrate a dawn ceremony 'to renew the life force of the dominant hill in the locality'. The event was heralded as 'the beginning of the renewing of the Dreaming', and was the first of many such ceremonies by 'Renewal People' or 'Dreamers' (as they call themselves) at 'places of power' in the eastern parts of Australia.[50] One 'Dreamer' acknowledged that the efforts were 'fumbling and hesitant' but that guidance could be found in 'our own Aboriginal Earth tradition'. Newton's examination of the counterculture movement in eastern Australia shows how it consciously embraced Aboriginality.[51] The 1983 Nimbin Lifestyle Festival in rural Australia held workshops on establishing dialogues with Aboriginal communities. At the event a non-Aboriginal women's group promoted Aboriginal women's knowledges, holding seminars on their land-based culture and on traditional birthing methods. Festival profits went to local Aboriginal groups and the event closed with a collective dance choreographed in a spiral to represent the Rainbow Serpent, a common Aboriginal Dreaming figure. Such events may be seen as fringe activities, but the concern with indigenous knowledges is now considered an important part of mainstream environmental politics. The national Ecopolitics Conference in Australia has in recent years regularly designated sessions concerned with 'First Peoples'.

In a recent publication Robert Lawlor provides transpersonal environmentalism with a treatise for survival. *Voices of the First Day* is a more spiritual version of *The Wisdom of the Elders*, developed explicitly through Australian Aboriginal culture. Lawlor is concerned with what he describes as the 'terminal crisis in the life cycle of the planet'. The 'spiritual guide' for recovery is 'the oldest known human culture . . . Australian Aborigines'. He invites the reader to enter into an Earth Dreaming, guided by Aboriginal Dreamings.[52] Lawlor has little sense of a need for boundary between Aboriginal knowledges and his New Age quest for the ecospiritual recovery of the planet. His publisher's preface attests to the way in which this volume conflates difference and denies history in the quest for ecospiritual rebirth:

> The Dreaming has no religious racial, or cultural boundaries, no governments or social castes. . . . Perception and Dreamtime are the two worlds of all Aboriginal people.[53]

Lawlor is only one of a number of ecospiritual revisionists who have turned to the Aboriginal Dreaming for inspiration and guidance. Matthew Fox, founder of a 'creation spirituality' movement, calls for a 'wilderness Dreamtime':

> Spirituality must begin with the land. This is basic to the entire Aboriginal consciousness. It is also basic to the environmental survival not just of our species but all the species with whom we share this planet.[54]

As in Lawlor, boundaries of difference are breached in this quest. Fox suggests that ecospiritualists call upon 'Australian Aboriginal peoples not only outside you but *in* you'. One of Fox's fellow travelers suggests that we must 'reclaim' Aboriginal sacred sites and Dreamings and think of the Aboriginal Dreaming 'as our root and foundations as Australians'.[55] Ecospiritualists evoke the possibility of an ultimate invasive colonial moment in which all Australians are able to claim an Aboriginality by way of an appropriated and reimagined Wilderness Dreaming. In his analysis of Lawlor's text, Thomas notes the presence of a New Age primitivism that constructs Aboriginality as culturally stable and ahistorical.[56] Within the ecological discourse of Lawlor and other environmentalists, primitivist essentialism adjudicates on what is authentically Aboriginal, problematizing the place of Aboriginal communities that are no longer 'traditional' on his road to ecological salvation.

In such practices Aborigines become both 'an otherness and an origin' in settler Australia's desire for ecological sensitivity.[57] Lattas argues that the ecospiritual alienation from the land that underpins environmentalism in Australia is part of a more pervasive and officially sanctioned discourse regarding the ecologically sound nation. Possessing Aboriginal knowledge is not only the final step in securing the Australian eco-nation, but also in a process of colonization, in which settler Australians can move from the status of aliens to that of indigenes.[58]

The land rights process has consolidated Aboriginal and environmentalist alliances. Many significant tracts of land are returned to Aborigines under land rights provisions *only* if they are then re-leased to National Park authorities. In other parts of Australia, Aborigines are *only* able to claim Unalienated Crown Land or designated National Parks.[59] While this does extend Aboriginal claims to land, it also confines Aboriginal use of the land to ecologically sanctioned options.[60] Under such legal confines, Aboriginal coalitions with environmentalists are as much a strategic necessity as they are a possible recognition of shared environmental objectives.

Indeed, not all Aborigines accept the idea that conservation is compatible with Aboriginal interests. The Aboriginal politician Michael Mansell complained when conservationists failed to seek Aboriginal approval to defend the Franklin River in Tasmania from damming and charged environmental activists with invading Aboriginal land.[61] In the conflict over a road being built through the World Heritage Listed Daintree Forest in northern Australia, Aborigines and environmentalist were far from sharing a 'wilderness dreaming'. While environmentalists spoke of how important the area was to local Aborigines, the very same Aborigines argued for the construction of the road to their poorly serviced and barely accessible settlement.[62] As Lee Sackett suggests, the view of Aborigines as the first conservationists is often based on a partial, romanticized and racist understanding of traditional Aboriginal associations with the land and the political action Aborigines may wish to take in relation to that land.[63]

Many environmentalists feel women are specially placed to pursue the goal of the econation. The assumption that women are 'natural' caregivers, not only of the immediate family but of the planet, permeates at a policy level in Australian environmentalism. In recent years the Australian government has been outlining a program for ecologically sustainable development. The National Women's Consultative Council, in calling for women to contribute to the consultation program, said this:

> Women are life givers. It is no accident they have led on environmental issues at all levels . . . locally and globally. Women's concern is rooted in concern for the health and well-being of our families and communities.[64]

The executive director of Australia's most mainstream conservation lobby group, the Australian Conservation Foundation, holds an equally essentialist position, arguing that 'women are more concerned about the environment than men' and that they alone in their role as nurturers have the capacity to 'sow the seeds for new attitudes and practices'.[65] Certainly, the women's movement in Australia and elsewhere gained new strength through coalitions with the environmental and peace movements.[66]

The joining of the women's movement with environmentalism coincided with a growing alliance between women's right activists and Aboriginal women.[67] This vision of a cooperative ecodevelopment between Aborigines (particularly women) and environmentally sound settler Australians (particularly women) is advocated by some Aboriginal spokespeople. Burnam Burnam argues that:

> it will be the female peace-keeping energy which will save the planet from destruction by old males. Females make up three-quarters of the Green movement. . . . And it is Aboriginal women who possess an indisputable connection with our mother the Earth. Her spiritual strength, born out of tradition, is also acquired from male abuse, mainly sexual.[68]

Yet coalitions between Aboriginal and non-Aboriginal women have been spo-radic and at times troubled.[69] The source of this conflict was non-Aboriginal women (and indeed some Aboriginal women) seeking to make rape within Aboriginal society (that is rape of Aboriginal women by Aboriginal men) a general political issue for the women's movement.[70] The women's movement saw such violence as evidence of the workings of patriarchy within another cul-tural setting, whereas Aboriginal women opposed the politization of rape in this manner arguing it set female solidarity ahead of racial solidarity. For Aboriginal women, colonization had meant an ongoing battle to protect the family, most starkly from government policies to forcibly remove children who were known to have non-Aboriginal parentage. The appropriation of the issue of rape within Aboriginal society into the political agenda of the women's movement was seen as yet another non-Aboriginal invasion into the Aboriginal family.[71] Such rifts point toward the limits of coalitional politics and suggest that these limits are grounded in the historical specificities of colonialism.

In the final part of this chapter I want to examine a recent development con-troversy in remote Central Australia, in which Aboriginal women, conserva-tionists, and feminists came together in a loose political coalition. I want to explore this coalition in the context of the critique of radical environmental-isms covered in the early part of the chapter. I think it is important to consider such political formations, for they reveal complexities and ambiguities that are often conveniently avoided when one's analytical field is confined to easy target texts such as Robert Lawlor's ecospiritualism or more extreme ecofeminist pre-scriptions against which charges of 'appropriation' are easily laid. Examining such a political alliance problematizes the notion of 'appropriation', which as Meaghan Morris notes, has become 'the model verb of all and any action' setting 'predation' as 'the universal rule of cultural exchange'.[72]

EARTH DREAMINGS: THE ARRERNTE LAND STRUGGLE

Since the early 1960s the Northern Territory government has been considering building a dam in the vicinity of landlocked Alice Springs, in central Australia. The dam was intended to offer both recreation amenities and flood mitigation for the occasions when the usually dry Todd River rages. In 1983 the Northern Territory government announced that a site on the Todd River north of the town and near the Old Telegraph Station had been selected as the most suitable dam location. The site is part of a historic reserve that incorporates the remains of the first European telegraph station and government outpost to be built in the area.

There was strong opposition to the proposed dam site from local Aborigines. As early as 1979 they had alerted the Aboriginal Land Council for the area of the presence of sacred sites in the proposed dam location. A special committee, the Welatye Therre Defence Committee, was established to assist in organizing support for the protection of the site. The most dramatic form of protest came in April 1983, when the traditional Aboriginal owners of that area, the Arrernte people, reoccupied the site. To the Arrernte people, it is the site of the 'Two Women Dreaming' songline, which traverses Australia from south to north. According to an Arrernte press release, the main site in the area is 'Welatye Therre' (Two Breasts), a place where 'women have danced and sung for thousands of years to assert and strengthen their unique relationship with the country'.[73]

Some fifty Arrernte men and women remained camped at the site for six months. An Aboriginal government official and leader, Charles Perkins, set up office at the site for a week in order to draw national media attention to the concerns of his Arrernte people.[74] Women's ceremonies were held at the site, during which Arrernte women were joined by other central Australian Aboriginal women, to reaffirm the significance of the country.[75] Aboriginal opposition was largely unsupported by the local non-Aboriginal population. Two prodevelopment petitions received by the government about the proposed dam contained over 5,000 signatures, accounting for some seventy-five per cent of the local urban voting population.[76] To resolve the conflict, the federal government called for an inquiry.

The Northern Territory government were not insensitive to the likelihood of Aboriginal sites being present in the proposed dam area. The authors of early feasibility studies had consulted with the relevant Aboriginal Lands Council, but had reported that there appeared to be no Aboriginal opposition to the flooding of known sacred sites in the area. But the confusion over Aboriginal approval of the proposal to flood the sites simply reenacted the anthropological practice of men's knowledges being privileged over that of women's. This gender bias had been carried into the emerging government structures to accommodate Aboriginal interests in the land: and early consultations were primarily 'by men and with men'.[77] The official inquiry into the dam deadlock guaranteed that future consultations about Aboriginal interests in the area acknowledged the rights of women. The Aboriginal Sacred Sites Protection Authority (ASSPA) arranged for female anthropologists to consult with local Aboriginal women. The importance of the area to women was recorded and the site, Welatye Therre, was placed on official registers of sites of significance to Aboriginal peoples.[78] Although both men and women know about the site, the responsibility for speaking for that country rested with the women.

The protection of Welatye Therre required details of its secret and sacred content to be revealed, at the very least to the official site-recording agents. Elsewhere I have discussed the political and cultural implications of such transferals of knowledge.[79] Within established land rights mechanisms 'traditional' land-based knowledge has become a key means of verifying the legitimacy of land claims. However, the passing over of such knowledge to government agents has the potential to undermine Aboriginal self-determination and particularly to enhance non-Aboriginal powers of arbitration over the 'authenticity' of Aboriginal claims, seriously disadvantaging those Aborigines who cannot or will not bring 'traditional' proofs of evidence to bear on land claims.

In the case of Welatye Therre, the Arrernte agreed to disclose information to the official site recording authorities on the condition such information was not widely circulated. This request was adhered to. But as the likelihood of the dam proceeding grew, it was the Arrernte themselves who reluctantly decided to make known that which should be unknowable to non-Aborigines. This caused considerable anxiety among the Arrernte, for such disclosures transgress important rules of secrecy surrounding such sites.[80] It is this process of disclosure and the political alliances that emerged around this disclosure that I want to concentrate on in the last part of this chapter.

The Arrernte women's opposition to the dam proposal was organized through the Welatye Therre Defence Committee. This group made public the Arrernte struggle throughout Australia and overseas, by means of press releases, pamphlets, a newsletter and a video which specifically targeted conservation and women's groups. The Arrernte deliberately allowed selected members of the press to see and photograph the site. Reports by the chosen journalists were sensationally explicit about the content of the site. In one report a group of Arrernte women are pictured 'cradling' sacred stones stored at the site. The report opens with this provocative evocation of the site's significance:

> The dry Todd River bed in Alice Springs conceals an ancient secret story of violence and rape. Only Aboriginal eyes which know the Dreaming can read and understand the story, laid out in rocky outcrops in the river bank.[81]

The narrative flirts with the knowability of the sacred content of this site. Simultaneously, readers are being told a story and being told it is a story they cannot know. The report continues, taking us into the explicit realms of the unknowable. I am not going to quote this section of the 1983 press report. This detail was released into the public domain under the specific pressures of development, not the conditions of the production of this chapter. My concern rests not with the explicit detail of the site (beyond the media designation of it as a 'rape site'), but with the knowability of the site, especially how non-Aboriginal interests come to know of it and demonstrate support for its protection.

While journalists were strategically led to view certain aspects of the site, the Arrernte still engaged in strategic nondisclosure, for there were 'other stones' nearby, that journalists were told of but not permitted to see. It was the presence of *these* ritual objects that was of paramount importance to the Arrernte women. A non-Aboriginal spokesperson suggested that if these objects were removed or flooded over, then sickness and death would occur among the elders.[82] Another warned that 'if they go ahead and build the dam here it will be no good for all the women in Australia'.[83]

Arrernte women were not insensitive to the resonance of their struggle with those of women elsewhere. Speaking of the sacred objects stored at the site, one Arrernte woman said:

> They are a vital part of being a women. Like you've got women's liberation, for hundred of years we've had ceremonies which control our conduct, how we behave and act and how we control our sexual lives. . . . They give spiritual and emotional health to Aboriginal women.[84]

The Welatye Therre Defence Committee campaign was successful: statements of support and donations poured in from across the country. It was indeed becoming an issue for all women. Support and donations were received from Women's Action Against Global Violence, the Feminist Antinuclear Group, Women's Health Centres (Adelaide and Sydney), the Feminist Bookshop (Sydney), a Sydney women's refuge, Women for Life and the Women's International League for Peace and Freedom.[85] The Arrernte women were keen to advertise this wider support for their cause: a broadsheet was released that listed and quoted many non-Aboriginal supporters.

Welatye Therre resonated with existing forms of feminism in a variety of ways. The disclosed content of this site hints at a premodern patriarchal violence against women. Designated as a 'rape site', it acts as an embodiment of the most violent act of male oppression. Under the pressure of development this violence is disclosed and threatens to be re-enacted through the dam construction as rape of the landscape. Pushed into the public sphere, the content of the site is opened to the gaze of all women (and men) and can be collectively claimed as a symbolic site of the violence of patriarchy. The site entered a discourse of universal patriarchal oppression. The Arrernte sites became proof of women as 'archetypal victims', spanning all time and all cultures.[86]

The violence this site and these women now faced reiterates the specific violence of colonialism.[87] This site and the struggle around its protection were absorbed as symbolic markers into a feminism that was struggling to come to grips with the concept of 'double oppression'; women's and black oppression added together.[88] Aboriginal women had ensured that the Australian women's movement was aware of the sexual as well as the racial violence of colonization.[89] In this adjustment the Aboriginal 'other' was included as a 'variegated amplification . . . of . . . global phallocentrism'.[90]

The alliances formed between women's groups and the Arrernte women may well be an example of a colonizing, self-aggrandizing feminism. But Welatye Therre is also a site whose violent content operates to provide guidance: it is a pedagogical site that teaches Aboriginal women and men about appropriate behaviors, in short, how to avoid the violence of patriarchy and how to care for the land. It calls into question a totalizing feminism and provides the type of template desired by ecofeminist visions. Yet even within this less totalizing conjuncture with feminism, it is difficult for the Arrernte struggle to remain untouched by the force of feminism.

Environmentalists too found that the concerns of the Arrernte women resonated with their own concerns. Statements of support were received from Greenpeace, Friends of the Earth, and other, more local, environmentalist groups. Extracts from some of the statements of support reveal how the political alliances around Welatye Therre were closely linked to an ecocentric/ecofeminist retrieval of indigenous wisdom. The Canberra-based Friends of the Earth wrote:

> The proposed Alice Springs dam will destroy a sacred site of great significance. It is a site where, for thousands of years, Aboriginal women have performed ceremonies to strengthen their special relationship with the land. . . . Aboriginal culture['s] ecological sensibility is exemplary. The Aboriginal relationship to the land, spanning 40,000 years of judicious ecological management, puts to shame 200 years of European pillage.[91]

The London-based Aboriginal Support Group made clear their sense of saving this site as part of a global indigenous knowledges project:

> We have all come to admire and respect the deep feeling Aboriginal people hold for their land and feel that we in Europe and people all over the world have much to learn from you in caring for the earth and its people whoever they are.[92]

Under the pressure of development, the Arrernte excessively express the nature of their Dreaming site: disclose it beyond unusual limits of disclosure and warn of an effect beyond the geography of their local land interests. This is not to say the women exaggerated the possible outcome of site destruction or invented the site. It is to say that this site has an amplified presence under the conditions of modernity, it is spoken (and not spoken) within the global geography not only of development but also of non-Aboriginal political agendas. In the modern discursive constitution of Welatye Therre the site's significance was amplified by the ways in which its specific characteristics as a women's site, a site of violence against women and a site belonging to 'indigenous nurturers' of the land intersected with non-Aboriginal environmentalisms and feminisms. Arrernte women's business, and its very localized expression in the sacred site of Welatye Therre, was being globalized through its intersection with planetary environmentalisms and feminisms.

The alliance between the Arrernte women and feminist and environmentalist groups is more complex than a process of appropriation of indigenous knowledges. For a start, the idea of appropriation is at the very least complicated by the issue of Arrernte women's agency: their strategic, albeit pressured, engagement with more universalist conservation and feminist agendas. But I think the complication of this alliance lies in some thing that is neither purely domination nor purely strategic agency. Nor does it reside satisfactorily in an explanation that presumes hybridization, that Aboriginal women's business is no longer 'purely traditional'. The importance of this alliance is that it maps a discursive interspace typical of race relations in settler countries like Australia.[93] It is that space formed out of a constant interplay of dominant constructions of Aboriginality and Aboriginal self definitions. The political alliances that formed around Welatye Therre may evidence some form of 'enunciative appropriation'. But the power dynamic of this process has a political ambiguity, suggesting that it is 'neither displaced identity, nor colonialist invasion, but a process that takes place in both', a struggle to 'fix the terms of reference'.[94]

The political problem of 'fixing the terms of reference' for the Aboriginal sacred is well illustrated by later developments in the ongoing efforts of the Northern Territory government to build a dam near Alice Springs. In the early stages of the controversy the disclosure of the content and effect of the Welatye Therre site was done reluctantly and strategically by the Arrernte. Some five years later the proposals for a dam re-emerged. A new location was considered, but it too encroached on land with sacred sites with 'sexual significance' relating to the Two Women Dreaming (as well as a men's Dreaming).[95] The Arrernte women seemed to take a more cautious approach to widespread disclosure in this second round of negotiations.

One Arrernte woman explained this caution to the second board of inquiry established to arbitrate on the deadlock:

> Only the Traditional owners used to hear these stories that their grandparents told them. Now they are going to hear this story all over the place. This dam has made the story really come out into the open, the story that used to be really secret. Now other tribes are going to hear about it . . . now everybody is going to learn, and the white people as well are going to learn about it. The country story that used to be hidden. It was like that for . . . Welatye Atherra. Now they know about that place all over the world, about the Dreaming as well. . . . We are giving away all our secrets now, and it will be heard all over the world, if there is a protest against building the dam. We'll have to give away our secrets again.[96]

A newspaper report on the second dam proposal evokes the Aboriginal interest in the land not by disclosing secrets that would not normally be disclosed, but by focusing on the impact of desecration and on secrecy itself. The *Age* newspaper reports:

> The sickness affects women, in ways that are so secret that only the half dozen older women who are its custodians are allowed to know the full dreaming story of the site and the implications of its destruction. . . . Aboriginal women will not discuss the site with men, and they will speak about it to a woman for publication only in generalities.[97]

While the detail of the site remained more carefully guarded in this second round of the controversy, the effect of damaging the site was again clearly put. Destruction of the site, an Arrernte spokeswoman is quoted as saying, would 'bring a curse on all women. . . . [n]ot just Aboriginal or local women, but all Australian women'.[98]

So far I have argued that detailed disclosure of the sacred content of sites assisted in the process of amplification of significance in a political interspace between Aboriginal land rights and its sympathizers. But part of the presentation of this women's Dreaming arises not out of a detailed elaboration of its content and geography, but instead out of quite the opposite; it is, in a Lacanian sense, the lack of representation. In the first stage of the dam controversy the explicit disclosure of the content of the site was accompanied by an act of nondisclosure: journalists were told some things but were also told there were other things they could not see and could not know. In the second part of the controversy even fewer details of the sites to be affected by development were disclosed. This hardened line on nondisclosure and the explicit statements by the Arrernte about the anxiety of disclosure had two effects. For non-sympathizers, the unknowability of the sacred opened the way for discrediting Arrernte claims. But for non-Aboriginal sympathizers the secrecy of the Arrernte sacred worked to intensify allegiance and, under the political force of this alliance, to finally ensure that the proposed dam did not proceed.

Secrecy around a sacred site is not simply a strategic measure: it accords with Aboriginal law. But within settler Australia secrecy has a strategic effect beyond the limits of Aboriginal society. Secrecy hints at an unknowable dimension of the women's concern for the Dreaming.[99] It is this unrepresentability that in a paradoxical sense authenticates the women's Dreaming for sympathizers and positively amplifies the significance of sites. It is under conditions of secrecy and partial disclosure that Welatye Therre becomes known. It becomes a sublime object, an embodiment of the lack in non-Aboriginal gender and environment relations. It is the 'half-seen' status of the women's sites that ensures their role in fulfilling the desires of contemporary sympathizers. Trinh argues that when non-colored feminists embrace 'the other' they seek the 'unspoiled', an 'image of the real native – the truly different'. She adds that 'the less accessible the product . . . the greater the desire to acquire and protect it'.[100] In the case of Welatye Therre the globalization of this local geography of the sacred was as much driven by the nostalgic desires of environmentalisms and feminisms as it was by the forces of development. And non-disclosure had a strategic effect with sympathizers by not only intensifying the authenticity of Aboriginal claims in their eyes but also by presenting the Aboriginal sacred as a lacuna that could be filled with their own political aspirations.

CONCLUSION

This chapter has attempted to understand the logic of Western environmentalist and feminist affiliations with if non-Western peoples. My analysis of the eco-centric and ecofeminist perspectives uncovered their colonialist and patriarchal subtexts, borne of a rearticulated desire of the West to possess indigenous knowledges held within a primitivist stereotype of the environmentally 'valid' and 'useful' indigene. It has been commonplace for postcolonial critiques to attack essentialisms like those in the primitivist or womanist subtexts of eco-centric and ecofeminist positions. Part of the presumption of this critique is that these essentialist idealizations are the constructions of colonial and neocolonial formations and may work to contain indigenous identities within a non-existent premodern identity. Within this discursive terrain, charges of appropriation are easily laid. It is possible to presume that 'predation' does indeed remain the dominant power dynamic of cultural exchange in settler states and that this is only negative in its effect, reenacting an ongoing process of invasion of Aboriginal knowledges and determining of Aboriginal identity.

Yet the Arrernte struggle unsettles this reading. The political alliances around their sacred sites do sustain the dynamic of appropriation, particularly in the sense that Aboriginal culture serves universalist environmentalist and feminist agendas. Yet the issue of secrecy and non-disclosure provides a key to an important complexity in the way 'appropriation' needs to be understood. Under the conditions of secrecy the desires of non-Aboriginal sympathizers to support Aboriginal rights did not diminish, but intensified. Secrecy may enhance desires of sympathizers, providing an unknowable space into which their imaginative desires about Aboriginality are projected. When one outcome of non-Aboriginal imaginative projections (such as the nostalgias of environmentalism and ecofeminism) is a political alliance that desires and does not discredit secrecy and assists in the acknowledgment of Aboriginal rights, then narrow adjudications of 'predatory appropriation' are problematized. They are not, however, eliminated. The disclosure of Arrernte business happened under the force of modernity. This includes the familiar pressures of development. It also includes the political imperative of harnessing the force of antidevelopment sympathizers. The sites were saved through such an alliance, but the politics of the alliance resonates with less sympathetic moments in the history of settler Australia.

It is the ambiguity of these sites, their ability to slip into and out of the universal issues of patriarchy and environmentalism, as well as an elusive premodern ecosensibility, which made them the loci of broader political coalitions. These sites contained a memory of universal oppression and exploitation as well as an unknowable hope of an alternative world. These sites became objects of desire for those who seek ecological salvation in the wisdom of the elders.

NOTES

1. Part of the title of this chapter is taken from a book that defines 'a new male sexuality' through a reconsideration of the relationship between masculinity and environmental ecology; see Robert Lawlor, *Earth Honouring The New Male Sexuality* (Newtown, Australia: Millennium Books, 1990).
2. Trinh T. Minh-ha, *Woman, Native, Other* (Bloomington: Indiana University Press, 1989), p. 52.
3. This has been a long-running dispute that reached final resolution only in 1992. My account focuses mainly on the early stages of the dispute in 1983–84 when there was concern for the site known as Welatye Therre.
4. Patrick Wolfe, 'On Being Woken Up: The Dreamtime in Anthropology and in Australian Settler Culture', *Comparative Studies in Society and History* 33 no. 2 (1991): pp. 197–224, esp. p. 198.

5. See, for example, Andree Collard, *Rape of the Wild: Man's Violence against Animals and the Earth* (Bloomington: Indiana University Press, 1989); Maria Mies, *Patriarchy and Accumulation* (London: Zed Books, 1989); Vandana Shiva, *Staying Alive: Women, Ecology and Development* (London: Zed Books, 1989); Susan Griffin, *Women and Nature: The Roaring Inside Her* (New York: Harper and Row, 1978); Carolyn Merchant, *The Death of Nature: Women, Ecology, and the Scientific Revolution* (San Francisco: Harper and Row, 1980), *Ecological Revolutions: Nature, Gender and Science in New England* (Chapel Hill: University of North Carolina Press, 1989; and *Radical Ecology: The Search for a Livable World* (New York: Routledge, 1992).

6. Robyn Eckersley, *Environmentalism and Political Theory: Towards an Ecocentric Approach* (London: UCL Press, 1992), p. 67.

7. See, for example, Arne Naess, 'The Shallow and the Deep, Long-Range Ecology Movement, a Summary', *Inquiry 16* (1989): pp. 95–100; Alan R. Drengson, *Beyond Environmental Crisis: From Technocrat to Planetary Person* (New York: Peter Lang, 1989); William R. Catton, Jr. and Riley E. Dunlap, 'A New Ecological Paradigm for Post-Exuberant Sociology', *American Behavioural Scientist 24* (1980): pp. 15–47; Warwick Fox, *Toward a Transpersonal Ecology: Developing New Foundations for Environmentalism* (Boston: Shambhala, 1990); and Mary Mellor, *Breaking the Boundaries: Towards a Feminist Green Socialism* (London: Virago Press, 1992).

8. See Eckersley, *Environmentalism and Political Theory*, Fox, *Toward a Transpersonal Ecology*; and Freye Mathews, *The Ecological Self* (London: Routledge, 1992).

9. Peter Knudston and David Suzuki, *Wisdom of the Elders* (Toronto: Allen and Unwin, 1992), pp. xiii–xiv.

10. David Suzuki, 'A Personal Foreword: The Value of Native Ecologies', in Knudston and Suzuki, *Wisdom of the Elders*, pp. xxi–xxxv, esp. xxxiv.

11. Knudston and Suzuki, *Wisdom of the Elders*, p. 46.

12. Julian Burger, *The Gaia Atlas of First Peoples* (Ringwood, Australia: Penguin Books, 1990), p. 6.

13. See Griffin, *Women and Nature*; Merchant, *The Death of Nature*; and Irene Diamond and Gloria Orenstien, eds., *Reweaving the World: The Emergence of Ecofeminism* (San Francisco: Sierra Club Books, 1990).

14. Eckersley, *Environmentalism and Political Theory*, p. 64.

15. Mellor, *Breaking the Boundaries*, p. 51.

16. Janet Biehl, *Finding Our Way: Rethinking Ecofeminist Politics* (Montreal: Black Rose Books, 1991), p. 15.

17. Charlene Spretnak, *The Politics of Women's Spirituality: Essays on the Rise of Spiritual Power within the Feminist Movement* (Garden City, NY: Anchor, 1982).

18. Eckersley, *Environmentalism and Political Theory*, p. 64.

19. Biehl, *Finding Our Way*. As a recent example, see Diamond and Orenstien, *Reweaving the World*.

20. Mellor, *Breaking the Boundaries*, p. 119.

21. Merchant, *Ecological Revolutions*.

22. Barbara Rogers, 'The Power to Feed Ourselves: Women and Land Rights', in *Reclaim the Earth: Women Speak Out for Life on Earth*, Leonie Caldecott and Stephanie Leland, eds. (London: Women's Press, 1983). pp. 101–106, esp. p. 103.

23. Ngahhuia, Te Awekotuku, 'He wahine, he whenua: Maori Women and the Environment', in *Reclaim the Earth*, Caldecott and Leland eds., pp. 136–140.

24. Vandana Shiva, *Staying Alive: Women, Ecology and Development* (London: Zed Books, 1989).

25. Biehl, *Finding Our Way*, p. 15.

26. Mellor, *Breaking the Boundaries*; Biehl, *Finding Our Way*.

27. George Bradford, *How Deep is Deep Ecology?* (Hadley, MA: Times Change Press, 1989.

28. Mellor, *Breaking Boundaries*, p. 47.

29. Judith Butler, *Gender Trouble*, (London: Routledge, 1990), esp. p. 35.

30. Winona LaDuke, 'Racism, Environmentalism and the New Age', *Green Left Notes 4* (1990): pp. 15–34, esp. p. 32.

31. Audre Lorde, 'The Master's Tools Will Never Dismantle the Master's House', in *This Bridge Called My Back: Writings by Radical Women of Color*, Cherrie Morraga and Gloria Anzaldua, eds. (Watertown, MA: Persphone Press, 1981), pp. 98–101, esp. p. 100.

32. Rogers, 'The Power to Feed Ourselves', pp. 101–6, esp. p. 101; Te Awekotuku, 'He wahine, he whenua', pp. 136–40.

33. Biehl, *Finding Our Way*, p. 130.

34. Andrew Lattas, 'Aborigines and Contemporary Australian Nationalism: Primordiality and the Cultural Politics of Otherness', in *Writing Australian Culture: Text, Society and National Identity*, Julie Marcus, ed. (Special issue *Social Analysis: Journal of Cultural and Social Practice 27*, pp. 50–69, esp. p. 58).

35. P. R. Hay, 'The Environmental Movement: Romanticsim Reborn?', *Island Magazine 14* (1981) pp. 10–17, esp. p. 13.

36. Merchant, cited in Virginia Westbury, 'Ecofeminism Australia', Bulletin, July 2, 1991, pp. 89–91, esp. p. 90.

37. Kay Schaffer, *Women and the Bush: Forces of Desire in the Australian Cultural Tradition* (Cambridge, UK: Cambridge University Press, 1988), esp. pp. 22, 77 and 79.

38. Lattas, 'Aborigines and Contemporary Australian Nationalism', pp. 50–69, esp. p. 58.

39. Brian Butcher and David Turnbull, 'Aborigines, Europeans and the Environment', in *A Most Valuable Acquisition: A People's History of Australia since 1788*, Verity Burgmann and Jenny Lee, eds. (Melbourne: McPhee Gribble/Penguin, 1988), pp. 13–28, esp. p. 28.

40. Adolphus P. Elkin, 'Introduction', in *Aboriginal Woman: Sacred and Profane*, Phyllis Kaberry, ed. (London: Routledge, 1989).

41. See Diane Bell, *Daughters of the Dreaming* (Sydney: McPhee Gribble/Allen and Unwin, 1983); Annette Hamilton, 'A Complex Strategical Situation: Gender and Power in Aboriginal Australia', in *Australian Women: Feminist Perspectives*, Norma Grieve and Patricia Grimshaw, eds. (Melbourne: Oxford University Press, 1981), pp. 69–85; Jane M. Jacobs, 'Women Talking Up Big: Aboriginal Women as Cultural Custodians', in *Women Rites and Sites: Aboriginal Women's Cultural Knowledge*, Peggy Brock, ed. (Sydney: Allen and Unwin, 1989), pp. 76–98.

42. Bell, *Daughters of the Dreaming*, pp. 36–7.

43. Deborah Bird Rose, *Dingo Makes Us Human: Life and Land in an Australian Aboriginal Culture* (Cambridge, UK: Cambridge University Press, 1992), p. 51.

44. Ibid.

45. Ibid., p. 218.

46. Tony Swaine, 'The Mother Earth Conspiracy: An Australian Episode', *Numen 38* (1992), pp. 3–26.

47. Rose, *Dingo Makes Us Human*, p. 90.

48. Ibid., pp. 90, 220, 232, 235.

49. Lee Sackett, 'Promoting Primitivism: Conservationist Depictions of Aboriginal Australians', *Australian Journal of Anthropology 2*, no. 2 (1991), pp. 233–46, esp. p. 235.

50. Chris Framer, 'Some People Say the Earth is Still Dreaming', *Habitat Australia 12*, no. 2 (1984): p. 32.

51. Janice Newton, 'Aborigines, Tribes and the Counterculture', *Social Analysis 25* (1988), pp. 53–71.

52. Robert Lawlor, *Voices of the First Day: Awakenings in the Aboriginal Dreamtime* (Rochester, VT: Inner Traditions, 1991), esp. p. 9.
53. Ehud Sperling, 'Preface', in Lawlor, *Voices of the First Day*, pp. xii–xvi, esp, p. xvi.
54. Matthew Fox, 'Creation Spirituality and the Dreaming', in *Creation, Spirituality and the Dreaming,* Matthew Fox, ed., (Newton, Australia: Millennium Books, 1991), pp. 1–20, esp. p. 7.
55. Elizabeth Cain, 'To Sacred Origins – Through Symbol and Story', in *Creation, Spirituality and the Dreaming*, Fox, ed., pp. 73–86, esp. p. 78.
56. Nicholas Thomas, *Colonialism's Culture* (Cambridge: UK: Polity Press, 1993).
57. Lattas, 'Aborigines and Contemporary Australian Nationalism', pp. 58, 63.
58. *Advertiser*, May 23, 1989, quoted in Lattas, 'Aborigines and Contemporary Australian Nationalism', p. 52.
59. See Tim Rowse, 'Hosts and Guests at Uluru', *Meanjin 51*, no. 2 (1992): pp. 265–76; Tony Birch, 'Nothing has changed: the Making and Unmaking of Koori Culture', *Meanjin 51*, no. 2 (1992), pp. 229–46; L. M. Baker and Mutitjulu Community', Comparing Two Views of the Landscape: Aboriginal Traditional Ecological Knowledge and Modern Scientific Knowledge', *Rangeland Journal 14*, no. 2 (1992): pp. 174–89; Jim Birkhead, Terry DeLacy and Laurajane Smith, eds., *Aboriginal Involvement in Parks and Protected Areas* (Canberra, Australia: Aboriginal Studies Press, 1992).
60. See Laura Beacroft, 'Conservation: Accommodating Aboriginal Interests or the New Competitor', *Aboriginal Law Bulletin 26* (1987), pp. 3–4; and Philip Toyne and Ross Johnston, 'Reconciliation or the New Dispossession?', *Habitat 19*, no. 3 (1991), pp. 8–10.
61. Michael Mansell, 'Comrades or Trespassers on Aboriginal Land', in *The Rest of the World is Watching*, Cassandra Pybus and Richard Flanagan, eds. (Melbourne, Australia: Sun Books, 1990), pp. 101–106, esp. p. 103.
62. Chris Anderson, 'Aborigines and Conservationism: The Daintree-Bloomfield Road', *Australian Journal of Social Issues 24* (1989), pp. 214–27.
63. Sackett, 'Promoting Primitivism'.
64. National Women's Consultative Committee, *What on Earth Can a Woman Do?* (Canberra, Australia: National Women's Consultative Committee, 1991), p. 4.
65. Patricia Caswell, 'Women and Ecologically Sustainable Development', *Australian Women's Book Review 4*, no. 4 (1992), pp. 15–17, esp. p. 15.
66. Curthoys, 'Doing It for Themselves', p. 426. Curthoys notes that one of the inputs to the 1980s women's movement in Australia was a visit by the ecofeminist Mary Daly.
67. Fay Gale, ed., *We Are Bosses Ourselves* (Canberra, Australia: Australian Institute of Aboriginal Studies, 1983); Jan Larbalestier, 'The 1980 Women and Labour Conference. Feminism as Myth: Aboriginal Women and the Feminist Encounter', *Refractory Girl*, nos. 20–21 (1980), pp. 31–9.
68. Burnam Burnam, 'Aboriginal Australia and the Green Movement', in *Green Politics in Australia*, D. Hutton, ed (Melbourne: Agnus and Robertson, 1987), pp. 91–104, esp. p. 92.
69. Curthoys, 'Doing It for Themselves: The Women's Movement since 1970', in *Gender Relations in Australia: Domination and Negotiation*, Kay Saunders and Raymond Evans, eds. (Sydney, Australia: Harcourt Brace Jovanovich, 1992); pp. 425–47, esp. p. 444.
70. Diane Bell and Topsy Napurrla Nelson, 'Speaking About Rape is Everyone's Business', *Women's Studies International Forum 12*, no. 4 (1989): pp. 403–16. For a summary of the debate, see Jan Larbalestier, 'The Politics of Representation: Aboriginal Women and Feminism', *Anthropological Forum*, 6, no. 2 (1990): pp. 143–57.
71. Heather Goodall and Jackie Huggins, 'Aboriginal Women are Everywhere: Contemporary Struggles', *Gender Relations in Australia*, Kay Saunders and

Raymond Evans, eds. (Sydney: Harcourt Brace Jovanovick, 1992), pp. 398–424 esp. pp. 401–02; Jackie Huggins, 'Black women and Women's Liberation', *Hecate* 13, no. 11 (1987): pp. 5–23.

72. Meaghan Morris, *Pirates Fiancee: Feminism Reading Postmodernism*. (London: Verso, 1988), esp. p. 267.

73. Welatye Therre Defence Committee, *Voices from Mparntwe*, newsletter. (Alice Springs, Australia: Welatye Therre Defence Committee, 1983).

74. *Australian*, May 14–15, 1983.

75. Justice Hal Wootton, *Significant Aboriginal Sites in Area of Proposed Junction Waterhole Dam. Alice Springs*, Report to the Minister for Aboriginal Affairs (Canberra, Australia: Aboriginal and Torres Strait Islander Commission, 1992), esp. pp. 25–6.

76. Robert Lloyd, Fay Gale and Minna Sitzler, *Report Alice Springs Recreation Lake*, vol. 1, (Alice Springs, Australia: Board of Inquiry into Alice Springs Recreation Lake, 1984), p. 15.

77. Diane Bell, 'Sacred Sites: The Politics of Protection', in *Aborigines, Land and Land Rights*, Nicholas Peterson and Marcia Langton, eds. (Canberra: Australian Institute of Aboriginal Studies, 1983), pp. 278–93, esp. p. 284.

78. Lloyd, Gale, and Sitzler, *Report*, p. 34.

79. Jane M. Jacobs, 'Politics and the Cultural Landscape: The Case of Aboriginal Land Rights' *Australian Geographical Studies* 26 (1988), pp. 249–63, and The Construction of Identity', in *Past and Present: The Construction of Aboriginality*, J. R. Beckett, ed. (Canberra, Australian Studies Press, 1988), pp. 31–44.

80. Lloyd, Gale and Sitzler, *Report*.

81. Age, April 22, 1983.

82. *Sydney Morning Herald*, July 21, 1984, p. 23.

83. Rosie Ferber, quoted in Welatye Therre Defence Committee, *Voices from Mparntwe*, n.p.

84. Welatye Therre Defence Committee, *Voices from Mpartwe*, n.p., cited in *Sun*, May 9, 1983, p. 13.

85. Lloyd, Gale and Sitzler, *Report*, pp. 7–8: Welatye Therre Defence Committee, *Voices from Mpartwe*.

86. Chandra Talpade Mohanty, 'Under Western Eyes: Feminist Scholarship and Colonialist Discourses', in *Third World Women and the Politics of Feminism*, Chandra Talpade Mohanty, Ann Russo and Lourdes Torres eds. (Bloomington: Indiana University Press, 1991), pp. 51–79, esp. pp. 58 and 71.

87. Jenny Sharpe, 'The Unspeakable Limits of Rape: Colonial Violence and Counterinsurgency', *Genders* 10 (1991), pp. 25–46; Roberta Sykes, 'Black Women in Australia', in *The Other Half: Women in Australian Society*, Jan Mercer, ed. (Melbourne: Penguin, 1975, pp. 313–21; Raymond Evans, 'Don't You Remember Black Alice, Sam Holt?' Aboriginal Women in Queensland History', Hecate 8, no. 2 (1982), pp. 7–21.

88. Curthoys, 'Doing It for Themselves', p. 443.

89. Goodall and Huggins, 'Aboriginal Women Are Everywhere', pp. 398–424.

90. Butler, *Gender Trouble*, p. 13.

91. Ian Watson, Friends of the Earth, letter to editor, *NT News*, May 25, 1983, p. 19.

92. Aboriginal Support Group, cited in Welatye Therre Defence Committee, *Voices from Mparntwe*.

93. What postcolonialist writers like Homi Bhabha and Edward Said might call the 'third space'. See Homi Bhabha, 'Introduction: Narrating the Nation', in *Nation and Narration*, Homi Bhabha, ed. (London: Routledge, 1990), pp. 1–7; and 'Postcolonial Authority and Postmodern Guilt', in *Cultural Studies*, Lawrence Grossberg, Cary Nelson and Paul Treichler, eds. (New York: Routledge, 1992), pp. 56–68; and Edward Said, 'Yeats and Decolonization', in *Nationalism, Colonialism and Literature*, Terry Eagleton, Frederick Jameson,

and Edward Said, eds. (Minneapolis: University of Minnesota Press, 1990, pp. 69–95.

94. Meaghan Morris, *The Pirate's Fiancée: Feminism Reading Postmodernism* (London: Verso, 1990), p. 259.
95. Rosemary West, 'Damning the River', *Age*, March 20, 1992, p. 9.
96. Cited in Wootton, *Significant Aboriginal Sites*, p. 74.
97. West, 'Damning the River', p. 9.
98. Ibid.
99. Slavoj Žižek, *The Sublime Object of Ideology* (London: Verso, 1989), p. 203.
100. Trinh, *Woman, Native, Other*, p. 88.

6.4

'GENDER AND COLONIAL SPACE'

Sara Mills

My aims in this article are to analyse the gendered nature of colonial space and to begin framework for a materialist-feminist postcolonial practice.[1] I will be drawing on theoretical work on gender and space which has been developed primarily by feminist geographers and anthropologists, and I will read this critical work through/against some of the theoretical material developed within postcolonial literary and cultural theory. I will attempt this fusion in order to analyse spatial relations without relying solely on the psychoanalytical models developed within postcolonial cultural theory which polarise and essentialise gender and racial divisions. The article thus begins with an examination of the possibility of developing a more materialist postcolonial theory/practice. I then critically examine the theoretical work which has been undertaken on space and gender, which generally considers the confinement of women to be the determining factor in women's sense of their position within spatial frameworks. I argue that the complexity of gendered spatial relations, particularly within the colonial context, cannot be encompassed within the notion of confinement. I then move to an analysis of the importance of viewing position for the construction of gendered spatial relations. Finally, I consider two levels of colonial space, the idealised level of distance and separation embodied within colonial architecture and town planning, and the 'contact zone' of sexualised colonial space. (Pratt, 1992). In this way, by being critical of the reductiveness of much psychoanalytical postcolonial theory, I hope to produce an analytical framework within

From: Sara Mills (1996), 'Gender and Colonial Space', pp. 125–47, in *Gender, Space and Culture*, vol. 3, no. 2.

which it is possible to make general statements about the gendered nature of colonial space, at the same time as being aware of the material specificity of different colonial contexts. Throughout this discussion I will examine briefly a number of primary texts written within different colonial contexts; my main focus of attention will be on India in the late nineteenth century.[2]

MATERIALIST FEMINISM AND COLONIAL SPATIAL RELATIONS

Like many critics working in the field of colonial discourse, I have felt politically committed to work on colonial material, but have not felt comfortable working within the frameworks currently in circulation. (See Young, 1990, 1995; Williams and Chrisman, 1993; and Ashcroft et al., 1995 for general surveys.) So ingrained is the use of psychoanalytical concepts within this type of theoretical work that it is difficult to engage in theoretical debates without, of necessity, reflecting the usage of certain terms to allow a more materialist analysis to develop. My principal objection to the reliance on psychoanalysis for the analysis of colonialism is that the specificity of the colonial context is lost – the materiality of invasion, discrimination, murder, rape, expropriation of land and also of resistance are erased. Instead of these material conditions being the focus of attention, within post-colonial theory, stereotype and fantasy have become the dominant realms of investigation. Whilst it is clear that stereotype/fantasy is crucial for an understanding of colonial relations, psychoanalytic models cannot account for the differential access to stereotypes/fantasies which people have and the differential use that they make of them; furthermore, this form of analysis attributes too great a stability to these stereotypes/fantasies, even whilst arguing for their ambivalence (Bhabha, 1994). Following Voloshinov, fantasy, and indeed the unconscious itself, should be seen to develop in reaction to and negotiation with material conditions (Voloshinov, 1986). In focusing attention on the colonial psyche, we risk ignoring the political and economic bases on which those psyches were constructed.

I will be focusing principally on social space as well as analysing the way that architectural space affects social space (King, 1976; Colomina, 1992; Wigley, 1992)[3]. It will thus be an attempt to move away from the rather abstract binary oppositions entailed in the notion of the Other, a concept which has received such critical attention within colonial and postcolonial discourse theory, and focus on a more material, multilayered view of power relations within the colonial period (see Ahmed, 1996). Indeed, perhaps rather than a simple Othering process, we need to examine the way that the process is one of racialisation, as McKendry has shown (McKendry, 1995). The term racialisation enables us to see the colonial context as one where a variety of processes were at work, and that they were processes which resulted in material practices rather than simply abstract psychoanalytical functions. I will be viewing space not as a given, but as a set of superimposed spatial frameworks, as many social spaces negotiated within one geographical place and time. Colonial space has often been described in monolithic terms, since it is the dominant spatial representations of British male colonists which have been examined. Instead of this monolithic view of space, I will attempt to examine the possibilities of developing a materialist-feminist analysis of representational space which will be aware of the way that women and men, colonised and coloniser, negotiate their positions in space through their interrogations with their respective social positions. Rather than simply arguing, for example, that British women have imposed upon them a spatial confinement within the colonial context, thus assuming that British males have complete freedom of movement, I will analyse the variety of spatial frameworks which are operating both for women and men within this context. I will be concerned to examine the way that discursive constraints work to produce often conflicting and contradictory spatial frameworks, where within certain colonial contexts, confinement for some women is the dominant mode of negotiating spatiality, whereas for other women, in other colonial contexts, transgressing these boundaries will be sanctioned. In still other situations, transgression will be a strategy of resistance. Indeed, I am concerned to examine whether spatial relations do not in fact determine the differences within gender and racial relations operating within a particular colonial context (Pratt and Hanson, 1994). As Massey has argued, 'it's not just that the spatial is socially constructed; the social is spatially constructed' (Massey, 1984, cited in Spain, 1992, p. 4).

It is important that materialist feminism intervenes in psychoanalytic postcolonial theory since, as Christine Delphy states, 'Materialist feminism . . . is an intellectual approach whose coming is crucial both for social movements, the feminist struggle and for knowledge' (Delphy 1981, p. 75). Materialist feminism can force a crisis in what we know about colonialism and imperialism and also what we know about gender. As Donna Landry and Gerald Maclean have argued:

> the material conditions of women's oppression and hence women's political interests, are themselves historically specific and therefore cannot be framed in terms of gender alone. A feminist politics projected exclusively in terms of women's equality cannot recognize, much less challenge, those . . . socio-political structures and institutional settings which divide women by class, race, sexuality, and ethnicity. (Landry and Maclean, 1993, p. 12).

A materialist-feminist analysis will thus be aware of the differences amongst women and men within the colonial context and will focus precisely upon the relations between these different agents.

A materialist-feminist analysis, as Landry and Maclean have shown, is one that 'takes the critical investigation, or reading, in the strong sense, of the artifacts of culture and social history, including literary and artistic texts, archival documents, and works of theory, to be a potential site of political contestation through critique' (Landry and Maclean, 1993, p. xi; see, also, Mills, 1992, 1995a). It is for this reason that I have chosen to refer to a number of primary texts written within a range of different colonial contexts: (British women travellers' texts within late nineteenth-century India and Africa; British male- and female-authored literary texts written about India and Africa in the late nineteenth century, together with critical and historical writing by current postcolonial theorists), in order to try to isolate the different subaltern and oppositional spaces existing within the colonial period. It may be objected that in analysing dominant cultural representations, I am simply reproducing dominant, and therefore Anglocentric, views of space and cannot therefore claim to be concerned with the spatial frameworks of Indian and African colonial subjects within the late nineteenth and early twentieth centuries. However, I am to show that the paucity of material produced by colonised subjects, itself symptomatic of colonial relations, forces us to examine a range of other textual and theoretical options in order to construe a range of spatial frameworks existing in conflict within colonial space.

It is important to try to construct these positions of agency in order that critical postcolonial analysis does not simply become a replication of the power of the empire.[4] The strategies which I have tried to develop are firstly to examine the colonial texts that I have chosen in a very literal way to see the ways in which they map out spatial relations between the coloniser and the colonised.[5] It is then possible to focus on the pressure exerted by the spatial frameworks of the colonised within these texts, in order to try to construct a different perspective, as Pratt has suggested (Pratt, 1992). As Chakrabarty has shown in his analysis of the conditions of working-crass Indians in the nineteenth century, 'ruling class documents . . . can be read both for what they say and their "silences" ' (Chakrabarty, 1988). Particularly in texts which are not simply reproducing dominant norms, for example, those written by subjects whose position within the dominant spatial framework is marginal or problematic, there may be the possibility for beginning to articulate a multiplicity of spatial frameworks.

A further objection to literary, non-literary, critical and historical texts being drawn upon in order to try to map the spatial frameworks in circulation within a particular historical period, may be that the period under consideration, late nineteenth-century British imperialism, is too complex to make specific assertions and that the texts themselves are too diverse to allow for generalisations. It is indeed the case that colonial and imperial contexts are marked by their diversity, as Hulme has shown (Hulme, 1986). However, what I am attempting there is to define some of the parameters within which spatial frameworks are constructed, rather than arguing that these frameworks are the same within each colonial context. Current feminist theory is engaged in developing models to engage with diversity, whilst not losing sight of the power relations informing differences, and it is this work which I will be drawing on here (Fuss, 1989; Butler, 1990). In recent years, feminist analysis has turned to the analysis of the colonial and postcolonial condition, and it is thus forced to engage with the diversity of positions which women and men forged for themselves in resisting or complying with colonial and imperial power (Callaway, 1987; Mohanty, 1988; Spivak, 1988, 1990, 1993; Mills, 1991; Minh-ha, 1989; Haggis, 1990; Sharpe, 1991, 1993; Chaudhuri and Strobel, 1992; Donaldson, 1992;

Ferguson, 1992, 1993; Suleri, 1992a, 1992b; Ware, 1992; Rajan, 1993; Blunt and Rose, 1994).

Before beginning this discussion of gender and colonial space, it is important to consider why such a study is necessary and how such a study can be carried out. Analysing such a problematic and difficult concept as space enables us to come to grips with the very complexity of theoretical analysis of the colonial context[6]; when only working with issues of representation in texts, for example, it is sometimes the case that a simple 'reading' will be produced which accords with the dominant views or which contests those views but which does not necessarily try to track down the multiplicity of the representations which inform the production of that text, and which determine its silences, its gaps and inconsistencies. With the analysis of space, that simplicity of reading is not possible, precisely because of the multiplicity of contextual factors which need to be considered. As Barnes and Duncan assert:

> just as written texts are not simply mirrors of a 'reality' outside them-
> selves, so cultural productions . . . are not 'about' something more real
> than themselves. But although not referential, such practices of significa-
> tion are intertextual in that they embody other cultural texts and, as
> a consequence, are communicative and productive of meaning. Such
> meaning is, however, by no means fixed; rather it is culturally and histor-
> ically and sometimes even individually and momentarily variable. (Barnes
> and Duncan, 1992, p. 7)

This type of analysis of space also needs to be undertaken in order to produce what I would like to call, drawing on Foucault's work, an 'archaeology of space' (Foucault, 1972); it is clear that within the postcolonial context in Britain and other countries, the spatial frameworks within which we are working are the legacy of, amongst many other factors, the colonial period and the norms and values which were developed and contested within that period. As Shohat and Stam have shown in their analysis of Eurocentrism, it is essen-tial to make visible the form of 'vestigal thinking which permeates and struc-tures contemporary practices and representations even after the formal end of colonialism', and which, as they have shown, is often characterised by precisely its invisibility or recalcitrance to analysis (Shohat and Stam, 1994, p. 2).

It is in order to try to develop strategies for resisting these colonial frame-works which are still active within current values that I feel that this type of analysis is necessary. How to go about this type of analysis is more complicated. It is often assumed that spatial analysis can simply be 'read off' textual repre-sentation; however, as Moore has shown, although it is possible to treat space as a text itself and then attempt to interpret its social and contextual history, the relation between texts themselves and spatial representation is not a simple one (Moore, 1986). As she states: 'meanings are not inherent in the organisa-tion of . . . space, but must be invoked through the activities of social actors' (Moore, 1986, p. 8); attempting to invoke these activities through the analysis of a range of texts whose horizons of interpretation are no longer extant poses considerable difficulties for analysis. But, as Moore goes on to say, 'What is inscribed in the organisation of space is not the actuality of past actions, but their meaning' (Moore, 1986, p. 81); thus I am not attempting to reach the 'reality' of spatial frameworks of the colonial period but simply the interpretive process at work on spatial frameworks within texts. Since texts, whether fiction or non-fictional, generally propose solutions to problems of interpretation, it is at this level I shall be trying to track down some of the conflicts and contradictions within colonial spatial frameworks.

SPACE AND GENDER

The relationship between gender and space has been the subject of rigorous enquiry, especially by feminist theorists (Ardener, 1981; Moore, 1986; Spain, 1992; Blunt and Rose, 1994; Massey, 1994). Early feminist work on women and space tended to focus on women's confinement and restriction in movement; for example Iris Marion Young's article 'Throwing like a girl' stressed the way that women learn to situate themselves and move in space in a way which is significantly more restricted than men – even simple actions like sitting or walking are ones where the female subject is self-consciously not allowing herself to transcend the limits of the body as an object (Young, 1989). Although Young's work is concerned with the production of femininity, it is clearly also concerned with female mobility. Similarly Marianne Wex has noted in a photographic essay on women in the public sphere, that women attempt to take up as little space as possible by positioning their bodies in a restricted and confining fashion (Wex, 1979). For Young, 'if there are particular modalities of feminine bodily comportment and motility, then it must follow that there are also particular modalities of feminine spatiality' (Young, 1989, p. 62). She goes on to argue that because of this sense of restrictedness on motility, women as a whole experience their position in space as enclosed and confining and they see themselves as precisely positioned in space, that is 'in its immanence and inhibition, feminine spatial existence is *positioned* by a system of coordinates which does not have its origin in her own intentional capacities' (Young, 1989, p. 64). This is a fairly conventional view of women as passive and as restricted, and it is clear from her article that her primary focus of attention is on Western, middle-class women, whilst her concluding remarks universalise this restriction to all women (see Donaldson, 1992, for a critique of such Western feminist universalising).

However, within the colonial sphere, this sense of restriction is not as clearly experienced as in the British context. In many of the accounts of women travelling and in autobiographical and fictional accounts, British women stress the freedom which they found within the colonial context, which seemed free of some of the constraints of British society; sport was very important for the maintenance of a sense of imperial fitness, and the imperial culture stressed leisure pursuits such as horse-riding for both women and men (Mangan,

1985).[7] Riding gave women a different relation to their own sense of control of and position within space. For many British women, travelling enabled them to abandon many of the social and spatial conventions enforced within the colonial city or within Britain, as Nina Mazuchelli states in her account of her travels through the Himalayas: 'How odd it will seem once more to return to the ways of civilisation and to home duties . . . to look spick and span and ladylike once more . . . Our return to Darjeeling [is] a thought that even now pursues me like a terrible nightmare' (Mazuchelli, 1876, p. 604). Mazuchelli here thus points to the differential spatial relations operating within one colonial context; the settled Anglo-Indian community of Darjeeling is seen as more confining than the 'freedom' of movement which was possible within the Himalayas.

It should also be noted that for Indian and African women within colonial society, their freedom was often curtailed not by their families within the harem or purdah, but through fear of attack or rape by British soldiers. Consider this oral account by Harry Bowen, a 16 year-old soldier stationed in Kanpur:

> There was one time I remember that an Indian woman strayed into the lines where we were barracked, and she got into very serious trouble. I don't know whether she'd come in by mistake or whether she was looking for business, but things must've got out of hand and she was passed from bed to bed and finished up as a dead body on the incinerator in the morning . . . There'd been about twenty four to thirty fellows involved, probably a lot more than that. She couldn't take it. It killed her. Of course the police came and they questioned a lot of people, but they couldn't pin it on any one person, so the whole thing petered out. (Bowen, reported in Gill, 1995, p. 73)

As I show later, colonial spatial relations were excessively sexualised. In this account, it is enough for an Indian woman to have 'strayed' into the wrong space, for her to be raped, without anyone being held responsible.[8]

The public/private sphere divide has been critically analysed by many feminist theorists, since the domestic is positioned as primarily a woman's space and her access to the public sphere is sometimes seen as marked or exceptional. Gillian Rose describes the work of feminist theorists who have charted the ways in which women's sense of place within the public sphere is bounded by a fear of physical attack. But she adds to this an account of the work feminist theorists have done to try to explode the notion of a clear-cut division between the private and the public. Milroy and Wismer have further developed this critique by showing the way that much of women's work cannot be fitted into this binary divide and that the spheres themselves are more interconnected than has previously been recognised; they thus argue for a disengagement of the conflation of gender and the private/public spheres (Milroy and Wismer, 1994). Certainly once one begins to move the analysis of the public/private sphere away from a concern with British middle-class women, the distinction becomes untenable.

This work clearly calls for a reappraisal of analysis of gender and colonialism where it is assumed that colonising and colonised women are confined to the private domestic sphere, whilst colonising and colonised men operate in the public sphere. As I hope to show in this article, colonised space troubles some of the simple binary oppositions of public and private spheres, since some of the values circulating within the colonised countries are profoundly at odds with the values of the imperial culture. There seem to be extreme forms of the public/private divide at an idealised, stereotypical level: for example, the perceived restriction of some Indian women in the private sphere within the harem or zenana, and the ultra-conservative spatial arrangements within the civil lines in British Indian cities (see Callan and Ardener, 1984). Yet at the same time, British women's travel writing in colonised countries, together with the accounts of British women in outpost situations, by their very presence alone in the public sphere destabilise notions of a clear female–private/male–public sphere divide (Mills, 1991; see also Paxton, 1992).

Space is in general encoded and policed/regulated in different ways for women and men. As Moore has noted, however, generally it is the dominant group's view of space which is considered to be the norm:

> The ruling or dominant group in society always present their culture both as natural and as the culture of the whole society . . . The plurality of culture and the existence of alternative interpretations and values are not usually emphasised in the symbolic analysis of space, or indeed in the symbolic analysis of any form of cultural representation. (Moore, 1986, p. 74)

It should be added that different groups of women have had different relations to space. Groups of women at various times in history have had to be chaperoned when in the public sphere, have seen the public sphere as a place of potential sexual attack and have been taught to consider the domestic as primarily a female space. However, this does not mean to say that women have not negotiated with those constraints. Nor does it mean that the public sphere is one which is threatening for all women. As Spain has shown, in many cultures where work takes place for all inhabitants outside the private sphere, for example, peasant farmers, the public sphere cannot be defined as a sexualised or threatening place (Spain, 1992). It is the particular conjuncture of industrial capitalism in the late nineteenth century which makes the public sphere problematic for British middle-class women. The colonial context troubles that simple binary divide, because the power relations inscribed therein are crosscut with other power relations, which British women can participate in.

Doreen Massey's work demonstrates the necessity of discussing women and men in space in materialistic terms, for she states that: 'what is at issue is not social phenomena in space but both social phenomena and space as constituted out of social relations, [we therefore need to think of] the spacial [as] social relations "stretched out"' (Massey, 1994, p. 2). This notion of space being imbricated with social relations is important in considering women in space, because it moves discussion away from simple notions of women as a group having a consistent relation to spatial frameworks. Whilst Massey's basic premise is essential for this kind of analysis, I have found it very difficult to forge a materialistic form of analysis from her work. Her lack of specificity in terms of different forms of spatial relation have led me to draw more on Henrietta Moore's anthropological work, since she has produced very detailed practical analyses (Moore, 1986). Thus, through an analysis of the socially constructed differences in women and men's access to the public and private sphere, it is possible to map out the differences this may entail for women and men when they negotiate spatial boundaries for themselves and for other subjects.

VIEWING POSITIONS: THE SUBLIME, KNOWLEDGE AND COLONIAL SPACE

In analysing space, it is important to consider not simply that which is represented spatially, but also the position from which that representation is produced. I would like to consider in this section the importance of viewing and knowing positions in constructing spatial relations. First, I will concentrate on the sublime as a supremely imperialist viewing/knowing position, and I will then move on to a consideration of knowledge itself.

Rose's work on the landscape has been very important in understanding Western women's different access to that position of intelligibility which is the viewer of landscape.[9] When describing fieldworkers and the landscape, Rose stresses that cultural geographers have begun to

> problematise the term 'landscape' as a reference to relations between society and environment . . . and they have argued that it refers not only to the relationship between different objects caught in the fieldworker's gaze, but that it also implies a specific way of looking. (Rose, 1993, p. 87).

This focus on a specific way of looking and a specific form of subjectivity is especially important in considering the way that spatiality is constructed. Rose goes on to argue that the 'domineering view of the single point of the omniscient observer of landscape' is one which is conventionally taken up by males and that women tend to see landscape in more relational ways; rather than seeking to subdue the landscape, in their writings they tend to see landscapes in relation to their domestic spaces and their networks of interaction. She describes the work of Pollock on women artists who abandon the conventional wide landscapes of male painters for more confined spatial representations; she states that they '[rearticulate] traditional space so that it ceases to function primarily as the space of sight for a mastering gaze, but becomes the locus of relationships' (Pollock, cited in Rose, 1993, p. 112). This seems an unnecessarily polarised view of gender and the gaze which cannot be seen to operate particularly well within the colonial setting. British women's gaze in this context is mastering, not in a simple aping of a male gaze, but in a more complex negotiation of their position within a power hierarchy instituted through colonisation.

The representation of experience of the sublime is crucial to a discussion of women's relation to landscape, since the sublime subject is one who locates himself/herself in a particular spatial and power framework. The sublime is, as Mellor states, 'probably [the] most important and simultaneously least attainable ideal. It is unattainable because the sublime ego seeks ultimately to collapse the difference between subject and object, self and other' (Mellor, 1993, p. 148). Mellor argues that the sublime ego is never achieved, simply because this fusion is impossible except at an imagined level. Generally, critics have argued that the sublime is a moment of confrontation between a solidarity individual ego and a landscape where these problems of conflict and otherness are resolved; it is a question of the subject controlling the landscape through controlling their visual sensations, thus consolidating their position as a unified seeing subject. Yaeger terms this encounter 'self-centred imperialism' (Yaeger, 1989, p. 192) and she states that the sublime is concerned with the attempt 'in words and feelings [to] transcend the normative, the human' (Yaeger, 1989, p. 192). In this process of transcendence, the sublime subject is aggrandised and is ratified in its position of power. Yet, it is clear that the sublime moment is one where the subject is engaging actively with a set of instutionalised beliefs and values, both about its own position within the terrain and within a larger set of beliefs about the way that society is organised. Whilst psychoanalytical theorising seems to find it necessary to characterise the sublime as a moment which the subject experiences in isolation from the wider society, it is clear that social forces are at work. Within the colonial context, the sublime moment is one where the power of the colonisers informs these seemingly transcendental moments.[10] So, whilst the sublime seems at first sight to be a concept only available for analysis using psychoanalytic theory, thus only focusing on the individual psyche, a materialist-feminist analysis would reinflect this concern to describe the differential access to that position of the sublime viewer.

There are particular types of sublime experience which Yaeger suggests are prototypically masculinist:

> Typically the male writing in the sublime mode will stage a moment of blockage which is followed by a moment of imagistic brilliance. That is, the mind fights back against the blocking source by representing its own ability to grasp the sublime object. This representation of inability becomes scriptive proof of the mind's percipience and stability – of the mind's willed relation to a transcendental order, and thus of the mind's powerful univocity – its potential for mental domination of the other. (Yaeger, 1989, p. 202)

Thus, the landscape is represented as Other and as problematic only in order for the subsequent control and transcendence to be brought to the fore.

The sublime moment is one in which the ego is represented as in isolation from other humans; it is a confrontation of the viewer and the landscape. Yet this spectatorial position in relation to an empty landscape recalls Mary Louise Pratt's work on colonial landscape, where the colonial male subject surveys the terrain from a panoramic position, and thus brings to bear the whole of the colonial enterprise in this encounter (Pratt, 1992). She states that the land in colonial writing presents itself to the viewer, it shows itself or unfolds beneath his gaze; the landscape is not seen to be one of human habitation or work, rather it is 'emptied' by the colonising 'improving' eye and 'made meaningful only in terms of a capitalist future and of their potential for producing a marketable surplus' (Pratt, 1992, p. 61). The moment of the sublime within the colonial landscape is thus an imposition of power relations, not of an individual and a colonised race, but of colonising institutions speaking through that colonising sublime subject. For example, consider Samuel Baker describing his 'discovery' of the source of the Nile:

> The day broke beautifully clear, and having crossed a deep valley between the hills, we toiled up the opposite slope. I hurried to the summit. The glory of our prize burst suddenly upon me! There, like a sea of quicksilver, lay far neath the grand expanse of water – a boundless sea horizon on the south and south-west, glittering in the noonday sun; and on the west, at fifty or sixty miles distance, blue mountains rose from the bosom of the lake to a height of about 7,000 feet above its level. It is impossible to describe the triumph of that moment; here was the reward for all our labour – for the years of tenacity with which we had toiled through Africa. England had won the sources of the Nile! . . . I thought how vainly mankind had sought these sources throughout so many ages, and reflected that I had been the humble instrument permitted to unravel this portion of the great mystery when so many greater than I had failed. . . . As an imperishable memorial of one loved and mourned by our gracious Queen and deplored by every Englishman, I called this great lake 'the Albert Nyanzan'. (Baker, 1866, in Hanbury-Tenison, 1993, pp. 182–3)

Here, the sublime subject vacillates between two uneasy positions: he takes up the conventional position of the sublime subject, overwhelmed by the grandeur and vastness of the visual stimulation, stressing distance, expanse and boundlessness; yet at the same time, this individual subject positions himself as a representative of colonial power, eliding himself with England ('England had won the sources of the Nile') and posing himself as Queen Victoria's emissary, naming the lake for her.

This sublime colonial subject position is one which is more available for British male viewers than British females for a number of reasons: because of the stereotypical difficulties of being alone in a landscape for women, because of the fear of sexual attack, fear of precisely not being alone, and the sense that the domestic is women's sphere rather than the public sphere, this colours women's experience of being in a natural environment in a way in which men's experience is not. As Hamner and Saunders state: 'women's sense of security is profoundly shaped by our inability to secure an undisputed right to occupy . . . [public] space' (cited in Rose, 1993, p. 34). However, this difficulty with assuming the sublime position can also be located within the material existence of British women within the colonial context, and, with changes in that context, there are concomitant changes in women's relation to the sublime. As Paxton states:

> Colonising British women could not so easily divorce themselves from the body and its desires, in part because they lived in a colonial economy that assigned white women the labour of reproduction but prohibited them from serving the Raj more directly by working in the military or civil service. (Paxton, 1992, p. 392)[11]

This difference in the way that women and men see their position in relation to the site of the sublime is bound to have effects on the way that landscape is represented and the way that men and women map out their spatial territories within colonialism. However, because of the power relations which British women negotiate within the colonial context, they are able to adopt this seemingly masculine sublime position. As Strobel states:

> women carved out a space amid the options available to them: options for the most part created by imperialism and limited by male dominance (and by class). As participants in the historical process of British expansion, they benefited from the economic and political subjugation of indigenous peoples and shared many of the accompanying attitudes of racism, paternalism, ethnocentricism and national chauvinism. (Strobel, 1991, p. xiii)

Thus it is possible to find representations within writing by British women which call into question the simple view of the sublime as stereotypically masculinist and imperialist; for example, Mary Kingsley represents herself alone in the middle of the West African jungle at midnight, taking a canoe and encountering a group of hippos in the middle of a lake.

> I was left in peace at about 11.30 p.m. and clearing off some clothes from the bench threw myself down and tried to get some sleep . . . Sleep impossible – mosquitoes! lice!! – at 12.40 I got up and slid aside my bark door . . . I went down them to our canoe and found it safe, high up among the Fan canoes on the stones, and then I slid a small Fan canoe off, and taking a paddle from a cluster stuck in the sand, paddled out on to the dark lake. It was a wonderfully quiet night with no light save that from the stars. One immense planet shone pre-eminent in the purple sky, throwing a golden path down onto the still waters. Quantities of big fish sprung out of the water, their glistening silver-white scales flashing so that they looked like slashing swords . . . I paddled leisurely across the lake to the shore on the right, and seeing crawling on the ground some large glow-worms, drove the canoes on to the bank among some hippo grass and got out to get them. While engaged on this hunt I felt the earth quiver under my feet and heard a soft big soughing sound, and looking around saw I

had dropped in on a hippo banquet. (Kingsley, 1897, pp. 253–4)

This type of representation is clearly written within the discursive frameworks of sublime encounters between the colonial individual (male), usually represented as overwhelming, strange and potentially dangerous. That it is possible for a female to represent herself as alone in such a scenario, given the discursive frameworks of British middle-class domesticity, can only be explained with reference to the difference of colonial femininity and hence spatiality. Yet, Kingsley does not wholeheartedly adopt this position of the sublime, since her representation of her ascent of the Peak of the Cameroons (Mungo Mah Etindeh) wavers between the sublime, (surveying the territory before her and setting herself in a lineage of European explorers) and the banal (detailing the difficulties of making tea, and the discomforts of climbing in torrential rain) (Kingsley, 1897, p. 555; see Mills, 1991 and Blunt, 1994). Many other women within the colonial context had much less problematic relations to the sublime, some of them able simply to adopt this position of spectatorial power because of their position within the colonial infrastructure, and some of them viewing their position as excluded from such power. It is material conditions and relations of power which determine viewing positions and hence spatial relations.

When considering viewing positions and spatiality, it is also important to analyse the relationship between positions of knowledge and space. As Michel Foucault has shown, there is a close relation between the production of power and the production of knowledge (Foucault, 1980). Within the British empire this is very clearly exemplified, as many critics have shown (Richards, 1993). Gillian Rose's work focuses on the interrelatedness of the spatial and power/ knowledge and examines the possibilities that exist within this model of spatiality for women to exploit (Rose, 1993, 1995). For her, whilst bodies are 'maps of the relation between power and identity', those maps do not simply trace subjection (Rose, 1993, p. 32). Rose also notes that women have tended to be represented as the space of the bodily; that male observers of nature do not do so from a bodily space but from a seeing space. This, as Rose goes on to show, is a space of power/knowledge, and this seeing position is more important in terms of the type of subject position that it maps out than for what is described.

Within the colonial context, as Mary Louise Pratt has shown, a particular type of knowledge was produced, what she terms planetary consciousness, that is:

> an orientation toward interior exploration and the construction of global-scale meaning through the descriptive apparatuses of natural history. This new planetary consciousness . . . is a basic element constructing modern Eurocentricism, that hegemonic reflex that troubles westerners even as it continues to be second nature to them. (Pratt, 1992, p. 15)

What characterised Linnaean typologies of natural history was their universal scope. The view of natural history led to Europeans travelling the globe in search of specimens and extracting those specimens from their meaning within indigenous systems of signification and functionality, in order for them to take their place within a Eurocentric and colonial system of knowledge. As John Noyes states in his analysis of German South West Africa: 'the colony is a space in which meaning is possible' (Noyes, 1992, p. 6). The position which a European traveller could adopt because of his or her role in the production of knowledge of natural history was one which was elided with the colonial state and, as Pratt states, travellers were 'central agents in legitimising scientific authority and its global project alongside Europe's other ways of knowing the world' (Pratt, 1992, p. 29). British women travellers in the same way as male travellers produced scientific knowledge which was fundamentally connected to European expansion and the promotion of a view of the world that sees European activities as essentially civilising. The naturalist figure may have had some appeal to women travellers since it seemed so innocent, in relation to an 'assumed guilt of conquest', as Pratt puts it (Pratt, 1992, p. 29). But this production of knowledge set up a network of spatial frameworks within which the colonised country is constructed as simply a repository of unusual specimens which Europeans may explore and plunder at will. The colonised country is produced as a space empty of systems of signification other than the order which European scientific knowledge imposes. Although imperial knowledge is generally thought of as masculine, women travellers played an important role in constructing a form of knowledge which, as Pratt shows, is a 'way of taking possession without subjugation and violence' (Pratt, 1992, p. 29).[12]

Thus, viewing positions and positions of knowledge are ones which are gendered, but not in simple oppositional terms: males have power/knowledge/sublime position; women do not. With contexts such as that of British imperialism where British women are differentially placed within the hierarchy of power, their access to these viewing positions and hence to particular spatial frameworks varies. These different inflections of gender, viewing and knowledge lead us to a consideration of different levels of colonial space.

LEVELS OF COLONIAL SPACE

In describing the gendered nature of colonial space it is important to examine a range of different spatial relations both at an ideal or stereotypical level, and at a more experiential level in what Mary Louise Pratt terms 'the contact zone' where 'disparate cultures meet, clash and grapple with each other, often in highly asymmetrical relations of domination and subordination' (Pratt, 1992, p. 38).[13]

Ideal/Stereotypical Level of Space

Although architectural space does not determine social relations, it may attempt to set out the parameters within which certain types of relation may be negotiated; as Spain states:

architecture itself does not directly determine how people act or how they see themselves and others. Yet the associations a culture establishes at any particular time between a 'model' or typical house and a notion of the model family do encourage certain roles and assumptions. (Spain, 1992, p. 108)

At an ideal level, British colonial space in India and Africa is primarily designed into clear-cut territories where distance between the colonised and the colonisers is emphasised. At an actual level, this distance is impossible to maintain and instead there develops what King has termed a third culture, that is, a very different form of cultural system to the colonial culture in Britain, modified as it is by the indigenous culture (King, 1976). Pratt has characterised this difference rather more amorphously as the 'contact zone' where the colonised and colonising culture mutually influence each others' norms and values, yet the notion of a distinct colonial culture embodied in King's term is more useful. In spatial terms, the notion of a distinct third culture helps us to develop an awareness of the interlocking and overlaid nature of spatial frameworks within this context.[14]

It is important here to analyse the built environment within the colonial period and consider the way in which architecture and town planning attempted to construct idealised forms of race relations (King, 1976; Dalrymple. 1994). I will focus here on colonial architecture in British India. As King has shown, the civil lines in India were generally located some way from the 'native' town; the justification for this distance was made on perceived health grounds, and colonial cities were designed to emphasise the distinction between ruler and ruled.[15] In contrast to what were seen as the sprawling accretions of the crowded 'native' town, the civil lines were generally planned with mathematical precision on a grid-plan, including strategically placed grand public buildings which dominated the cityscape and were easily viewed from a range of vistas, and wide, straight avenues which gave ease of access and visibility. Colonial residences were often set in spacious landscaped grounds and built on classical lines, emphasising the perceived imperial heritage of the inhabitants. Colonial town planning was an idealised embodiment of colonial relations. But this notion of the complete separation of the 'native' area from the British area is one which only holds at an ideal level, since the separated civil lines contained within them large numbers of indigenous people. Within each compound, there were servants' quarters; within the cantonment in British India, there was also a sizeable area reserved for Indian troops serving in the British Indian army, together with a 'serai' or accommodation for indigenous travellers which was not maintained by the cantonment.[16] There was also a special compound for prostitutes. Furthermore, in order to 'service' these large residences and the imperial infrastructure, within a caste system, it was necessary to allocate tasks to many different servants, which resulted in a large number of servants being present in the domestic space (see King, 1976; Ballhatchet, 1980). There was a great deal of crossing over of these clear-cut boundaries; British mensahibs shopping within the native town and traders visiting from house to house for example. British women worked in the 'native' town in missions and hospitals. British prostitutes worked both in the cantonment and sometimes in the 'native' town; some British women worked in bars in the 'native' town (Ballhatchet, 1980). Servants were given living quarters in the same compound as the colonisers, spending a great part of their time within the same domestic space as the colonisers, (particularly British women), making this ideal of distance and separation practically impossible. King has shown that there was a great deal of contact between Indians and British, but that the contact was between members of the British upper middle class and members of some of the lowest castes within Indian society. It is also true that the British often met with Indians of a far higher social status than themselves. However, it is clear that there were whole sections of Indian society, with whom the British had no contact (King, 1976).

Spatial segregation seems to be 'figured' around British females. As Ballhatchet notes:

> Improved conditions encouraged more English women to live in India, and in various ways their presence seems to have widened the distance between the ruling race and the people . . . As wives they hastened the disappearance of the Indian mistress. As hostesses they fostered the development of exclusive social groups in every civil station. As women they were thought by English men to be in need of protection from lascivious Indians. (Ballhatchet, 1980, p. 5)

This is the stereotypical representation of the memsahib, but as Ballhatchet shows, this figure of the distant mensahib is only invoked at moments when British colonial power is threatened, for example, in the case of the Ilbert Bill in 1883 and Gillies case of 1859 (see Chaudhuri and Strobel, 1992).[17]

The one space which seemed to be more clearly designed as a separate zone was interestingly enough the hill stations – those settlements which were built by the British so that women and children could escape from the heat of the plains during the summer. The hill station was built with the sole aim of providing protection and leisure opportunities for British women; there was usually only a small military presence, and often no administrative functions. They were not built on the site of Indian settlements and therefore it was possible to plan them without constraints. As King shows, whilst many servants lived in these hill stations and élite Indians had houses there, more than any other area in British India, the architecture and town planning reflected a concern to recreate a stereotypically 'British' space.[18] Indians were excluded from the clubs and they were also forbidden to use the main thoroughfare, which, as many of the photographs and illustrations of hill stations show, was used by the British as a space for socialising. As Frances Shebbeare states in an oral record about Simla:

There was a top road there which you used if you wanted to get from one side of town to the other. I used to use the bottom road if I was riding, but I wouldn't have gone there on my feet, not for anything. It was full of people crowded together, roasting corncobs, and there were horrible smells. It was the crowdedness I disliked. We lived in a refined, rarified atmosphere up at the top. (Shebbeare, reported in Gill, 1995, p. 99).

The hill station was a space where there were frequently more British women than men and where a great deal of time was devoted to leisure pursuits and the maintenance and regulation of communal ties (see Callan and Ardener, 1984).

Thus, architectural space and the planned space of British Indian towns and cities refracted some of the stereotypical values which circulated at an idealised level. This level of spatial design reaffirmed some of the stereotypical values circulating amongst the colonial third culture, but these values were themselves challenged by other discursive frameworks produced within the contact zone.

The Contact Zone: level of sexualized space

In literary writing about India and Africa, the contact zone is represented as a problematic arena where the meeting of the two cultures creates conflict. An emblematic text, such as Alice Perrin's short story, 'The Fakir's Island' (1901), represents the meeting of a British mensahib with an Indian fakir/beggar, as one where the woman is cursed, resulting in her developing smallpox (Perrin, in Cowasjee, 1990). Innumerable novels and short stories represent the contact zone as a space where there is mystery, barbarism, mutual incomprehension, conflict; the most prominent form of contact which underlies many other relations is sexual contact or the threat of sexual attack. Whilst the sexual contact was often between white males and indigenous females/males, this sexual contact was figured at an idealised/stereotypical level as between white women and indigenous males. The contact zone is sexualised, as novels such as E. M. Forster's A Passage to India demonstrate: entry into the contact zone is enough for there to be an assumption that sexual relations have taken place, and this assumption colours all other contact (Forster, 1924). As Frances Shebbeare states:

> A rather alarming thing you could do sometimes was to go down to the bazaar, to the Indian shops . . . I remember going a couple of times. I didn't like it at all. It was very uncomfortable. They had little tiny alleyways of streets, and everybody was crowding in on them. They weren't going to hit you or steal, really, but it was just rather frightening. One hardly even did it. If you wanted anything from the bazaar, you sent your bearer. (Shebbeare, in Gill, 1995, p. 98)

Here, there is no fear of violence, but simply a vague sense of ill-defined discomfort determined by this sexualising of space.

As the BBC2 series *Ruling Passions* (first aired during the spring of 1995) illustrated, whilst maintaining a strict policy of separation of the races because of fear of miscegenation and sexual contagion, in fact sexual contact was the norm rather than the exception, as is evidenced by the numbers of Anglo-Indians or people of mixed race and the stringent if ineffective legislation on sexually transmitted diseases, which continued in force in India long after the Contagious Diseases Acts had been repealed in Britain (Ballhatchet, 1980; Whitehead, 1995; Gill, 1995; Young, 1995; McClintock, 1995). As Hyam has shown, British males saw the colonial space as a sexualised one where 'sexual dynamics crucially underpinned the whole operation of British empire and Victorian expansion' (Hyam, 1990, p. 1). Hyam's study, like Gill's more popular 1995 analysis, is extremely problematic in viewing sexual activity only from the perspective of the British male, as Berger has shown, and neither study considers sexuality in the context of power relations (Berger, 1988; see also White, 1993). They characterise British male sexual activity within India and Africa as free from Victorian constraints, rather than determined by colonial power relations. However, Hyam's and Gill's analysis of British male sexuality serves as a contrast to the stereotypical view of sexualised space which centres on the need for protection of British women. Their work maps out the way in which heterosexual and homosexual British males sexually exploited colonised males, females and children and presented this sexual activity as something for which they did not need to take responsibility, as I showed earlier. The colonial presence justified and made 'natural' this form of exploitation; therefore, in most accounts of sexuality, British male activity is invisible.

At an ideal level, both British women and 'native' women are confined, either within the supposed safety of the civil lines, the safe 'British' space of the Indian hill station, or, in the case of the Indian woman, in the harem. This confined existence is characterised by many writers as a life of passivity, ennui and suffering for both Indian and British women. For British women in the civil lines in India, their children were either looked after by ayahs, or sent to the hill stations or to Britain for education; they were left to cultivate their gardens and supervise the servants. As one account states:

> The heat of the darkness seems almost intangible . . . the other sex lives and moves and has its being – on very early morning parades, in stuffy court houses all through the hottest hours, on the war-path after blackbuck over the plain at noon, on the tennis court, on the polo ground at sundown. But we women-folk seem simply to exist. (Anon, 1905, cited in King, 1976, p. 142)

But, as Jenny Sharpe has shown, this confinement of British women because of the fear of sexual attack has a history which is an integral part of the justification of colonial rule. Sharpe focuses on the fictional 'origins' of the image of the British woman subjected to rape by 'native' insurgents, in the 1857 Indian Uprising/Mutiny, and states that:

the idea of rebellion [in the 1857 revolt] was so closely imbricated with the violation of English womanhood that the Mutiny was remembered as a barbaric attack on innocent white women. Yet Magistrates commissioned to investigate the so-called eyewitness reports that could find no evidence to substantiate the rumours of rebels raping, torturing and multilating English women. (Sharpe, 1993, p. 2)

By meticulously examining the fictional accounts and historical records, she is able to document the way that this figure of woman serves to displace consideration of the oppressiveness of colonial rule and also to obscure its fragility in moments of conflict. She states that the 'savaged remains [of British women] display a fantasy of the native's savagery that screens the "barbarism" of colonialism' (Sharpe, 1993, p. 233) and also 'displaces attention away from the image of English men dying at the hands of native insurgents' (Sharpe, 1994, p. 231). She shows how focusing on representations of the rape of British women at times of conflict in colonial rule also has the effect of moving our attention away from political insurrection towards a concern with racial difference and Otherness. Thus, she stresses that it is important to see these images and the subsequent protection of British females as serving a function within the maintenance of colonial rule in a time of crisis (a crisis which was both a political crisis within India and also a wider crisis relating to the moral and ethical position of colonial rule) (see, also, Donaldson, 1992, and Sunder Rajan, 1994). This concern of rape and protection also had the effect of sexualising space for women.

Whilst this system of confinement and protection operates at an ideal level, it is therefore surprising that in British women's writing there are a variety of strategies adopted in relation to the fear of sexual attack. Some novelists, like Flora Annie Steel and Maud Diver represented the 1857 Mutiny/Uprising and focused on the assault of British women. Others, such as women travel writers, did not represent the threat of sexual attack; it seems to be the 'unsaid' of a wide range of women's texts, exerting a pressure and a tension on the writing but not manifesting itself. Women travellers seem to transgress the ideal spatial relations which colonialism establishes; they travel as honorary men, and they are allowed to enter places from which women are normally excluded. (For example, they dine with the men when indigenous women are excluded; they are allowed into places such as the harem from which British men are excluded. See, for example, Fanny Parkes, 1850.) One of their roles in representing these inaccessible places is to contribute to the imperial task of revealing the secrets of the colonised country. Thus, at an idealised and ideological level, British women are restricted to the civil lines, but in actuality their presence is transgressive of these spatial boundaries. The writings of British women travellers and novelists help to challenge the fixity of some of these idealised colonial boundaries.

A further factor which helps to complicate the picture of confinement within colonial space is the fact that although the memsahib is the archetypal 'figure' of British womanhood, there were many other women from different classes who lived and travelled in colonial India and Africa. Ballhatchet shows that British working-class women worked as prostitutes and in bars, amongst other professions, throughout the Empire. They also came to India and Africa as the wives of soldiers of the ranks and officers, and as missionaries and nurses (see Ballhatchet, 1980; Trollope, 1983; Young, 1995). This figure of the confined and 'rapable' mensahib needs therefore to be seen as one which is challenged by other representations of women which circulated within the Empire, and it also needs to be seen as a representation which occurred only at a particular time.[19]

Harem, Zenana, Suttee and the level of Subaltern Space

It is important to recognise that the confined spaces of Indian women operate at the ideal level of stereotype rather than the actual level. Whilst the concept of the stereotype is important, as Bhabha has shown, I would, however, like to question the monolithic quality of stereotype prevalent in psychoanalytic theorising, since these stereotypes changed over time and were challenged by other representations (Bhabha, 1994)[20]. As Moore has shown, stereotypes do not determine thinking, but need to be seen as forming part of a practice, which is developed in negotiation with other people and other practices:

> The organisation of space is not a direct reflection of cultural codes and meaning; it is above all a context developed through practice – that is, through the interaction of individuals. This context, or set of relationships, may have many meanings. These meanings . . . are in fact simultaneous. (Moore, 1986, p. 117)

This is not to deny that stereotypes exist, but simply to argue that stereotypes themselves are not so clearly defined as is often asserted, nor are they immutable; furthermore, they exist under conditions of constant negotiation and conflict with other representations and experience.

In discussing representations of Indian women, Rajaswari Sunder Rajan (1993) has shown that those confined to the harem were from a limited range of élite Indian women; and as Nair states, 'the zenana was confined to certain classes and regions: the upper and middle classes of north, northwestern and eastern India or where Moghul influence had been most direct and sustained' (Nair, 1990, p. 11). Furthermore the notion of confinement is problematic when one realises that the term harem simply means 'women's quarters' and that the restrictions generally apply to men entering the quarters rather than to women leaving them. If one read male-authored British colonial fiction literally, one would imagine that all Indian women were confined to the harem; consider Rudyard Kipling's short story 'Beyond the Pale' (1888), where contact between an Indian female confined to the harem and a British male results in the barbaric amputation of the woman's hands; this story is emblematic of the horror and mystery surrounding the harem for certain British males at a particular moment of colonial history. Representations of the harem preoccupied both European women and men alike, as Lewis has shown (Lewis, 1995). As Apter among others has shown, the harem was primarily imaged as a sexualised space for/by European meals (Apter, 1992). However, for British women, representations of the harem served different purposes, as Nair has shown, serving to critique colonised society and also to buttress the British notion of the family as part of a growing feminist awareness (Nair, 1990). Some British women wrote about the power which Indian women had within the harem but as Nair has shown, 'by stressing such power in a place that had long been dismissed as powerless and demonstrating only the urgency of change, Englishwomen successfully displaced the responsibility of the Raj for its stupendous failures and shifted it to the Indians themselves' (Nair, 1990, p. 21). She goes on to state: 'By making "visible" the woman of the colonies, they could successfully make "invisible" their own colonisation by English men' (Nair, 1990, p. 25).

In marked contrast to this vision of Indian women as confined within the harem is the other stereotypical vision of Indian women: suttee or sati, that display within the public sphere of submission in the widow's seemingly voluntary immolation on her husband's funeral pyre. Again in representational terms, this image of widow-sacrifice features large in many fictional representations and travel accounts of India. But as Rajan has shown, this practice is limited to defined social groups and its practitioners vary through time (Rajan, 1994). She also shows that, although British accounts have traditionally tried to demonstrate that sati is a form of utter devaluation of women and is thus barbaric, within Indian culture, sati, although much debated, within the nineteenth century, was a form of deification of women.[21]

It is important here to consider the notion of the subaltern subject, especially Gayatri Spivak's formulation, in order to examine the possibility of sketching out subaltern space/s (Spivak, 1988, 1990; Guha and Spivak, 1988). Just as colonial history is being rewritten through the matrices of race and gender, it is necessary to examine colonial spatial frameworks in order to construct subaltern spatiality (see Sangari and Vaid, 1990; Bhadra, 1988). Subaltern space within India and Africa can be defined as the complex where indigenous spatial frameworks and colonised evaluations of those frameworks collided, within the context of the imposition of imperial spatial frameworks. To colonised subjects, practices such as sati and the confinement of women, had been viewed differently before colonial rule, and once colonial rule was instituted colonised space was inflected differently. For many subjects, these practices figured large in nationalist struggles. It is not possible to 'retrieve' this subaltern space, but it may be possible to 'figure' it out from examining a range of representational practices, much as Rajan has done with her re-examination of sati (Rajan, 1993).

CONCLUSIONS

To sum up, I have argued that within the colonial sphere, British and indigenous women's interventions in the production and negotiation of spatial frameworks cannot simply be considered in terms of notions of confinement. The architectural constraints and ideological strictures on women's movement within the colonial zone were important in shaping a notion of a woman's place and contributed to a sexualising of space. Nevertheless, the spatial frameworks which developed as a result of the clash between these constraints and women as agents, as producers of knowledge and viewers of landscape meant that a variety of spatial roles existed for women. For example, British women's travel writing, with its ambivalent position, wavering between openly transgressive qualities and acceptance of the domestic sphere and protection, forces us to consider the complexity of the role of gender in mapping colonial space. Similarly, when considering colonised women and their spatial frameworks, it is not possible simply to consider the stereotypical representations of confinement in the harem. It is necessary to consider these representations together with critical subaltern re-evaluations of those spaces and alongside other representations of the majority of colonised women who were not confined. It is also necessary to consider the moment when spatial frameworks are overlaid or where they collide, for example, in Alice Perrin's short story 'Mary Jones', where an elderly, working-class 'British' woman is discovered on her death to have been an Anglo-Indian 'nautch' dancer (Perin, in Cowasjee, 1990). Thus, I have not been arguing that women have separate spatial frameworks, but that women negotiate meanings within the context of dominant discursive fields; whilst the dominant discourses may place emphasis on confinement, passivity and protection, these discourses are themselves challenged and reaffirmed by representations produced by both women and men. As Moore states:

> The fact that women may end up supporting the dominant male order in their efforts to value themselves within it does not imply that women's interests are ultimately identical with those of men. On the contrary women recognise the conflict of interests between themselves and men, but are trying to identify themselves as valuable, social individuals. The continuing dominance of the male order and the appropriation of apparently male values or interests by women are the result of the powerful and reinforced homology between what is socially valuable and what is male. (Moore, 1986, pp. 184–5)

I find this formulation helpful in that it enables us to examine both the ways in which colonial space is gendered and the ways in which it might be possible to discuss the existence of a range of spaces conflicting with the dominant representations of spatial relations; in so doing, it will then be possible to develop a practice which is more attuned to the specificities and complexities of colonial contexts.

NOTES

1. This article is a revised version of several short papers given at the Women and Space conference, Lancaster University, 1995; English Department, University of Umea, Sweden, 1995; and Culture and Colonialism conference, University College, Galway, Ireland, 1995. It forms part of a larger study of gender and colonial space which draws on a wider range of primary materials than could be included in this article. I would like to thank participants at the above conferences for their comments, particularly Alison Easton, Jackie Stacey and Margerie Toone; I would also like to thank Tony Brown for insightful comments on the various drafts of this article.

2. The analyses of the textual examples will of necessity be rather brief because of constraints of space. I hope merely to indicate the complexity of gendered colonial spatial relations.

3. I will be discussing spatial relations at a number of different levels and differentiating these relations from place as such, although I recognize that a clear-cut division is not possible, as Daphney Spain has shown in her cross-cultural analysis of the relation between the gendering of place and the gendering of spatial relations (Spain, 1992). Although I am primarily concerned with social space, it is also clear to me that geographical space cannot be ignored. As a linguist, rather than a geographer, my 'take' on these divisions may be slightly more relaxed than that of other critics.

4. I am not arguing that these positions of agency do not exist for colonised subjects or that colonised subjects did not themselves write accounts which could be drawn on in this account of spatial relations; however, as I will show in the section on the subaltern, it is clear that texts do not give access to some unmediated authentic experience, which could somehow be considered more 'real' or more 'true' than the biased accounts produced by the colonising subjects (see Spivak, 1993).

5. The notion of a simple literal reading is itself problematic since this is a reading position which I am constructing rather than simply 'recovering'; however, as I have argued in *Gendering the Reader* (1994a), there are positions which seem to proffer themselves as the dominant or, in Althusser's terms, the obvious reading for the text, and it is these seemingly 'obvious' readings which I shall concentrate on at certain times throughout these readings.

6. See Rose (1993) and Massey (1994) for discussions of the difficulty of defining space.

7. Many of the autobiographical accounts written during the imperial context stress the difficulty of being confined within the civil lines as an 'incorporated wife' with all of the attention to social hierarchy that this entailed, yet they also stress the freedom which was brought about through being in positions of power, which involved such upper middle-class British norms as riding alone, travelling unchaperoned and going on hunting expeditions (see Gill, 1995; Mangan, 1985).

8. What interests me most in this passage and many others which are drawn on by Gill in his account of sexual relations within the Raj is the fact that agency is meticulously avoided (Gill, 1995).

9. Again, it is assumed that women in general have limited access to the positions of power and intelligibility in relation to landscape. At an implicit level, the conditions of certain Western women are universalised to all women.

10. I am grateful to Tony Brown for this observation.

11. I would disagree with Paxton's view as a global representation of women's involvement in colonialism. Whilst British women were not employed by the colonial institutions, many women were employed by zenana hospitals as nurses, within missionary schools, and played an active role in the funding of colonial missions (see Trollope, 1983; Mills, 1994b).

12. British women produced a wide range of knowledges about colonised countries as

the essays in Chaudhuri and Strobel (1992) have shown, some of them similar to the knowledges produced by men and other specifically 'feminine', for example, knowledge of indigenous women. Some of these knowledges were devalued because they were concerned with domestic space, for example, Flora Annie Steel's *The Complete Indian Housekeeper and Cook* (1888), where Steel transforms the produce of India into simulacra of British cuisine. Spain (1992) argues that gendered spaces, such as the domestic, serve to exclude British women from positions of power, since the valued sphere is the one which British men inhabit. I discuss this book at more length in the wider study of gender and colonial space which I am currently engaged on.

13. I am cautious about the use of the word experiential here; I would like to contrast the stereotypical level with a level of representation which challenges stereotypes, but I do not want to infer that what is being discussed here is 'authentic' experience.

14. King describes the colonial third culture as different from the metropolitan culture, in that it is a culture without a working class and which requires indigenous labour to fulfil the functions normally carried out by that class. Because of its curious class composition (even those people who worked within British India and who did not come from the upper middle class tried to maintain the standards and ways of living of that class in Britain) and its conservatism, it developed significantly different ways of organising itself in terms of leisure, work and spatial arrangements. A further distinguishing factor about the third culture is its age profile, since most colonisers fell into a very limited age range. A fact which is very important in terms of gendering space is the fact that, within the colonial Civil Lines, there were very few children and no schools: children were generally educated in Britain or were educated in the hill stations. Those children below school age were taken care of by Indian 'ayahs'.

    However, one of the problems with King's work is that he does not develop a term for the indigenous culture which is transformed by contact with the colonial third culture; he somehow assumes that this culture remains the same. At the level of negative evaluation and spatial transformation, the indigenous culture differs markedly from, say, those cultures where colonialism has not taken place or where colonial relations are different.

15. King (1976) shows that town planning in the construction of the civil lines in Delhi was developed in line with then current views about the spread of disease through the air and through the air and through smell (so-called 'zymotic' diseases such as malaria). Colonial Civil Lines had to be built out of the line of prevailing winds coming from the indigenous town.

16. In 1863, there were 227,000 members of the colonial military stationed in India, 85,000 of them British/European, the rest of them being Indian (King, 1976, p. 98, citing Royal Commission 1863).

17. Under the Ilbert Bill, it would be possible for Indian judges to try Europeans; it is the image of the memsahib which is brought into play at this moment as a key factor in British resistance to growing Indian power. The Gilles case involved an Anglo-Indian gynaecologist whose British patient, Mrs Stonehouse, died of peritonitis; he was accused of negligence and ungentlemanly conduct and there was widespread debate about the employment of Indian or Anglo-Indian doctors for British women (Ballhatchet, 1980; Chaudhuri and Strobel, 1992).

18. But it is 'British' only at a stereotypical level; its architecture included neo-Gothic churches and streets based on The Mall, in London, but this was a model of the British spa town which was transformed by being transported out of the constraints of post-medieval town development in Britain, to the very different topographical constraints of an Indian mountain slope. I would like to thank Tony Brown for this observation.

19. It is clear that this sexualisation of space in this particular form is, as Sharpe has shown, determined by various political considerations. However, discursive structures have a continuity which does not map on to political events in such a clear-cut way, as I have shown in a discussion of discursive discontinuity and representations of rape in the context of apartheid (Mills, 1995b).

20. I am aware that Bhabha's notion of the stereotype is one which is riddled throughout with ambivalence and therefore should not be characterized as stable; however, the stereotype seems to have been analysed in isolation from its interaction with other discourses.

21. This is not an attempt to 'reclaim' sati as a place of power for Indian women, but simply to demonstrate that British accounts of sati were used to colonial purposes as many of the essays in Chaudhuri and Strobel's edited collection have shown (Chaudhuri and Strobel, 1992). Sati was also seized upon, as was clitoridectomy in Africa, as an essential part of the resistance and nationalist movement, thus figuring women within colonial space.

REFERENCES

Apter, E. (1992) 'Female trouble in the colonial harem', *differences*, 4, pp. 205–24.

Ahmed, S. (1996) 'Identifications, gender and racial difference: moving beyond the limits of a psychoanalytical account of subjectivity', in Rencka Shama, J. (ed.) *Representations of Gender and Identity Politics in South Asia*.

Ardener, S. (ed.) (1981) *Women and Space: ground rules and social maps* (London, Croom Helm).

Ashcroft, B., Griffiths, G. and Tiffin, H. (eds) (1995) *The Post-colonial Studies Reader* (London, Routledge).

Ballhatchet, K. (1980) *Race, Class and Sex under the Raj: imperial attitudes and policies and their critics 1793–1905* (London, Weidenfeld & Nicolson).

Barnes, T. J. and Duncan, J. S. (eds) (1992) *Writing Worlds: discourse, text and metaphor in the presentation of landscape* (London, Routledge).

Berger, M. (1988) 'Imperialism and sexual exploitation: a response to Ronald Hyams "Empire and sexual opportunity"', *Journal of Imperial and Commonwealth History*, 17, pp. 83–9.

Bhabha, H. (1994) 'The other question: stereotype, discrimination and the discourse of colonialism', in *The Location of Culture*, pp. 66–85 (London, Routledge).

Bhadra, G. (1988) 'Four rebels of eighteen-fifty-seven', in R. Guha and G. C. Spivak (eds) *Selected Subaltern Studies*, pp. 129–75 (New York, Oxford University Press).

Blunt, A. (1994) 'Mapping authorship and authority: reading Mary Kingsley's landscape descriptions' in A. Blunt and G. Rose (eds) *Writing Women and Space: colonial and postcolonial geographies*, pp. 51–73 (New York, Guilford Press).

Blunt, A. and Rose, G. (eds) (1994) *Writing Women and Space: colonial and postcolonial geographies* (New York, Guilford).

Butler, J. (1990) *Gender Trouble: feminism and the subversion of identity* (London, Routledge).

Callan, H. and Ardener, S. (eds) (1984) *The Incorporated Wife* (London, Croom Helm).

Callaway, H. (1987) Gender, Culture and Empire: European women in colonial Nigeria (Basingstoke, Macmillan).

Chakrabarty, D. (1988) 'Conditions for knowledge of working-class conditions: employers, government and the jute workers of Calcutta, 1890–1940', in R. Guha and G. C. Spivak (eds) *Selected Subaltern Studies* (New York, Oxford University Press).

Chaudhuri, N. and Strobel, M. (eds) (1992) *Western Women and Imperialism: complicity and resistance* (Bloomington, IN, Indiana University Press).

Colomina, B. (ed.) (1992) *Sexuality and Space* (Princeton, NJ, Princeton University).

Cowasjee, S. (ed.) (1990) *Women Writers of the Raj: short fiction from Kipling to Independence* (London, Grafton).

Dalrymple, W. (1994) *City of Djinns: a year in Delhi* (London, Flamingo).

Delphy, C. (1981) 'For a materialist feminism', *Feminist Issues*, 1, pp. 69–76.

Donaldson, L. (1992) *Decolonising Feminisms: race, gender and empire-building* (London, Routledge).

Ferguson, M. (1992) *Subject to Others: British women writers and colonial slavery, 1670–1834* (London: Routledge).

Ferguson, M. (1993) *Colonialism and Gender Relations from Mary Wollstonecraft to Jamaica Kincaid: East Caribbean connections* (New York, Columbia University Press).

Forster, E. M. (1989) *A Passage to India* (Harmondsworth, Penguin).

Foucault, M. (1972) *Archaeology of Knowledge*, tr. A. Sheridan Smith (New York, Harper Colophon) (first published in French, 1969).

Foucault, M. (1980) *Power/Knowledge: selected interviews*, C. Gordon (ed.) (Brighton, Harvester).

Fuss, D. (1989) *Essentially Speaking: feminism, nature and difference* (London, Routledge).

Gill, A. (1995) *Ruling Passions: sex, race and empire* (London, BBC Publications).

Guha, R. and Spivak, G. C. (eds) (1988) *Selected Subaltern Studies* (New York, Oxford University Press).

Haggis, J. (1990) 'Gendering colonialism or colonising gender? Recent women's studies approaches to white women and the history of British colonialism', *Women's Studies International Forum*, 13, pp. 105–15.

Hanbury-Tenison, R. (ed.) (1993) *The Oxford Book of Exploration* (Oxford, Oxford University Press).

Hennessy, R. (1993) *Materialist Feminism and the Politics of Discourse* (London, Routledge).

Hulme, P. (1986) *Colonial Encounters: Europe and the native Caribbean 1492–1797* (London, Methuen).

Hyam, R. (1990) *Empire and Sexuality: the British experience* (Manchester, Manchester University Press).

Kipling, R. (1987 [1888]) 'Beyond the Pale', in A. Rutherford (ed.) *Plain Tales from the Hills* (Oxford, Oxford University Press).

King, A. (1976) *Colonial Urban Development: culture, social power and environment* (London, Routledge & Kegan Paul).

Kingsley, M. (1897/1982) *Travels in West Africa* (London, Virago Press).

Landry, D. and Maclean, G. (1993) *Materialist Feminisms* (Oxford, Blackwell).

Lewis, R. (1995) 'Gendering Orientalism: the female Orientalist "'gaze"'', conference paper at the *Race and the Victorians Conference*, Leicester University, July.

McLintock, A. (1995) *Imperial Leather: race, gender and sexuality in the colonial contest* (London, Routledge).

McKendry, V. (1995) 'Royal maternalism and cultural imperialism: early images of Queen Victoria in the illustrated press', conference paper at the *Race and the Victorians Conference*, Leicester University, July.

Mangan, J. A. (1985) *The Games Ethic and Imperialism: aspects of the diffusion of an ideal* (Harmondsworth, Viking).

Massey, D. (1994) *Space, Place and Gender* (Cambridge, Polity Press).

Mazuchelli, N. (1876) *The Indian Alps and How We Crossed Them: being a narrative of two years residence in the Eastern Himalayas and a two month tour into the interior by a lady pioneer* (London, Longmans, Green & Co.).

Mellor, A. K. (1993) *Romanticism and Gender* (London and New York, Routledge).

Mills, S. (1991) *Discourses of Differences: women's travel writing and colonisation* (London, Routledge).

Mills, S. (1992) 'Knowing y/our place: a Marxist feminist stylistic analysis', in M.

Toolan (ed.) *Language, Text and Context: essays in stylistics*, pp. 182–208 (London, Routledge).

Mills, S. (ed.) (1994a) *Gendering the Reader* (Hemel Hempstead, Harvester/ Wheatsheaf).

Mills, S. (1994b) 'Knowledge, gender and empire', in A. Blunt & G. Rose (eds) *Writing Women and Space: colonial and postcolonial geographies*, pp. 29–50 (New York, Guilford).

Mills, S. (1995a) *Feminist Stylistics* (London, Routledge).

Mills, S. (1995b) 'Discontinuity and post/colonial discourse', *Ariel*, 26 (3), July 1995, pp. 73–88.

Milroy, B. M. and Wismer, S. (1994) 'Communities, work and public/private sphere-models', *Gender, Place and Culture*, 1, pp. 71–91.

Minh-ha, T. (1989) *Woman, Native, Other: writing postcoloniality and feminism* (Bloomington and Indianapolis, IN, Indiana University Press.

Mohanty, C. T. (1988) 'Under Western eyes: feminist scholarship and colonial discourses', *Feminist Review*, 30, pp. 66–88.

Moore, H. L. (1986) *Space, Text and Gender: an anthropological study of the Marakwet of Kenya* (Cambridge, Cambridge University Press).

Nair, J. (1990) 'Uncovering the zenana: visions of Indian womanhood in Englishwomen's writings 1813–1940', *Journal of Women's History*, 2, pp. 8–34.

Noyes, J. (1992) *Colonial Space: spatiality in the discourse of German South West Africa* (Chur, Harwood).

Parks, F. (1850) *Wanderings of a Pilgrim in Search of the Picturesque* (London, Pelham Richardson).

Paxton, N. (1992) 'Disembodied subjects: English women's autobiography under the Raj', in S. Smith and J. Watson (eds) *De/colonising the Subject: the politics of gender in women's autobiography* (Minneapolis, IN, University of Minnesota Press).

Pratt, G. and Hanson, H. (1994) 'Geography and the construction of difference', *Gender, Place and Culture*, 1, pp. 5–31.

Pratt, M. L. (1992) *Imperial Eyes: travel writing and transculturation* (London, Routledge).

Richards, T. (1993) *The Imperial Archive: knowledge and the fantasy of empire* (London, Verso).

Rose, G. (1993) *Feminism and Geography: the limits of geographical knowledge* (London, Polity Press).

Rose, G. (1995) 'Distance, surface, elsewhere: a feminist critique of the space of phallo-centric self/knowledge', paper given to the English and Geography Departments, University of Loughborough, February.

Sangari, K. and Vaid, S. (eds) (1990) *Recasting Women: Essays in Indian colonial history* (New Brunswick, NJ, Rutgers University Press).

Sharpe, J. (1991) 'The unspeakable limits of rape: colonial violence and counter-insurgency, *Genders*, 10, pp. 25–46.

Sharpe, J. (1993) *Allegories of Empire: the figure of woman in the colonial text* (Minneapolis, MN, University of Minnesota Press).

Shohat, E. and Stam, R. (1994) *Unthinking Eurocentrism: multiculturalism and the media* (London, Routledge).

Spain, D. (1992) *Gendered Species* (Chapel Hill, NC, University of North Carolina Press).

Spivak, G. C. (1988) *In Other Worlds: essays in cultural politics* (London, Routledge).

Spivak, G. C. (1990) *The Postcolonial Critic: interviews, strategies, dialogues*, S. Harasym (ed.) (London, Routledge).

Spivak, G. C. (1993) *Outside in the Teaching Machine* (London, Routledge).

Strobel, M. (1991) *European Women and the Second British Empire* (Indiana University Press, Bloomington).

Suleri, S. (1992a) 'Woman skin deep: feminism and the postcolonial condition', *Critical Inquiry*, 18, pp. 756–69.

Suleri, S. (1992b) *The Rhetoric of English India* (Chicago, IL., University of Chicago Press).

Trollope, J. (1983) *Britannia's Daughters: women of the British Empire* (London, Hutchinson).

Voloshinov, V. (1986 [1929]) *Marxism and the Philosophy of Language*, tr. L. Matejka and I. R. Titunik (Cambridge, MA, Harvard University Press).

Ware, V. (1992) *Beyond the Pale: white women, racism and history* (London, Verso).

Wex, M. (1979) *Let's Take Back our Space: female and male body language as a result of patriarchal structures* (Berlin, Frauenliteraturverlag Hermine Fees).

White, C. (1993) 'Women for breeding, boys for pleasure and melons for sheer delight: sexual colonisation and homosexual objects of desire', unpublished discussion paper, University of Loughborough.

Whitehead, J. (1995) 'Bodies clean and unclean: prostitution, sanitary legislation and respectable femininity in colonial North India', *Gender and History*, 7, pp. 41–63.

Wigley, M. (1992) 'Untitled: the housing of gender', in Colomina, B. (ed.) *Sexuality and Space*, pp. 327–89 (Princeton, NJ, Princeton University).

Williams, P. and Chrisman, L. (eds) (1993) *Colonial Discourse and Post-colonial Theory: a reader* (Hemel Hempstead, Wheatsheaf).

Yaeger, P. (1989) 'Toward a female sublime', in L. Kauffman (ed.) *Gender and Theory: dialogues on feminist criticism*, pp. 191–212 (Oxford, Blackwell).

Young, R. (1990) *White Mythologies: writing history and the west* (London, Routledge).

Young, R. (1995) *Colonial desire: hybridity in theory, culture and race* (London, Routlege).

Young, I. M. (1989) 'Throwing like a girl: a phenomenology of feminine bodily comportment, motility and spatiality', in J. Allen and I. M. Young (eds) *The Thinking Muse: feminism and modern French philosophy*, pp. 51–70 (Bloomington, IN, Indiana University Press).

6.5

'SPATIAL STORIES UNDER SIEGE: BRITISH WOMEN WRITING FROM LUCKNOW IN 1857'

Alison Blunt

Together with the rest of the British population in Lucknow, more than 200 women lived under siege for five months at the height of the Indian 'mutiny' in 1857. Events in India in 1857 posed an unprecedented threat to British rule in India, and graphic descriptions of the deaths and suffering of British women and children came to embody the severity of this threat (Sharpe, 1993; Tuson, 1998; Blunt, 2000). Most famously, more than 200 British women and children were killed at Cawnpore in July 1857, and their deaths were used to justify extreme levels of retribution. But, in contrast, only forty miles away, more than 200 British women and children survived the siege of Lucknow. This article examines six book-length diaries written by British women at Lucknow, four of which were published during the authors' lifetimes and two of which were first published one century after they had been written (Bartrum, 1858; Case, 1858; Harris, 1858; Inglis, 1892, Germon, 1957; Brydon, 1978). It is likely that other women also wrote diaries that did not survive the siege or the evacuation from Lucknow, were subsequently lost or destroyed, or remain in private collections. The surviving diaries describe daily domestic life under siege and inscribe a crisis of imperial rule on a domestic scale. But, unlike representations of embodied and domestic defilement that dominated other accounts and objectified British women as victims of the conflict, the diaries written by British women at Lucknow document their survival. Rather than explore representations *of* British women during the conflict, this article concentrates on repre-

From: Alison Blunt (2000), 'Spatial Stories Under Siege: British Women Writing from Lucknow in 1857', pp. 229–46, in *Gender, Place and Culture*, vol. 7, no. 3.

Table 1. *British women diarists at Lucknow, 1857*

Katherine Bartrum	Book-length diary published in 1858. Married to an army doctor with one young son. Travelled eighty miles from Gonda to Lucknow at the start of the siege. Her husband died as part of the first relief forces in September, and her son died in Calcutta in January 1858.
Colina Brydon	Book-length diary published for the first time in 1978. Married to an army doctor. Their two youngest children were at Lucknow during the siege while their five older children were living in Britain.
Adelaide Case	Book-length diary published in 1858. Married to Colonel Case of the Thirty-second Regiment, who was killed at Chinhut. No children.
Maria Germon	Book-length diary published for the first time in 1957. Married to a captain in the Indian Army. No children.
Katherine Harris	Book-length diary published in 1858. Married to the chaplain of the Thirty-second Regiment who, from August, was the only clergyman at Lucknow during the siege. No children.
Julia Inglis	Published a letter for private circulation, which included extracts from her diary, in 1858, and published a book-length diary in 1892. Married to Brigadier Inglis of the Thirty-second Regiment, who was in command of the defence of Lucknow for most of the siege. Their three young sons survived the siege.

sentations *by* British women themselves. Unlike more general studies of 'mutiny' writings by women (Sharpe, 1993; Robinson, 1996; Ghose, 1998; Tuson, 1998), a detailed focus on diaries written during the siege of Lucknow enables me to examine the differences as well as the similarities between accounts. While the diaries written by British women at Lucknow all describe five months of danger, discomfort and monotony, their different accounts of spatial confinement, unaccustomed servitude and domestic relief reinscribed a class hierarchy that existed not only between middle-class and working-class women at Lucknow, but also within the middle class itself.

Most of the women who lived under siege at Lucknow were married to soldiers, but sixty-nine 'ladies' were related to officers or officials (Innes, 1895). As Table 1 shows, the two most senior women at Lucknow both wrote diaries during the siege (Julia Inglis and Adelaide Case), as did the wives of two army doctors (Katherine Bartrum and Colina Brydon), the wife of a regimental chaplain (Katherine Harris) and the wife of a captain in the Indian Army (Maria Germon). British officers and officials in India, both military and civilian, have been described as emulating an aristocratic ruling class (Anderson, 1991). Their wives played important roles in establishing and maintaining a class hierarchy in domestic and social terms. As Margaret Strobel writes, '[a] wife who did not act in a manner appropriate to her husband's rank upset the entire community by disrupting the social order upon which European society was based' (Strobel, 1991, p. 13). The effectiveness of military organisation was thought to depend on the replication of a feudal hierarchy through the 'successful adaptation of gentry lifestyle and social relations to the messroom and barrack yard' (Trustram, 1984, p. 16). By providing for the physical, emotional, sexual and spiritual needs of soldiers, the regimental system came to encompass a range of domestic and familial as well as military roles (Trustram, 1984; Ballhatchet, 1990). The incorporation of British wives into regimental life not only reflected the domestic and familial functions of a regiment, but also reinforced the hierarchical basis of such functions both between, as well as among, officers and other ranks (Callan and Ardener, 1984). While the wives of soldiers often worked as cooks, seamstresses and washerwomen both for their husbands and the regiment, the wives of officers aspired to bourgeois and aristocratic ideals of feminine domesticity not only within their own families, but also in their familial relations with the regiment itself. While the siege of Lucknow and the 'mutiny' more generally disrupted the imperial order, it also disrupted the class hierarchy that underpinned it and was most tangibly enshrined in imperial regimental life. For British women diarists, the imperial and class disruption at Lucknow was felt most acutely in their domestic lives, and their diaries describe the severity of the imperial conflict on a household scale. This article traces the domestic geographies of imperial conflict and the intersections of gender, race and class on a household scale by exploring the spatial stories of disorder and reorder told in diaries by British women living under the siege at Lucknow.

Lucknow was the capital of the recently annexed province of Oudh in what is now the northern-central state of Uttar Pradesh. In May 1857, the increasing unrest in Lucknow meant that the wives and children of British soldiers were moved from barracks to the Residency compound in the centre of the 'native city'. This compound consisted of thirty-three acres of land around the residency building, which included many different houses and rooms that accommodated British officials. At the same time, eleven 'ladies' and fifteen children of the Thirty-second Regiment, including Julia Inglis and Adelaide Case, were invited to stay in cantonments in the house of Sir Henry Lawrence, the Chief Commissioner of Lucknow. On 25 May, these women were sent to the Residency compound because an uprising seemed imminent. They were joined there by women and children who had travelled from outlying settlements in Oudh, such as Katherine Bartrum. Following an uprising in cantonments and the final, unsuccessful British sortie at the battle of Chinhut on 30

June, the British population in Lucknow was confined to the Residency compound until late November. In September, an unsuccessful 'relief' provided reinforcements, and forces sent from Britain, under Sir Colin Campbell, relieved Lucknow for the second time on 17 November. This was followed by the evacuation of the Residency, first of the injured and then of women and children (and see Blunt, 1999a, for more on the diaries written by British women after their evacuation from Lucknow). Fighting continued until the British recaptured Lucknow in March 1858.

At the start of the siege, Katherine Bartrum wrote, 'My husband always consoled me with the promise that should things come to the worst he would destroy me with his own hand' (Bartrum, 1858, p. 10), and Julia Inglis recorded that 'several of the ladies had poison at hand' (Inglis, 1892, p. 101). In August, Maria Germon wrote, 'The future is a perfect blank, we are not able even to give a surmise as to what our fate may be – but we have all made up our minds never to give in, but to blow up all in the entrenchments sooner' (Germon, 1957, p. 75). While the future was 'a perfect blank' and the present was frightening and dangerous, the British women who wrote diaries during the siege of Lucknow recorded life as they feared death. In their diaries, they charted the passage of time by noting birthdays and anniversaries, described the spatial limits of life under siege and imagined their distant homes and families in Britain. Most of the diaries concentrated on day-to-day survival by focusing on the hardships of living under siege in domestic terms. As their diaries suggest, domestic and imperial disorder were intimately connected within the spatial confinement of life under siege at Lucknow. And yet, these diaries also chart the reinscription of domestic and imperial *order*, and the very act of writing a diary helped to impose some stability at a time of crisis. Most notably, although the first relief in September was unsuccessful, it provided some measure of domestic relief as more servants were available, mobility around the Residency increased and women were able to spend more time with their husbands. By considering residency at Lucknow in its broadest sense, I will explore the spatial confinement of British women in the Residency compound, their unaccustomed servitude as their servants left at the beginning of the siege and the domestic relief that helped British women to reinscribe the class differences that underpinned imperial regimental life.

SPATIAL STORIES

Many feminist and postcolonial critics have explored the gendered spatiality of imperial rule in their studies of the subordination and marginalisation of colonised men and women, imperial masculinities away from home and the contested place of white women in the empire (including Chaudhuri & Strobel, 1992; Driver, 1992; Foley et al., 1995; McClintock, 1995; Mills, 1996; Phillips, 1997; Midgley, 1998). Studies of white women and the spatiality of imperial power include accounts of their imperial travels and transgressions (Blunt, 1994; Mills, 1991) and the translation of feminine domesticity over imperial space (Sharpe, 1993; George, 1994; McClintock, 1995). They have shown how the travel accounts, diaries, letters, memoirs, household guides and novels written by women reflected and helped to shape their own and their readers' imaginative geographies of empire. By focusing on diaries by British women at Lucknow, I am seeking to privilege neither the written word nor the agency of white women over and above other representations, experiences and memories. Rather, it is important to interrogate the assumed transparency of whiteness not only to reveal the basis, exercise and self-legitimation of imperial power, but also to reveal the fissures and contradictions that destabilised imperial power from within. Moreover, these fissures and contradictions were often domesticated within imperial homes and embodied by white women at home in the empire (Stoler, 1995; Grewal, 1996; Metcalf, 1998; Blune, 1999b). In this article, I explore imperial domesticity at a time of crisis, dislocated from cantonments and civil lines to the Lucknow Residency for the duration of the five-month siege in 1857. Although many other spatial stories remain untold about the siege of Lucknow, the diaries written by British women provide the most detailed and extensive records to chart the domestic implications of the imperial crisis. Rather than represent the undifferentiated experiences of white women at Lucknow, these diaries also depict the disorder of imperial domesticity in class-specific terms.

Through a focus on the diaries written by British women at Lucknow, I examine not only the spatial limits of life under siege for white women during the imperial conflict, but also the gendered spatiality of diary narratives. More specifically, I explore the domestic geographies of these diaries in several, connected ways: the conditions under which they were written, the reasons for their publication and their content, which juxtaposed the dangers of life under siege with the domestic concerns of everyday life. Rather than depict siege life for all British women at Lucknow, these diaries were partial accounts, revealing the class differences that underpinned an imperial regimental hierarchy. This hierarchy was a crucial part of the imperial order, which was domesticated within regimental life and incorporated wives alongside their husbands. But this hierarchy was disrupted by the conflict in Lucknow and although the diarists described this disorder most directly in their domestic lives, their diary narratives also represent an imperial and domestic *reordering* as the siege continued. Most importantly, although the first 'relief' failed in military terms, it can be read through the diaries written by women as providing some measure of *domestic* relief that enabled the reinscription of class differences within and between the middle and working classes living under siege.

Diaries and other personal writings by women have attracted an increasing amount of critical attention in recent years because they provide detailed and diverse records of everyday life, feelings and events (Bunkers, 1987; Cooper, 1987; Huff, 1987; Nussbaum, 1989; Blodgett, 1991). Harriet Blodgett states that diaries and letters have been the most common form of women's writings for centuries, 'expressing a resilient creative impulse that through serial writing could find outlet in a sanctioned form' (Blodgett, 1991, p. 1). By the eighteenth century, diaries had come to include 'the serial record of personal memorabilia that gives us a sense of the diarist too' (Blodgett, 1991, p. 3) and provided a socially acceptable and often private channel for women to explore their feelings and experiences. And yet, this private channel for self-expression could act as an important site of resistance to gender norms in a patriarchal society. According to Suzanne Bunkers, 'a diary could become a place where the writer could generate a sense of self and establish its integrity, a place where she could contemplate her relationships with others and understand better what it meant to be a woman in her culture' (Bunkers, 1987, p. 9).

Diaries tell spatial as well as temporal stories, describing a period of time, often one day, in narrative space, and recording life not only at the time, but also in the place in which it is lived. Diaries can impose order on everyday life. But diaries can also record new experiences beyond the everyday, as shown by travel diaries about people and places far from home and by the importance of diaries written at times of war (see Frank, 1967; Baer, 1997; Weiner, 1997). Diaries have been described as sanctuaries, suggesting a textual space that is central to, but also separate from, daily life, providing an escape and textual freedom from confinement and captivity. Diaries have also been represented as confessionals, serving as a private, perhaps secret, narrative of thoughts and feelings. But diaries are not necessarily private, as a diarist may be conscious of the documentary value of their writings and may be recording events for a wider, future readership, not just for themselves alone.

Diary narratives reflect life and a sense of self as negotiated, complex and dynamic, rather than seamlessly coherent and static. In light of this, the spatiality of diary narratives has been interpreted in terms of mobility and travel in revealing ways. First, the words 'diary', 'journal' and 'journey' all originate from the Latin for 'daily', referring either to a daily record or a day's travel (Blythe, 1989). Writing a diary represents a journey over the course of a day, recording events and change over time in narrative space. Second, diaries and travel narratives both relate observational detail and the self-referentiality of the author: 'No form of expression more emphatically embodies the expresser: diaries are the flesh made word' (Mallon, 1984, p. xvii). Third, both diaries and travel accounts can simultaneously assert and undermine authorial authority by relating eyewitness accounts and observational detail alongside more personal, often emotional, content. The journey of self-discovery that is often implicit or explicit in travel accounts parallels a day's journey recorded in a diary (Hassam, 1990). As a central part of this article, I argue that, although the diaries written by British women at Lucknow told spatial stories under siege, they were not only narratives of confinement, but also of mobility. Once again, I focus here on class differences, charting the different experiences of confinement for women at Lucknow and tracing the reinscription of an imperial regimental hierarchy as women began to move more freely around the compound. Although the diaries written by British women at Lucknow represented both the disorder and reordering of imperial domesticity, they did so in class-specific terms and in different ways in different parts of the Residency compound.

DOCUMENTING SURVIVAL

The diaries by British women at Lucknow were written to record their daily lives for themselves and their families and friends at home. As Katherine Harris wrote:

> I have kept a rough sort of journal during the whole siege, often written under the greatest difficulties – part of the time with a child in my arms or asleep in my lap; but I persevered, because I knew if we survived you would like to live our siege life over in imagination, and the little details would interest you; besides the comfort of talking to you. (Harris, 1858, p. iii)

On their publication in London in 1858, the diaries of Katherine Harris, Katherine Bartrum and Adelaide Case reached an audience beyond the family and friends for whom they had been initially intended. Both Bartrum and Case were widowed during the siege of Lucknow and their books would have provided an important source of income in the first years after the 'mutiny'. Each author explained her decision to publish. Katherine Harris wrote:

> As no lady's diary has hitherto been given to the public, the friends of the writer have thought it might interest others, beyond the family circle, to communicate additional information on a subject in which the British nation feels so deep an interest. (Harris, 1858, p. iii)

Although Adelaide Case had kept a diary 'for the perusal of my relatives in England, and with no view whatever to publication' (Case, 1858, p. iii), she did, in the event, publish her diary, stating that she hoped to supplement official dispatches about Lucknow with her account of daily life. As she said, 'I have not attempted, by subsequent additions, to produce effect, or to aim at glowing descriptions, but have given it as it was written, in the simple narrative form, which the dangers and privations of the siege alone permitted' (Case, 1858, pp. iii–iv). Katherine Bartrum also wrote that her diary represented her personal experiences of daily life and domesticity under siege, stating in self-effacing terms that:

> It is not the wish of the writer of this little Volume, any more than it is in her power, to draw, in colours, a picture of sights and scenes through which it has been her lot to pass, but merely, at the desire of her friends, to give in simple truthfulness a detail of those domestic occurrences which fell immediately under her own observation during the siege of Lucknow. (Bartrum, 1858)

In contrast, although Julia Inglis published a letter to her mother in 1858 for private circulation, which included extracts from her diary, she did not publish her diary as a book until 1892. Some thirty-three years after the 'mutiny', she justified the publication of her diary because 'a thoroughly clear and accurate account has not been given' (Inglis, 1892, p. vi). Her diary was supplemented by notes written by Colonel Birch, her husband's aide-de-camp at Lucknow, and she wanted to avoid 'as much as possible all personal allusions' (Inglis, 1892, p. vii). Unlike the other published diaries by British women, Inglis sought to present an authoritative account of the defence of Lucknow and, as the wife of the commander of the defence, she was able to record strategic as well as personal information. On 5 October, she wrote, 'I was busy all the morning writing letters from Jon's dictation, which he was writing to Lord Canning (the Governor General of India). I read General Outram's order to our garrison, which was most handsome and gratifying' (Inglis, 1892, p. 176). Adelaide Case also read Outram's Order and noted that she had read Inglis's dispatch to Calcutta two days before, which 'gives a very clear and good account of the whole siege' (Case, 1858, p. 223). Adelaide Case also included a copy of Brigadier Inglis's *Narrative of the Defence of Lucknow* at the end of her published diary, because 'it supplies those interesting military details which cannot be looked for in a lady's journal' (Case, 1858, p. 332).

Supplementary material also helped to provide personal rather than strategic information. When Adelaide Case stopped writing her diary for one week following the death of her husband, her unmarried sister Caroline kept a record of events in the form of a letter to her cousin Gabrielle. This letter was subsequently published as part of Case's diary to provide a continuous record of daily life. Katherine Bartrum included extracts from letters written by her husband from the time that they parted in Gonda until his death in September 1857. Finally, Katherine Harris included several letters written after the evacuation of the Residency by her husband to his mother and sister in Britain, which concentrated on his work as chaplain during the siege, the hardships of siege life and the resilience of his wife. In a letter written from Allahabad to his mother in January 1858, James Harris wrote:

> My dear G [*sic*] behaved splendidly – never gave in – and constantly occupied herself in doing acts of kindness to others less able than herself. . . . G kept a sort of scrambling journal during the siege, which I hope to send to you soon; it was written under difficulties, with little hope that you would ever see it. (Harris, 1858, pp. 202–3)

Although the diaries written by British women at Lucknow primarily represented their own experiences of life under siege, they should be read as intertextual accounts, including other voices and sources that record strategic as well as personal events and information. However, this article will concentrate on the writings by the women diarists themselves, which documented their spatial confinement under siege, their unaccustomed servitude and the reinscription of a class hierarchy after the first 'relief'.

Spatial Confinement

The diaries written by British women at Lucknow were partial representations of life under siege, recording their experiences in particular places in the compound and among women of a similar social standing. The wives of soldiers – the majority of women at Lucknow – remain largely invisible and unrecorded in these diaries. Their social and spatial marginalisation was inseparable as they lived in the large underground room, or *tykhana*, beneath the Residency House. The only time that the women diarists lived in close proximity to the wives of soldiers was in late May, when they were ordered to move into the Residency House because an uprising was expected in the city. The wives of officers and officials occupied the upper storeys and several slept on the roof to escape the 'hot babel' (Germon, 1957, p. 35). The wives of soldiers lived in the underground, dark and overcrowded *tykhana*, which, despite its discomforts, was one of the safest places in the compound. The only contact recorded between these women was when the wives of officers visited with clothes and food. As Adelaide Case wrote:

> sometimes Mrs Inglis, Carry [Case's sister] and I go down into the Ty Khana, and see the women of the regiment, and any other poor creatures who may have been brought in there from different stations in the district. Mrs Inglis never goes down empty-handed. She is kind and considerate to every one, and often takes down some pudding or soup, which may have been at dinner, to a poor sick boy. A little tea, sugar, or any old clothes we can find to take with us to them is always very gratefully received, and it cheers their spirits to talk to them a little. (Case, 1858, p. 23)

For most of the siege, British women were confined indoors in a number of different houses and other buildings in the Residency compound that were known as 'garrisons'. This militaristic term reflects the location of these women in their new homes at the heart of an imperial conflict. Within the Residency compound, the location of different women reflected their social status. For most of the siege, British women diarists lived in the houses of officials, the Begum Kotie or rooms in Brigade Square.

Maria Germon and Katherine Harris were among the British residents numbering eleven 'ladies', six children and three men at the Fayrers' house during the siege. In late May Germon described life at the Fayrers' as a pleasant house party, writing that:

> our party here is a very agreeable one – we meet at *chota hazree* [early morning tea] and then after dressing, breakfast at ten – then have working, reading and music (there are some good performers amongst our party), *tiffin* [lunch] at two, dine at half-past seven and then the Padre reads a chapter and prayers and we retire. (Germon, 1957, p. 28)

Two days later, the wife of the 'Padre', Katherine Harris, described Dr and Mrs Fayrer as 'our host and hostess' and noted that 'The piano has been going on today a good deal; several of those here sing and play well' (Harris, 1858, p. 27). But, after the British defeat at Chinhut, the Fayrers' house became a place of danger rather than entertainment:

No sooner was the first gun fired than the ladies and children were all hurried downstairs into an underground room . . . damp, dark, and gloomy as a vault, and excessively dirty. Here we sat all day, feeling too miserable, anxious, and terrified to speak, the gentlemen occasionally coming down to reassure us and tell us how things were going on. (Harris, 1858, p. 75)

After a week, the British women and children moved upstairs to sleep in the dining room which, although lighter and less damp than the underground *tykhana*; afforded less privacy for the women and children. When she was unwell, Maria Germon wrote:

Dr Fayrer told me on no account to stir from bed – there I was in the dining room all open to the public, our gentlemen passing and repassing the door, but there was no help for it – it was the only room we could have a *punkah* [overhead fan] in. (Germon, 1957, p. 95)

Unlike the dangers and hardships of life at the Fayrers' house, the two most senior 'ladies' at Lucknow lived in safer and more private quarters in Brigade Square. Adelaide Case lived there with her unmarried sister, Julia Inglis, and the Inglis's three young children. Instead of the constant firing endured at the Fayrers', Inglis wrote, 'We have been in a particular safe place during the siege' (Inglis, 1858, p. 20). But even though its location was safer than that of the Fayrers' house, the Brigade Square was also dangerous and frightening. In August, Adeliade Case described their position under siege:

An attack is going on while I am writing, and I cannot help thinking what would be the feelings of any lady suddenly transported from quiet, peaceful England to this room, around which the bullets are whizzing, the round shot falling, and now and then a loud explosion, as if a mine were blowing up. (Case, 1858, p. 148)

In contrast to the seclusion and privacy enjoyed by Case and Inglis, Katherine Bartrum lived with her baby son in the Begum Kotie for the first two months of the siege before moving to the Ommanney's house to escape the threat of cholera. The Begum Kotie consisted of a large and crowded room that was shared by many women and children. Except at night, when fifteen women slept close together under the *punkah*, the communal room was divided into sections to demarcate space for each woman and her possessions. In the evenings, by candlelight, sitting on their mattresses and drinking weak tea, the women in the Begum Kotie remembered their homes and families:

We talked together of bygone days, of happy homes in England where our childhood had been spent, bringing from memory's stores tales to cheer the passing hour, and thinking of loved ones far away: of the father that knew not as yet that his child was captive in a foreign land: of the bright band of sisters and brothers who formed the household circle: but most of all of the husband fleeing perhaps for his life, whose heart was with his wife and child in their captivity, and who might even then be coming to their rescue. (Bartrum, 1858, p. 24)

Just as Julia Inglis and Adelaide Case visited solders' wives in the Residency Building at the beginning of the siege, Katherine Harris described her visit to the Begum Kothi on 18 June:

> [I visited] the poor women who came in from Seetapore, and gave them a few old dressing gowns and things of mine I thought would be useful ... They were very cheerful, and seemed quite to have got over their troubles. It is wonderful how little that class of people seem to feel things that would almost kill a lady. (Harris, 1858, p. 56)

For diarists such as Harris, any common experience as British women living under siege was lost in the face of class difference. By describing their philanthropic visits to other British women in the Residency compound, Adelaide Case and Katherine Harris helped to maintain class divisions that were starkly enshrined in a regimental hierarchy at the beginning of the siege (Prochaska, 1980). But as the siege continued, supplies became scarce, the mobility of women within the compound was increasingly curtailed and the opportunities to reaffirm class divisions through feminine philanthropy were reduced. The incorporated status of Julia Inglis and Adelaide Case as senior regimental 'ladies' was reflected by a number of soldiers' wives and other women asking them for food and clothes during the siege. Both Case and Inglis recorded a visit from Mrs Beale in August, whose late husband had been an overseer of roads:

> Yesterday afternoon a very respectable looking person, with a little baby in her arms, came to the door of our room, and after asking Mrs Inglis if she was 'the brigadier's lady', said she had come to beg a little milk for her child ... Her simple story, told in such a genuine honest manner, affected us all ... She said that her little baby was born on the first day of the attack; her husband ... was shot through the lungs, and died almost immediately. From grief and fretting she had lost all her milk, and had nothing to give the poor little thing. She told us that she had lost three children ... and was very anxious if she could to rear this one, to take it to her friends in England. Mrs Inglis asked her where her home was; she said, in Kent, and that her father is a clergyman there, and her husband's father was an officer in the army. She said she had every thing she wanted but nourishment for her child, and though many in this place are doubtless in this same sad plight, her plain tale, told without the slightest appearance of wishing to excite pity, made an impression on me I shall not easily forget. (Case, 1858, pp. 151–2)

The class difference between Adelaide Case and Mrs Beale is clearly evident. Even though Mrs Beale was 'a very respectable looking person', she was of the lower middle class and the widow of a man who 'had kept a large school in England, but came out to this country to try to make his fortune' (Inglis, 1892, pp. 117–8). But Julia Inglis was unable to spare any of the milk from her goats: 'It went to my heart to refuse her; but at this time I had just enough for my own children, and baby could not have lived without it. I think she understood that I would have given her some if I could' (Inglis, 1892, p. 117). Even though a clear class difference existed between Inglis and Case as regimental 'ladies' and Mrs Beale as an overseer's widow and a clergyman's daughter, they were all vulnerable during the siege and it was difficult to reinforce the class hierarchy buttressed by middle- and upper-class Victorian philanthropy.

UNACCUSTOMED SERVITUDE

At the beginning of the siege, whilst their Indian servants remained, there was some continuity not only of home life but also of imperial rule for British women diarists. But within a few days, most of the diaries recorded the desertion of their Indian servants. The only exceptions to this are the accounts by Adelaide Case and Julia Inglis, whose servants remained with them throughout the siege. As Inglis wrote, 'Our faithful servant, Curruk, was a great comfort to us . . . I am sure he kept all the other servants together, and in good spirits' (Inglis, 1892, p. 96). But, in contrast and reflecting the accounts of most women diarists, Katherine Harris described the desertion of her Indian servants in mid June:

> Our bearer [main servant], who has been with us almost ever since we came to India, and to whom James has been most kind, walked off, taking with him all his goods and chattels, and one of our punkah coolies to carry his bundle . . . People's servants seem to be deserting daily. We expect soon to be without attendants, and a good riddance it would be if this were a climate which admitted of one's doing without them; but if they all leave us, it will be difficult to know how we shall manage. Their impudence is beyond bounds; they are losing even the semblance of respect. I packed off my tailor yesterday: he came very late, and, on my remarking it, he gave me such an insolent answer and look, that I discharged him then and there; and he actually went off without waiting, or asking for his wages. (Harris, 1858, pp. 46–7)

For women like Harris, the desertion of household servants represented the severity of the imperial crisis on a domestic scale because previously established codes of deference, loyalty and respect had been disrupted. For the first time, many British women had to make tea, clean, wash their clothes and sometimes cook, although the wives of British soldiers were usually employed for this purpose. As Katherine Bartrum wrote in June, 'All our servants have deserted us, and now our trials have begun in earnest' (Bartrum, 1858, p. 21). But, by the next day, she wrote:

> We have found a woman who promises to cook for us once a day, and brings us hot water for breakfast and tea; if she will only make my baby's food, I shall be able to manage tolerably well. My time is fully occupied in nursing, and washing our clothes, together with cups and saucers, and fanning away the flies . . . I have taken it upon myself to keep the room somewhat neat and clean . . . even if I afford [my fellow-sufferers] amusement by giving them occasion to call me the servant-of-all work. (Bartrum, 1858, p. 22)

Even as the necessity of doing domestic work revealed the severity of the imperial crisis, it could also offer a diversion from the conflict. For Bartrum:

> In one way it was almost a blessing to have no servants, because it gave us so much occupation that we had less time to dwell upon our troubles and anxieties concerning those absent from us; and many a smile was drawn forth at the very absence of the comforts and even the necessaries of life. (Bartrum, 1858, p. 23)

For women such as Bartrum and Harris, imperial power was challenged most directly in a domestic sphere. By employing Indian servants, constructions of the racial and class superiority of British women enabled them to share in imperial power on a domestic scale, establishing what Rosemary Marangoly George has called an 'empire in the home' (George, 1994). But, by having to do domestic work themselves, constructions of racial and class superiority were destabilised and the basis of imperial legitimisation was threatened in the very arenas – home and daily life – on which it had previously relied. In his history of the 'mutiny', Sir John Kaye (1876, p. 354) wrote, 'our women were not dishonoured, save that they were made to feel their servitude' and, as Jenny Sharpe argues, 'the rebels had unsettled a colonial order to the degree of reversing its hierarchy of mastery and servitude' (Sharpe, 1993, p. 65). But such a reversal was clearly gender- and class-specific as it was only the wives of officers and senior officials who were made to feel an unaccustomed servitude. If British men had been positioned in this way, imperial self-legitimisation would have been completely compromised and, for the wives of British soldiers, such servitude was nothing new. As well as revealing the class hierarchy between women in the imperial aristocracy and the majority of women at Lucknow, accounts of the attempt to establish a new domestic order during the siege also reflected and reproduced inequalities among the 'ladies' themselves.

Most of the Indian servants left the Fayrers' house on the night of 2 July and, as Maria Germon noted two days later, 'Firing had been going on all night and it continued all day, but we were so engaged in kitchen duties we scarcely noticed it' (Germon, 1957, p. 59). While Katherine Harris's domestic duties came to include cleaning, nursing and caring for children, Maria Germon was responsible for making tea and distributing food. Writing in mid July, Germon recorded her daily routine, detailing her domestic duties under siege:

Rose a little before six and made tea for all the party, seventeen – then with Mrs Anderson gave out attah, rice, sugar, sago &c for the day's rations. While doing it a six pound shot came through the verandah above, broke down some plates and bricks and fell at our feet. Mrs Boileau and some children had a very narrow escape – they were sitting in the verandah at the time but no one was hurt. I then rushed at the *bheestie* [water carrier] who was passing and made him fill a tin can with water which I lugged upstairs then bathed and dressed. It was about half past eight when I was ready so I went to the front door to get a breath of fresh air – at nine down again to make tea again for breakfast which con-sisted of roast mutton, chupattees, rice and jam. I then sat and worked at Charlie's waistbands till nearly dinner time when I felt very poorly but it passed off. (Germon, 1957, p. 65)

Juxtaposing the dangers of life under siege with new experiences of domestic work, accounts like this represent the severity of the imperial conflict in domes-tic terms. And yet, the very act of writing a diary helped to create some order in everyday life even at its most disordered and frightening. Not only did domestic work provide a diversion from the danger and monotony of siege life, but recording such domestic work on a daily basis and charting a daily routine helped to impose a degree of order to life under siege.

Domestic Relief

Although the first relief of Lucknow did not end the siege, the reinforcements of officers, soldiers and servants that it provided relieved British women of some of their domestic work and enabled them to move more freely around the Residency. As Katherine Harris wrote:

James has got me a bearer, who relieves me of the dusting, and now we have our Madras man and the B[arwell]s have got a 'kit' (*Kitmutgar*, or table servant) there is no need for ladies to wash up cups and saucers, so I only superintend the general work and see that it is properly done. (Harris, 1858, pp. 140–1)

For Katherine Bartrum, 'the two servants that came up with my husband are a great comfort to me, they relieve me of the very hard work, and yet I have still plenty to do' (Bartrum, 1858, p. 50). While the diarists continued to record the impact of the imperial conflict on a domestic scale, the first relief also helped British women reinscribe a class hierarchy by visiting women of a similar social standing and receiving visits from officers in the relief force. So, for example, Maria Germon recorded on 27 September that 'Miss Nepean came over and several ladies were walking about – I walked down nearly to the gate of our compound the first time since Chinhut June 30th' (Germon, 1957, p. 99) and, in October, Colina Brydon wrote that she had 'a number of visitors in the evening. Mr and Mrs Barwell, who brought her baby to show me, and Mrs

Harris. We walked back with them to Dr Fayrer's[,] the first time I have been so far in that direction since the siege began' (Brydon, 1978, p. 52). Julia Inglis and Adelaide Case received several visitors on a daily basis from late September, with Case recording that 'Mrs Giddings, Mrs Orr, and Mrs Boileau passed through our square this evening' and, a week later, that 'Captain Wilson, Colonel Napier, and Captain Birch, came to drink tea with us yesterday evening' (Case, 1858, pp. 236 and 248).

The first relief of Lucknow also enabled several British women to spend more time alone with their husbands. As they moved more freely about the Residency, either with or to visit their husbands, such women saw the extent of the damage inflicted on the Residency compound for the first time. Captain Germon was posted on the Residency defences, but tried to visit his wife every day. On 4 October, Maria German visited her husband's post on the fortifications for the first time:

> I . . . was perfectly thunderstruck to see it such as mass of ruins . . . and even the centre room Charlie occupies has immense holes in the walls made by round shot . . . I enjoyed a cup of tea with him of course without milk or sugar but it seemed Paradise to be alone with him again. (Germon, 1957, pp. 103–4)

Despite the evident dangers of his position, Germon could spend time alone with her husband for the first time since the siege of Lucknow began. From this point, she continued to visit Charlie, even though 'Everyone thinks it very dangerous my going to his house but his room is tolerably safe, at all events as safe for me as him' (Germon, 1957, p. 112).

Despite her anxiety as the siege continued, Maria Germon wrote a long description of her sixth wedding anniversary on 21 October. This description contrasts with her usual accounts of a daily, domestic routine under siege by portraying her marriage to Charlie and rare moments alone with him as a sanctuary and escape. As such, her account provides a detailed and vivid impression of the reaffirmation of a loving marriage during the imperial conflict. This reaffirmation was inscribed in domestic terms. While Maria completed her usual domestic chores and sewed gifts for Charlie, Charlie obtained extra rations and made some 'sugar cakes'. For one day during the siege, the Germons were able to recreate a private space of marital, domestic peace on their anniversary.

> After dinner Charlie came for me as we were to spend the rest of the day together. I carried over a cup and saucer, teaspoon and wine-glass, the . . . coat and a book I had borrowed for Charlie. I found he had got a pint bottle of champagne, his rations for four days from the Brigade Mess (as sherry and port were all out). He would finish drinking it to our 'noble selves' and to our dear ones at home and he had made me with his own hands some sugar cakes, the remains of some sugar I had indented for

when I was ill – he had not been very successful but they were very sweet coming from his dear old hands. He then went and begged a little milk from one who possessed that luxury. I had two lumps of sugar given me as a present and having a little cocoa left of days gone by I set to work and made us each a cup which we thoroughly enjoyed. Charlie pronounced it capital and I enjoyed it much with the little cakes. We then chatted cosily till half past seven thinking of the grand dinner we had eaten at the Barackpore hotel that night six years ago and comparing it with our half rations in a battered garret. But I don't think it made either of us discontented, only thankful that our lives had been so mercifully preserved through such awful scenes. No one can see the battered condition of Charlie's house, an outpost, without feeling that he had been almost miraculously preserved. He walked home with me and about half past eight I went to bed. (Germon, 1957, pp. 109–10)

CONCLUSIONS

Many other spatial stories remain untold about the siege of Lucknow. This article has focused on the diaries written by six British women who belonged to the imperial aristocracy through their incorporation into imperial regimental life. In their diaries, these women recorded the spatial constraints that dictated their daily lives, the importance of class as well as gender in shaping everyday life under siege, and the domestication of the imperial conflict on a household scale. For British women at Lucknow, imperial power was challenged most directly in the domestic sphere. The intimate connections between domestic and imperial disorder were experienced most acutely by the middle-class diarists when many of their Indian servants left the Residency compound soon after the siege began.

In their descriptions of spatial confinement and unaccustomed servitude, the diaries written by British women living under siege helped to inscribe class differences not only between middle- and working-class women at Lucknow, but also within the middle class itself. The different locations of British women in the Residency compound reflected their status in an imperial regimental hierarchy. Most of the working-class wives of soldiers, who comprised the majority of women living under siege, remained socially and spatially marginal as they lived in the underground *tykhana* beneath the Residency House. Among the small elite that included the women diarists, the most senior women at Lucknow lived in more private and safer quarters than the wives of lower ranked officers and professional men. At the beginning of the siege, class differences were reinforced by the wives of officers and officials visiting soldiers' wives with gifts of clothes and food. But as the siege continued, as mobility became curtailed and as supplies became increasingly scarce, feminine traditions of philanthropy became harder to sustain. When many Indian servants left the Residency compound soon after the beginning of the siege, the middle-class women diarists were subjected to domestic work for the first time, and they wrote about the severity of the conflict in terms of their unaccustomed servitude. Although the siege disrupted the racial hierarchy between rulers and ruled on a domestic scale, it helped to reinscribe inequalities between middle- and working-class British women. While the diarists described their new routines of domestic work, they also employed the wives and widows of soldiers as cooks and children's nurses. From late September, the first relief of Lucknow enabled British women to move more freely around the Residency compound and to reaffirm class hierarchies by employing more servants, visiting women of a similar social standing and receiving visits from officers. Although the first 'relief' of Lucknow did not end the siege, it provided some measure of domestic relief.

Unlike more general studies of 'mutiny' writings by British women, this article has focused on the diaries written by six women at Lucknow to explore their differences, as well as similarities. While all of the diarists were white, middle class and married, some were widowed during the siege, some did not have children and others suffered the death of a child. Although all of the diaries record the spatial confinement and unaccustomed servitude of life under siege, they reflect diverse experiences in different rooms and houses in the Residency compound and according to the status of incorporated wives in an imperial regimental hierarchy. The diaries written by these women at Lucknow tell spatial as well as temporal stories, detailing the spatially-confined lives of elite women under siege, their different locations in the Residency compound and their place at the heart of an imperial conflict. At the same time, the diaries written by such women also provided a sanctuary away from the dangers and monotony of everyday life under siege, a channel for self-expression and self-determination and a space in which to imagine peaceful homes away from the conflict. In their diaries, the spatial stories of class difference and imperial domesticity written by British women during the siege of Lucknow depicted a crisis of imperial rule on a domestic scale, which both breached and reinforced imperial regimental hierarchies between middle- and working-class women and within the middle class itself.

ACKNOWLEDGEMENTS

Gill Valentine and three anonymous referees provided very helpful comments on this article, and Felix Driver, Derek Gregory, Cole Harris and Gerry Pratt all helped to improve a much earlier version. Thanks too to Lina Hall at the Cartographic Unit, University of Southampton.

NOTES

1. Estimates of the number of people under siege at Lucknow vary. Innes (1895) states that there were 3000 people under siege, of whom 1392 were Indian and 1608 were British and others of European descent. He also estimates that there were 1720 combatants and 1280 non-combatants. For more on the 'mutiny' and its implications, see Hibbert (1978) and Metcalf (1965).
2. The form and content of the diaries published in the nineteenth and twentieth cen-

turies are similar, suggesting that little editing took place. However, Maria Germon, whose diary remained unpublished in her lifetime, was the only diarist to describe discord among women living under siege. For example, she wrote, 'I rebelled against [keeping watching at night] – we had quite a fight about it during the day' (p. 64); 'I fought against sleeping in the dining room as I considered it dangerous but being the only one I was obliged to give in' (p. 80); and 'Mrs Helford [is] very angry at being turned out of her room to give place to the baby' (p. 77).

REFERENCES

Anderson, Benedict (1991) *Imagined Communities: reflections on the origins and spread of nationalism* (London, Verso).

Baer, Elizabeth (ed.) (1997) *Shadows on my Heart: the Civil War Diary of Lucy Rebecca Buck of Virginia* (Athens, GA, The University of Georgia Press).

Ballhatchet, Kennet (1980) *Race, Sex, and Class under the Raj* (London, Weidenfeld & Nicolson).

Bartrum, Katherine (1858) *A Widow's Reminiscences of the Siege of Lucknow* (London, James Nisbet).

Blodgett, Harriet (ed.) (1991) *'Capacious Hold-All': an anthology of Englishwomen's diary writings* (Charlottesville, VA, University of Virginia Press).

Blunt, Alison (1994) *Travel, Gender, and Imperialism: Mary Kingsley and West Africa* (New York, Guilford Press).

Blunt, Alison (1999a) 'The Flight from Lucknow: British women travelling and writing home, 1857–8' in J. Duncan and D. Gregory (eds) *Writes of Passage: reading travel writing* (London, Routledge).

Blunt, Alison (1999b) 'Imperial geographies of home: British domesticity in India, 1886–1925', *Transactions of the Institute of British Geographers*, 24, pp. 421–40.

Blunt, Alison (2000) 'Embodying war: British women and domestic defilement in the Indian 'Mutiny', 1857–8, *Journal of Historical Geography*, 26, pp. 403–28.

Blythe, Ronald (ed.) (1989) *The Penguin Book of Diaries* (London, Penguin).

Brydon, Colina (1978) *The Lucknow Siege Diary of Mrs C. M. Brydon* (edited and published by C. de L. W. fforde).

Bunkers, Suzanne (1987) 'Faithful friend: nineteenth–century Midwestern American women's unpublished diaries', *Women's Studies International Forum*, 10, pp. 7–17.

Callan, Hilary and Ardener, Shirley (eds) (1984) *The Incorporated Wife* (London, Croom Helm).

Case, Adelaide (1858) *Day by Day at Lucknow: a journal of the siege of Lucknow* (London, Richard Bentley).

Chaudhuri, Nupur and Strobel, Margaret (eds) (1992) *Western Women and Imperialism: complicity and resistance* (Bloomington, IN, Indiana University Press).

Cooper, Joanne (1987) 'Shaping meanings: women's diaries, journals and letters – the old and the new', *Women's Studies International Forum*, 10, pp. 95–9.

Driver, Felix (1992) 'Geography's empire: histories of geographical knowledge' *Environment and Planning D: Society and Space*, 10, pp. 23–40.

Foley, Timothy, Pilkington, Lionel, Ryder, Sean and Tilley, Elizabeth (eds) (1995) *Gender and Colonialism* (Galway, Ireland, Galway University Press).

Frank, Anne (1967) *The Diary of a Young Girl* (New York, Doubleday).

George, Rosemary Marangoly (1994) 'Homes in the empire, empires in the home', *Cultural Critique*, 15, pp. 95–127.

Germon, Maria (1957) *Journal of the Siege of Lucknow: an episode of the Indian Mutiny*, ed. Michael Edwardes (London, Constable).

Ghose, Indira (1998) *Women Travellers in Colonial India: the power of the female gaze* (Delhi, Oxford University Press).

Grewal, Inderpal (1996) *Home and Harem: nation, gender, empire and the cultures of travel* (Durham, NC, Duke University Press).

Harris, Katherine (1858) *A Lady's Diary of the Siege of Lucknow* (London, John Murray).

Hassam, Andrew (1990) '"As I write": narrative occasions and the quest for self-presence in the travel diary', *Ariel*, 21, pp. 33–47.

Hibbert, Christopher (1978) *The Great Mutiny: India 1857* (London, Penguin).

Huff, Cynthia (1987) 'Chronicles of confinement: reactions to childbirth in British women's diaries', *Women's Studies International Forum*, 10, pp. 63–8.

Inglis, Julia (1858) *Letters containing extracts from a journal kept by Mrs Julia Inglis during the siege of Lucknow* (London, privately printed; held at the Centre of South Asian Studies, University of Cambridge).

Inglis, Julia (1892) *The Siege of Lucknow, a Diary* (London, James R. Osgood).

Innes, MacLeod (1895) *Lucknow and Oude in the Mutiny: a narrative and a study* (London, A. D. Innes).

Kaye, John (1876) *A History of the Sepoy War in India 1857–8* (London, W. H. Allen).

Mallon, Thomas (1984) *A Book of One's Own: people and their diaries* (New York, Ticknor & Fields).

McClintock, Anne (1995) *Imperial Leather: race, gender and sexuality in the colonial contest* (New York, Routledge).

Metcalf, Thomas (1965) *The Aftermath of Revolt: India 1857–1870* (Princeton, NJ, Princeton University Press).

Metcalf, Thomas (1998) *Ideologies of the Raj* (New Delohi; Cambridge University Press).

Midgley, Claire (ed.) (1998) *Gender and Imperialism* (Manchester, Manchester University Press).

Mills, Sara (1991) *Discourses of Difference: an analysis of women's travel writing and colonialism* (London, Routledge).

Mills, Sara (1996) 'Gender and colonial space', *Gender, Place and Culture*, 3, pp. 125–48.

Nussbaum, Felicity (1989) *The Autobiographical Subject: gender and ideology in eighteenth century England* (Baltimore, MD, Johns Hopkins University Press).

Prochaska, Frank (1980) *Women and Philanthrophy in Nineteenth-century England* (Oxford, Clarendon Press).

Robinson, Jane (1996) *Angels of Albion: women of the Indian mutiny* (London, Viking).

Sharpe, Jenny (1993) *Allegories of Empire: the figure of woman in the colonial text* (Minneapolis, MN, University of Minnesota Press).

Stoler, Ann Laura (1995) *Race and the Education of Desire: Foucault's History of Sexuality and the colonial order of things* (Durham, NC; Duke University Press).

Strobel, Margaret (1991) *European Women and the Second British Empire* (Bloomington, IN, Indiana University Press).

Trustram, Myna (1984) *Women of the Regiment: marriage and the Victorian army* (Cambridge, Cambridge University Press).

Tuson, Penelope (1998) 'Mutiny narratives and the imperial feminine: European women's accounts of the rebellion in India in 1857', *Women's Studies International Forum*, 21, pp. 291–303.

Weiner, Marli (1997) *A Heritage of Woe: the Civil War Diary of Grace Brown Elmore, 1861–1868* (Athens GA, University of Georgia Press).

BIBLIOGRAPHY

Abu Odeh, L. (1993), 'Post-colonial feminism and the veil: thinking the difference', *Feminist Review*, 43, 26–37.

Amos, V. and P. Parmar (1984), 'Challenging imperial feminism', *Feminist Review*, 17, 3–19.

Ang, I. (1995), 'I'm a feminist but …: "Other" women and postnational feminism', in B. Caine and R. Pringle (eds), *Transitions: New Australian Feminisms*, Sydney: Allen and Unwin, 57–73.

Anzaldúa, G. (1987), *Borderlands/La Frontera: The New Mestiza*, San Francisco: Spinster Aunt Lute.

Apter, E. (1992), 'Female trouble in the colonial harem', *Differences*, 4, 205–24.

Ashcroft, B., G. Griffiths and H. Tiffin (eds) (1995), *The Post-Colonial Studies Reader*, London: Routledge.

Badran, M. (1996), *Feminists, Islam, and Nation*, Cairo: American University in Cairo Press.

Ballhatchet, K. (1980), *Race, Class and Sex under the Raj: Imperial Attitudes and Policies and their Critics 1793–1905*, London: Weidenfeld and Nicolson.

Baron, B. (1994), *The Women's Awakening in Egypt: Culture, Society and the Press*, New Haven, CT: Yale University Press.

Beaulieu, J. and M. Roberts (eds) (2002), *Orientalism's Interlocutors: Rewriting the Colonial Encounter*, Durham, NC: Duke University Press.

Benjamin, R. (ed.) (1997), *Orientalism: Delacroix to Klee*, Sydney: Art Gallery of New South Wales.

Bhabha, H. K. (1984), 'Of mimicry and men', *October*, 28, 125–33.

Bhatt, C. and Robert Lee (1997), 'Official knowledges: the free market, identity formation, sexuality and race in the HIV/AIDS sector', in J. Oppenheimer and R. Reckitt (eds), *Acting on AIDS: Sex Drugs and Politics*, London: Serpent's Tail.

Bhavnani, K. (2001), *Feminism and 'Race'*, Oxford: Oxford University Press.

Bhavnani, K. and M. Coulson (1986), 'Transforming socialist feminism: the challenge of racism', *Feminist Review*, 22, 81–92.

Blake, S. (1990), 'A woman's trek: or what difference does gender make?', *Women's Studies International Forum*, 13/4, 347–55.

Blank, D. R. (1999), 'A veil of controversy: the construction of a "Tchador Affair" in the French press', *Interventions*, vol. 1, no. 4, pp. 536–555.

Blunt, A. (2000), 'Spatial stories under siege: British women writing from Lucknow in 1857', *Gender, Place and Culture*, 7/3, 229–46.

Boone, J. (1995), 'Vacation cruises; or, the homoerotics of Orientalism', *PMLA*, January, 110/1, 89–107.

Brah, A. (1996), *Cartographies of Diaspora: Contesting Identities*, London: Routledge, chapter 8.

Bristow, J. (1991), *Empire Boys: Adventures in a Man's World*, London: HarperCollins.

Brown, H., M. Gilkes and A. Kaloski-Naylor (eds) (1999), *White? Women: Critical Perspectives on Race and Gender*, York: Raw Nerve Books.

Brownfoot, J. (1984), 'Memsahibs in colonial Malaya', in H. Callan and S. Ardener, *The Incorporated Wife*, London: Croom Helm.

Bryan, B., S. Dadzie and S. Scafe (eds) (1985), *The Heart of the Race: Black Women's Lives in Britain*, London: Virago.

Burton, A. (1992), 'The white woman's burden: British feminists and "the Indian woman" 1865–1915', in N. Chaudhuri and M. Strobel (eds), *Western Women and Imperialism: Complicity and Resistance*, Bloomington: Indiana University Press, 137–57.

Butler, J. (1990), *Gender Trouble*, London: Routledge.

Butler, J. (1997), *Excitable Speech: a Politics of the Performative*, London and New York: Routledge.

Carby, H. (1982), 'White woman listen! Black feminism and the boundaries of sisterhood', in Centre for Contemporary Cultural Studies (ed.), *The Empire Strikes Back: Race and Realism in 1970s Britain*, London: Hutchinson.

Carby, H. (1985), ' "On the threshold of woman's era": lynching, empire, and sexuality in Black feminist theory', *Critical Inquiry*, 12, 262–79.

(charles), H. (1992), 'Whiteness – the relevance of politically colouring the "non" ', in H. Hinds, A. Phoenix and J. Stacey (eds), *Working Out: New Directions for Women's Studies*, London: Falmer.

Chatterjee, P. (1990), 'The nationalist resolution of the women's question', in K. Sangari and S. Vaid (eds), *Recasting Women: Essays in Indian Colonial History*, New Brunswick, NJ: Rutgers University Press, 233–53.

Chaturvedi, V. (ed.) (2000), *Mapping Subaltern Studies and the Postcolonial*, London: Verso.

Chaudhuri, N. (1992), 'Shawls, jewellery, curry and rice in Victorian Britain', in N. Chaudhuri and M. Strobel (eds), *Western Women and Imperialism: Complicity and Resistance*, Bloomington: Indiana University Press, 231–47.

Chaudhuri, N. and M. Strobel (eds) (1992), *Western Women and Imperialism: Complicity and Resistance*, Bloomington: Indiana University Press.

Cherry, D. (2000), *Beyond the Frame: Feminism and Visual Culture, Britain 1850–1900*, London: Routledge.

Chow, R. (1994), 'Where have all the natives gone?', in Angelika Bammer (ed.),

Displacements: Cultural Identities in Question, Bloomington: Indiana University Press.

Codell, J. F. and Macleod D. Sachko (eds) (1998), *Orientalism Transposed: The Impact of the Colonies on British Culture*, Aldershot: Ashgate.

Copjec, J. (1994), *Read my Desire: Lacan Against the Historicists (October)*, Cambridge, MA: MIT Press.

Davis, A. (1982), *Women, Race and Class*, London: The Women's Press.

De Groot, J. (1998), 'Coexisting and conflicting identities: women and nationalisms in twentieth-century Iran', in R. Roach Pierson and N. Chaudhuri (eds), *Nation, Empire, Colony: Historicizing Gender and Race*, Bloomington: Indiana University Press.

Donnell, A. (1999), 'Editorial: Dressing with a difference: cultural representation, minority rights and ethnic chic', *Interventions, Special Topic, The Veil: Postcolonialism and the Politics of Dress*, 1/4, 489–99.

Dorkeno, R. (1994), *Cutting the Rose: Female Genital Mutilation: the Practice and its Prevention*, London: Minority Rights Publications.

Dyer, R. (1997), *White*, London: Routledge.

El Guindi , F. (1999), 'Veiling resistance' in *Fashion Theory*, 3/1, 51–80.

El Saadawi, N. (1980), *The Hidden Face of Eve: Women in the Arab World*, London: Zed Books.

El Saadawi, N. (1997), *The Nawal El Saadawi Reader*, London: Zed Books.

Fanon, F. (1959), 'Algeria unveiled' in *Studies in a Dying Colonialism*, trans. Haakon Chevalier, 1989, London: Earthscan.

Ferguson, M. (1992), *Subject to Others: British Women Writers and Colonial Slavery*, London: Routledge.

Foucault, M. (1980), *Power/Knowledge: Selected Interviews 1972–77*, ed. Colin Gordon, Brighton: Harvester.

Frankenberg, R. (1993), *White Women, Race Matters: The Social Construction of Whiteness*, London: Routledge.

Frankenberg, R. and L. Mani (1993), 'Crosscurrents, crosstalk: race, "postcoloniality" and the politics of location', *Cultural Studies*, 7/2, 292–310.

Gelder, K. and J. Jacobs (1998), *Uncanny Australia: Sacredness and Identity in a Postcolonial Nation*, Melbourne: Melbourne University Press.

Gilman, S. L. (1985), 'Black bodies, white bodies: towards an iconography of female sexuality in late nineteenth-century art, medicine and literature', *Critical Inquiry*, 12, 204–42.

Goçek, F. M. (1999), 'A veil of controversy: the contested location of gender in contemporary Turkey', *Interventions*, 1/4, 521–35.

Goldberg, D. (1993), *Racist Culture: Philosophy and the Politics of Meaning*, Oxford: Blackwell.

Graham-Brown, S. (1988), *Images of Women: the Portrayal of Women in Photography of the Middle East 1860–1950*, London: Quartet.

Grewal, I. (1996), *Home and Harem: Nation, Gender Empire and the Cultures of Travel*, Leicester: Leicester University Press.

Haggis, J. (1998), 'Women and imperialism: towards a non-recuperative history', in C. Midgley (ed.), *Gender and Imperialism*, Manchester: Manchester University Press, 45–75.

Hendricks, M. and P. Parker (eds) (1994), *Women, 'Race' and Writing in the Early Modern Period*, London: Routledge.

hooks, b. (1984), *Feminist Theory: From Margin to Center*, Boston: South End Press.

hooks, b. (1989), *Talking Back: Thinking Feminist Theory: Thinking Black*, London: Sheba Feminist Publishers.

hooks, b. (1992), *Black Looks: Race and Representation*, London: Turnaround.

Hosken, F. (1994), *The Hosken Report: Genital and Sexual Mutilation of Females*, Lexington, MA: Women's International Network News.

Hull, G. T. et al. (eds) (1982), *All the Women are White, All the Blacks are Men, But Some of Us are Brave: Black Women's Studies*, New York: The Feminist Press.

Hyam, R. (1990), *Empire and Sexuality: the British Experience*, Manchester: Manchester University Press.

Innes, L. (1994), 'Virgin territories and motherlands: colonial and nationalist representations of Africa,' *Feminist Review*, 47, 15–28.

Jacobs, J. (1994), 'Earth honoring: Western desires and indigenous knowledges', in A. Blunt and G. Rose (eds), *Writing Women and Space*, New York: Guilford, 169–96.

Jayawardena, K. (1995), *The White Woman's Other Burden: Western Women and South Asia During British Rule*, London: Routledge.

Jordan, G. and C. Weedon (1995), *Cultural Politics: Class, Gender, Race and the Postmodern World*, Oxford: Blackwell.

Kandiyoti, D. (1991), 'End of empire: Islam, nationalism and women in Turkey', in D. Kandiyoti (ed.), *Women, Islam and the State*, Basingstoke: Macmillan.

Keddie, N. R. (1991), 'Introduction: deciphering Middle Eastern women's history', in N. R. Keddie and B. Baron (eds), *Women in Middle Eastern History: Shifting Boundaries in Sex and Gender*, New Haven, CT: Yale University Press.

Kondo, D. (1997), *About Face: Performing Race and Fashion and Theater*, London: Routledge.

Lakoff, R. (2001), *The Language War*, Berkeley: University of California Press.

Levy, D. (1991), *Other Women: The Writing of Class, Race, and Gender, 1832–1898*, Princeton, NJ: Princeton University Press.

Lewis, R. (1996), *Gendering Orientalism: Race, Femininity and Representation*, London: Routledge.

Lewis, R. (1999), 'On veiling, vision and voyage: cross-cultural dressing and narratives of identity', *Interventions*, 1/4, 500–20.

Lightfoot-Klein, H. (1989), *Prisoners of Ritual: an Odyssey into Female Genital Mutilation*, New York: Haworth Press.

Lionnet, F. (1992), 'Feminisms and universalisms: "universal rights" and the legal debate around the practice of female excision in France', *Inscriptions, Special Issue, Orientalism and Cultural Differences*, 6, 97–113.

Loomba, A. (1993), 'Dead women tell no tales: issues of female subjectivity, subaltern agency and tradition in colonial and post-colonial writings on widow immolation in India', *History Workshop Journal*, 36, 209–27.

Lorde, A. (1983), 'The Master's Tools Will Never Dismantle the Master's House', in C. Moraga and G. Anzaldúa (eds), *This Bridge Called My Back: Writings by Radical Women of Colour*, New York: Kitchen Table Press.

Lowe, L. (1991), *Critical Terrains*, Ithaca, NY: Cornell University Press.

Mani, L. (1989), 'Multiple mediations: feminist scholarship in the age of multinational receptions', *Inscriptions*, 5, 1–23.

Mani, L. (1992), 'Cultural history, colonial texts: reading eyewitness accounts of widow burning', in L. Grossberg, C. Nelson and P. Treichler (eds), *Cultural Studies*, London: Routledge.

Massey, D. (1994), *Space, Place and Gender*, Cambridge: Polity Press.

McClintock, A. (1995), *Imperial Leather: Race, Gender and Sexuality in the Imperial Contest*, London: Routledge.

McEwan, C. (2000), *Gender, Geography and Empire: Victorian Women Travellers in West Africa*, London: Ashgate.

Melman, B. (1992), *Women's Orients: English Women and the Middle East, 1718–1918. Sexuality, Religion and Work*, Basingstoke: Macmillan.

Mernissi, F. (1985), *Beyond the Veil: Male-Female Dynamics in Muslim Society*, second edition, London: Al Saqi.

Meyer, S. L. (1989), 'Colonialism and the figurative strategy of *Jane Eyre*, *Victorian Studies*, 33/2, 247–68.

Micklewright, N. (1999), 'Public and private for Ottoman women of the nineteenth century', in D. Fairchild Ruggles (ed.), *Women and Self-Representation in Islamic Societies*, New York: State University of New York.

Midgley, C. (ed.) (1998), *Gender and Imperialism*, Manchester: Manchester University Press.

Miller, J. (1990), *Seductions: Studies in Reading and Culture*, London: Virago.

Mills, S. (1991), *Discourses of Difference: Women's Travel Writing and Colonialism*, London: Routledge.

Mills, S. (1996a), 'Post-colonial feminist theory', in S. Mills and L. Pearce (eds), *Feminist Readings/Feminists Reading*, second edition, London and New York: Prentice Hall, Harvester Wheatsheaf, 257–80.

Mills, S. (1996b), 'Gender and colonial space', *Gender, Place and Culture*, 3/2, 125–47.

Minh-ha, T. T. (1989), 'Difference: "a special third world women's issue"', in T. T. Minh-ha, *Women Native Other: Writing Postcoloniality and Feminism*, Bloomington: Indiana University Press, 79–118.

Mirza, H. S. (ed.) (1997), *Black British Feminism: A Reader*, London: Routledge.

Mohanty, C. (1984), 'Under Western eyes: feminist scholarship and colonial discourse', *Boundary 2*, 3, 333–58.

Moraga, C. and Anzaldúa, G. (eds) (1983), *This Bridge Called My Back: Writings by Radical Women of Color*, New York: Kitchen Table Press.

Morris, M. (1988), *The Pirate's Fiancée: Feminism Reading Postmodernism*, London: Verso.

Murray, A. (1998), 'Debt-bondage and trafficking: don't believe the hype', in K. Kempadoo and J. Doesema (eds), *Global Sex Workers: Rights, Resistance and Redefinition*, London: Routledge.

Murungi, K. (1994), 'Get away from my genitals!: A commentary on *Warrior Marks*', *Interstices*, 2/1, 11–15.

Nader, L. (1989), 'Orientalism, Occidentalism and the control of women', *Cultural Dynamics*, 2/3, 323–55.

Nair, J. (1990), 'Uncovering the zenana: vision of Indian womanhood in Englishwomen's writing, 1913–1940', *Journal of Women's History*, 2/1, Spring, 8–34.

Nanda, S. (1993), 'Hijras as neither man or woman', in Abelove et al. (eds), *The Lesbian and Gay Studies Reader*, London: Routledge.

Narayan, K. (1997), 'How native is a "native" anthropologist?', in L. Lamphere, H. Ragone and P. Zavella (eds), *Situated Lives: Gender and Culture in Everyday Life*, New York: Routledge, 23–41.

Nash, C. (1994), 'Remapping the body/land: new cartographies of identity, gender and landscape in Ireland', in A. Blunt and G. Rose (eds), *Writing Women and Space: Colonial and Post-colonial Geographies*, New York: Guilford.

Nelson, C. (1996), *Doria Shafik, Egyptian Feminist: A Woman Apart*, Cairo: American University in Cairo Press.

Nochlin, L. (1983), 'The imaginary Orient' in L. Nochlin, *The Politics of Vision*, Thames and Hudson, 1991.

Ong, A. (1995), 'State versus Islam: Malay families, women's bodies and the body politic in Malaysia', in A. Ong, *Bewitching Women – Pious Men: Gender and Politics in South East Asia*, University of California Press.

Paidar, P. (1996), 'Feminism and Islam in Iran', in D. Kandiyoti (ed.), *Women, Islam and the State*, Basingstoke: Macmillan.

Parker, A. et al. (eds) (1992), *Nationalisms and Sexualities*, London: Routledge.

Patton, C. (1992), 'From nation to family: containing "African AIDS"', in A. Parker et al. (eds), *Nationalisms and Sexualities*, London: Routledge.

Paxton, N. (1992), 'Disembodied subjects: English women's autobiography under the Raj', in S. Smith and J. Watson (eds), *Decolonising the Subject: the Politics of Gender in Women's Autobiography*, Minneapolis: University of Minnesota Press.

Peirce, L. (1993), *The Imperial Harem: Women and Sovereignty in the Ottoman Empire*, Oxford: Oxford University Press.

Phillips, R. (1997), *Mapping Men and Empire: A Geography of Adventure*, London: Routledge.

Pratt, M. L. (1992), *Imperial Eyes: Travel Writing and Transculturation*, London: Routledge.

Rahman, A. and Toubia, N. (eds) (2000), *Female Genital Mutilation: a Guide to Laws and Policies Worldwide*, London: Zed Books.

Rich, A. (1987), 'Notes toward a politics of location', in A. Rich, *Blood, Bread and Poetry: Selected Prose 1979–1985*, London: Virago.

Rifaat, A. (1990), 'Who will be the man?', in M. Badran and M. Cooke (eds), *Opening the Gates: A Century of Arab Feminist Writing*, London: Virago.

Rose, G. (1993), *Feminism and Geography: The Limits of Geographical Knowledge*, London: Polity.

Ryan, S. (1996), *The Cartographic Eye: How Explorers Saw Australia*, Melbourne: Cambridge University Press.

Sahgal, G. and Yuval-Davis, N. (1994), 'The uses of fundamentalism', *Women Against Fundamentalism Journal*, 5, 7–9.

Said, E. (1978), *Orientalism*, London: Routledge and Kegan Paul.

Sandoval, C. (1991), 'U.S. Third World feminism: the theory and method of oppositional consciousness in the postmodern world', *Genders*, 10, Spring, 1–24.

Sangari, K. and Vaid, S. (1990), *Recasting Women: Essays in Indian Colonial History*, New Brunswick, NJ: Rutgers University Press.

Schaffer, K. (1988), 'The bush and women', in K. Schaffer, *Women and the Bush: Forces of Desire in the Australian Cultural Tradition*, Cambridge: Cambridge University Press, 52–76.

Sharpe, J. (1993), *Allegories of Empire: The Figure of Woman in the Colonial Text*, Minneapolis: University of Minnesota Press.

Shohat, E. and Stam, R. (1994), *Unthinking Eurocentrism: Multiculturalism and the Media*, London: Routledge.

Sinha, M. (1995), *The 'Manly' Englishman and the Effeminate Bengali in the Late 19th Century*, Manchester: Manchester University Press.

Smith, B. (1983), *Home Girls: A Black Feminist Anthology*, New York, Kitchen Table: Women of Colour Press.

Spillers, H. (1988), 'Mama's baby, papa's maybe: an American grammar book', *Diacritics*, 17/2, Summer, 65–82.

Spivak, G. (1985), 'Three women's texts and a critique of imperialism', *Critical Inquiry* 12/1, 243–61.

Spivak, G. (1988), 'French Feminism in an international frame', in G. Spivak, *In Other Worlds: Essays in Cultural Politics*, London: Routledge.

Spivak, G. (1990a) (in discussion with S. Gunew and R. Sunder Rajan), 'Questions of multiculturalism', and 'The post-colonial critic', in G. Spivak, *The Post-colonial Critic*, ed. S. Harasym, London: Routledge, 59–74.

Spivak, G. (1990b), *The Post-colonial Critic: Interviews, Strategies, Dialogues*, ed. S. Harasym, London: Routledge.

Spivak, G. (1993a), 'Can the subaltern speak?', in P. Williams and L. Chrisman (eds), *Colonial Discourse and Post-Colonial Theory*, Hemel Hempstead: Harvester Wheatsheaf, 66–112.

Spivak, G. (1993b), *Outside in the Teaching Machine*, London: Routledge.

Spivak, G. (2000), 'The new subaltern: a silent interview', in V. Chaturvedi (ed.), *Mapping Subaltern Studies and the Postcolonial*, London: Verso.

Suleri, S. (1992a), 'Woman skin deep: feminism and the postcolonial condition', *Critical Inquiry*, 18, 756–69.

Suleri, S. (1992b), *The Rhetoric of English India*, Chicago: University of Chicago.

Sunder Rajan, R. (1993), 'The subject of sati', in R. Sunder Rajan, *Real and Imagined Women: Gender, Culture and Post-Colonialism*, London: Routledge, 15–39.

Toubia, N. F. (1997), 'The social and political implications of female circumcision: the case of the Sudan', in F. Warnock (ed.), *Women and Family in the Middle East: New Voices of Change*, Austin: University of Texas.

Visvanathan, N., L. Duggan, L. Nisonoff and N. Wiegersma (eds) (1997), *The Woman, Gender and Development Reader*, London: Zed.

Walker, A. and P. Palmer (1993), *Warrior Marks: Female Genital Mutilation and the Sexual Blinding of Women*, London: Harcourt Brace.

Ware, V. (1992), *Beyond the Pale: White Women, Racism and History*, London: Verso.

Wicomb, Z. (1994), 'Motherhood and the surrogate reader: race, gender and interpretation', in S. Mills (ed.), *Gendering the Reader*, Hemel Hempstead: Harvester Wheatsheaf, 99–127.

Wilkinson, S. and C. Kitzinger (eds) (1993), *Heterosexuality: A Feminism and Psychology Reader*, London: Sage.

Williams, P. and L. Chrisman (eds) (1993), *Colonial Discourse and Post-Colonial Theory: A Reader*, Hemel Hempstead: Harvester Wheatsheaf.

Woodhull, W. (1991), 'Unveiling Algeria', *Genders*, 10, Spring, 112–31.

Yeğenoğlu, M. (1998), *Colonial Fantasies: Towards a Feminist Reading of Orientalism*, Cambridge: Cambridge University Press.

Young, R. (2001), *Postcolonialism An Historical Introduction*, Oxford: Blackwell.

Zemon Davis, N. (1994), 'Iroquois women, European women', in M. Hendricks and P. Parker (eds), *Women, 'Race' and Writing in the Early Modern Period*, London: Routledge, 243–58.

Zonana, J. (1993), 'The sultan and the slave: feminist Orientalism and the structure of Jane Eyre', *Signs*, 18/3, Spring, 592–617.

INDEX